McDougal Littell

CLASSZONE

Visit classzone.com and get connected.

ClassZone resources provide instruction, practice and learning support for students and parents.

Literature and Reading Center

- Selection–specific content includes vocabulary practice, research links, and extension activities for writing and critical thinking
- Author Online provides information about each author, as well as in–depth author studies on selected writers
- English Learner support for a variety of languages includes audio summaries of selections and a Multi-Language Academic Glossary

Vocabulary and Spelling Center

- Vocabulary practice and games
- Spelling lessons

Writing and Grammar Center

- Quick–Fix Editing Machine provides grammar help in a student–friendly format
- Writing Templates and graphic organizers promote clear, orderly communication

Media Center

- Media Analysis Guides encourage critical thinking skills
- Project Ideas, Storyboards, and Production Templates inspire creative media projects

Access the online version of your textbook at classzone.com

Your complete text is available for immediate use!

McDougal Littell

Where Great Lessons Begin

Life is full of questions.
LITERATURE *helps you answer them.*

What if your whole **WORLD** *changed?*

When is there strength in **NUMBERS?**

Are there **TWO SIDES** *to every story?*

How strong is **PEER PRESSURE?**

Is **GOODNESS** *always rewarded?*

Can we ever **TAME** *what's wild?*

ACKNOWLEDGMENTS

INTRODUCTORY UNIT

Houghton Mifflin: Excerpt from *Number the Stars* by Lois Lowry. Copyright © 1989 by Lois Lowry. All rights reserved. Reprinted by permission of Houghton Mifflin Company.

Simon & Schuster: "Quilt" from *A Suitcase of Seaweed and Other Poems* by Janet S. Wong. Copyright © 1996 by Janet S. Wong. Reprinted with the permission of Margaret K. McElderry Books, an imprint of Simon & Schuster Children's Publishing Division.

PLAYS/Sterling Partners Inc.: Excerpt from "The Little Princess" by Frances Hodgson Burnett, adapted by Adele Than, from *Plays from Famous Stories and Fairy Tales* and *PLAYS, The Drama Magazine for Young People.* Copyright © 1989 and © 1985. Reprinted with the permission of the publisher PLAYS/Sterling Partners, Inc., P.O. Box 60016, Newton, MA 02460.

Sterling Lord Literistic: Excerpt from *Steven Spielberg: Crazy for Movies* by Susan Goldman Rubin. Copyright © 2001 by Susan Goldman Rubin. Reprinted by permission of Sterling Lord Literistic, Inc.

Francisco Jiménez: Excerpt from "The Circuit" by Francisco Jiménez from *Arizona Quarterly.* Autumn 1973. Reprinted by permission of Francisco Jiménez.

Continued on page R142

ART CREDITS

COVER, TITLE PAGE

Detail of *Tree Goddess* (1994), Jerry N. Uelsmann. © Jerry N. Uelsmann.

Continued on page R148

ISBN 13: 978-0-618-56864-2   ISBN 10: 0-618-56864-6

Printed in the United States of America.

4 5 6 7 8 0914 14 13 12 11 10   4500246245

McDougal Littell
LITERATURE

Janet Allen

Arthur N. Applebee

Jim Burke

Douglas Carnine

Yvette Jackson

Robert T. Jiménez

Judith A. Langer

Robert J. Marzano

Mary Lou McCloskey

Donna M. Ogle

Carol Booth Olson

Lydia Stack

Carol Ann Tomlinson

McDougal Littell

EVANSTON, ILLINOIS · BOSTON · DALLAS

SENIOR PROGRAM CONSULTANTS

JANET ALLEN Reading and Literacy Specialist; creator of the popular "It's Never Too Late"/"Reading for Life" Institutes. Dr. Allen is an internationally known consultant who specializes in literacy work with at-risk students. Her publications include *Tools for Content Literacy; It's Never Too Late: Leading Adolescents to Lifelong Learning; Yellow Brick Roads: Shared and Guided Paths to Independent Reading; Words, Words, Words: Teaching Vocabulary in Grades 4–12;* and *Testing 1, 2, 3 . . . Bridging Best Practice and High-Stakes Assessments.* Dr. Allen was a high school reading and English teacher for more than 20 years and has taught courses in both subjects at the University of Central Florida. She directed the Central Florida Writing Project and received the Milken Foundation National Educator Award.

ARTHUR N. APPLEBEE Leading Professor, School of Education at the University at Albany, State University of New York; Director of the Center on English Learning and Achievement. During his varied career, Dr. Applebee has been both a researcher and a teacher, working in institutional settings with children with severe learning problems, in public schools, as a staff member of the National Council of Teachers of English, and in professional education. Among his many books are *Curriculum as Conversation: Transforming Traditions of Teaching and Learning; Literature in the Secondary School: Studies of Curriculum and Instruction in the United States;* and *Tradition and Reform in the Teaching of English: A History.* He was elected to the International Reading Hall of Fame and has received, among other honors, the David H. Russell Award for Distinguished Research in the Teaching of English.

JIM BURKE Lecturer and Author; Teacher of English at Burlingame High School, Burlingame, California. Mr. Burke is a popular presenter at educational conferences across the country and is the author of numerous books for teachers, including *School Smarts: The Four Cs of Academic Success; The English Teacher's Companion; Reading Reminders; Writing Reminders;* and *ACCESSing School: Teaching Struggling Readers to Achieve Academic and Personal Success.* He is the recipient of NCTE's Exemplary English Leadership Award and was inducted into the California Reading Association's Hall of Fame.

DOUGLAS CARNINE Professor of Education at the University of Oregon; Director of the Western Region Reading First Technical Assistance Center. Dr. Carnine is nationally known for his focus on research-based practices in education, especially curriculum designs that prepare instructors of K–12 students. He has received the Lifetime Achievement Award from the Council for Exceptional Children and the Ersted Award for outstanding teaching at the University of Oregon. Dr. Carnine frequently consults on educational policy with government groups, businesses, communities, and teacher unions.

YVETTE JACKSON Executive Director of the National Urban Alliance for Effective Education. Nationally recognized for her work in assessing the learning potential of underachieving urban students, Dr. Jackson is also a presenter for the Harvard Principal Center and is a member of the Differentiation Faculty of the Association for Supervision and Curriculum Development. Dr. Jackson's research focuses on literacy, gifted education, and cognitive mediation theory. She designed the Comprehensive Education Plan for the New York City Public Schools and has served as their Director of Gifted Programs and Executive Director of Instruction and Professional Development.

ROBERT T. JIMÉNEZ Professor of Language, Literacy, and Culture at Vanderbilt University. Dr. Jiménez's research focuses on the language and literacy practices of Latino students. A former bilingual education teacher, he is now conducting research on how written language is thought about and used in contemporary Mexico. Dr. Jiménez has received several research and teaching honors, including two Fulbright awards from the Council for the International Exchange of Scholars and the Albert J. Harris Award from the International Reading Association. His published work has appeared in the *American Educational Research Journal, Reading Research Quarterly, The Reading Teacher, Journal of Adolescent and Adult Literacy,* and *Lectura y Vida.*

JUDITH A. LANGER Distinguished Professor at the University at Albany, State University of New York; Director of the Center on English Learning and Achievement; Director of the Albany Institute for Research in Education. An internationally known scholar in English language arts education, Dr. Langer specializes in developing teaching approaches that can enrich and improve what gets done on a daily basis in classrooms. Her publications include *Getting to Excellent: How to Create Better Schools* and *Effective Literacy Instruction: Building Successful Reading and Writing Programs.* She was inducted into the International Reading Hall of Fame and has received many other notable awards, including an honorary doctorate from the University of Uppsala, Sweden, for her research on literacy education.

ROBERT J. MARZANO Senior Scholar at Mid-Continent Research for Education and Learning (McREL); Associate Professor at Cardinal Stritch University in Milwaukee, Wisconsin; President of Marzano & Associates. An internationally known researcher, trainer, and speaker, Dr. Marzano has developed programs that translate research and theory into practical tools for K–12 teachers and administrators. He has written extensively on such topics as reading and writing instruction, thinking skills, school effectiveness, assessment, and standards implementation. His books include *Building Background Knowledge for Academic Achievement; Classroom Management That Works: Research-Based Strategies for Every Teacher;* and *What Works in Schools: Translating Research Into Action.*

DONNA M. OGLE Professor of Reading and Language at National-Louis University in Chicago, Illinois; Past President of the International Reading Association. Creator of the well-known KWL strategy, Dr. Ogle has directed many staff development projects translating theory and research into school practice in middle and secondary schools throughout the United States and has served as a consultant on literacy projects worldwide. Her extensive international experience includes coordinating the Reading and Writing for Critical Thinking Project in Eastern Europe, developing integrated curriculum for a USAID Afghan Education Project, and speaking and consulting on projects in several Latin American countries and in Asia. Her books include *Coming Together as Readers; Reading Comprehension: Strategies for Independent Learners; All Children Read;* and *Literacy for a Democratic Society.*

CAROL BOOTH OLSON Senior Lecturer in the Department of Education at the University of California, Irvine; Director of the UCI site of the National Writing Project. Dr. Olson writes and lectures extensively on the reading/writing connection, critical thinking through writing, interactive strategies for teaching writing, and the use of multicultural literature with students of culturally diverse backgrounds. She has received many awards, including the California Association of Teachers of English Award of Merit, the Outstanding California Education Research Award, and the UC Irvine Excellence in Teaching Award. Dr. Olson's books include *Reading, Thinking, and Writing About Multicultural Literature* and *The Reading/Writing Connection: Strategies for Teaching and Learning in the Secondary Classroom.*

CAROL ANN TOMLINSON Professor of Educational Research, Foundations, and Policy at the University of Virginia; Co-Director of the University's Institutes on Academic Diversity. An internationally known expert on differentiated instruction, Dr. Tomlinson helps teachers and administrators develop effective methods of teaching academically diverse learners. She was a teacher of middle and high school English for 22 years prior to teaching at the University of Virginia. Her books on differentiated instruction have been translated into eight languages. Among her many publications are *How to Differentiate Instruction in Mixed-Ability Classrooms* and *The Differentiated Classroom: Responding to the Needs of All Learners.*

ENGLISH LEARNER SPECIALISTS

MARY LOU McCLOSKEY Past President of Teachers of English to Speakers of Other Languages (TESOL); Director of Teacher Development and Curriculum Design for Educo in Atlanta, Georgia. Dr. McCloskey is a former teacher in multilingual and multicultural classrooms. She has worked with teachers, teacher educators, and departments of education around the world on teaching English as a second and foreign language. She is author of *On Our Way to English, Voices in Literature, Integrating English,* and *Visions: Language, Literature, Content.* Her awards include the Le Moyne College Ignatian Award for Professional Achievement and the TESOL D. Scott Enright Service Award.

LYDIA STACK International ESL consultant. Her areas of expertise are English language teaching strategies, ESL standards for students and teachers, and curriculum writing. Her teaching experience includes 25 years as an elementary and high school ESL teacher. She is a past president of TESOL. Her awards include the James E. Alatis Award for Service to TESOL (2003) and the San Francisco STAR Teacher Award (1989). Her publications include *On Our Way to English; Wordways: Games for Language Learning;* and *Visions: Language, Literature, Content.*

CURRICULUM SPECIALIST

WILLIAM L. McBRIDE Curriculum Specialist. Dr. McBride is a nationally known speaker, educator, and author who now trains teachers in instructional methodologies. A former reading specialist, English teacher, and social studies teacher, he holds a Masters in Reading and a Ph.D. in Curriculum and Instruction from the University of North Carolina at Chapel Hill. Dr. McBride has contributed to the development of textbook series in language arts, social studies, science, and vocabulary. He is also known for his novel *Entertaining an Elephant,* which tells the story of a burned-out teacher who becomes re-inspired with both his profession and his life.

MEDIA SPECIALISTS

DAVID M. CONSIDINE Professor of Instructional Technology and Media Studies at Appalachian State University in North Carolina. Dr. Considine has served as a media literacy consultant to the U.S. government and to the media industry, including Discovery Communications and Cable in the Classroom. He has also conducted media literacy workshops and training for county and state health departments across the United States. Among his many publications are *Visual Messages: Integrating Imagery into Instruction,* and *Imagine That: Developing Critical Viewing and Thinking Through Children's Literature.*

LARKIN PAULUZZI Teacher and Media Specialist; trainer for the New Jersey Writing Project. Ms. Pauluzzi puts her extensive classroom experience to use in developing teacher-friendly curriculum materials and workshops in many different areas, including media literacy. She has led media literacy training workshops in several districts throughout Texas, guiding teachers in the meaningful and practical uses of media in the classroom. Ms. Pauluzzi has taught students at all levels, from Title I Reading to AP English IV. She also spearheads a technology club at her school, working with students to produce media and technology to serve both the school and the community.

LISA K. SCHEFFLER Teacher and Media Specialist. Ms. Scheffler has designed and taught media literacy and video production curriculum, in addition to teaching language arts and speech. Using her knowledge of mass communication theory, coupled with real classroom experience, she has developed ready-to-use materials that help teachers incorporate media literacy into their curricula. She has taught film and television studies at the University of North Texas and has served as a contributing writer for the Texas Education Agency's statewide viewing and representing curriculum.

TEACHER ADVISORS

These are some of the many educators from across the country who played a crucial role in the development of the tables of contents, the lesson design, and other key components of this program:

Virginia L. Alford, MacArthur High School, San Antonio, Texas

Yvonne L. Allen, Shaker Heights High School, Shaker Heights, Ohio

Dave T. Anderson, Hinsdale South High School, Darien, Illinois

Kacy Colleen Anglim, Portland Public Schools District, Portland, Oregon

Beverly Scott Bass, Arlington Heights High School, Fort Worth, Texas

Jordana Benone, North High School, Torrance, California

Patricia Blood, Howell High School, Farmingdale, New Jersey

Marjorie Bloom, Eau Gallie High School, Melbourne, Florida

Edward J. Blotzer, Wilkinsburg Junior/Senior High School, Wilkinsburg, Pennsylvania

Stephen D. Bournes, Evanston Township High School, Evanston, Illinois

Barbara M. Bowling, Mt. Tabor High School, Winston-Salem, North Carolina

Kiala Boykin-Givehand, Duval County Public Schools, Jacksonville, Florida

Laura L. Brown, Adlai Stevenson High School, Lincolnshire, Illinois

Cynthia Burke, Yavneh Academy, Dallas, Texas

Hoppy Chandler, San Diego City Schools, San Diego, California

Gary Chmielewski, St. Benedict High School, Chicago, Illinois

Delorse Cole-Stewart, Milwaukee Public Schools, Milwaukee, Wisconsin

Kathy Dahlgren, Skokie, Illinois

Diana Dilger, Rosa Parks Middle School, Dixmoor, Illinois

L. Calvin Dillon, Gaither High School, Tampa, Florida

Dori Dolata, Rufus King High School, Milwaukee, Wisconsin

Jon Epstein, Marietta High School, Marietta, Georgia

Helen Ervin, Fort Bend Independent School District, Sugarland, Texas

Sue Friedman, Buffalo Grove High School, Buffalo Grove, Illinois

Chris Gee, Bel Air High School, El Paso, Texas

Paula Grasel, The Horizon Center, Gainesville, Georgia

Christopher Guarraia, Centreville High School, Clifton, Virginia

Rochelle L. Greene-Brady, Kenwood Academy, Chicago, Illinois

Michele M. Hettinger, Niles West High School, Skokie, Illinois

Elizabeth Holcomb, Forest Hill High School, Jackson, Mississippi

Jim Horan, Hinsdale Central High School, Hinsdale, Illinois

James Paul Hunter, Oak Park-River Forest High School, Oak Park, Illinois

Susan P. Kelly, Director of Curriculum, Island Trees School District, Levittown, New York

Beverley A. Lanier, Varina High School, Richmond, Virginia

Pat Laws, Charlotte-Mecklenburg Schools, Charlotte, North Carolina

Diana R. Martinez, Treviño School of Communications & Fine Arts, Laredo, Texas

Natalie Martinez, Stephen F. Austin High School, Houston, Texas

Elizabeth Matarazzo, Ysleta High School, El Paso, Texas

Carol M. McDonald, J. Frank Dobie High School, Houston, Texas

Amy Millikan, Consultant, Chicago, Illinois

Terri Morgan, Caprock High School, Amarillo, Texas

Eileen Murphy, Walter Payton Preparatory High School, Chicago, Illinois

Lisa Omark, New Haven Public Schools, New Haven, Connecticut

Kaine Osburn, Wheeling High School, Wheeling, Illinois

Andrea J. Phillips, Terry Sanford High School, Fayetteville, North Carolina

Cathy Reilly, Sayreville Public Schools, Sayreville, New Jersey

Mark D. Simon, Neuqua Valley High School, Naperville, Illinois

Scott Snow, Sequin High School, Arlington, Texas

Jane W. Speidel, Brevard County Schools, Viera, Florida

Cheryl E. Sullivan, Lisle Community School District, Lisle, Illinois

Anita Usmiani, Hamilton Township Public Schools, Hamilton Square, New Jersey

Linda Valdez, Oxnard Union High School District, Oxnard, California

Nancy Walker, Longview High School, Longview, Texas

Kurt Weiler, New Trier High School, Winnetka, Illinois

Elizabeth Whittaker, Larkin High School, Elgin, Illinois

Linda S. Williams, Woodlawn High School, Baltimore, Maryland

John R. Williamson, Fort Thomas Independent Schools, Fort Thomas, Kentucky

Anna N. Winters, Simeon High School, Chicago, Illinois

Tonora D. Wyckoff, North Shore Senior High School, Houston, Texas

Karen Zajac, Glenbard South High School, Glen Ellyn, Illinois

Cynthia Zimmerman, Mose Vines Preparatory High School, Chicago, Illinois

Lynda Zimmerman, El Camino High School, South San Francisco, California

Ruth E. Zurich, Brown Deer High School, Brown Deer, Wisconsin

CONTENTS IN BRIEF

Online LITERATURE CLASSZONE.COM

LITERATURE AND READING CENTER
- Author Biographies
- Additional Selection Background
- Literary Analysis Frames
- Power Thinking Activities

WRITING AND GRAMMAR CENTER
- Writing Templates and Graphic Organizers
- Publishing Options
- Grammar Arcade

MEDIA CENTER
- Production Templates
- Analysis Guides

VOCABULARY AND SPELLING CENTER
- Vocabulary Strategies and Practice
- Vocabulary Flip Cards
- Spelling Lessons
- Multi-Language Glossary of Academic Vocabulary

RESEARCH CENTER
- Web Research Guide
- Citation Guide

ASSESSMENT CENTER
- Assessment Practice and Test-Taking Tips
- SAT/ACT Practice and Tips

MORE TECHNOLOGY

eEdition
- Interactive Selections
- Audio Summaries

WriteSmart
- Writing Prompts and Templates
- Interactive Student Models
- Interactive Graphic Organizers
- Interactive Revision Lessons
- Rubric Generator

MediaSmart
- Media Lessons
- Interactive Media Studies

EssaySmart
- Online Essay Analyzer

UNIT 1

What's Happening?
PLOT, CONFLICT, AND SETTING
• IN FICTION • IN NONFICTION • IN POETRY • IN DRAMA • IN MEDIA

VOCABULARY STRATEGIES

Denotations and connotations, *p. 40*   Literal and figurative meanings, *p. 98*

Suffixes, *p. 60*   Prefixes and Latin roots: *ject, p. 120*

Synonyms, *p. 72*   Word origins, *p. 132*

Person to Person
ANALYZING CHARACTER AND POINT OF VIEW
• IN FICTION • IN NONFICTION • IN POETRY • IN MEDIA

VOCABULARY STRATEGIES

Easily confused words, *p. 189*

Words for *water, p. 202*

Figurative language, *p. 220*

Context clues, *p. 252*

Latin roots: *press, p. 264*

Prefixes that mean "not," *p. 278*

UNIT 3

The Big Idea
UNDERSTANDING THEME

• IN FICTION • IN POETRY

Skills and Standards

Fables,
Set a Purpose for Reading

Theme in Poetry, Visualize

Recurring Theme,
Make Inferences

Thesis, Evidence

Theme and Topic, Compare and
Contrast, Make Inferences

VOCABULARY STRATEGIES

Latin roots: *rupt, p. 326*

Noun-forming suffixes, *p. 346*

Slang, *p. 363*

Multiple-meaning words, *p. 376*

UNIT 4

Writer's Craft
MOOD, TONE, AND STYLE

• IN FICTION • IN NONFICTION • IN POETRY • IN DRAMA • IN MEDIA

Skills and Standards
Mood, Tone, Style, Elements of
Style, Comparing Styles

VOCABULARY STRATEGIES

Similes, *p. 435*   Latin roots: *pro, p. 476*
Compound words, *p. 460*   Dictionary usage labels, *p. 487*

UNIT

5

Word Pictures
THE LANGUAGE OF POETRY

VOCABULARY STRATEGIES

Specialized vocabulary, *p. 565*   Latin roots: *lect, p. 601*

UNIT 6

Timeless Tales
MYTHS, LEGENDS, AND TALES

VOCABULARY STRATEGIES

Context clues, *p. 654*   Connotations, *p. 707*

Reference aids, *p. 668*   General context clues, *p. 720*

Homonyms, *p. 686*   Base words, *p. 740*

UNIT 7

Life Stories
BIOGRAPHY AND AUTOBIOGRAPHY
• IN NONFICTION • IN POETRY • IN MEDIA

VOCABULARY STRATEGIES

Idioms, *p. 778*   Foreign Words in English, *p. 810*
Analogies, *p. 794*

UNIT 8

Know the Facts
INFORMATION, ARGUMENT, AND PERSUASION
• IN NONFICTION • IN MEDIA

VOCABULARY STRATEGIES

Word origins, *p. 854*   Synonyms, *p. 898*

Multiple-meaning words, *p. 862*   Context clues, *p. 907*

Word parts, *p. 878*   Connotations, *p. 913*

Investigation and Discovery
THE POWER OF RESEARCH

Student Resource Bank

Selections by Genre

READER'S WORKSHOPS

 LITERATURE CENTER at ClassZone.com

SPEAKING, LISTENING, AND VIEWING

 MEDIA CENTER at ClassZone.com

WRITING WORKSHOPS

 WriteSmart

MEDIA STUDY

MediaSmart DVD

VOCABULARY STRATEGIES

GRAMMAR AND WRITING

The Power of Ideas

INTRODUCING THE ESSENTIALS

- Literary Genres Workshop
- Reading Strategies Workshop
- Writing Process Workshop

What Are Life's Big Questions?

The challenges we face in life can raise many questions, including the ones shown here. Such questions get us thinking about ideas—such as friendship, freedom, and fitting in—that affect our lives. Through our attempts to find answers, we come closer to understanding our choices, actions, and mistakes. Sometimes, reading a powerful piece of literature can help us make sense of how we got where we are and where we want to go now.

What is a FRIEND?

There's nothing better than spending time with a true friend—whether that friend is someone your age, an older person with wisdom to share, or even a family pet. How do you know for certain that you have a friend you can count on in good and bad times? Many of the stories, poems, and plays you'll read in this book will help you think about what it takes to be a friend.

Who's really IN CHARGE?

Some people want to tell you how to live your life, giving opinions about everything from what you should wear to what you should be when you grow up. It's good to listen to advice, but how can you be sure you're charting your own course? In this book, you'll meet all kinds of characters and real people who have to decide who's *really* in charge.

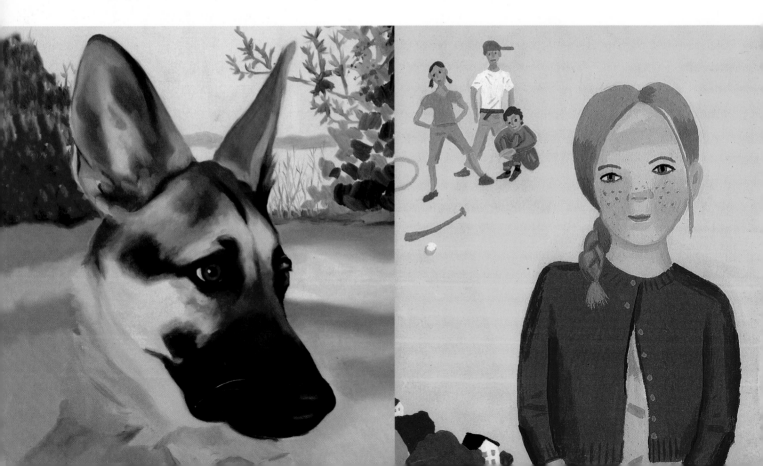

When is STRENGTH *more than muscle?*

Strength isn't always physical. Emotional strength and courage can be just as powerful. This book is filled with characters who find an inner source of strength when standing up to bullies, confronting deadly creatures, or experiencing impossible problems.

When is CHANGE *good?*

Change is all around you. Leaves turn from green to red, birds migrate from north to south, day turns to night. You deal with change at the start of each school year when you're faced with new classes, new friends, new problems. Why is change both exciting and scary? You'll consider this question as you read about people who confront changes, big and small.

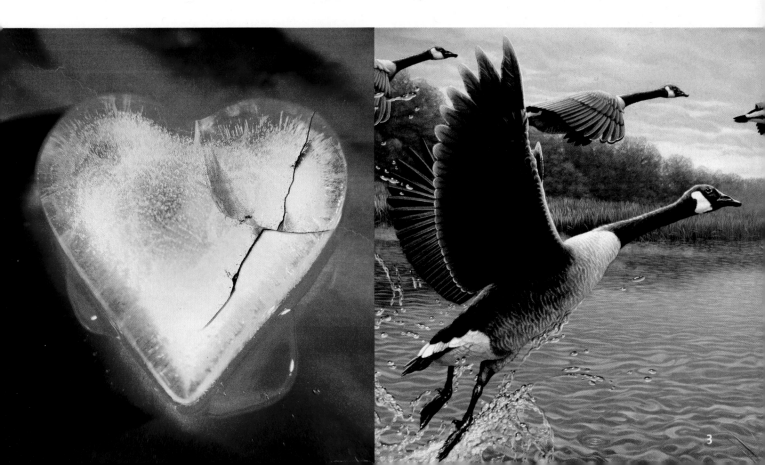

Reading Literature

You've been reading for most of your life, from your favorite childhood fairy tales to the novels, plays, and Web sites you encounter today. What more can you possibly learn about reading? In this book, you'll take your reading to a new level. Get started by discovering how literature can help you explore ideas that matter.

The Genres

Think about the ideas and questions that you talk about with your friends. For example, do you ever wonder about what it means to fit in or how it feels to be alone? You may be surprised to learn that writers often explore these same ideas, recording their thoughts for others to read and consider.

Writers use different forms to share their ideas with readers. Some writers dream up novels or poems, for instance. Others create blogs or movie screenplays. The main forms writers use are called **genres.**

GENRES AT A GLANCE

FICTION
Fiction refers to made-up stories about characters and events.
- short stories
- novels
- novellas
- folk tales

POETRY
Poetry is a type of literature in which words are chosen and arranged in a precise way to create specific effects.
- haiku
- limericks
- narrative poems

DRAMA
Dramas are stories that are meant to be performed.
- comedies
- historical dramas
- radio plays

NONFICTION
Nonfiction tells about real people, places, and events.
- autobiographies
- biographies
- essays
- speeches
- news articles
- reference articles

TYPES OF MEDIA

The word *media* refers to communication that reaches many people.
- TV shows
- advertising
- Web sites

READING FICTION

There's nothing quite like being swept away by a good work of fiction, whether it's a novel, a short story, or a folk tale. These strategies can help you make the most of your journey.

- **Make connections.** As you get to know the characters, ask yourself: Have I experienced similar situations or feelings in my own life?

- **Picture the scene.** Note descriptions of characters and settings. Use these descriptions to help you visualize a lifelike picture in your mind.

- **Predict what will happen.** At each twist and turn, ask: What's going to happen next? Then read on to find out if you guessed correctly.

- **Track the events.** Every story follows a **plot,** or a series of events that traces a problem. Keep track of the events in your notebook.

Read the Model *Number the Stars* is about a young girl named Annemarie, who lives in Denmark in 1943. German soldiers have taken over her city with the intent of imprisoning all Jewish people, including Annemarie's best friend Ellen. In this excerpt, Annemarie challenges Ellen to a race. Use the strategies to explore the **key idea** of fear.

from
Number the Stars

Novel by **Lois Lowry**

Annemarie outdistanced her friend quickly, even though one of her shoes came untied as she sped along the street called Østerbrogade, past the small shops and cafés of her neighborhood here in northeast Copenhagen. Laughing, she skirted an elderly lady in black who carried
5   a shopping bag made of string. A young woman pushing a baby in a carriage moved aside to make way. The corner was just ahead.

Annemarie looked up, panting, just as she reached the corner. Her laughter stopped. Her heart seemed to skip a beat.

"Halte!" the soldier ordered in a stern voice.

10   The German word was as familiar as it was frightening. Annemarie had heard it often enough before, but it had never been directed at her until now.

Close Read

1. What do you think the soldier will say to Annemarie? Make a prediction, based on what you've read so far.

2. **Key Idea: Fear** If you were in a scary situation like Annemarie's, would you be able to hide your **fear?** Would most people be able to? Explain.

rain
rattles
pane

READING POETRY

A red wheelbarrow, windshield wipers, war—a poet can create poems about anything. Yet, poets express their ideas differently than fiction writers do. For example, poets arrange their thoughts in **lines,** rather than sentences. Lines are often grouped into **stanzas,** instead of paragraphs. Use these strategies to fully appreciate any poem you read.

- **Examine the form.** First, notice how the poem looks on the page. Are the lines long or short? Are they grouped into stanzas?

- **Notice the punctuation.** In a poem, a single sentence can continue over many lines. Use the punctuation to help you figure out when to pause while reading.

- **Read the poem aloud.** Listen for the poem's musical rhymes or rhythms.

- **Form a mental picture.** Look for words and phrases that can help you imagine what's being described.

Read the Model As you read this poem, notice how the writer uses the description of an old quilt to explore the **key idea** of family.

ACADEMIC VOCABULARY FOR POETRY

- form
- line
- stanza
- rhythm
- rhyme

Quilt

Poem by
Janet S. Wong

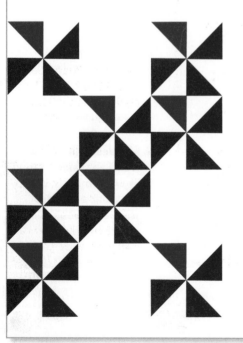

Our family
is a quilt

of odd remnants[1]
patched together

5   in a strange
pattern,

threads fraying,
fabric wearing thin—

but made to keep
10 its warmth

even in bitter
cold.

---

1. **remnants:** leftovers; remainders.

Close Read

1. Read the poem aloud, pausing only where there is punctuation. How many sentences are in this poem? How many lines and stanzas are there?

2. **Key Idea: Family** This poem compares a family with a quilt. How does this comparison help you understand the positive qualities of **family?**

READING DRAMA

A drama is meant to be acted out for an audience. However, it can be just as exciting on the page as it is on the stage. To read drama, you have to visualize the action in the theater of your mind. These strategies can help.

- **Read the play silently, then aloud with others.** Sometimes, hearing the dialogue can help you better understand what's happening.

- **Read the stage directions.** Often printed in *italic type,* **stage directions** are the writer's notes about everything from the setting and props to the characters' feelings and movements. Use these notes to help you picture the setting, action, and characters.

- **Get to know the characters.** Characters' words and actions tell you what they are like. Pay attention to their **dialogue,** or what they say, as well as the stage directions.

Read the Model Sara is treated like a princess at school because of her family's wealth. After her family fortune is lost, however, she must become a servant. In this excerpt, Becky, the school maid, comforts Sara. The two girls have always been friends, despite their different circumstances. What is the author suggesting about the **key idea** of differences?

ACADEMIC VOCABULARY FOR DRAMA

- plot
- character
- act
- scene
- dialogue
- stage directions

from

The Little Princess

Novel by **Frances Hodgson Burnett**
Dramatized by **Adele Thane**

Becky. I just wanted to ask you, miss—you've been such a rich young lady and been waited on hand and foot. What'll you do now, miss, without any maid? Please, would you let me wait on you after I'm done with my pots and kettles?

5   **Sara** (*with a sob*). Oh, Becky! Do you remember when I told you that we were just the same? Not a rich girl and a poor girl, but just two girls.
Becky. Yes, miss. You said it was an accident that I was not you and you were not me.
Sara. Well, you see how true it is, Becky. There's no difference now. I'm
10   not a princess any more. (BECKY *presses* SARA's *hand to her cheek.*)
Becky. Yes, miss, you are! Whatever happens to you, you'll be a princess just the same—and nothing could make it any different.

Close Read

1. How does Becky feel about Sara? How does Sara feel about Becky? How can you tell?

2. **Key Idea: Differences** Becky and Sara are friends, even though they come from different backgrounds. What other **differences** can people overcome in the name of friendship?

The Daily News
Today's Headlines

READING NONFICTION

From articles on the Web to front-page news, nonfiction is all around you. It includes not only informational texts like encyclopedia entries and news articles, but also autobiographies, essays, and speeches. By reading different types of nonfiction, you can learn about real people, places, events, and issues that matter.

ACADEMIC VOCABULARY FOR NONFICTION

- purpose
- organization
- main idea
- text features

TYPES OF NONFICTION

AUTOBIOGRAPHY/ BIOGRAPHY
The true story of a person's life, told by that person (autobiography) or by someone else (biography)

NEWS ARTICLE
Factual writing that reports on recent events

Homeless Dolphins to Get Back Together in Bahamas

JACKSON, Miss. (AP) — Several dolphins that were swept out to sea by Hurricane Katrina will soon be reunited at a resort in the Bahamas.

A resort on Paradise Island in the Bahamas will take on 17 dolphins from the Marine Life Oceanarium—eight of which were rescued from open water in September.

"The dolphins, I think, are a symbol of everything that's happened on the Gulf Coast and to find a new home for them—that's something that we hope will happen for everybody on the coast," said Howard Karawan, president and managing director of the company that owns the resort.

ESSAY
A short piece of writing about a single subject

What Video Games Can Teach Us
Emily Sohn

REFERENCE ARTICLE
Informative writing that provides facts and background on a specific subject

COYOTES
Wildlife Sense and Safety

SPEECH
An oral presentation of a speaker's ideas or beliefs

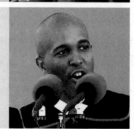

CONSUMER DOCUMENT
Printed material that usually comes with a product or a service

HOW TO USE YOUR DIGITAL MP3 PLAYER
A STEP-BY-STEP GUIDE

Strategies For Reading

- **Consider the purpose.** Is the writer trying to persuade, inspire, or inform? Understanding the purpose can help you know what to look for in the text.

- **Note the main ideas.** As you read, look for the **main ideas,** or the most important points about a topic. Record these ideas in a notebook to help you remember them.

- **Preview the text.** Some types of nonfiction have **text features,** like subheadings or captions. Before you read, look at the features to get a sense of what the text is about.

- **Examine the graphic aids.** Photographs and illustrations also convey information. Think about how they add to your understanding of a topic.

MODEL 1: READING A BIOGRAPHY

This excerpt is from a biography about Steven Spielberg, a famous movie director. How does it help you understand the **key idea** of inspiration?

from
Steven Spielberg:
Crazy *for* Movies

Biography by
Susan Goldman Rubin

When Steven Spielberg was ten, his father woke him up and took him out to the desert near where they lived in Phoenix, Arizona. They spread out a blanket and lay on their backs looking up at the sky. Steven's father, Arnold Spielberg, liked astronomy and hoped to see a comet
5 that was supposed to appear. Instead, they saw a meteor shower. "The stars were just tremendous," recalled Arnold. "They were so intense it was frightening." He gave Steven a scientific explanation of what was happening.

"But I didn't want to hear that," said Steven. "I wanted to think of
10 them as falling stars." That memory of falling stars stayed with him and inspired his first full-length movie, *Firelight*.

Close Read

1. What do you learn about Steven Spielberg from this excerpt?

2. **Key Idea: Inspiration** The memory of a meteor shower led Spielberg to create science-fiction films. What other experiences might **inspire** people to pursue certain careers?

MODEL 2: READING A REFERENCE ARTICLE

Turning a moment of inspiration into a life-long career takes more than just wishing on a falling star. Hard work and a curious mind are essential. As you read this Web article, think about the **key idea** of curiosity.

BACK FORWARD STOP REFRESH HOME PRINT

Meteors

Student reference article

Meteors are small particles of stone and <u>iron</u> that enter the earth's atmosphere at great speeds. <u>Friction</u> with the atmosphere causes intense heat, triggering the meteor to give off a brilliant light. This flying bright light creates the appearance of a shooting or falling star.

Meteorites

Most meteors burn up before they reach the earth's surface. Occasionally, though, very large meteors—called meteorites—make impact with the earth's surface.

This meteorite was found at the edge of the Kalahari Desert.

Close Read

1. What do you learn about this article simply by previewing the title, the subheading, and the photograph?

2. **Key Idea: Curiosity** People have always been fascinated by mysteries of science and nature. What scientific mysteries have sparked your **curiosity**?

READING THE MEDIA

Has an ad persuaded you to buy something you didn't need? Do you ever find yourself glued to the television or unable to tear yourself away from the Web? Media messages influence your life in all kinds of ways. That's why it's important to become **media literate**—that is, learn how to "read," analyze, and evaluate what you see and hear.

ACADEMIC VOCABULARY FOR MEDIA

- medium
- message
- target audience

TYPE OF MEDIA	STRATEGIES FOR VIEWING	
FILMS AND TV SHOWS Motion pictures, shown in movie theaters or broadcast on television, that tell stories	• **Know what's happening.** Ask a friend or an adult if you're confused about the plot. • **Spot the techniques.** Ask yourself: How does the director use sound and visuals to make the story more interesting?	
NEWS MEDIA Reports of recent events in newspapers and magazines and on TV, the radio, and the Web	• **Get the facts.** Make sure the report answers the questions *who, what, when, where, why,* and *how?* • **Evaluate the information.** Ask yourself: Can I trust what I'm seeing and hearing?	 **FIREFIGHTERS BATTLE BLAZE**
ADVERTISING The promotion of products, services, and ideas using print and broadcast media	• **Recognize the pitch.** Consider what the sponsor wants the audience to buy, believe, or do. • **Don't be duped by dazzle.** Visuals and sounds can be persuasive. Don't let flashy techniques influence your decisions.	
WEB SITES Collections of related pages on the World Wide Web; include hyperlinks and menus	• **Know the source.** Anyone can publish on the Web. Ask: Is this a good source of information? • **Don't get lost!** Always remember your purpose for visiting a site so you don't veer too far off course.	

Strategies That Work: Literature

❶ Ask Yourself the Right Questions

Sometimes, reading literature can be a challenge. That's why it helps to ask the right questions before, during, and after you read.

Stage of Reading	Kinds of Questions
Before Know what you're reading and why.	• What is this selection about? • Why am I reading? to be entertained? to learn something?
During Check your understanding.	• What's happening in the selection? Which parts are confusing to me? • What details help me to picture the scene in my mind?
After Analyze the selection and explore its key ideas.	• What might be the selection's theme, or its message about life? • What is unique about the author's style, or way of writing?

❷ Make Connections

Literature is more meaningful when you connect to it personally. Use these strategies to "get into" a text.

- **Connect to Your Life** Is fear paralyzing? What makes a family? Think about how your own experiences can help you understand the ideas in literature.

- **Connect to Other Subjects** The effects of fear, meteor showers, careers—the subjects you read about can help you learn more about the world. If a subject interests you, investigate it on the Web.

❸ Record Your Reactions

Jot down your questions, thoughts, and impressions in a **Reader's Notebook.** Try one of these formats.

JOURNAL

Write your reactions as you read.

> ### The Little Princess
> Becky treats Sara like a princess, even though Sara is no longer rich. It's interesting that Becky still views Sara the same way.

GRAPHIC ORGANIZER

After reading, create a graphic organizer to deepen your understanding of events and characters.

Becky's Traits	Evidence
polite	calls Sara "miss"
comforting	presses Sara's hand to her cheek
loyal	tells Sara she is still a princess no matter what

Becoming an Active Reader

To really appreciate stories, poems, plays, and articles, you have to be able to understand what you're reading. These strategies can help you unlock the meaning of all kinds of texts, including novels, newspapers, blogs, and even blockbuster movies. Which strategies do you recognize? Which are new to you?

SKILLS AND STRATEGIES FOR ACTIVE READING

Preview
Look at the title, the pictures, and the first paragraph. What do they tell you about what you're about to read?

Set a Purpose
Know *why* you are reading—for information, for enjoyment, or to understand a process?

Connect
Think about whether the characters or situations remind you of people or experiences in your own life.

Use Prior Knowledge
Jot down what you already know about a topic. Use these notes to help you make sense of what you read.

Predict
Guess what will happen next. Look for details in the selection that serve as clues.

Visualize
Picture the scene in your mind, using the writer's descriptions of settings, characters, and events.

Monitor
Check your understanding as you read.
- **Question** what is happening and why.
- **Clarify** what is unclear to you by rereading or asking for help.

Make Inferences
Make logical guesses about characters and events by considering details in the text and your own experiences.

Details in "The Circuit"	What I Know	My Inference
"Ito, the strawberry sharecropper, did not smile" when the season was ending.	People in charge get worried or unhappy when business slows down.	Ito is probably unhappy that the strawberry-picking season is over because that's how he makes a living.

Panchito is a young Mexican-American boy whose family frequently moves in search of farm work. The time has come for Panchito's family to move—again. How will he react? As you read an excerpt from this story, use the **Close Read** questions to practice the strategies you just learned.

from

The Circuit

Short story by **Francisco Jiménez**

I t was that time of year again. Ito, the strawberry sharecropper, did not smile. It was natural. The peak of the strawberry season was over and the last few days the workers, most of them *braceros,*[1] were not picking as many boxes as they had during the months of June and July.

5   As the last days of August disappeared, so did the number of *braceros.* Sunday, only one—the best picker—came to work. I liked him. Sometimes we talked during our half-hour lunch break. That is how I found out he was from Jalisco, the same state in Mexico my family was from. That Sunday was the last time I saw him.

10   When the sun had tired and sunk behind the mountains, Ito signaled us that it was time to go home. *"Ya esora,"*[2] he yelled in his broken Spanish. Those were the words I waited for twelve hours a day, every day, seven days a week, week after week. And the thought of not hearing them again saddened me.

15   As we drove home, Papa did not say a word. With both hands on the wheel, he stared at the dirt road. My older brother, Roberto, was also silent. He leaned his head back and closed his eyes. Once in a while he cleared from his throat the dust that blew in from outside.

    Yes, it was that time of year. When I opened the front door to the
20 shack, I stopped. Everything we owned was neatly packed in cardboard boxes. Suddenly I felt even more the weight of hours, days, weeks, and months of work. I sat down on a box. The thought of having to move to Fresno and knowing what was in store for me there brought tears to my eyes.

---

1. ***braceros*** (brä-sĕ'rôs) *Spanish*: Hispanic farm workers.
2. ***Ya esora***: a made-up spelling for the sharecropper's pronunciation of the Spanish expression *Ya es hora* (yä'ĕs-ô'rä), which means "It is time."

Close Read

1. **Monitor** Reread the boxed text. Why is Panchito sad to hear the words *Ya esora* this time?

2. **Connect** If you suddenly found out that you were moving, would you react as Panchito does? Consider whether you would get used to moving or dread it every time.

25 That night I could not sleep. I lay in bed thinking about how much I hated this move.

A little before five o'clock in the morning, Papa woke everyone up. A few minutes later, the yelling and screaming of my little brothers and sisters, for whom the move was a great adventure, broke the silence of 30 dawn. Shortly, the barking of the dogs accompanied them.

While we packed the breakfast dishes, Papa went outside to start the "Carcanchita." That was the name Papa gave his old '38 black Plymouth. He bought it in a used-car lot in Santa Rosa in the winter of 1949. Papa was very proud of his car. *"Mi Carcanchita,"* my little jalopy,[3] 35 he called it. He had a right to be proud of it. He spent a lot of time looking at other cars before buying this one. When he finally chose the "Carcanchita," he checked it thoroughly before driving it out of the car lot. He examined every inch of the car. He listened to the motor, tilting his head from side to side like a parrot, trying to detect any noises that 40 spelled car trouble. After being satisfied with the looks and sounds of the car, Papa then insisted on knowing who the original owner was. He never did find out from the car salesman. But he bought the car anyway. Papa figured the original owner must have been an important man, because behind the rear seat of the car he found a blue necktie.

45 Papa parked the car out in front and left the motor running. *"Listo,"*[4] he yelled. Without saying a word, Roberto and I began to carry the boxes out to the car. Roberto carried the two big boxes and I carried the smaller ones. Papa then threw the mattress on top of the car roof and tied it with ropes to the front and rear bumpers.

50 Everything was packed except Mama's pot. It was an old large galvanized pot she had picked up at an army surplus store in Santa Maria the year I was born. The pot was full of dents and nicks, and the more dents and nicks it had, the more Mama liked it. *"Mi olla,"*[5] she used to say proudly.

55 I held the front door open as Mama carefully carried out her pot by both handles, making sure not to spill the cooked beans. When she got to the car, Papa reached out to help her with it. Roberto opened the rear car door, and Papa gently placed it on the floor behind the front seat. All of us then climbed in. Papa sighed, wiped the sweat off his forehead 60 with his sleeve, and said wearily, *"Es todo."*[6]

As we drove away, I felt a lump in my throat. I turned around and looked at our little shack for the last time. . . .

---

3. **jalopy:** a shabby, old car.

4. *listo* (lē'stô) *Spanish:* ready.

5. *mi olla* (mē ô' yä) *Spanish:* my pot.

6. *Es todo* (ĕs tô'dô) *Spanish:* That's everything.

3. **Make Inferences** Reread lines 25–30. Why would younger kids—more than someone Panchito's age—view moving as an adventure?

4. **Visualize** What details in lines 31–44 help you to picture the family car and the father's initial inspection of it?

5. **Predict** Do you think Panchito will eventually adjust to life in Fresno? Try to guess what will happen once he arrives.

Strategies That Work: Reading

❶ Know Your Purpose

Determining ahead of time *why* you are reading can help you choose the right strategy to use. Consider these purposes and strategies.

Purpose	Strategy
For enjoyment	▶ Don't rush. Read at a comfortable pace for *you*.
To learn or become informed	▶ Take notes on the main ideas and supporting details as you read.
For research	▶ Skim the subheadings, captions, and graphics to quickly determine if a text has the information you're looking for.
To follow directions	▶ Be sure you understand each step. Use illustrations or photographs as guides.

❷ Take Notes

Jotting down your impressions as you read can deepen your understanding of a selection. In your notebook, create a two-column chart. In one column, write details or quotations from the selection. In the other, record your thoughts.

"The Circuit"	My Thoughts
Panchito worked "twelve hours a day, every day, seven days a week, week after week." (lines 12–13)	That seems like an impossible amount of work. I hope Panchito won't have to work so hard when his family moves to Fresno.

❸ Create a Personal Word List

When you encounter words that are unfamiliar to you, look them up. Start a list of these words and their meanings, and add new words as you come across them.

- **Choose your words.** Consider writing down the vocabulary words for each selection, as well as any other words you find challenging.
- **Know more than the definition.** Knowing synonyms (same), antonyms (opposite), and context (use in a sentence) adds to your total understanding of a word's meaning.
- **Practice makes perfect.** Visit the **Vocabulary Center** at **ClassZone.com** for more practice.

Word	Meaning
surplus (n.) "The Circuit," line 51	**Definition**: extra materials or supplies **Synonym**: excess **Antonym**: shortage **Sentence**: The owners donated the restaurant's <u>surplus</u> of canned goods to a local hospital.

Expressing Ideas in Writing

Writing is a way of discovering what you think and feel, and also a way to share ideas with others. You may write with a practical need—e-mailing a friend with a homework question, for example. Or, you may have a grander purpose, such as persuading a politician to see your viewpoint. Either way, writing can help you find your voice and share it with the world.

Consider Your Options

Are you writing a speech for your school assembly, a thank-you letter to a relative, or a message-board posting about last night's episode? Before you capture your ideas on paper, make sure you know your **purpose, audience,** and **format.**

PURPOSE	**AUDIENCE**	**FORMAT**
Why am I writing?	**Who are my readers?**	**Which format will best suit my purpose and audience?**
• to entertain	• classmates	• essay • journal entry
• to inform or explain	• teachers	• letter • research paper
• to persuade	• friends	• poem
• to describe	• myself	• short story • script
• to express thoughts and feelings	• community members	• review • power presentation
	• Web users	• speech • Web site
	• customer service at a company	

Continue the Process

Every writer eventually discovers the process that best suits his or her working style. The **Writing Workshops** in this book are designed to help you find the path to your best writing. The process described here can serve as your starting point.

THE WRITING PROCESS

What Should I Do?

What Does It Look Like?

PREWRITING
Explore your ideas in a graphic organizer or by freewriting. Then decide what you want to write about.

FREEWRITING

> It must be scary living in a town where soldiers patrol the streets. But some kids in the world deal with that in their daily lives. Maybe I will write about what it takes to be brave in scary situations.

DRAFTING
Turn your ideas into a first draft. If you're writing a formal essay, you may want to **draft from an outline.** If you're doing more informal writing, consider **drafting to discover,** letting your ideas take shape as you go.

OUTLINE

> 1. Being brave in the face of fear takes determination and a calm attitude.
>   A. Annemarie doesn't let the soldiers' presence stop her from racing her friend.
>   B. She remains calm when the soldier addresses her.

REVISING AND EDITING
Review what you've written. Are your ideas, style, and structure solid? Now is the time to do fine-tuning in all these areas.
- Check your work against a **rubric** (page 18).
- Ask a **peer** to give you feedback.
- **Proofread** for errors in spelling and grammar.

PEER SUGGESTIONS

> In <u>Number the stars</u>, the main character is brave.
> Suggestion: Why not begin with a more engaging sentence? Try: Annemarie must call on courage when she least expects to in Lois Lowry's novel <u>Number the Stars</u>.

PUBLISHING
Share your written ideas with a community of readers. Where you publish depends on your **purpose, audience,** and **format.**

Do a Self-Check

Even professional writers know there's always room for improvement. Use this rubric to determine if your draft is strong in all key trait categories.

KEY TRAITS RUBRIC

	Strong	Average	Weak
Ideas 1	• has a clear topic • supports statements with relevant details	• has a topic that needs more focus • includes some details but not enough	• has no clear topic • lacks details or includes ones that are unrelated to the topic
Organization 2	• begins with an interesting introduction and ends with a satisfying conclusion • uses transitions between ideas	• has an introduction and a conclusion, but they could be more interesting • needs more transitions to connect ideas	• has no introduction or conclusion • presents a confusing jumble of unrelated ideas
Voice 3	• reflects the writer's unique personality • has a tone that fits the audience and purpose	• shows a lack of interest in the topic • sounds too formal or informal at times	• has no life • uses a completely inappropriate tone
Word Choice 4	• uses vivid words • expresses ideas in a way that sounds natural	• uses words that are correct, but ordinary • sounds forced or awkward at times	• uses words that are too general or incorrect • fails to make the meaning clear
Sentence Fluency 5	• includes sentences of varying length and type	• varies sentence length and type somewhat, but not enough	• includes mostly short or overly long sentences
Conventions 6	• has few errors in grammar, usage, and mechanics	• includes some errors, but readers can still follow the ideas	• has so many errors that the writing is hard to understand

Strategies That Work: Writing

❶ Use Prewriting Strategies

Try different strategies to get your ideas flowing. Find one that works best for you and for the assignment.

- **Freewrite.** For ten minutes, jot down whatever crosses your mind.
- **Get graphic.** Generate ideas in a web or a chart.
- **Look and listen.** Carry a notebook while on the go each day. Record interesting sights and conversations.
- **Ask: What if?** What if kids were in charge of the town for a day? You could find an intriguing topic by answering a "what if" question.

❷ Get Friendly Feedback

Consider exchanging work with other writers. Feedback can help at any stage of the process, but remember these guidelines as you work.

When You're the Writer	When You're the Reader
• Ask for specific feedback. Do you want readers to comment on ideas, or simply check grammar and spelling? • Be open, patient, and polite when listening to others' suggestions. • Remember that the final decisions are yours. Consider all feedback, but only use what you find helpful.	• Tell the writer what you like, as well as what you think needs improvement. • Support all your feedback with specific examples. • Respect the writer. Know that the writer will make the final decisions about his or her work.

❸ Read, Read, Read

Reading work by other students, professional writers, and classic authors is a valuable way to develop your style. Seek out these sources.

LITERATURE

The literature in this book can serve as inspiration. You can also look to novels and daily news sources.

WRITING COMMUNITY

Start a writing group with your peers. Share your works-in-progress and the finished pieces you are proud of.

ONLINE RESOURCES

Visit the **Writing Center** at **ClassZone.com** for models and links to publication sites.

What's Happening?

PLOT, CONFLICT, AND SETTING

- In Fiction
- In Nonfiction
- In Poetry
- In Drama
- In Media

Share What You Know

How do you build a STORY?

A **story** can take many different shapes, but all stories share some basic elements. Like a bricklayer building a wall, a writer builds a story layer by layer. The writer might start with an interesting character and add an important event. Or, he or she might start by describing a place far away and see where that leads. If the writer is successful, the finished story will capture the reader's attention and never let go.

ACTIVITY Think of one of your favorite stories—it might be based on fact, such as a book about an ancient mystery, or pure fantasy, such as the classic story *Alice's Adventures in Wonderland*. Ask yourself these questions:

• What made the story interesting?

• What did the story make you feel?

• What part of the story do you remember most clearly?

In a small group, discuss your answers to the questions and consider what makes a story powerful.

Preview Unit Goals

LITERARY ANALYSIS	• Identify and analyze plot elements, conflicts, and setting • Identify foreshadowing • Analyze narrative nonfiction and narrative poetry
READING	• Develop strategies for reading, including monitoring, visualizing, and connecting • Make inferences, identify sequence, and trace chronological order • Use text features to comprehend informational text • Identify author's purpose
WRITING AND GRAMMAR	• Write a short story • Use commas correctly in dates, addresses, and letters • Maintain pronoun-antecedent agreement • Identify and correct sentence fragments and run-on sentences
SPEAKING, LISTENING, AND VIEWING	• Deliver a narrative speech • Identify and analyze visual and sound elements in film
VOCABULARY	• Understand and use base words, root words, and affixes • Understand and use synonyms
ACADEMIC VOCABULARY	• plot • text features • conflict • inferences • setting • chronological order • foreshadowing • author's purpose

What Makes a Good Story?

Can the hero save the city from danger? Will the lost hikers find their way home? Good stories have the power to capture our attention and to keep us wondering about what will happen next. Read on to discover the parts behind all good stories, whether those stories unfold on television, in conversations with friends, or on the pages of our favorite books.

Part 1: Parts of a Story

Think about two very different stories. One is about a city detective in charge of solving an important case. The other is about strange aliens that invade the planet. Even stories as different as these have something in common—the parts that make them tick. These parts are the setting, characters, and conflicts, which are described in the chart.

BASIC PARTS	EXAMPLES
SETTING Setting is the time and place of the action. The **time** can be the past, present, or future. It can also be a particular season or time of day. The **place** can be anywhere in the world or in your imagination.	• a rainy day on the planet Venus • a tropical island in the present day • a city park in the year 2086 • a palace in England in 1547
CHARACTERS Characters are the people, animals, or imaginary creatures who take part in the action. The most important characters are **main characters.** Less important characters are **minor characters.**	• a 12-year-old girl • a wizard with mysterious powers • a baseball coach • a family's pet dog
CONFLICT A conflict is the struggle that a character faces in a story. The struggle can be between characters or between a character and a force of nature, such as the weather. A conflict can also be within a character, as he or she struggles with difficult choices.	• A girl is made fun of by her friends. (girl vs. friends) • A family seeks shelter from a storm. (family vs. storm) • A boy must decide between telling the truth and lying to protect his friend's feelings. (telling the truth vs. lying)

MODEL 1: SETTING AND CHARACTERS

In this excerpt, a woman panics when her grandson Dewey disappears. Notice the details that describe the time and place of the action.

from Trouble River

Novel by **Betsy Byars**

She rose and moved to the open doorway where she looked out over the golden prairie.

"Dewey!" she called, her voice breaking with anxiety. "Deweeeeeee."

When there was no answer, she went back to her rocking chair.

5   "Dewey Martin," she called from her chair. "Oh, *Deweeee.*"

After a moment she went to stand in the doorway again. For as far as she could see there was only the prairie, the long waving line of grass on the horizon with not one single cabin or chimney in sight.

The sun was dropping behind the horizon, and she knew how quickly

10   darkness would cover the land, how quickly the colorful prairie would become desolate and cold.

Close Read

1. What can you tell about the setting in which the woman lives? Find two details that describe her surroundings. One detail has been boxed.

2. What do you learn about the woman from the way she reacts to her grandson's absence? Support your answer.

MODEL 2: CONFLICT

A boy named Aaron has just left his village to sell his family's goat. What unexpected conflict will he face on his journey?

from Zlateh the Goat

Short story by **Isaac Bashevis Singer**

The sun was shining when Aaron left the village. Suddenly the weather changed. A large black cloud with a bluish center appeared in the east and spread itself rapidly over the sky. A cold wind blew in with it. The crows flew low, croaking. At first it looked as if it would rain,

5   but instead it began to hail as in summer. It was early in the day, but it became dark as dusk. After a while the hail turned to snow.

In his twelve years Aaron had seen all kinds of weather, but he had never experienced a snow like this one. It was so dense it shut out the light of the day. In a short time their path was completely covered. The

10   wind became as cold as ice. The road to town was narrow and winding. Aaron no longer knew where he was.

Close Read

1. Find three details that convey the dangers of the weather. One detail has been boxed.

2. In your own words, describe the conflict that Aaron is facing. Whom or what is the conflict with?

Part 2: What Happens in a Story?

A story is more than its individual parts. The real power of a story comes from the action—what happens as the story develops. While the action varies from story to story, most stories follow a pattern called a plot. A **plot** is the series of events in a story. A typical plot begins by introducing a character who has a conflict. Suspense builds to a turning point as the character tries to resolve the conflict. Shortly after the conflict is resolved, the story comes to a close.

Most plots have five stages, which are described in the graphic. Learning about these stages can help you keep track of a story's events and answer the question "What happened?" when someone asks you what a story is about.

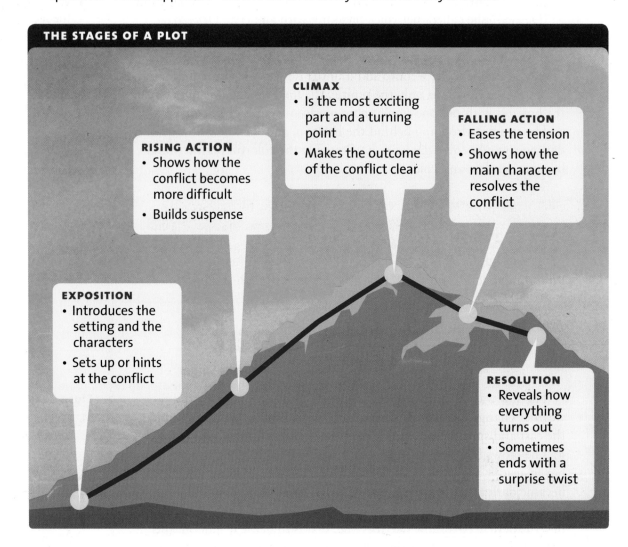

THE STAGES OF A PLOT

CLIMAX
- Is the most exciting part and a turning point
- Makes the outcome of the conflict clear

RISING ACTION
- Shows how the conflict becomes more difficult
- Builds suspense

FALLING ACTION
- Eases the tension
- Shows how the main character resolves the conflict

EXPOSITION
- Introduces the setting and the characters
- Sets up or hints at the conflict

RESOLUTION
- Reveals how everything turns out
- Sometimes ends with a surprise twist

MODEL 1: EXPOSITION

This story is about a young Japanese-American girl. What do you learn about the setting and the conflict in the exposition of the story?

from THE BRACELET

Short story by **Yoshiko Uchida**

It was April 21, 1942. The United States and Japan were at war, and every Japanese person on the West Coast was being evacuated by the government to a concentration camp. Mama, my sister Keiko, and I were being sent from our home, and out of Berkeley, and eventually out
5 of California.

The doorbell rang, and I ran to answer it before my sister could. I thought maybe by some miracle, a messenger from the government might be standing there, tall and proper and buttoned into a uniform, come to tell us it was all a terrible mistake; that we wouldn't have to
10 leave after all.

Close Read

1. Where and when does this story take place?

2. Reread the boxed details. Explain the conflict that the girl's family has. How does the girl feel about her situation?

MODEL 2: RISING ACTION

Billy is overjoyed when his mother buys him a bike for his birthday. What happens when Billy rides his prized possession to school? Find out by reading this excerpt from the rising action of the story.

from You're Not a **WINNER** Unless Your Picture's in the Paper

Short story by **Avi**

The racks were not sufficient for all the bikes, so lots of them were just dumped on the ground. Billy wouldn't do that to his bike. He leaned it carefully against a tree. The tree being in leaf, it shaded the bike from a too-hot sun.
5 On Wednesday, right after three o'clock dismissal, when Billy came to collect his bike, it was gone.
At first Billy thought he had just forgotten where he had left it, and went searching. But as more and more kids claimed their bikes and took off, it became obvious that his bike wasn't just gone, it had been *stolen*.

Close Read

1. Describe what you learn about Billy's conflict in the boxed lines. What is Billy's initial reaction?

2. In lines 8–9, Billy concludes that his problem is worse than he first realized. How does the conflict become more complicated?

Part 3: Analyze the Literature

Jenny has heard stories about a ferocious boar—a wild pig—that roams the woods near her home. Will she be the first person to come face-to-face with the dreaded creature? Use what you've learned in this workshop to analyze the plot, conflict, and setting of this suspenseful story.

BOAR OUT THERE

Short story by **Cynthia Rylant**

Everyone in Glen Morgan knew there was a wild boar in the woods over by the Miller farm. The boar was out beyond the splintery rail fence and past the old black Dodge that somehow had ended up in the woods and was missing most of its parts.

5　Jenny would hook her chin over the top rail of the fence, twirl a long green blade of grass in her teeth and whisper, "Boar out there."

And there were times she was sure she heard him. She imagined him running heavily through the trees, ignoring the sharp thorns and briars that raked his back and sprang away trembling.

10　She thought he might have a golden horn on his terrible head. The boar would run deep into the woods, then rise up on his rear hooves, throw his head toward the stars and cry a long, clear, sure note into the air. The note would glide through the night and spear the heart of the moon. The boar had no fear of the moon, Jenny knew, as she lay in bed,

15　listening.

One hot summer day she went to find the boar. No one in Glen Morgan had ever gone past the old black Dodge and beyond, as far as she knew. But the boar was there somewhere, between those awful trees, and his dark green eyes waited for someone.

20　Jenny felt it was she.

Close Read
Exposition (lines 1–15)

1. Where and when does this story take place? Find three details in lines 1–16 that help you to visualize the setting. One detail has been boxed.

Close Read
Rising Action (lines 16–46)

2. Explain what Jenny decides to do in lines 16–20. What conflict do you think might result from her plan of action?

Moving slowly over damp brown leaves, Jenny could sense her ears tingle and fan out as she listened for thick breathing from the trees. She stopped to pick a teaberry leaf to chew, stood a minute, then went on.

Deep in the woods she kept her eyes to the sky. She needed to be
25 reminded that there was a world above and apart from the trees—a world of space and air, air that didn't linger all about her, didn't press deep into her skin, as forest air did.

Finally, leaning against a tree to rest, she heard him for the first time. She forgot to breathe, standing there listening to the stamping of
30 hooves, and she choked and coughed.

Coughed!

And now the pounding was horrible, too loud and confusing for Jenny. Horrible. She stood stiff with wet eyes and knew she could always pray, but for some reason didn't.

35 He came through the trees so fast that she had no time to scream or run. And he was there before her.

His large gray-black body shivered as he waited just beyond the shadow of the tree she held for support. His nostrils glistened, and his eyes; but astonishingly, he was silent. He shivered and glistened and was
40 absolutely silent.

Jenny matched his silence, and her body was rigid, but not her eyes. They traveled along his scarred, bristling back to his thick hind legs. Tears spilling and flooding her face, Jenny stared at the boar's ragged ears, caked with blood. Her tears dropped to the leaves, and the only
45 sound between them was his slow breathing.

Then the boar snorted and jerked. But Jenny did not move.

High in the trees a bluejay yelled, and, suddenly, it was over. Jenny stood like a rock as the boar wildly flung his head and in terror bolted past her.
50 *Past* her. . . .

And now, since that summer, Jenny still hooks her chin over the old rail fence, and she still whispers, "Boar out there." But when she leans on the fence, looking into the trees, her eyes are full and she leaves wet patches on the splintery wood. She is sorry for the torn ears of the
55 boar and sorry that he has no golden horn.

But mostly she is sorry that he lives in fear of bluejays and little girls, when everyone in Glen Morgan lives in fear of him.

3. Reread lines 21–34. What details help to build suspense about what might happen next?

4. The conflict becomes clear in line 36. How do Jenny and the boar react to each other when they finally meet?

Close Read
Climax (lines 47–50)

5. What is surprising about what happens at the climax, or the turning point in the story?

Close Read
Falling Action and Resolution (lines 51–57)

6. The tension eases after Jenny's encounter with the boar. How has her impression of the boar changed?

The School Play
Short Story by Gary Soto

What do you FEAR most?

KEY IDEA Have you ever jumped at the sight of a harmless bug? Or, maybe you have waited a long time to ride a roller coaster only to change your mind when it was your turn? The things that frighten people range from big to small, from living to nonliving, from the seen to the unseen. In "The School Play," a student struggles to overcome a **fear** many people face.

SURVEY What are you most afraid of? Some of the most common fears people have are listed in the survey. Rank the fears from one to ten, with one being the thing you are most afraid of. Then survey the class to find out what is the most common fear in your classroom.

SURVEY

FACE YOUR FEARS!

Rank the following fears to see what scares you the most:

___ Heights

___ Spiders and Insects

___ Being in the Dark

___ Dentists

___ Thunder and Lightning

___ Failing a Test

___ Being Bullied

___ Airplane Rides

___ Public Speaking

___ Being in a Crowd

LITERARY ANALYSIS: PLOT

Everything in a story happens for a reason. The series of events is the story's **plot.** The plot usually follows a pattern.

- **Exposition** introduces the characters and **setting.** It may also hint at what the **conflict,** or problem, will be.
- **Rising action** shows how the conflict develops.
- The most exciting part, or turning point of the story, is the **climax.** The outcome of the conflict is decided at this time.
- Tension eases during the **falling action,** and events unfold as a result of the climax.
- The **resolution** is the final point in the plot, in which the reader learns how everything turns out.

As you read "The School Play," notice what occurs in each stage of the story's plot.

READING STRATEGY: MONITOR

Have you ever read halfway through a story and realized you've forgotten what you just read? To avoid this problem, **monitor** your reading by pausing occasionally to check your understanding. One way to monitor is to ask yourself questions about what you are reading. Sometimes you'll need to reread to find the answer. Other times you'll find the answer later on in the story.

As you read "The School Play," record questions about what is happening in a chart like the one shown.

My Questions	Answers
What is inside the cardboard box?	

VOCABULARY IN CONTEXT

Gary Soto uses the boldfaced words to help relate a student's experience in a school play. To see how many words you know, replace each boldfaced word with a different word or phrase.

1. Robert's friend gives the **narrative** about the background.
2. The audience's **relentless** talking distracts the actors.
3. A map of the West is the main **prop** in the play.
4. Belinda wanted to **smirk** when the actor forgot his lines.

Author Online

True to Life Gary Soto draws upon his childhood memories of his family and growing up in Fresno, California, as an inspiration for his writing. He is often asked what his family thinks about his

Gary Soto born 1952

writing. He jokes that they don't read much of his work, "so they're not fully aware of how they've been brought to the page."

A Star Is Born At age ten, Soto was cast in his school play. He had to remember one line: "I have the glasses." But he was so fascinated with the fake beard he was wearing that he forgot what to say.

 MORE ABOUT THE AUTHOR
For more on Gary Soto, visit the **Literature Center** at **ClassZone.com.**

Background

The Donner Party In the spring of 1846, a group of men, women, and children from Illinois and nearby states set out for California. George and Jacob Donner led the group.

While trying to cross the Sierra Nevada Mountains in eastern California, the Donner Party was trapped in a snowstorm. The travelers ran out of food, and members of the group began dying of starvation. In desperation, some of them ate the bodies of the dead. Only half the people made it through that grim winter.

The School play

Gary Soto

In the school play at the end of his sixth-grade year, all Robert Suarez
had to remember to say was, "Nothing's wrong. I can see," to a pioneer
woman, who was really Belinda Lopez. Instead of a pioneer woman,
Belinda was one of the toughest girls since the beginning of the world.
She was known to slap boys and grind their faces into the grass so
that they bit into chunks of wormy earth. More than once Robert had
witnessed Belinda staring down the janitor's pit bull, who licked his
frothing chops but didn't dare mess with her. **A**

The class rehearsed for three weeks, at first without costumes. Early
one morning Mrs. Bunnin wobbled into the classroom lugging a large
cardboard box. She wiped her brow and said, "Thanks for the help,
Robert."

Robert was at his desk scribbling a ballpoint tattoo that spelled DUDE
on the tops of his knuckles. He looked up and stared, blinking at his
teacher. "Oh, did you need some help?" he asked.

ANALYZE VISUALS
Examine the art on
page 33. In what way
do the exaggerated
details create a
humorous effect?

A **PLOT: EXPOSITION**
What background
information have you
learned about Robert?

She rolled her eyes at him and told him to stop writing on his skin. "You'll look like a criminal," she scolded.

Robert stuffed his hands into his pockets as he rose from his seat. "What's in the box?" he asked.

20 She muttered under her breath. She popped open the taped top and brought out skirts, hats, snowshoes, scarves, and vests. She tossed Robert a red beard, which he held up to his face, thinking it made him look handsome.

"I like it," Robert said. He sneezed and ran his hand across his moist nose.

His classmates were coming into the classroom and looked at Robert in awe. "That's bad," Ruben said. "What do I get?"

Mrs. Bunnin threw him a wrinkled shirt. Ruben raised it to his chest and said, "My dad could wear this. Can I give it to him after the play is done?"

30 Mrs. Bunnin turned away in silence.

Most of the actors didn't have speaking parts. They just got cutout crepe-paper snowflakes to pin to their shirts or crepe-paper leaves to wear.

During the blizzard in which Robert delivered his line, Belinda asked, "Is there something wrong with your eyes?" Robert looked at the audience, which at the moment was a classroom of empty chairs, a dented world globe that had been dropped by almost everyone, one limp flag, one wastebasket, and a picture of George Washington, whose eyes followed you around the room when you got up to sharpen your pencil. Robert answered, "Nothing's wrong. I can see."

40 Mrs. Bunnin, biting on the end of her pencil, said, "Louder, both of you."

Belinda stepped up, nostrils flaring so that the shadows on her nose quivered, and said louder, "Sucka, is there something wrong with your eye-balls?"

"Nothing's wrong. I can see."

"Louder! Make sure the audience can hear you," Mrs. Bunnin directed. She tapped her pencil hard against the desk. She scolded, "Robert, I'm not going to tell you again to quit fooling with the beard."

"It's itchy."

50 "We can't do anything about that. Actors need **props.** You're an actor. Now try again."

Robert and Belinda stood center stage as they waited for Mrs. Bunnin to call "Action!" When she did, Belinda approached Robert slowly. "Sucka face, is there anything wrong with your mug?" Belinda asked. Her eyes were squinted in anger. For a moment Robert saw his head grinding into the playground grass. **B**

"Nothing's wrong. I can see."

prop (prŏp) *n.* an object an actor uses in a play

B PLOT: RISING ACTION
Reread lines 42–56. What **conflict,** or struggle, is developing?

Robert giggled behind his red beard. Belinda popped her gum and **smirked.** She stood with her hands on her hips.

60 "What? What did you say?" Mrs. Bunnin asked, pulling off her glasses. "Are you chewing gum, Belinda?"

"No, Mrs. Bunnin," Belinda lied. "I just forgot my lines." **C**

Belinda turned to face the snowflake boys clumped together in the back. She rolled out her tongue, on which rested a ball of gray gum, depleted of sweetness under her **relentless** chomp. She whispered "sucka" and giggled so that her nose quivered dark shadows.

The play, *The Last Stand,* was about the Donner party just before they got hungry and started eating each other. Everyone who scored at least twelve out of fifteen on their spelling tests got to say at least one line.
70 Everyone else had to stand and be trees or snowflakes.

Mrs. Bunnin wanted the play to be a success. She couldn't risk having kids with bad memories on stage. The nonspeaking trees and snowflakes stood humming snow flurries, blistering wind, and hail, which they produced by clacking their teeth.

Robert's mother was proud of him because he was living up to the legend of Robert De Niro, for whom he was named. Over dinner he said, "Nothing's wrong. I can see," when his brother asked him to pass the dishtowel, their communal napkin. His sister said, "It's your turn to do dishes," and he said, "Nothing's wrong. I can see." His dog, Queenie,
80 begged him for more than water and a dog biscuit. He touched his dog's own hairy beard and said, "Nothing's wrong. I can see."

One warm spring night, Robert lay on his back in the backyard, counting shooting stars. He was up to three when David, a friend who was really his brother's friend, hopped the fence and asked, "What's the matter with you?"

"Nothing's wrong. I can see," Robert answered. He sat up, feeling good because the line came naturally, without much thought. He leaned back on his elbow and asked David what he wanted to be when he grew up. **D**

"I don't know yet," David said, plucking at the grass. "Maybe a fighter
90 pilot. What do you want to be?"

"I want to guard the president. I could wrestle the assassins and be on television. But I'd pin those dudes, and people would say, 'That's him, our hero.'" David plucked at a stalk of grass and thought deeply.

Robert thought of telling David that he really wanted to be someone with a supergreat memory, who could recall facts that most people thought were unimportant. He didn't know if there was such a job, but he thought it would be great to sit at home by the telephone waiting for scientists to call him and ask hard questions.

smirk (smûrk) *v.* to smile in an insulting way

C MONITOR
What is the actual line Belinda is supposed to say?

relentless (rĭ-lĕnt′lĭs) *adj.* refusing to stop or give up

D MONITOR
Reread lines 75–88. Why does Robert respond with his line when someone speaks to him at home?

The three weeks passed quickly. The day before the play, Robert felt
100   happy as he walked home from school with no homework. As he
turned onto his street, he found a dollar floating over the currents of wind.

"A buck," he screamed to himself. He snapped it up and looked for
others. But he didn't find any more. It was his lucky day, though. At
recess he had hit a home run on a fluke bunt—a fluke because the catcher
had kicked the ball, another player had thrown it into center field, and
the pitcher wasn't looking when Robert slowed down at third, then burst
home with dust flying behind him.

That night, it was his sister's turn to do the dishes. They had eaten
enchiladas with the works, so she slaved with suds up to her elbows.
110 Robert bathed in bubble bath, the suds peaked high like the Donner Pass.
He thought about how full he was and how those poor people had had
nothing to eat but snow. I can live on nothing, he thought and whistled
like wind through a mountain pass, raking flat the suds with his palm. **E**

The next day, after lunch, he was ready for the play, red beard in hand
and his one line trembling on his lips. Classes herded into the auditorium.
As the actors dressed and argued about stepping on each other's feet,
Robert stood near a cardboard barrel full of toys, whispering over and
over to himself, "Nothing's wrong. I can see." He was hot, itchy, and
confused when he tied on the beard. He sneezed when a strand of the
120 beard entered his nostril. He said louder, "Nothing's wrong. I can see,"
but the words seemed to get caught in the beard. "Nothing, no, no. I can
see great," he said louder, then under his breath because the words seemed
wrong. "Nothing's wrong, can't you see? Nothing's wrong. I can see you."
Worried, he approached Belinda and asked if she remembered his line.
Balling her hand into a fist, Belinda warned, "Sucka, I'm gonna bury your
ugly face in the ground if you mess up." **F**

"I won't," Robert said as he walked away. He bit a nail and looked into
the barrel of toys. A clown's mask stared back at him. He prayed that his
line would come back to him. He would hate to disappoint his teacher
130 and didn't like the thought of his face being rubbed into spiky grass.

The curtain parted slightly, and the principal came out smiling onto
the stage. She said some words about pioneer history and then, stern
faced, warned the audience not to scrape the chairs on the just-waxed
floor. The principal then introduced Mrs. Bunnin, who told the audience
about how they had rehearsed for weeks.

Meanwhile, the class stood quietly in place with lunchtime spaghetti
on their breath. They were ready. Belinda had swallowed her gum because
she knew this was for real. The snowflakes clumped together and began
howling.

E MONITOR
Think about how Robert
feels the day before the
play. How might this
affect his performance?

**F PLOT: RISING
ACTION**
How has the tension
increased now that it is
the day of the play?

140   Robert retied his beard. Belinda, smoothing her skirt, looked at him and said, "If you know what's good for you, you'd better do it right." Robert grew nervous when the curtain parted and his classmates who were assigned to do snow, wind, and hail broke into song.

    Alfonso stepped forward with his **narrative** about a blot on American history that would live with us forever. He looked at the audience, lost for a minute. He continued by saying that if the Donner party could come back, hungry from not eating for over a hundred years, they would be sorry for what they had done.

    The play began with some boys in snowshoes shuffling around the
150 stage, muttering that the blizzard would cut them off from civilization. They looked up, held out their hands, and said in unison,[1] "Snow." One stepped center stage and said, "I wish I had never left the prairie." Another one said, "California is just over there." He pointed, and some of the first graders looked in the direction of the piano.

    "What are we going to do?" one kid asked, brushing pretend snow off his vest.

    "I'm getting pretty hungry," another said, rubbing her stomach.

---

1. **in unison** (yōō′nĭ-sən): at the same time.

The audience seemed to be following the play. A ribbon of sweat ran down Robert's face. When his scene came up, he staggered to center stage
160 and dropped to the floor, just as Mrs. Bunnin had said, just as he had seen Robert De Niro do in that movie about a boxer. Belinda, bending over with an "Oh, my," yanked him up so hard that something clicked in his elbow. She boomed, "Is there anything wrong with your eyes?"

Robert rubbed his elbow, then his eyes, and said, "I can see nothing wrong. Wrong is nothing, I can see." **G**

"How are we going to get through?" she boomed, wringing her hands together at the audience, some of whom had their mouths taped shut because they were known talkers. "My husband needs a doctor." The drama advanced through snow, wind, and hail that sounded like
170 chattering teeth.

Belinda turned to Robert and muttered, "You mess-up. You're gonna hate life."

But Robert thought he'd done okay. At least, he reasoned to himself, I got the words right. Just not in the right order.

With his part of the play done, he joined the snowflakes and trees, chattering his teeth the loudest. He howled wind like a baying hound and snapped his fingers furiously in a snow flurry. He trembled from the cold.

The play ended with Alfonso saying that if they came back to life, the Donner party would be sorry for eating each other. "It's just not right,"
180 he argued. "You gotta suck it up in bad times." **H**

Robert figured that Alfonso was right. He remembered how one day his sister had locked him in the closet and he didn't eat or drink for five hours. When he got out, he hit his sister, but not so hard as to leave a bruise. He then ate three sandwiches and felt a whole lot better.

The cast then paraded up the aisle into the audience. Belinda pinched Robert hard, but only once because she was thinking that it could have been worse. As he passed a smiling and relieved Mrs. Bunnin, she patted Robert's shoulder and said, "Almost perfect."

Robert was happy. He'd made it through without passing out from fear.
190 Now the first and second graders were looking at him and clapping. He was sure everyone wondered who the actor was behind that smooth voice and red, red beard. ༄ **I**

G PLOT: CLIMAX
How is the delivery of Robert's line a turning point in the story?

H PLOT: FALLING ACTION
What effect does Robert's delivery of his lines have on the end of the play?

I PLOT: RESOLUTION
How do Robert, Belinda, and Mrs. Bunnin feel about Robert's performance?

Comprehension

1. **Clarify** Does repeating his line again and again when he is at home help Robert remember it?

2. **Clarify** Reread lines 86–98. What does Robert want to be when he grows up?

3. **Summarize** What happens on the day of the performance?

Literary Analysis

4. **Monitor** Review the chart you filled in as you read. Which questions and answers were most helpful for understanding the story? Explain your answer.

5. **Compare and Contrast** Do you think Belinda is nervous about performing in front of the student audience? Compare and contrast her actions with Robert's on the day of the play.

6. **Make Inferences** How does the audience react to the play? Support your answer with specific details from the story.

7. **Analyze Plot** The plot of "The School Play" centers on Robert's **fear** of forgetting his line. Go back through the story and make a list of important events. Place the events on a diagram like the one shown to identify what happens at each stage of the plot.

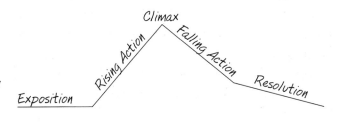

Extension and Challenge

8. **Creative Project: Drama** With a partner, choose a part of the story to act out. Rely on the details provided by Soto to accurately portray the characters. Present your performance to the class.

9. **Inquiry and Research** The Westward Expansion in the 1800s was mostly due to people's desire to own land. Pioneers followed specific trails from eastern states to territories in the West. Research to find the trail used by the Donner Party. Using a map you can write on, sketch the trail and label the Donner Pass, which Robert describes in line 110.

 RESEARCH LINKS
For more on the Donner Party, visit the **Research Center** at ClassZone.com.

Vocabulary in Context

VOCABULARY PRACTICE

Choose the letter of the word or phrase that has the same, or nearly the same, meaning as the boldfaced word.

1. a thrilling **narrative:** (a) argument, (b) story, (c) debate, (d) notice
2. **prop** for the play: (a) script, (b) costume, (c) object, (d) director
3. **relentless** noise: (a) constant, (b) deafening, (c) frightening, (d) occasional
4. to **smirk** at someone: (a) stare rudely, (b) laugh quietly, (c) yell loudly, (d) smile defiantly

VOCABULARY IN WRITING

If you had put on this play, how would you have designed the set? Write a paragraph describing your ideas. Use at least two vocabulary words in your description. Here is an example of how you might begin.

> **EXAMPLE SENTENCE**
>
> *I would have used some kind of **prop** for the snowflakes instead of people.*

VOCABULARY STRATEGY: DENOTATIONS AND CONNOTATIONS

A word's **denotation** is its literal meaning—that is, the meaning found in a dictionary definition. A word's **connotation** is the shades of meaning it may take on beyond its dictionary definition. It includes all the thoughts and feelings the word may bring to people's minds. For example, the vocabulary word *smirk* does mean "smile." But *smirk* also carries negative connotations of smugness or conceitedness. Recognizing connotations can improve both your reading and writing.

PRACTICE Using a dictionary, identify the denotative meanings of both words in each pair. Decide which of the two words has a negative connotation. Then use it in a sentence to show the negative meaning.

1. a (serious, dull) speech
2. her (funny, ridiculous) hat
3. (obsessed, enthusiastic) about the project
4. a (youthful, childish) outlook
5. (impatient, eager) to get started
6. a (tangy, bitter) taste

VOCABULARY PRACTICE
For more practice, go to the **Vocabulary Center** at **ClassZone.com.**

Reading-Writing Connection

Broaden your understanding of "The School Play" by responding to these prompts. Then complete the **Grammar and Writing** exercise.

A. Short Response: Write a Review
Drama critics write reviews of plays to give their opinion of a performance. In **one paragraph,** write a review of Robert's play for his school newspaper. Use your imagination to fill in the details.

A convincing review will . . .
- identify the play's strengths and weaknesses
- use evidence from the story to support your opinion

B. Long Response: Analyze the Ending
The way characters deal with conflict affects how the story ends. Write **two or three paragraphs** explaining how the resolution of the story would be different if Robert had not overcome his **fear** of being on stage.

An interesting analysis will . . .
- provide a different but believable climax
- explain the effect of the change on the falling action and resolution

GRAMMAR AND WRITING

AVOID SENTENCE FRAGMENTS A **sentence fragment** is exactly what it says it is—a piece of a sentence. A fragment lacks a **subject** (whom or what the sentence is about), a **predicate** (what the subject is or does), or both. Don't let the punctuation at the end of a fragment fool you. What might look like a sentence is still a fragment if a complete thought is not expressed. A fragment usually can be combined with the sentence before it to make a complete sentence.

Original: Robert was cast in a play. About the Donner Party.

Revised: Robert was cast in a play about the Donner Party.

PRACTICE Rewrite this paragraph, correcting the four sentence fragments.

The story would end very differently. If Robert had forgotten his line completely. He might run off the stage. Leaving Belinda to go on without him. Belinda would be angry. At Robert. However, Mrs. Bunnin would have another chance next year. To direct a perfect school play.

*For more help with fragments, see page R64 in the **Grammar Handbook.***

The Good Deed

Short Story by Marion Dane Bauer

Can first
IMPRESSIONS
be trusted?

KEY IDEA Whenever you meet someone, you form an **impression,** or idea of what that person is like. You base your opinion on how the person looks, talks, and acts. Sometimes, after you get to know the person, you realize that your first impression was wrong. In "The Good Deed," a young girl finds out whether her first impression of someone was accurate.

LIST IT Think of someone you have known for a year or two. Make a list of words that describe your first impression of that person. When you are finished, decide if your impression has changed. Make a second list of words describing how you currently feel about that person.

Antonio
1. Good listener
2.

● LITERARY ANALYSIS: CONFLICT

Have you ever noticed that at least one character in a story always faces some sort of problem or struggle? This struggle, or **conflict,** is what makes a story interesting. Many stories have more than one conflict. You can often identify conflicts by noticing when characters struggle with

- their thoughts or choices (internal)
- an outside force such as another character (external)

As you read "The Good Deed," look for examples of conflicts that affect the characters.

● READING STRATEGY: CONNECT

Stories introduce us to new people and sometimes to new places and times. However, as you read a story, you may find that you have had experiences or feelings similar to the characters. You then **connect,** or identify, with events or situations in the story. By connecting, you are better able to understand why the characters do what they do.

As you read, use a chart like the one shown to record the connections you make.

What Is Happening?	My Connection
Heather is scared to talk to Miss Benson.	I was nervous to meet my pen pal at the Senior Center for the first time.

▲ VOCABULARY IN CONTEXT

The author uses these words to show how powerful first **impressions** can be. See which ones you already know. Place each word in the correct column of a chart like the one shown.

WORD LIST	accusation	impaired	pert
	generic	incredibly	trite

Know Well	Think I Know	Don't Know

Author Online

Marion Dane Bauer
born 1938

A Life Spent Writing
Marion Dane Bauer spent much of her childhood making up stories. Her first written work was a poem dedicated to her teddy bear. For Bauer, writing is a habit. She says, "It's what I get up in the morning to do." In 1987 her efforts were rewarded when she received the Newbery Honor for her novel *On My Honor.*

Inspiration Many events in Bauer's life have inspired her writing. But she draws her stories less from real life than from her need to connect with someone else's feelings. "It may start with . . . a newspaper article, from something overheard in the grocery store, or told to me by a friend," she says. Then Bauer thinks about how to turn the information into a story. She explains, "It must first pass through my own thoughts and feelings. . . . And when it does, the story is true. Not because it 'really happened,' but because, for me, it is real."

 MORE ABOUT THE AUTHOR
For more on Marion Dane Bauer, visit the **Literature Center** at ClassZone.com.

The Good Deed

Marion Dane Bauer

Miss Benson was my good deed for the summer. Every girl in our scout troop was assigned someone. My friend Melody had Mr. Stengle. He's the oldest resident of the Riverview Nursing Home. He must be at least one hundred and two. He used to be a farmer, and all he ever talks about is the weather. Anne Marie got Mrs. Mechlenburg. Mrs. Mechlenburg has four children, all under five, and kind of bewildered, cocker spaniel eyes. Like maybe she doesn't know how they all got there. But I was assigned Miss Benson.

Miss Benson is old. Not old like Mr. Stengle, but old enough. And she's
10 blind. "Sight **impaired**, Heather," our scout leader said. But whether you say "sight impaired" or "blind," the truth is, Miss Benson can't see a thing.

ANALYZE VISUALS
What do the lines and colors in this painting lead you to focus on?

impaired (ĭm-pârd′)
adj. being in a less than perfect condition

"What do I do?" I asked. "What do I say?" **A**

"Start with 'hello,'" our scout leader said, like that was some kind of help. Then she added, "She's a retired teacher. I'll bet she'd just love it if you'd read to her." And she was off talking to Anne Marie about diapers.

The problem was I'd never been alone with a blind person before. Come to think of it, I don't suppose I'd ever even met one. And the thought of trying to talk to Miss Benson kind of scared me. Melody and

20 Anne Marie and I all had the same number of badges though, the most of anyone in the troop, and I wasn't about to let either of them get ahead of me. So the next day I called Miss Benson—she sounded normal enough on the phone—then I set out to meet her. **B**

Her place wasn't hard to find. She lived in the apartment building right next to the Piggly Wiggly, only a few blocks from my house. Which meant I got there really fast. Too fast. Then I kind of stood in front of her door, waiting, though I couldn't have said what I was waiting for. To figure out what I was going to say, I guess. After "hello," I mean. But before I even got around to knocking, the door across the hall from

30 Miss Benson's apartment popped open and this girl I'd never seen before stuck her head out.

"What do you want?" she said, like it was her door I was standing in front of.

"I'm visiting Miss Benson," I told her, which was perfectly obvious.

The girl had long brown hair. Kind of a reddish brown. But it was a tangled mess. I'll swear she'd pulled it into a ponytail that morning without ever passing it by a brush. "Why are you visiting her?" she wanted to know.

It would have sounded really dumb to say, "Because I'm a Girl Scout,

40 and she's my good deed for the summer." So I said instead, "I've come to read to her." And then I added, just in case this girl didn't know anything at all, "She's sight impaired, you know."

"No, she's not," the girl answered, with a toss of that tangled hair. "I've seen her. She's blind as a bat."

Behind the girl, from inside her apartment, a whole lot of noise was going on. It sounded like the beginnings of World War III. Or like a herd of runaway horses maybe. Just then two little kids came hurtling up to the doorway and stopped to peer out from each side of the girl. I couldn't tell whether they were boys or girls or one of each. They looked kind of

50 **generic.** Is that the word? Their hair wasn't combed either, and their noses were snotty. . . . I decided maybe reading to a blind woman wasn't so bad after all and turned to knock on the door.

A CONNECT
Reread lines 1–12. Think of a time when you felt nervous about meeting someone. What is adding to Heather's nervousness?

B CONFLICT
Reread lines 17–23. What conflict is Heather facing?

generic (jə-nĕr′ĭk) *adj.* having no particularly distinctive or noteworthy quality

"Wait," the girl said. "I'll come with you."

Just like that she said it, as though she'd been invited.

And the truth was, I didn't know whether to be annoyed at her for being so pushy or relieved that I didn't have to go in there alone. What if a good deed didn't count if you had help? But though there wasn't a reason in the world for me to do what that girl said, I found myself standing there with my hand in the air, waiting.

60 "Tell Mama I've gone across the hall," the girl told the two snotty-nosed kids. And she stepped out and closed the door behind herself.

"Mama," I heard the kids yodel as they stampeded back into the apartment. And then there was nothing left to do but to knock on Miss Benson's door.

The rest wasn't nearly as hard as I'd expected. After a moment a tall woman with curly, salt-and-pepper hair opened the door and said, "You must be Heather. Come in." I could tell she couldn't see me, because she looked right over my head like there was something interesting on the wall across the way, but her voice didn't *sound* blind.

70 I don't know what I mean by that exactly, except that she didn't sound like she was missing anything at all. And I guess she wasn't, because when the girl said, "Hi!" and followed me into the apartment Miss Benson asked right away, "Who's your friend?"

Of course, I didn't have a clue who my "friend" was, but she answered, just as **pert** as you please, "Risa. My mom and me and my little brothers"—so they *were* boys—"just moved in across the hall."

pert (pûrt) *adj.*
offensively bold; saucy

"Welcome, Risa," Miss Benson replied. Her voice sort of had a smile in it. "I'm glad to see you."

Just like that she said it. *I'm glad to see you!* Like she could.

80 Miss Benson led the way, one hand trailing lightly across the furniture she passed or sometimes just grazing the wall. "I hope you don't mind if we go to the kitchen," she called back. "It's the cheeriest place."

The kitchen was a cheery place. The sun was all spread out across a table made out of some kind of golden wood. And in the middle of the table, sweating coolness, sat a pitcher of lemonade and a big blue plate heaped with oatmeal-raisin cookies. There were glasses, too. Just two of them though.

"Mmmm, cookies," Risa said.

"Help yourselves, girls," Miss Benson told us. "I made them for you."

90 And it was a good thing she extended the invitation, because Risa already had one in her hand.

Miss Benson went to the cupboard and got out another glass and began to pour lemonade for everyone. She stopped pouring before she overflowed the glasses too, though I couldn't figure how she did it.

I expected Risa to gobble her cookie, just the way she had grabbed it off the plate without being invited, but she didn't. She just took a couple of nibbles, then tucked the rest into the pocket of her cutoffs. Can you imagine that? An oatmeal cookie in your pocket?

"Tell me about yourselves, girls," Miss Benson said, sitting across from us at the table, and before I could even open my mouth, Risa was off and running.

She told about her three little brothers—there was a baby I hadn't seen; he probably had a snotty nose too—and about how her mom had moved to Minnesota for a better job, only Risa didn't like her mom's new job because the boss wouldn't even let her take telephone calls from her children when she was at work.

ANALYZE VISUALS
Does the dining table in this painting seem as cheery as Miss Benson's kitchen? Explain.

Detail of *Breakfast Room II,* Marty Walsh. Oil on panel, 24″ × 24″. © Marty Walsh.

I told Miss Benson how many badges I'd earned and how my parents and I had gone to Disney World over spring break. I could tell, just by the way Risa looked at me, that she'd never been near any place like Disney World and that she hated me for saying I'd been there. But what was I supposed to do? It was the truth.

When Miss Benson pushed the cookies toward us and said "Help yourself" again, quick as a flash, Risa took another cookie and put that one into her pocket too. I figured she must be stashing them for the snotty-nosed brothers at home, and I was almost impressed. It was kind of nice of her, really, to think of her brothers that way. It made me wish I had a little brother or sister to take cookies home for, but if I had one, I'd teach mine how to use a tissue.

And then I offered to read, so Miss Benson sent me to her bedroom to check out her bookshelf. I found a tall blue book—it looked kind of tattered, so I figured it had been around awhile and was, maybe, a favorite—called *Stories That Never Grow Old.* There was a picture on the cover of a woman wearing a long dress reading a book to some children.

When I came back with the book, Risa looked at it and said low, under her breath, "Dummy. That one's for little kids."

I shrugged, like I didn't care, but still my cheeks went hot when I opened it and saw she was right. It was a lot of old-timey stories like "The Little Engine That Could" and "Hansel and Gretel" and "Why the Bear Has a Stumpy Tail," things like that. Probably not what a grown-up, even one who used to be a teacher, would want to hear.

But then Miss Benson asked, "What book did you get?" and when I told her, she clapped her hands and said, "Perfect!" So I shot Risa a look and started to read. "'Bruin, the young brown bear, was feeling very hungry.'" **C**

Risa leaned across the corner of the table so she could see the page too. She even started silently shaping the words with her mouth as I read, like she was tasting each one. I figured she must not be a very good reader though, because I'd given up reading with my lips when I was in the first grade.

As soon as I'd finished the story I knew I was right about her not being a good reader, because Miss Benson said, "Okay, Risa. Why don't you read the next one?"

While I was reading, she couldn't get close enough to the book, but suddenly she couldn't get away from it fast enough. "Oh no!" she said, pushing away from the table so hard that her chair screeched against the floor. "Anyway, you don't want to hear any more from that old thing. I'll do something else for you instead." **D**

C CONFLICT
Reread lines 124–134. What evidence is there that the tension between Heather and Risa has increased?

D CONFLICT
Why doesn't Risa want to read aloud?

Miss Benson's face was round and soft. "What do you want to do instead?" she asked, and she folded her hands in her lap, waiting.

150   For a moment Risa looked around, whipping that tangled ponytail back and forth like she was expecting to find an idea for something she could do hanging on the wall. Then it must have come to her, because her face lit up and she settled back in her chair. "How about," she said, "if I give you an eye bouquet."

"An eye bouquet?" The way Miss Benson leaned forward you could tell she was expecting something grand.

An eye bouquet? I thought. *How dumb!*

But Risa explained. "I'll make a picture for you with words."

"What a wonderful idea!" Miss Benson said.

160   And it was a wonderful idea. I wished I'd thought of something half as wonderful. Though Miss Benson seemed to like the story I'd read well enough.

Risa thought for a few seconds, then she began. "The lilac bushes are blooming in front of the apartments."

Miss Benson nodded. "It's been years since I've seen those old lilac bushes, but they're still there, are they?"

"Yes," Risa said. "And they're that shimmery color, halfway between silver and purple. You know what I mean?"

"Shimmery. Halfway between silver and purple." Miss Benson nodded
170 again. "That's it. That's it exactly. I can see them now."

I couldn't stand being bested by a girl who still read a little kiddy book with her lips, so I jumped in. I hadn't especially noticed the bushes she was talking about, but I'd seen lilac bushes all my life. "The leaves are shaped like little hearts," I said. "And they're green." I could see Miss Benson was waiting for something more, so I added, kind of feebly, "Green like grass."

But that wasn't any good, and I knew it. What could be more ordinary than "green like grass"? It's what my English teacher would call **trite.**

"The green of horses munching," Risa said, offering the words up like
180 a gift, and Miss Benson tipped her head back and laughed out loud.

"Well," I said, getting up so fast I had to catch my chair to keep it from tipping over. "I guess I'd better be going. My father"—I leaned heavily on the word since it was obvious Risa didn't have one of those—"told me he'd take me and my friends to the beach this weekend." **E**

It wasn't a lie. Daddy was taking me and Melody and Anne Marie to the beach, but not until Sunday afternoon. This was Saturday.

Miss Benson stood up too. "Thank you, Heather," she said, "for the nice visit. I enjoyed it. I enjoyed it very much."

trite (trīt) *adj.* boring because overused; not fresh or original

E CONNECT
Think of a time when you wanted to leave a place quickly. **Compare** and **contrast** how you left with how Heather leaves.

"I'll be back," I promised. "I'll come and read again on Monday."
190 *By myself,* I wanted to add, but I said instead, "I'll put your book away
before I go." And I carried it back to the bedroom.

When I got to the bookshelf I stood looking at the empty space where
the book had stood. *Risa lives right across the hall,* I was thinking. *What
if she decides to come back on her own? Maybe she'll even decide to read to
Miss Benson, and this is the book she'll want, one that doesn't have too many
big words.*

And then there I was, looking around for some place to put the book
where she wouldn't find it. After all, Miss Benson herself certainly wasn't
going to be wanting to look at it again while I was gone.

200 The wastebasket next to the bookshelf, rectangular and deep and
perfectly empty, was just the right size. I slipped the book inside. It would
be safe there, waiting for me. **F**

F CONFLICT
Reread lines 192–202.
Why does Heather
decide to hide the book?

When I got to the door, Risa was there, standing beside Miss Benson. She had to go home too, she said, though I knew she didn't have plans for going anywhere special like the beach. But I said all the polite things you're supposed to say to someone you've just met, to her and to Miss Benson too, and I left. My good deed was done for the day.

On my way out of the apartment building, I couldn't help but notice. The blooms on the lilac bushes were a crisp brown, the color of tea. So the girl was a liar, too, besides being a poor reader.

A couple of days later when I came to visit Miss Benson again, I stopped in front of her door, half expecting Risa to pop out of the apartment across the hall. All seemed quiet over there this time except for cartoons blaring from a TV. I breathed a sigh of relief and knocked on Miss Benson's door.

This time the blue plate on the table held sugar cookies, creamy white, just beginning to be brown at the edges, and sparkling with sugar.

"I'll get a book," I said, after we had each eaten a cookie and sipped some cocoa, chatting about this and that. And I hurried off to Miss Benson's bedroom to get *Stories That Never Grow Old*.

Only the book wasn't there.

I looked in the wastebasket, of course. I even picked it up and turned it upside down and shook it, as though something as big as a book could disappear. But the wastebasket was empty. Just the way it had been the first time I'd come into the room. I wondered, in fact, why Miss Benson had a wastebasket at all since she didn't seem to put anything into it.

Then I hurried to the shelf. Maybe Miss Benson had reached a hand into the basket and found it there and put it away herself. Or maybe someone who came and cleaned for her had discovered it. Now that I thought about it, a wastebasket was about the dumbest place in the world to hide a book.

The space left behind when I took *Stories That Never Grow Old* out, right between two fatter books—*A Literary History of England* and *The Oxford Companion to English Literature*—was still there, empty, accusing. *You did it!* the space said. *You've lost Miss Benson's book! Probably her favorite book in all the world.*

Did she empty her own wastebaskets? She wouldn't have been able to see what was in there. Or maybe somebody else emptied them for her and thought, seeing it there, that she meant to throw it away. My heart beat faster just thinking about the possibilities. **G**

There was nothing else to do, so I picked out another book, a collection of poems by Robert Frost, and brought that out instead.

G CONFLICT
Reread lines 227–240. How has Heather's conflict become more complicated?

"I have some poems," I told Miss Benson, and before she had a chance to say whether she was disappointed that I hadn't brought the blue book, I opened the collection and began to read.

"I'm going out to clean the pasture spring."[1]

She settled back to listen, a small smile tipping the corners of her mouth, but though she looked perfectly happy, I couldn't get past feeling that maybe she'd rather have heard *Stories That Never Grow Old.*

250 I read several poems—I especially liked the one about the boy who died after cutting himself with a chainsaw; it was so sad—but I kept feeling this weight in the pit of my stomach. The blue book was gone. Miss Benson had probably had it since she was a little kid.

I guess I quit reading without even noticing I'd stopped, because the next thing I knew Miss Benson was saying, "How about an eye bouquet now? What can you make me see?"

Her asking took me by surprise, because I'd already proven on Saturday that "eye bouquets" weren't really my thing. When I didn't answer right away though, she said, "I'll give you one first."

260 "All right," I said, though I couldn't help wondering what kind of eye bouquet a blind woman could come up with.

"Freckles," she said, "and hair the color of pulled taffy.[2] Green eyes, a misty green like the sea."

For a moment I just sat there, feeling dumb, until gradually what Miss Benson had said began to dawn. *I* had freckles, though I didn't like to think they were the first thing a person saw. And my hair . . . well, it's the color people like to call "dirty blond," though I always hated that description. I keep my hair as clean as anybody's. But if you were being real nice, you could say it's the color of pulled taffy. And my eyes? Were 270 they green like the sea? (I guess that would be better than green like horses munching.)

And then slowly, gradually, the truth dawned. Miss Benson had gotten her eye bouquet from . . .

"Risa's been here," I said. It came out sounding like an **accusation.**

"Yes. She came Sunday afternoon. She's a very nice girl. I'm sure the two of you are going to be great friends."

I ignored that, about Risa's being a nice girl and about the two of us being friends, because an idea was rising in me like dinner on a rocking boat. Risa had been in Miss Benson's apartment since the last time I'd 280 been there. The blue book was gone from the place where I'd hidden it. Risa had taken it. I already knew she was a liar. Now I knew she was a thief, too! ⓗ

accusation
(ăk′yōō-zā′shən) *n.* the act of charging someone with wrongdoing

ⓗ **CONFLICT**
Reread lines 272–282. How does Miss Benson's eye bouquet increase Heather's conflict with Risa?

---

1. **I'm going . . . pasture spring:** the first line of Robert Frost's poem "The Pasture." (See page 58.)
2. **pulled taffy:** a boiled candy usually of molasses or brown sugar that is stretched until light-colored.

ANALYZE VISUALS
Does the girl in this painting look more like Heather or Risa? Explain.

"Okay," I said, "I can give you an eye bouquet. Hair . . ." I was going to say *Hair that's never seen a brush,* but something stopped me. Instead I said, "Hair the color of chestnuts." I paused. That was pretty good. And Risa's hair was a nice reddish brown. "And eyes . . . eyes like little bits of sky." I didn't even know I'd noticed those things about Risa—what a rich color her hair was, tangled or not, and the brilliant blue of her eyes—until I'd named them, but even as I did, I was standing up.

290   "Sor . . . sorry," I said, stumbling over my feet and my tongue at the same time. "I'm afraid I've got to go. I mean, there's something I've got to do. But I'll be back. Tomorrow. I promise."

Miss Benson stood too. "Is your daddy taking you to the beach again?" she asked.

"No . . . no." I was backing toward the door. "Not today. He's working today. But"—I'd reached the front door—"he'll probably take us again next weekend."

"That's nice." Miss Benson had followed. "Come back anytime, dear. I like having you here."

300 *Come back anytime!* She wouldn't say that when she found out her book was missing. Then she would think I was the thief. Because I was the one who'd had the book last, wasn't I? She'd never think of suspecting Risa of stealing a book, Risa who'd refused to read, Risa with her pretty eye bouquets.

As soon as Miss Benson closed the door behind me, I stalked across the hall and knocked on Risa's door . . . hard. I could hear the television still, Road Runner³ cartoons, but no one answered. The girl was hiding from me!

I knocked again, harder, and when still no one came, I turned the
310 handle. Surprised to find the door unlocked—some people are **incredibly** careless!—I opened it slowly and peeked in. Two pairs of sky-blue eyes stared back at me from the couch. Without taking his thumb out of his mouth, one of the little boys mumbled, "Who're you?"

"I'm a friend of Risa's," I lied. "Is she here?"

They stared at one another and then, without answering, turned back to the TV.

"Where's Risa?" I said more loudly.

The one who had talked before pulled his thumb out of his mouth this time. "She took Andrew and went," he said. "She told us to sit right here."
320 He gave me a warning look. "She told us not to let anybody in, and we're not supposed to talk to strangers."

I stepped closer. Who was Andrew? The baby, probably. And where was their mother? Was she going to come marching in, demanding to know what I was doing in her apartment bullying her little kids? Not likely. This was Monday. She must be working. And Risa was supposed to be here taking care of the little boys. Well, so much for counting on her for anything. "When will she be back?" I demanded to know, stepping closer. "She's got something of mine."

No answer, so I moved between the couch and the coyote zooming
330 across the screen, facing down the two small, dirty-faced boys. And that's when I saw it. The tattered blue book lay on the couch between them, open to a picture of a cheerful train puffing up a steep hill.

I snatched up the book. "Where did you get this?"

---

3. **Road Runner:** a bird cartoon character who is constantly chased but never caught by Wile E. Coyote.

incredibly
(ĭn-krĕd′ə-blē) *adv.*
unbelievably

"Risa give it to us," the talker replied. The other one just leaned over until he had almost toppled onto his side, trying to peer around me to see the TV. Maybe he didn't know how to talk.

"I'll bet she did," I said. I could have burst. That buttinski girl who thought she was so great was a thief. Just as I'd thought. **I**

340 The voice came from the doorway behind me. "Miss Benson gave it to me, and I gave it to them." I whirled around to see Risa, standing there holding an armful of baby. He was asleep with a fat cheek pressed against her shoulder. Risa looked small under his weight.

"Miss Benson gave it to me," she said again, as though she knew I didn't believe her, "when I went over there on Sunday."

"Where did you find it?" I demanded to know.

"Why did you hide it?" she countered.

The question hung in the air. The instant she asked, I realized I couldn't answer. Why had I hidden the book anyway? Something about not wanting Risa to horn in[4] on my good deed. Was that it? **J**

350 I tried another attack. "How come you went off and left your little brothers? Something terrible could have—"

She interrupted. "Andrew was sick. His temperature got really high. I couldn't get hold of my mom, so I went looking for a doctor." As she said it, she kind of staggered, like she couldn't hold up that lump of a baby for another minute.

Suddenly I could see how scared she'd been, scared for the baby, scared to go off and leave her brothers, probably scared to walk into a strange doctor's office alone too. "Here," I said, moving toward her. "Let me take him. Is he going to be all right?"

360 When I lifted the baby away from her, I could feel how hot he was. And how heavy, too.

"Yeah." She rubbed her nose with the back of her hand. Had she been crying? "The doctor gave him a shot. And he called my mom too. Her boss didn't have any choice. He had to let the doctor talk to her. She's coming home real soon."

I walked over to the couch and laid the sleeping baby down beside the other two boys. His cheeks were bright red. I took a tissue out of my pocket and wiped his nose.

"I'll bet Miss Benson would have come over to watch the boys while 370 you went looking for the doctor," I said. And for a moment we both stood there, considering the word *watch*.

Risa nodded. "I didn't think of that," she said softly. But then she lifted her chin and added, like it was what we were talking about still, "I found her book in the wastebasket."

4. **horn in:** to push one's way in without invitation.

I CONNECT
What experiences have you had that help you understand Heather's actions?

J CONFLICT
Reread lines 346–349. How does Risa's question affect Heather?

"Did you tell her?"

Risa tossed her head. Her pretty chestnut hair had been brushed that morning, and it flowed with the movement like a horse's tail. "Of course not. What do you take me for?"

Something deep inside my chest loosened a bit. **K**

380   "Miss Benson said if I read out loud to my brothers it will help me get better. Better at reading, I mean." As Risa said it, a slow blush touched her cheeks, made her ears flame, even reached the roots of her hair. And that's why I knew she was telling the truth. Never in a thousand years would she have admitted that she needed help with reading except as a way of letting me know she hadn't stolen the book. "I'm going to read to her sometimes too," she added.

"That's . . . that's really great," I stammered. And I knew it was. Really. "You'll be helping her, and she'll be helping you. A kind of a good deed both ways."

390   "A good deed?" Risa laughed. "Is that what you call it?"

"Risa," one of the boys interrupted, the one I'd thought couldn't talk, "would you read to us some more?"

She looked sideways at me, and I knew that it was me—snotty me— who'd kept her from reading out loud before. "Why don't we take turns reading to them?" I said. "That would be fun."

Risa considered my offer long and carefully. "Okay," she said at last. "Just so it doesn't count as a good deed."

"It doesn't," I said. "I promise." ∾ **L**

K CONNECT
Think of a time when you realized your first impression of someone was wrong. How does that experience help you to understand how Heather is feeling?

L CONFLICT
What is the **resolution,** or end, of the conflict between Heather and Risa?

Heber Valley Pastures (2005), Douglas Aagard. Oil, 11″ × 14″. © 2005 Meyer-Milagros Gallery. All rights reserved.

The *Pasture*

Robert Frost

I'm going out to clean the pasture spring;
I'll only stop to rake the leaves away
(And wait to watch the water clear, I may):
I shan't be gone long.—You come too.

5 I'm going out to fetch the little calf
That's standing by the mother. It's so young
It totters when she licks it with her tongue.
I shan't be gone long.—You come too.

Comprehension

1. **Recall** How does Heather meet Risa?

2. **Clarify** Reread lines 260–274. Why is Miss Benson able to describe Heather?

3. **Represent** Sketch one of the eye bouquets described in "The Good Deed." Which of the author's words helped you form a mental picture of the image?

Literary Analysis

4. **Connect** Review the connections you made in your chart while reading "The Good Deed." How do they help you understand the characters' actions?

5. **Identify Conflicts** An **external conflict** is a character's struggle against an outside force. An **internal conflict** takes place inside a character's mind. Create a "portrait" of Heather like the one shown. Go back through the story and record examples of the internal and external conflicts she faces.

External Conflicts

1.
2.

Internal Conflicts

1. Heather wants to earn another badge, but she is scared to visit Miss Benson.

2.

6. **Make Inferences** Reread lines 274–276. Do you think Miss Benson is aware that there is a **conflict** between Heather and Risa?

7. **Evaluate Resolution** Do you think Heather accomplishes her "good deed" by the end of the story? Use examples to support your answer.

8. **Compare Literary Works** In line 246, Heather begins to read Robert Frost's poem "The Pasture" to Miss Benson. Reread the entire poem on page 58. Do you think the **speaker,** or the voice that talks to the reader, would treat Risa the way Heather did, or the way Miss Benson did? Support your opinion with examples from the poem and "The Good Deed."

Extension and Challenge

9. **Big Question Activity** In "The Good Deed," Heather says exactly what she thinks about Risa. But we don't always know what Risa is thinking. In a small group, discuss what Risa's first **impression** of Heather might have been. How might Risa's impression have changed throughout the story? Support your responses with examples from the story.

10. **Inquiry and Research** What challenges does a blind person face on a daily basis? Research the strategies, tools, and resources available to help them actively participate in every aspect of life, just as Miss Benson does.

RESEARCH LINKS
For more on challenges of the blind, visit the **Research Center** at ClassZone.com.

Vocabulary in Context

Show that you understand the vocabulary words by deciding if each statement is true or false.

1. A **generic** shirt is hard to find.
2. If you give a **pert** answer, other people will think you are quiet and shy.
3. A room that is **incredibly** noisy is very loud.
4. A **trite** statement usually suggests a new way of looking at something.
5. If my ability to hear is **impaired,** I can hear very well.
6. A false **accusation** against someone is likely to make that person angry.

accusation

generic

impaired

incredibly

pert

trite

VOCABULARY IN WRITING

What kinds of things might have made Heather nervous about meeting Miss Benson for the first time? Write a paragraph telling what you think, using at least two vocabulary words. You could start like this.

> **EXAMPLE SENTENCE**
>
> Because Miss Benson was a retired teacher, Heather might have been afraid that anything she said would sound **trite.**

VOCABULARY STRATEGY: SUFFIXES

A **suffix** is a word part that appears at the end of a root or base word to form a new word. Suffixes can change a word's part of speech. For example, the suffix in *accusation* changes the verb *accuse* to a noun. If you can recognize the base word, you can usually figure out the meaning of the new word. See the chart for common suffixes and their meaning.

Suffixes	Meanings
-er, -or	person or thing that
-ance, -ence, -ion, -tion, -ation	act or condition of

PRACTICE For each boldfaced word, identify the base word and its meaning. Then use your knowledge of the word and the information in the chart to define the boldfaced word.

1. The sudden noise broke his **concentration.**
2. Our swimming **instructor** was a teenager.
3. She received a weekly **allowance** for buying lunch.
4. I have always had a **fascination** with frogs and toads.

VOCABULARY PRACTICE
For more practice, go to the **Vocabulary Center** at **ClassZone.com.**

Reading-Writing Connection

Increase your understanding of "The Good Deed" by responding to these prompts. Then complete the **Grammar and Writing** exercise.

A. Short Response: Compare and Contrast
Outwardly, Heather treats Miss Benson differently than she treats Risa. Write **one paragraph** comparing Heather's behavior toward Miss Benson with her behavior toward Risa.

A strong response will ...
- include a topic sentence that evaluates Heather's behavior
- use examples from the story to support your topic sentence

B. Extended Response: Write a New Ending
What if Heather's **impression** of Risa had been correct and Risa had taken the book without asking Miss Benson? Write a **two- or three-paragraph summary** of a possible new ending to the story.

An effective ending will ...
- have a natural connection with the rest of the story
- tie up all loose ends in the story

GRAMMAR AND WRITING

AVOID RUN-ON SENTENCES A run-on sentence is two or more sentences written as one sentence. To correct the error, use a **period** to make two separate sentences, or use a **comma** and **coordinating conjunction** (*and, but, or*) to divide the parts of the run-on.

Original: Heather politely says goodbye to Miss Benson, she barges into Risa's home uninvited.

Revised: Heather politely says goodbye to Miss Benson, but she barges into Risa's home uninvited.

PRACTICE Rewrite the following sentences, making changes in punctuation and, if necessary, capitalization to correct the run-on sentences. Add coordinating conjunctions where needed.

1. Risa walked in the door, she asked me to give her the book.
2. I accused Risa of stealing the book, she blushed and looked down.
3. Risa told me she planned to return the book after she read it to her brothers, she asked me not to tell Miss Benson.
4. I wasn't sure what to do, I really liked Miss Benson.

*For more help with run-on sentences, see page R64 in the **Grammar Handbook**.*

All Summer in a Day

Short Story by Ray Bradbury

What if your whole WORLD *changed?*

KEY IDEA People often become comfortable in the familiar **world** of their family, friends, and daily routines. However, people move and traditions change. When your world changes, whether by a little or a lot, it can have an impact on your life. In "All Summer in a Day," a young girl feels lost in a new place.

SKETCH IT Think about the people, places, events, and ideas that are most precious to you. Create a sketch of your world, showing some of the things that make it a special place. How would you feel if any of these things disappeared?

● LITERARY ANALYSIS: SETTING

Setting is not only *where* a story takes place but also *when* it takes place. In **science fiction** stories, the setting is often the distant future. The imaginary world in which the characters live is based on real or possible scientific discoveries and inventions. This setting usually causes the events of the story to unfold in an unexpected way. As you read "All Summer in a Day," look for clues that tell you when and where the story takes place.

Review: **Conflict**

● READING SKILL: MAKE INFERENCES

As a reader you are a detective. Details, events, and dialogue in a story are your clues. You put the clues together with your own knowledge to **make inferences,** or make guesses.

As you read "All Summer in a Day," use an equation like the one shown to record the inferences you make about the characters' feelings and their actions.

Clues from the Story	+	My Knowledge	=	Inference
Margot is not part of the group.	+	Not being part of a group can make you feel sad.	=	Margot feels sad.

Review: **Identify Cause and Effect**

▲ VOCABULARY IN CONTEXT

Ray Bradbury uses these words as he creates a world that is very different from ours. Complete each sentence with an appropriate word from the list.

WORD LIST	apparatus	resilient	slacken
	immense	savor	tumultuously

1. The leaves shook _____, and we were scared.
2. The _____ planet offered many areas to explore.
3. The sturdy shelters are built to be _____.
4. After the storm, the wind began to _____.
5. The _____ used to open the hatch was broken.
6. She sat quietly to _____ everything around her.

Author On|ine

Vivid Imagination
As a boy in Illinois, Ray Bradbury had a passion for adventure stories, secret code rings, and comic strips. He started writing fiction to create his own imaginary worlds.

**Ray Bradbury
born 1920**

Creative Genius
While some of Bradbury's most famous stories are science fiction, he doesn't think of himself as a science fiction writer. Instead, he thinks of himself as someone who simply writes what he sees, just "through a different lens." Though he writes about future technology and space travel, Bradbury is a bit old-fashioned. He has never learned to drive a car, preferring to get around by riding a bicycle.

Background

Beyond Summer When Bradbury wrote "All Summer in a Day" in 1954, very little was known about Venus. The mysterious planet lay hidden beneath a very heavy layer of clouds. Scientists learned a few years later that this dense cloud cover did not result in constant rain, as occurs in Bradbury's story. Instead, the clouds appear to trap heat. The temperature at the surface of the planet is about 860°F, which is much too hot for rainfall.

MORE ABOUT THE AUTHOR AND BACKGROUND
To learn more about Ray Bradbury and the planet Venus, visit the **Literature Center** at ClassZone.com.

ALL SUMMER IN A DAY

RAY BRADBURY

ANALYZE VISUALS
What words would you use to describe this photograph?

"Ready?"

"Ready."

"Now?"

"Soon."

"Do the scientists really know? Will it happen today, will it?"

"Look, look; see for yourself!"

The children pressed to each other like so many roses, so many weeds, intermixed, peering out for a look at the hidden sun.

It rained.

10 It had been raining for seven years; thousands upon thousands of days compounded and filled from one end to the other with rain, with the drum and gush of water, with the sweet crystal fall of showers and the concussion[1] of storms so heavy they were tidal waves come over the islands. A thousand forests had been crushed under the rain and grown up a thousand times to be crushed again. And this was the way life was forever on the planet Venus, and this was the school room of the children of the rocket men and women who had come to a raining world to set up civilization and live out their lives. **A**

A SETTING
Reread lines 7–18. What do the **details** suggest about where and when the story takes place?

---

1. **concussion** (kən-kŭsh′ən): pounding.

It was gloomy

"It's stopping, it's stopping!"

20 "Yes, yes!"

Margot stood apart from them, from these children who could never remember a time when there wasn't rain and rain and rain. They were all nine years old, and if there had been a day, seven years ago, when the sun came out for an hour and showed its face to the stunned world, they could not recall. Sometimes, at night, she heard them stir, in remembrance, and she knew they were dreaming and remembering gold or a yellow crayon or a coin large enough to buy the world with. She knew that they thought they remembered a warmness, like a blushing in the face, in the body, in the arms and legs and trembling hands. But then they

30 always awoke to the tatting drum,[2] the endless shaking down of clear bead necklaces upon the roof, the walk, the gardens, the forest, and their dreams were gone.

All day yesterday they had read in class, about the sun. About how like a lemon it was, and how hot. And they had written small stories or essays or poems about it:

> "I think the sun is a flower,
> That blooms for just one hour."

That was Margot's poem, read in a quiet voice in the still classroom while the rain was falling outside.

40 "Aw, you didn't write that!" protested one of the boys.

"I did," said Margot. "I *did*."

"William!" said the teacher.

But that was yesterday. Now, the rain was **slackening,** and the children were crushed to the great thick windows.

"Where's teacher?"

"She'll be back."

"She'd better hurry, we'll miss it!"

They turned on themselves, like a feverish wheel, all tumbling spokes.

Margot stood alone. She was a very frail girl who looked as if she had

50 been lost in the rain for years and the rain had washed out the blue from her eyes and the red from her mouth and the yellow from her hair. She was an old photograph dusted from an album, whitened away, and if she spoke at all her voice would be a ghost. Now she stood, separate, staring at the rain and the loud wet world beyond the huge glass.

"What're *you* looking at?" said William.

Margot said nothing.

SCIENCE CONNECTION

Exploration of Venus began with a "flyby" spacecraft from the Soviet Union in 1961 and another from the United States in 1962. Since then, orbiting spacecraft and robotic equipment have provided pictures and information about conditions on Venus.

slacken (slăk′ən) *v.* to slow down or lessen

---

2. **tatting drum:** a continuous, soft, beating sound.

"Speak when you're spoken to." He gave her a shove. But she did not move; rather, she let herself be moved only by him and nothing else.

They edged away from her, they would not look at her. She felt them go away. And this was because she would play no games with them in the echoing tunnels of the underground city. If they tagged her and ran, she stood blinking after them and did not follow. When the class sang songs about happiness and life and games, her lips barely moved. Only when they sang about the sun and the summer did her lips move, as she watched the drenched windows.

And then, of course, the biggest crime of all was that she had come here only five years ago from Earth, and she remembered the sun and the way the sun was and the sky was, when she was four, in Ohio. And they, they had been on Venus all their lives, and they had been only two years old when last the sun came out, and had long since forgotten the color and heat of it and the way that it really was. But Margot remembered. **B**

"It's like a penny," she said once, eyes closed.

"No it's not!" the children cried.

"It's like a fire," she said, "in the stove."

"You're lying; you don't remember!" cried the children.

But she remembered and stood quietly apart from all of them and watched the patterning windows. And once, a month ago, she had refused to shower in the school shower-rooms, had clutched her hands to her ears and over her head, screaming the water mustn't touch her head. So after that, dimly, dimly, she sensed it, she was different and they knew her difference and kept away. **C**

There was talk that her father and mother were taking her back to Earth next year; it seemed vital to her that they do so, though it would mean the loss of thousands of dollars to her family. And so, the children hated her for all these reasons, of big and little consequence. They hated her pale, snow face, her waiting silence, her thinness and her possible future.

"Get away!" The boy gave her another push. "What're you waiting for?"

Then, for the first time, she turned and looked at him. And what she was waiting for was in her eyes.

"Well, don't wait around here!" cried the boy, savagely. "You won't see nothing!"

Her lips moved.

"Nothing!" he cried. "It was all a joke, wasn't it?" He turned to the other children. "Nothing's happening today. *Is* it?"

They all blinked at him and then, understanding, laughed and shook their heads. "Nothing, nothing!"

B CONFLICT
What is the conflict between Margot and her classmates?

C MAKE INFERENCES
Why does Margot refuse to take a shower?

"Oh, but," Margot whispered, her eyes helpless. "But, this is the day, the scientists predict, they say, they *know,* the sun . . ."

100   "All a joke!" said the boy, and seized her roughly. "Hey, everyone, let's put her in a closet before teacher comes!"

"No," said Margot, falling back.

They surged about her, caught her up, and bore her, protesting, and then pleading, and then crying, back into a tunnel, a room, a closet, where they slammed and locked the door. They stood looking at the door and saw it tremble from her beating and throwing herself against it. They heard her muffled cries. Then, smiling, they turned and went out and back down the tunnel, just as the teacher arrived. **D**

"Ready, children?" She glanced at her watch.

110   "Yes!" said everyone.

"Are we all here?"

"Yes!"

The rain slackened still more.

They crowded to the huge door.

The rain stopped.

It was as if, in the midst of a film concerning an avalanche, a tornado, a hurricane, a volcanic eruption, something had, first, gone wrong with the sound **apparatus,** thus muffling and finally cutting off all noise, all of the blasts and repercussions and thunders, and then, secondly, ripped
120   the film from the projector and inserted in its place a peaceful tropical slide which did not move or tremor. The world ground to a standstill. The silence was so **immense** and unbelievable that you felt that your ears had been stuffed or you had lost your hearing altogether. The children put their hands to their ears. They stood apart. The door slid back and the smell of the silent, waiting world came in to them.

The sun came out. **E**

It was the color of flaming bronze and it was very large. And the sky around it was a blazing blue tile color. And the jungle burned with sunlight as the children, released from their spell, rushed out, yelling, into the
130   summer-time.

"Now, don't go too far," called the teacher after them. "You've only one hour, you know. You wouldn't want to get caught out!"

But they were running and turning their faces up to the sky and feeling the sun on their cheeks like a warm iron; they were taking off their jackets and letting the sun burn their arms.

"Oh, it's better than the sun-lamps, isn't it?"

D CAUSE AND EFFECT
What happens to Margot as a result of the other children's dislike of her?

apparatus (ăp′ə-răt′əs) *n.* a device or set of equipment used for a specific purpose

immense (ĭ-měns′) *adj.* extremely big; huge

E SETTING
Reread lines 115–126. What do the children learn about their world when the sun comes out?

"Much, much better!"

They stopped running and stood in the great jungle that covered Venus, that grew and never stopped growing, **tumultuously,** even as you watched it. It was a nest of octopuses, clustering up great arms of flesh-like weed, wavering, flowering in this brief spring. It was the color of rubber and ash, this jungle, from the many years without sun. It was the color of stones and white cheeses and ink. **F**

The children lay out, laughing, on the jungle mattress, and heard it sigh and squeak under them, **resilient** and alive. They ran among the trees, they slipped and fell, they pushed each other, they played hide-and-seek and tag, but most of all they squinted at the sun until tears ran down their faces, they put their hands up at that yellowness and that amazing blueness, and they breathed of the fresh fresh air and listened and listened to the silence which suspended them in a blessed sea of no sound and no motion. They looked at everything and **savored** everything. Then, wildly, like animals escaped from their caves, they ran and ran in shouting circles. They ran for an hour and did not stop running. **G**

And then—

In the midst of their running, one of the girls wailed.

Everyone stopped.

The girl, standing in the open, held out her hand.

"Oh, look, look," she said, trembling.

They came slowly to look at her opened palm.

tumultuously
(tŏŏ-mŭl'chōō-əs'lē)
adv. in a wild or disorderly way

F SETTING
What is unusual about the plants on Venus?

resilient (rĭ-zĭl'yənt) *adj.*
flexible and springy

savor (sā'vər) *v.* to take great pleasure in

G CAUSE AND EFFECT
Reread lines 144–153. How do the children react to the change in the weather?

160 In the center of it, cupped and huge, was a single raindrop.
She began to cry, looking at it.
They glanced quickly at the sky.
"Oh. Oh."
A few cold drops fell on their noses and their cheeks and their mouths. The sun faded behind a stir of mist. A wind blew cool around them. They turned and started to walk back toward the underground house, their hands at their sides, their smiles vanishing away.

A boom of thunder startled them and like leaves before a new hurricane, they tumbled upon each other and ran. Lightning struck ten miles away,
170 five miles away, a mile, a half-mile. The sky darkened into midnight in a flash.

They stood in the doorway of the underground for a moment until it was raining hard. Then they closed the door and heard the gigantic sound of the rain falling in tons and avalanches everywhere and forever.
"Will it be seven more years?"
"Yes. Seven."
Then one of them gave a little cry.
"Margot!"
"What?"
180 "She's still in the closet where we locked her."
"Margot."

They stood as if someone had driven them, like so many stakes, into the floor. They looked at each other and then looked away. They glanced out at the world that was raining now and raining and raining steadily. They could not meet each other's glances. Their faces were solemn and pale. They looked at their hands and feet, their faces down.
"Margot."
One of the girls said, "Well . . . ?"
No one moved.
190 "Go on," whispered the girl.
They walked slowly down the hall in the sound of cold rain. They turned through the doorway to the room, in the sound of the storm and thunder, lightning on their faces, blue and terrible. They walked over to the closet door slowly and stood by it.
Behind the closet door was only silence.
They unlocked the door, even more slowly, and let Margot out. ❧ 🅗

🅗 MAKE INFERENCES
How might the children feel toward Margot now that they too have seen the sun?

Comprehension

1. **Recall** How often does the sun shine on Venus?

2. **Clarify** Why is Margot the only child who remembers the sun?

3. **Summarize** What happens to Margot while the teacher is out of the classroom?

Literary Analysis

4. **Make Inferences** Review the inferences that you recorded as you read the story. Were any of your ideas wrong or incomplete based on what you learned later on in the story? Adjust your equations as needed.

5. **Identify Cause and Effect** A cause-and-effect relationship occurs when one event causes another event to happen. What events in the story and prior to the story lead to Margot's unhappiness?

6. **Analyze Setting** Think about what happens on a sunny day in your **world.** How would that day be different from the one in the story? Use a Y chart to **compare and contrast** which details might stay the same and which might be different. Use your chart to explain how the setting affects the **plot,** or sequence of events, in "All Summer in a Day."

   Sunny Day on Earth

   Sunny Day on Venus
   The children prepare by doing activities about the sun.

   Similarities
   Children enjoy time in the sun.

7. **Examine Conflict** An **external conflict** is a struggle between a character and an outside force. An **internal conflict** happens when a character is at odds with his or her feelings. Reread lines 182–196. Are the children facing an external or internal conflict as they walk to the closet and unlock the door for Margot?

8. **Draw Conclusions** Considering what you know about Margot, how do you think she will respond to the other children when they open the closet door? Give examples from the story to support your answer.

Extension and Challenge

9. **SCIENCE CONNECTION** Venus and Earth have often been referred to as "twin planets." Research Venus and Earth to learn more about their similarities and differences.

   RESEARCH LINKS
   For more on Venus and Earth, visit the **Research Center** at **ClassZone.com.**

Venus   Earth

Vocabulary in Context

VOCABULARY PRACTICE

For each set, choose the word that differs most in meaning from the other words.

apparatus   savor
immense   slacken
resilient   tumultuously

1. (a) prepare, (b) appreciate, (c) enjoy, (d) savor
2. (a) appliance, (b) device, (c) apparatus, (d) operator
3. (a) slacken, (b) lessen, (c) decrease, (d) enlarge
4. (a) enormous, (b) immense, (c) gigantic, (d) distant
5. (a) tumultuously, (b) carefully, (c) thoughtfully, (d) cautiously
6. (a) elastic, (b) nervous, (c) flexible, (d) resilient

VOCABULARY IN WRITING

Pretend that you are one of Margot's classmates. What did you think would happen when the sun came out? Write a paragraph explaining your ideas, using two or more vocabulary words. You could start like this.

> **EXAMPLE SENTENCE**
>
> *I thought the rain would **slacken**, but I never believed that it would really stop.*

VOCABULARY STRATEGY: USE THE BEST SYNONYM

A **synonym** is a word that has the same or similar meaning to another word. Common words like *big* have many synonyms. However, not all of them mean exactly the same thing. In this story, for example, the word *immense* gives a more detailed sense of the setting than the common word *big* would give. In a **thesaurus** (a book or electronic tool used to find synonyms) or synonym finder, *immense* might be grouped with words like *enormous, gigantic, huge,* and *massive*.

Synonyms for *big*
hefty
oversized
spacious
vast

PRACTICE Choose the synonym from the box that best fits the meaning of each sentence. Use a dictionary or thesaurus if you need help.

1. The _____ poster did not fit into the small frame.
2. The _____ theater easily held the 600 students.
3. Fields of wheat stretched for miles across the _____ plains.
4. The _____ package was hard to lift.

VOCABULARY PRACTICE
For more practice, go to the **Vocabulary Center** at ClassZone.com.

Reading-Writing Connection

Explore the influence of setting in "All Summer in a Day" by responding to these prompts. Then complete the **Grammar and Writing** exercise.

WRITING PROMPTS

A. Short Response: Write a Letter

How might Margot see her **world** on Venus? Write a **one-paragraph letter** from Margot to her grandparents on Earth describing her new home.

SELF-CHECK

An engaging letter will . . .
- be consistent with details from the story
- use words and phrases that create a vivid description

B. Extended Response: Analyze Science Fiction

"All Summer in a Day" is considered **science fiction.** Reread the definition of science fiction on page 63. Then write **two or three paragraphs** that use details from the story to clearly explain why the story is an example of science fiction.

A logical response will . . .
- include a clear opening statement
- use specific examples to support your explanation

GRAMMAR AND WRITING

USE COMMAS CORRECTLY Be sure to put **commas** in the correct place when writing **dates, addresses,** and **letters.** Follow these guidelines:

- **In dates:** Use a comma between the day and the year. Use a comma after the year if the sentence continues.
- **In addresses:** Use a comma between the city or town and the state or country. Use a comma after the state or country if the sentence continues.
- **In letters:** Use a comma after the greeting of a casual letter and after the closing word before the signature in a casual or business letter.

Original:	We landed on Venus on March 21 3044 after months of travel.
Revised:	We landed on Venus on March 21, 3044, after months of travel.

PRACTICE Rewrite the letter and add the missing commas.

Dear Grandma and Grandpa

    I miss you. Mom and Dad say that I might return to Akron Ohio next year. The spacecraft leaves on May 10 3050. I can't wait to see you both.

Love

Margot

*For more help with commas, see page R49 in the **Grammar Handbook.***

Settling in Space

- Magazine Article, page 75
- Online Article, page 76
- Illustrations, page 80

Use with "All Summer in a Day," page 64.

What's the Connection?

In "All Summer in a Day," you read about people living in a colony on Venus. But what's Venus really like? What would it be like to live in a space colony? Study the articles and images on the next few pages to get the science facts about these science fiction settings.

Skill Focus: Use Text Features

Knowing how to use text features will help you find facts in an article. **Text features** are things such as titles and illustrations that call attention to important information. They can tell you what an article will be about, make key terms noticeable, and show the organization of a selection. For example:

- A **title** or **headline** identifies the topic.
- A **subheading**—a heading within an article—signals the start of a new topic or section and identifies what it will be about.
- **Bulleted lists** (like this one) distinguish items of equal importance.
- **Graphic aids**—such as illustrations, diagrams, and maps—may show people, places, things, or even ideas.

See what you can learn from the text features in the selections that follow. Take notes in a chart like the one shown here.

Selection	Text Feature	What I Learn or Infer
"Weather That's Out of This World"	Title: "Weather That's Out of This World!"	This article will probably be about wild weather or weather on another planet.
"Space Settlements"	Subheadings & Bulleted Items: 1. What is an Orbital Space Colony?	1. giant spacecraft that travels endlessly through space
"Artists' Views of a Space Colony"	Graphic Aid:	

Weather That's Out of This World! Alan Dyer

**If you think Earth's weather is wild,
just wait until you see what it's like elsewhere in the solar system.**

Hot, Sizzling Venus Ⓐ

"This is VTN—the Venus Television Network—with the latest forecast for the second planet from the Sun: hot today, hot tomorrow, and hot the following day. It will also be cloudy, with no sign of any sunshine. Take your glass umbrella—we're in for more acid rain."

If there were meteorologists on Venus, that's the kind of forecast they would have to give. Venus is a nasty place to live. Think of the hottest day you can remember. Then imagine what it would be like if it were 10 times hotter—that's what it's like on Venus.

10   Venus is the hottest planet in the solar system. The temperature at its surface is a searing 860 degrees Fahrenheit, day and night. The superhigh temperature surprised many astronomers, who once thought Mercury would be hotter, since it is closer to the Sun. But Venus has something very important that Mercury lacks—an atmosphere. Unlike Earth's atmosphere, which is made of oxygen and nitrogen, the air on Venus is mostly carbon dioxide gas, one of the so-called greenhouse gases. Like the glass in a greenhouse, carbon dioxide in the air traps heat coming from the Sun. With no place to go, the heat builds up. In the case of Venus, its thick carbon dioxide blanket has made the planet so hot that
20 some metals, such as lead, would melt on its surface.

Adding to Venus's unpleasant weather is a constant drizzle from the thick clouds that surround the planet. But it's not water that falls from the sky there. Instead, the rain is made of droplets of sulfuric acid, a corrosive liquid that burns anything it touches. Between the blistering heat and the sizzling acid rain, Venus's weather is much worse than anything we could find on Earth.

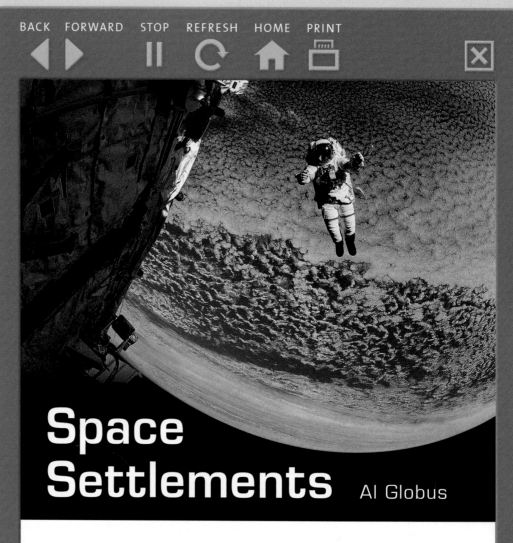

Space Settlements

Al Globus

B USE TEXT FEATURES
Preview this article to identify the **subheadings** in it. Write these in your chart, leaving space between them for notes. Then, as you read the article, jot down what you learn from the paragraphs that follow each subheading. Use **bullets** to list each key point.

What Is an Orbital Space Colony? **B**

An orbital space colony is a giant spacecraft big enough to live in. Orbital colonies will travel endlessly through space while the folks inside play, work, and socialize.

What Will Life Be Like?

Living inside a space colony will, in many ways, be like living on Earth. People will have houses or apartments. They will go to work and to school. There will be shops, sports teams, concerts, and movies. People will go to parties with their friends, just like 10 on Earth. However, there will also be many differences.

BACK FORWARD STOP REFRESH HOME PRINT

Today we live on the outside of a planet. Earth is thousands of kilometers across, so big that it looks like we are living on a flat surface. Instead of living on the outside of a huge planet, space settlers will live inside very large spacecraft. The spacecraft will be large enough for people to take a good walk, but not so big that it will look like you live on a flat surface. People will live on the inside of spheres, cylinders, and toruses (or donut shapes). These shapes are ideal for space colonies because colonies must rotate to produce pseudo-gravity, or false gravity.

20   The air and water we need to live is produced naturally here on Earth. On a space colony millions of times smaller than Earth, we will need to constantly monitor the air and water and take quick action if anything begins to go wrong. Otherwise, the entire population would be endangered within a matter of hours.

Here on Earth, many people feel they can use things and throw them away. There are plenty of materials all around us. On a space colony, every atom will be precious, so recycling will be a way of life. Nothing, except perhaps the most toxic wastes, will be thrown away. Everything will be endlessly recycled,
30 especially water. Waste water will run to the outside of the spacecraft, where sunlight will sterilize the waste, after which everything will be used again.

Agriculture will be different too. On Earth, huge farms take advantage of soil and water conditions to grow the food we need to live. On a space colony, food will be grown in small, carefully controlled rooms where conditions are kept perfect for the crops being grown. This will lead to abundant crops, so the area needed for agriculture will be far smaller than on Earth.

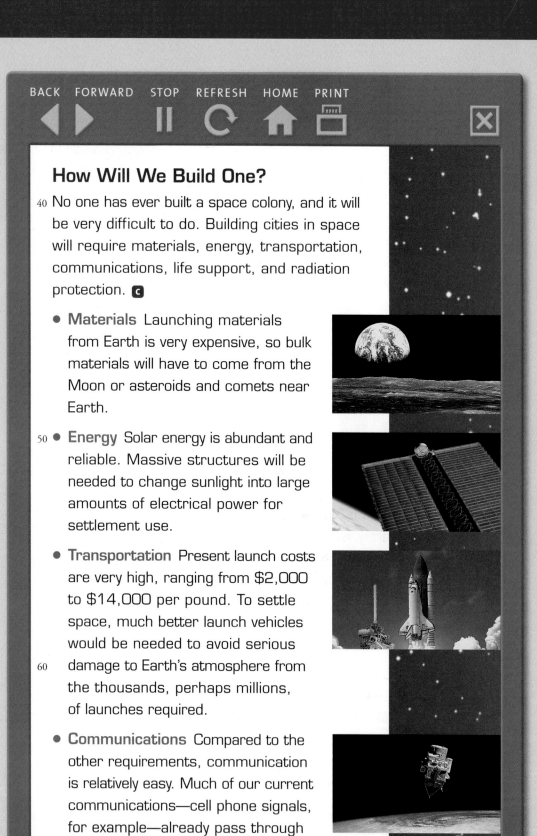

How Will We Build One?

40 No one has ever built a space colony, and it will be very difficult to do. Building cities in space will require materials, energy, transportation, communications, life support, and radiation protection. **C**

- **Materials** Launching materials from Earth is very expensive, so bulk materials will have to come from the Moon or asteroids and comets near Earth.

50 - **Energy** Solar energy is abundant and reliable. Massive structures will be needed to change sunlight into large amounts of electrical power for settlement use.

- **Transportation** Present launch costs are very high, ranging from $2,000 to $14,000 per pound. To settle space, much better launch vehicles would be needed to avoid serious
60 damage to Earth's atmosphere from the thousands, perhaps millions, of launches required.

- **Communications** Compared to the other requirements, communication is relatively easy. Much of our current communications—cell phone signals, for example—already pass through satellites.

C USE TEXT FEATURES
Reread the sentence in lines 41–44. Then skim the boldfaced terms in the **bulleted list** that follows it. What do you notice about the order of the terms in the list?

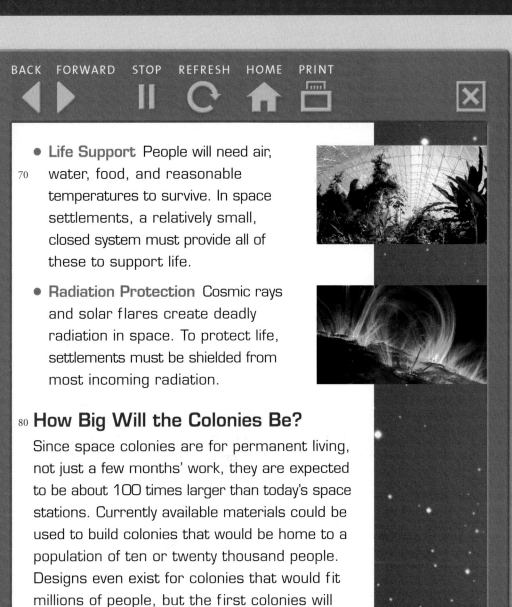

BACK   FORWARD   STOP   REFRESH   HOME   PRINT

- **Life Support** People will need air,
  70 water, food, and reasonable
  temperatures to survive. In space
  settlements, a relatively small,
  closed system must provide all of
  these to support life.

- **Radiation Protection** Cosmic rays
  and solar flares create deadly
  radiation in space. To protect life,
  settlements must be shielded from
  most incoming radiation.

80 ## How Big Will the Colonies Be?

Since space colonies are for permanent living,
not just a few months' work, they are expected
to be about 100 times larger than today's space
stations. Currently available materials could be
used to build colonies that would be home to a
population of ten or twenty thousand people.
Designs even exist for colonies that would fit
millions of people, but the first colonies will
almost certainly be smaller.

90   Right now, space colonies are just an idea,
but someday space colonies may crisscross
the solar system, providing homes for a trillion
people. What an achievement that will be. **D**

D **SCIENCE ARTICLE**
What do you think the
author's purpose was
for writing this science
article?

ARTISTS' VIEWS OF A
SPACE COLONY

As scientists explore the possibilities of how to colonize space, many of the concepts they present to the public can be difficult to visualize. For that reason, artists often work with scientists to help convey their ideas. Here, artists have illustrated inside and outside views of a possible space colony.

Exterior view of a space colony **E**

E **USE TEXT FEATURES**
What details of life in a space colony do these **graphic aids** help you visualize?

Interior view of a space colony

Comprehension

1. **Recall** What do you learn about Venus from the Venus Television Network "broadcast"?

2. **Summarize** Briefly describe the main features of the orbital space colony shown in the two illustrations on page 80.

Critical Analysis

3. **Use Text Features** "Space Settlements" is made up of several sections. Identify each section by its **subheading** and summarize its main ideas.

4. **Identify Characteristics of Form** What are three characteristics of "Space Settlements" that make it a **science article?** Explain.

5. **Draw Conclusions** Consider what you know of neighborhoods on Earth and what you have learned about orbital space colonies. Do you think the illustrations of an orbital space colony are realistic? Why or why not?

Read for Information: Compare and Contrast

WRITING PROMPT

When you **compare and contrast,** you identify the ways in which two or more subjects are alike and different. Compare and contrast one of the out-of-this-world settings in "Weather That's Out of This World!" and "Space Settlements" with the setting in Ray Bradbury's story "All Summer in a Day."

To answer this prompt, choose one of the two places you just read about—the real Venus or an orbital space colony. Then follow these steps:

1. Reread the information you gathered about the place you chose and Bradbury's description of the setting in "All Summer in a Day."

2. Using a Venn diagram, record details that describe each setting.

3. Look at your diagram to see whether there are more similarities or differences between the two settings.

4. In a sentence, tell whether your chosen setting and Bradbury's are more alike or more different. Then support your statement by pointing out specific similarities and differences.

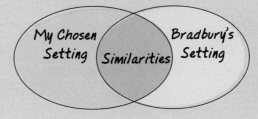

Lob's Girl

Short Story by Joan Aiken

How powerful is
LOYALTY?

KEY IDEA Has there ever been a time when someone stood by you when you really needed a friend? If so, then you know how important **loyalty,** or devotion, can be. A reliable friend or family member can help you overcome the toughest problems. In "Lob's Girl," a girl and her family discover just how powerful loyalty can be.

WEB IT Create a web of the people and things to which you are loyal. Then explain how you show your loyalty to each.

I listen to her.

Carla

Loyalty

● LITERARY ANALYSIS: FORESHADOWING

What is it that makes you want to continue reading a story? Sometimes writers build excitement and curiosity by providing a hint about something that will happen later in the story. This hint is known as **foreshadowing.** Foreshadowing may appear in

- what the characters say (*"I wish we could play with him every day."*)
- what the characters do (*Don came home very late and grim-faced.*)
- descriptions of setting (*narrow, steep, twisting hillroad*)

As you read "Lob's Girl," look for examples of foreshadowing.

● READING SKILL: IDENTIFY SEQUENCE

A story's events are presented in a specific order, or **sequence.** Certain words and phrases can help you identify the sequence of events, such as

the next day	at half-past nine	at the same moment
by that afternoon	then	a few minutes later

As you read, record the story's sequence of events on a timeline like the one shown. Above each event, record the clue words or phrases that signal it.

"It began"

Sandy meets Lob
on the beach.

▲ VOCABULARY IN CONTEXT

The boldfaced words help Joan Aiken tell the story of a very determined dog. To show how many you already know, provide a definition for each boldfaced word.

1. The **agitated** owner searches for his lost pet.
2. When they see the dog, the children **erupt** with joy.
3. The dog is **reluctant** to leave his new friends.
4. As he turns to leave, the dog looks **melancholy.**
5. The dog licks his owner as if to **atone** for running away.
6. He runs **decisively** toward his beloved new owner.

Author On**line**

Spinner of Tales
Joan Aiken grew up in England and was home-schooled by her mother until the age of 12. Since she was often alone as a child, she had trouble making friends when she left home for boarding school. Spending most of her free time writing, she completed her first novel by the time she was 16.

Joan Aiken
1924–2004

Royal Recognition As an adult, Aiken became famous for writing stories full of suspense, mystery, delightfully bad villains, charming heroes and heroines, and spooky surprises. In 1999 Queen Elizabeth II made Aiken a member of the Order of the British Empire in recognition of her contributions to children's literature.

> **MORE ABOUT THE AUTHOR**
> For more on Joan Aiken, visit the **Literature Center** at ClassZone.com.

Background

A Fishing Village Life in a fishing village revolves around the sea, and many of the village residents are fishermen. Some fishermen stay out at sea for days, while others set out each morning or evening, depending on the tide and weather. Tourism provides other jobs for the villagers. Tourists are attracted to the unspoiled beauty of the coastline and the charm of the village. In "Lob's Girl," the daughter of a fisherman meets a tourist who changes her life forever.

Lob's Girl

Joan Aiken

Some people choose their dogs, and some dogs choose their people. The Pengelly family had no say in the choosing of Lob; he came to them in the second way, and very **decisively.**

It began on the beach, the summer when Sandy was five, Don, her older brother, twelve, and the twins were three. Sandy was really Alexandra, because her grandmother had a beautiful picture of a queen in a diamond tiara and high collar of pearls. It hung by Granny Pearce's kitchen sink and was as familiar as the doormat. When Sandy was born everyone agreed that she was the living spit[1] of the picture, and so she was called Alexandra and
10 Sandy for short. A

On this summer day she was lying peacefully reading a comic and not keeping an eye on the twins, who didn't need it because they were occupied in seeing which of them could wrap the most seaweed around the other one's legs. Father—Bert Pengelly—and Don were up on the Hard[2] painting the bottom boards of the boat in which Father went fishing for pilchards.[3] And Mother—Jean Pengelly—was getting ahead with making the Christmas puddings because she never felt easy in her mind if they

---

decisively (dĭ-sī′sĭv′lē) *adv.* in a clear, definite way

A SEQUENCE
What clue words signal the first important event?

ANALYZE VISUALS
What can you **infer** about the dog based on the details in the image?

---

1. **the living spit:** an exact likeness, often worded as "the spitting image."
2. **Hard:** a landing place for boats.
3. **pilchards** (pĭl′chərdz): small fish similar to sardines.

weren't made and safely put away by the end of August. As usual, each member of the family was happily getting on with his or her own affairs.
20 Little did they guess how soon this state of things would be changed by the large new member who was going to **erupt** into their midst.

Sandy rolled onto her back to make sure that the twins were not climbing on slippery rocks or getting cut off by the tide. At the same moment a large body struck her forcibly in the midriff, and she was covered by flying sand. Instinctively she shut her eyes and felt the sand being wiped off her face by something that seemed like a warm, rough, damp flannel. She opened her eyes and looked. It was a tongue. Its owner was a large and bouncy young Alsatian, or German shepherd, with topaz eyes, black-tipped prick ears, a thick, soft coat, and a bushy, black-tipped tail.

30 "*Lob!*" shouted a man farther up the beach. "Lob, come here!"

But Lob, as if trying to **atone** for the surprise he had given her, went on licking the sand off Sandy's face, wagging his tail so hard while he kept on knocking up more clouds of sand. His owner, a gray-haired man with a limp, walked over as quickly as he could and seized him by the collar.

"I hope he didn't give you a fright?" the man said to Sandy. "He meant it in play—he's only young."

erupt (ĭ-rŭpt') *v.* to release one's anger or enthusiasm in a sudden, noisy way

atone (ə-tōn') *v.* to seek pardon; to make up for

ANALYZE VISUALS
What **details** do you notice in this illustration?

"Oh, no, I think he's *beautiful*," said Sandy truly. She picked up a bit of driftwood and threw it. Lob, whisking easily out of his master's grip, was after it like a sand-colored bullet. He came back with the stick, beaming,
40 and gave it to Sandy. At the same time he gave himself, though no one else was aware of this at the time. But with Sandy, too, it was love at first sight, and when, after a lot more stick-throwing, she and the twins joined Father and Don to go home for tea, they cast many a backward glance at Lob being led firmly away by his master.

"I wish we could play with him every day," Tess sighed.

"Why can't we?" said Tim.

Sandy explained. "Because Mr. Dodsworth, who owns him, is from Liverpool, and he is only staying at the Fisherman's Arms till Saturday."

"Is Liverpool a long way off?"

50 "Right at the other end of England from Cornwall, I'm afraid."

It was a Cornish[4] fishing village where the Pengelly family lived, with rocks and cliffs and a strip of beach and a little round harbor, and palm trees growing in the gardens of the little whitewashed stone houses. The village was approached by a narrow, steep, twisting hillroad and guarded by a notice that said LOW GEAR FOR 1½ MILES, DANGEROUS TO CYCLISTS. **B**

The Pengelly children went home to scones with Cornish cream and jam, thinking they had seen the last of Lob. But they were much mistaken. The whole family was playing cards by the fire in the front room after supper
60 when there was a loud thump and a crash of china in the kitchen.

"My Christmas puddings!" exclaimed Jean, and ran out.

"Did you put TNT in them, then?" her husband said.

But it was Lob, who, finding the front door shut, had gone around to the back and bounced in through the open kitchen window, where the puddings were cooling on the sill. Luckily only the smallest was knocked down and broken.

Lob stood on his hind legs and plastered Sandy's face with licks. Then he did the same for the twins, who shrieked with joy.

"Where does this friend of yours come from?" inquired Mr. Pengelly.

70 "He's staying at the Fisherman's Arms—I mean his owner is."

"Then he must go back there. Find a bit of string, Sandy, to tie to his collar." **C**

SOCIAL STUDIES CONNECTION

Cornwall is a county in southwestern England. Liverpool is a large city in northern England.

B FORESHADOWING
Reread line 56. How might this be an example of foreshadowing?

C SEQUENCE
What happens after Lob's owner takes him back to Fisherman's Arms? As you read, record the events on your timeline.

---

4. **Cornish:** in or from the English county Cornwall.

"I wonder how he found his way here," Mrs. Pengelly said, when the **reluctant** Lob had been led whining away and Sandy had explained about their afternoon's game on the beach. "Fisherman's Arms is right round the other side of the harbor."

reluctant (rĭ-lŭk′tənt)
adj. unwilling

Lob's owner scolded him and thanked Mr. Pengelly for bringing him back. Jean Pengelly warned the children that they had better not encourage Lob any more if they met him on the beach, or it would only lead to more
80 trouble. So they dutifully took no notice of him the next day until he spoiled their good resolutions by dashing up to them with joyful barks, wagging his tail so hard that he winded Tess and knocked Tim's legs from under him.

They had a happy day, playing on the sand.

The next day was Saturday. Sandy had found out that Mr. Dodsworth was to catch the half-past-nine train. She went out secretly, down to the station, nodded to Mr. Hoskins, the stationmaster, who wouldn't dream of charging any local for a platform ticket, and climbed up on the footbridge that led over the tracks. She didn't want to be seen, but she did want to see. She saw Mr. Dodsworth get on the train, accompanied by an
90 unhappy-looking Lob with drooping ears and tail. Then she saw the train slide away out of sight around the next headland, with a **melancholy** wail that sounded like Lob's last good-bye.

melancholy
(mĕl′ən-kŏl′ē) *adj.* sad;
gloomy

Sandy wished she hadn't had the idea of coming to the station. She walked home miserably, with her shoulders hunched and her hands in her pockets. For the rest of the day, she was so cross and unlike herself that Tess and Tim were quite surprised, and her mother gave her a dose of senna.[5]

A week passed. Then, one evening, Mrs. Pengelly and the younger children were in the front room playing snakes and ladders.[6] Mr. Pengelly and Don had gone fishing on the evening tide. If your father is
100 a fisherman, he will never be home at the same time from one week to the next.

Suddenly, history repeating itself, there was a crash from the kitchen. Jean Pengelly leaped up, crying, "My blackberry jelly!" She and the children had spent the morning picking and the afternoon boiling fruit.

But Sandy was ahead of her mother. With flushed cheeks and eyes like stars she had darted into the kitchen, where she and Lob were hugging one another in a frenzy of joy. About a yard of his tongue was out, and he was licking every part of her that he could reach.

"Good heavens!" exclaimed Jean. "How in the world did *he* get here?"
110 "He must have walked," said Sandy. "Look at his feet."

---

5. **senna** (sĕn′ə): medicine made from the leaves of senna, a tree or shrub that grows in warm regions.

6. **snakes and ladders**: a board game in which game pieces climb ladders and slide down.

They were worn, dusty, and tarry. One had a cut on the pad.

"They ought to be bathed," said Jean Pengelly. "Sandy, run a bowl of warm water while I get the disinfectant."

"What'll we do about him, Mother?" said Sandy anxiously.

Mrs. Pengelly looked at her daughter's pleading eyes and sighed.

"He must go back to his owner, of course," she said, making her voice firm. "Your dad can get the address from the Fisherman's tomorrow, and phone him or send a telegram. In the meantime he'd better have a long drink and a good meal."

120 Lob was very grateful for the drink and the meal, and made no objection to having his feet washed. Then he flopped down on the hearth rug and slept in front of the fire they had lit because it was a cold, wet evening, with his head on Sandy's feet. He was a very tired dog. He had walked all the way from Liverpool to Cornwall, which is more than four hundred miles.

The next day Mr. Pengelly phoned Lob's owner, and the following morning Mr. Dodsworth arrived off the night train, decidedly put out,[7] to take his pet home. That parting was worse than the first. Lob whined, Don walked out of the house, the twins burst out crying, and Sandy crept

130 up to her bedroom afterward and lay with her face pressed into the quilt, feeling as if she were bruised all over.

Jean Pengelly took them all into Plymouth to see the circus on the next day and the twins cheered up a little, but even the hour's ride in the train each way and the Liberty horses[8] and performing seals could not cure Sandy's sore heart.

She need not have bothered, though. In ten days' time Lob was back— limping this time, with a torn ear and a patch missing out of his furry coat, as if he had met and tangled with an enemy or two in the course of his four-hundred-mile walk.

140 Bert Pengelly rang up Liverpool again. Mr. Dodsworth, when he answered, sounded weary. He said, "That dog has already cost me two days that I can't spare away from my work—plus endless time in police stations and drafting newspaper advertisements. I'm too old for these ups and downs. I think we'd better face the fact, Mr. Pengelly, that it's your family he wants to stay with—that is, if you want to have him."

Bert Pengelly gulped. He was not a rich man, and Lob was a pedigreed dog.[9] He said cautiously, "How much would you be asking for him?"

---

7. **put out:** annoyed.

8. **Liberty horses:** groups of trained horses, often all white or all black, that perform simultaneously on vocal or visual command.

9. **pedigreed** (pĕd′ĭ-grēd′) **dog:** dog whose ancestry is known and recorded, making the dog more valuable.

"Good heavens, man, I'm not suggesting I'd *sell* him to you. You must have him as a gift. Think of the train fares I'll be saving. You'll be doing
150 me a good turn." **D**

"Is he a big eater?" Bert asked doubtfully.

By this time the children, breathless in the background listening to one side of this conversation, had realized what was in the wind and were dancing up and down with their hands clasped beseechingly.

"Oh, not for his size," Lob's owner assured Bert. "Two or three pounds of meat a day and some vegetables and gravy and biscuits—he does very well on that."

Alexandra's father looked over the telephone at his daughter's swimming eyes and trembling lips. He reached a decision. "Well, then, Mr.
160 Dodsworth," he said briskly, "we'll accept your offer and thank you very much. The children will be overjoyed and you can be sure Lob has come to a good home. They'll look after him and see he gets enough exercise. But I can tell you," he ended firmly, "if he wants to settle in with us, he'll have to learn to eat a lot of fish."

So that was how Lob came to live with the Pengelly family. Everybody loved him and he loved them all. But there was never any question who came first with him. He was Sandy's dog. He slept by her bed and followed her everywhere he was allowed.

Nine years went by, and each summer Mr. Dodsworth came back
170 to stay at the Fisherman's Arms and call on his erstwhile dog. Lob always met him with recognition and dignified pleasure, accompanied him for a walk or two—but showed no signs of wishing to return to Liverpool. His place, he intimated, was definitely with the Pengellys.

In the course of nine years Lob changed less than Sandy. As she went into her teens he became a little slower, a little stiffer, there was a touch of gray on his nose, but he was still a handsome dog. He and Sandy still loved one another devotedly. **E**

One evening in October all the summer visitors had left, and the little fishing town looked empty and secretive. It was a wet, windy dusk. When
180 the children came home from school—even the twins were at high school[10] now, and Don was a full-fledged fisherman—Jean Pengelly said, "Sandy, your Aunt Rebecca says she's lonesome because Uncle Will Hoskins has gone out trawling,[11] and she wants one of you to go and spend the evening with her. You go, dear; you can take your homework with you."

Sandy looked far from enthusiastic.

D SEQUENCE
What event finally leads Lob's owner to give him to the Pengelly family?

E SEQUENCE
Note on your timeline the nine-year break in the story after Lob came to live with the Pengellys. What do you think happened during that time?

---

10. **high school:** In Great Britain, students go to high school when they are about 11 years old.

11. **trawling** (trô′lĭng): fishing with a net pulled behind a boat along the sea bottom.

"Can I take Lob with me?"

"You know Aunt Becky doesn't really like dogs—Oh, very well." Mrs. Pengelly sighed. "I suppose she'll have to put up with him as well as you."

190 Reluctantly Sandy tidied herself, took her schoolbag, put on the damp raincoat she had just taken off, fastened Lob's lead to his collar, and set off to walk through the dusk to Aunt Becky's cottage, which was five minutes' climb up the steep hill.

The wind was howling through the shrouds[12] of boats drawn up on the Hard.

"Put some cheerful music on, do," said Jean Pengelly to the nearest twin. "Anything to drown that wretched sound while I make your dad's supper." So Don, who had just come in, put on some rock music, loud. Which was why the Pengellys did not hear the truck hurtle down the hill and crash against the post office wall a few minutes later.

200 Dr. Travers was driving through Cornwall with his wife, taking a late holiday before patients began coming down with winter colds and flu. He saw the sign that said STEEP HILL. LOW GEAR FOR 1½ MILES. Dutifully he changed into second gear.

"We must be nearly there," said his wife, looking out of her window. "I noticed a sign on the coast road that said the Fisherman's Arms was

---

12. **shrouds** (shroudz): ropes or cables on a boat's mast, the vertical pole that supports the sails.

F FORESHADOWING
Reread lines 189–192. Why might the narrator be drawing attention to the steep hill again?

G FORESHADOWING
Reread lines 195–199. What might the description of the crash suggest?

ANALYZE VISUALS
What **details** in the illustration suggest that the hill is steep?

two miles. What a narrow, dangerous hill! But the cottages are very pretty—Oh, Frank, stop, *stop!* There's a child, I'm sure it's a child—by the wall over there!"

Dr. Travers jammed on his brakes and brought the car to a stop. A little
210 stream ran down by the road in a shallow stone culvert,[13] and half in the water lay something that looked, in the dusk, like a pile of clothes—or was it the body of a child? Mrs. Travers was out of the car in a flash, but her husband was quicker.

"Don't touch her, Emily!" he said sharply. "She's been hit. Can't be more than a few minutes. Remember that truck that overtook us half a mile back, speeding like the devil? Here, quick, go into that cottage and phone for an ambulance. The girl's in a bad way. I'll stay here and do what I can to stop the bleeding. Don't waste a minute."

Doctors are expert at stopping dangerous bleeding, for they know the
220 right places to press. This Dr. Travers was able to do, but he didn't dare do more; the girl was lying in a queerly crumpled heap, and he guessed she had a number of bones broken and that it would be highly dangerous to move her. He watched her with great concentration, wondering where the truck had got to and what other damage it had done.

Mrs. Travers was very quick. She had seen plenty of accident cases and knew the importance of speed. The first cottage she tried had a phone; in four minutes she was back, and in six an ambulance was wailing down the hill.

Its attendants lifted the child onto a stretcher as carefully as if she were
230 made of fine thistledown.[14] The ambulance sped off to Plymouth—for the local cottage hospital did not take serious accident cases—and Dr. Travers went down to the police station to report what he had done.

He found that the police already knew about the speeding truck—which had suffered from loss of brakes and ended up with its radiator halfway through the post-office wall. The driver was concussed[15] and shocked, but the police thought he was the only person injured—until Dr. Travers told his tale.

At half-past nine that night Aunt Rebecca Hoskins was sitting by her fire thinking aggrieved thoughts about the inconsiderateness[16]
240 of nieces who were asked to supper and never turned up, when she was startled by a neighbor, who burst in, exclaiming, "Have you heard about Sandy Pengelly, then, Mrs. Hoskins? Terrible thing, poor little soul, and

---

13. **culvert** (kŭl'vərt): a gutter or tunnel that runs along or under a road.

14. **thistledown** (thĭs'əl-doun'): the soft, fluffy part of a thistle, a plant with a prickly stem and purple flowers.

15. **concussed** (kən-kŭsd'): suffering from a concussion, an injury that results from being struck in the head.

16. **aggrieved thoughts about the inconsiderateness:** offended feelings over the thoughtlessness.

they don't know if she's likely to live. Police have got the truck driver that hit her—ah, it didn't ought to be allowed, speeding through the place like that at umpty miles an hour, they ought to jail him for life—not that that'd be any comfort to poor Bert and Jean." **H**

Horrified, Aunt Rebecca put on a coat and went down to her brother's house. She found the family with white shocked faces; Bert and Jean were about to drive off to the hospital where Sandy had been taken, and the
250 twins were crying bitterly. Lob was nowhere to be seen. But Aunt Rebecca was not interested in dogs; she did not inquire about him. **I**

"Thank the Lord you've come, Beck," said her brother. "Will you stay the night with Don and the twins? Don's out looking for Lob and heaven knows when we'll be back; we may get a bed with Jean's mother in Plymouth." **J**

"Oh, if only I'd never invited the poor child," wailed Mrs. Hoskins. But Bert and Jean hardly heard her.

That night seemed to last forever. The twins cried themselves to sleep. Don came home very late and grim-faced. Bert and Jean sat in a waiting room of the Western Counties Hospital, but Sandy was unconscious,
260 they were told, and she remained so. All that could be done for her was done. She was given transfusions to replace all the blood she had lost. The broken bones were set and put in slings and cradles.

"Is she a healthy girl? Has she a good constitution?"[17] the emergency doctor asked.

"Aye, Doctor, she is that," Bert said hoarsely. The lump in Jean's throat prevented her from answering; she merely nodded.

"Then she ought to have a chance. But I won't conceal from you that her condition is very serious, unless she shows signs of coming out from this coma."[18]
270 But as hour succeeded hour, Sandy showed no signs of recovering consciousness. Her parents sat in the waiting room with haggard faces; sometimes one of them would go to telephone the family at home, or to try to get a little sleep at the home of Granny Pearce, not far away.

At noon next day Dr. and Mrs. Travers went to the Pengelly cottage to inquire how Sandy was doing, but the report was gloomy: "Still in a very serious condition." The twins were miserably unhappy. They forgot that they had sometimes called their elder sister bossy and only remembered how often she had shared her pocket money with them, how she read to them and took them for picnics and helped with their homework. Now
280 there was no Sandy, no Mother and Dad, Don went around with a gray, shuttered face, and worse still, there was no Lob. **K**

---

17. **constitution:** physical makeup.

18. **coma:** a sleeplike state in which a person cannot sense or respond to light, sound, or touch.

H SEQUENCE
What sequence of events caused the accident?

I FORESHADOWING
Where might Lob be?

J SEQUENCE
Who is out looking for Lob? Record this event on your timeline.

K SEQUENCE
How long has Lob been missing?

The Western Counties Hospital is a large one, with dozens of different departments and five or six connected buildings, each with three or four entrances. By that afternoon it became noticeable that a dog seemed to have taken up position outside the hospital, with the fixed intention of getting in. Patiently he would try first one entrance and then another, all the way around, and then begin again. Sometimes he would get a little way inside, following a visitor, but animals were, of course, forbidden, and he was always kindly but firmly turned out again. Sometimes the guard
290   at the main entrance gave him a pat or offered him a bit of sandwich— he looked so wet and beseeching and desperate. But he never ate the sandwich. No one seemed to own him or to know where he came from; Plymouth is a large city and he might have belonged to anybody.

At tea time Granny Pearce came through the pouring rain to bring a flask of hot tea to her daughter and son-in-law. Just as she reached the main entrance the guard was gently but forcibly shoving out a large, **agitated,** soaking-wet Alsatian dog.

agitated (ăj′ĭ-tāt′əd) *adj.* disturbed; upset **agitate** v.

"No, old fellow, you can *not* come in. Hospitals are for people, not for dogs."

300   "Why, bless me," exclaimed old Mrs. Pearce. "That's Lob! Here, Lob, Lobby boy!"

Lob ran to her, whining. Mrs. Pearce walked up to the desk.

"I'm sorry, madam, you can't bring that dog in here," the guard said.

Mrs. Pearce was a very determined old lady. She looked the porter in the eye.

"Now, see here, young man. That dog has walked twenty miles from St. Killan to get to my granddaughter. Heaven knows how he knew she was here, but it's plain he knows. And he ought to have his rights! He ought to get to see her! Do you know," she went on, bristling, "that dog has walked
310   the length of England—*twice*—to be with that girl? And you think you can keep him out with your fiddling rules and regulations?"

"I'll have to ask the medical officer," the guard said weakly.

"You do that, young man." Granny Pearce sat down in a determined manner, shutting her umbrella, and Lob sat patiently dripping at her feet. Every now and then he shook his head, as if to dislodge something heavy that was tied around his neck.

Presently a tired, thin, intelligent-looking man in a white coat came downstairs, with an impressive, silver-haired man in a dark suit, and there was a low-voiced discussion. Granny Pearce eyed them, biding her time.
320   "Frankly . . . not much to lose," said the older man. The man in the white coat approached Granny Pearce.

"It's strictly against every rule, but as it's such a serious case we are making an exception," he said to her quietly. "But only *outside* her bedroom door—and only for a moment or two."

Without a word, Granny Pearce rose and stumped upstairs. Lob followed close to her skirts, as if he knew his hope lay with her.

They waited in the green-floored corridor outside Sandy's room. The door was half-shut. Bert and Jean were inside. Everything was terribly quiet. A nurse came out. The white-coated man asked her something and she
330 shook her head. She had left the door ajar and through it could now be seen a high, narrow bed with a lot of gadgets around it. Sandy lay there, very flat under the covers, very still. Her head was turned away. All Lob's attention was riveted on the bed. He strained toward it, but Granny Pearce clasped his collar firmly.

"I've done a lot for you, my boy, now you behave yourself," she whispered grimly. Lob let out a faint whine, anxious and pleading.

At the sound of that whine, Sandy stirred just a little. She sighed and moved her head the least fraction. Lob whined again. And then Sandy turned her head right over. Her eyes opened, looking at the door.
340 "Lob?" she murmured—no more than a breath of sound. "Lobby, boy?"

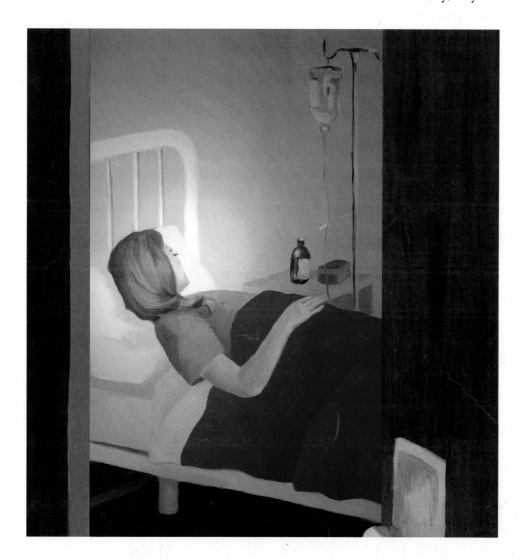

ANALYZE VISUALS
What **mood,** or feeling, does this illustration create?

The doctor by Granny Pearce drew a quick, sharp breath. Sandy moved her left arm—the one that was not broken—from below the covers and let her hand dangle down, feeling, as she always did in the mornings, for Lob's furry head. The doctor nodded slowly.

"All right," he whispered. "Let him go to the bedside. But keep a hold of him."

Granny Pearce and Lob moved to the bedside. Now she could see Bert and Jean, white-faced and shocked, on the far side of the bed. But she didn't look at them. She looked at the smile on her granddaughter's face as the groping fingers found Lob's wet ears and gently pulled them. "Good boy," whispered Sandy, and fell asleep again.

Granny Pearce led Lob out into the passage again. There she let go of him, and he ran off swiftly down the stairs. She would have followed him, but Bert and Jean had come out into the passage, and she spoke to Bert fiercely.

"*I* don't know why you were so foolish as not to bring the dog before! Leaving him to find the way here himself—"

"But, Mother!" said Jean Pengelly. "That can't have been Lob. What a chance to take! Suppose Sandy hadn't—" She stopped, with her handkerchief pressed to her mouth.

"Not Lob? I've known that dog nine years! I suppose I ought to know my own granddaughter's dog?"

"Listen, Mother," said Bert. "Lob was killed by the same truck that hit Sandy. Don found him—when he went to look for Sandy's schoolbag. He was—he was dead. Ribs all smashed. No question of that. Don told me on the phone—he and Will Hoskins rowed a half mile out to sea and sank the dog with a lump of concrete tied to his collar. Poor old boy. Still—he was getting on. Couldn't have lasted forever."

"*Sank him at sea?* Then what—?"

Slowly old Mrs. Pearce, and then the other two, turned to look at the trail of dripping-wet footprints that led down the hospital stairs.

In the Pengellys' garden they have a stone, under the palm tree. It says: "Lob. Sandy's dog. Buried at sea." ❧

Comprehension

1. **Recall** What causes the accident that injures Sandy?

2. **Clarify** Where does Mr. Dodsworth live?

3. **Summarize** How does Lob show his **loyalty** toward Sandy?

Literary Analysis

4. **Make Inferences** Reread lines 84–96. Why do you think Sandy wishes she had not gone to the train station to see Lob leave?

5. **Identify Sequence** Review your timeline to find the point in the story when you learned what happened to Lob. When did Sandy's brother Don most likely find Lob? Support your answer with evidence from the story.

6. **Identify Foreshadowing** Go back through the story to find details that foreshadow what happened to Lob. Record the hints and what happened to him in a diagram like the one shown.

Hints

"Every now and then he shook his head, as if to dislodge something heavy that was tied around his neck." (lines 315–316)

What Happened

7. **Analyze Setting** The setting has a strong influence on the events in the story. Compare and contrast the details of the setting on the day Sandy meets Lob and on the evening of the accident. How do the settings influence the **plot** of the story?

Extension and Challenge

8. **Readers' Circle** What if Mrs. Pengelly hadn't let Sandy take Lob with her to Aunt Rebecca's house? In a small group, discuss how this would affect the rest of the story. Support your responses with evidence from the story.

9. **SOCIAL STUDIES CONNECTION** Mr. Dodsworth has to travel from Liverpool to Cornwall every time Lob runs away to the Pengellys. Review the map on page 87. Research to find the names of other cities Mr. Dodsworth might travel through on his way to pick up Lob.

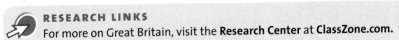

RESEARCH LINKS
For more on Great Britain, visit the **Research Center** at **ClassZone.com.**

Vocabulary in Context

VOCABULARY PRACTICE

Answer each question to show your understanding of the vocabulary words.

1. If a person is about to **erupt,** is that person angry or calm?
2. If I am **reluctant** to see a movie, have I heard good or bad things about it?
3. Does a baseball team **decisively** win a game by one run or six runs?
4. Do people show they are **agitated** by taking a nap or by yelling?
5. Would someone who is **melancholy** sit alone in a corner or dance?
6. Would you **atone** for an action that is praiseworthy or unlawful?

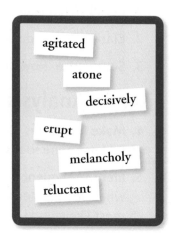

VOCABULARY IN WRITING

Have you known or read about another loyal pet or animal? Write a paragraph identifying the animal and explaining how its actions show loyalty. Use two or more vocabulary words. Here is a sample beginning.

> **EXAMPLE SENTENCE**
>
> My pet rabbit Hoppy is **reluctant** to go outside unless I go with him.

VOCABULARY STRATEGY: LITERAL AND FIGURATIVE MEANINGS

The **literal** meaning of a word is its most common and basic definition. Over time, though, some words take on **figurative** meanings that expand the basic definition. For example, the literal meaning of *erupt* is "to explode from a volcano with fire and noise." Now *erupt* is also used figuratively to refer to a person or animal "exploding" with emotion. When you encounter words that have both a literal and figurative meaning, use context clues to help you recognize which meaning the writer intends.

PRACTICE Explain the figurative meaning of each boldfaced word. Then explain how this meaning relates to the word's literal meaning.

1. After the candidate's support increased, he won by a **landslide.**
2. The family created a warm **cocoon** of affection in which their children thrived.
3. Everyone relied on Mrs. Casey to be the **pillar** of the volunteer group.
4. The children **stampeded** out of the classroom, happy that the school day was over.
5. Calling home daily was the **crutch** that helped Maria get through her loneliness.

VOCABULARY PRACTICE
For more practice, go to the **Vocabulary Center** at ClassZone.com.

Reading-Writing Connection

Broaden your understanding of "Lob's Girl" by responding to these prompts. Then complete the **Grammar and Writing** exercise.

A. Short Response: Write an Evaluation
Much of the story focuses on how Lob showed his **loyalty** toward Sandy. Do you think Sandy is equally loyal to Lob? In **one paragraph,** give your evaluation.

B. Extended Response: Write a Newspaper Article
Write a **two- or three-paragraph newspaper article** reporting how people respond to Sandy's curious recovery. Include reactions from the Pengelly family, Dr. Travers, and the hospital staff.

A strong evaluation will...
- make a judgment about Sandy's loyalty toward Lob
- support the evaluation with evidence from the text

An effective newspaper article will...
- include responses from a variety of people
- use specific details from the story

GRAMMAR AND WRITING

PUNCTUATE POSSESSIVES CORRECTLY The possessive form of a noun shows ownership or relationship. When forming a possessive noun, be sure to put the **apostrophe** in the correct place. A misplaced apostrophe can be confusing. Follow these guidelines for punctuating possessive nouns correctly:

- **Singular nouns:** Add an apostrophe and *s,* even if the word ends in *s* (*Sandy's dog, octopus's body*).
- **Plural nouns ending in *s:*** Add an apostrophe (*patients' beds*).
- **Plural nouns not ending in *s:*** Add an apostrophe and *s* (*fishermen's boat*).

   Original: Sandy was walking to her aunts' cottage. (*only one aunt*)

   Revised: Sandy was walking to her aunt's cottage.

PRACTICE Correct the possessive nouns in the following sentences.

1. Dr. Travers' wife called for an ambulance.
2. The familys' dog is missing.
3. Both nurses shifts at the hospital are ending.
4. The police said that the steep hill is a danger to peoples safety.

*For more help with possessives, see page R50 in the **Grammar Handbook.***

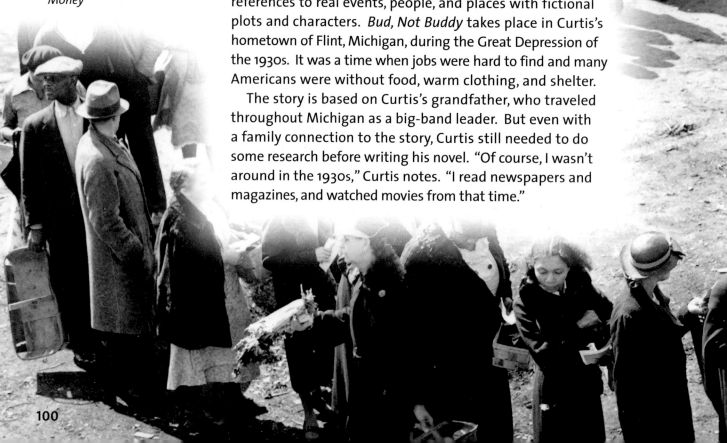

Great Reads

Bud, Not Buddy

Historical Novel by Christopher Paul Curtis

Christopher Paul Curtis
born 1954

Other Books by Christopher Paul Curtis

- *The Watsons Go to Birmingham—1963*
- *Mr. Chickee's Funny Money*

Meet Christopher Paul Curtis

Christopher Paul Curtis knew from an early age that he wanted to be a writer. "I must have been 10 or 11 years old," he remembers. "I said to my brothers and sisters, 'One day, I'm going to write a book.'" They just laughed at him. For a long time, it looked like Curtis's siblings were right. He worked full-time at an auto factory for 13 years and had little time to write.

Finally, Curtis's wife convinced him to quit his job. With time to focus on his life's dream, Curtis turned his attention to writing *The Watsons Go to Birmingham—1963*. The novel was named a Newberry Honor Book. *Bud, Not Buddy* received both the Newbery Medal and the Coretta Scott King Award.

Try a Historical Novel

Great **historical novels** make the past come alive by mixing references to real events, people, and places with fictional plots and characters. *Bud, Not Buddy* takes place in Curtis's hometown of Flint, Michigan, during the Great Depression of the 1930s. It was a time when jobs were hard to find and many Americans were without food, warm clothing, and shelter.

The story is based on Curtis's grandfather, who traveled throughout Michigan as a big-band leader. But even with a family connection to the story, Curtis still needed to do some research before writing his novel. "Of course, I wasn't around in the 1930s," Curtis notes. "I read newspapers and magazines, and watched movies from that time."

Read a Great Book

Times are hard when ten-year-old Bud, an orphan, runs away from a horrible foster home. With only a music flyer to guide him, he is determined to find the man he's convinced is his father. First, though, he has to get some much-needed food.

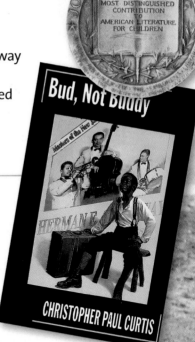

from

BUD, NOT BUDDY

CHRISTOPHER PAUL CURTIS

Uh-oh. My eyes opened and I could see the sun behind the branch of a Christmas tree.

I jumped up, folded my blanket inside my suitcase, hid it and started running the six or seven blocks down to the mission.

I turned the corner and said, "Whew!" There were still people lined up waiting. I started walking along the line. The end was a lot farther away than I thought. The line turned all the way around two corners, then crossed over one street before I saw the last person. Shucks. I walked up to get behind him.

10 He said, "Line's closed. These here folks are the last ones." He pointed at a man standing next to a woman who was carrying a baby.

I said, "But sir . . ."

He said, "But nothing. Line's closed. These here folks are the last ones."

It was time to start lying. If I didn't get any food now I'd have to steal something out of someone's garbage or I wouldn't be able to eat until the mission opened for supper.

I said, "Sir, I—"

The man raised his hand and said, "Look, kid, everybody's got
20 a story and everybody knows the rules. The line closes at seven o'clock. How's it fair to these people who been here since five o'clock that you can sleep until"—he looked at his wristwatch—"until seven-fifteen, then come busting down here expecting to eat?

You think you got some kind of special privilege just 'cause you're skinny and raggedy? Look in the line, there's lots of folks look just like you, you ain't the worst.

"Supper starts at six P.M., but you see how things is, if you plan on getting fed you better be in line by four. Now get out of here before I get rough with you."

30 Shucks, being hungry for a whole day is about as bad as it can get. I said, "But . . ."

He reached into his pocket and pulled something out that looked like a heavy black strap and slapped it across his hand. Uh-oh, here we go again.

He said, "That's it, no more talk, you opened your mouth one time too many. You rotten kids today don't listen to no one, but I'ma show you something that'll improve your hearing." He slapped the strap on his hand and started walking toward me.

I was wrong when I said being hungry for a day is about as bad as 40 it can get, being hungry plus having a big knot on your head from a black leather strap would be even worse.

I backed away but only got two steps before I felt a giant warm hand wrap around my neck from behind. I looked up to see whose doggone hand was so doggone big and why they'd put it around my neck.

A very tall, square-shaped man in old blue overalls looked down at me and said, "Clarence, what took you so long?"

I got ready to say, "My name's not Clarence and please don't choke me, sir, I'll leave," but as soon as I opened my mouth he gave 50 my head a shake and said, "I told you to hurry back, now where you been?" He gave me a shove and said, "Get back in line with your momma."

I looked up and down the line to see who was supposed to be my momma when a woman pointed her finger at her feet and said, "Clarence, you get over here right now." There were two little kids hanging on to her skirt.

I walked over to where she was and she gave me a good hard smack on the head. Shucks, for someone who was just pretending to be my momma she sure did slap me a good one.

60 I said, "Ow!"

The big square man who'd grabbed my neck looked at the man with the strap and said, ". . . Like you said, these kids today don't listen to nobody."

The strap man looked at the size of the man who called me Clarence and walked back to the end of the line.

When the overall man got back in line I said, 'Thank you, sir, I really tried to get—" But *he* popped me in the back of the head, hard, and said, "Next time don't be gone so long."

The two little kids busted out laughing and said, "Nyah-nyah-
70 nyah-nyah-nyah, Clarence got a lickin', Clarence got a lickin'."

I told them, "Shut up, and don't call me—" Then *both* my pretend poppa and my pretend momma smacked my head.

She looked at the people direct behind us and said, "Mercy, when they get to be this age . . ."

The people weren't too happy about me taking cuts in the line, but when they looked at how big my pretend daddy was and they saw how hard him and my pretend momma were going upside my head they decided they wouldn't say anything.

I was grateful to these people, but I wished they'd quit popping
80 me in the head, and it seems like with all the names in the world they could've come up with a better one for me than Clarence.

I stood in line with my pretend family for a long, long time. Everybody was very quiet about standing in line, even my pretend brother and sister and all the other kids. When we finally got around the last corner and could see the door and folks going in it seemed like a bubble busted and people started laughing and talking. The main thing people were talking about was the great big sign that was hanging over the building.

It showed a gigantic picture of a family of four rich white people
90 sitting in a car driving somewhere. You could tell it was a family 'cause they all looked exactly alike. The only difference amongst them was that the daddy had a big head and a hat and the momma had the same head with a woman's hat and the girl had two big yellow pigtails coming out from above her ears. They all had big shiny teeth and big shiny eyes and big shiny cheeks and big shiny smiles. Shucks, you'd need to squint your eyes if that shiny family drove anywhere near you.

You could tell they were rich 'cause the car looked like it had room for eight or nine more people in it and 'cause they had movie star clothes on. The woman was wearing a coat with a hunk of fur around the neck and the man was wearing a suit and a tie and the kids looked like they were wearing ten-dollar-apiece jackets.

Writ about their car in fancy letters it said, THERE'S NO PLACE LIKE AMERICA TODAY!

My pretend daddy read it and said, "Uh-uh-uh, well, you got to give them credit, you wouldn't expect that they'd have the nerve to come down here and tell the truth."

When we finally got into the building it was worth the wait. The first thing you noticed when you got inside was how big the place was, and how many people were in it and how quiet it was. The only sound you could hear was when someone scraped a spoon across the bottom of their bowl or pulled a chair in or put one back or when the people in front of you dragged their feet on the floor moving up to where they were spooning out the food.

After we'd picked up our spoons and bowls a lady dug a big mess of oatmeal out of a giant pot and swopped it down into our bowls. She smiled and said, "I hope you enjoy."

Me and my pretend family all said, "Thank you, ma'am." Then a man put two pieces of bread and a apple and a big glass of milk on your tray and said, "Please read the signs to your children. Thank you."

We all said, "Thank you, Sir." Then we walked past some signs someone'd stuck up on the wall.

One said, PLEASE DO NOT SMOKE, another said, PLEASE EAT AS QUICKLY AND QUIETLY AS POSSIBLE, another one said, PLEASE BE CONSIDERATE AND PATIENT—CLEAN UP AFTER YOURSELF—YOUR NEIGHBORS WILL BE EATING AFTER YOU, and the last one said, WE ARE TERRIBLY SORRY BUT WE HAVE NO WORK AVAILABLE.

My pretend daddy read the signs to my pretend brother and sister and we all sat at a long table with strangers on both sides of us.

The oatmeal was delicious! I poured some of my milk into it so it wouldn't be so lumpy and mixed it all together.

My pretend mother opened her pocketbook and took out a little brown envelope. She reached inside of it and sprinkled something on my pretend brother's and sister's oatmeal, then said to them, "I know that's not as much as you normally get, but I wanted to ask you if you minded sharing some with Clarence."

They pouted and gave me a couple of dirty looks. My pretend mother said, "Good," and emptied the rest of the envelope over my
140 oatmeal. Brown sugar!

Shucks, I didn't even mind them calling me Clarence anymore. I said "Thank you, Momma, ma'am."

She and my pretend daddy laughed and he said, "It took you long enough to catch on, Clarence." He acted like he was going to smack me again but he didn't.

After we'd finished all our food we put our bowls up and I thanked my pretend family again, I asked them, "Are you going to be coming back for supper?"

My pretend momma said, "No, dear, we only come here mornings.
150 But you make sure you get here plenty early, you hear?"

I said, "Yes, Momma, I mean, ma'am."

I watched them walking away. My pretend brother looked back at me and stuck out his tongue, then reached up and took my pretend mother's hand. I couldn't really blame him, I don't think I'd be real happy about sharing my brown sugar and my folks with any strange kids either. ☙

Keep Reading

Poor Bud—on his own, struggling to find food and a place to sleep. Think about what you have learned about Bud from his experience in the mission. Will he succeed in finding his father? Read the rest of *Bud, Not Buddy* to find out. As Bud continues on his journey, he will have to overcome hunger, fear, and prejudice. Will his struggle be worth it in the end?

from **Lemony Snicket's A Series of Unfortunate Events**

Film Clip on ⊙ **MediaSmart** DVD

What makes your heart
POUND?

KEY IDEA Movies have the power to pull an audience into an imaginary world. **Excitement** builds as characters face difficult problems in dangerous settings. You'll watch a scene from *Lemony Snicket's A Series of Unfortunate Events* to see how moviemakers brought an odd, interesting world to the big screen.

Background

Unhappily Ever After "If you are interested in stories with happy endings, you would be better off reading some other book."

So begins *The Bad Beginning,* the first book in *A Series of Unfortunate Events,* a popular group of novels by an author who calls himself Lemony Snicket. The unfortunate events of the title happen to the three Baudelaire children—Violet, Klaus, and Sunny—who are sent to live with a distant relative named Count Olaf when their parents are killed in a fire. Count Olaf is determined to get his hands on the children's inheritance, even if he has to take extreme measures to do so. In 2004, moviemakers brought the Baudelaires' adventures to movie theaters.

Media Literacy: Setting and Conflict in Movies

Writers often make their stories richer by vividly describing the **setting** where the events take place. For example, dangerous settings can add a sense of excitement and create more **conflict** for characters. In a movie, you don't have to rely on a written description. Moviemakers can use **visual and sound techniques** to reveal the setting and conflict to their audience. You get to watch and listen as the exciting events unfold before your eyes.

Close-up shot

Long shot

FILM TECHNIQUES	STRATEGIES FOR VIEWING
Visual A **shot** is a single, continuous view filmed by a camera. A shot includes all the action that happens until the movie cuts to the next shot.	• Look for **long shots,** which provide a wide view of a scene. They can be used to establish setting. Long shots can also make the conflict more exciting by showing danger approach from far away. • Watch for **close-up shots,** which show the details of a person or object. In an exciting scene, they can show the characters' emotions as the conflict builds. They can also focus on a small detail that can affect the plot. • Notice the use of **medium shots,** which show one or more characters from the waist up. They can be used to show how characters interact and how they feel about each other.
Sound The **sounds** in a movie consist of **music, sound effects,** and **dialogue.** Sound can be used to make you happy, sad, scared, or excited.	• Listen to the **music,** and notice how it changes. An exciting scene will often have fast, menacing music that increases your sense of danger. • Notice the **sound effects,** such as the rumbling noise of a train. As the danger builds in a scene, the sound effects may get faster and louder. • When listening to the **dialogue,** notice both what characters say and how they say it. Tone of voice can reveal emotions.

MediaSmart DVD

- **Film:** *Lemony Snicket's A Series of Unfortunate Events*
- **Director:** Brad Silberling
- **Genre:** Adventure fantasy
- **Running Time:** 4 minutes

Viewing Guide for

Lemony Snicket's A Series of Unfortunate Events

In this scene, the dastardly Count Olaf uses a remote control to lock the Baudelaire children in his car after parking it on train tracks. The children must use their wits and special talents to foil Olaf's plans. Violet is an inventor, Klaus has read many books on many subjects, and the baby, Sunny, has her own surprising skills.

Pay attention to the rising excitement as you watch the scene. You can watch the clip more than once, then use these questions to help you analyze it.

NOW VIEW

FIRST VIEWING: Comprehension

1. **Recall** Why doesn't Mr. Poe understand the danger the children are in when he talks to Violet on the car phone?

2. **Clarify** How do the children pull the track-switching lever so that the train misses the car?

CLOSE VIEWING: Media Literacy

3. **Identify Conflict** What is the conflict in the scene, and how do the children first become aware of the danger they are in?

4. **Analyze Shots** Think about the moment in the scene after Violet gets off the phone with Mr. Poe. The train is bearing down on the children and they can't get out of the car. Why do you think the director chose this moment to show a **close-up** of Violet?

5. **Evaluate Sound** Listen carefully to the **music** and **sound effects** in the scene. What part of the scene is the most exciting? What sound elements make it exciting?

6. **Analyze Setting** Throughout the movie, Violet, Klaus, and Sunny find themselves in dangerous places and situations. Which details in this scene's **setting** make it exciting to you?

Write or Discuss

Evaluate Suspense Think about the racing train scene you viewed. Do you think the moviemakers do a good job of building suspense? Are the film techniques you learned about used effectively? Write a brief evaluation of the scene. Is it as exciting as other movies you've enjoyed? Think about the following parts of the scene:

- the types of shots and the length of shots
- the use of music and sound effects
- the dangers in the setting that threaten the children

Produce Your Own Media

Create a Storyboard Imagine you're a director and you've been asked to make a movie based on one of the stories in this unit. Work with a partner to create a storyboard for the most exciting scene from a story you read. A **storyboard** is a device used to plan the shooting of a movie. It is made up of drawings and brief descriptions of what happens in each shot in a scene.

HERE'S HOW Here are a few suggestions for making your storyboard:

- Imagine the scene happening in your head before you begin. Describe what you see to your partner.
- Think about the characters' emotions and the setting. Use what you learned about **camera shots** to decide what types of shots will work best.
- Draw the shots that show what happens in four to six individual frames.
- Write a brief description of what is happening under each drawing. Include any **dialogue** or **sound effects** you'd hear.

MEDIA TOOLS

For help with creating a storyboard, visit the **Media Center** at **ClassZone.com**.

STUDENT MODEL

Klaus says, "Violet, I don't mean to rush you . . ."

The elf's head swings around the track switcher.

Close-up of Violet's smiling face.

Medium shot of Violet and Klaus pulling the strap.

Long shot of the approaching train. The music is fast and exciting.

The train rumbles by loudly. Medium shot of Klaus and Violet.

Tech Tip

Try using a computer drawing program to make the frames for the storyboard.

from **Woodsong**
Memoir by Gary Paulsen

Does nature demand RESPECT?

KEY IDEA Nature can be a powerful force. It might be a thunderstorm rumbling in the night, a wave crashing onto the beach, or a lion's mighty roar. In *Woodsong,* Gary Paulsen shares a lesson he learned about **respect** for nature.

QUICKWRITE Think about your most memorable or intense encounter with nature. Describe this experience in a journal entry. What did you learn from the experience?

● LITERARY ANALYSIS: SETTING IN NONFICTION

Like all authors of **memoirs,** Gary Paulsen writes about real events of his life. Since these events actually happened to him, Paulsen is able to give specific details about the **setting.** He includes descriptions of

- the location and changing seasons
- his surroundings in the remote wilderness of Minnesota

As you read, look for details that show you what it's like to live in the wilderness. Then think about how the setting affects Paulsen's daily life.

● READING SKILL: IDENTIFY AUTHOR'S PURPOSE

A person can have many reasons for writing. For example, a writer might aim to

- explain or provide information about a topic or event
- share thoughts or feelings about an issue or event
- persuade people to think or act in a certain way
- entertain the reader with a moving story

Even when writers have several goals, they often have one main reason for writing. This is called the **author's purpose.** As you read, use a chart to record clues about Paulsen's main purpose for writing his memoir.

Author's Purpose

Explain/Inform   Share Thoughts   Persuade   Entertain

▲ VOCABULARY IN CONTEXT

Gary Paulsen uses these words to help relate an event that taught him a lesson. For each numbered word or phrase, choose the word from the list that is closest in meaning.

WORD LIST	coherent	hibernation	scavenge
	eject	novelty	truce

1. throw out
2. agreement
3. find leftovers
4. new thing
5. sensible
6. sleep

Author Online

Gary Paulsen born 1939

Into the Woods
For Gary Paulsen, the woods were often an escape from an unhappy home in a small Minnesota town. According to Paulsen, "all the hassles of life were very quickly forgotten" in the woods. His wilderness adventures and love of nature appear in much of his work.

Another Escape Paulsen discovered the joy of reading during his teenage years. One very cold night, he ducked into a public library to warm up. The librarian offered him a library card and recommended a book. Paulsen discovered that books, like the woods, provided a way for him to get away from it all, explore new worlds, and learn about himself.

Back to Nature In his book *Woodsong*, Paulsen describes his life in the woods of northern Minnesota. In this region, people are scarce, but wild animals are plentiful. It is home to timber wolves, white-tailed deer, beavers, and black bears. Paulsen lived there with his wife and son in a cabin with no plumbing or electricity. During this time, Paulsen raised dogs and trained for the Iditarod, the famous trans-Alaska dogsled race.

 MORE ABOUT THE AUTHOR
For more on Gary Paulsen, visit the **Literature Center at ClassZone.com.**

Woodsong

Gary Paulsen

We have bear trouble. Because we feed processed meat to the dogs, there is always the smell of meat over the kennel. In the summer it can be a bit high[1] because the dogs like to "save" their food sometimes for a day or two or four—burying it to dig up later. We live on the edge of wilderness, and consequently the meat smell brings any number of visitors from the woods.

Skunks abound, and foxes and coyotes and wolves and weasels—all predators. We once had an eagle live over the kennel for more than a week, **scavenging** from the dogs, and a crazy group of ravens has pretty much taken over the puppy pen. Ravens are protected by the state, and they seem to know it. When I walk toward the puppy pen with the buckets of meat, it's a toss-up to see who gets it—the pups or the birds. They have actually pecked the puppies away from the food pans until they have gone through and taken what they want. **A**

---

1. **it can be a bit high:** the smell can be rather strong.

Ursus, Susan Brearey. Oil and wax on wood with beech leaf and birch bark, 11⅛″ × 11″ × 1⅜″. © Susan Brearey represented by Geraid Peters Gallery, Santa Fe, New Mexico.

ANALYZE VISUALS
Examine the painting closely. What do you see?

scavenge (skăv′ənj) *v.* to search for discarded scraps

A **SETTING**
Reread lines 1–14. What description does Paulsen give of life at the edge of the wilderness?

Golden Autumn (1901), Stanislav Joukovski. Oil on canvas, 87.5 cm × 107.5 cm. Museum of Art, Serpukhov, Russia. © Bridgeman Art Library.

ANALYZE VISUALS
What **details** in the painting suggest that the house is in the wilderness?

Spring, when the bears come, is the worst. They have been in **hibernation** through the winter, and they are hungry beyond caution. The meat smell draws them like flies, and we frequently have two or three around the kennel at the same time. Typically they do not bother us much—although my wife had a bear chase her from the garden to the house one morning—but they do bother the dogs.

They are so big and strong that the dogs fear them, and the bears trade on this fear to get their food. It's common to see them scare a dog into his house and take his food. Twice we have had dogs killed by rough bear swats that broke their necks—and the bears took their food.

We have evolved an uneasy peace with them, but there is the problem of familiarity. The first time you see a bear in the kennel it is a **novelty,** but when the same ones are there day after day, you wind up naming some of them (old Notch-Ear, Billy-Jo, etc.). There gets to be a too-relaxed attitude. We started to treat them like pets.

A major mistake.

There was a large male around the kennel for a week or so. He had a white streak across his head, which I guessed was a wound scar from some hunter—bear hunting is allowed here. He wasn't all that bad, so we didn't mind him. He would frighten the dogs and take their hidden stashes now and then, but he didn't harm them, and we became accustomed to him hanging around. We called him Scarhead, and now and again we would joke about him as if he were one of the yard animals. **B**

hibernation
(hī′bər-nā′shən) *n.* the state of being inactive through the winter

novelty (nŏv′əl-tē) *n.* something new and unusual

B AUTHOR'S PURPOSE
Why does Paulsen tell you about the family's nickname for the bear?

At this time we had three cats, forty-two dogs, fifteen or twenty chickens, eight ducks, nineteen large white geese, a few banty hens . . .
40 ten fryers which we'd raised from chicks and couldn't (as my wife put it) "snuff and eat," and six woods-wise goats. **C**

The bears, strangely, didn't bother any of the yard animals. There must have been a rule, or some order to the way they lived, because they would hit the kennel and steal from the dogs but leave the chickens and goats and other yard stock completely alone—although you would have had a hard time convincing the goats of this fact. The goats spent a great deal of time with their back hair up, whuffing and blowing snot at the bears— and at the dogs, who would *gladly* have eaten them. The goats never really believed in the **truce.**

50 There is not a dump or landfill to take our trash to, and so we separate it—organic, inorganic[2]—and deal with it ourselves. We burn the paper in a screened enclosure, and it is fairly efficient; but it's impossible to get all the food particles off wrapping paper, so when it's burned, the food particles burn with it.

And give off a burnt food smell.

And nothing draws bears like burning food. It must be that they have learned to understand human dumps—where they spend a great deal of time foraging. And they learn amazingly fast. In Alaska, for instance, the bears already know that the sound of a moose hunter's gun means there
60 will be a fresh gut pile when the hunter cleans the moose. They come at a run when they hear the shot. It's often a close race to see if the hunter will get to the moose before the bears take it away. . . . **D**

Because we're on the south edge of the wilderness area, we try to wait until there is a northerly breeze before we burn, so the food smell will carry south, but it doesn't always help. Sometimes bears, wolves, and other predators are already south, working the sheep farms down where it is more settled—they take a terrible toll[3] of sheep—and we catch them on the way back through. **E**

That's what happened one July morning.
70 Scarhead had been gone for two or three days, and the breeze was right, so I went to burn the trash. I fired it off and went back into the house for a moment—not more than two minutes. When I came back out, Scarhead was in the burn area. His tracks (directly through the tomatoes in the garden) showed he'd come from the south.

---

2. **organic, inorganic:** *Organic* refers to plant or animal material that breaks down naturally. *Inorganic* refers to man-made material that will not break down naturally.

3. **take a terrible toll:** destroy a large number.

C SETTING
Reread lines 38–41. What words show that Paulsen has a personal connection to the setting?

truce (trōōs) *n.* an agreement to end an argument or fight

D AUTHOR'S PURPOSE
Reread lines 56–62. Why do you think Paulsen wants you to know these facts about bears?

E SETTING
Reread lines 63–68. How is Paulsen's knowledge of the wilderness useful to him?

He was having a grand time. The fire didn't bother him. He was trying to reach a paw in around the edges of flame to get at whatever smelled so good. He had torn things apart quite a bit—ripped one side off the burn enclosure—and I was having a bad day, and it made me mad.

I was standing across the burning fire from him, and without
80 thinking—because I was so used to him—I picked up a stick, threw it at him, and yelled, "Get out of here."

I have made many mistakes in my life, and will probably make many more, but I hope never to throw a stick at a bear again.

In one rolling motion—the muscles seemed to move within the skin so fast that I couldn't take half a breath—he turned and came for me.

ANALYZE VISUALS
What words would you use to describe the bear in this work of art?

Close. I could smell his breath and see the red around the sides of his eyes. Close on me he stopped and raised on his back legs and hung over me, his forelegs and paws hanging down, weaving back and forth gently as he took his time and decided whether or not to tear my head off.

90   I could not move, would not have time to react. I knew I had nothing to say about it. One blow would break my neck. Whether I lived or died depended on him, on his thinking, on his ideas about me—whether I was worth the bother or not.

   I did not think then.

   Looking back on it, I don't remember having one **coherent** thought when it was happening. All I knew was terrible menace. His eyes looked very small as he studied me. He looked down on me for what seemed hours. I did not move, did not breathe, did not think or do anything.

   And he lowered.

100   Perhaps I was not worth the trouble. He lowered slowly and turned back to the trash, and I walked backward halfway to the house and then ran—anger growing now—and took the rifle from the gun rack by the door and came back out.

   He was still there, rummaging through the trash. I worked the bolt and fed a cartridge in and aimed at the place where you kill bears and began to squeeze. In raw anger, I began to take up the four pounds of pull necessary to send death into him. **F**

   And stopped.

   Kill him for what?

110   That thought crept in.

   Kill him for what?

   For not killing me? For letting me know it is wrong to throw sticks at four-hundred-pound bears? For not hurting me, for not killing me, I should kill him? I lowered the rifle and **ejected** the shell and put the gun away. I hope Scarhead is still alive. For what he taught me, I hope he lives long and is very happy, because I learned then—looking up at him while he made up his mind whether or not to end me—that when it is all boiled down, I am nothing more and nothing less than any other animal in the woods. ❧ **G**

coherent (kō-hîr′ənt) *adj.* clear; logical

F **AUTHOR'S PURPOSE**
Reread lines 100–107. What emotion is Paulsen feeling at this point in the story?

eject (ĭ-jĕkt′) *v.* to throw out from inside

G **AUTHOR'S PURPOSE**
Reread lines 111–118. What does Paulsen now think about his place in nature?

NEWSPAPER ARTICLE Gary Paulsen's love of nature is not limited to the wilderness. In this article, based on an interview with Caroline Scott, Paulsen describes a typical day on his sailboat, on which he lives alone most of the year.

A Life in the Day of
Gary Paulsen

At 5:30 A.M. I have a bowl of oatmeal, then I go to work. First up, I stow all the gear away. Then I take the covers off the sails and fire the engine up to get out of the harbor. I hate the motor—once it's off, there's silence. I have a steering vane so I can go below and cook or sit and write. Sailing is an inherently beautiful thing. To me it's like dancing with the wind and the water; it's like running with wolves—a perfect meeting of man and nature. . . .

On the boat there is nothing, and I know I work better that way. I think that the writer in the city, with the traffic and the parties and the theater, is at a disadvantage, because the distractions are so enormous. I work in the city when I have to, but I find it really hard. I don't need much. The way I live is nobody's idea of luxury, but that's the way I like it. I use a battery to charge my laptop and I just head out to sea. Sometimes I go 150 miles out and 150 miles back; sometimes I head out and keep right on going. . . .

I write all morning, then I have a two-hour break to answer mail. I get around 400 letters a day from children and I have a secretary in New York who helps me answer them all. I owe a great deal to dogs and a great deal to children, and I try to help both of those species. A lot of what I write is fiction based on my life. . . . I spent my whole childhood running away. A lot of kids know this through my books, so I look for mail from kids in the same situation. It helps them to know you care. I'll try and get in touch with their school to let them know this child is in trouble. I'm aware I might be the only person they've told. I got a letter once from a girl who said, "My only friends in the world are your books." . . .

I don't get lonely. There was a time when I [wished I had] somebody who I could turn to and say, "Look at that!" I'd be leaning over the bow strip to touch the dolphins swimming alongside the boat. One time, three of them somersaulted in the air and crashed into the water, which was golden with the sinking sun. It was the most beautiful thing, and I felt so happy I just wanted to tell someone. But I realized that I'm telling it through my writing the whole time. . . .

I used to think I should be fulfilled by awards or by earning a million dollars, but with age has come some kind of self-knowledge. My rewards are less tangible: they're the killer whales who reared up out of the water to look at me. Or a 15-knot wind across my beam. Those are my moments of pure joy.

Comprehension

1. **Recall** What smell draws the bears to Paulsen's cabin?

2. **Clarify** Why does Scarhead show up the day Paulsen burns the trash even though the wind is blowing away from the wilderness?

3. **Summarize** What happens when Paulsen confronts Scarhead?

Literary Analysis

4. **Make Inferences** Reread lines 42–49. Why don't the bears bother the yard animals?

5. **Examine Setting** Go back through the selection and find details that describe the setting. Keep track of the details in a chart like the one shown. Which of these details seem most vivid to you?

Details About Setting		
Location	Seasons	Surroundings

6. **Analyze Author's Purpose** Review the clues you recorded in your chart as you read *Woodsong*. What is Paulsen's main purpose for sharing his experience? Support your answer with examples from the memoir.

7. **Make Judgments** Reread lines 115–118. Do you agree with Paulsen regarding the lesson he learned about **respect** for nature? Explain your answer.

8. **Compare Literary Works** Consider the newspaper article on page 118. Paulsen's **setting** has changed, but has this affected the way he lives his life? **Compare and contrast** Paulsen's way of life in *Woodsong* with his description of his daily routine in "A Life in the Day of Gary Paulsen." Note specific examples from both selections.

Extension and Challenge

9. **Creative Project: Art** Sketch the area where Paulsen lives, using details found in the memoir.

10. **Inquiry and Research** Paulsen explains that bears are very hungry in the spring after hibernating through the winter. Research to find out more about the hibernation process. In two or three paragraphs, explain why a bear hibernates, how it prepares for hibernation, and what happens to its body.

RESEARCH LINKS For more on bears and hibernation, visit the **Research Center** at **ClassZone.com**.

Vocabulary in Context

Choose the letter of the word or phrase that best completes each sentence.

1. A **coherent** message (a) is very long, (b) makes sense, (c) is a surprise.
2. A bear might **scavenge** in (a) garbage, (b) streams, (c) caves.
3. **Hibernation** involves (a) growling, (b) eating, (c) resting.
4. Enemies who call a **truce** (a) go to war, (b) stop fighting, (c) sink a ship.
5. After I **eject** the CD-ROM, I (a) put it away, (b) play it, (c) buy it.
6. A bear would be a **novelty** in (a) a zoo, (b) the wilderness, (c) a house.

coherent

eject

hibernation

novelty

scavenge

truce

VOCABULARY IN WRITING

Why didn't Scarhead hurt Paulsen? Write a paragraph telling what you think, using two or more vocabulary words. You might begin this way.

> **EXAMPLE SENTENCE**
>
> *Scarhead called a **truce** when he turned away from Paulsen.*

VOCABULARY STRATEGY: PREFIXES AND THE LATIN ROOT *ject*

A **prefix** is a word part that appears at the beginning of a base word to form a new word. For example, consider the word *uneasy* (un + easy) in line 25 of *Woodsong. Un-* is a prefix that means "not," so *uneasy* means "not easy."

Prefixes may also be added to **roots,** which are word parts that can't stand alone. The vocabulary word *eject* contains the Latin root *ject,* which means "to throw." This root is combined with various prefixes to form English words. To understand the meaning of words containing *ject,* use your knowledge of the root's meaning and the meanings of the prefixes used with it.

Prefix	Meaning
e-, ex-	from; out of
in-	in; into
pro-	forward; in front of
re-	back; again
sub-	under; down

PRACTICE Use the information in the chart and the meaning of the root *ject* to write a definition for each boldfaced word.

1. The emperor **subjected** his people to a harsh government.
2. Dad keeps his antique movie **projector** in the basement.
3. This **injection** will protect you from the illness.
4. The actor **rejected** the role offered to him.

VOCABULARY PRACTICE
For more practice, go to the **Vocabulary Center** at **ClassZone.com.**

Reading-Writing Connection

Increase your understanding of *Woodsong* by responding to these prompts. Then complete the **Grammar and Writing** exercise.

A. Short Response: Analyze Author's Purpose
Paulsen says that the bear gave him more **respect** for nature and taught him that he is just another animal in the woods. In **one paragraph,** explain how this lesson might change the way Paulsen will interact with nature in the future.

A clear analysis will...
- include details about the setting
- demonstrate an understanding of the author's purpose

B. Extended Response: Write a Scene
What do you think Scarhead might have been thinking during the confrontation with Paulsen? In **two or three paragraphs,** rewrite the scene from Scarhead's perspective.

A creative scene will...
- refer to events from Paulsen's memoir
- be consistent with Scarhead's behavior in the memoir

GRAMMAR AND WRITING

MAINTAIN PRONOUN-ANTECEDENT AGREEMENT A **pronoun** is a word that is used in place of a noun or another pronoun. The word that the pronoun refers to is its **antecedent.** For example, notice how the pronoun *his* refers to the antecedent *Gary* in the following sentence: *Gary walked out of his house.*

Pronouns should always **agree in number** with their antecedents. Be careful when using antecedents like *anyone, nobody, no one,* and *somebody.* These words should always be paired with singular pronouns. In the revised sentence, notice how the singular pronoun (in yellow) and the singular antecedent (in green) agree in number.

Original: Somebody threw a stick, and they yelled, "Get out of here."

Revised: Somebody threw a stick, and he yelled, "Get out of here."

PRACTICE Correct the following pronoun-antecedent errors.

1. Anyone in this situation would have turned to face their enemy.
2. For what seemed like an hour, nobody moved from their spot.
3. Someone had to be reasonable. They would need to walk away.
4. No one wanted their life cut short that day.

*For more help with pronouns, see page R52 in the **Grammar Handbook.***

The Horse Snake

From the Memoir *The Land I Lost*
by Huynh Quang Nhuong

When is there strength in NUMBERS?

KEY IDEA No matter who you are, life will present you with challenges. Perhaps you'll face danger from a natural disaster. Perhaps you'll find you have more work than you can do. Or maybe you'll be asked to carry emotional burdens that seem impossibly heavy. Will you be strong enough to take on every challenge alone? In "The Horse Snake," a community depends on **teamwork** to face a threat that is too big for just one person.

LIST IT With a group of classmates, make a list of goals and challenges that would be easier to meet if you worked with a team rather than by yourself. Discuss why teamwork would help bring success in each situation.

● LITERARY ANALYSIS: NARRATIVE NONFICTION

Narrative nonfiction tells true stories about events that really happened. To make these events interesting, writers use many of the elements found in short stories, such as

- a **conflict,** or struggle between opposing forces
- **suspense,** or the feeling of excitement or tension that makes you eager to find out what happens next

"The Horse Snake" is a type of narrative nonfiction called a **memoir,** in which the writer tells true stories from his or her life. As you read, notice how the author explains the conflict and creates suspense.

Review: **Foreshadowing**

● READING SKILL: TRACE CHRONOLOGICAL ORDER

Often, writers of narrative nonfiction present events in the same order in which they happened in real life. This is called **chronological order,** or time order. To recognize time order, look for clue words that tell when events occurred, such as *a few seconds later, shortly after midnight,* or *the next day.*

As you read, use a timeline to track the order of events and the time of day each event occurred.

Friend bangs on door
←———•————————————→
Night

▲ VOCABULARY IN CONTEXT

The author uses the listed words to help show the fear caused by a dangerous snake. To see how many you know, complete each phrase with the correct word from the list.

WORD	assume	nocturnal	stealthily
LIST	gait	petrify	succumb

1. One look at the deadly snake could ____ anyone.
2. It was a ____ animal, so it was seldom seen in daylight.
3. We must ____ responsibility for killing the snake.
4. To be safe, make sure you approach the snake ____.
5. So you don't scare it, walk with a quiet, careful ____.
6. After a hard fight, you might get the animal to ____.

Author On|ine

Village Life
Growing up in a small village in Vietnam, Huynh Quang Nhuong was tending rice fields by the time he was six years old. He also watched over his family's water buffaloes, including his favorite, Tank.

**Huynh Quang Nhuong
1936–2001**

There were no stores, cars, or televisions in the village. For entertainment, Huynh, his family, and his neighbors listened to one another tell stories. When he was older, Huynh received a scholarship to Saigon University, and he left home. He planned to return to his village as a teacher.

Distant Memories Instead, Huynh was drafted into the army of South Vietnam in the 1960s. After being paralyzed by a bullet, he traveled to the United States for treatment. Huynh never returned to Vietnam. However, his memoirs, poems, and plays brought his memories of Vietnam and the stories he heard there to audiences in the United States.

Wildlife in the Highlands "The Horse Snake" is a chapter in Huynh's memoir *The Land I Lost.* The memoir is set in Huynh's childhood village, which was surrounded by jungle on one side and mountains on the other. Huynh describes the realities of living close to fascinating and dangerous animals.

 MORE ABOUT THE AUTHOR
For more on Huynh Quang Nhoung, visit the **Literature Center** at ClassZone.com.

THE HORSE SNAKE

Huynh Quang Nhuong

Despite all his courage there was one creature in the jungle that Tank always tried to avoid—the snake. And there was one kind of snake that was more dangerous than other snakes—the horse snake. In some areas people called it the bamboo snake because it was as long as a full-grown bamboo tree.[1] In other regions, the people called it the thunder or lightning snake, because it attacked so fast and with such power that its victim had neither time to escape nor strength to fight it. In our area, we called it the horse snake because it could move as fast as a thoroughbred.

ANALYZE VISUALS
What does this photo suggest about the importance of the horse snake in relation to the village?

---

1. **a full-grown bamboo tree:** Actually, a bamboo tree can grow as tall as 120 feet!

10   One night a frightened friend of our family's banged on our door and asked us to let him in. When crossing the rice field in front of our house on his way home from a wedding, he had heard the unmistakable hiss of a horse snake. We became very worried; not only for us and our friend, but also for the cattle and other animals we raised. **A**

It was too far into the night to rouse all our neighbors and go to search for the snake. But my father told my cousin to blow three times on his buffalo horn,[2] the signal that a dangerous wild beast was loose in the hamlet. A few seconds later we heard three long quivering sounds of a horn at the far end of the hamlet[3] answering our warning. We presumed
20 that the whole hamlet was now on guard. **B**

I stayed up that night, listening to all the sounds outside, while my father and my cousin sharpened their hunting knives. Shortly after midnight we were startled by the frightened neighing of a horse in the rice field. Then the night was still, except for a few sad calls of **nocturnal** birds and the occasional roaring of tigers in the jungle.

The next day early in the morning all the able-bodied men of the hamlet gathered in front of our house and divided into groups of four to go and look for the snake. My father and my cousin grabbed their lunch and joined a searching party. **C**
30 They found the old horse that had neighed the night before in the rice field. The snake had squeezed it to death. Its chest was smashed, and all its ribs broken. But the snake had disappeared.

Everybody agreed that it was the work of one of the giant horse snakes which had terrorized our area as far back as anyone could remember. The horse snake usually eats small game, such as turkeys, monkeys, chickens, and ducks, but for unknown reasons sometimes it will attack people and cattle. A fully grown horse snake can reach the size of a king python.[4] But, unlike pythons, horse snakes have an extremely poisonous bite. Because of their bone-breaking squeeze and fatal bite they are one of the
40 most dangerous creatures of the uplands.

The men searched all day, but at nightfall they gave up and went home. My father and my cousin looked very tired when they returned. My grandmother told them to go right to bed after their dinner and that she would wake them up if she or my mother heard any unusual sounds. **D**

A CHRONOLOGICAL ORDER
Reread lines 10–14. What is the first event in this selection? Record the event and the time of day on your timeline.

B NARRATIVE NONFICTION
What are the people in the hamlet in **conflict** with? Think about what they are guarding against.

nocturnal (nŏk-tûr′nəl) *adj.* active at night

C CHRONOLOGICAL ORDER
What words or phrases in this paragraph help you understand the order of events?

D NARRATIVE NONFICTION
Reread lines 41–45. In what way does the men's return at nightfall add to the **suspense?**

---

2. **buffalo horn:** The horns of water buffalo are sometimes used to produce music or other sounds.

3. **hamlet:** a small village.

4. **king python:** large, heavy snake that can grow to a length of 20 feet and kills its prey by squeezing it to death.

The men went to bed and the women prepared to stay up all night. My mother sewed torn clothing and my grandmother read a novel she had just borrowed from a friend. And for the second night in a row, they allowed my little sister and me to stay awake and listen with them for
50 as long as we could. But hours later, seeing the worry on our faces, my grandmother put aside her novel and told us a story:

Once upon a time a happy family lived in a small village on the shore of the South China Sea. They respected the laws of the land and loved their neighbors very much. The father and his oldest son were woodcutters. The father was quite old, but he still could carry home a heavy load of wood.

One day on his way home from the jungle he was happier than usual. He and his son had discovered a wild chicken nest containing twelve eggs. Now he would have something
60 special to give to his grandchildren when they pulled his shirtsleeves and danced around him to greet him when he came home.

The father looked at the broad shoulders of his son and his steady **gait** under a very heavy load of wood. He smiled. His son was a good son, and he had no doubt that when he became even older still his son would take good care of him and his wife.

As he was thinking this he saw his son suddenly throw the load of wood at a charging horse snake that had come out of
70 nowhere. The heavy load of wood crashed into the snake's head and stunned it. That gave them enough time to draw their sharp woodcutting knives. But instead of attacking the horse snake from the front, the elder shouted to his son to run behind the big bush of elephant grass nearby while he, who was a little too old to run fast, jumped into the front end of the bush. Each time the snake passed by him the old man managed to hit it with his knife. He struck the snake many times. Finally it became weak and slowed down; so he came out of his hiding place and attacked the snake's tail, while his
80 son attacked the snake's head. The snake fought back furiously, but finally it **succumbed** to the well-coordinated attack of father and son.

When the snake was dead, they grabbed its tail and proudly dragged it to the edge of their village. Everyone rushed out to

SOCIAL STUDIES CONNECTION

The uplands, or the central highlands, of Vietnam are a mountainous area bordering Laos and Cambodia.

gait (gāt) *n.* manner of walking or moving on foot

succumb (sə-kŭm′) *v.* to give in; die

see their prize. They all argued over who would have the honor of carrying the snake to their house for them.

The old woodcutter and his son had to tell the story of how they had killed the snake at least ten times, but the people never tired of hearing it, again and again. They all agreed that the old woodcutter and his son were not only brave but clever as well. Then and there the villagers decided that when their chief, also a brave and clever man, died, the old woodcutter was the only one who deserved the honor of replacing him. **E**

90

When my grandmother finished the story, my little sister and I became a bit more cheerful. People could defeat this dangerous snake after all. The silent darkness outside became less threatening. Nevertheless, we were still too scared to sleep in our room, so my mother made a makeshift bed in the sitting room, close to her and our grandmother.

E FORESHADOWING
What does the grandmother's story suggest about the way the **conflict** between the people and the snake might be resolved?

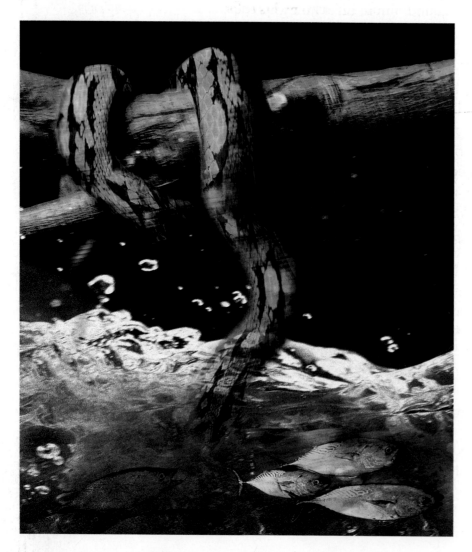

ANALYZE VISUALS
What **mood,** or feeling, does this work of art create?

100   When we woke up the next morning, life in the hamlet had almost returned to normal. The snake had not struck again that night, and the farmers, in groups of three or four, slowly filtered back to their fields. Then, late in the afternoon, hysterical cries for help were heard in the direction of the western part of the hamlet. My cousin and my father grabbed their knives and rushed off to help. **F**

   It was Minh, a farmer, who was crying for help. Minh, like most farmers in the area, stored the fish he had caught in the rice field at the end of the rainy season in a small pond. That day Minh's wife had wanted a good fish for dinner. When Minh approached his fish pond he heard
110 what sounded like someone trying to steal his fish by using a bucket to empty water from the pond. Minh was very angry and rushed over to catch the thief, but when he reached the pond, what he saw so **petrified** him that he fell over backward, speechless. When he regained control he crawled away as fast as he could and yelled loudly for help.

   The thief he saw was not a person but a huge horse snake, perhaps the same one that had squeezed the old horse to death two nights before. The snake had hooked its head to the branch of one tree and its tail to another and was splashing the water out of the pond by swinging its body back and forth, like a hammock. Thus, when the shallow pond became dry, it
120 planned to swallow all the fish.

   All the villagers rushed to the scene to help Minh, and our village chief quickly organized an attack. He ordered all the men to surround the pond. Then two strong young men approached the snake, one at its tail and the other at its head. As they crept closer and closer, the snake **assumed** a striking position, its head about one meter above the pond, and its tail swaying from side to side. It was ready to strike in either direction. As the two young men moved in closer, the snake watched them. Each man tried to draw the attention of the snake, while a third man crept **stealthily** to its side. Suddenly he struck the snake with his
130 long knife. The surprised snake shot out of the pond like an arrow and knocked the young man unconscious as it rushed by. It broke through the circle of men and went into an open rice field. But it received two more wounds on its way out. **G**

   The village chief ordered all the women and children to form a long line between the open rice field and the jungle and to yell as loudly as they could, hoping to scare the snake so that it would not flee into the jungle. It would be far easier for the men to fight the wounded snake in an open field than to follow it there.

   But now there was a new difficulty. The snake started heading toward
140 the river. Normally a horse snake could beat any man in a race, but since this one was badly wounded, our chief was able to cut off its escape by

F CHRONOLOGICAL ORDER
Reread lines 100–105. When are the cries for help heard? Mark the time and the event on your timeline.

petrify (pĕt′rə-fī′) v. to paralyze with astonishment or fear

VISUAL VOCABULARY

hammock n. canvas or heavy netting hung between two supports and used as a swinging bed

assume (ə-sōōm′) v. to take on

stealthily (stĕl′thə-lē) adv. secretly; sneakily

G NARRATIVE NONFICTION
Reread lines 121–133. At what points are you anxious or excited to learn what happens next? Note the details that create the **suspense**.

sending half his men running to the river. Blocked off from the river and jungle, the snake decided to stay and fight. **H**

  The hunting party surrounded the snake again, and this time four of the best men attacked the snake from four different directions. The snake fought bravely, but it perished. During the struggle one of the men received a dislocated shoulder, two had bruised ribs, and three were momentarily blinded by dirt thrown by the snake. Luckily all of them succeeded in avoiding the fatal bite of the snake.

150 We rejoiced that the danger was over. But we knew it would only be a matter of time until we would once again have to face our most dangerous natural enemy—the horse snake. ∾

H **NARRATIVE NONFICTION**
Why is this a turning point of the **conflict** between the people and the snake?

Comprehension

1. **Recall** Why is the horse snake more dangerous than other snakes?

2. **Clarify** Why does the grandmother tell the story about the father and son who face a horse snake?

3. **Represent** Reread lines 106–120. Use details from the selection to draw what Minh sees when he goes to his pond.

Literary Analysis

4. **Understand Chronological Order** Over what period of time do the events in this selection take place? Use your timeline to figure it out. Then note when most of the events occur.

5. **Make Inferences** Huynh does not directly state what he was doing during the battle with the horse snake. Reread lines 121–149. What do you think his role was in the battle? Support your inference with evidence from the selection.

6. **Analyze Narrative Nonfiction** In "The Horse Snake," each of the two forces that are in **conflict** has some advantages over the other. On a scale like the one shown, note the different qualities that make the snake and the community strong. How does the balance of qualities create **suspense?**

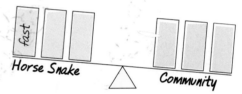

7. **Draw Conclusions** What role did **teamwork** play in defeating the snake? Use evidence from the selection to support your answer.

Extension and Challenge

8. **Creative Project: Music** Moviemakers often use music to add **suspense** to their films. If you were directing a movie of "The Horse Snake," what kind of music would you want to accompany each scene? Think about what instruments and rhythms should be used. Consider at what points the music should be loud or soft. As the director, write recommendations to your composer.

9.   **SOCIAL STUDIES CONNECTION** Read "Le Mat Village Holds On to Snake Catching Tradition" on page 133. Then do research to find out more about village life and cultural traditions in Vietnam. Display your findings in a poster.

> **RESEARCH LINKS**
> For more on Vietnam, visit the **Research Center** at **ClassZone.com**.

Vocabulary in Context

VOCABULARY PRACTICE

Choose the letter of the word or phrase that is not related in meaning to the other words.

1. (a) pace, (b) step, (c) gait, (d) feet
2. (a) stealthily, (b) secretly, (c) slyly, (d) swiftly
3. (a) frighten, (b) petrify, (c) confuse, (d) horrify
4. (a) sunny, (b) nocturnal, (c) moonlit, (d) dark
5. (a) take on, (b) move on, (c) undertake, (d) assume
6. (a) succumb, (b) reject, (c) refuse, (d) throw away

assume   petrify
gait   stealthily
nocturnal   succumb

VOCABULARY IN WRITING

If you lived in the village, what fears would you have about the horse snake? Write a paragraph telling what you think. Use at least two vocabulary words. Here is an example of how you might begin.

EXAMPLE SENTENCE

I would be most fearful of the horse snake entering my home **stealthily** *during the night.*

VOCABULARY STRATEGY: WORD ORIGINS

Many words that we use every day have interesting histories. For example, the vocabulary word *petrify* can be traced back to a Latin word that means "rock." If you saw something that petrified you, do you think it would make you freeze in place like a rock?

Dictionaries often provide information about a word's origin in an **etymology** at the end of the dictionary entry. Etymologies can help you understand the meaning of an English word by relating the unfamiliar word to something you know. The etymology is in brackets in the entry shown.

> **ballot** (băl′ət) *intr. v.* to cast a vote. [From Italian *ballotta*, small ball or pebble. Italian citizens once voted by casting a small ball or pebble into one of several boxes.]

PRACTICE Look up the etymology of each word in a dictionary. Then write the origin of each word and explain how the history will help you remember the meaning.

1. algorithm   2. hippopotamus   3. radar   4. safari

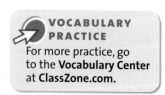

VOCABULARY PRACTICE
For more practice, go to the **Vocabulary Center** at **ClassZone.com**.

RADIO TRANSCRIPT In "The Horse Snake," villagers fight off a large snake that threatens their community. In the following radio transcript, you'll read about a modern Vietnamese village that prides itself on its tradition of catching snakes.

Le Mat Village Holds On to Snake Catching Tradition

Le Mat on the outskirts of Hanoi has long been famous for its tradition of catching snakes. Le Mat villagers, regardless of their age and gender, all know how to catch snakes. Although the trade is fading and many villagers now make a living from other jobs, local people's skills and love for catching snakes remain strong. Many can talk with visitors for hours about their village's unique tradition.

Legend has it that snake catching in the village dates back to the 11th century. King Ly Thai Tong's daughter was carried away by a giant snake when she was on a boat on the Duong River. The King announced that anyone who found his daughter's body would be rewarded.

A villager from Le Mat, Hoang Duc Trung, went to the part of the river where the princess was taken away. Trung killed the snake and brought back the princess's body. The King kept his promise and rewarded Trung, but he refused the reward and just asked the King to allow Le Mat's poor villagers to reclaim and settle in the area west of Thang Long Citadel. Under the leadership of the young man, villagers were able to turn a swampy area full of wild grass and poisonous snakes into a fertile and prosperous land. This is now the area of Ngoc Khanh, Lieu Giai, Cong Vi, and Kim Ma in Hanoi. Hoang Duc Trung taught the villagers how to catch snakes and was recognized as the Genie of Le Mat. . . .

Le Mat villagers know well the difference between poisonous and harmless snakes. They also know the characteristics of each snake species, and they all agree that snakes that do not react quickly are maybe the most dangerous. Despite the passage of time and changes in their lives, Le Mat people still love their special tradition and continue to catch any snake they see.

The Walrus and the Carpenter
Narrative Poem by Lewis Carroll

Have you ever been FOOLED?

KEY IDEA It can be fun to **trick** people—to watch their faces as you convince them to believe that something wacky is actually true. It can even be fun to be tricked. Has anyone ever told you that you were going somewhere boring when in fact you were headed to a surprise party? But not all tricks are fun or funny. In "The Walrus and the Carpenter," we see how easy it is to be fooled into doing something unwise.

CHART IT With a group of classmates, discuss what types of tricks are harmless and fun and what types of tricks can be harmful and cruel. Use a chart like the one shown to note your ideas.

Harmless	Harmful

LITERARY ANALYSIS: NARRATIVE POETRY

All poems use words carefully to create certain effects. "The Walrus and the Carpenter" is a **narrative poem,** which means that in addition to using words carefully, it tells a story. To do so, the poem uses the same narrative elements that any work of fiction does, such as

- setting   • characters   • plot

Identifying these elements will help you understand the ideas in a narrative poem.

As you read "The Walrus and the Carpenter," note details about the setting, characters, and plot events in a story map like the one shown.

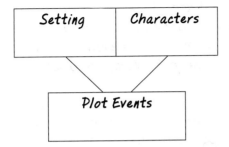

READING STRATEGY: VISUALIZE

You're about to read a poem with a vivid setting and some very unusual, fantastical characters. You'll probably enjoy the poem more and understand it better if you can **visualize,** or picture in your mind, the setting and characters. To visualize, follow these steps:

- Pay attention to the descriptions on the page.
- Take time to form mental images based on the words in the descriptions.
- Use your imagination to fill in the blanks.

As you read Lewis Carroll's poem, pay attention to details that will help you visualize the story the poem is telling.

Author Online

A New Name
In 1865 a British man named Charles Lutwidge Dodgson published his first book for children, *Alice's Adventures in Wonderland.* Instead of using his name, however, Dodgson chose a "pen name," a made-up name. The book was a huge success, and the pen name, Lewis Carroll, became very famous.

Lewis Carroll
1832–1898

Children's Entertainer Dodgson enjoyed entertaining children throughout his life. As the eldest son in a family of 11, he made up games for his brothers and sisters. As an adult, he told stories and drew pictures for the children he befriended—including a real-life Alice. By training, Dodgson was a mathematician, and even in this field he often focused on young people. He used his math skills to make up puzzles and brainteasers.

Poetic Lessons In the 1800s in Great Britain, children were often required to memorize long, boring poems that taught lessons about how young people should behave. In "The Walrus and the Carpenter," Carroll makes fun of this approach to education. But he might have slipped in a good lesson for children at the same time.

 MORE ABOUT THE AUTHOR
For more on Lewis Carroll, visit the **Literature Center** at ClassZone.com.

The Walrus and the Carpenter

Lewis Carroll

The sun was shining on the sea,
    Shining with all his might:
He did his very best to make
    The billows[1] smooth and bright—
5 And this was odd, because it was
    The middle of the night. **Ⓐ**

The moon was shining sulkily,[2]
    Because she thought the sun
Had got no business to be there
10   After the day was done—
"It's very rude of him," she said,
    "To come and spoil the fun!"

The sea was wet as wet could be,
    The sands were dry as dry.
15 You could not see a cloud because
    No cloud was in the sky:
No birds were flying overhead—
    There were no birds to fly. **Ⓑ**

ANALYZE VISUALS
How would you describe the **setting** in this illustration?

Ⓐ VISUALIZE
Reread lines 1–6. What words help you to visualize the scene?

Ⓑ NARRATIVE POETRY
What have you learned so far about the time, place, and weather conditions of the **setting?** Record details in your graphic organizer.

---

1. **billows:** large waves.
2. **sulkily:** in a gloomy, pouting way.

Illustrations by Sir John Tenniel from
Through the Looking-Glass by Lewis Carroll.

The Walrus and the Carpenter
20   Were walking close at hand:
They wept like anything to see
        Such quantities of sand:
"If this were only cleared away,"
        They said, "it *would* be grand!" **C**

25 "If seven maids with seven mops
        Swept it for half a year,
Do you suppose," the Walrus said,
        "That they could get it clear?"
"I doubt it," said the Carpenter,
30   And shed a bitter tear.

"O Oysters, come and walk with us!"
        The Walrus did beseech.[3]
"A pleasant walk, a pleasant talk,
        Along the briny[4] beach:
35 We cannot do with more than four,
        To give a hand to each."

The eldest Oyster looked at him,
        But never a word he said:
The eldest Oyster winked his eye,
40   And shook his heavy head—
Meaning to say he did not choose
        To leave the oyster-bed.

But four young Oysters hurried up,
        All eager for the treat:
45 Their coats were brushed, their faces washed,
        Their shoes were clean and neat—
And this was odd, because, you know,
        They hadn't any feet.

C **NARRATIVE POETRY**
What **characters** have you met? Note them in your graphic organizer. Add new characters as they are introduced in the poem.

---

3. **beseech:** to beg anxiously.
4. **briny:** containing a fair amount of salt.

Four other Oysters followed them,
50   And yet another four;
And thick and fast they came at last,
        And more, and more, and more—
All hopping through the frothy waves,
        And scrambling to the shore.

55 The Walrus and the Carpenter
        Walked on a mile or so,
And then they rested on a rock
        Conveniently low:
And all the little Oysters stood
60   And waited in a row. **D**

"The time has come," the Walrus said,
        "To talk of many things:
Of shoes—and ships—and sealing-wax—
        Of cabbages—and kings—
65 And why the sea is boiling hot—
        And whether pigs have wings."

"But wait a bit," the Oysters cried,
        "Before we have our chat;
For some of us are out of breath,
70   And all of us are fat!"
"No hurry!" said the Carpenter.
        They thanked him much for that.

"A loaf of bread," the Walrus said,
        "Is what we chiefly need:
75 Pepper and vinegar besides
        Are very good indeed—
Now, if you're ready, Oysters dear,
        We can begin to feed." **E**

D VISUALIZE
Reread lines 55–60. Tell what you see in your mind. Why might it be important that the rock is "conveniently low"?

E NARRATIVE POETRY
What's happening at this point in the poem? Note the **plot events** in your graphic organizer.

"But not on us!" the Oysters cried,
80   Turning a little blue.
"After such kindness, that would be
     A dismal[5] thing to do!"
"The night is fine," the Walrus said.
     "Do you admire the view?" **F**

85 "It was so kind of you to come!
     And you are very nice!"
The Carpenter said nothing but
     "Cut us another slice.
I wish you were not quite so deaf—
90   I've had to ask you twice!"

"It seems a shame," the Walrus said,
     "To play them such a trick.
After we've brought them out so far,
     And made them trot so quick!"
95 The Carpenter said nothing but
     "The butter's spread too thick!"

"I weep for you," the Walrus said:
     "I deeply sympathize."
With sobs and tears he sorted out
100   Those of the largest size,
Holding his pocket-handkerchief
     Before his streaming eyes. **G**

"O Oysters," said the Carpenter,
     "You've had a pleasant run!
105 Shall we be trotting home again?"
     But answer came there none—
And this was scarcely odd, because
     They'd eaten every one.

F NARRATIVE POETRY
The **climax** of a plot
is the turning point.
What do the Oysters
finally figure out in lines
79–80?

G VISUALIZE
Picture in your mind
the Walrus crying while
sorting the Oysters.
What details in the
poem help you to do so?

---

5. **dismal:** particularly bad; dreadful.

Comprehension

1. **Recall** What do the Walrus and the Carpenter invite the Oysters to do?

2. **Clarify** What **trick** do the Walrus and the Carpenter play on the Oysters?

Literary Analysis

3. **Make Inferences** Reread lines 37–42. Why might the eldest Oyster have lived longer than any of the other oysters in the oyster bed?

4. **Visualize** A **stanza** is a group of lines within a poem. Choose a stanza on page 138 and describe the mental picture you form when you read it. Then use a diagram like the one shown to note what helped you visualize.

5. **Identify Rhyme** The repetition of a sound at the ends of different words—as in *knows* and *rose*—is called **rhyme.** The words at the ends of lines 2, 4, and 6 rhyme. Which words in lines 7–12 rhyme? Which words rhyme in lines 13–18? Look through the rest of the poem and describe any pattern you notice.

6. **Evaluate Narrative Poetry** Using the story map that you created as you read, summarize "The Walrus and the Carpenter." Tell what happened, where it happened, and who took part. Do you find the events in the poem funny or disturbing? Explain your reaction.

7. **Interpret the Message** On the basis of this poem, what do you think Carroll might advise young people to do to avoid being tricked? Use evidence from the poem to support your answer.

> Words and Phrases from the Poem
>
> Details from My Imagination
>
> Description of the Picture in My Mind

Extension and Challenge

8. **Readers' Circle** With a partner, look over the fiction and nonfiction you have read in this unit. Decide which selection might serve as a good basis for a narrative poem and why. Then discuss how the selection would change if told in poem form. Would it be funnier, or more serious?

9. **Creative Project: Drama** Poems often lend themselves to being read aloud. Put together a cast of classmates to read "The Walrus and the Carpenter." Assign one person to be the narrator and others to perform the speaking parts. Then do a dramatic reading of the poem.

The Prince and the Pauper

Novel by Mark Twain

Dramatized by Joellen Bland

Who would you BE *if you could?*

KEY IDEA Most of us can name at least one person who has a life we sometimes envy. This person may be an actor, an athlete, a singer, or even a friend. However, you might not envy him or her if you knew what his or her life was really like. In *The Prince and the Pauper,* two characters learn unexpected lessons about themselves and each other when they **trade places.**

ROLE-PLAY With a classmate, choose two famous people whose lives you admire. Make a list of questions you would want to ask them and think of the answers the people would give. Be sure to go beyond the obvious—not everything in their lives would be perfect. Then take turns being the interviewer and present your interviews of the famous people to the class.

● LITERARY ANALYSIS: CONFLICT IN DRAMA

In drama, as in short stories, the **plot** revolves around a central **conflict.** Since drama is meant to be performed by actors, a drama's conflict usually unfolds through action and dialogue (conversation between characters).

Unlike a book, which has chapters, a play is divided into acts and scenes. The play you are about to read takes place in eight scenes that revolve around two boys who switch identities. As you read, notice how the conflict becomes more complicated.

● READING STRATEGY: READING A PLAY

In a drama, **stage directions** provide key information that readers would normally see or hear in a performance, such as

- the setting, scenery, and props (*Westminster Palace, England,* Scene 1, line 2)

- the music, sound effects, and lighting (*Fanfare of trumpets is heard,* Scene 3, line 282)

- the characters' movements, behavior, or ways of speaking (*surprised, standing up quickly,* Scene 4, line 345)

As you read the play, record examples of stage directions and tell what they help you to understand.

Stage Direction	Type of Direction	What It Tells Me
Fanfare of trumpets is heard (Scene 3, line 282)	Sound effects	Someone is entering.

▲ VOCABULARY IN CONTEXT

The boldfaced words help tell the story of two boys trading places. To see how many you know, replace each word with a different word or words that have the same meaning.

1. The king expected his son to be his **successor.**
2. Tom looked like a prince, but he was a **pauper.**
3. An **affliction** seemed to make the prince forgetful.
4. The king began to doubt that his son was **sane.**
5. The boy had no **recollection** of where he put the seal.
6. Was he the real prince or an **impostor?**

Author On|ine

Boyhood Adventures
Two of Mark Twain's best-known works focus on the adventures, or misadventures, of two young boys— Huckleberry Finn and Tom Sawyer. In developing these stories, Twain drew upon his own

**Mark Twain
1835–1910**

experiences and those of his childhood friends. Many of his tales take place along the Mississippi River, where Twain spent much of his time as a child and young adult.

Have Pen, Will Travel Twain loved to travel. His frequent trips throughout the United States and to Europe resulted in a series of funny and clever stories. Twain set some of his novels, including *The Prince and the Pauper,* in England, where he was greatly admired. Though he wrote *The Prince and the Pauper* as a novel, Joellen Bland later adapted the story as a play.

 MORE ABOUT THE AUTHOR
For more on Mark Twain, visit the **Literature Center** at ClassZone.com.

Background

True Royalty The prince in Twain's story is based on Edward, son of King Henry VIII of England. After Henry's death in 1547, the nine-year-old Edward took the throne, becoming King Edward VI.

THE
PRINCE AND THE
PAUPER

MARK TWAIN
Dramatized by Joellen Bland

CHARACTERS

Edward, Prince of Wales	**Justice**
Tom Canty, the Pauper	**Constable**
Lord Hertford	**Jailer**
Lord St. John	**Sir Hugh Hendon**
King Henry VIII	**Two Prisoners**
Herald	**Two Guards**
Miles Hendon	**Three Pages**
John Canty, Tom's father	**Lords and Ladies**
Hugo, a young thief	**Villagers**
Two Women	

SCENE ONE

Time: *1547.*

Setting: *Westminster Palace, England. Gates leading to courtyard are at right. Slightly to the left, off courtyard and inside gates, interior of palace anteroom[1] is visible. There is a couch with a rich robe draped on it, screen at rear, bellcord, mirror, chairs, and a table with bowl of nuts, and a large golden seal on it. Piece of armor hangs on one wall. Exits are rear and downstage.*

---

1. **anteroom** (ăn′tē-rōōm′): an outer room that leads to another room and is often used as a waiting room.

Photographs by Crown Media
Distribution, LLC.

At Curtain Rise: Two Guards—*one at right, one at left—stand in front of gates, and several*
10 Villagers *hover nearby, straining to see into courtyard where* Prince *may be seen through fence, playing.* Two Women *enter right.*

1st Woman. I have walked all morning just to have a glimpse of Westminster Palace.

2nd Woman. Maybe if we can get near enough to the gates, we can have a glimpse of the young Prince. (Tom Canty, *dirty and ragged, comes out of crowd and steps close to gates.*)

Tom. I have always dreamed of seeing a real
20 Prince! (*Excited, he presses his nose against gates.*)

1st Guard. Mind your manners, you young beggar! (*Seizes* Tom *by collar and sends him sprawling into crowd.* Villagers *laugh, as* Tom *slowly gets to his feet.*)

Prince (*rushing to gates*). How dare you treat a poor subject of the King in such a manner! Open the gates and let him in! (*As* Villagers *see* Prince, *they take off their hats and bow low.*)

Villagers (*shouting together*). Long live the
30 Prince of Wales! (Guards *open gates and* Tom *slowly passes through, as if in a dream.*)

Prince (*to* Tom). You look tired, and you have been treated cruelly. I am Edward, Prince of Wales. What is your name?

Tom (*looking around in awe*). Tom Canty, Your Highness.

Prince. Come into the palace with me, Tom. (Prince *leads* Tom *into anteroom.* Villagers *pantomime conversation, and all but a few exit.*)
40 Where do you live, Tom?

Tom. In the city, Your Highness, in Offal Court.

Prince. Offal Court? That is an odd name. Do you have parents?

Tom. Yes, Your Highness.

Prince. How does your father treat you?

Tom. If it please you, Your Highness, when I am not able to beg a penny for our supper, he treats me to beatings.

Prince (*shocked*). What! Beatings? My father
50 is not a calm man, but he does not beat me. (*looks at* Tom *thoughtfully*) You speak well and have an easy grace. Have you been schooled?

Tom. Very little, Your Highness. A good priest who shares our house in Offal Court has taught me from his books.

Prince. Do you have a pleasant life in Offal Court?

Tom. Pleasant enough, Your Highness, save when I am hungry. We have Punch and Judy
60 shows, and sometimes we lads have fights in the street.

Prince (*eagerly*). I should like that. Tell me more.

Tom. In summer, we run races and swim in the river, and we love to wallow in the mud.

Prince (*sighing, wistfully*). If I could wear your clothes and play in the mud just once, with no one to forbid me, I think I could give up the crown!

Tom (*shaking his head*). And if I could wear
70 your fine clothes just once, Your Highness . . .

Prince. Would you like that? Come, then. We shall change places. You can take off your rags and put on my clothes—and I will put on yours. (*He leads* Tom *behind screen, and they return shortly, each wearing the other's clothes.*) Let's look at ourselves in this mirror. (*leads* Tom *to mirror*)

Tom. Oh, Your Highness, it is not proper for me to wear such clothes.

80 **Prince** (*excitedly, as he looks in mirror*). Heavens, do you not see it? We look like brothers! We have the same features and bearing.[2] If we went about together, dressed alike, there is no one

---

2. **features and bearing:** parts of the face and ways of standing or walking.

who could say which is the Prince of Wales and which is Tom Canty!

Tom (*drawing back and rubbing his hand*). Your Highness, I am frightened. . . .

Prince. Do not worry. (*seeing* Tom *rub his hand*) Is that a bruise on your hand?

90 **Tom.** Yes, but it is a slight thing, Your Highness.

Prince (*angrily*). It was shameful and cruel of that guard to strike you. Do not stir a step until I come back. I command you! (*He picks up golden Seal of England[3] and carefully puts it into piece of armor. He then dashes out to gates.*) Open! Unbar the gates at once! (*2nd Guard opens gates, and as* Prince *runs out, in rags,* 1st Guard *seizes him, boxes him on the ear, and knocks him to the ground.*)

100 **1st Guard.** Take that, you little beggar, for the trouble you have made for me with the Prince. (Villagers *roar with laughter.*)

Prince (*picking himself up, turning on* Guard *furiously*). I am Prince of Wales! You shall hang for laying your hand on me!

1st Guard (*presenting arms; mockingly*). I salute Your Gracious Highness! (*Then, angrily,* 1st Guard *shoves* Prince *roughly aside.*) Be off, you mad bag of rags! (Prince *is surrounded* 110 *by* Villagers, *who hustle him off.*)

Villagers (*ad lib,[4] as they exit, shouting*). Make way for His Royal Highness! Make way for the Prince of Wales! Hail to the Prince! (*etc.*)

Tom (*admiring himself in mirror*). If only the boys in Offal Court could see me! They will

---

3. **Seal of England:** a device used to stamp a special design, usually a picture of the ruler, onto a document, thus indicating that it has royal approval.

4. **ad lib:** talk together about what is going on, but without an actual script.

not believe me when I tell them about this. (*looks around anxiously*) But where is the Prince? (*Looks cautiously into courtyard.* Two Guards *immediately snap to attention and salute.* 120 *He quickly ducks back into anteroom as* Lords Hertford *and* St. John *enter at rear.*)

Hertford (*going toward* Tom, *then stopping and bowing low*). My Lord, you look distressed. What is wrong?

Tom (*trembling*). Oh, I beg of you, be merciful. I am no Prince, but poor Tom Canty of Offal Court. Please let me see the Prince, and he will give my rags back to me and let me go unhurt. (*kneeling*) Please, be merciful and spare me!

130 **Hertford** (*puzzled and disturbed*). Your Highness, on your knees? To me? (*bows quickly, then, aside to* St. John) The Prince has gone mad! We must inform the King. (*to* Tom) A moment, your Highness. (Hertford *and* St. John *exit rear.*)

Tom. Oh, there is no hope for me now. They will hang me for certain! (Hertford *and* St. John *re-enter, supporting* King. Tom *watches in awe as they help him to couch, where he sinks* 140 *down wearily.*)

King (*beckoning* Tom *close to him*). Now, my son, Edward, my prince. What is this? Do you mean to deceive me, the King, your father, who loves you and treats you so kindly?

Tom (*dropping to his knees*). You are the King? Then I have no hope!

King (*stunned*). My child, you are not well. Do not break your father's old heart. Say you know me.

150 **Tom.** Yes, you are my lord the King, whom God preserve.

King. True, that is right. Now, you will not deny that you are Prince of Wales, as they say you did just a while ago?

Tom. I beg you, Your Grace, believe me. I am the lowest of your subjects, being born a **pauper,** and it is by a great mistake that I am here. I am too young to die. Oh, please, spare me, sire!

King (*amazed*). Die? Do not talk so, my child.
160 You shall not die.

Tom (*gratefully*). God save you, my king! And now, may I go?

King. Go? Where would you go?

Tom. Back to the alley where I was born and bred to misery.

King. My poor child, rest your head here. (*He holds* Tom's *head and pats his shoulder, then turns to* Hertford *and* St. John.) Alas, I am old and ill, and my son is mad. But this shall pass. Mad
170 or **sane,** he is my heir and shall rule England. Tomorrow he shall be installed and confirmed in his princely dignity! Bring the Great Seal!

Hertford (*bowing low*). Please, Your Majesty, you took the Great Seal from the Chancellor two days ago to give to His Highness the Prince.

King. So I did. (*to* Tom) My child, tell me, where is the Great Seal?

Tom (*trembling*). Indeed, my lord, I do not know.

180 **King.** Ah, your **affliction** hangs heavily upon you. 'Tis no matter. You will remember later. Listen, carefully! (*gently, but firmly*) I command you to hide your affliction in all ways that be within your power. You shall deny to no one that you are the true prince, and if your memory should fail you upon any occasion of state, you shall be advised by your uncle, the Lord Hertford.

Tom (*resigned*). The King has spoken. The
190 King shall be obeyed.

King. And now, my child, I go to rest. (*He stands weakly, and* Hertford *leads him off, rear.*)

Tom (*wearily, to* St. John). May it please your lordship to let me rest now?

St. John. So it please Your Highness, it is for you to command and us to obey. But it is wise that you rest, for this evening you must attend the Lord Mayor's banquet in your honor. (*He pulls bellcord, and* Three Pages *enter and kneel*
200 *before* Tom.)

Tom. Banquet? (*Terrified, he sits on couch and reaches for cup of water, but* 1st Page *instantly seizes cup, drops on one knee, and serves it to him.* Tom *starts to take off his boots, but* 2nd Page *stops him and does it for him. He tries to remove his cape and gloves, and* 3rd Page *does it for him.*) I wonder that you do not try to breathe for me also! (*Lies down cautiously.* Pages *cover him with robe, then back away and exit.*)

210 **St. John** (*to* Hertford, *as he enters*). Plainly, what do you think?

Hertford. Plainly, this. The King is near death, my nephew the Prince of Wales is clearly mad and will mount the throne mad. God protect England, for she will need it!

St. John. Does it not seem strange that madness could so change his manner from what it used to be? It troubles me, his saying he is not the Prince.

220 **Hertford.** Peace, my lord! If he were an **impostor** and called himself Prince, that would be natural. But was there ever an impostor, who being called Prince by the King and court, denied it? Never! This is the true Prince gone mad. And tonight all London shall honor him. (*Hertford and* St. John *exit.* Tom *sits up, looks around helplessly, then gets up.*)

Tom. I should have thought to order something to eat. (*sees bowl of nuts on table*) Ah! Here are
230 some nuts! (*looks around, sees Great Seal in armor, takes it out, looks at it curiously*) This will make a good nutcracker. (*He takes bowl of nuts, sits on couch and begins to crack nuts with Great Seal and eat them, as curtain falls.*)

SCENE TWO

Time: *Later that night.*

Setting: *A street in London, near Offal Court. Played before the curtain.*

At Curtain Rise: Prince *limps in, dirty and tousled. He looks around wearily. Several* Villagers *pass*
240 *by, pushing against him.*

Prince. I have never seen this poor section of London. I must be near Offal Court. If I can only find it before I drop! (John Canty *steps out of crowd, seizes* Prince *roughly.*)

Canty. Out at this time of night, and I warrant you haven't brought a farthing[5] home! If that is the case and I do not break all the bones in your miserable body, then I am not John Canty!

250 **Prince** (*eagerly*). Oh, are you his father?

Canty. *His* father? I am *your* father, and—

Prince. Take me to the palace at once, and your son will be returned to you. The King, my father, will make you rich beyond your wildest dreams. Oh, save me, for I am indeed the Prince of Wales.

Canty (*staring in amazement*). Gone stark mad! But mad or not, I'll soon find where the soft places lie in your bones. Come home! (*starts to*
260 *drag* Prince *off*)

Prince (*struggling*). Let me go! I am the Prince of Wales, and the King shall have your life for this!

Canty (*angrily*). I'll take no more of your madness! (*raises stick to strike, but* Prince *struggles free and runs off, and* Canty *runs after him*)

SCENE THREE

Setting: *Same as Scene 1, with addition of dining table, set with dishes and goblets, on raised*
270 *platform. Throne-like chair is at head of table.*

At Curtain Rise: *A banquet is in progress.* Tom, *in royal robes, sits at head of table, with* Hertford *at his right and* St. John *at his left.* Lords *and* Ladies *sit around table eating and talking softly.*

Tom (*to* Hertford). What is this, my Lord? (*holds up a plate*)

Hertford. Lettuce and turnips, Your Highness.

Tom. Lettuce and turnips? I have never seen them before. Am I to eat them?

280 **Hertford** (*discreetly*). Yes, Your Highness, if you so desire. (Tom *begins to eat food with his fingers. Fanfare of trumpets[6] is heard, and* Herald *enters, carrying scroll. All turn to look.*)

---

5. **farthing:** a former British coin worth one-fourth of a British penny.

6. **fanfare of trumpets:** a short tune or call, usually indicating that something important is about to occur.

Herald (*reading from scroll*). His Majesty, King Henry VIII, is dead! The King is dead! (*All rise and turn to* Tom, *who sits, stunned.*)

All (*together*). The King is dead. Long live the King! Long live Edward, King of England! (*All bow to* Tom. Herald *bows and exits.*)

290 **Hertford** (*to* Tom). Your Majesty, we must call the council. Come, St. John. (Hertford *and* St. John *lead* Tom *off at rear.* Lords *and* Ladies *follow, talking among themselves. At gates, down right,* Villagers *enter and mill about.* Prince *enters right, pounds on gates and shouts.*)

Prince. Open the gates! I am the Prince of Wales! Open, I say! And though I am friendless with no one to help me, I will not be driven from my ground.

300 **Miles Hendon** (*entering through crowd*). Though you be Prince or not, you are indeed a gallant lad and not friendless. Here I stand to prove it, and you might have a worse friend than Miles Hendon.

1st Villager. 'Tis another prince in disguise. Take the lad and dunk him in the pond! (*He seizes* Prince, *but* Miles *strikes him with flat of his sword.* Crowd, *now angry, presses forward threateningly, when fanfare of trumpets is heard offstage.* Herald,
310 *carrying scroll, enters up left at gates.*)

Herald. Make way for the King's messenger! (*reading from scroll*) His Majesty, King Henry VIII, is dead! The King is dead! (*He exits right, repeating message, and* Villagers *stand in stunned silence.*)

Prince (*stunned*). The King is dead!

1st Villager (*shouting*). Long live Edward, King of England!

Villagers (*together*). Long live the King!
320 (*shouting, ad lib*) Long live King Edward! Heaven protect Edward, King of England! (*etc.*)

Miles (*taking* Prince *by the arm*). Come, lad, before the crowd remembers us. I have a room at the inn, and you can stay there. (*He hurries off with stunned* Prince. Tom, *led by* Hertford, *enters courtyard up rear.* Villagers *see them.*)

Villagers (*together*). Long live the King! (*They fall to their knees as curtains close.*)

SCENE FOUR

Setting: *Miles' room at the inn. At right is table*
330 *set with dishes and bowls of food, a chair at each side. At left is bed, with table and chair next to it, and a window. Candle is on table.*

At Curtain Rise: Miles *and* Prince *approach table.*

Miles. I have had a hot supper prepared. I'll bet you're hungry, lad.

Prince. Yes, I am. It's kind of you to let me stay with you, Miles. I am truly Edward, King of England, and you shall not go unrewarded. (*sits at table*)

340 **Miles** (*to himself*). First he called himself Prince, and now he is King. Well, I will humor him. (*starts to sit*)

Prince (*angrily*). Stop! Would you sit in the presence of the King?

Miles (*surprised, standing up quickly*). I beg your pardon, Your Majesty. I was not thinking. (*Stares uncertainly at* Prince, *who sits at table, expectantly.* Miles *starts to uncover dishes of food, serves* Prince *and fills glasses.*)

350 **Prince.** Miles, you have a gallant way about you. Are you nobly born?

Miles. My father is a baronet,[7] Your Majesty.

Prince. Then you must also be a baronet.

Miles (*shaking his head*). My father banished me from home seven years ago, so I fought in

---

7. **baronet:** a rank of honor in Britain, below a baron and above a knight.

the wars. I was taken prisoner, and I have spent the past seven years in prison. Now I am free, and I am returning home.

Prince. You have been shamefully wronged! 360 But I will make things right for you. You have saved me from injury and possible death. Name your reward and if it be within the compass of my royal power, it is yours.

Miles (*pausing briefly, then dropping to his knee*). Since Your Majesty is pleased to hold my simple duty worthy of reward, I ask that I and my <u>successors</u> may hold the privilege of sitting in the presence of the King.

Prince (*taking Miles' sword, tapping him lightly* 370 *on each shoulder*). Rise and seat yourself. (*returns sword to Miles, then rises and goes over to bed*)

Miles (*rising*). He should have been born a king. He plays the part to a marvel! If I had not thought of this favor, I might have had to stand for weeks. (*sits down and begins to eat*)

Prince. Sir Miles, you will stand guard while I sleep? (*lies down and instantly falls asleep*)

Miles. Yes, Your Majesty. (*With a rueful look* 380 *at his uneaten supper, he stands up.*) Poor little chap. I suppose his mind has been disordered with ill usage. (*covers Prince with his cape*) Well, I will be his friend and watch over him. (*Blows out candle, then yawns, sits on chair next to bed, and falls asleep. John Canty and Hugo appear at window, peer around room, then enter cautiously through window. They lift the sleeping Prince, staring nervously at Miles.*)

Canty (*in loud whisper*). I swore the day he was 390 born he would be a thief and a beggar, and I won't lose him now. Lead the way to the camp Hugo! (*Canty and Hugo carry Prince off right, as Miles sleeps on and curtain falls.*)

SCENE FIVE

Time: *Two weeks later.*

Setting: *Country village street.*

Before Curtain Rise: Villagers *walk about.* Canty, Hugo, *and* Prince *enter.*

Canty. I will go in this direction. Hugo, keep my mad son with you, and see that he doesn't 400 escape again! (*exits*)

Hugo (*seizing Prince by the arm*). He won't escape! I'll see that he earns his bread today, or else!

Prince (*pulling away*). I will not beg with you, and I will not steal! I have suffered enough in this miserable company of thieves!

Hugo. You shall suffer more if you do not do as I tell you! (*raises clenched fist at Prince*) Refuse if you dare! (Woman *enters, carrying wrapped* 410 *bundle in a basket on her arm.*) Wait here until I come back. (Hugo *sneaks along after Woman, then snatches her bundle, runs back to Prince, and thrusts it into his arms.*) Run after me and call, "Stop, thief!" But be sure you lead her astray! (*Runs off.* Prince *throws down bundle in disgust.*)

Woman. Help! Thief! Stop, thief! (*rushes at* Prince *and seizes him, just as several Villagers enter*) You little thief! What do you mean by robbing a poor woman? Somebody bring the 420 constable! (Miles *enters and watches.*)

1st Villager (*grabbing Prince*). I'll teach him a lesson, the little villain!

Prince (*struggling*). Take your hands off me! I did not rob this woman!

Miles (*stepping out of crowd and pushing man back with the flat of his sword*). Let us proceed gently, my friends. This is a matter for the law.

Prince (*springing to Miles' side*). You have come just in time, Sir Miles. Carve this rabble to rags!

430 **Miles.** Speak softly. Trust in me and all shall go well.

Constable (*entering and reaching for* Prince). Come along, young rascal!

Miles. Gently, good friend. He shall go peaceably to the Justice.

Prince. I will not go before a Justice! I did not do this thing!

Miles (*taking him aside*). Sire, will you reject the laws of the realm, yet demand that your subjects respect them?

Prince (*calmer*). You are right, Sir Miles. Whatever the King requires a subject to suffer under the law, he will suffer himself while he holds the station of a subject. (Constable *leads them off right. Villagers follow. Curtain.*)

SCENE SIX

Setting: *Office of the Justice. A high bench is at center.*

At Curtain Rise: Justice *sits behind bench.* Constable *enters with* Miles *and* Prince, *followed by* Villagers. Woman *carries wrapped bundle.*

Constable (*to* Justice). A young thief, your worship, is accused of stealing a dressed pig from this poor woman.

Justice (*looking down at* Prince, *then* Woman). My good woman, are you absolutely certain this lad stole your pig?

Woman. It was none other than he, your worship.

Justice. Are there no witnesses to the contrary? (*All shake their heads.*) Then the lad stands convicted. (*to* Woman) What do you hold this property to be worth?

Woman. Three shillings and eight pence, your worship.

Justice (*leaning down to* Woman). Good woman, do you know that when one steals a thing above the value of thirteen pence, the law says he shall hang for it?

Woman (*upset*). Oh, what have I done? I would not hang the poor boy for the whole world! Save me from this, your worship. What can I do?

Justice (*gravely*). You may revise the value, since it is not yet written in the record.

Woman. Then call the pig eight pence, your worship.

Justice. So be it. You may take your property and go. (Woman *starts off, and is followed by* Constable. Miles *follows them cautiously down right.*)

Constable (*stopping* Woman). Good woman, I will buy your pig from you. (*takes coins from pocket*) Here is eight pence.

Woman. Eight pence! It cost me three shillings and eight pence!

Constable. Indeed! Then come back before his worship and answer for this. The lad must hang!

Woman. No! No! Say no more. Give me the eight pence and hold your peace. (Constable *hands her coins and takes pig.* Woman *exits, angrily.* Miles *returns to bench.*)

Justice. The boy is sentenced to a fortnight[8] in the common jail. Take him away, Constable! (Justice *exits.* Prince *gives* Miles *a nervous glance.*)

Miles (*following* Constable). Good sir, turn your back a moment and let the poor lad escape. He is innocent.

Constable (*outraged*). What? You say this to me? Sir, I arrest you in—

Miles. Do not be so hasty! (*slyly*) The pig you have purchased for eight pence may cost you your neck, man.

---

8. **fortnight:** 14 days.

Constable (*laughing nervously*). Ah, but I was merely jesting with the woman, sir.

Miles. Would the Justice think it a jest?

Constable. Good sir! The Justice has no more sympathy with a jest than a dead corpse! (*perplexed*) Very well, I will turn my back and see nothing! But go quickly! (*exits*)

510 **Miles** (*to* Prince). Come, my liege.[9] We are free to go. And that band of thieves shall not set hands on you again, I swear it!

Prince (*wearily*). Can you believe, Sir Miles, that in the last fortnight, I, the King of England, have escaped from thieves and begged for food on the road? I have slept in a barn with a calf! I have washed dishes in a peasant's kitchen, and narrowly escaped death. And not once in all my wanderings did I see a courier[10] searching for 520 me! Is it no matter for commotion and distress that the head of state is gone?

Miles (*sadly, aside*). Still busy with his pathetic dream. (*to* Prince) It is strange indeed, my liege. But come, I will take you to my father's home in Kent. We are not far away. There you may rest in a house with seventy rooms! Come, I am all impatience to be home again! (*They exit,* Miles *in cheerful spirits,* Prince *looking puzzled, as curtains close.*)

SCENE SEVEN

530 **Setting:** *Village jail. Bare stage, with barred window on one wall.*

At Curtain Rise: Two Prisoners, *in chains, are onstage.* Jailer *shoves* Miles *and* Prince, *in chains, onstage. They struggle and protest.*

Miles. But I tell you, I am Miles Hendon! My brother, Sir Hugh, has stolen my bride and my estate!

Jailer. Be silent! Impostor! Sir Hugh will see that you pay well for claiming to be his dead 540 brother and for assaulting him in his own house! (*exits*)

Miles (*sitting, with head in hands*). Oh, my dear Edith . . . now wife to my brother Hugh, against her will, and my poor father . . . dead!

1st Prisoner. At least you have your life, sir. I am sentenced to be hanged for killing a deer in the King's park.

2nd Prisoner. And I must hang for stealing a yard of cloth to dress my children.

550 **Prince** (*moved; to* Prisoners). When I mount my throne, you shall all be free. And the laws that have dishonored you shall be swept from the books. (*turning away*) Kings should go to school to learn their own laws and be merciful.

1st Prisoner. What does the lad mean? I have heard that the King is mad, but merciful.

2nd Prisoner. He is to be crowned at Westminster tomorrow.

Prince (*violently*). King? What King, good sir?

560 **1st Prisoner.** Why, we have only one, his most sacred majesty, King Edward the Sixth.

2nd Prisoner. And whether he be mad or not, his praises are on all men's lips. He has saved many innocent lives, and now he means to destroy the cruelest laws that oppress the people.

Prince (*turning away, shaking his head*). How can this be? Surely it is not that little beggar boy! (Sir Hugh *enters with* Jailer.)

Sir Hugh. Seize the impostor!

570 **Miles** (*as* Jailer *pulls him to his feet*). Hugh, this has gone far enough!

Sir Hugh. You will sit in the public stocks for two hours, and the boy would join you if he were not so young. See to it, jailer, and after

---

9. **my liege** (lēj): my lord.

10. **courier** (kŏŏr′ē-ər): messenger.

two hours, you may release them. Meanwhile, I ride to London for the coronation![11] (Sir Hugh *exits and* Miles *is hustled out by* Jailer.)

Prince. Coronation! What does he mean? There can be no coronation without me! (*curtain falls.*)

SCENE EIGHT

580 **Time:** *Coronation Day.*

Setting: *Outside gates of Westminster Abbey, played before curtain. Painted screen or flat at rear represents Abbey. Throne is in center. Bench is near it.*

At Curtain Rise: Lords *and* Ladies *crowd Abbey. Outside gates,* Guards *drive back cheering* Villagers, *among them* Miles.

Miles (*distraught*). I've lost him! Poor little chap! He has been swallowed up in the crowd!

590 (*Fanfare of trumpets is heard, then silence.* Hertford, St. John, Lords *and* Ladies *enter slowly, in a procession, followed by* Pages, *one of whom carries crown on a small cushion.* Tom *follows procession, looking about nervously. Suddenly,* Prince, *in rags, steps out from crowd, his hand raised.*)

Prince. I forbid you to set the crown of England upon that head. I am the King!

Hertford. Seize the little vagabond!

600 **Tom.** I forbid it! He is the King! (*kneels before* Prince) Oh, my lord the King, let poor Tom Canty be the first to say, "Put on your crown and enter into your own right again." (Hertford *and several* Lords *look closely at both boys.*)

Hertford. This is strange indeed. (*to* Tom) By your favor, sir, I wish to ask certain questions of this lad.

---

11. **coronation:** the act of crowning someone king or queen. In England coronations usually take place at a large church in London called Westminster Abbey.

Prince. I will answer truly whatever you may ask, my lord. .

610 **Hertford.** But if you have been well trained, you may answer my questions as well as our lord the King. I need a definite proof. (*thinks a moment*) Ah! Where lies the Great Seal of England? It has been missing for weeks, and only the true Prince of Wales can say where it lies.

Tom. Wait! Was the seal round and thick, with letters engraved on it? (Hertford *nods.*) I know where it is, but it was not I who put it there. The rightful King shall tell you. (*to* Prince)
620 Think, my King, it was the very last thing you did that day before you rushed out of the palace wearing my rags.

Prince (*pausing*). I recall how we exchanged clothes, but have no **recollection** of hiding the Great Seal.

Tom (*eagerly*). Remember when you saw the bruise on my hand, you ran to the door, but first you hid this thing you call the Seal.

Prince (*suddenly*). Ah! I remember! (*to* St. John)
630 Go, my good St. John, and you shall find the Great Seal in the armor that hangs on the wall in my chamber. (St. John *hesitates, but at a nod from* Tom, *hurries off.*)

Tom (*pleased*). Right, my King! Now the scepter[12] of England is yours again. (St. John *returns in a moment with Great Seal.*)

All (*shouting*). Long live Edward, King of England! (Tom *takes off his cape and throws it over* Prince's *rags. Trumpet fanfare is heard.* St.
640 John *takes crown and places it on* Prince. *All kneel.*)

Hertford. Let the small impostor be flung into the Tower!

Prince (*firmly*). I will not have it so. But for him, I would not have my crown. (*to* Tom) My poor boy, how was it that you could remember where I hid the Seal, when I could not?

Tom (*embarrassed*). I did not know what it was, my King, and I used it to . . . to crack nuts. (*All*
650 *laugh, and* Tom *steps back.* Miles *steps forward, staring in amazement.*)

Miles. Is he really the King? Is he indeed the sovereign of England, and not the poor and friendless Tom o' Bedlam[13] I thought he was? (*He sinks down on bench.*) I wish I had a bag to hide my head in!

1st Guard (*rushing up to him*). Stand up, you mannerless clown! How dare you sit in the presence of the King!

660 **Prince.** Do not touch him! He is my trusty servant, Miles Hendon, who saved me from shame and possible death. For his service, he owns the right to sit in my presence.

Miles (*bowing, then kneeling*). Your Majesty!

Prince. Rise, Sir Miles. I command that Sir Hugh Hendon, who sits within this hall, be seized and put under lock and key until I have need of him. (*beckons to* Tom) From what I have heard, Tom Canty, you have governed
670 the realm with royal gentleness and mercy in my absence. Henceforth, you shall hold the honorable title of King's Ward! (Tom *kneels and kisses* Prince's *hand.*) And because I have suffered with the poorest of my subjects and felt the cruel force of unjust laws, I pledge myself to a reign of mercy for all! (*All bow low, then rise.*)

All (*shouting*). Long live the King! Long live Edward, King of England! (*curtain*)

---

12. **scepter** (sĕp'tər): a baton or other emblem of royal authority.

13. **Tom o' Bedlam:** an insane person, such as someone hospitalized at St. Mary of Bethlehem Hospital, or Bedlam Hospital, in London.

Comprehension

1. **Recall** How do most of the adults explain the boys' claims that they are not who they appear to be?

2. **Clarify** Explain how the constable tricks the woman into selling the pig. How does Miles use the trick to get Edward released?

3. **Summarize** How has Edward's experience as a pauper influenced him?

Literary Analysis

4. **Make Inferences** Scan the play to find examples of how Miles treats the prince and how the members of the royal court treat Tom. What motivates their behavior toward the boys?

5. **Analyze Character** Tom's behavior at court leads people to believe the "prince" is mad. Why does Tom behave this way?

6. **Analyze Conflict in Drama** Use a chart like the one shown to summarize the main events of each scene. This will help you see how the conflict develops over the course of the play. In which scene is the conflict resolved?

> **Scene 1:** The guards mistake the Prince for Tom, and the King thinks that Tom is the Prince.
>
> **Scene 2:**

7. **Evaluate Stage Directions** Look over the stage directions you listed in your chart. Which ones seemed most necessary for understanding the play?

8. **Evaluate Resolution** What lessons did the boys learn about themselves and each other by **trading places?**

Extension and Challenge

9. **Inquiry and Research** During the time of Henry VIII and Edward VI, the British king was very powerful. Since then, the power of the royal family has decreased. Research Henry VIII's reign and compare it with that of Queen Elizabeth II. Focus on how royal powers and responsibilities have changed over time. Present your findings to the class.

King Henry VIII

 RESEARCH LINKS
For more on British royalty, visit the **Research Center** at **ClassZone.com.**

Writing Workshop

Short Story

What unusual places did the stories in this unit take you to? What strange characters did you meet there, and what conflicts did you find? In this workshop, you'll have a chance to invent a setting, characters, and a plot of your own. Follow each step in the **Writer's Road Map** to learn how.

WRITER'S ROAD MAP

Short Story

WRITING PROMPT 1

Writing from Your Imagination Write a short story set in an interesting place. Make sure that your story has a plot, a conflict, and one or more characters.

Settings to Consider

• an exotic place, such as a jungle or a desert island

• an everyday place where something unusual happens

• a place you have wanted to visit, such as the Pyramids or a space station

WRITING PROMPT 2

Writing from Literature Choose a story from this unit that you especially liked. Write a story that has a similar plot but different characters and a different setting.

Stories to Consider

• "The School Play" (characters participating in a school event, such as a science fair, a play, or a festival)

• "All Summer in a Day" (characters living in an alien world)

• "Lob's Girl" (extraordinary behavior of a pet)

WRITING TOOLS
For prewriting, revision, and editing tools, visit the **Writing Center** at **ClassZone.com**.

KEY TRAITS

1. IDEAS

• Creates clearly described **characters** and an interesting **plot**

• Uses **details** to help the reader picture the setting, characters, and events

• Has a **central conflict** and provides an ending for that conflict

• Includes **dialogue**

2. ORGANIZATION

• Follows a clear sequence of **events**

3. VOICE

• Has a consistent **point of view**

• Uses the **active voice**

4. WORD CHOICE

• Uses **sensory language**

5. SENTENCE FLUENCY

• Varies **sentence beginnings**

6. CONVENTIONS

• Uses **correct grammar, spelling, and punctuation**

Part 1: Analyze a Student Model

Sarah Edelstein
P.S. 129

Finding a Solution

One day last fall, Sarah was cutting through the park on the way home from school. She was daydreaming about big, shiny spaceships with bright lights, heat shields, and huge engines. In her mind, she stepped inside one of the spaceships. It was cold and shiny like a new
5 refrigerator but had dozens of flashing panels.

Sarah was still daydreaming when she heard a loud "Pssst" coming from behind some bushes. She stopped and noticed some red lights blinking. In the distance, she thought she saw a silver spaceship.

Shocked, Sarah just stood there until the same voice spoke again. It
10 said, "Don't be afraid. I'm harmless! And I need your help!"

Standing in front of Sarah was a light-blue spacewoman. Pale, pink eyes bulged from her large, oval head. Her tiny body was blinking blue and orange like a fast-food sign. She said to Sarah in a squeaky but firm voice, "I really need you. I have only enough Lekterol to last another
15 day. If I don't drink more soon, I'll stop blinking and die! You know, on my home planet, Utemore, Lekterol is just like water."

Sarah was so stunned that she couldn't move.

"Look," continued the spacewoman. "I'm Meena. I'm just like any Earth mom you know. I just want to get home to see my kids. I know
20 Lekterol can be made on your planet, and you've just got to get me some."

Once again, Sarah could barely speak. Meena seemed like an okay lady, and Sarah wanted to help. Still, where would Sarah ever find Lekterol? What was Lekterol, anyway? And how could she possibly
25 explain why she needed it?

Finally, Meena begged, "Please hurry! My life depends on it!"

KEY TRAITS IN ACTION

Uses **sensory language** and varies **sentence beginnings** to keep the reader interested.

Includes precise **details** to show the reader what the setting is like.

The story has clearly described **characters** and a **central conflict** (the spacewoman will die unless Sarah helps her).

Dialogue helps make the story dramatic and entertaining.

This time Sarah said, "Okay, I'll help you." Then she raced home and searched the Internet for information on Lekterol. She found only four hits, but one of them gave the formula. Then Sarah knew what to do. She would ask her Aunt Cindy, a scientist, to make the Lekterol in her lab.

Sarah raced to Xygen BioProducts. When she got to the lab, she was out of breath. "Aunt Cindy, you have to make something for me!" she panted.

Her aunt asked so many questions that Sarah had to explain why she needed the Lekterol. She could tell Aunt Cindy didn't believe her. Finally, her aunt gave in and said, "Okay, Sarah. I'm only going to do this because Lekterol is harmless, and I don't see how it can hurt anyone." Then she patted Sarah's shoulder gently and said, "But really, honey, you should try to get a grip on yourself."

"You're so right, Aunt Cindy," Sarah said in her most serious voice. Then she raced out of the lab.

Ten minutes later, Sarah was back at the spaceship.

"Oh, you wonderful Earthling!" Meena shouted when she saw Sarah waving two bottles of Lekterol.

In another minute, Meena had drunk the Lekterol and entered her spaceship. Before she closed the door, though, she called back, "You saved my life! Please visit me anytime on Utemore."

Sarah waved and said, "You bet I will." Then Sarah smiled and watched the spaceship disappear. She walked the rest of the way home, wondering how she could get to Utemore.

Keeps a consistent third-person **point of view** and uses the **active voice.**

Has an interesting **plot** with a clear **sequence of events.**

Provides an ending for the conflict.

2

Part 2: Apply the Writing Process

PREWRITING

What Should I Do?	What Does It Look Like?

1. Find an idea.
Make a long list of "what if" questions—on your own or with a friend. Highlight the one you like best.

See page 164: "What If" Questions

▶

What if a character got on a bus or train and got off on a strange island?

What if a spaceship landed right here in Colby Park?

What if my cat were leading a bunch of other cats to make a better world for them all?

What if I took a trip to the center of the Earth and found something new there?

2. Figure out what happens.
Jot down some ideas for the characters, setting, and plot of your story. Use a chart like this one to keep track of your thoughts.

▶

Characters	Setting
Sarah	the park
an alien	a lab

Plot
Sarah finds an alien in the park.
The alien is out of something she needs to get home. (What does the alien need?)
Sarah gets what the alien needs.
The alien returns home.

3. Map your story.
Think through the plot before you start writing. Then make a flow chart like the one shown here. If you prefer, you can make an outline or a list of events instead of a flow chart.

TIP Is it hard to come up with a great plot? Don't worry about making it perfect now. More ideas may come to you as you write, and you can always change plot details later.

▶

Meena says she needs Lekterol.
↓
Sarah finds out what Lekterol is.
↓
Sarah runs to the lab to get it made.
↓
Sarah goes back to the spaceship and saves Meena.

DRAFTING

What Should I Do?	What Does It Look Like?

1. Come up with a creative beginning.
Capture your reader's interest right away. You can use sensory details to introduce the setting or the characters, or you can start out with dialogue.

▶

Sensory language

Sarah was daydreaming about big, shiny spaceships with bright lights, heat shields, and huge engines.

Dialogue

"Pssst! I need your help!" a voice called from behind the bushes.

---

2. Decide on a point of view.
A character in your story can tell the story using *I*. This kind of **first-person narrator** draws your readers in. A **third-person narrator** is outside the story and refers to characters as *she*, *he*, and *they*. This type of narrator gives a broad view of characters and events.

TIP Either point of view is fine. Just be sure to stick to one or the other.

▶

First-person point of view

One day last fall, I was cutting through the park on my way home from school.

Third-person point of view

One day last fall, Sarah was cutting through the park on her way home from school.

---

3. Make the order of events clear.
Use words and phrases that tell your reader when things happened and how much time passed.

▶

Then she raced out of the lab.
Ten minutes later, Sarah was back at the spaceship.

---

4. Solve the central conflict.
A conflict is a problem to solve. If you don't have a conflict, you don't have a story. Remember that the story's ending must show how the conflict is resolved.

TIP Before revising, consult the key traits on page 158 and the rubric and peer-reader questions on page 164.

▶

In another minute, Meena had drunk the Lekterol and entered her spaceship. Before she closed the door, though, she called back, "You saved my life! Please visit me anytime on Utemore."

REVISING AND EDITING

| **What Should I Do?** | **What Does It Look Like?** |

1. Make the dialogue seem real.
- Read aloud the dialogue in your story. [Bracket] words and phrases that don't sound as if the characters would really say them.
- Revise your dialogue by adding contractions, slang, exclamations, or phrases that match the speaker's characteristics.

> *"Oh, you wonderful Earthling!" Meena shouted*
> *[~~"Thanks for your help," Meena said~~] when she saw Sarah waving two bottles of Lekterol.*

2. Make sure the sequence is clear.
- Ask a peer reader to <u>underline</u> places where the order of events is confusing.
- Add transitions to make the sequence clear.

See page 164: Ask a Peer Reader

> *When she got to the lab,*
> <u>*Sarah raced to Xygen BioProducts.*</u> *She was out of breath. "Aunt Cindy, you have to make something for me!" she panted.*

3. Use the active voice.
- When the subject acts (*Sarah wrote the story*), the verb is in the active voice. But if the subject is acted upon (*The story was written by Sarah*), the verb is in the passive voice—and that can make writing seem dull.
- Look for sentences you wrote in the passive voice. Consider changing them to active voice.

> Passive voice
> *The Internet was searched by Sarah, who was trying to find information on Lekterol.*

> Active voice
> *Sarah searched the Internet for information on Lekterol.*

4. Include descriptive details.
- Highlight descriptive details in your story.
- If you don't have much highlighting, add details to tell your reader what the setting and characters look like and how the events sound and feel.

> *Pale, pink eyes bulged from her large head.*
> *Standing in front of Sarah was a light-blue spacewoman. Her tiny body was blinking blue and orange like a fast-food sign.*
> *to Sarah in a squeaky but firm voice,*
> *She said, "I really need you."*

Apply the Rubric

A strong short story . . .

- ☑ has clearly described characters and an interesting plot
- ☑ uses dialogue
- ☑ makes the sequence of events easy to follow
- ☑ uses sensory language and specific details to show the characters, setting, and events
- ☑ keeps a consistent point of view
- ☑ varies how sentences begin
- ☑ uses the active voice most of the time
- ☑ includes a central conflict and an ending that resolves that conflict

Ask a Peer Reader

- What is the conflict in my story, and how is it resolved?
- What is believable or interesting about my characters?
- Do I need to make the sequence clearer? If so, where?
- Where do I need to add sensory language, dialogue, or details?

"What If" Questions

What if I set the story in an old castle?

What if I told the story from a stray dog's point of view?

What if the action took place in a laboratory under the sea?

What if a character walked through a wall into another universe?

What if it snowed every day for 15 years, and nobody knew why?

Check Your Grammar

- Most stories use the past tense.

> Sarah raced home. She searched the Internet for information on Lekterol. Then she knew what to do.

- Even if you describe events in the past tense, your characters may still speak in the present tense.

> "I just want to get home to see my kids."

Writing Online

PUBLISHING OPTIONS
For publishing options, visit the **Writing Center** at ClassZone.com.

ASSESSMENT PREPARATION
For writing and grammar assessment practice, go to the **Assessment Center** at ClassZone.com.

Telling a Story

Follow these guidelines to share the story you just wrote.

Planning the Story

1. **Decide on the mood.** Is your story scary? Funny? Suspenseful? Heartwarming? Think of a word or two that describe its overall mood. Keep that description in mind as you plan your presentation. Knowing the mood will help you decide what music or other effects to add, what to emphasize, and where to pause.

2. **Add effects.** What sound effects or music could you add to your presentation? For example, if you are trying to create a cheerful mood, you might play some happy music in the background. If you want to create a mood of fear, you might add eerie, creepy sounds. You might also use pictures—of spaceships, deep-sea creatures, or other animals or objects that match your story content.

3. **Learn your story.** Your goal is to tell, not read, your story. If you can, memorize your story. Create notes or cue cards to have ready in case you forget anything.

4. **Be dramatic.** Think of ways to keep your audience interested. You might include gestures, such as raising one arm as you descibe a spaceship taking off. Consider raising or lowering your voice when speaking dialogue that is especially dramatic or tension-filled.

Telling the Story

1. **Look at the audience.** Don't be afraid to refer to your notes or cards as you speak. Still, be sure to look at your audience most of the time. Practice holding the notes or cards in a way that allows you to keep your head up as you read them.

2. **Practice with your props.** Be sure to practice at least once with all your music or other props, so your timing will be smooth when you perform.

3. **Rehearse in front of someone.** Have someone listen to you as you rehearse. Ask for feedback. Repeat the rehearsals until you feel ready to tell your story to a real audience.

See page R80: Evaluate an Oral Presentation

Reading Comprehension

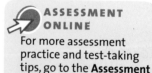

DIRECTIONS *Read this selection and answer the questions that follow.*

The Fish Story

Mary Lou Brooks

I know what I'm going to be when I grow up—unemployed. "Face it, Ernie," my dad always says. "The way you mess up every job, you have a great future—as a bum."

He's probably right. My first summer job was cutting the neighbor's lawn. The mower got away from me and ate ten tomato plants. Another time, I forgot to close the windows when I washed Mr. Hammer's car. The weeds I pulled out of Mrs. Miller's garden turned out to be flowers.

So I was really surprised when the Bensons asked me to look after their house while they were away on vacation. The Bensons are new on the
10 block. I guess they hadn't heard about me yet.

"We're leaving on Monday," explained Mrs. Benson. "You'll start on Tuesday. Just bring in the newspapers and the mail." That didn't sound too hard. Even *I* could probably handle this job.

"And feed Jaws once a day," Mrs. Benson added.

"*Jaws?*" I gulped. Did they have a pet shark or something?

Mrs. Benson laughed. "That's what the twins named their goldfish."

On Tuesday, I had baseball practice. So I was late getting to the Bensons'. I put the mail and the newspaper on the hall table. Then I headed for the fishbowl. Jaws was floating on top of the water.

20 I moaned. My first day on the job, and I killed the dumb fish! Not even the Army would want me now. That's what my dad would say—after he stopped yelling.

Now wait a minute, Ernie, I said to myself. This little fellow *could* still be alive. His eyes are open. He could be in a coma. I bent down very close to the water.

"Jaws!" I yelled. "It's me, Ernie, your babysitter. If you can hear me, blink once." He didn't.

I touched him with my finger. He was cold, stiff, and very slimy. "Face it, Ernie," I said out loud. "This is one dead fish you have here."

30 That night, I lay awake a long time trying to figure out why that dumb fish died. I didn't overfeed him. I never had a chance to feed him at all.

When I finally fell asleep, I had a nightmare. The shark from *Jaws* was chasing me. He was wearing a six-shooter. "You bumped off my kinfolk," he yelled. "Draw!"

I didn't tell my parents about Jaws. Every day, I went over to the Bensons' as though nothing was wrong. I had until Sunday. That's when the Bensons were coming home. Why rush things?

On Saturday, I remembered that Jaws was still in the fishbowl. I was about to toss him into the garbage. Suddenly, I had a great idea. I slipped
40 Jaws into a baggie and ran to the nearest pet store.

"I'd like another goldfish exactly like this one," I told the owner. Then I held up the baggie.

The owner glared at me. Half an hour later, he was still glaring. That's how long it took to find a perfect match. I paid the owner and headed back to the Bensons' house.

When I got there, I cleaned the fishbowl and added fresh water. Soon, Jaws II was in his new home. But instead of swimming around, he just stared at me.

"What you did was wrong," those tiny black eyes seemed to say.

50 The Bensons arrived home at 1:55 Sunday afternoon. I watched from my bedroom window as they piled out of their car. At 2:13, my mom called up the stairs.

"Ernie," she said, "Mrs. Benson is here." Caught! I trudged down the stairs to face the music.

Mrs. Benson was sitting at the kitchen table with my parents. "Here's the boy behind the Great Goldfish Switch," she said.

I felt like running. But Mrs. Benson put her arm around my shoulder.

"That was very thoughtful, Ernie," she said. "Monday was so crazy I didn't have time to pick up another fish. I've been dreading telling the
60 twins that Jaws died. Thanks to you, I won't have to."

She handed me money in an envelope. "This is for house-sitting," she said. "There's something extra for the new Jaws. You hear so many wild stories about kids these days. It's nice to know one who is responsible."

Mom looked so proud I thought she might cry. But Dad had a funny look on his face. I think he was trying not to laugh.

GO ON ➡

Comprehension

DIRECTIONS *Answer these questions about "The Fish Story."*

1. Which event causes a conflict for Ernie on his new job?

   A forgetting to feed Jaws

   B mowing over ten tomato plants

   C finding Jaws floating on top of the water

   D meeting the Bensons when they return from vacation

2. Which event happens first in the story?

   A Ernie has a nightmare about the shark from the movie *Jaws.*

   B Ernie runs to the pet store to buy a new fish.

   C Ernie learns how the fish got its name.

   D The Bensons go away for their vacation.

3. The setting of the story is

   A the Bensons' vacation home

   B a neighborhood

   C a fishing village

   D a local pet store

4. The climax of the story occurs when

   A Ernie goes downstairs to see Mrs. Benson and "face the music"

   B the new fish stares at Ernie with "those tiny black eyes"

   C Ernie dreams about "the shark from *Jaws*"

   D the weeds Ernie pulled up "turned out to be flowers"

5. What conflict does Ernie face after he buys the new fish?

   A He feels guilty for replacing Jaws.

   B The new fish doesn't look like Jaws.

   C He is sorry he took the job at the Bensons.

   D He wants to keep the new fish for himself.

6. What do you learn about Ernie in the exposition of the story?

   A He does not want to work when he grows up.

   B He has messed up several jobs.

   C He would like to go on vacation.

   D He loves to take care of fish.

7. During what time of year does the story take place?

   A summer   C winter

   B fall   D spring

8. You can infer that Mrs. Benson dreads telling the twins that the goldfish died because they might

   A refuse to believe her

   B figure it out for themselves

   C get upset at the news

   D blame Ernie for its death

9. When does Ernie run to the pet store?

   A when he sees the Bensons returning

   B the day before the Bensons return

   C as soon as he finds Jaws dead

   D after Mrs. Benson pays him

10. Which event happens in the resolution of the story?

   A Ernie buys a new fish.

   B Ernie's mom is proud of him.

   C The Bensons offer Ernie a job.

   D Ernie accepts the death of the fish.

11. Which event occurs during the rising action and increases the tension in the story?

   A Ernie goes to baseball practice before he goes to the Bensons' house.

   B Ernie's Dad looks like he has to keep himself from laughing.

   C The pet store owner takes a long time to find a matching fish.

   D Mrs. Benson hands Ernie an envelope with money in it.

12. When Ernie thinks, "Even I could probably handle this job," you can infer that he

   A is proud of his reputation

   B is unsure of himself

   C wants to impress Mrs. Benson

   D feels lucky to have a job

13. Which phrases in the story help you identify the order of events?

   A wait a minute, once a day, headed for

   B on Tuesday, on Saturday, at 2:13

   C blink once, long time, nearest pet store

   D going to be, coming home, getting to

Written Response

SHORT RESPONSE *Write two or three sentences to answer each question.*

14. What important events in the story lead up to Ernie's nightmare about the shark from the movie *Jaws?*

15. Identify two clues that show the story takes place in modern times.

EXTENDED RESPONSE *Write a short paragraph to answer this question.*

16. Describe the conflict Ernie feels in lines 1–13. With what thoughts or choices does he struggle?

GO ON ➤

Vocabulary

DIRECTIONS *Use context clues and your knowledge of synonyms to answer the following questions about words in "The Fish Story."*

1. Which word is a synonym for the underlined word in the following sentence?

   "'I've been <u>dreading</u> telling the twins that Jaws died.'"

   A anticipating   **C** fearing
   B avoiding   **D** planning

2. Which word is a synonym for the underlined word in the following sentence?

   "He was cold, stiff, and very <u>slimy</u>."

   A oily   **C** squashy
   B spongy   **D** bumpy

3. Which word is a synonym for the underlined word in the following sentence?

   "The owner <u>glared</u> at me."

   A looked   **C** gawked
   B scowled   **D** gazed

4. Which word is a synonym for the underlined word in the following sentence?

   "I <u>trudged</u> down the stairs to face the music."

   A clumped   **C** crept
   B galloped   **D** stole

DIRECTIONS *Use context clues and your knowledge of base words and suffixes to answer the following questions.*

5. What is the meaning of the word *probably* as it is used in line 4?

   "He's <u>probably</u> right."
   A in a certain way   **C** in all likelihood
   B not at all   **D** at some point

6. What is the meaning of the word *exactly* as it is used in line 41?

   "'I'd like another goldfish <u>exactly</u> like this one,' I told the owner."
   A in every way   **C** somewhat
   B greater than   **D** almost

7. What is the meaning of the word *thoughtful* as it is used in line 58?

   "'That was very <u>thoughtful</u>, Ernie,' she said."

   A acting with a strong purpose
   B having many thoughts on a topic
   C performing a task carelessly
   D showing concern for others

8. What is the meaning of the word *responsible* as it is used in line 63?

   "'It's nice to know one who is <u>responsible</u>.'"

   A able to be relied upon
   B likely to give an answer
   C forced to carry out a duty
   D ready to react to suggestions

Writing & Grammar

DIRECTIONS *Use your knowledge of writing and grammar to answer the following questions.*

1. Which one of the following sentences shows correct comma usage?

   A The Smiths stayed, in Orlando Florida with their friends.

   B The Smiths stayed in Orlando, Florida with their friends.

   C The Smiths stayed in Orlando Florida, with their friends.

   D The Smiths stayed in Orlando, Florida, with their friends.

2. Which one of the following sentences shows correct comma usage?

   A Benjamin Franklin was born, on January 17 1706 in Boston.

   B Benjamin Franklin was born on January 17 1706, in Boston.

   C Benjamin Franklin was born on January 17, 1706 in Boston.

   D Benjamin Franklin was born on January 17, 1706, in Boston.

3. What is the correct way to rewrite the following run-on sentence?

   > Big cars are nice they are expensive to own.

   A Big cars are nice, they are expensive to own.

   B Big cars are nice, but they are expensive to own.

   C Big cars are nice, But they are expensive to own.

   D Big cars are nice and they are expensive to own.

4. What is the correct way to rewrite the following run-on sentence?

   > Some apples are red some apples are green.

   A Some apples are red, some apples are green.

   B Some apples are red and, some apples are green.

   C Some apples are red, and some apples are green.

   D Some apples are red, Some apples are green.

5. Choose the correct pair of pronouns to complete the following sentences.

   > No one wanted to spend _____ time doing homework. The students wanted to leave _____ time free for other things.

   A their; his   **C** his; his

   B his; their   **D** their; their

6. Choose the correct pair of pronouns to complete the following sentences.

   > In the math contest, everybody had to turn in _____ answers. If a student didn't do this, _____ test would be disqualified.

   A her; her   **C** her; their

   B their; their   **D** their; her

More Great Reads

Ideas for Independent Reading

Which questions from Unit 1 made an impression on you?
Continue exploring with these books.

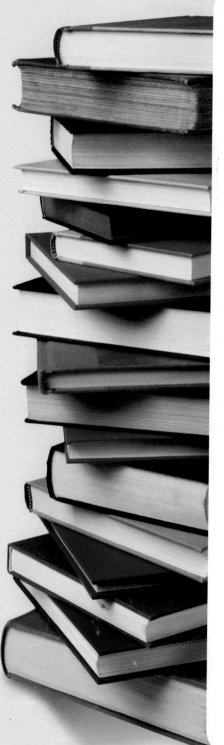

What do you fear most?

Before We Were Free
by Julia Alvarez

Anita's father is plotting to overthrow their country's cruel dictator. Now Anita has become a prisoner in her own house. Not even her diary is safe! What will happen now that everything has gone wrong?

Coraline
by Neil Gaiman

Coraline is bored in her family's huge old house. But then she finds a door that leads to another world. There she finds parents who look just like hers, but with some very scary differences.

Trouble Don't Last
by Shelley Pearsall

Eleven-year-old Samuel has been a slave all his life. Late one night, a slave named Harrison pulls Samuel from his bed. Together, they run north—to Canada and freedom. Their journey is one of joy and fear.

Can first impressions be trusted?

The Kidnapped Prince: Life of Olaudah Equiano
by Olaudah Equiano

Olaudah Equiano was just a little boy when he was stuffed into a sack and made a slave. Eleven years later he had won his freedom and gone on to write an autobiography that helped end slavery.

The View from Saturday
by E. L. Koningsburg

Nobody knows how Mrs. Olinski chose the four students on her sixth-grade academic bowl team, or what the secret to their success is. What connects these four students' lives and helps them unite as a real team?

When Zachary Beaver Came to Town
by Kimberly Willis Holt

When Zachary Beaver, the world's fattest boy, stops in Antler, Texas, Toby lines up to gawk at him. Zachary is snobby and rude and huge, but there's something else about him that will change Toby forever.

How powerful is loyalty?

The Incredible Journey
by Sheila Burnford

When the Hunters left their pets with a friend, they never suspected one of the dogs would get so homesick that he would try to return home. Can two dogs and a cat survive a 250-mile trek through the wilderness to get back to the family they love?

Tae's Sonata
by Haemi Balgassi

Taeyoung, an eighth-grade Korean American, wants to be like everyone else. She's embarrassed when she's assigned to work on a South Korea report with Josh, the most popular boy in school. Can she find a way to fit in while being loyal to her culture?

The Wee Free Men
by Terry Pratchett

Tiffany's little brother has been kidnapped by an evil queen. Armed with only a frying pan and a lot of common sense, Tiffany marches into Fairyland to fight its monsters, rescue her brother, and save her world.

Person to Person

2

ANALYZING CHARACTER AND POINT OF VIEW

- In Fiction
- In Nonfiction
- In Poetry
- In Media

Which CHARACTERS *are unforgettable?*

Some of the **characters** we meet in books and movies are so powerful that they become part of our culture. Think about fictional characters such as Little Red Riding-Hood, Aladdin, or Zorro. Their stories are told again and again, entertaining each new generation.

ACTIVITY In a small group, make a list of unforgettable characters from TV shows, books, or movies. Describe the appearance and behavior of each one. Then consider the following questions:

- What was your first impression of the character?

- Did your opinion of the character change as you learned more about him or her? If so, in what way?

- What makes a character unforgettable?

Preview Unit Goals

LITERARY ANALYSIS	• Identify and analyze first-person and third-person point of view • Identify and analyze character traits and characterization • Compare characters • Identify and analyze symbols
READING	• Develop reading strategies including visualizing, predicting, and connecting • Identify author's purpose • Take notes and generate research questions
WRITING AND GRAMMAR	• Write a description of a person • Use present, past, and future verb tenses correctly • Use comparative and superlative forms of adjectives and adverbs correctly • Use subject and object pronouns correctly
SPEAKING, LISTENING, AND VIEWING	• Conduct an interview • Analyze visual elements, sound, and dialogue in television • Analyze television techniques that establish character
VOCABULARY	• Understand and correctly use words that are easily confused • Use context clues to help determine the meaning of words and phrases • Use word roots and affixes to help determine word meaning
ACADEMIC VOCABULARY	• first-person point of view • character • third-person point of view • symbol • characterization • context clues

Character and Point of View

Characters in literature can be just as fascinating as people in your own life. Like real people, characters can be painfully shy, rude, or courageous. Some characters instantly draw you in, while others get on your nerves. Why do you react so strongly to the people you meet on the page? Character and point of view are the elements that influence your impressions.

Part 1: Who Tells the Story?

Suppose two of your closest friends got into a heated argument recently. You heard about the argument from each friend and from an innocent bystander who overheard every word. How would the three accounts differ? As this example shows, *who* tells a story is just as important as *what* that story is about. In literature, the **narrator** is the voice that tells the story. A writer's choice of narrator is known as **point of view.** This chart explains two points of view.

FIRST-PERSON POINT OF VIEW	THIRD-PERSON POINT OF VIEW
The narrator • is a character in the story • uses the words *I, me,* and *my* to refer to himself or herself • tells his or her own thoughts, opinions, and feelings • does not know what other characters are thinking and feeling	*The narrator* • is not a character in the story • uses words like *he, she,* and *they* to refer to the characters • can reveal the thoughts, opinions, and feelings of one or more characters
▼	▼
Example I was flying along when I spotted sparks exploding on the street below. The evil ShockBlaster was attacking innocent people! Time for me to come to the rescue again. Angry and annoyed, I realized that talented superheroes like me *never* get the day off.	*Example* As Dynamyte zoomed toward the explosion, a billion thoughts raced through his mind. He wondered why villains always started trouble on his day off. From a roof above the panicked crowd, ShockBlaster saw Dynamyte swooping across the sky toward him. "Him again?" ShockBlaster muttered.

MODEL 1: FIRST-PERSON POINT OF VIEW

The novel *Walk Two Moons* is about a 13-year-old girl named Salamanca. People call her Sal for short. One day, her mother leaves home forever, prompting Sal to deal with some confusing feelings.

from WALK TWO MOONS

Novel by **Sharon Creech**

When my mother left for Lewiston, Idaho, that April, my first thoughts were, "How could she do that? How could she leave me?"

As the days went on, many things were harder and sadder, but some things were strangely easier. When my mother had been there, I was like a mirror. If she was happy, I was happy. If she was sad, I was sad. For the first few days after she left, I felt numb, non-feeling. I didn't know how to feel. I would find myself looking around for her, to see what I might want to feel.

Close Read

1. Reread the boxed sentences. Find the pronouns that show the first-person point of view.

2. How does her mother's departure initially affect Sal? Find two details that reveal Sal's feelings.

MODEL 2: THIRD-PERSON POINT OF VIEW

Becky believes she was born to play golf. After practice one day, she encounters an elderly neighbor named Doña Carmen Maria. Notice what the third-person narrator reveals about Becky's thoughts.

from How Becky Garza Learned Golf

Short story by **Gary Soto**

Doña Carmen Maria reached for one of the clubs in the bag. She said it was like a sword. She poked the air and laughed to herself.

Becky didn't smile. She was hot, thirsty, and uneasy with the old woman who again started to play with the mole on her throat. But Becky's parents had always taught her to respect elders. And she had to respect Doña Carmen Maria because, if not, Becky feared the old woman would walk down the street and report her incivility. Becky could see herself grounded until she was as old as Doña Carmen Maria herself.

Close Read

1. How can you tell that this story is told from the third-person point of view? Support your answer.

2. Does Becky seem to like Doña Carmen Maria? Find details that describe Becky's thoughts and feelings about her neighbor.

Part 2: The People on the Page

When you meet someone for the first time, you form an impression based on certain clues, such as how the person looks, talks, or acts. Similar clues can help you get to know characters in literature. By noticing important details, you can infer a character's **traits,** or qualities, like shyness or friendliness. To form a complete picture of a character's personality, you have to consider all the details that the writer has included.

Writers use four methods to develop their characters. Use the questions and examples shown to help you understand one superhero's personality.

METHODS OF CHARACTERIZATION	EXAMPLES
CHARACTER'S PHYSICAL APPEARANCE **A character's look can influence your first impression of him or her. Ask:** • What does the character look like? • What facial expressions or gestures does he or she make?	Sparks of fire sizzled in Dynamyte's hair whenever he was getting ready to show off. He smiled confidently and flexed his muscles for the crowd.
CHARACTER'S THOUGHTS, SPEECH, AND ACTIONS **A character's own words and actions can reflect his or her personality. Ask:** • What is the character good at? bad at? • What kinds of things worry him or her? • How does he or she act toward others?	Dynamyte forgot about his day off when he realized how important he was to the city. "This is what happens when you're the *only* one capable of saving the world," he boasted as he prepared to show off some more.
OTHER CHARACTERS' REACTIONS **One way to learn about a character is to note how others feel about him or her. Ask:** • How do others treat the character? • What do they say about him or her?	ShockBlaster cringed in fear as he saw Dynamyte speeding toward him. "I must escape! I'll never win a battle against him."
NARRATOR'S DIRECT COMMENTS **The narrator may directly tell you about a character's personality. Ask:** • What qualities does the narrator say the character has? • Does the narrator admire the character?	Dynamyte's talent and skill made up for his bad attitude. He made saving the world look so easy!

METHOD 1: PHYSICAL APPEARANCE

In this fable, three princes compete for the love of a princess named Meliversa. As you read, look for descriptions of Meliversa's appearance.

from The Fable of the
Three Princes

Short story by **Isaac Asimov**

That night there was a great feast, and the three princes were the guests of honor.

The emperor, seated on a splendid throne at the head of the table, greeted them. Next to him was the princess Meliversa, and she was
5   indeed as beautiful as the sun. Her hair was long and the color of corn silk. Her eyes were blue and reminded everyone of the sky on a bright spring day. Her features were perfectly regular and her skin was flawless.

But her eyes were empty, and her face was expressionless.

Close Read

1. Find three details that describe Meliversa's beauty. One detail has been boxed.

2. Reread line 8. What do you learn about Meliversa from this description?

METHOD 2: THOUGHTS AND ACTIONS

Mary is supposed to be participating in Ta-Na-E-Ka, a custom of the Kaw Nation of Native Americans. Ta-Na-E-Ka is a test in which young people must survive five days alone in the woods. Mary thinks the tradition is silly, so she secretly spends the five days in a restaurant.

from **Ta-Na-E-Ka**

Short story by **Mary Whitebird**

I was sorry when the five days were over. I'd enjoyed every minute with Ernie. He taught me how to make Western omelets and to make Chili Ernie Style (still one of my favorite dishes). And I told Ernie all about the legends of the Kaw. I hadn't realized I knew so much about
5   my people.

But Ta-Na-E-Ka was over, and as I approached my house, at about nine-thirty in the evening, I became nervous all over again. What if Grandfather asked me about the berries and the grasshoppers? And my feet were hardly cut. I hadn't lost a pound and my hair was combed.
10   "They'll be so happy to see me," I told myself hopefully, "that they won't ask too many questions."

Close Read

1. Consider Mary's choice to secretly skip Ta-Na-E-Ka. What do her actions tell you about her?

2. Look at the boxed descriptions of Mary's thoughts. How does she feel about what she's done?

METHOD 3: OTHER CHARACTERS

In this excerpt, Cammy is listening to her cousin Patty Ann play the piano. As you read, notice how Cammy reacts to Patty Ann.

from **COUSINS**   Novel by **Virginia Hamilton**

   She [Cammy] couldn't sit still. Being there with her cousin made her as angry as she could be.

   Good at everything, Cammy thought to Patty Ann's back. In school, at home, at her piano. Miss Goody-goody. . . .

5   The music stopped abruptly. Patty Ann turned the page of a small notebook next to her music. The page was blank. She'd come to the end of her lessons. She closed the book. Closed her music books, too. She closed the piano top over the piano keys. To Cammy, everything she did was like chalk scraping on a blackboard.

Close Read

1. Does Cammy like Patty Ann? How can you tell?

2. Reread the boxed text. What impression of Patty Ann do you get from Cammy's reaction to her?

METHOD 4: NARRATOR'S COMMENTS

Sometimes, the narrator directly tells readers what a character is like. As you read this excerpt, think about how you would describe the soldier based on what the narrator tells you about him.

from **The King's Dragon**   Short story by **Jane Yolen**

   There was once a soldier who had fought long and hard for his king. He had been wounded in the war and sent home for a rest.

   Hup and one. Hup and two. He marched down the long, dusty road, using a crutch.

5   He was a member of the Royal Dragoons. His red-and-gold uniform was dirty and torn. And in the air of the winter's day, his breath plumed out before him like a cloud.

   Hup and one. Hup and two. Wounded or not, he marched with a proud step. For the Royal Dragoons are the finest soldiers in the land

10 and—they always obey orders.

Close Read

1. Look at the narrator's comments in the boxed sentences. Which word would you say does not describe the soldier?
   a. loyal
   b. lazy
   c. proud

2. Does the narrator seem to respect the soldier? Explain.

Part 3: Analyze the Literature

Meet Anastasia Krupnik, one of Lois Lowry's most memorable characters. For homework last night, Antastasia had to write a poem. Now, she must read it in front of her entire class. Use what you've learned to analyze this excerpt.

from ANASTASIA KRUPNIK

Novel by **Lois Lowry**

Anastasia had begun to feel a little funny, as if she had ginger ale inside of her knees. But it was her turn. She stood up in front of the class and read her poem. Her voice was very small, because she was nervous.

    hush   hush   the sea-soft night is aswim
5   with wrinklesquirm creatures
                                    listen (!)
    to them   move   smooth   in the moistly dark
               here in the   whisperwarm   wet

That was Anastasia's poem.

10   "Read that again, please, Anastasia, in a bigger voice," said Mrs. Westvessel.

So Anastasia took a deep breath and read her poem again. She used the same kind of voice that her father did when he read poetry to her, drawing some of the words out as long as licorice sticks, and making

15 some others thumpingly short.
The class laughed.
Mrs. Westvessel looked puzzled. "Let me see that, Anastasia," she said. Anastasia gave her the poem.
Mrs. Westvessel's ordinary, everyday face had about one hundred

20 wrinkles in it. When she looked at Anastasia's poem, her forehead and nose folded up so that she had two hundred new wrinkles all of a sudden.
"Where are your capital letters, Anastasia?" asked Mrs. Westvessel.
Anastasia didn't say anything.
"Where is the rhyme?" asked Mrs. Westvessel. "It doesn't rhyme at *all*."

25 Anastasia didn't say anything.
"What kind of poem *is* this, Anastasia?" asked Mrs. Westvessel. "Can you explain it, please?"
Anastasia's voice had become very small again, the way voices do, sometimes. "It's a poem of sounds," she said. "It's about little things that

30 live in tidepools, after dark, when they move around. It doesn't have sentences or capital letters because I wanted it to look on the page like small creatures moving in the dark."

Close Read

1. Is this story told from the first-person or the third-person point of view? How can you tell?

2. Is Anastasia someone who feels comfortable in front of large crowds? Cite details to support your answer.

3. What impression of Mrs. Westvessel do you get from the boxed details?

4. Reread lines 12–15 and 28–32. Would you describe Anastasia as a thoughtful, creative person or as someone who doesn't take her assignments seriously?

Eleven
Short Story by Sandra Cisneros

Is **AGE** *more than a number?*

KEY IDEA For some people, a birthday is an exciting, festive event. With each increase in **age,** they feel more mature. For others, a birthday is just the day they were born. Inside, they may not feel any different than they did the day before. In "Eleven," a young girl struggles with what it means to grow older.

WEB IT Think about what your age means to you. Create a web of meanings that you connect to being your age. Consider how the web would change if you were one year older or younger.

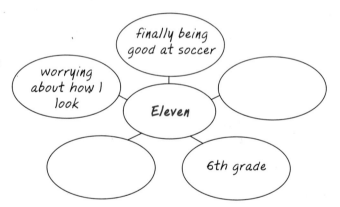

finally being good at soccer

worrying about how I look

Eleven

6th grade

LITERARY ANALYSIS: FIRST-PERSON POINT OF VIEW

Have you ever listened to a stranger tell a story? You often learn a great deal about the personality, experiences, and opinions of that person. When you read a story told from **first-person point of view,** the **narrator** is a character in the story. You learn what happens as the narrator experiences it.

As you read "Eleven," notice how the only information you receive comes from the narrator. Think about how that affects what you know about the characters and events.

READING STRATEGY: CONNECT

Characters, settings, and events in a story may remind you of people you know, places you've been, feelings you've had, or other stories you've read. When you **connect** with a story or parts of a story, you use your knowledge and experiences to help you better understand what you are reading.

As you read "Eleven," complete a chart like the one shown. Record details from the story and how they remind you of experiences from your own life.

Rachel's Birthday	My Connections
wakes up feeling like she's still ten	I remember that on my 11th birthday I didn't feel any different.

▲ VOCABULARY IN CONTEXT

Sandra Cisneros uses the words in the list to help tell the story of a young girl's difficult experience in school. Complete each phrase with the appropriate word from the list.

WORD LIST	alley	except	invisible	raggedy

1. _____ for math, the girl did well in school.
2. She felt _____ among the crowds of students.
3. Her old, _____ clothes embarrassed her.
4. After school, she ran home through the back _____.

Author Online

Escaping Through Fairy Tales Sandra Cisneros grew up in a bilingual home, speaking English to her mother and Spanish to her father. For that reason, different aspects of language became more noticeable to her.

Sandra Cisneros born 1954

As a child, Cisneros enjoyed reading fairy tales. She loved the style of language used, and in time she began writing her own stories and poems. Cisneros's mother made sure that her daughter had the space and quiet that she needed in order to write, even in a house with six brothers.

Writing to Be Heard Cisneros was shy as a child, much like Rachel in "Eleven." She compares who she was as a child—a quiet person who was never asked to speak in class—to the writer she is now. She notes, "I am finding that with words I have the power to make people listen, to make them think in a new way. . . . It's a powerful thing to make people listen to you."

MORE ABOUT THE AUTHOR
For more on Sandra Cisneros, visit the **Literature Center** at ClassZone.com.

ELEVEN

Sandra Cisneros

What they don't understand about birthdays and what they never tell you is that when you're eleven, you're also ten, and nine, and eight, and seven, and six, and five, and four, and three, and two, and one. And when you wake up on your eleventh birthday you expect to feel eleven, but you don't. You open your eyes and everything's just like yesterday, only it's today. And you don't feel eleven at all. You feel like you're still ten. And you are—underneath the year that makes you eleven.

Like some days you might say something stupid, and that's the part of you that's still ten. Or maybe some days you might need to sit on your
10 mama's lap because you're scared, and that's the part of you that's five. And maybe one day when you're all grown up maybe you will need to cry like if you're three, and that's okay. That's what I tell Mama when she's sad and needs to cry. Maybe she's feeling three.

Because the way you grow old is kind of like an onion or like the rings inside a tree trunk or like my little wooden dolls that fit one inside the other, each year inside the next one. That's how being eleven years old is.

You don't feel eleven. Not right away. It takes a few days, weeks even, sometimes even months before you say Eleven when they ask you. And you don't feel smart eleven, not until you're almost twelve. That's the way
20 it is. **A**

ANALYZE VISUALS
Based on the colors and details in this painting, how do you think the girl is feeling?

A **CONNECT**
The **narrator** shares her feelings and thoughts about her birthday. Have you ever felt like this?

Detail of *Room 13, Los Estudiantes* (2004), José Ramirez. Mixed media on canvas, 47″ × 19″.

Only today I wish I didn't have only eleven years rattling inside me like pennies in a tin Band-Aid box. Today I wish I was one hundred and two instead of eleven because if I was one hundred and two I'd have known what to say when Mrs. Price put the red sweater on my desk. I would've known how to tell her it wasn't mine instead of just sitting there with that look on my face and nothing coming out of my mouth.

"Whose is this?" Mrs. Price says, and she holds the red sweater up in the air for all the class to see. "Whose? It's been sitting in the coatroom for a month."

30 "Not mine," says everybody. "Not me."

"It has to belong to somebody," Mrs. Price keeps saying, but nobody can remember. It's an ugly sweater with red plastic buttons and a collar and sleeves all stretched out like you could use it for a jump rope. It's maybe a thousand years old and even if it belonged to me I wouldn't say so.

Maybe because I'm skinny, maybe because she doesn't like me, that stupid Sylvia Saldívar says, "I think it belongs to Rachel." An ugly sweater like that, all **raggedy** and old, but Mrs. Price believes her. Mrs. Price takes the sweater and puts it right on my desk, but when I open my mouth nothing comes out. **B**

40 "That's not, I don't, you're not . . . Not mine," I finally say in a little voice that was maybe me when I was four.

"Of course it's yours," Mrs. Price says. "I remember you wearing it once." Because she's older and the teacher, she's right and I'm not.

Not mine, not mine, not mine, but Mrs. Price is already turning to page thirty-two, and math problem number four. I don't know why but all of a sudden I'm feeling sick inside, like the part of me that's three wants to come out of my eyes, only I squeeze them shut tight and bite down on my teeth real hard and try to remember today I am eleven, eleven. Mama is making a cake for me for tonight, and when Papa comes home everybody 50 will sing Happy birthday, happy birthday to you.

But when the sick feeling goes away and I open my eyes, the red sweater's still sitting there like a big red mountain. I move the red sweater to the corner of my desk with my ruler. I move my pencil and books and eraser as far from it as possible. I even move my chair a little to the right. Not mine, not mine, not mine.

In my head I'm thinking how long till lunchtime, how long till I can take the red sweater and throw it over the schoolyard fence, or leave it hanging on a parking meter, or bunch it up into a little ball and toss it in the **alley**. **Except** when math period ends Mrs. Price says loud and in 60 front of everybody, "Now, Rachel, that's enough," because she sees I've shoved the red sweater to the tippy-tip corner of my desk and it's hanging all over the edge like a waterfall, but I don't care.

raggedy (răg'ĭ-dē) *adj.* tattered or worn out

B FIRST-PERSON POINT OF VIEW
What have you learned about the **narrator** so far?

alley (ăl'ē) *n.* a narrow street behind or between buildings

except (ĭk-sĕpt') *prep.* but; however

"Rachel," Mrs. Price says. She says it like she's getting mad. "You put that sweater on right now and no more nonsense."

"But it's not—"

"Now!" Mrs. Price says. **C**

This is when I wish I wasn't eleven, because all the years inside of me—ten, nine, eight, seven, six, five, four, three, two, and one—are pushing at the back of my eyes when I put one arm through one sleeve of the sweater that smells like cottage cheese, and then the other arm through the other and stand there with my arms apart like if the sweater hurts me and it does, all itchy and full of germs that aren't even mine.

That's when everything I've been holding in since this morning, since when Mrs. Price put the sweater on my desk, finally lets go, and all of a sudden I'm crying in front of everybody. I wish I was **invisible** but I'm not. I'm eleven and it's my birthday today and I'm crying like I'm three in front of everybody. I put my head down on the desk and bury my face in my stupid clown-sweater arms. My face all hot and spit coming out of my mouth because I can't stop the little animal noises from coming out of me, until there aren't any more tears left in my eyes, and it's just my body shaking like when you have the hiccups, and my whole head hurts like when you drink milk too fast. **D**

But the worst part is right before the bell rings for lunch. That stupid Phyllis Lopez, who is even dumber than Sylvia Saldívar, says she remembers the red sweater is hers! I take it off right away and give it to her, only Mrs. Price pretends like everything's okay. **E**

Today I'm eleven. There's a cake Mama's making for tonight, and when Papa comes home from work we'll eat it. There'll be candles and presents and everybody will sing Happy birthday, happy birthday to you, Rachel, only it's too late.

I'm eleven today. I'm eleven, ten, nine, eight, seven, six, five, four, three, two, and one, but I wish I was one hundred and two. I wish I was anything but eleven, because I want today to be far away already, far away like a runaway balloon, like a tiny *o* in the sky, so tiny-tiny you have to close your eyes to see it. ◑

70

80

90

C FIRST-PERSON POINT OF VIEW
What impression of Mrs. Price does Rachel give the reader?

invisible (ĭn-vĭz′ə-bəl) *adj.* not able to be seen

D CONNECT
Reread lines 67–82. Which of your own experiences help you to understand why Rachel gets so upset?

E FIRST-PERSON POINT OF VIEW
Reread lines 83–86. How does the first-person point of view affect what you know about Sylvia and Phyllis?

Comprehension

1. **Recall** Rachel uses many different comparisons to describe what it is like to grow older. Name one of the comparisons she makes.

2. **Recall** What thoughts does Rachel have about the sweater as she is putting it on?

3. **Clarify** How is the issue of the sweater finally settled?

Literary Analysis

4. **Make Inferences** What is it about growing older that Rachel finds disappointing? Use examples from the story to support your answer.

5. **Connect** Look at the chart you filled in as you read. How do the connections you made help you to understand Rachel's thoughts and experiences?

6. **Analyze Plot** Reread lines 35–41. Imagine that Rachel is bold instead of timid. How might she have reacted when Mrs. Price put the sweater on her desk?

7. **Analyze a Minor Character** Minor characters help carry out the action of a story. Mrs. Price is a minor character in "Eleven," but she plays an important part in the story. How do you think Mrs. Price would describe the incident with the sweater? Use details from the story to support your answer.

8. **Evaluate First-Person Point of View** As the **narrator** of the story, Rachel shares many of her thoughts and feelings. However, she is not able to tell us the thoughts and feelings of the other characters. Using a chart like the one shown, note what you learned through the story's first-person point of view and what you would still like to know.

What I Learned from Rachel	What I Would Like to Know

Extension and Challenge

9. **Creative Project: Art** The red sweater is an important part of "Eleven." How did you picture it in your mind as you read the story? Using colored pencils, markers, or crayons, create a picture of the sweater as you imagined it.

10. **Big Question Activity** Revisit the activity on page 182. This time, think about how Rachel might have filled out a web about her **age.** Use details from the story to complete Rachel's web.

Vocabulary in Context

VOCABULARY PRACTICE

Choose the letter of the word or phrase that is most closely related to the boldfaced word.

1. **except:** (a) not including, (b) with, (c) as well as, (d) plus
2. **invisible:** (a) impossible, (b) white, (c) unseen, (d) unwell
3. **alley:** (a) highway, (b) narrow path, (c) parking lot, (d) freeway
4. **raggedy:** (a) shabby, (b) tidy, (c) elegant, (d) beautiful

VOCABULARY IN WRITING

What surprised you more in this story, the way Mrs. Price behaved or the way Rachel behaved? Write a paragraph explaining what you think. Use at least two vocabulary words. You could start this way.

> **EXAMPLE SENTENCE**
>
> I was surprised that Mrs. Price caused so much trouble over a **raggedy** sweater.

VOCABULARY STRATEGY: EASILY CONFUSED WORDS

Some words sound or look so similar that it is easy to misuse them. An example of a confusing pair of words is the vocabulary word *except* and the word *accept*. Though these words have different meanings, you may have to be careful to choose the correct one. Other confusing pairs have similar meanings as well as similar spellings. If you are not sure which word you should be using, it is a good idea to check definitions in a dictionary.

PRACTICE Choose the word or phrase in parentheses that correctly completes each sentence.

1. The (affect, effect) of the hurricane was felt 150 miles away.
2. My father offered me some good (advise, advice), but I didn't listen to him.
3. Luis was (all ready, already) to have his photograph taken.
4. Washington's (capital, capitol) building is a beautiful sight.
5. Corinne's family moved (farther, further) away from the city.

VOCABULARY PRACTICE
For more practice, go to the **Vocabulary Center** at **ClassZone.com.**

Ghost of the Lagoon
Short Story by Armstrong Sperry

What makes a HERO?

KEY IDEA Many different people can be considered heroes. A person's heroes might include well-known sports figures, firefighters, survivors of disaster, teachers, or respected friends and relatives. A **hero,** with his or her bravery, inner strength, or kindness, gives us inspiration for our everyday lives. In "Ghost of the Lagoon," a boy faces a difficult situation with heroic skill and courage.

CHART IT Think of three heroic people you know. Write their names in a chart like the one shown. Then identify the actions and personal qualities that make them heroes to you.

Heroes		
Person	Actions	Qualities
1. Aunt Gwen	helps injured animals	kind, funny
2.		

● LITERARY ANALYSIS: THIRD-PERSON POINT OF VIEW

When a story is told from the **third-person point of view,** the **narrator** is not a character in the story but is observing from the outside. Because of this, the third-person narrator is often able to reveal more information about all the characters' thoughts, feelings, and actions than any single character from the story could reveal.

As you read "The Ghost of the Lagoon," look for details the narrator provides about the main character.

● READING STRATEGY: PREDICT

Writers often give their readers clues to help them **predict,** or make a reasonable guess about, what might happen in a story. As a reader, you combine details from the story with your own knowledge and experience to help you make predictions about what you are reading.

As you read, use a chart like the one shown to write down your predictions and the clues from the story that helped you make them.

My Prediction	Clues in Story
Mako will use his harpoon during the story.	Mako is clever, the harpoon he made is sharp and has five iron spears.

▲ VOCABULARY IN CONTEXT

Armstrong Sperry uses the boldfaced words to help tell an adventure story. Use context clues to figure out the meaning of each of the boldfaced words.

1. The boy ran off in **pursuit** of a frightening sea creature.
2. It had always made the calm, watery **lagoon** its home.
3. Creatures would sometimes hide in gaps in the **reef.**
4. The hunter was feeling **tense** from stress.
5. Mako had spent a **restless** night worrying.
6. He felt very **vulnerable** in his small, flimsy boat.

Author Online

Story Lover As a boy growing up in Connecticut, Armstrong Sperry loved listening to his grandfather's wonderful tales of the South Sea Islands. In 1925, after studying art in college and working

Armstrong Sperry
1897–1976

as an illustrator, Sperry headed to the South Pacific. He spent several months on the island of Bora Bora, charmed by the island's beauty and culture. He was inspired by its brave people, who rebuilt their island after it was destroyed by a hurricane during Sperry's time there.

World Traveler Sperry returned to the United States and settled in Vermont, but he couldn't resist going back to sea. He set sail again, traveling the world in search of ideas for stories. The books and stories Sperry wrote often have characters who, like the people of Bora Bora, overcome a great challenge with strength and courage.

 MORE ABOUT THE AUTHOR
For more on Armstrong Sperry, visit the **Literature Center** at ClassZone.com.

Background

Pacific Island Bora Bora, where this story takes place, is one of more than 100 small islands in French Polynesia in the southern Pacific Ocean. The island is almost completely surrounded by coral reefs and is known for the crystal clear waters of its lagoon.

GHOST of the LAGOON

Armstrong Sperry

The island of Bora Bora, where Mako lived, is far away in the South
Pacific. It is not a large island—you can paddle around it in a single
day—but the main body of it rises straight out of the sea, very high into
the air, like a castle. Waterfalls trail down the faces of the cliffs. As you
look upward, you see wild goats leaping from crag to crag.

Mako had been born on the very edge of the sea, and most of his waking
hours were spent in the waters of the **lagoon,** which was nearly enclosed by
the two outstretched arms of the island. He was very clever with his hands;
he had made a harpoon that was as straight as an arrow and tipped with
10 five pointed iron spears. He had made a canoe, hollowing it out of a tree.
It wasn't a very big canoe—only a little longer than his own height. It had
an outrigger, a sort of balancing pole, fastened to one side to keep the boat
from tipping over. The canoe was just large enough to hold Mako and his
little dog, Afa. They were great companions, these two. **A**

ANALYZE VISUALS
What sense does this
painting give you of
the story's **setting?**

lagoon (lə-gōōn') *n.* a
shallow body of water
separated from a
larger body of water by
sandbars or other barriers

A **THIRD-PERSON
POINT OF VIEW**
Reread lines 6–14.
What does the **narrator**
reveal about Mako?

Detail of *New Moon Rising*, Peter
Sickles. © Peter Sickles/SuperStock.

One evening Mako lay stretched at full length on the pandanus mats,[1] listening to Grandfather's voice. Overhead, stars shone in the dark sky. From far off came the thunder of the surf on the **reef.**

The old man was speaking of Tupa, the ghost of the lagoon. Ever since the boy could remember, he had heard tales of this terrible
20 monster. Frightened fishermen, returning from the reef at midnight, spoke of the ghost. Over the evening fires, old men told endless tales about the monster.

Tupa seemed to think the lagoon of Bora Bora belonged to him. The natives left presents of food for him out on the reef: a dead goat, a chicken, or a pig. The presents always disappeared mysteriously, but everyone felt sure that it was Tupa who carried them away. Still, in spite of all this food, the nets of the fishermen were torn during the night, the fish stolen. What an appetite Tupa seemed to have!

Not many people had ever seen the ghost of the lagoon. Grandfather
30 was one of the few who had.

"What does he really look like, Grandfather?" the boy asked, for the hundredth time.

The old man shook his head solemnly. The light from the cook fire glistened on his white hair. "Tupa lives in the great caves of the reef. He is longer than this house. There is a sail on his back, not large but terrible to see, for it burns with a white fire. Once, when I was fishing beyond the reef at night, I saw him come up right under another canoe—"

"What happened then?" Mako asked. He half rose on one elbow. This was a story he had not heard before.

40 The old man's voice dropped to a whisper. "Tupa dragged the canoe right under the water—and the water boiled with white flame. The three fishermen in it were never seen again. Fine swimmers they were, too." **B**

Grandfather shook his head. "It is bad fortune even to speak of Tupa. There is evil in his very name."

"But King Opu Nui has offered a reward for his capture," the boy pointed out.

"Thirty acres of fine coconut land, and a sailing canoe as well," said the old man. "But who ever heard of laying hands on a ghost?"

Mako's eyes glistened. "Thirty acres of land and a sailing canoe.
50 How I should love to win that reward!"

Grandfather nodded, but Mako's mother scolded her son for such foolish talk. "Be quiet now, son, and go to sleep. Grandfather has told you that it is bad fortune to speak of Tupa. Alas, how well we have learned that lesson! Your father—" She stopped herself.

---

1. **pandanus** (păn-dā′nəs) **mats:** mats made from the fiber of leaves from a palmlike tree.

reef (rēf) *n.* a ridge of rocks, sand, or coral that rises to the surface of a body of water

SOCIAL STUDIES CONNECTION

Bora Bora

Reef

PACIFIC OCEAN

Only six miles long, Bora Bora is one of the "Society Islands" of French Polynesia in the South Pacific.

B PREDICT
Reread lines 31–42. What kind of creature do you think Tupa is? Note this information on your chart.

Detail of *Fishermen, Finisterre* (1951), Keith Vaughan. Oil on canvas, 91.4 cm × 71.1 cm. Private collection. © Bridgeman Art Library. © 2008 Artists Rights Society (ARS), New York/DACS, London.

ANALYZE VISUALS
What do the **details** in this painting tell you about the three men?

"What of my father?" the boy asked quickly. And now he sat up straight on the mats.

"Tell him, Grandfather," his mother whispered.

The old man cleared his throat and poked at the fire. A little shower of sparks whirled up into the darkness.

60 "Your father," he explained gently, "was one of the three fishermen in the canoe that Tupa destroyed." His words fell upon the air like stones dropped into a deep well.

Mako shivered. He brushed back the hair from his damp forehead. Then he squared his shoulders and cried fiercely, "I shall slay Tupa and win the king's reward!" He rose to his knees, his slim body **tense**, his eyes flashing in the firelight. **C**

"Hush!" his mother said. "Go to sleep now. Enough of such foolish talk. Would you bring trouble upon us all?"

Mako lay down again upon the mats. He rolled over on his side 70 and closed his eyes, but sleep was long in coming.

The palm trees whispered above the dark lagoon, and far out on the reef the sea thundered.

tense (tĕns) *adj.* nervous; feeling strain

C PREDICT
Consider the conversation between the **characters** and what you know so far about Mako. What do you think is going to happen? Add this information to your chart.

The boy was slow to wake up the next morning. The ghost of Tupa had played through his dreams, making him **restless.** And so it was almost noon before Mako sat up on the mats and stretched himself. He called Afa, and the boy and his dog ran down to the lagoon for their morning swim.

When they returned to the house, wide-awake and hungry, Mako's mother had food ready and waiting.

80   "These are the last of our bananas," she told him. "I wish you would paddle out to the reef this afternoon and bring back a new bunch."

The boy agreed eagerly. Nothing pleased him more than such an errand, which would take him to a little island on the outer reef, half a mile from shore. It was one of Mako's favorite playgrounds, and there bananas and oranges grew in great plenty.

"Come, Afa," he called, gulping the last mouthful. "We're going on an expedition." He picked up his long-bladed knife and seized his spear. A minute later, he dashed across the white sand, where his canoe was drawn up beyond the water's reach.

90   Afa barked at his heels. He was all white except for a black spot over each eye. Wherever Mako went, there went Afa also. Now the little dog leaped into the bow of the canoe, his tail wagging with delight. The boy shoved the canoe into the water and climbed aboard. Then, picking up his paddle, he thrust it into the water. The canoe shot ahead. Its sharp bow cut through the green water of the lagoon like a knife through cheese. And so clear was the water that Mako could see the coral gardens, forty feet below him, growing in the sand. The shadow of the canoe moved over them.

A school of fish swept by like silver arrows. He saw scarlet rock cod 100 with ruby eyes and the head of a conger eel[2] peering out from a cavern in the coral. The boy thought suddenly of Tupa, ghost of the lagoon. On such a bright day it was hard to believe in ghosts of any sort. The fierce sunlight drove away all thought of them. Perhaps ghosts were only old men's stories, anyway!

Mako's eyes came to rest upon his spear—the spear that he had made with his own hands—the spear that was as straight and true as an arrow. He remembered his vow of the night before. Could a ghost be killed with a spear? Some night, when all the village was sleeping, Mako swore to himself that he would find out! He would paddle out to the reef and 110 challenge Tupa! Perhaps tonight. Why not? He caught his breath at the thought. A shiver ran down his back. His hands were tense on the paddle. **E**

restless (rĕst′lĭs) *adj.* unable to sleep or rest

D THIRD-PERSON POINT OF VIEW Reread lines 73–77. What is the **narrator** able to reveal about Mako that the other **characters** in the story wouldn't know?

VISUAL VOCABULARY

coral (kôr′əl) *n.* a type of marine animal, the skeletons of which build up a rocklike underwater structure called a reef

E THIRD-PERSON POINT OF VIEW Reread lines 105–111. How do you learn what Mako is thinking even though he hasn't spoken?

2. **rock cod . . . conger eel:** Rock cod is a type of saltwater fish, and a conger eel is a large eel.

As the canoe drew away from shore, the boy saw the coral reef that, above all others, had always interested him. It was of white coral—a long slim shape that rose slightly above the surface of the water. It looked very much like a shark. There was a ridge on the back that the boy could pretend was a dorsal fin, while up near one end were two dark holes that looked like eyes!

Times without number the boy had practiced spearing this make-believe shark, aiming always for the eyes, the most **vulnerable**
120 spot. So true and straight had his aim become that the spear would pass right into the eyeholes without even touching the sides of the coral. Mako had named the coral reef Tupa.

This morning, as he paddled past it, he shook his fist and called, "Ho, Mister Tupa! Just wait till I get my bananas. When I come back, I'll make short work of you!"

Afa followed his master's words with a sharp bark. He knew Mako was excited about something.

The bow of the canoe touched the sand of the little island where the bananas grew. Afa leaped ashore and ran barking into the jungle, now
130 on this trail, now on that. Clouds of sea birds whirled from their nests into the air with angry cries.

Mako climbed into the shallow water, waded ashore, and pulled his canoe up on the beach. Then, picking up his banana knife, he followed Afa. In the jungle the light was so dense and green that the boy felt as if he were moving underwater. Ferns grew higher than his head. The branches of the trees formed a green roof over him. A flock of parakeets fled on swift wings. Somewhere a wild pig crashed through the undergrowth while Afa dashed away in **pursuit**. Mako paused anxiously. Armed only with his banana knife, he had no desire to meet the wild pig.
140 The pig, it seemed, had no desire to meet him, either.

Then, ahead of him, the boy saw the broad green blades of a banana tree. A bunch of bananas, golden ripe, was growing out of the top.

At the foot of the tree he made a nest of soft leaves for the bunch to fall upon. In this way the fruit wouldn't be crushed. Then with a swift slash of his blade he cut the stem. The bananas fell to the earth with a dull thud. He found two more bunches.

Then he thought, "I might as well get some oranges while I'm here. Those little rusty ones are sweeter than any that grow on Bora Bora."

So he set about making a net out of palm leaves to carry the oranges.
150 As he worked, his swift fingers moving in and out among the strong green leaves, he could hear Afa's excited barks off in the jungle. That was just like Afa, always barking at something: a bird, a fish, a wild pig. He never caught anything, either. Still, no boy ever had a finer companion.

The palm net took longer to make than Mako had realized. By the time it was finished and filled with oranges, the jungle was dark and gloomy. Night comes quickly and without warning in the islands of the tropics.

Mako carried the fruit down to the shore and loaded it into the canoe. Then he whistled to Afa. The dog came bounding out of the bush, wagging his tail.

160 "Hurry!" Mako scolded. "We won't be home before the dark comes."

The little dog leaped into the bow of the canoe, and Mako came aboard. Night seemed to rise up from the surface of the water and swallow them. On the distant shore of Bora Bora, cook fires were being lighted. The first star twinkled just over the dark mountains. Mako dug his paddle into the water, and the canoe leaped ahead.

The dark water was alive with phosphorus.[3] The bow of the canoe seemed to cut through a pale liquid fire. Each dip of the paddle trailed streamers of light. As the canoe approached the coral reef, the boy called, "Ho, Tupa! It's too late tonight to teach you your lesson. But I'll come
170 back tomorrow." The coral shark glistened in the darkness. **G**

And then, suddenly, Mako's breath caught in his throat. His hands felt weak. Just beyond the fin of the coral Tupa, there was another fin—a huge one. It had never been there before. And—could he believe his eyes? It was moving.

The boy stopped paddling. He dashed his hand across his eyes. Afa began to bark furiously. The great white fin, shaped like a small sail, glowed with phosphorescent light. Then Mako knew. Here was Tupa—the real Tupa—ghost of the lagoon! **H**

His knees felt weak. He tried to cry out, but his voice died in his throat.
180 The great shark was circling slowly around the canoe. With each circle, it moved closer and closer. Now the boy could see the phosphorescent glow of the great shark's sides. As it moved in closer, he saw the yellow eyes, the gill slits in its throat.

Afa leaped from one side of the canoe to the other. In sudden anger Mako leaned forward to grab the dog and shake him soundly. Afa wriggled out of his grasp as Mako tried to catch him, and the shift in weight tipped the canoe on one side. The outrigger rose from the water. In another second they would be overboard. The boy threw his weight over quickly to balance the canoe, but with a loud splash Afa fell over into
190 the dark water.

Mako stared after him in dismay. The little dog, instead of swimming back to the canoe, had headed for the distant shore. And there was the great white shark—very near.

G THIRD-PERSON POINT OF VIEW
Reread lines 166–170. How would this paragraph be different if Mako were telling the story?

H PREDICT
What do you think Mako will do next? Write your prediction on your chart.

---

3. **phosphorus** (fŏs′fər-əs): a substance that glows with a yellowish or white light.

"Afa! Afa! Come back! Come quickly!" Mako shouted.

The little dog turned back toward the canoe. He was swimming with all his strength. Mako leaned forward. Could Afa make it? Swiftly the boy seized his spear. Bracing himself, he stood upright. There was no weakness in him now. His dog, his companion, was in danger of instant death.

Afa was swimming desperately to reach the canoe. The white shark had
200 paused in his circling to gather speed for the attack. Mako raised his arm, took aim. In that instant the shark charged. Mako's arm flashed forward. All his strength was behind that thrust. The spear drove straight and true, right into the great shark's eye. Mad with pain and rage, Tupa whipped about, lashing the water in fury. The canoe rocked back and forth. Mako struggled to keep his balance as he drew back the spear by the cord fastened to his wrist.

He bent over to seize Afa and drag him aboard. Then he stood up, not a moment too soon. Once again the shark charged. Once again Mako threw his spear, this time at the other eye. The spear found its mark.
210 Blinded and weak from loss of blood, Tupa rolled to the surface, turned slightly on his side. Was he dead?

ANALYZE VISUALS
How does the shark shown **compare** with your mental picture of Tupa?

Mako knew how clever sharks could be, and he was taking no chances. Scarcely daring to breathe, he paddled toward the still body. He saw the faintest motion of the great tail. The shark was still alive. The boy knew that one flip of that tail could overturn the canoe and send him and Afa into the water, where Tupa could destroy them.

Swiftly, yet calmly, Mako stood upright and braced himself firmly. Then, murmuring a silent prayer to the shark god, he threw his spear for the last time. Downward, swift as sound, the spear plunged into a white
220 shoulder. ◖I◗

Peering over the side of the canoe, Mako could see the great fish turn over far below the surface. Then slowly, slowly, the great shark rose to the surface of the lagoon. There he floated, half on one side.

Tupa was dead.

Mako flung back his head and shouted for joy. Hitching a strong line about the shark's tail, the boy began to paddle toward the shore of Bora Bora. The dorsal fin, burning with the white fire of phosphorus, trailed after the canoe.

Men were running down the beaches of Bora Bora, shouting as they
230 leaped into their canoes and put out across the lagoon. Their cries reached the boy's ears across the water.

"It is Tupa—ghost of the lagoon," he heard them shout. "Mako has killed him!"

That night, as the tired boy lay on the pandanus mats listening to the distant thunder of the sea, he heard Grandfather singing a new song. It was the song which would be sung the next day at the feast which King Opu Nui would give in Mako's honor. The boy saw his mother bending over the cook fire. The stars leaned close, winking like friendly eyes. Grandfather's voice reached him now from a great distance, "Thirty acres
240 of land and a sailing canoe . . ." ❧

◖I◗ PREDICT
How do you predict the story will end?

Comprehension

1. **Recall** Where does Mako spend most of his time?

2. **Recall** What weapon does Mako use in his battle with Tupa?

3. **Clarify** What makes Mako so determined to kill Tupa?

Literary Analysis

4. **Predict** Look at the chart you made while reading. Match the predictions you made with what happened in the story. Which of your predictions were correct?

5. **Understand Cause and Effect** A story's events are related by cause and effect when one event becomes the cause of another. Reread lines 147–156. What effect does Mako's decision to gather oranges have on the story?

6. **Examine Conflict** Mako's battle with the shark is an example of **external conflict,** the struggle between a character and an outside force. What **internal conflict,** or struggle within a character's mind, does Mako face when Afa falls into the water?

7. **Analyze Third-Person Point of View** Skim through the story, focusing on descriptions of Mako. Use a chart like the one shown to note information provided by the **narrator** that Mako might not have included if he were telling the story.

Mako's Thoughts	Mako's Feelings	Mako's Actions

8. **Evaluate Character** How does Mako demonstrate the qualities of a **hero?** Explain your answer using details from the story.

Extension and Challenge

9. **SOCIAL STUDIES CONNECTION** Bora Bora is one of more than 25,000 islands in the South Pacific. These islands are broken up into three major groups: Melanesia, Micronesia, and Polynesia. Do some research to learn more about the islands in one of these groups. Look for information about how the islands were formed, their climate and vegetation, and the cultural history of the people who live there.

> **RESEARCH LINKS**
> For more on the islands of the South Pacific, visit the **Research Center** at ClassZone.com.

Vocabulary in Context

VOCABULARY PRACTICE

Show that you understand the vocabulary words by deciding if each statement is true or false.

lagoon   restless

pursuit   tense

reef   vulnerable

1. A person who is **restless** has a hard time relaxing.
2. A **lagoon** is an enormous body of water.
3. If a vase is fragile, it is **vulnerable** to being damaged.
4. The leader in a race is the one in **pursuit** of the other racers.
5. A **reef** is a parking lot for cars.
6. A **tense** moment is one that makes people laugh.

VOCABULARY IN WRITING

Imagine you are Mako. Write a paragraph describing how you felt when you were fighting Tupa. Use at least three vocabulary words. Here is a sample of how you might begin.

EXAMPLE SENTENCE

*I felt very **vulnerable** while I was fighting Tupa.*

VOCABULARY STRATEGY: WORDS CONNECTED WITH WATER

THE VOCABULARY WORD *lagoon* is the name for a certain kind of water body. A *reef* is the name for a kind of structure found in the water. Learning other words connected with water can help you to be more specific when speaking and writing about the environment.

PRACTICE Match each word with its meaning, using a dictionary if needed.

1. current
2. levee
3. tide
4. canal
5. strait
6. bay

a. man-made waterway, dug across land
b. part of the sea extending into the land
c. directional flow of water
d. high bank to keep a river from overflowing
e. rise and fall of the ocean, caused by the pull of the moon
f. narrow waterway connecting two bodies of water

VOCABULARY PRACTICE

For more practice, go to the **Vocabulary Center** at **ClassZone.com**.

Reading-Writing Connection

Increase your understanding of "Ghost of the Lagoon" by responding to these prompts. Then complete the **Grammar and Writing** exercise.

WRITING PROMPTS

SELF-CHECK

A. Short Response: Make a Prediction
After the upcoming feast in his honor, Mako's life may change. Write a **one-paragraph prediction** about what Mako's future will hold now that he's seen as a **hero.** Use details from the story to support your writing.

A reasonable prediction will . . .
- show understanding of a hero's role in a community
- build on the ending of the story

B. Extended Response: Write a Scene
How would the story have been different if it had focused on the thoughts and feelings of a character other than Mako? Choose a scene in the story and, in **two or three paragraphs,** retell it through the eyes of Mother, Grandfather, or even Afa.

An effective scene will . . .
- show another side of the character
- be consistent with the rest of the story

GRAMMAR AND WRITING

USE CORRECT PRONOUN CASE Personal pronouns have subject and object cases, and the two are often used incorrectly, especially in compound subjects and compound objects. Use a **subject pronoun** (*I, she, he, we,* or *they*) if the pronoun is part of a compound subject. Use an **object pronoun** (*me, her, him, us,* or *them*) if the pronoun is part of a compound object. (*You* and *it* function as both subject and object pronouns.)

Original:	Afa and me are going to the island to get bananas.
Revised:	Afa and I are going to the island to get bananas. (*The pronoun is part of a compound subject, so it should be* I, *not* me.)

PRACTICE Choose the correct pronoun to complete each sentence.

1. (They, Them) and their families lived in fear of the "monster."
2. (He, Him) and Afa found Tupa that night.
3. The men shouted to Mako and (he, him).
4. (We, Us) and our families were glad that the monster was gone.

FOR MORE HELP WITH PRONOUN CASES, SEE PAGE R53 IN THE *Grammar Handbook.*

Tuesday of the Other June

Short Story by Norma Fox Mazer

How do you deal with a BULLY?

KEY IDEA A **bully** can turn your life into a nightmare. All your thoughts become focused on the next awful encounter. Advice for dealing with a bully is often to "walk away." When actually dealing with a bully, however, many people dream of standing up for themselves. In "Tuesday of the Other June," you'll read about a girl who becomes the target of a bully.

LIST IT Imagine that your best friend is being bothered by a bully and has come to you for help. What advice would you give? Prepare a short list of suggestions.

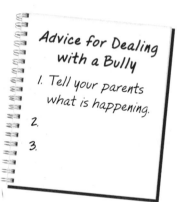

Advice for Dealing with a Bully
1. Tell your parents what is happening.
2.
3.

SECTION C THE STAR JOURNAL C5

For Better or For Worse by Lynn Johnston

MOM, BRAD LUGGSWORTH IS RUINING MY LIFE!

I'VE TRIED FIGHTING WITH HIM, I'VE TOLD ON HIM, I'VE TRIED JUST LEAVING HIM ALONE—BUT, HE STILL PICKS ON ME!

WELL... I THINK THIS CALLS FOR A NEW LINE OF DEFENSE!... CONFUSE THE ENEMY!

BE NICE TO HIM!

For Better or For Worse © 1983 Lynn Johnston Productions. Distributed by Universal Press Syndicate. Reprinted with permission. All rights reserved.

● LITERARY ANALYSIS: CHARACTERIZATION

Many stories hold our attention because we want to find out what happens to the characters. The way a writer creates and helps us get to know his or her characters is called **characterization.** For example, a writer may

- describe the character's appearance
- present the character's words, thoughts, and actions
- present other characters' thoughts about and reactions to the character
- make direct comments about the character's personality

As you read this story, notice what you learn about each character and how that information is presented.

● READING STRATEGY: VISUALIZE

Certain details in a story help you **visualize,** or form a mental picture of, what takes place. Notice ways in which the writer helps you picture in your mind the things being described. As you read, fill in a chart like the one shown.

Details	What I Visualize
Mother combs June's hair.	a mother combing her daughter's hair in front of a mirror and smiling

Review: **Predict**

▲ VOCABULARY IN CONTEXT

The boldfaced words help to tell the story of a girl's encounter with a bully. Restate each sentence using a different word or words for the boldfaced term.

1. The scary situation put her in a **daze.**
2. Her enemy loved to **torment** her.
3. Fear was reflected in her **emerald** eyes.
4. June had no **devoted** friends to help her out.
5. The young girl's body went **rigid** with terror.
6. Finally, she put on a **dazzling** display of courage.

Author Online

Writing for Pleasure
By the age of 13, Norma Fox Mazer knew that she wanted to become a writer. With that goal in mind, she became editor of her high school newspaper and served as a correspondent for her town's newspaper as well.

Norma Fox Mazer
born 1931

Success Mazer went on to write fiction, and after the success of her first book, she continued writing novels for young people. Today she is a well-known prize-winning writer of fiction for young adults. Viewing literature as a way of making sense of the world, she writes about the real problems teenagers face.

Building Characters Mazer carefully develops her characters before introducing them to her readers. She says, "There comes a time when I understand my characters so well that I know exactly how they will act and react at any moment, and that's wonderful." Mazer's sense of her characters helps them come alive in her writing.

 MORE ABOUT THE AUTHOR
For more on Norma Fox Mazer, visit the **Literature Center** at ClassZone.com.

Tuesday of the Other June

Norma Fox Mazer

"Be good, be good, be good, be good, my Junie," my mother sang as she combed my hair; a song, a story, a croon, a plea. "It's just you and me, two women alone in the world, June darling of my heart, we have enough troubles getting by, we surely don't need a single one more, so you keep your sweet self out of fighting and all that bad stuff. People can be little-hearted, but turn the other cheek, smile at the world, and the world'll surely smile back."

We stood in front of the mirror as she combed my hair, combed and brushed and smoothed. Her head came just above mine, she said when 10 I grew another inch she'd stand on a stool to brush my hair. "I'm not giving up this pleasure!" And she laughed her long honey laugh. **A**

My mother was April, my grandmother had been May, I was June. "And someday," said my mother, "you'll have a daughter of your own. What will you name her?"

"January!" I'd yell when I was little. "February! No, November!" My mother laughed her honey laugh. She had little <u>emerald</u> eyes that warmed me like the sun.

ANALYZE VISUALS
What sense do you get of the personalities of the two girls in this painting?

A VISUALIZE
Reread lines 8–11. What details help you form a mental picture of what is happening? Note them in your chart.

emerald (ĕm′ər-əld) *adj.* of a rich green color

Detail of *Fire and Ice* (2004), Brian Calvin. Acrylic on canvas, 48″ × 60″. Courtesy of Anton Kern Gallery, New York. © Brian Calvin.

Every day when I went to school, she went to work. "Sometimes I stop what I'm doing," she said, "lay down my tools, and stop everything,
20 because all I can think about is you. Wondering what you're doing and if you need me. Now, Junie, if anyone ever bothers you—"

"—I walk away, run away, come on home as fast as my feet will take me," I recited.

"Yes. You come to me. You just bring me your trouble, because I'm here on this earth to love you and take care of you." **B**

I was safe with her. Still, sometimes I woke up at night and heard footsteps slowly creeping up the stairs. It wasn't my mother, she was asleep in the bed across the room, so it was robbers, thieves, and murderers, creeping slowly . . . slowly . . . slowly toward my bed.

30 I stuffed my hand into my mouth. If I screamed and woke her, she'd be tired at work tomorrow. The robbers and thieves filled the warm darkness and slipped across the floor more quietly than cats. **Rigid** under the covers, I stared at the shifting dark and bit my knuckles and never knew when I fell asleep again. **C**

In the morning we sang in the kitchen. "Bill Grogan's goat! Was feelin' fine! Ate three red shirts, right off the line!" I made sandwiches for our lunches, she made pancakes for breakfast, but all she ate was one pancake and a cup of coffee. "Gotta fly, can't be late."

I wanted to be rich and take care of her. She worked too hard; her
40 pretty hair had gray in it that she joked about. "Someday," I said, "I'll buy you a real house, and you'll never work in a pot factory again." **D**

"Such delicious plans," she said. She checked the windows to see if they were locked. "Do you have your key?"

I lifted it from the chain around my neck.

"And you'll come right home from school and—"

"—I won't light fires or let strangers into the house, and I won't tell anyone on the phone that I'm here alone," I finished for her.

"I know, I'm just your old worrywart mother." She kissed me twice, once on each cheek. "But you are my June, my only June, the
50 only June."

She was wrong; there was another June. I met her when we stood next to each other at the edge of the pool the first day of swimming class in the Community Center.

"What's your name?" She had a deep growly voice.

"June. What's yours?"

She stared at me. "June."

"We have the same name."

B CHARACTERIZATION
Reread lines 24–25. What do the mother's words tell you about her?

rigid (rĭj′ĭd) *adj.* stiff; not moving

C VISUALIZE
Reread lines 26–34. What details help you picture the nights when June gets scared? Record them in your chart.

D CHARACTERIZATION
What do you learn about June through her descriptions of her mother?

"No we don't. June is my name, and I don't give you permission to use it. Your name is Fish Eyes." She pinched me hard. "Got it, Fish Eyes?"

60　The next Tuesday, the Other June again stood next to me at the edge of the pool. "What's your name?"

"June."

"Wrong. Your—name—is—Fish—Eyes."

"June."

"Fish Eyes, you are really stupid." She shoved me into the pool.

The swimming teacher looked up, frowning, from her chart. "No one in the water yet."

Later, in the locker room, I dressed quickly and wrapped my wet suit in the towel. The Other June pulled on her jeans. "You guys see that
70　bathing suit Fish Eyes was wearing? Her mother found it in a trash can."

Left panel of *Le Plongeur (Paper Pool 18)* (1978), David Hockney. Colored and pressed paper pulp. 72″x171″.
© David Hockney/Bradford Art Galleries and Museums, West Yorkshire, United Kingdom/Bridgeman Art Library.

"She did not!"

The Other June grabbed my fingers and twisted. "Where'd she find your bathing suit?"

"She bought it, let me go."

"Poor little stupid Fish Eyes is crying. Oh, boo hoo hoo, poor little Fish Eyes."

After that, everyone called me Fish Eyes. And every Tuesday, wherever I was, there was also the Other June—at the edge of the pool, in the pool, in the locker room. In the water, she swam alongside me, blowing and
80 huffing, knocking into me. In the locker room, she stepped on my feet, pinched my arms, hid my blouse, and knotted my braids together. She had large square teeth; she was shorter than I was, but heavier, with bigger bones and square hands. If I met her outside on the street, carrying her bathing suit and towel, she'd walk toward me, smiling a square, friendly smile. "Oh well, if it isn't Fish Eyes." Then she'd punch me, blam! her whole solid weight hitting me. **E**

I didn't know what to do about her. She was training me like a dog. After a few weeks of this, she only had to look at me, only had to growl, "I'm going to get you, Fish Eyes," for my heart to slink like a whipped dog
90 down into my stomach. My arms were covered with bruises. When my mother noticed, I made up a story about tripping on the sidewalk. **F**

My weeks were no longer Tuesday, Wednesday, Thursday, and so on. Tuesday was Awfulday. Wednesday was Badday. (The Tuesday bad feelings were still there.) Thursday was Betterday and Friday was Safeday. Saturday was Goodday, but Sunday was Toosoonday, and Monday— Monday was nothing but the day before Awfulday.

I tried to slow down time. Especially on the weekends, I stayed close by my mother, doing everything with her, shopping, cooking, cleaning, going to the laundromat. "Aw, sweetie, go play with your friends."
100 "No, I'd rather be with you." I wouldn't look at the clock or listen to the radio (they were always telling you the date and the time). I did special magic things to keep the day from going away, rapping my knuckles six times on the bathroom door six times a day and never, ever touching the chipped place on my bureau. But always I woke up to the day before Tuesday, and always, no matter how many times I circled the worn spot in the living-room rug or counted twenty-five cracks in the ceiling, Monday disappeared and once again it was Tuesday. **G**

The Other June got bored with calling me Fish Eyes. Buffalo Brain came next, but as soon as everyone knew that, she renamed me Turkey Nose.

E CHARACTERIZATION
Reread lines 77–86. What methods has the writer used to show readers what the characters are like?

F PREDICT
Based on what you know about June the narrator up to this point, how do you think she will deal with the Other June?

G VISUALIZE
Reread lines 97–107. What details about the house suggest that June and her mother don't have a lot of money? Record them in your chart.

110 Now at night it wasn't robbers creeping up the stairs, but the Other June, coming to **torment** me. When I finally fell asleep, I dreamed of kicking her, punching, biting, pinching. In the morning I remembered my dreams and felt brave and strong. And then I remembered all the things my mother had taught me and told me.

Be good, be good, be good; it's just us two women alone in the world . . . Oh, but if it weren't, if my father wasn't long gone, if we'd had someone else to fall back on, if my mother's mother and daddy weren't dead all these years, if my father's daddy wanted to know us instead of being glad to forget us—oh, then I would have punched the Other June with a frisky
120 heart, I would have grabbed her arm at poolside and bitten her like the dog she had made of me.

One night, when my mother came home from work, she said, "Junie, listen to this. We're moving!"

Alaska, I thought. Florida. Arizona. Someplace far away and wonderful, someplace without the Other June.

"Wait till you hear this deal. We are going to be caretakers, trouble-shooters for an eight-family apartment building. Fifty-six Blue Hill Street. Not janitors; we don't do any of the heavy work. April and June, Trouble-shooters, Incorporated. If a tenant has a complaint
130 or a problem, she comes to us and we either take care of it or call the janitor for service. And for that little bit of work, we get to live rent free!" She swept me around in a dance. "Okay? You like it? I do!"

So. Not anywhere else, really. All the same, maybe too far to go to swimming class? "Can we move right away? Today?"

"Gimme a break, sweetie. We've got to pack, do a thousand things. I've got to line up someone with a truck to help us. Six weeks, Saturday the fifteenth." She circled it on the calendar. It was the Saturday after the last day of swimming class.

Soon, we had boxes lying everywhere, filled with clothes and towels
140 and glasses wrapped in newspaper. Bit by bit, we cleared the rooms, leaving only what we needed right now. The dining-room table staggered on a bunched-up rug, our bureaus inched toward the front door like patient cows. On the calendar in the kitchen, my mother marked off the days until we moved, but the only days I thought about were Tuesdays—Awfuldays. Nothing else was real except the too fast passing of time, moving toward each Tuesday . . . away from Tuesday . . . toward Tuesday. . . . **H**

---

torment (tôr′mĕnt′) *v.* to cause severe distress to the body or mind

H VISUALIZE
Reread lines 139–147. Which words in the descriptions of the table and bureaus help you picture the objects in your mind? Add them to your chart.

And it seemed to me that this would go on forever, that Tuesdays would come forever and I would be forever trapped by the side of the pool, the Other June whispering Buffalo Brain Fish Eyes Turkey Nose into my ear, while she ground her elbow into my side and smiled her square smile at the swimming teacher.

And then it ended. It was the last day of swimming class. The last Tuesday. We had all passed our tests, and, as if in celebration, the Other June only pinched me twice. "And now," our swimming teacher said, "all of you are ready for the Advanced Class, which starts in just one month. I have a sign-up slip here. Please put your name down before you leave." Everyone but me crowded around. I went to the locker room and pulled on my clothes as fast as possible. The Other June burst through the door just as I was leaving. "Goodbye," I yelled, "good riddance to bad trash!" Before she could pinch me again, I ran past her and then ran all the way home, singing, "Goodbye . . . goodbye . . . goodbye, good riddance to bad trash!"

Later, my mother carefully untied the blue ribbon around my swimming class diploma. "Look at this! Well, isn't this wonderful! You are on your way, you might turn into an Olympic swimmer, you never know what life will bring."

"I don't want to take more lessons."

"Oh, sweetie, it's great to be a good swimmer." But then, looking into my face, she said, "No, no, no, don't worry, you don't have to."

The next morning, I woke up hungry for the first time in weeks. No more swimming class. No more Baddays and Awfuldays. No more Tuesdays of the Other June. In the kitchen, I made hot cocoa to go with my mother's corn muffins. "It's Wednesday, Mom," I said, stirring the cocoa. "My favorite day."

"Since when?"

"Since this morning." I turned on the radio so I could hear the announcer tell the time, the temperature, and the day.

Thursday for breakfast I made cinnamon toast, Friday my mother made pancakes, and on Saturday, before we moved, we ate the last slices of bread and cleaned out the peanut butter jar.

"Some breakfast," Tilly said. "Hello, you must be June." She shook my hand. She was a friend of my mother's from work; she wore big hoop earrings, sandals, and a skirt as **dazzling** as a rainbow. She came in a truck with John to help us move our things.

John shouted cheerfully at me, "So you're moving." An enormous man with a face covered with little brown bumps. Was he afraid his voice wouldn't travel the distance from his mouth to my ear? "You looking

dazzling (dăz′lĭng) *adj.* beautiful; amazing
dazzle *v.*

at my moles?" he shouted, and he heaved our big green flowered chair
190 down the stairs. "Don't worry, they don't bite. Ha, ha, ha!" Behind him
came my mother and Tilly balancing a bureau between them, and behind
them I carried a lamp and the round, flowered Mexican tray that was my
mother's favorite. She had found it at a garage sale and said it was as close
to foreign travel as we would ever get. ❶

The night before, we had loaded our car, stuffing in bags and boxes
until there was barely room for the two of us. But it was only when we
were in the car, when we drove past Abdo's Grocery, where they always
gave us credit,[1] when I turned for a last look at our street—it was only
then that I understood we were truly going to live somewhere else, in
200 another apartment, in another place mysteriously called Blue Hill Street.

Tilly's truck followed our car.

"Oh, I'm so excited," my mother said. She laughed. "You'd think
we were going across the country."

Our old car wheezed up a long steep hill. Blue Hill Street. I looked from
one side to the other, trying to see everything.

My mother drove over the crest of the hill. "And now—ta da!—our
new home."

❶ **CHARACTERIZATION**
Reread lines 190–194.
What does June's
mother's attitude about
the tray tell you about
her personality?

---

1. **credit:** an agreement to trust in someone's ability and intention to pay for something at a later date.

"Which house? Which one?" I looked out the window and what I saw was the Other June. She was sprawled on the stoop of a pink house, lounging back on her elbows, legs outspread, her jaws working on a wad of gum. I slid down into the seat, but it was too late. I was sure she had seen me.

My mother turned into a driveway next to a big white building with a tiny porch. She leaned on the steering wheel. "See that window there, that's our living-room window. . . and that one over there, that's your bedroom. . . ."

We went into the house, down a dim, cool hall. In our new apartment, the wooden floors clicked under our shoes, and my mother showed me everything. Her voice echoed in the empty rooms. I followed her around in a **daze.** Had I imagined seeing the Other June? Maybe I'd seen another girl who looked like her. A double. That could happen. **J**

"Ho yo, where do you want this chair?" John appeared in the doorway. We brought in boxes and bags and beds and stopped only to eat pizza and drink orange juice from the carton.

"June's so quiet, do you think she'll adjust all right?" I heard Tilly say to my mother.

"Oh, definitely. She'll make a wonderful adjustment. She's just getting used to things."

But I thought that if the Other June lived on the same street as I did, I would never get used to things.

That night I slept in my own bed, with my own pillow and blanket, but with floors that creaked in strange voices and walls with cracks I didn't recognize. I didn't feel either happy or unhappy. It was as if I were waiting for something.

Monday, when the principal of Blue Hill Street School left me in Mr. Morrisey's classroom, I knew what I'd been waiting for. In that room full of strange kids, there was one person I knew. She smiled her square smile, raised her hand, and said, "She can sit next to me, Mr. Morrisey."

"Very nice of you, June M. OK, June T, take your seat. I'll try not to get you two Junes mixed up."

I sat down next to her. She pinched my arm. "Good riddance to bad trash," she mocked.

I was back in the Tuesday swimming class, only now it was worse, because every day would be Awfulday. The pinching had already started. Soon, I knew, on the playground and in the halls, kids would pass me, grinning. "Hiya, Fish Eyes."

daze (dāz) *n.* a condition in which one cannot think clearly

J VISUALIZE
Reread lines 217–221. Which details help you picture what it looks like inside the house and how it feels to be there? Record them in your chart.

ANALYZE VISUALS
How does this painting compare with your mental picture of June's new neighborhood?

Detail of *Potrero* (2005), Michael Shankman. Oil on canvas, 18″ × 72″. © 2005 Michael Shankman. All rights reserved.

The Other June followed me around during recess that day, droning in my ear, "You are my slave, you must do everything I say, I am your master, say it, say, 'Yes, master, you are my master.'"

250 I pressed my lips together, clapped my hands over my ears, but without hope. Wasn't it only a matter of time before I said the hateful words?

"How was school?" my mother said that night.

"OK."

She put a pile of towels in a bureau drawer. "Try not to be sad about missing your old friends, sweetie; there'll be new ones."

The next morning, the Other June was waiting for me when I left the house. "Did your mother get you that blouse in the garbage dump?" She butted me, shoving me against a tree. "Don't you speak anymore, Fish Eyes?" Grabbing my chin in her hands, she pried open my mouth.

260 "Oh, ha ha, I thought you lost your tongue."

We went on to school. I sank down into my seat, my head on my arms. "June T, are you all right?" Mr. Morrisey asked. I nodded. My head was almost too heavy to lift.

The Other June went to the pencil sharpener. Round and round she whirled the handle. Walking back, looking at me, she held the three sharp pencils like three little knives.

Someone knocked on the door. Mr. Morrisey went out into the hall. Paper planes burst into the air, flying from desk to desk. Someone turned on a transistor radio. And the Other June, coming closer, smiled and

270 licked her lips like a cat sleepily preparing to gulp down a mouse. **K**

I remembered my dream of kicking her, punching, biting her like a dog.

Then my mother spoke quickly in my ear: Turn the other cheek, my Junie; smile at the world, and the world'll surely smile back.

But I had turned the other cheek and it was slapped. I had smiled and the world hadn't smiled back. I couldn't run home as fast as my feet would take me, I had to stay in school—and in school there was the Other June. Every morning, there would be the Other June, and every afternoon, and every day, all day, there would be the Other June. **L**

She frisked down the aisle, stabbing the pencils in the air toward me.

280 A boy stood up on his desk and bowed. "My fans," he said, "I greet you." My arm twitched and throbbed, as if the Other June's pencils had already poked through the skin. She came closer, smiling her Tuesday smile.

"No," I whispered, "no." The word took wings and flew me to my feet, in front of the Other June. "Nooooo." It flew out of my mouth into her surprised face.

The boy on the desk turned toward us. "You said something, my **devoted** fans?"

K VISUALIZE
Reread lines 267–270. How does this comparison help you to describe the scene and the Other June? Add this information to your chart.

L PREDICT
What does June's new attitude suggest about what might happen?

devoted (dĭ-vō'tĭd) *adj.* very loyal; faithful **devote** *v.*

Detail of *Fire and Ice* (2004), Brian Calvin. Acrylic on canvas, 48″ × 60″. Courtesy of Anton Kern Gallery, New York. © Brian Calvin.

"No," I said to the Other June. "Oh, no! No. No. No. No more." I pushed away the hand that held the pencils.

290 The Other June's eyes opened, popped wide like the eyes of somebody in a cartoon. It made me laugh. The boy on the desk laughed, and then the other kids were laughing, too.

"No," I said again, because it felt so good to say it. "No, no, no, no." I leaned toward the Other June, put my finger against her chest. Her cheeks turned red, she squawked something—it sounded like "Eeeraaghyou!"— and she stepped back. She stepped away from me.

The door banged, the airplanes disappeared, and Mr. Morrisey walked to his desk. "OK. OK. Let's get back to work. Kevin Clark, how about it?" Kevin jumped off the desk and Mr. Morrisey picked up a piece

300 of chalk. "All right, class—" He stopped and looked at me and the Other June. "You two Junes, what's going on there?"

I tried it again. My finger against her chest. Then the words. "No—more." And she stepped back another step. I sat down at my desk.

"June M," Mr. Morrisey said.

She turned around, staring at him with that big-eyed cartoon look. After a moment she sat down at the desk with a loud slapping sound.

Even Mr. Morrisey laughed.

And sitting at my desk, twirling my braids, I knew this was the last Tuesday of the Other June. ᑌ Ⓜ

Ⓜ **CHARACTERIZATION**
How has June changed since the beginning of the story?

PRIMER

RITA DOVE

In the sixth grade I was chased home by
the Gatlin Kids, three skinny sisters
in rolled-down bobby socks.[1] Hissing
Brainiac! And *Mrs. Stringbean!*, they trod my heel.
5 I knew my body was no big deal
but never thought to retort:[2] who's
calling *who* skinny? (Besides, I knew
they'd beat me up.) I survived
their shoves across the schoolyard
10 because my five-foot-zero mother drove up
in her Caddie[3] to shake them down to size.
Nothing could get me into that car.
I took the long way home, swore
I'd show them all: I would grow up.

---

1. **bobby socks:** 1940s and 1950s term for socks reaching just above
   the ankle.
2. **retort:** answer back in a sharp way.
3. **Caddie:** Cadillac, a type of car.

Comprehension

1. **Recall** What is June's mother's approach to dealing with life's difficulties?

2. **Recall** What unpleasant discovery does June make on moving day?

3. **Represent** Reread lines 92–96. Create a weekly calendar showing the days of the week and June's nickname for each.

Literary Analysis

4. **Visualize** Look at the chart you made as you read. Choose the detail that is clearest in your mind and sketch it. Explain how the information from your chart helped you to make your sketch.

5. **Identify Characterization** Think about the ways in which each of the two Junes is described in the story. Fill in a chart like the one shown using examples from the story.

	June	Other June
Appearance		
Character's Thoughts/Actions		-
Other Characters' Reactions/Comments		
Narrator's Direct Comments About Character		

6. **Analyze the Main Character** Think about the type of person June is. How does her personality affect the course of events in the story? Note whether the predictions you made about her actions were correct and whether they fit her personality.

7. **Evaluate Character Traits** A character's traits are the qualities shown by the character. You learn about a character through his or her thoughts, actions, appearance, and words. Based on what you know about the Other June's traits, does she seem like a believable character? Use examples from the story to support your answer.

8. **Compare Literary Works** Reread Rita Dove's poem on page 218. How is the **speaker,** or voice, of the poem like June the **narrator?** Use examples from each selection to support your answer.

Extension and Challenge

9. **Readers' Circle** Get together with a small group and discuss the way June deals with the Other June. Discuss the other ways she could have responded, as well as the way her mother might react to her behavior. Did June do the right thing?

10. **Big Question Activity** Look back at the list you created on page 204. If a friend came to you now and asked for advice, would you still give the same suggestions? If your ideas about dealing with **bullies** have changed, update your list. Explain in writing why your ideas have or have not changed.

Vocabulary in Context

VOCABULARY PRACTICE

Choose the letter of the word or phrase you would associate with each boldfaced vocabulary word.

1. **Emerald** is a shade of (a) gray, (b) blue, (c) green.
2. A person in a **daze** is (a) excited, (b) confused, (c) good at sports.
3. (a) An enemy, (b) A vacation, (c) A prize might **torment** you.
4. The **rigid** flagpole (a) sways in the wind, (b) does not move, (c) falls over.
5. A **dazzling** light is (a) dim, (b) harsh, (c) bright.
6. Someone who is **devoted** to you is (a) very fond of you, (b) confused by your decisions, (c) unwilling to stick up for you.

daze	emerald
dazzling	rigid
devoted	torment

VOCABULARY IN WRITING

Did you expect the Other June to react the way she did at the end of the story? Write a paragraph explaining your opinion, using two or more vocabulary words. Here is a sample of how you might begin.

> **EXAMPLE SENTENCE**
>
> *People who **torment** others are often cowards.*

VOCABULARY STRATEGY: FIGURATIVE LANGUAGE IN CONTEXT

Figurative language is language used to express ideas in an imaginative way. Often, one idea or thing is being compared to another. In this story, a character's skirt is said to be "as dazzling as a rainbow." This figurative comparison helps you see the skirt in a new and interesting way. At the same time, thinking of the qualities of a rainbow—its brightness and beauty—can help you understand what the word *dazzling* means. The comparison provides context clues to help you interpret the meaning of an unknown word.

PRACTICE Explain the comparison being made in each sentence. Then write a definition for each boldfaced word.

1. Jeremy was as **pugnacious** as a boxer preparing for a championship bout.
2. His dog was as **recalcitrant** as a child who refused to go to sleep.
3. The three young children were **loquacious,** like chattering monkeys.
4. That volcano is as **dormant** as a hibernating bear.

VOCABULARY PRACTICE
For more practice, go to the **Vocabulary Center** at **ClassZone.com.**

Reading-Writing Connection

Deepen your understanding of "Tuesday of the Other June" by responding to these prompts. Then complete the **Grammar and Writing** exercise.

WRITING PROMPTS

SELF-CHECK

A. Short Response: Analyze the Message
June seems to be unable to tell her mother about the **bullying** she is experiencing. Write a **one-paragraph letter** that June might write to her mother explaining what has been happening to her.

A good letter will . . .
- contain informal language that reflects their close relationship
- include specific details from the story

B. Extended Response: Write a Description
"Tuesday of the Other June" focuses on the main character's feelings of helplessness and anxiety. Imagine how June might feel after finally standing up to the Other June. Write **two or three paragraphs** describing June's thoughts, feelings, and actions after the encounter.

A strong description will . . .
- state specific words, thoughts, and actions of the character
- match what is already known about June's character traits

GRAMMAR AND WRITING

USE CORRECT VERB TENSE Verb tenses are used to show that events or actions occur at certain times. The **past tense** is used for an event or action that has already occurred. The **present tense** is used for an event or action that occurs in the moment or regularly. The **future tense** is used to refer to an event or action that has not yet occurred. When you write, it is important to use the correct tense and not switch it inappropriately.

Original: When the mother went to work, she thinks about June.

Revised: When the mother went to work, she thought about June.
(*The second part of the sentence needs a past tense verb.*)

PRACTICE Choose the correct verb tense to complete each sentence.

1. June wakes up every night worrying about robbers, but in the morning she and her mother (sing, sang) together.
2. June dreaded Tuesdays because she (has, had) to go to swimming class.
3. As her mother (drives, drove) over the hill, June sees the Other June.
4. June will meet up with the Other June soon, and she (handles, will handle) the situation differently.

FOR MORE HELP WITH VERB TENSES, SEE PAGE R56 IN THE *Grammar Handbook.*

The Problem with Bullies
Feature Article

Use with "Tuesday of the Other June," page 206.

What's the Connection?

In the short story you just read, a young girl becomes the target of a bully. In the **feature article** you are about to read, Sean Price takes a closer look at the problem of bullying.

Skill Focus: Take Notes

When you **take notes,** you record the most important information from whatever you are reading. You might record this information in a graphic organizer or in a simple outline. The choice is up to you. However, be sure to pick a format you can refer back to easily.

   Previewing the article—looking at its title, subheadings, topic sentences, and graphic aids—can help you decide on a format. For example, by previewing "The Problem with Bullies," you can see that this feature article covers the following information:

- statistics about bullying
- forms of bullying
- the roots of bullying
- the effects of bullying
- the stopping bullies

In preparation for taking notes on these subtopics, you might set up a graphic organizer like the one shown.

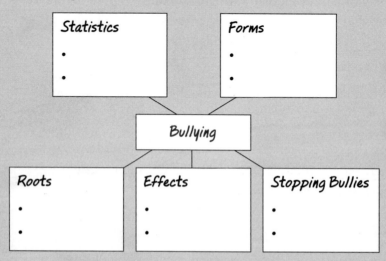

Handwritten sticky note:
- She was in 6th grade.
- She was adopted.
- She had one friend.

The PROBLEM with BULLIES by Susan Price

FOCUS ON FORM
"The Problem with Bullies" is a **feature article,** a nonfiction article found in a newspaper or magazine. It gives readers ideas and information about a high-interest topic.

By sixth grade, Karen had experienced her share of hardships. She had just been adopted by a family in Chattanooga, Tennessee, after spending six years in foster care. Naturally shy and quiet, Karen also struggled with a slight speech impediment.[1] She had only one good friend.

---

1. **speech impediment:** a physical condition that makes it difficult for a person to speak clearly.

All this made Karen (not her real name) an easy target for a bully. Her tormentor,[2] a popular girl at school, loved to taunt Karen about the way she spoke and about her home life.

"She made fun of the fact that I was a foster kid and that my mother

10 dic *She was bullied by another girl.* might shove Karen or

thr e other girl received

se g, she refused to give

Ka

by went through. A study

Human Development

fou rades 6-12 say that

th that they had been

bu

20 Another study found

tha ll be convicted of a

cri atural part of growing

up. Today, authorities see it as a serious health crisis. It is estimated that bullying keeps 160,000 kids out of school each day.

What Is Bullying?

Bullying takes many forms: gossip, snubbing, put-downs, threats, and violent attacks. Its roots lie in the difference of power between the bullies and their victims. Bullies tend to be confident, impulsive,
30 and popular. Victims tend to be withdrawn and have few friends. Many bullies come from homes where they are neglected or abused. Bullying allows them to exercise power that's denied to them at home.

Boys and girls bully differently. Boys tend to use threats and physical violence. Girl bullies rely more on backbiting (cruel comments), social exclusion, and spreading false rumors. Cyberbullying, a newer form of harassment, allows bullies to humiliate[3] their peers with e-mail and blog postings.

---

2. **tormentor:** a person who is the source of harrassment, annoyance, or pain.

3. **humiliate:** to lower the pride, dignity, or self-respect of another.

(F) OCUS ON FORM

"The Problem with Bullies" is a **feature article,** a nonfiction article found in a newspaper or magazine. It gives readers ideas and information about a high-interest topic.

The PROBLEM with BULLIES by Sean Price

By sixth grade, Karen had experienced her share of hardships. She had just been adopted by a family in Chattanooga, Tennessee, after spending six years in foster care. Naturally shy and quiet, Karen also struggled with a slight speech impediment.[1] She had only one good friend.

---

1. **speech impediment:** a physical condition that makes it difficult for a person to speak clearly.

A FEATURE ARTICLE
Reread lines 15–19.
Then reread the **Focus on Form** on page 223.
What makes bullying a good topic for a feature article? Explain.

B TAKE NOTES
In the appropriate section of your graphic organizer, restate the information in lines 20–22. Keep in mind that this study does not prove that being a bully *causes* a person to become a criminal.

All this made Karen (not her real name) an easy target for a bully. Her tormentor,[2] a popular girl at school, loved to taunt Karen about the way she spoke and about her home life.

"She made fun of the fact that I was a foster kid and that my mother didn't take care of me," says Karen.

Sometimes the abuse was physical. The bully might shove Karen or throw one of her shoes in the toilet. Even after the other girl received several suspensions and detentions for her bullying, she refused to give Karen a break.

Millions of U.S. teens understand what Karen went through. A study by the National Institute of Children's Health and Human Development found that more than 16 percent of students in grades 6–12 say that they have been bullied. Nineteen percent said that they had been bullies themselves. **A**

It's not just the victims who are hurt by bullying. Another study found that 60 percent of the bullies in grades 6–9 will be convicted of a criminal act by age 24! **B**

At one time, bullying was considered just a natural part of growing up. Today, authorities see it as a serious health crisis. It is estimated that bullying keeps 160,000 kids out of school each day.

What Is Bullying?

Bullying takes many forms: gossip, snubbing, put-downs, threats, and violent attacks. Its roots lie in the difference of power between the bullies and their victims. Bullies tend to be confident, impulsive, and popular. Victims tend to be withdrawn and have few friends. Many bullies come from homes where they are neglected or abused. Bullying allows them to exercise power that's denied to them at home.

Boys and girls bully differently. Boys tend to use threats and physical violence. Girl bullies rely more on backbiting (cruel comments), social exclusion, and spreading false rumors. Cyberbullying, a newer form of harassment, allows bullies to humiliate[3] their peers with e-mail and blog postings.

---

2. **tormentor:** a person who is the source of harrassment, annoyance, or pain.

3. **humiliate:** to lower the pride, dignity, or self-respect of another.

For victims, being bullied damages self-esteem. Bullying expert
40 Marlene Snyder says that fear of bullies also makes class time much
more trying for the victims. "They're sitting there trying to survive, not
being able to really learn," she says.

Karen's frequent complaints about the bullying finally brought her
some relief. She and her tormentor were given separate class
schedules for eighth grade.

Karen believes the other girl may have been threatened with
expulsion. Whatever happened, the bully now ignores Karen. Life is
easier to handle. And yet the bullying has left its mark.

"School's still stressful," Karen says. "I'm always on the watch to
50 see who's coming toward me." **C**

C TAKE NOTES
In your graphic
organizer, note the
effects of bullying that
are included in this
section.

Stopping Bullies

In recent years, many schools have implemented[4] effective antibullying programs. Denny Middle School in Seattle, Washington, launched such a program recently. Already there have been signs of progress. Craig Little, a student, saw a new student being taunted by a group of fellow seventh-graders. The lead bully wouldn't let the boy pass.

Instead of standing by, Craig acted. He said, "You guys leave him alone, and let him go." Craig then escorted the boy away from the group. The lead bully and the new student have since made up. "I talked
60 to both of them [later], and they're all right with each other," Craig said. "They're kind of becoming friends." **D**

4. **implemented:** put into effect or carried out.

D TAKE NOTES
What information does this section provide about stopping bullies? Take notes in your graphic organizer.

Comprehension

1. **Recall** How many students do authorities estimate are out of school each day because of bullying?

2. **Summarize** Briefly describe what happened to Karen and how the problem was resolved.

Critical Analysis

Boy/Girls

3. **Improve Your Notes** How might you use the topic sentence in line 34 to help you organize your notes? Explain what you would add to your graphic organizer and where you would add it.

4. **Evaluate a Feature Article** A strong feature article explores a topic of high interest and presents new ideas or useful information about the topic. In your opinion, is this feature article strong? Explain.

Read for Information: Develop Research Questions

WRITING PROMPT

Choose one of the following bulleted topics. Then develop a short list of research questions to learn more about it.

- statistics about bullying
- effects of bullying
- forms of bullying
- stopping bullies
- roots of bullying

Research questions are questions about a topic that really can't be answered with just a yes or a no. Follow these steps to help you select your topic and develop research questions about it.

1. Review your notes about each topic. Using a different color ink, add anything else you already know about the topic that you think is important or useful.

2. Choose the topic that interests you most, and write it at the top of a piece of paper.

3. Below your topic, write the words *Who, What, When, Where, Why,* and *How* in a column. Next to each, write the questions about your topic that begin with that word. Circle those that you are most interested in answering.

Topic:_____
- Who?
- What?
- When?
- Where?
- Why?
- How?

4. If time allows, use the questions you've developed to research your topic.

President Cleveland, Where Are You?
Short Story by Robert Cormier

Aaron's Gift
Short Story by Myron Levoy

What would you do for your FAMILY?

KEY IDEA The word *family* means different things to different people. It might mean parents, siblings, cousins, or grandparents. It can also mean close, trusted friends. Although you may not always understand or agree with the people you call family, you are there for them in times of need, and they are there for you. In each of the two stories you are about to read, a boy does something nice for someone in his family.

QUICKWRITE Think of a time when you helped someone through a hard time or when someone did something special for you. Write a few sentences about that experience.

● LITERARY ANALYSIS: CHARACTER

A good short story has believable characters. Usually the story focuses on one or two **main characters.** We observe a character's **traits,** or qualities, in a story in the same ways we observe someone's traits in life. We come to understand a story's characters through

- what they say, think, and do
- the conflicts they face
- the choices they make and the actions they take

In the stories you are about to read, pay attention to the traits, problems, and actions of each of the main characters.

● READING STRATEGY: SET A PURPOSE FOR READING

When you **set a purpose for reading,** you determine your reasons for reading one or more works. Your purpose for reading the following two stories is to find the similarities and differences between their main characters. After reading the first story, begin filling in the chart.

	Jerry	Aaron
What are the character's traits?		
What problems does he face?		
What choices does he make?		

Review: **Connect**

▲ VOCABULARY IN CONTEXT

Cormier and Levoy use the listed words to help tell the stories of two boys. To see which words you already know, fill in the chart. Then write a sentence using each word you know.

WORD LIST		
allot	frenzied	skirmish
assassinate	incredulous	stalemate
contempt	massacre	
divulge	obsess	

Know Well	Think I Know	Don't Know

Author Online

Robert Cormier: Young Poet

Robert Cormier 1925–2000

Robert Cormier was published for the first time at age 12, when a local paper printed some of his poems. Cormier later wrote for a newspaper before becoming one of the first writers to create literature for young adult readers.

Myron Levoy: Inspired Writer

Myron Levoy born 1930

While working at the New York Public Library when he was 16, Myron Levoy came across an exhibit of the original hand-written poems of Edwin Arlington Robinson. Upon seeing "Miniver Cheevy," which he had just studied in school, he knew instantly that he wanted to be a writer.

 MORE ABOUT THE AUTHOR For more on Robert Cormier and Myron Levoy, visit the **Literature Center** at **ClassZone.com.**

PRESIDENT CLEVELAND,
WHERE ARE YOU?

~ ROBERT CORMIER ~

That was the autumn of the cowboy cards—Buck Jones and Tom Tyler and Hoot Gibson and especially Ken Maynard.[1] The cards were available in those five-cent packages of gum: pink sticks, three together, covered with a sweet white powder. You couldn't blow bubbles with that particular gum, but it couldn't have mattered less. The cowboy cards were important—the pictures of those rock-faced men with eyes of blue steel. **A**

On those wind-swept, leaf-tumbling afternoons, we gathered after school on the sidewalk in front of Lemire's Drugstore, across from
10　St. Jude's Parochial School, and we swapped and bargained and matched for the cards. Because a Ken Maynard serial[2] was playing at the Globe every Saturday afternoon, he was the most popular cowboy of all, and one of his cards was worth at least ten of any other kind. Rollie Tremaine had a treasure of thirty or so, and he guarded them jealously. He'd match you for the other cards, but he risked his Ken Maynards only when the other kids threatened to leave him out of the competition altogether.

You could almost hate Rollie Tremaine. In the first place, he was the only son of Auguste Tremaine, who operated the Uptown Dry Goods Store, and he did not live in a tenement but in a big white birthday cake of a house on
20　Laurel Street. He was too fat to be effective in the football games between

A CHARACTER
Reread lines 1–7.
What do you learn
about the **narrator?**

ANALYZE VISUALS
Examine the photograph.
What can you **infer**
about the boys?

1.　**Buck Jones . . . Kent Maynard:** well-known movie cowboys who developed their skills in rodeos and Wild West shows or as stuntmen.

2.　**serial** (sîr′ē-əl): a movie appearing in weekly parts.

the Frenchtown Tigers and the North Side Knights, and he made us constantly aware of the jingle of coins in his pockets. He was able to stroll into Lemire's and casually select a quarter's worth of cowboy cards while the rest of us watched, aching with envy.

Once in a while I earned a nickel or dime by running errands or washing windows for blind old Mrs. Belander, or by finding pieces of copper, brass, and other valuable metals at the dump and selling them to the junkman. The coins clutched in my hand, I would race to Lemire's to buy a cowboy card or two, hoping that
30 Ken Maynard would stare boldly out at me as I opened the pack. At one time, before a disastrous matching session with Roger Lussier (my best friend, except where the cards were involved), I owned five Ken Maynards and considered myself a millionaire, of sorts.

One week I was particularly lucky; I had spent two afternoons washing floors for Mrs. Belander and received a quarter. Because my father had worked a full week at the shop, where a rush order for fancy combs had been received, he **allotted** my brothers and sisters and me an extra dime along with the usual ten cents for the Saturday-afternoon movie. Setting aside the movie fare, I found myself with a bonus of thirty-five cents, and I then
40 planned to put Rollie Tremaine to shame the following Monday afternoon.

Monday was the best day to buy the cards because the candy man stopped at Lemire's every Monday morning to deliver the new assortments. There was nothing more exciting in the world than a fresh batch of card boxes. I rushed home from school that day and hurriedly changed my clothes, eager to set off for the store. As I burst through the doorway, letting the screen door slam behind me, my brother Armand blocked my way. **B**

He was fourteen, three years older than I, and a freshman at Monument High School. He had recently become a stranger to me in many ways—indifferent to such matters as cowboy cards and the
50 Frenchtown Tigers—and he carried himself with a mysterious dignity that was fractured now and then when his voice began shooting off in all directions like some kind of vocal fireworks.[3]

"Wait a minute, Jerry," he said. "I want to talk to you." He motioned me out of earshot of my mother, who was busy supervising the usual after-school **skirmish** in the kitchen.

I sighed with impatience. In recent months Armand had become a figure of authority, siding with my father and mother occasionally. As the oldest son, he sometimes took advantage of his age and experience to issue rules and regulations. **C**

---

3. **his voice . . . vocal fireworks:** Because Armand's voice is changing, its pitch varies unexpectedly from high to low.

allot (ə-lŏt') *v.* to parcel out; distribute

B CONNECT
Think about a time when you were looking forward to something. Why do you think the narrator is so excited about the new cards?

skirmish (skûr'mĭsh) *n.* a minor battle or conflict

C CHARACTER
Reread lines 47–59. What does his attitude toward Armand tell you about Jerry?

60 "How much money have you got?" he whispered.

"You in some kind of trouble?" I asked, excitement rising in me as I remembered the blackmail plot of a movie at the Globe a month before.

He shook his head in annoyance. "Look," he said, "it's Pa's birthday tomorrow. I think we ought to chip in and buy him something . . ."

I reached into my pocket and caressed the coins. "Here," I said carefully, pulling out a nickel. "If we all give a nickel, we should have enough to buy him something pretty nice."

He regarded me with **contempt.** "Rita already gave me fifteen cents, and I'm throwing in a quarter. Albert handed over a dime—all that's left
70 of his birthday money. Is that all you can do—a nickel?"

"Aw, come on," I protested. "I haven't got a single Ken Maynard left, and I was going to buy some cards this afternoon."

"Ken Maynard!" he snorted. "Who's more important—him or your father?"

His question was unfair because he knew that there was no possible choice—"my father" had to be the only answer. My father was a huge man who believed in the things of the spirit. . . . He had worked at the Monument Comb Shop since the age of fourteen; his booming laugh—or grumble—greeted us each night when he returned from the factory.
80 A steady worker when the shop had enough work, he quickened with gaiety on Friday nights and weekends . . . and he was fond of making long speeches about the good things in life. In the middle of the Depression,[4] for instance, he paid cash for a piano, of all things, and insisted that my twin sisters, Yolande and Yvette, take lessons once a week.

I took a dime from my pocket and handed it to Armand.

"Thanks, Jerry," he said. "I hate to take your last cent."

"That's all right," I replied, turning away and consoling myself with the thought that twenty cents was better than nothing at all.

When I arrived at Lemire's, I sensed disaster in the air. Roger Lussier
90 was kicking disconsolately at a tin can in the gutter, and Rollie Tremaine sat sullenly on the steps in front of the store.

"Save your money," Roger said. He had known about my plans to splurge on the cards.

"What's the matter?" I asked.

"There's no more cowboy cards," Rollie Tremaine said. "The company's not making any more."

> **contempt** (kən-tĕmpt') *n.* the feeling produced by something disgraceful or worthless; scorn

---

4. **Depression:** During the 1930s, the United States suffered an economic crisis known as the Great Depression. Banks and businesses all over the country were forced to close, and poverty and unemployment were widespread.

"They're going to have President cards," Roger said, his face twisting with disgust. He pointed to the store window. "Look!"

A placard in the window announced: "Attention, Boys. Watch for the New Series. Presidents of the United States. Free in Each 5-Cent Package of Caramel Chew."

"President cards?" I asked, dismayed.

I read on: "Collect a Complete Set and Receive an Official Imitation Major League Baseball Glove, Embossed with Lefty Grove's[5] Autograph."

Glove or no glove, who could become excited about Presidents, of all things?

Rollie Tremaine stared at the sign. "Benjamin Harrison, for crying out loud," he said. "Why would I want Benjamin Harrison when I've got twenty-two Ken Maynards?"

I felt the warmth of guilt creep over me. I jingled the coins in my pocket, but the sound was hollow. No more Ken Maynards to buy.

"I'm going to buy a Mr. Goodbar," Rollie Tremaine decided.

I was without appetite, indifferent even to a Baby Ruth, which was my favorite. I thought of how I had betrayed Armand and, worst of all, my father.

"I'll see you after supper," I called over my shoulder to Roger

as I hurried away toward home. I took the shortcut behind the church, although it involved leaping over a tall wooden fence, and I zigzagged recklessly through Mr. Thibodeau's garden, trying to outrace my guilt. I pounded up the steps and into the house, only to learn that Armand had already taken Yolande and Yvette uptown to shop for the birthday present.

I pedaled my bike furiously through the streets, ignoring the indignant horns of automobiles as I sliced through the traffic. Finally I saw Armand and my sisters emerge from the Monument Men's Shop. My heart sank when I spied the long, slim package that Armand was holding. **D**

"Did you buy the present yet?" I asked, although I knew it was too late.

"Just now. A blue tie," Armand said. "What's the matter?"

"Nothing," I replied, my chest hurting.

Whelan's Drug Store, 44th Street and Eighth Avenue, Manhattan (February 7, 1936), Berenice Abbott.

D CHARACTER
Reread lines 123–132. Jerry is suddenly concerned about finding his brother. Why is he feeling this way?

---

5. **Lefty Grove's:** belonging to Lefty Grove, a Hall of Fame pitcher for the Philadelphia A's (Athletics) and the Boston Red Sox between 1925 and 1941.

He looked at me for a long moment. At first his eyes were hard, but then they softened. He smiled at me, almost sadly, and touched my arm. I turned away from him because I felt naked and exposed.

"It's all right," he said gently. "Maybe you've learned something."
140 The words were gentle, but they held a curious dignity, the dignity remaining even when his voice suddenly cracked on the last syllable.

I wondered what was happening to me, because I did not know whether to laugh or cry.

Sister Angela was amazed when, a week before Christmas vacation, everybody in the class submitted a history essay worthy of a high mark—in some cases as high as A minus. (Sister Angela did not believe that anyone in the world ever deserved an A.) She never learned—or at least she never let on that she knew—we all had become experts on the Presidents because of the cards we purchased at Lemire's. Each card contained a picture
150 of a President and, on the reverse side, a summary of his career. We looked at those cards so often that the biographies imprinted themselves on our minds without effort. Even our street-corner conversations were filled with such information as the fact that James Madison was called "The Father of the Constitution," or that John Adams had intended to become a minister.

The President cards were a roaring success, and the cowboy cards were quickly forgotten. In the first place, we did not receive gum with the cards, but a kind of chewy caramel. The caramel could be tucked into a corner of your mouth, bulging your cheek in much the same manner as wads of tobacco bulged the mouths of baseball stars. In the second place,
160 the competition for collecting the cards was fierce and frustrating—fierce because everyone was intent on being the first to send away for a baseball glove and frustrating because although there were only thirty-two Presidents, including Franklin Delano Roosevelt,[6] the variety at Lemire's was at a minimum. When the deliveryman left the boxes of cards at the store each Monday, we often discovered that one entire box was devoted to a single President—two weeks in a row the boxes contained nothing but Abraham Lincolns. One week Roger Lussier and I were the heroes of Frenchtown. We journeyed on our bicycles to the North Side, engaged three boys in a matching bout, and returned with five new Presidents,
170 including Chester Alan Arthur, who up to that time had been missing.

Perhaps to sharpen our desire, the card company sent a sample glove to Mr. Lemire, and it dangled, orange and sleek, in the window. I was half sick with longing, thinking of my old glove at home, which I had inherited from

---

6. **Franklin Delano Roosevelt:** president of the United States from 1933 to 1945; president at the time of this story.

Armand. But Rollie Tremaine's desire for the glove outdistanced my own. He even got Mr. Lemire to agree to give the glove in the window to the first person to get a complete set of cards, so that precious time wouldn't be wasted waiting for the postman. **E**

We were delighted at Rollie Tremaine's frustration, especially since he was only a substitute player for the Tigers. Once, after spending fifty
180 cents on cards—all of which turned out to be Calvin Coolidge—he threw them to the ground, pulled some dollar bills out of his pocket, and said, "The heck with it. I'm going to buy a glove!"

"Not that glove," Roger Lussier said. "Not a glove with Lefty Grove's autograph. Look what it says at the bottom of the sign."

We all looked, although we knew the words by heart: "This Glove Is Not For Sale Anywhere."

Rollie Tremaine scrambled to pick up the cards from the sidewalk, pouting more than ever. After that he was quietly **obsessed** with the Presidents, hugging the cards close to his chest and refusing to tell us how
190 many more he needed to complete his set. **F**

I too was obsessed with the cards, because they had become things of comfort in a world that had suddenly grown dismal. After Christmas, a layoff at the shop had thrown my father out of work. He received no paycheck for four weeks, and the only income we had was from Armand's after-school job at the Blue and White Grocery Store—a job he lost finally when business dwindled as the layoff continued.

Although we had enough food and clothing—my father's credit had always been good, a matter of pride with him—the inactivity made my father restless and irritable. . . . The twins fell sick and went to the hospital to
200 have their tonsils removed. My father was confident that he would return to work eventually and pay off his debts, but he seemed to age before our eyes.

When orders again were received at the comb shop and he returned to work, another disaster occurred, although I was the only one aware of it. Armand fell in love.

I discovered his situation by accident, when I happened to pick up a piece of paper that had fallen to the floor in the bedroom he and I shared. I frowned at the paper, puzzled.

"Dear Sally, When I look into your eyes the world stands still . . ."

The letter was snatched from my hands before I finished reading it.
210 "What's the big idea, snooping around?" Armand asked, his face crimson. "Can't a guy have any privacy?"

E CHARACTER
Reread lines 171–177. What do you learn about Jerry through his thoughts about the glove?

obsess (əb-sĕs′) *v.*
to occupy the mind of

F CONNECT
Think about a time when you were competing for something you really wanted. In what way does that experience help you understand how Jerry and his friends are feeling?

ANALYZE VISUALS
How does this photograph compare with your mental picture of Jerry and his friends?

He had never mentioned privacy before. "It was on the floor," I said. "I didn't know it was a letter. Who's Sally?"

He flung himself across the bed. "You tell anybody and I'll muckalize you," he threatened. "Sally Knowlton."

Nobody in Frenchtown had a name like Knowlton.

"A girl from the North Side?" I asked, **incredulous.**

He rolled over and faced me, anger in his eyes, and a kind of despair, too. "What's the matter with that? Think she's too good for me?" he asked.

220 "I'm warning you, Jerry, if you tell anybody . . ."

"Don't worry," I said. Love had no particular place in my life; it seemed an unnecessary waste of time. And a girl from the North Side was so remote that for all practical purposes she did not exist. But I was curious. "What are you writing her a letter for? Did she leave town or something?"

"She hasn't left town," he answered. "I wasn't going to send it. I just felt like writing to her."

I was glad that I had never become involved with love—love that brought desperation to your eyes, that caused you to write letters you did not plan to send. Shrugging with indifference, I began to search in the closet for the

230 old baseball glove. I found it on the shelf, under some old sneakers. The webbing was torn and the padding gone. I thought of the sting I would feel when a sharp grounder slapped into the glove, and I winced.

incredulous
(ĭn-krĕj′ə-ləs) *adj.*
unbelieving

"You tell anybody about me and Sally and I'll—"

"I know. You'll muckalize me."

I did not **divulge** his secret and often shared his agony, particularly when he sat at the supper table and left my mother's special butterscotch pie untouched. I had never realized before how terrible love could be. But my compassion was short-lived, because I had other things to worry about: report cards due at Eastertime; the loss of income from old Mrs. Belander, who had gone to live with a daughter in Boston; and, of course, the Presidents. **G**

Because a **stalemate** had been reached, the President cards were the dominant force in our lives—mine, Roger Lussier's and Rollie Tremaine's. For three weeks, as the baseball season approached, each of us had a complete set—complete except for one President, Grover Cleveland. Each time a box of cards arrived at the store, we hurriedly bought them (as hurriedly as our funds allowed) and tore off the wrappers, only to be confronted by James Monroe or Martin Van Buren or someone else. But never Grover Cleveland, never the man who had been the twenty-second and the twenty-fourth President of the United States. We argued about Grover Cleveland. Should he be placed between Chester Alan Arthur and Benjamin Harrison as the twenty-second President, or did he belong between Benjamin Harrison and William McKinley as the twenty-fourth President? Was the card company playing fair? Roger Lussier brought up a horrifying possibility—did we need two Grover Clevelands to complete the set?

Indignant, we stormed Lemire's and protested to the harassed storeowner, who had long since vowed never to stock a new series. Muttering angrily, he searched his bills and receipts for a list of rules.

"All right," he announced. "Says here you only need one Grover Cleveland to finish the set. Now get out, all of you, unless you've got money to spend."

Outside the store, Rollie Tremaine picked up an empty tobacco tin and scaled it across the street. "Boy," he said. "I'd give five dollars for a Grover Cleveland."

When I returned home, I found Armand sitting on the piazza[7] steps, his chin in his hands. His mood of dejection mirrored my own, and I sat down beside him. We did not say anything for a while.

"Want to throw the ball around?" I asked.

He sighed, not bothering to answer.

"You sick?" I asked.

---

7. **piazza** (pē-ăz′ə): a porch or balcony, usually with a roof.

divulge (dĭ-vŭlj′) v. to reveal, especially something private or secret

G **CHARACTER**
Reread lines 235–240. How does Jerry feel about Armand and his troubles?

stalemate (stāl′māt′) n. a situation in which no one playing a game is able to win

GROVER CLEVELAND

AMERICAN HEROES CARAMEL

He stood up and hitched up his trousers, pulled at his ear, and finally told me what the matter was—there was a big dance next week at the high school, the Spring Promenade, and Sally had asked him to be her escort.

I shook my head at the folly of love. "Well, what's so bad about that?"

"How can I take Sally to a fancy dance?" he asked desperately. "I'd have to buy her a corsage . . . And my shoes are practically falling apart. Pa's got too many worries now to buy me new shoes or give me money for flowers for a girl."

280   I nodded in sympathy. "Yeah," I said. "Look at me. Baseball time is almost here, and all I've got is that old glove. And no Grover Cleveland card yet . . ."

"Grover Cleveland?" he asked. "They've got some of those up on the North Side. Some kid was telling me there's a store that's got them. He says they're looking for Warren G. Harding."

"Holy smoke!" I said. "I've got an extra Warren G. Harding!" Pure joy sang in my veins. I ran to my bicycle, swung into the seat—and found that the front tire was flat.

"I'll help you fix it," Armand said.

290   Within half an hour I was at the North Side Drugstore, where several boys were matching cards on the sidewalk. Silently but blissfully I shouted: President Grover Cleveland, here I come!

After Armand had left for the dance, all dressed up as if it were Sunday, the small green box containing the corsage under his arm, I sat on the railing of the piazza, letting my feet dangle. The neighborhood was quiet because the Frenchtown Tigers were at Daggett's Field, practicing for the first baseball game of the season.

I thought of Armand and the ridiculous expression on his face when he'd stood before the mirror in the bedroom. I'd avoided looking at his 300 new black shoes. "Love," I muttered.

Spring had arrived in a sudden stampede of apple blossoms and fragrant breezes. Windows had been thrown open and dust mops had banged on the sills all day long as the women busied themselves with housecleaning. I was puzzled by my lethargy. Wasn't spring supposed to make everything bright and gay?

I turned at the sound of footsteps on the stairs. Roger Lussier greeted me with a sour face.

"I thought you were practicing with the Tigers," I said.

"Rollie Tremaine," he said. "I just couldn't stand him." He slammed his 310 fist against the railing. "Jeez, why did he have to be the one to get a Grover Cleveland? You should see him showing off. He won't let anybody even touch that glove. . . ."

I felt like Benedict Arnold[8] and knew that I had to confess what I had done.

"Roger," I said, "I got a Grover Cleveland card up on the North Side. I sold it to Rollie Tremaine for five dollars." **H**

"Are you crazy?" he asked.

"I needed that five dollars. It was an—an emergency."

"Boy!" he said, looking down at the ground and shaking his head.
320 "What did you have to do a thing like that for?"

I watched him as he turned away and began walking down the stairs.

"Hey, Roger!" I called.

He squinted up at me as if I were a stranger, someone he'd never seen before.

"What?" he asked, his voice flat.

"I had to do it," I said. "Honest."

He didn't answer. He headed toward the fence, searching for the board we had loosened to give us a secret passage.

I thought of my father and Armand and Rollie Tremaine and Grover
330 Cleveland and wished that I could go away someplace far away. But there was no place to go.

Roger found the loose slat in the fence and slipped through. I felt betrayed: Weren't you supposed to feel good when you did something fine and noble? **I**

A moment later, two hands gripped the top of the fence and Roger's face appeared. "Was it a real emergency?" he yelled.

"A real one!" I called. "Something important!"

His face dropped from sight and his voice reached me across the yard: "All right."

340 "See you tomorrow!" I yelled.

I swung my legs over the railing again. The gathering dusk began to soften the sharp edges of the fence, the rooftops, the distant church steeple. I sat there a long time, waiting for the good feeling to come. ❧

H CHARACTER
Reread lines 313–316. What does Jerry's confession tell you about the kind of person he is?

I CONNECT
What connection can you make that helps you understand how Jerry is feeling?

---

8. **Benedict Arnold:** an American general who became a traitor to his country during the Revolutionary War.

Comprehension

1. **Recall** Why is each of the boys eager to gather a complete set of President cards?

2. **Recall** What is the name of the drugstore where the Frenchtown boys usually buy the President cards?

3. **Clarify** How does Jerry get the Grover Cleveland card?

Literary Analysis

4. **Describe the Main Character** Think about how you would describe Jerry to someone who hasn't read "President Cleveland, Where Are You?" What are his most important **traits?**

5. **Examine Motivation** Through the events in his **family** life, Jerry is developing a sense of values. What do you think is Jerry's motivation, or reason, for selling the card? Focus on his thoughts, feelings, and actions.

6. **Analyze a Minor Character** Minor characters help carry out the action of a story. They also help you learn more about the main character. Armand is a minor character, yet he plays a major role in the story. How does Armand's character help you learn more about Jerry?

7. **Analyze the Main Character** At a turning point in the story, Armand says to Jerry, "It's all right. Maybe you've learned something." What do you think Jerry has learned by the end of the story?

Comparing Characters

Now that you have read about Jerry, start filling in your chart. Add information that helps you understand Jerry's character.

	Jerry	Aaron
What are the character's traits?		
What problems does he face?	whether to spend his money on his father's present or buy cards	
What choices does he make?	to sell the card to Rollie	

AARON'S GIFT

Myron Levoy

Aaron Kandel had come to Tompkins Square Park to roller-skate, for the streets near Second Avenue were always too crowded with children and peddlers and old ladies and baby buggies. Though few children had bicycles in those days, almost every child owned a pair of roller skates. And Aaron was, it must be said, a Class A, triple-fantastic roller skater. **Ⓐ**

Aaron skated back and forth on the wide walkway of the park, pretending he was an aviator in an air race zooming around pylons,[1] which were actually two lampposts. During his third lap around the racecourse, he noticed a pigeon on the grass, behaving very strangely.
10 Aaron skated to the line of benches, then climbed over onto the lawn.

The pigeon was trying to fly, but all it could manage was to flutter and turn round and round in a large circle, as if it were performing a **frenzied** dance. The left wing was only half open and was beating in a clumsy, jerking fashion; it was clearly broken.

Luckily, Aaron hadn't eaten the cookies he'd stuffed into his pocket before he'd gone clacking down the three flights of stairs from his apartment, his skates already on. He broke a cookie into small crumbs and tossed some toward the pigeon. "Here pidge, here pidge," he called. The pigeon spotted the cookie crumbs and, after a moment, stopped
20 thrashing about. It folded its wings as best it could, but the broken wing still stuck half out. Then it strutted over to the crumbs, its head bobbing forth-back, forth-back, as if it were marching a little in front of the rest of the body—perfectly normal, except for that half-open wing which seemed to make the bird stagger sideways every so often.

---

1. **pylons** (pī'lŏnz'): towers marking turning points for airplanes in a race.

Ⓐ CHARACTER
What do you learn about the main character in the first paragraph?

frenzied (frĕn'zēd) *adj.* wildly excited; frantic

ANALYZE VISUALS
Examine the painting. What can you **infer** about the people and their location?

The pigeon began eating the crumbs as Aaron quickly unbuttoned his shirt and pulled it off. Very slowly, he edged toward the bird, making little kissing sounds like the ones he heard his grandmother make when she fed the sparrows on the back fire escape.

Then suddenly Aaron plunged. The shirt, in both hands, came down
30 like a torn parachute. The pigeon beat its wings, but Aaron held the shirt to the ground, and the bird couldn't escape. Aaron felt under the shirt, gently, and gently took hold of the wounded pigeon.

"Yes, yes, pidge," he said, very softly. "There's a good boy. Good pigeon, good."

The pigeon struggled in his hands, but little by little Aaron managed to soothe it. "Good boy, pidge. That's your new name. Pidge. I'm gonna take you home, Pidge. Yes, yes, *ssh.* Good boy. I'm gonna fix you up. Easy, Pidge, easy does it. Easy, boy." **B**

Aaron squeezed through an opening between the row of benches and
40 skated slowly out of the park, while holding the pigeon carefully with both hands as if it were one of his mother's rare, precious cups from the old country. How fast the pigeon's heart was beating! Was he afraid? Or did all pigeons' hearts beat fast?

It was fortunate that Aaron was an excellent skater, for he had to skate six blocks to his apartment, over broken pavement and sudden gratings and curbs and cobblestones. But when he reached home, he asked Noreen Callahan, who was playing on the stoop, to take off his skates for him. He would not chance going up three flights on roller skates this time.

"Is he sick?" asked Noreen.
50 "Broken wing," said Aaron. "I'm gonna fix him up and make him into a carrier pigeon[2] or something."

"Can I watch?" asked Noreen.

"Watch what?"

"The operation. I'm gonna be a nurse when I grow up."

"OK," said Aaron. "You can even help. You can help hold him while I fix him up."

Aaron wasn't quite certain what his mother would say about his newfound pet, but he was pretty sure he knew what his grandmother would think. His grandmother had lived with them ever since his
60 grandfather had died three years ago. And she fed the sparrows and jays and crows and robins on the back fire escape with every spare crumb she could find. In fact, Aaron noticed that she sometimes created crumbs

B CHARACTER
What do you learn about Aaron through his treatment of the pigeon?

VISUAL VOCABULARY

cobblestone
(kŏb'əl-stōn') *n.* a stone used to pave roads or walkways

2. **carrier pigeon:** a pigeon trained to carry messages from place to place.

where they didn't exist, by squeezing and tearing pieces of her breakfast roll when his mother wasn't looking.

Aaron didn't really understand his grandmother, for he often saw her by the window having long conversations with the birds, telling them about her days as a little girl in the Ukraine. And once he saw her take her mirror from her handbag and hold it out toward the birds. She told Aaron that she wanted them to see how beautiful they were. Very strange. But
70 Aaron did know that she would love Pidge, because she loved everything.

To his surprise, his mother said he could keep the pigeon, temporarily, because it was sick, and we were all strangers in the land of Egypt,[3] and it might not be bad for Aaron to have a pet. *Temporarily.*

The wing was surprisingly easy to fix, for the break showed clearly and Pidge was remarkably patient and still, as if he knew he was being helped. Or perhaps he was just exhausted from all the thrashing about he had done. Two Popsicle sticks served as splints, and strips from an old undershirt were used to tie them in place. Another strip held the wing to the bird's body. **C**

80 Aaron's father arrived home and stared at the pigeon. Aaron waited for the expected storm. But instead, Mr. Kandel asked, "Who *did* this?"

"Me," said Aaron. "And Noreen Callahan."

"Sophie!" he called to his wife. "Did you see this! Ten years old and it's better than Dr. Belasco could do. He's a genius!"

As the days passed, Aaron began training Pidge to be a carrier pigeon. He tied a little cardboard tube to Pidge's left leg and stuck tiny rolled-up sheets of paper with secret messages into it: The Enemy Is Attacking at Dawn. Or: The Guns Are Hidden in the Trunk of the Car. Or: Vincent DeMarco Is a British Spy. Then Aaron would set Pidge down
90 at one end of the living room and put some popcorn at the other end. And Pidge would waddle slowly across the room, cooing softly, while the ends of his bandages trailed along the floor.

At the other end of the room, one of Aaron's friends would take out the message, stick a new one in, turn Pidge around, and aim him at the popcorn that Aaron put down on his side of the room.

And Pidge grew fat and contented on all the popcorn and crumbs and corn and crackers and Aaron's grandmother's breakfast rolls.

Aaron had told all the children about Pidge, but he only let his very best friends come up and play carrier pigeon with him. But telling
100 everyone had been a mistake. A group of older boys from down the block

---

3. **we were all . . . Egypt:** a Bible reference: "Love ye therefore the stranger: for ye were strangers in the land of Egypt" (Deuteronomy 10:19).

SOCIAL STUDIES CONNECTION

Now a country in eastern Europe, Ukraine was under the rule of Russia during the late nineteenth and early twentieth centuries.

C CONNECT
Think of a time you saw an animal in need. Why do you think Aaron decides to help Pidge?

had a club—Aaron's mother called it a gang—and Aaron had longed to join as he had never longed for anything else. To be with them and share their secrets, the secrets of older boys. To be able to enter their clubhouse shack on the empty lot on the next street. To know the password and swear the secret oath. To belong. **D**

About a month after Aaron had brought the pigeon home, Carl, the gang leader, walked over to Aaron in the street and told him he could be a member if he'd bring the pigeon down to be the club mascot. Aaron couldn't believe it; he immediately raced home to get Pidge. But his mother told Aaron to stay away from those boys, or else. And Aaron, miserable, argued with his mother and pleaded and cried and coaxed. It was no use. Not with those boys. No. **E**

110

Aaron's mother tried to change the subject. She told him that it would soon be his grandmother's sixtieth birthday, a very special birthday indeed, and all the family from Brooklyn and the East Side would be coming to their apartment for a dinner and celebration. Would Aaron try to build something or make something for Grandma? A present made with his own hands would be nice. A decorated box for her hairpins or a crayon picture for her room or anything he liked.

120

In a flash Aaron knew what to give her: Pidge! Pidge would be her present! Pidge with his wing healed, who might be able to carry messages for her to the doctor or his Aunt Rachel or other people his grandmother seemed to go to a lot. It would be a surprise for everyone. And Pidge would make up for what had happened to Grandma when she'd been a little girl in the Ukraine, wherever that was.

130

Often, in the evening, Aaron's grandmother would talk about the old days long ago in the Ukraine, in the same way that she talked to the birds on the back fire escape. She had lived in a village near a place called Kishinev[4] with hundreds of other poor peasant families like her own. Things hadn't been too bad under someone called Czar Alexander the Second,[5] whom Aaron always pictured as a tall handsome man in a gold uniform. But Alexander

D CHARACTER
Reread lines 98–105. What do you learn about Aaron?

E CONNECT
Reread lines 106–112. Think about why Aaron is so upset. What connection can you make that helps you understand his reaction?

---

4. **Kishinev** (kĭsh′ə-nĕf′): a city that is now the capital of the country of Moldova and is known today as Chisinau.

5. **Czar** (zär) **Alexander the Second:** emperor of Russia from 1855 to 1881.

the Second was **assassinated,** and Alexander the Third,[6] whom Aaron pictured as an ugly man in a black cape, became the czar. And the Jewish people of the Ukraine had no peace anymore.

140   One day, a thundering of horses was heard coming toward the village from the direction of Kishinev. "The Cossacks! The Cossacks!" someone had shouted. The czar's horsemen! Quickly, quickly, everyone in Aaron's grandmother's family had climbed down to the cellar through a little trap door hidden under a mat in the big central room of their shack. But his grandmother's pet goat, whom she'd loved as much as Aaron loved Pidge and more, had to be left above, because if it had made a sound in the cellar, they would never have lived to see the next morning. They all hid under the wood in the woodbin and waited, hardly breathing.

        Suddenly, from above, they heard shouts and calls and screams at a
150 distance. And then the noise was in their house. Boots pounding on the floor, and everything breaking and crashing overhead. The smell of smoke and the shouts of a dozen men.

        The terror went on for an hour, and then the sound of horses' hooves faded into the distance. They waited another hour to make sure, and then the father went up out of the cellar and the rest of the family followed. The door to the house had been torn from its hinges, and every piece of furniture was broken. Every window, every dish, every stitch of clothing was totally destroyed, and one wall had been completely bashed in. And on the floor was the goat, lying quietly. Aaron's grandmother, who was
160 just a little girl of eight at the time, had wept over the goat all day and all night and could not be consoled.

        But they had been lucky. For other houses had been burned to the ground. And everywhere, not goats alone, nor sheep, but men and women and children lay quietly on the ground. The word for this sort of **massacre,** Aaron had learned, was *pogrom.* It had been a pogrom. And the men on the horses were Cossacks. Hated word. Cossacks. **F**

        And so Pidge would replace that goat of long ago. A pigeon on Second Avenue where no one needed trap doors or secret escape passages or woodpiles to hide under. A pigeon for his grandmother's sixtieth
170 birthday. *Oh wing, heal quickly so my grandmother can send you flying to everywhere she wants!*

        But a few days later, Aaron met Carl in the street again. And Carl told Aaron that there was going to be a meeting that afternoon in which a map was going to be drawn up to show where a secret treasure lay buried on

---

6. **Alexander the Third:** emperor of Russia from 1881 to 1894.

assassinate (ə-săs′ə-nāt′) *v.* to murder by surprise attack for political reasons

massacre (măs′ə-kər) *n.* the act of killing a number of helpless humans or animals

F CHARACTER What does Aaron's interest in his grandmother's childhood tell you about him?

Head with a Bird II (1971), Pablo Picasso. Oil on canvas, 55 cm × 46 cm. Private collection.
© Bridgeman Art Library © 2008 Estate of Pablo Picasso/Artists Rights Society (ARS), New York.

the empty lot. "Bring the pigeon and you can come into the shack. We got a badge for you. A new kinda membership badge with a secret code on the back."

Aaron ran home, his heart pounding almost as fast as the pigeon's. He took Pidge in his hands and carried him out the door while his
180 mother was busy in the kitchen making stuffed cabbage, his father's favorite dish. And by the time he reached the street, Aaron had decided to take the bandages off. Pidge would look like a real pigeon again, and none of the older boys would laugh or call him a bundle of rags. **G**

G CHARACTER
Reread lines 167–183. What does Aaron's choice to join the boys tell you about him?

Gently, gently he removed the bandages and the splints and put them in his pocket in case he should need them again. But Pidge seemed to hold his wing properly in place.

When he reached the empty lot, Aaron walked up to the shack, then hesitated. Four bigger boys were there. After a moment, Carl came out and commanded Aaron to hand Pidge over.

190   "Be careful," said Aaron. "I just took the bandages off."

"Oh sure, don't worry," said Carl. By now Pidge was used to people holding him, and he remained calm in Carl's hands.

"OK," said Carl. "Give him the badge." And one of the older boys handed Aaron his badge with the code on the back. "Now light the fire," said Carl.

"What . . . what fire?" asked Aaron.

"The fire. You'll see," Carl answered.

"You didn't say nothing about a fire," said Aaron. "You didn't say nothing to—"

"Hey!" said Carl. "I'm the leader here. And you don't talk unless I tell
200 you that you have p'mission. Light the fire, Al."

The boy named Al went out to the side of the shack, where some wood and cardboard and old newspapers had been piled into a huge mound. He struck a match and held it to the newspapers.

"OK," said Carl. "Let's get 'er good and hot. Blow on it. Everybody blow."

Aaron's eyes stung from the smoke, but he blew alongside the others, going from side to side as the smoke shifted toward them and away.

"Let's fan it," said Al.

In a few minutes, the fire was crackling and glowing with a bright yellow-orange flame.

210   "Get me the rope," said Carl.

One of the boys brought Carl some cord and Carl, without a word, wound it twice around the pigeon, so that its wings were tight against its body.

"What . . . what are you *doing!*" shouted Aaron. "You're hurting his wing!"

"Don't worry about his wing," said Carl. "We're gonna throw him into the fire. And when we do, we're gonna swear an oath of loyalty to—"

"No! *No!*" shouted Aaron, moving toward Carl. ⓗ

"Grab him!" called Carl. "Don't let him get the pigeon!"

220   But Aaron had leaped right across the fire at Carl, taking him completely by surprise. He threw Carl back against the shack and hit out at his face with both fists. Carl slid down to the ground, and the pigeon rolled out of his hands. Aaron scooped up the pigeon and ran, pretending he was on roller skates so that he would go faster and faster. And as he ran across the lot he

ⓗ **CHARACTER**
Reread lines 211–218.
What does Aaron's
reaction to the boys'
plan reveal about him?

pulled the cord off Pidge and tried to find a place, *any* place, to hide him. But the boys were on top of him, and the pigeon slipped from Aaron's hands.

"Get him!" shouted Carl.

Aaron thought of the worst, the most horrible thing he could shout at the boys. "Cossacks!" he screamed. "You're all Cossacks!"

230 Two boys held Aaron back while the others tried to catch the pigeon. Pidge fluttered along the ground just out of reach, skittering one way and then the other. Then the boys came at him from two directions. But suddenly Pidge beat his wings in rhythm, and rose up, up, over the roof of the nearest tenement, up over Second Avenue toward the park.

With the pigeon gone, the boys turned toward Aaron and tackled him to the ground and punched him and tore his clothes and punched him some more. Aaron twisted and turned and kicked and punched back, shouting "Cossacks! Cossacks!" And somehow the word gave him the strength to tear away from them.

240 When Aaron reached home, he tried to go past the kitchen quickly so his mother wouldn't see his bloody face and torn clothing. But it was no use; his father was home from work early that night and was seated in the living room. In a moment Aaron was surrounded by his mother, father, and grandmother, and in another moment he had told them everything that had happened, the words tumbling out between his broken sobs. Told them of the present he had planned, of the pigeon for a goat, of the gang, of the badge with the secret code on the back, of the shack, and the fire, and the pigeon's flight over the tenement roof.

And Aaron's grandmother kissed him and thanked him for his present 250 which was even better than the pigeon.

"What present?" asked Aaron, trying to stop the series of sobs.

And his grandmother opened her pocketbook and handed Aaron her mirror and asked him to look. But all Aaron saw was his dirty, bruised face and his torn shirt.

Aaron thought he understood, and then, again, he thought he didn't. How could she be so happy when there really was no present? And why pretend that there was?

Later that night, just before he fell asleep, Aaron tried to imagine what his grandmother might have done with the pigeon. She would have fed 260 it, and she certainly would have talked to it, as she did to all the birds, and . . . and then she would have let it go free. Yes, of course Pidge's flight to freedom must have been the gift that had made his grandmother so happy. Her goat has escaped from the Cossacks at last, Aaron thought, half dreaming. And he fell asleep with a smile. ❧

Comprehension

1. **Recall** What is Aaron doing when he finds the wounded pigeon?

2. **Recall** How do Aaron's mother and father react when he brings the pigeon home?

3. **Summarize** What happens when Aaron goes to the shack?

Literary Analysis

4. **Describe the Main Character** Through his thoughts, feelings, and actions, what have you learned about Aaron's values and personality **traits?**

5. **Examine Motivation** What is Aaron's motivation, or reason, for giving Pidge to his grandmother as a gift?

6. **Analyze Flashback** The story of Aaron's grandmother's past is a flashback—a description of a conversation or event that took place before the beginning of the story. How is the flashback important to your understanding of Aaron's **family**—and of the events in the story?

7. **Interpret** Reread lines 65–70. In this passage, Aaron tells us that his grandmother would hold a mirror toward birds so that they could see how beautiful they were. Why, at the end of the story, does she hold a mirror out for Aaron?

Comparing Characters

Now that you have read about Aaron, finish filling in your chart. Add the final question and answer it.

	Jerry	Aaron
What are the character's traits?		
What problems does he face?	whether to spend his money on his father's present or buy cards.	to join the club or obey his mother
What choices does he make?	to sell the card to Rollie	• to fix the bird's wing • to join the boys' club
In what ways are the characters similar and different?		

Vocabulary in Context

VOCABULARY PRACTICE

Synonyms are two or more words that have the same meaning. **Antonyms** are words that have opposite meanings. Decide whether the words in each pair are synonyms or antonyms.

1. skirmish/battle
2. massacre/slaughter
3. stalemate/progress
4. incredulous/believing
5. frenzied/calm
6. divulge/expose
7. contempt/admiration
8. allot/dispense
9. assassinate/kill
10. obsess/worry

VOCABULARY IN WRITING

Think about someone you know who is similar to either Jerry or Aaron. Describe the person using three or more vocabulary words from the list. You could start this way.

> **EXAMPLE SENTENCE**
>
> *Just like Jerry, my friend Andre will* **obsess** *over things like trading cards.*

VOCABULARY STRATEGY: CONTEXT CLUES

Context clues may be found in the words, sentences, and paragraphs that surround an unknown word. These clues can help you interpret unfamiliar words and ideas in stories that you read. **Examples** are one type of context clue. In "Aaron's Gift," for instance, you can figure out the meaning of *frenzied* from the other descriptions of the bird's movements. Example clues are introduced by signal words like *such as, especially, including, like,* and *for example*.

PRACTICE Use the example clue to help you define each boldfaced word.

1. Look for a **periodical,** such as a weekly or monthly magazine.
2. He was guilty of many **peccadillos,** including letting the screen door slam shut.
3. She was fond of quoting **maxims** like "Haste makes waste."
4. Elena loves **crudités,** especially celery sticks and baby carrots.

VOCABULARY PRACTICE
For more practice, go to the **Vocabulary Center** at **ClassZone.com.**

Writing for Assessment

1. READ THE PROMPT

You've just read two stories about boys making difficult choices. In writing assessments, you will often be asked to compare and contrast two works that are similar in some way, such as two short stories with similar characters.

PROMPT

In three paragraphs, compare Jerry in "President Cleveland, Where Are You?" to Aaron in "Aaron's Gift." Consider each character's traits, the conflicts he faces, and the choice or choices he has to make. Use details from each of the two stories to support your response.

◀ **STRATEGIES IN ACTION**

1. I need to identify the **similarities and differences** between the two boys.

2. I should include **examples** from the stories about the boys' personal **qualities**, **problems**, and **choices** to support my ideas.

2. PLAN YOUR WRITING

Using the chart you filled in as you read, identify the ways in which the characters are alike and different. Then think about how to present these similarities and differences.

- Decide on a main idea for your response.

- Review the stories to find details that support your ideas.

- Create an outline to organize your response. This sample outline shows one way to organize your paragraphs.

I. Introduce Characters and Main Idea

II. Compare Conflicts They Face

III. Compare Choices They Make

3. DRAFT YOUR RESPONSE

Paragraph 1 Include the title and author of each story. Introduce each main character and summarize his traits. Also include your main idea.

Paragraph 2 Explain the problems that each character faces, using examples from the stories. Include your position on whether the boys' conflicts are similar or different.

Paragraph 3 Explain the choices each character makes. Then explain how the boys are similar and different based on the choices they make.

Revision Make sure it's always clear which boy you are writing about by using names when appropriate and not overusing the pronoun *he*.

from **Smallville**

Television Clip on ⊙ *MediaSmart* DVD

What is a character's true IDENTITY?

KEY IDEA One of the most enjoyable things about watching TV is getting to know interesting characters. Think about your favorite TV character. What makes him or her seem like a real person? To explore how TV makes characters believable, you will watch a scene that shows a **superhero** deal with a problem you may have faced yourself.

Background

Teen of Steel Fans of Superman know him as the "man of steel." He uses his amazing powers to save ordinary people from disaster. The TV series *Smallville* is about Superman before he became a hero. The show focuses on his secret identity of Clark Kent. It portrays Clark as a real teenager struggling to fit in, rather than as a perfect hero.

Clark has been raised by his adoptive parents in Smallville, Kansas. They found him as a toddler after he crashed to Earth in a spaceship. Now Clark is a teenager, and doesn't always agree with his parents' advice on how to control his newly developed superpowers.

Media Literacy: TV Characters

When studying film or TV, it helps to think of moviemakers as storytellers who use pictures as well as words. Writers use physical description, dialogue, and characters' thoughts and actions to make them real. Visual storytellers use facial expressions, body language, and camera shots and

DEVELOPING TV CHARACTERS

Physical Appearance
- facial expressions
- body language
- costumes
- height, weight, and build

Camera Shots
- **close-up shot:** a detailed view that can focus on a person's face or hand
- **medium shot:** showing one or more characters from the waist up

Behavior
- actions
- dialogue
- attitude
- interactions with others

Camera Movement
- follows the action of a scene
- changes the view of a character to reveal emotion

movement to bring their characters to life.

STRATEGIES FOR ANALYZING CHARACTER DEVELOPMENT

- Follow a character's emotions throughout a scene. The actor's **facial expressions** and **body language** will reveal how he or she feels about people and events.
- Pay attention to the actors' **costumes.** In a TV show, clothing can give you clues to a character's personality and background.
- Be aware of the types of shots the director chooses. **Close-ups** are often used to reveal a character's feelings. **Medium shots** can show how characters react to others.
- Watch for **camera movement.** Notice the camera move in close to focus on a facial expression as a character's mood changes or emotion rises.

⊙ MediaSmart DVD

- **TV Series:** *Smallville*
- **Director:** Greg Beeman
- **Genre:** Sci-fi adventure
- **Running Time:** 4 minutes

Viewing Guide for

Smallville

The *Smallville* series begins when Clark Kent is just starting to develop the superpowers that will make him Superman. He struggles to control his powers and act like a normal teenager. His parents have decided that the best thing for him is to keep his gifts a secret, so that he can grow up to live a normal life.

As you watch the scene, pay attention to changes in Clark's emotions. Watch his facial expressions and body language. Notice when he stands tall and proud, and when he slouches. Watch the scene several times, and keep these questions in mind.

NOW VIEW

FIRST VIEWING: Comprehension

1. **Clarify** Why doesn't Clark's father want him to join the football team?

2. **Recall** What causes Clark to use his powers to score the touchdown the second time he gets the ball?

CLOSE VIEWING: Media Literacy

3. **Identify Body Language** When Clark runs onto the football field, he stands tall, with his chest puffed out. How do you think he feels at this moment?

4. **Identify Emotion** In the barn with his father, Clark goes through many emotions. Give an example of one and describe how you know what he is feeling. Consider the **acting** and the **camera shots** and **movement**.

5. **Analyze Character** Even though they are in an argument, it is clear that Clark loves and respects his father. How is that shown in the scene? Think about these points:
   - the actors' **body language** and **tone of voice** when they argue
   - Clark's **facial expressions** when he talks to his father
   - the reason the coach yells at Clark

Write or Discuss

Evaluate Character You've read that the creators of *Smallville* set out to make Clark Kent a real teen with real problems. Think about the scene you viewed. Use what you learned about **appearance, behavior,** and **camera work** to write a brief evaluation of Clark's character. Do you think the show's creators succeeded in making Clark seem like a real teen? Did he react the way you would have in his situation? Think about

- changes in Clark's emotions
- Clark's relationship with his dad
- Clark's decision to play football

Produce Your Own Media

MEDIA TOOLS

For help with creating a character gallery, visit the **Media Center** at **ClassZone.com.**

Create a Character Gallery Imagine you've been hired to cast the actors for a new TV show. You will need actors who can show many different emotions. Create a photo gallery using your classmates as stars of the new show. Take four different pictures of a classmate, showing four different emotions.

HERE'S HOW Use these tips as you create and present your gallery:

- Have your actors use the **facial expressions** and **body language** techniques you noticed in the *Smallville* scene.
- Think about **close-ups** and **medium shots.** Close-ups are perfect for capturing facial expressions. Medium shots work better for posture and other body language.
- Have the rest of the class try to guess the actors' emotions.

Tech Tip

Try using a computer graphics program to present the galleries as a slideshow.

STUDENT MODEL

Role-Playing and Discovery
Personal Essay by Jerry Pinkney

What makes a perfect SATURDAY?

KEY IDEA At the beginning of each week, some people are already looking forward to Saturday. For many, Saturday is a welcome break from their weekday routine. It's a time to relax and spend their **free time** with family and friends. Read "Role-Playing and Discovery" to learn what Jerry Pinkney has to say about some of the best Saturdays of his youth.

DISCUSS With your classmates, talk about your favorite weekend activities. Take turns explaining why each activity is important to you. Then rank the activities to see which are the most popular.

● LITERARY ANALYSIS: PERSONAL ESSAY

Nonfiction writing includes many forms. For example, there are biographies and autobiographies that tell us about the lives of famous people. There are articles that give us information about the world around us. There are also essays. An **essay** is a short nonfiction work that deals with a single subject. An essay in which a writer presents his or her thoughts or feelings about a subject is called a **personal essay.**

As you read "Role-Playing and Discovery," look for the ways Jerry Pinkney expresses his thoughts or feelings.

● READING SKILL: IDENTIFY AUTHOR'S PURPOSE

The **author's purpose** is the reason or reasons that an author has for writing a particular work. Authors write to inform or explain, to express thoughts or feelings, to persuade, or to entertain. Identifying the author's purpose will help you better understand what you are reading.

As you read, find reasons or clues that suggest the author's purpose for writing this essay. Record each reason or clue in the proper column of a chart like the one shown.

To Inform or Explain	To Express Thoughts or Feelings	To Persuade	To Entertain

▲ VOCABULARY IN CONTEXT

In "Role-Playing and Discovery," Jerry Pinkney uses the boldfaced words to help him write about part of his childhood. To see which ones you know, substitute a word with a similar meaning for each boldfaced term.

1. The **impressionable** child was easily convinced.
2. The crowd's **intensity** increased with each touchdown.
3. She answered his question with a **resounding** "No!"
4. The blizzard had a **profound** effect on the small town.

Role-Playing and Discovery

JERRY PINKNEY

On Saturdays, after household chores were finished, I would meet up with my best friends. Off we would rush to the movies. Tickets were ten cents, and there was always a double feature. I was most excited when there were westerns. As a young boy growing up in Philadelphia, Pennsylvania, I dreamed of exploring the early frontier.

My friends and I played at being cowboys and explorers. With much enthusiasm and **intensity,** we inhabited the characters portrayed on the silver screen. We fashioned our costumes and gear from what we could find at home or purchase from the local five-and-dime store. I would whittle out of wood a bowie knife modeled after the one Jim Bowie had at his side while defending the Alamo. I would then take my turn at being Roy Rogers, the cowboy, or Daniel Boone,[1] the famous pioneer, journeying through the rugged wilderness. **A**

ANALYZE VISUALS
What can you **infer** about Bill Pickett from this poster?

intensity (ĭn-tĕn'sĭ-tē) *n.* extreme amount of energy or feeling

A AUTHOR'S PURPOSE
Notice the **details** the author provides. Why does he offer readers this information?

---

1. **Jim Bowie . . . Roy Rogers . . . Daniel Boone:** Bowie (1796–1836) and Boone (1734–1820) were famous historical figures of the American West. Roy Rogers (1911–1998) was a movie and television cowboy from the 1930s through the 1960s.

The Bull-dogger (1923), Ritchey Lithography Corporation. Library of Congress.

If anyone had asked at that time if my excitement was due to an early interest in history, my answer would have been a **resounding**, "No!" However, looking back, I realize that answer would not have been entirely true. Yes, we did have fun, and yes, our flights into the past seemed to be more about action than about learning history, but that role-playing seeded my interest in discovery. When
20 I learned as an adult that one out of three cowboys was black or Mexican, that discovery was moving and **profound**.

I do wonder, though, how we would have been affected as young boys if, at that **impressionable** time, we had known about Nat Love, a cowboy; Bill Pickett, a rodeo cowboy; Jim Beckwourth, a fur trader; or Jean Baptiste Du Sable, the explorer—all persons of African descent. ✎ **B**

important

resounding
(rĭ-zound'ĭng) *adj.*
unmistakable; loud

profound (prə-found')
adj. very deep or great

impressionable
(ĭm-prĕsh'ə-nə-bəl) *adj.*
easily influenced

B **PERSONAL ESSAY**
Reread lines 22–26.
Why did Pinkney save
such a strong statement
for the last paragraph?

NAT LOVE
(1854–1921)
Love became famous
for his skill as a range
rider and marksman.
He was also fluent in
Spanish, and he had his
autobiography published
in 1907.

JEAN BAPTISTE POINTE DU SABLE
(1745–1818)
Du Sable, a trapper
and trader, was born in
Haiti. He is credited
as being the founder of
the city of Chicago.

JIM BECKWOURTH
(1800–1866)
Beckwourth worked
as a trapper and
fur trader, as well
as a scout and mule
driver for the
U.S. Army.

Comprehension

1. **Recall** Who did Jerry Pinkney and his friends pretend to be?

2. **Recall** What was Jean Baptiste Du Sable most famous for?

3. **Clarify** Where did the author and his friends get their costumes?

Literary Analysis

4. **Make Inferences** Reread lines 22–26. If, as a young boy, Pinkney had known about the men "of African descent" he mentions, how do you think it might have affected him?

5. **Identify Author's Purpose** Look back at the notes you made on your chart. What do you think was the author's purpose for writing this essay?

6. **Analyze Cause and Effect** One cause can have many effects. What effects did role-playing have on the author? Make a diagram like the one shown, and fill in the empty boxes using information from the essay.

CAUSE
Attends cowboy movies with his friends in his **free time**

Effect
Role-plays the movie cowboys and explorers with his friends

Effect

Effect

7. **Evaluate a Personal Essay** In most personal essays, the author uses an informal, conversational style to express his or her thoughts and feelings. Do you think Pinkney does this? Explain your answer using details from the essay for support.

Extension and Challenge

8. **Creative Project: Music** Some stories about life in the American West have been kept alive through songs. Create your own song telling about one of the cowboys or explorers mentioned in the essay, or choose another. Present your piece to the class.

9. **Inquiry and Research** Many people became famous figures of the American West. The actors who portrayed them on stage and screen became famous, too. Read the newspaper article on page 265. Then do some research to learn about famous men and women of the American West. Choose one person and find out what made him or her notable. Share your findings with the class.

Annie Oakley, cowgirl

 RESEARCH LINKS
For more on famous men and women of the American West, visit the **Research Center** at **ClassZone.com.**

Vocabulary in Context

VOCABULARY PRACTICE

Choose the letter of the phrase that best connects with each boldfaced word.

1. **impressionable:** (a) an old woman sewing, (b) a van filled with camping supplies, (c) an eager young student
2. **intensity:** (a) a severe thunderstorm, (b) a relaxing piece of music, (c) a tired factory worker
3. **profound:** (a) a very noisy crowd, (b) a very moving story, (c) a very mild infection
4. **resounding:** (a) a nervous speaker, (b) a loud cheer, (c) a relaxing walk

VOCABULARY IN WRITING

Think back to playing your favorite game when you were a child. Did it influence the ideas or interests you have now? Write about the game and how it affected you, using at least two vocabulary words. You could start like this.

> **EXAMPLE SENTENCE**
>
> As a child, I played checkers with great **intensity**.

VOCABULARY STRATEGY: THE LATIN ROOT *press*

The vocabulary word *impressionable* contains the Latin root *press*, which means "to push down." This root is used to form a large number of English words. Use your knowledge of what this root means, along with context clues in the sentence or paragraph, to infer the meaning of unfamiliar words.

```
        impressionable      pressure

                                           depression
                          press
        compressor

                                         repressive
                         suppress
```

PRACTICE Choose the word from the web that best completes each sentence. Consider what you know about the Latin root and the other word parts shown. Refer to a dictionary if you need help.

1. The _____ policies of the government caused the people to rebel.
2. Many students _____ themselves to excel in both sports and school.
3. The lawyer got in trouble for trying to _____ important evidence.
4. If a(n) _____ is punctured, air or gas may leak out.
5. After his father's death, he suffered from severe _____.

VOCABULARY PRACTICE
For more practice, go to the **Vocabulary Center** at **ClassZone.com.**

MAGAZINE ARTICLE In "Role-Playing and Discovery," you read about the heroes who influenced Jerry Pinkney. The following magazine article will tell you more about African-American cowboys in history and in film.

Invisible Hero

BY BILL GWALTNEY

The image of the American cowboy has become synonymous with the West. Yet decades of Hollywood westerns, popular tales, and even operas and classical music have given the world an impression of cowboys that is incorrect in many ways. One major inaccuracy is the absence of black cowboys. It is estimated that there were as many as 9,000 cowboys working cattle in the West during the 1800s.

Historian Kenneth Wiggins Porter located lists of trail herd outfits that prove, on the average, cowboys were 63 percent white, 25 percent African American, and about 12 percent Mexican American. A documented 1877 trail outfit listed seven white cowboys, two black cowboys, a black cook, and a Mexican-American horse wrangler (a cowboy who herds saddle horses). An 1874 cattle crew was made up entirely of black cowboys with a white trail boss.

Life as a cowboy answered the call for adventure, the need for regular pay, and a chance to live the free life of a "cowpuncher." The nature of the job made it difficult for racism to take hold as it had in many other aspects of American life.

As the country warmed to western heroes, however, African Americans saw themselves written out of the script. It would be up to people such as black film director Oscar Micheaux to create black westerns. One actor who became widely known in black America was singing cowboy Herb Jeffries, whose movie nickname was the "Bronze Buckaroo." Jeffries's movies included plots similar to those of white westerns and even included a sidekick.

As the 1960s changed America, so too did they change the western movie. Many Hollywood westerns, including Lonesome Dove, Silverado, and The Quick and the Dead, have depicted African Americans as a regular part of their story lines.

The Red Guards

From the Memoir *Red Scarf Girl*
by Ji-li Jiang

What happens when FREEDOM *vanishes?*

KEY IDEA The United States is known as "the land of the free." Its laws state that citizens can travel where they like, worship as they wish, and enjoy whatever music and books they choose. But what if those laws suddenly changed? In "The Red Guards," you'll read about a girl struggling with the loss of **freedoms** she once took for granted.

DISCUSS With a group of classmates, talk about the freedoms that you most cherish. Do you read a newspaper each day? Do you watch the television programs you want to? Can you go into a bookstore and buy any book you choose? Talk about what it means to be able to do these things—and what it would mean to not be able to.

● LITERARY ANALYSIS: AUTHOR'S PERSPECTIVE

An author's personal feelings about a subject affect the way he or she writes about it. The combination of ideas, values, feelings, and beliefs that shape the way an author looks at a topic is called the **author's perspective.** In nonfiction, you can identify the author's perspective by paying attention to

- direct statements by the author that tell what he or she thinks, feels, or cares about
- words he or she uses to describe people, events, and things

As you read "The Red Guards," look for ways the author shows her perspective on events in her childhood.

● READING STRATEGY: IDENTIFY SYMBOL

A **symbol** is a person, place, or thing that stands for something else. A sunrise, for example, might be a symbol of hope or a new beginning. To identify symbols, look for

- things that the author mentions over and over
- objects that seem to have great importance to the author

As you read "The Red Guards," look for objects that serve as symbols. Think about the ideas each symbol represents. Record your thoughts in a chart like the one shown.

Symbol	Stands For
butterfly	freedom, beauty

Review: **Make Inferences**

▲ VOCABULARY IN CONTEXT

The words in Column A help tell about a frightening event. To see how many you know, match each word in Column A with the word in Column B that is closest in meaning.

Column A	Column B
1. zealous	a. harsh
2. indistinct	b. threateningly
3. leniency	c. take
4. aggressively	d. unclear
5. acrid	e. mercy
6. confiscate	f. enthusiastic

Author Online

Tough Times
Ji-li Jiang's (jē-lē jyäng) happy childhood in Shanghai, China, became one of fear when Mao Zedong (mou' dzŭ'dŏng') took over China. Because of their wealth, Jiang and her family were treated harshly by supporters of the Chinese government for years.

Ji-li Jiang born 1954

Bridging the Gap Jiang moved to the United States in 1984. She wrote *Red Scarf Girl* to share her childhood memories of the Cultural Revolution. "By telling my story," Jiang says, "I hope that people will learn about the Cultural Revolution and make sure that such a terrible event will never happen again."

Background

The Cultural Revolution In 1966 Communist Chairman Mao Zedong began his attempt to transform China's government. He enlisted the help of teenage students known as the Red Guards. Squads of Red Guards went from house to house seeking to get rid of all "fourolds"— anything that represented old ideas, old culture, old customs, and old habits. These searches went on for several years and destroyed millions of lives.

MORE ABOUT THE AUTHOR AND BACKGROUND
For more on Ji-li Jiang and the Cultural Revolution, visit the **Literature Center** at ClassZone.com.

THE RED GUARDS

Ji-li Jiang

In the following excerpt, Ji-li Jiang is 12 years old, and the Cultural Revolution is underway. At first a loyal follower of Chairman Mao, Ji-li's perspective changes after her late grandfather's status as a wealthy landlord becomes known. Mao's government considers landlords and their families possible enemies of the people. Now classified by the Red Guards as having "suspicious status," the Jiang family lives in fear.

Mom got home from work that evening looking nervous. She whispered to Dad and Grandma, and as soon as we finished dinner, she told us to go outside and play.

"We have something to take care of," she said. I knew this had something to do with the Cultural Revolution. I wished she would just say so. We were too old to be fooled like little children. But I didn't say anything and went outside with the others. **Ⓐ**

When it was nearly dark, Ji-yun and I went back home, leaving Ji-yong[1] with his friends.

As we entered the apartment, I smelled smoke, **acrid** and choking. I looked around in alarm. But Grandma was sitting alone in the main room, showing no sign of worry.

"Grandma, is there a fire?" we shouted anxiously. "Don't you smell the smoke?"

---

1. **Ji-yun** (jē-yŭn) . . . **Ji-yong** (jē-yŏng): the author's younger sister and brother.

Ⓐ AUTHOR'S PERSPECTIVE
The author is an adult but writes the events as a young girl. Why might this help the reader better understand her perspective than if she had written the events as an adult?

acrid (ăk'rĭd) *adj.* harsh and sharp in taste or odor

ANALYZE VISUALS
What **mood,** or feeling, do the colors in this painting help create?

September (2003), Hung Liu. Oil on canvas, 66″ × 66″. © Hung Liu.

"Hush, hush!" Grandma pulled us to her quickly. "It's nothing. They're just burning some pictures." We looked puzzled. "Your mother heard today that photos of people in old-fashioned long gowns and mandarin jackets are considered fourolds.² So your parents are burning them in the bathroom."

20 "Can we go watch?" I loved looking at pictures, especially pictures of all those uncles and aunts I had never met.

Grandma shook her head. I winked at Ji-yun, and we both threw ourselves into her arms, begging and pleading. As always, she gave in, and went to the bathroom door to ask Mom and Dad.

Mom opened the door a crack and let us in.

The bathroom was filled with thick smoke that burned our eyes and made us cough. Dad passed us a glass of water. "We can't open the window any wider," he said. "The neighbors might notice the smoke and report us."

30 Mom and Dad were sitting on small wooden stools. On the floor was a tin washbowl full of ashes and a few pictures disappearing into flames. At Dad's side was a stack of old photo albums, their black covers stained and faded with age. Dad was looking through the albums, page by page, tearing out any pictures that might be fourolds. He put them in a pile next to Mom, who put them into the fire.

I picked up one of the pictures. It was of Dad, sitting on a camel, when he was about six or seven years old. He was wearing a wool hat and pants with suspenders, and he was laughing. Grandma, looking very young and beautiful and wearing a fur coat, was standing beside him. **B**

40 "Mom, this one doesn't have long gowns or anything," Ji-yun said. "Can't we keep it?"

"The Red Guards might say that only a rich child could ride a camel. And besides, Grandma's wearing a fur coat." She threw it into the fire.

Mom was right, I thought. A picture like that was fourolds.

The flames licked around the edges of the picture. The corners curled up, then turned brown. The brown spread quickly toward the center, swallowing Grandma, then the camel, and finally Dad's woolen hat.

Picture after picture was thrown into the fire. Each in turn curled, melted, and disappeared. The ashes in the washbowl grew deeper. Finally 50 there were no more pictures left. Mom poured the ashes into the toilet and flushed them away. **C**

That night I dreamed that the house was on fire. . . .

B MAKE INFERENCES
Reread lines 36–39. What does this information suggest about how Ji-li's father used to live?

C IDENTIFY SYMBOL
Consider what the photographs symbolize to the Red Guards. What might the photographs symbolize to the Jiang family? Record this information in your chart.

---

2. **mandarin jackets . . . fourolds:** Mandarin jackets are fancy jackets with narrow, stand-up collars. They were one of the "fourolds"—old ideas, old culture, old customs, and old habits—that were forbidden during the Cultural Revolution.

Early in the morning Song Po-po[3] rushed upstairs to tell us the news. All the neighbors were saying that a knife had been found in the communal[4] garbage bin. The Neighborhood Dictatorship Group had declared this to be an illegal weapon, so the entire bin had been searched and some incompletely burned pictures found. In one of them they recognized my Fourth Aunt.[5] Because my Fourth Uncle had fled to Hong Kong right before Liberation, her family was on the Neighborhood
60 Party Committee's list of black families.[6] The weapon was automatically associated with the pictures, and that was enough for Six-Fingers[7] to report to the powerful Neighborhood Party Committee.[8]

All day we were terrified. Grandma and the three of us went to the park immediately after breakfast. This time none of us wanted to play. We just sat together on Grandma's bench.

"Will the Red Guards come?" Ji-yun asked.

"Maybe they will, sweetie," Grandma answered. "We just don't know."

She took out her knitting. I tried to to do the same, but I kept finding myself staring into space with no idea of where I was in the pattern. Ji-yun
70 and Ji-yong ran off to play but always came back to the bench after a few minutes. At four o'clock Grandma sent me to see if anything was happening at home.

I cautiously walked into the alley, alert for anything unusual, but there was no sound of drums or gongs or noise at all. The mop was still on the balcony.[9] I looked into our lane. There were no trucks. Everything seemed calm, and I told Grandma it was safe to go home. **D**

Mom and Dad both came home earlier than usual. Dinner was short and nearly silent. Soon after dinner we turned the lights off and got into bed, hoping that the day would end peacefully after all. I lay for a long
80 while without sleeping but finally drifted into a restless doze. When I heard pounding on the door downstairs, I was not sure whether it was real or a dream.

It was real.

I heard my cousin You-mei ask bravely, "Who's there?"

D AUTHOR'S PERSPECTIVE
Reread lines 63–76. What words and phrases show the intense feeling the author experienced that day?

---

3. **Song Po-po** (sông pō-pō): Jiang family's downstairs neighbor, friend, and former housekeeper.

4. **communal:** used by everyone in the building.

5. **Fourth Aunt:** Ji-li Jiang's aunt. "Fourth" means the fourth child born to the parents.

6. **Because my . . . black families:** The author's uncle had gone to Hong Kong (at that time independent from China) just before Chairman Mao established his government. Because of this, the Communist Party officers in charge of the neighborhood listed the family as opponents of Communism.

7. **Six-Fingers:** the nickname for Mr. Ni, chairman of the Neighborhood Dictatorship Group, who had six fingers on one of his hands.

8. **Neighborhood Party Committee:** the Communist Party officers in charge of a neighborhood.

9. **The mop . . . balcony:** a signal used by the Jiangs to indicate to family members returning home that the Red Guards were not in the house.

Detail of *Women Warriors I* (2004), Hung Liu. Oil on canvas, 24″ × 42″. © Hung Liu.

ANALYZE VISUALS
Does this painting give you a positive or negative sense of the Red Guards?

Six-Fingers's voice replied, "The Red Guards. They're here to search your house. Open up!"

They rushed into Fourth Aunt's apartment downstairs.

At first we could not hear much. Then we heard more: doors slamming, a cry from Hua-hua,[10] crash after crash of dishes breaking
90 overhead, and the **indistinct** voices of the Red Guards.

By this time we were all awake, but no one turned on a light or said anything. We all lay and held our breaths and listened, trying to determine what was going on downstairs. No one even dared to turn over. My whole body was tense. Every sound from my Fourth Aunt's room made me stiffen with dread.

Thirty minutes passed, then an hour. In spite of the fear I began to feel sleepy again.

I was jolted awake by shouts and thunderous knocks. Someone was shouting Dad's name. "Jiang Xi-reng![11] Get up! Jiang Xi-reng!"

indistinct
(ĭn′dĭ-stĭngkt′) *adj.*
not clearly recognizable or understandable

---

10. **Hua-hua** (hwä-hwä): You-mei's daughter; Fourth Aunt's granddaughter.

11. **Jiang Xi-reng** (jyäng shē-rĕng): Ji-li's father, like other people in China, is called by his surname first.

100   Dad went to the door. "What do you want?"

"Open up!" Six-Fingers shouted. "This is a search in passing! The Red Guards are going to search your home in passing."

We often asked somebody to buy something in passing or get information in passing, but I had never heard of searching a house in passing.

Dad opened the door.

The first one in was Six-Fingers, wearing an undershirt and dirty blue shorts and flip-flops. Behind him were about a dozen teenaged Red Guards. Though the weather was still quite warm, they all wore tightly belted army uniforms. Their leader was a **zealous**, loud-voiced girl with
110 short hair and large eyes. **E**

"What's your relationship with the Jiangs living downstairs?" the girl yelled, her hand **aggressively** on her hip.

"He is her brother-in-law," Six-Fingers answered before Dad could open his mouth.

"Oh, so you're a close relative," she said, as if she only now realized that. "**Leniency** for confession, severity for resistance! Hand over your weapons now, or we will be forced to search the house." She stood up straight and stared at Dad.

"What weapons?" Dad asked calmly. "We have no—"
120   "Search!" She cut Dad off with a shouted order and shoved him aside. At the wave of her arm the Red Guards behind her stormed in. Without speaking to each other, they split into three groups and charged toward our drawers, cabinets, and chests. The floor was instantly strewn with their contents.

They demanded that Mom and Dad open anything that was locked, while we children sat on our beds, staring in paralyzed fascination. To my surprise, it was not as frightening as I had imagined through the weeks of waiting. Only Little White[12] was panicked by the crowd and the noise. She scurried among the open chests until she was kicked by a Red Guard.
130 Then she ran up into the attic and did not come down. **F**

I watched one boy going through the wardrobe. He took each piece of clothing off its hanger and threw it onto the floor behind him. He went carefully through a drawer and unrolled the neatly paired socks, tossing them over his shoulder one by one.

I turned my head and saw another boy opening my desk drawer. He swept his hand through it and jumbled everything together before removing the drawer and turning it upside down on the floor. Before he could examine the contents, another one called him away to help move a chest.

---

12. **Little White:** the Jiang family's cat.

zealous (zĕl′əs) *adj.* eager and enthusiastic

E MAKE INFERENCES
Reread lines 106–110. Why do you think the Red Guard is made up mostly of teenagers?

aggressively (ə-grĕs′ĭv-lē) *adv.* in a manner showing readiness to attack

leniency (lē′nē-ən-sē) *n.* tolerance; gentleness

F MAKE INFERENCES
Reread lines 125–130. Jiang stares "in paralyzed fascination." Why is the experience not as frightening as she had imagined it would be?

140   All my treasures were scattered on the floor. The butterfly fell out of its glass box; one wing was crushed under a bottle of glass beads. My collection of candy wrappers had fallen out of their notebook and were crumpled under my stamp album.

    My stamp album! It had been a birthday gift from Grandma when I started school, and it was my dearest treasure. For six years I had been getting canceled stamps from my friends, carefully soaking them to get every bit of envelope paper off. I had collected them one by one until I had complete sets. I had even bought some inexpensive sets with my own allowance. I loved my collection, even though I knew I should not. With
150 the start of the Cultural Revolution all the stamp shops were closed down, because stamp collecting was considered bourgeois.[13] Now I just knew something terrible was going to happen to it. **G**

    I looked at the Red Guards. They were still busy moving the chest. I slipped off the bed and tiptoed across the room. If I could hide it before they saw me . . . I stooped down and reached for the book.

    "Hey, what are you doing?" a voice demanded. I spun around in alarm. It was the Red Guard leader.

    "I . . . I didn't do anything," I said guiltily, my eyes straying toward the stamp album.
160   "A stamp album." She picked it up. "Is this yours?"

    I nodded fearfully.

    "You've got a lot of fourolds for a kid," she sneered as she flipped through it. "Foreign stamps too," she remarked. "You little xenophile."[14]

    "I . . . I'm not . . ." I blushed as I fumbled for words.

    The girl looked at Ji-yong and Ji-yun, who were still sitting on their beds, watching, and she turned to another Red Guard. "Get the kids into the bathroom so they don't get in the way of the revolution." She threw the stamp album casually into the bag of things to be **confiscated** and went back downstairs. She didn't even look at me. **H**
170   Inside the bathroom we could still hear the banging of furniture and the shouting of the Red Guards. Ji-yun lay with her head in my lap, quietly sobbing, and Ji-yong sat in silence.

    After a long time the noise died down. Dad opened the bathroom door, and we fearfully came out.

    The apartment was a mess. The middle of the floor was strewn with the contents of the overturned chests and drawers. Half of the clothes had been taken away. The rest were scattered on the floor along with some old

G AUTHOR'S PERSPECTIVE
Reread lines 140–152. What do you learn about the author's attitude toward the Cultural Revolution?

confiscate (kŏn′fĭ-skāt′) v. to take and keep something that belongs to someone else

H IDENTIFY SYMBOL
The stamp album symbolizes something different to Jiang than it does to the leader of the Red Guards. In your chart, record what it symbolizes to each of them.

---

13. **bourgeois** (bŏŏr-zhwä′): related to members of the middle class—that is, to people like merchants or professionals. Those labeled *bourgeois* were considered suspicious by the Communist Party.

14. **xenophile** (zĕn′ə-fīl′): person who loves foreigners and foreign objects.

copper coins. The chests themselves had been thrown on top of each other when the Red Guards decided to check the walls for holes where weapons could be hidden. Grandma's German clock lay upside down on the floor with the little door on its back torn off.

I looked for my things. The wing of the butterfly had been completely knocked off the body. The bottle holding the glass beads had smashed, and beads were rolling all over the floor. The trampled candy wrappers looked like trash.

And the stamp album was gone forever. ∾ ⒤

⒤ **IDENTIFY SYMBOL**
How does the stamp album act as a symbol here, not only for Jiang, but also for the reader?

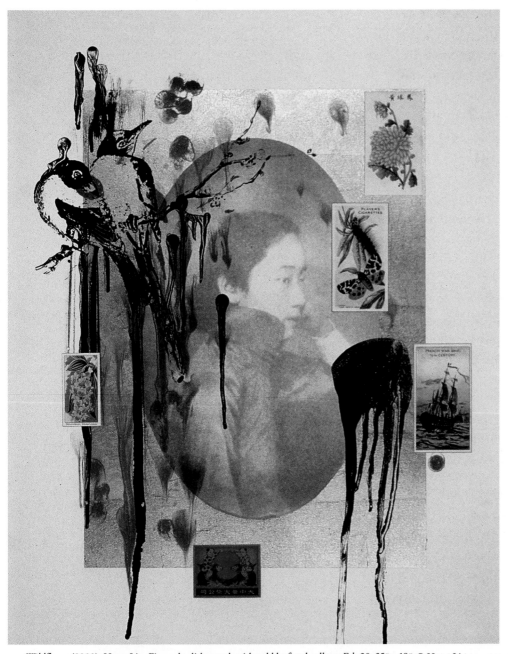

Wildflower (2003), Hung Liu. Five-color lithograph with gold leaf and collage, Ed. 20, 25″ × 19″. © Hung Liu.

ANALYZE VISUALS
What **details** in this piece of art are also mentioned in the **memoir?**

Reading for Information

INTERVIEW In "The Red Guards," you read about some of Ji-li Jiang's experiences during the Cultural Revolution. In the following interview, she explains her reasons for sharing her story with young readers.

BACK   FORWARD   STOP   REFRESH   HOME   PRINT

AN INTERVIEW WITH JI-LI JIANG

Why did you write Red Scarf Girl for young people instead of adults?

In 1984 I moved to the States. The first year, I lived with an American family. They were very interested in my life in China. Using my limited English, I shared some of my stories with them. One day they gave me a present, a book, The Diary of Anne Frank. Inside they wrote: "In the hope that one day we will read the diary of Ji-li Jiang." Of course, I was very moved by the story, and also, I was inspired to write my own story through a little girl's eyes, instead of as an adult looking back. Honestly speaking, I didn't target my readers before I wrote it, but I am glad it turned out to be a children's book. I used to be a teacher in China. If my book has an impact on the kids who read it, I will feel most rewarded . . .

Why did you leave China?

After the Cultural Revolution, things didn't change much. Rigid policies and restrictions kept me from achieving my dream: to enter the Shanghai Drama Institute. I was not allowed to audition. When the universities re-opened, I passed the exam, but because of my family's political situation, I was only accepted into a less prestigious university. After frustration upon frustration, when America opened the door to students from China, I decided to go to the United States. At that time, my only option was to go overseas and study in America. . . .

Ji-li means "lucky and beautiful," a name your parents carefully selected for you. Do you consider yourself lucky?

Yes, I consider myself quite lucky. Despite everything I experienced in China, I have never lacked for love from my family, my friends, and also God. After surviving the Cultural Revolution, I find myself more sensitive to the beauty of nature and the human spirit. I am grateful for having my mind in peace, grateful to have experienced other cultures and lifestyles, and especially grateful that I have been able to do something meaningful and enjoyable to me.

Comprehension

1. **Recall** Why do Ji-li Jiang's mother and father burn the photographs?

2. **Recall** What are the author, her grandmother, and her brother and sister worrying about while they're at the park?

3. **Clarify** Why do the Red Guards search Fourth Aunt's apartment?

Literary Analysis

4. **Draw Conclusions** The lives of Ji-li Jiang and her family have changed because of the Cultural Revolution. What personal rights and **freedoms** have they lost?

5. **Examine Author's Purpose** Reread the interview with Ji-li Jiang on page 276. Was Ji-li Jiang's reason for writing her **memoir** to inform or explain, to persuade, to entertain, or a combination of these? Support your answer with information from the selection.

6. **Identify Author's Perspective** On a chart like the one shown, describe the author's perspective on each topic.

7. **Analyze Symbol** Look at the diagram you completed while reading "The Red Guards." Explain how the symbols and what they mean help you to understand the events that Jiang is writing about.

Topic	Perspective
her family's experience	
the Cultural Revolution	

Extension and Challenge

8. **Inquiry and Research** In her memoir, Ji-li Jiang calls her stamp collection her "dearest treasure." Stamp collecting is a common pastime, but people collect all sorts of items. Do research to find out some of the other items that people collect. Present your findings to the class.

9. **SOCIAL STUDIES CONNECTION** The Cultural Revolution began in China in 1966. This set up a period of chaos and bloodshed that lasted for years. Conduct research to find out what life is like in China today. How have things changed? When did they change? Share your findings with your classmates.

> **RESEARCH LINKS**
> For more on modern Chinese culture, visit the **Research Center** at **ClassZone.com**.

Street in modern-day
Shanghai, China

Vocabulary in Context

VOCABULARY PRACTICE

Choose the word in each item that is not related in meaning to the other words.

1. (a) sharp, (b) bitter, (c) acrid, (d) bland
2. (a) leniency, (b) displeasure, (c) patience, (d) forgiveness
3. (a) calmly, (b) aggressively, (c) coolly, (d) peacefully
4. (a) excited, (b) eager, (c) zealous, (d) prejudiced
5. (a) correct, (b) confiscate, (c) seize, (d) claim
6. (a) unclear, (b) blurred, (c) inspect, (d) indistinct

acrid

aggressively

confiscate

indistinct

leniency

zealous

VOCABULARY IN WRITING

Imagine you are Ji-li Jiang. In one paragraph, explain the worst part about the Red Guards' visit using at least two vocabulary words. Here is a sample beginning.

> **EXAMPLE SENTENCE**
>
> *To see strangers **confiscate** my belongings was terrible.*

VOCABULARY STRATEGY: PREFIXES THAT MEAN "NOT"

A prefix is a word part that appears at the beginning of a base word to form a new word. One example is the vocabulary word *indistinct* (in + distinct). The prefix *in-* is one of several prefixes that can mean "not." Look at the chart to see other prefixes that can mean "not," and to see what other meanings these prefixes may have. To figure out the meaning of a word that contains a prefix and a base word, think of the meaning of each word part separately. Then use this information, as well as any context clues that might be available, to define the word.

Prefix	Meanings
dis-	not; opposite of
in-	not; in
un-	not
mis-	not; incorrectly or badly
non-	not; opposite of

PRACTICE Use these strategies to determine the meaning of each numbered word. Then use each word in a sentence that shows its meaning.

1. disagree
2. nonfiction
3. unlikely
4. incurable
5. misunderstand

VOCABULARY PRACTICE
For more practice, go to the **Vocabulary Center** at ClassZone.com.

Reading-Writing Connection

Deepen your understanding of "The Red Guards" by responding to these prompts. Then complete the **Grammar and Writing** exercise.

A. Short Response: Evaluate Perspective
How does Ji-li Jiang react to her loss of **freedom** at the hands of the Red Guards? Write **one paragraph** describing her thoughts and feelings.

A strong evaluation will . . .
- include a summary of her reactions
- use examples from the selection

B. Extended Response: Write a News Article
The author's description of events in her childhood is full of emotion. The description would be different if a journalist from the United States, for example, were writing about it years later. Write a **two- or three-paragraph news article** about the Red Guards searching the Jiang family home.

A reliable news article will . . .
- present the facts clearly and logically
- answer the questions *Who? What? When? Where? Why?* and *How?*

GRAMMAR AND WRITING

COMPARE CORRECTLY Adjectives and adverbs have special forms that are used to make comparisons. Use the **comparative form** to compare two people or things. Use the **superlative form** to compare three or more people or things. For most one-syllable adjectives and adverbs, add *er* to form the comparative and *est* to form the superlative. For most two-syllable adjectives and adverbs, use *more* instead of *er* and *most* instead of *est*.

Original: Ji-yun was the youngest of the two girls.

Revised: Ji-yun was the younger of the two girls.

PRACTICE Complete the following sentences with the correct form of the adjective or adverb.

1. Of all her cousins, You-mei was the (braver, bravest).
2. Ji-yun and Ji-yong were both sleeping, but Ji-li was (more, most) restless.
3. One girl yelled (more loudly, loudlier) than the other.
4. Out of all her possessions, the stamp album was what Ji-li was (sadder, saddest) about losing.

FOR MORE HELP WITH COMPARATIVE AND SUPERLATIVE FORMS, SEE PAGE R58 IN THE *Grammar Handbook.*

Life Doesn't Frighten Me
Poem by Maya Angelou

On Turning Ten
Poem by Billy Collins

How do we know we're GROWN UP?

KEY IDEA When we hear someone described as **"grown up,"** we know it refers to more than just the person's age. Along with age come new responsibilities, greater independence, and, sometimes, hesitation. The poems you're about to read explore the excitement—and challenges—that growing up can present.

QUICKWRITE What are some ways you think you've grown up over the last few years? Consider any responsibilities you've taken on, such as caring for a pet or doing certain chores. Write these down in your journal. Then describe how you feel in general about growing up.

● LITERARY ANALYSIS: SPEAKER

Just as a short story has a **narrator,** a poem has a **speaker,** or voice that "talks" to the reader. The speaker may be the poet or a fictional character. (Be aware that even when a poem uses the pronouns *I* or *me,* it does not always mean the poet is the speaker.) Identifying the speaker, and understanding his or her situation, is an essential part of discovering the meaning of a poem.

As you read each poem that follows, look for clues in the title and in individual lines that help you determine who the speaker is and what his or her situation is like.

● READING STRATEGY: READING POETRY

A poem can tell a tale or provide a message, just as a short story can. To gain a better understanding of what a poem is saying, use these strategies:

- **Reread the poem.** After reading the poem the first time, read it again. With each reading, you may discover images or ideas you hadn't noticed before.

- **Read the poem aloud.** Poetry is meant to be heard as well as read. Reading it aloud will help you hear the poem's song-like qualities and understand the importance of line breaks.

- **Take notes.** Record any words, phrases, or lines you find particularly interesting. Jot down comments or questions you might have about the speaker or the poem's meaning.

Read "Life Doesn't Frighten Me" and "On Turning Ten" three times. During each reading, use a chart like the one shown to record any images or ideas that help you understand the speaker and the poem's meaning.

	"Life Doesn't Frighten Me"	"On Turning Ten"
1st Reading	The speaker seems pretty brave.	
2nd Reading		
3rd Reading (aloud)		

Life Doesn't Frighten Me

Maya Angelou

Shadows on the wall
Noises down the hall
Life doesn't frighten me at all
Bad dogs barking loud
5 Big ghosts in a cloud
Life doesn't frighten me at all.

Mean old Mother Goose
Lions on the loose
They don't frighten me at all **Ⓐ**
10 Dragons breathing flame
On my counterpane[1]
That doesn't frighten me at all,

ANALYZE VISUALS
Does the girl in this photograph look frightened? Explain.

Ⓐ SPEAKER
Reread lines 1–9. What **details** give clues about the age of the speaker?

---

1. **counterpane:** a bedspread.

I go boo
Make them shoo
15 I make fun
Way they run
I won't cry
So they fly
I just smile
20 They go wild **B**
Life doesn't frighten me at all.

Tough guys in a fight
All alone at night
Life doesn't frighten me at all.

25 Panthers in the park
Strangers in the dark
No, they don't frighten me at all.

That new classroom where
Boys all pull my hair
30 (Kissy little girls
With their hair in curls)
They don't frighten me at all.

Don't show me frogs and snakes
And listen for my scream,
35 If I'm afraid at all
It's only in my dreams.

I've got a magic charm
That I keep up my sleeve,
I can walk the ocean floor
40 And never have to breathe. **C**

Life doesn't frighten me at all
Not at all
Not at all.
Life doesn't frighten me at all.

B READING POETRY
Read lines 13–20 aloud.
Notice how the poem's
structure changes here,
with the lines becoming
shorter. What effect
does this change have
on your reading?

C SPEAKER
Reread lines 37–40.
What do these lines tell
you about the speaker's
personality?

On Turning Ten
Billy Collins

The whole idea of it makes me feel
like I'm coming down with something,
something worse than any stomach ache
or the headaches I get from reading in bad light—
5 a kind of measles of the spirit,
a mumps of the psyche,[1]
a disfiguring chicken pox[2] of the soul. ◖D◗

D **SPEAKER**
Reread the **title** and
lines 1–7. What emotions
is the speaker feeling,
and why?

1. **psyche** (sī′kē): the spirit or soul.
2. **disfiguring chicken pox:** Like measles and mumps, chicken pox was once
   a common childhood disease. It caused pockmarks to appear on the skin,
   sometimes leaving scars behind.

You tell me it is too early to be looking back,
but that is because you have forgotten
10 the perfect simplicity of being one
and the beautiful complexity introduced by two. **E**
But I can lie on my bed and remember every digit.
At four I was an Arabian wizard.
I could make myself invisible
15 by drinking a glass of milk a certain way.
At seven I was a soldier, at nine a prince.

But now I am mostly at the window
watching the late afternoon light.
Back then it never fell so solemnly
20 against the side of my tree house,
and my bicycle never leaned against the garage
as it does today,
all the dark blue speed drained out of it. **F**

This is the beginning of sadness, I say to myself,
25 as I walk through the universe in my sneakers.
It is time to say good-bye to my imaginary friends,
time to turn the first big number.

It seems only yesterday I used to believe
there was nothing under my skin but light.
30 If you cut me I would shine.
But now when I fall upon the sidewalks of life,
I skin my knees. I bleed. **G**

E SPEAKER
To whom do you think
the speaker is talking
in lines 8–11?

F READING POETRY
Reread lines 17–23.
What feelings do
these lines convey?

G SPEAKER
Reread lines 31–32.
What does the speaker
learn about himself?

Comprehension

1. **Recall** In "Life Doesn't Frighten Me," what are three things the **speaker** isn't afraid of?

2. **Recall** In the first **stanza,** or group of lines, in "On Turning Ten," what is turning ten being compared to?

3. **Summarize** How does the speaker of "On Turning Ten" feel about turning one year older?

Literary Analysis

4. **Make Inferences** How might the poems' speakers answer the question "How do we know we're **grown up?**"

5. **Interpret Lines** The speaker in "On Turning Ten" says, "At four I was an Arabian wizard" and "At seven I was a soldier, at nine a prince." What is the speaker referring to in these lines?

6. **Monitor Understanding** Look back at the chart of your first, second, and third readings of the poems. Explain how your understanding of the poems and their speakers changed with each reading. Which lines, words, or phrases had the greatest effect on you?

7. **Compare and Contrast Speakers** Think about the situation each speaker faces and the attitude each one expresses. In what ways are the speakers alike and different? Use a chart like the one shown to record your thoughts.

	"Life Doesn't Frighten Me"	"On Turning Ten"
Who is the speaker?	I think the speaker is a girl.	
What situation does he or she face?		

8. **Make Judgments** Do you think the speaker of "Life Doesn't Frighten Me" isn't really afraid? Use examples from the poem to support your answer.

Extension and Challenge

9. **Speaking and Listening** Based on what you've learned about the poems' speakers, how do you think their voices would sound? Perform a reading of one of the poems for your class. Use a tone of voice that allows the speaker's attitude to come across in your reading.

Writing Workshop

Describing a Person

Have you ever read a description of a person or a character and said, "I know someone just like that!" Maybe you have read a short story like "Eleven" or "President Cleveland, Where Are You?" and wished that you could meet one of the characters because they are described so vividly. To learn how to describe a person or a character, follow the **Writer's Road Map.**

WRITER'S ROAD MAP

Describing a Person

WRITING PROMPT 1

Writing from Your Life Write a focused description of a person. Your description should have many details and should tell why the person is important to you.

People to Consider

- a person you know very well
- a person who has influenced you
- a family member or neighbor who helped you

WRITING PROMPT 2

Writing from Literature The literature in this unit is full of vivid characters. Choose one of the characters you read about. Describe that person as clearly as you can.

Characters to Consider

- Mako in "Ghost of the Lagoon"
- June, the narrator in "Tuesday of the Other June"
- Jerry in "President Cleveland, Where Are You?"

 WRITING TOOLS
For prewriting, revision, and editing tools, visit the **Writing Center** at ClassZone.com.

KEY TRAITS

1. IDEAS
- **Identifies** the person or character
- Focuses on a **main impression** of the person or character

2. ORGANIZATION
- Has a clear **organization,** with an introduction, a body, and a conclusion
- Uses **transitions** to connect ideas
- Provides any **background information** the reader may need

3. VOICE
- Has a direct and respectful **tone**

4. WORD CHOICE
- Uses **sensory details** to show the reader what the person or character is like

5. SENTENCE FLUENCY
- Varies the **lengths of sentences** to make the description lively and interesting

6. CONVENTIONS
- Uses **correct grammar, spelling, and punctuation**

Part 1: Analyze a Student Model

Billy Mayhew
Andrew Jackson Middle School

Uncle Edward

When my friends see me, they say, "Hey, Billy!" or "What's happening?" They smile, and sometimes they pat me on the shoulder. When my uncle Edward sees me, he looks me straight in the eye and says, "William." He says it without a smile. It's as if he's trying out the
5   name for the first time and making sure it fits me. The way he greets me is just the way he always is—serious and in control.

Uncle Edward is a stern man in his sixties. He has wavy silver hair, which is the only soft-looking part of him. He stands as straight as a chimney. Even when Uncle Edward watches TV, he sits straight in his
10   chair and never even leans back. His shirts feel as stiff as cardboard, and you'll never catch him with his shirt untucked. In fact, he looks like a soldier, even though he was never in the military.

The way Uncle Edward stands and moves lets you know that he isn't the kind of guy you call Eddie, or even Ed. All the people I know call
15   him Edward, or else they call him Mr. Mayhew. I'm guessing he never got slapped on the back either. Probably the closest anyone came to doing that was giving him a good, firm handshake.

Uncle Edward has always been the kind of guy who makes the rules or makes sure that no one else breaks them. He used to be a foreman
20   at McKinley Chemical in Lawson, so he got good at barking out orders. The workers there probably did everything he said, the minute he said it. He has the voice of a general, too. It's loud and couldn't be clearer. When he tells me what to do, it never sounds like maybe. For example, when Uncle Edward says to me, "Get me that book" or "Answer the
25   door," I always jump right up. I don't ever wait to find out what would happen if I took my time.

KEY TRAITS IN ACTION

Introduction **identifies** the person and gives a **main impression** of him: he is serious and in control.

The highlighted **sensory details** show rather than tell what Uncle Edward is like. The **tone** is respectful without being stuffy.

Background information gives the reader interesting details about Uncle Edward.

No one in our family ever seems to go against what Uncle Edward says. He makes the decisions. When we're at the family picnic, if Uncle Edward says it's time to eat, it's time to eat. If he says it's time for the annual relay race, then we start the annual relay race. Every Thanksgiving, we eat when Uncle Edward likes to eat, 4:00 sharp. My mom always says, "Oh, Billy, it doesn't really matter to us, but it matters to him."

Although Uncle Edward is tough on the outside, he has a soft center just like my favorite candy bar. Nobody could tell that from his voice or looks. Still, I know it's there because I can tell he wants me to come see him. For example, he always has my favorite cookies in the house, but he never eats any himself. He also always asks me about my life. He'll even smile if I tell him I got a good grade or a great hit at the last baseball game. When I leave, I know he's sorry to see me go. Even though he might not show it, when he says "William," I think he really means "Good to see you, Billy."

Different **sentence lengths** keep the writing from sounding choppy or droning.

Transitions connect ideas and help make the overal **organization** clear.

The **conclusion** summarizes the description and presents a new way of looking at Uncle Edward.

2

Part 2: Apply the Writing Process

PREWRITING

What Should I Do?	What Does It Look Like?

1. Think of a person to write about.
Make a list of people who stand out in your memory. Jot down what is special or important about each. Highlight the one you want to write about.

TIP Think about people you love, people who drive you crazy, and people you respect. Consider fictional characters and famous people, too.

> | Person | What Is Important |
> |---|---|
> | Grandma Liz | smart and kind |
> | Uncle Edward | stern and serious |
> | Mrs. Romanek | terrific, creative teacher |
> | Scott | loyal friend who really knows me |

2. Find a focus.
What is the main point you want to make about this person? For example, is he funny and interesting? Is she a great athlete? Freewrite about your subject.

> **serious, in control all the time**
> - doesn't smile when he says hello
> - sounds like a general or something
> - tells everybody what to do at the family picnic

3. Gather information.
Make a list of what the person does and says. Be sure each detail in your lists helps to show the focus you decided on in step 2.

TIP If you are writing about someone you know, you might want to interview him or her. See page 295 for interviewing tips.

> **Words:** "William" (not "Billy"), "Answer the door," "It's time to eat"
>
> **Actions:** makes the rules, gives commands, sits up straight even when he's watching television

4. Think about sensory details.
What sounds, sights, and other details does this person bring to mind? List details that will make your reader want to keep reading.

TIP Avoid clichés, which are overused expressions. See page 294 for examples of clichés and of fresh, original expressions.

> sight: stands and sits straight, has wavy hair
>
> sound: loud, clear voice that barks out orders
>
> Uncle Edward
>
> touch: stiff shirts

What Should I Do?	What Does It Look Like?

1. Capture your reader's attention.
Make a bold beginning. Use sensory details, exciting dialogue, a quotation, or a contrast to invite your reader to read on.

> **TIP** Are you stuck trying to come up with a great beginning? Try writing the rest of your paper first and then coming back to the introduction.

▶

Sensory details

He stands straight, walks tall, and shouts commands. My Uncle Edward is the most serious person I know.

Contrast

When my friends see me, they say, "Hey, Billy!" or "What's happening?" They smile. When my uncle Edward sees me, he looks me straight in the eye and says, "William." He says it without a smile.

2. Show, don't tell.
Don't just write "he is nice" or "she is weird." Instead, quote words, such as "I'll do that for you, Martha," or describe actions, such as drinking milk with gravy in it. In this excerpt, the writer shows how his uncle can seem a little bit scary.

▶

When he tells me what to do, it never sounds like maybe. For example, when Uncle Edward says to me, "Get me that book," or "Answer the door," I always jump right up.

3. Include some sensory details.
Add some of the details you listed while prewriting. Be sure to use more than just visual details. For example, you might include sounds and textures you associate with the person.

▶

Uncle Edward is a stern man. He has wavy silver hair. This is the only soft-looking part of him. He stands as straight as a chimney. His shirts feel as stiff as cardboard, and you'll never catch him with his shirt untucked.

4. Write a satisfying conclusion.
Your ending can be a final bit of description. It can reveal a lesson that the person taught you. It can also add a new but related idea.

> **TIP** Before revising, consult the key traits on page 288 and the rubric and peer-reader questions on page 294.

▶

Although Uncle Edward is tough on the outside, he is really a kind person. I can tell he wants me to come see him. He also always asks me about my life. When I leave, I know he's sorry to see me go. Even though he might not show it, when he says "William," I think he really means "Good to see you, Billy."

REVISING AND EDITING

What Should I Do?	*What Does It Look Like?*
1. Stick to what's important. • Reread your essay. Do all the details relate to the main idea you want to give your reader about this person? • Cross out unrelated information so that your description stays focused on your main idea.	▶ He makes the decisions. When we're at the family picnic, if Uncle Edward says it's time to eat, it's time to eat. ~~Uncle Edward loves Mom's barbecued ribs.~~ If he says it's time for the annual relay race, then we start the annual relay race.
2. Add background information. • Sometimes writers leave out information that the reader needs. Ask a peer reader to [bracket] parts of your essay that are unclear. • Add explanations or details to help your reader follow your thinking. **See page 294:** Ask a Peer Reader	▶ Peer reader's question: How old is Uncle Edward? Uncle Edward is a stern man, in his sixties. Peer reader's question: What kind of work did Uncle Edward do? He used to be a foreman at McKinley Chemical, so He got good at barking out orders. [The workers there probably did everything he said, the minute he said it.]
3. Strike the right tone. • Read your essay aloud. Do parts seem too formal or slangy? • Choose words that make your description respectful and thoughtful.	▶ ~~He acts all strict and stuff, but I know he's a good guy.~~ Although Uncle Edward is tough on the outside, he has a soft center just like my favorite candy bar.
4. Add variety to your sentences. • Choose a paragraph and count the number of words in each sentence. Are most sentences about the same length? • Revise or combine sentences to create a pleasing rhythm of long and short sentences.	▶ Uncle Edward has wavy silver hair, which ~~This is~~ the only soft-looking part of him. He stands as straight as a chimney.

Apply the Rubric

A strong description of a person or character . . .

- ☑ identifies the person or character and focuses on a main impression of him or her
- ☑ has an introduction, a body, and a conclusion
- ☑ uses sensory details to show rather than tell about the person or character
- ☑ includes helpful background information
- ☑ maintains a tone that is direct and respectful
- ☑ shows how ideas are related by using transitions
- ☑ keeps the description lively by varying sentence lengths

Ask a Peer Reader

- What is important about the person or character I have described?
- Is my description clearly organized? If not, which parts do I need to improve?
- Do I need to add background information? If so, where?

Avoid Clichés

Cliché: Uncle Edward has **a big heart.**

Rewrite: Although Uncle Edward is tough on the outside, he has a soft center just like my favorite candy bar.

Cliché: He is **neat as a pin.**

Rewrite: You'll never catch him with his shirt untucked.

Cliché: He **calls the shots.**

Rewrite: If Uncle Edward says it's time to eat, it's time to eat.

Check Your Grammar

- Use a comma after an introductory phrase.

  In fact, he looks like a soldier.

- Use a comma in a compound sentence.

  He always has my favorite cookies in the house, but he never eats any himself.

See page R49: Quick Reference: Punctuation

Writing Online

PUBLISHING OPTIONS
For publishing options, visit the **Writing Center** at ClassZone.com.

ASSESSMENT PREPARATION
For writing and grammar assessment practice, go to the **Assessment Center** at ClassZone.com.

Conducting an Interview

When you interview someone, you see the world through his or her eyes. Read on to find out how to get the most out of an interview.

Planning the Interview

1. **Find a person to interview.** Choose someone who truly interests you. For example, if you like iguanas, you might interview the owner of a local pet store. If you want to know more about your family history, you might interview a grandparent.

2. **Set up the interview.** Call, write, or e-mail the person. Give your name, your school, and your reason for the interview. If you want to make a video or audio recording, be sure to ask permission for that, too. If the person agrees, ask when and where you can do the interview. You might meet the person in a public place or conduct the interview by telephone, e-mail, or instant message.

3. **Prepare for the interview.** If necessary, read about your subject. Write a long list of questions. Avoid questions that can be answered with a simple "yes" or "no." Ask, "How did you feel during your first day at sea?" not, "Did you like your first day at sea?"

Conducting the Interview

1. **Listen carefully.** Take notes, even if you are recording the interview. If you are conducting the interview in person, make frequent eye contact with the person during the questions and the answers. It's okay to ask, "Can you give me a moment to write that down?"

2. **Ask follow-up questions.** During the interview, remember to say, "Please tell me more about that," or to ask "Why?"

3. **Be courteous.** Show interest and enthusiasm during the interview. When you are done, say thank you. Send the person a handwritten thank-you note afterward.

4. **Write it up.** Your teacher will tell you how to do this. Your work might take the form of a summary, a transcript (a word-for-word "script" telling what was said), or a self-assessment of what went right or wrong.

See page R82: Evaluate an Interview

Reading Comprehension

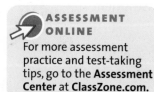

DIRECTIONS *Read these selections and answer the questions that follow.*

from Phoenix Farm

Jane Yolen

So we got ready to head for Grandma's farm up in the valley, with only the clothes we'd been wearing; our cat, Tambourine; and Mama's track medals, all fused together. She found them when the firefighters let us go back upstairs to sort through things. Nicky grabbed a souvenir, too. His old basketball. It was flat and blackened, like a pancake someone left on the stove too long.

I looked around and there was nothing I wanted to take. Nothing. All that I cared about had made it through the fire: Mama, Nicky, and Tam. It was as if we could start afresh and all the rest of it had been
10 burned away. But as we were going down the stairs—the iron stairs, not the wooden ones inside, which were all gone—I saw the most surprising thing. On the thirteenth step up from the bottom, tucked against the riser, was a nest. It was unburnt, unmarked, the straw that held it the rubbed-off gold of a wheat field. A piece of red string ran through it, almost as if it had been woven on a loom. In the nest was a single egg.

It didn't look like any egg I'd ever seen before, not dull white or tan like the eggs from the store. Not even a light blue like the robin's egg I'd found the one summer we'd spent with Grandma at the farm. This was a shiny, shimmery gray-green egg with a red vein—the red
20 thread—cutting it in half.

"Look!" I called out. But Mama and Nicky were already in the car, waiting. So without thinking it all the way through—like, what was I going to do with an egg, and what about the egg's mother, and what if it broke in the car or, worse, hatched—I picked it up and stuck it in the pocket of my jacket. Then, on second thought, I took off the jacket and made a kind of nest of it, and carefully carried the egg and my jacket down the rest of the stairs.

When I got into the car, it was the very first time I had ever ridden in the back all alone without complaining. And all the way to the farm,
30 I kept the jacket-nest and its egg in my lap. All the way.

Dallas and Florida, a brother and sister, have come from an orphanage where they were badly treated. They are staying in the home of Sairy and Tiller.

from Ruby Holler

Sharon Creech

"Look at this place!" Dallas said. "You ever seen anything so amazing? All these trees? All these hills? Is that a creek over there?"

"Dallas, don't you go falling for sweet talk and trees and creeks. We've got to be ready to flee for the hills and catch that train, you hear?"

"I hope you don't mind the sleeping arrangements," Sairy said, as they stepped onto the front porch.

"Where are you putting us?" Florida asked. "In the hog pen?"

"The hog pen?" Tiller said. "I'm afraid we don't have a cockamamie hog pen. I suppose we could build you one though, if you wanted."

10 "You got a snake pit?"

"A snake pit?" Tiller said. "You hankering after a slimy snake pit?"

"No," Florida said.

"Don't mind that sagging porch," Sairy said, leading the way inside. "And our place is kind of small, I know." She paused to smooth a quilt covering a chair. "You'll be upstairs."

"In the attic?" Florida said. "You got a dusty cobwebby attic up there?"

Sairy motioned to the wooden ladder. "It's a loft. See? Up there—it's kind of open to everything down below. I hope you don't mind. All our kids slept up there together. I'm sorry we don't have separate rooms for you."

20 Florida and Dallas scrambled up the ladder into the light, airy loft. Windows overlooked the trees outside and the deep blue mountains beyond. There were four beds in the room, each covered with a brightly colored quilt: hundreds of patches of red and orange and yellow and brilliant green stitched together.

Dallas gazed out at the trees. *It's like a treehouse up here. A treehouse with beds.*

"Up here? Is this where you mean?" Florida called down to Sairy. "In this big huge place? Or is there a cupboard? You going to put us in a cupboard?"

GO ON ➡

30   "I thought you might sleep in those beds. Well, not all of them. Two of them. I hope that's okay," Sairy said. "I hope you'll be comfortable up there."

Dallas sank onto one soft bed. "Florida, this is like floating on a cloud. Try one."

Florida stretched out on another bed. "Probably has bugs in it," she said, jumping up again. "What's the catch? Are they going to fatten us up like Hansel and Gretel and stick us in the oven?"

"Dallas, Florida, could you please come down here?"

"See?" Florida said. "I bet they're going to put us to work now. We're probably going to have to dig a well or something."

40   Downstairs, Sairy and Tiller had laid the table with a yellow tablecloth. Spread across it was a sliced ham, warm applesauce sprinkled with cinnamon, hot corn bread, and green beans. Four places were set.

It's a feast, Dallas thought. *For kings and queens and very important people.*

"You having company? We have to go outside now?" Florida said.

"This is for us," Sairy said. "For the four of us. Two of us and two of you."

Comprehension

DIRECTIONS *Answer these questions about the excerpt from the story "Phoenix Farm."*

1. Which one of these details helps you visualize the destruction from the fire?

   A "Mama's track medals, all fused together" (lines 2–3)

   B "his old basketball" (line 5)

   C "a piece of red string" (line 14)

   D "the jacket-nest and its egg" (line 30)

2. Which phrase from the story helps you visualize the egg?

   A "tucked against the riser" (lines 12–13)

   B "woven on a loom" (line 15)

   C "not even a light blue" (line 17)

   D "shiny, shimmery gray-green" (line 19)

3. You can tell that this story is told from the first-person point of view because the narrator

   A calls herself "I"

   B does not take part in the story's action

   C knows what other characters are feeling

   D is not a character in the story

4. If this story were told from the third-person point of view,

   A the reader would learn about the characters from an outside observer

   B the story would include more descriptive details

   C the narrator would be a character in the story

   D all of the information would come from the main character

5. When the narrator makes a nest for the egg, she shows that she

A loves her home

B acts before she thinks

C needs a pet to care for

D is gentle and caring

DIRECTIONS *Answer these questions about the excerpt from the novel* Ruby Holler.

6. You can tell that this story is told from the third-person point of view because the narrator

A includes all the characters' dialogue

B is not a character in the story

C reveals one character's actions

D describes his or her own thoughts

7. The questions Florida asks Sairy show that she and Dallas

A have had problems in life

B are alike in many ways

C have a close relationship

D have learned to trust people

8. The way Sairy treats the children shows that she is

A selfish   **C** gruff

B timid   D kind

9. The description of the quilts on the children's beds in lines 22–24 helps you visualize a home that is

A simple but welcoming

B too fancy for children

C dusty and run down

D crowded with old furniture

10. Which detail helps you visualize the loft in Sairy and Tiller's house?

A "slimy snake pit" (line 11)

B "dusty cobwebby attic" (line 16)

C "treehouse with beds" (lines 25–26)

D "big huge place" (line 28)

DIRECTIONS *Answer this question about both selections.*

11. Which experience do the main characters in both excerpts have in common?

A eating a feast

B moving to new homes

C losing their homes to fire

D finding old souvenirs

Written Response

SHORT RESPONSE *Write two or three sentences to answer this question.*

12. In "Phoenix Farm," what does the narrator reveal about herself when she says, "All that I cared about had made it through the fire: Mama, Nicky, and Tam"?

EXTENDED RESPONSE *Write a short paragraph to answer this question.*

13. In *Ruby Holler,* how do Dallas and Florida react to their new home? Use examples from the story to support your answer.

GO ON ➡

Vocabulary

DIRECTIONS *Use context clues to answer the following questions.*

1. What is the most likely meaning of the word *fused* in line 3 of the excerpt from "Phoenix Farm"?

   A tied
   B melted
   C knotted
   D nailed

2. What is the most likely meaning of the word *shimmery* in line 19 of the excerpt from "Phoenix Farm"?

   A shaky
   B fragile
   C precious
   D gleaming

3. What is the most likely meaning of the word *flee* in line 4 of the excerpt from *Ruby Holler?*

   A climb
   B march
   C run
   D hide

4. What is the most likely meaning of the word *scrambled* in line 20 of the excerpt from *Ruby Holler?*

   A climbed quickly
   B shouted loudly
   C walked clumsily
   D crawled slowly

DIRECTIONS *Use context clues to help you answer the following questions about words that are easily confused.*

5. Choose the correct word to fill in the blank in the following sentence.

   The teacher wrote the answers on a clean _____ of paper.

   A piece
   B peace
   C peas
   D appease

6. Choose the correct word to fill in the blank in the following sentence.

   Sophie wanted a treat, _____.

   A two
   B to
   C too
   D tow

7. Choose the correct word to fill in the blank in the following sentence.

   The white marble had a thin blue _____ across the middle.

   A vein
   B vane
   C vain
   D van

Writing & Grammar

DIRECTIONS *Read this passage and answer the questions that follow.*

(1) I had a horrible week. (2) On Monday, I was the <u>sadder</u> girl in my class. (3) My dog Ziggy <u>eats</u> garbage and was ill. (4) The next day, <u>me and my friends</u> got in trouble for talking. (5) The school called our parents, and <u>us and our parents</u> had to meet with the teacher. (6) I am <u>cheerfuller</u> today than I was yesterday, though. (7) The sun is shining, and Ziggy <u>wagged</u> his tail. (8) After school, <u>him and me</u> will go to the park together. (9) He is the <u>most great</u> dog ever!

1. Choose the correct superlative to replace the underlined word in sentence 2.

    A most sadder   **C** more sadder

    B most saddest   **D** saddest

2. Choose the correct verb tense to replace the underlined word in sentence 3.

    A ate   **C** is eating

    B will be eating   **D** will eat

3. Choose the correct way to rewrite the underlined words in sentence 4.

    A them and me

    B they and me

    C my friends and me

    D my friends and I

4. Choose the correct way to rewrite the underlined words in sentence 5.

    A us and them

    B we and our parents

    C us and they

    D our parents and us

5. Choose the correct comparative to replace the underlined word in sentence 6.

    A most cheerful

    B more cheerful

    C cheerfullest

    D more cheerfuller

6. Choose the correct verb tense to replace the underlined words in sentence 7.

    A will wag   **C** is wagging

    B had wagged   **D** was wagging

7. Choose the correct way to rewrite the underlined words in sentence 8.

    A he and me   **C** him and I

    B he and I   **D** me and him

8. Choose the correct superlative to replace the underlined words in sentence 9.

    A most greatest   **C** greater

    B more great   **D** greatest

More Great Reads

Ideas for Independent Reading

Which questions from Unit 2 made an impression on you? Continue exploring with these books.

What makes a hero?

The Breadwinner
by Deborah Ellis

Parvana is only 11 when the Taliban orders all the girls and women in Afghanistan to stay in their houses. When her father is arrested, someone must feed her family. Will Parvana be able to do it?

Heck, Superhero
by Martine Leavitt

Heck's mom needs a hero to help her out. But Heck is only a kid, and sometimes even the most wonderful good deed in the world can't change a boy into a superhero—or can it?

A Single Shard
by Linda Sue Park

Tree-ear, an orphan in 12th-century Korea, is a potter's apprentice. When something goes wrong on a journey to the King's Court, Tree-ear must learn that there's more than one way to show true courage.

How do you deal with a bully?

Blubber
by Judy Blume

Jill doesn't really think about it when her whole class picks on Linda. She even helps. But when Wendy, the class leader, makes Jill the next target, Jill gets a taste of bullying from the victim's side.

Indigo's Star
by Hilary McKay

On Indigo's first day back at school, the bullies are already waiting for him. He is saved by the distraction of Tom, a new boy in his class. Will the two be able to work together to survive?

Molly Moon's Incredible Book of Hypnotism
by Georgia Bying

Nobody likes Molly Moon—not even the other orphans. They call her Bog Eyes and Drono. She's also always getting punished. Then one day Molly finds a book on hypnotism that changes her life.

What would you do for your family?

Artemis Fowl
by Eoin Colfer

Twelve-year-old Artemis is the genius son of a criminal mastermind. He decides to steal the fairies' gold to restore his family's fortune and finance his father's rescue operation—if his father is still alive.

Bird
by Angela Johnson

What would you do to get your father back? Bird leaves her mother and takes a bus to Acorn, Alabama, to hide out in a shed and spy on her stepfather. Will she get him to come home?

The Mouse and His Child
by Russell Hoban

Does a wind-up mouse need a mother? This one thinks he does. Follow a toy mouse and his father as they hide from the evil Manny Rat and search for a family all their own.

The Big Idea

UNDERSTANDING THEME

- In Fiction
- In Poetry

What are life's big
LESSONS?

What do you think of when you hear the word *lessons?* You might picture a chalkboard and a textbook, or start sweating at the thought of a quiz. But it is also possible to learn valuable lessons on a Saturday while hanging out with your friends. For instance, you might learn the importance of nurturing a friendship in order to help it grow. You can even learn lessons while reading a powerful book or watching a gripping movie. The messages about life and human nature that writers and directors convey through their work are called **themes.** The themes they share can keep you from having to learn lessons the hard way.

ACTIVITY Choose a book, poem, or movie that taught you one of life's big lessons. Share your choice with a small group and talk about why this message is important to you. Have other members of the group learned similar lessons?

Preview Unit Goals

LITERARY ANALYSIS	• Understand the difference between a topic and a theme • Identify and analyze theme and recurring theme • Read and evaluate historical fiction • Analyze characters, including traits, words, and actions
READING	• Develop strategies for reading, including predicting, visualizing, and setting a purpose • Make inferences • Compare and contrast • Identify main ideas and details; synthesize information
WRITING AND GRAMMAR	• Write an analysis essay • Combine sentences by using compound subjects and predicates • Use commas and coordinating conjunctions correctly when combining sentences
SPEAKING, LISTENING, AND VIEWING	• Participate in a group discussion
VOCABULARY	• Use context clues to determine the meaning of words with multiple meanings • Understand and use base words and suffixes to determine word meaning
ACADEMIC VOCABULARY	• topic • main idea and details • theme • synthesize • recurring theme • sentence combining

Understanding Theme

"Winning isn't everything." "Follow your heart." You've probably learned lessons like these at one time or another. Your own experience is usually the best teacher, but literature can also communicate important truths, or themes. A **theme** is a message about life or human nature that a writer wants readers to understand. In this workshop, you'll learn how to figure out what the stories, poems, and plays you read *really* mean.

Part 1: Topic Versus Theme

Have you heard the fairy tale about the duckling who doesn't fit in? His siblings call him the "ugly duckling" because he looks different from them. In the end, the duckling discovers that he is actually a beautiful swan.

The story of the ugly duckling is about being different. But this is not the theme of the story. It is simply a topic—one or two words that sum up what the story is about. The theme is the writer's message *about* the topic. "It's important to accept people for who they are" or "Differences are what make people special" are two possible themes of the story.

While a topic can be described in a word or two, it takes a complete sentence to describe a theme, as you'll notice in the following example.

EXAMPLE

The Drum
Poem by Nikki Giovanni

daddy says the world is
a drum tight and hard
and i told him
i'm gonna beat
out my own rhythm

TOPICS
• individuality
• being yourself

THEME STATEMENTS
• It's important to be yourself.
• People should march to their own rhythm.
• Individuality is about doing your own thing.

MODEL 1: THEME IN A STORY

Many fables teach lessons about human nature through the actions of animal characters. These lessons communicate important themes. As you read this fable, notice the mistake the dog makes.

The Dog and His Reflection

Fable by **Aesop**

A dog who thought he was very clever stole a steak from a butcher shop. As he ran off with it in his teeth, he crossed a bridge that spanned a small, still river.

As he looked over the side of the bridge and into the water, he saw his
5 own reflection, but he thought it was another dog.

"Hmm," thought the dog, "that other dog has a nice, juicy steak almost as good as the one I have. He's a stupid-looking dog. If I can scare him, perhaps he'll drop his steak and run."

This seemed to the dog to be a perfect plan. But as he opened his
10 mouth to bark, he dropped his steak into the water and lost it.

Close Read

1. Explain how the dog loses the steak he stole from the butcher.

2. What lesson can readers learn from the dog's failed plan to get another steak when he already had one? State the theme of this fable in a sentence.

MODEL 2: THEME IN A POEM

This poem has a message about the topic of beauty.

The Stray Cat

Poem by **Eve Merriam**

It's just an old alley cat
that has followed us all the way home.

It hasn't a star on its forehead,
or a silky satiny coat.

5 No proud tiger stripes, no dainty tread,
no elegant velvet throat.

It's a splotchy, blotchy
city cat, not a pretty cat,
a rough little tough little bag of old bones.

10 "Beauty," we shall call you.
"Beauty, come in."

Close Read

1. Notice the way the cat is described. Would most people consider this cat beautiful? Explain.

2. Reread the boxed lines. Choose the statement that best expresses this poem's theme.
   a. Beauty is something that everyone can agree on.
   b. Different people have different ideas about what is beautiful.

Part 2: Clues to Theme

In some folk tales and stories, the theme is directly stated by a character or the narrator. In most works of literature, though, the theme is not usually revealed in the form of a direct statement. As a reader, you need to **infer,** or guess, the theme. To make a reasonable guess, you have to consider certain clues. The elements in the chart can all serve as clues.

THE CLUES

TITLE

▶ **The title may hint at a theme by highlighting an important idea, setting, or character. Ask:**
- To what in the story does the title refer?
- What ideas does the title emphasize?

PLOT AND CONFLICT

▶ **A story's plot often focuses on a conflict that is important to the theme. Ask:**
- What conflicts do the characters face?
- How are the conflicts resolved?

CHARACTERS

▶ **Characters can reflect a theme by how they act and what they learn. Ask:**
- What are the main characters like? (Notice what they do and say.)
- How do the characters deal with the conflicts?
- How do the characters change?
- What lessons do the characters learn?

SETTING

▶ **A setting can suggest a theme because of the conflicts it creates for the characters. Ask:**
- What conflicts does the setting create?
- How do the characters feel about their surroundings?

Part 3: Analyze the Literature

As you read this folk tale, use the clues you just learned about to help you uncover the theme. The **Close Read** questions will guide you.

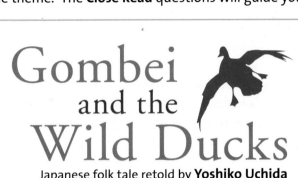

Gombei and the Wild Ducks

Japanese folk tale retold by **Yoshiko Uchida**

Once long ago, in a small village in Japan, there lived a man whose name was Gombei. He lived very close to a wooded marsh where wild ducks came each winter to play in the water for many long hours. Even when the wind was cold and the marsh waters were frozen, the ducks came in great clusters, for they liked Gombei's marsh, and they often stayed to sleep on the ice.

Just as his father had done before him, Gombei made his living by trapping the wild ducks with simple loops of rope. When a duck stepped into a loop, Gombei simply pulled the rope tight and the duck was caught. And like his father before him, Gombei never trapped more than one duck each day.

"After all, the poor creatures come to the marsh never suspecting that they will be caught," Gombei's father had said. "It would be too cruel to trap more than one at a time."

And so for all the years that Gombei trapped, he never caught more than one duck a day.

One cold winter morning, however, Gombei woke up with a dreary ache in his bones. "I am growing too old to work so hard, and there is no reason to continue as my father did for so many years," he said to himself. "If I caught one hundred ducks all at once, I could loaf for ninety-nine days without working at all."

Gombei wondered why he hadn't done this sooner. "It is a brilliant idea," he thought.

The very next morning, he hurried out to the marsh and discovered that its waters were frozen. "Very good! A fine day for trapping," he murmured, and quickly he laid a hundred traps on the icy surface. The sun had not yet come up and the sky was full of dark clouds. Gombei knelt behind a tree and clutched the ends of the hundred rope traps as he shivered and waited for the ducks to come.

Close Read

1. Which character does the title suggest is important to watch? As you read, look for details that show what this character is like and how he changes.

2. Reread the boxed text. What impression do you have of Gombei? Explain whether you see any problems with his plan.

30   Slowly the sky grew lighter and Gombei could see some ducks flying toward his marsh. He held his breath and watched eagerly as they swooped down onto the ice. They did not see his traps at all and gabbled noisily as they searched for food. One by one as the ducks stepped into his traps, Gombei tightened his hold on the ropes.

35   "One—two—three—" he counted, and in no time at all, he had ninety-nine ducks in his traps. The day had not even dawned and already his work was done for the next ninety-nine days. Gombei grinned at his cleverness and thought of the days and weeks ahead during which he could loaf.

40   "One more," he said patiently, "just one more duck and I will have a hundred."

The last duck, however, was the hardest of all to catch. Gombei waited and waited, but still there was no duck in his last trap. Soon the sky grew bright for the sun had appeared at the rim of the wooded

45   hills, and suddenly a shaft of light scattered a rainbow of sparkling colors over the ice. The startled ducks uttered a shrill cry and almost as one they fluttered up into the sky, each trailing a length of rope from its legs.

Gombei was so startled by their sudden flight, he didn't let go of the

50   ropes he held in his hands. Before he could even call for help, he found himself swooshed up into the cold winter sky as the ninety-nine wild ducks soared upward, pulling him along at the end of their traps. . . .

Soon one hand began to slip, a little at first, and then a little more. He was losing his grip on the ropes! Slowly Gombei felt the ropes slide

55   from his numb fingers and finally, he was unable to hold on any longer. He closed his eyes tight and murmured a quick prayer as he plummeted pell-mell down to earth. The wild ducks, not knowing what had happened, flew on trailing their ropes behind like ribbons in the sky.

As Gombei tumbled toward the ground, however, a very strange

60   thing began to take place. First, he sprouted a bill, and then feathers and wings, and then a tail and webbed feet. By the time he was almost down to earth, he looked just like the creatures he had been trying to trap. Gombei wondered if he were having a bad dream. But no, he was flying and flapping his wings, and when he tried to call out, the only

65   sound that came from him was the call of the wild duck. He had indeed become a wild duck himself. Gombei fluttered about frantically, trying to think and feel like a duck instead of a man. At last, he decided there was only one thing to do.

"If I am to be a wild duck, I must live like one," he thought, and he

70   headed slowly toward the waters of a marsh he saw glistening in the sun.

Close Read

3. What happens to Gombei as a result of his actions?

4. In lines 69–70, Gombei returns to a familiar setting—a marsh—but there is nothing familiar about the situation he's in. What conflict do you think he's about to have?

He was so hungry he simply had to find something to eat, for he had not even had breakfast yet. He swooped down to the marsh and looked about hungrily. But as he waddled about thinking only of his empty stomach, he suddenly felt a tug at his leg. He pulled and pulled, but he
75 could not get away. Then he looked down, and there wound around his leg was the very same kind of rope trap that he set each day for the wild ducks of his marsh.

"I wasn't harming anything. All I wanted was some food," he cried. But the man who had set the trap could not understand what Gombei
80 was trying to say. He had been trapped like a wild animal and soon he would be plucked and eaten.

"Oh-h-h-h me," Gombei wailed, "now I know how terrible it is for even one wild duck to be trapped, and only this morning I was trying to trap a hundred poor birds. I am a wicked and greedy man," he thought,
85 "and I deserve to be punished for being so cruel."

As Gombei wept, the tears trickled down his body and touched the rope that was wound tightly about his leg. The moment they did, a wonderful thing happened. The rope that was so secure suddenly fell apart and Gombei was no longer caught in the trap.

90 "I'm free! I'm free!" Gombei shouted, and this time he wept tears of joy. "How good it is to be free and alive! How grateful I am to have another chance," he cried.

As the tears rolled down his face, and then his body, another strange and marvelous thing happened. First, his feathers began to disappear,
95 and then his bill, and then his tail and his webbed feet. Finally he was no longer a duck, but had become a human being once more. . . .

"Never again will I ever trap another living thing," Gombei vowed when he reached home safely. Then he went to his cupboard and threw out all his rope traps and burned them into ash.
100 "From this moment on, I shall become a farmer," he said. "I will till the soil and grow rice and wheat and food for all the living creatures of the land." And Gombei did exactly that for the rest of his days.

As for the wild ducks, they came in ever-increasing numbers, for now they found grain and feed instead of traps laid upon the ice, and they
105 knew that in the sheltered waters of Gombei's marsh they would always be safe.

Close Read

5. Examine the boxed text. What does Gombei realize about himself and his plan? Explain what has caused the change in his attitude.

6. Reread lines 97–102. Why does Gombei decide to become a farmer after he is magically freed?

7. Think about the lesson that Gombei has learned. Choose a topic shown and write a statement that expresses a theme of the story.
   • freedom
   • treatment of others
   • understanding others' problems

The Dog of Pompeii
Short Story by Louis Untermeyer

What would you RISK *for someone else?*

KEY IDEA Some people take **risks** for the excitement of it, whether they are trying a new skateboarding trick or auditioning for a play. Others, such as a student entering a spelling bee, take risks hoping to gain a reward. In "The Dog of Pompeii," one character risks his life simply to help someone else.

LIST IT Brainstorm a list of situations in which you would be willing to take a risk for another person. Compare your lists with those of your classmates. What differences and similarities do you see?

• LITERARY ANALYSIS: THEME VERSUS TOPIC

Most stories center around a **theme,** or an overall message about life that the writer shares with readers. A story's theme is different from its **topic,** or what the story is about.

	Length	Example
Topic	can usually be stated in a word or two	love
Theme	more complex than a topic; usually described in a sentence	Love can help people solve their differences.

One topic of "The Dog of Pompeii" is friendship. As you read, look for the larger message the author wants to share.

● READING STRATEGY: READING HISTORICAL FICTION

Writers of **historical fiction** use a combination of real and made-up settings, events, and characters from the past. The story you are about to read uses a real place, the town of Pompeii, as its **setting.** It also describes a real event— a volcanic eruption. As you read, make a list of details that the author uses to make the story's setting and events come alive. Be sure to include information about food, clothing, transportation, houses, entertainment, and so on.

Review: **Monitor**

▲ VOCABULARY IN CONTEXT

Louis Untermeyer uses the following words to craft his tale of an ancient city. To see how many you know, try to complete each phrase with the appropriate word.

WORD	agonize	dislodge	ponder
LIST	corrupt	emerge	

1. The shaking is able to _____ huge boulders.
2. The citizens _____ over what is happening in their town.
3. They wonder when they can _____ from hiding.
4. The lava begins to _____ the soil, making it unusable.
5. Modern archaeologists _____ the town's ruins.

Author Online

Louis Untermeyer
1885–1977

Passion for Poetry
Though as a young man he worked several jobs within his family's jewelry business, Louis Untermeyer was also constantly writing. He eventually retired from the jewelry business in order to devote more time to writing. Although Untermeyer wrote many stories, poetry was his true passion. During his lifetime, he published more than 100 books and developed friendships with famous poets such as Robert Frost and E. E. Cummings.

Background

Mount Vesuvius Erupts In the year A.D. 79, the volcanic mountain Vesuvius (vĭ-sōō′vē-əs) erupted in southern Italy. It poured burning lava and ashes over the countryside and buried the nearby cities of Pompeii (pŏm-pā′) and Herculaneum (hûr′kyə-lā′nē-əm). Of Pompeii's estimated population of 20,000, at least 2,000 were killed. Pompeii lay undisturbed for almost 1,700 years, until its ruins were discovered in the late 1500s. The remains of the city, preserved by volcanic ash, present a picture of life in the Roman Empire, as if it had been frozen in time.

MORE ABOUT THE AUTHOR AND BACKGROUND
To learn more about Louis Untermeyer and Mount Vesuvius, visit the **Literature Center** at **ClassZone.com.**

The Dog of Pompeii

Louis Untermeyer

Tito and his dog Bimbo lived (if you could call it living) under the wall where it joined the inner gate. They really didn't live there; they just slept there. They lived anywhere. Pompeii was one of the gayest of the old Latin towns, but although Tito was never an unhappy boy, he was not exactly a merry one. The streets were always lively with shining chariots and bright red trappings;[1] the open-air theaters rocked with laughing crowds; sham battles and athletic sports were free for the asking in the great stadium. Once a year the Caesar[2] visited the pleasure city, and the fireworks lasted for days; the sacrifices in the forum[3] were better than a
10 show. But Tito saw none of these things. He was blind—had been blind from birth. He was known to everyone in the poorer quarters. But no one could say how old he was, no one remembered his parents, no one could tell where he came from. Bimbo was another mystery. As long as people could remember seeing Tito—about twelve or thirteen years—they had seen Bimbo. Bimbo had never left his side. He was not only dog but nurse, pillow, playmate, mother, and father to Tito. **A**

ANALYZE VISUALS
Make inferences about life in Pompeii based on the details in this image.

A HISTORICAL FICTION
Reread lines 3–10. Which **details** in this passage tell you that this story takes place in the past?

---

1. **trappings:** ornamental coverings or decorations.
2. **the Caesar:** the Roman emperor.
3. **forum:** the public square or marketplace of an ancient Roman city.

Illustrations © 1997 by Greg Ruhl.

Did I say Bimbo never left his master? (Perhaps I had better say comrade, for if anyone was the master, it was Bimbo.) I was wrong. Bimbo did trust Tito alone exactly three times a day. It was a fixed
20 routine, a custom understood between boy and dog since the beginning of their friendship, and the way it worked was this: Early in the morning, shortly after dawn, while Tito was still dreaming, Bimbo would disappear. When Tito woke, Bimbo would be sitting quietly at his side, his ears cocked, his stump of a tail tapping the ground, and a fresh-baked bread— more like a large round roll—at his feet. Tito would stretch himself; Bimbo would yawn; then they would breakfast. At noon, no matter where they happened to be, Bimbo would put his paw on Tito's knee, and the two of them would return to the inner gate. Tito would curl up in the corner (almost like a dog) and go to sleep, while Bimbo, looking quite
30 important (almost like a boy), would disappear again. In half an hour he'd be back with their lunch. Sometimes it would be a piece of fruit or a scrap of meat; often it was nothing but a dry crust. But sometimes there would be one of those flat, rich cakes, sprinkled with raisins and sugar, that Tito liked so much. At suppertime the same thing happened, although there was a little less of everything, for things were hard to snatch in the evening with the streets full of people. Besides, Bimbo didn't

ANALYZE VISUALS
Compare and contrast this image with your mental picture of the city of Pompeii.

approve of too much food before going to sleep. A heavy supper made boys too restless and dogs too stodgy—and it was the business of a dog to sleep lightly with one ear open and muscles ready for action. **B**

40　　But whether there was much or little, hot or cold, fresh or dry, food was always there. Tito never asked where it came from and Bimbo never told him. There was plenty of rainwater in the hollows of soft stones; the old egg-woman at the corner sometimes gave him a cupful of strong goat's milk; in the grape season the fat winemaker let him have drippings of the mild juice. So there was no danger of going hungry or thirsty. There was plenty of everything in Pompeii if you knew where to find it—and if you had a dog like Bimbo.

As I said before, Tito was not the merriest boy in Pompeii. He could not romp with the other youngsters and play hare and hounds and I 50 spy and follow-your-master and ball-against-the-building and jackstones and kings and robbers with them. But that did not make him sorry for himself. If he could not see the sights that delighted the lads of Pompeii, he could hear and smell things they never noticed. He could really see more with his ears and nose than they could with their eyes. When he and Bimbo went out walking, he knew just where they were going and exactly what was happening.

　　"Ah," he'd sniff and say as they passed a handsome villa, "Glaucus Pansa is giving a grand dinner tonight. They're going to have three kinds of bread, and roast pigling, and stuffed goose, and a great stew—I think 60 bear stew—and a fig pie." And Bimbo would note that this would be a good place to visit tomorrow.

　　Or, "H'm," Tito would murmur, half through his lips, half through his nostrils. "The wife of Marcus Lucretius is expecting her mother. She's shaking out every piece of goods in the house; she's going to use the best clothes—the ones she's been keeping in pine needles and camphor[4]—and there's an extra girl in the kitchen. Come, Bimbo, let's get out of the dust!"

　　Or, as they passed a small but elegant dwelling opposite the public baths,[5] "Too bad! The tragic poet is ill again. It must be a bad fever this time, for they're trying smoke fumes instead of medicine. Whew! I'm glad 70 I'm not a tragic poet!"

　　Or, as they neared the forum, "Mm-m! What good things they have in the macellum today!" (It really was a sort of butcher-grocer-marketplace, but Tito didn't know any better. He called it the macellum.) "Dates from

B THEME VERSUS TOPIC
How does Bimbo show his loyalty to Tito?

SOCIAL STUDIES CONNECTION

The city of Pompeii was located in what is now southern Italy. In the year A.D. 79, this region was part of the Roman Empire.

---

4. **camphor** (kăm′fər): a strong-smelling substance used to keep moths away.

5. **public baths:** large public complexes with locker rooms, steam rooms, and bathing pools kept at different temperatures. In many parts of the Roman Empire, a trip to the public baths was a daily ritual for many people.

Africa, and salt oysters from sea caves, and cuttlefish, and new honey, and sweet onions, and—ugh!—water-buffalo steaks. Come, let's see what's what in the forum." And Bimbo, just as curious as his comrade, hurried on. Being a dog, he trusted his ears and nose (like Tito) more than his eyes. And so the two of them entered the center of Pompeii. **C**

80   The forum was the part of the town to which everybody came at least once during each day. It was the central square, and everything happened here. There were no private houses; all was public—the chief temples, the gold and red bazaars, the silk shops, the town hall, the booths belonging to the weavers and jewel merchants, the wealthy woolen market, the shrine of the household gods. Everything glittered here. The buildings looked as if they were new—which, in a sense, they were. The earthquake of twelve years ago had brought down all the old structures, and since the citizens of Pompeii were ambitious to rival Naples and even Rome, they had seized the opportunity to rebuild the whole town. And they had done it all within a dozen years. There was scarcely a building that was older than Tito.

90   Tito had heard a great deal about the earthquake, though being about a year old at the time, he could scarcely remember it. This particular quake had been a light one—as earthquakes go. The weaker houses had been shaken down; parts of the outworn wall had been wrecked; but there was little loss of life, and the brilliant new Pompeii had taken the place of the old. No one knew what caused these earthquakes. Records showed they had happened in the neighborhood since the beginning of time. Sailors said that it was to teach the lazy city folk a lesson and make them appreciate those who risked the dangers of the sea to bring them luxuries and protect their town from invaders. The priests said that the gods took

100   this way of showing their anger to those who refused to worship properly and who failed to bring enough sacrifices to the altars and (though they didn't say it in so many words) presents to the priests. The tradesmen said that the foreign merchants had **corrupted** the ground and it was no longer safe to traffic in imported goods that came from strange places and carried a curse with them. Everyone had a different explanation—and everyone's explanation was louder and sillier than his neighbor's.

    They were talking about it this afternoon as Tito and Bimbo came out of the side street into the public square. The forum was the favorite promenade[6] for rich and poor. What with the priests arguing with the

110   politicians, servants doing the day's shopping, tradesmen crying their wares, women displaying the latest fashions from Greece and Egypt, children playing hide-and-seek among the marble columns, knots of

C THEME VERSUS TOPIC
What **details** help you **infer** that Bimbo is important to Tito?

corrupt (kə-rŭpt') v. to cause something to change from good to bad

---

6. **promenade** (prŏm'ə-nād'): a public place for walking and socializing.

soldiers, sailors, peasants from the provinces—to say nothing of those who merely came to lounge and look on—the square was crowded to its last inch. His ears even more than his nose guided Tito to the place where the talk was loudest. It was in front of the shrine of the household gods that, naturally enough, the householders were arguing. 🅓

"I tell you," rumbled a voice which Tito recognized as bath master Rufus's, "there won't be another earthquake in my lifetime or yours. There
120 may be a tremble or two, but earthquakes, like lightnings, never strike twice in the same place."

"Do they not?" asked a thin voice Tito had never heard. It had a high, sharp ring to it, and Tito knew it as the accent of a stranger. "How about the two towns of Sicily that have been ruined three times within fifteen years by the eruptions of Mount Etna? And were they not warned? And does that column of smoke above Vesuvius mean nothing?"

"That?" Tito could hear the grunt with which one question answered another. "That's always there. We use it for our weather guide. When the smoke stands up straight, we know we'll have fair weather; when it
130 flattens out, it's sure to be foggy; when it drifts to the east—"

"Yes, yes," cut in the edged voice. "I've heard about your mountain barometer.[7] But the column of smoke seems hundreds of feet higher than usual, and it's thickening and spreading like a shadowy tree. They say in Naples—"

"Oh, Naples!" Tito knew this voice by the little squeak that went with it. It was Attilio, the cameo[8] cutter. "*They* talk while we suffer. Little help we got from them last time. Naples commits the crimes, and Pompeii pays the price. It's become a proverb with us. Let them mind their own business."

"Yes," grumbled Rufus, "and others, too."

140 "Very well, my confident friends," responded the thin voice, which now sounded curiously flat. "We also have a proverb—and it is this: Those who will not listen to men must be taught by the gods. I say no more. But I leave a last warning. Remember the holy ones. Look to your temples. And when the smoke tree above Vesuvius grows to the shape of an umbrella pine, look to your lives."

Tito could hear the air whistle as the speaker drew his toga about him, and the quick shuffle of feet told him the stranger had gone.

"Now what," said the cameo cutter, "did he mean by that?"

"I wonder," grunted Rufus. "I wonder."

150 Tito wondered, too. And Bimbo, his head at a thoughtful angle, looked as if he had been doing a heavy piece of **pondering**. By nightfall the

🅓 HISTORICAL FICTION
Reread lines 108–115. Note important details about the forum. What does the description tell you about life in Pompeii?

ponder (pŏn′dər) *v.* to think seriously about; reflect on

---

7. **mountain barometer:** A barometer is an instrument for measuring the pressure of air and predicting weather changes. The people of Pompeii used the smoke from the volcano as a sort of barometer.

8. **cameo:** a shell or gem with a picture carved on it.

argument had been forgotten. If the smoke had increased, no one saw it in the dark. Besides, it was Caesar's birthday, and the town was in holiday mood. Tito and Bimbo were among the merrymakers, dodging the charioteers who shouted at them. A dozen times they almost upset baskets of sweets and jars of Vesuvian wine, said to be as fiery as the streams inside the volcano, and a dozen times they were cursed and cuffed. But Tito never missed his footing. He was thankful for his keen ears and quick instinct—most thankful of all for Bimbo.

160   They visited the uncovered theater, and though Tito could not see the faces of the actors, he could follow the play better than most of the audience, for their attention wandered—they were distracted by the scenery, the costumes, the by-play, even by themselves—while Tito's whole attention was centered in what he heard. Then to the city walls, where the people of Pompeii watched a mock naval battle in which the city was attacked by the sea and saved after thousands of flaming arrows had been exchanged and countless colored torches had been burned. Though the thrill of flaring ships and lighted skies was lost to Tito, the shouts and cheers excited him as much as any, and he cried out with the loudest of them.

170   The next morning there were *two* of the beloved raisin and sugar cakes for his breakfast. Bimbo was unusually active and thumped his bit of a tail until Tito was afraid he would wear it out. The boy could not imagine whether Bimbo was urging him to some sort of game or was trying to tell him something. After a while, he ceased to notice Bimbo. He felt drowsy. Last night's late hours had tired him. Besides, there was a heavy mist in the air—no, a thick fog rather than a mist—a fog that got into his throat and scraped it and made him cough. He walked as far as the marine gate to get a breath of the sea. But the blanket of haze had spread all over the bay, and even the salt air seemed smoky. **E**

180   He went to bed before dusk and slept. But he did not sleep well. He had too many dreams—dreams of ships lurching in the forum, of losing his way in a screaming crowd, of armies marching across his chest, of being pulled over every rough pavement of Pompeii.

    He woke early. Or, rather, he was pulled awake. Bimbo was doing the pulling. The dog had dragged Tito to his feet and was urging the boy along. Somewhere. Where, Tito did not know. His feet stumbled uncertainly; he was still half asleep. For a while he noticed nothing except the fact that it was hard to breathe. The air was hot. And heavy. So heavy that he could taste it. The air, it seemed, had turned to powder, a warm

190 powder that stung his nostrils and burned his sightless eyes.

    Then he began to hear sounds. Peculiar sounds. Like animals under the earth. Hissings and groanings and muffled cries that a dying creature might make **dislodging** the stones of his underground cave.

E THEME VERSUS TOPIC
Reread lines 170–174. Notice the way Tito reacts to Bimbo's behavior. In what way does his reaction suggest that something has changed?

dislodge (dĭs-lŏj′) *v.* to move from a settled position

There was no doubt of it now. The noises came from underneath. He not only heard them—he could feel them. The earth twitched; the twitching changed to an uneven shrugging of the soil. Then, as Bimbo half pulled, half coaxed him across, the ground jerked away from his feet and he was thrown against a stone fountain.

The water—hot water—splashing in his face revived him. He got to
200 his feet, Bimbo steadying him, helping him on again. The noises grew louder; they came closer. The cries were even more animal-like than before, but now they came from human throats. A few people, quicker of foot and more hurried by fear, began to rush by. A family or two—then a section—then, it seemed, an army broken out of bounds. Tito, bewildered though he was, could recognize Rufus as he bellowed past him, like a water buffalo gone mad. Time was lost in a nightmare. **F**

ANALYZE VISUALS
What kind of **mood,** or feeling, do the colors and facial expressions in this illustration create?

F MONITOR
Reread lines 196–199.
Clarify why the water in the fountain is so hot.

THE DOG OF POMPEII   **321**

It was then the crashing began. First a sharp crackling, like a monstrous snapping of twigs; then a roar like the fall of a whole forest of trees; then an explosion that tore earth and sky. The heavens, though Tito could not see them, were shot through with continual flickerings of fire. Lightnings above were answered by thunders beneath. A house fell. Then another. By a miracle the two companions had escaped the dangerous side streets and were in a more open space. It was the forum. They rested here awhile— how long he did not know.

Tito had no idea of the time of day. He could *feel* it was black—an unnatural blackness. Something inside—perhaps the lack of breakfast and lunch—told him it was past noon. But it didn't matter. Nothing seemed to matter. He was getting drowsy, too drowsy to walk. But walk he must. He knew it. And Bimbo knew it; the sharp tugs told him so. Nor was it a moment too soon. The sacred ground of the forum was safe no longer. It was beginning to rock, then to pitch, then to split. As they stumbled out of the square, the earth wriggled like a caught snake, and all the columns of the temple of Jupiter came down. It was the end of the world—or so it seemed. **G**

G **HISTORICAL FICTION**
Reread lines 207–224. Which **details** show you how the eruption has affected the forum and the town?

ANALYZE VISUALS
What do the actions of the people in this illustration suggest about the eruption?

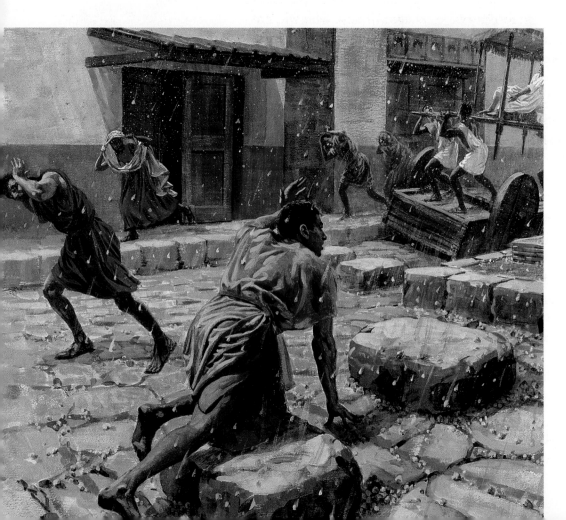

To walk was not enough now. They must run. Tito was too frightened to know what to do or where to go. He had lost all sense of direction. He started to go back to the inner gate; but Bimbo, straining his back to the last inch, almost pulled his clothes from him. What did the creature want? Had the dog gone mad?

230 Then, suddenly, he understood. Bimbo was telling him the way out—urging him there. The sea gate,[9] of course. The sea gate—and then the sea. Far from falling buildings, heaving ground. He turned, Bimbo guiding him across open pits and dangerous pools of bubbling mud, away from buildings that had caught fire and were dropping their burning beams. Tito could no longer tell whether the noises were made by the shrieking sky or the **agonized** people. He and Bimbo ran on—the only silent beings in a howling world.

New dangers threatened. All Pompeii seemed to be thronging toward the marine gate; and, squeezing among the crowds, there was the chance 240 of being trampled to death. But the chance had to be taken. It was growing harder and harder to breathe. What air there was choked him. It was all dust now—dust and pebbles, pebbles as large as beans. They fell on his head, his hands—pumice stones[10] from the black heart of Vesuvius. The mountain was turning itself inside out. Tito remembered a phrase that the stranger had said in the forum two days ago: "Those who will not listen to men must be taught by the gods." The people of Pompeii had refused to heed the warnings; they were being taught now—if it was not too late.

Suddenly it seemed too late for Tito. The red hot ashes blistered his 250 skin; the stinging vapors tore his throat. He could not go on. He staggered toward a small tree at the side of the road and fell. In a moment Bimbo was beside him. He coaxed. But there was no answer. He licked Tito's hands, his feet, his face. The boy did not stir. Then Bimbo did the last thing he could—the last thing he wanted to do. He bit his comrade, bit him deep in the arm. With a cry of pain, Tito jumped to his feet, Bimbo after him. Tito was in despair, but Bimbo was determined. He drove the boy on, snapping at his heels, worrying his way through the crowd; barking, baring his teeth, heedless of kicks or falling stones. Sick with hunger, half dead with fear and sulphur[11] fumes, Tito pounded on, pursued by Bimbo. How long he never 260 knew. At last he staggered through the marine gate and felt soft sand under him. Then Tito fainted. . . . ▯

agonize (ăg'ə-nīz') v. to suffer extreme physical or mental pain

SCIENCE CONNECTION

Mount Vesuvius is a type of volcano called a composite volcano. When composite volcanoes erupt, they release not only pieces of rock but also clouds of hot ash and toxic gases.

H MONITOR
Clarify why Bimbo bites Tito in line 255.

---

9. **sea gate:** a gate in the city wall, leading to the sea.

10. **pumice** (pŭm'ĭs) **stones:** lightweight rocks formed from lava.

11. **sulphur** (sŭl'fər): a pale yellow substance that produces a choking fume when burned.

Someone was dashing seawater over him. Someone was carrying him toward a boat.

"Bimbo," he called. And then louder, "Bimbo!" But Bimbo had disappeared.

Voices jarred against each other. "Hurry—hurry!" "To the boats!" "Can't you see the child's frightened and starving!" "He keeps calling for someone!" "Poor boy, he's out of his mind." "Here, child—take this!"

They tucked him in among them. The oarlocks creaked; the oars splashed; the boat rode over toppling waves. Tito was safe. But he wept continually.

"Bimbo!" he wailed. "Bimbo! Bimbo!"

He could not be comforted.

Eighteen hundred years passed. Scientists were restoring the ancient city; excavators were working their way through the stones and trash that had buried the entire town. Much had already been brought to light—statues, bronze instruments, bright mosaics,[12] household articles; even delicate paintings had been preserved by the fall of ashes that had taken over two thousand lives. Columns were dug up, and the forum was beginning to **emerge.**

It was at a place where the ruins lay deepest that the director paused.

"Come here," he called to his assistant. "I think we've discovered the remains of a building in good shape. Here are four huge millstones that were most likely turned by slaves or mules—and here is a whole wall standing with shelves inside it. Why! It must have been a bakery. And here's a curious thing. What do you think I found under this heap where the ashes were thickest? The skeleton of a dog!"

"Amazing!" gasped his assistant. "You'd think a dog would have had sense enough to run away at the time. And what is that flat thing he's holding between his teeth? It can't be a stone."

"No. It must have come from this bakery. You know it looks to me like some sort of cake hardened with the years. And, bless me, if those little black pebbles aren't raisins. A raisin cake almost two thousand years old! I wonder what made him want it at such a moment." ❶

"I wonder," murmured the assistant. ∾

emerge (ĭ-mûrj′) v. to come into view

❶ THEME VERSUS TOPIC
Reread lines 288–294. What do Bimbo's last actions tell you about him?

---

12. **mosaics** (mō-zā′ĭks): designs formed from inlaid pieces of stone or glass.

Comprehension

1. **Recall** When does Bimbo leave Tito alone?

2. **Recall** Why is the stranger in the forum worried about the column of smoke coming from Vesuvius?

3. **Clarify** What is the source of the fumes and ashes that hurt Tito?

Literary Analysis

4. **Make Inferences** Reread lines 288–290. Why didn't Bimbo have "sense enough to run away" when Mount Vesuvius erupted?

5. **Understand Historical Fiction** Look back at the list of details you recorded as you read the story. Explain why the **setting** is so important in the story.

6. **Identify Theme** Keeping the **topic** of friendship in mind, note important details about Tito and Bimbo's thoughts and actions in a web like the one shown. Then, in the center, write a sentence expressing the story's theme.

Detail:

Detail:

Theme:

Detail:
Bimbo wakes Tito
after Vesuvius

Detail:

7. **Analyze Foreshadowing** A clue or hint about something that will happen later on in a story is called foreshadowing. Reread the conversation between Rufus and the stranger in the forum in lines 118–134. What events are foreshadowed in this passage?

8. **Evaluate a Character** Although historical fiction can contain made-up details and characters, the story should seem as though it really could have happened. Consider whether Bimbo's behavior, both before and after the volcano erupts, is believable. Support your answer.

Extension and Challenge

9. **SCIENCE CONNECTION** There are many famous volcanoes in the world with long and vivid histories. Many are at **risk** of erupting again in the near or distant future. Research one of these volcanoes, and prepare a brief description of one eruption and its effects. Explain the ways in which this eruption was similar to or different from the one that destroyed Pompeii. Share your description with the class.

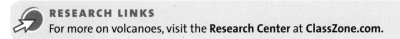

RESEARCH LINKS
For more on volcanoes, visit the **Research Center** at **ClassZone.com**.

Vocabulary in Context

VOCABULARY PRACTICE

Choose the letter of the situation you would connect with each boldfaced word.

1. **agonize:** (a) go on a long, boring drive, (b) suffer through a death in the family, (c) listen to an amusing speaker
2. **corrupt:** (a) a dad working overtime, (b) a politician taking bribes, (c) a child swimming
3. **dislodge:** (a) visit a national park, (b) loosen a stone from a wall, (c) lend a friend cash
4. **emerge:** (a) birds building nests, (b) tulips growing in spring, (c) cars entering a tunnel
5. **ponder:** (a) making a hard decision, (b) canoeing in a lake, (c) missing a meeting

VOCABULARY IN WRITING

Suppose that you are in Pompeii, and the volcano is beginning to erupt. Write about how you feel and what you must do, using two or more vocabulary words. You could start like this.

> **EXAMPLE SENTENCE**
>
> *There is no time to **ponder** the best escape route from this city.*

VOCABULARY STRATEGY: THE LATIN ROOT *rupt*

The vocabulary word *corrupt* contains the Latin root *rupt,* which means "to break." (This root is also found in the story in the word *eruption.*) The root *rupt* is used to form a number of English words. To understand the meaning of words with *rupt,* use your knowledge of what this root means. If you need more help, look for context clues in the sentence or paragraph.

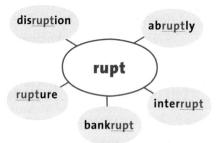

PRACTICE Choose a word from the web that best completes each sentence. Use context clues or, if necessary, a dictionary.

1. He got so far into debt that he went _____.
2. Because she was angry, she ended the conversation _____.
3. They would not stop talking, so finally I had to _____ them.
4. The _____ in the water pipe caused liquid to leak out.
5. A bee flew in the open window, causing a(n) _____ in the classroom.

VOCABULARY PRACTICE
For more practice, go to the **Vocabulary Center** at **ClassZone.com.**

Reading-Writing Connection

Show your understanding of "The Dog of Pompeii" by responding to the following prompts. Then complete the **Grammar and Writing** exercise.

WRITING PROMPTS

A. Short Response: Create a Dialogue
Suppose Bimbo had the ability to speak and had told Tito about his plan to **risk** another trip into Pompeii. What kind of conversation would he and Tito have had? Think about the characters' friendship and the story's theme. Then write a **brief dialogue** in which the two friends share their thoughts at that moment.

B. Extended Response: Write a News Report
Imagine what a person living in a town near Pompeii would have seen or heard when Vesuvius erupted. Write a **two-to-three-paragraph news report** about the tragic event. Be sure to include the major events of the day, as well as details about the warning signs.

SELF-CHECK

A strong dialogue will . . .
- draw on evidence from the story about how the two characters felt about each other
- have Tito express himself in a way similar to the way he speaks in the story

A detailed response will . . .
- use specific details from the story
- give readers an accurate picture of the situation

GRAMMAR AND WRITING

PUNCTUATE DIALOGUE CORRECTLY Correctly punctuated **dialogue** helps readers know which character in a story is speaking. Dialogue is set off from the rest of the text with **quotation marks.** It is often preceded or followed by phrases like *he said* or *she asked,* separated from the quotations by a **comma.** A **period** or comma at the end of a sentence of dialogue should be placed inside the end quotation marks.

Original: Tito said I don't want you to go, Bimbo.

Revised: Tito said, "I don't want you to go, Bimbo."

PRACTICE Rewrite the following sentences. Correct the misplaced punctuation marks and insert any missing marks.

1. "Bimbo, I need you to be my eyes said Tito."
2. Bimbo said, "You will make other friends".
3. Tito said "You are my best friend."
4. I will always be your friend, Bimbo replied.

FOR MORE HELP WITH PUNCTUATING DIALOGUE, SEE PAGE R50 IN THE *Grammar Handbook.*

Pompeii and Vesuvius

- Nonfiction Book Excerpt, page 329
- Online Article, page 334

Use with "The Dog of Pompeii," page 314.

What's the Connection?

You've just read "The Dog of Pompeii," a story that takes place on the day that Mount Vesuvius erupts and buries Pompeii in ash. Now you will learn more about this historical event and what the future may hold for those currently living in the shadow of Mount Vesuvius.

Skill Focus: Synthesize

When you learn something about a topic, you add the new information to your overall knowledge. In other words, you **synthesize** information—or put together facts, details, and ideas from different sources—to gain a better understanding of a topic than you would have if you relied only on one source.

On the next few pages, you will be asked to synthesize information about Pompeii and Mount Vesuvius. To get started, summarize what you learned about the city of Pompeii and the eruption of Vesuvius from "The Dog of Pompeii." Then gather additional facts and details from the selections that follow. Also, notice how your original understanding of the story changes. Record your notes in a chart like the one started here.

Source	Information About Pompeii	Information About Mount Vesuvius
"The Dog of Pompeii"	• It was a rich and lively city filled with open-air theaters, shops, golden chariots, and tourists. • It often had earthquakes.	• A column of smoke usually stood above it, which the people of Pompeii used to tell the weather. • Before the eruption, the column got much taller and thicker.
In Search of Pompeii		
"Italians Trying to Prevent a Modern Pompeii"		

from IN SEARCH OF POMPEII
BY GIOVANNI CASELLI

F OCUS ON FORM
An **informational text** is written material that provides factual information. News articles, encyclopedia entries, timelines, and nonfiction books are examples of informational texts.

Pompeii: The Evidence

Much of our knowledge of Roman life comes from the evidence uncovered at Pompeii. Splendid houses, beautiful paintings, sculptures of bronze and marble, fine glass, metal, and pottery bear witness not only to a city that perished in one day, but also to a long-vanished civilization.

A visit to Pompeii is like entering a time machine: you can see wide streets still with the ruts cut in the paving stones by the wheels of chariots, the entrance to a shop with graffiti on the wall beside it, the baths and grand houses with their wall paintings and
10 colonnaded gardens. But, above all, there are the people of Pompeii, overwhelmed as they tried to escape the horror that overtook their city. Across nearly 2,000 years, their twisted bodies are vivid witnesses of what happened on August 24, A.D. 79. **A**

A SYNTHESIZE
What do you learn about the city of Pompeii in this passage? Record this information in your chart.

FORUM BATHS
Much of Pompeii had running water, carried in by lead pipes under the streets. Public bath complexes used central furnaces to heat the water.

House of the Tragic Poet

Vesuvian gate   Central baths

Temple of Jupiter (Capitol)

Temple of Venus

Stabian baths

Government buildings

Gladiator barracks

B SYNTHESIZE
In "The Dog of Pompeii," Tito and Bimbo rest for a time in the forum. Locate the forum on the diagram. How far away from the forum does the nearest sea gate appear to be? What other places on the diagram do you recall from the story?

FORUM
The Forum was Pompeii's main public space. Crowds gathered to shop in the marketplace, worship at the temples, listen to speeches, or visit government offices and courthouses. **B**

TEMPLE OF ISIS
Ancient Pompeiians participated in a variety of religions. This temple was dedicated to an Egyptian goddess.

Uncovering Pompeii

In December 1860, Victor Emmanuel II, king of the newly united Italy, appointed Giuseppe Fiorelli Director of the Excavations at Pompeii. The era of scientific excavation had begun.

Fiorelli divided the city into quarters, or regions, and gave every block and building a number—a system which is still used today. Archaeologists from all over the world came to see Fiorelli's work at
20 Pompeii.

Slowly and carefully, soil and volcanic debris were removed. The position of every fragment of plaster and brickwork was recorded and then restored to its original place. Charred wood was replaced by fresh timber.

Nola gate

Unexcavated

Sarno gate

Grand palestra

Unexcavated

Swimming pool

Nucerian gate

AMPHITHEATER
The amphitheater was where thousands of Pompeiians gathered to see gladiators, athletic competitions, and other forms of entertainment. **C**

C SYNTHESIZE
In "The Dog of Pompeii," Tito and Bimbo attend the performance of a play in an "uncovered theater." What do the photo and caption here add to your understanding of this place?

A Tragic Day

When the volcano Vesuvius erupted on August 24, A.D. 79, it destroyed a rich and thickly populated part of southern Italy. We know this from the archaeological discoveries at Herculaneum and Pompeii. But, more remarkably, we know what the disaster was actually like for the people who lived in the region.

30   The young Roman nobleman Pliny the Younger witnessed the eruption and wrote a letter that is the earliest known account of such a tragedy. As people screamed and struggled to escape the horror, Pliny described the eruption as looking like "a pine tree, for it shot up to a great height in the form of a trunk, which extended itself at the top into several branches."

COMPOSITE VOLCANO

A composite volcano is a cone-shaped volcano built up of layers of lava and layers of rock fragments. Composite volcanoes have violent eruptions for two reasons. First, expanding gases trapped in rising magma tend to cause explosions. Second, hardened lava from earlier eruptions often plugs openings in these volcanoes. This rock must be blown out of the way before any more magma can escape.

During an eruption, volcanic gases can mix with rock fragments and stay near the ground. The mixture forms a pyroclastic flow, which is a dense cloud of superhot gases and rock fragments that races downhill. **D**

D SYNTHESIZE
In "The Dog of Pompeii," Tito experiences intense heat. What does the caption here reveal about the scientific reasons for this heat?

Magma Core

A Survivor's Letter

"Ashes now fall upon us, though as yet not in great quantity. I looked behind me; gross darkness pressed upon our rear, and came rolling over the land after us like a torrent . . . darkness overspread us, not like that of a moonless or cloudy night, but of a room when it is shut up, and the lamp is put out. You could hear the shrieks of women, the crying of children, and the shouts of men; some were seeking their children, others their parents, others their wives or husbands . . . one lamenting his own fate, another that of his family . . . many lifting their hands to the gods; but the greater part imagining that there were no gods left and that the last and eternal night was come upon the world." **E**

This description from Pliny the Younger's letter to Tacitus is as vivid now as when he wrote it almost 2,000 years ago.

E SYNTHESIZE
What details from Pliny's letter give you a sense of what Pompeii was like during the A.D. 79 eruption? Record this information in your chart.

Italians Trying to Prevent a Modern Pompeii

by Ellen Hale, USA TODAY

SAN SEBASTIANO AL VESUVIO, Italy — Concerned that too many people now crowd the sides of the active volcano, authorities here have launched a bold plan to prevent a repeat of the catastrophic explosion that wiped out Pompeii and smothered thousands of its residents nearly 2,000 years ago.

Authorities hope to thin the ranks of residents so they can be evacuated when Mount Vesuvius erupts again. They are doing this by offering cash incentives to move, demolishing the illegal buildings that have sprouted on its flanks, and establishing a national park at
10 its top.

It's only a matter of time before the volcano does erupt, scientists say.

"It won't be tomorrow, it won't be next month, and maybe it won't be next year. But it is overdue," says Giovanni Macedonio, director of Vesuvius Observatory, the institute responsible for monitoring the volcano. When it blows, Macedonio warns, it could be with the power of "tens of hundreds of atomic bombs."

Vesuvius last erupted in 1944. Lava destroyed some orchards and homes and 26 people were killed. . . . Residents put pots on their heads to protect against rocks shooting through the air, but the
20 rumblings soon stilled. Vesuvius has been quiet since. . . .

During the volcano's 60-year slumber, however, sprawl from nearby Naples has spilled out; nearly 600,000 people now live in the 18 towns in the shadow of the volcano. **F**

F SYNTHESIZE
Add information about modern-day Mount Vesuvius and the surrounding towns to your chart. Consider whether the modern situation is similar to or different from the situation in ancient times.

Comprehension

1. **Recall** According to the online article, how many people could be affected by an eruption of Mount Vesuvius today?

2. **Clarify** Reread page 331. Describe the system Fiorelli used for labeling Pompeii during its excavation.

3. **Summarize** Write a brief summary of the events Pliny the Younger describes in his letter on page 333.

Critical Analysis

4. **Make Inferences About Informational Text** Reread the description of composite volcanoes on page 332. Based on the details in Pliny's letter, what part of the volcano's eruption might he have witnessed? Explain.

5. **Synthesize** Based on everything you have read, predict the future of the region around Mount Vesuvius. Support your prediction using details and examples from the selections.

Read for Information: Evaluate Historical Fiction

WRITING PROMPT

"The Dog of Pompeii" is a made-up story. However, Louis Untermeyer includes real people, places, and events to help bring his story to life. Based on the information you have just read, evaluate Louis Untermeyer's accuracy in describing Pompeii before, during, and after Mount Vesuvius erupted.

To answer this prompt, you will need to do the following:

1. Skim through "The Dog of Pompeii" to create a list of the main events and descriptive details Untermeyer includes.

2. Review the informational texts to see whether the events and descriptive details in the story match what is thought to have occurred in Pompeii when Vesuvius actually erupted.

3. Rate the story's accuracy. Support your rating with evidence from the story and informational texts.

Story Event or Detail	True to the Facts?	Support for Decision
1. The Forum was the central square.	X yes __ no	Map on page 330
2. _____	__ yes __ no	_____

Nadia the Willful

Short Story by Sue Alexander

Can MEMORIES
keep the past alive?

KEY IDEA Memories are how we hold on to people we have known, places we have been, and things we have done. As time goes by, those memories can fade unless we find ways to keep them fresh. In "Nadia the Willful," a character takes action to make sure that a precious memory will last.

QUICKWRITE Think about a happy or important occasion you want to remember. It might be a wedding, a birthday, or a day spent with friends. Write down some ideas about how you can preserve this memory.

Keeping Memories Alive
1. Take photos
2. Make a scrapbook

● LITERARY ANALYSIS: CONFLICT AND THEME

If you have a **conflict,** it means you have a struggle. The struggle might be with someone else, with nature, or even with yourself. In a story, the main conflict affects what the characters think and do, so the conflict often helps express a **theme,** or message about life. To see how a conflict relates to a story's theme, ask yourself the following questions:

- What conflicts does the character face?
- How does the character respond to these conflicts?
- How are the conflicts resolved?

As you read "Nadia the Willful," notice these conflicts and what they reveal about the story's theme.

● READING SKILL: COMPARE AND CONTRAST

When you **compare and contrast,** you identify the ways in which two or more things are alike and different. Comparing and contrasting **characters** can help you better understand a story. For example, in "Nadia the Willful," the character Nadia shares some traits with her family and other members of her community. Other parts of Nadia's personality are unique.

As you read the story, use a graphic organizer like the one shown to record similarities and differences between Nadia, Tarik, and Hamed.

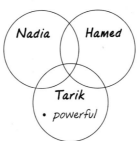

▲ VOCABULARY IN CONTEXT

Sue Alexander uses the following words to help tell how one family deals with sorrow. To see how many words you know, rewrite each sentence using a different word or phrase in place of the vocabulary word.

WORD LIST	banish	clan	console	graciousness

1. Nadia lives in a close-knit family **clan.**
2. Her father's **graciousness** fades away in his sorrow.
3. She wants someone to **console** her after her brother's death.
4. Nadia does not want her father to **banish** anyone.

Author Online

Writing from Life Sue Alexander wrote "Nadia the Willful" to express her sadness about the death of her own brother. She was afraid that if she set the story in the present day, it would be too painful to write.

Sue Alexander born 1933

She knew that it "would have to take place somewhere far away, preferably in another culture." The story took about four months to write, except for the first paragraph, which took much longer. Alexander says, "I must have rewritten it 50 times before I found the right words for that paragraph."

> **MORE ABOUT THE AUTHOR**
> For more on Sue Alexander, visit the **Literature Center** at ClassZone.com.

Background

The Sahara Desert The Sahara, which is the setting for this story, is the largest desert in the world. It is located in northern Africa and covers about 3.5 million square miles—an area about as large as the United States. It is sometimes called "the sea without water." Food and water are scarce, sandstorms are common, and temperatures can reach 130° Fahrenheit during the day. Despite its harsh climate, the Sahara supports approximately 2.5 million people, as well as many kinds of plants and animals.

NADIA THE WILLFUL

SUE ALEXANDER

In the land of the drifting sands where the Bedouin move their tents to follow the fertile grasses, there lived a girl whose stubbornness and flashing temper caused her to be known throughout the desert as Nadia the Willful.

Nadia's father, the sheik[1] Tarik, whose kindness and **graciousness** caused his name to be praised in every tent, did not know what to do with his willful daughter.

Only Hamed, the eldest of Nadia's six brothers and Tarik's favorite son, could calm Nadia's temper when it flashed.

10 "Oh, angry one," he would say, "shall we see how long you can stay that way?" And he would laugh and tease and pull at her dark hair until she laughed back. Then she would follow Hamed wherever he led. **A**

One day before dawn, Hamed mounted his father's great white stallion and rode to the west to seek new grazing ground for the sheep. Nadia stood with her father at the edge of the oasis[2] and watched him go.

Hamed did not return.

1. **sheik** (shēk): a leader of an Arab family or village.
2. **oasis**: a fertile or green spot in a desert or wasteland, made so by the presence of water.

ANALYZE VISUALS
What can you **infer** about the girl in this image?

graciousness
(grā'shəs-nəs) *n.* the condition of being pleasant, courteous, and generous

A **COMPARE AND CONTRAST**
Reread lines 8–12. What do you learn about the personalities of Nadia and Hamed?

Nadia rode behind her father as he traveled across the desert from oasis to oasis, seeking Hamed.

Shepherds told them of seeing a great white stallion fleeing before the
20 pillars of wind that stirred the sand. And they said that the horse carried no rider.

Passing merchants, their camels laden with spices and sweets for the bazaar,[3] told of the emptiness of the desert they had crossed.

Tribesmen, strangers, everyone whom Tarik asked, sighed and gazed into the desert, saying, "Such is the will of Allah."[4]

At last Tarik knew in his heart that his favorite son, Hamed, had been claimed, as other Bedouin before him, by the drifting sands. And he told Nadia what he knew—that Hamed was dead.

Nadia screamed and wept and stamped the sand, crying, "Not even
30 Allah will take Hamed from me!" until her father could bear no more and sternly bade her to silence.

Nadia's grief knew no bounds. She walked blindly through the oasis, neither seeing nor hearing those who would **console** her. And Tarik was silent. For days he sat inside his tent, speaking not at all and barely tasting the meals set before him. **B**

Then, on the seventh day, Tarik came out of his tent. He called all his people to him, and when they were assembled, he spoke. "From this day forward," he said, "let no one utter Hamed's name. Punishment shall be swift for those who would remind me of what I have lost."

40 Hamed's mother wept at the decree. The people of the **clan** looked at one another uneasily. All could see the hardness that had settled on the sheik's face and the coldness in his eyes, and so they said nothing. But they obeyed.

Nadia, too, did as her father decreed, though each day held something to remind her of Hamed. As she passed her brothers at play, she remembered games Hamed had taught her. As she walked by the women weaving patches for the tents and heard them talking and laughing, she remembered tales Hamed had told her and how they had made her laugh. And as she watched the shepherds with their flock, she remembered the
50 little black lamb Hamed had loved.

Each memory brought Hamed's name to Nadia's lips, but she stilled the sound. And each time that she did so, her unhappiness grew until, finally, she could no longer contain it. She wept and raged at anyone and anything that crossed her path. Soon everyone at the oasis fled at her approach. And she was more lonely than she had ever been before. **C**

SOCIAL STUDIES
CONNECTION

The Bedouin are a tribe of people who live in the deserts of Africa and the Middle East. They are nomads, or wanderers, who live in tents and move from place to place seeking pasture for their livestock.

console (kən-sōl´) v. to ease someone's sorrow; to comfort

B COMPARE AND CONTRAST
Note the similarities and differences between how Nadia and Tarik react to Hamed's death.

clan (klăn) n. a family group; a group united by common interests or qualities

C CONFLICT AND THEME
Reread lines 51–55. What conflict does Tarik's decree cause for Nadia?

---

3. **bazaar** (bə-zär´): in Middle Eastern countries, an outdoor market of small shops.

4. **Allah** (ăl´ə): the name for God in the Islamic religion.

One day, as Nadia passed the place where her brothers were playing, she stopped to watch them. They were playing one of the games that Hamed had taught her. But they were playing it wrong.

Without thinking, Nadia called out to them. "That is not the way!
60 Hamed said that first you jump this way and then you jump back!"

Her brothers stopped their game and looked around in fear. Had Tarik heard Nadia say Hamed's name? But the sheik was nowhere to be seen.

"Teach us, Nadia, as our brother taught you," said her smallest brother.

And so she did. Then she told them of other games and how Hamed had taught her to play them. And as she spoke of Hamed, she felt an easing of the hurt within her.

So she went on speaking of him.

She went to where the women sat at their loom[5] and spoke of Hamed. She told them tales that Hamed had told her. And she told how he had
70 made her laugh as he was telling them.

At first the women were afraid to listen to the willful girl and covered their ears, but after a time, they listened and laughed with her.

"Remember your father's promise of punishment!" Nadia's mother warned when she heard Nadia speaking of Hamed. "Cease, I implore you!"

Nadia knew that her mother had reason to be afraid, for Tarik, in his grief and bitterness, had grown quick-tempered and sharp of tongue. But she did not know how to tell her mother that speaking of Hamed eased the pain she felt, and so she said only, "I will speak of my brother! I will!" And she ran away from the sound of her mother's voice. **D**

80 She went to where the shepherds tended the flock and spoke of Hamed. The shepherds ran from her in fear and hid behind the sheep. But Nadia went on speaking. She told of Hamed's love for the little black lamb and

---

5. **loom:** a tool used for making thread or yarn into cloth by weaving strands together at right angles.

D CONFLICT AND THEME
Reread lines 69–79. How has Nadia changed her response to Tarik's order?

ANALYZE VISUALS
What kind of **mood,** or feeling, do the details in this image create?

how he had taught it to leap at his whistle. Soon the shepherds left off their hiding and came to listen. Then they told their own stories of Hamed and the little black lamb.

The more Nadia spoke of Hamed, the clearer his face became in her mind. She could see his smile and the light in his eyes. She could hear his voice. And the clearer Hamed's voice and face became, the less Nadia hurt inside and the less her temper flashed. At last, she was filled with peace.

90 But her mother was still afraid for her willful daughter. Again and again she sought to quiet Nadia so that Tarik's bitterness would not be turned against her. And again and again Nadia tossed her head and went on speaking of Hamed.

Soon, all who listened could see Hamed's face clearly before them.

One day, the youngest shepherd came to Nadia's tent, calling, "Come, Nadia! See Hamed's black lamb; it has grown so big and strong!"

But it was not Nadia who came out of the tent.

It was Tarik.

On the sheik's face was a look more fierce than that of a desert hawk, 100 and when he spoke, his words were as sharp as a scimitar.

"I have forbidden my son's name to be said. And I promised punishment to whoever disobeyed my command. So shall it be. Before the sun sets and the moon casts its first shadow on the sand, you will be gone from this oasis—never to return."

"No!" cried Nadia, hearing her father's words.

"I have spoken!" roared the sheik. "It shall be done!" **E**

Trembling, the shepherd went to gather his possessions.

And the rest of the clan looked at one another uneasily and muttered among themselves.

110 In the hours that followed, fear of being **banished** to the desert made everyone turn away from Nadia as she tried to tell them of Hamed and the things he had done and said.

And the less she was listened to, the less she was able to recall Hamed's face and voice. And the less she recalled, the more her temper raged within her, destroying the peace she had found. **F**

By evening, she could stand it no longer. She went to where her father sat, staring into the desert, and stood before him.

"You will not rob me of my brother Hamed!" she cried, stamping her foot. "I will not let you!"

120 Tarik looked at her, his eyes colder than the desert night.

But before he could utter a word, Nadia spoke again. "Can you recall Hamed's face? Can you still hear his voice?"

Tarik started in surprise, and his answer seemed to come unbidden to his lips. "No, I cannot! Day after day I have sat in this spot where I last saw Hamed, trying to remember the look, the sound, the happiness that was my beloved son—but I cannot."

And he wept.

Nadia's tone became gentle. "There is a way, honored father," she said. "Listen."

130 And she began to speak of Hamed. She told of walks she and Hamed had taken and of talks they had had. She told how he had taught her games, told her tales, and calmed her when she was angry. She told many things that she remembered, some happy and some sad.

And when she was done with the telling, she said gently, "Can you not recall him now, Father? Can you not see his face? Can you not hear his voice?"

Tarik nodded through his tears, and for the first time since Hamed had been gone, he smiled. **G**

"Now you see," Nadia said, her tone more gentle than the softest of the 140 desert breezes, "there is a way that Hamed can be with us still."

The sheik pondered what Nadia had said. After a long time, he spoke, and the sharpness was gone from his voice.

"Tell my people to come before me, Nadia," he said. "I have something to say to them."

When all were assembled, Tarik said, "From this day forward, let my daughter Nadia be known not as willful, but as wise. And let her name be praised in every tent, for she has given me back my beloved son."

And so it was. The shepherd returned to his flock, kindness and graciousness returned to the oasis, and Nadia's name was praised in 150 every tent. And Hamed lived again—in the hearts of all who remembered him. ❧

G COMPARE AND CONTRAST
Reread lines 130–138. Does this passage show more of Nadia and Tarik's similarities or their differences?

Comprehension

1. **Recall** What is Hamed doing when he disappears?

2. **Clarify** Why does Tarik forbid his people to talk about Hamed?

3. **Summarize** What happens to make Tarik send the shepherd away?

Literary Analysis

4. **Make Inferences** Reread lines 145–147. What does Tarik mean when he says that Nadia "has given me back my beloved son"?

5. **Compare and Contrast Characters** Look again at the graphic organizer you filled in as you read. Think about Nadia's and Tarik's personalities, attitudes, reactions, and roles in the story. Are they more similar or more different? Support your answer.

6. **Analyze Conflict and Theme** Recall that the conflict of a story often helps express the story's theme. Use a chart like the one shown to explore the conflict in "Nadia the Willful." Then write a theme statement for the story.

Conflict	How Characters Respond to Conflict	How Conflict Is Resolved
Nadia wants to talk about Hamed, but Tarik forbids it.		

Theme Statement:

7. **Evaluate Theme** A theme should be more than just the author's opinion. It should also express an idea about human nature that everyone can understand. Does Sue Alexander's message about **memories** work well as a theme? Explain why or why not.

Extension and Challenge

8. **Speaking and Listening** Nadia found that the best way to keep her brother's memory alive was to tell stories about him. With a partner, create your own memorable stories. Take turns interviewing each other about interesting parts of your lives. Then choose one or two stories about your partner to share with the class.

9. **SOCIAL STUDIES CONNECTION** Modern life threatens to change the traditional lifestyle of the nomadic Bedouin. Research how the Bedouin way of life has changed over time. What traditions have they been able to keep?

> **RESEARCH LINKS**
> For more on Bedouin culture, visit the **Research Center** at ClassZone.com.

Vocabulary in Context

VOCABULARY PRACTICE

Choose the letter of the word or phrase that means about the same as each boldfaced vocabulary word.

1. member of the **clan:** (a) neighborhood, (b) troop, (c) club, (d) family
2. **console** the sad child: (a) punish, (b) comfort, (c) praise, (d) tease
3. the host's **graciousness:** (a) idea, (b) kindness, (c) schedule, (d) memory
4. **banish** the traitor: (a) force out, (b) catch, (c) trick, (d) ignore

banish

clan

console

graciousness

VOCABULARY IN WRITING

"Nadia the Willful" shows how family members can learn from one another. Write a paragraph about a time you learned something from someone in your family. Use at least one vocabulary word. You could start this way.

> **EXAMPLE SENTENCE**
>
> I didn't think anyone could **console** me after my cat died.

VOCABULARY STRATEGY: NOUN-FORMING SUFFIXES

Suffixes are word parts that are added to the ends of words to form new words. Many common suffixes change adjectives or verbs into nouns. For example, the noun-forming suffix *-ness* can be added to the adjective *gracious* to form the noun *graciousness*. See the chart for other noun-forming suffixes and their meanings.

When you read words with these suffixes, use their base words to figure out their meanings. Remember that sometimes a final *e* is dropped from the base word, or a final letter is changed. For instance, *y* may change to *i*.

Suffixes	Meanings
-cy	state of; quality of being
-dom	
-ity	
-ment	
-ness	
-ship	

PRACTICE Identify the base word and noun-forming suffix in each boldfaced word. Then write a definition of the word.

1. People in charge of **security** in an airport seldom stand out from the crowd.
2. The coach told me not to worry if the **accuracy** of my fastball was a little off.
3. The principal made an **announcement** about the school's new lunchroom policy.
4. Jack's **outrageousness** caused the teacher to punish our whole class.
5. Their **partnership** lasted for many years.

VOCABULARY PRACTICE
For more practice, go to the **Vocabulary Center** at ClassZone.com.

Reading-Writing Connection

Show your understanding of "Nadia the Willful" by responding to these prompts. Then complete the **Grammar and Writing** exercise.

WRITING PROMPTS

A. Short Response: Identify Cause and Effect
Hamed's death begins a long chain of events that results in changes for the entire clan. In **one paragraph,** explain the effect that each event after Hamed's death has on the members of his clan.

SELF-CHECK

A strong analysis will . . .
- identify multiple events caused by Hamed's death
- clearly show how each event led to a change

B. Extended Response: Write Journal Entries
Using the voice of Nadia, write **three brief journal entries.** Describe Nadia's feelings and **memories,** first after Hamed's death, then after Tarik's decree, and finally after Tarik has changed his mind.

Creative journal entries will . . .
- accurately reflect Nadia's personality
- mention key events in the story

GRAMMAR AND WRITING

COMBINE SENTENCES If your sentences seem choppy or repetitious, you may want to try combining them. Look for two sentences that have the same **subject** or **predicate** (what the subject does). If the sentences share a subject, delete the subject from the second sentence. Then insert a word such as *and, or,* or *but* to combine the two predicates. If the sentences share a predicate, delete the predicate from the second sentence. Then combine the two subjects.

> *Original:* Hamed made me happy. Hamed calmed my temper.
>
> *Revised:* Hamed made me happy and calmed my temper. (*Use and to form one sentence with two predicates.*)

PRACTICE Combine the sentences in each item.

1. "Nadia the Willful" discusses the topic of grief. "Nadia the Willful" demonstrates the power of memory.
2. Nadia cried when Hamed died. Her mother cried when Hamed died.
3. Nadia often behaves stubbornly. Nadia treats people nicely sometimes.
4. She traveled in the desert. Tarik traveled in the desert.

FOR MORE HELP WITH COMPOUND SUBJECTS AND PREDICATES, SEE PAGE *R60* IN THE *Grammar Handbook.*

Scout's Honor

Short Story by Avi

When is a trip an ADVENTURE?

KEY IDEA When we think of an **adventure,** we usually think of something big, like an African safari. But even a trip across town can be an adventure, if you're going somewhere you've never been before. In the short story "Scout's Honor," three boys get more adventure than they bargained for when they try to earn a new merit badge.

SKETCH IT How could a simple trip—a visit to a distant relative, for example—become an adventure? Think about what might happen and who you might meet along the way. Sketch a timeline with labels to show how you imagine your potential adventure.

● LITERARY ANALYSIS: CHARACTER AND THEME

When you read a story, you often feel as though you are experiencing the events along with its **characters.** Characters can often help reveal the **theme,** or message about life, that a writer wishes to share with the reader. You can find clues to the theme in

- what the characters say and do
- what lessons the characters learn
- whether the characters change in any way

As you read "Scout's Honor," study the characters to see how they help express the story's theme.

● READING STRATEGY: PREDICT

Predicting what will happen next is one of the things that makes reading exciting. When you **predict,** you use details and clues from a story to make a reasonable guess about events in the story that haven't happened yet.

As you read, use a graphic organizer like the one shown to record important details and clues and what you predict will happen based on the clues.

Clues	Predictions
The narrator has never left Brooklyn before.	→ He might get lost.
	→

▲ VOCABULARY IN CONTEXT

Avi uses the words listed here to help tell the story of a camping **adventure.** To see how many you know, place each word under the heading "Know Well," "Think I Know," or "Don't Know." Then write a brief definition of each word you know.

WORD LIST		
congeal	khaki	retrieve
discard	retort	simultaneously

Know Well	Think I Know	Don't Know

Author Online

Avi
born 1937

A Struggle to Write
From an early age, Avi loved reading. Writing, however, was difficult for him. He had trouble with English classes in school, and some of his teachers thought he was not intelligent. He received failing grades at his first high school and then went to a different one, where he got help from a writing tutor. Avi recalls that the tutor told him, "You know, you're really very interesting. If you wrote better, people would know about it." From that point on, Avi says, "I wanted to write."

Learning from His Mistakes
As an adult, Avi discovered that his problems with writing were partially caused by a learning disability called dysgraphia (dĭs-grăf'ē-ə). People with dysgraphia reverse letters, misspell words, and confuse left and right. Now, Avi often shows his book manuscripts, "which are covered in red marks," to students with learning disabilities. He hopes that by showing students that even a best-selling author makes mistakes, he might inspire them to believe that they, too, can write.

 MORE ABOUT THE AUTHOR
For more on Avi, visit the **Literature Center** at ClassZone.com.

SCOUT'S
HONOR

AVI

Back in 1946, when I was nine, I worried that I wasn't tough enough. That's why I became a Boy Scout. Scouting, I thought, would make a man of me. It didn't take long to reach Tenderfoot rank. You got that for joining. To move up to Second Class, however, you had to meet three requirements. Scout Spirit and Scout Participation had been cinchy. The third requirement, Scout Craft, meant I had to go on an overnight hike in the *country*. In other words, I had to leave Brooklyn, on my own, for the first time in my life.

Since I grew up in Brooklyn in the 1940s, the only grass I knew was in
10 Ebbets Field[1] where the Dodgers played. Otherwise, my world was made of slate pavements, streets of asphalt (or cobblestone), and skies full of tall buildings. The only thing "country" was a puny pin oak tree at our curb, which was noticed, mostly, by dogs. **A**

---

1. **Ebbets Field:** The Los Angeles Dodgers were the Brooklyn Dodgers until the late 1950s. They played in the Ebbets Field stadium.

A PREDICT
Reread lines 7–13. Make a prediction about how easy camping will be for the **narrator.**

11th Floor Water Towers Looking East (2005), Sonya Sklaroff. Oil on panel, 48″ × 48″. Private Collection. © 2005 Sonya Sklaroff. www.goartonline.com.

I asked Scoutmaster Brenkman where I could find some country. Now, whenever I saw Mr. Brenkman, who was a church pastor, he was dressed either in church black or Scout **khaki.** When he wore black, he'd warn us against hellfire. When he wore khaki, he'd teach us how to build fires.

"Country," Scoutmaster Brenkman said in answer to my question, "is
20 anywhere that has lots of trees and is not in the city. Many boys camp in the Palisades."

"Where's that?"

"Just north of the city. It's a park in Jersey."

"Isn't that a zillion miles from here?"

"Take the subway to the George Washington Bridge, then hike across."

I thought for a moment, then asked, "How do I prove I went?"

Mr. Brenkman looked deeply shocked. "You wouldn't *lie,* would you? What about Scout's honor?"

30 "Yes, sir," I replied meekly. **B**

My two best friends were Philip Hossfender, whom we nicknamed Horse, and Richard Macht, called Max because we were not great spellers. They were also Scouts, Tenderfoots like me.

Horse was a skinny little kid about half my size whose way of arguing was to ball up his fist and say, "Are you saying . . . ?" in a threatening tone.

Max was on the pudgy side, but he could talk his way out of a locked room. More importantly, he always seemed to have pocket money, which gave his talk real power.

40 I wasn't sure why, but being best friends meant we were rivals too. One of the reasons for my wanting to be tougher was a feeling that Horse was a lot tougher than I was, and that Max was a little tougher.

"I'm going camping in the Palisades next weekend," I casually informed them.

"How come?" Max challenged.

"Scout Craft," I replied.

"Oh, *that,*" Horse said with a shrug.

"Look," I said, "I don't know about you, but I don't intend to be a Tenderfoot all my life. Anyway, doing stuff in the city is for sissies.
50 Scouting is real camping. Besides, I like roughing it."

"You saying I don't?" Horse snapped.

"I'm not saying nothing," I said.

khaki (kăk'ē) *n.* cloth made of light yellowish brown cotton or wool

⬤ **SOCIAL STUDIES**
⊻ **CONNECTION**

Brooklyn is one of New York City's five major sections, or boroughs. It is located south of Manhattan.

B **PREDICT**
What do you predict will happen? Record this and your other predictions in your graphic organizer.

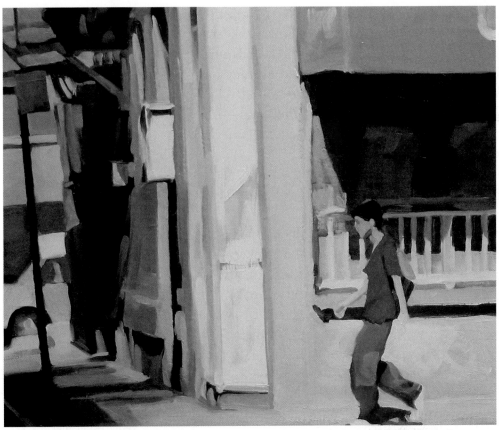

Lafayette Street Morning (2005), Lisbeth Firmin. Oil on panel, 16″ × 16″. Courtesy of Klaudia Marr Gallery, Santa Fe, New Mexico.

ANALYZE VISUALS
Explain in what ways this painting does or does not match your mental picture of the **narrator** leaving for the camping trip.

They considered my idea. Finally, Horse said, "Yeah, well, I was going to do that, but I didn't think you guys were ready for it." **C**

"I've been ready for *years*," Max protested.

"Then we're going, right?" I said.

They looked around at me. "If you can do it, I can do it," Max said.

"Yeah," Horse said thoughtfully.

The way they agreed made me nervous. Now I really was going to have

60 to be tough.

We informed our folks that we were going camping overnight (which was true) and that the Scoutmaster was going with us—which was a lie. We did remember what Mr. Brenkman said about honesty, but we were baseball fans too, and since we were prepared to follow Scout law—being loyal, helpful, friendly, courteous, kind, obedient, cheerful, thrifty, brave, clean, *and* reverent—we figured a 900 batting average[2] was not bad. **D**

C CHARACTER AND THEME
Reread lines 31–54. What do you learn about Horse and Max based on what they say?

D CHARACTER AND THEME
Why do the boys think it is okay that they are telling a lie?

---

2. **900 batting average:** In baseball, a batting average is the number of times a batter gets a hit compared to the number of times he bats. A batting average of .900 is nearly perfect, since it means the batter gets a hit 90% of the time. The boys use this term to mean that since they have followed most of Scout law, they are above-average Scouts, even if they tell a lie.

So Saturday morning we met at the High Street subway station. I got there first. Stuffed in my dad's army surplus knapsack was a blanket, a pillow, and a paper bag with three white-bread peanut-butter-and-jelly sandwiches—that is, lunch, supper, and Sunday breakfast. My pockets were full of stick matches. I had an old flashlight, and since I lived by the Scout motto—Be Prepared—I had brought along an umbrella. Finally, being a serious reader, I had the latest Marvel Family comics.

Horse arrived next, his arms barely managing to hold on to a mattress that seemed twice his size. As for food, he had four cans of beans jammed into his pockets.

Max came last. He was lugging a new knapsack that contained a cast-iron frying pan, a packet of hot dogs, and a box of saltine crackers—plus two bottles. One bottle was mustard, the other, celery soda. He also had a bag of Tootsie Rolls and a shiny hatchet. "To build a lean-to,"[3] he explained.

Max's prize possession, however, was an official Scout compass. "It's really swell," he told us. "You can't ever get lost with it. Got it at the Scout store."

"I hate that place," Horse informed us. "It's all new. Nothing real."

"This compass is real," Max **retorted.** "Points north all the time. You can get cheaper ones, but they point all different directions."

"What's so great about the north?" Horse said.

"That's always the way to go," Max insisted. **E**

"Says who?" I demanded.

"Mr. Brenkman, dummy," Horse cried. "Anyway, there's always an arrow on maps pointing the way north."

"Cowboys live out west," I reminded them. They didn't care.

On the subway platform, we realized we did not know which station we were heading for. To find out, we studied the system map, which looked like a noodle factory hit by a bomb. The place we wanted to go (north) was at the top of the map, so I had to hoist Horse onto my shoulders for a closer look. Since he refused to let go of his mattress—or the tin cans in his pockets—it wasn't easy. I asked him—in a kindly fashion—to put the mattress down.

No sooner did he find the station—168th Street—than our train arrived. We rushed on, only to have Horse scream, "My mattress!" He had left it on the platform. Just before the doors shut, he and I leaped off. Max, however, remained on the train. Helplessly, we watched as his

VISUAL VOCABULARY

compass *n.* a device used to determine geographic direction

retort (rĭ-tôrt') *v.* to reply, especially in a quick or unkind way

E PREDICT
The boys feel that they are prepared with enough food and supplies for their trip. How effective do you predict the boys' camping gear will be?

---

3. **lean-to:** a shelter with a flat, sloping roof.

horror-stricken face slid away from us. "Wait at the next station!" I bellowed. "Don't move!"

The next train took forever to come. Then it took even longer to get to the next stop. There was Max. All around him—like fake snow in a glass ball—were crumbs. He'd been so nervous he had eaten all his crackers.

"Didn't that make you thirsty?"

"I drank my soda."

I noticed streaks down his cheeks. Horse noticed them too. "You been crying?" he asked.

"Naw," Max said. "There was this water dripping from the tunnel roof. But, you said don't move, right? Well, I was just being obedient."

By the time we got on the next train—with all our possessions—we had been traveling for an hour. But we had managed to go only one stop.

During the ride, I got hungry. I pulled out one of my sandwiches. With the jelly soaked through the bread, it looked like a limp scab.

Horse, envious, complained *he* was getting hungry.

"Eat some of your canned beans," I suggested.

He got out one can without ripping his pocket too badly. Then his face took on a mournful look.

"What's the matter?" I asked.

"Forgot to bring a can opener."

Max said, "In the old days, people opened cans with their teeth."

"You saying my teeth aren't strong?"

"I'm just talking about history!"

"You saying I don't know history?"

Always kind, I plopped half my sandwich into Horse's hand. He squashed it into his mouth and was quiet for the next fifteen minutes. It proved something I'd always believed: The best way to stop arguments is to get people to eat peanut butter sandwiches. They can't talk.

Then we became so absorbed in our Marvel Family comics we missed our station. We got to it only by coming back the other way. When we reached street level, the sky was dark.

"I knew it," Max announced. "It's going to rain."

"Don't worry," Horse said. "New Jersey is a whole other state. It probably won't be raining there."

"I brought an umbrella," I said smugly, though I wanted it to sound helpful.

As we marched down 168th Street, heading for the George Washington Bridge, we looked like European war refugees.[4] Every few paces, Horse

---

4. **European war refugees:** people who fled Europe to escape World War II (1939–1945) and its effects.

cried, "Hold it!" and adjusted his arms around his mattress. Each time we paused, Max pulled out his compass, peered at it, then announced, "Heading north!"

150   I said, "The bridge goes from east to west."

"Maybe the bridge does," Max insisted with a show of his compass, "but guaranteed, *we* are going north."

About then, the heel of my left foot, encased in a heavy rubber boot over an earth-crushing Buster Brown shoe, started to get sore. Things weren't going as I had hoped. Cheerfully, I tried to ignore the pain.

The closer we drew to the bridge, the more immense it seemed. And the clouds had become so thick, you couldn't see the top or the far side.

Max eyed the bridge with deep suspicion. "I'm not so sure we should go," he said. **F**

160   "Why?"

"Maybe it doesn't have another side."

We looked at him.

"No, seriously," Max explained, "they could have taken the Jersey side away, you know, for repairs."

F PREDICT
What do you predict the boys will do at this point?

Detail of *The George Washington Bridge Seen from the Upper West Side,* (ca. 1940), Louis Aston Knight. Oil on board, 10.8″ × 17″. Photo courtesy of Spanierman Gallery, LLC, New York.

ANALYZE VISUALS
What **mood**, or feeling, do the colors in this painting create?

"Cars are going across," I pointed out.

"They could be dropping off," he suggested.

"You would hear them splash," Horse argued.

"I'm going," I said. Trying to look brave, I started off on my own. My bravery didn't last long. The walkway was narrow. When I looked down, I saw only fog. I could feel the bridge tremble and sway. It wasn't long before I was convinced the bridge was about to collapse. Then a ray of hope struck me: Maybe the other guys had chickened out. If they had, I could quit because of *them*. I glanced back. My heart sank. They were coming. **G**

After they caught up, Horse looked me in the eye and said, "If this bridge falls, I'm going to kill you."

A quarter of a mile farther across, I gazed around. We were completely fogged in.

"I think we're lost," I announced.

"What do we do?" Horse whispered. His voice was jagged with panic. That made me feel better.

"Don't worry," Max said. "I've got my compass." He pulled it out.

"North is that way," he said, pointing in the direction we had been going.

G CHARACTER AND THEME
Reread lines 158–174. In what ways do the boys try to hide their fear from one another?

170

180

Horse said, "You sure?"

"A Scout compass never lies," Max insisted.

"*We* lied," I reminded him.

"Yeah, but this is an *official* Scout compass," Max returned loyally.

"Come on," Max said and marched forward. Horse and I followed. In moments, we crossed a metal bar on the walkway. On one side, a sign
190 proclaimed: NEW YORK; on the other, it said: NEW JERSEY.

"Holy smoke,"[5] Horse said with reverence as he straddled the bar. "Talk about being tough. We're in two states at the same time."

It began to rain. Max said, "Maybe it'll keep us clean."

"You saying I'm not clean?" Horse shot back.

Ever friendly, I put up my umbrella.

We went on—Max on one side, Horse on the other, me in the middle—trying to avoid the growing puddles. After a while, Max said, "Would you move the umbrella? Rain is coming down my neck."

"We're supposed to be roughing it," I said.

200 "Being in the middle isn't roughing it," Horse reminded me.

I folded the umbrella up so we all could get soaked equally.

"Hey!" I cried. "Look!" Staring up ahead, I could make out tollbooths[6] and the dim outlines of buildings.

---

5. **Holy smoke:** an old slang expression meaning "My goodness."
6. **tollbooths:** booths at which drivers must stop to pay a toll, or small fee.

Ⓗ CHARACTER AND THEME
Reread lines 195–201. What do the boys' definitions of "roughing it" tell you about them?

ANALYZE VISUALS
What **details** do you notice in this painting of a campsite?

Tent (1984), Christopher Brown. Oil on canvas, 72″ × 96″. Private collection.

"Last one off the bridge is a rotten egg!" Horse shouted and began to run. The next second, he tripped and took off like an F-36 fighter plane. Unfortunately, he landed like a Hell-cat dive-bomber[7] as his mattress unspooled before him and then slammed into a big puddle.

Max and I ran to help. Horse was damp. His mattress was soaked. When he tried to roll it up, water cascaded like Niagara Falls.

210   "Better leave it," Max said.

"It's what I sleep on at home," Horse said as he slung the soaking, dripping mass over his shoulder.

When we got off the bridge, we were in a small plaza. To the left was the roadway, full of roaring cars. In front of us, aside from the highway, there was nothing but buildings. Only to the right were there trees.

"North is that way," Max said, pointing toward the trees. We set off.

"How come you're limping?" Horse asked me. My foot *was* killing me. All I said, though, was, "How come you keep rubbing your arm?"

220   "I'm keeping the blood moving."

We approached the grove of trees. "Wow," Horse exclaimed. "Country." But as we drew closer, what we found were **discarded** cans, bottles, and newspapers—plus an old mattress spring.

"Hey," Max cried, sounding relieved, "this is just like Brooklyn." ❶

I said, "Let's find a decent place, make camp, and eat."

It was hard to find a campsite that didn't have junk. The growing dark didn't help. We had to settle for the place that had the least amount of garbage.

Max said, "If we build a lean-to, it'll keep us out of the rain." He and
230 Horse went a short distance with the hatchet.

Seeing a tree they wanted, Max whacked at it. The hatchet bounced right out of his hand. There was not even a dent in the tree. Horse **retrieved** the hatchet and checked the blade. "Dull," he said.

"Think I'm going to carry something sharp and cut myself?" Max protested. They contented themselves with picking up branches.

I went in search of firewood, but everything was wet. When I finally gathered some twigs and tried to light them, the only thing that burned was my fingers.

Meanwhile, Horse and Max used their branches to build a lean-to
240 directly over me. After many collapses—which didn't help my work—they finally got the branches to stand in a shaky sort of way.

discard (dĭ-skärd') *v.* to throw away

❶ **CHARACTER AND THEME**
Max is relieved to find the campsite is full of garbage. Why?

retrieve (rĭ-trēv') *v.* to get back again

---

7. **Hell-cat dive-bomber:** a World War II plane that took off from and returned to an aircraft carrier.

"Uh-oh," Horse said. "We forgot to bring something for a cover."

Max eyed me. "Didn't you say you brought a blanket?"

"No way!" I cried.

"All in favor of using the blanket!"

Horse and Max both cried, "Aye."

Only after I built up a mound of partially burned match sticks and lit
them, did I get the fire going. It proved that where there's smoke there
doesn't have to be much fire. The guys meanwhile draped my blanket over
250 their branch construction. It collapsed twice.

About an hour after our arrival, the three of us were gathered inside
the tiny space. There was a small fire, but more light came from my
flickering flashlight.

"No more rain," Horse said with pride.

"Just smoke," I said, rubbing my stinging eyes.

"We need a vent hole," Horse pointed out.

"I could cut it with the hatchet," Max said.

"It's my mother's favorite blanket."

"And you took it?" Max said.

260 I nodded.

"You *are* tough," Horse said.

Besides having too much smoke in our eyes and being wet, tired, and in
pain, we were starving. I almost said something about giving up, but as far
as I could see, the other guys were still tough. **J**

Max put his frying pan atop my smoldering smoke. After dumping
in the entire contents of his mustard bottle, he threw in the franks.
Meanwhile, I bolted down my last sandwich.

"What am I going to eat?" Horse suddenly said.

"Your beans," I reminded him.

270 Max offered up his hatchet. "Here. Just chop off the top end of
the can."

"Oh, right," Horse said. He selected a can, set it in front of him, levered
himself onto his knees, then swung down—hard. There was an explosion.
For a stunned moment, we just sat there, hands, face, and clothing
dripping with beans.

Suddenly Max shouted, "Food fight! Food fight!" and began to paw the
stuff off and fling it around.

Having a food fight in a cafeteria is one thing. Having one in the
middle of a soaking wet lean-to with cold beans during a dark, wet New

J PREDICT
Reread lines 262–264.
Make a prediction about
whether the **narrator's**
statement will turn out
to be true.

280 Jersey night is another. In seconds, the lean-to was down, the fire kicked over, and Max's frankfurters dumped on the ground.

"The food!" Max screamed, and began to snatch up the franks. Coated with mustard, dirt, grass, and leaves, they looked positively prehistoric. Still, we wiped the franks clean on our pants then ate them—the franks, that is. Afterward, we picked beans off each other's clothes—the way monkeys help friends get rid of lice.

For dessert, Max shared some Tootsie Rolls. After Horse swallowed his sixteenth piece, he announced, "I don't feel so good."

The thought of his getting sick was too much. "Let's go home," I said,
290 ashamed to look at the others. To my surprise—and relief—nobody objected.

Wet and cold, our way lit by my fast-fading flashlight, we gathered our belongings—most of them, anyway. As we made our way back over the bridge, gusts of wind-blown rain pummeled us until I felt like a used-up punching bag. By the time we got to the subway station, my legs were melting fast. The other guys looked bad too. Other riders moved away from us. One of them murmured, "Juvenile delinquents." To cheer us up, I got out my comic books, but they had **congealed** into a lump of red, white, and blue pulp.

300 With the subways running slow, it took hours to get home. When we emerged from the High Street Station, it was close to midnight.

Before we split up to go to our own homes, we just stood there on a street corner, embarrassed, trying to figure out how to end the day gracefully. I was the one who said, "Okay, I admit it. I'm not as tough as you guys. I gave up first."

Max shook his head. "Naw. I wanted to quit, but I wasn't tough enough to do it." He looked to Horse.

Horse made a fist. "You saying I'm the one who's tough?" he demanded. "I hate roughing it!" **K**

310 "Me too," I said quickly.

"Same for me," Max said.

Horse said, "Only thing is, we just have to promise not to tell Mr. Brenkman."

Grinning with relief, we **simultaneously** clasped hands. "No matter what," Max reminded us.

To which I added, "Scout's Honor." ❧

congeal (kən-jēl') v. to make into a solid mass

K CHARACTER AND THEME
Reread lines 302–309. Pay attention to how Horse and Max react to the **narrator's** confession. In what ways have their attitudes changed?

simultaneously (sī'məl-tā'nē-əs-lē) adv. at the same time

Comprehension

1. **Recall** Why do the boys need to take a camping trip?

2. **Recall** What makes the **narrator** decide it is time to go home?

3. **Represent** Create a diagram of the boys' route to their campsite. Be sure to include all of the important places mentioned in the story. Use the map on page 352 to help you.

Literary Analysis

4. **Predict** Review the graphic organizer you made as you read. Notice which events in the story you were able to predict. Which events were surprises?

5. **Compare and Contrast Characters** Compare and contrast the three boys. In what way is the **narrator** different from his friends? Support your answer with examples from the story.

6. **Analyze Character and Theme** Fill in a chart like the one shown with information about the story's characters. Record each character's important statements and actions, what lessons he learns, and how he changes. Then, restate the story's message as a theme statement.

	Narrator	Horse	Max
Statements/ Actions	"I like roughing it."		
What He			
How He Changes			

Theme Statement:

7. **Evaluate Plot** Do you think the boys' experience of going to the "country" could be called an **adventure?** Explain.

Extension and Challenge

8. **SOCIAL STUDIES CONNECTION** Read the requirements for earning the Wilderness Survival Merit Badge on page 365. Choose three of the requirements. For each one, state whether the boys in "Scout's Honor" met that requirement. Explain why or why not.

Vocabulary in Context

VOCABULARY PRACTICE

Synonyms are words that mean the same thing, while **antonyms** are words that mean the opposite. Examine the words in each pair and identify whether they are synonyms or antonyms.

1. retrieve/lose
2. retort/reply
3. discard/keep
4. khaki/cloth
5. congeal/separate
6. simultaneously/together

congeal

discard

khaki

retort

retrieve

simultaneously

VOCABULARY IN WRITING

Would a group of kids today go camping the way the boys in "Scout's Honor" did? Write a paragraph explaining why or why not. Use two or more vocabulary words. Here is a sample beginning.

> **EXAMPLE SENTENCE**
>
> *To go camping today, you need more than **khaki** and comic books.*

VOCABULARY STRATEGY: IDENTIFYING SLANG

When you talk to a group of your friends, you probably use some slang. **Slang** expressions are words and phrases that have a new or special meaning within a particular group of people. For example, the word *cool* usually means "neither warm nor very cold." To many people, though, *cool* can also be used to mean "good." Most slang terms, such as the expression *holy smoke* used in line 191 of "Scout's Honor," remain popular for only a short time. When you encounter unfamiliar slang, use context clues to help you figure out the meaning.

PRACTICE Identify the slang word or expression in each sentence. Then use context clues to help you supply a definition for it.

1. You may believe his story, but I think he is all wet.
2. I don't think you should pay much attention to her monkeyshines.
3. Arlene was bothering me, so I told her to take a powder.
4. Dad decided to lie down and catch some Z's.

VOCABULARY PRACTICE
For more practice, go to the **Vocabulary Center** at **ClassZone.com**.

Reading-Writing Connection

Increase your understanding of "Scout's Honor" by responding to these prompts. Then complete the **Grammar and Writing** exercise.

WRITING PROMPTS	SELF-CHECK
A. Short Response: Write a Letter Consider how the characters in "Scout's Honor" might describe their camping trip to others. Would they tell about it truthfully or change the details to make it sound better? Choose either Horse or Max and write a **brief letter** in which he describes the **adventure** to a friend or family member.	***An interesting letter will . . .*** • include details about the trip • show an understanding of the character's attitude as seen in the story
B. Extended Response: Evaluate Characters Did you find the characters in "Scout's Honor" to be realistic? Consider the dialogue, the ways in which the characters change, and the ways they react to situations. Then write a **two- to three-paragraph summary** of your evaluation.	***A strong evaluation will . . .*** • include a clearly-stated opinion • provide examples from the story

GRAMMAR AND WRITING

COMBINE SENTENCES On page 347, you learned how to join two subjects or two predicates to combine sentences. Another way to connect two sentences is to use a **comma** and a **coordinating conjunction,** such as *and, but, or, nor, yet, so,* or *for.* Here is an example:

Original: Max was a fast talker. He always had pocket money.

Revised: Max was a fast talker, and he always had pocket money.

PRACTICE Join these sentences by inserting a comma and the correct coordinating conjunction.

1. Horse could carry his mattress. He could leave it behind.
2. It was raining when we reached the bridge. We crossed it anyway.
3. Our stomachs were growling. We ate all of our food.
4. Horse used his hatchet to open the beans. The can exploded.

FOR MORE HELP WITH COORDINATING CONJUNCTIONS, SEE PAGE R47 IN THE *Grammar Handbook.*

HANDBOOK EXCERPT The characters in "Scout's Honor" find that meeting the Scout Craft requirement isn't as easy as it seems. Read the following excerpt to find out what today's Boy Scouts must do to earn a similar merit badge.

Wilderness Survival

1. From memory, describe the priorities for survival in a backcountry or wilderness location.

2. Describe ways to (a) avoid panic and (b) maintain a high level of morale when lost.

3. Show that you know first aid for injuries or illnesses likely to occur in backcountry outings, including hypothermia, hyperthermia, heat stroke, heat exhaustion, frostbite, dehydration, sunburn, stings, ticks, snakebite, blisters, and hyperventilation.

4. Tell what you would do to survive in the following environments:

   a. Cold and snowy
   b. Wet (forest)
   c. Hot and dry (desert)
   d. Windy (mountains or plains)
   e. Water (ocean or lake)

5. Make up a small survival kit and be able to explain how each item in it is useful.

6. Show that you can start fires using three methods other than matches.

7. Do the following:

   a. Tell five different ways of attracting attention when lost.
   b. Show how to use a signal mirror to attract attention when lost.
   c. From memory, describe five international ground-to-air signals and tell what they mean.

8. Show that you can find and improvise a natural shelter minimizing the damage to the environment.

9. Spend a night in your shelter.

10. Explain how to protect yourself against insects, reptiles, rodents, and bears.

11. Show three ways to purify water.

12. Show that you know the proper clothing to be worn in your area on an overnight in extremely hot weather and extremely cold weather.

13. Explain why it usually is not wise to eat edible wild plants or wildlife in a wilderness survival situation.

Ant and Grasshopper

Traditional Fable by Aesop

Retold by James Reeves

The Richer, the Poorer

Modern Fable by Dorothy West

Should you LIVE *for the present or the future?*

KEY IDEA People have different ideas about **saving** and spending. Some people prefer to save as much as possible. That way, the money will be there when they really need it. Others prefer to spend what they have right away, so that they can enjoy it. In the fables you are about to read, four characters struggle with their decisions to save or spend.

DISCUSS Is it better to save for the future or enjoy yourself in the present? Find a partner and debate this question. Be sure that you and your partner each take a different side. Provide reasons to support your response.

● LITERARY ANALYSIS: FABLE

Fables teach us lessons about life. A **traditional fable** like "Ant and Grasshopper" often uses animal characters to tell a story. It ends with a **moral,** or a clever, memorable statement of the fable's message. A **modern fable** like "The Richer, the Poorer" is more likely to use human characters. It has a **theme** that readers have to determine on their own. As you read the two fables, pay attention to the characters and the lessons they learn.

● READING STRATEGY: SET A PURPOSE FOR READING

When you were younger, you might have read fables for entertainment. In this lesson, your **purpose for reading** is to find similarities and differences between two fables. As you read, record details about characters' key **traits,** their words and actions, and what they consider important.

	"Ant and Grasshopper"		"The Richer, the Poorer"	
	Ant	Grass-hopper	Lottie	Bess
Key Traits	hard-working	fun-loving		
Words and Actions				
Character's Priority				

▲ VOCABULARY IN CONTEXT

Dorothy West uses the listed words to help tell her fable about **saving.** To see how many you know, match each word with the numbered term closest in meaning.

WORD	clarity	frugal	intolerable
LIST	enhance	inefficient	lean

1. scanty
2. wasteful
3. clearness
4. improve
5. unbearable
6. thrifty

Ant and Grasshopper

Aesop
Retold by James Reeves

All summer the ant had been working hard, gathering a store of corn for the winter. Grain by grain she had taken it from the fields and stowed it away in a hole in the bank, under a hawthorn bush.

One bright, frosty day in winter Grasshopper saw her. She was dragging out a grain of corn to dry it in the sun. The wind was keen, and poor Grasshopper was cold. **A**

"Good morning, Ant," said he. "What a terrible winter it is! I'm half dead with hunger. Please give me just one of your corn grains to eat. I can find nothing, although I've hopped all over the farmyard. There isn't a
10 seed to be found. Spare me a grain, I beg."

"Why haven't you saved anything up?" asked Ant. "*I* worked hard all through the summer, storing food for the winter. Very glad I am too, for as you say, it's bitterly cold."

"I wasn't idle last summer, either," said Grasshopper.

"And what did you do, pray?"

"Why, I spent the time singing," answered Grasshopper. "Every day from dawn till sunset I jumped about or sat in the sun, chirruping to my heart's content." **B**

"Oh you did, did you?" replied Ant. "Well, since you've sung all
20 summer to keep yourself cheerful, you may dance all winter to keep yourself warm. Not a grain will I give you!"

And she scuttled off into her hole in the bank, while Grasshopper was left cold and hungry.

IN GOOD TIMES PREPARE FOR WHEN THE BAD TIMES COME. ❧

ANALYZE VISUALS
What can you **infer** about these two illustrations by viewing them next to each other?

A FABLE
Reread lines 1–6. What indicates that this is a **traditional fable?**

B FABLE
Why does Grasshopper think he has kept busy all summer? Note how this is different from Ant's idea of being busy.

From *Aesop's Fables.* © 2000 by Jerry Pinkney. Used with permission of Chronicle Books LLC, San Francisco.

The Richer, the Poorer

Dorothy West

O ver the years Lottie had urged Bess to prepare for her old age. Over the years Bess had lived each day as if there were no other. Now they were both past sixty, the time for summing up. Lottie had a bank account that had never grown **lean**. Bess had the clothes on her back, and the rest of her worldly possessions in a battered suitcase. **C**

Lottie had hated being a child, hearing her parents' skimping and scraping. Bess had never seemed to notice. All she ever wanted was to go outside and play. She learned to skate on borrowed skates. She rode a borrowed bicycle. Lottie couldn't wait to grow up and buy herself the best 10 of everything.

As soon as anyone would hire her, Lottie put herself to work. She minded babies; she ran errands for the old.

She never touched a penny of her money, though her child's mouth watered for ice cream and candy. But she could not bear to share with Bess, who never had anything to share with her. When the dimes began to add up to dollars, she lost her taste for sweets.

By the time she was twelve, she was clerking after school in a small variety store. Saturdays she worked as long as she was wanted. She decided to keep her money for clothes. When she entered high school, she would 20 wear a wardrobe that neither she nor anyone else would be able to match.

But her freshman year found her unable to indulge so frivolous a whim, particularly when her admiring instructors advised her to think seriously of college. No one in her family had ever gone to college, and certainly Bess would never get there. She would show them all what she could do, if she put her mind to it.

She began to bank her money, and her bankbook became her most private and precious possession.

lean (lēn) *adj.* having little to spare; thin

C FABLE
Reread lines 1–5. Consider the ways this passage is similar to the first two paragraphs of "Ant and Grasshopper." What do you think will happen in the rest of the story?

In her third year in high school she found a job in a small but expanding restaurant, where she cashiered from the busy hour until closing. In her
30 last year in high school the business increased so rapidly that Lottie was faced with the choice of staying in school or working full time.

She made her choice easily. A job in hand was worth two in the future.

Bess had a beau[1] in the school band, who had no other ambition except to play a horn. Lottie expected to be settled with a home and family while Bess was still waiting for Harry to earn enough to buy a marriage license.

That Bess married Harry straight out of high school was not surprising. That Lottie never married at all was not really surprising either. Two or three times she was halfway persuaded, but to give up a job that paid well for a homemaking job that paid nothing was a risk she was incapable of taking.
40 Bess's married life was nothing for Lottie to envy. She and Harry lived like gypsies,[2] Harry playing in second-rate bands all over the country, even getting himself and Bess stranded in Europe. They were often in rags and never in riches.

D FABLE
Reread lines 26–32.
What is Lottie's priority in life?

ANALYZE VISUALS
Describe the **mood**, or feeling, that each of these paintings conveys.

---

1. **beau:** boyfriend.
2. **gypsies:** people who move from place to place.

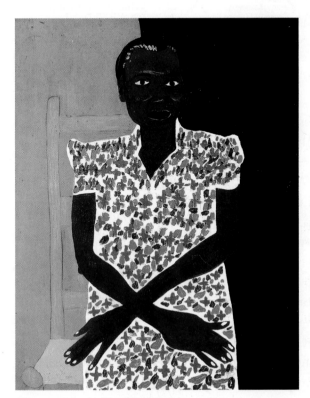

Woman in Calico (1944), William H. Johnson. © Smithsonian American Art Museum, Washington, D.C./Art Resource, New York.

Mom and Dad (1944), William H. Johnson. Oil on paperboard, 31″ × 25³/₈″. Gift of the Harmon Foundation. © Smithsonian American Art Museum, Washington, D.C./Art Resource, New York.

Street Life, Harlem (1940), William H. Johnson. © Smithsonian American Art Museum, Washington, D.C./Art Resource, New York.

ANALYZE VISUALS
Which of the sisters would you be more likely to **connect** to the woman in this painting?

Bess grieved because she had no child, not having sense enough to know she was better off without one. Lottie was certainly better off without nieces and nephews to feel sorry for. Very likely Bess would have dumped them on her doorstep. **E**

That Lottie had a doorstep they might have been left on was only because her boss, having bought a second house, offered Lottie his first
50 house at a price so low and terms so reasonable that it would have been like losing money to refuse.

She shut off the rooms she didn't use, letting them go to rack and ruin.[3] Since she ate her meals out, she had no food at home, and did not encourage callers, who always expected a cup of tea.

Her way of life was mean and miserly, but she did not know it. She thought she lived **frugally** in her middle years so that she could live in comfort and ease when she most needed peace of mind.

E **FABLE**
Reread lines 44–47. Why does Lottie approve of the fact that Bess never had children?

frugal (frōō′gəl) *adj.* avoiding waste; thrifty

---

3. **go to rack and ruin:** become shabby or wrecked.

The years, after forty, began to race. Suddenly Lottie was sixty, and retired from her job by her boss's son, who had no sentimental feeling about keeping her on until she was ready to quit.

She made several attempts to find other employment, but her dowdy appearance made her look old and **inefficient.** For the first time in her life Lottie would gladly have worked for nothing, to have some place to go, something to do with her day.

Harry died abroad, in a third-rate hotel,[4] with Bess weeping as hard as if he had left her a fortune. He had left her nothing but his horn. There wasn't even money for her passage home.

Lottie, trapped by the blood tie, knew she would not only have to send for her sister, but take her in when she returned. It didn't seem fair that Bess should reap the harvest of Lottie's lifetime of self-denial. **F**

It took Lottie a week to get a bedroom ready, a week of hard work and hard cash. There was everything to do, everything to replace or paint. When she was through the room looked so fresh and new that Lottie felt she deserved it more than Bess.

She would let Bess have her room, but the mattress was so lumpy, the carpet so worn, the curtains so threadbare that Lottie's conscience pricked her. She supposed she would have to redo that room, too, and went about doing it with an eagerness that she mistook for haste.

When she was through upstairs, she was shocked to see how dismal downstairs looked by comparison. She tried to ignore it, but with nowhere to go to escape it, the contrast grew more **intolerable.**

She worked her way from kitchen to parlor, persuading herself she was only putting the rooms to rights to give herself something to do. At night she slept like a child after a long and happy day of playing house. She was having more fun than she had ever had in her life. She was living each hour for itself.

There was only a day now before Bess would arrive. Passing her gleaming mirrors, at first with vague awareness, then with painful **clarity,** Lottie saw herself as others saw her, and could not stand the sight.

She went on a spending spree from specialty shops to beauty salon, emerging transformed into a woman who believed in miracles. **G**

inefficient (ĭn'ĭ-fĭsh'ənt) *adj.* not able to produce without wasting time or energy

F FABLE
Note Lottie's reaction to sharing her home with Bess. How is this similar to or different from what happens in "Ant and Grasshopper"?

intolerable (ĭn-tŏl'ər-ə-bəl) *adj.* unbearable; too much to be endured

clarity (klăr'ĭ-tē) *n.* the quality of being clear

G FABLE
Reread lines 75–92. Based on the changes Lottie has made, would you **predict** that her attitude toward Bess will change too?

---

4. **third-rate hotel:** a hotel of poor quality.

She was in the kitchen basting a turkey when Bess rang the bell.
Her heart raced, and she wondered if the heat from the oven was
responsible.

She went to the door, and Bess stood before her. Stiffly she suffered
Bess's embrace, her heart racing harder, her eyes suddenly smarting from
the onrush of cold air.

"Oh, Lottie, it's good to see you," Bess said, but saying nothing about
100 Lottie's splendid appearance. Upstairs Bess, putting down her shabby
suitcase, said, "I'll sleep like a rock tonight," without a word of praise for
her lovely room. At the lavish table, top-heavy with turkey, Bess said, "I'll
take light and dark, both," with no marveling at the size of the bird, or
that there was turkey for two elderly women, one of them too poor to buy
her own bread.

With the glow of good food in her stomach, Bess began to spin stories.
They were rich with places and people, most of them lowly, all of them
magnificent. Her face reflected her telling, the joys and sorrows of her
remembering, and above all, the love she lived by that **enhanced** the
110 poorest place, the humblest person.

Then it was that Lottie knew why Bess had made no mention of her
finery, or the shining room, or the twelve-pound turkey. She had not even
seen them. Tomorrow she would see the room as it really looked, and
Lottie as she really looked, and the warmed-over turkey in its second-day
glory. Tonight she saw only what she had come seeking, a place in her
sister's home and heart. **H**

She said, "That's enough about me. How have the years used you?"

"It was me who didn't use them," said Lottie wistfully. "I saved for
them. I saved for them. I forgot the best of them would go without my
120 ever spending a day or a dollar enjoying them. That's my life story in
those few words, a life never lived.

"Now it's too near the end to try."

Bess said, "To know how much there is to know is the beginning of
learning to live. Don't count the years that are left us. At our time of life
it's the days that count. You've too much catching up to do to waste a
minute of a waking hour feeling sorry for yourself."

Lottie grinned, a real wide-open grin, "Well, to tell the truth I felt sorry for
you. Maybe, if I had any sense, I'd feel sorry for myself, after all. I know I'm
too old to kick up my heels, but I'm going to let you show me how. If I land
130 on my head, I guess it won't matter. I feel giddy already, and I like it." ∾ **I**

enhance (ĕn-hăns′) v.
to increase in value or
quality

H FABLE
Reread lines 106–116.
What does Bess consider
her highest priority?

I FABLE
Reread lines 127–130.
Contrast Lottie's attitude
in this passage with her
attitude at the beginning
of the fable.

Comprehension

1. **Recall** Why does Grasshopper need to ask Ant for food?

2. **Recall** Why does Bess come to live with her sister Lottie?

3. **Summarize** What does Lottie do to prepare for Bess's arrival?

Literary Analysis

4. **Analyze Cause and Effect** Consider the actions that Ant and Grasshopper take and the results of those actions. Then suggest the ways in which either character might have changed the fable's ending.

5. **Analyze Characters** Think about which of the characters in the two fables changed and which ones did not. Identify who changed and explain in what ways he or she changed.

6. **Evaluate Fables** Which fable does a better job of teaching a lesson about **saving** and spending? Support your opinion using examples from the fables.

Compare Fables

Now that you've read both fables, add a new row to the chart you filled out as you read. Use the answers to the questions to help you identify the **theme** of "The Richer, the Poorer."

| | "Ant and Grasshopper" | | "The Richer, the Poorer" | |
	Ant	Grasshopper	Lottie	Bess
Key Traits	hard-working, plans for future	fun-loving, lives for today		
Words and Actions				
Character's Priority				

Moral: In good times prepare for when the bad times come.

Theme:

Vocabulary in Context

VOCABULARY PRACTICE

Choose the letter of the word that has a different meaning from the other words.

1. (a) enable, (b) enhance, (c) improve, (d) increase
2. (a) unjust, (b) prejudiced, (c) unfair, (d) inefficient
3. (a) quick, (b) sparing, (c) frugal, (d) thrifty
4. (a) lean, (b) sparse, (c) scanty, (d) lengthy
5. (a) generosity, (b) kindness, (c) charity, (d) clarity
6. (a) impractical, (b) unenjoyable, (c) intolerable, (d) terrible

clarity
enhance
frugal
inefficient
intolerable
lean

VOCABULARY IN WRITING

Think of a simple lesson you could teach with a story about two animals. Write your story using at least two vocabulary words. You could start this way.

EXAMPLE SENTENCE

*Trevor Frog always had an **inefficient** way of doing things.*

VOCABULARY STRATEGY: MULTIPLE MEANING WORDS

Many English words have more than one meaning. You may have known, for example, that *lean* can mean "rest the body against something for support." But you may not have been familiar with its use in "The Richer, the Poorer," where the word means "having little to spare; thin."

If a word does not seem to make sense in context, look at the rest of the sentence to figure out what other meaning the word might have. If you are still not sure of the meaning, check a dictionary.

PRACTICE Use context clues or a dictionary to define the boldfaced words.

1. She **cast** her hat and scarf aside when she got home.
2. The golfer used an **iron** to make the shot.
3. Instead of making a decision, she chose to **hedge** for a while longer.
4. To swing the bat better, **plant** your feet solidly yet comfortly.

VOCABULARY PRACTICE
For more practice, go to the **Vocabulary Center** at ClassZone.com.

Writing for Assessment

1. READ THE PROMPT

The two fables you've just read handle a similar idea in very different ways. In writing assessments, you will often be asked to compare and contrast similar characters or themes in two stories, poems, or fables.

PROMPT

In three paragraphs, compare the traditional fable "Ant and Grasshopper" with the modern fable "The Richer, the Poorer." Consider the moral or theme of each fable and the traits, actions, and priorities of each character. Support your ideas using details from the fables.

◀ **STRATEGIES IN ACTION**

1. I have to identify the **similarities and differences** between the fables.

2. I need to describe what the **characters** say, do, and think, and any **lessons** they learn.

3. I need to include **details and examples** from the fables to support my ideas.

2. PLAN YOUR WRITING

Using the chart you filled in as you read, identify the ways in which the fables are alike and different. Then think about how to present these similarities and differences.

- Decide on a main idea, or position statement, for your response.

- Review the fables to find examples and details that support your position.

- Create an outline to organize your response. This sample outline shows one way to organize your three paragraphs.

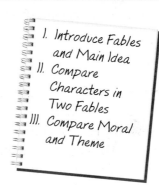

I. Introduce Fables and Main Idea
II. Compare Characters in Two Fables
III. Compare Moral and Theme

3. DRAFT YOUR RESPONSE

Paragraph 1 Provide the titles and authors of both fables, as well as a sentence telling what each fable is about. Also include your main idea.

Paragraph 2 Explain how the four characters are similar or different. Support your position with examples of what they say, do, or think.

Paragraph 3 Provide the moral or theme of each fable. Explain how the messages are similar or different. Use supporting details from the fables.

Revision Make sure you've used transition words such as *similarly, also, however, instead,* or *unlike* to show similarities and differences.

Esperanza Rising

Novel by Pam Muñoz Ryan

Pam Muñoz Ryan
born 1951

Other Books by Pam Muñoz Ryan

- *Becoming Naomi León*
- *Riding Freedom*
- *California, Here We Come!*

Meet Pam Muñoz Ryan

Award-winning author Pam Muñoz Ryan grew up in a family with a rich tradition of storytelling. Ryan inherited some of the family's most interesting stories from her grandmother, with whom she spent a lot of time. Her grandmother's own life story—leaving behind wealth and luxury in Mexico for a life of hard work in the United States during the Great Depression—inspired Ryan to write *Esperanza Rising*.

Even without the family history, Ryan would have no problem sympathizing with a young girl who feels out of place. When Ryan entered middle school, her family moved and she had to change schools. Feeling like an outsider, Ryan found comfort in books. In fact, when asked why she writes for children, Ryan says, "Books influenced me so much in middle school and junior high. So I want to write for the same age."

Try a Coming-of-Age Novel

Think of a time when you suddenly felt much older, or when your responsibilities became more serious. Chances are it happened when you were facing a situation or challenge for the first time. When a novel centers on a young person becoming more mature as a result of a challenging experience, it is often called a **coming-of-age novel**. *Esperanza Rising* is an example of this type of novel.

Read a Great Book

Esperanza Rising tells the story of Esperanza Ortega, a rich, pampered girl who must give up her carefree life in Mexico for a life of hardship in the United States. After Esperanza's father is murdered, her devious uncle, Tío Luis, demands that her mother marry him. By marrying her, he hopes to gain control of the family's riches. In the excerpt you are about to read, you'll discover the extremes to which Tío Luis will go to make Esperanza's mother accept his proposal.

from

Esperanza Rising

The wind blew hard that night and the house moaned and whistled. Instead of dreaming of birthday songs, Esperanza's sleep was filled with nightmares. An enormous bear was chasing her, getting closer and closer and finally folding her in a tight embrace. Its fur caught in her mouth, making it hard to breathe. Someone tried to pull the bear away but couldn't. The bear squeezed harder until it was smothering Esperanza. Then when she thought she would suffocate, the bear grabbed her by the shoulders and shook her until her head wagged back and forth.

10   Her eyes opened, then closed again. She realized she was dreaming and for an instant, she felt relieved. But the shaking began again, harder this time.

Someone was calling her.

"Esperanza!"

She opened her eyes.

"Esperanza! Wake up!" screamed Mama. "The house is on fire!"

Smoke drifted into the room.

"Mama, what's happening?"

"Get up, Esperanza! We must get Abuelita!"

20   Esperanza heard Alfonso's deep voice yelling from somewhere downstairs.

"Señora Ortega! Esperanza!"

"Here! We are here!" called Mama, grabbing a damp rag from the washbowl and handing it to Esperanza to put over her mouth and nose. Esperanza swung around in a circle looking for something, anything, to save. She grabbed the doll. Then she and Mama hurried down the hall toward Abuelita's room, but it was empty.

"Alfonso!" screamed Mama. "Abuelita is not here!"

30   "We will find her. You must come now. The stairs are beginning to burn. Hurry!"

Esperanza held the towel over her face and looked down the stairs. Curtains flamed up the walls. The house was enveloped in a fog that thickened toward the ceiling. Mama and Esperanza crouched down the stairs where Alfonso was waiting to lead them out through the kitchen.

In the courtyard, the wooden gates were open. Near the stables, the *vaqueros* were releasing the horses from the corrals. Servants scurried everywhere. Where were they going?

40   "Where's Abuelita? Abuelita!" cried Mama.

Esperanza felt dizzy. Nothing seemed real. Was she still dreaming? Was this her own imagination gone wild?

Miguel grabbed her. "'Where's your mother and Abuelita?"

Esperanza whimpered and looked toward Mama. He left her, stopped at Mama, then ran toward the house.

The wind caught the sparks from the house and carried them to the stables. Esperanza stood in the middle of it all, watching the outline of her home silhouetted in flames against the night sky.

Someone wrapped a blanket around her. Was she cold? She did
50 not know.

Miguel ran out of the burning house carrying Abuelita in his arms. He laid her down and Hortensia screamed. The back of his shirt was on fire. Alfonso tackled him, rolling him over and over on the ground until the fire was out. Miguel stood up and slowly took off the blackened shirt. He wasn't badly burned.

Mama cradled Abuelita in her arms.

"Mama," said Esperanza, "Is she . . . ?"

"No, she is alive, but weak and her ankle . . . I don't think she can walk," said Mama.

60 Esperanza knelt down.

"Abuelita, where were you?"

Her grandmother held up the cloth bag with her crocheting and after some minutes of coughing, whispered, "We must have something to do while we wait."

The fire's anger could not be contained. It spread to the grapes. The flames ran along the deliberate rows of the vines, like long curved fingers reaching for the horizon, lighting the night sky.

Esperanza stood as if in a trance and watched El Rancho de las Rosas burn.

❧

70 Mama, Abuelita, and Esperanza slept in the servants' cabins. They really didn't sleep much, but they didn't cry either. They were numb, as if encased in a thick skin that nothing could penetrate. And there was no point in talking about how it happened. They all knew that the uncles had arranged the fire.

At dawn, still in her nightgown, Esperanza went out among the rubble. Avoiding the smoldering piles, she picked through the black wood, hoping to find something to salvage. She sat on an adobe block near what used to be the front door, and looked over at Papa's rose garden. Flowerless stems were covered in soot. Dazed
80 and hugging herself, Esperanza surveyed the surviving victims: the

twisted forms of wrought-iron chairs, unharmed cast-iron skillets, and the mortars and pestles from the kitchen that were made from lava rock and refused to burn. Then she saw the remains of the trunk that used to sit at the foot of her bed, the metal straps still intact. She stood up and hurried toward it, hoping for *un milagro,* a miracle. She looked closely, but all that remained were black cinders.

There was nothing left inside, for someday.

❧

90 ⁓Esperanza saw her uncles approaching on horseback and ran to tell the others. Mama waited on the steps of the cabin with her arms crossed, looking like a fierce statue. Alfonso, Hortensia, and Miguel stood nearby.

"Ramona," said Tío Marco, remaining on his horse. "Another sadness in so short a time. We are deeply sorry."

"I have come to give you another chance," said Tío Luis. "If you reconsider my proposal, I will build a bigger, more beautiful house and I will replant everything. Of course, if you prefer, you can live here with the servants, as long as another tragedy does not happen to their homes as well. There is no main house or fields 100 where they can work, so you see that many people's lives and jobs depend upon you. And I am sure you want the best for Esperanza, do you not?"

Mama did not speak for several moments. She looked around at the servants who had gathered. Now, her face did not seem so fierce and her eyes were damp. Esperanza wondered where the servants would go when Mama told Tío Luis no.

Mama looked at Esperanza with eyes that said, "forgive me." Then she dropped her head and stared at the ground. "I will consider your proposal," said Mama.

110 Tío Luis smiled. "I am delighted! I have no doubt that you will make the right decision. I will be back in a few days for your answer." ❧

Keep Reading

You have just been introduced to three generations of Ortega women. Whose behavior surprised you the most, and why? As you continue to read *Esperanza Rising*, you will follow the Ortega family through hardship, injustice, and serious illness. Esperanza learns to triumph over the challenges she and her family face, while the strength of her mother and grandmother helps her grow into a remarkable young woman.

Words Like Freedom

Dreams

Poems by Langston Hughes

How do POSSIBILITIES *become reality?*

KEY IDEA You've probably heard the saying "The sky's the limit." It means that anything is possible if we try hard enough. Even if we have unlimited **possibilities,** though, achieving our goals may require more than hard work. We may also need a strong desire to succeed and the help of people around us. In his poems "Words Like Freedom" and "Dreams," Langston Hughes describes some of the difficulties involved in living up to our potential.

WEB IT Think of a person who, in your opinion, is very successful. It could be a celebrity or someone you know. What helps this person to achieve his or her goals? Record your thoughts in an idea web like the one shown.

He has friends who support him.

My Uncle Steven

LITERARY ANALYSIS: THEME IN POETRY

Although a poem looks very different from a short story, it often contains a **theme,** or message about life. To identify a poem's theme, keep the following clues in mind:

- A poem's **title** sometimes helps you determine the theme by suggesting what the poem will focus on.
- Repeated words and phrases tell you how the **speaker,** or voice of the poem, feels.

As you read "Words Like Freedom" and "Dreams," look for the repeated words and phrases that help you determine the theme in each poem.

READING STRATEGY: VISUALIZE

When you **visualize,** you form a mental picture based on a written description. Since poetry often expresses its meaning using fewer words than other forms of literature, readers sometimes need to rely on key words and phrases to visualize a setting, character, or an event.

As you read each poem, use a chart like the one shown to record the words and phrases that help you form specific mental pictures.

	Words and Phrases	Mental Picture
"Words Like Freedom"	1. "On my hearstrings freedom sings" (line 3)	1. someone singing out "freedom" with great feeling
"Dreams"		

Author Online

Writer from Harlem
In 1925, Langston Hughes left three of his poems with a famous author who was eating in the restaurant where Hughes worked. Sharing those poems led to his first book, *The Weary Blues.*

Langston Hughes
1902–1967

Much of Hughes's writing focuses on the experiences of the people who lived around him in Harlem. "I knew only the people I had grown up with," he once said, "and they weren't people whose shoes were always shined. . . . But they seemed to me good people, too."

The Music of Poetry Growing up, Hughes fell in love with jazz and the blues. He expressed this love by using blues themes, images, and rhythms in his poetry. In the 1950s, Hughes made a recording of his poems set to jazz.

Renaissance Man Langston Hughes was one of the strongest voices of a cultural movement called the Harlem Renaissance, which took its name from the Harlem neighborhood in New York City and the time period called the Renaissance, which means "rebirth." During this period, which lasted for most of the 1920s, African-American artists, writers, and musicians worked to establish a proud and vibrant cultural identity.

 MORE ABOUT THE AUTHOR
For more on Langston Hughes, visit the **Literature Center** at **ClassZone.com.**

WORDS LIKE FREEDOM

Langston Hughes

There are words like *Freedom*
Sweet and wonderful to say.
On my heartstrings freedom sings
All day everyday.

5 There are words like *Liberty* **A**
That almost make me cry.
If you had known what I know
You would know why.

A **THEME**
Why does the **speaker** choose to repeat the words in lines 1 and 5?

La Grande Famille (1947), René Magritte. Oil on canvas, 100 cm × 81 cm. Private collection. © 2008 C. Herscovici, Brussels/Artists Rights Society (ARS), New York.

DREAMS

Langston Hughes

Hold fast[1] to dreams
For if dreams die
Life is a broken-winged bird
That cannot fly.

5 Hold fast to dreams
For when dreams go
Life is a barren field
Frozen with snow. **B**

B VISUALIZE
How does the mental picture of "a barren field frozen with snow" add to your understanding of the poem?

---

1. **Hold fast:** grasp tightly; stick firmly.

Comprehension

1. **Recall** What line is repeated in "Dreams"? / —

2. **Recall** What do words like *liberty* make the **speaker** do?

Literary Analysis

3. **Make Inferences** Reread the last two lines of "Words Like Freedom." What can you infer about the people the **speaker** is addressing?

4. **Visualize** Reread the chart you filled in as you read. Then underline the words and phrases that had the strongest effect on you. Which poem was more effective at helping you visualize?

5. **Analyze Visuals** Compare the details, colors, and subject matter of the paintings on pages 387 and 388. Do these paintings create the same **mood,** or feeling, when you look at them?

6. **Identify Theme** As you read, you looked for the ways in which titles and repeated words could lead you to a poem's theme. Use a diagram like the one shown to write theme statements for Hughes's poems.

Title of Poem	Repeated Words and Phrases	Theme Statement
"Words Like Freedom"	there are words like	If you had known what I know you would know why
"Dreams"	hold fast to dreams	when dreams go life is a barren field frozen with snow.

7. **Compare and Contrast Stanzas** Compare and contrast the two **stanzas,** or groups of lines, in "Words Like Freedom." How are they similar and different?

Extension and Challenge

8. **Creative Project: Art** Like a piece of literature, a piece of visual art can mean different things to different people. Choose either "Words Like Freedom" or "Dreams" and create an original work of art to go with the poem. For inspiration, think about the poem's subject, details, and most of all, how the poem made you feel.

9. **Inquiry and Research** Research the civil rights movement to create a timeline of the important civil rights rulings and events that happened during Langston Hughes's lifetime (1902–1967). How might these events have affected Hughes's view of his **possibilities?**

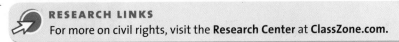

RESEARCH LINKS
For more on civil rights, visit the **Research Center** at **ClassZone.com.**

Same Song
Poem by Pat Mora

Without Commercials
Poem by Alice Walker

Can how you LOOK change who you are?

KEY IDEA Advertisers suggest that a new pair of jeans will make you more popular or that a new hair color will make you more attractive. But are those claims really true? Your **appearance** might affect how you look to others, but can it really change who you are? The two poems you are about to read discuss some of the ways and reasons people try to change the way they look.

QUICKWRITE Consider some of the things that people might do when they want a new appearance. This could mean getting a haircut or a new sweater. Are there times, however, when changes to appearance can be harmful? Write a brief paragraph to answer that question, including at least two harmful changes.

2 Street
Station

B D F Q 7

LITERARY ANALYSIS: RECURRING THEME

The lessons learned from common life experiences are often expressed as themes in literature. When the same theme appears in more than one piece of literature, it is called a **recurring theme.**

The two poems you are about to read both express a recurring theme about the importance of appearance. However, each poet expresses her message in a different way. To get at the poets' shared theme, ask yourself the following questions as you read the poems:

- What is the subject being presented?
- What words tell you how the speaker feels?
- What images stand out in your mind as you read?

READING SKILL: MAKE INFERENCES

When you **make inferences,** you make logical guesses based on two things: clues in the selection and what you already know from reading or from experience. As you read "Same Song" and "Without Commercials," use a chart like the one shown to record your inferences.

My Inferences	Clues from the Poems	What I Know
The girl in "Same Song" spends a lot of time getting ready each morning.	"stumbles into the bathroom at six a.m.," "curls," "strokes," "smoothes," "outlines"	It takes my sister a long time to do her hair and makeup.

Author Online

Pat Mora: Border Woman Pat Mora grew up feeling as though she didn't belong to either Mexican or American culture. She was born in El Paso, Texas, near the Mexican border. She later wrote in a poem that she was "an American to Mexicans / a Mexican to Americans." Mora has said that she writes to help give Hispanic ideas and issues a larger place in American literature and because she is "fascinated by the pleasure and power of words."

Pat Mora
born 1942

Alice Walker: Solitary Observer At the age of eight, Alice Walker was blinded in one eye by a shot from her brother's BB gun. The accident left horrible scars, but Walker later said that the emotions she went through during that time helped her to become a writer. Walker went on to become a highly influential author. In 1983, she became the first African-American woman to win the Pulitzer Prize in fiction for her novel *The Color Purple*.

Alice Walker
born 1944

 MORE ABOUT THE AUTHOR
For more on Pat Mora and Alice Walker, visit the **Literature Center** at **ClassZone.com.**

Same Song

Pat Mora

While my sixteen-year-old son sleeps,
my twelve-year-old daughter
stumbles into the bathroom at six a.m.
plugs in the curling iron
5 squeezes into faded jeans
curls her hair carefully
strokes Aztec Blue shadow on her eyelids
smoothes Frosted Mauve blusher on her cheeks
outlines her mouth in Neon Pink
10 peers into the mirror, mirror on the wall
frowns at her face, her eyes, her skin,
not fair. **A**

At night this daughter
stumbles off to bed at nine
15 eyes half-shut while my son
jogs a mile in the cold dark
then lifts weights in the garage
curls and bench presses[1]
expanding biceps, triceps, pectorals,
20 one-handed push-ups, one hundred sit-ups
peers into that mirror, mirror and frowns too. **B**

for Libby

A MAKE INFERENCES
Reread lines 10–12.
What does the **speaker's**
daughter think is unfair?

B RECURRING THEME
Notice the phrase
"mirror, mirror" in lines
10 and 21. What fairy
tale does this phrase
remind you of?

---

1. **curls and bench presses:** weight-lifting activities. Curls are done with the hands,
   wrists, and forearms. Bench presses involve lifting a weight with both arms while
   lying face-up.

Lipsticks II, Philip Le Bas. Enamel
paints on panel, 20 cm × 20 cm. Portal
Gallery. © Bridgeman Art Library.

WITHOUT COMMERCIALS

ALICE WALKER

Listen,
stop tanning yourself
and talking about
fishbelly
5 white.
The color white
is not bad at all.
There are white mornings
that bring us days.
10 Or, if you must,
tan only because
it makes you happy
to be brown,
to be able to see
15 for a summer
the whole world's
darker
face
reflected
20 in your own. **C**

Stop unfolding
your eyes. **D**
Your eyes are
beautiful.
25 Sometimes
seeing you in the street
the fold zany[1]
and unexpected
I want to kiss
30 them
and usually
it is only
old
gorgeous
35 black people's eyes
I want
to kiss.

C MAKE INFERENCES
Reread the first **stanza.**
Who is the **speaker**
addressing?

D MAKE INFERENCES
Reread lines 21–22.
What is meant by
"unfolding your eyes"?

---

1. **zany:** silly in an outrageous sort of way.

Detail of *Bessie's Blues: The American Collection #5* (1997), Faith Ringgold. Acrylic on canvas, painted, tie-dyed, and pieced fabric, 76⅞″ × 79¼″. Robert Allerton Endowment, 2002.381, The Art Institute of Chicago. Faith Ringgold © 1997.

Stop trimming
your nose.
40 When you
diminish
your nose
your songs
become little
45 tinny, muted
and snub.
Better you should
have a nose
impertinent[2]
50 as a flower,
sensitive
as a root;
wise, elegant,
serious and deep.
55 A nose that
sniffs
the essence
of Earth. And knows
the message
60 of every
leaf. **E**

Stop bleaching
your skin
and talking
65 about
so much black
is not beautiful.
The color black
is not bad
70 at all.
There are black nights
that rock
us
in dreams.
75 Or, if you must,
bleach only
because it pleases you

E **RECURRING THEME**
What are the qualities of a nose that has not been "trimmed"?

2. **impertinent:** bold; beyond what is proper.

to be brown,
to be able to see
80　for as long
as you can bear it
the whole world's
lighter face
reflected
85　in your own. **F**

As for me,
I have learned
to worship
the sun
90　again.
To affirm
the adventures
of hair. **G**

For we are all
95　*splendid*
descendants
of Wilderness,
Eden:[3]
needing only
100　to see
each other
without
commercials
to believe. **H**

105　Copied skillfully
as Adam.

Original

as Eve.

F RECURRING THEME
According to lines 75–85, what would be the only good reason to bleach one's skin?

G MAKE INFERENCES
Reread lines 86–93. What do these lines tell you about the **speaker's** attitude toward her own appearance?

H MAKE INFERENCES
What can you **infer** about the "commercials" mentioned here and in the **title?** Add this information to your chart.

---

3. **Eden:** reference to the biblical Garden of Eden, the first home of the first humans.

Comprehension

1. **Recall** To whom does the **speaker** compare everyone in "Without Commercials"?

2. **Clarify** In "Same Song," why does the daughter "stumble off to bed at nine" with her "eyes half shut"?

3. **Paraphrase** Rewrite lines 94–108 of "Without Commercials" in words and length similar to those in the poem.

Literary Analysis

4. **Make Inferences** Look again at the inferences you recorded in your chart as you read. Which were most helpful in understanding each poem?

5. **Analyze Word Choice** Does "Without Commercials" present a mostly negative or mostly sympathetic view of people who try to change their natural **appearance?** Cite specific words and phrases as examples.

6. **Compare Poems** In "Same Song," how do you think the **speaker** feels about the work her children do to change the way they look? Compare and contrast this with the speaker's attitude in "Without Commercials."

7. **Analyze Recurring Theme** Use a chart like the one shown to gather information about the two poems. Then state in your own words the recurring theme they share about appearance.

	"Same Song"	"Without Commercials"
Subject Presented	looks	commericals
Words That Tell How Speaker Feels	frowns at her face	your eyes are beautieul
Images That Stand Out in My Mind	peers into mirror and crowns	lighter face reflected in your own

Theme About Appearance: You are beautiful

Extension and Challenge

8. **Creative Project: Writing** Keeping the **recurring theme** in mind, write an extra stanza for "Without Commercials" in which the **speaker** addresses the children from "Same Song." What advice would she give them?

Writing Workshop

Analyzing a Story

Stories like the ones in this unit can help you enter other lives and other worlds—without even leaving home. Analyzing the familiar and unfamiliar parts of a story can help you understand it better and enjoy it more. The **Writer's Road Map** will guide you as you write an analysis of a story.

WRITER'S ROAD MAP

Analyzing a Story

WRITING PROMPT 1

Writing from Literature Analyzing a story means figuring out meanings that you did not notice at first. Choose a short story and write an analysis that helps a reader understand it better. Examine one or two literary elements in the story, such as plot, characters, conflict, setting, theme, or point of view.

Literature and Literary Elements to Consider

- plot in "The Dog of Pompeii"
- characters in "Scout's Honor"
- conflict in "Eleven"

WRITING PROMPT 2

Writing from the Real World Great stories are everywhere, not just in literature. Think of a story that you recently viewed or read. Write an essay that briefly summarizes the story and analyzes an important aspect of it.

Places to Look

- television shows that have strong characters
- action movies with fast-moving plots
- true-life adventure stories in magazines

 WRITING TOOLS
For prewriting, revision, and editing tools, visit the **Writing Center** at ClassZone.com.

KEY TRAITS

1. IDEAS
- Includes a **thesis statement** that gives the key points the writer will discuss
- Supports key points with **evidence**—details, examples, or quotations

2. ORGANIZATION
- Identifies the author and title of the work in the **introduction**
- Gives enough **details** about the story so the reader can understand the analysis
- Summarizes the ideas in a **conclusion** and tells why the story is special or important

3. VOICE
- Has an appropriate **tone** for the audience and purpose

4. WORD CHOICE
- Uses **precise language** to examine and explain the work

5. SENTENCE FLUENCY
- Uses different **sentence types** (statements, questions, and exclamations) where appropriate

6. CONVENTIONS
- Uses **correct grammar, spelling, and punctuation**

Part 1: Analyze a Student Model

Paola Arroyo
San Gabriel Middle School

Characters and Conflict in "Nadia the Willful"

When I started reading "Nadia the Willful" by Sue Alexander, I didn't think I would be interested in this stubborn desert girl who doesn't get along with anybody except her brother. By the time I finished the story, though, her wisdom and courage made me want to be just like her.

5 This story has a very important theme—that we should never forget the people we love, even after they die. The author gets this message across by showing us the conflict between Nadia and her father.

The story's title tells us a lot about the conflict before we even begin reading. Nadia has a terrible temper. Even her important and powerful

10 father can't control her. Only her brother Hamed can "laugh and tease and pull at her dark hair until she laughed back." When he dies, the whole family feels terrible grief. Nadia cries, but her father just sits, "speaking not at all." Finally, he orders everyone never to mention Hamed's name again. Nadia obeys her father. She can't stop thinking

15 about her brother, though, and she gets angrier and sadder.

In the middle of the story, the conflict heats up. Nadia becomes so miserable that she ignores her father's order and begins talking about Hamed. Do you think she pays attention when her mother begs her to stop or even when her father punishes a shepherd who says Hamed's

20 name? No. She keeps on talking about Hamed even after everyone stops listening. Nadia finally stands up to her father directly. "You will not rob me of my brother Hamed!" she shouts. "I will not let you!"

At the end of the story, this direct conflict makes the theme clear. At first, Nadia's father looks at her with eyes that are "colder than the

25 desert night." I thought he might banish her, because that's what he did

KEY TRAITS IN ACTION

Strong introduction identifies the author and title of the story.

Clear thesis statement focuses on how two literary elements (theme and conflict) affect the story's meaning.

Important **details** help the reader understand the analysis. **Evidence** from the story supports the idea that the conflict is important.

Precise language makes the essay clear and lively.

Different **sentence types** help to hold the reader's interest.

to the shepherd who talked about Hamed. However, Nadia gently helps her father realize that he is already beginning to forget what Hamed was like. By sharing her memories, she shows her father that talking about a dead person is a way to keep that person alive in our hearts. We

30 know this message is the lesson the author wants us to learn because, after hearing it, the father tells everyone, "From this day forward, let my daughter Nadia be known not as willful but as wise."

Nadia realizes that we never lose the people we love as long as we remember them. During the conflict of the story, she teaches her father,

35 the other characters in the story, and all its readers this important lesson. I'm glad I got to know this strong, wise character who stands up for what she believes.

Tone is serious enough for the story's theme and is appropriate for the writer's classmates and teacher.

Conclusion restates the story's theme, summarizes how the author gets the theme across, and tells what the writer learned.

2

Part 2: Apply the Writing Process

PREWRITING

What Should I Do?

1. Think about the different parts of the story.
If you are analyzing a short story, what did you notice about the characters, the plot, the conflict, the setting, the point of view, or the theme? If you are analyzing a different kind of story, what did you notice about the events, the pacing (fast or slow), or the overall message? Make a chart listing your ideas.

2. Do some freewriting.
Jot down your thoughts, feelings, and questions as you think about the story.

3. Put your thesis into words.
Write a sentence or two explaining the main point you want to make in your essay. Don't worry about saying it perfectly. Just get your ideas down for now.

TIP Make sure you are doing what the prompt asks you to. For example, if you chose Prompt 1, your thesis should name one or two literary elements and tell how they work in the story.

4. Go back to the story for evidence.
Read (or watch) the story again. List quotations and examples that support your thesis.

What Does It Look Like?

Characters	Conflict	Theme
• Nadia • Her father • Her brother Hamed	Nadia won't obey her father.	It's important to remember people who have died. That way they stay alive in our memories.

I like Nadia . . . she stands up to her father, even though he is really stern.

Why won't the father talk about his son? Nadia's right. He should remember the good times with Hamed.

Working Thesis Statement:

The main conflict in the story is between Nadia and her father. The conflict teaches us the theme, which is that we should remember the people we love, even after they die.

My Main Points	Supporting Evidence
After Hamed dies, Nadia and her father react in different ways.	Nadia cries, but her father just sits without talking.
Nadia stands up to her father.	"You will not rob me of my brother Hamed!"

What Should I Do?	**What Does It Look Like?**
1. Organize your analysis. Make a list or an outline of the points you plan to cover. The writer of the student model organized her essay in the order of the events in the story. **TIP** Another way to organize your analysis is to discuss the end of the story first, and then trace how the author arrived at that ending.	▶ *Introduction and thesis* *Beginning of story* • *Conflict: Nadia is stubborn, and her father is strict.* • *Theme (never forget the people we love): The father is sad, so he tries to forget his dead son.* *Middle of story* • *Conflict: Nadia ignores her father's order not to talk about Hamed.* • *Theme: "You will not rob me of my brother Hamed!"* *End of story* • *Conflict: Nadia helps her father realize that he is starting to forget Hamed.* • *Theme: Nadia's father says that it is wise to remember the people we love.* *Conclusion*
2. Think about your audience. Is your reader familiar with this story, or is it new to him or her? Give enough background information so that your reader can understand the points you are making.	▶ *The story's title tells us a lot about the conflict before we even begin reading. Nadia has a terrible temper. Even her important and powerful father can't control her. Only her brother Hamed can "laugh and tease and pull at her dark hair until she laughed back." When he dies, the whole family feels bad.*
3. Include details that support your ideas. You don't need to include every event of the story. Choose quotations or examples that help readers understand the points you are making. **TIP** Before revising, review the **key traits** on page 398 and the **rubric** and **peer-reader questions** on page 404.	▶ *Nadia finally stands up to her father directly.* ⟩—Key idea *"You will not rob me of my brother Hamed!" she shouts. "I will not let you!"* ⟩—Quotation that supports the key idea

REVISING AND EDITING

What Should I Do?	*What Does It Look Like?*

1. Make your introduction memorable.

- <u>Underline</u> the first sentence or two of your analysis. Ask a peer reader, "Does this introduction make you want to keep reading? Why or why not?"

- If your introduction is weak, think about including a quotation, a question, or a strong personal statement.

See page 404: Ask a Peer Reader

> ▶ ~~"Nadia the Willful" is a short story by Sue~~ ~~Alexander. I didn't like it at first, but then it got~~ ~~really interesting.~~ When I started reading "Nadia the Willful" by Sue Alexander, I didn't think I would be interested in this stubborn desert girl. By the time I finished the story, though, her wisdom and courage made me want to be just like her.

2. Use exact words.

- (Circle) words such as *nice, good, bad, okay,* and *interesting.* These words give your reader little or no information.

- Replace vague words with specific terms that help your reader understand your analysis.

> ▶ When he dies, the whole family feels (bad) terrible grief.

> By sharing her memories, she shows her father that talking about a dead person is (okay) a way to keep that person alive in our hearts.

3. Include different types of sentences.

- Draw a ⎡box⎤ around questions or exclamations in your analysis.

- If your analysis has no boxes, consider adding a question or exclamation for variety.

TIP Too many questions can make you seem confused. Too many exclamations can make you seem overexcited. Use them sparingly.

> ▶ Do you think
> She pays no attention when her mother begs her to stop or even when her father punishes a shepherd who says Hamed's name? No.

4. End strongly.

- Read your conclusion aloud. Does it tie your main ideas together?

- Revise so that the ending summarizes your ideas and reminds readers of the story's meaning or importance.

> ▶ Nadia realizes that we never lose the people we love as long as we remember them. ~~That's important.~~ During the conflict of the story, she teaches her father, the other characters in the story, and all its readers this important lesson. I'm glad I got to know this strong, wise character who stands up for what she believes.

Apply the Rubric

A strong analysis of a story . . .

☑ has an introduction that identifies the story's title and author

☑ includes a thesis statement that gives the key points of the essay

☑ provides examples, quotations, or other evidence to support those key points

☑ provides details about the story to help the reader understand the analysis

☑ uses exact, specific language

☑ creates a tone that is right for the essay's purpose and audience

☑ occasionally varies sentence types

☑ ends by summarizing the key points and explaining why the story is worthwhile

Ask a Peer Reader

• How can I improve my introduction?

• How would you describe the key points in your own words?

• Do any points need more evidence or explanation? If so, which ones?

Check Your Grammar

• Punctuate quotations correctly. Copy statements from the story exactly as they appear. Put quotation marks at the beginning and end, with periods, commas, and exclamation points inside the quotation marks.

> Nadia cries, but her father just sits, "speaking not at all."

> "You will not rob me of my brother Hamed!" she shouts. "I will not let you!"

> The father tells everyone, "From this day forward, let my daughter Nadia be known not as willful but as wise."

See page R49: Quick Reference: Punctuation

• Make sure that pronouns agree with their antecedents.

> We never lose the people we love as long as we remember him. them.

See page R52: Agreement with Antecedent

Writing Online

 PUBLISHING OPTIONS
For publishing options, visit the **Writing Center** at ClassZone.com.

ASSESSMENT PREPARATION
For writing and grammar assessment practice, go to the **Assessment Center** at ClassZone.com.

Holding a Discussion

Part of the fun of analyzing a story is sharing your thoughts with others. When you take part in a discussion, you expand your understanding and appreciation of what you have read.

Planning the Discussion

1. **Gather in a group.** Form a discussion group with two or three other students who have read the same story. Then ask for a volunteer to lead the group and for another volunteer to record the main points of the discussion.
2. **Agree on some basic rules.** Group members should speak clearly, listen without interrupting, and ask thoughtful questions.
3. **Review the story and your opinions about it.** Reread the analysis you have written. Write down one or two points you would like to make during the discussion.

Holding the Discussion

1. **Get started.** Have the group leader begin by identifying the story and its author and asking a question for the group to respond to. Here's an example: "Which character do you think is most important to the story? Why?"
2. **Share your ideas.** Give all group members a chance to respond to the first question and to comment on what other members have to say.

> *"I agree that Nadia is a main character. If Hamed hadn't died, though, none of the other events in the story would have happened. That's why I think he is the most important character."*

3. **Keep comments and questions focused on the story.** If someone gets off the topic, the discussion leader should gently bring the discussion back to the story.
4. **Bring it to a close.** The group leader should summarize what you have discussed and then thank everyone for participating. If your teacher asks groups to report to the class, have the member who recorded your discussion present a summary.

   See page R81: Group Discussion

Reading Comprehension

DIRECTIONS *Read these selections and answer the questions that follow.*

The Wolf and the House Dog

Aesop

There once was a Wolf who got very little to eat because the Dogs of the village were so wide awake and watchful. He was really nothing but skin and bones, and it made him very downhearted to think of it.

One night this Wolf happened to fall in with a fine fat House Dog who had wandered a little too far from home. The Wolf would gladly have eaten him then and there, but the House Dog looked strong enough to leave his marks should he try it. So the Wolf spoke very humbly to the Dog, complimenting him on his fine appearance.

"You can be as well-fed as I am if you want to," replied the Dog. "Leave
10 the woods; there you live miserably. Why, you have to fight hard for every bite you get. Follow my example and you will get along beautifully."

"What must I do?" asked the Wolf.

"Hardly anything," answered the House Dog. "Chase people who carry canes, bark at beggars, and fawn on the people of the house. In return you will get tidbits of every kind, chicken bones, choice bits of meat, sugar, cake, and much more besides, not to speak of kind words and caresses."

The Wolf had such a beautiful vision of his coming happiness that he almost wept. But just then he noticed that the hair on the Dog's neck was worn and the skin was chafed.

20 "What is that on your neck?"

"Nothing at all," replied the Dog.

"What! Nothing!"

"Oh, just a trifle!"

"But please tell me."

"Perhaps you see the mark of the collar to which my chain is fastened."

"What! A chain!" cried the Wolf. "Don't you go wherever you please?"

"Not always! But what's the difference?" replied the Dog.

"All the difference in the world! I don't care a rap for your feasts and I wouldn't take all the tender young lambs in the world at that price." And
30 away ran the Wolf to the woods.

There is nothing worth so much as liberty.

Your World

Georgia Douglas Johnson

Your world is as big as you make it
I know, for I used to abide
In the narrowest nest in a corner
My wings pressing close to my side.

5 But I sighted the distant horizon
Where the sky-line encircled the sea
And I throbbed with a burning desire
To travel this immensity.

I battered the cordons around me
10 And cradled my wings on the breeze
Then soared to the uttermost reaches
With rapture, with power, with ease!

Comprehension

DIRECTIONS *Answer these questions about "The Wolf and the House Dog."*

1. Which statement compares the way the Wolf and the House Dog feel at the beginning of the fable?

   A Both want to change the way they live.

   B The House Dog is lonely; the Wolf is scared.

   C The House Dog is satisfied; the Wolf is unhappy.

   D The House Dog is angry; the Wolf is friendly.

2. The House Dog probably avoids talking about the mark on his neck because he

   A does not know he has a mark

   B is vain about his appearance

   C feels ashamed to wear a collar

   D thinks the Wolf will hurt him

3. What is the topic of this fable?

   A freedom

   B vanity

   C greed

   D friendship

4. What can you infer about the Wolf's feelings at the end of the fable?

   A He is sad that the House Dog has to wear a collar and chain.

   B He envies the House Dog, even though he wouldn't want to be him.

   C He is glad he found out about the chain before moving into a house.

   D He is sure he will find something to eat soon.

5. What is the main difference between the attitude of the House Dog and that of the Wolf?

   A The House Dog is boastful; the Wolf is humble.

   B The House Dog prefers to be cared for; the Wolf prefers to be on his own.

   C The House Dog likes people; the Wolf dislikes them.

   D The House Dog is a good hunter; the Wolf is not.

6. What comparison can you make between the Wolf and the House Dog based on their physical appearance?

   A The Wolf has a hard life; the House Dog has an easy life.

   B The Wolf has a good life; the House Dog is mistreated.

   C The Wolf is gray; the House Dog is spotted.

   D The Wolf lives outdoors; the House Dog lives indoors.

7. Why doesn't the Wolf eat the House Dog?

   A The Wolf isn't hungry that day.

   B The Dog looks stronger than the Wolf.

   C Other good food is available nearby.

   D The Dog's owners chase the Wolf away.

DIRECTIONS *Answer these questions about "Your World."*

8. What is the topic of this poem?

   A leaving home

   B choosing independence

   C enjoying nature

   D making friends

9. From the description in lines 2–4 you can infer that the speaker's life used to be

   A safe and predictable

   B happy and comfortable

   C lonely and harsh

   D busy and exciting

10. The description in lines 11–12 suggests that the speaker has

    A become an important person

    B experienced new adventures

    C lived a life of luxury

    D decided to return home

11. Which statement best describes the theme of this poem?

    A Sometimes it is good to live alone.

    B Happiness comes from traveling.

    C Experience is the best teacher.

    D You are as free as you want to be.

12. Reread line 9: "I battered the cordons around me." You can infer that the speaker

    A did not want to change

    B needed to feel safe in life

    C had to overcome obstacles

    D traveled around the world

DIRECTIONS *Answer this question about both selections.*

13. A message about life found in both selections is that

    A being well fed is the key to survival

    B liberty is more important than security

    C the truth will come out in the end

    D some things are too good to be true

Written Response

SHORT RESPONSE *Write two or three sentences to answer this question.*

14. "The Wolf and the House Dog" and "Your World" are both about making choices. Compare the choices that the characters and the speaker make in these selections.

EXTENDED RESPONSE *Write a short paragraph to answer this question.*

15. In what way is the speaker in "Your World" like the Wolf in Aesop's fable? Use details from the selections to support your answer.

GO ON ➤

Vocabulary

DIRECTIONS *Use context clues and your knowledge of suffixes to answer the following questions.*

1. What is the most likely meaning of the word *immensity* as it is used in line 8 of "Your World"?

   A hugeness
   B growing
   C bigger
   D largely

2. What is the most likely meaning of the word *rapture* as it is used in line 12 of "Your World"?

   A ecstatic
   B enchant
   C bliss
   D happily

3. What is the most likely meaning of the word *appearance* as it is used in line 8 of "The Wolf and the House Dog"?

   A groomed
   B handsome
   C nicely
   D looks

4. What is the most likely meaning of the word *miserably* as it is used in line 10 of "The Wolf and the House Dog"?

   A sadness
   B unhappily
   C crying
   D depress

DIRECTIONS *Use context clues and your knowledge of multiple-meaning words to answer the following questions.*

5. Which meaning of the word *rap* is used in line 28 of "The Wolf and the House Dog"?

   "I don't care a <u>rap</u> for your feasts. . . ."

   A tap
   B bit
   C discussion
   D punishment

6. Which meaning of the word *trifle* is used in line 23 of "The Wolf and the House Dog"?

   "Oh, just a <u>trifle</u>!"

   A small thing
   B custard dessert
   C tiny amount
   D shiny trinket

7. Which meaning of the word *abide* is used in lines 2–3 of "Your World"?

   "I know, for I used to <u>abide</u>
   In the narrowest nest in a corner"

   A tolerate
   B await
   C comply
   D live

Writing & Grammar

DIRECTIONS *Read this passage and answer the questions that follow.*

(1) Call me when you get to Sue's my mom said nervously. (2) This was my first train trip on my own. (3) It was a big event in our family. (4) I was leaving Chicago. (5) I was going to my aunt's house in New York.

(6) My parents had said You're too young to travel alone. (7) They didn't want me to go by myself. (8) I convinced them to let me go, anyway. (9) I knew this would be a journey worth taking.

1. Choose the correct way to punctuate the dialogue in sentence 1.

  A "Call me when you get to Sue's", my mom said nervously.

  B "Call me when you get to Sue's" my mom said nervously.

  C Call me when you get to Sue's, my mom said nervously.

  D "Call me when you get to Sue's," my mom said nervously.

2. Choose the correct coordinating conjunction to combine sentences 2 and 3.

  A or   **C** for

  B so   **D** but

3. Choose the correct way to combine sentences 4 and 5 by using one subject and two predicates.

  A I was leaving Chicago; I was going to my aunt's house in New York.

  B I was leaving Chicago and going to my aunt's house in New York.

  C I was leaving Chicago, and I was going to my aunt's house in New York.

  D My aunt and I were leaving Chicago and going to her house in New York.

4. Choose the correct way to punctuate the dialogue in sentence 6.

  A My parents had said "You're too young to travel alone."

  B My parents had said, You're too young to travel alone.

  C My parents had said, "You're too young to travel alone."

  D My parents had said "You're too young to travel alone".

5. Choose the correct coordinating conjunction to combine sentences 7 and 8.

  A or   **C** but

  B for   **D** so

More Great Reads

Ideas for Independent Reading

Which questions from Unit 3 made an impression on you?
Continue exploring with these books.

Can memories keep the past alive?

The Color of My Words
by Lynn Joseph

Anna Rosa is only 12, but she knows she's a writer. She soon learns that writing is powerful as well as dangerous. She also realizes that writing someone's story will help keep his memory alive.

Locomotion
by Jacqueline Woodson

Lonnie's parents are dead and he can't live with his sister. Everything seems bad—but every day, in Ms. Marcus's class, he writes poems about the people he loves so he'll never forget them. Slowly, things begin to get better.

Up on Cloud Nine
by Anne Fine

Stolly is in a coma and Ian can't help him, so Ian sits next to his friend's bed and starts writing down everything he remembers about Stolly's life. Will Ian's memories help Stolly understand his past when he wakes up?

When is a trip an adventure?

Gregor the Overlander
by Suzanne Collins

Gregor is so bored that a trip to the laundry room in the basement seems exciting. Before their clothes are dry, however, he and his sister are sucked into the Underland and have to fight their way back home.

Hatchet
by Gary Paulsen

Brian is on a small plane going to visit his father the summer after his parents' divorce. Suddenly, the pilot has a heart attack and Brian finds himself alone in the Canadian wilderness. How will he survive?

Journey to the River Sea
by Eva Ibbotson

Maia is nervous and excited when she sets off from England to live with relatives in Brazil. She doesn't realize that her sea voyage and a trip on the Amazon are only the beginning of a bigger adventure.

Should you live for the present or the future?

The Fire-Eaters
by David Almond

Bobby's life has just gone bad: He has cruel teachers, a sick father, and the United States is about to enter a nuclear war. Then Bobby meets McNulty, a fire-eater. Can believing in miracles help Bobby see hope for the future?

Gentle's Holler
by Kerry Madden

Dreaming of the future, Livy sees herself standing on the Great Wall of China, not up in a tree in North Carolina watching her little sisters. After a terrible accident, Livy has to decide if her dreams are more important than her family.

Listening for Lions
by Gloria Whelan

When her parents die during an epidemic in Africa, Rachel's deceitful neighbors send her to England in their dead daughter's place. Will Rachel be stuck living a lie or will she be able to return to the country she loves?

Writer's Craft

MOOD, TONE, AND STYLE

- In Fiction
- In Nonfiction
- In Poetry
- In Drama
- In Media

Who has STYLE?

Picture some people you know. How do they look? What are they wearing? Perhaps one person has neatly trimmed hair and wears a button-down shirt. Another is dressed in an old T-shirt and flip-flops, and has ten bracelets on each wrist. However these people look or act, each is displaying a personal **style**—the choices that make him or her unique. Writers, filmmakers, and artists also have a unique style. They display this style through how they choose to tell their stories or express their ideas.

ACTIVITY Think of a television or movie character who has a distinct personal style. Get together with a few classmates and describe your character's style without naming him or her. Can the others guess your choice?

Lion King (1999), William Wegman. Color Polaroid, 24″ × 20″.

Reader (1999), William Wegman. Color Polaroid, 24″ × 20″.

Glamour Puss (1999), William Wegman. Color Polaroid, 24″ × 20″.

Preview Unit Goals

LITERARY ANALYSIS
- Identify and analyze tone
- Identify, analyze, and compare mood
- Identify and analyze elements of style, including point of view, dialogue, word choice, similes, sentence structure, and imagery
- Identify and analyze elements of style in fiction and nonfiction
- Identify and analyze imagery

READING
- Identify and analyze author's purpose
- Develop strategies for reading, including monitoring, connecting, visualizing, and setting a purpose
- Take notes and summarize

WRITING AND GRAMMAR
- Write a compare-and-contrast essay
- Identify and correctly punctuate declarative, interrogative, imperative, and exclamatory sentences
- Use commas correctly with adjectives and items in a series

SPEAKING, LISTENING, AND VIEWING
- Prepare and deliver a power presentation
- Identify and analyze color, line, shape, and texture in illustrations
- Compare and contrast the style of illustrations

VOCABULARY
- Identify the meaning of compound words
- Use context clues to help determine word meaning

ACADEMIC VOCABULARY
- mood
- tone
- elements of style
- author's purpose
- summarize
- take notes

Mood, Tone, and Style

Every story has its own unmistakable personality—one that you respond to either positively or negatively. In this workshop, you'll learn about the elements that make up a story's personality. These elements are mood, tone, and style.

Part 1: What's the Difference?

Mood is the feeling that a writer creates for readers. **Tone** is a writer's attitude toward his or her subject. This example can help you understand the difference between the two: Your soccer team is playing a rival. In the final seconds of the game, you score the winning goal. The crowd cheers, and your teammates rush toward you. The mood is one of excitement.

Later, a player from the other team says to you, "Great game." Is she bitter or sincere? You could determine her attitude, or tone, by noticing *how* she says "Great game."

So, how can you identify mood and tone in a work of literature? A mood is often revealed through the description of a setting or of a character's feelings. A writer's tone comes across through his or her choice of words and details. Take a closer look at the examples shown.

MOOD
Words to Describe Mood
• joyful   • threatening   • exciting
• scary   • peaceful   • eerie

Example: Peaceful Mood
The highlighted descriptions of the setting help to create a peaceful mood.

They were standing in a sunlit field, and the air about them was moving with the delicious fragrance that comes only on the rarest of spring days when the sun's touch is gentle . . .

—from *A Wrinkle in Time*
by Madeleine L'Engle

TONE
Words to Describe Tone
• mocking   • disgusted   • sarcastic
• humorous   • serious   • sentimental

Example: Mocking Tone
The highlighted details help you understand that the writer is making fun of his clumsiness.

. . . I worked in construction, mostly hitting my fingers with a hammer and making serious attempts at cutting something off my body with power saws while I tried to build houses. . . .

—from *My Life in Dog Years*
by Gary Paulsen

MODEL 1: MOOD

A young Chinese immigrant named Moon Shadow comes to San Francisco to join his father. Shortly after Moon Shadow arrives, he follows his father on a mysterious nighttime mission. As you read, notice the details used to describe the setting and create a mood.

from DRAGONWINGS
Novel by **Laurence Yep**

I counted to ten before I followed him outside. It was a night when the thick fog drifted through the streets and I could not see more than an arm's length before me, and everything seemed unreal, as if I were asleep and dreaming. The gaslights showed in the fog only as dull spots of
5   light—like ghosts hovering. A building would appear out of the grayness and then disappear. The whole world seemed to have become unglued. If ever there was a night for monsters to be out, this was the night.

Close Read

1. The boxed detail helps readers to picture the nighttime setting. Find three more details that describe the setting.

2. Review the details you found. What mood do they help to create?

MODEL 2: TONE

In his memoir, author Jerry Spinelli shares his memories of growing up in Pennsylvania. Read on to find out what Spinelli remembers about one important subject—his family's garbage can!

from Knots in My Yo-Yo String
Memoir by **Jerry Spinelli**

To lift the lid off the garbage can was to confront all the horrors of the creepiest movie: dead, rotting matter; teeming colonies of pale, slimy creeping things; and a stench that could be survived only in the smallest whiffs.
5   Ironically, the garbage can was never more disgusting than the day *after* garbage collection—for the collection was never quite complete. The garbage man would snatch the can from our curbside and overturn it into the garbage truck's unspeakable trough. He would bang it once, maybe twice, against the trough wall. This would dislodge most of the
10 garbage, including a rain of maggots, but not the worst of it, not the very bottom of it, the most persistent, the oldest, the rottenest, the vilest.

Close Read

1. Many details, including the one in the box, help you to see or smell the garbage. Identify three other descriptive details.

2. Read aloud lines 1–4 as you think Spinelli would sound saying them. Would you describe his tone as amused, irritated, joking, or something else?

Part 2: What Is Style?

You've seen how mood and tone can affect your reaction to a story. Style, though, is what really gives a story its one-of-a-kind personality. **Style** refers to a writer's unique way of communicating ideas. It is the result of many elements, including word choice, sentence structure, imagery, point of view, and dialogue. You'll learn about some of these elements as you examine two excerpts by authors with different styles.

E. L. KONIGSBURG'S STYLE

Claudia and Jamie awoke very early the next morning. It was still dark. Their stomachs felt like tubes of toothpaste that had been all squeezed out. Giant economy-sized tubes. They had to be out of bed and out of sight before the museum staff came on duty.

—from *From the Mixed-up Files of Mrs. Basil E. Frankweiler*

JEAN CRAIGHEAD GEORGE'S STYLE

Miyax pushed back the hood of her seal-skin parka and looked at the Arctic sun. It was a yellow disc in a lime-green sky, the colors of six o'clock in the evening and the time when the wolves awoke. Quietly she put down her cooking pot and crept to the top of a dome-shaped frost heave, one of the many earth buckles that rise and fall in the crackling cold . . .

—from *Julie of the Wolves*

WORD CHOICE
Word choice, or a writer's use of language, is a basic element of style.

- Konigsburg: Uses casual, informal language like *giant* and *squeezed out*.
- George: Uses precise, descriptive adjectives, such as *lime-green* and *dome-shaped*.

SENTENCE STRUCTURE
Sentence structure refers to the lengths and types of sentences a writer uses.

- Konigsburg: Writes in short, simple sentences, creating a straightforward style.
- George: Uses longer, complex sentences that are packed with descriptions.

IMAGERY
Some writers are known for their use of **imagery**, language that appeals to readers' senses.

- Konigsburg: Includes a humorous image— stomachs *like tubes of toothpaste.* This creates a playful style.
- George: Uses vivid images like *yellow disc in a lime-green sky.*

MODEL 1: COMPARING STYLES

Buried riches, greedy pirates, and wild adventures are all part of Robert Louis Stevenson's novel *Treasure Island*. In this excerpt, a boy and his mother open a sea chest that once belonged to a ship captain. An evil blind man is in pursuit of the chest. As you read, you'll examine the elements that help to create Stevenson's dramatic and formal style.

from Treasure Island

Novel by **Robert Louis Stevenson**

When we were about half-way through, I suddenly put my hand upon her arm; for I had heard in the silent, frosty air, a sound that brought my heart into my mouth—the tap-tapping of the blind man's stick upon the frozen road. It drew nearer and nearer, while we sat
5 holding our breath. Then it struck sharp on the inn door, and then we could hear the handle being turned, and the bolt rattling as the wretched being tried to enter; and then there was a long time of silence both within and without.

Close Read

1. One element of Stevenson's style is his use of imagery. Find three images that help you to hear what's happening. One example has been boxed.

2. Would you describe Stevenson's sentences as short and simple or as long and complex? Support your answer.

MODEL 2: COMPARING STYLES

The characters in this modern story are also startled by a sound at their door. As you read, you'll look closely at the elements that make Bruce Coville's style lighter and more informal than Stevenson's.

from Duffy's Jacket

Short story by **Bruce Coville**

"There's something at the door," I said frantically. "Maybe it's been lurking around all day, waiting for our mothers to leave. Maybe it's been waiting for years for someone to come back here."

Scratch, scratch.

5 "I don't believe it," said Duffy. "It's just the wind moving a branch. I'll prove it."

He got up and headed for the door. But he didn't open it. Instead he peeked through the window next to it. When he turned back, his eyes looked as big as the hard-boiled eggs we had eaten for supper.

Close Read

1. How do the boxed sentences compare with the sentences in *Treasure Island*?

2. Informal dialogue is one element of Coville's style. Reread the dialogue in lines 1–6. Which words or phrases make this sound like an everyday conversation?

Part 3: Analyze the Literature

Now, you'll apply what you've learned by analyzing two excerpts. Both excerpts describe summer days, but they are strikingly different. Read on to see how mood, tone, and style help to create these differences.

The first excerpt is from the beginning of the novel *Tuck Everlasting*. Don't worry if you don't know exactly what's happening. This is an intentional choice by the author, and it's meant to draw you into the story.

from
Tuck Everlasting

Novel by **Natalie Babbitt**

The first week of August hangs at the very top of summer, the top of the live-long year, like the highest seat of a Ferris wheel when it pauses in its turning. The weeks that come before are only a climb from balmy spring, and those that follow a drop to the chill of autumn, but the first
5   week of August is motionless, and hot. It is curiously silent, too, with blank white dawns and glaring noons, and sunsets smeared with too much color. Often at night there is lightning, but it quivers all alone. There is no thunder, no relieving rain. These are strange and breathless days, the dog days, when people are led to do things they are sure to be
10 sorry for after.

One day at that time, not so very long ago, three things happened and at first there appeared to be no connection between them.

At dawn, Mae Tuck set out on her horse for the wood at the edge of the village of Treegap. She was going there, as she did once every ten
15 years, to meet her two sons, Miles and Jesse.

At noontime, Winnie Foster, whose family owned the Treegap wood, lost her patience at last and decided to think about running away.

And at sunset a stranger appeared at the Fosters' gate. He was looking for someone, but he didn't say who.
20 No connection, you would agree. But things can come together in strange ways. The wood was at the center, the hub of the wheel. All wheels must have a hub. A Ferris wheel has one, as the sun is the hub of the wheeling calendar. Fixed points they are, and best left undisturbed, for without them, nothing holds together. But sometimes people find
25 this out too late.

Close Read

1. One aspect of Babbitt's style is her use of colorful imagery. What images in lines 1–10 tell you what the first week of August is like?

2. The writer's tone might be described as both conversational and secretive. What words and phrases in lines 11–12 and 20–25 contribute to this tone?

3. Reread the boxed detail, in which the narrator delivers a strange warning. Also review the images you found in lines 1–10. What mood do these elements create?

The summer days that Jewell Parker Rhodes describes in "Block Party" are ones that she herself experienced as a child. As you read this excerpt, you'll analyze some of the elements that make Rhodes's description so different from Babbitt's.

from

BLOCK PARTY

Memoir by **Jewell Parker Rhodes**

        Summer block parties were the best. We'd close off traffic and sometimes the Fire Department would open the hydrants and we'd dance and sing while water gushed at us. A spray of wet beneath the moon and stars. Tonie, Aleta, and I pushed boxes together to make
5 a stage and lipsynched to the record player, pretending we were The Supremes. *"Stop, in the name of love! Before you break my heart. Think it o-o-over! . . ."* and we'd giggle as the grown-ups clapped and the other children squealed, and everyone danced, even fat Charlie who could boogie so well you'd swear there was magic in his shoes.
10   The best block parties happened for no reason. Anyone—even a child—could wake up one day and call for "Block Party Day." And we'd share ribs, corn, chicken, tater pie, and collard greens, and Miss Sarah who never married always made punch with vanilla ice cream and it would melt into a swishy mess. Finally, when legs wouldn't move
15 another dance step, then the record player was taken away, the street was swept. There were cries and whispers of good night. My real family and I, we'd go into the house. Grandma, Grandpa, Aunt, and Daddy would tuck us in bed and kiss me, Tonie, and Aleta good night. And I would wait until Tonie and Aleta were asleep in the small twin beds (I didn't
20 want them to think I was off my head) and I'd go to the window. Then, peeking over the ledge, I'd whisper my own private "G'night" to the rest of my family, tucked in their beds inside the tall houses all along my street, there in the city where the three rivers meet.

Close Read

1. What images in lines 1–14 help to establish the joyful mood of the summer scene?

2. Reread the boxed text. Notice that Rhodes packs many thoughts into one long sentence, using a series of *and*'s. Identify another sentence that reflects this style.

3. Words like *G'night* in line 21 help to create a conversational style. Find two other informal words or phrases.

4. How would you describe Rhodes's tone, or attitude, toward the block parties?
   a. humorous and sarcastic
   b. warm and reflective
   c. sad and regretful

The All-American Slurp
Short Story by Lensey Namioka

Are people more ALIKE or different?

KEY IDEA Have you ever been somewhere and found that the language, food, or customs were different than what you were used to? You may have felt out of place. Or perhaps you discovered that you actually had a lot in common with the people you met. In "The All-American Slurp," a Chinese-American girl learns that people can share **similarities** even when they appear very different at first.

SURVEY Complete this survey. Then form a group with two or three people you don't know well. Share your surveys to see how much you do (or don't) have in common.

Survey:

Choose Your Favorites

Choose your favorite from each grouping. Then find out how your classmates answered.

Music
- Rock 'n' Roll
- Country
- Classical

Food
- Desserts
- Spicy Foods
- Salty Snacks

Holidays
- Thanksgiving
- Halloween
- Valentine's Day
- Fourth of July

Movies
- Dramas
- Comedies
- Musicals
- Sci-Fi

Seasons
- Winter
- Spring
- Summer
- Fall

● LITERARY ANALYSIS: TONE

Stories can express a writer's **tone,** or attitude toward a subject. The tone might be described in a single word, such as *sarcastic, silly,* or *sentimental.*

This story is about the challenges people face when adjusting to life in a new country. Lensey Namioka establishes a humorous tone toward this subject through

- characters' thoughts, words, and actions
- the narrator's descriptions
- the order of events

As you read "The All-American Slurp," look for these elements as the family faces a series of awkward situations.

● READING STRATEGY: SUMMARIZE

One way to check your understanding of a story is to **summarize** it. A good summary provides a brief retelling of the main ideas. It uses your own words but does not include your opinions about the subject. As you read "The All-American Slurp," record the key events of the story in a log like the one shown.

> ### Key Events
> - *Lin family emigrates from China to the United States.*
> -

▲ VOCABULARY IN CONTEXT

Lensey Namioka uses the listed words to help tell a story about people's differences. To see how many you know, complete each sentence with a word from the list.

WORD	consumption	etiquette	mortified
LIST	cope	lavishly	revolting

1. Follow proper _____ when you meet someone new.
2. I'm _____ when I can't remember someone's name.
3. Their sofa was _____ decorated with fancy pillows.
4. That weird stew was absolutely _____!
5. The waiter had to _____ with the loud guests.
6. _____ of too many spicy foods makes me feel ill.

Author Online

Outsiders' Stories
Lensey Namioka says that her stories tell about people who feel like "outsiders." This is true whether the story is set in present-day Seattle or 16th-century Japan. To write these stories, she draws upon her own experiences.

Lensey Namioka born 1929

Growing Up on the Outside Namioka grew up in China. When war broke out in 1937, her family moved to western China, where the food was very spicy and the dialect (regional form of a language) was hard to understand. This made her feel like an outsider in her own country. Before the war ended, her family moved to the United States. The strange customs, food, and language of her new country made her feel even more like an outsider.

Living in Two Worlds At first, Namioka's father charged everyone in the family a fine for each English word used at home. He did so because he did not want his family to forget the Chinese language. Namioka's mother ended the fines when she refused to pay. "Besides," says Namioka, "there were words that just had no Chinese translation. How do you say 'cheeseburger' in Chinese, for instance?"

 MORE ABOUT THE AUTHOR
For more on Lensey Namioka, visit the **Literature Center** at ClassZone.com.

The All-American Slurp

Lensey Namioka

The first time our family was invited out to dinner in America, we disgraced ourselves while eating celery. We had emigrated to this country from China, and during our early days here we had a hard time with American table manners.

In China we never ate celery raw, or any other kind of vegetable raw. We always had to disinfect the vegetables in boiling water first. When we were presented with our first relish tray, the raw celery caught us unprepared.

We had been invited to dinner by our neighbors, the Gleasons. After
10 arriving at the house, we shook hands with our hosts and packed ourselves into a sofa. As our family of four sat stiffly in a row, my younger brother and I stole glances at our parents for a clue as to what to do next. **Ⓐ**

Mrs. Gleason offered the relish tray to Mother. The tray looked pretty, with its tiny red radishes, curly sticks of carrots, and long, slender stalks of pale green celery. "Do try some of the celery, Mrs. Lin," she said. "It's from a local farmer, and it's sweet."

Mother picked up one of the green stalks, and Father followed suit. Then I picked up a stalk, and my brother did too. So there we sat, each with a stalk of celery in our right hand.

20 Mrs. Gleason kept smiling. "Would you like to try some of the dip, Mrs. Lin? It's my own recipe: sour cream and onion flakes, with a dash of Tabasco sauce."

Ⓐ TONE
Reread lines 1–12. What words and phrases help create a humorous tone toward the subject of the story?

Most Chinese don't care for dairy products, and in those days I wasn't even ready to drink fresh milk. Sour cream sounded perfectly **revolting**. Our family shook our heads in unison.

Mrs. Gleason went off with the relish tray to the other guests, and we carefully watched to see what they did. Everyone seemed to eat the raw vegetables quite happily.

Mother took a bite of her celery. *Crunch.* "It's not bad!" she whispered.

30   Father took a bite of his celery. *Crunch.* "Yes, it *is* good," he said, looking surprised.

I took a bite, and then my brother. *Crunch, crunch.* It was more than good; it was delicious. Raw celery has a slight sparkle, a zingy taste that you don't get in cooked celery. When Mrs. Gleason came around with the relish tray, we each took another stalk of celery, except my brother. He took two.

There was only one problem: long strings ran through the length of the stalk, and they got caught in my teeth. When I help my mother in the kitchen, I always pull the strings out before slicing celery.

40   I pulled the strings out of my stalk. *Z-z-zip, z-z-zip.* My brother followed suit. *Z-z-zip, z-z-zip, z-z-zip.* To my left, my parents were taking care of their own stalks. *Z-z-zip, z-z-zip, z-z-zip.* **B**

Suddenly I realized that there was dead silence except for our zipping. Looking up, I saw that the eyes of everyone in the room were on our family. Mr. and Mrs. Gleason, their daughter Meg, who was my friend, and their neighbors the Badels—they were all staring at us as we busily pulled the strings of our celery.

That wasn't the end of it. Mrs. Gleason announced that dinner was served and invited us to the dining table. It was **lavishly** covered with
50   platters of food, but we couldn't see any chairs around the table. So we helpfully carried over some dining chairs and sat down. All the other guests just stood there.

Mrs. Gleason bent down and whispered to us, "This is a buffet dinner. You help yourselves to some food and eat it in the living room."

Our family beat a retreat back to the sofa as if chased by enemy soldiers. For the rest of the evening, too **mortified** to go back to the dining table, I nursed[1] a bit of potato salad on my plate. **C**

Next day Meg and I got on the school bus together. I wasn't sure how she would feel about me after the spectacle[2] our family made at the party.
60   But she was just the same as usual, and the only reference she made to the party was, "Hope you and your folks got enough to eat last night. You certainly didn't take very much. Mom never tries to figure out how

---

1. **nursed**: very slowly ate.
2. **spectacle**: public display of bad behavior.

revolting (rĭ-vōl'tĭng) *adj.* causing disgust **revolt** *v.*

B TONE
Using a word that sounds like what it means is called **onomatopoeia** (ŏn'ə-măt'ə-pē'ə). Notice the word *z-z-zip* in lines 40–42. How does this word add humor to the story?

lavishly (lăv'ĭsh-lē) *adv.* in a rich or plentiful way; abundantly

mortified (môr'tə-fīd') *adj.* ashamed, humiliated **mortify** *v.*

C SUMMARIZE
What happened at the Gleason's dinner party to make the narrator feel as if her family members disgraced themselves? Record the events in your log.

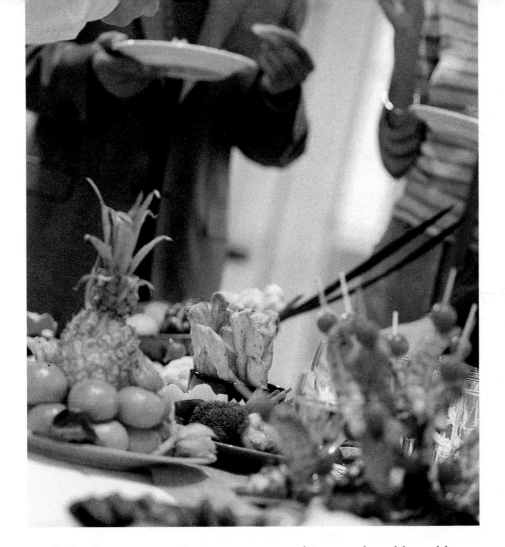

ANALYZE VISUALS
Based on the food shown, what can you **infer** about the event pictured here?

much food to prepare. She just puts everything on the table and hopes for the best."

I began to relax. The Gleasons' dinner party wasn't so different from a Chinese meal after all. My mother also puts everything on the table and hopes for the best.

Meg was the first friend I had made after we came to America. I eventually got acquainted with a few other kids in school, but Meg
70 was still the only real friend I had.

My brother didn't have any problems making friends. He spent all his time with some boys who were teaching him baseball, and in no time he could speak English much faster than I could—not better, but faster.

I worried more about making mistakes, and I spoke carefully, making sure I could say everything right before opening my mouth. At least I had a better accent than my parents, who never really got rid of their Chinese accent, even years later. My parents had both studied English in school before coming to America, but what they had studied was mostly written English, not spoken.

80   Father's approach to English was a scientific one. Since Chinese verbs have no tense, he was fascinated by the way English verbs changed form according to whether they were in the present, past imperfect, perfect, pluperfect, future, or future perfect tense. He was always making diagrams of verbs and their inflections,[3] and he looked for opportunities to show off his mastery of the pluperfect and future perfect tenses, his two favorites. "I shall have finished my project by Monday," he would say smugly.[4]

      Mother's approach was to memorize lists of polite phrases that would cover all possible social situations. She was constantly muttering things

90   like "I'm fine, thank you. And you?" Once she accidentally stepped on someone's foot, and hurriedly blurted, "Oh, that's quite all right!" Embarrassed by her slip, she resolved to do better next time. So when someone stepped on *her* foot, she cried, "You're welcome!" **D**

      In our own different ways, we made progress in learning English. But I had another worry, and that was my appearance. My brother didn't have to worry, since Mother bought him blue jeans for school, and he dressed like all the other boys. But she insisted that girls had to wear skirts. By the time she saw that Meg and the other girls were wearing jeans, it was too late. My school clothes were bought already, and we didn't have money

100   left to buy new outfits for me. We had too many other things to buy first, like furniture, pots, and pans.

      The first time I visited Meg's house, she took me upstairs to her room, and I wound up trying on her clothes. We were pretty much the same size, since Meg was shorter and thinner than average. Maybe that's how we became friends in the first place. Wearing Meg's jeans and T-shirt, I looked at myself in the mirror. I could almost pass for an American—from the back, anyway. At least the kids in school wouldn't stop and stare at me in the hallways, which was what they did when they saw me in my white blouse and navy blue skirt that went a couple of inches below the knees.

110   When Meg came to my house, I invited her to try on my Chinese dresses, the ones with a high collar and slits up the sides. Meg's eyes were bright as she looked at herself in the mirror. She struck several sultry poses, and we nearly fell over laughing.

      The dinner party at the Gleasons' didn't stop my growing friendship with Meg. Things were getting better for me in other ways too. Mother finally bought me some jeans at the end of the month, when Father got his paycheck. She wasn't in any hurry about buying them at first, until

D TONE
Reread lines 88–93. Why does a character's awkward situation add to the story's humorous tone?

SOCIAL STUDIES CONNECTION

The Chinese dress Meg tries on is a *cheongsam* (chông'säm') or *qipao* (kī'pä-ō'). *Cheongsam* is from the Cantonese dialect and translates as "long dress." *Qipao* is Mandarin for "banner gown."

---

3. **inflections** (ĭn-flĕk'shənz): different tenses.
4. **smugly**: with self-satisfaction; self-righteously.

I worked on her. This is what I did. Since we didn't have a car in those days, I often ran down to the neighborhood store to pick up things for her.
120 The groceries cost less at a big supermarket, but the closest one was many blocks away. One day, when she ran out of flour, I offered to borrow a bike from our neighbor's son and buy a ten-pound bag of flour at the big supermarket. I mounted the boy's bike and waved to Mother. "I'll be back in five minutes!"

Before I started pedaling, I heard her voice behind me. "You can't go out in public like that! People can see all the way up to your thighs!"

"I'm sorry," I said innocently. "I thought you were in a hurry to get the flour." For dinner we were going to have pot-stickers (fried Chinese dumplings), and we needed a lot of flour.

130 "Couldn't you borrow a girl's bicycle?" complained Mother. "That way your skirt won't be pushed up."

"There aren't too many of those around," I said. "Almost all the girls wear jeans while riding a bike, so they don't see any point buying a girl's bike."

We didn't eat pot-stickers that evening, and Mother was thoughtful. Next day we took the bus downtown and she bought me a pair of jeans. In the same week, my brother made the baseball team of his junior high school, Father started taking driving lessons, and Mother discovered rummage sales. We soon got all the furniture we needed, plus a dart board
140 and a 1,000-piece jigsaw puzzle (fourteen hours later, we discovered that it was a 999-piece jigsaw puzzle). There was hope that the Lins might become a normal American family after all. **E**

Then came our dinner at the Lakeview Restaurant.

The Lakeview was an expensive restaurant, one of those places where a headwaiter dressed in tails conducted you to your seat, and the only light came from candles and flaming desserts. In one corner of the room a lady harpist played tinkling melodies.

Father wanted to celebrate, because he had just been promoted. He worked for an electronics company, and after his English started improving,
150 his superiors decided to appoint him to a position more suited to his training. The promotion not only brought a higher salary but was also a tremendous boost to his pride.

Up to then we had eaten only in Chinese restaurants. Although my brother and I were becoming fond of hamburgers, my parents didn't care much for Western food, other than chow mein.[5]

E SUMMARIZE
What key events lead the narrator to say, "There was hope that the Lins might become a normal American family after all"? Record the events in your log.

---

5. **chow mein** (chou′ mān′): Chinese-American dish of vegetables and meat served over fried noodles.

But this was a special occasion, and Father asked his coworkers to recommend a really elegant restaurant. So there we were at the Lakeview, stumbling after the headwaiter in the murky dining room.

At our table we were handed our menus, and they were so big that to 160 read mine I almost had to stand up again. But why bother? It was mostly in French, anyway. **F**

Father, being an engineer, was always systematic. He took out a pocket French dictionary. "They told me that most of the items would be in French, so I came prepared." He even had a pocket flashlight, the size of a marking pen. While Mother held the flashlight over the menu, he looked up the items that were in French.

"*Pâté en croûte,*" he muttered. "Let's see . . . *pâté* is paste . . . *croûte* is crust . . . hmm . . . a paste in crust."

The waiter stood looking patient. I squirmed and died at least fifty times. 170 At long last Father gave up. "Why don't we just order four complete dinners at random?" he suggested.

"Isn't that risky?" asked Mother. "The French eat some rather peculiar things, I've heard."

"A Chinese can eat anything a Frenchman can eat," Father declared.

The soup arrived in a plate. How do you get soup up from a plate? I glanced at the other diners, but the ones at the nearby tables were not on their soup course, while the more distant ones were invisible in the darkness.

Fortunately my parents had studied books on Western **etiquette** before 180 they came to America. "Tilt your plate," whispered my mother. "It's easier to spoon the soup up that way."

She was right. Tilting the plate did the trick. But the etiquette book didn't say anything about what you did after the soup reached your lips. As any respectable Chinese knows, the correct way to eat your soup is to slurp. This helps to cool the liquid and prevent you from burning your lips. It also shows your appreciation.

We showed our appreciation. *Shloop,* went my father. *Shloop,* went my mother. *Shloop, shloop,* went my brother, who was the hungriest.

The lady harpist stopped playing to take a rest. And in the silence, our 190 family's **consumption** of soup suddenly seemed unnaturally loud. You know how it sounds on a rocky beach when the tide goes out and the water drains from all those little pools? They go *shloop, shloop, shloop.* That was the Lin family, eating soup.

At the next table a waiter was pouring wine. When a large *shloop* reached him, he froze. The bottle continued to pour, and red wine flooded the tabletop and into the lap of a customer. Even the customer didn't notice anything at first, being also hypnotized by the *shloop, shloop, shloop.*

etiquette (ĕt′ĭ-kĕt′) *n.* the practice of social manners

consumption (kən-sŭmp′shən) *n.* the act of taking in, eating, or drinking **consume** *v.*

It was too much. "I need to go to the toilet," I mumbled, jumping to my feet. A waiter, sensing my urgency, quickly directed me to the ladies' room.

I splashed cold water on my burning face, and as I dried myself with a paper towel, I stared into the mirror. In this perfumed ladies' room, with its pink-and-silver wallpaper and marbled sinks, I looked completely out of place. What was I doing here? What was our family doing in the Lakeview Restaurant? In America?

The door to the ladies' room opened. A woman came in and glanced curiously at me. I retreated into one of the toilet cubicles and latched the door.

Time passed—maybe half an hour, maybe an hour. Then I heard the door open again, and my mother's voice. "Are you in there? You're not sick, are you?"

There was real concern in her voice. A girl can't leave her family just because they slurp their soup. Besides, the toilet cubicle had a few drawbacks as a permanent residence. "I'm all right," I said, undoing the latch.

Mother didn't tell me how the rest of the dinner went, and I didn't want to know. In the weeks following, I managed to push the whole thing into the back of my mind, where it jumped out at me only a few times a day. Even now, I turn hot all over when I think of the Lakeview Restaurant. **G**

G SUMMARIZE
Many things embarrass the narrator during the dinner at the Lakeview Restaurant. Record the key events in your log.

ANALYZE VISUALS
Does this meal look inviting or intimidating? Explain.

But by the time we had been in this country for three months, our family was definitely making progress toward becoming Americanized. I remember my parents' first PTA[6] meeting. Father wore a neat suit and tie, and Mother put on her first pair of high heels. She stumbled only once. They met my homeroom
230 teacher and beamed as she told them that I would make honor roll soon at the rate I was going. Of course Chinese etiquette forced Father to say that I was a very stupid girl and Mother to protest that the teacher was showing favoritism toward me. But I could tell they were both very proud.

The day came when my parents announced that they wanted to give a
240 dinner party. We had invited Chinese friends to eat with us before, but this dinner was going to be different. In addition to a Chinese-American family, we were going to invite the Gleasons.

"Gee, I can hardly wait to have dinner at your house," Meg said to me. "I just *love* Chinese food."

That was a relief. Mother was a good cook, but I wasn't sure if people who ate sour cream would also eat chicken gizzards[7] stewed in soy sauce.

Mother decided not to take a chance with chicken gizzards. Since we had Western guests, she set the table with large dinner plates, which we never used in Chinese meals. In fact we didn't use individual plates at all, but
250 picked up food from the platters in the middle of the table and brought it directly to our rice bowls. Following the practice of Chinese-American restaurants, Mother also placed large serving spoons on the platters.

The dinner started well. Mrs. Gleason exclaimed at the beautifully arranged dishes of food: the colorful candied fruit in the sweet-and-sour pork dish, the noodle-thin shreds of chicken meat stir-fried with tiny peas, and the glistening pink prawns[8] in a ginger sauce.

---

6. **PTA:** Parent Teacher Association.

7. **gizzards:** A gizzard is the muscular pouch behind a bird's stomach that helps with its digestion.

8. **prawns** (prônz): large seafood, similar to shrimp.

At first I was too busy enjoying my food to notice how the guests were doing. But soon I remembered my duties. Sometimes guests were too polite to help themselves and you had to serve them with more food.

I glanced at Meg, to see if she needed more food, and my eyes nearly popped out at the sight of her plate. It was piled with food: the sweet-and-sour meat pushed right against the chicken shreds, and the chicken sauce ran into the prawns. She had been taking food from a second dish before she finished eating her helping from the first!

Horrified, I turned to look at Mrs. Gleason. She was dumping rice out of her bowl and putting it on her dinner plate. Then she ladled prawns and gravy on top of the rice and mixed everything together, the way you mix sand, gravel, and cement to make concrete.

I couldn't bear to look any longer, and I turned to Mr. Gleason. He was chasing a pea around his plate. Several times he got it to the edge, but when he tried to pick it up with his chopsticks, it rolled back toward the center of the plate again. Finally he put down his chopsticks and picked up the pea with his fingers. He really did! A grown man! ⓗ

All of us, our family and the Chinese guests, stopped eating to watch the activities of the Gleasons. I wanted to giggle. Then I caught my mother's eyes on me. She frowned and shook her head slightly, and I understood the message: the Gleasons were not used to Chinese ways, and they were just **coping** the best they could. For some reason I thought of celery strings.

When the main courses were finished, Mother brought out a platter of fruit. "I hope you weren't expecting a sweet dessert," she said. "Since the Chinese don't eat dessert, I didn't think to prepare any."

"Oh, I couldn't possibly eat dessert!" cried Mrs. Gleason. "I'm simply stuffed!"

Meg had different ideas. When the table was cleared, she announced that she and I were going for a walk. "I don't know about you, but I feel like dessert," she told me, when we were outside. "Come on, there's a Dairy Queen down the street. I could use a big chocolate milkshake!"

Although I didn't really want anything more to eat, I insisted on paying for the milkshakes. After all, I was still hostess.

Meg got her large chocolate milkshake and I had a small one. Even so, she was finishing hers while I was only half done. Toward the end she pulled hard on her straws and went *shloop, shloop*.

"Do you always slurp when you eat a milkshake?" I asked, before I could stop myself.

Meg grinned. "Sure. All Americans slurp." ꙮ ⓘ

ⓗ **TONE**
Reread lines 257–273. Is it the Gleasons' actions, the narrator's responses, or both that add humor to the story? Explain.

cope (kōp) *v.* to struggle to overcome difficulties

ⓘ **SUMMARIZE**
What does the narrator learn the night of her parents' dinner party? Include this key event in your log.

Comprehension

1. **Recall** What two types of food served at the Gleasons' dinner party are unusual for the Lin family?

2. **Recall** How does each member of the Lin family learn English?

3. **Clarify** Why do the Lins slurp their soup in the French restaurant?

4. **Represent** Create a timeline to show the order of events in the story.

Literary Analysis

5. **Summarize** Review the log you created while reading. Cross out any events that don't seem as important now that you have read the entire story. Write a story summary using the remaining information.

6. **Understand Analogy** An analogy is a comparison of two things that are alike in some way. The writer describes one thing to help readers understand the other. Reread the analogy in lines 190–193. What does the comparison help you understand?

7. **Compare and Contrast Characters** Find examples of **similarities** and differences between the Lin family and the Gleasons. Do you think the narrator feels more like or different from her neighbors by the end of the story? Support your answer with evidence from the story.

8. **Evaluate Tone** Give examples of the characters' thoughts, words, and actions that contribute to the humorous tone of "The All-American Slurp." Record the examples in a chart like the one shown. Which details do you think have the strongest effect on the tone of the story?

Thoughts	Words	Actions

Extension and Challenge

9. **Speaking and Listening** It is sometimes easier to understand the intended **tone** of a story if it is read out loud. In a group, reread lines 221–238 aloud as if you are rehearsing for a play. Be sure to emphasize key words to maintain a humorous tone.

10. **SOCIAL STUDIES CONNECTION** Reread lines 1–57. Use the description of the Gleasons' dinner party and the information in the article on page 437 to write an etiquette guide for someone who is attending his or her first buffet meal in the United States. Explain how the food is arranged, what utensils should be used, and the overall behavior the newcomer can expect to see.

Vocabulary in Context

VOCABULARY PRACTICE

Choose the letter of the item you would associate with each vocabulary word as it is used in "The All-American Slurp."

1. **revolting:** (a) a borrowed sweater, (b) a spoiled sandwich, (c) an old car
2. **lavishly:** (a) a generous amount, (b) a large classroom, (c) a crowded train station
3. **mortified:** (a) playing a trick, (b) going to a meeting, (c) falling down in public
4. **etiquette:** (a) fixing a bicycle, (b) writing a thank-you note, (c) baking a dessert
5. **consumption:** (a) taking an elevator, (b) finding a lost hat, (c) eating lunch
6. **cope:** (a) get angry, (b) finish a project, (c) manage

consumption

cope

etiquette

lavishly

mortified

revolting

VOCABULARY IN WRITING

Using three or more vocabulary words, write a paragraph in which Mrs. Lin describes her French dinner. You might begin your paragraph like this.

> **EXAMPLE SENTENCE**
>
> *I thought I knew everything about **etiquette**, but I was wrong.*

VOCABULARY STRATEGY: SIMILES AS CONTEXT CLUES

When writers want to compare two things, they sometimes use similes. **Similes** are comparisons that use the words *like* or *as*. In "The All-American Slurp," the narrator's family leaves the buffet table at a party "*as* if chased by enemy soldiers." The simile here is humorous and helps the writer emphasize how quickly the family left.

   Similes can also give you context clues to help you figure out the meanings of unfamiliar words. If you can form a mental picture of the comparison, you understand the meaning of the unfamiliar word.

PRACTICE Use the simile in each sentence as a context clue to help you define the boldfaced word.

1. She was stepping as **gingerly** as the parent of a sleeping baby.
2. Storm clouds **loomed** like Friday's spelling test.
3. He felt like a caged bird in the house's **confining** guest room.
4. Her sloppy handwriting was as **cryptic** as any secret code.
5. The awkward fit of his clothes made him feel **gawky,** like a newborn giraffe.

VOCABULARY PRACTICE

For more practice, go to the **Vocabulary Center** at **ClassZone.com**.

Reading-Writing Connection

Explore the meaning of "The All-American Slurp" by responding to these prompts. Then complete the **Grammar and Writing** exercise.

A. Short Response: Write a Journal Entry
In lines 253–283, the Lins serve Chinese food to the Gleasons. Write a **one-paragraph journal entry** as if you were Meg. What **similarities** or differences might she notice compared to dining at home? Explain how the night affected her.

A well-written entry will . . .
- refer to specific events in the story
- be consistent with Meg's character as revealed in the story

B. Extended Response: Write About Etiquette
The Lin family learned American etiquette the hard way. Read "American Lifestyles and Habits" on page 437. In **two or three paragraphs,** explain what information from the article would have helped the Lins.

A strong response will . . .
- demonstrate understanding of cultural differences
- combine information from the story and the article

GRAMMAR AND WRITING

AVOID CLAUSES AS FRAGMENTS A clause is a group of words that has a subject and a verb. If a clause states a complete thought and can stand alone as a sentence, it is called an **independent clause.** Fragments, or incomplete sentences, occur when **dependent clauses** (subordinate clauses) are used on their own. To correct such a fragment, simply join the dependent clause to an independent clause. Here is an example with the independent clause highlighted in yellow and the dependent clause highlighted in green:

Original: I put down my chopsticks. Because everyone was staring.

Revised: I put down my chopsticks because everyone was staring.

PRACTICE Find four fragments in the following paragraph. Then fix the fragments by correctly combining independent and dependent clauses.

> The Lins invited us to a Chinese dinner at their house. Because we had them over for dinner. I wasn't expecting any surprises. Since we ate at Chinese restaurants all the time. I piled a heap of the sweet-and-sour meat on my plate with all the other food. As Mrs. Lin passed the dish around. Most of the food was pretty good. Dad didn't embarrass me. Although he picked up a pea with his fingers.

FOR MORE HELP WITH INDEPENDENT AND DEPENDENT CLAUSES, SEE PAGE R62 IN THE *Grammar Handbook.*

ONLINE ARTICLE In "The All-American Slurp," you read about a Chinese family adjusting to customs in the United States. The following article offers advice to visitors and immigrants about American etiquette.

BACK   FORWARD   STOP   REFRESH   HOME   PRINT

American Lifestyles & Habits   Project Harmony

Etiquette and traditions for guests in an American family

There are some significant differences between cultures concerning etiquette and hospitality. The role of the guest is quite different in America than it is in other countries. In America, guests are generally urged to "make themselves at home." Americans believe that both guests and hosts are most comfortable when neither is anxious about being too polite or reserved. For instance, if you are hungry you should not wait for your host to offer you food. It's perfectly normal to ask for a snack, or to make one yourself! . . .

The types of food that Americans eat shock many people and it sometimes takes time to adjust. If you are longing for some "normal" food, you should offer to cook a national meal. Americans are almost always interested in trying new foods and would be honored if their guest(s) offered to cook a dinner.

When you are sitting at the table, you will generally have to help yourself. You may be offered food once, and if you refuse, it will not be offered again. As mentioned before, Americans tend to give honest, straightforward answers rather than feign politeness. While in your country it may be considered polite to answer "no" when food is first offered, American hosts will take "no" as exactly that and will not offer you the food again. If there is something additional that you would like at the table, you should ask for it or just take it.

When it comes to food, you may find that Americans

- Love vegetarian, low-fat salads with different salad dressings
- Eat most of their food quickly, and often take a meal with them to eat en route somewhere
- Put ice in almost all beverages—one American favorite is ICED tea!
- Use lots of spices and often like ethnic foods
- Eat dinner as the main meal of the day
- Often eat little or no breakfast—so be sure to ask for food in the **morning**

The True Story of the Three Little Pigs
Storybook Parody by Jon Scieszka

Are there TWO SIDES
to every story?

KEY IDEA "That's not how it happened. Let me tell it!" When you hear **two sides** to a story, the differences between the two often outweigh the similarities. Because people sometimes see things differently, the details in each version often depend on which person is telling the story. In "The True Story of the Three Little Pigs," you'll discover what it's like when someone clearly stretches the truth.

QUICKWRITE Think about a time when you either read or heard two sides to the same story, either in real life, in a book, or in a movie. How did the versions differ? Write a brief summary of each side. Then explain why you think there were two sides to the story.

LITERARY ANALYSIS: PARODY

Sometimes books, movies, or songs are so good or interesting that they just beg to be copied. The copies are called parodies. A **parody** pokes fun at what it is imitating by using the same style or content in a new and humorous way. Often, the purpose of a parody is to show a different view of the original work.

In "The True Story of the Three Little Pigs," the wolf is now the **narrator** telling the story. As a result, the reader hears the familiar tale with a new version of "the truth." As you read the parody, record examples of how the wolf's role as narrator adds a humorous twist to the tale.

Line Numbers	Funny Sentence
10–11	"If cheeseburgers were cute, folks would probably think you were Big and Bad, too."

READING SKILL: IDENTIFY CAUSE AND EFFECT

As in real life, events in a story plot are often linked by **cause and effect.** One event (the cause) makes another event (the effect) happen. Sometimes, an effect then becomes the cause of another event, creating a cause-and-effect chain.

The following graphic organizer shows how an event from the original "Three Little Pigs" story creates a cause-and-effect chain. As you read "The True Story of the Three Little Pigs," use a chain graphic organizer like the one shown to identify **cause-and-effect relationships** in the story.

Cause

Pig builds straw house.

Effect/Cause

Wolf easily blows house down.

Effect

House falls down on pig.

Author Online

**Jon Scieszka
born 1954**

Tales with a Twist
Jon Scieszka (chěs'-kä) originally had trouble getting "The True Story of the Three Little Pigs" published because its humor was considered too mature. But Scieszka knew young people would appreciate it, saying that "nothing cracks them up like a joke that turns stuff upside down."

Friends and Partners Scieszka and illustrator Lane Smith have been friends and work partners for many years. Sharing a similar sense of humor and love for the absurd made the two a natural fit. "The True Story of the Three Little Pigs" was the first book they worked on together.

> **MORE ABOUT THE AUTHOR**
> For more on Jon Scieszka, visit the **Literature Center** at ClassZone.com.

Background

The Original "Three Little Pigs" In the classic tale, the first and second little pigs built their houses from straw and sticks. When the pigs wouldn't let the wolf in, he blew their houses down and ate the pigs. The third little pig built his house from bricks. When the wolf couldn't blow the house down, he went down the chimney. The pig had a pot of boiling water waiting for him, though, so the third little pig had wolf stew for dinner.

THE TRUE STORY OF THE THREE LITTLE PIGS

A. Wolf
As Told to Jon Scieszka

Everybody knows the story of the Three Little Pigs. Or at least they think they do. But I'll let you in on a little secret. Nobody knows the real story, because nobody has ever heard *my* side of the story.

I'm the wolf. Alexander T. Wolf.

You can call me Al.

I don't know how this whole Big Bad Wolf thing got started, but it's all wrong.

Maybe it's because of our diet.

Hey, it's not my fault wolves eat cute little animals like bunnies and
10 sheep and pigs. That's just the way we are. If cheeseburgers were cute, folks would probably think you were Big and Bad, too.

But like I was saying, the whole Big Bad Wolf thing is all wrong. The real story is about a sneeze and a cup of sugar. **A**

ANALYZE VISUALS
What **details** do you notice about the wolf in this illustration?

A PARODY
What humorous words and phrases does the author use to let you know that this story is a parody?

Illustrations by Lane Smith.

THIS IS THE REAL STORY.

Way back in Once Upon a Time time, I was making a birthday cake for my dear old granny.

I had a terrible sneezing cold.

I ran out of sugar.

So I walked down the street to ask my neighbor for a cup of sugar.

20 Now this neighbor was a pig.

And he wasn't too bright, either.

He had built his whole house out of straw.

Can you believe it? I mean who in his right mind would build a house of straw?

So of course the minute I knocked on the door, it fell right in. I didn't want to just walk into someone else's house. So I called, "Little Pig, Little Pig, are you in?" No answer. **B**

I was just about to go home without the cup of sugar for my dear old granny's birthday cake.

30 That's when my nose started to itch.

I felt a sneeze coming on.

Well I huffed.

And I snuffed.

And I sneezed a great sneeze.

And you know what? That whole darn straw house fell down. And right in the middle of the pile of straw was the First Little Pig—dead as a doornail. **C**

He had been home the whole time.

40 It seemed like a shame to leave a perfectly good ham dinner lying there in the straw. So I ate it up.

Think of it as a big cheeseburger just lying there.

I was feeling a little better. But I still didn't have my cup of sugar. So I went to the next neighbor's house.

This neighbor was the First Little Pig's brother.

50 He was a little smarter, but not much.

He had built his house of sticks.

I rang the bell on the stick house.

Nobody answered.

I called, "Mr. Pig, Mr. Pig, are you in?"

He yelled back, "Go away wolf. You can't come in. I'm shaving the hairs on my chinny chin chin."

B **PARODY**
Reread lines 19–27. What does the wolf say to make readers think it's the pig's fault that the door fell in?

C **CAUSE AND EFFECT**
According to the wolf, what causes the death of the first pig? Create a cause-and-effect chain that shows the series of events.

I had just grabbed the doorknob when I felt another sneeze coming on.
I huffed. And I snuffed. And I tried to cover my mouth, but I sneezed
60 a great sneeze.

And you're not going to believe it, but this guy's house fell down just
like his brother's.

When the dust cleared, there was the Second Little Pig—dead as a doornail. Wolf's honor.

Now you know food will spoil if you just leave it out in the open.

So I did the only thing there was to do. I had dinner again.

Think of it as a second helping. **D**

I was getting awfully full.

But my cold was feeling a little better.

70　And I still didn't have that cup of sugar for my dear old granny's birthday cake.

So I went to the next house.

This guy was the First and Second Little Pigs' brother.

He must have been the brains of the family.

He had built his house of bricks.

I knocked on the brick house. No answer.

I called, "Mr. Pig, Mr. Pig, are you in?"

And do you know what that rude little porker answered?

"Get out of here, Wolf. Don't bother me again."

80　Talk about impolite!

He probably had a whole sackful of sugar.

And he wouldn't give me even one little cup for my dear sweet old granny's birthday cake.

What a pig!

I was just about to go home and maybe make a nice birthday card instead of a cake, when I felt my cold coming on.

I huffed.

And I snuffed.

And I sneezed once again.

90　Then the Third Little Pig yelled, "And your old granny can sit on a pin!"

Now I'm usually a pretty calm fellow. But when somebody talks about my granny like that, I go a little crazy. **E**

When the cops drove up, of course I was trying to break down this Pig's door. And the whole time I was huffing and puffing and sneezing and making a real scene.

The rest, as they say, is history.

D PARODY
Reread lines 40–44 and 65–67. What words or phrases make the wolf's reasons for eating the pigs funny?

E CAUSE AND EFFECT
Reread lines 90–93. What are the cause and effect identified in these lines? Use the graphic organizer to show this relationship.

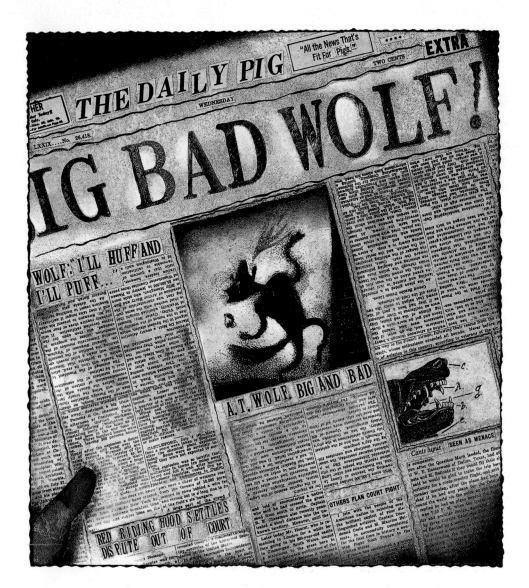

The news reporters found out about the two pigs I had for dinner. They figured a sick guy going to borrow a cup of sugar didn't sound very exciting.

So they jazzed up the story with all of that "Huff and puff and blow your house down."

And they made me the Big Bad Wolf.

That's it.

The real story. I was framed. **F**

But maybe you could loan me a cup of sugar. ∽

F PARODY
Reread lines 98–105. Explain how the author's choice of **narrator** adds a playful twist to the original story's ending.

Comprehension

1. **Recall** Why is the wolf telling his story?

2. **Recall** At the beginning of the story, what two things does the wolf say the "real story" is about?

3. **Clarify** Why does the wolf think it's the first pig's fault that the straw house fell down?

4. **Summarize** What happens at the house of the third pig?

Literary Analysis

5. **Examine Parody** Throughout his parody, Jon Scieszka makes several references to lines that appear in the original "Three Little Pigs" story. In a chart like the one shown, contrast the original version's lines with those that appear in the parody. This will help you to see how Scieszka is poking fun at the original tale.

Original	Parody
Big Bad Wolf	
Little pig, little pig, let me come in.	
Not by the hair of my chinny chin chin.	
He huffed, and he puffed, and he blew the house down.	

6. **Compare Cause-and-Effect Relationships** While reading the **parody,** you recorded cause-and-effect relationships. Think back to what you know about the original "Three Little Pigs" story. Explain how the parody's cause-and-effect relationships are different from those in the original tale.

7. **Make Judgments About the Narrator** How convincing is the wolf as a narrator? Explain why you do or do not trust his retelling of the story.

Extension and Challenge

8. **Big Question Activity** Think of another classic tale like "The Three Little Pigs" that could be told from **two sides.** Select a character who might tell the story differently and write a new version with that character acting as narrator.

9. **Creative Project: Drama** With a group of classmates, perform for your class a traditional version of "The Three Little Pigs," followed by "The True Story of the Three Little Pigs." Consider how the characters' voices and behavior might change between the two performances.

Jeremiah's Song

Short Story by Walter Dean Myers

When is a story a TREASURE?

KEY IDEA Some stories are forgotten as soon as the words leave the storyteller's lips. Other stories are passed from one generation to the next. Think about what makes a story a **treasure**—something worth remembering and sharing with others. Does it matter if it is funny, sad, or scary? Does the story have to teach you something? In "Jeremiah's Song," the young characters consider the value of an older man's stories.

QUICKWRITE In a journal entry, briefly describe a story that is meaningful to you. The story can be one you have heard, read, or seen. Explain why this story is important to you.

● LITERARY ANALYSIS: STYLE

Each writer's **style,** or way of communicating ideas, is unique—like a fingerprint. It is often the writer's style that makes a story memorable. In this story, Walter Dean Myers's style comes across through elements such as

- **Point of view**—Myers chooses to tell the story from a first-person point of view, using a child as the narrator.
- **Dialogue**—Myers brings the characters to life by re-creating the way they actually speak.
- **Word choice**—Myers uses precise descriptions, vivid adjectives, and unusual comparisons to create memorable images.

As you read "Jeremiah's Song," notice how Myers uses these style elements.

● READING STRATEGY: MONITOR

To avoid becoming confused as you read, it is good to occasionally check, or **monitor,** your understanding. One way to monitor is to **clarify** what you've read. This means you stop and make sure that you can clearly explain what has happened. If not, reread and look for clues in the selection to help you restate the information in your own words.

As you read, pause to clarify meaning. It may help to use a chart like the one shown.

This Confuses Me	My Words

▲ VOCABULARY IN CONTEXT

Myers uses the boldfaced words to help tell the story of an older man. To see how many you know, restate each sentence using a different word or phrase in place of the boldfaced word.

1. Grandpa has a serious **condition,** but it can be treated.
2. The doctor made a **diagnosis** about what was wrong.
3. He couldn't move his arm after he had a **stroke.**
4. Getting a cold was only a small **setback** in his recovery.

Author Online

Role Models
Walter Dean Myers once said that people should have role models with whom they can identify. Myers's foster father and grandfather were his role models. Both were gifted storytellers, and

Walter Dean Myers
born 1937

Myers has followed in their footsteps. Throughout his writing career, Myers has introduced his readers to fictional and real African-American role models.

Getting to Know His Characters
Pictures are important to Myers's writing experience. When he is working on a story, he cuts out pictures of people who look the way he imagines his characters should look. His wife creates a collage of the pictures, and he hangs it over his computer. When Myers sits down to write each day, he sees the characters and feels as if he is getting to know them better all the time.

 MORE ABOUT THE AUTHOR
For more on Walter Dean Myers, visit the **Literature Center** at ClassZone.com.

Background

Storytelling Tradition Storytelling has a long history in the African-American community. Stories of family ties, folklore, faith, and struggles for civil rights create strong bonds from one generation to the next. In "Jeremiah's Song," Grandpa Jeremiah shares the stories of his ancestors with the young people in his life.

JEREMIAH'S Song

WALTER DEAN MYERS

I knowed my cousin Ellie was gonna be mad when Macon Smith come around to the house. She didn't have no use for Macon even when things was going right, and when Grandpa Jeremiah was fixing to die I just knowed she wasn't gonna be liking him hanging around. Grandpa Jeremiah raised Ellie after her folks died and they used to be real close. Then she got to go on to college and when she come back the first year she was different. She didn't want to hear all them stories he used to tell her anymore. Ellie said the stories wasn't true, and that's why she didn't want to hear them.

10   I didn't know if they was true or not. Tell the truth I didn't think much on it either way, but I liked to hear them stories. Grandpa Jeremiah said they wasn't stories anyway, they was songs.

"They the songs of my people," he used to say.

I didn't see how they was songs, not regular songs anyway. Every little thing we did down in Curry seemed to matter to Ellie that first summer she come home from college. You couldn't do nothin' that was gonna please her. She didn't even come to church much. 'Course she come on Sunday or everybody would have had a regular fit, but she didn't come on Thursday nights and she didn't come on Saturday even though she used

20   to sing in the gospel choir. **A**

"I guess they teachin' her somethin' worthwhile up there at Greensboro," Grandpa Jeremiah said to Sister Todd. "I sure don't see what it is, though."

ANALYZE VISUALS
What kind of music do you think this person is playing? Explain your answer.

A **MONITOR**
Reread lines 1–20.
Clarify the relationship between Grandpa Jeremiah and Ellie. When and how did it change? Record your answer in your chart.

Howling Duet (Musical Interlude) (1998), Benny Andrews. Oil and collage on paper, 29 8/10″ × 22½″. Courtesy of ACA Galleries, New York. © Estate of Benny Andrews/Licensed by VAGA, New York.

"You ain't never had no book learning, Jeremiah," Sister Todd shot back. She wiped at where a trickle of sweat made a little path through the white dusting powder she put on her chest to keep cool. "Them old ways you got ain't got nothing for these young folks."

"I guess you right," Grandpa Jeremiah said.

He said it but I could see he didn't like it none. He was a big man with a big head and had most all his hair even if it was white. All that summer, instead of sitting on the porch telling stories like he used to when I was real little, he would sit out there by himself while Ellie stayed in the house and watched the television or read a book. Sometimes I would think about asking him to tell me one of them stories he used to tell but they was too scary now that I didn't have nobody to sleep with but myself. I asked Ellie to sleep with me but she wouldn't.

"You're nine years old," she said, sounding real proper. "You're old enough to sleep alone."

I *knew* that. I just wanted her to sleep with me because I liked sleeping with her. Before she went off to college she used to put cocoa butter on her arms and face and it would smell real nice. When she come back from college she put something else on, but that smelled nice too.

It was right after Ellie went back to school that Grandpa Jeremiah had him a **stroke** and Macon started coming around. I think his mama probably made him come at first, but you could see he liked it. Macon had always been around, sitting over near the stuck window at church or going on the blueberry truck when we went picking down at Mister Gregory's place. For a long time he was just another kid, even though he was older'n me, but then, all of a sudden, he growed something fierce. I used to be up to his shoulder one time and then, before I could turn around good, I was only up to his shirt pocket. He changed too. When he used to just hang around with the other boys and play ball or shoot at birds he would laugh a lot. He didn't laugh so much anymore and I figured he was just about grown. When Grandpa got sick he used to come around and help out with things around the house that was too hard for me to do. I mean, I could have done all the chores, but it would just take me longer. **B**

When the work for the day was finished and the sows[1] fed, Grandpa would kind of ease into one of his stories and Macon, he would sit and listen to them and be real interested. I didn't mind listening to the stories when Grandpa told them to Macon because he would be telling them in the middle of the afternoon and they would be past my mind by the time I had to go to bed. **C**

---

1. **sows:** adult female hogs.

stroke (strōk) *n.* a sudden, severe attack; a sudden loss of blood flow to the brain, often leading to physical or mental damage

B STYLE
By using **first-person point of view**, Myers can share the **narrator's** thoughts. What do we learn about the narrator through his description of Macon in lines 47–55?

C MONITOR
Reread lines 58–61. What does the narrator mean when he says that the stories "would be past my mind by the time I had to go to bed"?

Macon had an old guitar he used to mess with, too. He wasn't too bad on it, and sometimes Grandpa would tell him to play us a tune. He could play something he called "the Delta Blues" real good, but when Sister Todd or somebody from the church come around he'd play "Precious Lord" or "Just a Closer Walk With Thee."

Grandpa Jeremiah had been feeling poorly from that stroke, and one of his legs got a little drag to it. Just about the time Ellie come from school the next summer he was real sick. He was breathing loud so you could
70 hear it even in the next room, and he would stay in bed a lot even when there was something that needed doing or fixing.

"I don't think he's going to make it much longer," Dr. Crawford said. "The only thing I can do is to give him something for the pain."

"Are you sure of your **diagnosis?**" Ellie asked. She was sitting around the table with Sister Todd, Deacon[2] Turner, and his little skinny wife.

Dr. Crawford looked at Ellie like he was surprised to hear her talking. "Yes, I'm sure," he said. "He had tests a few weeks ago and his **condition** was bad then."

"How much time he got?" Sister Todd asked.
80 "Maybe a week or two at best," Dr. Crawford said.

When he said that, Deacon Turner's wife started crying and goin' on and I give her a hard look but she just went on. I was the one who loved Grandpa Jeremiah the most and she didn't hardly even know him so I didn't see why she was crying.

Everybody started tiptoeing around the house after that. They would go in and ask Grandpa Jeremiah if he was comfortable and stuff like that or take him some food or a cold glass of lemonade.

Sister Todd come over and stayed with us. Mostly what she did is make supper and do a lot of praying, which was good because I figured that
90 maybe God would do something to make Grandpa Jeremiah well. When she wasn't doing that she was piecing on[3] a fancy quilt she was making for some white people in Wilmington.

Ellie, she went around asking everybody how they felt about Dr. Crawford and then she went into town and asked about the tests and things. Sister Jenkins asked her if she thought she knowed more than Dr. Crawford, and Ellie rolled her eyes at her, but Sister Jenkins was reading out her Bible and didn't make no notice of it.

Then Macon come over.

He had been away on what he called "a little piece of a job" and hadn't
100 heard how bad off Grandpa Jeremiah was. When he come over he talked

---

2. **Deacon:** a term used for church members who assist their church's priest or minister.

3. **piecing on:** mending or adding blocks of fabric.

SOCIAL STUDIES CONNECTION

MISSISSIPPI

LOUISIANA

New Orleans

Mississippi R.

Mississippi Delta

The type of music known as the Delta Blues originated in the Delta region of Mississippi. Musicians performed soulful songs accompanied only by a guitar or harmonica. This style of music soon spread across the country.

diagnosis (dĭ′əg-nō′sĭs) *n.* the identification of a disease through examination of a patient

condition (kən-dĭsh′ən) *n.* a disease or state of health

Detail of *Cookin Hog Cracklin* (1995), Jessie Coates. Acrylic on masonite. Private collection.
© Jessie Coates/SuperStock.

ANALYZE VISUALS
What can you **infer** about the people in this painting?

to Ellie and she told him what was going on and then he got him a soft drink from the refrigerator and sat out on the porch and before you know it he was crying. **D**

You could look at his face and tell the difference between him sweating and the tears. The sweat was close against his skin and shiny and the tears come down fatter and more sparkly. **E**

Macon sat on the porch, without saying a word, until the sun went down and the crickets started chirping and carrying on. Then he went in to where Grandpa Jeremiah was and stayed in there for a long time.

110 Sister Todd was saying that Grandpa Jeremiah needed his rest and Ellie went in to see what Macon was doing. Then she come out real mad.

"He got Grandpa telling those old stories again," Ellie said. "I told him Grandpa needed his rest and for him not to be staying all night."

He did leave soon, but bright and early the next morning Macon was back again. This time he brought his guitar with him and he went on in to Grandpa Jeremiah's room. I went in, too.

Grandpa Jeremiah's room smelled terrible. It was all closed up so no drafts could get on him and the whole room was smelled down with disinfect[4] and

D MONITOR
Reread lines 88–103. In your chart, record how Sister Todd, Ellie, and Macon deal with Grandpa Jeremiah's illness.

E STYLE
Reread lines 104–106. What **adjectives** does Myers use to create a vivid image of Macon?

---

4. **disinfect:** short for *disinfectant*, a chemical that destroys germs and bacteria.

medicine. Grandpa Jeremiah lay propped up on the bed and he was so
gray he looked scary. His hair wasn't combed down and his head on the
pillow with his white hair sticking out was enough to send me flying if
Macon hadn't been there. He was skinny, too. He looked like his skin got
loose on his bones, and when he lifted his arms, it hung down like he was
just wearing it instead of it being a part of him. **F**

Macon sat slant-shouldered with his guitar across his lap. He was
messin' with the guitar, not making any music, but just going over the
strings as Grandpa talked.

"Old Carrie went around out back to where they kept the pigs penned up
and she felt a cold wind across her face. . . ." Grandpa Jeremiah was telling
the story about how a old woman out-tricked the Devil and got her son
back. I had heard the story before, and I knew it was pretty scary. "When
she felt the cold breeze she didn't blink nary[5] an eye, but looked straight
ahead. . . ."

All the time Grandpa Jeremiah was talking I could see Macon fingering
his guitar. I tried to imagine what it would be like if he was actually
plucking the strings. I tried to fix my mind on that because I didn't like
the way the story went with the old woman wrestling with the Devil.

We sat there for nearly all the afternoon until Ellie and Sister Todd
come in and said that supper was ready. Me and Macon went out and ate
some collard greens, ham hocks, and rice. Then Macon he went back in
and listened to some more of Grandpa's stories until it was time for him to
go home. I wasn't about to go in there and listen to no stories at night.

Dr. Crawford come around a few days later and said that Grandpa
Jeremiah was doing a little better.

"You think the Good Lord gonna pull him through?" Sister Todd asked.

"I don't tell the Good Lord what He should or should not be doing,"
Dr. Crawford said, looking over at Sister Todd and at Ellie. "I just said
that *my* patient seems to be doing okay for his condition."

"He been telling Macon all his stories," I said.

"Macon doesn't seem to understand that Grandpa Jeremiah needs his
strength," Ellie said. "Now that he's improving, we don't want him to have
a **setback**."

"No use in stopping him from telling his stories," Dr. Crawford said.
"If it makes him feel good it's as good as any medicine I can give him."

I saw that this didn't set with Ellie, and when Dr. Crawford had left
I asked her why.

"Dr. Crawford means well," she said, "but we have to get away from the
kind of life that keeps us in the past." **G**

---

5. **nary:** not one; not any.

F STYLE
Reread lines 122–124.
What words and phrases
does Myers use to create
a **precise description**
of how skinny Grandpa
Jeremiah is?

setback (sĕt′băk′) *n.*
an unexpected stop in
progress; a change from
better to worse

G MONITOR
Reread lines 155–158.
What does Ellie mean
by her response to the
narrator's question?

She didn't say why we should be trying to get away from the stories and
160 I really didn't care too much. All I knew was that when Macon was sitting
in the room with Grandpa Jeremiah I wasn't nearly as scared as I used to
be when it was just me and Ellie listening. I told that to Macon.

"You getting to be a big man, that's all," he said.

That was true. Me and Macon was getting to be good friends, too. I didn't
even mind so much when he started being friends with Ellie later. It seemed
kind of natural, almost like Macon was supposed to be there with us instead
of just visiting.

Grandpa wasn't getting no better, but he wasn't getting no worse,
either.

170 "You liking Macon now?" I asked Ellie when we got to the middle of
July. She was dishing out a plate of smothered chops⁶ for him and I hadn't
even heard him ask for anything to eat.

"Macon's funny," Ellie said, not answering my question. "He's in there
listening to all of those old stories like he's really interested in them. It's
almost as if he and Grandpa Jeremiah are talking about something more
than the stories, a secret language."

I didn't think I was supposed to say anything about that to Macon, but
once, when Ellie, Sister Todd, and Macon were out on the porch shelling
butter beans after Grandpa got tired and was resting, I went into his room
180 and told him what Ellie had said.

"She said that?" Grandpa Jeremiah's face was skinny and old looking
but his eyes looked like a baby's, they was so bright. **H**

"Right there in the kitchen is where she said it," I said. "And I don't
know what it mean but I was wondering about it."

"I didn't think she had any feeling for them stories," Grandpa Jeremiah
said. "If she think we talking secrets, maybe she don't."

"I think she getting a feeling for Macon," I said.

"That's okay, too," Grandpa Jeremiah said. "They both young."

"Yeah, but them stories you be telling, Grandpa, they about old people
190 who lived a long time ago," I said.

"Well, those the folks you got to know about," Grandpa Jeremiah said.
"You think on what those folks been through, and what they was feeling,
and you add it up with what you been through and what you been feeling,
then you got you something."

"What you got Grandpa?"

"You got you a bridge," Grandpa said. "And a meaning. Then when
things get so hard you about to break, you can sneak across that bridge
and see some folks who went before you and see how they didn't break. **I**

H STYLE
Consider Myers's **word choice** to describe Grandpa Jeremiah's eyes. Why is this an unusual comparison?

I MONITOR
Reread lines 189–198. Why are the stories important to Grandpa Jeremiah? Add this information to your chart.

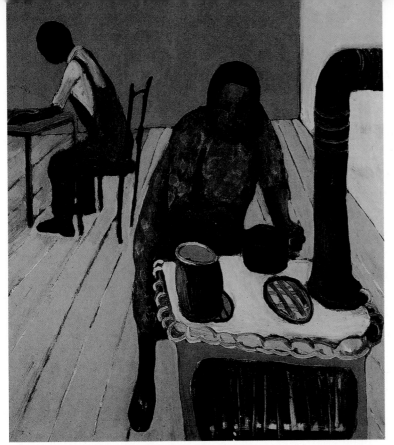

The Poverty of It All (1965), Benny Andrews. Oil and collage on canvas, 26″ × 22″. Courtesy of ACA Galleries, New York. © Estate of Benny Andrews/Licensed by VAGA, New York.

ANALYZE VISUALS
What do the colors in this picture suggest about how the people are feeling?

Some got bent and some got twisted and a few fell along the way, but they
200 didn't break."

"Am I going to break, Grandpa?"

"You? As strong as you is?" Grandpa Jeremiah pushed himself up on his
elbow and give me a look. "No way you going to break, boy. You gonna be
strong as they come. One day you gonna tell all them stories I told you to
your young'uns and they'll be as strong as you."

"Suppose I ain't got no stories, can I make some up?"

"Sure you can, boy. You make 'em up and twist 'em around. Don't
make no mind. Long as you got 'em."

"Is that what Macon is doing?" I asked. "Making up stories to play on
210 his guitar?"

"He'll do with 'em what he see fit, I suppose," Grandpa Jeremiah said.
"Can't ask more than that from a man." ⓙ

It rained the first three days of August. It wasn't a hard rain but it
rained anyway. The mailman said it was good for the crops over East
but I didn't care about that so I didn't pay him no mind. What I did mind
was when it rain like that the field mice come in and get in things like the
flour bin and I always got the blame for leaving it open.

When the rain stopped I was pretty glad. Macon come over and sat with
Grandpa and had something to eat with us. Sister Todd come over, too.

ⓙ STYLE
Reread lines 201–212.
What do you learn
through the **dialogue**
about how Grandpa
Jeremiah views stories?

220   "How Grandpa doing?" Sister Todd asked. "They been asking about him in the church."

    "He's doing all right," Ellie said.

    "He's kind of quiet today," Macon said. "He was just talking about how the hogs needed breeding."

    "He must have run out of stories to tell," Sister Todd said. "He'll be repeating on himself like my father used to do. That's the way I *hear* old folks get."

    Everybody laughed at that because Sister Todd was pretty old, too. Maybe we was all happy because the sun was out after so much rain.
230 When Sister Todd went in to take Grandpa Jeremiah a plate of potato salad with no mayonnaise like he liked it, she told him about how people was asking for him and he told her to tell them he was doing okay and to remember him in their prayers.

    Sister Todd came over the next afternoon, too, with some rhubarb pie with cheese on it, which is my favorite pie. When she took a piece into Grandpa Jeremiah's room she come right out again and told Ellie to go fetch the Bible.

It was a hot day when they had the funeral. Mostly everybody was there. The church was hot as anything, even though they had the window
240 open. Some yellowjacks flew in and buzzed around Sister Todd's niece and then around Deacon Turner's wife and settled right on her hat and stayed there until we all stood and sang "Soon-a Will Be Done."

    At the graveyard Macon played "Precious Lord" and I cried hard even though I told myself that I wasn't going to cry the way Ellie and Sister Todd was, but it was such a sad thing when we left and Grandpa Jeremiah was still out to the grave that I couldn't help it.

    During the funeral and all, Macon kind of told everybody where to go and where to sit and which of the three cars to ride in. After it was over he come by the house and sat on the front porch and played on his guitar.
250 Ellie was standing leaning against the rail and she was crying but it wasn't a hard crying. It was a soft crying, the kind that last inside of you for a long time. **K**

    Macon was playing a tune I hadn't heard before. I thought it might have been what he was working at when Grandpa Jeremiah was telling him those stories and I watched his fingers but I couldn't tell if it was or not. It wasn't nothing special, that tune Macon was playing, maybe halfway between them Delta Blues he would do when Sister Todd wasn't around and something you would play at church. It was something different and something the same at the same time. I watched his fingers go over that
260 guitar and figured I could learn that tune one day if I had a mind to. ∾

K STYLE
Evaluate how Myers's use of a child **narrator** affects the type of details you get about the funeral. What observations does the narrator make that an adult might not have made?

Comprehension

1. **Recall** Which members of the community take an interest in Grandpa Jeremiah's health?

2. **Clarify** The **narrator** describes a younger Macon in lines 44–55. How has Macon changed?

3. **Summarize** What evidence is there that Ellie begins to like Macon?

Literary Analysis

4. **Monitor** Review the chart you created as you read. Choose three entries and explain what clues helped you **clarify** the information.

5. **Make Inferences** By the end of the story, which characters do you think **treasure** Grandpa Jeremiah's stories?

6. **Identify Mood** The feeling that a piece of literature creates for the reader is called the mood. What words would you use to describe the overall mood of "Jeremiah's Song"? Support your response by noting specific places in the text that create this feeling.

7. **Analyze Style** Recall that Myers's **first-person narrator** in this story is a child. Find three examples of narration that seem especially typical of how a child might tell a story. Record them in a diagram like the one shown. How does the choice of a child narrator affect the story?

Example: "I was the one who loved Grandpa Jeremiah the most and she didn't hardly even know him so I didn't see why she was crying." (lines 82–84)	Example:	Example:

Effect on the Story:

8. **Evaluate** Do you think "Jeremiah's Song" is an appropriate title for the story? Use examples from the selection to support your opinion.

Extension and Challenge

9. **SOCIAL STUDIES CONNECTION** Research Macon's favorite music—the Delta Blues—and the musicians who made it famous. Focus your search on one musician, such as Muddy Waters, Robert Johnson, Son House, or Charley Patton. Share your findings with the class.

> **RESEARCH LINKS**
> For more on Delta Blues musicians, visit the **Research Center** at **ClassZone.com**.

Muddy Waters

Vocabulary in Context

VOCABULARY PRACTICE

Show that you understand the vocabulary words by deciding whether each statement is true or false.

1. You usually get a **diagnosis** from a doctor.
2. A **setback** during a long project is very exciting.
3. Having a heart **condition** means that you have strong feelings.
4. After having a **stroke,** you might not be able to speak as clearly.

condition

diagnosis

setback

stroke

VOCABULARY IN WRITING

Suppose Jeremiah invented a story of his experiences after having a stroke. What might he have said? Write Jeremiah's story using at least two vocabulary words. You might begin like this.

> **EXAMPLE SENTENCE**
>
> *Before this **setback**, I was as fit and healthy as a young man.*

VOCABULARY STRATEGY: COMPOUND WORDS

When two or more words are combined to have one meaning, they are called **compound words.** You can understand some compound words, like *firefighter*, by looking at the meanings of the combined words. For others, like the vocabulary word *setback*, you may need help from context clues or a dictionary to fully understand the meaning of the word.

PRACTICE Use context clues to figure out the meaning of each boldfaced compound word. Then write the definition. Use a dictionary if necessary.

1. It was the first time he had broken a rule, so we chose to **overlook** it.
2. She tries to pay closer attention to things, but she is still a **scatterbrain.**
3. As the **ringleader** of the neighborhood baseball team, he was responsible for gathering the players and setting the rules.
4. I became good friends with the **shopkeeper** who sold used books.
5. Once the cottage was fixed up, it was a lovely **getaway** from busy city life.

VOCABULARY PRACTICE
For more practice, go to the **Vocabulary Center** at **ClassZone.com.**

Reading-Writing Connection

Demonstrate your understanding of "Jeremiah's Song" by responding to
these prompts. Then complete the **Grammar and Writing** exercise.

A. Short Response: Analyze a Character
Consider Macon's relationship with Jeremiah,
Ellie, and the narrator. In **one paragraph,**
summarize how Macon becomes part of the
family. Include at least one reason why you
think he **treasures** Jeremiah's stories.

A strong analysis will . . .
- show an understanding
  of Macon's character
- use specific details and
  events from the story to
  support your ideas

B. Extended Response: Write a Narrative
The narrator describes Grandpa Jeremiah's
funeral in lines 238–260 the way he sees it.
In **two to three paragraphs,** rewrite the funeral
scene as Ellie sees it.

*A successful narrative
will . . .*
- include possible details not
  mentioned by the story's
  narrator
- keep Ellie's character traits
  in mind

GRAMMAR AND WRITING

USE CORRECT SENTENCE TYPE In order for your sentences to communicate
the meaning and emotions you intend, it is important to use the correct
sentence type. A **declarative** sentence makes a statement and ends with a
period. An **interrogative** sentence asks a question and ends with a question
mark. An **imperative** sentence makes a request or gives a command and
usually ends with a period. An **exclamatory** sentence shows strong feeling
and ends with an exclamation point.

PRACTICE Identify the sentence type for each of the following sentences and
punctuate it correctly.

1. Oh, what a comfort that is to me
2. I cried when I heard Macon play the guitar
3. Ladies, please sit down
4. What song is Macon playing on the porch

FOR MORE HELP WITH SENTENCE TYPES, SEE PAGE R60 IN THE *Grammar
Handbook.*

Maniac Magee

Novel by Jerry Spinelli

Jerry Spinelli
born 1941

Other Books by Jerry Spinelli

- *Knots in My Yo-Yo String*
- *Milkweed*
- *Report to the Principal's Office!*
- *Space Station Seventh Grade*
- *Stargirl*

Meet Jerry Spinelli

Growing up, Jerry Spinelli dreamed of being a major league baseball player. Luckily for his readers, by the time Spinelli finished high school, his dream had changed: He wanted to become a writer. He wrote four novels in 12 years while also working as a magazine editor. All four novels were rejected, but Spinelli was not about to give up. He wrote another novel, *Space Station Seventh Grade*. This time, children's publishers loved it. Spinelli's career as a published writer had begun.

What has Spinelli learned from his many years of writing? For one thing, he says that if you "write what you care about,... you stand the best chance of doing your best writing." Spinelli takes his own advice. "The first 15 years of my life turned out to be one big research project," Spinelli explains. "I thought I was simply growing up in Norristown, Pennsylvania; looking back, now I can see that I was also gathering material that would one day find its way into my books."

Try a Humorous Novel

After *Space Station Seventh Grade* launched Spinelli into the publishing world, Maniac Magee secured his success. Spinelli describes the novel as "a blending of tall tale and actuality." The tale of Maniac's life is so amazing that fiction and reality merge "to the point where it makes no difference which is which," Spinelli notes. Like many other **humorous novels**, *Maniac Magee* offers its readers more than just a great laugh. It uses humor to address some tough issues, particularly racism.

Read a Great Book

Not many homeless 12-year-olds end up becoming legends; but then again, there is only one Jeffrey Lionel Magee. As Jerry Spinelli writes, "The history of a kid is one part fact, two parts legend, and three parts snowball." Part tall tale, part novel, *Maniac Magee* follows the many adventures of Jeffrey as he searches for a place to call home. In the excerpt you are about to read, Jeffrey begins a new life in Two Mills, Pennsylvania.

from

Maniac Magee

Everybody knows that Maniac Magee (then Jeffrey) started out in Hollidaysburg and wound up in Two Mills. The question is: What took him so long? And what did he do along the way?

Sure, two hundred miles is a long way, especially on foot, but the year that it took him to cover it was about fifty-one weeks more than he needed—figuring the way he could run, even then.

The legend doesn't have the answer. That's why this period is known as The Lost Year.

And another question: Why did he stay here? Why Two Mills?

10   Of course, there's the obvious answer that sitting right across the Schuylkill is Bridgeport, where he was born. Yet there are other theories. Some say he just got tired of running. Some say it was the butterscotch Krimpets. And some say he only intended to pause here but that he stayed because he was so happy to make a friend.

If you listen to everybody who claims to have seen Jeffrey-Maniac Magee that first day, there must have been ten thousand people and a parade of fire trucks waiting for him at the town limits. Don't believe it. A couple of people truly remember, and here's what 20 they saw: a scraggly little kid jogging toward them, the soles of both sneakers hanging by their hinges and flopping open like dog tongues each time they came up from the pavement.

But it was something they heard that made him stick in their minds all these years. As he passed them, he said, "Hi." Just that— "Hi"—and he was gone. They stopped, they blinked, they turned, they stared after him, they wondered: *Do I know that kid?* Because people just didn't say that to strangers, out of the blue.

❧

As for the first person to actually stop and talk with Maniac, that would be Amanda Beale. And it happened because of a 30 mistake.

It was around eight in the morning, and Amanda was heading for grade school, like hundreds of other kids all over town. What made Amanda different was that she was carrying a suitcase, and that's what caught Maniac's eye. He figured she was like him, running away, so he stopped and said, "Hi."

Amanda was suspicious. Who was this white stranger kid? And what was he doing in the East End, where almost all the kids were black? And why was he saying that?

But Amanda Beale was also friendly. So she stopped and said 40 "Hi" back.

"Are you running away?" Jeffrey asked her.

"Huh?" said Amanda.

Jeffrey pointed at the suitcase.

Amanda frowned, then thought, then laughed. She laughed so hard she began to lose her balance, so she set the suitcase down and sat on it so she could laugh more safely. When at last she could speak, she said, "I'm not running away. I'm going to school."

She saw the puzzlement on his face. She got off the suitcase and opened it up right there on the sidewalk.

50   Jeffrey gasped. "Books!"

Books, all right. Both sides of the suitcase crammed with them. Dozens more than anyone would ever need for homework.

Jeffrey fell to his knees. He and Amanda and the suitcase were like a rock in a stream; the school-goers just flowed to the left and right around them. He turned his head this way and that to read the titles. He lifted the books on top to see the ones beneath. There were fiction books and nonfiction books, who-did-it books and let's-be-friends books and what-is-it books and how-to books and how-not-to books and just-regular-kid books. On the bottom was a
60 single volume from an encyclopedia. It was the letter A.

"My library," Amanda Beale said proudly.

Somebody called, "Gonna be late for school, girl!"

Amanda looked up. The street was almost deserted. She slammed the suitcase shut and started hauling it along. Jeffrey took the suitcase from her. "I'll carry it for you."

Amanda's eyes shot wide. She hesitated; then she snatched it back. "Who *are* you?" she said.

"Jeffrey Magee."

"Where are you from? West End?"

70   "No."

She stared at him, at the flap-soled sneakers. Back in those days the town was pretty much divided. The East End was blacks, the West End was whites. "I know you're not from the East End."

"I'm from Bridgeport."

"Bridgeport? Over there? *That* Bridgeport?"

"Yep."

"Well, why aren't you there?"

"It's where I'm from, not where I am."

80   "Great. So where do you *live?*"

Jeffrey looked around. "I don't know . . . maybe . . . here?"

"*Maybe?*" Amanda shook her head and chuckled. "*Maybe* you better go ask your mother and father if you live here or not."

She speeded up. Jeffrey dropped back for a second, then caught up with her. "Why are you taking all these books to school?"

Amanda told him. She told him about her little brother and sister at home, who loved to crayon every piece of paper they could find, whether or not it already had type all over it. And about the dog, Bow Wow, who chewed everything he could get his teeth on. And that, she said, was why she carried her whole library to and from school every day.

First bell was ringing; the school was still a block away. Amanda ran. Jeffrey ran.

"Can I have a book?" he said.

"They're mine," she said.

"Just to read. To borrow."

"No."

"Please. What's your name?"

"Amanda."

"Please, Amanda. Any one. Your shortest one."

"I'm late now and I'm not gonna stop and open up this thing again. Forget it."

He stopped. "Amanda!"

She kept running, then stopped, turned, glared. What kind of kid was this, anyway? All grungy. Ripped shirt. Why didn't he go back to Bridgeport or the West End, where he belonged? Bother some white girl up there? And why was she still standing here?

"So what if I loaned you one, huh? How am I gonna get it back?"

"I'll bring it back. Honest! If it's the last thing I do. What's your address?"

"Seven twenty-eight Sycamore. But *you* can't come there. You can't even be *here*."

Second bell rang. Amanda screamed, whirled, ran.

"Amanda!"

She stopped, turned. "*Ohhhh*," she squeaked. She tore a book from the suitcase, hurled it at him—"*Here!*"—and dashed into school.

The book came flapping like a wounded duck and fell at Jeffrey's feet. It was a story of the Children's Crusade. Jeffrey picked it up, and Amanda Beale was late to school for the only time in her life.

∾

Jeffrey made three other appearances that first day.

The first came at one of the high school fields, during eleventh-grade gym class. Most of the students were playing soccer. But about a dozen were playing football, because they were on the varsity, and the gym teacher happened to be the football coach. The star quarterback, Brian Denehy, wound up and threw a sixty-yarder to his favorite receiver, James "Hands" Down, who was streaking a
130 fly pattern down the sideline.

But the ball never quite reached Hands. Just as he was about to cradle it in his big brown loving mitts, it vanished. By the time he recovered from the shock, a little kid was weaving upfield through the varsity football players. Nobody laid a paw on him. When the kid got down to the soccer field, he turned and punted the ball. It sailed back over the up-looking gym-classers, spiraling more perfectly than anything Brian Denehy had ever thrown, and landed in the outstretched hands of still stunned Hands Down. Then the kid ran off.

140 There was one other thing, something that all of them saw but no one believed until they compared notes after school that day: up until the punt, the kid had done everything with one hand. He had to, because in his other hand was a book. ∾

Keep Reading

Jeffrey seems like an unusual boy the minute he hits town, so why do you think Amanda lets him borrow her book? To find out how Jeffrey turns into the legendary Maniac Magee, read the rest of the novel. As the hilarious plot unfolds, Maniac continues to search for a home—and for a way to heal the conflicts he finds in Two Mills.

The Jacket
Essay by Gary Soto

What builds CONFIDENCE?

KEY IDEA If you have **confidence,** that means you believe in yourself and in what you can accomplish. Confidence can help you speak in front of a group, meet new people, or make difficult choices. Real confidence comes from within. Still, as Gary Soto expresses in "The Jacket," outside pressures can sometimes bring you down.

LIST IT Brainstorm with a small group of classmates to make a list of the kinds of experiences that can build confidence. Then identify some ways that a person's confidence can be damaged.

Confidence Builders	Confidence Busters
doing well on a test	

● LITERARY ANALYSIS: TONE IN NONFICTION

As in fiction, nonfiction writers often express an attitude toward their subjects. This is known as **tone**. One of the ways writers express tone is by using similes. A **simile** is a comparison of unlike things using the word *like* or *as*. Look at the following example from "The Jacket":

I stared at the jacket, like an enemy, thinking bad things before I took off my old jacket. . . .

The simile "like an enemy" reveals Soto's tone of anger toward the jacket. Other similes Soto uses in the essay reveal other emotions and attitudes. Look for these similes as you read and notice what they help the reader understand.

● READING STRATEGY: CONNECT

Suppose you tell a friend about a bad day, and your friend says, "I know how you feel—the same thing happened to me." This instantly makes you feel understood.

You do a similar thing when you **connect** your own experiences and knowledge to what you read. When you make connections, you may have a stronger understanding of the writer's message. As you read "The Jacket," use a graphic organizer to record the connections you make.

Event in "The Jacket"	+	My Experience	=	What I Understand About the Event
The character is in sixth grade.	+	I am in the sixth grade.	=	I know what things are important to a sixth grader.

▲ VOCABULARY IN CONTEXT

Gary Soto uses the boldfaced words to help tell about a jacket he hated. To see how many you know, replace each boldfaced word with a word or phrase that means the same thing.

1. Gary Soto remembers looking at his **profile** in the mirror, hoping to look cool in his new jacket.

2. He spun each arm like a **propeller** to see how silly the jacket looked.

3. Eventually the jacket began to **shrivel** and no longer fit.

4. Soto remembers the **vicious** thoughts he had about it.

THE
JACKET
GARY SOTO

My clothes have failed me.

I remember the green coat that I wore in fifth and sixth grades when you either danced like a champ or pressed yourself against a greasy wall, bitter as a penny toward the happy couples.

When I needed a new jacket and my mother asked what kind I wanted, I described something like bikers wear: black leather and silver studs[1] with enough belts to hold down a small town. We were in the kitchen, steam on the windows from her cooking. She listened so long while stirring dinner that I thought she understood for sure the kind I wanted. The next day when I got home from school, I discovered draped on my bedpost a jacket the color of day-old guacamole.[2] I threw my books on the bed and approached the jacket slowly, as if it were a stranger whose hand I had to shake. I touched the vinyl sleeve, the collar, and peeked at the mustard-colored lining.

10

---

1. **studs:** small ornamental metal buttons mounted on fabric.
2. **guacamole** (gwä′kə-mō′lē): a thick paste made from avocados, citrus juice, onions, and seasoning, often served as a dip.

ANALYZE VISUALS
Examine the facial expression of the boy in this photograph. What kind of attitude does he seem to have?

A CONNECT
Reread lines 5–14. Think of a time when you felt your parents hadn't understood you. How does this help you understand Soto's disappointment?

From the kitchen mother yelled that my jacket was in the closet. I closed the door to her voice and pulled at the rack of clothes in the closet, hoping the jacket on the bedpost wasn't for me but my mean brother. No luck. I gave up. From my bed, I stared at the jacket. I wanted to cry because it was so ugly and so big that I knew I'd have to wear it a long time. I was a
20 small kid, thin as a young tree, and it would be years before I'd have a new one. I stared at the jacket, like an enemy, thinking bad things before I took off my old jacket whose sleeves climbed halfway to my elbow.

I put the big jacket on. I zipped it up and down several times, and rolled the cuffs up so they didn't cover my hands. I put my hands in the pockets and flapped the jacket like a bird's wings. I stood in front of the mirror, full face, then **profile,** and then looked over my shoulder as if someone had called me. I sat on the bed, stood against the bed, and combed my hair to see what I would look like doing something natural. I looked ugly. I threw it on my brother's bed and looked at it for a long time before I slipped it on
30 and went out to the backyard, smiling a "thank you" to my mom as I passed her in the kitchen. With my hands in my pockets I kicked a ball against the fence, and then climbed it to sit looking into the alley. I hurled orange peels at the mouth of an open garbage can and when the peels were gone I watched the white puffs of my breath thin to nothing. **B**

I jumped down, hands in my pockets, and in the backyard on my knees I teased my dog, Brownie, by swooping my arms while making bird calls. He jumped at me and missed. He jumped again and again, until a tooth sunk deep, ripping an L-shaped tear on my left sleeve. I pushed Brownie away to study the tear as I would a cut on my arm. There was no blood,
40 only a few loose pieces of fuzz. Dumb dog, I thought, and pushed him away hard when he tried to bite again. I got up from my knees and went to my bedroom to sit with my jacket on my lap, with the lights out.

That was the first afternoon with my new jacket. The next day I wore it to sixth grade and got a D on a math quiz. During the morning recess Frankie T., the playground terrorist, pushed me to the ground and told me to stay there until recess was over. My best friend, Steve Negrete, ate an apple while looking at me, and the girls turned away to whisper on the monkey bars.[3] The teachers were no help: they looked my way and talked about how foolish I looked in my new jacket. I saw their heads bob with
50 laughter, their hands half-covering their mouths. **C**

Even though it was cold, I took off the jacket during lunch and played kickball in a thin shirt, my arms feeling like braille[4] from goose bumps. But when I returned to class I slipped the jacket on and shivered until I

profile (prō'fīl') *n.* a side view of an object, especially of the human head

B TONE
Identify the **simile** in line 25. How does this comparison tell you how Soto feels?

C CONNECT
In your chart, describe a moment when you worried that everyone was looking at you. What does this help you understand about how Soto is feeling?

---

3. **monkey bars:** a structure of poles and bars for climbing, often found in playgrounds.

4. **braille** (brāl): a system of writing or printing for blind people, made up of arrangements of raised dots representing letters and numbers.

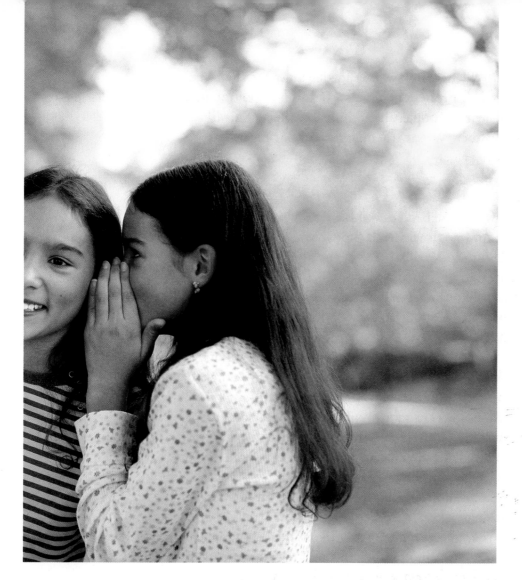

ANALYZE VISUALS
What can you **infer** about the two girls in this image and the secret they are sharing?

was warm. I sat on my hands, heating them up, while my teeth chattered like a cup of crooked dice. Finally warm, I slid out of the jacket but a few minutes later put it back on when the fire bell rang. We paraded out into the yard where we, the sixth graders, walked past all the other grades to stand against the back fence. Everybody saw me. Although they didn't say out loud, "Man, that's ugly," I heard the buzz-buzz of gossip and even
60 laughter that I knew was meant for me.

A nd so I went, in my guacamole-colored jacket. So embarrassed, so hurt, I couldn't even do my homework. I received Cs on quizzes, and forgot the state capitals and the rivers of South America, our friendly neighbor. Even the girls who had been friendly blew away like loose flowers to follow the boys in neat jackets. **D**

I wore that thing for three years until the sleeves grew short and my forearms stuck out like the necks of turtles. All during that time no love came to me—no little dark girl in a Sunday dress she wore on Monday.

D TONE
How does the **simile** in the last sentence of the paragraph help you to understand Soto's frustration?

At lunchtime I stayed with the ugly boys who leaned against the chainlink
70 fence and looked around with **propellers** of grass spinning in our mouths.
We saw girls walk by alone, saw couples, hand in hand, their heads like
bookends pressing air together. We saw them and spun our propellers so
fast our faces were blurs.

I blame that jacket for those bad years. I blame my mother for
her bad taste and her cheap ways. It was a sad time for the heart. With
a friend I spent my sixth-grade year in a tree in the alley, waiting for
something good to happen to me in that jacket, which had become the
ugly brother who tagged along wherever I went. And it was about that
time that I began to grow. My chest puffed up with muscle and, strangely,
80 a few more ribs. Even my hands, those fleshy hammers, showed bravely
through the cuffs, the fingers already hardening for the coming fights.
But that L-shaped rip on the left sleeve got bigger, bits of stuffing coughed
out from its wound after a hard day of play. I finally Scotch-taped it
closed, but in rain or cold weather the tape peeled off like a scab and more
stuffing fell out until that sleeve **shriveled** into a palsied arm.[5] That
winter the elbows began to crack and whole chunks of green began to fall
off. I showed the cracks to my mother, who always seemed to be at the
stove with steamed-up glasses, and she said that there were children in
Mexico who would love that jacket. I told her that this was America and
90 yelled that Debbie, my sister, didn't have a jacket like mine. I ran outside,
ready to cry, and climbed the tree by the alley to think bad thoughts and
watch my breath puff white and disappear. **ⓔ**

But whole pieces still casually flew off my jacket when I played hard,
read quietly, or took **vicious** spelling tests at school. When it became so
spotted that my brother began to call me "camouflage," I flung it over the
fence into the alley. Later, however, I swiped the jacket off the ground and
went inside to drape it across my lap and mope.

I was called to dinner: steam silvered my mother's glasses as she said
grace;[6] my brother and sister with their heads bowed made ugly faces at
100 their glasses of powdered milk. I gagged too, but eagerly ate big rips of
buttered tortilla that held scooped-up beans. Finished, I went outside with
my jacket across my arm. It was a cold sky. The faces of clouds were piled
up, hurting. I climbed the fence, jumping down with a grunt. I started up
the alley and soon slipped into my jacket, that green ugly brother who
breathed over my shoulder that day and ever since. **∾**

propeller (prə-pĕl'ər) *n.*
a spinning blade used to
move a boat or airplane
forward   **propel** *v.*

shrivel (shrĭ'vəl) *v.* to
shrink or wrinkle

ⓔ TONE
Reread lines 83–85.
In what way does the
simile "like a scab" help
express Soto's attitude
toward the jacket?

vicious (vĭsh'əs) *adj.*
severe or fierce

VISUAL VOCABULARY

camouflage
(kăm'ə-flāzh') *n.* fabric
dyed to make the
wearer blend in with
the environment

---

5. **palsied** (pôl'zēd) **arm:** a paralyzed or weakened arm.

6. **grace:** a short prayer or blessing said before or after a meal.

Comprehension

1. **Clarify** Reread lines 104–105. What does Soto mean when he calls his jacket an "ugly brother who breathed over my shoulder"?

2. **Summarize** Why is Soto disappointed by his sixth-grade year?

3. **Represent** Using details from the essay, sketch the jacket Soto wanted to have. Then create a series of sketches showing the jacket his mother actually gives him, and how the jacket changes over time.

Literary Analysis

4. **Compare and Contrast** What are the similarities and differences between the jacket Soto asked for and the one he received? Explain how what he wanted affected his attitude toward what he got.

5. **Make Connections** Review your chart of connections to find parts of the essay that were similar to your own experience. How do these connections affect your understanding of the story?

6. **Identify Symbol** A symbol is a person, place, thing, or activity that stands for something beyond itself. Explain what Soto's jacket might be a symbol for, and why.

7. **Identify Tone** Create a chart like the one shown to gather the **similes** Soto uses in "The Jacket." Then decide what overall tone these comparisons convey.

Simile	Basic Description	Positive or Negative
"I stared at the jacket, like an enemy" (line 21)	he stared meanly or cautiously at it	negative

8. **Evaluate** Reread lines 61–74. Do you agree with Soto that the jacket is responsible for his "bad years"? Give examples from the essay to support your answer.

Extension and Challenge

9. **Big Question Activity** With a group of classmates, reread lines 43–50. Take turns discussing the effect the jacket had on Soto's **confidence.**

10. **Reader's Circle** Soto blames his jacket for his awkwardness in the sixth grade. In a small group, discuss the ways in which Soto's attitude might have made wearing the jacket seem worse than it actually was. What are some things he could have done to overcome the effects of the jacket?

Vocabulary in Context

VOCABULARY PRACTICE

Use context clues to choose the vocabulary word that best completes each sentence.

1. The airplane made an emergency landing when its _____ broke.
2. It was sad to see my favorite sweater _____ and shrink with each wash.
3. I know he was upset, but he didn't need to be so _____.
4. Many portraits show only the person's _____, not the whole face.

profile

propeller

shrivel

vicious

VOCABULARY IN WRITING

Write a paragraph describing a piece of clothing, like Soto's jacket, that you really don't like to wear. Use at least two vocabulary words. You might start like this.

> **EXAMPLE SENTENCE**
>
> *Having to wear my itchy mittens makes me **vicious**.*

VOCABULARY STRATEGY: THE LATIN ROOT *pro*

The vocabulary words *profile* and *propellers* both contain the Latin root *pro*, which means "forth" or "forward." You can find the word root *pro* combined with other roots and base words in many English words. When you come across an unfamiliar word containing *pro*, use context clues, as well as your knowledge of the root, to figure out the meaning.

progress

profuse

pro

prominent

projector

promote

PRACTICE Choose the word from the web that best completes each sentence. Use a dictionary if necessary. Explain how the root *pro* helps give meaning to each word.

1. After five years, the company decided to _____ him from assistant to manager.
2. We couldn't see the movie because the _____ wasn't working.
3. His _____ and detailed thank-you note was four pages long!
4. They were pleased to make such good _____ on their report.
5. He has become a very _____ man since running for town mayor.

VOCABULARY PRACTICE
For more practice, go to the **Vocabulary Center** at **ClassZone.com.**

Reading-Writing Connection

Increase your understanding of "The Jacket" by responding to these prompts.
Then complete the **Grammar and Writing** exercise.

WRITING PROMPTS

A. Short Response: Explore Tone
Write a **one-paragraph description** of the jacket as if you were Soto's mother. Use a **simile** to help express her attitude toward the jacket. Your description should have a different tone from the one in the essay.

SELF-CHECK

A strong description will . . .
- show the jacket from the mother's point of view
- create a tone that matches the mother's attitude

B. Extended Response: Evaluate Ideas
"The Jacket" tells about a time in Soto's life when he lacked **confidence.** Does he seem to have more confidence as an adult looking back? In **two or three paragraphs,** explain the ways in which Soto has or hasn't changed since the years when he wore the green jacket.

An interesting response will . . .
- compare Soto's adult way of thinking with his attitude as a sixth-grader
- use examples from the essay as support

GRAMMAR AND WRITING

USE COMMAS CORRECTLY When writing a sentence that includes a list of three or more items, use **commas** to help make the sentence's meaning clear. Place commas after every **item in a series** except the last item. To separate two or more **adjectives** describing the same noun, use a comma after all but the last adjective.

Original: Soto remembers the embarrassment sadness and awkwardness of having an ugly jacket.

Revised: Soto remembers the embarrassment, sadness, and awkwardness of having an ugly jacket.

PRACTICE Insert commas where needed in the following sentences.

1. His mother bought cheap sturdy and practical clothes for the kids.
2. He uses humorous vivid familiar images to describe the jacket's ugliness.
3. The jacket resulted in poor grades no girlfriend and ugly friends for Soto.
4. Thinking of the jacket brings back memories of poverty disappointments and loneliness.

FOR MORE HELP WITH COMMAS, SEE PAGE R49 IN THE *Grammar Handbook.*

The First Skateboard in the History of the World

Memoir by Betsy Byars

How strong is PEER PRESSURE?

KEY IDEA Friends and classmates can have a big influence on you. They may encourage you to make decisions—good or bad. The pressure you feel to please or fit in with people your age is called **peer pressure.** Standing up to peer pressure can be difficult, but giving into it can cause trouble. In "The First Skateboard in the History of the World," Betsy Byars recalls her bumps and bruises from a time when peer pressure was too hard to resist.

WEB IT Think about the different ways peer pressure affects us. What things might a person do in order to fit in? Create a word web to gather your ideas.

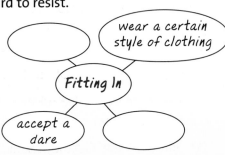

SECTION C   THE STAR JOURNAL   C4

LOOK, IF YOU'RE GOING TO HANG OUT WITH US, FIRST THING YOU GOTTA' DO IS LOSE THE BELL.

● LITERARY ANALYSIS: STYLE IN NONFICTION

Think about the many styles of clothing people wear. Some people dress in a simple way without fussing over jewelry, hats, or "just the right" pair of shoes. Other people enjoy adding many different accessories. Similarly, each writer has a unique **style,** or way of communicating his or her ideas.

In "The First Skateboard in the History of the World," Betsy Byars achieves a casual, friendly style through

- a humorous **tone,** or attitude toward her subject
- **sentence structure** that includes short, direct sentences and fragments, or parts of sentences
- realistic **dialogue,** or conversations

As you read, notice how Byars uses these elements to create a specific style.

● READING STRATEGY: ANALYZE AUTHOR'S PURPOSE

A writer may have many reasons for writing a particular piece. Each of these reasons is referred to as the **author's purpose.** A writer typically writes a **memoir,** or true account of personal experiences, for one or more of these reasons:

- to inform the reader about his or her life
- to share thoughts and feelings
- to entertain readers with a good story

As you read "The First Skateboard in the History of the World," note the passages in which Byars achieves these goals. Record them in a chart.

Inform	Share Thoughts or Feelings	Entertain

▲ VOCABULARY IN CONTEXT

Betsy Byars uses the boldfaced words to help tell a story about risk taking. To see how many you know, substitute a different word or phrase for each one.

1. Riding a skateboard requires **agility** as well as bravery.
2. The neighborhood kids never **protest** anything Bee says.
3. Betsy didn't get any **acclaim** for her tremendous efforts.
4. No one offered to **administer** first aid to the injured rider.

479

THE
FIRST SKATEBOARD
IN THE
HISTORY OF THE WORLD

BETSY BYARS

S ince none of my friends knew I was scared of anything, I was thought to be a tough little kid.

My bravery (and the rest of me) was about seven years old when I was selected by the neighborhood to test ride The First Skateboard in the History of the World. **A**

I didn't even know what a skateboard was. This was the summer of 1935. Skateboards hadn't been invented back then. But that did not stop our neighborhood from making one.

Here's what went into The First Skateboard in the History of the World:

10   One board.

Forty-two assorted nails.

One roller skate.

Back then, roller skates were made out of metal and could be adjusted to stretch waaaay out for long feet, which a lot of us had. We stretched this skate out so far that it came apart. This suited us just fine. We nailed the front half of the skate to the front of the board and the back half to the back.

A AUTHOR'S PURPOSE
Reread lines 1–5. For what purpose do you suppose Byars wrote this passage? Record this information in the appropriate column of your chart.

ANALYZE VISUALS
Describe as many **details** in this illustration as you can.

Illustrations by Juliette Borda.

Bee →

915 Magnolia Ave.

Red Hill

monkey bars

Betsy Alice Cromer

Then we turned the board over and hammered the tips of the nails (which had come through the board) down—hard. We had a deep respect for nails. We had all stepped on nails at one time or another, and even though we **protested** all the way to the doctor's office, "It wasn't rusty! I swear it wasn't rusty! If you don't believe me ask Skrunky! He'll tell you it wasn't rusty!" we still got a shot. We also had a deep respect for shots. **B**

The whole construction took less than five minutes, and the skateboard was ready to go. By this time we knew it was a skateboard because the leader of the neighborhood—a sixth grade girl named Bee—said, "Who wants to go first on the skateboard?"

There was a silence.

Then Bee answered her own question. "Betsy will."

There was a sort of echo from the rest, "Betsy will-ill-ill-ill-ill."

And that was how I—seven-year-old Betsy Alice Cromer—got the honor of testing The First Skateboard in the History of the World.

At the time it didn't seem like an honor, more like a military duty.

20

30

protest (prə-tĕst′) *v.* to argue about or object to something

B STYLE IN NONFICTION
Reread lines 18–23. Which words or phrases create a humorous **tone** in this paragraph?

The FIRST Skateboard

ONE BOARD

42 assorted nails

one Hammer

One Roller Skate

However, we always did what Bee told us to do. The explanation "Bee told me to" often made my mother explode with, "And if Bee told you to stick your head in a lion's mouth, would you?" "If Bee told you to jump off the Empire State Building,[1] would you?" Well . . . I was glad it never came to those things. **C**

We took the skateboard to the top of Magnolia Avenue, which was the street I lived on. Magnolia Avenue was not a steep hill, but the sidewalk had been buckled by the roots of old trees, and it was considered challenging for a skater.

We put the skateboard down on the sidewalk.

Bee said, "Go ahead, Betsy."

I said, "I will."

Fortunately we were unfamiliar with skateboards, and we didn't know you were supposed to stand up on them, so I sat down. Otherwise I wouldn't be alive today. **D**

I sat, put my feet up on the skateboard, and held on to the sides with both hands.

Somebody gave me a push.

I rolled a few inches but came to a stop at the first wide crack in the sidewalk.

They pushed again—harder.

Same disappointing ride. **E**

"This hill isn't steep enough," Bee complained, "I vote we take it to Red Hill."

"Red Hill-ill-ill-ill," came the echo.

The echo had a scary ring to it this time because Red Hill was the Alps, the Himalayas, and Mount Everest[2] all rolled into one.

We weren't allowed to roller-skate down Red Hill. We weren't even allowed to ride our bikes down it. But nobody had told us we couldn't *skateboard* down it.

We set off in a silence, tense with excitement. My throat was dry. I had recently recovered from a broken arm—the result of a daring feat on the monkey bars in Dilworth Park.

See, we had been having a contest to see who could hang on to the bars by one hand the longest, and I held on so long that my body began to angle out to the side, as if I were doing a gymnastic display of **agility,**

C AUTHOR'S PURPOSE
Why might Byars have chosen to include her mother's comments? Record this information in your chart.

D STYLE IN NONFICTION
Reread lines 46–48. What words or phrases help create the humorous **tone?**

E STYLE IN NONFICTION
Reread lines 51–55. How do the short sentences and sentence fragment help Byars create a casual style?

agility (ə-jĭl′ĭ-tē) *n.* quickness or ease of movement

---

1. **Empire State Building:** a skyscraper in New York City, once the world's tallest building.

2. **the Alps, the Himalayas, and Mount Everest:** The Alps and the Himalayas are mountain ranges located in Europe and Asia, respectively. Mount Everest, located on the border between Nepal and Tibet, is the highest mountain in the world.

70 which I wasn't. When I finally let go, I was horizontal to the ground and landed on my left elbow, which showed its displeasure by snapping in two. (I did win the contest, but neither of my parents congratulated me on the win.)

By the time we reached the top of Red Hill, my left arm was throbbing a warning like jungle drums.

And we reached the top of Red Hill very quickly.

"Sit down," Bee said.

I didn't want to, but I had to. Bee had told me to. I sat down on the skateboard. I said, "Now don't push me till I'm ready and I'm not ready
80 yet so don't push me till I say I'm ready, till I say 'Go.' Then when I say 'Go,' I only want Wilma to push me"—Wilma was the weak link in the gang—"and until I say 'Go,' everybody stay back and leave me—"

The neighborhood gang heard only the "Go" and they pushed. And I went.

The first thing that happened was that all the skin was scraped off my knuckles. (I was holding onto the sides of the board and my weight in the center of the board brought it closer to the road than anticipated.)

The next thing that happened was a three-part miracle.

The skate broke off the back of the board, the back of the board acted
90 as a brake, and The First Skateboard in the History of the World ground to a halt twenty feet down Red Hill.

There were cries of disappointment and of determination to renail the skate and start all over again, but these cries were drowned out by my own.

"I knew it wasn't going to work! Look what it did to my fingers! If you don't know how to make skateboards, don't make skateboards! Anyway, there is no such thing as a skateboard and there never will be!"

I stormed down the hill. My shouts of outrage turned to whimpers of pain as I got out of the gang's earshot and saw the damage to my knuckles.
100 I grew silent as I got within earshot of 915 Magnolia Avenue, my home. I liked to **administer** my own first-aid treatments because I was the only one who would stop administering if it hurt.

"What have you done now?" my mother asked, seeing me at the bloodied basin.

I gave my usual answer. "Nothing."

"What—have—you—done—now?" My mother always added the word *now* to give the impression that I did a lot of things.

administer
(ăd-mĭn′ĭ-stər) *v.* to give or apply

"I went down Red Hill on a skateboard."

"A what?"

110 "A board with a skate on the bottom."

"I suppose Bee told you to."

Silence.

"And if Bee told you to catch a train to Timbuktu,³ would you?"

Probably. **F**

So the test ride of the skateboard came and went without notice, without <u>acclaim.</u> I never got on another one. I never will.

But when I see kids on skateboards doing 180 ollies, ollie impossibles, lipslides, and G-turns,⁴ I think to myself, You guys would never believe it to look at me now, but I actually test rode The First Skateboard in the
120 History of the World. 〰 **G**

F **STYLE IN NONFICTION**
Reread lines 103–114. How does Byars's use of realistic **dialogue** help show what she and her mother are feeling?

acclaim (ə-klām') *n.* enthusiastic praise

G **AUTHOR'S PURPOSE**
Read lines 115–120. What does Byars want her readers to know about her?

---

3. **Timbuktu** (tĭm´bŭk-tōō´): a city located in central Mali, in West Africa.

4. **180 ollies . . . G-turns:** a series of complicated and even dangerous tricks and jumps done by experienced skateboarders.

Comprehension

1. **Recall** Who is the leader of the neighborhood?

2. **Recall** Why did the group decide to take the skateboard to Red Hill?

3. **Clarify** Do the other kids know Betsy is afraid to ride the skateboard?

Literary Analysis

4. **Make Inferences** Reread lines 24–38. Which words and phrases show that it is **peer pressure,** not pure bravery, that is leading Betsy to be daring?

5. **Examine Style** Reread lines 39–73. Find examples of Byars's casual, friendly style by looking at her use of short sentences, fragments, realistic **dialogue,** and humorous **tone.** What effect do these elements have on you as the reader? Record your answers in a chart like the one shown.

	Example	Effect on Reader
Short Sentences or Fragments		
Realistic Dialogue		
Humorous Tone	Lines 72–73: "I did win the contest, but neither of my parents congratulated me on the win."	Helps me laugh with Byars as she looks back on the foolish things she did as a child.

6. **Analyze Memoir** Go back through the selection and find references to specific places. What might be the purpose of including these details?

7. **Analyze Author's Purpose** Review the chart you completed as you read. What do you think was the author's main purpose for writing her memoir? Support your answer.

8. **Draw Conclusions** Byars begins by saying that she was "thought to be a tough little kid." Do you think she is tough? Explain.

Extension and Challenge

9. **Inquiry and Research** Research the history of skateboarding. Create a timeline that traces trends in skateboarding, changes in the design of skateboards, and the development of skateboarding tricks.

RESEARCH LINKS
For more on skateboarding, visit the **Research Center** at **ClassZone.com.**

Vocabulary in Context

VOCABULARY PRACTICE

Choose the vocabulary word that best completes each sentence.

1. The diver proved his _____ by doing a backflip.
2. I continually _____ against my early bedtime.
3. Our Neighborhood Watch program received _____ for its success.
4. It is a superhero's job to _____ justice.

acclaim

administer

agility

protest

VOCABULARY IN WRITING

Should Betsy have tried harder to avoid riding the skateboard? Write a paragraph explaining your opinion. Use at least two vocabulary words. Here's an example of how you might begin.

> **EXAMPLE SENTENCE**
>
> *In my opinion, Betsy's need for **acclaim** made her do something foolish.*

VOCABULARY STRATEGY: DICTIONARY USAGE LABELS

The meanings of words can shift slowly over time. In line 65, Betsy Byars uses the word *feat* to mean "a notable act or deed, especially an act of courage." If you were to look up the word *feat* in a dictionary, you would find that it also has a definition with the usage label OBSOLETE at the beginning or end of the entry. This label lets you know that one meaning of the word *feat,* "a specialized skill," is never used anymore.

Here are some other usage labels that dictionaries frequently use:

ARCHAIC: a word that is rarely used anymore

INFORMAL: a word or expression used in everyday speech and writing, but not in formal situations

SLANG: a word or expression appropriate in casual conversation with friends

PRACTICE Look up each term in a dictionary and note the usage label you find. Also note the definition given with that label.

1. eke
2. smoosh
3. case
4. fried
5. mop
6. skedaddle

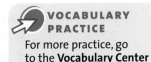

VOCABULARY PRACTICE
For more practice, go to the **Vocabulary Center** at **ClassZone.com**.

Use with "The First Skateboard in the History of the World," page 480.

Skateboard Science
Science Article

What's the Connection?

When Betsy Byars test rode "The First Skateboard in the History of the World," she had two simple goals: stay on and don't get hurt. Now, skateboarders aim to do acrobatic leaps, dizzying mid-air spins, and other tricks that look nearly impossible. In this lesson, you will read a **science article** that explains one of these "moves."

Skill Focus: Trace the Steps in a Process

The skateboarding move described on the next few pages is usually completed in one fluid motion. The writers break it down into steps to explain exactly how the skateboarder makes it happen and the science principles at work. Use these strategies to follow along:

- Read the steps in **numerical order.** Don't skip around.
- Notice **transitional words and phrases** such as *during, as,* and *meanwhile.* These identify when each event occurs.
- Focus on the vivid verbs, adverbs, and adjectives to **visualize** each step.
- Before leaving a step, **compare** your visualization of the step to the illustration included with it. Does your mental picture match? If not, reread the text to discover what you may have missed or read incorrectly.

Finally, to make certain you truly understand these steps, explain each one in your own words in a chart like the one shown.

Review: **Use Text Features, Take Notes**

	My Own Words
Before the Ollie	Three forces are acting on the rider and his board. Weight and gravity pull the board and rider down. The ground pushes them up. These forces cancel each other out, so nothing speeds up the skateboard or stops it from rolling.
Step 1	
Step 2	

BACK FORWARD STOP REFRESH HOME PRINT

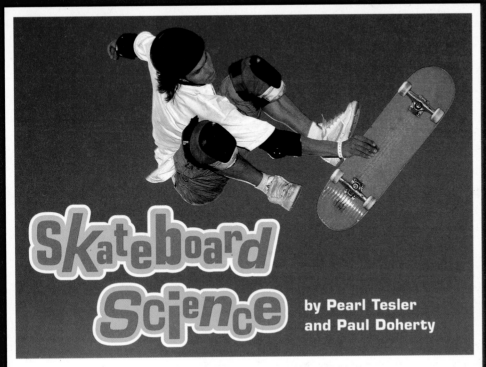

Skateboard Science

by Pearl Tesler and Paul Doherty

In the Beginning, Skateboarding Was Simple. . . . Ⓐ

With nothing more than a two-by-four on roller-skate wheels, the sidewalk surfers of the 30s, 40s, and 50s had a straightforward mission: Start at the top of a hill and ride down. The primary goal was just to stay on and avoid collisions; given the humble equipment and rough road conditions, it was no small challenge. Now, thanks in part to improvements in design and materials, skateboarders have a higher calling.

In a blur of flying acrobatics, skaters leap and skid over and onto obstacles, executing flips and turns of ever increasing
10 complexity—all at top speeds. For onlookers and beginners, it can be hard to follow the action, let alone answer the question that springs naturally to mind: How on earth do they do that? While it may seem that modern skateboarders are defying the laws of physics, the truth is that they're just using them to their advantage. Let's take a closer look at a fundamental skateboarding move and the physics principles behind it.

B TAKE NOTES
Use the article's **subheadings** as topics for notes, leaving space beneath them. Then, as you read, jot down key information about the topics in the appropriate spaces.

C SCIENCE ARTICLE
Why do you need to read lines 30–36 to fully understand the illustration?

BACK FORWARD STOP REFRESH HOME PRINT

Jumping: The Ollie **B**

Invented in the late 1970s by Alan "Ollie" Gelfand, the ollie has become a skateboarding fundamental, the basis for many other
20 more complicated tricks.

In its simplest form, the ollie is a jumping technique that allows skaters to hop over obstacles and onto curbs. What's so amazing about the ollie is the way the skateboard seems to stick to the skater's feet in midair. Seeing pictures of skaters performing soaring four-foot ollies, many people assume that the board is somehow attached to a skater's feet. It's not. What's even more amazing about the ollie is that to get the skateboards to jump up, the skaters push down on the board! . . . Let's take a closer look.

Forces in the Ollie

30 Imagine a skater rolling along a flat surface. As he does so, there are three forces acting on the skateboard. One of these forces is the weight of the rider. Another is the force of gravity on the board itself. The third is the force of the ground pushing up on the skateboard. Since these three forces balance out to zero, the skateboard doesn't speed up or slow down. It rolls along at a constant speed. **C**

As the skater gets ready to perform an ollie, he crouches down. This will help him jump
40 high when the time comes. (Don't believe it? Stand perfectly straight and try jumping without crouching . . . you didn't get very high, did you?) Now let's follow the changing forces that go into making an ollie.

BACK   FORWARD   STOP   REFRESH   HOME   PRINT

1 The skater pushes himself upward by explosively straightening his legs and raising his arms. During the jump, his rear foot exerts a much greater force on the tail of the board than his front foot does on the nose. This causes the board to pivot counterclockwise about the rear wheel, which means the tail of the board touches the ground. **D**

2 As the tail strikes the ground, the ground pushes back. The result of this upward force is that the board bounces up and begins to pivot clockwise, this time around its center of mass, which is the center of the board.

3 With the board now completely in the air, the skater slides his front foot forward, using the friction between his foot and the rough surface of the board to drag the board upward even higher.

4 The skater then begins to push his front foot down, raising the rear wheels and leveling out the board. Meanwhile, he lifts his rear leg to get it out of the way of the rising tail of the board. If he times this motion perfectly, his rear foot and the rear of the board rise in perfect unison, seemingly "stuck" together.

D STEPS IN A PROCESS
Why do you suppose the illustrator chose to include arrows in these illustrations?

5 The board is now level at its maximum height. With both feet touching the board, the skater and board begin to fall together under the influence of gravity.

6 Gravity eventually wins out and the skater bends his legs to absorb the impact of the landing. **E**

E STEPS IN A PROCESS
Notice how many steps there are in an ollie according to this article. Be sure to restate the same number of steps in your chart.

F SCIENCE ARTICLE
Why might the authors have chosen to include a glossary of terms with this article?

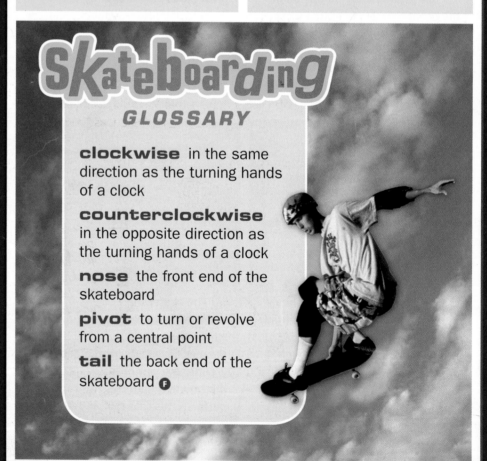

Skateboarding
GLOSSARY

clockwise in the same direction as the turning hands of a clock

counterclockwise in the opposite direction as the turning hands of a clock

nose the front end of the skateboard

pivot to turn or revolve from a central point

tail the back end of the skateboard **F**

Comprehension

1. **Recall** How did the ollie get its name?

2. **Clarify** What are some of the ways skateboarding has changed since the 1930s, 1940s, and 1950s?

Critical Analysis

3. **Analyze Strategies for Tracing Steps** Take a moment to recall the strategies you used to trace the steps in the process described in the article. Then identify one you found particularly helpful and explain how and where you used it.

4. **Evaluate a Science Article** A strong science article interests readers, makes the science easy for its target audience to understand, and is, of course, accurate. Would you say that "Skateboard Science" is a strong science article? Support your conclusion with details from the selection.

Read for Information: Create Instructions

WRITING PROMPT

In the science article you just read, Pearl Tesler and Paul Doherty explain the science behind the ollie. Use the relevant information from their article to create a simple set of instructions a skateboarder could use to perform an ollie. Write directly to the reader, addressing the reader as "you."

To answer this prompt, follow these steps:

1. In the chart you completed while reading the article, you restated each of the six steps. Now write each step as a direction to a skateboarder, leaving out the scientific details.

2. Review your instructions to see if they are clear. You might need to add transitional words and phrases to indicate when the skateboarder should do each part of the move.

How to Do an Ollie

1. From a crouched position on top of your skateboard, quickly straighten your legs and raise your arms.

3. Arrange your directions in a logical order. (You may choose to combine or add steps.) Use numbers to show the order.

4. Sketch at least two illustrations to go with your directions. You can use a stick figure for the rider. Include an arrow to show the direction of movement.

Poem: The Morning Walk
Poem by Mary Oliver

There Is No Word for Goodbye
Poem by Mary Tall Mountain

When are WORDS
not enough?

KEY IDEA Sometimes it's not what you *say* that is important but what you *do*. Saying "good game" may mean more if you also shake your opponent's hand. Saying "hello" may mean more if you also smile. Actions often add deeper meaning to simple **words.** In "The Morning Walk" and "There Is No Word for Goodbye," two poets explore the limitations of language.

QUICKWRITE Think of a time when using an electronic form of communication, such as e-mail or instant messaging, led to a misunderstanding. Explain briefly how talking in person could have made your meaning clearer.

LITERARY ANALYSIS: MOOD

Whenever you read a poem, you should ask yourself, "How does this poem make me feel?" A poem can make you feel many different ways, such as sad, joyful, thoughtful, or even frightened. The feeling readers get from a poem is called the poem's **mood.** Poets take great care to create mood in their poems. Often they use **imagery,** or description that appeals to the reader's sense of sight, touch, taste, smell, or hearing.

- "the dark blanket of sky" (sense of sight)
- "leaves crunched under Jeb's feet" (sense of hearing)

The two poems you are about to read focus on the meanings of words. However, the feeling the reader gets from each poem is different. As you read each poem, look for examples of imagery and any other interesting words and phrases to help you identify the mood.

READING STRATEGY: SET A PURPOSE FOR READING

In this lesson, your **purpose for reading** is to compare and contrast the moods of two poems. To help you do this, pay attention to your feelings as you read.

After you've read the poems once, read them again. This time, fill in a chart like the one shown. You will be asked to do more with this chart after you finish reading.

	"The Morning Walk"	"There Is No Word for Goodbye"
Which descriptions appeal to your sense of sight?		
Which descriptions appeal to your sense of hearing?		
Which descriptions appeal to your sense of touch?		
What other words or phrases stand out?		

Review: **Make Inferences**

Author Online

Mary Oliver: Nature Guide
Walking in the woods near her Massachusetts home often provides inspiration for Mary Oliver's poetry. But one day, Oliver forgot to bring a pencil on her walk and

Mary Oliver born 1935

was frustrated that she could not write down her ideas. To make sure this didn't happen again, she later returned to the woods and hid pencils among the trees. Oliver has said that a writer's duty begins with "the powers of observing."

Mary Tall Mountain: Divided Poet
Through her poetry, Mary Tall Mountain rediscovered the home and heritage she lost as a child, bringing her two worlds together. Tall Mountain was only six years old when her mother

Mary Tall Mountain 1918–1997

died, an event that caused her to be adopted by white Americans and taken away from her village. From then on, she felt torn between her new home and her Native-American community in Alaska. She once said, "Wherever I can find a place to sit down and write, that is my home."

MORE ABOUT THE AUTHOR
For more on these poets, visit the **Literature Center** at ClassZone.com.

Poem: *The Morning Walk* Mary Oliver

There are a lot of words meaning *thanks*.
Some you can only whisper.
Others you can only sing.
The pewee whistles instead.
5 The snake turns in circles,
the beaver slaps his tail
on the surface of the pond.
The deer in the pinewoods stamps his hoof.
Goldfinches shine as they float through the air. **A**
10 A person, sometimes, will hum a little Mahler.[1]
Or put arms around old oak tree.
Or take out lovely pencil and notebook to find a few
touching, kissing words.

ANALYZE VISUALS
Notice the colors in this painting. What effect do they have on the **mood** of the painting?

A MOOD
Reread lines 4–9. What mood do the **descriptions** of the animals create?

---

1. **Mahler:** Gustav Mahler (gōōs′täf mä′lər) (1860–1911); composer and conductor of classical music.

Detail of *Stag on Alert, In Wooded Clearing*, Rosa Bonheur. © SuperStock.

There Is No Word for *Goodbye*

Mary Tall Mountain

Sokoya,[1] I said, looking through
    the net of wrinkles into
    wise black pools
    of her eyes. **B**

5 What do you say in Athabaskan[2]
    when you leave each other?
    What is the word
    for goodbye?

    A shade of feeling rippled
10   the wind-tanned skin.
    Ah, nothing, she said,
    watching the river flash. **C**

B MOOD
Reread lines 1–4. What feeling do you get from the way the **speaker,** or voice of the poem, describes her aunt?

C MAKE INFERENCES
What might the aunt be experiencing in lines 9–12?

---

1. **Sokoya** (sə-koi′yə): word meaning "aunt on the mother's side."
2. **Athabaskan** (ăth′ə-băs′kən): a language spoken by Native American tribes in parts of Canada, Alaska, Oregon, and California.

Detail of *Bluebells in Shakespeare's Wood* (2004), Timmy Mallett. Acrylic. © Timmy Mallett.

She looked at me close.
   We just say, Tlaa. That means,
15   See you.
   We never leave each other.
   When does your mouth
   say goodbye to your heart? **D**

She touched me light
20   as a bluebell.
   You forget when you leave us,
   You're so small then.
   We don't use that word.

We always think you're coming back,
25   but if you don't,
   we'll see you some place else.
   You understand.
   There is no word for goodbye. **E**

D MAKE INFERENCES
Reread lines 14–18. What does the aunt mean by the question she asks at the end of this section?

E MOOD
Reread the poem to find other places where the word *goodbye* appears. How does the **repetition** of *goodbye* affect the mood of the poem?

Comprehension

1. **Recall** In Mary Oliver's poem, what are the different animals all expressing through their sounds and actions?

2. **Clarify** In Mary Tall Mountain's poem, why does the aunt not tell the poem's speaker how to say *goodbye* in her language?

3. **Clarify** What does the word *tlaa* mean?

Literary Analysis

4. **Make Inferences** Explain why Mary Oliver might have decided to call her poem "The Morning Walk."

5. **Analyze Sensory Details** Which sensory details in "The Morning Walk" are most vivid? What feeling do you think these details create?

6. **Analyze Characters** Reread lines 19–28 in "There Is No Word for Goodbye." How would you describe the relationship between the characters?

7. **Analyze Mood** Would you describe the mood of "There Is No Word for Goodbye" as angry, hopeful, sad, joyful, or thoughtful? You may choose more than one word. Support your choices with details from the poem.

8. **Draw Conclusions** In "There Is No Word for Goodbye," what do you learn about Athabaskan people and how they view one another?

Comparing Mood

Now that you have read both poems and answered some questions about them, fill in a chart like the one shown.

	"The Morning Walk"	"There Is No Word for Goodbye"
Which descriptions appeal to your sense of sight?	The snake turns in circles	
Which descriptions appeal to your sense of hearing?	whisper, sing	
Which descriptions appeal to your sense of touch?		
What other words or phrases stand out?	thanks	
What is the mood of the poem?	joyful	

Writing for Assessment

1. READ THE PROMPT

Poems usually include words that are full of emotion. Recognizing these feelings and how the poet created them is an important part of appreciating poems. In writing assessments, you will often be asked to **compare and contrast** the mood or feeling created in two poems or stories.

PROMPT

In three paragraphs, compare "The Morning Walk" and "There Is No Word for Goodbye." Describe the mood of each poem and tell whether the moods are more similar or different. Support your ideas using details from the poems.

◀ **STRATEGIES IN ACTION**

1. I need to describe the **similarities and differences** between the poems.

2. I need to describe the **feeling** I get from each poem and decide if the feelings are more alike or different.

3. I need to include **examples** of words and descriptions from the poems that help support my ideas.

2. PLAN YOUR WRITING

Study the chart you filled in to review your ideas about the mood of each poem. Then think about how to present your ideas.

- Decide on the main idea, or focus, for your response.
- Reread the poems to find more examples and details.
- Create an outline to organize your paragraphs. This sample outline shows one way you might organize them.

I. Introduce poems and main idea
II. Describe mood in first poem
III. Describe mood in second poem and compare with first poem

3. DRAFT YOUR RESPONSE

Paragraph 1 Include the titles of the poems and the names of the poets. Describe what happens in each poem. Then state your opinion about whether the moods are mostly similar or different.

Paragraph 2 Describe the mood in the first poem. Explain which words and descriptions create the mood.

Paragraph 3 Describe the mood in the second poem. Explain which words and descriptions create the mood. Tell how the mood in this poem is similar to or different from the mood in the first poem.

Revision Double check that you have included enough details as support.

The Phantom Tollbooth, Act One
Novel by Norton Juster

Dramatized by Susan Nanus

When is logic not LOGICAL?

KEY IDEA Has there ever been a time when you thought you were making perfect sense, but no one understood what you meant? In *The Phantom Tollbooth,* a boy travels to a land where no one and nothing make sense. There he finds that what he thinks is **logical** really isn't.

QUICKWRITE Imagine that one day you arrived at school to find everyone behaving differently and nothing as it normally is. What kinds of changes do you imagine taking place? Write one or two paragraphs describing people's behavior, how things look, and how you would feel.

DANGER
SOFT SAND

● LITERARY ANALYSIS: HUMOR

Writers often use **humor** to increase interest and entertain readers. Writers add humor in a number of different ways. They may

- have the characters speak and act in funny ways
- create events that lead to funny situations
- add puns for comic effect. A **pun** is a deliberate confusion of similar-sounding words or phrases that have different meanings. For example, in *The Phantom Tollbooth,* the Whether Man says that "it's more important to know whether there will be weather than what the weather will be." (pun: *whether* and *weather*)

As you read Act One of *The Phantom Tollbooth,* notice how these elements add humor to the play.

● READING STRATEGY: VISUALIZE

Details that tell you how something looks, sounds, smells, feels, or tastes help you **visualize,** or form a mental picture, as you read. In plays, these sensory details are often provided in stage directions, which give information about the setting, characters' speech and behavior, sound effects, and lighting.

As you read, create a log like the one shown to record the stage directions that help you visualize what's happening.

See	Hear	Smell	Touch	Taste
	ticking			

▲ VOCABULARY IN CONTEXT

The numbered words help tell the story of a boy's journey to a strange land. Match these words with their definitions, and then write a sentence using the word correctly.

1. crag	**a.** unhurried
2. dejectedly	**b.** where a person is going
3. destination	**c.** make a guess
4. ferocious	**d.** fierce
5. leisurely	**e.** cliff
6. surmise	**f.** unhappily

Background

Words Versus Numbers Just as Norton Juster balances words and numbers in his life, so, too, does the fantasy land featured in *The Phantom Tollbooth.* One king rules Dictionopolis, the kingdom of words, and another rules Digitopolis, the kingdom of numbers. A long-standing feud divides the two: Are words or numbers more important?

Juster wrote *The Phantom Tollbooth* as a novel. Susan Nanus later adapted the story as a play.

The
Phantom Tollbooth

Norton Juster Dramatized by Susan Nanus

CAST

(*in order of appearance*)

The Clock	Three Word Merchants
Milo, a boy	The Letterman (Fourth Word Merchant)
The Whether Man	Spelling Bee
Six Lethargarians	The Humbug
Tock, the Watchdog (same as The Clock)	The Duke of Definition
Azaz the Unabridged, King of Dictionopolis	The Minister of Meaning
The Mathemagician, King of Digitopolis	The Earl of Essence
Princess Sweet Rhyme	The Count of Connotation
Princess Pure Reason	The Undersecretary of Understanding
Gatekeeper of Dictionopolis	A Page

Photographs taken at The Kennedy Center, 2007.
© Carol Pratt.

The Set

It is recommended that the setting be either a platform set, employing vertical pipes from which banners, etc., are hung for various scenes, or a book set, with the spine UC, the leaves of the book being painted drops[1] which are turned like book leaves whenever the scene changes.

The settings should be impressionistic rather than realistic:

1. **Milo's bedroom:** *With shelves, pennants, pictures on the wall, as well as suggestions of the characters of the Land of Wisdom.*

2. **The road to the Land of Wisdom:** *A forest, from which the* Whether Man *and the* Lethargarians *emerge.*

3. **Dictionopolis:** *A marketplace full of open air stalls as well as little shops. Letters and signs should abound. There may be street signs and lampposts in the shapes of large letters (large O's and Q's) and all windows and doors can be in the shape of H's and A's.*

Act One **Scene 1**

The stage is completely dark and silent. Suddenly the sound of someone winding an alarm Clock *is heard, and after that, the sound of loud ticking is heard.*

Lights up on the Clock, *a huge alarm clock. The* Clock *reads 4:00. The lighting should make it appear that the* Clock *is suspended in mid-air (if possible). The* Clock *ticks for 30 seconds.*

Clock. See that! Half a minute gone by. Seems
10 like a long time when you're waiting for something to happen, doesn't it? Funny thing is, time can pass very slowly or very fast, and sometimes even both at once. The time now? Oh, a little after four, but what that means should depend on you. Too often, we do something simply because time tells us to. Time for school, time for bed, whoops, 12:00, time to be hungry. It can get a little silly, don't you think? Time is important, but it's what you do
20 with it that makes it so. So my advice to you is to use it. Keep your eyes open and your ears perked. Otherwise it will pass before you know it, and you'll certainly have missed something!

Things have a habit of doing that, you know. Being here one minute and gone the next. In the twinkling of an eye. In a jiffy. In a flash!

I know a girl who yawned and missed a
30 whole summer vacation. And what about that caveman who took a nap one afternoon, and woke up to find himself completely alone. You see, while *he* was sleeping, someone had invented the wheel and everyone had moved to the suburbs. And then of course, there is Milo. (*Lights up to reveal* Milo's *bedroom. The* Clock *appears to be on a shelf in the room of a young boy—a room filled with books, toys, games, maps, papers, pencils, a bed, a desk. There*
40 *is a dartboard with numbers and the face of the* Mathemagician, *a bedspread made from* King Azaz's *cloak, a kite looking like the* Spelling Bee, *a punching bag with the* Humbug's *face, as well as records, a television, a toy car, and a large box that is wrapped and has an envelope taped to the top. The sound of footsteps is heard, and then enter* Milo **dejectedly.** *He throws down his books and coat, flops into a chair, and sighs loudly.*) Who never knows what to do
50 with himself—not just sometimes, but always. When he's in school, he wants to be out, and when he's out, he wants to be in. (*During the following speech,* Milo *examines the various toys, tools, and other possessions in the room, trying*

---

1. **painted drops:** cloths that are painted to look like scenery, or, in this case, the pages of a book.

them out and rejecting them.) Wherever he is, he wants to be somewhere else—and when he gets there, so what. Everything is too much trouble or a waste of time. Books—he's already read them. Games—boring. T.V.—dumb. So what's 60 left? Another long, boring afternoon. Unless he bothers to notice a very large package that happened to arrive today.

Milo. (*Suddenly notices the package. He drags himself over to it, and disinterestedly reads the label.*) "For Milo, who has plenty of time." Well, that's true. (*sighs and looks at it*) No. (*walks away*) Well . . . (*Comes back. Rips open envelope and reads.*)

Voice. "One genuine turnpike tollbooth, easily 70 assembled at home for use by those who have never traveled in lands beyond."

Milo. Beyond what? (*continues reading*)

Voice. "This package contains the following items:" (Milo *pulls the items out of the box and sets them up as they are mentioned.*) "One (*1*) genuine turnpike tollbooth to be erected according to directions. Three (*3*) precautionary signs to be used in a precautionary fashion. Assorted coins for paying tolls. One (*1*) map, 80 strictly up to date, showing how to get from here to there. One (*1*) book of rules and traffic regulations which may not be bent or broken. Warning! Results are not guaranteed. If not perfectly satisfied, your wasted time will be refunded."

Milo (*skeptically*). Come off it, who do you think you're kidding? (*walks around and examines tollbooth*) What am I supposed to do with this? (*The ticking of the* Clock *grows loud* 90 *and impatient.*) Well . . . what else do I have to do. (Milo *gets into his toy car and drives up to the first sign. NOTE: The car may be an actual toy car propelled by pedals or a small motor, or simply*

a cardboard imitation that Milo *can fit into, and move by walking.*)

Voice. "HAVE YOUR **DESTINATION** IN MIND."

Milo (*pulls out the map*). Now, let's see. That's funny. I never heard of any of these places. 100 Well, it doesn't matter anyway. Dictionopolis. That's a weird name. I might as well go there. (*Begins to move, following map. Drives off.*)

Clock. See what I mean? You never know how things are going to get started. But when you're bored, what you need more than anything is a rude awakening.

(*The alarm goes off very loudly as the stage darkens. The sound of the alarm is transformed into the honking of a car horn, and then is joined* 110 *by the blasts, bleeps, roars and growls of heavy highway traffic. When the lights come up, Milo's bedroom is gone and we see a lonely road in the middle of nowhere.*)

Act One **Scene 2**
The Road to Dictionopolis

Enter Milo *in his car.*

Milo. This is weird! I don't recognize any of this scenery at all. (*A sign is held up before* Milo, *startling him.*) Huh? (*reads*) WELCOME TO EXPECTATIONS. INFORMATION, PREDICTIONS AND ADVICE 120 CHEERFULLY OFFERED. PARK HERE AND BLOW HORN. (Milo *blows horn.*)

Whether Man (*A little man wearing a long coat and carrying an umbrella pops up from behind the sign that he was holding. He speaks very fast and excitedly*). My, my, my, my, my, welcome, welcome, welcome, welcome to the Land of Expectations, Expectations, Expectations! We don't get many travelers these days; we certainly

don't get many travelers. Now what can I do
for you? I'm the Whether Man.

Milo (*referring to map*). Uh . . . is this the right
road to Dictionopolis?

Whether Man. Well now, well now, well now, I
don't know of any *wrong* road to Dictionopolis,
so if this road goes to Dictionopolis at all, it
must be the right road, and if it doesn't, it must
be the right road to somewhere else, because
there are no wrong roads to anywhere. Do you
think it will rain?

Milo. I thought you were the Weather Man.

Whether Man. Oh, no, I'm the Whether Man,
not the weather man. (*pulls out a sign or opens
a flap of his coat, which reads: "WHETHER"*)
After all, it's more important to know whether
there will be weather than what the weather
will be.

Milo. What kind of place is Expectations?

Whether Man. Good question, good question!
Expectations is the place you must always go to
before you get where you are going. Of course,
some people never go beyond Expectations, but
my job is to hurry them along whether they
like it or not. Now what else can I do for you?
(*opens his umbrella*)

Milo. I think I can find my own way.

Whether Man. Splendid, splendid, splendid!
Whether or not you find your own way,
you're bound to find some way. If you
happen to find my way, please return it. I
lost it years ago. I imagine by now it must be
quite rusty. You did say it was going to rain,
didn't you? (*escorts Milo to the car under the
open umbrella*) I'm glad you made your own
decision. I do so hate to make up my mind

about anything, whether it's good or bad, up
or down, rain or shine. Expect everything, I
always say, and the unexpected never happens.
Goodbye, goodbye, goodbye, good . . . (*A
loud clap of thunder is heard.*) Oh dear! (*He
looks up at the sky, puts out his hand to feel for
rain, and runs away.* Milo *watches puzzledly
and drives on.*)

Milo. I'd better get out of Expectations, but
fast. Talking to a guy like that all day would
get me nowhere for sure. (*He tries to speed up,
but finds instead that he is moving slower and
slower.*) Oh, oh, now what? (*He can barely
move. Behind* Milo, *the* Lethargarians[2] *begin to
enter from all parts of the stage. They are dressed
to blend in with the scenery and carry small
pillows that look like rocks. Whenever they fall
asleep, they rest on the pillows.*) Now I really am
getting nowhere. I hope I didn't take a wrong
turn. (*The car stops. He tries to start it. It won't
move. He gets out and begins to tinker with it.*)
I wonder where I am.

Lethargarian 1. You're . . . in . . . the . . . Dol . . .
drums[3] . . . (Milo *looks around.*)

Lethargarian 2. Yes . . . the . . . Dol . . . drums . . .
(*A yawn is heard.*)

Milo (*yelling*). WHAT ARE THE
DOLDRUMS?

Lethargarian 3. The Doldrums, my friend, are
where nothing ever happens and nothing ever
changes. (*Parts of the scenery stand up or six
people come out of the scenery colored in the same
colors of the trees or the road. They move very
slowly and as soon as they move, they stop to rest
again.*) Allow me to introduce all of us. We are
the Lethargarians at your service.

---

2. **Lethargarians** (lĕth'ər-jâr'ē-ənz): a made-up name based on the word *lethargy*. A *Lethargarian* would
   thus be dull, inactive, or uncaring.

3. **in the doldrums** (dōl'drəmz'): the condition of being depressed or listless; here, *the Doldrums* refers to
   an imaginary land.

Milo (*uncertainly*). Very pleased to meet you. I think I'm lost. Can you help me?

Lethargarian 4. Don't say think. (*He yawns.*) It's against the law.

Lethargarian 1. No one's allowed to think in the Doldrums. (*He falls asleep.*)

Lethargarian 2. Don't you have a rule book? It's local ordinance[4] 175389-J. (*He falls asleep.*)

210 **Milo** (*pulls out rule book and reads*). Ordinance 175389-J: "It shall be unlawful, illegal and unethical to think, think of thinking, **surmise,** presume, reason, meditate or speculate while in the Doldrums. Anyone breaking this law shall be severely punished." That's a ridiculous law! Everybody thinks.

All the Lethargarians. We don't!

Lethargarian 2. And most of the time, you don't, that's why you're here. You weren't thinking and you weren't paying attention either.
220 People who don't pay attention often get stuck in the Doldrums. Face it, most of the time, you're just like us. (*Falls, snoring, to the ground. Milo laughs.*)

Lethargarian 5. Stop that at once. Laughing is against the law. Don't you have a rule book? It's local ordinance 574381-W.

Milo (*opens the rule book and reads*). "In the Doldrums, laughter is frowned upon and smiling is permitted only on alternate
230 Thursdays." Well, if you can't laugh or think, what can you do?

Lethargarian 6. Anything as long as it's nothing, and everything as long as it isn't anything. There's lots to do. We have a very busy schedule . . .

Lethargarian 1. At 8:00 we get up and then we spend from 8 to 9 daydreaming.

Lethargarian 2. From 9:00 to 9:30 we take our early midmorning nap . . .

240 **Lethargarian 3.** From 9:30 to 10:30 we dawdle and delay . . .

---

4. **ordinance:** a rule or law designed to control or govern behavior.

Lethargarian 4. From 10:30 to 11:30 we take our late early morning nap . . .

Lethargarian 5. From 11:30 to 12:00 we bide our time[5] and then we eat our lunch.

Lethargarian 6. From 1:00 to 2:00 we linger and loiter . . .

Lethargarian 1. From 2:00 to 2:30 we take our early afternoon nap . . .

250 **Lethargarian 2.** From 2:30 to 3:30 we put off for tomorrow what we could have done today . . .

Lethargarian 3. From 3:30 to 4:00 we take our early late afternoon nap . . .

Lethargarian 4. From 4:00 to 5:00 we loaf and lounge until dinner . . .

Lethargarian 5. From 6:00 to 7:00 we dilly-dally . . .

Lethargarian 6. From 7:00 to 8:00 we take our early evening nap and then for an hour before 260 we go to bed, we waste time.

Lethargarian 1 (*yawning*). You see, it's really quite strenuous doing nothing all day long, and so once a week, we take a holiday and go nowhere.

Lethargarian 5. Which is just where we were going when you came along. Would you care to join us?

Milo (*yawning*). That's where I seem to be going, anyway. (*stretching*) Tell me, does everyone here do nothing?

270 **Lethargarian 3.** Everyone but the terrible Watchdog. He's always sniffing around to see that nobody wastes time. A most unpleasant character.

Milo. The Watchdog?

Lethargarian 6. THE WATCHDOG!

All the Lethargarians (*yelling at once*). RUN! WAKE UP! RUN! HERE HE COMES! THE WATCHDOG! (*They all run off. Enter a large dog with the head, feet, and tail of a dog, and* 280 *the body of a clock, having the same face as the character the* Clock.)

Watchdog. What are you doing here?

Milo. Nothing much. Just killing time. You see . . .

Watchdog. KILLING TIME! (*His alarm rings in fury.*) It's bad enough wasting time without killing it. What are you doing in the Doldrums, anyway? Don't you have anywhere to go?

Milo. I think I was on my way to Dictionopolis 290 when I got stuck here. Can you help me?

Watchdog. Help you! You've got to help yourself. I suppose you know why you got stuck.

Milo. I guess I just wasn't thinking.

Watchdog. Precisely. Now you're on your way.

Milo. I am?

Watchdog. Of course. Since you got here by not thinking, it seems reasonable that in order to get out, you must *start* thinking. Do you mind if I get in? I love automobile rides. (*He gets in.* 300 *They wait.*) Well?

Milo. All right. I'll try. (*screws up his face and thinks*) Are we moving?

Watchdog. Not yet. Think harder.

Milo. I'm thinking as hard as I can.

Watchdog. Well, think just a little harder than that. Come on, you can do it.

Milo. All right, all right. . . . I'm thinking of all the planets in the solar system, and why water expands when it turns to ice, and all the words

---

5. **bide our time:** an expression that means "to wait for further developments."

310 that begin with "q," and . . . (*The wheels begin to move.*) We're moving! We're moving!

Watchdog. Keep thinking.

Milo (*thinking*). How a steam engine works and how to bake a pie and the difference between Fahrenheit and Centigrade . . .[6]

Watchdog. Dictionopolis, here we come.

Milo. Hey, Watchdog, are you coming along?

Tock. You can call me Tock, and keep your eyes on the road.

320 **Milo.** What kind of place is Dictionopolis, anyway?

Tock. It's where all the words in the world come from. It used to be a marvelous place, but ever since Rhyme and Reason[7] left, it hasn't been the same.

Milo. Rhyme and Reason?

Tock. The two princesses. They used to settle all the arguments between their two brothers who rule over the Land of Wisdom. You see,
330 Azaz is the king of Dictionopolis and the Mathemagician is the king of Digitopolis and they almost never see eye to eye on anything. It was the job of the Princesses Sweet Rhyme and Pure Reason to solve the differences between the two kings, and they always did so well that both sides usually went home feeling very satisfied. But then, one day, the kings had an argument to end all arguments. . . .

(*The lights dim on* Tock *and* Milo, *and come up*
340 *on* King Azaz *of Dictionopolis on another part of the stage.* Azaz *has a great stomach, a grey beard reaching to his waist, a small crown and a long robe with the letters of the alphabet written all over it.*)

Azaz. Of course, I'll abide by the decision of Rhyme and Reason, though I have no doubt as to what it will be. They will choose *words*, of course. Everyone knows that words are more important than numbers any day of the week.

350 (*The* Mathemagician *appears opposite* Azaz. *The* Mathemagician *wears a long flowing robe covered entirely with complex mathematical equations, and a tall pointed hat. He carries a long staff with a pencil point at one end and a large rubber eraser at the other.*)

Mathemagician. That's what you think, Azaz. People wouldn't even know what day of the week it is without *numbers*. Haven't you ever looked at a calendar? Face it, Azaz. It's numbers
360 that count.

Azaz. Don't be ridiculous. (*to audience, as if leading a cheer*) Let's hear it for WORDS!

Mathemagician (*to audience, in the same manner*). Cast your vote for NUMBERS!

Azaz. A, B, C's!

Mathemagician. 1, 2, 3's! (*A fanfare[8] is heard.*)

Azaz and Mathemagician (*to each other*). Quiet! Rhyme and Reason are about to announce their decision.

370 (Rhyme *and* Reason *appear.*)

Rhyme. Ladies and gentlemen, letters and numerals, fractions and punctuation marks— may we have your attention, please. After careful consideration of the problem set before us by King Azaz of Dictionopolis (Azaz *bows.*) and the Mathemagician of Digitopolis (Mathemagician *raises his hands in a victory salute.*) we have come to the following conclusion:

---

6. **Fahrenheit** (făr'ən-hīt') **and Centigrade** (sĕn'tĭ-grād'): *Fahrenheit* is a temperature scale on which water freezes at 32° and boils at 212°. On the *Centigrade* (or *Celsius*) scale, water freezes at 0° and boils at 100°.

7. **Rhyme and Reason:** sense or explanation. The princesses try to establish order. When they disappear, there is "neither Rhyme nor Reason in this kingdom."

8. **fanfare:** a loud blast of trumpets.

Reason. Words and numbers are of equal value, for in the cloak of knowledge, one is the warp and the other is the woof.[9]

Rhyme. It is no more important to count the sands than it is to name the stars.

Rhyme and Reason. Therefore, let both kingdoms, Dictionopolis and Digitopolis, live in peace. (*The sound of cheering is heard.*)

Azaz. Boo! is what I say. Boo and Bah and Hiss!

Mathemagician. What good are these girls if they can't even settle an argument in anyone's favor? I think I have come to a decision of my own.

Azaz. So have I.

Azaz and Mathemagician (*to the* Princesses). You are hereby banished from this land to the Castle-in-the-Air. (*to each other*) And as for you, KEEP OUT OF MY WAY! (*They stalk off in opposite directions.*)

(*During this time, the set has been changed to the Market Square of Dictionopolis. Lights come up on the deserted square.*)

Tock. And ever since then, there has been neither Rhyme nor Reason in this kingdom. Words are misused and numbers mismanaged. The argument between the two kings has divided everyone and the real value of both words and numbers has been forgotten. What a waste!

Milo. Why doesn't somebody rescue the Princesses and set everything straight again?

Tock. That is easier said than done. The Castle-in-the-Air is very far from here, and the one path which leads to it is guarded by **ferocious** demons. But hold on, here we are. (*A man appears, carrying a gate and a small tollbooth.*)

Gatekeeper. AHHHHREMMMM! This is Dictionopolis, a happy kingdom, advantageously located in the foothills of Confusion and caressed by gentle breezes from the Sea of Knowledge. Today, by royal proclamation, is Market Day. Have you come to buy or sell?

Milo. I beg your pardon?

Gatekeeper. Buy or sell, buy or sell. Which is it? You must have come here for a reason.

---

9. **warp and . . . woof:** In weaving, the *warp* is made of parallel threads stretched on a loom. The *woof* is made of threads that wind between the warp threads to make cloth.

Milo. Well, I . . .

Gatekeeper. Come now, if you don't have a reason, you must at least have an explanation or certainly an excuse.

430 **Milo** (*meekly*). Uh . . . no.

Gatekeeper (*shaking his head*). Very serious. You can't get in without a reason. (*thoughtfully*) Wait a minute. Maybe I have an old one you can use. (*pulls out an old suitcase from the tollbooth and rummages through it*) No . . . no . . . no . . . this won't do . . . hmmm . . .

Milo (*to* Tock). What's he looking for? (Tock *shrugs.*)

Gatekeeper. Ah! This is fine. (*Pulls out a*
440 *medallion on a chain. Engraved in the medallion is:* "*WHY NOT?*") Why not. That's a good reason for almost anything . . . a bit used, perhaps, but still quite serviceable. There you are, sir. Now I can truly say: Welcome to Dictionopolis.

(*He opens the gate and walks off.* Citizens *and* Merchants *appear on all levels of the stage, and* Milo *and* Tock *find themselves in the middle of a noisy marketplace. As some people buy and sell their*
450 *wares, others hang a large banner which reads:* WELCOME TO THE WORD MARKET.)

Milo. Tock! Look!

Merchant 1. Hey-ya, hey-ya, hey-ya, step right up and take your pick. Juicy tempting words for sale. Get your fresh-picked "if's," "and's" and "but's"! Just take a look at these nice ripe "where's" and "when's."

Merchant 2. Step right up, step right up, fancy, best-quality words here for sale. Enrich your
460 vocabulary and expand your speech with such elegant items as "quagmire,"[10] "flabbergast,"[11] or "upholstery."

Merchant 3. Words by the bag, buy them over here. Words by the bag for the more talkative customer. A pound of "happy's" at a very reasonable price . . . very useful for "Happy Birthday," "Happy New Year," "happy days," or "happy-go-lucky." Or how about a package of "good's," always handy for "good morning,"
470 "good afternoon," "good evening," and "goodbye."

Milo. I can't believe it. Did you ever see so many words?

Tock. They're fine if you have something to say. (*They come to a Do-It-Yourself Bin.*)

Milo (*to* Merchant 4 *at the bin*). Excuse me, but what are these?

Merchant 4. These are for people who like to make up their own words. You can pick
480 any assortment you like or buy a special box complete with all the letters and a book of instructions. Here, taste an "A." They're very good. (*He pops one into* Milo's *mouth.*)

Milo (*tastes it hesitantly*). It's sweet! (*He eats it.*)

Merchant 4. I knew you'd like it. "A" is one of our best-sellers. All of them aren't that good, you know. The "Z," for instance—very dry and sawdusty. And the "X"? Tastes like a trunkful of stale air. But most of the others
490 aren't bad at all. Here, try the "I."

Milo (*tasting*). Cool! It tastes icy.

Merchant 4 (*to* Tock). How about the "C" for you? It's as crunchy as a bone. Most people are just too lazy to make their own words, but take it from me, not only is it more fun, but it's also *de*-lightful, (*holds up a "D"*) *e*-lating,[12] (*holds up an "E"*) and extremely *u*seful! (*holds up a "U"*)

---

10. **quagmire** (kwăg'mīr'): has two meanings: land with a soft, muddy surface; a difficult situation.

11. **flabbergast:** to cause to be overcome with astonishment; astound.

12. **elating** (ĭ-lā'tĭng): making a person proud or joyful.

Milo. But isn't it difficult? I'm not very good at making words.

(*The* Spelling Bee, *a large colorful bee, comes up from behind.*)

Spelling Bee. Perhaps I can be of some assistance . . . a-s-s-i-s-t-a-n-c-e. (*The three turn around and see him.*) Don't be alarmed . . . a-l-a-r-m-e-d. I am the Spelling Bee. I can spell anything. Anything. A-n-y-t-h-i-n-g. Try me. Try me.

Milo (*backing off,* Tock *on his guard*). Can you spell goodbye?

Spelling Bee. Perhaps you are under the misapprehension[13] . . . m-i-s-a-p-p-r-e-h-e-n-s-i-o-n that I am dangerous. Let me assure you that I am quite peaceful. Now, think of the most difficult word you can, and I'll spell it.

Milo. Uh . . . o.k. (*At this point,* Milo *may turn to the audience and ask them to help him choose a word or he may think of one on his own.*) How about . . . "Curiosity"?

Spelling Bee (*winking*). Let's see now . . . uh . . . how much time do I have?

Milo. Just ten seconds. Count them off, Tock.

Spelling Bee (*as* Tock *counts*). Oh dear, oh dear. (*just at the last moment, quickly*) C-u-r-i-o-s-i-t-y.

Merchant 4. Correct! (*All cheer.*)

Milo. Can you spell anything?

Spelling Bee (*proudly*). Just about. You see, years ago, I was an ordinary bee minding my own business, smelling flowers all day, occasionally picking up part-time work in people's bonnets. Then one day, I realized that I'd never amount to anything without an education, so I decided that . . .

Humbug (*coming up in a booming voice*). BALDERDASH![14] (*He wears a lavish coat, striped pants, checked vest, spats and a derby hat.*) Let me repeat . . . BALDERDASH! (*swings his cane and clicks his heels in the air*) Well, well, what have we here? Isn't someone going to introduce me to the little boy?

Spelling Bee (*disdainfully*). This is the Humbug. You can't trust a word he says.

Humbug. NONSENSE! Everyone can trust a Humbug. As I was saying to the king just the other day . . .

Spelling Bee. You've never met the king. (*to* Milo) Don't believe a thing he tells you.

Humbug. Bosh, my boy, pure bosh. The Humbugs are an old and noble family, honorable to the core. Why, we fought in the Crusades with Richard the Lionhearted,[15] crossed the Atlantic with Columbus, blazed trails with the pioneers. History is full of Humbugs.

Spelling Bee. A very pretty speech . . . s-p-e-e-c-h. Now, why don't you go away? I was just advising the lad of the importance of proper spelling.

Humbug. BAH! As soon as you learn to spell one word, they ask you to spell another. You can never catch up, so why bother? (*puts his arm around* Milo) Take my advice, boy, and forget about it. As my great-great-great-grandfather George Washington Humbug used to say . . .

---

13. **misapprehension** (mĭs-ăp'rĭ-hĕn'shən): the misunderstanding of something.

14. **balderdash:** nonsense.

15. **Crusades with Richard the Lionhearted:** The Crusades were journeys undertaken by European Christians in the eleventh through thirteenth centuries to fight the Muslims for control of the Holy Land. Richard the Lionhearted was an English king who led the Third Crusade (1190–1192).

Spelling Bee. You, sir, are an impostor i-m-p-o-s-t-o-r who can't even spell his own name!

Humbug. What? You dare to doubt my word?
570 The word of a Humbug? The word of a Humbug who has direct access to the ear of a King? And the king shall hear of this, I promise you . . .

Voice 1. Did someone call for the king?

Voice 2. Did you mention the monarch?

Voice 3. Speak of the sovereign?

Voice 4. Entreat the emperor?

Voice 5. Hail his highness?

(*Five tall, thin gentlemen regally dressed in silks*
580 *and satins, plumed hats and buckled shoes appear as they speak.*)

Milo. Who are they?

Spelling Bee. The King's advisors. Or in more formal terms, his cabinet.

Minister 1. Greetings!

Minister 2. Salutations!

Minister 3. Welcome!

Minister 4. Good afternoon!

Minister 5. Hello!

590 **Milo.** Uh . . . Hi.

(*All the* Ministers, *from here on called by their numbers, unfold their scrolls and read in order.*)

Minister 1. By the order of Azaz the Unabridged[16] . . .

Minister 2. King of Dictionopolis . . .

---

16. **unabridged:** containing the original content; not shortened.

Minister 3. Monarch of letters . . .

Minister 4. Emperor of phrases, sentences, and miscellaneous figures of speech . . .

600 **Minister 5.** We offer you the hospitality of our kingdom . . .

Minister 1. Country

Minister 2. Nation

Minister 3. State

Minister 4. Commonwealth

Minister 5. Realm

Minister 1. Empire

Minister 2. Palatinate

Minister 3. Principality.

Milo. Do all those words mean the same thing?

610 **Minister 1.** Of course.

Minister 2. Certainly.

Minister 3. Precisely.

Minister 4. Exactly.

Minister 5. Yes.

Milo. Then why don't you just use one? Wouldn't that make a lot more sense?

Minister 1. Nonsense!

Minister 2. Ridiculous!

Minister 3. Fantastic!

620 **Minister 4.** Absurd!

Minister 5. Bosh!

Minister 1. We're not interested in making sense. It's not our job.

Minister 2. Besides, one word is as good as another, so why not use them all?

Minister 3. Then you don't have to choose which one is right.

Minister 4. Besides, if one is right, then ten are ten times as right.

630 **Minister 5.** Obviously, you don't know who we are. (*Each presents himself and* Milo *acknowledges the introduction.*)

Minister 1. The Duke of Definition.

Minister 2. The Minister of Meaning.

Minister 3. The Earl of Essence.

Minister 4. The Count of Connotation.

Minister 5. The Undersecretary of Understanding.

All Five. And we have come to invite you to the
640 Royal Banquet.

Spelling Bee. The banquet! That's quite an honor, my boy. A real h-o-n-o-r.

Humbug. DON'T BE RIDICULOUS! Everybody goes to the Royal Banquet these days.

Spelling Bee (*to the* Humbug). True, everybody does go. But some people are invited and others simply push their way in where they aren't wanted.

Humbug. HOW DARE YOU? You buzzing
650 little upstart, I'll show you who's not wanted . . . (*raises his cane threateningly*)

Spelling Bee. You just watch it! I'm warning w-a-r-n-i-n-g you! (*At that moment, an ear-shattering blast of trumpets, entirely off-key, is heard, and a* Page *appears.*)

Page. King Azaz the Unabridged is about to begin the Royal Banquet. All guests who do not appear promptly at the table will automatically lose their place. (*A huge table*
660 *is carried out with* King Azaz *sitting in a large chair, carried out at the head of the table.*)

Azaz. Places. Everyone take your places. (*All the characters, including the* Humbug *and the* Spelling Bee, *who forget their quarrel, rush to take their places at the table.* Milo *and* Tock *sit near the* King. Azaz *looks at* Milo.) And just who is this?

Milo. Your Highness, my name is Milo and this is Tock. Thank you very much for inviting
670 us to your banquet, and I think your palace is beautiful!

Minister 1. Exquisite.

Minister 2. Lovely.

Minister 3. Handsome.

Minister 4. Pretty.

Minister 5. Charming.

Azaz. SILENCE! Now tell me, young man, what can you do to entertain us? Sing songs? Tell stories? Juggle plates? Do tumbling tricks?
680 Which is it?

Milo. I can't do any of those things.

Azaz. What an ordinary little boy. Can't you do anything at all?

Milo. Well . . . I can count to a thousand.

Azaz. AARGH, numbers! Never mention numbers here. Only use them when we absolutely have to. Now, why don't we change the subject and have some dinner? Since you are the guest of honor, you may
690 pick the menu.

Milo. Me? Well, uh . . . I'm not very hungry. Can we just have a light snack?

Azaz. A light snack it shall be!

(Azaz *claps his hands. Waiters rush in with covered trays. When they are uncovered, shafts of light pour out. The light may be created through the use of battery-operated flashlights which are secured in the trays and covered with a false bottom. The guests help themselves.*)

700 **Humbug.** Not a very substantial meal. Maybe you can suggest something a little more filling.

Milo. Well, in that case, I think we ought to have a square meal . . .

Azaz (*claps his hands*). A square meal it is! (*Waiters serve trays of colored squares of all sizes. People serve themselves.*)

Spelling Bee. These are awful. (Humbug *coughs and all the guests do not care for the food.*)

Azaz (*claps his hands and the trays are removed*).
710 Time for speeches. (*to Milo*) You first.

Milo (*hesitantly*). Your Majesty, ladies and gentlemen, I would like to take this opportunity to say that . . .

Azaz. That's quite enough. Musn't talk all day.

Milo. But I just started to . . .

Azaz. NEXT!

Humbug (*quickly*). Roast turkey, mashed potatoes, vanilla ice cream.

Spelling Bee. Hamburgers, corn on the cob,
720 chocolate pudding p-u-d-d-i-n-g. (*Each guest names two dishes and a dessert.*)

Azaz (*the last*). Pate de fois gras, soupe a l'oignon, salade endives, fromage et fruits et demi-tasse.[17] (*He claps his hands. Waiters serve each guest his words.*) Dig on. (*to Milo*) Though I can't say I think much of your choice.

Milo. I didn't know I was going to have to eat my words.

Azaz. Of course, of course, everybody here does.
730 Your speech should have been in better taste.

Minister 1. Here, try some somersault. It improves the flavor.

Minister 2. Have a rigamarole.[18] (*offers breadbasket*)

Minister 3. Or a ragamuffin.[19]

Minister 4. Perhaps you'd care for a synonym bun.

Minister 5. Why not wait for your just desserts?

Azaz. Ah yes, the dessert. We're having a special
740 treat today . . . freshly made at the half-bakery.

Milo. The half-bakery?

Azaz. Of course, the half-bakery! Where do you think half-baked ideas come from? Now, please don't interrupt. By royal command, the pastry chefs have . . .

Milo. What's a half-baked idea?

(*Azaz gives up the idea of speaking as a cart is wheeled in and the guests help themselves.*)

Humbug. They're very tasty, but they don't
750 always agree with you. Here's a good one. (*Humbug hands one to Milo.*)

Milo (*reads*). "The earth is flat."

Spelling Bee. People swallowed that one for years. (*picks up one and reads*) "The moon is made of green cheese." Now, there's a half-baked idea.

(*Everyone chooses one and eats. They include: "It Never Rains but Pours," "Night Air Is Bad Air," "Everything Happens for the Best," "Coffee*
760 *Stunts Your Growth."*)

Azaz. And now for a few closing words. Attention! Let me have your attention! (*Everyone leaps up and exits, except for* Milo, Tock *and the* Humbug.) Loyal subjects and friends, once again on this gala occasion, we have . . .

Milo. Excuse me, but everybody left.

Azaz (*sadly*). I was hoping no one would notice. It happens every time.

770 **Humbug.** They've gone to dinner, and as soon as I finish this last bite, I shall join them.

Milo. That's ridiculous. How can they eat dinner right after a banquet?

---

17. **pate de fois gras . . . demi-tasse:** *French: pâté de fois gras* (pä-tä də fwä grä'): a paste made from goose liver; *soupe a l'oignon* (sō̅o̅p ä läɴ'nôn): onion soup; *salade endives* (sä-läd' ĕn'dīv'): lettuce salad; *fromage et fruits* (frō'mäj ĕ frō̅o̅'ē): cheese and fruit; *demitasse* (dĕm'ē-täs'): a small cup of strong, black coffee.

18. **rigamarole** (rĭg'ə-mə-rōl'): has two meanings: confused or rambling conversation; a complicated set of procedures. Here, the writer is playing off the word *roll*, as in *dinner roll*.

19. **ragamuffin** (răg'ə-mŭf'ĭn): a shabbily dressed, dirty child. Here, the writer is playing off the word *muffin*.

Azaz. SCANDALOUS! We'll put a stop to it at once. From now on, by royal command, everyone must eat dinner before the banquet.

Milo. But that's just as bad.

Humbug. Or just as good. Things which are equally bad are also equally good. Try to look 780 at the bright side of things.

Milo. I don't know which side of anything to look at. Everything is so confusing, and all your words only make things worse.

Azaz. How true. There must be something we can do about it.

Humbug. Pass a law.

Azaz. We have almost as many laws as words.

Humbug. Offer a reward. (Azaz *shakes his head and looks madder at each suggestion.*) Send for 790 help? Drive a bargain? Pull the switch? Lower the boom?[20] Toe the line? (*As Azaz continues to scowl, the* Humbug *loses confidence and finally gives up.*)

Milo. Maybe you should let Rhyme and Reason return.

Azaz. How nice that would be. Even if they were a bother at times, things always went so well when they were here. But I'm afraid it can't be done.

800 **Humbug.** Certainly not. Can't be done.

Milo. Why not?

Humbug (*now siding with* Milo). Why not, indeed?

Azaz. Much too difficult.

Humbug. Of course, much too difficult.

Milo. You could, if you really wanted to.

Humbug. By all means, if you really wanted to, you could.

Azaz (*to* Humbug). How?

810 **Milo** (*also to* Humbug). Yeah, how?

Humbug. Why . . . uh, it's a simple task for a brave boy with a stout heart, a steadfast dog and a serviceable small automobile.

Azaz. Go on.

Humbug. Well, all that he would have to do is cross the dangerous, unknown countryside between here and Digitopolis, where he would have to persuade the Mathemagician to release the Princesses, which we know to be 820 impossible because the Mathemagician will never agree with Azaz about anything. Once achieving that, it's a simple matter of entering the Mountains of Ignorance from where no one has ever returned alive, an effortless climb up a two-thousand-foot stairway without railings in a high wind at night to the Castle-in-the-Air. After a pleasant chat with the Princesses, all that remains is a **leisurely** ride back through those chaotic **crags** where the frightening 830 fiends have sworn to tear any intruder from limb to limb and devour him down to his belt buckle. And finally after doing all that, a triumphal parade! If, of course, there is anything left to parade . . . followed by hot chocolate and cookies for everyone.

Azaz. I never realized it would be so simple.

Milo. It sounds dangerous to me.

Tock. And just who is supposed to make that journey?

840 **Azaz.** A very good question. But there is one far more serious problem.

Milo. What's that?

Azaz. I'm afraid I can't tell you that until you return.

---

20. **lower the boom:** a sailing term that refers to the *boom* of a sailboat, the long poll that extends from the mast and holds or extends the foot of the sail. To *lower the boom* is to put the boom of the sailboat down. The phrase can also be slang for "scold harshly."

Milo. But wait a minute, I didn't . . .

Azaz. Dictionopolis will always be grateful to you, my boy and your dog. (Azaz *pats* Tock *and* Milo.)

Tock. Now, just one moment, sire . . .

850 **Azaz.** You will face many dangers on your journey, but fear not, for I can give you something for your protection. (Azaz *gives* Milo *a box.*) In this box are the letters of the alphabet. With them you can form all the words you will ever need to help you overcome the obstacles that may stand in your path. All you must do is use them well and in the right places.

Milo (*miserably*). Thanks a lot.

860 **Azaz.** You will need a guide, of course, and since he knows the obstacles so well, the Humbug has cheerfully volunteered to accompany you.

Humbug. Now, see here . . . !

Azaz. You will find him dependable, brave, resourceful and loyal.

Humbug (*flattered*). Oh, Your Majesty.

Milo. I'm sure he'll be a great help. (*They approach the car.*)

870 **Tock.** I hope so. It looks like we're going to need it.

(*The lights darken and the King fades from view.*)

Azaz. Good luck! Drive carefully! (*The three get into the car and begin to move. Suddenly a thunderously loud noise is heard. They slow down the car.*)

Milo. What was that?

Tock. It came from up ahead.

Humbug. It's something terrible, I just know it.

880 Oh, no. Something dreadful is going to happen to us. I can feel it in my bones. (*The noise is repeated. They all look at each other fearfully as the lights fade.*)

(*end Act One*)

Comprehension

1. **Recall** Why does Milo receive the unusual package?

2. **Recall** What forbidden activity does Milo perform in order to get himself out of the Doldrums?

3. **Summarize** Briefly explain the events that led to the banishment of Rhyme and Reason.

Literary Analysis

4. **Visualize** Review your log of **stage directions.** Use the details you listed to visualize the characters or settings they describe. Which details are most effective at helping you visualize?

5. **Examine a Character** How has Milo's life changed from the beginning of Act One to the end of Act One?

6. **Analyze Humor** Review the definition of a **pun** on page 503. Then use a chart like the one shown to record examples of puns that appear in the play. For each pun you list, explain the different meanings the word or words can have. Use a dictionary or thesaurus for help.

Pun	Real Meaning	Humorous Meaning
watchdog	a dog that watches over people or a place	a dog that has the body of a clock (like a watch)

7. **Make Judgments** Whom do you regard as the most **logical** character or characters in the play, and why? Support your answer with evidence from the play.

8. **Evaluate Message** What message about communication does the play convey? Give examples to support your answer.

Extension and Challenge

9. **Creative Project: Art** Sketch a character or a setting in the play based on the details you used earlier to help you **visualize.**

10. **Readers' Circle** Literature that contains at least one unreal or impossible element is called **fantasy.** In a small group, make a list of elements that show why *The Phantom Toolbooth* is a work of fantasy.

What gives an artist STYLE?

KEY IDEA When you were younger, did you have favorite picture books that you looked at again and again? If so, it's likely that you admired the style, or the special look, of the illustrations. In this lesson, you'll take a close look at the work of two artists. You'll explore the elements that give an illustration a unique **style.**

Background

Drawing Attention The first two illustrations you'll examine are by Carmen Lomas Garza. She's known for portraying the joys of everyday life. The book in which these images first appeared is entitled *In My Family*. The third illustration is by Benny Andrews from the book *Pictures for Miss Josie*. He's known for creating art in many forms. Both artists have won high praise for their ability to draw viewers into the worlds they create.

Media Literacy: Style in Illustrations

Style is the uniquely personal way in which creators express ideas. For example, you've seen how a writer crafts a style by using **word choice, sentence structure,** and **imagery.**

To create a style in illustrations, artists use the basic elements of design—**color, line, shape,** and **texture.** Becoming familiar with these elements can help you interpret the style of an illustration.

ANALYZING ELEMENTS OF DESIGN

La Bendición en el Día de la Boda (1993), Carmen Lomas Garza. Alkyds on canvas, 24″ × 32″. © 1993 Carmen Lomas Garza. Collection of Smith College Museum, Northampton, Massachusetts. Photo by M. Lee Fatheree.

❶ Artists use hues or shades of **color** for different reasons. Color makes objects stand out or blend into the background. Color also creates emotional connections. For example, the color blue can suggest a peaceful feeling.

❷ **Shape** is the outline of an object or image. Starting with a simple square, circle, or triangle, an artist can add details to form real-looking objects. In this image, notice how the doorway is basically a rectangle.

❸ A **line** is a stroke or mark that can be thick, thin, long, curvy, smooth, or blurred. Lines can help to "frame" the objects in an illustration. Where do you see a strong use of lines in this image? How many different types of lines do you see?

❹ **Texture** is the surface quality or appearance of an image. Adding texture helps an object look more real. For example, an artist might create a smooth, shiny texture for an apple or a bumpy texture for a basketball.

La Llorona (1989), Carmen Lomas Garza. Gouache, 18″ × 26″. © 1989 Carmen Lomas Garza. Collection of Sonia Saldivar-Hull and Felix Hull, Austin, Texas. Photo by Wolfgang Dietze.

Illustration by Benny Andrews. © 2003 Benny Andrews.

Viewing Guide for

Artists and Style

Use the DVD to look at each illustration at a larger size. Each illustration presents a scene of family or friends. On this page you see another illustration by Carmen Lomas Garza and one by Benny Andrews.

In looking at each image, think about what first catches your eye. Jot down any single words or phrases that describe what you see. Then study each image carefully. Examine the smaller details. Look for the use of **color, line, shape,** and **texture.** Answer these questions to help you understand each illustrator's style.

NOW VIEW

FIRST VIEWING: Comprehension

1. **Identify** What is the subject of each painting?

2. **Clarify** In this illustration, how do you know that what the mother is saying is interesting?

CLOSE VIEWING: Media Literacy

3. **Analyze Color** In this illustration, children listen as a mother tells a mysterious tale. What colors give the illustration a mood of mystery?

4. **Analyze Shape** Focus on the illustration on page 523. Where do you see objects that are shaped like triangles?

5. **Analyze Texture** In the illustration of a father and son, identify any part of the image that seems to have a rough texture.

6. **Interpret the Style** Choose one of the illustrations from this lesson. In your own words, write a statement that describes anything you can about the artist's style. Think about

- the subject matter of the image
- the design elements that you see
- the feelings you think the image expresses

Write or Discuss

Compare Styles Carmen Lomas Garza says most of her illustrations "are from my recollections of my childhood in south Texas where I was born and raised." The illustrations of Benny Andrews are often based on his early life in Georgia. Look closely at the illustrations that appear in this lesson. In a few sentences, compare the styles of each artist. Think about

- the special ways each illustrator uses **color, line, shape,** or **texture**
- the feeling or feelings each illustration communicates to you

Produce Your Own Media

MEDIA TOOLS

For help with creating an illustration, visit the **Media Center** at **ClassZone.com.**

Create an Illustration Plan and create your own illustration, in any style you would like to try. You might create an illustration that fits the subject of "family and friends" or base your creation on any topic that inspires you.

HERE'S HOW Follow these suggestions to create the illustration.

- What colors will you choose? Will you draw shapes using bold lines or soft? Decide what design elements will work best for you.
- Choose your paint, pencils, crayons, chalk, or markers. You might even form images out of pieces of cut up paper or fabric.
- Show your illustration to a partner. Imagine that your illustration is part of a larger picture book, and tell the story that the images would tell.

STUDENT MODEL

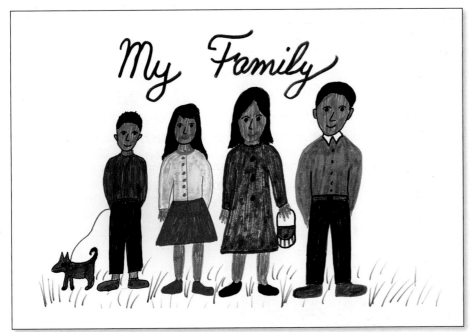

Tech Tip

Use a drawing program to make an illustration or to add a new style.

Writing Workshop

Comparison-Contrast Essay

Some of the selections in this unit made you laugh. Others made you stop and think. What do the unit selections have in common? How are they different? In this workshop, you will learn how to discuss likenesses and differences in an orderly, interesting way.

WRITER'S ROAD MAP

Comparison-Contrast Essay

WRITING PROMPT 1

Writing from Literature Write an essay that compares and contrasts two literary selections or two characters. Your essay should explain why you chose those selections or characters.

Ideas for Comparisons and Contrasts

- two poems, such as "There Is No Word for Goodbye" and "Words Like Freedom"
- two short stories, such as "The All-American Slurp" and "Scout's Honor"
- two selections by the same author, such as "The Jacket" and "The School Play" (by Gary Soto)

WRITING PROMPT 2

Writing from Your Life Write a comparison-contrast essay about two people, places, objects, or actions that are familiar to you. Explain why you chose those subjects.

Subjects to Compare and Contrast

- two people you know very well
- games or manners or family rituals from two different cultures
- two places you have lived
- two fast-food restaurants

 WRITING TOOLS
For prewriting, revision, and editing tools, visit the **Writing Center** at **ClassZone.com.**

KEY TRAITS

1. IDEAS

- Identifies the **subjects** being compared and contrasted
- Presents a **thesis statement** that identifies similarities, differences, or both
- Supports key points with **examples**

2. ORGANIZATON

- Includes a strong **introduction** and a **conclusion** that summarizes the key points
- Connects ideas with **transitions**

3. VOICE

- Uses language that is **appropriate** for the audience and purpose

4. WORD CHOICE

- Uses **precise words** to explain similarities and differences

5. SENTENCE FLUENCY

- Varies **sentence beginnings**

6. CONVENTIONS

- Uses **correct grammar, spelling, and punctuation**

Part 1: Analyze a Student Model

Cody Parcell
Carbondale Middle School

Same Story, Different Styles

"I'll huff, and I'll puff, and I'll blow your house down!" Most people know this line from the story of the Three Little Pigs. When I started reading Jon Scieszka's version of the story, I thought it was the same old fairy tale. However, "The True Story of the Three Little Pigs" is
5 different from the classic version in two important ways. The newer version has an unusual narrator and a humorous tone.

In both "The True Story of the Three Little Pigs" and the classic version, a wolf destroys the houses of two little pigs but can't wreck the third pig's house. In the version that most people know, none of the
10 characters talk directly to the reader. In contrast, "The True Story of the Three Little Pigs" has a surprising narrator—the wolf! "Nobody has ever heard my side of the story," says Alexander T. Wolf. He adds, "You can call me Al." He actually sounds friendly. Because the wolf is telling the story, readers know right away that this version will be different.

15 Having the wolf tell the story makes an important change in the tone. When I first heard the classic version, I thought it had a serious tone. The message of the classic version is, if you don't plan ahead, bad things can happen to you. Also, the wolf in the classic story is vicious. He wrecks houses because he wants to eat the pigs who live there.
20 Scieszka's wolf, on the other hand, gives lots of excuses for his behavior. "Hey, it's not my fault wolves eat cute little animals like bunnies and sheep and pigs. That's just the way we are," he says. The only reason he bothered the pigs was to borrow some sugar to bake a cake for his "dear old granny." According to Al Wolf, two of the pigs are
25 stupid, and the third is rude. The tone in "The True Story of the Three Little Pigs" made me laugh and also feel a little bit sorry for the wolf.

KEY TRAITS IN ACTION

A lively **introduction** identifies the **subjects**— two versions of a story. The highlighted **thesis statement** explains how the versions differ.

Highlighted **transitions** show how ideas are related. **Precise words** such as *destroys, wreck,* and *friendly* make those ideas clear.

A variety of **sentence beginnings** helps to keep the essay interesting.

Scieszka's tone means that his version of the story is much funnier than the classic version. Even though the wolf is huge and scary and likes to eat pigs, he claims that wrecking the straw house was

30 an accident. "It seemed like a shame to leave a perfectly good ham dinner lying there in the straw," he says. The Scieszka version is full of humorous comments like these. "What a pig!" the wolf jokes when describing the third pig's rudeness. Also, the idea of a scary wolf making a birthday present for his grandma is funny because it's unexpected.

35 "The True Story of the Three Little Pigs" and the classic Three Little Pigs story are different in many ways. Jon Scieszka surprises readers by making the wolf the narrator and by using a humorous tone. By making these changes, he lets readers look at an old story in a new way.

Quotations and other **examples** support the idea that Scieszka's version is funnier. Language is lighthearted but not slangy— **appropriate** for the writer's teacher and classmates.

Conclusion summarizes the key ideas of the essay.

2

Part 2: Apply the Writing Process

PREWRITING

What Should I Do?	*What Does It Look Like?*

1. Carefully study the prompt.
Read the prompt at least twice. (Circle) the kind of writing you have to do, such as an essay or a letter. <u>Underline</u> your purpose, such as explaining a process or telling a story. Think about your **audience**—the person or people who will read your essay.

> **TIP** If the prompt does not name an audience, write for your teacher and classmates.

▶ **WRITING PROMPT** Write an (essay) that <u>compares and contrasts two literary selections or two characters</u>. Your essay should <u>explain why you chose those selections or characters</u>.

> What kind of comparison and contrast would my teacher and classmates enjoy reading? I liked the story about the pigs. Maybe I should compare that version of the story with the classic version.

2. Think of similarities and differences.
Think about how the subjects you have chosen are alike and different. (If you chose Prompt 1, reread the stories or poems you chose.) Then create a Venn diagram or a two-column chart to organize your thoughts.

> **TIP** If you can't think of many similarities or differences, choose two new subjects.

▶ **Classic Version**
* Characters don't talk to reader.
* Wolf is bad.

Both
* 3 pigs
* Wolf
* Houses blow down.

"True Story"
* Wolf tells the story.
* Wolf says he's good and the pigs are stupid.

3. List support for each key point.
Be sure you can explain and support each similarity or difference. List at least one example or explanation you might present for each key point.

▶ **Key point**: Having the wolf tell the story makes a big difference in the writer's attitude (the tone).

Support: In the classic story, the wolf is horrible. In Scieszka's version, the wolf tells the reader, "Hey, it's not my fault wolves eat cute little animals."

4. Write a draft thesis.
Your thesis should name your subjects and sum up how they are alike and/or different. You can also briefly state your main points in the order that you will explain them.

> **TIP** Your thesis doesn't have to be perfect. You can always revise it later.

▶ "The True Story of the Three Little Pigs" is not the same as the classic version of the story.
1. In the new version, the wolf is the narrator.
2. The tone is different—it's much funnier.

What Should I Do?	What Does It Look Like?

1. Put your thoughts in a sensible order.
Study these two ways to organize a comparison-contrast essay. Choose the one that works better for you. The writer of the student model chose the point-by-point approach.

- **Point-by-Point Organization**
  Discusses the key points one by one, explaining how they relate to each subject

- **Subject-by-Subject Organization**
  Makes and discusses all the points about the first subject and then moves on to the second subject

POINT BY POINT

Point 1: Narrator
  Classic Version:
    Characters don't talk to reader.
  "True Story": Wolf tells story.
Point 2: Tone
  Classic Version: Wolf is mean, not funny.
  "True Story": Wolf makes excuses and is really funny.

SUBJECT BY SUBJECT

Subject A: Classic version
  Point 1: Characters don't talk to reader.
  Point 2: Wolf is mean, not funny.
Subject B: "True Story"
  Point 1: Wolf tells the story.
  Point 2: Wolf makes excuses, and is really funny.

2. Explain and support your key points.
Stating "This story is funnier than that one" is not enough. Use details or quotations to show your reader what you mean.

Scieszka's tone means that his version of the story is much funnier than the classic version. — Key point

"What a pig!" the wolf jokes when describing the third pig's rudeness. Also, the idea of a scary wolf making a birthday present for his grandma is funny because it's unexpected. — Support: quotation and explanation

3. Link ideas with transitions.
Transitions show your reader that you are moving from one idea to the next. Transitions also help you vary your sentence beginnings.

See page 532: Add Transitions

TIP Before revising, review the key traits on page 526 and the rubric and peer-reader questions on page 532.

Because the wolf is telling the story, readers know right away that this version will be different.
Scieszka's wolf, on the other hand, gives lots of excuses for his behavior.

REVISING AND EDITING

What Should I Do?	What Does It Look Like?

1. Create a strong introduction.
(Circle) your first sentence or two. Think about whether this introduction would make you want to keep reading. If not, add a quotation, a surprising fact or detail, a question, or a bit of dialogue.

▶ ~~(There are two versions of the Three Little Pigs story, and they are very different.)~~

"I'll huff, and I'll puff, and I'll blow your house down!" Most people know this line from the story of the Three Little Pigs.

2. Be on the lookout for vague words.
Reread your essay. Draw a box around vague words such as *nice, really, very, many,* and *happy.* Replace them with fresher or more forceful words.

TIP Look for places to substitute stronger verbs instead of using *does* or *says* all the time.

▶ Even though the wolf is ~~not very nice,~~ he ~~says~~ that ~~doing anything~~ to the straw house was an accident.

Even though the wolf is huge and scary and likes to eat pigs, he claims that wrecking the straw house was an accident.

3. Notice how you begin sentences.
Do most of your sentences start out with *The* or with a noun or pronoun? If so, try starting a few of them with a transition, an adjective, an adverb, or a word that ends with "ing."

▶ In contrast,
"The True Story of the Three Little Pigs" has a surprising narrator—the wolf!

~~The wolf tells the story. That's an important difference.~~ Having the wolf tell the story makes an important change in the tone.

4. Have a peer reader double-check your conclusion.
Ask a peer reader to restate your conclusion. If your peer reader has trouble figuring out the key points of your essay, you may need to add details or make your conclusion more specific.

See page 532: Ask a Peer Reader

▶ "The True Story of the Three Little Pigs" and the classic Three Little Pigs story are different in many ways. Jon Scieszka surprises readers by making the wolf the narrator and by using a humorous tone. By making these changes, he lets readers look at an old story in a new way.

Comparison-Contrast Essay

Apply the Rubric

A strong comparison-contrast essay . . .

- ☑ has a strong introduction that names the subjects being compared and contrasted
- ☑ includes a thesis that tells the reader the key points of the essay
- ☑ supports key points with examples and details
- ☑ uses appropriate language and precise words when making comparisons and contrasts
- ☑ varies sentence beginnings
- ☑ includes transitions that show how ideas are related
- ☑ concludes by summarizing key points

Ask a Peer Reader

- Which two subjects am I comparing and contrasting?
- What key points do I make about how the subjects are alike and different?
- What, if anything, should I do to strengthen my conclusion?

Add Transitions

For Comparing	For Contrasting
both	however
in addition	in contrast
like	on the other hand
neither	unlike

Check Your Grammar

- Correct fragments by adding a subject, a verb, or other words that form a complete thought.

> *Because the wolf is telling the story, readers know right away that this version will be different.*

See page R64: Correcting Fragments

- Run-on sentences confuse your reader.

> *According to Al Wolf, two of the pigs are*
> *and*
> *stupid, the third is rude.*

See page R64: Correcting Run-On Sentences

Writing Online

PUBLISHING OPTIONS
For publishing options, visit the **Writing Center** at ClassZone.com.

ASSESSMENT PREPARATION
For writing and grammar assessment practice, go to the **Assessment Center** at ClassZone.com.

Producing a Power Presentation

You can share your essay with the class by turning it into a power presentation. That means using a computer to project the key points of your essay on a screen as you explain them.

Planning the Presentation

1. **Stick to the big ideas.** Create one slide for your introduction, one for your conclusion, and at least one for each key point or body paragraph. Each slide you make should have a headline, which gives the main idea of the slide, and at least two bullet points that give supporting ideas. Be sure that the slides are in a logical order.

2. **Decide on colors and fonts.** You can select a template (preset fonts and colors) from the program you are using, or you can choose your own fonts and colors. The type should be easy to read, even from far away.

3. **Practice the presentation.** Learn how to use the equipment. Instead of just reading the words on the slide, explain and expand on the ideas you are presenting (as you did when you wrote the essay). Make sure that your points are logical and that all words are spelled correctly.

Delivering the Presentation

1. **Watch your pacing.** Even if you are nervous, don't race through your presentation. Ask a friend to sit at the back of the room and signal if you are talking too quickly or too slowly.

2. **Request feedback.** When you are done, ask the audience to tell you what they liked and what they understood best. Think about what you will do differently when you make your next presentation.

Reading Comprehension

DIRECTIONS *Read these selections and answer the questions that follow.*

from Alan Mendelsohn, the Boy from Mars

Daniel Pinkwater

I got off to a bad start at Bat Masterson Junior High School. My family had moved from my old school district during the summer, and I didn't know a single kid at the school. On top of that, it turned out that kids at Bat Masterson put a lot of emphasis on how you look. This created a problem—I am a short, portly kid, and I wear glasses. Every other kid in the school was tall, had a suntan, and none of them wore glasses. Also clothes wrinkle up on me. I don't know why this should be—five minutes after I get dressed in the morning, everything is wrinkled. It looks like I slept in my clothes.

10 Not only did I not know anybody on my first day, not only did I find out that a short, portly, wrinkled kid with glasses is an outcast in that school, but I also sat down on somebody's half-finished Good Humor bar in the school yard. That reduced my confidence. Then it turned out that the school was not expecting me. My records, and grades, and whatever the old school was supposed to send, they had not sent—or they had sent them to the wrong place—or they had gotten lost.

So I had to sit on this bench in the office for most of the morning, sort of sticking to the bench because of the leftover Good Humor on the seat of my pants. Finally they gave me this big pile of cards to fill out. Then I
20 had to run all over the school getting teachers to sign the cards. Three or four times I had to go back to the office with notes from teachers saying that their class was full, or it was the wrong class, or it conflicted with another class I was supposed to take.

And each time I entered a classroom, the class would giggle at me. Then the teacher would ask my name. It was written right at the top of every one of the cards—but the teacher would ask me to say it anyway. "Leonard Neeble," I would say, and the kids in the class would just go wild. I don't know why, but my name gets them every time.

At lunchtime I walked around the school yard. All the kids looked
30 sort of grown-up and unwrinkled. Some of the girls even had lipstick on.

The kids stood around in groups, talking and laughing. Some guys were showing off, walking on top of benches, and chasing each other, and hollering. Nobody looked at me or said anything to me. I had the feeling that if I tried to talk to anybody, they wouldn't have been able to hear me. I looked for a quiet spot to eat my tuna fish sandwich.

Sparky
Earl Nightingale

I came across a story about a boy named Sparky. School was all but impossible for Sparky. He failed every subject in the eighth grade. He flunked physics in high school. Receiving a flat zero in the course, he distinguished himself as the worst physics student in the school's history. He also flunked Latin and algebra and English. He didn't do much better in sports. Although he did manage to make the school golf team, he promptly lost the only important match of the year. There was a consolation match. He lost that, too.

Throughout his youth Sparky was awkward socially. He was not
10 actually disliked by the other students; no one cared that much. He was astonished if a classmate ever said hello to him outside school hours. No way to tell how he might have done at dating. In high school, Sparky never once asked a girl out. He was too afraid of being turned down.

Sparky was a loser. He, his classmates—everyone knew it. So he rolled with it. Sparky made up his mind early in life that if things were meant to work out, they would. Otherwise he would content himself with what appeared to be his inevitable mediocrity.

But one thing was important to Sparky: drawing. He was proud of his own artwork. Of course, no one else appreciated it. In his senior year
20 of high school, he submitted some cartoons to the editors of his class yearbook. They were turned down. Despite this particularly painful rejection, Sparky was so convinced of his ability that he decided to become a professional artist.

Upon graduating from high school, he wrote a letter to Walt Disney Studios. He was told to send some samples of his artwork, and the subject

GO ON ➡

matter for a cartoon was suggested. Sparky drew the proposed cartoon. He spent a great deal of time on it and on the other drawings. Finally the reply from Disney Studios came—he had been rejected once again. Another loss for the loser.

30   So Sparky wrote his own autobiography in cartoons. He described his childhood self, a little-boy loser and chronic underachiever. The cartoon character would soon become famous all over the world. For Sparky, the boy who failed every subject in the eighth grade and whose work was rejected again and again, was Charles Schulz. He created the "Peanuts" comic strip and the little cartoon boy whose kite would never fly and who never succeeded in kicking the football—Charlie Brown.

Comprehension

DIRECTIONS *Answer these questions about the excerpt from* Alan Mendelsohn, the Boy from Mars.

1. The author's main purpose in this excerpt is to

  A persuade readers to be kind to new students

  B explain how to be popular in a new school

  C entertain readers by describing a situation they can understand

  D give information about Bat Masterson Junior High School

2. The author gives the excerpt a humorous tone in his description of

  A girls wearing lipstick

  B Leonard sitting on an ice cream bar

  C teachers signing a pile of cards

  D boys showing off in the schoolyard

3. In describing Leonard's first day at school, the author creates a mood of

  A loneliness   **C** sorrow

  B anger   **D** suspense

4. Which sentence best expresses the mood of the excerpt?

  A "Also clothes wrinkle up on me." (lines 6–7)

  B "Finally they gave me this big pile of cards to fill out." (line 19)

  C "The kids stood around in groups, talking and laughing." (line 31)

  D "Nobody looked at me or said anything to me." (line 33)

DIRECTIONS *Answer these questions about* "Sparky."

5. Which word best describes the author's attitude toward Sparky?

  A indifferent   **C** sentimental

  B admiring   **D** sarcastic

6. The author's main purpose in telling Sparky's story is to

   A express ideas about art and education

   B entertain readers with funny stories about Charlie Brown

   C inform readers about someone who turned failure into success

   D persuade readers that "Peanuts" is a world-famous cartoon

7. Which statement most clearly expresses the author's purpose in telling Sparky's story?

   A "He was not actually disliked by the other students; no one cared that much." (lines 9–10)

   B "Sparky made up his mind early in life that if things were meant to work out, they would." (lines 15–16)

   C "Finally the reply from Disney Studios came—he had been rejected once again." (lines 27–28)

   D "For Sparky, the boy who failed every subject in the eighth grade and whose work was rejected again and again, was Charles Schulz." (lines 32–34)

8. The author tells the story of Sparky's failures mainly in

   A sentences with flowery words

   B sentence fragments

   C short, direct sentences

   D realistic dialogue

9. Which words in the selection help to create a casual style?

   A distinguished, mediocrity

   B awkward, underachiever

   C chronic, inevitable

   D flunked, loser

DIRECTIONS *Answer this question about both selections.*

10. Which statement is true about the tone of both selections?

   A Poetic language is used to create a formal tone.

   B The tone changes from playful to gloomy.

   C Vivid details add a mysterious tone to the narrative.

   D The author has a sympathetic tone toward the person he writes about.

Written Response

SHORT RESPONSE *Write two or three sentences to answer this question.*

11. Name two events in *Alan Mendelsohn, the Boy from Mars* that contribute to the mood of the excerpt.

EXTENDED RESPONSE *Write a short paragraph to answer this question.*

12. Why do you think Earl Nightingale waits until the end to reveal Sparky's identity? As you write your answer, think about the author's purpose in telling Sparky's story.

537

Vocabulary

DIRECTIONS *Use context clues and your knowledge of similes to answer the following questions about the underlined words.*

> When she tripped in front of the class, Carmen felt as <u>awkward</u> as a ballerina in boots.

1. The word *awkward* means

A unhappy

B comfortable

C special

D clumsy

> For city drivers, traffic jams are as <u>inevitable</u> as the sunrise.

2. The word *inevitable* means

A early in the day

B sure to happen

C hard to handle

D far away

> His <u>mediocrity</u> made him feel as common as a weed along the roadside.

3. The word *mediocrity* means

A average ability

B great strength

C artistic skills

D sense of humor

DIRECTIONS *Use context clues and your knowledge of compound words to answer the following questions.*

4. The word *outcast* in line 11 of the excerpt from *Alan Mendelsohn, the Boy from Mars* refers to someone who

A looks after others

B rebels against authority

C is not accepted into a group

D gets rid of old ideas

5. The word *yearbook* in line 21 of "Sparky" refers to a publication that

A shows student activities and class photos from the past school year

B explains what students will learn in the coming school year

C helps teachers plan lessons and homework assignments for the year

D tries to persuade students to improve each year

6. The word *underachiever* in line 31 of "Sparky" refers to someone who

A works hard but doesn't succeed

B performs worse than expected

C does well under pressure

D wants to get ahead in life

Writing & Grammar

DIRECTIONS *Use your knowledge of writing and grammar to answer the following questions.*

1. In which sentence are the commas correctly placed?

   A Tasty food good friends and lively music made her birthday party, a great success.

   B Tasty food, good friends, and lively music made her birthday party a great success.

   C Tasty food good friends and lively music, made her birthday party a great success.

   D Tasty food, good friends, and lively music, made her birthday party a great success.

2. How might you rewrite the following sentence to make it declarative?

   Does Sam take guitar lessons?

   A Sam, take guitar lessons.

   B Sam takes guitar lessons.

   C Sam even takes guitar lessons!

   D When does Sam take guitar lessons?

3. How might you rewrite the following sentence to make it exclamatory?

   The movie was scary.

   A Watch the scary movie.

   B I was scared by the movie.

   C How scary was the movie?

   D The movie was scary!

4. In which sentence are the commas correctly placed?

   A His kind, friendly, and generous, nature drew people to him.

   B His kind friendly, and generous nature drew people to him.

   C His kind, friendly, and generous nature drew people to him.

   D His kind, friendly, and generous nature, drew people to him.

5. How might you rewrite the following sentence to make it interrogative?

   Maria ate all the food.

   A Did Maria eat all the food?

   B Tell Maria not to eat all the food.

   C I can't believe Maria ate all the food!

   D Don't eat all the food, Maria.

6. In which sentence are the commas correctly placed?

   A Grandpa's stories, were exciting, colorful and full of adventure.

   B Grandpa's stories, were exciting, colorful, and full, of adventure.

   C Grandpa's stories were exciting colorful, and, full of adventure.

   D Grandpa's stories were exciting, colorful, and full of adventure.

STOP

More Great Reads

Ideas for Independent Reading

Which questions from Unit 4 made an impression on you?
Continue exploring with these books.

What builds confidence?

Becoming Naomi León
by Pam Muñoz Ryan

Naomi is shy. She's only comfortable when she's carving soap. When Naomi's mother tries to take her away from her grandmother and brother, the three run away to Mexico, where Naomi finally learns about her father's legacy and herself.

The Bicycle Man
by David L. Dudley

Carissa, a 12-year-old in rural Georgia in 1927, can't seem to do anything right. One day, old Bailey stops in front of her house with his bicycle. He teaches Carissa and her mother how to find their balance, which helps them move forward on their own.

Surviving the Applewhites
by Stephanie S. Tolan

Jake's last chance before juvenile hall is a home school run by the chaotic and eccentric Applewhite family. Jake thinks he'll be out of there in a week. Can a group of self-involved artists help a "bad" boy discover who he really is?

How strong is peer pressure?

I Walk in Dread
by Lisa Rowe Fraustino

In the winter of 1691, four girls in Salem, Massachusetts, accuse people of being witches and a trial begins. As more and more people are accused, more girls claim to be victims. Who is telling the truth?

Sixth-Grade Glommers, Norks, and Me
by Lisa Papademetriou

Allie is starting sixth grade at a new school. When her best friend, Tamara, wants Allie to change so she can be popular, Allie questions her own choices. Will she be able to survive middle school alone?

Stitches
by Glen Huser

Travis wants to be a puppeteer, and his best friend is a girl who walks with a limp. Neither of these things makes life easy at his junior high, where boys are expected to take shop class and play sports. Will Travis change?

When are words not enough?

Missing May
by Cynthia Rylant

Six months after Aunt May's death, 12-year-old Summer worries that sadness will pull her little family apart. Together, she and Uncle Ob search for a message from May, some sign that will tell them how they can live without her.

Pictures of Hollis Woods
by Patricia Reilly Giff

Hollis always wanted to be part of a family. But when she got one, she messed it up. She only has her drawings to remember how happy she was. Now she has a second chance, and she'll do anything to make it work.

Samir and Yonatan
by Daniella Carmi

Samir, a Palestinian, lies in an Israeli hospital waiting for an operation. All day long he's angry, homesick, and lonely. But every night, Yonatan, an Israeli in the next bed, whispers stories to him about Mars. Will the stories bring Samir peace?

Word Pictures

THE LANGUAGE OF POETRY

541

Where can you find a POEM?

Is a jump-rope rhyme a **poem?** What about the lyrics of your favorite song, or the jingle that a fast-food chain uses to sell you a burger? Not every poem has to come out of a book. In fact, once you start looking for poems, you'll find that they are all around you. You may have written some yourself!

ACTIVITY Make a list of all the places and forms in which you can find a poem. Then ask yourself the following questions:

• How did you know each form of writing on your list was a poem?

• What do they have in common? How are they different?

Compare lists with a partner. Discuss what makes a group of words a poem.

I asked my mother
for fifty cents
To see the elephant
jump the fence.
He jumped so high
he touched the sky,
And didn't come back
'til the Fourth of July.

Preview Unit Goals

LITERARY ANALYSIS	• Identify and analyze sound devices, including rhyme, rhythm, repetition, alliteration, and onomatopoeia • Identify and analyze figurative language, including metaphor, simile, and personification • Identify and interpret imagery • Identify and compare tone
READING	• Make inferences • Take notes and organize information • Develop reading strategies, including visualizing and monitoring
WRITING AND GRAMMAR	• Write a personal response to a poem • Maintain subject-verb agreement
SPEAKING, LISTENING, AND VIEWING	• Deliver an oral interpretation of a poem
VOCABULARY	• Understand and use specialized vocabulary • Use knowledge of Latin word roots to determine word meaning
ACADEMIC VOCABULARY	• sound devices • metaphor • imagery • rhyme • simile • tone • repetition • personification • onomatopoeia • figurative language

Reader's Workshop

Appreciating Poetry

Poetry is everywhere, not just within the pages of this book. Song lyrics, greeting-card messages, and commercial jingles can all be considered poetry. You might describe some poems as clever, others as inspiring, and still others as sappy. Every so often, though, you might encounter a poem that gets inside your heart and mind. How does a poem do that? Read on to find out.

Part 1: What Makes Poetry Different?

One difference between poetry and fiction has to do with **form,** or the way a poem looks on the page. While short stories and novels consist of sentences and paragraphs, poems are made up of lines. A **line** can be a single word, a sentence, or part of a sentence. In many poems, lines are arranged into groups called **stanzas.** The way a poet chooses to arrange lines and stanzas can affect a poem's meaning.

Poetry is different from fiction in another way. While a story or a novel has a narrator who tells the story, every poem has a **speaker**—a voice that "talks" to readers. It's important to remember that the speaker is not necessarily the poet, as you can see from this humorous poem.

A Fine Head of Lettuce
Poem by **Jack Prelutsky**

I'm a fine head of lettuce,
a handsome romaine.
I haven't a cranium
made for a brain.

I'm simple and shy.
I remain on my own.
I'm known in the garden
as lettuce alone.

STUDY THE POEM

- Who is the **speaker?** In this poem, the speaker directly tells you about itself. Usually, you have to infer a speaker's identity and personality using details in the poem.

- How many **stanzas** does the poem have?

- How many **lines** are in each stanza? Notice that the lines are all about the same length.

MODEL: FORM AND SPEAKER

The poem "Losing Face" is more serious than "A Fine Head of Lettuce."
At a quick glance, you can see that it also looks different from Jack
Prelutsky's poem. That's because the lines and stanzas in "Losing
Face" vary in length. The poem sounds different too—more like
conversation. As you read the poem, take a closer look at its form.
Also think about what each stanza reveals about the speaker.

LoSiNg FAce

Poem by **Janet S. Wong**

Finally Mother is proud
of something
I have done.
"My girl won
5   the art contest,"
she tells the world,
smiling so big
and laughing so loud
her gold tooth
10   shows.

I'm the only one
who knows
how I drew so well,
erasing the perfect lines
15   I traced,
drawing worse ones
on purpose
in their place.
I feel awful.
20   I want to tell.

But I don't want to lose
Mother's glowing
proud face.

Close Read

1. Who is the speaker of
   this poem? Describe the
   conflict she is having.

2. All three stanzas
   work together to help
   you understand the
   speaker's feelings.
   In your own words,
   summarize what each
   stanza is about.

3. Reread the boxed
   section. It is the only
   place where each line
   contains a complete
   sentence. Why might
   the poet have chosen to
   emphasize these lines?

4. Reread the last stanza.
   Why doesn't the speaker
   want to admit what
   she's done?

Part 2: What Brings a Poem to Life?

Think about the comforting melody of a lullaby, the contagious beat of a certain song, or those few words in a poem that perfectly capture how you're feeling. The power of a poem comes from more than its form and its speaker. Sound devices, imagery, and figurative language are the elements that can make a poem simply unforgettable.

SOUND DEVICES

Most poems are meant to be heard, not just read. So, a poem's sounds are often as carefully chosen as its words. Poets use these sound devices to make music, to emphasize ideas, or to remind you of the subjects they are describing.

SOUND DEVICES	EXAMPLES
RHYME the repetition of sounds at the ends of words, as in *thing* and *sing*, *cry* and *sky* **RHYTHM** the beat you hear as you read a poem aloud. This beat is affected by which syllables are stressed (ˊ) and which are unstressed (˘). Stressed words are read with more emphasis.	**The rhyme and rhythm in this poem help to create a singsong sound.** Some people talk and talk and never say a thing Some people look at you and birds begin to sing. Some people laugh and laugh and yet you want to cry. Some people touch your hand and music fills the sky. —"People" by Charlotte Zolotow

REPETITION
 	
the use of a word, phrase, sound, or line more than once, such as the repeated use of *The rain* and *pools*
 	
ALLITERATION
 	
the repetition of consonant sounds at the beginning of words, such as the *s* in *sleep-song*
	The repetition in these lines suggests a steady downpour. The alliteration mimics the rain's soothing sounds.
	
	The rain makes still pools on
	    the sidewalk.
	The rain makes running pools
	    in the gutter.
	The rain plays a little sleep-song on our
	    roof at night—
	
	And I love the rain.
	
	    —from "April Rain Song" by
	    Langston Hughes

MODEL 1: RHYME AND REPETITION

In "Pete at the Zoo," a young speaker considers an important question: Do zoo animals ever get lonely? Read the poem aloud, paying particular attention to the use of rhyme and repetition.

PETE AT THE ZOO

Poem by **Gwendolyn Brooks**

I wonder if the elephant
Is lonely in his stall
When all the boys and girls are gone
And there's no shout at all,
5   And there's no one to stamp before,
No one to note his might.
Does he hunch up, as I do,
Against the dark of night?

Close Read

1. Examine the words at the ends of the lines. Which words rhyme?

2. Notice the repeated words and phrases in the boxed lines. What does the repetition help to emphasize about nighttime at the zoo?

MODEL 2: RHYTHM AND ALLITERATION

What kinds of sounds do you associate with fireworks? In this poem, rhythm and alliteration help you to hear some of these sounds. Read the poem aloud to get the full effect.

Fireworks

Poem by **Valerie Worth**

First
A far thud,
Then the rocket
Climbs the air,
5   A dull red flare,
To hang, a moment,
Invisible, before
Its shut black shell cracks
And claps against the ears,
10 Breaks and billows into bloom,
Spilling down clear green sparks, gold spears,
Silent sliding silver waterfalls and stars.

Close Read

1. Stressed and unstressed syllables are marked in lines 8–10. Read these lines aloud, emphasizing the stressed words. What does the rhythm remind you of?

2. The use of alliteration in the boxed line helps you to hear the noise of the fireworks after they've exploded. Find another example of alliteration.

IMAGERY AND FIGURATIVE LANGUAGE

Suppose the poet who wrote "Fireworks" had described her subject as "loud and colorful." Her poem might not have had the same impact on you. Instead, the sound is "a far thud," and the colors are "clear green sparks" and "gold spears." These are examples of **images,** words and phrases that call up pictures in your mind. Images appeal to your senses of sight, hearing, smell, taste, and touch. They help you to clearly imagine what a poem describes.

One way that poets create images is through **figurative language,** the use of creative comparisons to describe familiar things in new ways. Review the three types of figurative language in the graphic. What does each example tell you about the autumn leaves?

SIMILE

a comparison between two unlike things that includes the word *like* or *as*

In a high wind the
leaves don't
fall but fly
straight out of the
tree like birds

—"Poem" by A. R. Ammons

METAPHOR

a comparison between two unlike things that does not include the word *like* or *as*

The fallen leaves are cornflakes
That fill the lawn's wide dish,

—from "December Leaves" by
Kaye Starbird

PERSONIFICATION

a description of an object, an animal, or an idea as if it were human or had human qualities and reactions

New sounds to
walk on
today,

dry
leaves
talking
in hoarse
whispers
under bare trees.

—"New Sounds" by Lilian Moore

Part 3: Analyze the Literature

In this poem, Eve Merriam transports you to a familiar scene—a dinner table. You'll see how Merriam uses many of the techniques you just learned about to help you understand the speaker's relationship with his or her parents.

LIKE BOOKENDS

Poem by **Eve Merriam**

Like bookends
my father at one side
my mother at the other

propping me up
5 but unable to read
what I feel.

Were they born with clothes on?
Born with rules on?

When we sit at the dinner table
10 we smooth our napkins into polite folds.
How was your day dear
Fine
And how was yours dear
Fine
15 And how was school
The same

Only once in a while
when we're not trying so hard
when we're not trying at all
20 our napkins suddenly whirl away
and we float up to the ceiling
where we sing and dance until it hurts from laughing

and then we float down
with our napkin parachutes
25 and once again spoon our soup
and pass the bread please.

Close Read

1. Notice the simile in lines 1–6. How are the mother and father like bookends?

2. The use of repetition in lines 7–8 emphasizes the speaker's frustration with his or her parents. What other examples of repetition can you find?

3. Examine the two boxed images. What contrasting dinner scenes do they bring to mind?

4. Line 22 is the longest one in the poem. Why might Merriam have chosen to make this line stand out? (Hint: Think about the mood at this particular moment.)

5. How would you describe the speaker's relationship with his or her parents? Support your answer.

Analysis of Baseball
Poem by May Swenson

Alone in the Nets
Poem by Arnold Adoff

Why do we love SPORTS?

KEY IDEA Many people consider **sports** an important part of their life, whether they play sports or just watch. Athletes enjoy being part of a team and competing with their peers. Fans enjoy watching games to see the skill and endurance of the athletes. The following poems present two views of the excitement of sports, both on and off the field.

LIST IT Think about the sports that play a part in your life. With a small group, pick one sport and come up with a list of the top ten reasons to play or watch that sport. Compare your list with the lists of other groups in the class.

LITERARY ANALYSIS: LINE

One of the first things you will notice about poems is that they are made up of lines. A **line** of poetry can be a complete sentence, part of a sentence, or even a single word. The length of the lines in a poem can help develop the poem's rhythm and support its meaning. Line length can also give a poem its shape, or **form,** which affects how the poem is read.

- Short lines might give a poem a fast, choppy **rhythm,** or beat. Long lines might give it a smoother, slower rhythm.
- Poets use **line breaks,** or the places where lines of poetry end, to add emphasis to certain words or phrases.

As you read the following poems, pay attention to how the line length, line breaks, and overall form contribute to your understanding of a sport and a player.

READING STRATEGY: READING POETRY ALOUD

Usually, poetry is meant to be heard as well as read. Many poems have **rhyming words,** or repeated sounds at the ends of words, that are easier to notice when the poem is **read aloud.** Poets might also include words such as *bang* or *thump* to give the reader the sense of a noise being made. In addition to being pleasant to hear, these elements can help emphasize a poem's meaning.

   Read "Analysis of Baseball" and "Alone in the Nets" aloud. In a chart like the one shown, record places in the poems where you notice rhyming words or repeated words and phrases. Also record any "noise" words you find.

	"Analysis of Baseball"	"Alone in the Nets"
Rhyming Words	hits/it/mitt	
Repeated Words and Phrases		
Noise Words		

ANALYSIS OF BASEBALL

May Swenson

It's about
the ball,
the bat,
and the mitt.
5 Ball hits
bat, or it
hits mitt.
Bat doesn't
hit ball, bat
10 meets it.
Ball bounces
off bat, flies
air, or thuds
ground (dud)
15 or it
fits mitt.

Bat waits
for ball
to mate.
20 Ball hates
to take bat's
bait. Ball
flirts, bat's
late, don't
25 keep the date.
Ball goes in
(thwack) to mitt,
and goes out
(thwack) back
30 to mitt.

Ball fits
mitt, but
not all
the time.
35 Sometimes
ball gets hit
(pow) when bat
meets it,
and sails
40 to a place
where mitt
has to quit
in disgrace. **A**
That's about
45 the bases
loaded,
about 40,000
fans exploded.

It's about
50 the ball,
the bat,
the mitt,
the bases
and the fans. **B**
55 It's done
on a diamond,
and for fun.
It's about
home, and it's
60 about run.

A READING POETRY
ALOUD
Reread lines 11–43 aloud.
What do the noise
words in parentheses
add to the experience of
reading the poem?

B LINE
Reread lines 49–54.
What words do the **line
breaks** help emphasize?

Alone in the Nets

Arnold Adoff

I
am
alone   of   course,
    in the nets, on this cold and raining afternoon, **C**
5   and our best defending fullback[1]
    is lying on the wet ground   out of position.
    Half the opposition is pounding
               down the field,
        and their lead forward[2] is gliding
10   so fast, she can just barely keep
        the ball in front of her   sliding
                foot.

Her cleats[3] are expensive,
and her hair $b_o{}^u{}_n{}^c{}_e{}^s$
15   neatly
like the   after
    girls   in the shampoo commercials.
      There   is   a   big   grin
           on her face.

20 Now: In This Frozen Moment   On This Moving World Through Space

    is the right time to ask   why am I here just standing
                in my frozen place?
Why   did I get up on time this morning?
Why   did I get up at all?
25 Why   did I listen to the coach and agree to play
    this strange position in a   r e a l   game
    in a strange town   on this   wet   and   moving world?

---

1. **defending fullback:** In soccer, this refers to a player whose position is near the defensive goal or goal line.

2. **lead forward:** the primary, or main, player on the offensive line in the game of soccer.

3. **cleats:** shoes with pieces of metal or hard rubber sticking out from the soles.

Why   is it raining?
Why   is it raining so h a r d?
30 Where
            are all of our defenders?
Why   do all of our players
            do all of the falling
                            down?

35   Why am I here? **D**

But Frozen Moments Can Unfreeze   And I Can Stretch

and reach for the ball   flying to the corner of
                                              our
                                              goal.

40 I can reach   and jump
                and dive   into the s p a c e
                            between my out
                                    stretched
                                    hands

45 and the outside poles
            of the nets.

My fears evaporate   like my sweat in this chilling
                                        breeze,

and I can move with this moving world
50 and pace my steps
    like that   old
                    movie
                high
                noon sheriff in his just
55   right
                                time.

That grinning forward gets her shot away too soon,
and I am there, on my own time, in the air,
                        to meet the ball,
60 and fall on it
    for the save.

I wave my happy ending wave and get up.
            The game goes on. **E**

D READING POETRY ALOUD
Reread lines 28–35. How does the arrangement of the words and letters help convey the meaning in these lines?

E LINE
How are lines 62–63 different from the ones just before them?

Comprehension

1. **Clarify** Reread lines 58–60 of "Analysis of Baseball." What do these lines mean?

2. **Clarify** What happens to the forward's shot at the end of "Alone in the Nets"?

3. **Represent** Choose one group of lines from "Alone in the Nets" and create a sketch based on the details given in the poem.

Literary Analysis

4. **Understand Form in Poetry** Sometimes poets arrange letters and words in unusual ways based on the subject of the poem. In a chart like the one shown, record places in "Alone in the Nets" where Arnold Adoff does this. How do these lines help you understand the poem?

Word, Phrase, or Line	Shape	Effect of the Shape
a r e a l game	stretched out, made to be long like the game itself	makes me read the line more slowly and put emphasis on **real**

5. **Analyze Line** Choose one **stanza,** or group of lines, from "Analysis of Baseball." Rewrite the stanza, changing the **line breaks** so that each line ends with a comma or period. Compare your version to the original. How does changing line breaks change the effect of the stanza?

6. **Evaluate Poetry** Look at the chart you completed as you read aloud to find places where you noticed repeated words or sounds. In what way does the repetition seem to connect to the action in the poems?

Extension and Challenge

7. **Creative Project: Writing** Rewrite "Alone in the Nets" as an article for your school newspaper. You may want to read the magazine article on page 557 first to see an example of **sports** writing. Be sure to include team names, player names, the date of the game, and the final score.

8. **Speaking and Listening** When a poem is divided up between several readers and spoken aloud, it is called a **choral reading.** In a small group, perform a choral reading of one of the poems.

MAGAZINE ARTICLE The poems "Analysis of Baseball" and "Alone in the Nets" give you a sense of two different sports. In the following article, you will read about the challenges and benefits of becoming a professional athlete.

Teen Athletes:
MANY KIDS DREAM OF PLAYING IN THE BIG LEAGUES. BUT AT WHAT COST?
Victor Landauro

Becoming a famous athlete may look easy, but it's not. Just ask an Olympic gold medalist or a pro soccer player. They will tell you that playing sports well means hard work and discipline.

"I've made a lot of sacrifices," gymnast Carly Patterson told *Junior Scholastic.*

The 16-year-old won Olympic gold in the all-around competition, her sport's premier event. Despite achieving Olympic glory, Carly is actually jealous of her 14-year-old sister's "regular" life. "[Jordan] goes to public school, has sleepovers with friends, and eats junk food," says Carly. "I can't do that because I need to rest and eat healthy."

Freddy Adu, who plays forward for the D.C. United soccer team, knows firsthand what Carly is talking about. "I love playing, but I work very hard at soccer," the 15-year-old told *JS.* "I hear fans cheer for me, and it definitely makes me train harder.". . .

Not Fun Anymore

Almost everyone agrees that athletics are good for most kids. Several studies show that playing sports can lead to better physical and emotional health. Through athletics, children learn important lessons in sportsmanship, discipline, teamwork, and leadership.

But critics worry that those benefits are getting lost in the chase to become the next star. Too many kids are either pushing—or being pushed by coaches and parents—to reach the top of their sport.

"Many kids who quit sports typically say, 'It's not fun anymore,'" says Avery Faigenbaum, a professor of exercise science and physical education at the College of New Jersey. "They would rather play on a losing team than sit on the bench of a winning team.". . .

Life Beyond Sports

Upon retirement, many professional athletes seek new challenges. There is even a Baseball Hall of Famer on Capitol Hill: Kentucky Senator Jim Bunning. Other athletes have become judges, lawyers, business leaders, and teachers.

"It's important to have multiple dreams," says Jay Coakley, a sociologist who studies sports. "Dream of a life that is outside of sports, too."

That advice weighs heavily on Carly Patterson. "I want to go to college, and maybe become a singer," she says. "I'm going to keep on working and see what happens."

Sea-Fever
Poem by John Masefield

The Village Blacksmith
Poem by Henry Wadsworth Longfellow

When is your WORK *your life?*

KEY IDEA What do you think of when you hear the word **work?**
If your experience with projects or chores hasn't been pleasant,
then words like *boring* and *dull* might come to mind. When you
love what you do, however, work can become more than just a job.
It can be an exciting or challenging way to spend your time. For
the people in the following two poems, the work they do each day
becomes a large part of who they are.

DISCUSS What jobs might be interesting enough to build your
life around? With a small group, discuss the characteristics
that would make a job mean more to you than just
a paycheck.

● LITERARY ANALYSIS: RHYME

One method poets have for creating sounds that appeal to readers and listeners is to use rhyme. **Rhyme** is the repetition of sounds at the ends of words. A poet may develop a pattern of rhyme that stays much the same throughout a poem. In this example from "The Village Blacksmith," lines that rhyme are labeled with the same letter:

Under a spreading chestnut-<u>tree</u>	*a*
The village smithy <u>stands</u>;	*b*
The smith, a mighty man is <u>he</u>,	*a*
With large and sinewy <u>hands</u>;	*b*

As you read "Sea-Fever" and "The Village Blacksmith," record rhyming words in a log like the one shown.

"Sea-Fever"	"The Village Blacksmith"
	tree/he

● READING SKILL: RECOGNIZE RHYTHM

Poems and songs often have a distinct **rhythm,** or beat. It is created by putting stress, or emphasis, on some syllables and not on others. Read the first line of "Sea-Fever." Notice the pattern of stressed (´) and unstressed (˘) syllables.

Ĭ mús̆t gŏ dówn tŏ thĕ séas ăgáin, tŏ thĕ lónĕlý séa ănd thĕ ský,

As you read the following poems, notice their patterns of rhythm.

Review: **Paraphrase**

▲ VOCABULARY IN CONTEXT

The poets use the following words in their poems about **work.** Match each numbered word or phrase with the vocabulary word that is closest in meaning.

WORD LIST	brawny	repose	sinewy	vagrant

1. strong and muscular
2. lean and tough
3. moving from place to place
4. freedom from work

Author Online

John Masefield: Poet of the Sea
John Masefield's love of the ocean began in childhood. He received part of his education at a floating school, on a ship called the HMS *Conway*. His first job was a position on the crew of an ocean liner. An illness eventually forced him to return to dry land, but his love of the water continued to play an important role in his life and his writing.

John Masefield
1878–1967

Henry Wadsworth Longfellow: American Original
Henry Wadsworth Longfellow got an early start on college—at age 14. By graduation, he had published nearly 40 poems. Poems such as "The Song of Hiawatha" and "Paul Revere's Ride" made Longfellow one of the most popular American poets of his time. When he died, the British government gave Longfellow a memorial in Westminster Abbey's Poets' Corner, where the greatest British poets are buried. He was the first American to receive this honor.

Henry Wadsworth Longfellow
1807–1882

MORE ABOUT THE AUTHOR
For more on these poets, visit the **Literature Center** at ClassZone.com.

Sea-Fever

John Masefield

I must go down to the seas again, to the lonely sea and
    the sky,
And all I ask is a tall ship and a star to steer her by,
And the wheel's kick and the wind's song and the white
    sail's shaking,
And a grey mist on the sea's face and a grey dawn breaking. **Ⓐ**

5 I must go down to the seas again, for the call of the
    running tide
Is a wild call and a clear call that may not be denied;
And all I ask is a windy day with the white clouds flying,
And the flung spray and the blown spume,[1] and the
    sea-gulls crying.

I must go down to the seas again to the **vagrant** gypsy life,
10 To the gull's way and the whale's way where the wind's like
    a whetted[2] knife;
And all I ask is a merry yarn[3] from a laughing fellow-rover,
And a quiet sleep and a sweet dream when the long
    trick's[4] over.

Ⓐ RHYME
Reread lines 1–4, paying
attention to the pattern
of rhyming words.
Record any rhyming pairs
or groups in your log.

vagrant (vā′grənt) *adj.*
wandering from place
to place; unrestrained

---

1. **spume** (spyo͞om): foam or froth on a liquid.
2. **whetted** (hwĕt-ĭd): sharpened.
3. **yarn:** long, entertaining tale.
4. **trick:** term of work or duty.

Unnamed clipper ship, Claude Marks. Private
collection. Photo © Bridgeman Art Library.

THE VILLAGE BLACKSMITH

Henry Wadsworth Longfellow

The Blacksmith, (1909), James Carroll
Beckwith. Oil on canvas, 52¼″ × 32¼″.
Photo © Smithsonian American Art
Museum, Washington, D.C./Art
Resource, New York.

Under a spreading chestnut-tree
  The village smithy stands;
The smith, a mighty man is he,
  With large and **sinewy** hands;
5 And the muscles of his **brawny** arms
  Are strong as iron bands.

His hair is crisp, and black, and long,
  His face is like the tan;
His brow is wet with honest sweat,
10   He earns whate'er he can,
And looks the whole world in the face,
  For he owes not any man. **Ⓑ**

Week in, week out, from morn till night,
  You can hear his bellows[1] blow;
15 You can hear him swing his heavy sledge,
  With measured beat and slow,
Like a sexton[2] ringing the village bell,
  When the evening sun is low.

sinewy (sĭn′yōō-ē) *adj.*
lean and tough

brawny (brô′nē) *adj.*
strong and muscular

Ⓑ RHYME
Reread the first two
stanzas, or groups of
lines. What pattern of
rhyming words do you
see?

---

1. **bellows:** a device for providing air to feed a fire.

2. **sexton:** an employee of a church, responsible for maintaining
the building and ringing the church bells.

And children coming home from school
20   Look in at the open door;
They love to see the flaming forge,
        And hear the bellows roar,
And catch the burning sparks that fly
        Like chaff from a threshing-floor.[3]

25 He goes on Sunday to the church,
        And sits among his boys;
He hears the parson pray and preach,
        He hears his daughter's voice,
Singing in the village choir,
30   And it makes his heart rejoice. **C**

It sounds to him like her mother's voice,
        Singing in Paradise!
He needs must think of her once more,
        How in the grave she lies;
35 And with his hard, rough hand he wipes
        A tear out of his eyes.

Toiling, —rejoicing, —sorrowing,
        Onward through life he goes;
Each morning sees some task begin,
40   Each evening sees it close;
Something attempted, something done,
        Has earned a night's **repose.** **D**

Thanks, thanks to thee, my worthy friend,
        For the lesson thou hast taught!
45 Thus at the flaming forge of life
        Our fortunes must be wrought;
Thus on its sounding anvil[4] shaped
        Each burning deed and thought.

C **RECOGNIZE RHYTHM**
Write out lines 25–28
and label each syllable
with a stressed or
unstressed mark. What
do you notice about the
pattern of the rhythm?

repose (rĭ-pōz') *n.*
freedom from work or
worry; rest

D **PARAPHRASE**
Reread lines 37–42.
Then rewrite the stanza
line by line, using your
own words.

---

3. **chaff from a threshing-floor:** Chaff is the dry coating on grains
   of wheat. It is discarded during threshing, when the wheat and
   straw are separated.

4. **sounding anvil:** An anvil is a heavy block of iron on which metals
   are hammered into shape. *Sounding* refers to the ringing noise
   the hammering makes.

Comprehension

1. **Clarify** What "call" is the **speaker,** or voice of the poem, answering in "Sea-Fever"?

2. **Recall** List three physical characteristics of the village blacksmith.

3. **Clarify** Explain what the blacksmith thinks about when he hears his daughter sing.

Literary Analysis

4. **Identify Repetition** Note which words and phrases are repeated in each **stanza** in "Sea-Fever." In each case, why do you think the poet chose to repeat those words?

5. **Identify Theme** What theme, or message about life or human nature, does Henry Wadsworth Longfellow communicate in "The Village Blacksmith"? Support your answer with examples from the poem.

6. **Analyze Poetry** Reread line 37 of "The Village Blacksmith." In what way is this line a summary of the entire poem?

7. **Analyze Rhythm** Write down a few lines from each poem and mark the stressed and unstressed syllables, as shown on page 559. Now read the lines aloud. What effect does the rhythm have on each line?

8. **Evaluate Rhyme** In addition to creating a pattern of sound, rhyme helps emphasize important ideas or words in a poem. Look back at the chart you filled in as you read. Consider the groups of rhyming words that appear in "Sea-Fever." Why might the poet have chosen to emphasize these words in his poem about sailing?

9. **Draw Conclusions** How does the speaker in "The Village Blacksmith" feel about the blacksmith? In the center of a web like the one shown, record whether you think the speaker's view of the blacksmith is positive or negative. Then fill out the web with words and phrases from the poem that support your opinion.

"worthy friend"

Speaker's View:

Extension and Challenge

10. **Big Question Activity** Think back to the discussion you had about **work** (see page 558) and the characteristics your ideal job would have. Which of the poems comes closer to your idea of what makes a job worthwhile? Explain your choice, using examples from the poems.

Vocabulary in Context

VOCABULARY PRACTICE

To show your understanding of the vocabulary words, answer the following questions.

1. If you wanted a day's **repose,** would you go to a cabin in the woods or a busy train station?
2. Who would more likely be described as **sinewy,** a pie-eating champion or a track star?
3. Does a **brawny** person have a slender build or large muscles?
4. Does a **vagrant** cat wander from yard to yard or sit on the windowsill?

brawny
repose
sinewy
vagrant

VOCABULARY IN WRITING

Which person could you **visualize** more clearly: the sailor in "Sea-Fever" or the blacksmith in "The Village Blacksmith"? Write a paragraph explaining your choice, using at least two vocabulary words. You might start this way.

EXAMPLE SENTENCE

I pictured the **sinewy** *blacksmith more clearly than the sailor in "Sea-Fever."*

VOCABULARY STRATEGY: SPECIALIZED VOCABULARY

Some jobs or professions seem to have a vocabulary all their own. Doctors use special terms associated with disease and health. Sailors, like the speaker in "Sea-Fever," have specialized terms for elements of their job. We often think of the word *trick,* for example, as meaning "prank" or "illusion." For a sailor, however, it refers to a term of duty at sea. Understanding these specialized words can help to give you a better sense of life at sea.

PRACTICE Match each numbered word with its definition in the second column. If you need help, use a dictionary.

1. rigging   **a.** a small boat, usually towed by a larger one
2. dinghy   **b.** the kitchen of a ship
3. pier   **c.** a flap on the bottom of a ship, used for steering
4. rudder   **d.** a platform over water at which ships can unload
5. galley   **e.** the arrangement of sails and ropes on a ship

VOCABULARY PRACTICE
For more practice, go to the **Vocabulary Center** at ClassZone.com.

Something Told the Wild Geese

Poem by Rachel Field

Change

Poem by Charlotte Zolotow

What are NATURE'S *mysteries?*

KEY IDEA The natural world is full of both power and beauty. A terrifying tornado or earthquake might be followed by a lovely rainbow or sunset. Many of these fascinating displays of **nature** are also mysterious. We are not always certain how or why they occur. The poems you are about to read explore two of these mysteries—the changes in seasons and the changes in ourselves.

QUICKWRITE What natural mystery do you find most amazing? Think of a remarkable or unusual animal, plant, or natural event you have seen or heard about and write a paragraph explaining why it fascinates you.

LITERARY ANALYSIS: IMAGERY

Imagery is the use of words and phrases that appeal to the senses of sight, hearing, touch, smell, and taste. Poets will often use imagery to create vivid descriptions or express a strong idea in only a few words or lines.

The winter
still stings
clean and cold and white

In these lines from "Change," the word *white* appeals to your sense of sight, while the words *stings* and *cold* appeal to your sense of touch. As you read "Something Told the Wild Geese" and "Change," record examples of imagery and note the sense or senses each example appeals to.

	Taste	Sight	Touch	Smell	Hearing
"Something Told the Wild Geese"					
"Change"		"white"	"stings," "cold"		

READING SKILL: UNDERSTAND REPETITION

When you read a poem, you will sometimes come across the same word, phrase, sound, or line several times. Poets often use **repetition** to emphasize a particular word or idea. Repetition can also help develop a poem's rhythm, or beat, and support its meaning.

For example, similar pairs of lines appear at the beginning and end of "Something Told the Wild Geese":

Something told the wild geese
  It was time to go. (lines 1–2)

Something told the wild geese
  It was time to fly,— (lines 13–14)

Repeating these lines emphasizes that the geese must leave. The repetition also suggests that like the lines, the migration of the geese is something that repeats.

As you read the following poems, look for repeated words, phrases, and lines. Consider why the poet might have chosen to repeat them.

Author Online

Rachel Field: Late Bloomer As a child, Rachel Field enjoyed listening to her mother read aloud, but she was not interested in learning to read on her own. In fact, Field did not learn to read until she was ten years

Rachel Field
1894–1942

old. Eventually she found reading and writing more enjoyable and began writing essays for her friends. Field's writing skills helped her to enter Radcliffe College, a part of Harvard University. In 1929 Field became the first woman to win the Newbery Medal for children's literature.

Charlotte Zolotow: Natural Observer As a young woman, Charlotte Zolotow worked for a publishing company. Walking to work each day, she passed a park. Zolotow saw how the park changed

Charlotte Zolotow
born 1915

with the seasons and told her boss that it might be a good topic for a children's book. The boss asked Zolotow to write the book, and she did. That was the first book of many in a writing career that has lasted more than 70 years.

 MORE ABOUT THE AUTHOR
For more on these poets, visit the **Literature Center** at **ClassZone.com**.

SOMETHING TOLD THE WILD GEESE

RACHEL FIELD

Something told the wild geese
    It was time to go.
Though the fields lay golden
    Something whispered,—"Snow."
5 Leaves were green and stirring,
    Berries, luster-glossed,[1]
But beneath warm feathers
    Something cautioned,—"Frost."
All the sagging orchards
10   Steamed with amber spice,
But each wild breast stiffened
    At remembered ice. **A**
Something told the wild geese
    It was time to fly,—
15 Summer sun was on their wings,
    Winter in their cry.

ANALYZE VISUALS
Do the geese in this image seem to be coming or going? Explain.

A IMAGERY
Reread lines 5–12. How many of the five senses (sight, hearing, taste, touch, and smell) do the **details** in these lines appeal to? Record your answers in your chart.

---

1. **luster-glossed:** having a bright or shiny coating.

Change

Charlotte Zolotow

The summer
still hangs
heavy and sweet
with sunlight
5 as it did last year.

The autumn
still comes
showering gold and crimson
as it did last year.

10 The winter
still stings
clean and cold and white
as it did last year. **B**

The spring
15 still comes
like a whisper in the dark night.

It is only I
who have changed.

ANALYZE VISUALS
What **details** in this painting suggest change?

B **UNDERSTAND REPETITION**
Reread the poem's first three **stanzas,** or groups of lines. Why do you think the poet chose to repeat the line at the end of each stanza?

The Farewell (1952), Bernard Perlin. Photo © Smithsonian American Art Museum, Washington, D.C./Art Resource, New York.

Comprehension

1. **Recall** According to the speaker in "Change," which season comes "like a whisper in the dark night"?

2. **Clarify** In what season does "Something Told the Wild Geese" take place?

3. **Represent** Divide a piece of paper into fourths and sketch the mental picture you get of each season based on the descriptions in "Change."

Literary Analysis

4. **Compare and Contrast Imagery** Compare and contrast the descriptions of **nature** in the two poems. Do the images in "Something Told the Wild Geese" create a different impression of the seasons than those in "Change"? Support your answer.

5. **Understand Repetition** In a chart like the one shown, record repeated lines, words, and phrases from each poem. In what way does repetition help emphasize meaning in the two poems?

"Something Told the Wild Geese"	"Change"
"It was time"	

6. **Analyze Imagery** Look back at the chart you completed as you read. Note which of your five senses the poems appeal to most often. Which seasons in the poems seem to appeal most to the sense of touch, and which ones appeal more to the sense of sight?

7. **Draw Conclusions** In "Something Told the Wild Geese," why do you think the poet chose not to say what the "something" is? Explain.

Extension and Challenge

8. **Creative Project: Poem** A **lyric poem** is a short poem in which a speaker expresses personal thoughts and feelings. Write a lyric poem about your favorite or least favorite season. Try to include **imagery** that appeals to as many of the five senses as possible.

9. **Inquiry and Research** Do some research on the science behind why birds such as wild geese migrate. Why do some kinds of birds migrate while others do not? Present your findings to the class.

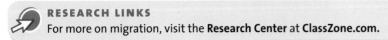
RESEARCH LINKS
For more on migration, visit the **Research Center** at **ClassZone.com**.

Reading-Writing Connection

Increase your understanding of the poems "Something Told the Wild Geese" and "Change" by responding to these prompts. Then complete the **Grammar and Writing** exercise.

A. Short Response: Analyze Poetry
Reread the descriptions of summer and winter in "Something Told the Wild Geese," paying attention to the speaker's attitude in each description. In a **one-paragraph response,** decide what season the speaker seems to prefer. Explain why you think so.

B. Extended Response: Describe Seasons
We often connect the seasons to the activities or events that take place in them. Choose a season and write **two or three paragraphs** to explain what, for you, signals that the season has arrived. Think about changes both in **nature** and in your life.

A strong analysis will . . .
- identify the speaker's attitude toward each season
- use examples from the poem for support

A vivid description will . . .
- draw on real-life experiences
- use imagery that appeals to the reader's senses

GRAMMAR AND WRITING

MAINTAIN SUBJECT-VERB AGREEMENT The verb in a sentence must always **agree in number** with the subject of the sentence. This means that if a subject is singular, its verb must have a singular form. If the subject is plural, its verb must have a plural form. Be especially careful when forming sentences that begin with *here* or *there,* and when forming questions.

Original: There was too many leaves to count.

Revised: There were too many leaves to count. (*The subject* leaves *is plural, so the verb should be plural too.*)

PRACTICE Choose the verb form that agrees in number with the subject in each of the following sentences.

1. Here (comes, come) the new season.
2. (Is, Are) the leaves starting to change color?
3. My sister (rakes, rake) the leaves in the yard.
4. There (is, are) no colors prettier than autumn's colors.

*For more help with subject-verb agreement, see page R65 in the **Grammar Handbook.***

Message from a Caterpillar
Poem by Lilian Moore

Fog
Poem by Carl Sandburg

Two Haiku
Poems by Bashō

How much can one WORD *say?*

KEY IDEA Sometimes a single word can pack a powerful punch. Words like *peace, freedom, friendship,* and *love* can represent strong feelings, ideas, and memories. In each of the following short poems, the poet has worked as much **meaning** as possible into the smallest number of words.

WEB IT What are some small words that are big on meaning? Choose a word that you find expressive. Create a web with the word at the center. In the outer part of the web, write the feelings, ideas, and memories that you connect to that word.

LITERARY ANALYSIS: WORD CHOICE

Though some poems may look alike or share a subject, no two are ever the same. One way writers make their poems unique is by choosing their words carefully. Through **word choice,** poets make each word work toward expressing a poem's overall meaning.

For an example of the effect of word choice, read the following lines from "Message from a Caterpillar":

> *Don't shake this*
> *bough.*
> *Don't try*
> *to wake me*
> *now.*

The poem begins with the commands "Don't shake" and "Don't try." These commands set up a strong message: the caterpillar is not to be interrupted. The contraction *Don't* suggests that the caterpillar's message is urgent, as well—there is no time to say "do not." As you read each of the following short poems, be aware of how carefully each word has been chosen by the poet.

READING STRATEGY: VISUALIZE

Poetry has the power to "paint" a picture with words. When you read a poem, use the details in it to **visualize,** or form a mental picture of, what is being described.

As you read each of the following poems, note the mental pictures that you form and the words and phrases that helped you create them. Record these notes in a chart like the one shown.

Mental Pictures	Words and Phrases
tree branch	

Author Online

Lilian Moore: Lifelong Writer Some of Lilian Moore's earliest memories were of hanging out in her neighborhood and making up stories to tell her friends. Writing simple, vivid stories and poems for young readers eventually became her life's work.

Lilian Moore
1909–2004

Carl Sandburg: Informal Poet Carl Sandburg adopted an informal style in his poetry, believing that formal poetry had "the skill of a solved crossword puzzle." He thought of poetry as a glimpse, leaving readers "to guess about what is seen during a moment."

Carl Sandburg
1878–1967

Matsuo Bashō: Wandering Poet Matsuo Bashō is considered one of Japan's greatest poets. He set the rules for haiku, poems that describe a single moment, feeling, or object in three unrhymed lines.

Matsuo Bashō
1644–1694

MORE ABOUT THE AUTHOR
For more on these poets, visit the
Literature Center at ClassZone.com.

Message from a Caterpillar

Lilian Moore

Don't shake this
bough.
Don't try
to wake me
5 now.

6 In this cocoon
I've work to
do.
Inside this silk
10 I'm changing
things.

I'm worm like now
but in this
dark
15 I'm growing
wings. Ⓐ

Ⓐ VISUALIZE
Reread lines 12–16. What
words help you form a
mental picture of what
is going on inside the
cocoon?

Fog

Carl Sandburg

The fog comes
on little cat feet. **B**

It sits looking
over harbor and city
5 on silent haunches[1]
and then moves on.

B WORD CHOICE
Reread lines 1–2 without
the word *little*. Does this
change the meaning of
the poem? Explain.

---

1. **haunches:** the hind legs of a
   four-legged animal.

Two Haiku Bashō

Winter solitude—
in a world of one color
the sound of the wind.

A field of cotton—
as if the moon
had flowered. **C**

C VISUALIZE
Reread the second haiku.
What **images** does the
poem create in your
mind? Record the key
words and phrases in
your chart.

Comprehension

1. **Clarify** Why doesn't the caterpillar in "Message from a Caterpillar" want to be awakened?

2. **Clarify** In the first haiku, what does "a world of one color" refer to?

3. **Represent** Sketch the image the second haiku creates in your mind.

Literary Analysis

4. **Make Inferences** How would you describe the speaker's personality in "Message from a Caterpillar"?

5. **Analyze Metaphor** Carl Sandburg bases his poem "Fog" on a single metaphor, or comparison of two things. To what does Sandburg compare the fog? Explain how the comparison helps you **visualize** the fog.

6. **Visualize Haiku** A traditional haiku written in Japanese has only three lines and 17 syllables. The first and third lines have five syllables, and the second line has seven. (Haiku translated into English may not follow this pattern exactly.) Within these strict rules, the poet tries to capture a moment in time. Look at the words and phrases you noted in your chart as you read the haiku by Bashō. Which poem created a more vivid picture?

7. **Examine Word Choice** Traditional haiku usually do not have titles. Choose a title for each of the haiku by Bashō. Your titles could refer to the poems' subjects, their **meanings,** or the feelings and images they create. Explain how your titles reinforce the poet's word choice.

8. **Compare and Contrast Poems** Compare and contrast "Fog" with the first haiku by Bashō. In what ways are they similar and different? Record your responses in a Venn diagram.

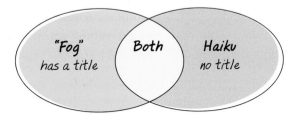

Extension and Challenge

9. **Big Question Activity** Look back at the word web you created on page 574. Using the web for ideas, write a haiku of your own. Try to express as much as you can in three short lines.

10. **Inquiry and Research** From 1912 to 1917, a group of poets called the imagists formed and became famous. Do research to find out how they were influenced by Japanese poetry such as haiku. Share your findings with the class.

RESEARCH LINKS
For more on imagists and haiku, visit the **Research Center** at **ClassZone.com.**

Windshield Wiper

Poem by Eve Merriam

Night Journey

Poem by Theodore Roethke

How do you SEE *the world?*

KEY IDEA When you stand on your head, the world looks very different, even unfamiliar. Turning upside down is one way of changing your **perspective,** or your way of seeing something. Perspective can also be a mental outlook, or a way of responding to things that happen. The poems you are about to read involve both physical and mental perspective. Both poems are written from the perspective of looking out a window, but they capture two very different responses.

LIST IT To get a sense of perspective, try looking a little differently at something you see every day. Roll a piece of paper to form a tube, and look through it at what's around you. Make a list of everything you see. Did you notice anything that you hadn't noticed before?

LITERARY ANALYSIS: SOUND DEVICES

You may have heard or read poems that sound almost like songs. Poetry gets many of its musical qualities from **sound devices.** Sound devices can also suggest meaning or add emphasis. Three commonly used sound devices are

- **repetition,** or the use of a word, phrase, or line several times (*Example: It was a good song, a sad song, a sweet song.*)
- **onomatopoeia** (ŏn'ə-măt'ə-pē'ə), or the use of words that sound like their meanings (*Examples: buzz, zap*)
- **alliteration,** or the repetition of the same consonant sound at the beginning of words (*Example: magical mountain mist*)

A poet might use these devices to draw attention to a particular line or idea. As you read "Windshield Wiper" and "Night Journey," record examples of these devices.

Repetition	Onomatopoeia	Alliteration
tissue paper/ tissue paper		

READING SKILL: UNDERSTAND FORM

Poets do more than just choose their words carefully. They also pay special attention to how the words are arranged on a page. This is called **form.** The form of a poem can affect how it sounds when you read it aloud. It can also affect the poem's meaning.

To understand a poem, ask yourself these questions:

- Are the **lines** short or long? Are they interrupted by extra **space?**
- How would you describe the overall **shape** of the poem on the page?
- In reading the poem aloud, how does line length and overall shape affect the speed of your reading?

Each of the following poems describes a moving object. As you read each poem, notice how form helps reflect the subject of the poem.

Author On|ine

Eve Merriam: Lover of Language

Eve Merriam's advice on how to appreciate poetry was "Eat it, drink it, enjoy it, and share it." Merriam began writing poetry at age seven. She loved rhythm and rhyme and the way poems came to life when read aloud. After college, she continued to write poetry while working as a writer in advertising and radio. Merriam particularly enjoyed sharing her love of poetry with young readers.

Eve Merriam
1916–1992

Theodore Roethke: Reluctant Poet

Theodore Roethke spent his childhood reading and longed to write beautifully, but he struggled with the idea of becoming a poet. Worried about fitting in, he went to law school—but quickly decided to become a poet after all. Roethke eventually won a Pulitzer Prize for his poetry. Much of his work explores the natural world and memories of his childhood.

Theodore Roethke
1908–1963

MORE ABOUT THE AUTHOR
For more on Eve Merriam and Theodore Roethke, visit the **Literature Center** at **ClassZone.com.**

WINDSHIELD WIPER

Eve Merriam

fog smog	fog smog
tissue paper	tissue paper
clear the blear	clear the smear **A**
fog more	fog more
splat splat	downpour
rubber scraper	rubber scraper
overshoes	macintosh[1]
bumbershoot[2]	muddle on
slosh through	slosh through
drying up	drying up
sky lighter	sky lighter
nearly clear	nearly clear
clearing clearing veer **B**	
clear here clear	

5 (line number for "splat splat")
10 (line number for "drying up")

A UNDERSTAND FORM
How would you read lines 1–3, across each line or down one column then down the other? Explain.

B SOUND DEVICES
How does the **repetition** in these lines reflect the subject of the poem?

1. **macintosh:** raincoat.
2. **bumbershoot:** umbrella.

NIGHT JOURNEY

THEODORE ROETHKE

Now as the train bears west,
Its rhythm rocks the earth,
And from my Pullman berth[1]
I stare into the night
5   While others take their rest. **C**
Bridges of iron lace,
A suddenness of trees,
A lap of mountain mist
All cross my line of sight,
10 Then a bleak wasted place,
And a lake below my knees.
Full on my neck I feel
The straining at a curve;
My muscles move with steel,
15 I wake in every nerve.
I watch a beacon swing
From dark to blazing bright;
We thunder through ravines
And gullies washed with light.
20 Beyond the mountain pass
Mist deepens on the pane;
We rush into a rain
That rattles double glass. **D**
Wheels shake the roadbed stone,
25 The pistons jerk and shove,
I stay up half the night
To see the land I love.

C UNDERSTAND FORM
Roethke often breaks long sentences up into several **lines.** If he wrote this poem using longer lines, how might that affect your reading of it?

D SOUND DEVICES
Reread lines 22–23. What sound device appears in these lines? Record your answer in your chart.

---

1. **Pullman berth:** A Pullman is a type of railroad car invented by George Pullman (1831–1897). The sleeping car featured private beds called berths.

Comprehension

1. **Recall** Name three things that the speaker sees in "Night Journey."

2. **Clarify** What are the "bridges of iron lace" in line 6 of "Night Journey"?

3. **Clarify** What kinds of weather are described in "Windshield Wiper"?

Literary Analysis

4. **Understand Form** Take another look at the unusual way in which "Windshield Wiper" is arranged on the page. The **spacing** in the center of each line mimics the movement of actual windshield wipers. What does it mean when that space disappears in lines 13 and 14?

5. **Examine Word Choice** Skim "Night Journey" and list all the words you can find that convey movement. Compare lists with a partner.

6. **Analyze Sound Devices** Look at the chart you filled in as you read. For each poem, which sound device is used most often, **repetition, onomatopoeia,** or **alliteration?**

7. **Analyze Rhyme** Create a chart like the one shown, and list the rhyming words or phrases in each poem. In which poem does rhyme have a more important role?

	"Windshield Wiper"	"Night Journey"
Rhyming Words and Phrases	blear / smear	

Extension and Challenge

8. **Big Question Activity** Reread the list of observations you made for the activity on page 580. Now look at the same scene again, without the paper tube. Make a new list of everything you notice, and compare it with your first list. Did your observations change when you changed your **perspective?**

9. **SOCIAL STUDIES CONNECTION** Read the excerpt from *A Long Hard Journey* that begins on page 588. What further information does the excerpt provide about the speaker's trip in "Night Journey"?

Reading-Writing Connection

Increase your appreciation of "Windshield Wiper" and "Night Journey" by responding to these prompts. Then complete the **Grammar and Writing** exercise.

WRITING PROMPTS

A. Short Response: Analyze Poetry
Would you say that "Windshield Wiper" appeals more to your mind or to your senses? Explain your opinion in a **one-paragraph response,** using examples from the poem.

B. Extended Response: Create a Travel Journal
"Night Journey" describes a train going west. Think of a journey you have taken and write about it in a **two- or three-paragraph journal entry.** Describe the scenery, your form of transportation, and who went with you. End by telling whether the trip changed your **perspective**—on your home, your destination, or travel itself—in any way.

SELF-CHECK

A strong analysis will . . .
- express an opinion about the poem
- include words and lines from the poem for support

An engaging entry will . . .
- clearly state where you were going and why
- use details to bring the journey to life

GRAMMAR AND WRITING

MAINTAIN SUBJECT-VERB AGREEMENT You have already learned that a verb must agree with its subject in number. A **compound subject** is made up of two or more subjects joined by a **conjunction,** such as *and* or *or.* This conjunction is the clue that tells you whether to use a singular or plural verb in the sentence. A compound subject joined by *and* usually takes a plural verb. If a compound subject is joined by *or*, the verb should agree with the part of the subject closer to it.

Original: Bells or the train whistle mean the train is arriving.

Revised: Bells or the train whistle means the train is arriving.

PRACTICE Choose the verb form that agrees with each compound subject.

1. A dining car or comfortable seats (makes, make) the trip more enjoyable.
2. My mother and I (plays, play) board games to pass the time.
3. My uncle and my grandparents (was, were) there to meet the train.
4. The conductor or the engineer (rings, ring) the whistle as the train leaves.

*For more help with subject-verb agreement with compound subjects, see page R65 in the **Grammar Handbook.***

from A Long Hard Journey: The Story of the Pullman Porter
Informational Text

Use with "Night Journey," page 584.

What's the Connection?

In the poem "Night Journey," the speaker describes what it's like to view the American landscape at night through the window of a Pullman car on a speeding train. Now you will read an **informational text** about the luxurious interiors of Pullman cars and about the people whose services made the ride enjoyable for passengers.

Skill Focus: Gather and Organize Information

In 1867, George Pullman's Palace Car Company began employing ex-slaves as porters. The Pullman Company operated successfully well into the mid-1900s. During most of that time, porters were exclusively African Americans. The selection you are about to read describes the elegant furnishings and modern conveniences built into the Pullman Palace cars and "Hotel Cars." It also discusses the benefits of the porters' job and some of the challenges they faced while making sure each passenger's experience was exceptional.

As you read the excerpt from *A Long Hard Journey*, gather and organize information about Pullman-car furnishings, conveniences, porters, and passengers. You can do this by recording facts, descriptive details, and other information in a chart like the one shown.

	Facts, Descriptive Details, and Other Information
Furnishings	
Conveniences	
Porters	workers on the train
Passengers	customers on the train.

A Long Hard Journey: The Story of the Pullman Porter

by Patricia and Fredrick McKissack

FOCUS ON FORM
An **informational text** is written material that provides factual information. Newspaper and encyclopedia articles, timelines, and nonfiction books are all considered informational texts.

When Pullman cars first became popular, steam locomotives like this one were used to pull the cars.

The early porters were called "Travelin' Men." They were highly respected, even revered by their contemporaries.[1] A young woman considered herself fortunate to be courted by a porter, and with good reason. They were pillars of their community; they made a decent living and had experiences other men only dreamed about. As a popular song of that day indicated, some women preferred a railroad husband over all others. **A**

A GATHER AND ORGANIZE INFORMATION
What do you learn about Pullman porters from this introduction? Record the information in your chart.

---

1. **contemporaries:** other people who were living in that time period.

A railroader, a railroader
A railroader for me.
10 *If ever I marry in this wide world,*
A railroader's bride I'll be. . . .

Nineteenth-century porters traveled to faraway places, mingled with wealthy, well-educated travelers, and worked in elegant surroundings. In 1867, the *Western World* magazine described the Pullman porter's work environment:

> The furniture is of black walnut, handsomely carved and ornamented and upholstered with royal purple velvet plush imported from England expressly for this purpose. The finest Axminster carpets cover the floor. The night curtains for the
> 20 berths are of heaviest silk; splendid chandeliers are pendent overhead; elegant mirrors grace the walls. Luxurious beds invite repose by night and when made up for the day the cars betray no trace of the eating or sleeping uses to which they can be put. The total cost of each car is $30,000. . . . **B**

Since most of their neighbors had never seen such luxury, the porters formed an almost exclusive brotherhood bonded by their common experiences. It has been said they had more in common with each other than they did with family, friends, and neighbors. Fathers did so well that they encouraged their sons to become porters.
30 Uncles helped nephews, and brothers spoke for brothers.

Porters saw in their travels what most of their neighbors could only dream about. But on a more realistic level, having a steady job allowed them to marry, buy homes, and raise their children with dignity. . . . **C**

Meanwhile, George Pullman continued to make it possible for ordinary passengers to experience some of the pleasures and privileges generally reserved for the wealthy. His "Hotel Cars" were designed to give passengers the benefits of fine hotel food, service, and a comfortable bed, all on wheels. Pullman later designed and built the dining car which boasted "every variety of meats, vegetables, and pastry" that could be
40 "cooked on the cars, according to the best style of culinary art."[2]

The *Delmonico* was the first Pullman dining car, introduced in 1868. All passengers, whether using Pullman sleeping-car arrangements or not, could now eat in the diners. That also meant the hiring of more

---

2. **culinary art:** cooking of high quality and skill.

B GATHER AND ORGANIZE INFORMATION
Reread lines 12–24. Note any specific information in the appropriate rows of your chart.

C GATHER AND ORGANIZE INFORMATION
Reread lines 25–33. Which benefits of the job can you **infer** were more important to the porters?

Pullman lounge cars offered elegant furniture, carved ceilings, and all the comforts of home.

blacks as waiters, cooks, and stewards—although these positions were not exclusively black, as porter jobs were.

In 1870, the first all-Pullman train, called the *Board of Trade Special,* made its run from Boston to California. A baggage car contained iceboxes to keep the wines cool and the vegetables fresh. There was even a printing press on board that issued a daily newspaper, the *Trans-Continental.* It is
50 no wonder James Norman Hall, author of *The Caine Mutiny,* said, "I can no more conceive of a world without railroads and trains to run on them than I can imagine wishing to live in such a world." **D**

In spite of his plush surroundings, the porter's job was anything but glamorous. He was viewed as a servant. At first these travelin' men didn't mind playing the role George Pullman had cast for them. They wore the mask very well.

Dressed in well-tailored blue uniforms,[3] the Pullman porters adhered to very specific rules of conduct issued by the Pullman Company. Although a pleasant "good morning" or "good afternoon" when greeting each boarding
60 passenger was all that was originally required, many porters took the time to learn the names of their regular passengers and greeted them by name— "Good morning, Mr. Smith"—and *always* with a broad smile. . . .

D GATHER AND ORGANIZE INFORMATION
Reread lines 46–52. What additional conveniences did Pullman introduce on the *Board of Trade Special?*

---

3. **well-tailored blue uniforms:** According to the Pullman Company rule book, porters were required to wear navy blue uniform coats, along with hats, ties, and polished black shoes, whenever they helped passengers outside the train. Inside the train, porters wore starched white jackets. In warmer weather, an all-white uniform was often worn.

Once the passengers were comfortably seated and their bags were stored, the porter attended to special requests. He might be handing out newspapers, helping a mother with restless children, or pointing out geographic points of interest to first-time travelers or foreign visitors.

The Pullman porter's primary focus was the customer's welfare. He was instructed—and very often tested—to answer all calls promptly and courteously, no matter what time the calls were made. **E**

Porters were expected to follow numerous rules for dress and behavior. On the train, a spotless white coat was required at all times. From the moment a train pulled into the station, a porter was "on call" to meet the passengers' every need.

When it was time to make the beds, the porter was expected to move with speed and agility. The company rule book was precise. According to Nathaniel Hall, a porter, the rule book specified "the proper handling of the linen closet—the proper method of folding and putting away clean linen and blankets, the correct way of stacking laundry bags and dirty, discarded bedding. A sheet, towel, or pillowcase once unfolded cannot be used again, although it may be spotless. Technically, it is dirty and must make a round trip to the laundry before it can reenter the service."

Porters were not allowed to make noise. "Noise was tabooed," reported Hall. "And even a soft knock on the top of the berth [was] forbidden. A porter must gently shake the curtains on the bedding from without."

Pullman demanded that all passengers were made to feel special. . . . Porters' salaries were deliberately kept low so they'd be dependent upon the tip to make ends meet.

The public knew that on a Pullman coach, the customer was always right. No exceptions. **F**

E GATHER AND ORGANIZE INFORMATION

In your chart, note how the porters were expected to act. What kinds of conveniences did these rules make possible?

F INFORMATIONAL TEXT

Review the facts in this informational text. Do you think most of them can be verified? Why or why not?

Comprehension

1. **Recall** Who was allowed to eat in the *Delmonico* dining car?

2. **Clarify** Reread line 56. What does this line mean?

Critical Analysis

3. **Evaluate an Informational Text** Would you describe this selection as well-researched and balanced? Support your answer.

4. **Organize Information** Review the information about porters that you gathered in your chart. How might you further organize this information into different categories? Explain.

Read for Information: Use Information to Write a Poem

> **WRITING PROMPT**
>
> Write a poem about traveling on a Pullman train from the point of view of a porter, a passenger, or even the train itself. Use sound devices in your poem, as well as details from the informational text.

To answer this prompt, choose a point of view. Then follow these steps:

1. Use the notes in your chart to help you imagine what your activities might be. Also decide on the thoughts, feelings, or concerns you might have as the speaker. Try to include the sounds, sights, and other sensations you might notice.

2. Write a first draft of your poem.

3. Read your first draft aloud to yourself, listening for places where you can use **repetition, onomatopoeia,** or **alliteration** to re-create sounds or add emphasis. Revise your poem to include these sound devices and any other changes.

4. Have a classmate recite your poem. Did he or she read it the way you had imagined? If not, you might need to change your punctuation or line breaks to better show how you want your poem to be read.

I'm Nobody! Who are You?

Poem by Emily Dickinson

Is the Moon Tired?

Poem by Christina Rossetti

Mooses

Poem by Ted Hughes

When do ATTITUDES *need adjusting?*

KEY IDEA When you're in a bad state of mind, even ordinary situations can seem awful. Then, when your state of mind, or **attitude,** changes, things no longer seem so bad. You might have heard people say that someone "needs an attitude adjustment." It usually means that the person makes himself or herself unhappy all the time. As you read the following poems, consider whether anyone in them might benefit from a little adjustment.

DISCUSS Think about something you generally have a bad attitude about—your chores, for example, or a visit to relatives you don't care for. Think about how your attitude affects your behavior. In a small group, come up with five ways to improve your attitude.

SECTION C   THE STAR JOURNAL   C9

Garfield

● LITERARY ANALYSIS: FIGURATIVE LANGUAGE

To describe people, places, or events in memorable ways, writers often use **figurative language,** or words used to express something more than their usual meanings. Three common types of figurative language are defined here:

- A **simile** is a comparison of two things, using the words *like* or *as.* (*Her eyes were like green emeralds.*)
- A **metaphor** is a comparison of two things without the words *like* or *as.* (*Her eyes were green emeralds.*)
- **Personification** is the technique of giving human qualities to an object, animal, or idea. (*The tea kettle sang happily.*)

As you read the following three poems, look for examples of figurative language and its effects.

Review: **Sound Devices**

● READING SKILL: MAKE INFERENCES

When you read poetry, you will sometimes have to **make inferences,** or make logical guesses, about the meaning of the poem. You can combine your own knowledge and experience with the language used in the poem to figure out any confusing lines. As you read, record each inference you make in a graphic organizer like the one shown.

Lines in Poem		My Knowledge		Inference
"I'm Nobody!" (line 1)	+	The word "nobody" could mean "nobody special."	=	The speaker isn't well-known.

▲ VOCABULARY IN CONTEXT

In the poems you are about to read, the following words are used to express different **attitudes.** To see how many you already know, use them to complete the sentences.

> **WORD LIST**   blunder   cackle   dreary   lectern

1. The lonely, awkward moose lives a _____ life.
2. He is big and sturdy, like a _____.
3. Often, he imagines he has heard the world _____ at him.
4. Clumsy and lost, he'll _____ on through the woods.

Detail of *The Son of Man* (1964), René Magritte.
© 2008 C. Herscovici, Brussels/Artists Rights Society
(ARS), New York. Photo © Christie's Images/Corbis.

I'm Nobody!
Who are You?

Emily Dickinson

I'm Nobody! Who are you?
Are you—Nobody—Too?
Then there's a pair of us!
Don't tell! they'd advertise—you know!

5 How **dreary**—to be—Somebody!
How public—like a Frog—
To tell one's name—the livelong June—
To an admiring Bog!¹ Ⓐ

dreary (drîr'ē) *adj.*
dismal, bleak, or boring

Ⓐ **FIGURATIVE
LANGUAGE**
In lines 5–8, the poet
compares a public
person—"Somebody"—
to a frog. In what ways
is this comparison
accurate?

---

1. **bog:** an area of soft, waterlogged ground.

Detail of *The Masterpiece on the Mysteries* (1955),
René Magritte. Oil on canvas. © 2008 C. Herscivici,
Brusssels/Artists Rights Society (ARS), New York.
Photo © Christie's Images/SuperStock.

Is the Moon
Tired?

Christina Rossetti

Is the moon tired? she looks so pale
Within her misty veil: **B**
She scales the sky from east to west,
And takes no rest.

5 Before the coming of the night
The moon shows papery white;
Before the dawning of the day
She fades away. **C**

B MAKE INFERENCES
What is the "misty veil"
mentioned in line 2?

**C FIGURATIVE
LANGUAGE**
What human qualities
does Rossetti give to the
moon?

Mooses

Ted Hughes

The goofy Moose, the walking-house frame, **D**
Is lost
In the forest. He bumps, he **blunders,** he stands.

With massy bony thoughts sticking out near his ears—
5 Reaching out palm upwards, to catch whatever might be
    falling from heaven—
He tries to think,
Leaning their huge weight
On the **lectern** of his front legs.

10 He can't find the world!
Where did it go? What does a world look like?
The Moose
Crashes on, and crashes into a lake, and stares at the
    mountain and cries
15 "Where do I belong? This is no place!"

He turns and drags half the lake out after him
And charges the **cackling** underbrush—

He meets another Moose.
He stares, he thinks "It's only a mirror!"

D **FIGURATIVE LANGUAGE**
Reread line 1. Explain why you think the poet makes this comparison.

blunder (blŭn′dər) v. to move clumsily

lectern (lĕk′tərn) n. a stand that holds books, a laptop computer, or papers for someone giving a speech or lecture

cackle (kăk′əl) v. to make a sound of shrill laughter or chatter

Splash, Nancy Glazier. Oil, 26″ × 34″.

20 "Where is the world?" he groans, "O my lost world!
And why am I so ugly?
And why am I so far away from my feet?"

He weeps.
Hopeless drops drip from his droopy lips. **E**

25 The other Moose just stands there doing the same.

Two dopes of the deep woods. **F**

E SOUND DEVICES
How does the **alliteration** in line 24 help you to picture the moose?

F MAKE INFERENCES
Who might the speaker be referring to in the last line?

Comprehension

1. **Recall** In "Mooses," what does the moose think when he meets another moose?

2. **Clarify** According to the speaker in "I'm Nobody! Who are You?" what does a person do when he or she is a "Somebody"?

3. **Clarify** In "Is the Moon Tired?" what does the speaker think made the moon tired and pale?

Literary Analysis

4. **Understand Figurative Language** Choose one of the **metaphors** in "Mooses" and rewrite it as a **simile.**

5. **Analyze Form** What is unusual about the punctuation and capitalization in "I'm Nobody! Who are You?" Explain the effect of the punctuation on your reading of the poem.

6. **Compare and Contrast** The poems by Emily Dickinson and Christina Rossetti have the same number of lines and **stanzas,** or groups of lines. What are their other similarities? What are their differences?

7. **Interpret Symbol** A symbol is a person, place, or thing that stands for something other than itself. What might the moose in "Mooses" symbolize? Think about the way he is described and the **attitude** he expresses in the poem. Explain your answer.

8. **Evaluate Inferences** Look back at the graphic organizers you filled in as you read. Which of the three poems were you able to infer the most about? Tell why it might have been easier to make logical guesses about the meanings in that poem.

9. **Make Judgments** Reread "Mooses" and use a web like the one shown to record details in the poem that are funny or sad. Is "Mooses" a mostly sad poem or a mostly humorous one? Support your opinion.

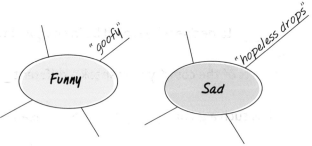

Extension and Challenge

10. **Creative Project: Writing** We often think of the things around us, such as cars, computers, or pets, as having personalities of their own. Choose an animal or object. Using **personification,** write a poem that shows how the animal or object you chose has human qualities. Share your poem with the class.

Vocabulary in Context

VOCABULARY PRACTICE

To show your understanding of the vocabulary words, choose the letter
of the term that is most closely related to the boldfaced word.

1. **blunder:** (a) dance, (b) cook, (c) stumble, (d) mumble
2. **lectern:** (a) voter, (b) guide, (c) desk, (d) chair
3. **cackle:** (a) laugh, (b) gather, (c) cry, (d) punish
4. **dreary:** (a) heavy, (b) gloomy, (c) ready, (d) old

VOCABULARY IN WRITING

Suppose the second moose in "Mooses" could speak. Write a short paragraph
in which he gives advice to his fellow moose. Use at least two vocabulary
words. You might want to start like this.

> **EXAMPLE SENTENCE**
>
> *Life as a moose doesn't have to be so **dreary**.*

VOCABULARY STRATEGY: THE LATIN ROOT *lect*

The vocabulary word *lectern* contains the Latin root *lect,* which
means "to choose" or "to read." This root appears in many English
words. You can use other word parts and context clues to figure
out the meaning of words containing the root *lect*.

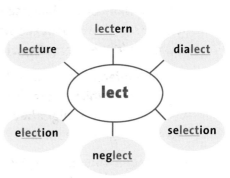

PRACTICE Choose the word from the web shown that best
completes each sentence. Use context clues, or, if necessary,
use a dictionary.

1. We held a(n) _____ to decide who would be in charge of the
   Student Council.
2. People in other parts of the country may speak a different _____
   of English.
3. Since this store has such a great _____, you can buy nearly anything
   here.
4. The teacher's _____ on literature was long, but interesting.
5. The house had been abandoned for years and showed signs of _____.

VOCABULARY PRACTICE
For more practice, go
to the **Vocabulary Center**
at **ClassZone.com.**

who knows if the moon's
Poem by E. E. Cummings

Two Limericks
Poems by Edward Lear and Ogden Nash

Can LANGUAGE *surprise you?*

KEY IDEA Writers inform us, entertain us, and often persuade us to see the world in a new light. Much of what people read daily—such as newspaper articles—is written to achieve a serious goal. Still, you can always find some literature that is meant to be fun! The three poems you are about to read take a playful look at **language.**

WEB IT Try using language in an unexpected way. Think of something to describe, such as the sky. Instead of writing about the way it looks, try to describe how it sounds, feels, tastes, or smells. Create a spider map to organize your response.

LITERARY ANALYSIS: FORM IN POETRY

The way a poem looks on the page, with its shape and number of lines, is called its **form.** A poem's form is one of the things that give the poem its sound and meaning. The poems you are about to read have different forms.

- The poem by E. E. Cummings is an example of **free verse.** This form does not contain regular patterns of rhythm, rhyme, or line length.
- The poems by Edward Lear and Ogden Nash are limericks. A **limerick** is a short, five-line poem about something silly or lighthearted. Read the limericks out loud and notice their fun, singsong rhythm.

As you read "who knows if the moon's" and the two limericks, pay attention to any differences and similarities among them.

READING STRATEGY: MONITOR

Some things you read will require you to work harder to understand them. One way to do this is to **monitor,** or check, your understanding as you read. Use the following tips:

- Stop occasionally and try to restate what you've just read.
- When you come across a word or idea that you don't understand, **reread** the passage.
- To **clarify** a confusing detail, or make it more understandable, look at the surrounding words and phrases for clues to the detail's meaning.

As you read the poems, use a graphic organizer like the one shown to record phrases or lines that give you trouble. Also note what meanings become clearer as you reread or clarify them.

Phrases or Lines	Why It's Confusing	My Notes
"in the sky—filled with pretty people?" (Cummings, line 3)	Are the people in the sky or in the balloon?	Rereading the first two lines tells me that the people are in the balloon.

Author Online

E. E. Cummings: A New Kind of Poet From age 8 to age 22, E. E. Cummings wrote one poem a day. While in college, he began to experiment with his writing. He ignored "proper" grammar and punctuation to write in a way that he felt best expressed his feelings.

E.E. Cummings 1894–1962

Edward Lear: An Accidental Poet Edward Lear considered himself an artist, and he first became famous for his drawings. Then he began writing limericks to entertain his employer's grandchildren. Lear's skill at writing these five-line nonsense poems was key to his lasting fame.

Edward Lear 1812–1888

Ogden Nash: A Humorous Success Odgen Nash's early serious poems were rarely published. When he started writing humorous verse, however, Nash quickly found success.

Ogden Nash 1902–1971

 MORE ABOUT THE AUTHOR For more on these poets, visit the **Literature Center at ClassZone.com.**

who knows
if the moon's

E. E. Cummings

who knows if the moon's
a balloon,coming out of a keen city
in the sky—filled with pretty people?
(and if you and i should

5 get into it,if they
should take me and take you into their balloon,
why then
we'd go up higher with all the pretty people **A**

than houses and steeples and clouds:
10 go sailing
away and away sailing into a keen
city which nobody's ever visited,where

always
          it's
15   Spring)and everyone's
in love and flowers pick themselves **B**

A MONITOR
Reread lines 4–8. What would happen if "you and i" got into the balloon?

B FORM IN POETRY
Reread lines 13–16. Why do you think Cummings broke these lines the way he did?

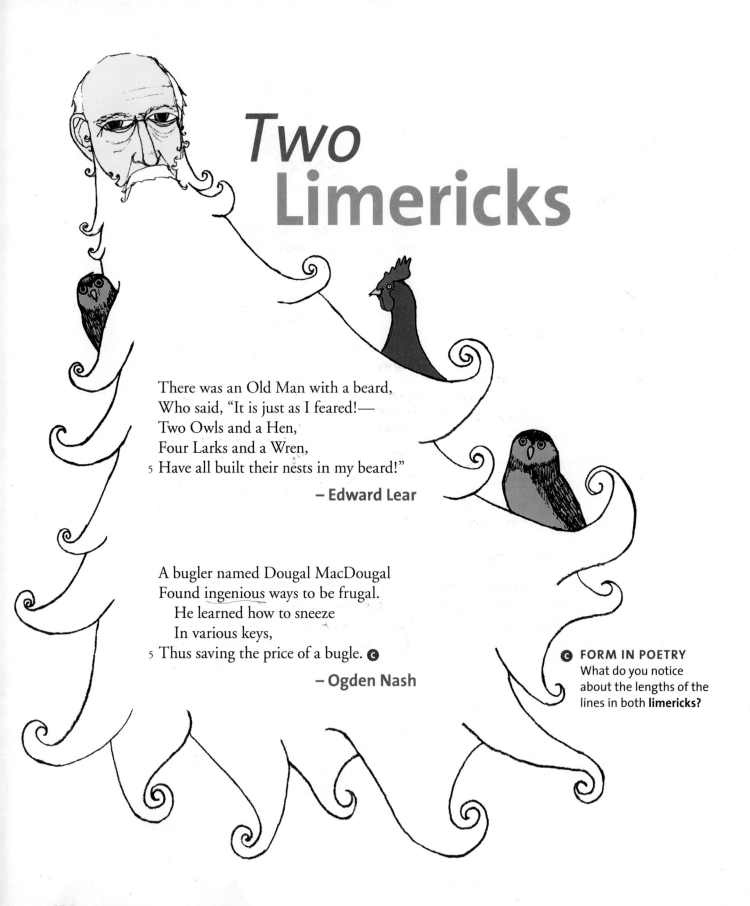

Two Limericks

There was an Old Man with a beard,
Who said, "It is just as I feared!—
Two Owls and a Hen,
Four Larks and a Wren,
5 Have all built their nests in my beard!"

– Edward Lear

A bugler named Dougal MacDougal
Found ingenious ways to be frugal.
   He learned how to sneeze
   In various keys,
5 Thus saving the price of a bugle. **C**

– Ogden Nash

C FORM IN POETRY
What do you notice about the lengths of the lines in both **limericks?**

Comprehension

1. **Recall** In "who knows if the moon's," to what does the speaker compare the moon?

2. **Recall** In the first limerick, what does the Old Man find in his beard?

3. **Clarify** In the second limerick, why doesn't Dougal need a bugle?

Literary Analysis

4. **Monitor** Look back at the graphic organizer you completed as you read. What parts of "who knows if the moon's" were you able to understand better after **rereading?**

5. **Compare and Contrast Form** Using a chart like the one shown, compare and contrast the forms of the poems.

6. **Analyze Humor** A **limerick** is a nonsense poem, meant to amuse its readers and poke fun at its subjects. What is especially funny in each of the limericks on page 606?

7. **Analyze Free Verse** Does the free verse **form** work well with the subject matter of "who knows if the moon's"? Explain why or why not.

	"who knows if the moon's"	Two Limericks
Rhythm and Rhyme	no regular rhythm or rhyme	regular rhythm, regular rhyme pattern (aabba)
Lines and Stanzas		
Shape		

Extension and Challenge

8. **Big Question Activity** Look back at the spider map you filled out on page 602 to experiment with **language.** Using the descriptions you recorded there, write your own limerick or free verse poem. If you choose to write a **limerick,** give it a regular rhythm and follow the limerick rhyme pattern (*aabba*). Recall that **free verse** should not have a regular rhythm or pattern of rhyme.

9. **Speaking and Listening** In a poetry slam, people take turns getting up and reading their poetry to an audience. The readers must focus both on what they are saying and how they are saying it. Using the poems you and your classmates wrote for question 8, start a poetry slam in the classroom. Use your voice to add emphasis to important words in your poem.

Good Hotdogs / Ricos Hot Dogs
Poem by Sandra Cisneros

Ode to an Artichoke / Oda a la Alcachofa
Poem by Pablo Neruda

When is FOOD more than fuel?

KEY IDEA If **food** were only useful for keeping us alive, people would probably just eat the same thing day after day. However, food serves many purposes. Sitting down to eat allows us to spend time with family and friends, celebrate important events, and build traditions. For the two writers whose poems you are about to read, food sparks memories and the imagination as well as nourishing the body.

DISCUSS In a small group, discuss the meals your family prepares on special occasions such as holidays or birthdays. Explain how these foods became part of your family traditions. What emotions and memories do you connect with each traditional meal?

● LITERARY ANALYSIS: TONE

Imagine a friend said to you, "Hey, nice shoes." You would know whether this comment was honest or sarcastic based on your friend's tone, or the attitude in his or her voice.

Recognizing tone is also important when you want to know the meaning of a poem. The **tone** of a poem is the poet's attitude toward the subject. Tone can usually be described with a single word, such as *humorous, respectful,* or *sarcastic.* Poets create tone by using words and details to describe the subject and by creating a speaker, or voice that tells the poem.

The two poems in this lesson are about food. As you read, use these clues to identify each poet's attitude:

- Identify the **subject.** Ask, "Is the poet writing about something more than food?"

- Notice the **images** and descriptions. Are they serious, silly, frightening, or something else?

- Decide how the **speaker** feels. Does the speaker seem happy, sad, angry, or amused?

Review: **Personification**

● READING STRATEGY: SET A PURPOSE FOR READING

Your **purpose for reading** "Good Hotdogs" and "Ode to an Artichoke" is to identify the tone of each poem and then compare and contrast the tones. Read the poems twice. First read them to understand what they are about. The second time you read, look for images and descriptions that are clues to tone. Record the clues in a chart like the one shown. You will be asked to do more with this chart later.

	"Good Hotdogs"	"Ode to an Artichoke"
What is the subject of the poem?	memories of sharing hot dogs with a friend	the life of an artichoke
Which images and descriptions stand out?	"We'd run/ Straight from school"	
How does the speaker feel?		

Author Online

Sandra Cisneros: Doubly Rich Writer
As a young child, Sandra Cisneros spoke English to her mother and Spanish to her father. Cisneros says bilingual speakers are "doubly rich. You have two ways of looking at the world."

Sandra Cisneros born 1954

Pablo Neruda: Poet from the Start Growing up in Chile, Ricardo Basoalto was inspired by his country's plants and trees. By age ten, he was already thinking of himself as a poet. At age 13, he published his poetry—after renaming himself Pablo Neruda. In 1971 Neruda received the Nobel Prize for literature.

Pablo Neruda 1904–1973

 MORE ABOUT THE AUTHOR
For more on these poets, visit the **Literature Center** at ClassZone.com.

Background

Reading Poetry in Translation
Sometimes a poem written in one language is translated into another one so that more readers can enjoy it. A translation will not always have the same rhyme or rhythm as the original poem, but it re-creates the same feelings and ideas.

GOOD HOTDOGS

Sandra Cisneros

for Kiki

Fifty cents apiece
To eat our lunch
We'd run
Straight from school
5 Instead of home
Two blocks   Ⓐ
Then the store
That smelled like steam
You ordered
10 Because you had the money
Two hotdogs and two pops for here
Everything on the hotdogs
Except pickle lily[1]
Dash those hotdogs
15 Into buns and splash on
All that good stuff
Yellow mustard and onions
And french fries piled on top all

Ⓐ **TONE**
Reread lines 1–6. Which
words in these lines
show that the **speaker**
and her friend are
eager to eat hot dogs
together?

---

1. **pickle lily:** or piccalilli, a type of relish.

RICOS HOT DOGS

Sandra Cisneros

para Kiki

Cincuenta centavos cada uno
Para almorzar
Corríamos
Directo de la escuela
5 Sin pasar por la casa
Dos cuadras
Y a la tienda
Que olía a vapor
Tú los pedías
10 Porque traías el dinero
Dos *hot dogs* y dos sodas
Los *hot dogs* con todo
Menos pepinillos
Pon de volada las salchichas
15 En los panes y échales
Todo lo rico
Mostaza y cebolla
Y papas fritas encima todo

Rolled up in a piece of wax
20 Paper for us to hold hot
In our hands
Quarters on the counter
Sit down
Good hotdogs
25 We'd eat
Fast till there was nothing left
But salt and poppy seeds even
The little burnt tips
Of french fries
30 We'd eat
You humming
And me swinging my legs **B**

B TONE
Which words and descriptions in lines 19–32 might hint at a joyful attitude?

Envuelto en papel
20 Encerado para agarrarlo calientito
En las manos
Pesetas en el mostrador
Y a sentarnos
Ricos *hot dogs*
25 Nos los comíamos
Rápido hasta que no quedaba nada
Más que sal y semillas hasta
Las puntitas quemadas
De las papas
30 Nos las comíamos
Tú tarareando
Y yo columpiando las piernas

Translated into Spanish by Liliana Valenzuela

ODE TO AN ARTICHOKE

Pablo Neruda

The soft-hearted
artichoke
put on armor,
stood at attention, raised
5 a small turret[1]
and kept itself
watertight
under
its scales. **C**
10 Beside it,
the fertile plants
tangled,
turned into
tendrils, cattails,
15 moving bulbs.
In the subsoil
the red-whiskered
carrot slept,
the grapevine
20 parched the shoots
that wine climbs up,
the cabbage
busied itself
with trying on skirts,
25 the marjoram[2]
with making the world smell sweet, **D**

C TONE
Reread lines 1–9.
What ideas about the
artichoke do you get
from these lines?

D PERSONIFICATION
Reread lines 1–26. What
human qualities does
Pablo Neruda give the
artichoke, the carrot,
and the cabbage?

---

1. **turret:** a small tower.

2. **marjoram** (mär′jər-əm): a sweet herb used in cooking.

ODA A LA ALCACHOFA

Pablo Neruda

La alcachofa
de tierno corazón
se vistió de guerrero,
erecta, construyó
5 una pequeña cúpula,
se mantuvo
impermeable
bajo
sus escamas,
10 a su lado
los vegetales locos
se encresparon,
se hicieron
zarcillos, espadañas,
15 bulbos conmovedores,
en el subsuelo
durmió la zanahoria
de bigotes rojos,
la viña
20 resecó los sarmientos
por donde sube el vino,
la col
se dedicó
a probarse faldas,
25 el orégano
a perfumar el mundo,

and the gentle
artichoke
in the kitchen garden,
30 equipped like a soldier,
burnished[3]
like a grenade,
was full of itself.
And one day,
35 packed with others,
in big willow
baskets, it marched
through the market
to act out its dream—
40 the militia.[4]
It was never as martial[5]
in rows
as at the fair.
Among the vegetables,
45 men in white shirts
were
the artichokes'
marshals,
closed ranks,
50 commands, **E**

E **TONE**
Which **images** in lines
27–50 help you imagine
the artichoke as a soldier
going into battle?

---

3. **burnished:** polished.
4. **militia** (mə-lĭsh′ə): military force used in emergencies.
5. **martial** (mär′shəl): relating to the armed forces.

y la dulce
alcachofa
allí en el huerto,
30 vestida de guerrero,
bruñida
como una granada,
orgullosa,
y un día
35 una con otra
en grandes cestos
de mimbre, caminó
por el mercado
a realizar su sueño:
40 la milicia.
En hileras
nunca fue tan marcial
como en la feria,
los hombres
45 entre las legumbres
con sus camisas blancas
eran
mariscales
de las alcachofas,
50 las filas apretadas,

the explosion
of a falling crate;
but
then
55 Maria
shows up
with her basket,
fearlessly
chooses
60 an artichoke,
studies it, squints at it
against the light like an egg,
buys it,
dumps it
65 into her bag
with a pair of shoes,
a white cabbage and
a bottle
of vinegar
70 till
she enters the kitchen
and drowns it
in the pot. **F**
And so
75 this armored vegetable
men call an artichoke
ends its career
in peace.
Later,
80 scale by scale,
we strip
this delight
and dine on
the peaceful pulp
85 of its green heart. **G**

Translated into English by Cheli Durán

F TONE
Which **images** and
descriptions in lines
55–73 create the most
vivid picture?

G TONE
Reread lines 74–85. How
can you tell that the
speaker feels sympathy
and respect for the
artichoke?

las voces de comando,
y la detonación
de una caja que cae,
pero
55 entonces
viene
María
con su cesto,
escoge
60 una alcachofa,
no le teme,
la examina, la observa
contra la luz como si fuera un huevo,
la compra,
65 la confunde
en su bolsa
con un par de zapatos,
con un repollo y una
botella
70 de vinagre
hasta
que entrando a la cocina
la sumerge en la olla.
Así termina
75 en paz
esta carrera
del vegetal armado
que se llama alcachofa,
luego
80 escama por escama
desvestimos
la delicia
y comemos
la pacífica pasta
85 de su corazón verde.

Comprehension

1. **Recall** In "Good Hotdogs," how much does a hot-dog lunch cost?

2. **Summarize** In "Ode to an Artichoke," what happens to the artichoke after Maria buys it?

Literary Analysis

3. **Analyze Word Choice** Which words and phrases in "Good Hotdogs" give you a vivid picture of the two friends eating **food** together?

4. **Draw Conclusions** Are there any clues in "Good Hotdogs" about the ages of the **speaker** and the speaker's friend? Decide how old you think they are. Support your conclusion with details from the poem.

5. **Compare and Contrast** How is the artichoke different from the other vegetables in the garden?

6. **Make Judgments** Reread lines 74–78 of "Ode to an Artichoke." Does the artichoke end "its career in peace"? Explain your ideas.

7. **Analyze an Ode** A traditional ode is a serious poem written to praise a person, an event, or something in nature in a dignified way. How is "Ode to an Artichoke" like a traditional ode? How is it different?

Comparing Tone

Now that you have read both poems, you can finish filling in your chart. Be sure to add the two final questions to your chart.

	"Good Hotdogs"	*"Ode to an Artichoke"*
What is the subject of the poem?	memories of sharing hot dogs with a friend	the life of an artichoke
Which images and descriptions stand out?	"We'd run/Straight from school" "The store/That smelled like steam"	
How does the speaker feel?	enthusiastic, warm, happy	
What is the tone, or the poet's attitude?		
Do the poems have similar or different tones?		

Writing for Assessment

1. READ THE PROMPT

Tone is an important element in any piece of writing. In writing assessments, you may be asked to compare and contrast the tone of two poems, stories, or essays.

PROMPT

Although "Good Hotdogs" and "Ode to an Artichoke" both touch on the subject of food, their tones are not exactly the same. In three paragraphs, compare the two poems. Describe the tone of each poem, and explain whether the tones are more similar or different. Support your response by using details from the poems.

◀ **STRATEGIES IN ACTION**

1. I need to identify the **similarities and differences** between the poems.
2. I need to describe each poet's **attitude** toward the subject and decide if those attitudes are more alike or different.
3. I need to include **examples** of images, descriptions, and the speaker's feelings to support my ideas.

2. PLAN YOUR WRITING

Using the chart you filled out for the two poems, consider how the tones of the poems are similar and different. Then think about how to set up your response.

I. Introduce poems and main idea
II. Describe tone in 1st poem
III. Describe tone in 2nd poem and compare to 1st poem

- Decide on a main idea for your response.
- Reread the poems and your chart to make sure you have enough examples to support your ideas.
- Make an outline to help organize your response. This sample outline shows one way you might organize your three paragraphs.

3. DRAFT YOUR RESPONSE

Paragraph 1 Include the titles of the poems and the names of the poets. State whether the tones of the poems are more similar or different.
Paragraph 2 Describe the subject and tone of the first poem. Identify the images, descriptions, and speaker's feelings that help develop the tone.
Paragraph 3 Describe the subject and tone of the second poem. Explain which images, descriptions, and speaker's feelings help develop the tone. Tell how the tone is similar to and different from the tone of the first poem.
Revision Ask two classmates to read your response and look for errors such as sentence fragments and run-on sentences. Revise your writing as needed.

Writing Workshop

Personal Response to a Poem

Poems like the ones in this unit can help you see the world in new ways. Writing down your response to a poem can help you appreciate the work and share your feelings, too. Get started on your own response to a poem by following the **Writer's Road Map**.

WRITER'S ROAD MAP
Personal Response to a Poem

WRITING PROMPT 1

Writing from Literature Choose a poem that you especially liked, a poem that you strongly disliked, or a poem that puzzled you. Write a personal response that explains how you reacted to the poem. Briefly describe the poem so that readers who don't know it will understand your ideas.

Poems to Explore

- "Something Told the Wild Geese"
- "I'm Nobody! Who are You?"
- "Good Hotdogs / Ricos Hot Dogs"

WRITING PROMPT 2

Writing from the Real World Songs are poems, too. Write an essay about a song lyric that is especially meaningful to you. Give specific examples and details from the song so that readers will know why the song matters to you.

Music to Explore

- a favorite song
- a traditional song from your culture
- a song that tells a story, such as a ballad or a rap

 WRITING TOOLS
For prewriting, revision, and editing tools, visit the **Writing Center at ClassZone.com.**

KEY TRAITS

1. IDEAS
- Clearly presents an **overall response** to the poem or song
- Gives **details and quotations** to support the key ideas

2. ORGANIZATON
- Begins by **identifying** the poem or song
- Provides enough **information** about the poem or song so readers can understand the response
- Uses **transitions** to show how ideas are related

3. VOICE
- Has a **tone** that shows the writer's honest response

4. WORD CHOICE
- Uses **precise words** to explain the response

5. SENTENCE FLUENCY
- Varies **sentence lengths**

6. CONVENTIONS
- Uses **correct grammar, spelling, and punctuation**

Part 1: Analyze a Student Model

Vicki C. Brennan
Oakton Charter School

Why I Like "who knows if the moon's"

Sometimes I dream about flying to the moon, but I always wake up before I can go exploring. That's why I really liked the poem "who knows if the moon's" by E. E. Cummings. I liked the way the poet played with words and line lengths. The poem showed me one possible
5 ending to my dream and made me want to keep on dreaming—about the moon and anything else.

The poem talks about the moon as a big balloon "filled with pretty people" and invites readers to sail away to a place where "everyone's / in love and flowers pick themselves." I really liked that image a lot. First,
10 it made me feel light and happy. After all, people have to leave their problems behind when they're up in a balloon. The image also surprised me, because I had never thought of the moon as a balloon before. I had never pictured a balloon filled with people. Also, I definitely had never heard of flowers picking themselves. This poem is full of surprises, I
15 thought.

When I looked at the form of the poem, I got more surprises. First of all, Cummings doesn't capitalize words the way most people do. For example, none of the words in the title start with capital letters. Then, at the end of the first stanza, he writes the pronoun *I* as *i*. The only word
20 that begins with a capital letter in the whole poem is *Spring,* a word that isn't usually capitalized. Because the poem had so few capital letters, I felt a little bit unsteady, like I was up in this strange balloon.

KEY TRAITS IN ACTION

Begins by **identifying** the poem and author. Presents an **overall response** that explains how much the writer liked it and why.

The highlighted sentence gives **information** about the poem. The other sentences explain the personal response to that information. A mix of **sentence lengths** keeps the response interesting.

Transitions make the response easier to understand.

The lines are all different lengths, too. They don't stop at the end of a thought, the way I expected them to. For instance, the first line of the poem, "who knows if the moon's," just left me hanging. In the second stanza, there's a line with nine words, then one with two words, and then another one with nine. The lines that start with "it's" and "Spring" don't even begin at the left of the page. Reading these lines made me feel like I was swaying back and forth in the basket of a hot-air balloon. Maybe that's why Cummings wrote them that way.

I also noticed the rhyming words *moon* and *balloon,* and *city* and *pretty.* These made me feel bouncy because of their sound. The surprise was that they weren't all at the ends of the lines, the way rhyming words usually are in poems. They bobbed me around when I wasn't expecting it, like a balloon floating on the air.

By the end of the poem, I felt like I was soaring in the air in a magic moon world. Cummings did such surprising things with words and lines that I was ready to believe that the moon is a balloon, that flowers do pick themselves, and that anything I imagine can come true.

Details and **quotations** help to show how the poem's unusual line lengths affected the personal response.

Precise words make the personal response clear.

Admiring **tone** shows the writer's positive reaction to the poem.

2

REVISING AND EDITING

What Should I Do?	**What Does It Look Like?**

1. Enliven how you start.
- Ask a peer reader, "Does my introduction grab your attention?"
- To make a stronger first impression, consider adding a personal story, a quotation, or a question.

See page 628: Ask a Peer Reader

▶ *Sometimes I dream about flying to the moon, but I always wake up before I can go exploring. That's why ₍ᴧ₎I really liked the poem "who knows if the moon's" by E. E. Cummings. I liked the way the poet played with words and line lengths. The poem showed me one possible ending to my dream and made me want to keep on dreaming—about the moon and anything else.*

2. Pick specific words.
- <u>Underline</u> vague words—*interesting, good, bad, nice, dumb, weird, maybe, thing, stuff, kind of, sort of*—that don't tell your reader exactly what you mean.
- Replace them with precise words.

▶ *also surprised me,*
The image <u>was interesting</u> because I had never thought ₍ᴧ₎of the moon as a balloon before.

I also noticed the rhyming words <u>moon</u> and <u>balloon</u>, and <u>city</u> and <u>pretty</u>. These made me feel <u>good.</u> bouncy because of their sound.

3. Think about sentence length.
- Reread your essay, this time focusing on sentence length.
- If you don't have a mix of long and short sentences, combine or divide some sentences to give readers variety.

▶ ~~In the second stanza, there's a line with nine words. Then there's one with two words. After that, there's one with nine words again.~~

In the second stanza, there's a line with nine words, then one with two words, and then another one with nine.

4. Help your reader by using transitions.
- Draw a box around each transition. How many did you use?
- If necessary, add transitions that show your reader how your ideas are related.

▶ *First, it made me feel light and happy.*

By the end of the poem,
₍ᴧ₎I felt like I was soaring in the air in a magic moon world.

Personal Response to a Poem

Apply the Rubric

A strong personal response to a poem . . .

☑ names the poem or song and tells the writer's overall response to it

☑ includes enough information about the poem or song to make the response understandable

☑ supports key ideas with details and quotations

☑ has a tone that shows the writer's response to the poem or song

☑ links ideas with transitions

☑ uses exact, specific words

☑ adds variety by using short and long sentences

Ask a Peer Reader

• Do you understand why I responded to the work the way I did? Why or why not?

• What details might make my introduction livelier?

• Do you need more information about this song or poem? If so, what?

Literary Terms

form—the distinctive way a poem is laid out on the page

free verse—poetry with no regular patterns of rhythm or rhyme

rhythm—beat caused by stressed and unstressed words

rhyme—repeated sounds at the ends of words

speaker—the voice that "talks" to the reader (like a narrator in fiction)

stanza—group of lines in a poem

Check Your Grammar

When quoting poems or songs, copy the words exactly as the author wrote them. Put quotation marks at the beginning and end of the quotation. Use a slash (/) to show where one line ends and another begins.

> The poem talks about the moon as a big balloon "filled with pretty people" and invites readers to sail away to a place where "everyone's / in love and flowers pick themselves."

Writing Online

PUBLISHING OPTIONS
For publishing options, visit the **Writing Center** at **ClassZone.com.**

ASSESSMENT PREPARATION
For writing and grammar assessment practice, go to the **Assessment Center** at **ClassZone.com.**

Oral Interpretation of a Poem

Poems and songs are meant to be heard. By giving an oral interpretation, you can let your audience hear the poem or song you chose.

Planning the Oral Interpretation

1. **Read the poem or song aloud.** Listen for places you can change your volume or speed to make the meaning clearer. Also, think about what gestures or facial expressions you could make to help your audience understand the meaning.

2. **Make a script.** Copy the poem or song, leaving space between the lines. Use highlighters to mark places where you will speak more loudly, softly, quickly, or slowly. Add notes showing when to make gestures or facial expressions.

> (and if you and i should
> get into it, if they
> should take me and take you into their
> balloon, why then
> we'd go up higher with all the pretty people
> than houses and steeples and clouds:
>
> *Notes*
>
> Green = Say softly. Blue = Speed up, raise arms, and look up.

3. **Practice your presentation.** Read it in front of a mirror and to a friend or family member.

Performing the Oral Interpretation

1. **Stay calm.** Look up from your script often and make eye contact with your audience. Remember that you're an expert on this poem or song.

2. **Act naturally.** Use a normal tone of voice and keep your gestures simple. This will help your audience stay focused on the poem or song, not on you.

3. **Ask for feedback.** Ask one or two classmates what they thought of your interpretation. Use their comments to plan how to improve your next presentation.

See page R80: Evaluate an Oral Interpretation

Reading Comprehension

DIRECTIONS *Read these poems and answer the questions that follow.*

Rain Sizes

John Ciardi

Rain comes in various sizes.
Some rain is as small as a mist.
It tickles your face with surprises,
And tingles as if you'd been kissed.

5 Some rain is the size of a sprinkle
And doesn't put out all the sun.
You can see the drops sparkle and twinkle,
And a rainbow comes out when it's done.

Some rain is as big as a nickle[1]
10 And comes with a crash and a hiss.
It comes down too heavy to tickle.
It's more like a splash than a kiss.

When it rains the right size and you're wrapped in
Your rainclothes, it's fun out of doors.
15 But run home before you get trapped in
The big rain that rattles and roars.

---

1. **nickle:** a spelling variation of the word *nickel*.

Rain in Ohio

Mary Oliver

The robin cries: *rain!*
The crow calls: *plunder!*

The blacksnake climbing
in the vines halts
5 his long ladder of muscle

while the thunderheads whirl up
out of the white west,

their dark hooves nicking
the tall trees as they come.

10 *Rain, rain, rain!* sings the robin
frantically, then flies for cover.

The crow hunches.
The blacksnake

pours himself swift and heavy
15 into the ground.

Comprehension

DIRECTIONS *Answer these questions about "Rain Sizes."*

1. Which statement describes the pattern of rhyme in this poem?

    A The first and third and the second and fourth lines in each stanza rhyme.

    B The first and second lines in each stanza rhyme.

    C All four lines in each stanza have the same rhyme.

    D The first and second and the third and fourth lines in each stanza rhyme.

2. Which description of rain is a simile?

    A "Rain comes in various sizes." (line 1)

    B "Some rain is the size of a sprinkle" (line 5)

    C "And a rainbow comes out when it's done." (line 8)

    D "Some rain is as big as a nickle" (line 9)

3. The simile in line 4 compares misty rain to

    A someone's face

    B a kiss

    C a surprise

    D rainbows

4. Which phrase is an example of onomatopoeia?

    A "tickles your face" (line 3)

    B "put out all the sun" (line 6)

    C "run home before" (line 15)

    D "rattles and roars" (line 16)

5. Which image appeals to your sense of hearing?

    A "Some rain is as small as a mist."

    B "You can see the drops sparkle and twinkle,"

    C "And comes with a crash and a hiss."

    D "It comes down too heavy to tickle."

6. You can infer that the speaker in "Rain Sizes"

    A does not notice the rain

    B enjoys all types of rain

    C stays indoors when it rains

    D wishes the sun would come out

DIRECTIONS *Answer these questions about "Rain in Ohio."*

7. The metaphor in line 5, "his long ladder of muscle," emphasizes the snake's

    A length and power

    B speed and cunning

    C size and dangerousness

    D scaly skin and strong back

8. Reread lines 6–9. The thunderheads with "their dark hooves nicking" are being compared to

    A tumbleweeds rolling

    B wagons rumbling

    C horses galloping

    D trees swaying

9. Reread lines 10–11. You can infer that when the robin sings *"Rain, rain, rain!"* in line 10 it is

   A expressing joy

   B sounding a warning

   C signaling its location

   D looking for a mate

10. The metaphor in lines 13–15 compares the blacksnake's movement to

   A flowing liquid

   B distant thunder

   C heavy rains

   D the still air

11. How do the birds and the snake seem to feel about the approaching storm?

   A curious

   B confused

   C happy

   D fearful

DIRECTIONS *Answer this question about both poems.*

12. In both poems, the descriptions of rain

   A are scientific

   B include vivid imagery

   C use the same metaphors

   D have rhyming words

Written Response

SHORT RESPONSE *Write two or three sentences to answer each question.*

13. In "Rain Sizes," what idea does the speaker emphasize by repeating the phrase "some rain is"?

14. Do you think "Rain in Ohio" describes the approach of a wild thunderstorm or a gentle rain? Give two examples from the poem to support your idea.

EXTENDED RESPONSE *Write a short paragraph to answer this question.*

15. Find three images in "Rain in Ohio" that describe how the robin, the crow, and the blacksnake react to the storm. Are their reactions the same or different? Explain.

GO ON ➡

Vocabulary

DIRECTIONS *Use context clues to help you answer the following questions about specialized vocabulary words.*

1. The word *mist* in line 2 of "Rain Sizes" means

   A something that hides

   B a single drop of liquid

   C a haze that makes it hard to see

   D fine drops of water in the air

2. The word *sprinkle* in line 5 of "Rain Sizes" means a

   A light rainfall

   B scattering of items

   C sudden downpour

   D little piece of candy

3. The word *rainbow* in line 8 of "Rain Sizes" means

   A an unrealistic hope

   B a brightly colored fish

   C a wide assortment or collection

   D an arc of colors that appears in the sky

4. The word *thunderheads* in line 6 of "Rain in Ohio" means

   A loud noises heard in a storm

   B swollen parts of storm clouds

   C flashes of lightning shaped like a bolt

   D mythical birds that are thought to cause storms

DIRECTIONS *Use context clues and the definitions of Latin words and roots to answer the following questions.*

5. The Latin word *quiritare* means "to shriek or scream." Which word in the poems most likely comes from the word *quiritare?*

   A cries

   B calls

   C rattles

   D roars

6. The Latin word *assisa* means "a fixed quantity." Which word in the poems most likely comes from the word *assisa?*

   A swift

   B plunder

   C size

   D long

7. The prefix *co-* means "with," and the Latin word *operire* means "to close completely." Which word in the poems most likely comes from the Latin word *cooperire?*

   A crow

   B cover

   C home

   D ground

Writing & Grammar

DIRECTIONS *Use your knowledge of writing and grammar to answer the following questions.*

1. Which sentence shows correct subject-verb agreement?

   A My cousin play a midfield position in lacrosse.

   B My cousins plays a midfield position in lacrosse.

   C My cousin do play a midfield position in lacrosse.

   D My cousin plays a midfield position in lacrosse.

2. Which sentence shows correct subject-verb agreement?

   A There are stars out tonight.

   B There are star out tonight.

   C There is stars out tonight.

   D There was stars out tonight.

3. Which sentence shows correct subject-verb agreement?

   A Is the boat at the dock?

   B Are the boat at the dock?

   C Is the boats at the dock?

   D Was the boats at the dock?

4. Which sentence shows correct subject-verb agreement?

   A A coin and shells was in his pocket.

   B A coin and shells is in his pocket.

   C Coins and shells was in his pocket.

   D A coin and shells are in his pocket.

5. Which sentence shows correct subject-verb agreement?

   A Either the guides or the teacher explain the owl's diet.

   B Either the guide or the teacher explain the owl's diet.

   C Either the guide or the teacher explains the owl's diet.

   D Either the guide or the teachers explains the owl's diet.

6. Which sentence shows correct subject-verb agreement?

   A My brother and sisters sings in the chorus.

   B My brother and sisters is singing in the chorus.

   C My brother and sisters sing in the chorus.

   D My brothers and sister sings in the chorus.

7. Which sentence shows correct subject-verb agreement?

   A Was there empty seats on the bus?

   B Are there empty seats on the bus?

   C Are there an empty seat on the bus?

   D Is there empty seats on the bus?

STOP

Ideas for Independent Reading

Which questions from Unit 5 made an impression on you? Continue exploring with these books.

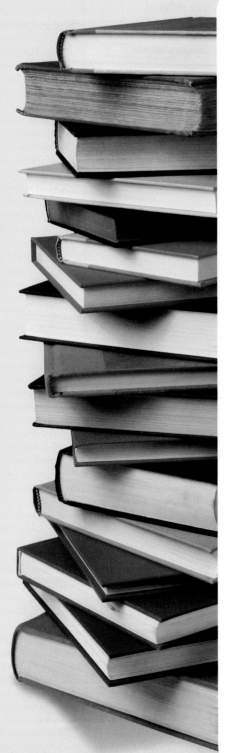

Why do we love sports?

Crash
by Jerry Spinelli

Sports can bring out the best or the worst in people. Crash Coogan, seventh-grade football star and part-time bully, is no different from anyone else—that is, until his grandfather, Scooter, comes for a visit and decides to stay.

Slam Dunk: Poems About Basketball
edited by Lillian Morrison

Forty-two poems describe such things as the brush of the ball as it leaves the tips of the fingers, the tension as the ball circles the rim, and the way the ball looks clinging to the side of the net as it goes in.

Strike Two
by Amy Goldman Koss

Gwen and Jess are ready for a summer of softball, but when the staff at the town newspaper goes on strike, things get ugly. Can Gwen hatch a plan that will bring the town and her team together again?

What are nature's mysteries?

Airborn
by Kenneth Oppel

A year after Matt pulled a dying balloonist onto his airship, he meets the man's granddaughter, Kate. Now he has to choose between loyalty to his captain and the desire to help Kate find proof of the fantastic creatures in her grandfather's journal.

Carver: A Life in Poems
by Marilyn Nelson

George Washington Carver was born a slave in 1864. His curiosity about nature pushed him to go to places African Americans had never been. By the time of his death in 1943, he had become an artist, an educator, and a world-renowned scientist.

Fossil Fish Found Alive: Discovering the Coelacanth
by Sally M. Walker

In 1938, Marjorie Courtenay-Latimer discovers a strange blue fin in a pile of specimens for her museum in South Africa. She thinks it is from a fish that was believed to be extinct.

When do attitudes need adjusting?

The Crow-Girl
by Bodil Bredsdorff

Before the Crow-Girl's grandmother died, she told the girl that some people feed you by looking at you, but others leave you ice-cold even in front of a roaring fire. Now that the girl is alone, will her grandmother's advice help her survive?

Technically, It's Not My Fault: Concrete Poems
by John Grandits

Robert is an ordinary boy with extraordinary ideas. One time he re-created Galileo's gravity experiment by using a tomato and a concrete block. It really wasn't his fault that the experiment went wrong.

The Penderwicks
by Jeanne Birdsall

When four eccentric sisters, their naturalist father, a canine escape-artist, two rabbits, a boy, and a gardening competition all come together, it's a summer no one can forget—even if Mrs. Tifton wishes she could.

Timeless Tales

MYTHS, LEGENDS, AND TALES

Why do we tell STORIES?

Think of a movie that taught you about a historical event, a television program that inspired you in some way, or a novel that kept you laughing from the first page to the last. **Stories** are told for many reasons—some simply entertain us, while others teach us a lesson. Many stories are told year after year to pass on cultural values and traditions from one generation to the next.

ACTIVITY Recall an experience you've had or a story you've heard that you'd like to share with others. Now get together with a small group. As you take turns telling stories, consider these questions:

- Why do you think each person decided to tell the story he or she did?

- Which story do you think you will remember and retell? Why?

Preview Unit Goals

LITERARY ANALYSIS	• Identify and analyze characteristics of myths, legends, tall tales, and folk tales • Identify cultural values in traditional literature • Identify and analyze universal themes
READING	• Develop strategies for reading, including visualizing and predicting • Identify cause-effect relationships • Summarize plot • Identify main ideas and supporting details; create an outline
WRITING AND GRAMMAR	• Write a problem-solution essay • Write a compare-contrast essay • Use capitalization correctly • Combine clauses to form compound and complex sentences
SPEAKING, LISTENING, AND VIEWING	• Create a class newspaper
VOCABULARY	• Use context clues, base words, and affixes to figure out the meanings of words • Use a dictionary, thesaurus, or synonym finder to find synonyms for words • Identify and use connotative meanings of words
ACADEMIC VOCABULARY	• myth • folk tale • cultural values • legend • tall tale • universal themes

Myths, Legends, and Tales

A young girl lives happily ever after, thanks to a fairy godmother and a glass slipper. A lion learns the value of a small friend. A knight defeats a hideous monster. Many stories that are still popular today, such as Aesop's fables and medieval legends, were first told hundreds, even thousands of years ago. Handed down by word of mouth and later recorded in writing, these stories do more than entertain. They help us to understand and appreciate other times and cultures.

Part 1: What Stories Live On?

In this unit, you will read many traditional stories that have stood the test of time, such as myths and several kinds of folk tales. Before you can learn from these stories, you need to know what to expect from them. Examine this graphic to discover the characteristics of myths, legends, and tall tales.

TRADITIONAL STORIES

MYTH
Story that was created to explain mysteries of the universe

- Often explains how something connected with humans or nature came to be
- Usually features gods, goddesses, and other beings with supernatural powers as well as human flaws

LEGEND
Story handed down from the past that is believed to be based on real people and events

- Tells about a hero or heroine with special powers and admirable qualities
- Describes the hero's or heroine's struggle against a powerful force

TALL TALE
Humorous story about events and characters that are exaggerated

- Often features a character who is "larger than life"—stronger, louder, or more extraordinary than a regular person
- Includes details that make events and the character's qualities seem unbelievable

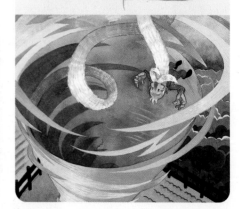

This myth comes from the Creek, a Native American tribe from the southern United States. What mysteries of the natural world does the myth explain?

How Day and Night Came

Creek myth retold by **Virginia Pounds Brown** and **Laurella Owens**

The question was: how shall day and night be divided? Some wanted it always to be daytime; others wanted it always to be night.

After much talk, the chipmunk said: "I see that the raccoon has rings on his tail divided equally, first a dark color and then a light color. I

5 think day and night should be divided like the rings on the raccoon's tail."

The animals were surprised at the wisdom of the chipmunk. They adopted his plan and divided day and night like the rings on the raccoon's tail, one succeeding the other in regular order.

10 The bear was so envious of the chipmunk's wisdom and of the attention given that small creature, that he attacked him. He scratched the chipmunk's back so deeply that even today chipmunks have stripes on their backs.

Close Read

1. Describe the plan the chipmunk devises to divide day and night.

2. In addition to the origin of day and night, what other mystery of the natural world does this myth explain?

MODEL 2: TALL TALE

Now read this excerpt from a tall tale about a character named Sal Fink.

from SAL FINK

Hi-i-i-i-i-i-ow-ow-ow-who-whooh!

Tall tale retold by **Robert D. San Souci**

. . . Mississippi River boatman Mike Fink had one daughter, Sal, who was a "ring-tailed roarer" in her own right. In fact, she became known far and wide as the "Mississippi Screamer," because of the way she would bellow "*Hi-i-i-i-i-i-ow-ow-ow-who-whooh!*" when she was feeling high-

5 spirited or ready for a fight. Up and down the river she was known for fighting a duel with a thunderbolt, riding the river on the back of an alligator while "standen upright an' dancing 'Yankee Doodle,'" and even outracing a steamboat poling her own keelboat with a hand-picked crew.

Close Read

1. What qualities make Sal Fink "larger than life"?

2. The boxed detail describes one unbelievable feat that Sal has accomplished. What else has Sal done that seems unbelievable or exaggerated?

Part 2: What Can Stories Teach Us?

The Creek myth you just read does more than explain two mysteries of the natural world. It also teaches readers about the qualities that mattered most to the Creek. One such quality is wisdom. Did you notice that all the animals, except for the jealous bear, respected the chipmunk? Read between the lines of most traditional stories, and you can draw conclusions about the **cultural values**—ideas and beliefs—that were honored by that culture.

Consider this Vietnamese folk tale about two brothers named Kim and De. Kim is a hard-working man who is embarrassed by De's laziness. Notice how asking yourself a few questions can help you make inferences about Vietnamese cultural values.

from # The Beggar in the Blanket

Vietnamese folk tale retold by **Gail B. Graham**

. . . Kim's wife was a gentle and thoughtful woman, and she felt sorry for De.

"It's been more than a month since we've seen your brother," she said to Kim one night. "Why don't you ask him to come and have dinner
5 with us?"

Kim was surprised. "What would Nguyen and Ton and Cao and Duc and all my other friends think if they came in and found that good-for-nothing brother of mine sitting at our table?" he asked. "They would be insulted! They would never come to my house again!"
10 "So much the worse for them," replied his wife. "Friends are not the same as a brother."

"And it's a good thing they're not!" Kim retorted. "The whole village would starve if all my friends were as lazy as De."

Kim's wife could see that it was no use arguing with her stubborn
15 husband. Nevertheless she vowed that she would make Kim understand the value of a brother, even a poor and lazy brother like De.

QUESTIONS TO ASK

Which characters have admirable qualities, and which have flaws?
Kim's "thoughtful" wife is described positively. However, her husband is "stubborn"; De is "lazy."

What lessons do the characters learn?
Kim's wife vows to teach her husband a lesson about the importance of family.

What can you infer about this culture's values?
The people who told this tale valued family over everything else. They also believed in working hard.

MODEL 1: CULTURAL VALUES IN A MYTH

In this ancient Greek myth, two gods disguise themselves as humans and travel from door to door in search of food and shelter. Baucis and Philemon, a poor couple, welcome the strangers into their home. Find out what happens when the gods reveal their identity to their hosts.

from BAUCIS AND PHILEMON
Greek myth retold by **Olivia E. Coolidge**

"Philemon, you have welcomed us beneath your roof this day when richer men refused us shelter. Be sure those shall be punished who would not help the wandering stranger, but you shall have whatever reward you choose. Tell us what you will have."

5 The old man thought for a little with his eyes bent on the ground, and then he said: "We have lived together here for many years, happy even though the times have been hard. But never yet did we see fit to turn a stranger from our gate or to seek reward for entertaining him. To have spoken with the immortals face to face is a thing few men can

10 boast of. . . ."

Close Read

1. Consider how the gods respond to Philemon's actions. What can you infer about the kinds of behavior that were rewarded in ancient Greek culture?

2. Reread the boxed text. What does it tell you about how the Greeks felt about their gods?

MODEL 2: CULTURAL VALUES IN A LEGEND

Many movies and novels tell about the daring deeds of Robin Hood, a hero of medieval legend. Though he was an outlaw, Robin Hood was celebrated by many because he fought to help the helpless.

from Robin Hood of Sherwood Forest
Legend retold by **Ann McGovern**

Life in those olden days was oftentimes cruel and unjust for the good yeomen and poor folk who were made to pay large sums of money to the nobles and the rich. High taxes, outrageous rents, and fines made the poor even poorer as they tried to scratch a life out of the fields and forests.

5 Indeed, the laws of the rich were such that whosoever stepped into the King's forest to kill a deer to keep their families from starving or cut wood to keep from freezing were guilty of crime and, if caught, could be hanged.

So it was that men, such as Robin Hood, Will Stutely, Midge the

10 Miller's son, and others as honest as these, were called outlaws through no wish or fault of their own.

Close Read

1. Which details suggest that the people who first told this legend were fed up with the unfair laws of the rich?

2. Reread the boxed details, noting how the characters are described. What qualities do you think were valued in medieval times?

Part 3: Analyze the Literature

Ancient Greek myths are more than 3,000 years old, so why are we still drawn to them? With their mighty heroes, flawed gods and goddesses, and supernatural events, Greek myths still have the power to entertain. At the same time, they help us to understand the values and beliefs of the people who first told them. Use what you've learned in this workshop to analyze "Orion," one of several Greek myths that you will read in this unit.

ORION

Greek myth retold by **Alice Low**

Orion was a giant and a brave hunter. He could walk on water, a gift given him by his father, Poseidon, god of the sea.

One day Orion walked across the water to the island of Chios. There he fell in love with the king's daughter, Merope.

5   Orion said to the king, "I wish to marry your daughter, for I have fallen deeply in love with her. Tell me what I must do to gain her hand."

"Very well," said the king. "Since you are famous as a mighty hunter, you must rid my island of lions and bears and wolves. Only then will I give you my precious daughter's hand in marriage."

10   Orion strode through the hills and killed all the wild animals with his sword and his club. Then he brought their skins to the king and said, "Now I have finished my task. Let us set a day for the wedding."

But the king did not want to part with his daughter and kept putting off the wedding date. This angered Orion, and he tried to carry off

15   Merope.

Close Read

1. Reread the boxed details. What qualities and powers make Orion special?

Her father retaliated.[1] He called on the god of wine, Dionysus, to put Orion into a deep sleep. Then the king blinded Orion and flung him onto the sand by the sea.

When Orion awoke sightless, he cried out, "I am blind and helpless.
20 How shall I ever hunt again or win Merope for my bride?"

In his despair, Orion consulted an oracle,[2] which answered him, "O Orion, you shall regain your sight if you travel east to the place where the sun rises. The warm rays of the sun shall heal your eyes and restore their power."

25 But how could a blind man find his way to that distant place? Orion followed the sound of the Cyclopes'[3] hammers to the forge of the god Hephaestus.[4] When the god saw the blind hunter, he took pity on him and gave him a guide to lead him to the sun, just as it was rising.

Orion raised his eyes to the sun and, miraculously, he could see again.
30 After thanking the sun, Orion set off for the island of Chios to take revenge on the king. But the king and his daughter had fled, possibly to Crete, and Orion went there to look for them. He never found them, but he met up with Artemis, goddess of the hunt, and spent days hunting with her. They were a happy pair, roving through the woods,
35 until Artemis's brother, Apollo, became jealous.

Apollo sent a scorpion to attack Orion. Orion could not pierce the scorpion's tough body with his arrows, but he dodged the poisonous insect and strode far out to sea.

Apollo was bent on destroying Orion, and he called to Artemis,
40 "See that rock way out there in the sea? I challenge you to hit it."

Artemis loved a challenge. She drew her bow and aimed carefully. Her first arrow hit the mark, and Apollo congratulated her on her skill.

But when the waves brought Orion's body to the shore, Artemis moaned with grief. "I have killed my beloved companion. I shall never
45 forget him. And the world shall never forget him, either."

She lifted his body up into the sky, where he remains among the stars to this day—the mighty hunter, one of the most brilliant constellations,[5] with his sword and his club and three bright stars for his belt.

---

1. **retaliated:** got revenge.
2. **oracle:** in ancient Greece, a wise person who was said to be able to communicate with the gods and predict the future.
3. **Cyclopes:** one-eyed monsters.
4. **Hephaestus:** the god of fire, responsible for creating armor, sculptures, and other objects by shaping hot metal with a hammer.
5. **constellations:** groupings of stars in the sky.

Close Read

2. Whom does Orion turn to for help with his problem? Explain what his actions in lines 21–27 suggest about ancient Greek beliefs.

3. Review lines 16–18 and 25–28. In what ways do the gods play a role in Orion's life?

4. Reread lines 34–44. What human qualities or emotions do Apollo and Artemis display?

5. How does Apollo trick Artemis into "destroying Orion"?

6. What mystery of the universe does this myth explain?

The Story of Ceres and Proserpina

Classical Myth Retold by Mary Pope Osborne

How powerful is LOVE?

KEY IDEA **Love** can be a powerful force in people's lives, shaping the decisions they make and the actions they take. In this myth, you'll read about a mother's deep affection for her daughter and how it affects the people and places around her.

LIST IT Make a list of three people you care about deeply. You can include relatives, friends, or other special people who have been meaningful in your life. Under each name, note at least one way in which the person has shown his or her love.

> Ways People Show Love
> 1. Mom
>   Always tells me that she is proud of me
> 2.
> 3.

● LITERARY ANALYSIS: CHARACTERISTICS OF MYTHS

Classical myths are ancient stories that were used to explain the world and the gods and goddesses who ruled over it, shaping the lives of all humans. Passed down by word of mouth for generations, these myths

- explain how something in the world, such as the seas or the mountains, came to be
- feature gods, goddesses, and other beings with extraordinary powers. However, these beings often have the same emotions and weaknesses as humans.

As you read "The Story of Ceres and Proserpina," notice what it explains about the natural world and the behavior of the gods.

● READING SKILL: RECOGNIZE CAUSE AND EFFECT

The events of a story are often linked by cause-and-effect relationships. That is, one event acts as a **cause,** directly bringing about another event, or **effect.** The effect might, in turn, be the cause of another effect, creating a chain of events. As you read "The Story of Ceres and Proserpina," look for cause-and-effect relationships. Record them in a graphic organizer like the one shown.

Cause	Effect/Cause	Effect
Proserpina goes to look at a beautiful flower.	→ She gets too far away from her mother.	→ Proserpina is kidnapped by Pluto.

▲ VOCABULARY IN CONTEXT

Mary Pope Osborne uses the listed words to help create a vivid setting for this myth. Choose the word that best completes each sentence.

WORD LIST	barren	chariot	fertile	shrouded

1. The _____ field produced an enormous crop of corn.
2. Two horses pulled a golden _____.
3. The _____ mountain was difficult to see.
4. The sandy desert was dry and _____.

Author Online

Adventure Seeker

Mary Pope Osborne grew up in a military family. By the time she was 15, she had lived in Austria, as well as a number of places in the United States. She continued to travel as an adult and once spent many months traveling through Asia. "I craved the adventure and changing scenery of our military life," Osborne said.

Mary Pope Osborne
born 1949

Time Travel As children, Osborne and her brothers sought adventures everywhere they went. These adventures became the basis for Osborne's most popular fiction series, *The Magic Tree House,* about a brother and sister who find books that transport them to distant times and places.

Background

Classical Mythology The myths told by the ancient Greeks and Romans are known as classical mythology. The earliest Greek myths appeared almost 3,000 years ago. When Rome conquered Greece around 178 B.C., the Romans adopted the Greek myths but changed the names of the gods to Roman names.

 MORE ABOUT THE AUTHOR AND BACKGROUND
To learn more about Mary Pope Osborne and classical mythology, visit the **Literature Center** at ClassZone.com.

THE STORY OF
CERES AND PROSERPINA

RETOLD BY MARY POPE OSBORNE

One day Proserpina, the young maiden of spring, was picking
wildflowers with her mother, Ceres, the goddess of grain. Entering
the cool moist woods, Proserpina filled her basket with lilies and violets.
But when she spied the white petals of the narcissus flower, she strayed far
from her mother.

Just as Proserpina picked a beautiful narcissus, the earth began to
rumble. Suddenly the ground cracked open, splitting fern beds and
ripping flowers and trees from their roots. Then out of the dark depths
sprang Pluto, god of the underworld. **Ⓐ**

10   Standing up in his black **chariot,** Pluto ferociously drove his stallions
toward Proserpina. The maiden screamed for her mother, but Ceres was
far away and could not save her.

Pluto grabbed Proserpina and drove his chariot back into the earth.
Then the ground closed up again, leaving not even a seam.

When the mountains echoed with Proserpina's screams, her mother
rushed into the woods, but it was too late—her daughter had disappeared.

Beside herself with grief, Ceres began searching for her kidnapped
daughter in every land. For nine days the goddess did not rest, but carried
two torches through the cold nights, searching for Proserpina.

ANALYZE VISUALS
What can you tell
about the girl's
emotions, based on
her body positioning
and the fuzziness
of the illustration?

Ⓐ MYTHS
Reread lines 6–9. What
extraordinary power is
Pluto exhibiting?

chariot (chăr′ē-ət) *n.*
a two-wheeled vehicle
used in ancient times

Illustrations by Leonid Gore.

20   On the tenth day, Hecate, goddess of the dark of the moon, came
to Ceres. Holding up a lantern, the **shrouded** goddess said, "I also heard
your daughter's screams, but I didn't see her. Let us fly to Helios, the sun
god, and ask him what happened."

shrouded (shroud′əd)
adj. concealed or hidden

    Ceres and Hecate flew to Helios, the sun god; and weeping, Ceres
asked Helios if he'd seen her daughter while he was shining down upon
the woods.

    "I pity you, Ceres," said Helios, "for I know what it is to lose a child.
But I know the truth. Pluto wanted Proserpina for his wife, so he asked
his brother, Jupiter, to give him permission to kidnap her. Jupiter gave
30 his consent, and now your daughter reigns over the land of the dead
with Pluto."

    Ceres screamed in rage and thrust her fist toward Mount Olympus,[1]
cursing Jupiter for aiding in the kidnapping of his own daughter. Then
she returned to earth, disguised as an old woman, and began wandering
from town to town. **B**

B MYTHS
Reread lines 24–35.
What human emotions
is Ceres experiencing?

    One day as she rested by a well, Ceres watched four princesses gathering
water. Remembering her own daughter, she began to weep.

    "Where are you from, old woman?" one princess asked.

    "I was kidnapped by pirates, and I escaped," said Ceres. "Now I know
40 not where I am."

    Feeling pity for her, the princesses brought Ceres home to their palace.
At the palace, their mother, the queen, took an immediate liking to Ceres
when she noticed how good she was with her baby son the prince. When
she asked Ceres if she would live with them and be his nurse, the goddess
gladly consented.

    Ceres grew deeply fond of the child. The thought that he would
someday grow old and die was too much for her to bear. So she decided
to change him from a mortal to a god. Every night, when everyone else
was asleep, she poured a magic liquid on the body of the baby prince and
50 held him in a fire. Soon the prince began to look like a god; everyone was
amazed at his beauty and strength. The queen, disturbed by the changes
in her child, hid in the nursery and watched Ceres and the boy. And when
she saw Ceres place the child into the fire, she screamed for help.

    "Stupid woman!" shouted Ceres, snatching the baby from the fire.
"I was going to make your son a god! He would have lived forever! Now
he'll be a mere mortal and die like the rest of you!"

    The king and queen then realized that the boy's nurse was Ceres,
the powerful goddess of grain, and they were terrified.

---

1. **Mount Olympus** (ə-lĭm′pəs): the highest point in Greece and home of the gods and goddesses.

"I will only forgive you," said Ceres, "if you build a great temple
60 in my honor. Then I will teach your people the secret rites to help the
corn grow." **C**

At dawn the king ordered a great temple be built for the goddess.
But after the temple was completed, Ceres did not reveal the secret
rites. Instead she sat by herself all day, grieving for her kidnapped daughter.
She was in such deep mourning that everything on earth stopped growing.
It was a terrible year—there was no food, and people and animals began
to starve. **D**

Jupiter grew worried—if Ceres caused the people on earth to die, there
would be no more gifts and offerings for him. Finally he sent gods from
70 Mount Olympus to speak with her.

The gods came to Ceres and offered her gifts and pleaded with her to
make the earth **fertile** again.

"I never will," she said, "not unless my daughter is returned safely to me."

Jupiter had no choice but to bid his son, Mercury, the messenger god,
to return Proserpina to her mother.

Wandering the underworld, Mercury passed through dark smoky
caverns filled with ghosts and phantoms, until he came to the misty

C CAUSE AND EFFECT
Reread lines 46–61.
What are the effects
of the queen's scream?

D MYTHS
What extraordinary
abilities has Ceres
displayed?

fertile (fûr'tl) *adj.*
able to produce farm
crops or other vegetation

ANALYZE VISUALS
What **mood,** or feeling,
is conveyed through this
illustration?

throne room of Pluto and Proserpina. Though
the maiden was still frightened, she had grown
80 accustomed to her new home and had almost
forgotten her life on earth.

"Your brother, Jupiter, has ordered you
to return Proserpina to her mother," Mercury
told Pluto. "Otherwise, Ceres will destroy
the earth."

Pluto knew he could not disobey Jupiter, but
he didn't want his wife to leave forever, so he
said, "She can go. But first, we must be alone."

When Mercury left, Pluto spoke softly to
90 Proserpina: "If you stay, you'll be queen of
the underworld, and the dead will give you
great honors."

As Proserpina stared into the eyes of the
king of the dead, she dimly remembered the
joy of her mother's love. She remembered
wildflowers in the woods and open sunlit
meadows. "I would rather return," she
whispered.

Pluto sighed, then said, "All right, go. But before you leave, eat this
100 small seed of the pomegranate fruit. It is the food of the underworld—
it will bring you good luck."

Proserpina ate the tiny seed. Then Pluto's black chariot carried her
and Mercury away. The two stallions burst through the dry ground
of earth—then galloped over the **barren** countryside to the temple
where Ceres mourned for her daughter.

When Ceres saw her daughter coming, she ran down the hillside,
and Proserpina sprang from the chariot into her mother's arms. All day
the two talked excitedly of what had happened during their separation,
but when Proserpina told Ceres about eating the pomegranate seed,
110 the goddess hid her face and moaned in anguish.

"What have I done?" cried Proserpina.

"You have eaten the sacred food of the underworld," said Ceres. "Now
you must return for half of every year to live with Pluto, your husband." **E**

And this is how the seasons began—for when fall and winter come,
the earth grows cold and barren because Proserpina lives in the
underworld with Pluto, and her mother mourns. But when her daughter
comes back to her, Ceres, goddess of grain, turns the world to spring and
summer: The corn grows, and everything flowers again. ⌒

barren (băr′ən) *adj.*
unable to produce or
without vegetation

E CAUSE AND EFFECT
What are the effects
of the trick Pluto plays
on Proserpina?

Comprehension

1. **Recall** How long does Ceres search for Proserpina before Hecate visits her?

2. **Summarize** How does the myth explain the changing of the seasons?

3. **Represent** Ceres, Pluto, Hecate, Helios, and Mercury are each the god or goddess of something. Create a chart or diagram showing what each controls.

Literary Analysis

4. **Draw Conclusions** The gods in mythology are not equal in rank or power. Make a chart like the one shown. Using details from the myth, note the powers that each of the three gods has. Then explain which god in this myth has the greatest power.

Jupiter	Ceres	Pluto

5. **Identify Cause and Effect** Look at the cause-effect chains you created while reading "The Story of Ceres and Proserpina." Think about how the events in the plot are connected to each other. Which events in the plot create cause-effect chains?

6. **Analyze Characteristics of Myths** In what ways does this myth demonstrate the gods' influence over people on Earth? Explain.

7. **Evaluate** Why might a story about the power of **love** and loss be used to help explain the change of seasons?

Extension and Challenge

8. **Creative Project: Writing** Imagine that the gods and goddesses used the same methods of communication that we use today. Compose a few of the e-mails that Ceres and Proserpina might have sent to each other during Proserpina's second visit to the underworld.

9. **Inquiry and Research** Research one of the gods or goddesses from "The Story of Ceres and Proserpina." What additional information did you find about that character? Share your findings with the class.

RESEARCH LINKS
For more on Roman mythology, visit the **Research Center** at **ClassZone.com.**

Vocabulary in Context

VOCABULARY PRACTICE

Show that you understand the vocabulary words by deciding if each
statement is true or false.

1. A **barren** hillside is covered with trees and flowers.
2. If there is a **shrouded** opening to a castle, it is easy to see it clearly.
3. In **fertile** soil, crops usually grow easily.
4. A **chariot** has four wheels and a powerful engine.

barren

chariot

fertile

shrouded

VOCABULARY IN WRITING

Using two or more vocabulary words, write a paragaph explaining how Ceres
learned that her daughter Proserpina had been kidnapped. Here is a sample
of how you might begin.

> **EXAMPLE SENTENCE**
>
> *A **shrouded** goddess named Hecate took Ceres to talk to Helios.*

VOCABULARY STRATEGY: CONTEXT CLUES

Sometimes you can figure out the meaning of a word you don't know
by reading the words and sentences around it. For example, a clue to the
meaning of *barren* in the myth you just read is when Pluto's stallions "burst
through the dry ground" to gallop over the "barren countryside." The phrase
"dry ground" gives us a clue to the meaning of the word *barren*.

PRACTICE Use context clues to write the definition of each boldfaced word.

1. Though already an **octogenarian,** Sally claimed she was still in her
   seventies.
2. Fred is **mercenary** because he'll do anything for money.
3. The roast beef **leavings** were fed to the dog.
4. Though he worked hard, Hank's **pittance** was not enough to pay all
   his bills.
5. In **hindsight,** Brandon realized that his demanding teacher had only
   wanted him to do his best.
6. Instead of staying on the topic, the speaker went off on a **tangent.**

**VOCABULARY
PRACTICE**
For more practice, go
to the **Vocabulary Center**
at **ClassZone.com.**

Reading-Writing Connection

Demonstrate your understanding of "The Story of Ceres and Proserpina" by responding to these prompts. Then complete the **Grammar and Writing** exercise.

WRITING PROMPTS	SELF-CHECK
A. Short Response: Write a Journal Entry What were Proserpina's thoughts and feelings about being kidnapped and taken to the underworld? Write a **one-paragraph journal entry** in which Proserpina describes her feelings about being taken away from her home and the mother she **loves.**	**A realistic journal entry will . . .** • describe events as they occurred • reveal the character's thoughts and feelings
B. Extended Response: Analyze a Character Why was Ceres unable to go to the underworld and bring Proserpina back? In **two or three paragraphs,** explain why Ceres' power to rescue her daughter was limited.	**A strong analysis will . . .** • explain Ceres's powers and limits as a goddess • be supported by details from the myth

GRAMMAR AND WRITING

CAPITALIZE CORRECTLY Be sure to capitalize a **family relationship** word, such as *mother, father,* or *uncle,* when it is used as a name or directly before a name. Do not capitalize a family relationship word when it follows a possessive pronoun like *her* or *my* or an article like *a, an,* or *the.*

> *Original:* Proserpina and her Mother were very close.

> *Revised:* Proserpina and her mother were very close.

PRACTICE Correct the capitalization errors in each sentence.

1. Proserpina said, "I long for the days when mother and I were together."
2. It was clear that Ceres missed her Daughter.
3. "I'll find an Aunt to look after you," Jupiter said.
4. Mercury said, "I'd be happy to send a message for you, father."

*For more help with capitalization, see page R51 in the **Grammar Handbook.***

Apollo's Tree: The Story of Daphne and Apollo
Classical Myth Retold by Mary Pope Osborne

Arachne
Classical Myth Retold by Olivia E. Coolidge

Can PRIDE ever hurt you?

KEY IDEA It's good to have **pride** in yourself as well as in your accomplishments. But when pride turns to conceit and boasting, it can get you into trouble. Some classical myths, such as the two you are about to read, serve as warnings about the dangers of being overly sure of yourself.

DISCUSS With a group of classmates, discuss a time when you or someone you know witnessed the bad side of pride. What were the consequences? Take turns discussing the effect it had on those involved.

LITERARY ANALYSIS: CULTURAL VALUES IN MYTHS

Cultural values are the standards of behavior that a society expects from its people. **Myths** reflect the cultural values of the societies in which they were first told. Some values often taught in Greek and Roman myths are

- respecting your elders
- respecting and obeying the gods, who are often involved in humans' everyday lives
- knowing your place

As you read "Apollo's Tree" and "Arachne," notice what happens to the characters who do not maintain these values. Then determine what lessons are being taught by the myths.

READING STRATEGY: PREDICT

When you **predict,** you make reasonable guesses about what will happen next based on clues in a story and your own experiences. Predicting is a way of becoming more involved in a story and gaining more enjoyment from reading. As you read each of the myths that follow, create a chart like the one shown to record your predictions.

Myth	My Predictions	Clues in Story	What Really Happens
"Apollo's Tree"	Cupid will shoot Apollo with an arrow.		

VOCABULARY IN CONTEXT

These words help tell the stories of people trapped by pride. Make a chart like the one shown. Put each vocabulary word in the appropriate column. Then write a brief definition of each word you know or think you know.

WORD LIST		
distorted	indignantly	ominous
exquisite	obscure	sacred
immensely	obstinacy	

Know Well	Think I Know	Don't Know at All

Author Online

Mary Pope Osborne: Inspired Traveler While on an extended journey through Asia, Mary Pope Osborne became ill and ended up in a hospital in Nepal. During her stay, she read J. R. R. Tolkien's

Mary Pope Osborne born 1949

trilogy *The Lord of the Rings*. Osborne has said that in those three books, she "encountered worlds of light and worlds of darkness." Reading them "planted seeds of the imagination that led directly to my being an author of children's books." (For more information about Mary Pope Osborne, see page 647.)

Olivia E. Coolidge: Historical Writer Born in England, Olivia E. Coolidge eventually became a U.S. citizen. After World War II, she began writing biographical and historical books for young people. "My general purpose,"

Olivia E. Coolidge born 1908

Coolidge once explained about her writing, ". . . is to give a picture of life." She went on to add that "a good book should excite, amuse, and interest."

MORE ABOUT THE AUTHOR
For more on the authors, visit the **Literature Center** at ClassZone.com.

Apollo's Tree

The Story of Daphne and Apollo

Retold by Mary Pope Osborne

One day when Apollo, the god of light and truth, was a young man, he came upon Cupid, the god of love, playing with one of his bows. "What are you doing with my bow?" Apollo asked angrily. "Don't try to steal my glory, Cupid! I've slain a great serpent with that weapon. Play with your own little bow and arrows!"

"Your arrows may slay serpents, Apollo," said the god of love, "but *my* arrows can do worse harm! Even you can be wounded by them!"

With that **ominous** threat, Cupid flew into the sky and landed on top of a high mountain. Then he pulled two arrows from his quiver:[1] One had
10 a blunt tip filled with lead. Whomever was hit by this arrow would run from anyone professing love. The second arrow was sharp and made of gold. Whomever was hit with this arrow would instantly fall in love. **A**

Cupid aimed his first arrow at Daphne, a beautiful nymph[2] hunting deep in the woods. Daphne was a follower of Diana, Apollo's twin sister and the goddess of wild things. Like Diana, Daphne loved her freedom, as she roamed the woods and fields with her hair in wild disarray and her limbs bare to the sun and rain.

Cupid pulled the bowstring back and shot the blunt-tipped arrow at Daphne. When the arrow flew through the air, it became invisible. And
20 when it pierced Daphne's heart, she felt a sharp pain, but knew not why.

Holding her hands over her wound, Daphne rushed to her father, the river god. "Father!" she shouted. "You must make me a promise!"

"What is it?" called the god who stood in the river, surrounded by water nymphs.

---

ominous (ŏm'ə-nəs) *adj.* threatening; frightening

A PREDICT
Reread lines 1–12. What do you think Cupid is going to do? Add your prediction to your chart.

ANALYZE VISUALS
Examine the painting of Cupid. What **details** do you notice?

---

1. **quiver** (kwĭv'ər): a portable case for holding arrows.

2. **nymph** (nĭmf): any of a number of minor gods represented as beautiful maidens in Greek and Roman mythology.

Detail of *Cupid,* manner of Jean-Baptiste Greuze. Oil on canvas. © Christie's Images/SuperStock.

"Promise I will never have to get married!" Daphne cried.

The river god, confused by his daughter's frantic request, called back, "But I wish to have grandchildren!"

"No, Father! No! I *never* want to get married! Please, let me always be as free as Diana!"

30   "But I want you to marry!" cried the god.

"No!" screamed Daphne. And she beat the water with her fists, then rocked back and forth and sobbed.

"All right!" shouted the river god. "Do not grieve so, Daphne! I promise I'll never make you marry!" **B**

"And promise you'll help me escape my suitors!" cried the huntress.

"I promise, I will!" called the river god.

After Daphne secured this promise from her father, Cupid aimed his second arrow—the sharp, gold-tipped one—at Apollo, who was wandering in the woods. Just as the young god came
40   upon Daphne, Cupid pulled back the tight string of his bow and shot the golden arrow into Apollo's heart.

The god instantly fell in love with Daphne. Even though the huntress's hair was wild and she wore only rough animal skins, Apollo thought she was the most beautiful woman he'd ever seen.

"Hello!" he cried. But Daphne gave him a startled look, then bolted into the woods like a deer.

Apollo ran after her, shouting, "Stay! Stay!" But Daphne fled as fast as the wind.

"Don't run, please!" cried Apollo. "You flee like a dove flees an eagle.
50   But I'm not your enemy! Don't run from me!"

Daphne continued to run.

"Stop!" Apollo cried.

Daphne did not slow down.

"Do you know who I am?" said the god. "I am not a farm boy or a shepherd. I am Lord of Delphi! Son of Jupiter! I've slain a great serpent with my arrow! But alas, I fear Cupid's weapons have wounded me worse!"

Daphne continued to run, her bare limbs lit by the sun and her soft hair wild in the wind.

Apollo grew tired of begging her to stop, so he began to pick up
60   speed. On the wings of love, running more swiftly than he'd ever run before, the god of light and truth gave the girl no rest, until soon he was close upon her. **C**

Her strength gone, Daphne could feel Apollo's breath on her hair. "Help me, Father!" she cried to the river god. "Help me!"

B CULTURAL VALUES
Reread lines 25–34. In what way does Daphne's behavior show disrespect toward elders?

C PREDICT
How do you think the myth will end?

Apollo and Daphne (1565–1570), Paolo Veronese. Oil on canvas, 109.4 cm × 113.3 cm.
© San Diego Museum of Art, San Diego, California/Bridgeman Art Library.

ANALYZE VISUALS
How do the people in this painting **compare** with your mental picture of Apollo and Daphne?

No sooner had she spoken these words, than her arms and legs grew heavy and turned to wood. Then her hair became leaves, and her feet became roots growing deep into the ground. She had become a laurel tree;[3] and nothing was left of her, but her **exquisite** loveliness.

Apollo embraced the tree's branches as if they were Daphne's arms.
70 He kissed her wooden flesh. Then he pressed his hands against the tree's trunk and wept.

"I feel your heart beating beneath this bark," Apollo said, tears running down his face. "Since you can't be my wife, you'll be my **sacred** tree. I'll use your wood for my harp and for my arrows. I'll weave your branches into a wreath for my head. Heroes and scholars will be crowned with your leaves.[4] You'll always be young and green—my first love, Daphne." ∾ **D**

exquisite (ĕk'skwĭ-zĭt) *adj.* of extraordinary beauty or charm

sacred (sā'krĭd) *adj.* worthy of great respect; holy

D CULTURAL VALUES
Think about what happens to Apollo. What lessons does the myth teach?

---

3. **laurel tree:** a Mediterranean evergreen tree with fragrant leaves and small, blackish berries.

4. **Heroes and scholars . . . your leaves:** In ancient times, a wreath of laurel leaves was often given to poets, heroes, and victors in athletic contests as a mark of honor.

ARACHNE

Retold by Olivia E. Coolidge

rachne was a maiden who became famous throughout Greece, though she was neither wellborn nor beautiful and came from no great city. She lived in an **obscure** little village, and her father was a humble dyer of wool. In this he was very skillful, producing many varied shades, while above all he was famous for the clear, bright scarlet which is made from shellfish and which was the most glorious of all the colors used in ancient Greece. Even more skillful than her father was Arachne. It was her task to spin the fleecy wool into a fine, soft thread and to weave it into cloth on the high-standing loom within the cottage. Arachne
10 was small and pale from much working. Her eyes were light and her hair was a dusty brown, yet she was quick and graceful, and her fingers, roughened as they were, went so fast that it was hard to follow their flickering movements. So soft and even was her thread, so fine her cloth, so gorgeous her embroidery,[1] that soon her products were known all over Greece. No one had ever seen the like of them before.

obscure (ŏb-skyŏŏr′) *adj.* far from cities or other areas of human population

ANALYZE VISUALS
What can you **infer** about the woman in this illustration?

---

1. **embroidery:** the decoration of fabric with needlework.

Illustrations by Blair Drawson.

At last Arachne's fame became so great that people used to come from far and wide to watch her working. Even the graceful nymphs would steal in from stream or forest and peep shyly through the dark doorway, watching in wonder the white arms of Arachne as she stood at the
20 **loom** and threw the shuttle[2] from hand to hand between the hanging threads or drew out the long wool, fine as a hair, from the distaff[3] as she sat spinning. "Surely Athena herself must have taught her," people would murmur to one another. "Who else could know the secret of such marvelous skill?"

Arachne was used to being wondered at, and she was **immensely** proud of the skill that had brought so many to look on her. Praise was all she lived for, and it displeased her greatly that people should think anyone, even a goddess, could teach her anything. Therefore, when she heard them murmur, she would stop her work and turn round **indignantly** to say,
30 "With my own ten fingers I gained this skill, and by hard practice from early morning till night. I never had time to stand looking as you people do while another maiden worked. Nor if I had, would I give Athena credit because the girl was more skillful than I. As for Athena's weaving, how could there be finer cloth or more beautiful embroidery than mine? If Athena herself were to come down and compete with me, she could do no better than I." E

One day when Arachne turned round with such words, an old woman answered her, a grey old woman, bent and very poor, who stood leaning on a staff and peering at Arachne amid the crowd of onlookers.
40 "Reckless girl," she said, "how dare you claim to be equal to the immortal gods themselves? I am an old woman and have seen much. Take my advice and ask pardon of Athena for your words. Rest content with your fame of being the best spinner and weaver that mortal eyes have ever beheld."

"Stupid old woman," said Arachne indignantly, "who gave you a right to speak in this way to me? It is easy to see that you were never good for anything in your day, or you would not come here in poverty and rags to gaze at my skill. If Athena resents my words, let her answer them herself. I have challenged her to a contest, but she, of course, will not come.
50 It is easy for the gods to avoid matching their skill with that of men." F

At these words the old woman threw down her staff and stood erect. The wondering onlookers saw her grow tall and fair and stand clad in long robes of dazzling white. They were terribly afraid as they realized

---

2. **shuttle:** a device used in loom weaving to carry thread back and forth between other threads held lengthwise.

3. **distaff:** an attachment for a spinning wheel that holds unspun wool, cotton, or flax.

VISUAL VOCABULARY

loom *n.* a device for making cloth by weaving strands of yarn or thread together

immensely (ĭ-mĕns′lē) *adv.* extremely; very

indignantly (ĭn-dĭg′nənt-lē) *adv.* angrily; in annoyance

E PREDICT
Reread lines 16–36. Based on Arachne's boasting, what do you predict will happen next?

F CULTURAL VALUES
Reread lines 37–50. What value is Arachne showing no respect for? Explain.

that they stood in the presence of Athena. Arachne herself flushed red for a moment, for she had never really believed that the goddess would hear her. Before the group that was gathered there she would not give in; so pressing her pale lips together in **obstinacy** and pride, she led the goddess to one of the great looms and set herself before the other. Without a word both began to thread the long woolen strands that hung from the rollers and between which the shuttle would move back and forth. Many skeins[4] lay heaped beside them to use, bleached white, and gold, and scarlet, and other shades, varied as the rainbow. Arachne had never thought of giving credit for her success to her father's skill in dyeing, though in actual truth the colors were as remarkable as the cloth itself. **G**

Soon there was no sound in the room but the breathing of the onlookers, the whirring of the shuttles, and the creaking of the wooden frames as each pressed the thread up into place or tightened the pegs by which the whole was held straight. The excited crowd in the doorway began to see that the skill of both in truth was very nearly equal but that, however the cloth might turn out, the goddess was the quicker of the two. A pattern of many pictures was growing on her loom. There was a border of twined branches of the olive, Athena's favorite tree, while in the middle, figures began to appear. As they looked at the glowing colors, the spectators realized that Athena was weaving into her pattern a last warning to Arachne. The central figure was the goddess herself, competing with Poseidon[5] for possession of the city of Athens; but in the four corners were mortals who had tried to strive with gods and pictures of the awful fate that had overtaken them. The goddess ended a little before Arachne and stood back from her marvelous work to see what the maiden was doing.

Never before had Arachne been matched against anyone whose skill was equal, or even nearly equal, to her own. As she stole glances from time to time at Athena and saw the goddess working swiftly, calmly, and always a little faster than herself, she became angry instead of frightened, and an evil thought came into her head. Thus, as Athena stepped back a pace to watch Arachne finishing her work, she saw that the maiden had taken for her design a pattern of scenes which showed evil or unworthy actions of the gods, how they had deceived fair maidens, resorted to trickery, and appeared on earth from time to time in the form of poor and humble people. When the goddess saw this insult glowing in bright colors on Arachne's loom, she did not wait while the cloth was judged but stepped forward, her grey eyes blazing with anger, and tore Arachne's work across.

60

70

80

90

obstinacy
(ŏb′stə-nə-sē) *n.* the act of being stubborn or disobedient

G PREDICT
Who do you think will win the weaving contest? Add this prediction to your chart.

---

4. **skeins** (skānz): lengths of thread or yarn wound in long, loose coils.

5. **Poseidon** (pō-sīd′n): in Greek mythology, the god of waters, earthquakes, and horses.

ANALYZE VISUALS
What human qualities do you see in this illustration of Arachne as a spider?

Then she struck Arachne across the face. Arachne stood there a moment, struggling with anger, fear, and pride. "I will not live under this insult," she cried, and seizing a rope from the wall, she made a noose and would have hanged herself. **H**

The goddess touched the rope and touched the maiden. "Live on, wicked girl," she said. "Live on and spin, both you and your descendants.[6] When men look at you, they may remember that it is not wise to strive with Athena." At that the body of Arachne shriveled up; and her legs grew tiny, spindly, and **distorted**. There before the eyes of the spectators hung a little dusty brown spider on a slender thread.

All spiders descend from Arachne, and as the Greeks watched them spinning their thread wonderfully fine, they remembered the contest with Athena and thought that it was not right for even the best of men to claim equality with the gods. ∾

H CULTURAL VALUES
In what ways does Arachne's behavior show disrespect for the gods?

distorted (dǐ-stôrt′əd) *adj.* twisted out of shape; misshapen

---

6. **descendants** (dǐ-sĕn′dənts): persons whose ancestry can be traced to a particular individual.

Comprehension

1. **Recall** In "Apollo's Tree," what is special about each of Cupid's two arrows?

2. **Recall** In addition to her skill as a weaver, what makes Arachne's work so beautiful?

3. **Clarify** What final warning does Athena try to give Arachne through the designs she weaves into her cloth?

Literary Analysis

4. **Interpret** Reread lines 1–12 and 54–56 of "Apollo's Tree." What does Apollo mean when he says that the wounds from Cupid's weapons are worse than those from his own arrows? Explain your answer.

5. **Identify Cultural Values in Myths** People living in ancient Greece didn't always behave as expected. Make a chart like the one shown. Under each of the three values, list details that show how characters demonstrate or disregard the value in each myth.

Ancient Greek Values		
Respect Elders	Respect the Gods	Know Your Place

6. **Analyze Predictions** Look at the chart you filled in while reading "Apollo's Tree" and "Arachne." Complete the chart by noting what actually happened in the story. Which of your predictions were correct?

7. **Analyze Characters** What human qualities do the god Apollo and the goddess Athena demonstrate? Include examples from the myths to support your answer.

8. **Draw Conclusions** In what ways does Arachne's **pride** bring about her downfall?

Extension and Challenge

9. **Reader's Circle** Does Arachne deserve the punishment she receives? Get together with a small group and discuss whether Athena's treatment of Arachne is fair.

10. **Creative Project: Art** In "Arachne," Athena and Arachne include designs in their weavings that are intended as messages for each other. Sketch how you imagine these designs look, using the descriptions in the myth as your guide.

Vocabulary in Context

VOCABULARY PRACTICE

Choose the vocabulary word that best completes each sentence.

1. The funhouse mirror made her body look strangely____.
2. The ____ town couldn't be found on her map.
3. Her positive attitude made Kiana ____ popular.
4. The site of the grave was considered ____ by the mourners.
5. When asked if she was lying, Lola denied it ____.
6. The ____ diamond sparkled brightly.
7. Kyle's ____ often got him in trouble at school.
8. The ____ clouds carried with them a terrible thunderstorm.

distorted   obscure
exquisite   obstinacy
immensely   ominous
indignantly   sacred

VOCABULARY IN WRITING

Which character in these myths is the most stubborn? Write an explanation, using three or more vocabulary words. You might begin like this.

> **EXAMPLE SENTENCE**
>
> *Arachne's **obstinacy** created many problems for her.*

VOCABULARY STRATEGY: USE REFERENCE AIDS

To express ideas clearly and correctly, you need to choose your words carefully. Sometimes this means that you need to replace a vague or general word with a more specific **synonym.** Synonyms are words with similar meanings. For example, a synonym for *exquisite* is *gorgeous.* To find a synonym for a word, look in a **reference aid,** or information resource, such as

- a dictionary, in which synonyms are listed after the definition or definitions of a word

  exquisite (ĕk′skwĭ-zĭt) *adj.* of extraordinary beauty or charm: *They watched the exquisite sunset.* **syn** BEAUTIFUL, GORGEOUS, FLAWLESS, SUPERB

- a reference book of synonyms, such as a thesaurus or a synonym finder. Many word processing programs feature an electronic thesaurus tool.

  exquisite *adjective* beautiful, gorgeous, flawless, superb

PRACTICE Use a dictionary or thesaurus to find a synonym for each word. Note the synonym as well as the reference aid you used to find it.

1. bravery   2. battle   3. naughty   4. calm

VOCABULARY PRACTICE For more practice, go to the **Vocabulary Center** at **ClassZone.com.**

Reading-Writing Connection

Increase your understanding of "Apollo's Tree" and "Arachne" by responding to these prompts. Then complete the **Grammar and Writing** exercise.

WRITING PROMPTS

A. Short Response: Write a Letter
Imagine that you are a friend of Arachne and you are concerned that her behavior will eventually get her into trouble. Write a **short letter** in which you urge her to be less boastful.

B. Extended Response: Write an Explanation
How does the myth of Apollo and Daphne connect to the Big Question on page 656? Write a **two- or three-paragraph explanation** of how **pride** hurt each of the characters.

SELF-CHECK

An effective letter will . . .
- summarize Arachne's bad behavior
- present convincing arguments for changing

A good explanation will . . .
- show an understanding of the characters' attitudes and behavior
- include specific examples

GRAMMAR AND WRITING

USE CORRECT SENTENCE STRUCTURE An **independent clause** contains a subject and a verb and can stand alone as a sentence. A **simple sentence** contains one independent clause. A **compound sentence** contains two or more independent clauses. The clauses are joined either by a comma and a coordinating conjunction such as *and, or, but,* or *so,* or by a semicolon.

> *Original:* Cupid played with Apollo's bows. Apollo became angry. (*Each simple sentence contains one independent clause.*)

> *Revised:* Cupid played with Apollo's bows, and Apollo became angry. (*The compound sentence contains two independent clauses joined by a comma and a coordinating conjunction.*)

PRACTICE Combine each pair of simple sentences to form a compound sentence. Use the coordinating conjunction that most clearly shows the relationship between the two ideas.

1. The arrow hits Daphne. She feels a sharp pain.
2. Apollo falls in love with Daphne. Daphne runs away from him.
3. Arachne is a skillful weaver. Athena is a better weaver.
4. Arachne is rude to Athena. The goddess turns her into a spider.

For more help with simple and compound sentences, see page R63 in the **Grammar Handbook.**

Spider Webs
Online Science Article

ARACHNE

Use with "Apollo's Tree:
The Story of Daphne and
Apollo" and "Arachne,"
pages 658 and 662.

What's the Connection?

One of the the two Greek myths you've just read was about the origin of spiders and their webs. You will now read a **science article** to learn about the different kinds of webs spiders weave.

Skill Focus: Identify Main Idea and Details

In nonfiction, the **main idea** is the most important idea that a writer wants to communicate to readers. The main idea is not just the topic or subject of the writing, it is a position statement about the topic or subject. A writer may state the main idea directly or only imply it, leaving readers to infer the main idea based on supporting details. **Supporting details** are the reasons, facts, statistics, examples, statements from experts, and other details a writer uses to back up his or her main idea.

As you read "Spider Webs," try to find a direct statement of its main idea. To help identify the main idea, focus on the kinds of details the author presents. Create a chart like the one shown to list details from the article about spiders and their webs. You will use this information later.

Details About Spiders	Details About Webs
1.	1.
2.	2.
3.	3.

SPIDER WEBS

You know there are many kinds of spiders, but did you know there are also many kinds of spider webs? In fact, a spider web can be a big clue to the kind of spider that made it. When you know the different kinds of webs that spiders commonly make, you can make a pretty accurate guess about the kind of spider that created it. **A**

▲ The kind of web that you are probably most familiar with is made by **ORB SPIDERS** (*Araneidae* family). Their webs are shaped like spirals on lines and are often very beautiful. To maintain that beauty, orb spiders have to repair their webs at least once every day. As the web loses its stickiness, the spider will eat it as it spins new threads. **B**

F OCUS ON FORM
A **science article** is a short piece of nonfiction on a scientific subject. The author's purpose for writing a science article is usually to inform or explain. Science articles often use photographs and boldfaced type to point out subtopics and to clarify ideas and information.

A MAIN IDEA AND DETAILS
Preview the article title and first paragraph. Is the title the topic or the main idea of the article? Explain.

B SCIENCE ARTICLE
Notice the orb spiders' Latin family name in parentheses. Why is it helpful to have this information?

BACK   FORWARD   STOP   REFRESH   HOME   PRINT

▲ **TRIANGLE SPIDERS** (*Uloboridae* family) make triangular webs. These webs resemble a slice of the webs made by orb spiders.

▲ **FUNNEL SPIDERS** (*Agelenidae* family) make webs that might look like a bird's nest made of silk. The spiders make sheets of silk and shape them into funnels. The funnels have one big opening to catch prey. They also have one small opening in the back in case the spider needs to escape. These webs are not actually sticky. The spiders that make them are just better at moving around in the smooth funnel shape than their prey.

Sometimes, funnel spider webs aren't cupped. Instead, spiders may make flat sheets with a small funnel-shaped retreat off to one side. **C**

C MAIN IDEA AND DETAILS
What do you learn about funnel spiders and their webs? Record the details in your chart.

BACK FORWARD STOP REFRESH HOME PRINT

▲ **Cobweb spiders** (*Theriidae* family) make small, random messes of silk string that are attached to their surroundings by long strings. Cobweb spiders are also called comb-footed spiders.

▲ **Meshweb spiders** (*Dictynidae* family) make webs that are similar to those of cobweb spiders but have a little more structure. The spiders are usually found in small, messy webs at the tips of vegetation, especially in grassy fields. They can also be found under stones and dead leaves. **D**

D MAIN IDEA AND DETAILS
Reread this photo caption. Add what you learn about meshweb spiders to your chart.

BACK   FORWARD   STOP   REFRESH   HOME   PRINT

▶ **SHEETWEB SPIDERS**
(*Linyphiidae* family) make many kinds of webs that are formed out of sheets of silk. The sheets are a maze of threads, and don't have many large gaps.

There are several kinds of sheetweb spiders. *Platform spiders* make thickly interwoven sheets of silk. *Filmy dome spiders* make dome-shaped sheets that are secured by a network of silk strings. *Bowl and doily*[1] *spiders* make unusual webs. The tops look like bowls that are secured by strings to something above them. The bowl appears to be sitting on a doily that is the second part of the web and is attached horizontally. These kinds of webs make very effective booby-traps for unsuspecting insects. **E**

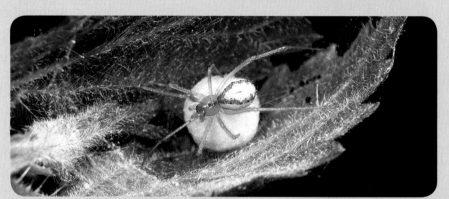

▲ Spider webs are a sign that spiders have been nearby, but they aren't the only sign. Spiders also spin webs to protect their eggs and developing young. These **EGG CASES** look like eggs but actually contain hundreds of tiny spider eggs.

Some spiders don't make webs at all. However, these spiders do use silk to make a little hiding place for themselves, especially females with eggs. **F**

---

1. **doily** (doi′lē): a small mat, often round and made of lace, that is used as a protective or decorative cover on furniture.

E MAIN IDEA AND DETAILS
Reread this caption on sheetweb spiders. What is the main idea the author is trying to get across to readers?

F SCIENCE ARTICLE
What two text features often used by science writers appear in this article?

Comprehension

1. **Recall** What is another name for a cobweb spider?

2. **Recall** What are the three kinds of sheetweb spiders mentioned in the article?

Critical Analysis

3. **Make Inferences** From the information in the article, what inference can you make about how spiders get their names?

4. **Identify the Main Idea** Review your list of details about spiders and their webs. Then determine the main idea of the article by asking yourself, "What idea does this information support?"

5. **Evaluate a Science Article** A strong science article is interesting, accurate, and makes science easy to understand. Do you think "Spider Webs" is a strong science article? Support your opinion with details from the selection.

Read for Information: Create an Outline

WRITING PROMPT

Create an outline of the science article "Spider Webs." Be sure your outline contains all of the most important ideas and information from the article.

To answer this prompt, do as follows:

1. Title your outline with a statement of the article's main idea. All of your entries should support or develop this idea.

2. Review the article and note the boldfaced labels for each type of spider. Use these as outline subheadings.

3. Use a Roman numeral to label each subheading under the title.

4. Under each subheading, list supporting details that you collected as you read. Label each supporting detail with a capital letter.

Main Idea of Article
I. Subheading
   A. Supporting detail
   B. Supporting detail
II. Subheading
   A. Supporting detail
   B. Supporting detail
III. Subheading
   A. Supporting detail
   B. Supporting detail

*For more help with outlining, see page R4 in the **Reading Handbook.***

The Chenoo

Native American Legend Retold by Joseph and James Bruchac

Is FEAR *ever fun?*

KEY IDEA What do scary movies, amusement park haunted houses, and roller coasters have in common? Though they cause chills, screams, and **fear,** we turn to them again and again because they are fun. In the following Native American legend, you'll meet a monster—so prepare yourself for some fearful fun.

CHART IT Make a chart listing the fearful activities you've experienced. Then rate their fear and fun levels on a scale of 1 to 5 (with 5 being the highest). Compare your answers with those of your classmates.

Activity	Fun Level	Fear Level
roller coaster	4	3
reading a scary story		

● LITERARY ANALYSIS: CHARACTERISTICS OF LEGENDS

A **legend** is a tale about heroes and heroines and their extraordinary deeds. Many legends are based on real people and events from history. However, as a story is repeated over time, details are added or changed to make it more exciting. In most legends, events occur that could not actually take place in the real world.

Usually, the hero or heroine in a legend shows uncommon courage and cleverness in working against a powerful person or force causing a problem. As you read "The Chenoo," notice the way the heroine in the legend handles a frightening intruder.

● READING SKILL: MAKE INFERENCES

When you **make inferences** as you read, you make logical guesses about the events or characters in a story. For example, you might infer that a character is kind and considerate if that character helps someone in need.

As you read "The Chenoo," use a chart to record the inferences you make about Nolka based on her words and actions.

Nolka's Words and Actions	Inferences About Nolka
cleans an elk hide and heats rocks for a sweat lodge	She is hard-working and takes good care of her brothers.

▲ VOCABULARY IN CONTEXT

The Bruchacs use the listed words to help tell the story of an encounter with a monster. Choose the word that best completes each sentence.

WORD LIST	clearing	inspect	proceed	sibling

1. The brothers were worried about their _____, Nolka.
2. They walked through the forest into a _____.
3. She wanted to _____, but she was frozen by fear.
4. Awasos stooped to _____ the tracks on the ground.

Author Online

Joseph Bruchac: Keeper of Culture Joseph Bruchac (brōō'shăk) has devoted his life to educating people about Native American culture. Bruchac, who is part Abenaki, has produced more than 70 books and is well known as a storyteller.

Joseph Bruchac III born 1942

James Bruchac: The Next Generation James Bruchac felt lucky to grow up as the son of storyteller Joseph Bruchac. Of the many Native American legends he heard as a child, his favorites were monster stories. James works with his father and younger brother to help preserve Native American culture.

James Bruchac

 MORE ABOUT THE AUTHOR For more on the authors, visit the **Literature Center** at ClassZone.com.

Background

Scary Stories Monster stories are a popular type of legend passed down in Native American culture. In many monster stories, a hero or heroine defeats a foe by using his or her wits and courage. Often, the lesson of these stories is that bravery and intelligence can triumph over evil.

THE CHENOO

Retold by Joseph and James Bruchac

Long ago, during the Moon of Falling Leaves,[1] a woman and her two brothers traveled to the north to set up a hunting camp. Hoping to bring back enough furs and meat for the winter, they went far away from their village, much farther than anyone had gone in a long time.

During the first two days after making camp the hunting was very good. Each day the two brothers would go hunting. The sister, whose name was Nolka, would stay behind to tend their camp and prepare any game caught the day before. On the third day, however, while out hunting, the brothers came across a very large set of footprints. Those
10 footprints were over two feet long and ten feet apart. Kneeling down, Awasos, the older of the two brothers, carefully **inspected** each track. **A**

"Great-grandfather told me of a creature that makes tracks like this. It is called a Chenoo."[2] Awasos lifted his head to scan the forest around them.

"Yes, I remember," answered Kasko, Awasos's younger brother. "He said they were giant cannibals[3] with sharp teeth and hearts made of ice. Consuming the spirit of a human being makes them stronger."

ANALYZE VISUALS
What **mood** does this photograph convey?

inspect (ĭn-spĕkt′) v. to examine carefully

A MAKE INFERENCES
What inference can you make about the footprints?

---

1. **Moon of Falling Leaves:** In many Native American cultures, the Moon of Falling Leaves is the name given to the tenth of the thirteen cycles of the moon each year. The Moon of Falling Leaves usually begins in October.

2. **Chenoo** (chā′nōo)

3. **cannibals:** people or animals that feed on others of their own kind.

Looking closer at the tracks, the two men realized the huge footprints were headed in the direction of their camp.

"We must return and check on our sister," said Awasos. Both men
20 began to run back toward camp.

Meanwhile, back at camp, unaware of any danger, Nolka was busy cleaning an elk hide. Several yards away, in a large fire pit, a pile of rocks was being heated up for her brothers' evening sweat lodge.

Having finished the hide, Nolka slowly stood up to add more wood to the fire. As she did so, she heard a sudden sound of breaking branches. She turned and looked up. There stood a huge Chenoo. Its large gray body was covered with pine pitch[4] and leaves, and it wore a necklace of human skulls. Its legs and arms were as thick as tree stumps. Its open mouth revealed a sharp set of teeth, and its eyes were darker than a starless
30 night. The Chenoo raised its arms, preparing to grasp Nolka in its long, bony fingers. **B**

Knowing there was nowhere to hide, Nolka thought quickly.

"Grandfather!" she said with a smile. "Where have you been?"

"GRANDFATHER?" the Chenoo growled. It stopped in its tracks and looked confused. No human being had ever dared to speak to it this way before. **C**

"Yes, Grandfather. I have been waiting here all day for you. Don't you even remember me?" Nolka said. There was a long pause. Nolka did her best to appear calm.

40 "GRANDDAUGHTER?!" roared the Chenoo. "I HAVE A GRANDDAUGHTER?!"

"Yes, of course you do. I have been preparing this sweat lodge for you all day," Nolka said, motioning toward the large pile of rocks glowing in the fire. She hoped to delay the Chenoo from trying to eat her until her brothers returned from hunting. So far the plan was working. **D**

"Grandfather, please come into the lodge," she said, lifting up the door flap.

"THANK YOU, GRANDDAUGHTER," the Chenoo rumbled as it walked over to the sweat lodge and bent down. Crawling in on its hands and knees, the giant squeezed through the door. Sitting down, his legs
50 around the fire pit, the Chenoo filled the entire lodge.

Walking over to the fire, Nolka picked up a large forked stick and carried one hot rock after another and began placing them in the center of the lodge. She was just pulling another rock out of the fire when she heard someone coming.

---

4. **pine pitch:** the thick, sticky sap of a pine tree.

SOCIAL STUDIES CONNECTION

A sweat lodge, or sweathouse, is a structure used by many Native Americans to induce sweating as a cleansing ritual. It is heated by pouring water over hot stones.

B **LEGENDS**
What **details** show how powerful the Chenoo is?

C **MAKE INFERENCES**
Why is Nolka speaking to the Chenoo in such an unusual way?

D **MAKE INFERENCES**
Reread lines 37–44. Though Nolka appears calm and in control, what feelings is she probably experiencing?

"Sister, what are you doing?" called Awasos as he and Kasko, both completely out of breath, came running into the **clearing.**

"We saw huge tracks headed toward our camp," Kasko said. "We were afraid that you—"

Nolka held up a hand to her mouth, and her brothers stopped talking.
60 She looked over toward the lodge.

"Our grandfather has finally arrived!" Nolka said. "Come and greet him." Then she picked up another glowing rock. As she walked over to the lodge, her brothers, totally confused, followed her. **E**

"Grandfather, your grandsons have returned to greet you," said Nolka to the Chenoo, through the door of the lodge.

clearing (klîr'ĭng) *n.* an open area of land, as in the middle of a forest

E LEGENDS
What courageous qualities does Nolka show?

ANALYZE VISUALS
In what way is this photograph like the Chenoo's necklace?

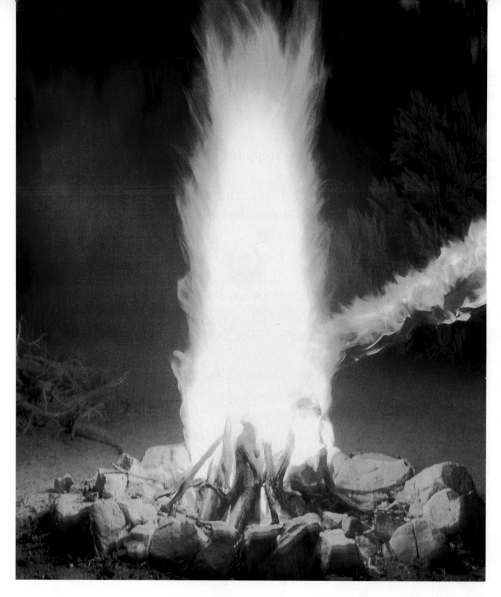

"GRANDSONS? I HAVE GRANDSONS?" roared the Chenoo. Looking into the lodge, Awasos and Kasko could not believe it. There sat the very same monster whose tracks they had seen headed toward camp.

"HELLO, MY GRANDSONS!" the Chenoo rumbled.

70 "Oh, ah, yes. Hello, grandfather . . . it is good to see you," Kasko said, after being nudged in the ribs by Nolka.

"THIS LODGE FEELS GOOD. BRING ME MORE ROCKS!"

"Yes, Grandfather," Kasko said.

The two men and their sister piled one glowing rock after another in the center of the lodge. Then, after placing a large birch-bark bucket full of water just inside the door of the lodge, they closed the flap. Moments later, a loud hissing sound came from inside the lodge as the Chenoo began to pour water on the rocks.

"Now is our chance to make a run for it," Nolka whispered to her
80 brothers. The three of them began to quietly sneak out of camp. But they had not moved quickly enough.

"MORE ROCKS! BRING ME MORE ROCKS! OPEN THE DOOR!" roared the Chenoo.

Nolka ran over and swung open the flap of the lodge. Awasos and Kasko **proceeded** to bring in four more loads of rocks. Then, after the fourth load, the flap to the lodge was again closed. As soon as the door was closed, the sound of hissing steam came again from within the lodge. And just as before, just when they began to sneak away, the Chenoo shouted for them again.

90   "OPEN THE DOOR. MORE ROCKS, MORE WATER!"

"Yes, Grandfather. We are coming!"

Quickly Awasos and Kasko brought more rocks as Nolka ran to a nearby stream to refill the birch-bark bucket. When they opened the door to the lodge, huge gusts of steam flowed out so thickly that the only thing in the lodge they could see was the Chenoo's huge arm as it reached out to grab the freshly filled bucket of water.

Closing the flap again, all three **siblings** agreed it was no use trying to run. The Chenoo would only call for them again. And sure enough, it did.

"OPEN THE DOOR. MORE ROCKS. MORE WATER."

100   This time, they brought in every rock from the fire, even the rocks from the fire circle. They hoped the heat would be so great that the Chenoo would pass out. Standing by the lodge, they listened closely. But, to their surprise, as the hissing sound of the water hitting the rocks got louder and louder, the Chenoo began to sing.

"WAY-YAA, WAY-YAA, WAY-YAA, HOOO!!

WAY-YAA, WAY-YAA, WAY-YAA, HOOO!!"

Then it paused to pour more water on the rocks before it sang again.

"WAY-YAA, WAY-YAA, WAY-YAA, HOOO!!

WAY-YAA, WAY-YAA, WAY-YAA, HOOO!!"

110   This time, as the Chenoo sang, they noticed that its voice did not seem as loud. Again they heard the sounds of steam rising as water was poured on the stones.

"WAY-YAA, WAY-YAA, WAY-YAA, HOOO!!

WAY-YAA, WAY-YAA, WAY-YAA, HOOO!!"

That voice was much softer now, so soft that it sounded like the voice of an old man.

"WAY-YAA, WAY-YAA, WAY-YAA, HOOO!!

WAY-YAA, WAY-YAA, WAY-YAA, HOOO!!"

Then it was silent.

120   "Grandchildren, open the door," a little voice called from inside the sweat lodge.

proceed (prō-sēd´) v. to go forward or onward; continue

sibling (sĭb´lĭng) n. a brother or sister

ANALYZE VISUALS
What part of the legend does this photograph represent?

Awasos lifted up the door flap. A huge gust of steam blew out from the lodge, knocking him backward. As the steam rose into the air, a little old man crawled out from the lodge. As he stood up, the little old man began to cough. He coughed and coughed until he coughed up a huge piece of ice in the shape of a human heart. Falling to the ground, the heart-shaped piece of ice that was the bad spirit of the Chenoo shattered on a rock.

"Thank you, my grandchildren. You have saved me. I am no longer a monster. Now I am truly your grandfather," said the old man with 130 a smile. **F**

S o Nolka and her two brothers took the old man who had been a Chenoo as their grandfather. They brought him back to their village, where he quietly and peacefully lived out the rest of his days. ~

F LEGENDS
Reread lines 122–130. What extraordinary event has occurred?

Comprehension

1. **Recall** What does Nolka do while her brothers are hunting?

2. **Recall** Why do the brothers rush back to camp when they see a set of large footprints?

3. **Clarify** How do the three plan to escape from the Chenoo?

Literary Analysis

4. **Make Inferences** Look at the chart you created as you read. In what ways does Nolka demonstrate the qualities of a heroine?

5. **Examine Characteristics of Legends** Which details about the characters and events in "The Chenoo" seem real, and which do not? Make a chart like the one shown. Fill in each square using details from the legend.

	Character	Event
Real		
Not Real		

6. **Identify Theme** In many legends, the hero slays a monster; but in this legend, the hero saves a monster. What lessons about human nature and behavior does this story seem to teach?

7. **Analyze Symbol** Reread lines 122–127. What might the heart of ice that the Chenoo coughs up symbolize?

Extension and Challenge

8. **Big Question Activity** Although "The Chenoo" is about a life-and-death battle of wits with a monster that inspires **fear,** the story also has a humorous element. On a chart like the one on page 676, record how you think Nolka, Kasko, and Awasos would rate their ordeal. Do you think that at any point Nolka and her brothers were having fun applying their courage and quick wits to the unusual situation? Explain.

9.   **SOCIAL STUDIES CONNECTION** Storytelling has always been an important part of Native American culture. Turn to page 687 to learn more about the people who first told the story of the Chenoo. Then choose another Native American legend to read. Share a summary of the story with the class.

> **RESEARCH LINKS**
> For more on Native American legends, visit the **Research Center** at **ClassZone.com.**

Vocabulary in Context

VOCABULARY PRACTICE

Choose the letter of the word or phrase that is most closely related to the boldfaced word.

1. **proceed:** (a) continue, (b) halt, (c) pause
2. **sibling:** (a) friend, (b) father, (c) brother
3. **inspect:** (a) ignore, (b) refuse, (c) examine
4. **clearing:** (a) grove of trees, (b) open land, (c) thick jungle

clearing

inspect

proceed

sibling

VOCABULARY IN WRITING

Using two or more vocabulary words, write a paragraph from Nolka's point of view explaining what she was thinking when she first saw the Chenoo. You could start like this.

> **EXAMPLE SENTENCE**
>
> When the monster came into the **clearing**, I didn't know what to do.

VOCABULARY STRATEGY: HOMONYMS

Words with the same spelling and pronunciation but different meanings and origins are called **homonyms.** One example is the word *hide*.

Read the following dictionary entries for the word *hide*. The number at the upper right of the word signals that the word has more than one origin.

hide[1] (hīd) *v.* to put or keep out of sight [middle English *hidden*, cover]

hide[2] (hīd) *n.* the skin or pelt of an animal [old English *hyd*, skin]

If you read a word that is used in a way that is unfamiliar to you, check a dictionary to see if it is a homonym.

PRACTICE Each of the following words has one or more homonyms. Look up the word in a dictionary, and write its different definitions.

1. pick   3. duck   5. die
2. band   4. reel   6. flat

VOCABULARY PRACTICE
For more practice, go to the **Vocabulary Center** at **ClassZone.com.**

MAP "The Chenoo" is a legend from the Passamaquoddy people. This map illustrates the location where the Passamaquoddy lived in the past, and where many live today.

Lands of the Passamaquoddy

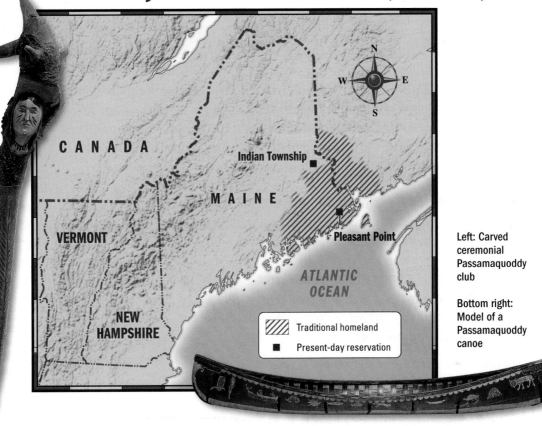

Left: Carved ceremonial Passamaquoddy club

Bottom right: Model of a Passamaquoddy canoe

The legend of "The Chenoo" has been passed down from generation to generation by the Passamaquoddy people of northeastern North America. The early Passamaquoddy moved from place to place throughout the year to follow the herds of animals they hunted.

Despite their frequent movement, the Passamaquoddy remained within one general region. Their eastern location allowed them to be among the first to see the rising sun each day. Because of this, they became known as "People of the Dawn."

Today, Passamaquoddy reservations are located in eastern Maine in two locations: Pleasant Point and Indian Township. These reservations are within the same region where previous generations of Passamaquoddy people lived and traveled.

Damon and Pythias
Greek Legend Dramatized by Fan Kissen

What is true FRIENDSHIP?

KEY IDEA It's often said that actions speak louder than words. This is certainly the case when it comes to **friendship.** It's important for people to *show* that they're your friends and not just *say* it. In *Damon and Pythias,* you'll read about a man who is willing to pay the ultimate price to help a friend.

WEB IT Think about what types of behavior reflect true **friendship**—the ways people prove to each other that they're loyal and trustworthy. Then use a web diagram like the one shown to record your thoughts.

True Friendship

loyalty

stick up for each other

encourage each other

● LITERARY ANALYSIS: CULTURAL VALUES IN LEGENDS

What does it take to be a hero? In many cases, a hero is someone who shows great bravery. In legends, though, a hero is expected not only to be brave but also to uphold the **cultural values** of a society. These are the behaviors a society wants its people to have. In ancient Greece, two important cultural values were

- loyalty, or devotion to friends and family

- honesty

As you read *Damon and Pythias*, look for examples of how the main characters demonstrate these values.

● READING STRATEGY: READING A PLAY

In some plays, a **narrator,** or teller of the story, helps guide the audience through the action. The narrator supplies background information, explains what's happening, and tells about conversations and events not included in the dialogue. The narrator might also explain characters' thoughts and feelings and why they act as they do.

As you read the play, use a chart like the one shown to summarize the information the narrator provides and how it helps you understand the play.

Narrator's Information	How It Helps
lines 10–12: The king is cruel and shows no mercy for anyone.	tells me what kind of person the king is

▲ VOCABULARY IN CONTEXT

Fan Kissen uses the words in Column A to help tell the story of two men fighting a cruel king. Match the words in Column A with their meanings in Column B.

Column A
1. desperately
2. harsh
3. persuade
4. proclaim
5. tyrant

Column B
a. convince
b. dictator
c. urgently
d. rough
e. announce

Author Online

**Fan Kissen
1904–1978**

Radio Writer
From the 1940s to the 1960s, Fan Kissen had a radio series called *Tales from the Four Winds*. Kissen dramatized world folk tales and legends, such as *Damon and Pythias*, for the series. Though the majority of her writing consists of plays written in radio script format, Kissen also produced several biographies of little-known historical figures for young people.

Background

Legendary Friendship *Damon and Pythias* is an ancient Greek legend, adapted as a radio play. The story takes place around the 4th century B.C., and the relationship between Damon and Pythias has remained a model of true friendship throughout the centuries.

MORE ABOUT THE AUTHOR AND BACKGROUND
To learn more about Fan Kissen and Greek legends, visit the **Literature Center** at **ClassZone.com**.

DAMON AND PYTHIAS

Dramatized by Fan Kissen

CAST OF CHARACTERS

Narrator	Pythias	Mother
First Voice	King	First Robber
Second Voice	Damon	Second Robber
Soldier	Third Voice	

Narrator. Long, long ago there lived on the island of Sicily[1] two young men named Damon and Pythias.[2] They were known far and wide for the strong friendship each had for the other. Their names have come down to our own times to mean true friendship. You may hear it said of two persons:

First Voice. Those two? Why, they're like Damon and Pythias!

10 **Narrator.** The king of that country was a cruel **tyrant**. He made cruel laws, and he showed no mercy toward anyone who broke his laws. Now, you might very well wonder:

Second Voice. Why didn't the people rebel?

Narrator. Well, the people didn't dare rebel because they feared the king's great and powerful army. No one dared say a word against the king or his laws—except Damon and Pythias. One day a soldier overheard 20 Pythias speaking against a new law the king had **proclaimed**.

Soldier. Ho, there! Who are you that dares to speak so about our king?

Pythias (*unafraid*). I am called Pythias.

Soldier. Don't you know it is a crime to speak against the king or his laws? You are under

---

1. **Sicily** (sĭs′ə-lē): large island off the southern tip of Italy.

2. **Damon** (dā′mən) . . . **Pythias** (pĭth′ē-əs).

Poseidon and Apollo. Detail from *Poseidon, Apollo and Artemis.* Relief from the east frieze of the Parthenon, Athens. Inv. 856. Acropolis Museum, Athens. © Erich Lessing/Art Resource, New York.

arrest! Come and tell this opinion of yours to the king's face!

(*music: a few short bars in and out*)

30 **Narrator.** When Pythias was brought before the king, he showed no fear. He stood straight and quiet before the throne.

King (*hard, cruel*). So, Pythias! They tell me you do not approve of the laws I make.

Pythias. I am not alone, Your Majesty, in thinking your laws are cruel. But you rule the people with such an iron hand that they dare not complain.

King (*angry*). But you have the daring to 40 complain for them! Have they appointed you their champion?

Pythias. No, Your Majesty. I speak for myself alone. I have no wish to make trouble for anyone. But I am not afraid to tell you that the people are suffering under your rule. They want to have a voice in making the laws for themselves. You do not allow them to speak up for themselves.

King. In other words, you are calling me a tyrant! Well, you shall learn for yourself how 50 a tyrant treats a rebel! Soldier! Throw this man into prison!

Soldier. At once, Your Majesty! Don't try to resist, Pythias!

Pythias. I know better than to try to resist a soldier of the king! And for how long am I to remain in prison, Your Majesty, merely for speaking out for the people?

King (*cruel*). Not for very long, Pythias. Two weeks from today, at noon, you shall be put 60 to death in the public square as an example to anyone else who may dare to question my laws or acts. Off to prison with him, soldier!

(*music: in briefly and out*)

Narrator. When Damon heard that his friend Pythias had been thrown into prison and the severe punishment that was to follow, he was heartbroken. He rushed to the prison and **persuaded** the guard to let him speak to his friend.

70 **Damon.** Oh, Pythias! How terrible to find you here! I wish I could do something to save you!

Pythias. Nothing can save me, Damon, my dear friend. I am prepared to die. But there is one thought that troubles me greatly.

Damon. What is it? I will do anything to help you.

Pythias. I'm worried about what will happen to my mother and my sister when I'm gone.

Damon. I'll take care of them, Pythias, as if 80 they were my own mother and sister.

Pythias. Thank you, Damon. I have money to leave them. But there are other things I must arrange. If only I could go to see them before I die! But they live two days' journey from here, you know.

Damon. I'll go to the king and beg him to give you your freedom for a few days. You'll give your word to return at the end of that time. Everyone in Sicily knows you for a man who 90 has never broken his word.

Pythias. Do you believe for one moment that the king would let me leave this prison, no matter how good my word may have been all my life?

Damon. I'll tell him that I shall take your place in this prison cell. I'll tell him that if you do not return by the appointed day, he may kill me in your place!

Pythias. No, no, Damon! You must not do 100 such a foolish thing! I cannot—I will not— let you do this! Damon! Damon! Don't go! (*to himself*) Damon, my friend! You may find yourself in a cell beside me!

(*music: in briefly and out*)

Damon (*begging*). Your Majesty! I beg of you! Let Pythias go home for a few days to bid farewell to his mother and sister. He gives his word that he will return at your appointed time. Everyone knows that his word can be trusted.

110 **King.** In ordinary business affairs—perhaps. But he is now a man under sentence of death. To free him even for a few days would strain his honesty—any man's honesty—too far. Pythias would never return here! I consider him a traitor, but I'm certain he's no fool.

Damon. Your Majesty! I will take his place in the prison until he comes back. If he does not return, then you may take my life in his place.

King (*astonished*). What did you say, Damon?

120 **Damon.** I'm so certain of Pythias that I am offering to die in his place if he fails to return on time.

King. I can't believe you mean it!

Damon. I do mean it, Your Majesty.

King. You make me very curious, Damon, so curious that I'm willing to put you and Pythias to the test. This exchange of prisoners will be made. But Pythias must be back two weeks from today, at noon.

130 **Damon.** Thank you, Your Majesty!

King. The order with my official seal shall go by your own hand, Damon. But I warn you, if your friend does not return on time, you shall surely die in his place! I shall show no mercy!

(*music: in briefly and out*)

Narrator. Pythias did not like the king's bargain with Damon. He did not like to leave his friend in prison with the chance that he might lose his life if something went wrong. But

140 at last Damon persuaded him to leave, and Pythias set out for his home. More than a week went by. The day set for the death sentence drew near. Pythias did not return. Everyone in the city knew of the condition on which the king had permitted Pythias to go home. Everywhere people met, the talk was sure to turn to the two friends.

First Voice. Do you suppose Pythias will come back?

150 **Second Voice.** Why should he stick his head under the king's axe, once he's escaped?

Third Voice. Still, would an honorable man like Pythias let such a good friend die for him?

First Voice. There's no telling what a man will do when it's a question of his own life against another's.

Second Voice. But if Pythias doesn't come back before the time is up, he will be killing his friend.

Third Voice. Well, there's still a few days' time.

160 I, for one, am certain that Pythias will return in time.

Second Voice. And I am just as certain that he will *not*. Friendship is friendship, but a man's own life is something stronger, I say!

165 **Narrator.** Two days before the time was up, the king himself visited Damon in his prison cell.

(*sound: iron door unlocked and opened*)

King (*mocking*). You see now, Damon, that you were a fool to make this bargain. Your friend

170 has tricked you! He will not come back here to be killed! He has deserted you!

Damon (*calm and firm*). I have faith in my friend. I know he will return.

King (*mocking*). We shall see!

(*sound: iron door shut and locked*)

Narrator. Meanwhile, when Pythias reached the home of his family, he arranged his business affairs so that his mother and sister would be able to live comfortably for the rest of their

180 years. Then he said a last farewell to them before starting back to the city.

Mother (*in tears*). Pythias, it will take you only two days to get back. Stay another day, I beg you!

Pythias. I dare not stay longer, Mother. Remember, Damon is locked up in my prison cell while I'm gone. Please don't make it harder for me! Farewell! Don't weep for me. My death may help to bring better days for all our people.

Narrator. So Pythias began his return journey in
190 plenty of time. But bad luck struck him on the very first day. At twilight,[3] as he walked along a lonely stretch of woodland, a rough voice called:

First Robber. Not so fast there, young man! Stop!

Pythias (*startled*). Oh! What is it? What do you want?

Second Robber. Your money bags.

Pythias. My money bags? I have only this small bag of coins. I shall need them for some last favors, perhaps, before I die.

200 **First Robber.** What do you mean, before you die? We don't mean to kill you, only to take your money.

Pythias. I'll give you my money, only don't delay me any longer. I am to die by the king's order three days from now. If I don't return to prison on time, my friend must die in my place.

First Robber. A likely story! What man would be fool enough to go back to prison, ready to die?

Second Robber. And what man would be fool
210 enough to die for you?

First Robber. We'll take your money, all right. And we'll tie you up while we get away.

Pythias (*begging*). No! No! I must get back to free my friend! (*fade*) I must go back!

Narrator. But the two robbers took Pythias' money, tied him to a tree, and went off as fast as they could. Pythias struggled to free himself. He cried out for help as loud as he could for

a long time. But no one traveled through
220 that lonesome woodland after dark. The sun had been up for many hours before he finally managed to free himself from the ropes that had tied him to the tree. He lay on the ground, hardly able to breathe.

(*music: in briefly and out*)

Narrator. After a while Pythias got to his feet. Weak and dizzy from hunger and thirst and his struggle to free himself, he set off again. Day and night he traveled without stopping,
230 **desperately** trying to reach the city in time to save Damon's life.

(*music: up and out*)

Narrator. On the last day, half an hour before noon, Damon's hands were tied behind his back, and he was taken into the public square. The people muttered[4] angrily as Damon was led in by the jailer. Then the king entered and seated himself on a high platform.

(*sound: crowd voices in and hold under single
240 voices*)

Soldier (*loud*). Long live the king!

First Voice (*low*). The longer he lives, the more miserable our lives will be!

King (*loud, mocking*). Well, Damon, your lifetime is nearly up. Where is your good friend Pythias now?

Damon (*firm*). I have faith in my friend. If he has not returned, I'm certain it is through no fault of his own.

250 **King** (*mocking*). The sun is almost overhead. The shadow is almost at the noon mark. And still your friend has not returned to give you back your life!

Damon (*quiet*). I am ready, and happy, to die in his place.

---

3. **twilight:** the time of day between sunset and dark. The darker stage of twilight is often called dusk.

4. **mutter:** to speak in low tones, especially to complain.

Reception in the Senate, detail from the Arch of Trajan (100s). Marble. Benevento, Campania, Italy. © Bridgeman Art Library.

King (*harsh*). And you shall, Damon! Jailer, lead the prisoner to the—

(*sound: crowd voices up to a roar, then under*)

First Voice (*over noise*). Look! It's Pythias!

260 **Second Voice** (*over noise*). Pythias has come back!

Pythias (*breathless*). Let me through! Damon!

Damon. Pythias!

Pythias. Thank the gods I'm not too late!

Damon (*quiet, sincere*). I would have died for you gladly, my friend.

Crowd Voices (*loud, demanding*). Set them free! Set them both free!

King (*loud*). People of the city! (*crowd voices out*)

270 Never in all my life have I seen such faith and friendship, such loyalty between men. There are many among you who call me **harsh** and cruel. But I cannot kill any man who proves such strong and true friendship for another. Damon and Pythias, I set you both free. (*roar of approval from crowd*) I am king. I command a great army. I have stores[5] of gold and precious jewels. But I would give all my money and my power for one friend like Damon or Pythias!

280 (*sound: roar of approval from crowd up briefly and out*)

(*music: up and out*)

---

5. **stores:** great quantities.

Comprehension

1. **Recall** Why is Pythias arrested?

2. **Clarify** Why is the king willing to strike such an unusual bargain with Damon?

3. **Summarize** What causes Pythias to return so late?

Literary Analysis

4. **Make Inferences** Reread lines 165–173. What does Damon's response to the king's mockery tell you about the nature of his **friendship** with Pythias?

5. **Reading a Play** Look at the chart you filled in while reading. Explain how the play would be different without the **narrator's** comments. What key pieces of information would be missing?

6. **Identify Cultural Values in a Legend** How do Damon and Pythias prove their honesty and their loyalty to each other? Make a list of their important words and actions.

Examples of Honesty and Loyalty
1. Damon immediately rushes to prison to see Pythias.
2.

7. **Analyze a Character** Pythias tells his mother not to weep, saying, "My death may help to bring better days for all our people" (lines 187–188). Explain what he means. What does the statement reveal about his character?

8. **Make Judgments** Throughout Sicily, Pythias was known for being a trustworthy person. Why do you think some people still doubted that he would return in time to save Damon?

Extension and Challenge

9. **Creative Project: Drama** In a small group, record your own "radio broadcast" of *Damon and Pythias*. Be sure to include in your recording any music or other sound effects mentioned in the play. Then play your recording for the class.

10. **SOCIAL STUDIES CONNECTION** The character of the king is based on Dionysius the Elder (also known as Dionysius I), a real ruler of Syracuse, Sicily. Use encyclopedias and the Internet to do research on him. Share your findings with the class.

> **RESEARCH LINKS**
> For more on Dionysius the Elder, visit the **Research Center** at **ClassZone.com**.

Reading-Writing Connection

Expand your knowledge of *Damon and Pythias* by responding to these prompts. Then complete the **Grammar and Writing** exercise.

WRITING PROMPTS

A. Short Response: Examine a Cultural Value
Think about how the value of loyalty is presented in the play. Write a **one-paragraph response** that identifies who is the most loyal character in the play and why.

B. Extended Response: Write Dialogue
Imagine the conversation Damon and Pythias have after Pythias agrees to let Damon take his place in prison. Write the conversation as a **half-page dialogue.** (Use the play as an example of how to write dialogue.)

SELF-CHECK

A thoughtful response will . . .
• identify a loyal character
• use examples from the play as support

A realistic dialogue will . . .
• reflect the men's deep **friendship**
• use speech similar to what the characters say in the play

GRAMMAR AND WRITING

USE CORRECT SENTENCE STRUCTURE An **independent clause** can stand alone as a sentence. A **dependent clause** is a group of words that contains a subject and a verb but cannot stand alone as a sentence. Dependent clauses begin with words and phrases such as *because, even though, if, since, that,* and *when.* When a dependent clause and an independent clause are combined, they form a **complex sentence.**

Original: Pythias criticizes the king. Even though he knows he will be punished for it. (*The first clause is independent. The second clause is dependent and cannot stand alone.*)

Revised: Pythias criticizes the king even though he knows he will be punished for it. (*Together, the clauses form a complex sentence.*)

PRACTICE Form a complex sentence by combining the two clauses.

1. Pythias promises to return. After he visits his family.
2. Most people probably wouldn't return. If they were in his position.
3. Damon never gave up his faith. Because he completely trusted Pythias.
4. The crowd was happy. That Damon and Pythias would both be free.

For more help with dependent clauses and complex sentences, see page R64 in the Grammar Handbook.

Uncle Septimus's Beard

Tall Tale by Herbert Shippey

Why do we
EXAGGERATE?

KEY IDEA Have you ever claimed you were hungry enough to eat a horse, or said that you waited in the rain until you were soaked to the bone? Sometimes, in order to express feelings or describe adventures, people **exaggerate.** As you will see in the tale that follows, exaggeration can add humor to a story and make everyday experiences sound more interesting.

QUICKWRITE Think of a time when you or someone you know exaggerated in order to make a point or make a story more exciting. Then write a brief version of each—the real story, and the exaggerated version. Share your writing with your classmates.

● LITERARY ANALYSIS: CHARACTERISTICS OF A TALL TALE

A **tall tale** is a humorous story in which the characters and events are exaggerated. This means that the characters and events are made to seem bigger, louder, or greater in some way than they really are. For example:

Eventually the beard reached down to his toes and began to drag on the ground. Then he had to wash it out every evening to get rid of the dust and grit that would collect during the day. Aunt Rachel was rather pleased with this new development, because she no longer had to sweep the floor, except under the beds.

As you read "Uncle Septimus's Beard," look for other examples of exaggeration.

● READING STRATEGY: VISUALIZE

Tall tales are often so full of exaggerated action and description that you can **visualize,** or picture in your mind, many of their characters and scenes. As you read "Uncle Septimus's Beard," make a list of descriptive words and phrases that help you create a strong mental picture of the tale's events.

Vivid Descriptions
1. Beard used to sweep floor
2. Beard used as a jump rope

▲ VOCABULARY IN CONTEXT

Herbert Shippey uses the boldfaced words to help tell the story of a man's unbelievable beard. Try to figure out what each boldfaced word means within its sentence.

| **WORD LIST** | assert | imposing | incident | inspiration |

1. Everyone remembers an **incident** involving the beard.
2. No one knew Septimus's **inspiration** for growing it.
3. People **assert** that it was the greatest beard ever.
4. The **imposing** beard was the talk of the town.

Author Onine

Weeding and Reading As a teenager, it was Herbert Shippey's job to weed his family's garden. He would often take rests from his work in the hot Georgia sun to read Henry David Thoreau's *Walden.*

Herbert Shippey
born 1944

He says that reading opened his mind to "imaginative possibilities." Later, when deciding upon a career, Shippey chose to combine work with pleasure by becoming an English teacher.

MORE ABOUT THE AUTHOR
For more on Herbert Shippey, visit the **Literature Center** at ClassZone.com.

Background

Campfire Stories Folk tales are stories that have been handed down from one generation to the next and are about common people, or folk. When a folk tale is about extraordinary events and characters, it is called a **tall tale.** Some of the first tall tales were told around campfires in the American West of the 1800s.

Humorous Tales To help cope with their difficult lives, some early American settlers created and told humorous stories. Some of the heroes and heroines of these stories were imaginary characters. Others were real people who were known for their strength and courage. As the stories of these people's deeds were retold, they often became exaggerated, and the people became larger than life.

Uncle Septimus's Beard

Herbert Shippey

No one knows exactly why Uncle Septimus began growing a beard. Aunt Rachel always said that she admired a man with hair on his chin. Her grandfather, a circuit-riding Methodist preacher, was noted for having a long beard. Whenever he stood at the pulpit,[1] pounding his fists and preaching hellfire and brimstone, some people thought he looked like Moses in their Bible pictures. So maybe this **imposing** image, recalled so vividly by Aunt Rachel, was the **inspiration** for Uncle Septimus's decision. Or maybe one day he just got tired of shaving.

Moreover, no one knew why everyone—including his grandchildren—
10 called him "Uncle." Perhaps his blue eyes sparkled with such good humor and he did so many neighborly deeds that he seemed like an uncle to half the county.

When his beard extended to his waist, Uncle Septimus tucked it beneath the bib of his overalls to keep from dribbling milk, gravy, or cane syrup on it when he sat down to eat. Sometimes, though, he'd forget, and after a meal he'd have to walk to the back porch to shake out the crumbs and bacon rinds. The shakings alone were enough to keep his bird dogs and chickens fat and happy. **Ⓐ**

ANALYZE VISUALS
In what ways does the illustration add humor to the **tall tale?**

imposing (ĭm-pō′zĭng)
adj. impressive; grand

inspiration
(ĭn′spə-rā′shən)
n. something that motivates or influences

Ⓐ **TALL TALE**
Reread lines 9–18. What details about Septimus and his beard seem exaggerated?

---

1. **pulpit:** raised platform or stand used in preaching or leading a religious service.

Illustrations by Joel Priddy.

Eventually the beard reached down to his toes and began to drag
20 on the ground. Then he had to wash it out every evening to get rid
of the dust and grit that would collect during the day. Aunt Rachel
was rather pleased with this new development, because she no longer
had to sweep the floor, except under the beds.

The beard grew longer and longer. It became so long that it dragged
several feet behind Uncle Septimus, but he refused to trim it. Sometimes
at family dinners he fell asleep in his favorite chair beneath the pecan tree
in the front yard. Then the grandchildren took the beard and used it as
a jump rope. They swung it round and round and took turns jumping,
but Uncle Septimus never seemed to notice. On other occasions, he
30 looped the beard up in his own hands and let the children swing on it.

The grandchildren all loved the beard, and they enjoyed examining it
while he slept, because they found marvelous surprises. Since the beard
was so long, all kinds of things became entangled in it. One summer
morning two of the grandchildren pulled out a robin's egg, a broken
arrowhead made from caramel-colored flint, six chicken feathers, two
swirled marbles, a silver dollar, and two green lizards that had set up
housekeeping, not to mention tons of cockleburs and beggar lice.[2] **B**

Later that same day Uncle Septimus went fishing at the creek with his
sons. He sat on a log and carefully removed his beard from beneath the
40 bib of his overalls. Handful by handful, he drew the beard out, letting
the end down into the water and then allowing the current to carry
it downstream. It steadily unreeled the way a harpoon rope uncoils when
it has stuck firmly in a sounding whale. Septimus's sons watched the long
gray strand floating downstream until the whole mass was quivering
underwater like seaweed.

Uncle Septimus sat still for several minutes, and then the sons waded
into the creek and began drawing the beard in. Coil after dripping coil
fell upon the sand, and the fish tangled in the beard flopped onto the
bank. Soon there were catfish, bluegills, largemouth bass, pike, jack, gar,
50 snapping turtles, and even a water moccasin.[3] There were so many fish
that Uncle Septimus gave a fish fry for the whole community.

Oftentimes on a cold winter night Uncle Septimus wrapped his beard
around himself to keep warm in bed. If Aunt Rachel wanted to wake him
up, she just asked one of her hefty sons to jerk the end of the beard, and
out he would come, rolling like a bolt of fabric tossed on a store counter.

B VISUALIZE
What information
about the uses of the
beard helps you picture
it in your mind? Add this
information to your list.

---

2. **cockleburs and beggar lice:** any of several plants having small, prickly fruits that cling to clothing
   or animal fur.
3. **catfish . . . water moccasin:** catfish, bluegills, largemouth bass, pike, jack, and gar are all types
   of freshwater fish. The water moccasin, also known as a cottonmouth, is a poisonous water snake
   found in the southeastern and south central United States.

Sometimes Uncle Septimus wrapped the beard round and round himself
when he sat at his deer stand before daybreak on a frosty winter morning.
In the uncertain predawn light, it looked as if a large, gray boa constrictor
had attacked him. Uncle Septimus claimed, though, that winding the
beard around himself allowed him to walk through the woods without
getting it tangled in the branches and briars. But there was a drawback.
It took him most of the night just to entwine[4] himself, and he had
to be careful to leave openings for his arms so that he could shoot.
Needless to say, going to the bathroom was a problem. So most of the
time he preferred just to let the beard drag behind him on the ground. **C**

You could always tell where Uncle Septimus had been. Old man
Marchant said that one time he went to Drothers's store, hoping to find
Uncle Septimus. He needed to see him about a hog that had broken out.
So he said to Bill Drothers, "I see Septimus has just left because yonder goes
his beard dragging out the front door. If I run, maybe I can catch him."

But Bill Drothers, sitting by the stove and reading the weekly paper,
didn't even look up. "You needn't bother," he said. "Septimus left over
an hour ago, and his beard's been unwinding ever since. Most likely
he's home now, sitting on his front porch and chewing tobacco while
one of his boys hauls in the beard."

The beard did create problems. One time Uncle Septimus walked
several times around the yard raking leaves, and the beard got all
fouled up. It had wrapped around a tree several times, and you could
no longer see the well for the beard. And the chicken coop was completely
covered. It took his boys three days to untangle him, and all that time the
chickens didn't lay a single egg because they thought it was night. Uncle
Septimus sat there the whole time, complaining about how he missed his
fried eggs.

Aunt Rachel kept saying, "Septimus, if you don't cut off that beard,
it's going to be the death of you! One of these days you're going to get
so tangled up, ain't nobody going to be able to get to you."

After that **incident,** Septimus's sons rigged up a windlass[5] and wrapped
the beard around it. That way he could work around the yard, and his
boys could wind the beard back up after he was finished. The beard didn't
completely unwind unless he went a long ways. Aunt Rachel also found
the windlass useful. Whenever she needed her husband, all she had to do
was start turning the handle, and eventually she'd see him coming down
the road, led by his beard. **D**

C TALL TALE
Reread lines 52–65.
In what way does the
simile "rolling like a bolt
of fabric tossed on
a store counter" create
a humorous effect?

incident (ĭn'sĭ-dənt)
n. a single event or
occurrence

D VISUALIZE
Reread lines 87–93.
What details do you
find amusing when you
visualize this scene?

---

4. **entwine** (ĕn-twīn'): to twist or coil together.

5. **windlass:** a machine used for pulling and lifting, usually on ships.

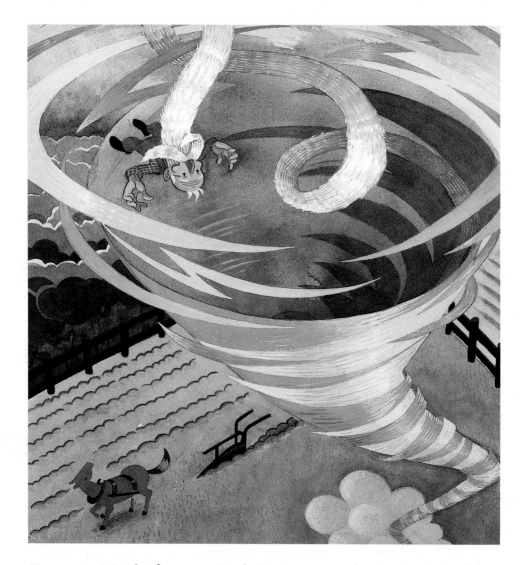

ANALYZE VISUALS
What similarities do you see between the tornado and Uncle Septimus's beard in this illustration?

Late one March afternoon, Uncle Septimus was plowing in the back field. The wind had been blowing all day, and the beard went streaming off downwind. Everything worked all right for a while. Uncle Septimus simply plowed upwind, and the beard didn't get in his way. It was a big field, and the beard had plenty of room to swish back and forth. But not quite enough room. There was a fence at the edge of the field, and the beard
100 backed up behind the fence and didn't go flowing off into the next county.

Well, Uncle Septimus got nearly forty acres plowed that afternoon, but the wind was blowing so hard he couldn't hear Aunt Rachel standing on the back porch calling him to supper. The boys came out and yelled to get their daddy's attention. But to their horror, the family saw a funnel cloud form over the woods beyond the field and start moving in Uncle Septimus's direction.

That tornado was twisting around, pulling up trees and stumps by the roots and tossing them in the air, and Uncle Septimus, not noticing

anything, just kept on plowing. At first it seemed the twister would miss
110 him. But though it had passed Uncle Septimus by, it was heading straight
for the beard pile behind the fence.

What happened next was simply amazing. The tornado caught that beard
and began winding it up round and round until Uncle Septimus himself
shot off into the cloud like a yo-yo snatched up by a child. That twister
began to roar louder and louder, and the lightning flashed all around.
Hail the size of hen eggs fell. Then the twister began to make a peculiar
high-pitched noise that gradually dwindled to a low hum. Finally, the thing
squeaked once and fell silent, like a man who's choked on a piece of tobacco.
That cloud swelled out like it would bust. It turned green and then gray and
120 purple and black. It swayed back and forth, uncertain which way to go.
And then the thing just blew up. Rain, hail, and clouds flew off in all
directions, leaving a clear evening sky with the full moon shining through.
Even a rip-snorting tornado couldn't deal with that much beard. **E**

Nobody knows what happened to Uncle Septimus. He just disappeared.
Some folks say he was carried up into heaven like the prophet Elijah.
Others say he was blown clean to Texas or some other place out West.
They speculate that even now he's trying to find his way back home.
Others say that he got blown to the Great Smoky Mountains and that he's
living up there today on top of Clingman's Dome,[6] and that a lot of times
130 when we look up and see a jet contrail,[7] it's not really vapor but Uncle
Septimus's beard. On windy days, they say, he goes up to the highest peak
and lets the wind catch that beard and stretch it out across the sky, just
to give it a good airing. Other people **assert** that what we take to be
Spanish moss hanging on the oaks in southern Georgia and northern
Florida may really be pieces of Uncle Septimus's beard.

Aunt Rachel preferred to take that view. She'd ride down the road beneath
the oak trees and say, "You know, it's kind of comforting to see the Spanish
moss. In a way it's kind of like Septimus never really left home. Seems all I'd
have to do is start tugging on one of those moss tips, and pretty soon here
140 would come Septimus back from Texas or Tennessee or wherever he's gone."

You may take whichever view you prefer. But one thing is for certain.
Uncle Septimus's beard was the most wonderful ever, and it's unlikely
people in this part of the country will ever stop talking about it. Probably
in the future they'll say he was kidnapped by aliens and that the tail of
Halley's comet[8] is really just his beard stretching across the night sky. ∾ **F**

---

6. **Clingman's Dome:** a mountain located on the border of North Carolina and Tennessee. It is the highest
peak in the Great Smoky Mountains.

7. **jet contrail:** a visible trail of water vapor or ice crystals that sometimes forms behind a jet plane.

8. **Halley's comet:** a bright, heavenly body with a cloudy tail that is visible from Earth about every 76 years.

E VISUALIZE
Reread lines 112–123.
Which descriptive words
and phrases help you
visualize the scene?

assert (ə-sûrt´) v. to put
into words with force or
confidence; maintain

VISUAL VOCABULARY

Spanish moss n. a plant
of the southeastern
United States with gray,
threadlike stems that
droop in long clusters

F TALL TALE
In what ways has Uncle
Septimus become larger
than life?

Comprehension

1. **Recall** Reread lines 24–30. How do Uncle Septimus's grandchildren make use of his beard?

2. **Clarify** What are some of the advantages and disadvantages of the beard?

3. **Summarize** What happens to the beard during the tornado?

Literary Analysis

4. **Visualize** Look at the list you made while reading. Which description makes it easiest for you to visualize the beard? Explain.

5. **Identify Characteristics of a Tall Tale** As the beard grows, so does the unbelievability of the events. How do the events surrounding the beard become more and more **exaggerated?** Make a timeline like the one shown to trace the way the uses for the beard change with its increasing length.

6. **Examine a Character** Aunt Rachel has both positive and negative feelings about Septimus's beard. Skim through the story and note her reactions to the beard. Are her feelings about Septimus and his beard more positive or negative overall? Explain your answer.

7. **Analyze a Character** Uncle Septimus was not a hero in the usual sense, yet he was a much-celebrated character. What made him special to the people around him? Cite examples from the story.

Extension and Challenge

8. **Creative Project: Music** Many American folk heroes, such as John Henry and Pecos Bill, had songs written about them. With a group of classmates, write a song about Uncle Septimus and his incredible beard. Present your song to the rest of the class.

9. **Inquiry and Research** Some characters who appear in tall tales were real people. Research American folk literature and find a character from a tall tale who was based on a real person. Why did he or she become the subject of a tale? Share your findings with your classmates.

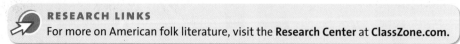

RESEARCH LINKS
For more on American folk literature, visit the **Research Center** at ClassZone.com.

Vocabulary in Context

VOCABULARY PRACTICE

Choose the vocabulary word that best completes each sentence.

1. Len's unusual height and large build made him an ____ figure.
2. The winner of the race was an ____ to her fans.
3. In one embarrassing ____, Stella tripped on the stairs.
4. Lisa's parents ____ that she is a gifted pianist.

assert

imposing

incident

inspiration

VOCABULARY IN WRITING

Imagine you lived near Uncle Septimus at the time of the story. Write a paragraph about an encounter you had with him. You might start like this.

> **EXAMPLE SENTENCE**
>
> *In one **incident**, Septimus got his beard stuck in a briar bush.*

VOCABULARY STRATEGY: CONNOTATIONS AND MEANING

A word's **connotations** are the different shades of meaning that are suggested by the word. These trigger different thoughts and feelings than the **denotation,** or dictionary definition, of the word does. For example

- The vocabulary word *assert* means "to put into words with confidence," but it carries a positive connotation of directness or support. (*The citizen* asserted *that she had the right to vote.*)

- *Argue* also means "to put into words with confidence," but it usually carries a negative connotation of conflict. (*He* argued *that it was a foolish thing to do.*)

It is important to consider the connotations of the words you choose when you write. They can affect how well your ideas are understood.

PRACTICE Decide which word in each pair has a positive connotation. Then write a sentence that shows its positive meaning. Use a dictionary if needed.

1. quaint/strange
2. stench/aroma
3. colorful/gaudy
4. slender/skinny
5. fussy/careful
6. energetic/wild

VOCABULARY PRACTICE
For more practice, go to the **Vocabulary Center** at ClassZone.com.

The Crane Maiden
Japanese Folk Tale Retold by Rafe Martin

Aunty Misery
Puerto Rican Folk Tale Retold by Judith Ortiz Cofer

When is it time to LET GO?

KEY IDEA There are times when we have to say goodbye—to someone or something we love, or to feelings that are no longer helpful. There may also be times when we have to choose to **release** someone from a promise or sense of responsibility. The following two folk tales demonstrate different kinds of letting go.

DISCUSS With a group of classmates, make a list of stories or movies in which a character has to give up someone or something. Discuss which situation was the most difficult, and why.

Story or Movie	Character	What Character Lets Go Of
1.		
2.		

● LITERARY ANALYSIS: CHARACTERISTICS OF FOLK TALES

Folk tales are stories that have been passed down from one generation to another by being told aloud. They often feature both human and animal characters. In most folk tales

- a character represents one or more qualities—for example, greed, honesty, kindness, or cleverness
- supernatural beings and events are part of the story
- a lesson or message about life is presented

As you read "The Crane Maiden" and "Aunty Misery," notice which of these characteristics are present in each folk tale.

● READING STRATEGY: SUMMARIZE

When you **summarize,** you retell, using fewer words, the main ideas and most important details of something you've read or heard. Though a summary doesn't include your own opinions or ideas, you do need to decide which ideas and information are most important to include.

As you read each of the following folk tales, create a chart like the one shown to record key information. This will help you summarize the folk tales later.

Setting	Characters	Key Events

▲ VOCABULARY IN CONTEXT

These boldfaced words are used to help convey the messages in these two folk tales. To see how many of the words you already know, write a definition of each.

WORD	hospitality	mournful	taunt
LIST	inevitable	snare	

1. Neighborhood children **taunt** and tease the old woman.
2. Her **hospitality** made the visitor feel welcome in her home.
3. He found the poor animal trapped in a **snare.**
4. It was **inevitable** that the girl would have to leave.
5. They were **mournful** about the loss of their daughter.

Author Online

Rafe Martin: Writer and Storyteller Rafe Martin started out as a writer. But after he had children and began reading aloud to them, he discovered the full power of storytelling:

Rafe Martin born 1946

"I began to get a sense that the telling of stories was really how they were passed on, and the power lay in finding voice and sharing stories." Martin continues to write and has produced over 20 books based on traditional tales.

Judith Ortiz Cofer: Writer from Two Cultures As a child, Judith Ortiz Cofer moved back and forth between her family's native Puerto Rico and their home in Paterson, New Jersey. In Puerto Rico, Cofer learned traditional storytelling from her

Judith Ortiz Cofer born 1952

grandmother. In Paterson, she spent much of her free time at the public library. Cofer read the library's entire section of folk literature. In her own stories, Cofer blends her love of language with her experience of growing up in two cultures.

MORE ABOUT THE AUTHOR
For more on the authors, visit the **Literature Center** at ClassZone.com.

THE
CRANE
MAIDEN

Retold by Rafe Martin

Once, long ago, an old couple lived all alone near the edges of a marsh.[1] They were hard-working but poor.

One day the man had been gathering marsh plants, cattails, and such for his wife to cook. As he walked back along the trail, he heard a sharp cry and the sounds of someone—or something—struggling. Parting the long grasses by the trail's edge, he walked carefully into the marsh. The sounds—a clacking and a flapping, whirring noise—came from up ahead. Frightened but still curious, he stepped forward and looked. There on the ground before him lay a great white crane. Its leg was trapped
10 in a **snare** and it was flapping desperately about trying to get free. Its beak was clacking open and shut. Its eye was wild with pain and fear. Its wings were muddied. Never had the man seen such desperation in a wild creature. His heart was moved. Speaking soothingly he drew closer. Somehow the crane seemed to sense his intent and grew calm. Gentle and slow were the man's movements as he approached. Then, bending down, he loosened the snare from the crane's leg and backed away. **A**

---

1. **marsh:** a wet, low-lying area, often thick with tall grasses.

snare (snâr) *n.* a trap for catching small animals and birds

A SUMMARIZE
What have you learned so far about the **setting** and **characters**?

Crane (about 1800), Kano Yosen'in Korenobu. Hanging scroll. Photo © 2007 Museum of Fine Arts, Boston.

The crane stood up. Flexing its injured leg, it stood there gazing directly at the man. Then opening its wings, it flapped once, twice, lifted up off the muddy ground, and flew away.

20 The man stood gazing after the great white bird as it made its way across the sky. Tears came to his eyes with the beauty of it. "I must see this clearly, and remember it, every detail," he said to himself. "How my wife will enjoy hearing of this adventure. I shall weave every detail into words for her, so she too will see."

"You are late," his wife said when her husband returned. "I have been worried. Are you all right?"

"I am better than all right, dear wife. I have had an adventure. I have seen such a sight. Wait, let me remove my sandals and sit down. I shall tell you all."

30 Then he told her of his finding the trapped crane, of the bird's panic and pain, and of the great joy he felt as he watched the white bird fly away.

"Dear husband, I am so glad you helped that wild creature. Truly it must have been a wondrous sight to see the crane rise up from the muddied ground and soar into the heavens."

"It was. It was. I have told it to you as best I could. For when I saw it fly I knew it was a sight you would have loved. And I wanted to share it with you." **B**

"Thank you, husband." Then she steamed the plants he had gathered and they ate their rice and drank their tea and, when it grew late and 40 the moon rose up in the blackness and sailed across the night sky, they let the fire sink down and they slept. **C**

The next morning they heard a knocking at the door. The woman opened the door and there stood a young girl.

"I am lost," she said. "May I come in?"

"Of course. Come in, dear child," the old woman said. "Have a cup of tea. Sit down."

So the girl came in. She was alone in this world, she said, "Let me confess," she added, after drinking the tea and eating the rice the old couple gave her, "I would like to stay here with you. I am a hard worker. 50 I no longer wish to be alone. You are kind people. Please let me stay."

The old couple had always wanted a daughter, and so it was agreed.

"Thank you," the girl said. "I do not think you will regret it." She peered curiously around the house. She looked into an adjoining room. Her face lit up. "I see you have a loom.² May I use it from time to time?"

B FOLK TALES
What quality or qualities have the old man and his wife demonstrated?

C SUMMARIZE
What has happened in the story so far? Record the main events in your chart.

---

2. **loom:** a device for making cloth by weaving strands of yarn or thread together.

ANALYZE VISUALS
How does the girl in this work of art **compare** with your image of the young girl in the story?

"Daughter," the woman said, "all that we have is yours. Of course you may use the loom."

"I am a shy weaver," the girl said. "Please, Mother, please, Father, when I am weaving do not look into the room until I am done. Will you promise me this?"

60 "It will be as you wish, child."

The next day their new daughter said she would go into the weaving room. The door was to be shut and neither her father nor her mother were to look in until her work was completed.

All day the girl sat at the loom. And all day the old couple heard the clacking and the whirring of the shuttle, the spinning of the bobbins[3] of thread.

When the sun was setting the girl emerged, pale and worn. But in her hands she held the most splendid cloth the old couple had ever seen. The pattern was perfect, the colors glowing. Images of the marsh, the sun,
70 the flight of cranes flowed elegantly through the finely woven material.

"Mother, Father, please take this cloth to the market and sell it. With the money your life will become easier. I want to do this for you."

The old people were astonished at their daughter's skill. The next day the man brought the cloth to the town. Immediately people began to bid for the beautiful cloth, which was sold at last for three ryo[4] of gold—an unheard of sum.

That night the old couple and their daughter, dressed in new kimonos,[5] ate a wonderful meal—all bought with a small bit of the gold. For several months life was easy. But then the money was gone.

80 Once more the daughter entered the room, closed the door, and began to weave. *Clack clack clack, whirr whirr whirr.* Hours later she emerged, pale and worn. In her arms was a cloth that shone like silver, filled with patterns of the moon and stars, patterns of sunlight and moonlight shining on water. The old couple had never imagined a material of such stunning beauty.

But once again the girl said, "Mother, Father, do not keep the cloth. I can make more. Please sell it and use the money to care for your old age."

So again the man took the cloth to town. The merchants were astonished. They bid furiously, one against the other, until the cloth
90 had been sold for six ryo of gold. **D**

D SUMMARIZE
In your chart, summarize what has happened in the story since the young girl arrived at the old couple's home.

---

3. **shuttle . . . bobbins:** A shuttle is a device used in loom weaving to carry thread back and forth between other threads held lengthwise. A bobbin is a spool that holds thread or yarn for weaving.

4. **ryo** (ryō): a gold piece used as currency in Japan until the mid-1800s.

5. **kimonos** (kə-mō′nōz): long, wide-sleeved Japanese robes worn most often by women.

For many months the family lived happily together. But in time, that money too was gone. The daughter went once again to the loom. But this time her mother and father were curious. Why must they not look? They couldn't bear it. They decided that they would take just a peek through a crack in the wall. If their daughter could not see them, they reasoned, it would not disturb her at all. **E**

Clack clack clack, whirr whirr whirr. The man and the woman walked softly along the wall, knelt down, and peered through a thin crack in the paper wall. At the loom sat a white crane pulling feathers from its own breast and wings with its long bill. It was weaving with those feathers. The crane turned toward the crack and looked with a great black **mournful** eye. The man and the woman tumbled backward. But it was too late. They had been seen.

Later, when the door of the room opened, their daughter emerged, pale and worn. In her arms she held a most magnificent cloth. On it were images of the setting sun, the rising moon, the trees in autumn, the long migrations of the cranes. On it too were the images of a man and a woman watching a white crane fly away.

"Father, Mother," she said, "I had hoped to stay with you always. But you have seen me as I truly am. I am the crane you saved, Father, from the trap. I wanted to repay you for your kindness. I shall never forget you, but now that you know this truth, I cannot stay with you." **F**

The man and the woman wept. They begged and pleaded, "We love you. Do not leave us. We do not care that you are a crane! You are our daughter. We shall tell no one."

"It is too late," whispered the girl. "The marshes call to me. The sky calls to me. The wind in the trees whispers my name. And I must follow. Perhaps all is as it should be. The debt has been repaid. I shall never forget you. Farewell."

She walked from the hut and stood out in the open air. The man and the woman watched in wonder as before their eyes their beautiful pale daughter became a beautiful white crane. Flapping her wings once, twice, three times, the great crane rose slowly up off the ground and, circling the hut, flew away. **G**

"Farewell," said the man and the woman, watching the crane disappear over the marsh. "We shall miss you, daughter. But we are glad that you are free." **H**

After that, every year when the cranes migrated, the old couple left a silver dish of grain out before their door. And every year a beautiful crane came to eat that grain.

So the story goes. ❧

E FOLK TALES
In folk tales, events often occur in sets of three. How many times has the girl gone to the loom?

mournful (môrn'fəl) *adj.* feeling or expressing sorrow or grief

F FOLK TALES
What quality or qualities might the crane represent?

G FOLK TALES
What supernatural abilities does the crane demonstrate?

H FOLK TALES
What is the old couple meant to learn from this experience?

AUNTY MISERY

Retold by Judith Ortiz Cofer

This is a story about an old, very old woman who lived alone in her little hut with no other company than a beautiful pear tree that grew at her door. She spent all her time taking care of her pear tree. But the neighborhood children drove the old woman crazy by stealing her fruit. They would climb her tree, shake its delicate limbs, and run away with armloads of golden pears, yelling insults at "Aunty Misery," as they called her.

One day, a pilgrim[1] stopped at the old woman's hut and asked her permission to spend the night under her roof. Aunty Misery saw that 10 he had an honest face and bade the traveler come in. She fed him and made a bed for him in front of her hearth. In the morning while he was getting ready to leave, the stranger told her that he would show his gratitude for her **hospitality** by granting her one wish.

"There is only one thing that I desire," said Aunty Misery.

"Ask, and it shall be yours," replied the stranger, who was a sorcerer[2] in disguise.

"I wish that anyone who climbs up my pear tree should not be able to come back down until I permit it."

"Your wish is granted," said the stranger, touching the pear tree as he 20 left Aunty Misery's house. ❶

---

1. **pilgrim:** a traveler.
2. **sorcerer:** a wizard or magician.

ANALYZE VISUALS
What **mood** does this painting suggest?

hospitality
(hŏs′pĭ-tăl′ĭ-tē) *n.*
the friendly, generous treatment of guests

❶ FOLK TALES
Which characteristics of folk tales are in the story so far?

716 UNIT 6: MYTHS, LEGENDS, AND TALES

Detail of *Windy Day Gribun,
Isle of Mull*, John Lowrie-Morrison.
© John Lowrie-Morrison/Getty Images.

And so it happened that when the children came back to **taunt** the old woman and to steal her fruit, she stood at her window watching them. Several of them shimmied[3] up the trunk of the pear tree and immediately got stuck to it as if with glue. She let them cry and beg her for a long time before she gave the tree permission to let them go, on the condition that they never again steal her fruit or bother her. **J**

Time passed and both Aunty Misery and her tree grew bent and gnarled with age. One day another traveler stopped at her door. This one looked suffocated and exhausted, so the old woman asked him what he wanted in her village. He answered her in a voice that was dry and hoarse, as if he had swallowed a desert: "I am Death, and I have come to take you with me."

Thinking fast, Aunty Misery said, "All right, but before I go I would like to pluck some pears from my beloved pear tree to remember how much pleasure it brought me in this life. But, I am a very old woman and cannot climb to the tallest branches where the best fruit is; will you be so kind as to do it for me?"

With a heavy sigh like wind through a catacomb,[4] Death climbed the pear tree. Immediately he became stuck to it as if with glue. And no matter how much he cursed and threatened, Aunty Misery would not give the tree permission to release Death.

Many years passed and there were no deaths in the world. The people who make their living from death began to protest loudly. The doctors claimed no one bothered to come in for examinations or treatments anymore, because they did not fear dying; the pharmacists' business suffered too because medicines are, like magic potions, bought to prevent or postpone the **inevitable;** the priests and undertakers[5] were unhappy with the situation also, for obvious reasons. There were also many old folks tired of life who wanted to pass on to the next world to rest from the miseries of this one.

Aunty Misery realized all this, and not wishing to be unfair, she made a deal with her prisoner, Death: if he promised not ever to come for her again, she would give him his freedom. He agreed. And that is why so long as the world is the world, Aunty Misery will always live. ∾ **K**

taunt (tônt) *v.*
to mock or insult

J SUMMARIZE
How does Aunty Misery solve her problem? Add these events to your chart.

inevitable
(ĭn-ĕv′ĭ-tə-bəl) *adj.*
impossible to avoid or prevent

K FOLK TALES
What qualities does Aunty Misery demonstrate through her actions?

---

3. **shimmied:** shinnied, or scooted.

4. **catacomb** (kăt′ə-kōm′): an underground cemetery made up of tunnels full of graves.

5. **undertakers:** funeral directors.

Comprehension

1. **Recall** In "The Crane Maiden," what does the old man do to help the crane?

2. **Recall** What does the man do with the cloth the girl makes?

3. **Clarify** In "Aunty Misery," how does the old woman save her own life?

Literary Analysis

4. **Make Inferences** Why do you think the crane, once discovered, needs to leave the man and woman?

5. **Analyze a Character** In the second folk tale, why do the children name the woman Aunty Misery? Explain whether the name is appropriate for her.

6. **Summarize** Look at the chart you created while reading the folk tales. Choose one of the stories and, using your chart, retell the tale briefly. Be sure to include key events and important details.

7. **Identify Characteristics of Folk Tales** Use a chart to list the characteristics of folk tales found in the stories you just read.

	"The Crane Maiden"	"Aunty Misery"
Qualities Characters Represent		
Supernatural Beings/Events		
Story Lesson or Message		

8. **Examine Figurative Language Personification** is a kind of figurative language in which an animal, an object, or an idea is given the qualities of a human. What human qualities does Death have in "Aunty Misery"?

Extension and Challenge

9. **Creative Project: Drama** Choose either "The Crane Maiden" or "Aunty Misery" and, with a group of classmates, write it as a play. Perform your play for the rest of the class.

10. **Big Question Activity** Consider whether Aunty Misery makes the right choice when she decides to **release** Death. Does this situation turn out for the best? Discuss your views with a small group of classmates.

Vocabulary in Context

VOCABULARY PRACTICE

Decide whether the words in each pair are synonyms—words with similar meanings—or antonyms—words with opposite meanings.

1. hospitality/rudeness
2. inevitable/expected
3. mournful/cheerful
4. snare/trap
5. taunt/defend

hospitality
inevitable
mournful
snare
taunt

VOCABULARY IN WRITING

Using three or more vocabulary words, write a paragraph describing Aunty Misery's life after she made the deal with Death. Here is a sample of how you might begin.

> **EXAMPLE SENTENCE**
>
> It was **inevitable** that Aunty Misery would have extra time on her hands.

VOCABULARY STRATEGY: GENERAL CONTEXT CLUES

When you come across an unfamiliar word in your reading, try rereading what's around the word to figure out its meaning. **Context clues** may be found in the same sentence as the unfamiliar word or in one or more other sentences in the paragraph. For example, "its leg was trapped in a snare" is a clue to the meaning of the vocabulary word *snare* in "The Crane Maiden." From this context clue, we know that a snare is a type of trap.

PRACTICE Use context clues to write the definition of each boldfaced word.

1. After the crime, the **malefactor** was sent to prison.
2. The dark, heavy curtains will **occlude** all light from coming through the window.
3. Isabel's **propensity** to talk out of turn often got her in trouble.
4. I was **ravenous** because I hadn't eaten since yesterday.
5. The sickly child was **susceptible** to frequent colds and other illnesses.

VOCABULARY PRACTICE
For more practice, go to the **Vocabulary Center** at **ClassZone.com**.

Reading-Writing Connection

Demonstrate your understanding of "The Crane Maiden" and "Aunty Misery" by responding to these prompts. Then complete the **Grammar and Writing** exercise.

WRITING PROMPTS

SELF-CHECK

A. Short Response: Compare and Contrast Characters

Both Aunty Misery and the old couple in "The Crane Maiden" face situations in which they have to **release** something. Write **one paragraph** comparing and contrasting the ways in which the couple and Aunty Misery behave.

A strong paragraph will . . .
- explain the characters' similarities and differences
- use examples from each folk tale

B. Extended Response: Write a Monologue

Imagine that Aunty Misery and the old man and old woman in "The Crane Maiden" each decided to tell the story of his or her experiences. Choose one of the three characters and write the story in the form of a **one-page monologue**.

An effective monologue will . . .
- tell the story from the character's point of view
- reveal the character's thoughts and motivations

GRAMMAR AND WRITING

USE COMMAS CORRECTLY To avoid confusing your readers, be sure to use a comma after an **introductory word,** such as *finally* or *meanwhile*. Also, insert a comma after an **introductory phrase.**

> *Example:* On his way home, the old man found a trapped crane.

PRACTICE In each sentence, insert a comma where it is needed.

1. Until then the old man had been gathering cattails.
2. Through the crack the old couple saw a crane sitting at the loom.
3. Eventually their time together would have to end.
4. After saying goodbye the crane flew away.

*For more help with punctuating introductory words and phrases, see page R49 in the **Grammar Handbook**.*

Yeh-Shen: A Cinderella Story from China

Folk Tale Retold by Ai-Ling Louie

Sootface: An Ojibwa Cinderella Story

Folk Tale Retold by Robert D. San Souci

Is GOODNESS *always rewarded?*

KEY IDEA Have you ever heard someone being accused of living in a "fairy-tale world"? In this kind of world, everything works out for the best and **goodness** triumphs over evil. Unfortunately, life often doesn't turn out this way in the real world. Stories with happy endings, however, can give comfort and hope. They can encourage people to be kind even when life is cruel. The following tales from two cultures present different versions of a familiar story.

LIST IT Get together with a small group and make a list of as many classic tales as you can think of. How many have an ending in which goodness is rewarded? Compare lists with other groups in your class.

● LITERARY ANALYSIS: UNIVERSAL THEME

A **universal theme** is a message that is meaningful to people living in any country and at any time. The universal themes found in folk tales usually state simple ideas about life.

You might be familiar with the tale of Cinderella. There are more than 900 versions of this folk tale from cultures around the world. The tales are not identical, but they share similar plots and themes.

As you read the following two Cinderella tales, think about their characters, events, and lessons. Use this information to determine their universal theme.

● READING STRATEGY: SET A PURPOSE FOR READING

In this lesson, your **purpose for reading** is to compare two stories and to identify the universal theme they share. To help you do this, take notes in a chart like the one shown.

	"Yeh-Shen"	"Sootface"
Who are the characters?	• main character: Yeh-Shen • helpful characters: • mean characters:	• main character: Sootface • helpful characters: • mean characters:
What are the key events?		
What lesson does the tale teach?		

▲ VOCABULARY IN CONTEXT

The boldfaced words help tell two Cinderella stories. See how many you already know. Make a chart like the one shown, and put each vocabulary word in the appropriate column.

WORD LIST	banquet	eldest	glistening
	collapse	embrace	

Know Well	Think I Know	Don't Know at All

Author On|ine

Ai-Ling Louie: Storyteller

Ai-Ling Louie born 1949

The grandmother of Ai-Ling Louie (ī-lǐng lōō'ē) heard the tale of Yeh-Shen in China and passed it down within her family. While working as a teacher, Louie wrote the story down to share it with her class and other readers.

Robert D. San Souci: Voice of Many Cultures

Robert D. San Souci born 1946

Through his retellings of traditional tales, award-winning author Robert D. San Souci (săn sōō'sē) helps his readers "discover how much we share in common with people around the world."

> **MORE ABOUT THE AUTHOR**
> For more on Ai-Ling Louie and Robert D. San Souci, visit the **Literature Center** at **ClassZone.com.**

Background

Popular Tale In the version of the Cinderella story most Americans know, Cinderella goes to the prince's ball, where she loses a glass slipper. The prince seeks out the owner of the slipper, eventually returning it to Cinderella, and the two marry.

YEH-SHEN

A Cinderella Story from China

Retold by Ai-Ling Louie

In the dim past, even before the Ch'in and the Han dynasties,[1] there lived
a cave chief of southern China by the name of Wu. As was the custom
in those days, Chief Wu had taken two wives. Each wife in their turn had
presented Wu with a baby daughter. But one of the wives sickened and died,
and not too many days after that Chief Wu took to his bed and died too.

Yeh-Shen, the little orphan, grew to girlhood in her stepmother's home.
She was a bright child and lovely too, with skin as smooth as ivory and dark
pools for eyes. Her stepmother was jealous of all this beauty and goodness,
for her own daughter was not pretty at all. So in her displeasure, she gave
10 poor Yeh-Shen the heaviest and most unpleasant chores.

The only friend that Yeh-Shen had to her name was a fish she had
caught and raised. It was a beautiful fish with golden eyes, and every day
it would come out of the water and rest its head on the bank of the pond,
waiting for Yeh-Shen to feed it. Stepmother gave Yeh-Shen little enough
food for herself, but the orphan child always found something to share
with her fish, which grew to enormous size. **Ⓐ**

ANALYZE VISUALS
This painting shows
a scene and its reflection
in the water. Identify
where the water begins
and ends.

Ⓐ UNIVERSAL THEME
Reread lines 11–16.
What do you learn about
Yeh-Shen from the way
she treats her friend?

---

1. **Ch'in** (chĭn) **and the Han** (hän) **dynasties** (dī′nə-stēz): groups that held power in China. The Ch'in
   dynasty ruled from 221 to 206 B.C., and the Han dynasty ruled from 206 B.C. to A.D. 220.

Detail of *The Moonlight* (2001),
Chen Jia Qi. Watercolor. Red Lantern
Folk Art, Mukashi Collection.
© The Mukashi Collection/SuperStock.

Somehow the stepmother heard of this. She was terribly angry to discover that Yeh-Shen had kept a secret from her. She hurried down to the pond, but she was unable to see the fish, for Yeh-Shen's pet wisely hid itself. 20 The stepmother, however, was a crafty woman, and she soon thought of a plan. She walked home and called out, "Yeh-Shen, go and collect some firewood. But wait! The neighbors might see you. Leave your filthy coat here!" The minute the girl was out of sight, her stepmother slipped on the coat herself and went down again to the pond. This time the big fish saw Yeh-Shen's familiar jacket and heaved itself onto the bank, expecting to be fed. But the stepmother, having hidden a dagger[2] in her sleeve, stabbed the fish, wrapped it in her garments, and took it home to cook for dinner. **B**

When Yeh-Shen came to the pond that evening, she found her pet had disappeared. Overcome with grief, the girl **collapsed** on the ground and 30 dropped her tears into the still waters of the pond.

"Ah, poor child!" a voice said.

Yeh-Shen sat up to find a very old man looking down at her. He wore the coarsest of clothes, and his hair flowed down over his shoulders.

"Kind uncle, who may you be?" Yeh-Shen asked.

"That is not important, my child. All you must know is that I have been sent to tell you of the wondrous powers of your fish."

"My fish, but sir . . ." The girl's eyes filled with tears, and she could not go on.

The old man sighed and said, "Yes, my child, your fish is no longer 40 alive, and I must tell you that your stepmother is once more the cause of your sorrow." Yeh-Shen gasped in horror, but the old man went on. "Let us not dwell on things that are past," he said, "for I have come bringing you a gift. Now you must listen carefully to this: The bones of your fish are filled with a powerful spirit. Whenever you are in serious need, you must kneel before them and let them know your heart's desire. But do not waste their gifts."

Yeh-Shen wanted to ask the old sage[3] many more questions, but he rose to the sky before she could utter another word. With heavy heart, Yeh-Shen made her way to the dung heap to gather the remains of her friend.

50 Time went by, and Yeh-Shen, who was often left alone, took comfort in speaking to the bones of her fish. When she was hungry, which happened quite often, Yeh-Shen asked the bones for food. In this way, Yeh-Shen managed to live from day to day, but she lived in dread that her stepmother would discover her secret and take even that away from her. **C**

B UNIVERSAL THEME
Why does the stepmother kill the fish?

collapse (kə-lăps') v. to fall down

C UNIVERSAL THEME
Many Cinderella stories include supernatural elements. What supernatural elements are in this story?

---

2. **dagger:** a short, pointed weapon.
3. **sage:** someone known for his or her wisdom.

So the time passed and spring came. Festival time was approaching: It was the busiest time of the year. Such cooking and cleaning and sewing there was to be done! Yeh-Shen had hardly a moment's rest. At the spring festival young men and young women from the village hoped to meet and to choose whom they would marry. How Yeh-Shen 60 longed to go! But her stepmother had other plans. She hoped to find a husband for her own daughter and did not want any man to see the beauteous Yeh-Shen first. When finally the holiday arrived, the stepmother and her daughter dressed themselves in their finery and filled their baskets with sweetmeats.⁴ "You must remain at home now, and watch to see that no one steals fruit from our trees," her stepmother told Yeh-Shen, and then she departed for the **banquet** with her own daughter. **D**

As soon as she was alone, Yeh-Shen went to speak to the bones of her fish. "Oh, dear friend," she said, kneeling before the precious bones, "I long to go to the festival, but I cannot show myself in these rags. 70 Is there somewhere I could borrow clothes fit to wear to the feast?" At once she found herself dressed in a gown of azure blue,⁵ with a cloak of kingfisher feathers draped around her shoulders. Best of all, on her tiny feet were the most beautiful slippers she had ever seen. They were woven of golden threads, in a pattern like the scales of a fish, and the **glistening** soles were made of solid gold. There was magic in the shoes, for they should have been quite heavy, yet when Yeh-Shen walked, her feet felt as light as air.

"Be sure you do not lose your golden shoes," said the spirit of the bones. Yeh-Shen promised to be careful. Delighted with her transformation, she bid a fond farewell to the bones of her fish as she slipped off to join 80 in the merrymaking. **E**

That day Yeh-Shen turned many a head as she appeared at the feast. All around her people whispered, "Look at that beautiful girl! Who can she be?"

But above this, Stepsister was heard to say, "Mother, does she not resemble our Yeh-Shen?"

Upon hearing this, Yeh-Shen jumped up and ran off before her stepsister could look closely at her. She raced down the mountainside, and in doing so, she lost one of her golden slippers. No sooner had the shoe fallen from her foot than all her fine clothes turned back to rags. Only one thing remained—a tiny golden shoe. Yeh-Shen hurried to the 90 bones of her fish and returned the slipper, promising to find its mate. But now the bones were silent. Sadly Yeh-Shen realized that she had lost her only friend. She hid the little shoe in her bedstraw, and went outside to cry. Leaning against a fruit tree, she sobbed and sobbed until she fell asleep. **F**

banquet (băng'kwĭt) *n.* a dinner honoring a particular guest or occasion

D UNIVERSAL THEME
Reread lines 55–66. Why doesn't Yeh-Shen's stepmother allow her to go to the festival?

glistening (glĭs'ən-ĭng) *adj.* sparkling

E UNIVERSAL THEME
Reread the warning in line 77. What do you **predict** will happen to the golden slippers?

F UNIVERSAL THEME
What effect does losing the slipper have on Yeh-Shen?

---

4. **sweetmeats:** sweet food, such as candy.

5. **azure blue** (ăzh'ər bloo): a light purplish blue.

Celebration (1996), Pang Gui Chen. Watercolor. Red Lantern Folk Art, Mukashi Collection.
© The Mukashi Collection/SuperStock.

The stepmother left the gathering to check on Yeh-Shen, but when she returned home she found the girl sound asleep, with her arms wrapped around a fruit tree. So thinking no more of her, the stepmother rejoined the party. Meantime, a villager had found the shoe. Recognizing its worth, he sold it to a merchant, who presented it in turn to the king of the island kingdom of T'o Han.

100   The king was more than happy to accept the slipper as a gift. He was entranced by the tiny thing, which was shaped of the most precious of metals, yet which made no sound when touched to stone. The more he marveled at its beauty, the more determined he became to find the woman to whom the shoe belonged. A search was begun among the ladies of his

ANALYZE VISUALS
Choose a figure from this painting that reminds you of one of the story's characters. Which character does the figure remind you of, and why?

own kingdom, but all who tried on the sandal found it impossibly small. Undaunted, the king ordered the search widened to include the cave women from the countryside where the slipper had been found. Since he realized it would take many years for every woman to come to his island and test her foot in the slipper, the king thought of a way to get the right woman to come forward. He ordered the sandal placed in a pavilion[6] by the side of the road near where it had been found, and his herald announced that the shoe was to be returned to its original owner. Then from a nearby hiding place, the king and his men settled down to watch and wait for a woman with tiny feet to come and claim her slipper.

All that day the pavilion was crowded with cave women who had come to test a foot in the shoe. Yeh-Shen's stepmother and stepsister were among them, but not Yeh-Shen—they had told her to stay home. By day's end, although many women had eagerly tried to put on the slipper, it still had not been worn. Wearily, the king continued his vigil[7] into the night. **G**

It wasn't until the blackest part of night, while the moon hid behind a cloud, that Yeh-Shen dared to show her face at the pavilion, and even then she tiptoed timidly across the wide floor. Sinking down to her knees, the girl in rags examined the tiny shoe. Only when she was sure that this was the missing mate to her own golden slipper did she dare pick it up. At last she could return both little shoes to the fish bones. Surely then her beloved spirit would speak to her again.

Now the king's first thought, on seeing Yeh-Shen take the precious slipper, was to throw the girl into prison as a thief. But when she turned to leave, he caught a glimpse of her face. At once the king was struck by the sweet harmony of her features, which seemed so out of keeping with the rags she wore. It was then that he took a closer look and noticed that she walked upon the tiniest feet he had ever seen. **H**

With a wave of his hand, the king signaled that this tattered creature was to be allowed to depart with the golden slipper. Quietly, the king's men slipped off and followed her home.

All this time, Yeh-Shen was unaware of the excitement she had caused. She had made her way home and was about to hide both sandals in her bedding when there was a pounding at the door. Yeh-Shen went to see who it was—and found a king at her doorstep. She was very frightened at first, but the king spoke to her in a kind voice and asked her to try the

G **UNIVERSAL THEME**
How does the king react when he receives Yeh-Shen's missing slipper as a gift?

H **UNIVERSAL THEME**
Reread lines 121–133. Why does the king first think Yeh-Shen is a thief?

---

6. **pavilion** (pə-vĭl′yən): a decorated tent.

7. **vigil** (vĭj′əl): a period of observing.

golden slippers on her feet. The maiden did as she was told, and as she stood in her golden shoes, her rags were transformed once more into the feathered cloak and beautiful azure gown.

Her loveliness made her seem a heavenly being, and the king suddenly knew in his heart that he had found his true love.

N ot long after this, Yeh-Shen was married to the king. But fate was not so gentle with her stepmother and stepsister. Since they had been unkind to his beloved, the king would not permit Yeh-Shen to bring them
150 to his palace. They remained in their cave home, where one day, it is said, they were crushed to death in a shower of flying stones. ⌒ ❶

❶ UNIVERSAL THEME
How is Yeh-Shen rewarded in the story?

Shadow Puppets, Chen Lian Xing. Watercolor. Red Lantern Folk Art, Mukashi Collection.
© The Mukashi Collection/SuperStock.

ANALYZE VISUALS
Notice how the figures in this painting are dressed. **Compare** them with how you imagined Yeh-Shen and the king looked.

Comprehension

1. **Recall** Who is Yeh-Shen's only friend?

2. **Recall** What does Yeh-Shen's stepmother do to trick the fish?

3. **Summarize** How does the king find the owner of the golden slipper?

Literary Analysis

4. **Analyze Characters** In the beginning of the story, Yeh-Shen is described as having "beauty and goodness." What details about her thoughts and actions show her goodness?

5. **Make Judgments** Reread lines 147–151. Do the stepmother and Yeh-Shen get what they deserve at the end of the story? Support your ideas with details from the folk tale.

6. **Evaluate Theme** Consider the message in this folk tale about how people should be treated. Is this message still important today? Explain.

Comparing Universal Theme

Now that you have read the first folk tale, finish filling in the "Yeh-Shen" column of your chart.

	"Yeh-Shen"	"Sootface"
Who are the characters?	• main character: Yeh-Shen • helpful characters: • mean characters: stepmother	• main character: Sootface • helpful characters: • mean characters:
What are the key events?		
What lesson does the tale teach?		

Sootface

AN OJIBWA CINDERELLA STORY

Retold by Robert D. San Souci

Once, an Ojibwa man whose wife had died raised three daughters alone. They lived in a village beside a lake, deep in a forest of birch.

The sisters were supposed to share the work of gathering firewood, cooking food, and sewing clothes from skins their father provided.

The two older girls, though pretty enough, were lazy and bad-tempered. When their father was away hunting, they gave most of the work to their youngest sister. The flames from the cooking fire singed her hair and burned her skin. Sometimes her sisters beat her and smeared her face with ashes. Then they made fun of her and called her Sootface.

10 Poor Sootface's eyes were always sad and tired, but her sisters only gave her more work. At evening her **eldest** sister cried, "Hurry, lazy Sootface! Fetch some wood to make a fire. Cook the deer meat, for we are hungry."

In the morning, her middle sister said, "Hurry, lazy Sootface! Clean the ashes from last night's fire. Brush the mats, gather berries, and bring fresh water. Our father will soon return from hunting." Ⓐ

ANALYZE VISUALS
What do the **details** in this illustration help you to **infer** about the girl?

eldest (ĕl′dĭst) *adj.* oldest

Ⓐ **UNIVERSAL THEME**
What terrible situation is Sootface in?

When the hunter returned, he saw poor Sootface and asked, "What has happened to my youngest child?"

The eldest sister said, "That one is so clumsy, she fell over her own feet and rolled through the ashes."

20 And the middle sister said, "We tell her to be careful, not to go too near the fire, but she will not heed us."

Sootface was too afraid of her sisters to argue; she just kept on working. All the while, she sang a little song to herself:

> *Oh, I am thinking,*
> *Oh, I am dreaming,*
> *That even ugly as I am,*
> *I will someday find a husband.* **B**

Her sisters took the best skins to make dresses and moccasins for themselves. Sootface had only scraps to sew into a skirt and a worn-out 30 pair of her father's moccasins, grown stiff with age. When she walked to the lake to fetch water, the young men would nudge each other and point and laugh.

N ow, there was a mighty warrior who lived with his sister in a wigwam across the lake from the village. A great medicine man had given him the power to make himself invisible. No one from the village had ever seen him, though they saw his white moccasins when his sister hung them beside the door flap. They saw the flap rise and fall when he entered or left his wigwam.

The villagers knew he was a great hunter, for they watched his sister 40 skin and dry all the deer, elk, and other game that her brother brought her. Though no one but his sister could see him, the women of the village were sure that he was very handsome.

One day, the invisible warrior told his sister, "Go to the village across the water, and say that I will marry the woman who can see me. This means that she has a kind and honest heart. Each day I will carry my magic bow. The woman who tells you what my bow and bowstring are made of will be my bride." **C**

His sister brought this message to the village people. One by one the young women came to visit the lone wigwam. Each carefully 50 braided her hair, dressed in her softest deerskin skirt and moccasins, and wore her finest necklaces of shells or beads.

The invisible hunter's sister greeted each young woman kindly. But when she asked them to tell her what her brother looked like,

B UNIVERSAL THEME
Reread lines 16–27.
Why doesn't Sootface's father help her?

VISUAL VOCABULARY

wigwam (wĭg′wŏm′) *n.* a Native American dwelling, usually having an arched or conelike shape

C UNIVERSAL THEME
Reread lines 43–47.
Who do you **predict** will pass this test?

and what his bow and bowstring were made of, each young woman failed the test, and was sent home.

This went on for a long time. At last, Sootface's eldest sister said that she was going to visit the invisible hunter.

She brushed her hair until it gleamed, and had Sootface braid it for her. Then she went on her way, wrapped in her best deerskin robe and wearing 60 her finest beaded moccasins. She met the hunter's sister beside the lake. Soon they saw white moccasins approaching.

"Can you see my brother?" asked his sister.

"Oh, yes," lied the eldest sister.

"Of what is his bow made?"

"Birch."

"And with what is it strung?"

"Rawhide."

"You did not see my brother," the other woman said.

The eldest sister went home in a bad temper. She yelled at Sootface 70 and gave her more work to do.

The middle sister, who thought herself clever, decided to try her luck. She hung strings of pale shells at her throat and had Sootface weave some into her long braids. Off she went, sure she would become the lucky bride.

As she walked with the hunter's sister, she saw the white moccasins approaching. Quickly, she said, "Here comes your brother now."

"Of what is his bow made?" asked the hunter's sister.

ANALYZE VISUALS
What do you notice about the shadows in this illustration?

"Horn," said the middle sister, thinking of the finest bow she could imagine.

"And with what is it strung?"

80 "Braided horsehair," said the middle sister, pleased at her own cleverness. But the other woman shook her head. "You have not seen my brother." **D**

The middle sister arrived home in a fury. She scolded Sootface and smeared more ashes on her face.

The next day, Sootface decided to visit the hunter's lodge as her sisters had done. She begged her eldest sister, "Sister, let me wear your white shell necklace, softest skirt, and moccasins. I want to go and seek a husband."

But her sister refused, saying, "You would only make my clothes as sooty as yourself."

Then Sootface begged her second sister, "Sister, help me wash and braid
90 my hair, so I may go and seek a husband."

But her sister said, "The fire has burned your hair too short to braid. And I do not want my hands dirtied by the ash that clings to you."

Sootface was stung by their unkindness. But she was determined to present herself to the warrior and his sister. She went alone into the woods. There she said, "Sister birch tree, share your soft white skin with me. Then I can wear a new skirt when I go to seek a husband."

Sootface took strips of birch bark and sewed them together to make a skirt. She wove herself a necklace of wildflowers, and soaked her old, stiff moccasins in a spring until they grew softer. Next, she washed her
100 face and hair as best she could. Her hair was too short to braid, so she added flowers to it, all the while singing:

Soon, I am thinking,
Soon, I am dreaming,
That I will find a husband.
I am sure it will be so.

But when she passed through the village, dressed in the finery the forest had provided, her eldest sister cried, "You are so ugly and foolish-looking, go inside at once!"

"You will shame us before the hunter and his sister," called Sootface's
110 middle sister.

But Sootface walked on as though they were no more than chattering birds in the trees. **E**

D UNIVERSAL THEME
Why can't the two sisters see the warrior's bow and bowstrings?

E UNIVERSAL THEME
Reread lines 93–112. Based on what you have read so far, how would you describe Sootface?

ANALYZE VISUALS
Based on her facial expression in the illustration, how would you describe Sootface's reaction to her sisters' comments?

When her sisters saw that she would not listen to them, they began to laugh at her. To friends and neighbors, the eldest sister said, "Come, see little Sootface. Her clothes are birch bark and weeds. Her moccasins are stiff and cracked. Yet she goes to find a husband!"

Next the middle sister shouted, "Look at little Sootface! Her hair is burned too short for braids. The smell of cook fires clings to her. Still she hopes to find a husband!"

120   Soon all the village was laughing at her. But the young woman continued on her way, never once looking back.

After a time Sootface met the hunter's sister, who was drawing water from the lake. She greeted Sootface kindly, and they began talking.

Suddenly, Sootface said, "There is a handsome man walking toward us. Do you know him?"

The hunter's sister said, "You can see him?"

"Yes, he is carrying a beautiful bow."

"Of what is his bow made?"

"A rainbow!"

130   "And how is it strung?"

"With white fire, like the Milky Way, the Path of Souls."

The hunter's sister **embraced** Sootface, crying, "You are going to be my brother's bride and my own sister!"

She led Sootface to the wigwam. There she poured water into a big pot and mixed in sweet-smelling herbs. Sootface found her hurt and sadness washed away as easily as the ashes from her face.

The hunter's sister gave her a dress of soft white buckskin decorated with beads and quillwork. Then she combed Sootface's hair with a magic comb that made it long and thick and shiny as a blackbird's wing. This
140 she plaited[1] into braids.

"You have made me beautiful," said Sootface when she looked at her reflection in the pot of water.

"Your beauty was merely hidden beneath the scars and ashes," said the other woman kindly. Then she called her brother into the lodge.

"What is your name?" the young man asked gently.

"Sootface," the girl said, blushing.

He smiled and shook his head. "Your eyes shine with such joy that I will call you Dawn-Light. Today I will carry a gift of game to your family as a sign of our betrothal."[2]
150 Then his sister said, "Come, radiant Dawn-Light, and sit beside my brother. Claim the wife's place by the door flap. From now on this is your home."

At these words, Dawn-Light exclaimed:

Now, I am happy,
Now, I am certain,
That I have found my husband,
My new sister and new home.

They were married soon after. Everyone was pleased, except Dawn-Light's two older sisters, who had to do all the cooking and
160 cleaning themselves now. ❧ **F**

---

1. **plaited:** folded or braided.
2. **betrothal:** a promise to marry.

Comprehension

1. **Recall** Why do the older sisters mistreat Sootface?

2. **Recall** What are the warrior's bow and bowstring made of?

3. **Clarify** What kind of woman does the warrior want to marry?

Literary Analysis

4. **Analyze Setting** What details in "Sootface" tell you that it takes place in the distant past?

5. **Evaluate Folk Tales** "Sootface" is an Ojibwa folk tale. Which traits do you think are more important to the Ojibwa: kindness and honesty, or beauty and cleverness? Use story details to support your ideas.

6. **Compare and Contrast Characters** In what ways are Sootface and Yeh-Shen similar? How are they different?

Comparing Universal Theme

Finish filling in your chart with information from "Sootface." Then add the final question to your chart and try to answer it.

	"Yeh-Shen"	"Sootface"
Who are the characters?	• main character: Yeh-Shen • helpful characters: • mean characters: stepmother	• main character: Sootface • helpful characters: • mean characters: sisters
What are the key events?	• gets married • step-sisters get punished	• gets married • step-sisters get punished
What lesson does the tale teach?	goodness and hope can overcome harm	goodness and hope can overcome harm
What is the universal theme?	Good things always happen to those who wait.	

Vocabulary in Context

VOCABULARY PRACTICE

Choose the letter of the word or words that have a meaning similar to the boldfaced word.

1. a wedding **banquet:** (a) performance, (b) tuxedo, (c) dinner, (d) ring
2. the **eldest** sibling: (a) prettiest, (b) loudest, (c) smartest, (d) oldest
3. **embrace** the child: (a) hold, (b) feed, (c) reward, (d) scold
4. a **glistening** dress: (a) sparkling, (b) fading, (c) hanging, (d) flowing
5. it might **collapse:** (a) rebuild, (b) fall down, (c) dance, (d) wave

VOCABULARY IN WRITING

Using two or more vocabulary words, write a paragraph telling why the king was attracted to Yeh-Shen or why the hunter was attracted to Sootface. You might start like this.

> **EXAMPLE SENTENCE**
>
> Yeh-Shen's <u>glistening</u> shoes got the attention of the king.

VOCABULARY STRATEGY: RECOGNIZING BASE WORDS

You've already learned that it's easier to understand an unfamiliar word that has **affixes**—word parts added to the beginning (prefix) or end (suffix) of a **base word**— if you first identify the base word. However, sometimes the base word is spelled differently when affixes are added. For example, the word *reception* contains the base word *receive* and the suffix *-tion*. If you're having problems recognizing the base word, try using context clues to figure out the meaning of the unfamiliar word.

Suffixes	Meanings
-able	capable of being
-ance	state of being
-ion, -tion	result of being

PRACTICE For each boldfaced word, identify the base word and the suffix. Then define the word. Use a dictionary if necessary.

1. Mr. Stine made a large **contribution** to the school.
2. She had a **considerable** advantage over the other players.
3. He had a negative **perception** of what she was trying to say.
4. Lily's **remembrance** of her vacation brought a smile to her face.
5. She received **recognition** for her accomplishments at work.

VOCABULARY PRACTICE

For more practice, go to the **Vocabulary Center** at **ClassZone.com**.

Writing for Assessment

1. READ THE PROMPT

The two Cinderella stories you've just read express the same universal theme. In writing assessments, you often will be asked to compare and contrast two works that are similar in some way, such as these two folk tales.

PROMPT

The folk tales "Yeh-Shen" and "Sootface" express the same universal theme. However, each tale expresses the theme in a different way. In three paragraphs, compare and contrast the way in which the two tales express their message. Support your response by using details from each tale.

◀ **STRATEGIES IN ACTION**

1. I need to make sure I understand the **message** both folk tales express.

2. I need to identify the **similarities and differences** in how the tales express the message.

3. I need to include **specific information** from the tales to help support my ideas.

2. PLAN YOUR WRITING

Review the chart you filled in as you read. Add any missing information about characters, events, or lessons. Use the chart to determine how each tale expresses the universal theme. Then think about how you will set up your response.

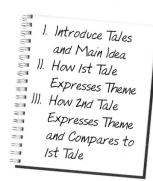

I. Introduce Tales and Main Idea
II. How 1st Tale Expresses Theme
III. How 2nd Tale Expresses Theme and Compares to 1st Tale

- Decide what your main idea will be.

- On your chart, mark the most important similarities and differences between the two tales.

- Create an outline to organize your ideas. This sample outline shows one way to organize your paragraphs.

3. DRAFT YOUR RESPONSE

Paragraph 1 Include the titles of the folk tales and the names of the authors who retold them. Tell what universal theme is expressed in the tales. Then state your main idea, which should say something about the similarities or the differences in how the tales present the theme.

Paragraph 2 Describe how the theme is expressed in the first folk tale through characters, events, and lessons.

Paragraph 3 Describe how the theme is expressed in the second folk tale and how it is similar to or different from the first tale.

Revision Make sure you vary the length of your sentences to keep your writing interesting. For example, try to create compound sentences.

Writing Workshop

Problem-Solution Essay

Are you as good at facing challenges as Nolka from "The Chenoo" or the old woman from "Aunty Misery"? To improve your problem-solving skills, write your own problem-solution essay. Use the **Writer's Road Map** as your guide.

WRITER'S ROAD MAP

Problem-Solution Essay

WRITING PROMPT 1

Writing for the Real World Choose a problem that deeply interests you. Write an essay in which you explain the problem, examine its causes, and explore possible solutions.

Problems to Explore

- litter and graffiti you see on the way to school
- a disagreement that two of your friends are having
- a situation involving school lockers or a lack of lockers

WRITING PROMPT 2

Writing from Literature Some of the myths, legends, and tales in this unit are about solving problems. Choose a tale that interests you. In an essay, explain the problem and describe the solution.

Selections to Explore

- "The Chenoo" (avoiding danger)
- "The Crane Maiden" (repaying a kindness)
- The two Cinderella stories (escaping cruel treatment)
- "Damon and Pythias" (staying true to a friend)

WRITING TOOLS
For prewriting, revision, and editing tools, visit the **Writing Center at ClassZone.com.**

KEY TRAITS

1. IDEAS

- **Presents the problem** in a clear thesis statement
- Explains the **causes and effects** of the problem
- Gives **details** to help explain the **solution** to the problem

2. ORGANIZATION

- Captures the reader's attention in the **introduction**
- Uses **transitions** to connect ideas
- **Concludes** by summing up the solution

3. VOICE

- **Tone** is suited to topic, audience, and purpose

4. WORD CHOICE

- Uses **precise words** to express the importance of the problem

5. SENTENCE FLUENCY

- Varies **sentence types** (statements, questions, and exclamations)

6. CONVENTIONS

- Uses **correct grammar, spelling, and punctuation**

Part 1: Analyze a Student Model

Bobby Velez
Waresboro Junior High School

Who's Watching What?

What do you get when you have only one television and five people who each want to watch different television programs? You have a big problem. In my family, we usually end up watching the program my parents or my older brother and sister want to see. That doesn't work
5 well for me, though, because I'd rather do chores than watch old movies, love stories, and game shows. My family needs to find a fair way to share the TV set.

Because of this problem, there have been many arguments in the family. We usually get along well and treat each other with respect.
10 When it comes to who gets to hold the remote control for the TV, however, we forget all about that. "What kind of person would watch anything so stupid and boring?" my brother screamed at my sister the other day. It's almost like we turn into strangers and enemies. Everyone is unhappy about this situation and would like it to change. It would be
15 nice if we could afford another TV set, but that's just not possible right now. After thinking about the problem, I came up with an answer. My solution is to make up a "Who's Watching What" schedule. This would give everyone a chance to see at least one favorite program and a certain number of other programs a week.

20 How would it work? We would set up a dry-erase board in the kitchen. Each person would write down his or her three favorite TV programs and the days and times they come on. If favorite programs were on at the same time, then the people would have to discuss the situation and come to an agreement. Maybe they could alternate weeks.
25 One person also might decide to watch a favorite program at a friend's house or to sign up for his or her next-favorite program instead.

KEY TRAITS IN ACTION

Introduction includes an interesting question to get the reader's attention. Highlighted thesis statement **presents the problem** clearly.

Clearly describes the **causes and effects** of the problem. Uses **precise words** to explain why having only one TV is a problem for the family.

Suggests a logical, practical **solution.**

Includes different **sentence types.**

Highlighted **transitions** show the reader how ideas are related. Specific **details** help the reader understand how the solution would work.

This solution has many advantages. Each of us would know in advance which shows our family would watch. I could do my chores the night my sister watched her soap opera, and she could do her chores

30 during my favorite reality show. Even if we disagreed about what to watch, we could settle it long before the show started. Getting into a fight that lasts for half the show is the worst.

The best part of this solution is that the schedule wouldn't be permanent. We could change it whenever we all agreed to do so. We

35 could erase shows at any time. We could also make up a new schedule every month or whenever anyone asked for one. This would work especially well during the holiday season because many special programs are on then. If some of us tried to change the schedule too often, or if we kept arguing about what to watch, our parents could just remind

40 us of the way things used to be. Nobody would want to go back to fighting all the time. Also, nobody would want Mom and Dad to say that we can't watch TV at all!

Putting my "Who's Watching What" schedule to work would solve a big problem at my house. It would give everyone equal TV time. It

45 would get us working together. Also, it would mean that we could watch arguments on soap operas instead of having them in our family.

> Positive and informal **tone** is appropriate for the topic, purpose, and audience.

> Summarizes the proposed solution in a funny and clever **conclusion.**

2

Part 2: Apply the Writing Process

PREWRITING

What Should I Do?

1. Read and understand the prompt.
Choose one of the prompts and read it at least twice. <u>Underline</u> the parts that tell you what tasks you have to do. Start thinking about how you will find a topic.

TIP Be sure that you do everything the prompt asks you to do. This prompt asks you to choose a problem, describe it, discuss what caused it, and suggest how to solve it.

2. Think of some interesting problems.
If you chose Prompt 1, make a chart or list of problems that bother you and that you would like to try to solve. If you chose Prompt 2, make a chart or list of difficult or surprising problems from literature. For either prompt, choose one problem and highlight it.

3. Consider possible solutions.
Make a cluster diagram to help you explore several solutions to the problem that you have chosen. You don't have to include all of these possible solutions in your essay. Just pick the best ones.

4. Find details to support your solution.
Telling your reader "This is the best solution" is not enough. For Prompt 1, list facts, reasons, and other details that explain why your solution will work. For Prompt 2, find evidence in the literature that shows why the solution worked or did not work.

What Does It Look Like?

WRITING PROMPT <u>Choose a problem</u> that deeply interests you. <u>Write an essay in which you explain the problem, examine its causes, and explore possible solutions.</u>

I can think of lots of problems. Maybe I should divide them into problems at home, in school, and in the neighborhood.

Home	School	Neighborhood
• too many chores	• short lunch periods	• lack of bike paths
• fights over TV	• not enough computers	• noisy car alarms

everyone is unhappy about this situation. *lots of homework* *nowhere to play.*

What to Do if Two Programs Conflict
• *Watch on alternate weeks.*
• *Watch at a friend's house.*
• *Watch next-favorite show instead.*

What Should I Do?	**What Does It Look Like?**

1. State the problem and tell why it's important.

Clearly explain what the problem is and what makes it a problem. Try starting with a question or a surprising fact to make your reader interested.

TIP Include any background information readers will need to understand the situation.

What do you get when you have only one TV set and five people who each want to watch different television programs? You have a big problem. In my family, we usually end up watching the program my parents or my older brother and sister want to see.

2. Make an informal outline.

One way to organize your essay is to discuss the problem first and then give your solution, as the writer of the student model did. You could also state the problem and solution right away and then go on to explain both.

1. Introduction and thesis

Here's the problem: We have only one TV and five people who want to watch it.

2. Details about problem

We have fights, and everybody is unhappy.

3. Proposed solution

We should make up a TV schedule. We could call it "Who's Watching What."

4. Details about proposed solution

Each of us picks our favorite shows and writes them on the schedule. We will have to learn to compromise if favorite shows are on at the same time.

5. Conclusion

This solution will get our family working together.

3. Explain the causes and effects of the problem.

Be sure you understand what caused this problem and what effects it has had. Describe these causes and effects clearly, using facts, examples, or quotations.

See page 748: Add Transitions

Causes	Effects
• only one TV	• arguments
• five people with different likes and dislikes	• brother yelling "What kind of person would watch anything so stupid and boring?"
	• everybody wanting change

REVISING AND EDITING

What Should I Do?	**What Does It Look Like?**
1. Make sure details truly support your statements. • Reread your rough draft. Draw a box around your supporting details and reasons. • If you don't have many boxes, or if the details are weak or don't make sense, add strong, solid supporting information.	▶ The best part of this solution is that the schedule will work really well, wouldn't be permanent. We could change it whenever we all agreed to do so. We could erase shows at any time. We could also make up a new schedule every month or whenever anyone asked for one.
2. Use strong, specific verbs. • Circle verbs like *is, are, has,* and *do* that don't give readers much information. • Replace some of these verbs with precise action verbs.	▶ Maybe they could do something different, alternate weeks. ▶ Putting my "Who's Watching What" schedule to work would be a good change, solve a big problem at my house.
3. Link ideas with transitions. • Ask a peer reader to read your draft and put a star next to sentences that are not connected logically. • Add transitions to show how the ideas are related. **See page 748:** Ask a Peer Reader	▶ Favorite programs might be on at the same time. People would have to discuss the situation and come to an agreement. ✳ If favorite programs were on at the same time, then the people would have to discuss the situation and come to an agreement.
4. Sum up the solution. • Reread your concluding paragraph. Does it clearly restate the solution? • If not, revise it to include a summary and to leave readers with something to think about.	▶ Putting my Who's-Watching-What schedule to work would solve a big problem at my house. It would give everyone equal TV time. It would get us working together. Also, it would mean that we could watch arguments on soap operas instead of having them in our family.

Problem-Solution Essay

Apply the Rubric

A strong problem-solution essay . . .

- ☑ introduces the problem in an attention-getting way
- ☑ clearly identifies the problem in a thesis statement
- ☑ uses precise words to tell why the problem matters
- ☑ explores the causes and effects of the problem
- ☑ has a tone that matches the topic, audience, and purpose
- ☑ includes an occasional question or exclamation for variety
- ☑ connects ideas with transitions
- ☑ includes details that fully describe the solution
- ☑ accurately sums up the solution in the conclusion

Ask a Peer Reader

- Do any of my ideas lack clear connections to the rest of the essay? If so, which ones?
- Which point in my essay is the strongest? Why?
- Do you think my proposed solution will work? Why or why not?

Add Transitions

accordingly	for that reason
after	if . . . then
as a result	since
because	so
before	therefore
consequently	thus

Check Your Grammar

When should you use *who*, and when should you use *whom*?

- If you can put the subject pronoun *he*, *she*, or *it* in place of *who* or *whom*, then use *who*.

  > Who likes to watch sports on TV?
  > She likes to watch sports on TV.

- If you can answer the question with the object pronoun *me*, *him*, *her*, or *them*, then use *whom*.

  > Whom should I thank for this TV schedule? Thank him.

Writing Online

PUBLISHING OPTIONS
For publishing options, visit the **Writing Center** at ClassZone.com.

ASSESSMENT PREPARATION
For writing and grammar assessment practice, go to the **Assessment Center** at ClassZone.com.

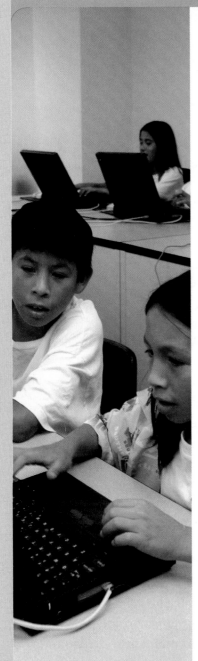

Creating a Class Newspaper

You can create a class newspaper to share the solution you developed.

Planning the Class Newspaper

1. **Decide what articles to include.** Ask volunteers to write articles about different topics. Some students may want to write articles based on their problem-solution essays.
2. **Design your newspaper.** Think of a name for the paper. Decide how many pages it will have. Consider whether you will add photographs, cartoons, charts, or graphs.

Producing the Class Newspaper

1. **Input or scan the articles and visuals into a computer.** Make sure the text is complete and that all words are spelled correctly. If necessary, write captions for the visuals.
2. **Put it together.** Use a page layout program or a template from a word processing program to help you place each article and visual.

> ⚡ **GRADE 6 NEWS FLASH** ⚡
>
> NEWS FROM MR. NELSON'S CLASS • *FREE*
>
> ## Who's Watching What?
>
> by **Bobby Velez**
>
> What do you have with only one television and five people who want to watch different TV programs? You have a big problem.
>
>

3. **Print and distribute your newspaper.** Congratulations— you're a publisher! Give copies of your paper to your teacher and classmates. You could also post a copy on the bulletin board. Ask readers to let you know what they liked and didn't like so you can create a better newspaper next time.

Reading Comprehension

DIRECTIONS *Read this selection and answer the questions that follow.*

Cassiopeia

Retold by Alice Low

Cassiopeia, wife of King Cepheus of Ethiopia, boasted to the sea nymphs, "I and my daughter, Andromeda, are far more beautiful than you. You are plain next to us."

The lovely sea nymphs swam to Poseidon, god of the sea, to tell him about Cassiopeia's insult. "You must punish Cassiopeia," they said. "She must not get away with such boasting."

Poseidon acted quickly. He sent a huge and hungry sea monster to Ethiopia to devour scores of King Cepheus's people.

King Cepheus was distraught, and he asked an oracle,[1] "What must
10 I do to rid my country of this ferocious monster?"

The oracle replied, "Chain your daughter, Andromeda, to a rock by the sea. Leave her there for the sea monster to feast upon. Only in this way shall you be rid of it."

To his wife's despair, King Cepheus did as he was told, and poor Andromeda awaited her fate, chained and helpless. But as the sea monster was about to devour her, the hero Perseus flew overhead in Hermes' winged sandals. Just in time, he landed on the monster's back and thrust his sword into it repeatedly. After a raging battle, Perseus killed the monster and carried away the lovely Andromeda, who became his bride.
20 Perseus and Andromeda lived happily together, but the sea nymphs never forgot Cassiopeia's insult. Many years later, when Cassiopeia died, the sea nymphs again begged Poseidon to punish her.

This time Poseidon did so by setting Cassiopeia in the north sky in a most uncomfortable position. She sits in a high-backed chair that looks like a *W*—but during part of the year, the chair hangs upside down.

Near Cassiopeia, Athena placed the constellation Andromeda, and Andromeda's brave husband, Perseus, stands not far from her in the Milky Way. Cepheus is there, too, though dimmer, and so is Cetus, the sea monster, also called the Whale.

---

1. **oracle:** a person through whom a god is believed to speak.

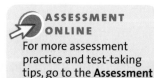

Comprehension

DIRECTIONS *Answer these questions about the myth "Cassiopeia."*

1. Cassiopeia shows disrespect for a cultural value when she

    A disobeys Poseidon's orders

    B becomes upset with King Cepheus

    C rewards Andromeda with lavish gifts

    D insults the sea nymphs by bragging

2. Why does King Cepheus chain his daughter, Andromeda, to a rock by the sea?

    A He hopes to save Cassiopeia.

    B He thinks that Perseus will save her.

    C He wants to get rid of the sea monster.

    D He has to punish Andromeda.

3. Which statement best summarizes lines 14–19?

    A Cassiopeia is sad because Cepheus chains Andromeda to a rock.

    B Perseus rescues Andromeda just as the sea monster is about to eat her.

    C Hermes gives his winged sandals to Perseus.

    D Andromeda happily marries Perseus.

4. Why does Poseidon set Cassiopeia in an uncomfortable position in the sky?

    A The sea monster will stop eating people if Cassiopeia is upside down.

    B Poseidon wants to punish her for insulting the sea nymphs.

    C Cassiopeia will be able to see her family from that position.

    D King Cepheus needs a warning for his false statements.

Written Response

SHORT RESPONSE *Write two or three sentences to answer this question.*

5. Classical myths often explain how something in the universe came to be. What natural wonder does this myth explain?

EXTENDED RESPONSE *Write a short paragraph to answer this question.*

6. Summarize what happens to Andromeda in this myth.

GO ON ➡

DIRECTIONS *Read this selection and answer the questions that follow.*

Castor and Pollux

Retold by Alice Low

Castor and Pollux were inseparable twin brothers. Their father was Zeus, and their mother was a mortal, Leda of Sparta.

They were strong, athletic young men. Castor was renowned as a soldier and tamer of horses, and Pollux was an outstanding boxer. Both entered the Olympic games and won many competitions. They were worshipped as gods by athletes, soldiers, and sailors.

Castor and Pollux were among the Argonauts, who aided Jason in his quest for the Golden Fleece. But after their return, they had a dispute with two young men. A terrible battle followed, and Castor, who was

10 mortal, was killed. Pollux, who was immortal, wept over the body of his twin. He cried to his father, Zeus, "Please let me kill myself and follow my brother to the underworld. I feel that half of myself is gone, and the half that remains is but a shadow."

Zeus took pity on Pollux and said, "Though I cannot enable you to die, for you are immortal, I shall allow you and Castor to be together always. Together you shall spend alternate days in the underworld and on Olympus. And because of your great love for your brother, I shall raise your images into the sky. There you shall shine next to each other forever."

And Castor and Pollux became the twin stars, forming the constellation

20 Gemini.

Comprehension

DIRECTIONS *Answer these questions about the myth "Castor and Pollux."*

7. Why are Castor and Pollux separated?

   A They participate in different Olympic sports.

   B Zeus decides that they must spend days apart.

   C Castor is killed in a battle, but Pollux is immortal.

   D Pollux is unhappy about decisions Castor makes.

8. Which human emotion does the god Zeus feel toward the troubled Pollux?

   A jealousy

   B affection

   C adoration

   D compassion

9. In this myth, Zeus has the power to

   A help Castor and Pollux win many Olympic competitions

   B make it possible for Castor and Pollux to remain together forever

   C let Pollux become human so that he can join his brother

   D give Castor immortality so that he can always live on Olympus with his brother

10. What cultural value does Pollux honor?

   A brotherly love

   B obedience to the gods

   C respect for his elders

   D honorable living

11. What happens when Zeus agrees to help Pollux?

   A The constellation Gemini appears in the sky.

   B Castor loses his life in a fierce battle.

   C Pollux suffers through a time of great sadness.

   D Everyone praises the Argonauts who looked for the Golden Fleece.

Written Response

SHORT RESPONSE *Write two or three sentences to answer this question.*

12. Reread lines 3–6. Identify two cultural values in this myth that seem to be important to the Greeks.

EXTENDED RESPONSE *Write a short paragraph to answer this question.*

13. According to the myth, how was the Gemini constellation formed?

GO ON ➤

Vocabulary

DIRECTIONS *Use context clues and your knowledge of connotation to answer the following questions.*

1. The word *devour* in lines 8 and 16 of "Cassiopeia" has a connotation of
   A selfishness
   B confusion
   C hugeness
   (D) greediness

2. The word *ferocious* in line 10 of "Cassiopeia" has a connotation of
   (A) cruelty
   B sadness
   C stupidity
   D ugliness

3. The word *thrust* in line 17 of "Cassiopeia" has a connotation of
   A uncertainty
   B playfulness
   C powerfulness
   (D) bravery

4. The word *renowned* in line 3 of "Castor and Pollux" has a connotation of
   (A) admiration
   B fear
   C authority
   D disgrace

DIRECTIONS *Use the dictionary entry to answer the following questions.*

> **shadow** (shăd'ō) *noun* **1.** An area that is not lit up. **2.** The rough image cast by an object blocking rays of light. **3.** An imperfect imitation or copy. **4.** A nearby region. *verb* **1.** To make gloomy or dark. **2.** To darken in a painting or drawing. **3.** To follow, especially in secret; trail.
> **Synonyms:** *noun:* shade, trace, phantom; *verb:* darken, cloud, follow.

5. Which definition best matches the meaning of the word *shadow* as it is used in line 11 of "Castor and Pollux"?
   A noun definition 1
   (B) noun definition 2
   C noun definition 3
   D noun definition 4

6. Which word is a synonym for the word *shadow* in the following sentence?

   They sat in the <u>shadow</u> of a leafy tree.
   (A) shade   C trace
   B cloud   D phantom

7. In which sentence is the word *shadow* used as a verb?
   A Tracking the fawn was like chasing a <u>shadow</u>.
   B The setting sun cast a dark <u>shadow</u>.
   (C) Six detectives <u>shadow</u> the spy.
   D We grew up in the <u>shadow</u> of the temple.

Writing & Grammar

DIRECTIONS *Read this passage and answer the questions that follow.*

> (1) Every year, my brothers and my mom help uncle Harry and aunt Lea make maple syrup. (2) "Sugaring" takes place in the early spring. (3) The whole season lasts only one or two months. (4) My uncle and my brother Seth drill holes into the trees, and mom and aunt Lea attach buckets to them. (5) The buckets then collect the sap. (6) Every day, Seth brings the sap to the sugarhouse. (7) I boil off the water. (8) Maple syrup is a treat. (9) We must work very hard to make just a small batch of it. (10) It takes about 40 gallons of maple sap to produce one gallon of maple syrup!

1. Which words should be capitalized in sentence 1?

   A brothers, mom   C uncle, aunt

   B mom, uncle   D mom, aunt

2. How might you combine sentences 2 and 3 to form one compound sentence?

   A "Sugaring" takes place in the early spring, and the whole season lasts only one or two months.

   B "Sugaring" takes place in the early spring, when the whole season lasts only one or two months.

   C "Sugaring" takes place in the early spring, the whole season lasts only one or two months.

   D "Sugaring" takes place in the early spring the whole season lasts only one or two months.

3. Which words should be capitalized in sentence 4?

   A brother, uncle   C mom, aunt

   B uncle, aunt   D brother, mom

4. How might you combine sentences 6 and 7 to form one compound sentence?

   A Every day, Seth brings the sap to the sugarhouse, I boil off the water.

   B Every day, Seth brings the sap to the sugarhouse, and I boil off the water.

   C Every day, Seth brings the sap to the sugarhouse, where I boil off the water.

   D Every day, Seth brings the sap to the sugarhouse I boil off the water.

5. How might you combine sentences 8 and 9 to form one compound sentence?

   A Maple syrup is a treat, but we must work very hard to make just a small batch of it.

   B Maple syrup is a treat we must work very hard to make just a small batch of it.

   C Maple syrup is a treat that we must work very hard to make just a small batch of it.

   D Maple syrup is a treat, we must work very hard to make just a small batch of it.

STOP

More Great Reads

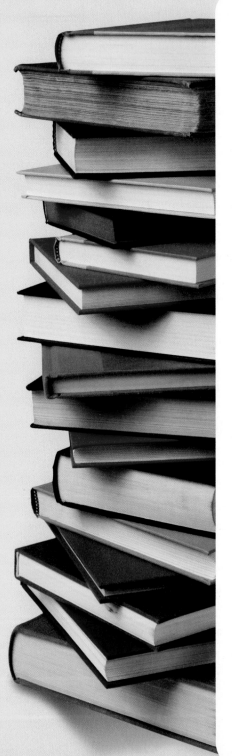

Ideas for Independent Reading

Which questions from Unit 6 made an impression on you?
Continue exploring with these books.

Why do we exaggerate?

American Tall Tales
by Mary Pope Osborne

Davy Crockett carries thunder in his fist and lightning flies from his fingers. Paul Bunyan carves the Grand Canyon with his pickax. Stories of these larger-than-life characters captured the adventurous spirit of early American pioneers.

Montmorency: Thief, Liar, Gentleman
by Eleanor Updale

Montmorency, a thief who wants to be a gentleman, copies the manners and clothing of the rich when he gets out of jail. But that isn't enough. He must become a member of the group he once hated.

Ruby Electric
by Theresa Nelson

Ruby writes screenplays to escape her life. In her movies, dads are part of their daughters' lives and moms don't have secrets. Then, suddenly, her father reappears, and Ruby has to cope with the truth about her family.

When is it time to let go?

Dybbuk: A Version
by Barbara Rogasky

Konin, a poor scholar, is in love with Leah. When Leah's father decides she must marry a rich man, Konin searches for a way to make his fortune. Can Konin and Leah's love endure the trials they will face?

Home Is East
by Many Ly

Everyone in St. Petersburg's small Cambodian community told Amy Lin her mother would run away, but it still hurt when she left. Now Amy and her father live in California, and Amy keeps hoping her mother will return.

The Liberation of Gabriel King
by K. L. Going

Gabriel is scared of 38 things, including moving up to the fifth grade. His best friend, Frita, comes up with a plan to free him of his fears before school starts. Will he be able to let his fears go?

Is goodness always rewarded?

Goddess of Yesterday
by Caroline B. Cooney

Anaxandra pretends to be a princess when she is rescued by King Menelaus. Now she is trapped within the walls of Troy as Menelaus's army arrives to reclaim his wife, Helen. Anaxandra soon finds that the lives of many people depend on her.

Stand Tall
by Joan Bauer

At six feet three inches tall, Tree is the tallest 12-year-old most people have met. Because of his size, many people expect too much of him. But when disaster strikes his family and town, Tree surprises everyone, even himself.

The Sea of Trolls
by Nancy Farmer

Jack is only 11 when Norse warriors called the beserkers kidnap him and his sister. After they are taken to a cruel, half-troll queen, Jack sets out on a dangerous quest in order to save his sister's life.

Life Stories

BIOGRAPHY AND AUTOBIOGRAPHY

- In Nonfiction
- In Poetry
- In Media

What makes a person larger than LIFE?

Martin Luther King Jr., Anne Frank, George Washington—why are these people remembered? Each person comes from a very different time and place. Yet they are alike in that their words and actions shaped the lives of the people of their time, and continue to influence people today. Each one is larger than **life.**

ACTIVITY Think of someone who has had a strong impact on you. It might be a historical figure, a celebrity, or someone you know. In a small group, discuss the following questions to decide what makes this person larger than life:

• What is the person best known for?

• How has he or she influenced your life, or the lives of others?

• Might his or her words and actions affect the future? How?

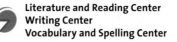
Preview Unit Goals

LITERARY ANALYSIS
- Identify the form and characteristics of a biography and autobiography
- Analyze a biography and autobiography
- Identify and analyze imagery

READING
- Identify main ideas and supporting details
- Trace chronological order using signal words
- Synthesize information from multiple sources
- Identify author's purpose

WRITING AND GRAMMAR
- Write a personal narrative
- Use colons correctly to introduce a list
- Capitalize proper nouns correctly

SPEAKING, LISTENING, AND VIEWING
- Create a video documentary
- Identify and analyze elements of a documentary
- Compare print and film versions

VOCABULARY
- Recognize the origins and meanings of frequently used foreign words in English
- Use context clues to understand the meanings of idioms and analogies

ACADEMIC VOCABULARY
- biography
- autobiography
- main idea
- supporting details
- chronological order
- synthesize
- imagery
- author's
- purpose

Biography and Autobiography

The magician Harry Houdini thrilled audiences with his escapes from deadly traps. How did he develop his tricks? Young Helen Keller overcame tremendous odds to discover the mystery of language. How did she feel when she could suddenly communicate with others? Most people are curious about the lives of others, from Houdini and Helen Keller to today's athletes and stars. Biographies and autobiographies can let you in on the lives of many fascinating people.

Part 1: Life Stories

Both biographies and autobiographies tell the stories of people's lives. So, what makes them different from each other? The most important difference has to do with *who* does the writing.

A **biography** is written by someone other than the subject. The writer, or **biographer,** reports on the events, achievements, and struggles in a subject's life. An **autobiography,** however, is written by the subject. In many ways, an autobiography gives you an inside look. You get to hear all about the subject's life directly from the source.

Here are some other differences between biographies and autobiographies.

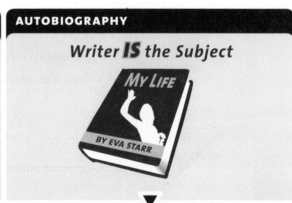

BIOGRAPHY	AUTOBIOGRAPHY
*Writer **IS NOT** the Subject*	*Writer **IS** the Subject*

Characteristics
- is written from the third-person point of view, using pronouns such as *she, he, his, her, they,* and *them* to refer to the subject
- is often based on information from many sources, including books about the subject, the subject's journals or letters, and interviews
- sometimes includes details provided by the subject himself or herself

Characteristics
- is written from the first-person point of view, using pronouns such as *I, me, my, we,* and *us* to refer to the subject
- describes the subject's thoughts, feelings, and opinions about his or her life
- is based primarily on details that come from the subject's own memories
- may include information from other sources, such as the subject's family and friends

MODEL 1: BIOGRAPHY

Years ago, readers worldwide first fell in love with the wizard Harry Potter. Soon after, J. K. Rowling became a household name. This excerpt is from a biography of Rowling, the author of the *Harry Potter* series.

from
J. K. Rowling

Biography by **Bradley Steffens**

J. K. Rowling, as she was becoming known to the world, was pretty well prepared to handle life's ups and downs. She had equipped herself with a good education, traveled and lived abroad, been married and divorced, given birth to a child, and lost a parent. She had struggled
5   through grim poverty and realized a lifelong dream of publishing a book. Yet nothing could have prepared her for what was about to happen. Within five years she would become one of the richest and most recognizable women in the world. The media would report on her every move. . . . Most important, hundreds of millions of people—children
10 and adults alike—would read and reread her books.

Close Read

1. How can you tell that this excerpt is from a biography rather than an autobiography?

2. What was Rowling's life like before she became famous? Name two specific things you learn about her from this excerpt.

MODEL 2: AUTOBIOGRAPHY

As a Jew growing up in Poland, Anita Lobel was only five when World War II began. At that time, Nazi Germany had invaded Poland with the intent of imprisoning and killing Jewish people. Lobel and her brother spent days in hiding from German soldiers before they were captured.

from
No Pretty Pictures: *A Child of War*

Autobiography by **Anita Lobel**

Walking as we did down the middle of the bridge, I hoped that we were hidden from view. Under our feet this short, solid stone walkway felt like a tightrope. I held my brother's hand. We will get across, I thought. We will. We had squeaked by in other situations. This was just
5   another adventure. Already, with every step, the distance to the safe side was shrinking. The guards were not looking in our direction. Not yet.

Close Read

1. What pronouns in the first sentence let you know that this is an autobiography?

2. In the boxed text, Lobel describes what she was thinking when she was crossing the bridge. Where else does she share her thoughts or feelings?

Part 2: Reading Life Stories

Picture this situation: You're in the library or on the Web, trying to find out more about a person who interests you. Perhaps that person is a former president, a professional athlete, or the genius who invented the cell phone. How can you learn as much as possible about that person's life, personality, and accomplishments?

The best way to get to know any person—whether he or she is a historical figure or a rising star—is to consult both autobiographies and biographies. Here are some important questions to keep in mind as you read.

QUESTIONS TO ASK

Who *wrote the work?*
In an autobiography, the writer is the subject. You get to hear about the subject's life from his or her own point of view. In a biography, you learn about the subject from someone who has consulted many sources. Sometimes, a biography can give you a more complete picture of a subject's life.

When *was the work written?*
Was the work written early on in the subject's life or 100 years after his or her death? *When* an autobiography or biography is written affects the kind of information it includes.

What *does the work focus on?*
Some works focus on a single period in a subject's life—a wacky childhood or a championship season in an athletic career, for instance. Other works give a broader overview of the major moments in a subject's life.

How *is the subject described?*
The writer of any life story makes choices about how to describe the subject and what details to include. These details can affect how you feel about the subject. Ask yourself: Am I getting a positive, negative, or neutral impression?

MODEL 1: READING A BIOGRAPHY

Tony Hawk is a professional skateboarder. By the time he was 16, Hawk was taking the skateboarding world by storm and winning all kinds of competitions. This article was published in 1986, when Hawk was 18.

from **Chairman of the Board**

Sports Illustrated magazine article by **Armen Keteyian**

When Hawk swoops down from the top of a U-shaped bowl and starts digging into his bag of tricks—720s, 360 varial inverts, finger flips—he's a sight to see, an aerialist who is equal parts gymnast, acrobat and ballet dancer. He often concludes his show with an
5   electrifying 720 aerial; Hawk is the only skater in the world who can complete two midair somersaults and somehow still land on a 31- by 10-inch hunk of hardwood.

Close Read

1. If you knew nothing about Tony Hawk except for what you've just read, how would you describe him?

2. Examine the boxed details. Do they give you a positive or negative impression of Hawk?

MODEL 2: READING AN AUTOBIOGRAPHY

In 1999 Hawk retired from competitive skateboarding. However, he has managed to stay involved in the sport that brought him fame. Hawk has developed his own line of skateboards and even has video games named after him. In this autobiography, Hawk looks back on his childhood and his career.

from

TONY HAWK: PROFESSIONAL SKATEBOARDER

Autobiography by **Tony Hawk** with Sean Mortimer

I got picked on. I was less than five feet tall when I entered eighth grade, and weighed less than eighty pounds. I was so skinny that I resembled a set of toothpicks walking awkwardly down the hallway. Only my legs had a hint of muscle on them. If I flexed my bicep
5   nothing would pop up—muscle or fat. And, I was short. If I had to be skinny, at least someone could have given me height. I was a seriously late bloomer and in school nothing is more noticeable than that.

Close Read

1. In what way does this excerpt change your impression of the champion skater described in the magazine article?

2. How would you describe Hawk's personality?

Part 3: Analyze the Literature

Marian Anderson, an African-American singer, rose to fame in the 1930s. She performed for audiences across the country. However, she was banned from singing at Constitution Hall because she was black. Outraged, some people arranged for Anderson to give a free concert at the Lincoln Memorial in Washington, D.C. On April 9, 1939, Anderson performed for 75,000 people.

Author Russell Freedman writes about Anderson's life in *The Voice That Challenged a Nation,* published 11 years after her death.

from

The Voice That Challenged a Nation
Marian Anderson and the Struggle for Equal Rights

Biography by **Russell Freedman**

Marian Anderson never expected to become an activist in the struggle for equal rights. Away from the concert stage she valued her privacy and preferred a quiet family life. She disliked confrontations. And she never felt comfortable as the center of a public controversy.

5 "I would be fooling myself to think that I was meant to be a fearless fighter," she said in her autobiography. "I was not, just as I was not meant to be a soprano instead of a contralto."[1]

Actually, Anderson had to fight hard to win her place in American music history. As she pursued her career, she was forced to challenge
10 racial barriers simply to succeed as a singer. . . .

It was only after she toured Europe to great acclaim in the early 1930s that her artistry was recognized in her own homeland. And even then, Anderson's fame could not easily overcome the racial prejudice that she confronted as a black singer touring America. Well into her career, she
15 was turned away from restaurants and hotels.

Anderson's exceptional musical gifts and her uncompromising artistic standards made it possible for her to break through racial barriers. She became a role model, inspiring generations of African American performers who followed her. But it was the strength of her character,
20 her undaunted[2] spirit and unshakable dignity, that transformed her from a singer to an international symbol of progress in the advancement of human rights.

---

1. **soprano . . . contralto:** terms used to describe a singer's vocal range.
2. **undaunted:** courageously determined, especially during difficult times.

Close Read

1. How can you tell that this excerpt is from a biography?

2. What do you learn about Anderson's personality in lines 1–4?

3. What source of information does the biographer cite in this excerpt?

4. What details does the writer include to give you a positive impression of Anderson? One detail is boxed.

Now read this excerpt from Anderson's autobiography, which was published in 1956. In the excerpt, Anderson remembers that April day in 1939 when she sang at the Lincoln Memorial.

from

My Lord, What a Morning

Autobiography by **Marian Anderson**

There seemed to be people as far as the eye could see. The crowd stretched in a great semicircle from the Lincoln Memorial around the reflecting pool on to the shaft
5 of the Washington Monument. I had a feeling that a great wave of good will poured out from these people, almost engulfing me. And when I stood up to sing our National Anthem I felt for a moment as though I were choking. For a desperate second I thought that the words, well
10 as I know them, would not come.

I sang, I don't know how. There must have been the help of professionalism I had accumulated over the years. Without it I could not have gone through the program. I sang—and again I know because I consulted a newspaper clipping—"America," the aria "O mio Fernando,"
15 Schubert's "Ave Maria," and three spirituals—"Gospel Train," "Trampin'," and "My Soul Is Anchored in the Lord."

I regret that a fixed rule was broken, another thing about which I found out later. Photographs were taken from within the Memorial, where the great statue of Lincoln stands, although there was a tradition
20 that no pictures could be taken from within the sanctum.[1]

It seems also that at the end, when the tumult[2] of the crowd's shouting would not die down, I spoke a few words. I read the clipping now and cannot believe that I could have uttered another sound after I had finished singing. "I am overwhelmed," I said. "I just can't talk.
25 I can't tell you what you have done for me today. I thank you from the bottom of my heart again and again."

It was the simple truth. But did I really say it?

---

1. **sanctum:** a sacred place.
2. **tumult:** commotion.

Close Read

1. What thoughts and feelings does Anderson recall having before she started to sing?

2. In lines 13–14 and 22–24, Anderson admits that she consulted a newspaper for help with remembering details about the day. Why might she have had trouble recalling a day she experienced firsthand?

3. What picture of Anderson do you have after reading both excerpts? Explain how this picture would be different if you had not read her autobiography.

Matthew Henson at the Top of the World

Biography by Jim Haskins

Why attempt the IMPOSSIBLE?

KEY IDEA Sailing across the ocean. Taking a walk on the moon. Once, these things were thought to be **impossible.** Then someone had the courage to try what had never been done. In the following selection, you will see how a young explorer's determination helped him go where nobody had gone before.

WEB IT What do you want to accomplish in your lifetime? Write down one of your biggest ambitions in the center of a word web like the one shown. Then brainstorm different things you could do to make that achievement possible.

take astronomy classes

study all I can about outer space

read books about space

Become an Astronaut

visit NASA

● LITERARY ANALYSIS: BIOGRAPHY

A **biography** is the true account of a person's life, written by another person. No two writers are the same, so every biography is unique—even if many are about the same person. Still, all biographies share a few characteristics.

- They are written from the **third-person point of view.**
- They explain how events, people, and experiences shaped the person's life.
- They include quotations from people who knew him or her.

As you read this biography of Matthew Henson, look for these elements.

● READING SKILL: COMPARE AND CONTRAST

When you **compare and contrast,** you identify the ways in which two or more subjects are alike or different. As you read the following biography, use a Venn diagram to compare and contrast the explorers Matthew Henson and Robert Peary. Some points you may want to consider are family background, education, and personal motivation.

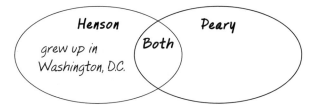

Review: **Recognize Cause-and-Effect Relationships**

▲ VOCABULARY IN CONTEXT

Jim Haskins uses the following boldfaced words to tell about a journey. To see how many you know, try to substitute a different word or phrase for each one.

1. Matthew Henson was an **ardent** adventurer.
2. His difficult early years taught him **resourcefulness.**
3. His lack of money was a **manifestation** of prejudice.
4. Their **expedition** to the North Pole began in 1908.
5. First, Henson studied the **feasibility** of the expedition.
6. If they succeeded, they would win **prestige** and fame.

Background

Arctic Exploration The Arctic is the area north of the Arctic Circle, 66° north latitude. The Dutch and the English began exploring the Arctic in the early 1500s. They hoped to find a trade route to Asia. In early Arctic exploration, ships often became trapped in the ice, and many sailors lost their lives.

By the late 1800s, nearly all of the Arctic had been explored. Groups began to set records, pushing farther north each time. The race to reach the North Pole became an international competition.

MATTHEW HENSON AT THE TOP OF THE WORLD

Jim Haskins

W hile the explorers of the American West faced many dangers in their travels, at least game and water were usually plentiful; and if winter with its cold and snow overtook them, they could, in time, expect warmth and spring. For Matthew Henson, in his explorations with Robert Peary at the North Pole, this was hardly the case. In many ways, to forge ahead into the icy Arctic took far greater stamina[1] and courage than did the earlier explorers' travels, and Henson possessed such hardiness. As Donald MacMillan, a member of the **expedition,** was later to write: "Peary knew Matt Henson's real worth. . . . Highly respected

10 by the Eskimos, he was easily the most popular man on board ship. . . . Henson . . . was of more real value to our Commander than [expedition members] Bartlett, Marvin, Borup, Goodsell and myself all put together. Matthew Henson went to the Pole with Peary because he was a better man than any one of us." **A**

Matthew Henson was born on August 8, 1866, in Charles County, Maryland, some forty-four miles south of Washington, D.C. His parents were poor, free tenant farmers[2] who barely eked a living from the sandy soil. The Civil War had ended the year before Matthew was born, bringing with it a great deal of bitterness on the part of former slave-

20 owners. One **manifestation** of this hostility was the terrorist activity on the part of the Ku Klux Klan in Maryland. Many free and newly freed blacks had suffered at the hands of this band of night riders. Matthew's

---

1. **stamina** (stăm′ə-nə): physical strength or endurance.
2. **tenant farmers:** farmers who rent the land they work and live on and pay rent in cash or crops.

father, Lemuel Henson, felt it was only a matter of time before the Klan turned its vengeful eyes on his family. That, and the fact that by farming he was barely able to support them, caused him to decide to move north to Washington, D.C. **B**

At first, things went well for the Henson family, but then Matthew's mother died and his father found himself unable to care for Matthew. The seven-year-old boy was sent to live with his uncle, a kindly man
30 who welcomed him and enrolled him in the N Street School. Six years later, however, another blow fell; his uncle himself fell upon hard times and could no longer support Matthew. The boy couldn't return to his father, because Lemuel had recently died. Alone, homeless, and penniless, Matthew was forced to fend for himself.

Matthew Henson was a bright boy and a hard worker, although he had only a sixth-grade education. Calling upon his own **resourcefulness,** he found a job as a dishwasher in a small restaurant owned by a woman named Janey Moore. When Janey discovered that Matthew had no place to stay, she fixed a cot for him in the kitchen; Matthew had found a home again.
40 Matthew Henson didn't want to spend his life waiting on people and washing dishes, however, no matter how kind Janey was. He had seen enough of the world through his schoolbooks to want more, to want adventure. This desire was reinforced by the men who frequented the restaurant—sailors from many ports, who spun tales of life on the ocean and of strange and wonderful places. As Henson listened, wide-eyed, to their stories, he decided, as had so many boys before him, that the life of a sailor with its adventures and dangers was for him. Having made up his mind, the fourteen-year-old packed up what little he owned, bade good-bye to Janey, and was off to Baltimore to find a ship. **C**
50 Although Matthew Henson's early life seems harsh, in many ways he was very lucky. When he arrived in Baltimore, he signed on as a cabin boy on the *Katie Hines,* the master of which was a Captain Childs. For many sailors at that time, life at sea was brutal and filled with hard work, deprivation, and a "taste of the cat": whipping. The captains of many vessels were petty despots,[3] ruling with an iron hand and having little regard for a seaman's health or safety. Matthew was fortunate to find just the opposite in Childs.

Captain Childs took the boy under his wing. Although Matthew of course had to do the work he was assigned, Captain Childs took a
60 fatherly interest in him. Having an excellent private library on the ship, the captain saw to Matthew's education, insisting that he read widely in geography, history, mathematics, and literature while they were at sea.

B RECOGNIZE CAUSE-AND-EFFECT RELATIONSHIPS
Why does Henson's father move his family to Washington, D.C.?

resourcefulness
(rĭ-sôrs′fəl-nĕs) *n.* the ability to act effectively, even in difficult situations

C BIOGRAPHY
What inspired Matthew Henson to become an explorer?

---

3. **petty despots** (dĕs′pəts): leaders who insist on absolute power and mistreat people.

ANALYZE VISUALS
Compare and contrast
the ship in this
photograph with
what you know
about modern ships.

The years on the *Katie Hines* were good ones for Matthew Henson. During that time he saw China, Japan, the Philippines, France, Africa, and southern Russia; he sailed through the Arctic to Murmansk. But in 1885 it all ended; Captain Childs fell ill and died at sea. Unable to face staying on the *Katie Hines* under a new skipper, Matthew left the ship at Baltimore and found a place on a fishing schooner bound for Newfoundland. **D**

70 Now, for the first time, Henson encountered the kind of unthinking cruelty and tyranny so often found on ships at that time. The ship was filthy, the crew surly and resentful of their black shipmate, and the captain a dictator. As soon as he was able, Matthew left the ship in Canada and made his way back to the United States, finally arriving in Washington, D.C., only to find that things there had changed during the years he had been at sea.

Opportunities for blacks had been limited when Henson had left Washington in 1871, but by the time he returned they were almost nonexistent. Post–Civil War reconstruction had failed, bringing with its failure a great deal of bitter resentment toward blacks. Jobs were scarce, and the few available were menial ones. Matthew finally found a job as
80 a stock clerk in a clothing and hat store, B. H. Steinmetz and Sons, bitterly wondering if this was how he was to spend the rest of his life. But his luck was still holding.

Steinmetz recognized that Matthew Henson was bright and hardworking. One day Lieutenant Robert E. Peary, a young navy officer, walked into the store, looking for tropical hats. After being shown a number of hats, Peary unexpectedly offered Henson a job as his personal servant. Steinmetz had recommended him, Peary said, but the job wouldn't be easy. He was bound for Nicaragua to head an engineering survey team. Would Matthew be willing to put up with the discomforts and hazards of such a trip?

D BIOGRAPHY
Reread lines 63–68.
What **details** does the
author provide about
Henson's first job on a
ship?

90 Thinking of the adventure and opportunities offered, Henson eagerly said yes, little realizing that a partnership had just been formed that would span years and be filled with exploration, danger, and fame.

Robert E. Peary was born in Cresson, Pennsylvania, in 1856, but was raised in Maine, where his mother had returned after his father's death in 1859. After graduating from Bowdoin College, Peary worked as a surveyor[4] for four years and in 1881 joined the navy's corps of civil engineers. One result of his travels for the navy and of his reading was an **ardent** desire for adventure. "I shall not be satisfied," Peary wrote to his mother, "until my name is known from one end of the earth to the other."
100 This was a goal Matthew Henson could understand. As he later said, "I recognized in [Peary] the qualities that made me willing to engage myself in his service." In November 1887, Henson and Peary set sail for Nicaragua, along with forty-five other engineers and a hundred black Jamaicans. **E**

Peary's job was to study the **feasibility** of digging a canal across Nicaragua (that canal that would later be dug across the Isthmus of Panama). The survey took until June of 1888, when the surveying party headed back to the United States. Henson knew he had done a good job for Peary, but, even as they started north, Peary said nothing to him about continuing on as his servant. It was a great surprise, then, when
110 one day Peary approached Henson with a proposition. He wanted to try to raise money for an expedition to the Arctic, and he wanted Henson to accompany him. Henson quickly accepted, saying he would go whether Peary could pay him or not.

"It was in June, 1891, that I started on my first trip to the Arctic regions, as a member of what was known as the 'North Greenland Expedition,'" Matthew Henson later wrote. So began the first of five expeditions on which Henson would accompany Peary.

During this first trip to Greenland, on a ship named *Kite,* Peary discovered how valuable Henson was to any expedition. He reported
120 that Henson was able to establish "a friendly relationship with the Eskimoes, who believed him to be somehow related to them because of his brown skin. . . ." Peary's expedition was also greatly aided by Henson's expert handling of the Eskimoes, dogs, and equipment. Henson also hunted with the Eskimoes for meat for the expedition and cooked under the supervision of Josephine Peary, Robert's wife. On the expedition's return to New York, September 24, 1892, Peary wrote, "Henson, my faithful colored boy, a hard worker and apt at anything, . . . showed himself . . . the equal of others in the party." **F**

ardent (är'dnt)
adj. having strong enthusiasm or devotion

E COMPARE AND CONTRAST
Reread lines 97–103. Compare and contrast the reasons that Peary and Henson wanted to become explorers. Record your answers in your diagram.

feasibility
(fē'zə-bĭl-ə-tē') *n.* the possibility of something's being accomplished

F BIOGRAPHY
According to Robert Peary, what qualities made Henson a valuable member of the expedition team?

---

4. **surveyor:** one who measures the boundaries of lands, areas, or surface features.

This first expedition to the Arctic led to several others, but it was with the 1905 expedition that Peary first tried to find that mystical[5] point, the North Pole, the sole goal of the 1908 expedition.

On July 6, 1908, the *Roosevelt* sailed from New York City. Aboard it were the supplies and men for an expedition to reach the North Pole. Accompanying Peary were Captain Robert Bartlett and Ross Marvin, who had been with Peary on earlier expeditions; George Borup, a young graduate from Yale and the youngest member of the group; Donald MacMillan, a teacher; and a doctor, J. W. Goodsell. And, of course, Matthew Henson. In Greenland the group was joined by forty-one Eskimos and 246 dogs, plus the supplies. "The ship," Henson wrote, "is now in a most perfect state of dirtiness." On September 5, the *Roosevelt* arrived at Cape Sheridan and the group began preparing for their journey, moving supplies north to Cape Columbia by dog sled to establish a base camp. Peary named the camp Crane City in honor of Zenas Crane, who had contributed $10,000 to the expedition.

The plan was to have two men, Bartlett and Borup, go ahead of the rest of the group to cut a trail stretching from the base camp to the North Pole. On February 28, the two men set out, and on March 1, the remainder of the expedition started north, following the trail Bartlett and Borup had cut the day before. At first, trouble seemed to plague them. On the first day, three of the sledges broke, Henson's among them. Fortunately, Henson was able to repair them, despite the fact that it was nearly 50 degrees below zero.

As the days passed, further trouble came the way of the expedition. Several times they encountered leads—open channels of water—and were forced to wait until the ice closed over before proceeding. On March 14, Peary decided to send Donald MacMillan and Dr. Goodsell back to the base camp. MacMillan could hardly walk, because he had frozen a heel when his foot had slipped into one of the leads. Dr. Goodsell was exhausted. As the expedition went on, more men were sent back due to exhaustion and frostbite. George Borup was sent back on March 20, and, on the 26th, so was Ross Marvin.

Although the expedition had encountered problems with subzero temperatures, with open water, and in handling the dogs, they had had no real injuries. On Ross Marvin's return trip to the base camp, however, he met with tragedy. On his journey, Marvin was accompanied by two Eskimos. He told them that he would go ahead to scout the trail. About an hour later, the Eskimos came upon a hole in the ice; floating in it was Marvin's coat. Marvin had gone through thin ice and, unable to save himself, had drowned or frozen. The Peary expedition had suffered its first—and fortunately its last—fatality.

SCIENCE CONNECTION

Peary and Henson were looking for the North Pole, or the top point of the axis on which Earth rotates. The red line represents the route they traveled. The pole is located on the Arctic ice cap, a layer of ice approximately ten feet thick and floating on the ocean's surface.

---

5. **mystical:** associated with a sense of wonder or mystery.

By April 1, Peary had sent back all of the original expedition except for
four Eskimos and Matthew Henson. When Bartlett, the last man to be sent
back, asked Peary why he didn't also send Henson, Peary replied, "I can't get
along without him." The remnant of the original group pushed on. **G**

> *We had been travelling eighteen to twenty hours out of every twenty-four.*
> *Man, that was killing work! Forced marches all the time. From all our other*
> *expeditions we had found out that we couldn't carry food for more than fifty*
> *days, fifty-five at a pinch. . . .*
> *We used to travel by night and sleep in the warmest part of the day. I was*
> *ahead most of the time with two of the Eskimos.*

So Matthew Henson described the grueling[6] journey. Finally, on the
morning of April 6, Peary called a halt. Henson wrote: "I was driving ahead
and was swinging around to the right. . . . The Commander, who was about
50 feet behind me, called to me and said we would go into camp. . . ." In
fact, both Henson and Peary felt they might have reached the Pole already.
That day, Peary took readings with a sextant and determined that they were
within three miles of the Pole. Later he sledged ten miles north and found
he was traveling south; to return to camp, Peary would have to return north
and then head south in another direction—something that could only
happen at the North Pole. To be absolutely sure, the next day Peary again
took readings from solar observations. It was the North Pole, he was sure.

---

6. **grueling** (grōō'ə-lĭng): physically or mentally demanding; exhausting.

G **BIOGRAPHY**
What impact did
Peary's decision have
on Henson's life?

VISUAL VOCABULARY

sextant (sĕk'stənt) *n.* a
tool that measures one's
location based on the
position of the sun, the
moon, or a star

Explorers hold the flags of their countries as they stand on the Arctic ice.

ANALYZE VISUALS
What do the **details** in
this illustration suggest
about Arctic exploration
in Henson's time?

190 On that day Robert Peary had Matthew Henson plant the American flag at the North Pole. Peary then cut a piece from the flag and placed it and two letters in a glass jar that he left at the Pole. The letters read:

90 N. Lat., North Pole
April 6, 1909
Arrived here today, 27 marches from C. Columbia.
I have with me 5 men, Matthew Henson, colored, Ootah, Egingwah, Seegloo, and Ooqueah, Eskimos; 5 sledges and 38 dogs. My ship, the S.S. Roosevelt, is in winter quarters at Cape Sheridan, 90 miles east of Columbia.
The expedition under my command which has succeeded in reaching the
200 *Pole is under the auspices[7] of the Peary Arctic Club of New York City, and has been fitted out and sent north by members and friends of the Club for the purpose of securing this geographical prize, if possible, for the honor and* **prestige** *of the United States of America.*
The officers of the Club are Thomas H. Hubbard of New York, President; Zenas Crane, of Mass., Vice-president; Herbert L. Bridgman, of New York, Secretary and Treasurer.
I start back for Cape Columbia tomorrow.
Robert E. Peary
United States Navy

210 *90 N. Lat., North Pole*
April 6, 1909
I have today hoisted the national ensign[8] of the United States of America at this place, which my observations indicate to be the North Polar axis of the earth, and have formally taken possession of the entire region, and adjacent,[9] for and in the name of the President of the United States of America.
I leave this record and United States flag in possession.
Robert E. Peary
United States Navy

Having accomplished their goal, the small group set out on the return
220 journey. It was, Matthew Henson wrote, "17 days of haste, toil, and misery. . . . We crossed lead after lead, sometimes like a bareback rider in the circus, balancing on cake after cake of ice." Finally they reached the *Roosevelt,* where they could rest and eat well at last. The Pole had been conquered!

During the return trip to New York City, Henson became increasingly puzzled by Peary's behavior. "Not once in [three weeks]," Henson wrote,

prestige (prĕ-stēzh′) *n.* recognition; fame

---

7. **auspices** (ô′spĭ-sĭz): protection or support.

8. **hoisted the national ensign:** raised the flag.

9. **adjacent** (ə-jā′sənt): close to or next to.

"did he speak a word to me. Then he . . . ordered me to get to work. Not a word about the North Pole or anything connected with it." Even when the *Roosevelt* docked in New York in September of 1909, Peary remained withdrawn and silent, saying little to the press and quickly withdrawing to
230 his home in Maine.

The ostensible reason for his silence was that when the group returned to New York, they learned that Dr. Frederick A. Cook was claiming that *he* had gone to the North Pole—and done so before Peary reached it. Peary told his friends that he wished to wait for his own proofs to be validated by the scientific societies before he spoke. He felt sure that Cook would not be able to present the kinds of evidence that he could present, and so it proved. **H**

On December 15, Peary was declared the first to reach the North Pole; Cook could not present adequate evidence that he had made the discovery. Peary and Bartlett were awarded gold medals by the National Geographic
240 Society; Henson was not. Because Henson was black, his contributions to the expedition were not recognized for many years.

After 1909, Henson worked in a variety of jobs. For a while, he was a parking-garage attendant in Brooklyn, and at the age of forty-six, he became a clerk in the U.S. Customs House in Lower Manhattan. In the meantime, friends tried again and again to have his contributions to the expedition recognized. At last, in 1937, nearly thirty years after the expedition, he was invited to join the Explorers Club in New York, and in 1944, Congress authorized a medal for all of the men on the expedition, including Matthew Henson. **I**
250 After his death in New York City on March 9, 1955, another lasting tribute was made to Henson's endeavors. In 1961, his home state of Maryland placed a bronze tablet in memory of him in the State House. It reads, in part:

MATTHEW ALEXANDER HENSON
Co-Discoverer of the North Pole
with
Admiral Robert Edwin Peary
April 6, 1909
Son of Maryland, exemplification of courage, fortitude[10] and patriotism,
260 *whose valiant deeds of noble devotion under the command of Admiral Robert Edwin Peary, in pioneer arctic exploration and discovery, established everlasting prestige and glory for his State and Country. . . .* ◐

H RECOGNIZE CAUSE-AND-EFFECT RELATIONSHIPS
Reread the explanation Peary gives for being "withdrawn and silent" on the trip back to New York. What other reasons might he have had for behaving this way toward Henson?

I COMPARE AND CONTRAST
Compare and contrast the way Peary treated Henson during the expedition and the way the public treated him upon their return.

---

10. **fortitude:** strength of mind; courage.

Comprehension

1. **Recall** Why was Henson forced to take care of himself at age 13?

2. **Recall** Where did Henson first meet Robert Peary?

3. **Clarify** Why didn't Frederick Cook get credit for discovering the Pole?

Literary Analysis

4. **Make Inferences** Reread lines 109–113. What does this passage tell you about Henson's goals as an explorer?

5. **Compare and Contrast** Look back at the Venn diagram you completed as you read. Notice the ways in which Peary and Henson are similar and different. Why do you think they made a good team as they attempted the **impossible?**

6. **Identify Cause-and-Effect Relationships** What events in Matthew Henson's life helped him become an explorer? In a cause-and-effect chain like the one shown, trace the events that led to Henson's career.

Cause		Effect/Cause		Effect/Cause
Henson's uncle can't support him.	→	Henson finds a job.	→	Henson's job lets him meet many sailors.

7. **Analyze Biography** Biographies draw their information from a variety of reliable sources. These sources may include diaries, letters, reference books, or even photographs. List some of the sources Jim Haskins uses in "Matthew Henson at the Top of the World." In what ways do they add to the picture of Henson's life?

Extension and Challenge

8. **Inquiry and Research** Find out more about the life and work of author Jim Haskins. Do the details of his life give you any hints about why he wrote the biography of Matthew Henson? Decide whether the **author's purpose** was primarily to inform, to entertain, to persuade, or to share personal thoughts and feelings.

9. **SCIENCE CONNECTION** Now that the North Pole has been discovered, why do present-day explorers still go there? Use the Internet and Will Steger's journal entries on pages 781–784 to write a paragraph about modern North Pole expeditions and their goals.

RESEARCH LINKS
For more on North Pole exploration, visit the **Research Center** at ClassZone.com.

Vocabulary in Context

VOCABULARY PRACTICE

Choose the word that best completes each sentence.

1. After getting lost three times, we abandoned our _____ to the lake.
2. Bill is a(n) _____ fan of that writer and has read all of her books.
3. Lucy's _____ helped her find her way back to the camp.
4. Fame and _____ are not the only reasons to be ambitious.
5. The project's _____ depends upon how much time is available.
6. The time she gives to her students is one _____ of her love of teaching.

ardent

expedition

feasibility

manifestation

prestige

resourcefulness

VOCABULARY IN WRITING

From the point of view of Matthew Henson, write a one-paragraph journal entry about a day on the *Katie Hines*. Try to use at least two vocabulary words. Here is an example of how you might begin.

> **EXAMPLE SENTENCE**
>
> *Today I am excited, because we are beginning a new **expedition**.*

VOCABULARY STRATEGY: IDIOMS

In the selection you have just read, the phrase "took the boy under his wing" (line 58) doesn't mean that Captain Childs had wings. It means that Captain Childs took care of Matthew Henson. Expressions like these are called **idioms.** Though the words in an idiom do not have the meaning you might expect, you often can figure out what the expression means by looking at context clues. Otherwise, a dictionary will help.

PRACTICE Write a brief definition for the boldfaced idiom in each sentence.

1. I don't know anything else about it now, but I'll **keep you posted.**
2. She's good at **breaking the ice** when she meets someone new.
3. Arnold **hit the roof** when someone stole his bicycle.
4. I can't make any definite plans—can we just **play it by ear?**
5. That exam next week is **nothing to sneeze at,** so you'd better study.

VOCABULARY PRACTICE
For more practice, go to the **Vocabulary Center** at **ClassZone.com.**

Reading-Writing Connection

Increase your understanding of "Matthew Henson at the Top of the World" by responding to these prompts. Then complete the **Grammar and Writing** exercise.

WRITING PROMPTS

SELF-CHECK

A. Short Response: Analyze Biography
What do you think was Matthew Henson's most important contribution? In a **one-paragraph response,** explain your opinion using examples from the biography.

A strong analysis will . . .
- clearly state an opinion
- combine details from the biography with your own interpretation

B. Extended Response: Write a Letter
Write a **two- or three-paragraph letter** to the National Geographic Society, persuading its members to honor Matthew Henson for his accomplishments. Discuss his willingness to try the **impossible** and his great skill in helping others on the expedition to the North Pole.

A persuasive letter will . . .
- list several reasons for honoring Henson
- support these reasons with details from the selection

GRAMMAR AND WRITING

USE COLONS CORRECTLY A **colon** is a punctuation mark used to introduce a list of items. If a list follows a verb or preposition, however, do not use a colon.

Example: On the expedition, they took the following items: sleds, dogs, and food.

Example: On the expedition, they took sleds, dogs, and food.

PRACTICE Rewrite the following sentences, inserting or deleting colons as needed.

1. The only things he could see were: snow, ice, and his companions.
2. Henson was: ambitious, helpful, and skilled at repairs.
3. They were confronted with: a broken sled, thin ice, and frostbite.
4. Those who were sent back included the following Borup, Marvin, and Bartlett.

*For more help with colons, see page R50 in the **Grammar Handbook.***

Over the Top of the World
Journal Entries

Use with "Matthew Henson at the Top of the World," page 768.

What's the Connection?

In "Matthew Henson at the Top of the World," you learned about some of the challenges faced by Arctic explorers in the early 1900s. In the **journal entries** you are about to read, you will learn how present-day explorers tackle the same journey.

Skill Focus: Synthesize

When you **synthesize** information, you put together facts, details, and ideas from different sources. Using information from multiple sources can give you a better understanding of a topic than you would have if you relied on only one source.

As you read the journal kept by William Steger during his 1995 trek to the North Pole, synthesize the information about modern Arctic expeditions with what you know about earlier journeys. Notice the ways in which technology has changed how people explore the North Pole.

To begin, record what you learned from "Matthew Henson at the Top of the World" in a chart like the one shown. Sort the information into categories such as "Weather and Geography," "How They Traveled," and "Challenges They Faced." Then add details from Steger's journal to the chart.

Source	Weather and Geography	How They Traveled	Challenges They Faced
"Matthew Henson at the Top of the World"	• temperature drops to –50 degrees • crisscrossed by open channels of water called leads	• sailed to Arctic with supplies • hunted for meat and cooked along the way	• explorers sent back due to exhaustion and frostbite • could run out of supplies
from "Over the Top of the World"			

F **OCUS ON FORM**
A **journal** is a personal record of thoughts, activities, and feelings. While a journal reveals a lot about the person writing, it can also give information about the time and place in which it was written.

from Over the Top of the World by Will Steger

APRIL 10

Here are the conditions we face most days: The ice is more than three years old and thick, so leads are usually less than three feet wide. Each time we come to one we have to decide whether to try to cross over it or find a way around. There's roughly two feet of snow covering the ice, and we're traveling through an area filled with 10-to-15-foot-tall pressure ridges. . . .

APRIL 16

The temperatures continue to drop, and today was a very cold,
10 difficult day. . . . By day's end, we and the dogs were all very tired.
Our goal now is to reach land in Canada sometime in July. That will mean another 100 days living in tents, eating the same frozen food, rarely bathing or changing clothes. I see why some people can't understand why we do these expeditions! **A**

A **SYNTHESIZE**
Reread lines 8–14. What **details** does Steger supply in this journal entry? Record them in your chart.

APRIL 17

We passed 89 degrees north latitude, which means we are less than 60 miles from the pole! Unlike explorers who traveled to the North Pole at the turn of the century, we are able to find out exactly where we are at any moment using a handheld computer called a Global
20 Positioning System, or GPS. By communicating with a satellite orbiting Earth, in just minutes it can tell us our exact latitude and longitude. We use it every night to see how far we've traveled—and every morning to see how far we've drifted. . . . **B**

B SYNTHESIZE
What is important about the GPS device Steger describes in lines 17–23?

APRIL 22

We have reached the North Pole exactly as planned, on Earth Day. It's been nine years since I first dogsledded here, and I've seen and learned a lot since then. I've now traveled to both poles, North and South, and find something calm and peaceful about being at the top, or the bottom, of the world. . . .
30   We were greeted by a small group of friends who had flown up for the occasion with our resupply. We spent the morning having our pictures taken while our fingers and toes nearly froze. . . .

Our friends have brought supplies with them, including letters and small gifts from our families, whom we haven't seen for two months. In addition, they carried with them 15 more days of food and fuel, a half-dozen waterproof bags, and some boards and plastic necessary for repairing our sleds, which have been quite punished by the rough ice. . . . But I got the best present—an apple pie baked by my mother back in Minneapolis. **C**

C SYNTHESIZE
What conveniences do Steger and his team get to enjoy on Earth Day? Note these in the correct column of your chart.

APRIL 24
40
So far, the most surprising aspect of the whole trip is all the snow. Most years the Arctic is like a desert, with very little precipitation. This year is different. It snows almost every day! Even when the skies are

clear, there is a light sprinkling. Some storms dump five or six inches overnight. On top of that, the winds have been incredible.
50 Temperatures have gone as low as –40°F, but the average is –20°F. Since we left Siberia, the warmest temperature was 0°F. . . . **D**

MAY 3

Outside this morning it's clear, –20°F, with a north wind, which is good because it is at our back. I'm looking forward to the days now, as are the dogs, who are strong and excited. It's a very simple existence we lead when we're traveling like this. . . .

One of the reasons we're here is to draw attention to the environmental problems that affect the Arctic. We are collecting snow samples along the way for scientists back home to test.
60 On most days it's hard to believe there's pollution out here in the middle of the Arctic Ocean. But there is. In the air, the water, and the ice and, unfortunately, in the wildlife.

The pollution problems that scientists study in the Arctic are created in big industrial cities and on farms in North America, Asia, and Europe. Pollution travels through the air and water, carried by wind, river, and ocean currents. Once in the Arctic, pollutants "live" longer because of the cold conditions. Studies have shown that man-made pollutants are starting to show up in Arctic animals, like seals and polar bears. So we're not affecting
70 just the air and the water, but the animals, too. . . .

MAY 13

Early this morning, at 4 o'clock, we were awakened by the sound of dogs howling. All 22 of them in unison. They don't howl for no reason, so I was sure there was a polar bear nearby.

They soon quieted down, though, and I fell back asleep—only to be awakened again a half-hour later when a gigantic snap in the ice sent a shockwave rolling through camp. A tremor lifted our tents, like an earthquake rolling right beneath our sleeping bags. The air was filled with a thundering, grinding, rumbling
80 roar, a very frightening sound, one we had not heard before. I shot out of my bag and quickly unzipped the tent door, ready to jump out in my long underwear to pull the tent to safety.

D **SYNTHESIZE**
What do you learn from the April 24 entry about the Arctic climate and the conditions Steger's team faces? Add this information to your chart.

What I saw amazed me. A wall of ice, 20 feet tall and as long as a football field, was moving our way as if being pushed by the blade of a giant bulldozer. Blocks of ice as big as cars were falling off the top of the moving wall and being crushed beneath it. It moved toward us, threatening to crush us, too.

The dogs were in shock, standing perfectly still and quiet. All five of us were out of our tents, and we, too, were in shock. All we could 90 do was watch, helplessly. Just as suddenly as it began, the wall of ice stopped, only 100 feet from our tents.

Julie has compared traveling on the Arctic Ocean to traveling on a big, floating jigsaw puzzle. This morning we watched as some of the bigger pieces shifted around. It was very powerful, and very beautiful, too. And, I admit, quite frightening. . . . **E**

JUNE 24

Another miserable day of hauling. It snowed throughout the day, dumping more than a foot, resulting in deep drifts coming up over our knees. All day long we slaved in a complete whiteout, pulling the 100 sleds forward just inches at a time. In six hours, we made only three miles. No one is saying it out loud, but we're all wondering if we'll ever make it to land. . . .

JULY 3

Our last morning was spent pulling the canoe-sleds up a 200-foot ridge and then riding them down the other side like toboggans. I was on the front, pushing with one leg as if I were riding a scooter, and Victor was sitting in the back, pushing with his ski poles and yelling like a little boy. It was a perfect way to end the trip—slipping and sliding and laughing.

110 As we pulled the last couple of miles, I could feel all the tension of the past months lift off my shoulders. I picked up the first stones I saw and rolled them in my hand, feeling their smooth hardness. When we finally saw dirt and small flowers, we kneeled and pulled them to our faces. It was perhaps the best smell I have ever had! We made it! We were all safe, finally on solid ground. **F**

E JOURNAL
Reread lines 88–95. What are Steger's thoughts and feelings about the event described in the May 13 entry?

F SYNTHESIZE
What does Steger write about Arctic geography and weather in his June 24 and July 3 entries? Add this information to your chart.

Comprehension

1. **Clarify** Reread the May 3 entry. What are the sources of Arctic pollution?

2. **Summarize** According to the April 24 entry, what is Arctic weather usually like, and how is the weather different this year?

Critical Analysis

3. **Make Inferences** Reread lines 103–115. What might you infer from this journal entry about the overall attitudes of Steger and his team members?

4. **Analyze a Journal** A **primary source** is anything that provides firsthand information about a person, place, time, or event. Identify a research topic for which you could use Steger's journal as a primary source. Then use the journal to give an example of information on that topic.

5. **Synthesize** Based on Jim Haskins's and Will Steger's accounts of North Pole expeditions, in what ways have such expeditions changed over time? Use details from the selections to support your response.

Read for Information: Draw Conclusions

WRITING PROMPT

A **conclusion** is a judgment or belief about something. To reach a solid conclusion, you need to use sound reasoning, evidence, and experience. In a paragraph, state and support a conclusion you have reached about one of the following topics:

- why some people become explorers
- how present-day explorers compare with explorers such as Henson and Peary
- the joys and dangers of traveling in the Arctic

The following steps can help you arrive at and support a solid conclusion:

1. Choose a topic and jot down ideas and information about it.

2. Use this information to draw a conclusion about the topic.

3. Pick out specific evidence from both the biography and the journal for support.

4. State your conclusion in a topic sentence. Then present the reasons and evidence that support the conclusion.

MY CONCLUSION

Support from Biography	Support from Journal
• detail • detail	• detail • detail

from **The Story of My Life**
Autobiography by Helen Keller

Do we have to accept *our* LIMITS?

KEY IDEA Sometimes the things we most want to do are the hardest to accomplish. It can be discouraging to discover our **limits** and frustrating to find ourselves facing unexpected challenges. Fortunately, many serious obstacles can be overcome with creativity and determination. In this excerpt from *The Story of My Life,* Helen Keller describes triumphing over her limitations.

QUICKWRITE Helen Keller found a way to succeed despite being both blind and deaf. Think of someone else—from your life, a book, or a movie—who also had to deal with some type of limitation. Write a brief paragraph describing this person and his or her efforts to conquer a major difficulty.

● LITERARY ANALYSIS: AUTOBIOGRAPHY

If someone asked you to write your life story, you would be writing an autobiography. An **autobiography** is the story of a person's life, written by that person. In biographies, the subject is a person other than the writer. In autobiographies, the writer is the subject. Autobiographies

- are told from the **first-person point of view**
- include descriptions of people and events that have influenced the writer
- share the writer's personal thoughts and feelings about his or her experiences

As you read *The Story of My Life,* notice the information the author decides to include about herself.

● READING STRATEGY: MONITOR

Monitoring is the process of checking your understanding as you read. One way to do this is to **clarify** ideas, or to pause and think about what you have just read.

As you read Helen Keller's autobiography, note any passages that you find confusing. Record them in a chart like the one shown. Next to each passage, write what you think it means.

Keller's Words	My Words
"Anger and bitterness had preyed upon me" (line 14)	She couldn't stop feeling angry and bitter.

▲ VOCABULARY IN CONTEXT

Helen Keller uses the following words to tell how she came to understand the world around her. To see how many you know, match each vocabulary word from the Word List with the numbered word or phrase closest in meaning.

WORD LIST	consciousness	sensation	uncomprehending
	repentance	tangible	

1. not understanding   3. feeling   5. regret
2. awareness   4. touchable

The Story of My Life

Helen Keller

The most important day I remember in all my life is the one on which my teacher, Anne Mansfield Sullivan, came to me. I am filled with wonder when I consider the immeasurable contrasts between the two lives which it connects. It was the third of March, 1887, three months before I was seven years old.

On the afternoon of that eventful day, I stood on the porch, dumb,[1] expectant. I guessed vaguely from my mother's signs and from the hurrying to and fro in the house that something unusual was about to happen, so I went to the door and waited on the steps. The afternoon

10 sun penetrated the mass of honeysuckle that covered the porch, and fell on my upturned face. My fingers lingered almost unconsciously on the familiar leaves and blossoms which had just come forth to greet the sweet southern spring. I did not know what the future held of marvel or surprise for me. Anger and bitterness had preyed upon me continually for weeks and a deep languor had succeeded[2] this passionate struggle. **A**

Have you ever been at sea in a dense fog, when it seemed as if a **tangible** white darkness shut you in, and the great ship, tense and

ANALYZE VISUALS
What can you **infer** about the relationship between Helen Keller and Anne Sullivan by looking at this photograph of them?

A AUTOBIOGRAPHY
Reread lines 6–15. In what way does the **first-person point of view** help show Keller's thoughts and feelings?

tangible (tăn′jə-bəl) *adj.* possible to touch; real

---

1. **dumb:** unable to speak; mute.
2. **deep languor had succeeded:** a complete lack of energy had followed.

anxious, groped her way toward the shore with plummet and sounding-
line,[3] and you waited with beating heart for something to happen? I was
like that ship before my education began, only I was without compass
or sounding-line, and had no way of knowing how near the harbor was.
"Light! Give me light!" was the wordless cry of my soul, and the light
of love shone on me in that very hour. **B**

I felt approaching footsteps. I stretched out my hand as I supposed to
my mother. Someone took it, and I was caught up and held close in the
arms of her who had come to reveal all things to me, and, more than all
things else, to love me.

The morning after my teacher came she led me into her room and gave
me a doll. The little blind children at the Perkins Institution had sent it
and Laura Bridgman[4] had dressed it; but I did not know this until afterward.
When I had played with it a little while, Miss Sullivan slowly spelled into my
hand the word "d-o-l-l." I was at once interested in this finger play and tried
to imitate it. When I finally succeeded in making the letters correctly I was
flushed with childish pleasure and pride. Running downstairs to my mother
I held up my hand and made the letters for *doll*. I did not know that I was
spelling a word or even that words existed; I was simply making my fingers
go in monkey-like imitation. In the days that followed I learned to spell in
this **uncomprehending** way a great many words, among them *pin, hat, cup*
and a few verbs like *sit, stand* and *walk*. But my teacher had been with me
several weeks before I understood that everything has a name. **C**

One day, while I was playing with my new doll, Miss Sullivan put
my big rag doll into my lap also, spelled "d-o-l-l" and tried to make me
understand that "d-o-l-l" applied to both. Earlier in the day we had had
a tussle over the words "m-u-g" and "w-a-t-e-r." Miss Sullivan had tried
to impress it upon me that "m-u-g" is *mug* and that "w-a-t-e-r" is *water*, but
I persisted in confounding the two. In despair she had dropped the subject
for the time, only to renew it at the first opportunity. I became impatient
at her repeated attempts and, seizing the new doll, I dashed[5] it upon the
floor. I was keenly delighted when I felt the fragments of the broken doll
at my feet. Neither sorrow nor regret followed my passionate outburst.
I had not loved the doll. In the still, dark world in which I lived there was
no strong sentiment or tenderness. I felt my teacher sweep the fragments
to one side of the hearth, and I had a sense of satisfaction that the cause of

B MONITOR
Reread lines 16–23.
To **clarify**, rephrase
what Keller is saying
about how she felt
before her education
began. Record this
information in your
chart.

uncomprehending
(ŭn'kŏm-prĭ-hĕn'dĭng)
adj. not understanding

C MONITOR
What does Keller not
understand about the
words she is spelling?

---

3. **plummet and sounding-line:** a weighted rope used to measure the depth of water.

4. **Perkins Institution . . . Laura Bridgman:** The Perkins Institution was a school for the blind, located
   in Massachusetts. Laura Bridgman (1829–1889), a student at the Perkins Institution, was the first
   deaf and blind child to be successfully educated. Like Keller, Bridgman became quite famous for her
   accomplishments.

5. **dashed:** threw or knocked with sudden violence.

my discomfort was removed. She brought me my hat, and I knew I was going out into the warm sunshine. This thought, if a wordless 60 **sensation** may be called a thought, made me hop and skip with pleasure.

We walked down the path to the well-house, attracted by the fragrance of the honeysuckle with which it was covered.

This house on the Keller property was where Sullivan often took Helen for lessons.

70 Someone was drawing water and my teacher placed my hand under the spout. As the cool stream gushed over one hand she spelled into the other the word *water,* first slowly, then rapidly. I stood still, my whole attention fixed upon the motions of her fingers. Suddenly I felt a misty **consciousness** as of something forgotten—a thrill of returning thought; and somehow the mystery of language was revealed to me. I knew then that "w-a-t-e-r" meant the wonderful cool something that was flowing over my hand. That living word awakened my soul, gave it light, hope, joy, set it free! There were barriers still, it is true, but barriers that could in time be swept away. **D**

I left the well-house eager to learn. Everything had a name, and each 80 name gave birth to a new thought. As we returned to the house every object which I touched seemed to quiver with life. That was because I saw everything with the strange, new sight that had come to me. On entering the door I remembered the doll I had broken. I felt my way to the hearth and picked up the pieces. I tried vainly[6] to put them together. Then my eyes filled with tears; for I realized what I had done, and for the first time I felt **repentance** and sorrow. **E**

I learned a great many new words that day. I do not remember what they all were; but I do know that *mother, father, sister, teacher* were among them— words that were to make the world blossom for me, "like Aaron's rod, with 90 flowers."[7] It would have been difficult to find a happier child than I was as I lay in my crib at the close of that eventful day and lived over the joys it had brought me, and for the first time longed for a new day to come. ～

6. **vainly:** without success.

7. **like Aaron's rod, with flowers:** a reference to a story in the Bible in which a wooden staff suddenly sprouts flowers.

ANALYZE VISUALS
Compare Helen's description of the well-house (lines 64–69) to this photograph of it. What do you learn from each source?

sensation (sĕn-sā'shən) *n.* a feeling

consciousness (kŏn'shəs-nĭs) *n.* awareness of one's own thoughts

D AUTOBIOGRAPHY
Reread lines 64–78. Which **details** in this passage might not have been included in a biography?

repentance (rĭ-pĕn'təns) *n.* sorrow or regret

E MONITOR
Reread lines 79–86. **Clarify** why Keller suddenly feels sorry for breaking the doll.

LETTER Throughout her life, Helen Keller came into contact with many famous Americans. In this letter, the president of the United States sends Keller his good wishes and congratulates her on her accomplishments.

THE WHITE HOUSE
WASHINGTON

February 24, 1938

My dear Miss Keller:

I send you my very best wishes as you prepare to observe the fiftieth anniversary of your first meeting with your devoted teacher-liberator, Anne Sullivan Macy. This anniversary will bring precious memories to you of an association which was to be such a blessing to you. Your faith and optimism and high courage and helpful work in behalf of others have made you a greatly beloved figure.

Your determination to carry on the work of your friend and teacher is a fortunate thing for all those who sit in darkness. In this noble undertaking I wish you all success.

Very sincerely yours,

Franklin D. Roosevelt

Franklin D. Roosevelt

Miss Helen Keller
American Foundation for the Blind, Inc.,
15 West 16th Street,
New York, N.Y.

Courtesy of the Helen Keller archives,
American Foundation for the Blind.

Comprehension

1. **Recall** How does Helen Keller know that something unusual is happening on the day Anne Sullivan arrives?

2. **Recall** What is the first word Sullivan tries to teach Keller?

3. **Summarize** How does Keller's world change once she begins to understand the connection between language and meaning?

Literary Analysis

4. **Monitor** Look back at the chart you used to help you **clarify** ideas as you read. Choose one passage that you found difficult to understand, and explain what clues helped you to rephrase it as you did.

5. **Identify Sensory Details** Although Keller lacked the senses of sight and hearing, she was able to observe many things using her remaining senses. In a graphic organizer like the one shown, record words and phrases that Keller used to help her readers understand what she was describing.

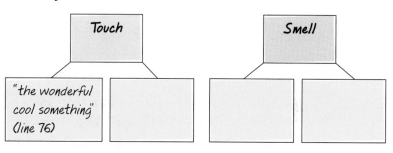

6. **Analyze Autobiography** Consider what Keller shares about her experiences. How would the story of Keller's life be different if Anne Sullivan had written it?

7. **Evaluate Analogy** Keller was aware that many of her readers would never experience the challenge of missing one or more senses. Reread lines 16–23, focusing on the **analogy,** or point-by-point comparison, in which Keller describes herself as a ship lost in the fog. Is this an effective way for her to share her feelings? Explain.

8. **Compare Literary Works** Reread the letter to Helen Keller from Franklin D. Roosevelt on page 792. Roosevelt calls Anne Sullivan a "liberator"—a person who frees a prisoner or captive. Would Keller agree with this description? Support your response.

Extension and Challenge

9. **Inquiry and Research** In the 1800s, blind and deaf people had few resources. Many were confined to hospitals. Fortunately, this is no longer the case. Research two or three of the technological advances that now help people overcome their physical **limits.** Share your discoveries with the class.

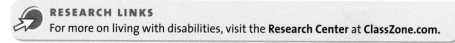

RESEARCH LINKS
For more on living with disabilities, visit the **Research Center** at ClassZone.com.

Vocabulary in Context

VOCABULARY PRACTICE

Complete each sentence using the appropriate vocabulary word.

1. After the ride ended, he still had the _____ of being upside-down.
2. Her happiness was _____, like a warm blanket wrapped around her.
3. The teacher looked at him in a(n) _____ way, so he repeated himself.
4. A feeling of _____ is natural after you do something hurtful or wrong.
5. When I hit my head, I lost _____ and my mind went blank.

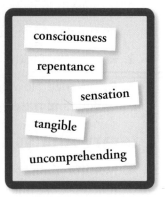

consciousness
repentance
sensation
tangible
uncomprehending

VOCABULARY IN WRITING

Write a paragraph from the point of view of Anne Sullivan, describing her thoughts and feelings just after Helen begins to understand language. Use at least two vocabulary words. You might start like this.

EXAMPLE SENTENCE

*Helen is starting to understand that each **sensation** means something.*

VOCABULARY STRATEGY: ANALOGIES AS CONTEXT CLUES

An **analogy** is a comparison that helps readers understand more than they might from a simple explanation. Writers use analogies to make their ideas clearer by relating them to something familiar.

Analogies can also provide **context clues** to the meanings of difficult words. When you come across an unfamiliar term in an analogy, look at the rest of the comparison for words and phrases that might describe the unknown term.

PRACTICE Define the boldfaced word in each of the following analogies. Then identify the context clues that helped you figure out the meaning.

1. **Petrified** by the frightening scene, I stopped in my tracks like a deer in headlights.
2. Good friends **sustain** a person the way strong pillars support a bridge.
3. She was **jostled** by the crowd like a boat caught in a current.
4. Like a candle that lights up the room, knowledge **illuminates** the mind.

VOCABULARY PRACTICE
For more practice, go to the **Vocabulary Center** at **ClassZone.com**.

Reading-Writing Connection

Extend your understanding of *The Story of My Life* by responding to these prompts. Then complete the **Grammar and Writing** exercise.

WRITING PROMPTS	SELF-CHECK
A. Short Response: Write a Letter Write a **brief letter** from Helen Keller to Anne Sullivan in which Keller thanks Sullivan for helping her to move past her **limits.**	*An effective letter will...* • show an understanding of how Keller felt about Sullivan • include details from the selection
B. Extended Response: Evaluate Autobiography Do you believe that Helen Keller really remembered all of the details she included in *The Story of My Life?* Why or why not? In **two or three paragraphs,** discuss which details in the autobiography you think are an accurate record of the events, and which ones might not be.	*A strong evaluation will...* • express a clear opinion • include examples from the selection as support

GRAMMAR AND WRITING

CAPITALIZE CORRECTLY A **common noun** is a general name for a person, place, or thing. Common nouns, such as *street* or *girl,* are not capitalized. Specific names, such as *Main Street* or *Helen,* are **proper nouns.** These are always capitalized. Words that indicate family relationships (*my father, her uncle*) are only capitalized when they are used as names (*Hi, Dad!*) or before names (*Uncle Bob*).

> *Example:* Keller wouldn't forget the name of her teacher. (*common noun*)

> *Example:* Anne Sullivan changed my life. (*proper noun*)

PRACTICE Rewrite the following sentences, correcting the errors in capitalization.

1. I could tell from my Mother's actions that something was happening.
2. Children at the perkins institution sent me a doll.
3. You taught me to spell words such as *Pin* and *hat.*
4. I could not wait to show father what I had learned.

*For more help with capitalization, see page R51 in the **Grammar Handbook.***

Under the Royal Palms: A Childhood in Cuba

Memoir by Alma Flor Ada

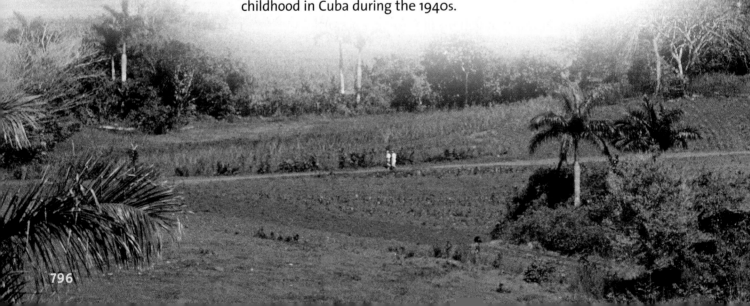

Alma Flor Ada
born 1938

Other Books by Alma Flor Ada

- *Alma Flor Ada and YOU*
- *Choices and Other Stories from the Caribbean*
- *The Gold Coin*
- *Where the Flame Trees Bloom*

Meet Alma Flor Ada

By the time she was three, Alma Flor Ada had already learned to read. She had also learned that she was born into a family of storytellers. It is no surprise, then, that she would grow up to become a storyteller herself.

Ada writes to share some of "the joy, the excitement, the surprise" she felt reading books and hearing stories as a child. Seeing her books in the hands of readers is one of her greatest joys. Another is using her writing to help children from different cultures understand one another. Ada writes many of her books in both English and Spanish, hoping that her readers will learn "to not only celebrate but also deeply respect and appreciate others."

Try a Memoir

A **memoir** is a form of nonfiction in which a person tells about significant events in his or her life. Unlike an autobiography, which generally covers a person's entire life, a memoir may describe just one particular time period or experience. Alma Flor Ada's memoir describes the experiences that shaped her childhood in Cuba during the 1940s.

The award-winning memoir *Under the Royal Palms* paints a vivid picture of growing up in Cuba. Alma Flor Ada grew up on her family's ranch, which was called *La Quinta Simoni*. In the excerpt you are about to read, Alma and her cousins are led by their imaginations to explore an unfamiliar area. They quickly find themselves lost in their "jungle" playground. What will happen to them?

from

Under the Royal Palms:

A Childhood in Cuba

Life at *La Quinta Simoni* provided constant invitations for adventure. One morning I met my cousins Jorge and Virginita by the fallen tree. It was a huge poplar, possibly uprooted by a hurricane. But the tree had refused to die and, although fallen, had sprouted new branches. These new branches, covered with heart-shaped leaves, projected upward like spears pointed at the sky. The tree was an excellent place for playing. Sometimes it became our pirate ship: On it, we crossed the Caribbean while the wind filled our green sails. At other times it was a castle, and 10 from its turrets we defended our fortress from invading warriors. Or perhaps it was a covered wagon crossing the plains, or a sleigh racing across the Russian steppes pursued by a wolf pack.

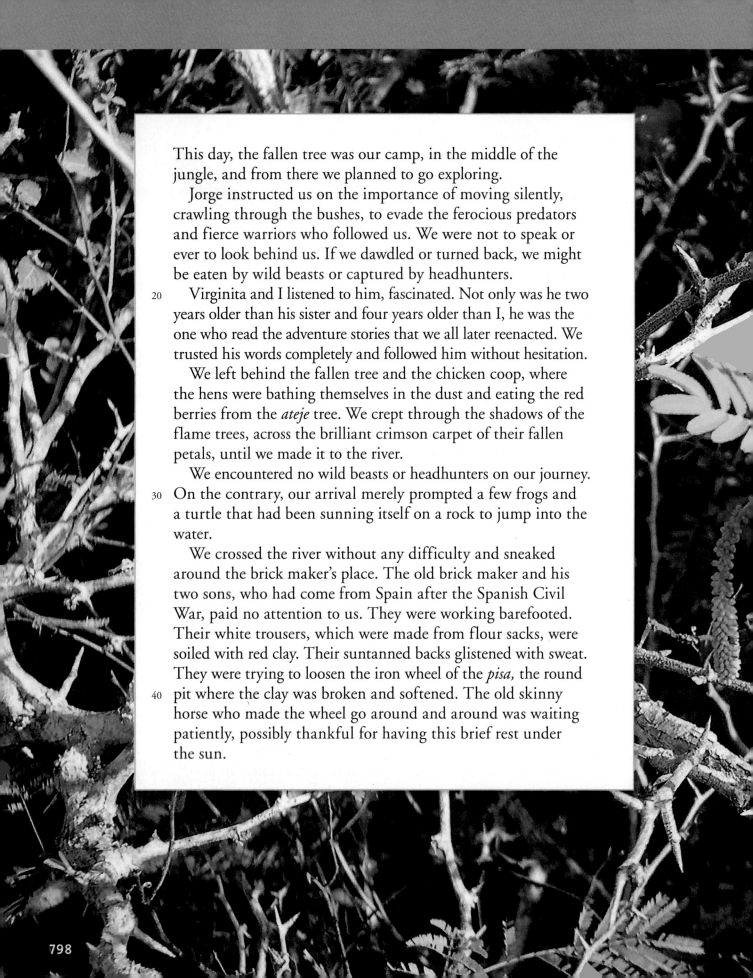

This day, the fallen tree was our camp, in the middle of the jungle, and from there we planned to go exploring.

Jorge instructed us on the importance of moving silently, crawling through the bushes, to evade the ferocious predators and fierce warriors who followed us. We were not to speak or ever to look behind us. If we dawdled or turned back, we might be eaten by wild beasts or captured by headhunters.

20   Virginita and I listened to him, fascinated. Not only was he two years older than his sister and four years older than I, he was the one who read the adventure stories that we all later reenacted. We trusted his words completely and followed him without hesitation.

We left behind the fallen tree and the chicken coop, where the hens were bathing themselves in the dust and eating the red berries from the *ateje* tree. We crept through the shadows of the flame trees, across the brilliant crimson carpet of their fallen petals, until we made it to the river.

We encountered no wild beasts or headhunters on our journey.
30 On the contrary, our arrival merely prompted a few frogs and a turtle that had been sunning itself on a rock to jump into the water.

We crossed the river without any difficulty and sneaked around the brick maker's place. The old brick maker and his two sons, who had come from Spain after the Spanish Civil War, paid no attention to us. They were working barefooted. Their white trousers, which were made from flour sacks, were soiled with red clay. Their suntanned backs glistened with sweat. They were trying to loosen the iron wheel of the *pisa,* the round
40 pit where the clay was broken and softened. The old skinny horse who made the wheel go around and around was waiting patiently, possibly thankful for having this brief rest under the sun.

Beyond the brick maker's place, the thorny bushes began. They say that the *marabú* plant was brought to Cuba by a countess who loved its flowers, which resemble pink powder puffs. But the bush did not want to remain locked up in a garden, so it slowly spread out across the fields.

Once *marabú* takes hold of a field, it is difficult to clear it. Its roots intertwine under the soil, forming a net that is almost impossible to pull out. One must plow the field to turn over the earth and then rake it, making sure that every last piece of root is removed. Otherwise, it will sprout again.

A *marabú* field is impenetrable unless a path is opened with a machete. The thorny branches form a barrier open only at ground level.

And it was at that level that we began to cross the *marabú* field. Jorge showed us how easy it could be if we simply crawled between and around the thin trunks. It was easy enough, indeed. But soon we had lost him. Because it was impossible to stand up or even to turn, we did not stop. Virginita and I continued, trying to follow the route plotted by our chief explorer, who was by now far ahead and out of sight. . . .

As we moved farther into the *marabú* field, the trees seemed to grow closer and closer together, the branches more intertwined. The thorns caught on our dresses, tore at our hair. But there was nothing we could do. With Jorge's order never to turn back still fresh in our minds, and with a desperate desire to escape the *marabú* jungle, we struggled on, hoping to find our leader at some turn of the maze. . . .

For hours, Virginita and I crawled through the *marabú*, avoiding when we could the dead thorny branches that had fallen on the ground, leaving behind pieces of our dresses and strands of our hair.

Meanwhile, at home, everyone was alarmed. The girls were lost! Jorge, who had returned a long time ago, had moved on to other pastimes. Nobody knew where to find us.

My parents went to the river. They talked to the brick makers. But not for a minute did they imagine we would have entered the marabú field. Jorge, to avoid a scolding, said only that he had left us playing at the other side of the river.

Late in the afternoon, with our clothes in tatters and our faces covered with muddy tears, we finally emerged at the other end of the marabú field. We were immediately surrounded by a group of children, half naked and as dirty as we were by then, who invited us to play hide-and-seek. Of course we were much too exhausted to accept.

Hearing us crying, the parents of the children appeared at the doors of their huts.

"Poor little ones," one of the women said kindly. "They are lost." She took me in her arms and asked Virginita to follow her.

With water from an old tin basin, she washed our faces and arms, all covered with scratches. Then she opened an old lard can, which she used as her cupboard, and took out two crackers—thick, large sailors' crackers. She sprinkled them with coarse brown sugar—poor people's way of fooling their bodies into believing they had eaten when there was no more substantial food to be had. Then she gave one to each of us.

"Eat, little ones, eat," she said, coaxing us. "Don't worry. We'll take you home."

And from the doorway, the children looked at us with big, open eyes, trying to imagine what we possibly could have done to merit such a generous and unexpected treat. ◐

Keep Reading

How do you think Alma's parents will react when she and her cousin return home? As you continue reading her memoir, you'll meet the rest of her extended family and share in her adventures, her joys, and her sorrows. Most of all, you will have the chance to see how every event shapes Alma, as she grows from a child into a young woman.

from Spellbinder: The Life of Harry Houdini

Biography by Tom Lalicki

Can you BELIEVE *your eyes?*

KEY IDEA If you've ever watched a movie full of incredible stunts and outrageous special effects, then you know you can't always believe what you see. Still, sometimes it's fun to play along with an **illusion,** even when we know the truth. In the following biography, you will read about Harry Houdini, an entertainer who thrilled audiences with his daring tricks—some of which weren't illusions at all!

DISCUSS Sometimes it's simple to figure out how a trick is done. When an illusion is really impressive, however, it can be hard to convince yourself that it isn't real. With a small group, talk about some illusions you've seen that you just can't explain.

● ELEMENTS OF NONFICTION: MAIN IDEA AND DETAILS

Much of what we know about famous or historical figures comes from their **biographies,** or the stories of their lives. Writers of biography cover the main events of a person's life and often reveal their own ideas about what kind of person the subject was. Writers back up their **main ideas** with **supporting details** such as the following:

- **anecdotes,** or brief stories from the person's life that reveal something about his or her character
- **examples** of the person's thoughts, feelings, or behavior
- **statements** made by or about the person
- **descriptions** of life-changing experiences and events

As you read *Spellbinder,* look for Tom Lalicki's main ideas about Houdini and the details he includes to back up his views.

● READING SKILL: TRACE CHRONOLOGICAL ORDER

Many biographies present the events of a person's life in **chronological order,** or the order in which they happened. For clues to the order of events, look for words and phrases that identify specific times, such as *before, first, two years earlier,* or *meanwhile.*

As you read *Spellbinder,* track the major events in Houdini's early career on a timeline like the one shown.

Date or Time Period   1894

Event   performs in Dime Museums

▲ VOCABULARY IN CONTEXT

Tom Lalicki uses the following words to help tell the story of a master of illusion. To see how many you already know, place each word in the appropriate column.

WORD LIST	certify	commence	devise	obstacle

Know Well	Think I Know	Don't Know at All

Author On|ine

Writing History and Mystery Tom Lalicki started out as a filmmaker, but a love of history eventually led him to become a writer. Lalicki's work includes biographies of scientists Dian Fossey and Alexander Graham Bell. He has also written a mystery novel featuring Harry Houdini.

**Tom Lalicki
born 1949**

Background

Escape Artist Harry Houdini (1874–1926), whose real name was Erik Weisz, was born in Hungary. His family immigrated to the United States when he was a child. As a young man, Weisz changed his name to Houdini and began performing as an escape artist. Houdini mostly used his strength and skill to open locks, though on occasion he hid tools on his body or in his clothes. Houdini often boasted about his strength— but this boast may have contributed to his death. After a tiring performance, Houdini allowed a young man to punch him in the stomach to challenge his strength. Unfortunately, Houdini did not know he was suffering from an infected appendix, which the punches may have made worse. He died of the infection shortly afterward.

MORE ABOUT THE AUTHOR AND BACKGROUND
To learn more about Tom Lalicki and Harry Houdini, visit the **Literature Center** at ClassZone.com.

SPELLBINDER: THE LIFE OF HARRY HOUDINI

Tom Lalicki

Vaudeville, the variety stage show, was the premier family entertainment at the end of the 19th century. Singers, comedians, dancers, impersonators,[1] comedy singers, comedy dancers, and magicians filled out affordable three-hour shows for growing audiences. . . .

Promoters built lavish theaters, decorated with huge chandeliers, pillars, and murals that gave audiences comfortable places to relax and see first-rate shows. There were several tiers[2] of vaudeville theaters. The best acts played the Keith-Albee Circuit of theaters on the East Coast and the Orpheum Circuit on the West. But in 1894, the husband-and-wife team
10 of Bess and Harry Houdini were far from prime-time players.

Ranked below vaudeville were the Dime Museums, an outgrowth of P. T. Barnum's Museums.[3] There magicians, jugglers, and puppeteers were jumbled together with curiosity, or "curio," acts like sword swallowers, fire eaters, midgets, giants, and fat ladies. Performers did from twelve to twenty shows a day for very low wages. Even recent immigrants could understand and afford these shows. **A**

ANALYZE VISUALS
What information does this poster provide about Houdini?

A MAIN IDEA AND DETAILS
Reread lines 1–16. What do these details about vaudeville and the Dime Museums help you understand about Bess and Harry Houdini?

---

1. **impersonators:** performers who mimic the voices or appearances of other people, usually famous people.

2. **tiers:** ranks or levels.

3. **P. T. Barnum's Museums:** The stage promoter P. T. Barnum (1810–1891) ran a series of traveling museums that featured performers and "oddities"—including the fake mummified body of a mermaid. Barnum's exhibitions eventually became the Barnum and Bailey Circus.

Handcuff King Poster, 1906. The Granger Collection, New York.

The bottom rung of urban entertainment was the beer hall, where noisy and not very interested patrons enjoyed corny one-act plays and sentimental songs. Small-town folk needed entertainment, too, and that was offered by circuses and medicine shows.[4]

20 Between 1894 and 1899, the Houdinis learned the craft of showmanship by performing in all these arenas, struggling to make ends meet the whole time. To get bookings, they did a song-and-dance act and appeared in very bad plays. Houdini performed as "Projea, the Wild Man" in an animal cage and did a mind-reading act and onstage séances.[5] . . .

A less determined, less confident man would have given up entirely and taken a job. The closest Houdini came to that was opening a correspondence school[6] for magicians in his mother's apartment. He offered all his secrets for sale. Luckily, nobody thought the tricks worth
30 buying.

The problem with Houdini's act was that he hadn't yet discovered the real Houdini. He performed as "The King of Cards," "The King of Billiard Balls," even as "The Paper Tearing King," without much success. Audiences loved the Metamorphosis escape[7] but did not love Houdini's magic tricks. He worked constantly to develop new ones. He watched and studied hundreds of other performers to learn showmanship. He improved his grammar and stage speech. Most importantly, he invented brilliant ways to promote the act. But none of his efforts opened the door to stardom. **B**

In 1895, Houdini let audience members handcuff him (with their own
40 handcuffs) as part of Metamorphosis. He escaped. Then he let the police of Gloucester, Massachusetts, lock him in their handcuffs. And he escaped. In Woonsocket, Rhode Island, police and newspaper reporters shackled Houdini with six sets of handcuffs and locked him in a room. He escaped in eighteen seconds. **C**

It was terrific advertising in those relatively small towns, but it went no farther. In the days before national news magazines, radio, and television, Houdini's escape from police handcuffs in Woonsocket was purely local news. . . .

Another trademark trick that Houdini developed during this time was
50 the straitjacket escape—a stunning feat of strength and agility nobody else could match. . . .

B MAIN IDEA AND DETAILS
Reread lines 31–38. What main idea do the details in these lines support?

C CHRONOLOGICAL ORDER
Reread lines 39–44. What two time-order clues does the author use to indicate the order of Houdini's early handcuff escapes?

---

4. **medicine shows:** traveling groups common in the 1800s that provided entertainment and sold "miracle cures" (usually phony) for a variety of illnesses and pains.

5. **séances** (sā'än-səz'): meetings at which people attempt to receive messages from ghosts or spirits.

6. **correspondence school:** a school that sends lessons and exams to students by mail.

7. **Metamorphosis escape:** In this trick, Bess would lock Harry, handcuffed, inside a trunk. On the count of three, Houdini would free himself—and Bess would be locked inside the trunk.

During a Canadian tour, Houdini visited a mental hospital and [witnessed the use of straitjackets]. Determined to escape from a straitjacket himself, Houdini borrowed one
60 and had Bess wrap him in it. She restrained him in the jacket seven times before he **devised** a technique for escaping. It left him swollen, bruised, and bloody.

Onstage, the cabinet curtain was drawn closed

ANALYZE VISUALS
This photograph shows Houdini completing a straitjacket escape. Why might Houdini have chosen to perform this trick upside down?

as the straitjacketed Houdini twisted, turned, and rolled on the floor
70 until, free, he opened the curtain holding the empty canvas coat. This stunt didn't catch on right away, either. Audiences thought it was a cheat. Nobody could escape from a real straitjacket, so they assumed Houdini's was rigged. The trick was a flop.

Houdini didn't give up on either the handcuff or the straitjacket escape. Houdini never gave up on a good idea. If audiences didn't like an escape *he* liked, he tried to improve the presentation. He had the patience and determination to keep going back over a problem until it was solved.

devise (dǐ-vīz′) *v.* to plan or design

W hile playing a Minneapolis hall in the spring of 1899, lightning struck Houdini's floundering[8] career. Martin Beck, who ran the
80 entire Orpheum vaudeville circuit, liked Metamorphosis and the handcuff escape. He told Houdini to drop the card, billiard ball, and paper-tearing tricks from the act. Beck wanted Houdini to do a twenty-minute turn in the top vaudeville theaters for sixty dollars a week—more than he had ever earned before. Houdini wrote that the offer "changed my whole Life's journey." **D**

Like a jewel under a bright light, Houdini responded to attention by revealing brilliant new facets.[9] Now he played only two shows a day, not twelve. He stayed in cities for a week or more, not one night. This gave him the time and the platform to experiment with his act and impress his
90 audience. **E**

D CHRONOLOGICAL ORDER
When and how did Houdini meet Martin Beck? Add this information to your timeline.

E MAIN IDEA AND DETAILS
In what ways was meeting Martin Beck a life-changing experience for Houdini?

---

8. **floundering:** struggling or stumbling.

9. **facets:** a flat, polished surface on a jewel. The word *facets* also refers to different sides of a personality.

He constantly improved Metamorphosis. He sometimes borrowed a suit jacket from the audience, which he would put on before going into the trunk. After the switch, Bess would emerge wearing the borrowed jacket. Sometimes he took people into the trunk who escaped with him.

Responding to an accusation that he used keys to open handcuffs, Houdini went to a San Francisco police station on July 13, 1899. [His clothes were removed] and examined by a police surgeon who **certified** that he was hiding nothing. His mouth was taped shut, his wrists and ankles were shackled in ten sets of police handcuffs. For good measure, 100 the ankle cuffs were attached to the handcuffs with an eleventh pair before he was locked into an interrogation room.[10] Five minutes later Houdini walked out, still "n——" (the way most polite newspapers spelled the word *naked* then), carrying all the cuffs in his hands. **F**

In April 1900, again [unclothed], he took just three minutes to escape from a doubly locked jail cell in Kansas City. He repeated these escapes wherever the police allowed. Each police force added new **obstacles,** almost desperate not to be embarrassed by this upstart magician. But they always were. And as Houdini knew, the stories written about him by big-city newspapers were the most valuable and cheapest advertising available.

110 The public commotion he caused generated massive interest in his stage act and sold tickets. His $60 salary rapidly increased to $250 a week—half the total yearly income of an average American worker.

Houdini also introduced another new trick that, like Metamorphosis, would continue to thrill audiences for his entire career. To perform the East Indian Needles, Houdini called an audience committee onstage to look into his nose and throat. Nothing hidden there. He swallowed a handful of sewing needles, loudly chewing on them and washing them down with water. Next, he swallowed a ball of sewing thread. Then he put his hand into his mouth and slowly drew out the thread with the 120 needles threaded onto it.

Although profoundly successful, Houdini needed more. The Houdini legend was started and continuously reinforced by a tireless engine churning out mountains of promotion. The engine was Houdini's mind. A 1900 flyer he sent to theater managers announced: WHERE THE POSSIBILITY CEASES, THE IMPOSSIBILITY **COMMENCES**! . . . HARRY HOUDINI, "KING OF HANDCUFFS," DEFIES DUPLICATION, EXPLANATION, IMITATION OR CONTRADICTION. ∾

certify (sûr′tə-fī′) *v.* to confirm as true or genuine

F MAIN IDEA AND DETAILS
Reread lines 95–103. Explain what this **anecdote** reveals about Houdini's character.

obstacle (ŏb′stə-kəl) *n.* something that stands in the way or prevents progress

commence (kə-mĕns′) *v.* to begin

---

10. **interrogation room:** a secure room in which police officers question suspects.

Comprehension

1. **Recall** What names did Harry Houdini perform under before becoming famous as "The King of Handcuffs"?

2. **Recall** What advice did Martin Beck give Houdini?

3. **Summarize** How did Houdini try to prove that he wasn't cheating during his performances?

Critical Analysis

4. **Make Inferences** Reread lines 121–127. What does Houdini's method of advertising his performances tell you about him?

5. **Identify Supporting Details**
One of the author's main ideas in this selection is that "Houdini never gave up on a good idea" (line 75). Skim the selection to find supporting details that back up this statement. Record the details in a diagram like the one shown.

Main Idea:
"Houdini never gave up on a good idea."

Detail:
He kept working on his escapes until people liked them.

Detail:

Detail:

6. **Analyze Main Idea** What do you think is the main idea of the entire selection? List details from the selection to support your answer.

7. **Evaluate Chronological Order** Look back at the timeline you made as you read. In what way does the use of chronological order help you understand the path Houdini took in order to become famous?

Extension and Challenge

8. **Readers' Circle** What was the key to Harry Houdini's success? With a small group, discuss which was most useful to Houdini during his early career—his personality, his skills, or the help of people around him. Use examples from the selection to support your opinion.

9. **Inquiry and Research** The stunts and escapes that amazed Houdini's audiences might have looked magical, but they were actually the result of strength, skill, and constant practice. Choose one of Houdini's famous **illusions** and research how it was done. Present your findings to the class in the form of a poster.

RESEARCH LINKS
For more on Houdini's illusions, visit the **Research Center** at **ClassZone.com**.

Houdini prepares to escape from a locked milk can.

Vocabulary in Context

VOCABULARY PRACTICE

Show that you understand the vocabulary words by deciding whether each statement is true or false.

1. When you **commence** a project, you are almost done.
2. When teachers **devise** homework assignments, they are grading them.
3. If someone can **certify** a claim, you ought to believe it.
4. Something that helps you achieve your goals is an **obstacle.**

certify

commence

devise

obstacle

VOCABULARY IN WRITING

Suppose you have just seen Houdini perform. Using at least two vocabulary words, write a brief review of his show. Here is a sample beginning.

> **EXAMPLE SENTENCE**
>
> *I don't think there's any **obstacle** that can stop Houdini.*

VOCABULARY STRATEGY: FOREIGN WORDS IN ENGLISH

As an English speaker, you might be surprised to learn that many of the words we regularly use actually come from other languages. For example, the word *vaudeville* comes from a French word meaning "humorous songs." Understanding how languages share words can add to your knowledge of word meanings.

PRACTICE Use a dictionary to find the original language and meaning of each of the boldfaced words.

1. We always have **macaroni** for dinner on Wednesday nights.
2. If you want to perform in the **ballet,** you will have to practice.
3. He prefers to eat **tofu** rather than chicken or beef.
4. I went to the **opera** with my grandparents last year.
5. She enjoys having breakfast out on the **patio.**

VOCABULARY PRACTICE
For more practice, go to the **Vocabulary Center** at **ClassZone.com.**

Reading-Writing Connection

Increase your appreciation of *Spellbinder* by responding to these prompts. Then complete the **Grammar and Writing** exercise.

A. Short Response: Write a Promotional Flyer
As you read in lines 121–127, Harry Houdini often used flyers to promote his performances. Choose one of the **illusions** described in the selection and write a **one-paragraph flyer** persuading people to attend.

A creative flyer will . . .
- use persuasive language
- include details about Houdini's act as described in the selection

B. Extended Response: Evaluate Ideas
On his deathbed, Houdini told his doctor, "I am nothing but a fake, while you do great things for your fellow man." Do you agree or disagree with Houdini's opinion of himself? Respond in **two or three paragraphs.**

A strong response will . . .
- state a clear opinion
- use information from the selection as support

GRAMMAR AND WRITING

CAPITALIZE CORRECTLY **Proper nouns,** as well as any adjectives made from those nouns, are always capitalized. Some specific types of proper nouns to watch for are

- names and titles of people (*Dr. Jackson, Mr. Lewis Smith*)
- countries (*France, Germany*)
- nationalities and ethnicities (*Korean, my Italian-American uncle*)
- languages (*Spanish, Russian*)
- religions (*Christianity, Islam*)

    Example: Harry Houdini, who was Jewish, was born in Hungary.

PRACTICE Rewrite the following sentences, capitalizing all proper nouns.

1. Often, mrs. houdini was part of harry's act.
2. Houdini learned to use a straitjacket while on a canadian tour.
3. He worked hard to improve his english.
4. Houdini earned more than the average american worker.

*For more help with capitalization, see page R51 in the **Grammar Handbook.***

How do you UNLOCK a mystery?

KEY IDEA True stories fascinate people. It's exciting to hear an astonishing tale and learn how it actually happened. In this lesson, you'll view a documentary about the amazing Harry Houdini. You'll also explore the tools moviemakers used to tell the story of Houdini's life and his many death-defying **escapes.**

Background

Stranger Than Fiction Harry Houdini led a more interesting life than many fictional characters we know from books and movies. He captivated audiences around the world with his incredible escapes. In his time, Houdini was as famous as any major professional athlete or movie star today.

Even though Houdini died in 1926, he's still one of the world's most famous magicians. People are curious to learn about his life and the details of his legendary feats. This makes him a great subject for a documentary film. In this documentary, you'll get a chance to see Houdini perform, and you'll even learn the secrets behind some of his extraordinary escapes.

Media Literacy: Documentary

A **documentary** is a nonfiction film that gives viewers information about important people or historical events. Documentaries are made for several purposes. They can inform and entertain. They can take the viewer "behind the scenes" and provide the full story behind an interesting person or event. Documentary filmmakers gather factual material about their subjects and use it to tell their stories. This material is presented through footage, interviews, and voice-over narration.

FEATURES OF A DOCUMENTARY	STRATEGIES FOR VIEWING
Footage is recorded material that gives information about a subject. Documentary filmmakers combine different types of footage to tell their subject's story. Footage can include • film clips • photographs • news reports • interviews	Think about why the particular footage was chosen. Does it • show details of a historical time? • create an emotional response? • reveal the filmmakers' point of view?
Interviews are a type of footage usually filmed specially for the documentary. Filmmakers may interview experts on the subject or topic. They might also interview people who knew the person or were involved in the event the documentary is about.	Think about why the person was chosen to be interviewed. Does he or she • have special knowledge about the subject? • present another side to the story?
Voice-over narration is the voice of an unseen speaker that is heard in a documentary. The voice-over can provide important facts about the subject. It can also help explain the footage.	Listen to the voice-over narration for additional information about the footage. Also listen for clues to what's most important about the subject.

Viewing Guide for

Houdini: The Great Escape

The amazing things Harry Houdini did make many people want to know the whole story. They want to see him perform his escapes, and to learn the secrets behind them. With this documentary, you'll get to do just that.

Think about the documentary features as you view the clip. Notice how they work together to tell Houdini's story. View the clip more than once, thinking about the footage, interviews, and voice-over narration.

NOW VIEW

FIRST VIEWING: Comprehension

1. **Recall** During his performances, what did Houdini ask the audience to do just before he had himself locked in the milk can?

2. **Summarize** In your own words, describe how Houdini escaped from the packing crate lowered into the river.

CLOSE VIEWING: Media Literacy

3. **Examine Voice-Over Narration** Think about the **voice-over narration** that plays over the film footage of Houdini hanging upside down and escaping from the straitjacket. What details do you learn from the narration that you couldn't get from just watching the footage?

4. **Analyze Interviews** What type of people do the filmmakers **interview** for the documentary? Why do you think these people were chosen to talk about Houdini?

5. **Evaluate Footage** The documentary uses film clips, photographs, newspaper articles, and posters from Houdini's time. Which type of **footage** best helps you understand Houdini? Give a reason for your choice.

Write or Discuss

Compare the Film and Essay You've now read a biography of Harry Houdini and seen a documentary about him. Think about what you learned from the essay, and what you learned from the film. What are the strengths of each? Write a paragraph that compares the two. Think about

- the amount of detail you learned about Houdini's life from the essay
- the **footage** of Houdini performing his tricks
- the descriptions of Houdini's tricks in the **interviews**
- the information given by the **voice-over narration**

Produce Your Own Media

MEDIA TOOLS

For help with planning a photo documentary, visit the **Media Center** at **ClassZone.com.**

Create a Photo Documentary Think about how you would make a documentary about an ordinary person. To keep the audience interested, you'd want to focus on the most fascinating parts of that person's life. What sets him or her apart from everyone else? Choose an ordinary person you know, and shoot a series of photographs to tell the behind-the-scenes story of his or her life. Attach your photographs to a bulletin board or poster board and present them to the class.

HERE'S HOW Here are a few suggestions for shooting your photo documentary:

- First, do your research. Interview your subject to find out about his or her life. Choose the most interesting parts to focus on.
- Think of your photos as documentary footage. Take shots of important people, locations, and objects in your subject's daily life.
- If you don't have a camera, take notes as you follow your subject through his or her day. Write a description of the most interesting events of the day.

STUDENT MODEL

Tech Tip

If available, use computer software to create a slideshow presentation of your photo documentary.

In a Neighborhood in Los Angeles
Poem by Francisco X. Alarcón

For Gwen, 1969
Poem by Margaret Walker

How would you like to be REMEMBERED?

KEY IDEA Suppose you and your family were moving to another state. How would you want to be **remembered** by your friends and classmates? Would you like them to remember something you accomplished, the way you looked, or how you treated others? The poems you are about to read recollect the lasting impact of a special grandmother and an important American poet.

LIST IT Divide a sheet of paper in half. Use one half to list what you remember about a person who has had a significant effect on your life. On the other half of the page, make a list of the ways you hope to be remembered.

How I Remember _____	How I Want to Be Remembered
1.	1.
2.	2.

● LITERARY ANALYSIS: CHARACTERIZATION IN POETRY

In just a few lines, a poem can paint a portrait of a memorable character. To create great characters, poets use four methods of **characterization** similar to those used for fiction and nonfiction. Those methods are

- describing the character's physical appearance
- presenting the character's thoughts, words, and actions
- presenting the thoughts, words, and actions of other characters
- having the speaker of the poem comment directly on the character

As you read the following poems, look for places where the poets use these methods of characterization. Record the examples in a chart like the one shown.

	Grandmother	Gwen
What does the character look like?		
What does she think, say, and do?	"mijito don't cry" (lines 4–5)	
What do others say about her?		

● READING SKILL: IDENTIFY IMAGERY

Many poets use imagery to create vivid descriptions. **Imagery** is made up of words and phrases that appeal to one of the reader's five senses: touch, sight, taste, smell, and hearing. These **sensory details** help to hint at different ideas and emotions surrounding the poem's subject or setting.

As you read "In a Neighborhood in Los Angeles" and "For Gwen, 1969," pay attention to the words and phrases each poet uses to appeal to your senses. Consider what ideas or emotions these details might suggest.

In a Neighborhood in Los Angeles

Francisco X. Alarcón

I learned
Spanish
from my grandma

mijito[1]
5 don't cry
she'd tell me **Ⓐ**

on the mornings
my parents
would leave

10 to work
at the fish
canneries

my grandma
would chat
15 with chairs

sing them
old
songs

dance
20 waltzes with them
in the kitchen **Ⓑ**

Ⓐ CHARACTERIZATION
What do the grandmother's words in lines 4–6 tell us about her? Record this information in your characterization chart.

Ⓑ CHARACTERIZATION
Reread lines 13–21. What can you **infer** about the grandmother's personality from this description of her actions?

---

1. *mijito* (mē-hē'tō): Spanish for "my little child." A contraction of the phrase *mi hijito*.

when she'd say
niño barrigón[2]
she'd laugh

25 with my grandma
I learned
to count clouds

to point out
in flowerpots
30 mint leaves

my grandma
wore moons
on her dress

Mexico's mountains
35 deserts
ocean

in her eyes
I'd see them
in her braids

40 I'd touch them
in her voice
smell them

one day
I was told:
45 she went far away

but still
I feel her
with me

whispering
50 in my ear
mijito

C IDENTIFY IMAGERY
What **sensory details**
in lines 31–42 help you
visualize, or form a
mental picture of, the
speaker's grandmother?

2. *niño barrigón* (nēn'yō
   bär-rē-gōn'): a Spanish phrase
   meaning "potbellied little boy."

Rain Slicked Avenue (2004), Lisbeth Firmin. Oil on panel, 20″ × 20″. Klaudia Marr Gallery, Santa Fe, New Mexico.

For Gwen, 1969 (Gwendolyn Brooks)

Margaret Walker

The slender, shy, and sensitive young girl
is woman now,
her words a power in the Ebon land.[1]
Outside her window on the street
5 a mass of life moves by.
Chicago is her city. **D**
Her heart flowers with its flame—
old stockyards, new beaches
all the little storefront churches
10 and the bar on the corner.
Dreamer and seer of tales
She witnesses rebellion,
struggle and sweat.
The people are her heartbeat—
15 In their footsteps pulsate daily
all her black words of fire and blood. **E**

D CHARACTERIZATION
Reread lines 1–6. What do you learn about Gwen in these lines?

E IDENTIFY IMAGERY
What senses do the details in lines 14–16 appeal to?

---

1. **Ebon land:** a reference to African-American society and culture.

MAGAZINE ARTICLE In "For Gwen, 1969," Margaret Walker celebrates the successes of her friend, Gwendolyn Brooks. Brooks remained successful and influential for 30 years after 1969. This article traces her impressive career.

A Way with Words

James C. Hall

Gwendolyn Brooks liked to say that African-American poetry is the story of a community learning "to lift its face unashamed." Poetry's emotion and commitment to powerful, memorable language made it ideal for writers who wanted to transform how people felt about the possibilities of the future. Gwendolyn Brooks has always successfully tapped the ability of poetry to affect our sense of life's possibilities. . . .

By paying close attention to the lives of common folk in the Chicago neighborhoods around her, Brooks discovered a way to draw attention to the unjust conditions in which they lived and to celebrate the fact that they did so with courage and purpose. Keeping families together, caring for loved ones, educating, and teaching were all necessary parts of the struggle—parts that most definitely deserved celebration. . . . Yet, at the same time, Brooks's poetry did not reduce the complex nature of human beings to social problems.

Her book *Annie Allen* was granted the Pulitzer Prize in 1950, and Brooks became the first African American to win that award. Brooks's poetry was elaborate in its use of symbolism and its reference to other writing. However, she always managed to tell the story of individuals whose lives and struggles were easy to recognize and respect. Human lives were always complicated in a Brooks poem, but a reader rarely leaves her work puzzled or unaffected.

Brooks was born in 1917 and died in 2000. For most of her life, Chicago was home, and she had always been one of its model cultural ambassadors. . . .

In the final decades of Brooks's life, she worked to cultivate an interest in poetry among schoolchildren. She recognized how underserved Chicago's children were and how often poetry and the arts were the first activities to be cut in an underfunded school system. With her own resources, she sponsored a poetry contest for children of all backgrounds and creatively drew attention to the skills and ability that might be lost. As effectively as any writer in the African-American tradition, Brooks managed to model a life and create a body of work that made known the necessity of "lifting one's face unashamed."

Comprehension

1. **Recall** What is Gwen's "heartbeat" in "For Gwen, 1969"?

2. **Clarify** What happens to the speaker's grandmother at the end of "In a Neighborhood in Los Angeles"?

3. **Represent** Based on the details in "In a Neighborhood in Los Angeles," create a sketch of the speaker's grandmother.

Literary Analysis

4. **Make Inferences About Character** Reread lines 1–3 of "For Gwen, 1969." What can you infer about the speaker's feelings toward Gwen?

5. **Identify Author's Purpose** What do you think is the author's main purpose in each poem—to inform, to entertain, to persuade, or to share personal thoughts and feelings? Support your answer with details from the poems.

6. **Analyze Characterization** Look back at the chart you filled in as you read. Which methods of characterization does the poet rely on most in "In a Neighborhood in Los Angeles"?

7. **Analyze Imagery** The poem "In a Neighborhood in Los Angeles" uses imagery to describe the speaker's grandmother. In a web like the one shown, write down the details from the poem that appeal to each of the five senses. Then note the feelings or ideas this imagery helps the speaker express.

8. **Evaluate Characterization** Which **character** do you think is more powerfully presented, the grandmother or Gwen? Explain.

Extension and Challenge

9. **Big Question Activity** With a small group of classmates, compare and contrast the ways in which the poems describe their subjects. Do you think the women would be happy with the way they are **remembered?**

10. **SOCIAL STUDIES CONNECTION** Reread the article about Gwendolyn Brooks on page 822, then do some research on Chicago during the 1960s. Why might Margaret Walker have chosen the year 1969 as the **setting** for her poem about Brooks?

Writing Workshop

Personal Narrative

Just like Matthew Henson, Helen Keller, and other writers in this unit, you have a life story, too. Even if you aren't famous, you can still turn events in your life into great stories. Find out how to create a personal narrative from one of your own experiences by following the **Writer's Road Map.**

WRITER'S ROAD MAP

Personal Narrative

WRITING PROMPT 1

Writing from Your Life Think of a special event in your life, and write a narrative to describe it. Include details to help your reader understand what the event was like. Be sure to explain why the event was important to you.

Events to Consider

- your first day at a new school or in a new neighborhood
- the day you got a pet
- a special vacation

WRITING PROMPT 2

Writing from Literature Choose an event from a literary work that reminds you of something in your own life. Describe the event and tell what similar thing happened to you.

Events and Literary Works to Consider

- a time when you learned something that changed your life (*The Story of My Life*)
- a loving relationship with someone ("In a Neighborhood in Los Angeles")
- a performance you can't forget (*Spellbinder: The Life of Harry Houdini*)

 WRITING TOOLS
For prewriting, revision, and editing tools, visit the **Writing Center** at **ClassZone.com.**

KEY TRAITS

1. IDEAS
- Focuses on a **single experience**
- Uses **dialogue** to re-create the experience

2. ORGANIZATION
- Has an attention-getting **introduction**
- Uses **transitions** to make the **order of events** clear
- Shows the **importance** of the experience in the **conclusion**

3. VOICE
- Shows the writer's individual **style**

4. WORD CHOICE
- Uses **descriptive language** to make the experience come alive for the reader

5. SENTENCE FLUENCY
- Uses a variety of **sentence types** (statements, questions, and exclamations)

6. CONVENTIONS
- Uses **correct grammar, spelling, and punctuation**

Part 1: Analyze a Student Model

Veronica Alley
Rancho Santa Margarita
Intermediate School

There's No Place Like Home

Hesitantly, I hopped out of the big van into the chilly air. I watched as my younger cousin Andrew hopped out, too. Then the van spat a cloud of exhaust in my face as my aunt drove around the corner.

"She's not coming back to pick us up, is she?" I asked in despair.

5 "Nope. We're walkin' home," Andrew chirped joyously through his thick Eastern accent.

We were walking home, in a city like this, at this time of day? My heart sank. What was Aunt Carol thinking? Whatever apprehension I felt dissolved like sugar in my mouth when I saw the candy store.

10 Andrew and I exchanged glances and rushed in. Oh, the choices! We left munching on chocolate bars and crunching cherry-flavored candy canes.

It was dark now, but the uneven sidewalks of Chicago were still used by a vastly different, and slightly frightening, array of people. My

15 anxiety returned.

"Um . . . y-you know how to get to your house, right?"

"Of course I know how to get to my house," Andrew smirked.

Looking around me, I saw graffiti-covered buildings, chewing-gum-littered sidewalks, and scary-looking children. Passersby kept glaring at

20 me, their faces snarling at me from the shadows, as if they could smell my fear. The only things back home that could smell anxiety were dogs, bees, and my glitchy computer. I suddenly missed my quiet city in California. I decided that talking with Andrew would maybe take my mind off our surroundings.

KEY TRAITS IN ACTION

Introduction begins the action and creates interest. The entire narrative is about a **single experience** (the walk to Andrew's home).

The writer varies **sentence types.** Including some questions and an exclamation keeps her narrative lively and appealing.

The highlighted **transition** helps the reader understand the **order of events**—in other words, what happened when.

Vivid and exciting **descriptive language** helps to pull the reader into the narrative. The writer's **style** is dramatic.

25   "So, how's school?" I began casually.

"Fifth grade is fun. My teacher lets us do all kinds of things we weren't allowed to do last year."

"Anything interesting happen lately?"

"Well, somebody drowned in the school swimming pool the other
30 day," he said indifferently.

"Somebody drowned?"

"Yup. The state made them fill the pool in with concrete so it couldn't happen again."

I was liking this city less and less by the minute. Then I heard a big,
35 loud bang. I screamed and looked around frantically.

"What was that?" I shrieked at Andrew.

"Oh, that's probably just Justin who lives a block down from us. He sets off a lot of fireworks."

I wanted to go home. The home I once regarded as boring was
40 suddenly very appealing, not to mention safe. I imagined myself at home, sitting on my warm, comfortable sofa watching my favorite television show while drinking a cold can of my favorite soda. There would be no more possible criminals snarling at me, no more fireworks, and no more children drowning in swimming pools. I began gnawing
45 madly at my chocolate bar.

Andrew stared at me and said, "You okay? What's wrong?"

"I'm okay. I'm just tired and thirsty," I muttered.

"Well, we're almost at my house."

I sighed in relief. We turned the corner, and I recognized the large
50 house, its warm, bright windows making me long to open the door. In my mad desire to be inside, I dashed to the front steps, my cheeks red from the cold and running. Andrew followed behind me and opened the door. A choir of angels sang in my head as I stepped into the warm, safe house.

Dialogue gives the reader a "you are there" feeling.

The **conclusion** shows the **importance** of the experience: Being in a strange place made the narrator appreciate familiar things.

2

Part 2: Apply the Writing Process

PREWRITING

What Should I Do?	What Does It Look Like?

1. Decide what you want to write about.
Make a list of special things that have happened to you. Think of important times and events in your life. If you are responding to Prompt 2, you must think of an event from a literary work and a similar event from your life. (Circle) your best idea.

TIP Focus on just one experience. If you write about several things, you will confuse your reader.

▶

my first roller coaster ride

the day we moved to our new apartment

(*getting scared while walking in Chicago*)

going fishing with Grandma G.

when I broke my arm playing soccer

winning the kite-flying competition

getting my green belt in tae kwon do

camping during a thunderstorm

---

2. List all the details you remember.
Try to remember as many details as you can. Write them down. You don't need to use them all in your narrative, but writing down details will help you remember the experience more clearly.

▶

Details about the walk:

dark sidewalks	*even kids seemed scary*
loud BANG!	*chocolate bar*
graffiti	*not like California*
Andrew's accent	*wanting to go home*
smelly exhaust fumes	*crunchy candy canes*
shadows	*Aunt Carol's van*
the candy store	*Andrew's house*

---

3. Use descriptive language.
Choose a person, place, or object that is an important part of your narrative. Think of creative, descriptive words that will help your reader understand him, her, or it.

▶

What Should I Do?	What Does It Look Like?
1. Make a plan. Like any great story, a narrative has characters, a setting, and a plot. A narrative can have dialogue and suspense, too. Creating a story map will help you plan the elements of your narrative. **TIP** Make sure your map gets the sequence of events right. Your reader will want to know what happened first, next, and last.	**Title:** *A Scary Walk Home* **Setting:** *Chicago, last October* **Events:** *1. Aunt Carol drops us off.* *2. We go to the candy store.* *3. We start walking and I get scared.* *4. There's a big, loud bang.* *5. We reach Andrew's house.* **Effect on me:** *It made me want to be back home.*
2. Set the scene for your reader. In a narrative, the **introduction** usually gives readers information about the time, place, and characters. Some introductions describe a place or a character in great detail. Others start the action right away.	**Event 1 from story map:** *Aunt Carol drops us off.* **First draft of introduction:** *I got out of the car. Andrew got out, too. It was chilly, and I didn't want to leave the car, but I did. Then Aunt Carol drove off and left us there alone.*
3. Use dialogue effectively. You don't need to reproduce every word that each person said. However, dialogue can bring your characters to life and move the action along. You can use sentence fragments and slang if that's what people actually said at the time. **See page 830:** Check Your Grammar **TIP** Before revising, consult the **key traits** on page 824 and the **rubric** and **peer-reader questions** on page 830.	**What I want to tell my reader:** *I was scared when we left the candy store.* **How I could show that by including dialogue:** *"Um . . . y-you know how to get you house, right?"* *"Of course I know how to get to my house," Andrew smirked.* **What I want to tell my reader:** *Chicago seemed dangerous.* **How I could show that by including dialogue:** *"What was that?" I shrieked at Andrew.* *"Oh, that's probably just Justin who lives a block down from us. He sets off a lot of fireworks."*

REVISING AND EDITING

What Should I Do?	*What Does It Look Like?*

1. Double-check the sequence of events.
- Ask a peer reader to <u>underline</u> places where the order of events is confusing.
- Decide if you need to change the order or add transitions.

See page 830: Ask a Peer Reader

> <u>We were walking home, in a city like this, at this time of day? My heart sank. What was Aunt Carol thinking? Whatever apprehension I felt dissolved like sugar in my mouth. Andrew and I exchanged glances and rushed in.</u>
>
> when I saw the candy store.

2. Enrich your narrative with descriptive details.
- Draw a box around each descriptive word or phrase you used in your story.
- Add details to help your reader see, hear, taste, smell, or feel what you experienced.

> We left the store happy, munching on chocolate bars and crunching cherry-flavored candy canes.

> Looking around me, I saw scary stuff, graffiti-covered buildings, chewing-gum-littered sidewalks, and scary-looking children.

3. Have you used different sentence types?
- An occasional question or exclamation adds variety to your writing.
- If all your sentences end in periods, consider using an exclamation or a question where it makes sense to do so.

> ~~I worried about walking home at this time of day.~~ We were walking home, in a city like this, at this time of day? My heart sank. What was Aunt Carol thinking?

> ~~There were lots of different kinds of candy.~~ Oh, the choices!

4. Show how the experience affected you.
- Does your narrative include details that show your inner thoughts and reactions?
- [Bracket] details that show the overall effect of the experience. If necessary, add information about why this experience matters to you.

> [I wanted to go home.] The home I once regarded as boring was suddenly very appealing, not to mention safe. I imagined myself at home, sitting on my warm, comfortable sofa watching my favorite television show while drinking a cold can of my favorite soda.

Personal Narrative

Apply the Rubric

A strong personal narrative . . .

- ☑ focuses on a single experience
- ☑ describes events in a logical order
- ☑ sparks reader interest with a surprising or appealing introduction
- ☑ includes dialogue and vivid descriptions
- ☑ uses transitions where needed
- ☑ varies sentence types, occasionally using questions or exclamations
- ☑ has a style that shows the writer's personality
- ☑ explains the significance of the experience in the conclusion

Ask a Peer Reader

- What experience did I describe, and what effect did it have on me?
- Do I need to make the sequence of events clearer? If so, what should I change?
- Do I need to add descriptive details or background information? If so, where?

Check Your Grammar

- Punctuate dialogue correctly. Enclose the speaker's words in quotation marks. Use a comma to separate a speaker's statement from the words that name the speaker.

> *"I'm okay. I'm just tired and thirsty," I muttered.*

- If the speaker's words end with a question mark or an exclamation point, don't include a comma.

> *"What was that?" I shrieked at Andrew.*

- Begin a new paragraph each time the speaker changes.

> *"Anything interesting happen lately?"*
>
> *"Well, somebody drowned in the school swimming pool the other day," he said indifferently.*
>
> *"Somebody drowned?"*

See page R49: Quick Reference: Punctuation

Writing Online

PUBLISHING OPTIONS
For publishing options, visit the **Writing Center** at **ClassZone.com.**

ASSESSMENT PREPARATION
For writing and grammar assessment practice, go to the **Assessment Center** at **ClassZone.com.**

Creating a Video Documentary

A **documentary** is a video program about true-life events. You can create a documentary based on the narrative you just wrote or on a different event.

Planning the Documentary

1. **List ideas and resources.** Your documentary should be three to five minutes long. Jot down ideas that would fill that time—brief events, not your life story. For example, you might explain how to solve a problem between siblings. If you prefer, you could create a humorous documentary, such as one that shows a day in the life of your pet goldfish. List places where you could film and people who could be in the documentary or operate the camera.
2. **Find out what equipment is available.** Your school may have video cameras. Ask your school's computer expert if video-editing software is available. If not, you will need to shoot the scenes of your documentary in order.
3. **Create a storyboard.** Sketch what you want viewers to see alongside notes about what you want them to hear. For an example of a storyboard, see page 109.
4. **Write a script.** Your script can include dialogue, narration, or both. **Dialogue** means words that someone says on camera. **Narration** means words that someone says off-camera. You can hear the person, but you can't see him or her.

Producing the Documentary

1. **Rehearse before you shoot.** Do the narration and dialogue make sense? Are the scenes in the right order?
2. **Roll camera and then review.** Try to include a mixture of **close-ups** (head and shoulders only) and **medium shots** (from head to waist). After watching what you have filmed, you may decide to reshoot some parts.
3. **Screen your masterpiece.** Ask viewers which parts worked well and which could be improved in your next documentary.

Assessment
Practice

DIRECTIONS *Read this selection and answer the questions that follow.*

*In 1962, the astronaut John Glenn became the first American to orbit the earth. In
1998, at age 77, he again joined the crew of a space shuttle, this time as the oldest
person ever to travel in space.*

from John Glenn: A Memoir

John Glenn with Nick Taylor

I especially enjoyed being with my father, whom most people called
Herschel, while I grew up being called Bud. He could turn very serious
at times, . . . but most of the time he was lighthearted. He joked a lot
and made me laugh. Part of the fun of being with him was that he was
curious. He always wanted to learn about new things, and he would
go out of his way to investigate them. Although the Glenn Plumbing
Company grew into a successful business of which he was very proud,
I think he recognized the limitations of his education. He wanted to give
me the curiosity and sense of unbounded possibility that could come
10 from learning.

The summer I turned eight, Dad took me along to Cambridge one day
when he went to check on a plumbing job. It was the time of year when
wildflowers bloomed on the roadsides and in the farm fields where cattle
grazed. He checked on the job, and as we drove past a grass-field airport
outside of town, he spotted a plane there and we stopped.

We got out of the car to look. A man had an old open-cockpit
biplane—it was a WACO, but I didn't know that then—and he was
taking people up. He was a Steve Canyon–type pilot, a helmet-and-
goggles sort of guy right out of the comics. We were leaning against the
20 car and watching him, and my dad said, "You want to go up, Bud?"

I almost died. Flying was a great adventure. Everybody knew about
Charles Lindbergh's transatlantic flight two years before. When Lindy
came home, the papers had chronicled his every move. Dad had read
that he would be flying by Cambridge and New Concord on his way to
Columbus, and soon after that we were on a farm outside of town when
a silver plane flying west passed high overhead. I'd always imagined it

was him. I probably was scared at the idea of going up, but there wasn't any doubt about it—I wanted to do it. I thought it would be the greatest thing that ever happened. "You mean it?" I said.

30   "I sure do," Dad replied. "In fact, if you don't want to do it, I'm going anyway. So you better come unless you want to sit down here and watch."

    We walked over to the plane. It was bigger than I had thought, with two cockpits, one in front of the other. Dad handed the guy some money. He climbed into the backseat, and the pilot helped me up after him. Dad was big, but the seat was wide enough for the two of us, and one strap fit across us both. I could barely see out. The pilot got in front and revved the engine. We bounced down that grass strip and then we were in the air. The plane banked, and I could look straight down. We flew around Cambridge a couple of times. Dad kept trying to point things out to
40 me, but I couldn't catch his words over the sound of the engine and the rushing air. We turned back and landed.

    When I got out of the plane I was elated. I couldn't get the view from the air out of my mind, and the feeling of being suspended without falling. We had gone so high, and everything on the ground looked so small, like the buildings and trees in a toy train set you'd see in a store window.

    As we drove home, Dad asked me if I'd liked the flight. I told him that I had. He said he had, too. He said he'd wanted to see what flying was like ever since he'd been in France in World War I and had seen biplanes
50 dogfighting over the lines. I realized later that it wasn't simply fun for him. Flying was progressive, just the kind of thing he would have wanted to experience so he could speak with authority about what it felt like and, just as likely, what it meant. His eagerness to experiment was one of the most important lessons of my youth.

Comprehension

DIRECTIONS *Answer these questions about the excerpt from* John Glenn: A Memoir.

1. Which sentence tells you that the selection is an autobiography?

   A "Flying was a great adventure." (line 21)

   B "Everybody knew about Charles Lindbergh's transatlantic flight two years before." (lines 21–22)

   C "The pilot got in front and revved the engine." (lines 36–37)

   D "I realized later that it wasn't simply fun for him." (line 50)

2. Which detail in this excerpt might not have been included in a biography?

   A John Glenn's childhood nickname

   B the name of Herschel Glenn's business

   C information about Charles Lindbergh

   D the description of how John Glenn felt after his first plane ride

3. Herschel Glenn's reply in lines 30–31 supports the idea that he

   A had a spirit of adventure

   B was a serious person

   C knew a lot about flying

   D owned a successful business

4. Which phrases show the order of events?

   A at times; where cattle grazed; around Cambridge

   B the summer I turned eight; two years before; when I got out of the plane

   C out of his way; past a grass-field airport; one in front of the other

   D his every move; my youth; got in front

5. Which quotation expresses the main idea of the excerpt?

   A "I especially enjoyed being with my father, whom most people called Herschel, while I grew up being called Bud." (lines 1–2)

   B "I couldn't get the view from the air out of my mind, and the feeling of being suspended without falling." (lines 42–44)

   C "As we drove home, Dad asked me if I'd liked the flight. I told him that I had." (lines 47–48)

   D "His eagerness to experiment was one of the most important lessons of my youth." (lines 53–54)

6. Which statement tells you this excerpt is from an autobiography rather than a biography?

   A It is written from a first-person point of view.

   B It includes quotations from people who knew John Glenn.

   C It explains how events shaped John Glenn's life.

   D It talks about other people who were alive at the time.

7. The description of the pilot in lines 18–19 reminds the reader that

   A children often confuse fantasy and reality

   B early pilots were not concerned about safety

   C John Glenn liked to read when he was young

   D this memory is recalled from a child's point of view

8. Which sentence reveals John Glenn's personal feelings?

A "He could turn very serious at times, . . . but most of the time he was lighthearted." (lines 2–3)

B "He always wanted to learn about new things, and he would go out of his way to investigate them." (lines 5–6)

C "It was the time of year when wildflowers bloomed on the roadsides and in the farm fields where cattle grazed." (lines 12–14)

D "I probably was scared at the idea of going up, but there wasn't any doubt about it—I wanted to do it." (lines 27–28)

9. In this selection, the statement "When Lindy came home, the papers had chronicled his every move" (lines 22–23) supports the idea that

A airplanes made transatlantic travel possible

B people were eager to learn about flying

C news coverage in the past was better than it is today

D World War I dogfighters made flying seem easy

10. Which event would come first in a timeline of John Glenn's life?

A John Glenn takes his first plane ride.

B Herschel Glenn stops his car near a biplane outside of town.

C John Glenn and his father drive to Cambridge.

D Charles Lindbergh flies across the Atlantic Ocean.

11. John Glenn's father first wondered what flying was like when he saw

A biplanes dogfighting during World War I

B an airplane on a grass-field airport near town

C a newspaper article about Charles Lindbergh

D a silver plane flying overhead

12. If this excerpt were taken from a biography instead of an autobiography, it would have to be a true account of John Glenn's life

A told from the first-person point of view

B written by someone else

C based on details from Glenn's memories

D published during Glenn's lifetime

Written Response

SHORT RESPONSE *Write two or three sentences to answer this question.*

13. Find two details in the excerpt to support the idea that Glenn's father was curious about flying.

EXTENDED RESPONSE *Write a short paragraph to answer this question.*

14. Rewrite lines 11–15 as if they were from a biography instead of an autobiography.

GO ON ➡

Vocabulary

DIRECTIONS *Use context clues and your knowledge of word origins to answer the following questions.*

1. The word *investigate* comes from the Latin word *vestigare,* which means "to track." What is the meaning of *investigate* as it is used in line 6?

   A to grab hold of
   B to give money to
   C to examine in detail
   D to turn upside down

2. The word *limitations* comes from the Latin word *limes,* which means "border." What is the meaning of *limitations* as it is used in line 8?

   A details
   B outlines
   C requirements
   D shortcomings

3. The prefix *un-* means "not," and the Old English word *bindan* means "to bind or hold captive." What is the meaning of *unbounded* as it is used in line 9?

   A not realistic
   B not restricted
   C not known
   D not complicated

4. The Latin prefix *bi-* means "two." A *biplane* (line 17) has

   A extra-wide seats
   B large propellers
   C a powerful engine
   D a double pair of wings

5. The Latin prefix *trans-* means "across." A *transatlantic* flight (line 22) travels

   A from one side of the Atlantic Ocean to the other
   B just over the horizon of the Atlantic Ocean
   C along the natural shoreline of the Atlantic Ocean
   D to the middle of the Atlantic Ocean and back again

6. The word *chronicle* comes from *khronos,* the Greek word for "time." What is the meaning of *chronicled* as it is used in line 23?

   A refused to report on
   B made a historical record of
   C questioned the reasons for
   D attached great importance to

7. The word *suspended* comes from the Latin word *pendere,* which means "to hang." What is the meaning of *suspended* as it is used in line 43?

   A attached to the ground with bolts
   B removed from a position or team
   C interrupted for a period of time
   D held in the air without support

8. The Latin prefix *pro-* means "forward." What is the meaning of the word *progressive* as it is used in line 51?

   A modern
   B changeable
   C popular
   D risky

Writing & Grammar

DIRECTIONS *Read this passage and answer the questions that follow.*

(1) John herschel glenn was born in 1921. (2) His parents raised him and his sister jean in a small town in ohio. (3) Throughout his lifetime, Glenn has held several positions Marine pilot, astronaut, businessman, and politician. (4) In february 1962, while flying aboard the spacecraft friendship 7, he became the first american to orbit the earth. (5) He was elected and re-elected to the U.S. Senate in the following years 1974, 1980, 1986, and 1992. (6) In Congress he devoted much of his time to three causes creating a research station in space, funding scientific education, and limiting the development of nuclear weapons. (7) In 1998, at age 77, mr. Glenn returned to space aboard the shuttle discovery.

1. Choose the correct way to capitalize the name in sentence 1.
   - **A** john Herschel Glenn
   - **B** John Herschel Glenn
   - **C** John herschel Glenn
   - **D** john herschel Glenn

2. Which nouns should be capitalized in sentence 2?
   - **A** parents, sister
   - **B** parents, ohio
   - **C** sister, jean
   - **D** jean, ohio

3. In sentence 3, a colon should be placed after which word?
   - **A** has
   - **B** Throughout
   - **C** held
   - **D** positions

4. Which nouns should be capitalized in sentence 4?
   - **A** february, spacecraft
   - **B** february, friendship, american
   - **C** spacecraft, friendship, american
   - **D** february, american

5. In sentence 5, a colon should be placed after which word?
   - **A** years
   - **B** in
   - **C** re-elected
   - **D** to

6. In sentence 6, a colon should be placed after which word?
   - **A** time
   - **B** devoted
   - **C** causes
   - **D** to

7. Which nouns should be capitalized in sentence 7?
   - **A** mr., shuttle
   - **B** space, shuttle
   - **C** mr., discovery
   - **D** space, discovery

STOP

More Great Reads

Ideas for Independent Reading

Which questions from Unit 7 made an impression on you? Continue exploring with these books.

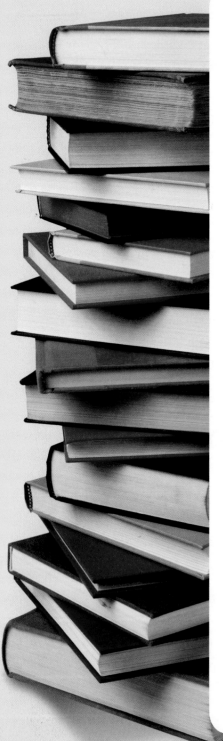

Why attempt the impossible?

The Man Who Went to the Far Side of the Moon
by Bea Uusma Schyffert

While Neil Armstrong and Buzz Aldrin walked on the moon, Michael Collins was alone in the team's spacecraft, separated from everyone he knew by the vast darkness of space.

Shipwreck at the Bottom of the World
by Jennifer Armstrong

Sir Ernest Shackleton sails from England to Antarctica in 1914. Almost two years later, his crew is stranded hundreds of miles from any port. Will Shackleton be able to save them all?

With Courage and Cloth
by Ann Bausum

Before 1920, most Americans thought the idea of a woman voting was ridiculous. It had taken over 70 years for activists like Alice Paul to convince the president and other lawmakers to give women the right to vote.

How do you unlock a mystery?

At Her Majesty's Request
by Walter Dean Myers

Sarah was born an African princess. After her village is destroyed, a British commander saves Sarah. He brings her to England as a gift for the queen. What will life be like for the rescued orphan?

Hana's Suitcase
by Karen Levine

When children visiting a Holocaust museum in Tokyo ask questions about a suitcase, Fumiko decides to find some answers. Two years later, she knows the suitcase belonged to a little girl—and she has found the girl's brother.

The Longitude Prize
by Joan Dash

In the 1700s, sailors die every year because they lose their way at sea. John Harrison, a carpenter and clockmaker, knows he can save them with his idea. He just has to get the Royal Society to believe that it will work.

How would you like to be remembered?

Don't Hold Me Back
by Winfred Rembert

He didn't lead marches, but Winfred Rembert was part of the Civil Rights Movement. He and his parents were farm workers and often treated like slaves. But Rembert's paintings record stories of courage and hope.

Girls Think of Everything
by Catherine Thimmesh

Mary Anderson invented the windshield wiper after a terrifying streetcar ride. Grace Hopper created the first computer language that used English. Female inventors are responsible for many of the things we use every day.

The Lost Garden
by Laurence Yep

As a boy in 1950s San Francisco, Laurence Yep didn't fit in. He felt American, but the other kids said he wasn't. He hated going to Chinatown because he couldn't speak Chinese. Writing helped him find his place.

Know the Facts

INFORMATION, ARGUMENT, AND PERSUASION

- In Nonfiction
- In Media

Can INFORMATION *be trusted?*

Newspapers, the Internet, television commercials—all of these sources and more are constantly bombarding you with **information.** But not all the information you receive is as reliable as a fingerprint or as trustworthy as an X-ray. How do you know when to trust what you are reading and hearing?

ACTIVITY Get together with a small group. Take turns naming sources that you use to get information. Then discuss whether you can trust each source that is mentioned. Consider the following questions:

• Who created the source? Is that person or group reliable?

• How current is the information?

• Why is the information being provided?

Preview Unit Goals

READING	• Identify main ideas and supporting details • Summarize main ideas • Analyze an argument, including claim, support, and counterargument • Identify and analyze persuasive techniques • Identify and analyze text features • Use text features to locate information • Use and evaluate graphic aids • Evaluate and compare information
WRITING AND GRAMMAR	• Use capitalization, quotation marks, and italics to punctuate titles correctly • Write a persuasive essay
SPEAKING, LISTENING, AND VIEWING	• Identify and analyze persuasive techniques in advertising • Compare and contrast presentation of news reports • Deliver a persuasive speech
VOCABULARY	• Use base words and affixes to help figure out word meaning • Use context clues to help figure out word meaning
ACADEMIC VOCABULARY	• argument • text features • persuasive techniques • summarize

Reading for Information

What were the first Olympic Games like? Which bus will take you where you need to go? People are always in search of information to satisfy their curiosity, help them make a decision, or learn something new. With all the newspapers, magazines, and Web sites out there, how do you even begin to find answers? In this workshop, you'll learn how to read and understand a world of information.

Part 1: What's the Big Picture?

Have you ever felt overwhelmed by a magazine article or a Web site that was packed with information? To guide readers through informational articles and Web pages, writers use **text features,** or special design elements. Text features include subheadings, captions, boldfaced words, and sidebars. These elements help readers to see useful information at a glance.

Consider the following article. Previewing its text features can help you to understand the "big picture" before you read every word.

1 The **title** describes the topic of the article.

2 **Subheadings** identify the foods that the article focuses on.

3 A **caption** describes what is shown in the photograph.

4 A **sidebar** provides additional information.

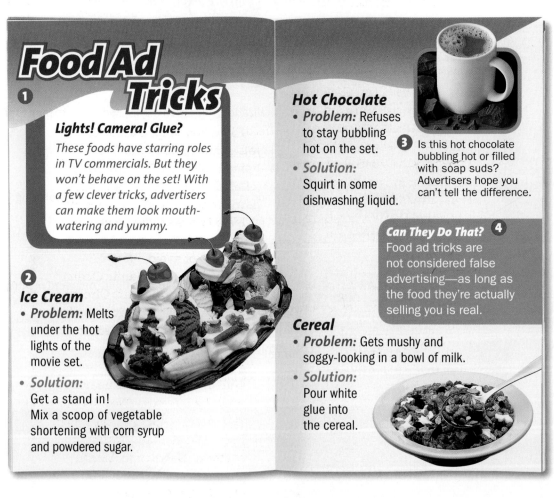

Food Ad Tricks

1

Lights! Camera! Glue?

These foods have starring roles in TV commercials. But they won't behave on the set! With a few clever tricks, advertisers can make them look mouth-watering and yummy.

2
Ice Cream
- **Problem:** Melts under the hot lights of the movie set.
- **Solution:** Get a stand in! Mix a scoop of vegetable shortening with corn syrup and powdered sugar.

Hot Chocolate
- **Problem:** Refuses to stay bubbling hot on the set.
- **Solution:** Squirt in some dishwashing liquid.

3 Is this hot chocolate bubbling hot or filled with soap suds? Advertisers hope you can't tell the difference.

Can They Do That? **4**
Food ad tricks are not considered false advertising—as long as the food they're actually selling you is real.

Cereal
- **Problem:** Gets mushy and soggy-looking in a bowl of milk.
- **Solution:** Pour white glue into the cereal.

Preview the title, subheadings, caption, and sidebar in this magazine article. What kind of information do you think the article will provide? Now read the article closely and answer the questions.

Swimmers *Beware:*
Jellyfish Are Everywhere!

Magazine article by **Susan Jaques**

What Are Jellyfish?

Jellyfish are not fish at all. They are invertebrates, relatives of corals and sea anemones 5 (uh-NEH-muh-neez). A jelly has no head, brain, heart, eyes, or ears. It has no bones, either. . . .

To capture prey for food, jellies have a net of tentacles 10 that contain poisonous, stinging cells. When the tentacles brush against prey (or, say, a person's leg), thousands of tiny stinging cells explode, launching barbed 15 stingers and poison into the victim.

Feared by many beachgoers, bell-shaped **sea nettles** are known for their painful stings.

Where Danger Lurks

All jellies sting, but not all jellies have poison that hurts 20 humans. Of the 2,000 species of jellyfish, only about 70 seriously harm or occasionally kill people.

Listed here are the more dangerous jellies and where you 25 can find—or avoid—them.

- *Lion's mane*—Atlantic Ocean from above the Arctic Circle to Florida; Gulf of Mexico; Pacific Ocean from Alaska to southern California
- 30 *Portuguese man-of-war*— Gulf of Mexico; Caribbean Sea near the Bahamas; West Indies
- *Sea nettle*—Chesapeake Bay; 35 Pacific Ocean from Alaska to southern California; Atlantic Ocean from Massachusetts to Florida; Gulf of Mexico

DON'T GET STUNG

1. Take note of jellyfish warning signs posted on the beach.

2. Be careful around jellies washed up on the sand. Some still sting if their tentacles are wet.

3. If you are stung, wash the wound with vinegar or rubbing alcohol.

Close Read

1. Which part of this article focuses on the world's most dangerous jellyfish and where they prowl? Identify the text feature that helped you to locate this information.

2. Read the boxed caption. What do you learn about the kind of jellyfish shown in the photograph?

3. Identify another text feature and explain how it helped you to quickly find information.

Part 2: Reading to Learn

After you've gotten the big picture, you're ready to jump into a text and read it more closely. Use these strategies to make sure you're picking up on the most important information.

FIND THE MAIN IDEAS

Main ideas are the most important ideas about a topic that a writer wants to convey to readers. A writer will include **supporting details,** such as statistics and examples, to further explain each main idea. Often, the main idea of a paragraph or a section is directly stated in a **topic sentence** at the beginning or end of that paragraph or section. Sometimes, however, the main idea is **implied,** or not directly stated. In such a case, you have to ask yourself: What do all the supporting details add up to?

Examine this paragraph from the article about jellyfish. Notice that the main idea is directly stated.

> All jellies sting, but not all jellies have poison that hurts humans. Of the 2,000 species of jellyfish, only about 70 seriously harm or occasionally kill people.

This **topic sentence** states the main idea of the paragraph: that not all jellyfish stings are harmful to humans.

This fact **supports** the main idea. It shows that only a relatively few kinds of jellyfish are harmful.

TAKE NOTES

Taking notes as you read can help you track the main ideas in a text and remember them after you've finished reading. Your notes can take any number of forms, such as an **outline,** a **bulleted list,** or a **graphic organizer.** Try to include only the most important ideas, along with the details that support those ideas. Remember to restate the ideas in your own words.

Bulleted List
1. *All jellyfish sting.*
• *Some have deadly stings.*
• *They capture food with tentacles that release poison.*
• *Only 70 kinds of jellyfish can harm or kill humans.*
2. *People can avoid being stung.*
• *Look for signs on the beach.*
• *Don't step on jellies on the sand.*

Graphic Organizer

- lion's mane
- Portuguese man-of-war
- Most Dangerous Jellyfish
- sea nettle

Part 3: Analyze the Text

Read this Web article, using what you've learned in this workshop to help you understand the information. The **Close Read** questions will help you take notes on the most important ideas.

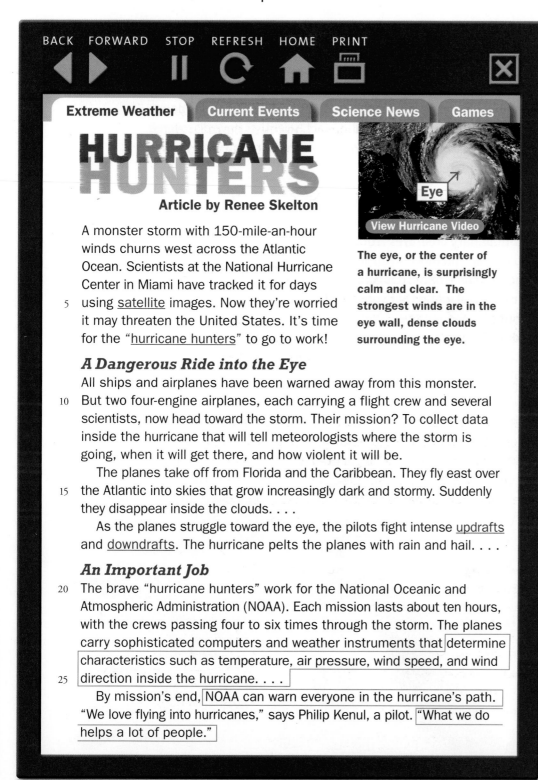

BACK   FORWARD   STOP   REFRESH   HOME   PRINT

Extreme Weather   Current Events   Science News   Games

HURRICANE HUNTERS
Article by Renee Skelton

Eye

View Hurricane Video

The eye, or the center of a hurricane, is surprisingly calm and clear. The strongest winds are in the eye wall, dense clouds surrounding the eye.

A monster storm with 150-mile-an-hour winds churns west across the Atlantic Ocean. Scientists at the National Hurricane Center in Miami have tracked it for days
5   using <u>satellite</u> images. Now they're worried it may threaten the United States. It's time for the "<u>hurricane hunters</u>" to go to work!

A Dangerous Ride into the Eye

All ships and airplanes have been warned away from this monster.
10   But two four-engine airplanes, each carrying a flight crew and several scientists, now head toward the storm. Their mission? To collect data inside the hurricane that will tell meteorologists where the storm is going, when it will get there, and how violent it will be.

The planes take off from Florida and the Caribbean. They fly east over
15   the Atlantic into skies that grow increasingly dark and stormy. Suddenly they disappear inside the clouds. . . .

As the planes struggle toward the eye, the pilots fight intense <u>updrafts</u> and <u>downdrafts</u>. The hurricane pelts the planes with rain and hail. . . .

An Important Job

20   The brave "hurricane hunters" work for the National Oceanic and Atmospheric Administration (NOAA). Each mission lasts about ten hours, with the crews passing four to six times through the storm. The planes carry sophisticated computers and weather instruments that determine characteristics such as temperature, air pressure, wind speed, and wind
25   direction inside the hurricane. . . .

By mission's end, NOAA can warn everyone in the hurricane's path. "We love flying into hurricanes," says Philip Kenul, a pilot. "What we do helps a lot of people."

Caption

Close Read

1. Where is the eye of a hurricane located? Identify the text feature that helped you to answer this question.

2. The main idea of the first section (lines 8–18) is shown here. In your notebook, copy the main idea and write three details that support it.

    1. Hurricane hunters have a dangerous job.
    •
    •
    •

3. Reread lines 19–28, noting the subheading and the boxed details. What is the main idea of this section? Complete your notes by writing the main idea and supporting details.

    2. Main idea: _____
    •
    •
    •

SuperCroc

Magazine Article by Peter Winkler

Are MONSTERS *real?*

KEY IDEA Monsters have always existed in the world of the imagination. Yet fierce, deadly creatures that could be considered **monsters** exist in reality as well. In fact, scientists have discovered a prehistoric creature so terrifying that even dinosaurs may have feared it.

CHART IT Make a chart that shows your favorite monsters. In one column, list imaginary creatures from stories you've read and movies you've seen. In the other, list some of the dangerous creatures from the real world that you have learned about from books, television programs, and nature magazines. Share your chart with your classmates. Which list is more frightening?

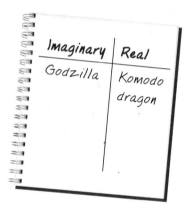

Imaginary	Real
Godzilla	Komodo dragon

● ELEMENTS OF NONFICTION: TEXT FEATURES

Text features are design elements that help to organize information visually. They highlight key ideas and provide additional information. Some common text features are

- **subheadings,** or section titles, which identify the main idea or topic of the information that follows
- **graphic aids,** such as maps, photographs, or graphs
- **captions,** which provide information about a graphic aid

As you read "SuperCroc," identify the text features it contains, and notice the information they provide.

● READING STRATEGY: SUMMARIZE

When you **summarize,** you use your own words to retell the main ideas of a spoken or written work. A summary is generally no more than one-third the length of the original work.

As you read "SuperCroc," use a chart like the one shown to record key information from each section of the article. You will use this information later when you write your summary.

Section	Key Information
Introduction	scientists studying dinosaur fossils in Niger
What Makes This Croc So Super?	

▲ VOCABULARY IN CONTEXT

Peter Winkler uses the boldfaced words to help tell about the discovery of a real-life monster from the past. To see how many you know, substitute a different word or phrase for each one.

1. Paul Sereno is a dinosaur **expert.**
2. Dinosaurs have been **extinct** for millions of years.
3. His team found more than just one **fossil.**
4. This **species** of crocodile was previously unknown.
5. The **predator** could have eaten anything it wanted.

Author Online

Adventure School
Peter Winkler is a freelance writer from Long Island, New York. He once realized he was in over his head—literally—when he was unable to climb back into an overturned kayak in the cold waters

**Peter Winkler
born 1963**

of the Pacific Ocean. He ended up having to swim to shore. Winkler's assignment had been to cover the Presidio Adventure Racing Academy. He realized later that although the experience was frightening, "somehow I'd still learned the key lesson of adventure school: Stretch yourself, and life will take shapes you never imagined."

National Geographic Writer Peter Winkler has been writing for the National Geographic Society since 1987. His writings include Web features, science articles for young people, television scripts, educational materials, and three books. He has also written about movies for CineFan, an online movie database.

 MORE ABOUT THE AUTHOR
For more on Peter Winkler, visit the **Literature Center** at **ClassZone.com.**

SUPERCROC

PETER WINKLER

O ut of Africa comes a giant reptile that lived with dinosaurs—and ate them.

"We're stuck again!" Scientist Paul Sereno and his team said those words many times as they drove into a rugged part of Africa. Desert sand kept stopping their vehicles.

It took 10 hours to go just 87 miles.

That long crawl ended at Gadoufaoua,[1] a dry region in the country of Niger.[2] To most eyes, the place looked empty.
10 There was sand. There was wind. There was nothing else. Or so it seemed.

But Sereno saw much more. He saw a chance to find dinosaurs. Sereno, a paleontologist, knew that the region contains countless **fossils** from ancient dinosaurs. Gadoufaoua is one of

The country of Niger is in West Africa. **A**

fossil (fŏs′əl) *n.* the remains of a living thing, preserved in soil or rock

A TEXT FEATURES
What information does this map provide about Gadoufaoua?

---

1. **Gadoufaoua** (gə-dōō′fä′wŏh).
2. **Niger** (nī′jər).

Africa's richest sources of dino fossils.

Sereno found some fossils there in 1997. He came back in 2000 to seek more. The team spent four months in the desert. Crew members woke at 6:00 each morning, then explored the sand dunes for about 12 hours. They worked even when the temperature hit 125°F.

And they found fossils. By the end of the expedition, Sereno and his team had collected 20 tons of bones. Most of the fossils came from dinosaurs, including types never seen before. Others came from turtles, fish, and crocodiles.

One of those crocodiles was *Sarcosuchus imperator,*[3] a name that means "flesh crocodile emperor." Sereno's team nicknamed it "SuperCroc." **B**

Using SuperCroc's jaw bone and their own bodies, Sereno (fourth from front) and his team demonstrate SuperCroc's estimated length.

What Makes This Croc So Super? **C**

In a word, size. The skull alone was six feet long. Sereno says it's "about the biggest I've ever seen."

Naturally, Sereno wondered how big SuperCroc was overall. The team found only part of its skeleton, so Sereno had to make an estimate. To do that, he looked at crocodiles that live today. He and other **experts** compared the animals' skull and body sizes.

Based on his research, Sereno concluded that an adult SuperCroc could grow to be 40 feet long and probably weighed as much as 10 tons. That's heavier than an African elephant.

Those measurements make SuperCroc one of the largest crocodiles ever to walk Earth. Today's biggest crocs grow to about 20 feet. **D**

---

3. *Sarcosuchus imperator* (sär′kō-sōo′kĭs ĭm-pîr′ā-tôr).

B SUMMARIZE
What have you learned about SuperCroc so far? Note this information in your chart.

C TEXT FEATURES
Preview the article's **subheadings.** What do you think the article will tell you about SuperCroc?

expert (ĕk′spûrt′) *n.* one who is skilled in or knowledgeable about a particular thing

D SUMMARIZE
What have you learned from this section of the article? Record this information in your chart.

extinct (ĭk-stĭngkt') *adj.*
no longer existing

predator (prĕd'ə-tər) *n.*
an animal that feeds
on other animals

species (spē'shēz) *n.*
a variety or type
of something

E SUMMARIZE
What have you learned
about SuperCroc's
appearance? Add this
information to your
chart.

A Different-Looking Beast

SuperCroc's long head is wider in front
than in the middle. That shape is unique.
No other croc—living or **extinct**—has
a snout quite like it.

At the front of SuperCroc's head is a big
60 hole. That's where the nose would be. That
empty space may have given the ancient
predator a keen sense of smell. Or perhaps
it helped SuperCroc make noise to
communicate with other members of its **species.**

Illustration of SuperCroc

SuperCroc wore serious armor. Huge plates of bone, called scutes,
covered the animal's back. Hundreds of them lay just below the
skin. A single scute from the back could be a foot long! **E**

When Did SuperCroc Live?

Estimating a fossil's age is a challenge. Sereno and his team looked
70 carefully at the group of fossils they had found. They compared the
fossils to others whose ages the scientists did know. Based on those
comparisons, Sereno
believes SuperCroc
lived about 110 million
years ago.

Gadoufaoua looked
a bit different in those
days. What is now a
desert was a land of
80 winding rivers. Plenty
of trees grew along the
banks. Huge fish swam
the rivers, while various
dinosaurs lived in the
forests.

Five or more
crocodile species lurked
in the rivers. SuperCroc,
Sereno says, was "the
90 monster of them all." **F**

Paul Sereno brushes sand from "sabercroc,"
another of several species of crocodile fossils
found at Gadoufaoua.

F SUMMARIZE
Reread lines 68–90.
Note what you learned
in this section in your
chart.

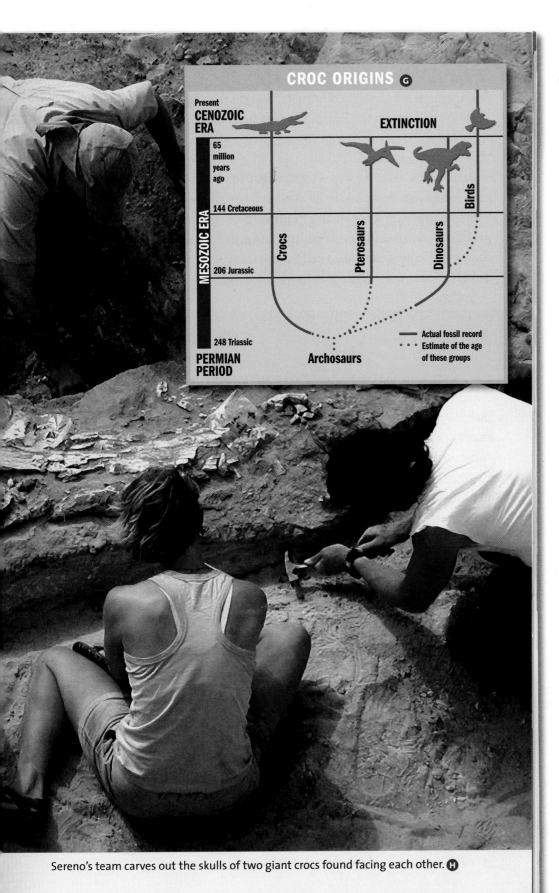

CROC ORIGINS G

Present
CENOZOIC ERA

EXTINCTION

MESOZOIC ERA

65 million years ago

144 Cretaceous

206 Jurassic

248 Triassic

PERMIAN PERIOD

Crocs

Pterosaurs

Dinosaurs

Birds

Archosaurs

—— Actual fossil record
• • • Estimate of the age of these groups

Sereno's team carves out the skulls of two giant crocs found facing each other. H

G **TEXT FEATURES**
What information does this **graph** provide about crocodiles?

H **TEXT FEATURES**
What information do this **photograph** and its **caption** add to the article?

SUPERCROC **851**

What Did SuperCroc Eat?

"Anything it wanted," Sereno says. SuperCroc's narrow jaws held about 130 teeth. The teeth were short but incredibly strong. SuperCroc's mouth was "designed for grabbing prey[4]—fish, turtles, and dinosaurs that strayed too close."

SuperCroc likely spent most of its life in the river. Water hid the creature's huge body. Only its eyes and nostrils poked above the surface.

After spotting a meal, the giant hunter moved quietly toward the animal. Then—*wham!* That huge mouth locked onto its prey.
100   SuperCroc dragged the stunned creature into the water. There the animal drowned. Then it became food. **I**

I SUMMARIZE
Reread lines 91–101. What does this section tell you about SuperCroc?

A crowd gathers around the first life-sized model of SuperCroc at the Australian Museum in Sydney, Australia. **J**

J TEXT FEATURES
What does the **caption** help you understand about the photograph?

K SUMMARIZE
Why didn't SuperCroc survive? Add this information to your chart.

What Happened to SuperCroc?

The giant beast probably lived only a few million years. That raises a huge question: Why didn't SuperCroc survive?

Sereno suspects that SuperCrocs were fairly rare. After all, a monster that big needs plenty of room in which to live. Disease or disaster could have wiped out the species pretty quickly. But no one knows for sure what killed SuperCroc. That's a mystery for future scientists. **K**

---

4. **prey:** animals that become the food of another animal.

Comprehension

1. **Recall** Why are Paul Sereno and his team interested in Gadoufaoua?

2. **Recall** What length does Sereno estimate SuperCroc could have grown to be?

3. **Clarify** What did Sereno and his team find in Gadoufaoua other than crocodile fossils?

Critical Analysis

4. **Summarize** Look at the chart you filled in while reading "SuperCroc." Use the information to write a brief summary of the article.

5. **Compare Information** Skim through "SuperCroc" to find information about how SuperCroc compares to crocodiles of today. Create a Venn diagram like the one shown to record the information you find.

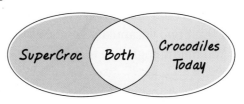

6. **Examine Text Features** Review the article's photographs and captions. What kind of information can photographs and captions provide that the regular text usually cannot?

7. **Draw Conclusions** Reread the section subtitled "When Did SuperCroc Live?" on page 850. Judging by the way Sereno and his team estimated the age of SuperCroc's fossils, what conclusions can you draw about how scientists determine the age of ancient creatures?

Extension and Challenge

8. **Big Question Activity** With a small group of classmates, examine the **monster** charts you created before reading "SuperCroc." Recall the list of creatures you chose as the most frightening. Has reading "SuperCroc" changed the way you feel? Take turns discussing whether you would still make the same choice, and explain your reasons why.

9. **Inquiry and Research** Paleontologists like Paul Sereno don't just dig for fossils in the desert. Conduct some research to discover how a person becomes a paleontologist. Find out what a paleontologist might have to do in order to prepare for an expedition, and what happens after the expedition is finished. Present your findings to the class.

 RESEARCH LINKS
For more on paleontology, visit the **Research Center** at **ClassZone.com.**

Vocabulary in Context

VOCABULARY PRACTICE

Choose the letter of the word that is not related in meaning to the other words.

1. (a) skeleton, (b) fossil, (c) bone, (d) alive
2. (a) expert, (b) inexperienced, (c) authority, (d) knowledgeable
3. (a) kind, (b) species, (c) type, (d) desert
4. (a) extinct, (b) living, (c) active, (d) breathing
5. (a) slayer, (b) admirer, (c) predator, (d) killer

VOCABULARY IN WRITING

Imagine that you are part of Paul Sereno's team. What would you find most exciting? Using at least two vocabulary words, write a paragraph describing your experience. You might begin like this.

> **EXAMPLE SENTENCE**
>
> *Finding a **fossil** in the middle of the desert is extremely exciting!*

VOCABULARY STRATEGY: WORD ORIGINS

Many common words in the English language have interesting histories. For example, the vocabulary word *fossil* comes from the Latin word *fossilis*, which means "dug up." It makes sense, then, that a fossil is something that is uncovered, or dug up, from rock or earth.

Information about a word's origin can be found in most dictionaries. Understanding the **etymology,** or history of a word, can help you connect the word's meaning to something you already know. An example of an etymology is shown here:

argue (är′gyo͞o) *v.* to disagree or quarrel [from Latin *argutare,* to babble, chatter]

PRACTICE Look up the etymology of each word in a dictionary. Write the word's origin, and explain how knowing the word's history can help you remember its meaning.

1. nominate
2. agriculture
3. regime
4. segregate
5. panorama
6. coif

VOCABULARY PRACTICE
For more practice, go to the **Vocabulary Center** at **ClassZone.com.**

Reading-Writing Connection

Demonstrate your understanding of "SuperCroc" by responding to these prompts. Then complete the **Grammar and Writing** exercise.

A. Short Response: Write a Description
Imagine that you could go back in time and see SuperCroc with your own eyes. Write a **one-paragraph description** of the prehistoric **monster** and its surroundings.

A strong description will . . .
- provide information about SuperCroc's environment
- include details about the creature's appearance

B. Extended Response: Evaluate an Article
Decide whether "SuperCroc" is a well-written article. Does the author present his information clearly and in a style that holds your interest? Write a **two- or three-paragraph evaluation** of the article.

A thorough evaluation will . . .
- offer a clear statement of your opinion
- provide specific examples from the article

GRAMMAR AND WRITING

CAPITALIZE CORRECTLY The **titles** of magazine articles, books, poems, and short stories must all be **capitalized** correctly. When writing a title, capitalize the first and last words, any important words, and all verbs. Do not capitalize conjunctions, articles, or prepositions of fewer than five letters.

Original: Finding Fossils In The Desert Dunes

Revised: Finding Fossils in the Desert Dunes

PRACTICE Rewrite each title by correcting any capitalization errors.

1. Monsters of The Past, The Present, and The Future
2. The day Godzilla met the gila monster
3. Silent Predator Of The African Waters
4. the scientist and the giant fossil

*For more help with capitalizing titles, see page R51 in the **Grammar Handbook**.*

Bird Brains

Online Article by Gareth Huw Davies

How SMART are animals?

KEY IDEA Who doesn't love watching animals? Whether they are performing tricks on command or displaying their behavior in the wild, animals continually demonstrate their unique **intelligence.** In the article you are about to read, you'll learn about birds who do surprisingly clever things, including playing tricks on humans.

QUICKWRITE Write an anecdote, or brief story, about a time you saw—or heard about—an animal doing something that showed its cleverness. Share the story with your classmates.

● ELEMENTS OF NONFICTION: MAIN IDEA AND DETAILS

In a work of nonfiction, the **main idea** is the most important idea that the work communicates about a topic. Main ideas can be stated directly or simply implied, or suggested. To determine the main idea, start by looking at the title and the subheadings.

Supporting details give more information about the main idea. They include reasons, facts, expert opinions, examples, and anecdotes—brief stories with a specific point. As you read, look for details that support the article's main idea.

● READING SKILL: EVALUATE INFORMATION

When you **evaluate information,** you examine and judge the details that are offered in support of a main idea. You might ask the following questions:

- Is the information from **reliable,** or trustworthy, sources?
- Are all the details **relevant,** or connected in some way, to the main idea?
- Are there an **adequate** number of supporting examples?

As you read "Bird Brains," record examples of supporting details in a chart like the one shown. Use check marks to note whether the information seems reliable and relevant.

Supporting Detail	Reliable?	Relevant?
Crows drop nuts in front of cars.		

▲ VOCABULARY IN CONTEXT

The listed words help explain birds' intelligence. Choose the word that best completes each sentence.

WORD LIST	complexity	mimic	variation
	engage	perception	

1. She found a way to ____ the bird in conversation.
2. Our ____ of birds is often not accurate.
3. A parrot isn't a ____ that only repeats what it hears.
4. The ____ of their behavior shows their intelligence.
5. Some birds play a ____ of a trick known to humans.

Author Online

Gareth Huw Davies
born 1948

Nature Writer
Gareth Huw Davies has been a journalist since his first article was published in London's *Sunday Times* newspaper in 1976. Though his writing specialties include wildlife and the environment, he has also written articles about technology, music, medicine, and travel. He is the author of two books and has been nominated for a number of awards for his work.

British Bird Journalist Born in Swansea, Wales, Davies typically writes for various British newspapers and magazines. However, "Bird Brains" is one of a number of articles he wrote for *The Life of Birds,* a series that appeared on the PBS (Public Broadcasting Service) Web site.

MORE ABOUT THE AUTHOR
For more on Gareth Huw Davies, visit the **Literature Center** at **ClassZone.com.**

A carrion crow waits for traffic before placing a walnut on the road, then enjoys a meal.

CLEVER CROWS Ⓐ

At a traffic light crossing on a university campus in Japan, carrion crows and humans line up patiently, waiting for the traffic to halt.

When the lights change, the birds hop in front of the cars and place walnuts, which they picked from the adjoining trees, on the road. After the lights turn green again, the birds fly away and vehicles drive over the nuts, cracking them open. Finally, when it's time to cross again, the crows join the pedestrians and pick up their meal.

If the cars miss the nuts, the birds sometimes hop back and put
10 them somewhere else on the road. Or they sit on electricity wires and drop them in front of vehicles. . . .

The crows in Japan have only been cracking nuts this way since about 1990. They have since been seen doing it in California. Researchers believe they probably noticed cars driving over nuts fallen from a walnut tree overhanging a road. The crows already knew about dropping clams from a height on the seashore to break them open. The birds found this did not work for walnuts because of their soft green outer shell. . . . Ⓑ

Ⓐ **MAIN IDEA AND DETAILS**
Preview the subheadings in this article. What do they suggest about the contents of the article?

Ⓑ **MAIN IDEA AND DETAILS**
Reread lines 1–17. What details in this section support the main idea suggested by the subheading?

TALK TO ME

Another sign of intelligence, thought to be absent in most non-human
20 animals, is the ability to **engage** in complex, meaningful communication.
The work of Professor Irene Pepperberg of the University of Arizona, Tucson,
has now shown the general **perception** of parrots as mindless **mimics**
to be incorrect.

The captive African grey parrot Alex is one of a number of parrots and
macaws now believed to have the intelligence and emotional make-up of
a 3- to 4-year-old child. Under the tutelage[1] of Professor Pepperberg, he
acquired a vocabulary of over 100 words. He could say the words for colors
and shapes and, apparently, use them meaningfully. He has learned the
labels for more than 35 different objects. He also knows when to use "no,"
30 and phrases such as "Come here," "I want X," and "Wanna go Y." . . . **C**

---

1. **tutelage** (tōōt'l-ĭj): instruction; teaching.

Professor Irene Pepperberg interacts with her research subject, Alex.

engage (ĕn-gāj') *v.*
to involve; participate

perception
(pər-sĕp'shən) *n.*
an impression or feeling

mimic (mĭm'ĭk) *n.* one
who imitates the speech
and gestures of others

C EVALUATE
INFORMATION
Do you think the
information in this
section is likely to be
reliable? Explain.

PLAYING GAMES WITH HUMANS

Some birds seem to indulge in "intelligent" play. The kea, a New Zealand parrot, has been filmed ripping (inedible[2]) windshield wipers off cars. Young keas, in a neat **variation** of ringing the doorbell and running away, are known to drop rocks on roofs to make people run outside.

Jack the jackdaw was raised by wildlife film producer John Downer. As soon as Jack was mature, he was released into the wild. However, he couldn't stay away. "One thing he is totally fascinated by is telephones," said Downer. "He knows how to hit the loudspeaker button and preset
40 dial button. Once we came into the office to find him squawking into the telephone to the local travel agent."

Jack also likes to fly down onto the mirror of the production car when he sees somebody going out. "He turns into the wind, gets his head down and surfs on the air current until we reach about 30 mph when he gives up. . . . **D**

ADJUSTING TO OTHERS

Scientists believe it is not physical need that drives creatures to become smarter, but social necessity. The **complexities** of living together require a higher level of intelligence. . . .

The African honeyguide, for example, lures badgers to bees' nests,
50 and feeds on the leftovers. To humans they offer their services as paid employees. They call and fly backward and forward to draw local tribespeoples'[3] attention to the location of honeycombs. They are then rewarded with a share of the takings for their trouble.

Of course, the bird world has its share of "bird brains." There are the birds that build three nests behind three holes under a flower pot because they can't remember which is which. There are also birds that attack their own reflections. . . .

The level of intelligence among birds may vary. But no living bird is truly stupid. Each generation of birds that leaves the protection of
60 its parents to become independent has the inborn genetic information that will help it to survive in the outside world and the skills that it has learned from its parents. It's just that some have more than others. **E**

---

2. **inedible** (ĭn-ĕd'ə-bəl): not suitable or safe for eating.

3. **tribespeople:** the people of a particular tribe, or group.

Side notes

variation (vâr'ē-ā'shən) *n.* a slightly different form of something

D EVALUATE INFORMATION
Reread lines 36–44. Are the details about Jack **relevant** to the article's main idea?

complexity (kəm-plĕk'sĭ-tē) *n.* the quality of being complicated

E MAIN IDEA AND DETAILS
Reread lines 45–62. What is the main idea of this section?

Comprehension

1. **Recall** Why do the crows drop walnuts in front of cars?

2. **Recall** How do African honeyguides help humans?

3. **Clarify** What behaviors do scientists interpret as being signs of intelligence in birds?

Critical Analysis

4. **Identify Main Idea and Details** Reread the section "Playing Games with Humans" on page 860. State the main idea of the section. What details are included to support the main idea?

5. **Analyze Text Features** Look back at the article's photographs and captions. How do these features affect your understanding of the article?

6. **Evaluate Information** Look over the chart you completed while reading "Bird Brains." Did the author provide an **adequate** number of **reliable** and **relevant** details to support his main idea? Using examples from the article, write a paragraph explaining your opinion.

7. **Make Judgments** Which of the birds in the article seems to be the most **intelligent?** Make a chart like the one shown and note the activities or abilities of the various birds in the article. Then, using the information in your chart, explain which bird or type of bird you think is the most intelligent, and why.

Bird	Activity or Ability

Extension and Challenge

8. **SCIENCE CONNECTION** Crows are known for being clever animals. Search the Internet for information about crow habits and behaviors. Take note of any information that supports the idea that crows are especially intelligent. Present your findings to the class.

> **RESEARCH LINKS**
> For more on crows, visit the **Research Center** at **ClassZone.com.**

A clever crow takes a drink.

Vocabulary in Context

VOCABULARY PRACTICE

Show that you understand the vocabulary words by deciding if each statement is true or false.

1. The game of softball is a **variation** of baseball.
2. If you **engage** in conversation, you do not speak.
3. A **complexity** makes something more complicated or difficult.
4. To **mimic** people, you need to study how they move and speak.
5. A **perception** is based only on facts, never on feelings.

complexity

engage

mimic

perception

variation

VOCABULARY IN WRITING

What did this article teach you about birds? Write a paragraph explaining what you learned. You might start like this.

> **EXAMPLE SENTENCE**
>
> My **_perception_** of birds changed a lot because of this article.

VOCABULARY STRATEGY: MULTIPLE-MEANING WORDS

Many English words have more than one meaning. For example, you might know that the vocabulary word *engage* can refer to a promise of marriage. Given this, you may have been confused by its use in this article. Here it means "to involve" or "to participate."

When you come across a familiar word that suddenly does not make sense to you, look at the words and sentences around it for clues to a different meaning for the word. If you are still unsure, check a dictionary.

PRACTICE Define the boldfaced words using context clues or a dictionary.

1. Gina wanted to rid her computer of all its stored **cookies.**
2. Isabel waited patiently for her tea to **steep.**
3. Starting his first job, Owen was considered **green.**
4. Wayne looked **sour** after his team's crushing defeat.
5. The landscaping crew was asked to **poll** any trees near electrical wires.

VOCABULARY PRACTICE
For more practice, go to the **Vocabulary Center** at **ClassZone.com.**

Reading-Writing Connection

Increase your understanding of "Bird Brains" by responding to these prompts. Then complete the **Grammar and Writing** exercise.

A. Short Response: Write a Summary
A summary is a restatement of the main ideas and details of a selection. Identify the main idea and supporting details in this article. Then write a **one-paragraph summary** of "Bird Brains."

A successful summary will . . .
- state the main idea of the article
- include the most important supporting details

B. Extended Response: Write a Letter
Pretend that you are trying to persuade a publisher that its new book on **intelligent** animals should include a chapter about birds. Write a **two- or three-paragraph letter** stating your case. Use the information from the article to make your argument.

A convincing letter will . . .
- contain a clear statement of your opinion
- include strong reasons and examples

GRAMMAR AND WRITING

PUNCTUATE TITLES CORRECTLY Be sure to punctuate titles correctly when you write. Use **quotation marks** for the titles of shorter works, such as short stories, essays, articles, songs, and poems. Use **italics** (or underlining) to set off titles of longer works, including books, plays, magazines, newspapers, movies, and TV series.

> *Examples:* The book *Are You My Mother?* is about a confused baby bird.
>
> "Kookaburra" is one of many songs about birds.

PRACTICE Rewrite each sentence, correctly punctuating the titles.

1. The TV series The Life of Birds was carefully researched.
2. This month's issue of Nature focuses entirely on birds.
3. I learned a lot from Joan Anderson's essay Cardinal Companion.
4. Robert Frost's poem A Dust of Snow mentions a crow.

*For more help with punctuating titles, see page R50 in the **Grammar Handbook.***

The First Emperor
Book Excerpt from *The Tomb Robbers* by Daniel Cohen

Digging Up the Past: Discovery and Excavation of Shi Huangdi's Tomb
Magazine Article by Helen Wieman Bledsoe

How can we uncover the PAST?

KEY IDEA To learn about the recent **past,** we might ask older friends and relatives to recall events they lived through, or to talk about the way life used to be. To explore the very distant past, we have to dig deeper—literally! The two selections you are about to read describe an amazing discovery that has uncovered an important part of China's ancient history.

QUICKWRITE Think about a time period you wish you knew more about. It might be when your parents were children, when your grandparents were children, or even thousands of years ago. Write down what span of years you would like to learn more about and why.

● ELEMENTS OF NONFICTION: MULTIPLE SOURCES OF INFORMATION

Have you ever wondered how there can be dozens, even hundreds, of resources available on the same topic? Sharing a topic doesn't mean that each source presents the same **information,** however. For example, one source may cover a large span of time and present only the most important facts and events. Another source may focus on a shorter period of time and take a closer look.

As you read "The First Emperor" and "Digging Up the Past," you'll notice that they are about the same topic. Try to figure out the focus of each selection.

● READING STRATEGY: SET A PURPOSE FOR READING

Your **purpose for reading** these two selections is to **make comparisons.** Look for similarities and differences in the information given. A chart can help you.

What do you learn about ...	"The First Emperor"	"Digging Up the Past"
... the emperor?		
... the history of the tomb?		
... the excavation of the tomb?		

▲ VOCABULARY IN CONTEXT

Make a chart like the one shown. Write each vocabulary word in the appropriate column, and then write a brief definition of each word you already know.

WORD LIST		
ancestor	disintegrate	reconstruction
archaeological	excavation	surpass
barbarian	immortality	
dedicate	preservation	

Know Well	Think I Know	Don't Know at All

Author Online

Daniel Cohen: Ghost Writer Though Daniel Cohen has written about world history, music, and nature, he is best known for his books of ghost stories. Research for these books led him to creep

Daniel Cohen
born 1936

around houses believed by some to be haunted. He even spent "a damp and chilly night in an English churchyard."

Helen Wieman Bledsoe: Magazine Writer Helen Wieman Bledsoe is a freelance writer whose articles have been published in more than 20 magazines. She also enjoys art, history, and travel.

Helen Wieman
Bledsoe

 MORE ABOUT THE AUTHOR
For more on the authors, visit the **Literature Center** at ClassZone.com.

Background

A Matter of Time The information contained in a nonfiction work is often affected by the time period in which the piece was written. "The First Emperor" was written when the excavation of the emperor's tomb was just beginning. "Digging Up the Past" was written some years later, when more information was available.

Ch'in Shih Huang Ti (1700s). Chinese painting. © British Library/The Art Archive.

THE FIRST EMPEROR Ⓐ

Daniel Cohen

There is what may turn out to be the greatest **archaeological** find of modern times, one that may ultimately outshine even the discovery of the tomb of Tutankhamun.[1] It is the tomb of the emperor Ch'in Shih Huang Ti.[2] Now admittedly the name Ch'in Shih Huang Ti is not exactly a household word in the West. But then neither was Tutankhamun until 1922. The major difference is that while Tutankhamun himself was historically insignificant, Ch'in Shih Huang Ti was enormously important in Chinese history. In many respects he was really the founder of China.

---

1. **Tutankhamun** (tōōt′äng-kä′mən): Egyptian pharaoh whose tomb was found intact in 1922.
2. **Ch'in Shih Huang Ti** (chĭn shĭh hwäng′ dē): The use of the word *Ch'in* (or *Qin*) at the beginning of the emperor's name is a formal title that refers to the place from which the emperor came.

10 The future emperor started out as the king of the small state Ch'in. At the time, the land was divided up among a number of small states, all constantly warring with one another. Ch'in was one of the smallest and weakest. Yet the king of Ch'in managed to overcome all his rivals, and in the year 221 B.C. he proclaimed himself emperor of the land that we now know as China. From that date until the revolution of 1912, China was always ruled by an emperor. The name China itself comes from the name Ch'in. **B**

Shih Huang Ti ruled his empire with ferocious efficiency. He had the Great Wall of China built to keep out the northern
20 **barbarians.** The Great Wall, which stretches some fifteen hundred miles, is a building project that rivals and perhaps **surpasses** the Great Pyramid.³ The Great Wall took thirty years to build and cost the lives of countless thousands of laborers. Today the Great Wall remains China's number one tourist attraction.

As he grew older, Shih Huang Ti became obsessed with the prospect of his own death. He had survived several assassination attempts and was terrified of another. He traveled constantly between his 270 different palaces, so that no one could ever be sure where he was going to be. He never slept in the same room for two

---

3. **Great Pyramid:** massive four-sided monument built around a tomb by people in ancient Egypt.

B MULTIPLE SOURCES
What is the focus of the information presented in lines 10–17?

barbarian (bär-bâr′ē-ən) *n.* a person considered by those of another group to have a primitive culture

surpass (sər-păs′) *v.* to become greater than; to go beyond

Shih Huang Ti's Empire

CHINA

The Great Wall

Shih Huang Ti's Tomb

Xi'an

▢ Empire of Shih Huang Ti
— Current border of China

ANALYZE VISUALS
Compare the man
in the carriage with
your mental image
of Shih Huang Ti.

Emperor Ch'in Shih Huang Ti Travelling in a Palanquin (1600s). Chinese School. Color on silk.
© Bibliothèque Nationale, Paris/Bridgeman Art Library.

immortality
(ĭm'ôr-tăl'ĭ-tē) *n.*
endless life

ancestor (ăn'sĕs'tər) *n.*
a person from whom
another person or group
is descended

C SET A PURPOSE
FOR READING
What do you learn
about Shih Huang Ti
in lines 32–40? Record
this information in
your chart.

30 nights in a row. Anyone who revealed the emperor's whereabouts
was put to death along with his entire family.

Shih Huang Ti searched constantly for the secret of
immortality. He became prey to a host of phony magicians and
other fakers who promised much but could deliver nothing.

The emperor heard that there were immortals living on some
far-off island, so he sent a huge fleet to find them. The commander
of the fleet knew that if he failed in his mission, the emperor would
put him to death. So the fleet simply never returned. It is said that
the fleet found the island of Japan and stayed there to become the
40 **ancestors** of the modern Japanese. **C**

In his desire to stay alive, Shih Huang Ti did not neglect the
probability that he would die someday. He began construction
of an immense tomb in the Black Horse hills near one of his
favorite summer palaces. The tomb's construction took as long
as the construction of the Great Wall—thirty years.

The emperor, of course, did die. Death came while he was visiting the eastern provinces.[4] But his life had become so secretive that only a few high officials were aware of his death. They contrived to keep it a secret until they could consolidate their
50 own power. The imperial procession[5] headed back for the capital. Unfortunately, it was midsummer and the emperor's body began to rot and stink. So one of the plotters arranged to have a cart of fish follow the immense imperial chariot to hide the odor of the decomposing corpse. Finally, news of the emperor's death was made public. The body, or what was left of it, was buried in the tomb that he had been building for so long. . . .

There are two contradictory stories about the tomb of Ch'in Shih Huang Ti. The first says that it was covered up with earth to make it resemble an ordinary hill and that its location
60 has remained unknown for centuries.

But a more accurate legend holds that there never was any attempt to disguise the existence of the tomb. Ch'in Shih Huang Ti had been building it for years, and everybody knew where it was. After his death the tomb was surrounded by walls enclosing an area of about five hundred acres. This was to be the emperor's "spirit city." Inside the spirit city were temples and all sorts of other sacred buildings and objects **dedicated** to the dead emperor.

Over the centuries the walls, the temples, indeed everything above ground was carried away by vandals. The top of the tomb
70 was covered with earth and eventually came to resemble a large hill. Locally the hill is called Mount Li. But still the farmers who lived in the area had heard stories that Mount Li contained the tomb of Ch'in Shih Huang Ti or of some other important person. . . . **D**

In the spring of 1974 a peasant plowing a field near Mount Li uncovered a life-sized clay statue of a warrior. Further digging indicated that there was an entire army of statues beneath the ground. Though **excavations** are not yet complete, Chinese authorities believe that there are some six thousand life-sized clay statues of warriors, plus scores of life-sized statues of horses.

---

4. **provinces:** districts, or parts, of a country.
5. **imperial procession:** a group of people traveling with an emperor.

dedicate (dĕd'ĭ-kāt')
v. to set apart for
a particular use

D SET A PURPOSE
FOR READING
What have you learned
so far about the tomb?
Add this information
to your chart.

excavation
(ĕk'skə-vā'shən) *n.*
the act or process of
exposing by digging
away a covering

A worker tries to piece together the broken terra-cotta statues.

80 Most of the statues are broken, but some are in an absolutely remarkable state of **preservation.** Each statue is finely made, and each shows a distinct individual, different from all the others.

This incredible collection is Shih Huang Ti's "spirit army." At one time Chinese kings practiced human sacrifice so that the victims could serve the dead king in the next world. Shih Huang Ti was willing to make do with models. Men and horses were arranged in a military fashion in a three-acre underground chamber. The chamber may have been entered at some point. The roof certainly collapsed. But still the delicate figures have survived surprisingly well.

90 Most of the damage was done when the roof caved in. That is why the Chinese archaeologists are so hopeful that when the tomb itself is excavated, it too will be found to have survived surprisingly well.

The Chinese are not rushing the excavations. They have only a limited number of trained people to do the job. After all, the tomb has been there for over two thousand years. A few more years won't make much difference. **E**

Though once denounced as a tyrant, Ch'in Shih Huang Ti is now regarded as a national hero. His name is a household word in China. The Chinese government knows that it may have an 100 unparalleled ancient treasure on its hands, and it wants to do the job well. Over the next few years we should be hearing much more about this truly remarkable find.

E SET A PURPOSE FOR READING
In your chart, note what you have learned from this selection about the excavation of the tomb.

Comprehension

1. **Recall** Why did Shih Huang Ti have the Great Wall built?

2. **Recall** What steps did Shih Huang Ti take to protect himself against people who might want to harm him?

3. **Clarify** What makes Shih Huang Ti an important person from the **past?**

Critical Analysis

4. **Identify the Main Idea** Consider the information that the author emphasizes in "The First Emperor." In one or two sentences, state the main idea of the selection.

5. **Examine Cause and Effect** Reread lines 18–24. What were the effects of building the Great Wall of China?

6. **Analyze Text Features** What information do the map and its labels on page 867 provide that the regular text does not?

7. **Evaluate Information** Skim through the selection, and note the details that support its main idea. Then explain whether you think the author provided enough information to support the main idea.

Comparing Information

Look over the chart you began to fill in as you read. Add notes about each kind of information presented in "The First Emperor."

What do you learn about . . .	"The First Emperor"	"Digging Up the Past"
. . . the emperor?	He had the Great Wall of China built.	
. . . the history of the tomb?		
. . . the excavation of the tomb?	There is an army of statues in it.	

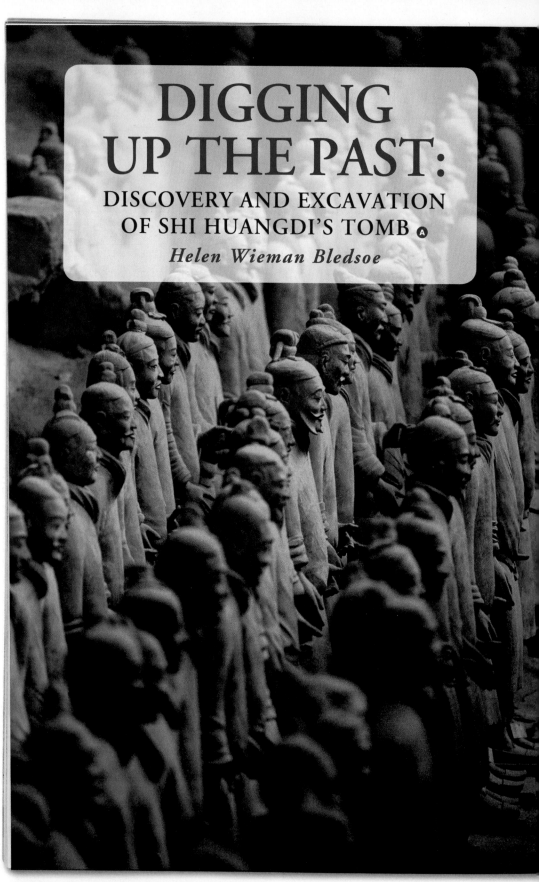

DIGGING UP THE PAST:
DISCOVERY AND EXCAVATION OF SHI HUANGDI'S TOMB Ⓐ

Helen Wieman Bledsoe

Ⓐ **MULTIPLE SOURCES**
Preview the article's title and graphic aids. What do you think the article will focus on?

ANALYZE VISUALS
These terra-cotta soldiers are only a small number of the thousands of statues unearthed at the sight of Shi Huangdi's tomb. What **details** do you notice in the rows of statues?

In March 1974, Chinese peasants digging a well near Xi'an in the central province of Shaanxi[1] found some unusual pottery fragments. Then, deeper down at 11 feet, they unearthed a head made of terra-cotta. They notified the authorities, and excavation of the site began immediately. To date, workers have dug up about 8,000 sculpted clay soldiers, and the site has proved to be one of the greatest archaeological discoveries of all time.

For over 2,000 years, these clay warriors have been guarding the tomb of Shi Huangdi,[2] the First Emperor of China. Tradition says that the
10 First Emperor began building his tomb when he ascended to the throne at age 13, and that it was unfinished at his death, 36 years later. The Chinese historian Sima Qian wrote in the *Shiji*, "Historical Records," that the emperor forced 700,000 laborers to work on his elaborate tomb.

The warriors stand guard in three pits (a fourth was found to be empty) that cover five-and-a-half acres and are 16 to 24 feet deep. The largest one contains 6,000 terra-cotta soldiers marching in military formation in 11 trenches, each as long as a football field. At the western end of the formation is a vanguard[3] of archers and bowmen. At the head of six of the trenches stand the remnants of
20 chariots, each with four life-sized horses and 18 soldiers. The wooden chariots have largely **disintegrated,** unlike the well-preserved terra-cotta horses and men. Last come row upon row of soldiers. **B**

Despite the enormous number of men, no two faces are alike. Their expressions display dignity, steadfastness, and intelligence. Each is tall, standing five-and-a-half to six feet high. Some people think the terra-cotta soldiers portray real-life men from the vast army of the First Emperor.

The warriors' legs are solid columns of clay, with square-toed sandals on their feet. The hollow bodies are of coiled clay. The head
30 and hands of each soldier were carefully molded and attached to the body in assembly-line fashion. Traces of pink, yellow, purple, blue, orange, green, brown, and black pigment show that the figures were once brightly painted. The horses were roan (reddish-brown), brown, or black with pink mouths.

disintegrate
(dĭs-ĭn'tĭ-grāt') *v.*
to break down into
smaller parts

B **MULTIPLE SOURCES**
What is the focus
of the information
presented in lines
14–22?

---

1. **Xi'an** (shē'än') . . . **Shaanxi** (shän'shē'): Xi'an is a city of central China. The former capital
   of the Qin (also called Ch'in) dynasty, it is now the capital of China's Shaanxi province.
2. **Shi Huangdi** (also **Shih Huang Ti**): The spelling of Chinese names and places can vary.
3. **vanguard** (văn'gärd): the troops that move at the head of an army.

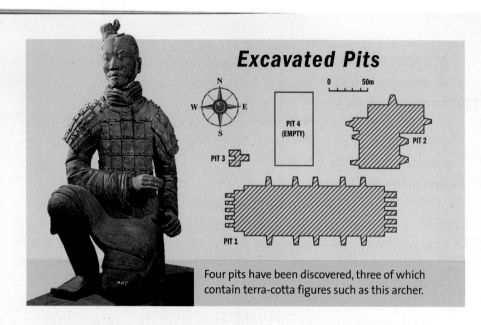

Excavated Pits

N W E S

0   50m

PIT 4 (EMPTY)

PIT 3

PIT 2

PIT 1

Four pits have been discovered, three of which contain terra-cotta figures such as this archer.

The warriors' hair styles and topknots, and the tassels trimming their garments, denote their military rank. Many do not wear helmets or carry shields, a mark of bravery in battle. Their armor was probably of lacquered[4] leather; some pieces look like baseball catchers' pads. The soldiers' hands are positioned to hold weapons, but most of the
40 weapons have disappeared. Very likely they were stolen when the pits were looted after the fall of the Qin Dynasty (the Dynasty founded by Shi Huangdi). Even so, bronze spears, halberds (a combination spear and battle-ax), swords, daggers, and about 1,400 arrowheads remain. Some of the blades are still very sharp.

A second pit, only partially excavated, contains about 1,400 more soldiers. While the first pit holds mostly infantry,[5] the second has a more mobile attack force of horses and chariots. A third pit is thought to hold the high command of the army. The chariot of the Commander-in-Chief survives, with men surrounding it in
50 protective formation. **C**

Covered by a wooden roof and ten feet of earth, these figures were not intended to be seen. When the pits were looted and burned, the roof fell in and damaged most of the sculptures. **Reconstruction** is a slow, delicate task. Today, a visitor to the site can walk on long wooden platforms 16 feet above the pits and gaze down with astonishment at the thousands of sculptured soldiers below.

C SET A PURPOSE FOR READING
Summarize what you have learned so far about the contents of the tomb. Add this information to your chart.

reconstruction
(rē′kən-strŭk′shən) *n.* the act of building or assembling again

---

4. **lacquered** (lăk′ərd): covered with a glossy, protective coating.

5. **infantry:** foot soldiers.

Approximately a mile away from the pits is a gently sloping, rounded mountain covered with trees—the burial mound of the First Emperor. The four-sided, rammed-earth mound covers three 60 quarters of a square mile and is 156 feet high. It once stood at 400 feet. Of the two great walls that enclosed the funerary park[6] only rubble remains. The perimeter[7] of the outer wall is almost four miles. Set into the strong thick walls were four gates and four corner towers. Inside the walls were gardens, pavilions,[8] and a sacrificial palace, in addition to the burial mound. The burial chamber itself is still untouched, its contents as yet unknown.

Tradition based on the *Shiji* says that the emperor's body was buried in a suit of small jade pieces sewed together with gold thread and covered with a pearl and jade shroud. Also in the burial 70 mound were bronze models of Shi Huangdi's palaces and government offices. These replicas featured such details as pearls to represent the sun and moon, and pools of mercury[9] to recreate rivers and seas.

---

6. **funerary park:** the place of a burial.

7. **perimeter:** the boundary or border of something.

8. **pavilions** (pǝ-vǐl'yǝnz): open-sided buildings used for shelter or recreation.

9. **mercury:** quicksilver; a chemical element that is a silvery liquid at room temperature.

Over 1,000 of the more than 6,000 soldiers and horses in Pit 1 have been restored.

Terra-cotta archers in Pit 2 wait for restoration.

D SET A PURPOSE
FOR READING
Reread lines 67–76.
What do you learn
about the emperor
and his tomb, based
on the *Shiji* and the
items that have been
excavated so far?
Add your findings
to your chart.

According to the ancient Chinese, the soul of the dead continued living and therefore required all of life's necessities within the tomb. Kings especially needed many luxuries and that is why their tombs are treasure houses of jewels, gold, silver, and bronze. **D**

The *Shiji* states that in order to prevent people from robbing the tomb, "Craftsmen built internal devices that would set off arrows should anyone pass through the tunnels." Because Sima Qian wrote
80 his history a century after the death of the First Emperor, the accuracy of his statements is questionable. In fact, grave robbers did enter and loot Shi Huangdi's tomb for 30 years after the fall of the Qin Dynasty (four years after the Emperor's death). During this time, many precious relics most likely were stolen.

In 1980, additional smaller pits were discovered. One contains pottery coffins with bones of exotic birds and animals, probably from the royal zoo. Another has vessels inscribed with the words, "Belonging to the Officials in Charge of Food at Mount Li," and must be where food and sacrifices were offered to the dead emperor.
90 Uncovered in the nearby Hall of Slumber were clothes and everyday objects for use by the soul of the Emperor. As the excavations continue, each find serves to remind us of the tremendous energy and genius of Shi Huangdi and his people.

Comprehension

1. **Recall** How was Shi Huangdi's tomb discovered?

2. **Recall** What happened to the tomb after the fall of the Qin dynasty?

3. **Represent** Sketch a diagram of the burial mound and the structures surrounding it, based on the descriptions in the article.

Critical Analysis

4. **Identify the Main Idea** Review "Digging Up the Past," and note the most important details of the article. What main idea do these details support?

5. **Evaluate Graphic Aids** Look back at the diagram on page 874. Does the diagram demonstrate what the tomb looks like more effectively than the text? Explain your answer.

6. **Draw Conclusions** Why do you think Shi Huangdi chose to have such an elaborate tomb built? Explain, using information from "The First Emperor" and "Digging Up the Past" for support.

Comparing Information

Now that you have read both selections, finish filling in your chart. Add the final question and answer it. This will help you identify the focus of each selection.

What do you learn about . . .	"The First Emperor"	"Digging Up the Past"
. . . the emperor?	He had the Great Wall of China built.	He ascended to the throne at age 13.
. . . the history of the tomb?		
. . . the excavation of the tomb?	There is an army of statues in it.	Each pit is 16 to 24 feet deep.
What do you learn the most about in each selection?		

Vocabulary in Context

VOCABULARY PRACTICE

Choose the word or phrase that is closest in meaning to each boldfaced word.

1. **preservation:** (a) demolition, (b) protection, (c) destruction
2. **disintegrate:** (a) fall apart, (b) combine with, (c) match up
3. **reconstruction:** (a) elimination, (b) cancellation, (c) restoration
4. **ancestor:** (a) older sister, (b) great-grandmother, (c) youngest daughter
5. **surpass:** (a) go beyond, (b) turn around, (c) fall back
6. **dedicate:** (a) dislike, (b) devote, (c) daydream
7. **barbarian:** (a) associate, (b) brute, (c) partner
8. **immortality:** (a) everlasting life, (b) short life, (c) temporary life
9. **archaeological:** (a) historical, (b) comical, (c) mystical
10. **excavation:** (a) an injury, (b) a vehicle, (c) a dig

ancestor

archaeological

barbarian

dedicate

disintegrate

excavation

immortality

preservation

reconstruction

surpass

VOCABULARY IN WRITING

Imagine you are writing a letter to a friend after a visit to Shi Huangdi's tomb. Using at least three vocabulary words, describe what you saw at the site. You might start like this.

EXAMPLE SENTENCE

*The work that goes into the **preservation** of this enormous tomb is amazing!*

VOCABULARY STRATEGY: WORD PARTS

Sometimes you can figure out the meaning of an unfamiliar word by breaking the word into parts. For example, the vocabulary word *reconstruction* has three parts: the prefix *re-* ("again"), the base word *construct* ("to build"), and the suffix *-ion* ("action or process").

When you combine the three meanings, you will find that *reconstruction* means "the action of building again." Knowing the meaning of one or more parts of a word will help you determine the meaning of the complete word.

PRACTICE Identify the word parts in each word. Then try to define the word. If you need help, use a dictionary.

1. unfortunate
2. disappearance
3. unfairness
4. irreversible

Prefixes	Meanings
dis-	apart
ir-	not
un-	the opposite of

Suffixes	Meanings
-ance, -ness	condition, state
-ate	to act upon
-ible	able, inclined to

VOCABULARY PRACTICE
For more practice, go to the **Vocabulary Center** at **ClassZone.com.**

Writing for Assessment

1. READ THE PROMPT

The two selections you've just read provide different kinds of information on the same topic. In writing assessments, you will often be asked to compare nonfiction selections that deal with a similar topic in different ways.

PROMPT

In three paragraphs, compare the focus of "The First Emperor" and "Digging Up the Past." Remember that the topic of each piece of writing is the same, but each presents different information. Support your comparison using details from each.

◀ **STRATEGIES IN ACTION**

1. I need to identify the **similarities and differences** in the focus of each selection.
2. I need to determine the **type** of information in each selection.
3. I should include **examples** from the selections to support my ideas.

2. PLAN YOUR WRITING

Using the chart you filled in as you read, identify the ways in which the selections are alike and different. Then think about how to present these similarities and differences.

- Decide on a main idea, or position statement, for your response.
- Review the selections to find details and examples that support your comparison.
- Create an outline to organize your ideas. This sample outline shows one way to organize your three paragraphs.

I. Introduction and focus of 1st selection
II. Focus of 2nd selection
III. Compare focus of selections

3. DRAFT YOUR RESPONSE

Paragraph 1 Provide the title and author of each selection, as well as a sentence explaining the topic they share. State the focus of the first selection. Include details from the book excerpt as examples.

Paragraph 2 State the focus of the second selection. Include details from the magazine article as examples.

Paragraph 3 Compare the types of information presented in each selection. Support your comparison with examples from each.

Revision Include transition words such as *also, however, instead,* or *unlike* to demonstrate similarities and differences.

Media Study

News Reports

TV Newscast Clip/Newspaper Report on *MediaSmart* DVD

What's the FULL *news story?*

KEY IDEA Whether you watch news on TV or turn to a newspaper, you want to have all the details. In other words, you want your news reports to be **thorough.** In this lesson, you'll examine two news stories. You'll learn a technique for figuring out how much important information a news story provides.

Background

Dolphin Crossing In August of 2005, a tropical storm began a path of destruction along the Gulf Coast section of the United States. Hurricane Katrina first struck Florida and grew more powerful as it neared the states of Alabama, Texas, Mississippi, and Louisiana. The hurricane brought **storm surges,** high winds that lift waves above sea level. Flooding caused many thousands to flee their homes.

Humans were not the only ones seeking a safer place. The two news reports in this lesson are about eight bottle-nosed dolphins that once lived in a marine park in Gulfport, Mississippi. As the hurricane raged, a storm surge swept these tame dolphins into the strange waters of the Gulf of Mexico.

880

Media Literacy: The 5 *W*'s and *H* of the News

To be **thorough** or complete, a news report should answer six basic questions—**who, what, when, where, why,** and **how.** Reporters often use the 5 *W*'s and *H* as an outline for writing reports. The best news reports answer these questions and include additional information.

THE 5 *W*'S AND *H* OF NEWS REPORTS

WHO?
Who is the report about?

WHAT?
What happened?

WHEN?
When did the event take place?

WHERE?
Where was the scene of the happenings?

WHY?
Why did the event occur?

HOW?
How did the event unfold?

SECTION E   THE STAR JOURNAL   E 5

Homeless Dolphins to Get Back Together in Bahamas

JACKSON, Miss. (AP) — Several dolphins that were swept out to sea by Hurricane Katrina will soon be reunited at a resort in the Bahamas.

A resort on Paradise Island in the Bahamas will take on 17 dolphins from the Marine Life Oceanarium—eight of which were rescued from open water in September.

"The dolphins, I think, are a symbol of everything that's happened on the Gulf Coast and to find a new home for them—that's something that we hope will happen for everybody on the coast," said Howard Karawan, president and managing director of the company that owns the resort.

STRATEGIES FOR ANALYZING THOROUGHNESS

- Search a news story for important details. They can be found beyond the **lead,** the first lines or paragraphs of a story. Details can be found within the first 30 seconds of a TV news report. Knowing these details can help you cover at least three of the 5 *W*'s.
- Be aware that the "why" and "how" details about an event are often shared in **interviews.** On TV, the brief statements made by experts or witnesses are called **sound bites.** In printed news, they're called **quotes.**

MediaSmart DVD

- **News Format 1:** "Rescue Mission"
- **Genre:** TV newscast
- **Running Time:** 2.5 minutes
- **News Format 2:** "Homeless Dolphins to Get Back Together in Bahamas"
- **Genre:** Newspaper report

Viewing Guide for
News Reports

Watch an ABC network news report that was first broadcast in the weeks after Hurricane Katrina had struck. Then read a newspaper report that appeared some time later. In analyzing each report, look or listen for any details that help you answer the 5 *W*'s and the *H* questions. Record your answers. Use these questions to guide you as you examine each report.

NOW VIEW

FIRST VIEWING: Comprehension

1. **Summarize** Refer to any notes that answer the 5 *W*'s and *H* questions. Use your answers to write a brief summary of either the TV news or newspaper report.

2. **Clarify** The TV newscast report appeared in August of 2005. How much later did the newspaper report appear?

CLOSE VIEWING: Media Literacy

3. **Identifying Details** The TV newscast focuses on only two of the dolphins. In the newspaper report, what more recent news do you learn about the condition of the dolphins?

4. **Analyze Sound Bites** In your opinion, were the **interviews** in the newscast helpful to you in answering the 5 *W*'s and *H* questions? Explain. Think about
   - the introduction by the news anchor at the beginning
   - the details given by the reporter at the rescue

5. **Compare News Forms** Use your notes on the news reports to fill out a chart like this one. Then compare your notes with another student's to see how well they match.

	Who?	What?	When?	Where?	Why?	How?
"Rescue Mission"						
"Homeless Dolphins"						

Write or Discuss

Evaluate News Reports You've analyzed two news reports. Choose either the TV news report or the newspaper report. Briefly express your opinion of how good a job the report does of providing complete information about the dolphins. Think about

- how well it answers the **5 *W*'s and *H*** questions
- how easy or difficult it was to find the important details
- any additional information in the report that added interest

Produce Your Own Media

Create Nursery Rhyme News Recall the stirring events surrounding such nursery rhyme characters as Jack and Jill or Humpty Dumpty. Or think of how tales like "Little Red Riding Hood" or "The Three Little Pigs" might be reported as news. Choose any rhyme or tale that's familiar to your class. Rewrite the tale as a news story and add more imaginative details. Have a partner check that your report delivers all the necessary information. If two or more students choose the same characters, plan each additional report as a news update.

HERE'S HOW Follow these suggestions for your report.

- Write the news report by using the **5 *W*'s and *H*** questions as an outline.
- Include **sound bites** or **quotes** from the characters.
- Take the role of a reporter to present your nursery news reports to the class. Each student can take turns reading aloud from a "news" desk.

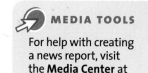

MEDIA TOOLS

For help with creating a news report, visit the **Media Center** at **ClassZone.com.**

STUDENT MODEL

Tech Tip

If available, add clip art to the news reports.

SCIENTISTS DISCOVER STAR

NEW YORK—In a press conference this morning, scientists announced the discovery of a new star. Its common name is Twinkle, Twinkle.

The lead scientist, Dr. Ester Esteban, is still amazed. "I wonder why it has taken billions and billions of years to find this star," Dr. Esteban said. "It sparkles like a diamond in the sky."

Argument and Persuasion

Think about all the choices and decisions that you make during a single day. For instance, you might choose to volunteer at an animal shelter, buy a new pair of shoes, or cast your vote for student-council president. Which persuasive messages influence your decisions? In this unit, you'll learn how to analyze editorials, ads, and speeches, many of which affect your beliefs and actions.

Part 1: What Is an Argument?

"Can't you just *listen* to me?" "This is so unfair!" When you hear the word *argument,* you may think of angry people shouting heated statements like these. In formal speaking and writing, however, a good argument is not emotional. It is a carefully stated claim supported by reasons and evidence. A strong argument is made up of two important parts.

- a **claim,** or a writer's position on a problem or an issue
- **support,** or the reasons and evidence that help to prove the claim. A writer may include many kinds of evidence, including eye-opening statistics, compelling anecdotes, or relevant examples.

Take a look at the parts of an argument in the following example.

CLAIM
Teens who use the Internet for different kinds of tasks are developing important life skills.

Support **1** Support **2** Support **3**

Support **1**
Using the Internet for research can help teens become experts at finding information. For example, looking up homework help and comparison-shopping online both require savvy research abilities.

Support **2**
Teens are learning how to multi-task. One study found that 30 percent of teens do more than one thing when they are on the Internet—for instance, surf the Web *and* e-mail friends at the same time.

Support **3**
The immediate responses required by e-mails and instant messages can help teens learn to type faster and to process information quickly. These abilities are critical in school and in business.

MODEL: PARTS OF AN ARGUMENT

This article is from *Humane Teen,* a Web site intended to educate students about important issues involving animal rights and the environment. As you begin reading the article, look for the author's claim.

STOP   REFRESH   PRINT   BOOKMARKS

http://www.humaneteen.org   ☒

Issues   **Projects**   **Message Board**   **Links**

POWER IN NUMBERS
WHY STUDENT CLUBS ARE SO EFFECTIVE

One person can do a lot for animals and the Earth. So, what's the point of starting a club? That's simple. When people work as a team, they can accomplish much more. Here's why:

- A group has more people to make calls, write letters, hand out
5   flyers, and get the word out about pressing <u>issues</u>.

- Trying to solve problems by yourself can be difficult and frustrating. But when you're part of a club, you get support and encouragement from other club members.

- A group of people speaking with one voice often has more influence
10   than a single person. People sit up and take notice when many individuals come together to champion an important cause.

- A club taps the wide range of skills and talents of its members. If you have a flair for art, you could design animal-protection posters or environmental T-shirts. Another member—someone who has a
15   way with words—could write <u>public service announcements</u> or letters to newspaper editors. Other club members might be dynamic speakers, thorough researchers, or good organizers. Your projects will be successful because of the efforts, experience, and creativity of all your club's members.

Find Clubs Near You   **E-mail Article**   **Print Article**

Close Read

1. Look at the title of this article and reread the first paragraph. What is the author's claim?

2. In your own words, restate two of the reasons that the author gives to support the claim.

3. One of the author's reasons has been boxed. What examples are given to back up this reason?

Part 2: The Power of Persuasion

What kinds of persuasive messages have made a lasting impression on you? Perhaps you remember a stirring speech that inspired you to support a cause or an alarming ad that made you vow to save the planet. In these cases, it probably wasn't just a well-supported claim that persuaded you. Most likely, you were reacting to the **persuasive techniques,** or the specific methods that were used to sway your heart and mind.

The persuasive techniques shown in the chart can make strong arguments even more powerful. However, you should keep in mind that they can also disguise flaws in weak arguments.

Appeals by Association	Emotional Appeals	Loaded Language
"Sell" a product or an idea by linking it with something or someone positive or influential	**Use strong feelings, rather than facts and evidence, to persuade**	**Relies on words with strongly positive or negative associations**

Bandwagon
Taps into people's desire to belong to a group

> Don't miss the fundraiser that everyone's talking about!

Testimonial
Relies on the backing of a celebrity, an expert, or a satisfied customer

> As the lead singer of Destination Home, I know good sound when I hear it. That's why I won't go anywhere without my FX portable music player.

Appeal to Fear
Makes people feel as if their safety, security, or health is in danger

> If a hurricane hit tomorrow, would your family be safe?

Appeal to Vanity
Uses flattery to win people over

> We're looking for talented athletes like you. Join our after-school running club.

Words with Positive Associations
Bring to mind something exciting, comforting, or desirable

> Sparkling waters, silky sands, and breezy air all await you at Shongum Lake Park.

Words with Negative Associations
Call up unpleasant images, experiences, or feelings

> The calves were raised in cramped, filthy stalls.

MODEL 1: PERSUASION IN WRITING

In this editorial, the author discusses a serious problem facing your generation. What persuasive techniques does he use to win you over?

A RECIPE FOR DISASTER
WHY TODAY'S TEENS NEED TO SHAPE UP

Magazine editorial by **Luis Frontera**

Picture this situation. You've just gotten home from a long day at school. You're not ready to start your homework, so you decide to kick back and watch TV. After seeing ads for greasy French fries, sugary soft drinks, and salty chips, you head to the kitchen to fix yourself
5   an enormous (and unhealthy) snack. With the TV blaring in the background, you then waste hours on the Web.

If you think there's nothing wrong with this lazy lifestyle, think again. Today's teens are the most overweight and inactive generation in history, largely because of poor eating habits, lack of exercise, and
10   exposure to mindless media. If teens don't break these damaging habits, they will increase their risk of developing life-threatening diseases, such as diabetes and hypertension.

Close Read

1. What kind of emotional appeal does the author use to convince you of his position?

2. Two examples of loaded language have been boxed. Find three additional examples.

MODEL 2: PERSUASION IN ADVERTISING

If you flip through your favorite magazine or turn on the TV, you'll most likely encounter ads that are targeting *you.* As you examine this public service ad, think about how the creators might want you to react to its message.

These teens have taken their health and well-being into their own hands.

WILL YOU JOIN THEM OR SIT ON THE SIDELINES?

Campaign for Fit Teens America

Close Read

1. Identify the persuasive technique that is used in this ad. Why might the creators have used this technique to target teens? Explain.

2. How does the photograph in this ad help to enhance the message? Support your answer.

Part 3: Analyze the Texts

Now, you'll apply what you've learned in this workshop as you analyze two texts—an editorial and a poster. Both texts are about pit bulls, but their similarities end there. As you read each text, notice the argument that is being presented.

DANGEROUS THREAT?
No—Loving Pet!

Editorial by **Lisa Epstein**

Recently, pit bulls have become the targets of negative media coverage. All pit bulls have the urge to attack people, some articles state. They are a danger to children, a few experts say. And, they are just *too* violent to be household pets, some lawmakers believe. As the educated owner of a
5 pit bull, I can say that these reports are false. Pit bulls are not necessarily violent toward humans. In fact, they can make affectionate, loving pets.

So where did the misperception come from? More than 200 years ago, pit bulls were bred to compete in fights with other dogs. For that reason, pit bulls had certain qualities—such as aggression and
10 determination—that were important for fighting. Pit bulls today still have these same qualities, but they have other qualities as well: loyalty, friendliness, and a desire to please.

It's true that some pit bulls, such as those featured in news stories, *are* violent. However, this is because of bad owners, not because they're
15 a violent breed. Some irresponsible owners train their pit bulls to fight or attack, and because pit bulls want to please their owners, they act accordingly. In contrast, owners who treat pit bulls with love are rewarded with endless affection in return.

People who still need proof that pit bulls aren't violent can look at
20 recent studies. For example, the American Temperament Test Society (ATTS) is an organization that rates all breeds of dogs based on qualities like shyness and friendliness. In one study, pit bulls got a better overall rating than golden retrievers, whom many people view as the friendliest dogs around.
25 So, don't believe the unfair reports about how violent pit bulls are. In reality, they don't want to attack us; they want to curl up at our feet.

Close Read

1. Reread lines 1–6. What is the author's claim?

2. Review the persuasive techniques listed on page 886. Which technique does the author use in the boxed sentence?

3. What reason does the author give in the third paragraph to support her claim? Explain this reason in your own words.

4. In lines 19–24, the author reveals that current studies help to prove her claim. What specific evidence does she cite?

Not everyone agrees that pit bulls are cuddly, harmless creatures. What do the creators of this poster want viewers to know about pit bulls?

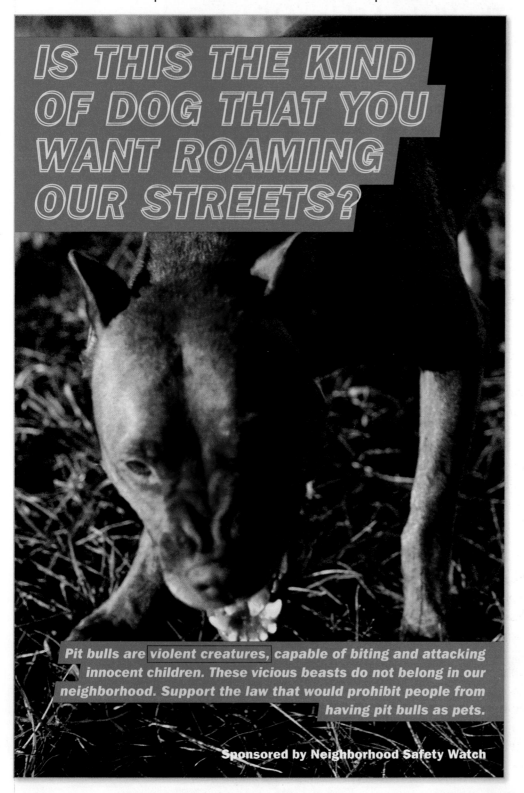

IS THIS THE KIND OF DOG THAT YOU WANT ROAMING OUR STREETS?

Pit bulls are violent creatures, capable of biting and attacking innocent children. These vicious beasts do not belong in our neighborhood. Support the law that would prohibit people from having pit bulls as pets.

Sponsored by Neighborhood Safety Watch

Close Read

1. In your own words, describe the claim that this poster makes.

2. What persuasive technique is used to convince the intended audience—responsible neighbors—of the claim? How can you tell?

3. One example of loaded language has been boxed. Find two additional examples.

4. How do the photograph and the page design add to the persuasive power of the poster? Explain your answer.

What Video Games Can Teach Us
The Violent Side of Video Games

Magazine Articles by Emily Sohn

Can a GAME play YOU?

KEY IDEA How often have you heard the reminder "It's only a **game**"? It's meant to warn us that games shouldn't be taken too seriously. But suppose a game could help you learn, or change the way you act. Would it still be "only a game"? Many people think that video games, in particular, can have a powerful effect on their players. The following articles will show you some of the ways in which video games can be helpful or harmful.

DISCUSS Gather in a small group to discuss your video game habits. Take turns answering such questions as "How much time do you spend playing video games each week?" "What kinds of games do you play?" and "Do you think video games have a positive or negative effect on you?" When you are done, compare your results with those of the other groups.

● ELEMENTS OF NONFICTION: ARGUMENT

An **argument** consists of a **claim,** or position on an issue or problem, supported by **reasons** and **evidence.** A basic argument might look like this.

Claim: *Dogs are smart.*

Support: *My dog knows his name and does tricks.*

A strong argument also raises possible objections to the claim and offers **counterarguments,** or arguments made to prove that the opposing viewpoint is wrong. As you read the following articles on video games, look for these elements.

● READING SKILL: EVALUATE SUPPORT

To avoid being easily swayed by a weak argument, it is a good idea to evaluate the **support** and reasoning a writer includes. Watch for these weaknesses:

- **Vague language**—statements that are unclear
- **Irrelevant examples**—examples that do not directly relate to the claim
- **Overgeneralizations**—statements too broad to be accurate. Overgeneralizations often use words such as *always, never, everyone,* or *none.*

As you read each article, record examples of strong support and weak support in a chart like the one shown.

"What Video Games Can Teach Us"	
Strong Support	Weak Support
	Vague language: "a number of young gamers" (line 33)

▲ VOCABULARY IN CONTEXT

Emily Sohn uses the following words to present some of the pros and cons of playing video games. To see how many you know, write definitions for the boldfaced words.

1. Video games **captivate** many people.
2. Some people worry about games that **simulate** violence.
3. Video game players learn to make **precise** movements.
4. The opinions of different experts **complicate** the issue.

Author Online

Emily Sohn

A Mind for Science
A specialist in health and science, Emily Sohn has written for a number of publications, including *Health, U.S. News & World Report, Smithsonian,* and *Outside.* She has also written for the student Web site for *Science News.*

On Assignment Though she is based in Minneapolis, Minnesota, Sohn's work as a freelance writer has taken her to faraway and fascinating places. Sohn has traveled to Cuba, Turkey, the Peruvian Amazon, and Sweden in order to research her stories. She is also the science correspondent for Project Exploration, a "living classroom" founded by paleontologist Dr. Paul Sereno and educator Gabrielle Lyon. Sohn went to the Sahara Desert in Niger to report on the project's Dinosaur Expedition 2005.

Free Time When she's not writing or traveling, Sohn enjoys rock climbing, camping, and exploring. She loves being outside.

 MORE ABOUT THE AUTHOR
For more on Emily Sohn, visit the **Literature Center** at ClassZone.com.

What Video Games Can Teach Us

Emily Sohn

HERE'S SOME NEWS FOR YOU TO SHARE WITH YOUR PARENTS AND TEACHERS: VIDEO GAMES MIGHT ACTUALLY BE GOOD FOR YOU.

Whenever a wave of teenage violence strikes, movies, TV, or video games often take the heat. Some adults assume that movies, TV, and video games are a bad influence on kids, and they blame these media[1] for causing various problems. A variety of studies appear to support the link between media violence and bad behavior among kids.

But media don't necessarily *cause* violence, says James Gee. Gee
10 is an education professor at the University of Wisconsin, Madison. "You get a group of teenage boys who shoot up a school—of course they've played video games," Gee says. "Everyone does. It's like blaming food because we have obese people."

Video games are innocent of most of the charges against them, Gee says. The games might actually do a lot of good. Gee has written a book titled *What Video Games Have to Teach Us About Learning and Literacy.* Ⓐ

Ⓐ **ARGUMENT**
Reread lines 1–17 and locate the author's **claim.** What **reasons** does she provide as **support** for it?

---

1. **media:** a general term that includes television, films, magazines, newspapers, and video games.

A growing number of researchers agree with Gee. If used in the right way, video and computer games have the potential to inspire learning.
20 And they can help players improve coordination[2] and visual skills.

Attention-Getting Games

A good video game is challenging, entertaining, and **complicated**, Gee says. It usually takes 50 to 60 hours of intense concentration to finish one. Even kids who can't sit still in school can spend hours trying to solve a video or computer game. . . .

The **captivating** power of video games might lie in their interactive nature. Players don't just sit and watch. They get to participate in the action and solve problems. Some games even allow players to make changes in the game, allowing new possibilities.

And kids who play computer games often end up knowing more
30 about computers than their parents do. "Kids today are natives in a culture in which their parents are immigrants," Gee says.

In his 2 to 3 years of studying the social influences of video games, Gee has seen a number of young gamers become computer science majors in college. One kid even ended up as a teaching assistant during his freshman year because the school's computer courses were too easy for him. **B**

Screen Reading

Video games can enhance reading skills too. In the game *Animal Crossing,* for instance, players become characters who live in a town full of animals. Over the course of the game, you can buy a house, travel
40 from town to town, go to museums, and do other ordinary things. All the while, you're writing notes to other players and talking to the animals. Because kids are interested in the game, they often end up reading at a level well above their grade, even if they say they don't like to read.

Games can inspire new interests. After playing a game called *Age of Mythology,* Gee says, kids (like his 8-year-old son) often start checking out mythology books from the library or join Internet chat groups about mythological characters. History can come alive to a player participating in the game. . . .

---

2. **coordination:** the ability to make multiple muscle groups work smoothly together.

complicate (kŏm′plĭ-kāt′) *v.* to make difficult or complex

captivate (kăp′tə-vāt′) *v.* to attract and hold interest

B EVALUATE SUPPORT
Reread lines 32–36. Why might the author have chosen to use **vague language** to make this point?

Improved Skills

Video games might also help improve visual skills. That was what
50 researchers from the University of Rochester in New York recently found.

In the study, frequent game players between the ages of 18 and 23
were better at monitoring what was happening around them than those
who didn't play as often or didn't play at all. They could keep track
of more objects at a time. And they were faster at picking out objects
from a cluttered environment.

"Above and beyond the fact that action video games can
be beneficial," says Rochester neuroscientist[3] Daphne Bavelier,
"our findings are surprising because they show that the learning
induced by video game playing occurs quite fast and generalizes
60 outside the gaming experience." **C**

The research might lead to better ways to train soldiers or treat
people with attention problems, the researchers say, though they
caution against taking that point too far.

Says Bavelier, "We certainly don't mean to convey the message
that kids can play video games instead of doing their homework!"

If Gee gets his way, though, teachers might some day start
incorporating computer games into their assignments. Already,
scientists and the military use computer games to help **simulate**
certain situations for research or training, he says. Why shouldn't
70 schools do the same thing? . . . **D**

Researchers at the Massachusetts Institute of Technology have
started a project they describe as the "Education Arcade." The
project brings together researchers, scholars,[4] game designers and
others interested in developing and using computer games in the
classroom. . . .

Looking at the bright side of video and computer games could
also help bring kids and adults closer together. Playing games can
be a social activity, during which kids and adults learn from one
another. By opening up lines of communication and understanding,
80 maybe one day we'll praise video games for saving society, not
blame them for destroying it.

---

3. **neuroscientist** (nŏŏrʹō-sīʹən-tĭst): a scientist who studies the brain and the nervous system.

4. **scholars:** people who study a particular subject.

C EVALUATE SUPPORT
Does the support the
author provides in lines
51–60 seem strong?
Explain why or why not.

simulate (sĭmʹyə-lātʹ)
v. to imitate

D EVALUATE SUPPORT
What **irrelevant
example** does the
author use in lines
66–70? Record this
information in your
chart.

The Violent Side of Video Games
Emily Sohn

WHEN I WAS A KID, I WAS OBSESSED WITH VIDEO GAMES.

I saved my allowance to buy new games every month. I read Nintendo magazines for tips about solving the Super Mario Brothers adventures. I played so many hours of *Tetris* that I used to dream about little blocks falling perfectly into place.

There were physical effects too. My thumbs turned into machines, quick and **precise**. During especially difficult levels of play, my palms would sweat. My heart would race. I'd have knots in my stomach from anxiety. It was the same feeling I'd sometimes get from watching scary
10 movies or suspenseful TV shows.

After a while, I started to think that looking at screens and playing games all the time might be affecting me in ways I didn't even suspect. It turns out that I was probably right. **E**

Scientists are discovering that playing video and computer games and watching TV and movies can change the way we act, think, and feel. Whether these changes are good or bad has become a subject of intense debate.

Concerns About Violence

Violence is one of the biggest concerns, especially as computer graphics and special effects become more realistic. Some parents
20 and teachers blame . . . aggressive behavior on media violence— as seen in TV programs, movies, and video games.

"If you've ever watched young children watching kickboxing," says child psychologist[1] John Murray, "within a few minutes they start popping up and pushing and shoving and imitating the actions." Murray is at Kansas State University in Manhattan, Kansas.

There's also evidence that people become less sensitive to violence after a while, Murray says. In other words, you get so used to seeing it that you eventually think it's not such a big deal. **F**

---

1. **child psychologist** (sī-kŏl'ə-jĭst): a person trained to study thought and behavior patterns in children.

precise (prĭ-sīs') *adj.* exact or correct

E ARGUMENT
Reread the title of the selection, followed by lines 1–13. What **claim** does the author make?

F EVALUATE SUPPORT
Reread lines 22–28. Does John Murray make any **overgeneralizations** to support his point?

Then there's the "mean world syndrome."[2] If you watch lots
of violence, you may start to think the world is a bad place. I still
sometimes have trouble falling asleep if I watch the news on TV
or read the newspaper right before going to bed. **G**

Still, it's hard to prove that violence on TV leads to violence in real
life. It might be possible, for example, that people who are already
aggressive for other reasons are more drawn to violent games and
TV shows. . . .

Video Power

Most of the research has focused on TV and movie violence, mainly
because TV and movies have been around much longer than video
games, says psychologist Craig Anderson of Iowa State University
in Ames, Iowa. Anderson has a Web site dedicated to looking at the
link between video games and violence.

In his own research and in analyses[3] of research by others,
Anderson says that he has detected a connection between violent
video games and violent behavior. He has found that people who
repeatedly play violent games have aggressive thoughts and become
less helpful and sociable. Physically, their heart rates accelerate.

Video games might have an even more powerful effect on the
brain than TV does, Murray says. Players actively participate in the
violence. . . .

Next time you play a violent video game, Murray suggests, check
your pulse just before and after each round as one way to see how
the game affects you.

"Ninety-nine percent of the time, I'll bet your heart rate will have
increased rather dramatically while playing one," Murray says. "This
indicates that . . . you are being affected." **H**

Three teenagers from Puerto Rico have data to back up that
observation. With the help of a school nurse, the high school seniors
found that people of all ages showed a rise in blood pressure and
heart rate after playing a superviolent game. Playing an active,
nonviolent game did not have the same effect.

G EVALUATE SUPPORT
Reread lines 29–32.
What is the **irrelevant example** in these lines meant to support?

H EVALUATE SUPPORT
Reread lines 47–55.
Does the **evidence** in this section provide strong support for the **claim?** Explain why or why not.

2. **syndrome** (sĭn'drōm'): a group or pattern of symptoms that make up a disease or condition.
3. **analyses** (ə-năl'ĭ-sēz'): examinations of different information or experimental results.

Comprehension

1. **Recall** According to "What Video Games Can Teach Us," why is the military using computer games for training?

2. **Clarify** According to "The Violent Side of Video Games," what is the "mean world syndrome"?

3. **Summarize** Reread lines 37–46 in "The Violent Side of Video Games." Then write a summary of Craig Anderson's discoveries.

Critical Analysis

4. **Understand Generalizations** A hasty generalization occurs when a person jumps to a conclusion based on too little **evidence**. Reread lines 44–48 of "What Video Games Can Teach Us." Why might the information in this paragraph be considered a hasty generalization?

5. **Analyze an Argument** Take note of the **claim** Sohn makes about video games in "What Video Games Can Teach Us." In a graphic organizer like the one shown, list the **reasons** Sohn gives for her position, and the **evidence** she uses to support it.

Claim: Video games can be good for you.

Reason: They enhance reading skills.

Reason:

Reason:

Support: A game called *Animal Crossing* teaches players to read above grade level.

Support:

Support:

6. **Examine Evidence** One common type of evidence is **expert testimony,** or quotes from people who are knowledgeable about whatever subject is being argued. Look over the articles to find the experts who are quoted in each one. Why might the author have chosen these particular experts?

7. **Evaluate Support** Look back at the chart you filled in as you read. Which article better supported its **claim?** Explain your answer.

Extension and Challenge

8. **Big Question Activity** Review the results of the group activity on page 890. Did you notice any patterns in the **games** your classmates like to play, or in the effect the games have on people? Write a short paragraph that explains whether the results seem to support the first article, the second article, or parts of each.

Vocabulary in Context

VOCABULARY PRACTICE

Choose the letter of the word or phrase that best completes each sentence.

1. You **complicate** directions by (a) adding steps, (b) explaining them, (c) writing them down.
2. To **simulate** eating, you (a) buy food, (b) pretend to chew, (c) think of dinner.
3. A movie can **captivate** you, making you want to (a) get popcorn, (b) chat, (c) watch closely.
4. A **precise** measurement is (a) estimated, (b) correct, (c) unreliable.

VOCABULARY IN WRITING

Were you surprised by any of the effects of video games described in these two articles? Answer this question in a short paragraph, using at least two vocabulary words. You might start like this.

> **EXAMPLE SENTENCE**
>
> I wasn't surprised to learn that video games often **simulate** violent scenes.

VOCABULARY STRATEGY: CHOOSE THE BEST SYNONYM

Words that have the same or similar meanings are called **synonyms.** A word can have many synonyms, so a writer has to choose carefully. For example, the vocabulary word *captivating* describes a video game that holds or captures interest better than its synonym *interesting* would. In a thesaurus (a book or electronic tool for finding synonyms), the word *captivating* is also grouped with words such as *fascinating* or *spellbinding*.

PRACTICE For each sentence, choose the synonym in parentheses that best replaces the boldfaced word in the context provided. Consult a dictionary or thesaurus for help.

1. The abandoned factory was dark and **empty.** (deserted, unfilled)
2. After the marathon, he **drank** as much water as he could. (sipped, gulped)
3. The room was **large** and airy. (spacious, massive)
4. The kittens **hit** a ball of yarn back and forth. (batted, smacked)
5. By the end of the five-mile hike, we were all **tired.** (sleepy, exhausted)

VOCABULARY PRACTICE
For more practice, go to the **Vocabulary Center** at **ClassZone.com.**

Reading-Writing Connection

Show your understanding of Emily Sohn's two articles by responding to these prompts. Then complete the **Grammar and Writing** exercise.

WRITING PROMPTS	SELF-CHECK
A. Short Response: Revise an Argument Provide a sample of vague language, overgeneralization, or an irrelevant example from either article. Rewrite the **paragraph** in which your example appears, correcting the weak reasoning.	*A successful revision will . . .* • identify an example of weak or faulty reasoning • use strong reasoning to rewrite the example
B. Extended Response: Write an Editorial A newspaper editorial is a short piece of writing that expresses an opinion. Write a **two- or three-paragraph editorial** stating whether young people should be allowed to play video **games** as a classroom exercise. Support your argument using examples from the articles.	*A convincing editorial will . . .* • contain a clear statement presenting your opinion • provide logical reasons and examples

GRAMMAR AND WRITING

AVOID MISPLACED MODIFIERS A **prepositional phrase** begins with a preposition—such as *from, in, on, under,* or *with*—and ends with a noun or pronoun. Prepositional phrases **modify,** or give information about, another word in the sentence. For example, in the sentence "The mouse is under the table," *under the table* modifies *mouse.* If a prepositional phrase is placed too far from the word it modifies, the sentence's meaning may be unclear.

Original: Anderson connected video games with behavior in his research.

Revised: In his research, Anderson connected video games with behavior.

PRACTICE Move each prepositional phrase to the correct position.

1. Much has been said about violent video games in the news media.
2. Video games can have a more powerful effect than TV on the brain.
3. You can learn a lot from video games with patience and concentration.
4. Emily Sohn talks about playing many video games in her article.

*For more help with misplaced modifiers, see page R59 in the **Grammar Handbook.***

Should Wild Animals Be Kept as Pets?

Persuasive Essay by the Humane Society of the United States

Can we ever TAME what's wild?

KEY IDEA Would you like to have a wolf for a pet? How about a monkey? Owning a wild animal may sound exciting, but unfortunately, people who keep wild animals as pets often run into trouble when they are trying to **tame** them. In the essay you are about to read, you'll discover some of the challenges that can come with having an unusual pet.

LIST IT Is there a particular wild animal you wish you could own? Make a list of what you think might be the advantages and disadvantages of keeping that type of animal. Compare your lists with those of your classmates.

Monkey	
Advantages	**Disadvantages**
I could teach it to play games.	It might break things.

● ELEMENTS OF NONFICTION: PERSUASIVE TECHNIQUES

If you make an argument for or against something, you are trying to persuade other people using reasons and facts. But there are other ways to persuade people to adopt an opinion or take action. These **persuasive techniques** include

- **Emotional appeals**—messages that create strong feelings, such as pity or fear
- **Appeals to authority**—references to people who are experts on a subject
- **Loaded language**—words with strongly positive or strongly negative connotations, or shades of meaning

As you read "Should Wild Animals Be Kept as Pets?" notice the persuasive techniques used in the essay. Record examples in a chart like the one shown.

Emotional Appeals	Appeals to Authority	Loaded Language

■ READING STRATEGY: PREVIEW

When you **preview,** you examine a text for clues to what it is about and how it is organized. One way to preview is to **skim text features,** quickly looking over such elements as the title, subheadings, footnotes, vocabulary definitions, and graphic aids. As you read the essay, notice how previewing the text features helps you focus on the most important ideas.

▲ VOCABULARY IN CONTEXT

The words in Column A help to explain the Humane Society's position on the issue of keeping wild animals. See how many you know by matching each vocabulary word in Column A with the word in Column B that is closest in meaning.

Column A

1. captivity
2. domesticate
3. instinctive
4. unsuitable

Column B

a. inborn
b. tame
c. confinement
d. improper

Background

Animal Protector
Founded in 1954, the Humane Society of the United States is the world's largest animal-protection organization. Members of the Humane Society are tireless in their efforts on behalf of the country's many dogs, cats, and other pets. However, the Humane Society also works to protect wildlife, animals raised for food, and animals used in research.

Policies and a Vision The Humane Society works to help make the public more aware of the proper treatment of animals, as well as enforcing laws that help to protect animals. The organization has a vision of a world in which humans and animals live in harmony. It believes that we have a moral duty to protect the animals whose habitats we share.

 BUILDING BACKGROUND
To learn more about the Humane Society of the United States, visit the **Literature Center** at ClassZone.com.

Ocelot

captivity (kăp-tĭv′ĭ-tē) *n.* the condition of being confined or not free

Should Wild Animals Be Kept as Pets? A

The Humane Society of the United States

The Humane Society of the United States strongly opposes keeping wild animals as pets. This principle[1] applies to both native and nonnative species, whether caught in the wild or bred in **captivity**. The overwhelming majority[2] of people who obtain these animals are unable to provide the care they require.

---

1. **principle:** a policy or rule.
2. **overwhelming majority:** most or almost all.

Caring for Wild Animals Is Difficult or Impossible B

B **PREVIEW**
Preview the article's **subheadings.** Why do you think they have been included in the essay?

Despite what animal sellers may say, appropriate care for wild animals requires considerable expertise,[3] specialized facilities,[4] and lifelong dedication to the animals. Their nutritional and social needs are demanding to meet and, in many cases, are unknown. They often grow to be larger, stronger, and more dangerous than owners expect or can manage. Small cats such as ocelots and bobcats can be as deadly to children as lions and tigers. Wild animals also pose a danger to human health and safety through disease and parasites.[5]

Baby Animals Grow Up

Baby animals can be irresistibly adorable—until the cuddly baby becomes bigger and stronger than the owner ever imagined. The **instinctive** behavior of the adult animal replaces the dependent behavior of the juvenile, resulting in biting, scratching, or displaying destructive behaviors without provocation[6] or warning. Such animals typically become too difficult to manage and are confined to small cages, passed from owner to owner, or disposed of in other ways. There are not enough reputable sanctuaries[7] or other facilities to properly care for unwanted wild animals. They can end up back in the exotic pet trade.[8] Some may be released into the wild where, if they survive, they can disrupt the local ecosystem.[9] C

instinctive
(ĭn-stĭngk'tĭv) *adj.* of or about the natural behaviors of a type of animal

Wild Animals Spread Disease

C **PERSUASIVE TECHNIQUES**
Reread lines 15–26. What **emotional appeals** are used in this section? Add this information to your chart.

The Centers for Disease Control and Prevention[10] discourages direct contact with wild animals for a simple reason: They can carry diseases that are dangerous to people, such as rabies, herpes B virus, and Salmonella. The herpes B virus commonly found among macaque monkeys can be fatal to humans. Thousands of people

---

3. **considerable expertise:** a great deal of knowledge and experience.
4. **specialized facilities:** places that are created and used for a specific function.
5. **parasites** (păr'ə-sīts'): animals that live on or in other animals and feed off of them.
6. **provocation** (prŏv'ə-kā'shən): something done to cause anger or irritation.
7. **reputable sanctuaries** (rĕp'yə-tə-bəl săngk'chōō-ĕr'ēz): trustworthy and reliable places that provide protected areas for animals.
8. **exotic pet trade:** the business of buying and selling wild, and sometimes rare, animals.
9. **ecosystem:** a community of living things, together with their environment.
10. **The Centers . . . Prevention:** One of 13 groups that are part of the U.S. Department of Health and Human Services, which works to protect the health and safety of Americans. Also referred to by its acronym: CDC.

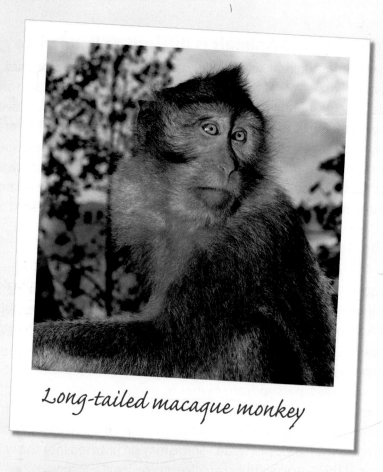

Long-tailed macaque monkey

D **PERSUASIVE TECHNIQUES**
Reread lines 27–38.
In your chart, note the persuasive techniques used in this section.

domesticate
(də-mĕs′tĭ-kāt′) *v.*
to tame a wild species of animal over generations

unsuitable
(ŭn-sōō′tə-bəl) *adj.* not appropriate or fitting

get Salmonella infections each year from contact with reptiles or amphibians, causing the CDC to recommend that these animals be kept out of homes with children under five. A recent outbreak of monkeypox[11] was set in motion when small mammals carrying the disease were imported for the pet trade and infected native prairie dogs, which were also sold as pets. **D**

Domestication Takes Thousands of Years

40 Wild animals are not <u>domesticated</u> simply by being captive-born or hand-raised. It's a different story with dogs and cats, who have been domesticated by selective breeding for desired traits over thousands of years. These special animal companions depend on humans for food, shelter, veterinary care, and affection. Wild animals, by nature, are self-sufficient and fare best without our interference. The instinctive behavior of these animals makes them <u>unsuitable</u> as pets.

---

11. **monkeypox:** a virus first found in monkeys, which is harmful and sometimes fatal to both humans and animals.

Capturing Wild Animals Threatens Their Survival

When wild-caught animals are kept as pets, their suffering may begin with capture—every year millions of birds and reptiles
50 suffer and die on the journey to the pet store. Even after purchase, their lives are likely to be filled with misery. If they survive, they may languish[12] in a cramped backyard cage or circle endlessly in a cat carrier or aquarium. More often, they become sick or die because their owners are unable to care for them properly. The global wild pet trade continues to threaten the existence of some species in their native habitats. **E**

Having any animal as a pet means being responsible for providing appropriate and humane care. Where wild animals are concerned, meeting this responsibility is usually impossible. 13
60 People, animals, and the environment suffer the consequences.

12. **languish** (lăng′gwĭsh): suffer in a state of neglect or indifference.

E PERSUASIVE TECHNIQUES
Reread lines 47–56. Record examples of the **loaded language** used in this section in your chart.

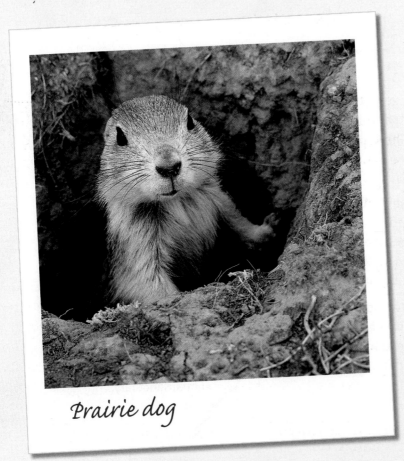

Prairie dog

Comprehension

1. **Recall** What three things are required in order to properly care for a wild animal?

2. **Clarify** Reread lines 15–26. What can happen to wild animals when their owners are no longer able to manage them?

3. **Clarify** Reread lines 39–46. Describe the process by which animals become domesticated.

Critical Analysis

4. **Examine Author's Purpose** Why do you think the Humane Society is trying to persuade people not to keep wild animals as pets? Explain your answer.

5. **Monitor Previewing** In what way did previewing the **text features** help you better understand the essay? Explain.

6. **Evaluate Persuasive Techniques** Review the chart that you filled in as you read. Then explain which of the three persuasive techniques used in the essay was the most effective and why.

7. **Draw Conclusions** According to the essay, there are distinct differences between wild animals and domesticated, or **tame,** animals. In a chart like

Wild	Tame

the one shown, note the unique traits of each category of animal. Then explain which traits make wild animals most unsuitable as pets.

Extension and Challenge

8. **Speaking and Listening** Imagine that you have been asked to film a public service announcement explaining the responsibilities and challenges that come with having an exotic pet. With a partner, write the script for your announcement. Then present it to the class.

9. **Inquiry and Research** Research to find out about wildlife sanctuaries, rescue centers, and other facilities in your area that aid in the survival and protection of animals. Choose one and summarize the work done there. Present your findings to the class.

An alligator at an exotic animal sanctuary

RESEARCH LINKS
For more on wildlife protection, visit the **Research Center** at ClassZone.com.

Vocabulary in Context

VOCABULARY PRACTICE

Show your understanding of the vocabulary words by deciding whether each statement is true or false.

1. An **instinctive** behavior is one that an animal learns as it grows.
2. You cannot **domesticate** an animal in a day.
3. Animals in **captivity** are never kept in cages.
4. If something meets a person's needs, it is considered **unsuitable.**

captivity

domesticate

instinctive

unsuitable

VOCABULARY IN WRITING

Using at least three vocabulary words, explain how a wild animal might feel about being kept as a pet. You might begin this way.

> **EXAMPLE SENTENCE**
>
> I really don't want to be kept in **captivity.**

VOCABULARY STRATEGY: CONTEXT CLUES

You can sometimes figure out the meaning of an unfamiliar word by finding **context clues** in the same sentence, or within the surrounding paragraph. This can be particularly helpful when you are reading nonfiction about an unfamiliar topic. For example, a clue to the meaning of the vocabulary word *domesticate* can be found in line 42: "selective breeding for desired traits." Using context clues, we can infer the meaning of *domesticate.*

PRACTICE Use context clues to write a definition of each boldfaced word.

1. Bulldozers **graded** the land so that it was smooth and level for the new road.
2. Ice will **liquefy** if the temperature is above 32 degrees.
3. Everyone got sick as the **contagion** was passed from one person to the next.
4. A **miscellany** of tools, including satellites, radar, and barometers, help people predict the weather.
5. Over the course of the season, the basketball player has had many free throw opportunities but has scored points only **sporadically.**

VOCABULARY PRACTICE
For more practice, go to the **Vocabulary Center** at **ClassZone.com.**

No Thought of Reward

Speech by Mawi Asgedom

What good comes from a GOOD DEED?

KEY IDEA You have probably heard the saying "It's better to give than to receive." Sometimes even the smallest **good deeds** can have an enormous effect on the lives of others—and on the life of the giver, as well. In the speech you are about to read, Mawi Asgedom shares what his father taught him about giving to others.

DISCUSS Is it sensible to do good deeds just for the sake of doing good, or is it reasonable to expect something good in return? Discuss this question with your classmates.

● ELEMENTS OF NONFICTION: AUTHOR'S MESSAGE

An **author's message** in a piece of nonfiction is like the theme of a story. It's the main point the writer wants to get across to his or her readers. Often an author's message is expressed by

- the title of a work
- a statement in the introduction or conclusion
- supporting details, such as the actions or comments of people in the selection

As you read "No Thought of Reward," look at these elements to identify the author's message.

● READING SKILL: ANALYZE PERSUASION

Persuasion is the art of leading others to accept a certain idea or take a specific action. To persuade someone, writers often start by building a logical, well-supported argument. Then, they might use persuasive devices to strengthen the argument.

In his persuasive speech, Mawi Asgedom supports his position with **examples** from personal experience. He also uses **rhetorical questions,** or questions that have an obvious answer. Asgedom uses these questions to suggest that anyone with common sense must agree with him. As you read the speech, record the personal examples and rhetorical questions he uses in a chart like the one shown.

Personal Examples	Rhetorical Questions
Tewolde supported a homeless man.	"Whom do you value: the person who takes from you or the person who gives to you?"

▲ VOCABULARY IN CONTEXT

Mawi Asgedom uses the boldfaced words to tell how he learned the value of good deeds. Restate each sentence using a different word or phrase for the boldfaced term.

1. Asgedom came to the United States as an **immigrant.**
2. Babay wanted his sons to **contribute** to their town.
3. At first, the boys didn't **appreciate** their father's advice.
4. They later admired his **dedication** to helping others.

Author Online

Inspiring Others
Motivational speaker Mawi Asgedom (mou'ē ŏz'gə'dŏm) travels the country inspiring American teenagers to become successful, caring people. He has produced several CDs and books, including *Of Beetles and Angels,* a memoir of his early life.

Mawi Asgedom
born 1976

A Young Refugee Asgedom arrived in the United States at the age of seven. His family had escaped from civil war in their native Ethiopia, and then suffered through three years in a refugee camp. In the United States, Asgedom had to overcome the challenges of poverty, a new language, and cruel teasing. Nevertheless, he worked hard in school and was accepted to Harvard University with a full scholarship.

Little Deeds of Kindness Asgedom is often moved by small acts of kindness. In his graduation speech at Harvard, Asgedom said, "Any one of us, however small and helpless we may feel, can spark unimagined changes.... Quite often, it will be the small things that . . . will have the most impact."

 MORE ABOUT THE AUTHOR
For more on Mawi Asgedom, visit the **Literature Center** at ClassZone.com.

NO THOUGHT OF REWARD

Mawi Asgedom

When we were kids, my brother Tewolde and I always looked forward to the weekend. Our father made us get up at 5:00 A.M. every weekday to exercise, so all we wanted to do Saturday morning was sleep late.

But our father, whom we called Babay, would have none of that. At the crack of dawn, his voice would echo all around our house.

"SELAMAWI, TEWOLDE, GET THE CLEANING BRUSHES," our father would order us. "IT'S TIME TO
10 REMOVE THE LEAVES FROM THE DRIVEWAY."

This wasn't just any driveway—the driveway that separated our house from our neighbors' must have been 100 feet long. Raking it took hours, and if that weren't bad enough, we barely even used it—it really belonged to our neighbors.

Tewolde and I would protest with every possible argument: "Come on, Babay! It's early in the morning. It's cold outside. Our family uses only a small part of the driveway. No one expects us to rake the whole thing! Why
20 can't our neighbors rake their own part?"

Our father's firm tone told us we had no choice.

"I KNOW YOU ARE MAD NOW, MY CHILDREN. BUT I AM TEACHING YOU HOW TO LIVE WELL WITH YOUR NEIGHBORS. YOU NEED TO LEARN, STARTING NOW, HOW TO GIVE TO OTHERS WITHOUT THOUGHT OF REWARD FOR YOURSELF." **A**

For a long time, we thought our father was crazy. Who in their right mind woke up early on a Saturday morning to
30 clear someone else's driveway for free?

But as we grew older, my brother Tewolde took our father's words to heart. Tewolde continued to rake the

A **AUTHOR'S MESSAGE**
Reread lines 22–27. Notice how the author repeats the idea stated in his title. Based on this repetition, what can you conclude is the author's message?

neighbors' leaves and also gave much more: He supported a homeless man who had no one else to turn to, gave to his classmates through kind words and actions, and even sent hundreds of dollars a year to support a child in South America—without telling anyone.

Years later, when Tewolde died, and again, when my father passed away, I was stunned by the number of folks
40 who came to honor their memories. The funeral-home directors said they had never witnessed such turnouts, not even for community leaders. **B**

How was it that my brother and father—poor, black **immigrants** in a wealthy, white town—had meant something special to so many folks? *It was because they had given so much without expecting anything in return.*

See, most of us walk around thinking: *How can I make myself happy? What can I get? How can I get other people to hook me up?*

50 But what if we instead thought: *What can I give to those around me? How can I* **contribute** *to my school, to my family, to my friends, to my neighbors?*

Wouldn't we mean something special to other people? Wouldn't other people want to give back to us, too?

Just think about your own life. Whom do you value: the person who takes from you, or the person who gives to you?

If you give your school everything you have—hard work, a great attitude, respect for others—won't your teachers and counselors[1] be more likely to **appreciate** you?
60 If you give your friends love, kindness, and support, won't they be more likely to give it back to you?

If you give your sports team effort, **dedication,** and a great attitude, won't your coaches more likely give you playing time? If you were the coach, wouldn't you want to give back to those who gave the most? I know I would. **C**

So if you want to mean something special to others, don't just focus on what you can get. Start by focusing on what you can give—without expecting any reward.

---

1. **counselors:** people responsible for giving students help and advice.

B ANALYZE PERSUASION
How do these **examples** of Tewolde's actions— and their results—help prove his father's point?

immigrant (ĭm′ĭ-grənt) *n.* a person who leaves one country to live in another

contribute (kən-trĭb′yo͞ot) *v.* to offer a gift or a service

appreciate (ə-prē′shē-āt′) *v.* to admire or value

dedication (dĕd′ĭ-kā′shən) *n.* commitment or devotion

C ANALYZE PERSUASION
Reread lines 53–65, recording any **rhetorical questions** in your chart. What is the effect of these questions?

Comprehension

1. **Recall** Why did Mawi Asgedom and his brother look forward to the weekend?

2. **Recall** Name two of Tewolde's good deeds.

3. **Clarify** In the author's opinion, why did large numbers of people go to Babay's and Tewolde's funerals?

Critical Analysis

4. **Examine Author's Message** Notice the various places in the speech where Asgedom repeats or restates his message. What reason might he have had for doing this?

5. **Identify Cause-and-Effect Relationships** Throughout his speech, Asgedom provides examples of cause-and-effect situations. Identify the cause-and-effect statements in the speech, and create a graphic organizer like the one shown for each example.

| Cause: Give your sports team effort. | → | Effect: Get more playing time. |

6. **Analyze Persuasive Devices** Look back at the chart you filled in as you read. Note the point at which Asgedom begins to include **rhetorical questions.** Do these questions strengthen or weaken his argument?

7. **Make Judgments** Reread the instructions Asgedom gives in lines 66–68 and compare them to Babay's original statement in lines 23–27. Notice that Asgedom's version begins with "if you want to mean something special to others." Why do you think he uses this approach?

8. **Evaluate Persuasion** Was Asgedom's speech successful in persuading you to accept his idea? Explain why or why not.

Extension and Challenge

9. **Big Question Activity** Now that you have read the speech, think back to the discussion activity on page 908. Make a list of at least five **good deeds** that you could do to improve the lives of others. Which of these activities do you think you would find most rewarding?

Vocabulary in Context

VOCABULARY PRACTICE

Show that you understand the boldfaced vocabulary words by answering the following questions.

1. Would an arriving **immigrant** be more likely to carry a small bag or a large suitcase?
2. Would you **contribute** to a charity by asking for help or by donating money?
3. Which shows more **dedication,** turning in homework or coming late to class?
4. If you **appreciate** classical music, do you like to listen to it?

VOCABULARY IN WRITING

What kinds of good deeds have people in your community done? Using at least two vocabulary words, write a paragraph about a neighbor, group, or organization that helps people in your area. You might start like this.

> **EXAMPLE SENTENCE**
>
> In my neighborhood, people always **contribute** to the local food pantry.

VOCABULARY STRATEGY: CONNOTATIONS

The **connotation** of a word includes all of the thoughts and feelings that people connect with that word. Connotations are especially important in persuasive writing because the writer wants to be sure the words match his or her message. For example, the vocabulary word *appreciate* has a positive connotation that suggests both enjoyment and respect.

PRACTICE Complete each sentence using a word from the parentheses. Choose the word with connotations that best fit within the positive or negative context of the sentence.

1. You should (accept, embrace) the challenge of trying to help others.
2. The customers (ate, gobbled) their sandwiches and left in a hurry.
3. Our backyard was empty except for brown grass and a (slender, spindly) tree.
4. A group of weary-looking people (strode, trudged) into the hotel.
5. The kitchen quickly filled with the (smell, aroma) of rich spices.

VOCABULARY PRACTICE
For more practice, go to the **Vocabulary Center** at ClassZone.com.

Persuasive Techniques in Commercials

TV Commercials on ⊙ *MediaSmart* DVD

How do you CAPTURE a customer?

KEY IDEA Sometimes, it seems a commercial was made just for you. Your eyes stay glued to the screen as you find out all the details about a product. When you react to an ad in this way, it's likely that you're part of what is called a **target audience.** In this lesson, you'll watch two commercials and study how advertisers direct their messages to very specific groups.

Background

Customer Awareness Each year, corporations spend billions of dollars to advertise their products. This money buys television or radio airtime or magazine, newspaper, or billboard advertising. They know that directing the right message to the right people increases the likelihood of success.

A **target audience** is a specific population or group of people an advertiser hopes to persuade. People who share certain likes or dislikes or who are the same age usually buy the same products. **Demographics** are the characteristics a group of people have in common. Advertisers study demographic data to research the interests, activities, and spending habits of a target audience. Then advertisers develop products, packaging, and ads that are designed to appeal to that audience.

Media Literacy: Target Audience

Demographic data help advertisers to determine when and where to advertise products. For example, it's likely the products that are advertised during your favorite TV programs appeal to people your own age. It's less likely that products advertised during the shows your parents watch are things you'd want to buy with your money.

To help you determine the target audience of any commercial, look at the elements the advertisers include and ask questions about their choices.

ELEMENTS OF COMMERCIALS	STRATEGIES FOR VIEWING
Images of People Advertisers want their target audience to respond favorably to any people who appear in the ad. The people might be "regular folks," actors, and even animated characters.	**Ask Yourself** • Who is shown in the ad? What ages are represented? What genders? • What group would relate to these people? • What are the people doing in the ad?
Visuals and Words In commercials, there are visual images that show the product and words that describe its features. The images and words are chosen to appeal to a specific group. You might also spot a **slogan,** a simple, carefully worded phrase intended to give a positive impression of the product. Slogans might be spoken near the end of a commercial.	**Ask Yourself** • How does the product appear in the ad? What shapes and colors are used? What words describe the product? • To whom would the visuals appeal? Are they designed for someone my age or someone older? • Are any special effects in use? What do they add to the emotional impact?
Sounds Sounds might be the **dialogue** or **narration** that give details about a product, or the **music** that sets a certain mood. Sound effects might be added to make the product appealing.	**Ask Yourself** • If there's **music** in the ad, what's the style? Who would the music appeal to the most? • What information is given in the **dialogue?** • Is there a **voice-over,** a voice of an unseen narrator? To whom is this voice speaking?

Viewing Guide for
TV Commercials

Prepare to watch the Apple iPod commercial first and then the one for Microsoft Windows XP. To analyze each commercial, look or listen closely for clues that reveal the target audience. In addition, look for techniques that make the ads appealing. Take notes. Use these questions to guide your analysis of the ads.

NOW VIEW

FIRST VIEWING: Comprehension

1. **Identify** What are the people doing in the iPod commercial?

2. **Clarify** Which ad doesn't describe the product through voice-over narration?

CLOSE VIEWING: Media Literacy

3. **Analyze Images** The iPod commercial shows outlines of people that appear against colorful backgrounds. While the people and backgrounds change, what remains the same?

4. **Analyze Target Audience** What audience do you think the makers of the iPod commercial are targeting? Explain.

5. **Draw Conclusions** The Windows XP commercial has the look and feel of a fairy tale. This might be a clue that the commercial is targeted to a young audience. Explain who else might be a target audience for this ad. Think about
   - what Windows XP allows young people to do
   - who might be inspired by the girl's qualities and abilities

6. **Compare Commercials** Both the iPod and Windows XP ads use music. How else are they alike or different? Compare and contrast the elements of these ads. Use your notes about the commercials to fill in a Venn diagram like this one.

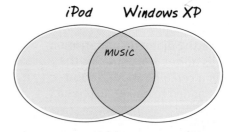

iPod   Windows XP
music

Write or Discuss

Analyze Persuasive Techniques The iPod and Windows XP commercials were made with a single goal in mind—to capture customers. You've analyzed two commercials to find clues about the target audience and the elements that advertisers design to be appealing. Now focus on one of the commercials. Describe a persuasive technique that impresses you, even though you've watched the ad a number of times. Think about

- any people that are presented in the commercial
- the use of any **graphics, special effects,** or **music**
- any image or fact that would stay in viewers' minds after watching the ad

Produce Your Own Media

Create a Storyboard Before shooting a commercial, advertisers plan it on a **storyboard.** This device presents images and brief descriptions of a product. In small groups, create a storyboard for a commercial. Begin by brainstorming the type of product and its most important features. Determine what segment of the population you'll target as your audience. Then map out the first six frames of the storyboard. Instead of planning an entire commercial, use a few frames to highlight the product and show who would use it.

HERE'S HOW Use these suggestions as you create the storyboard.

- Use each visual to cover one main point of your ad.
- Include a graphic image that shows the product and a **slogan** to make the product memorable.
- Catch viewers' eyes by showing images from different angles.
- Keep your descriptions brief. You can even replace them by writing out spoken dialogue (or voice-over narration).

MEDIA TOOLS
For help with creating a product storyboard, visit the **Media Center** at **ClassZone.com.**

Tech Tip
If available, use a camera to photograph the basic actions.

STUDENT MODEL

"When I want a deliciously healthy snack..."

"I dunk!"

"I dunk the easy way with Fruit Dunkers!"

"Fruit Dunkers is perfect for active kids like me."

"They combine yogurt with your favorite fruit!"

"Just dip and dunk!"

Persuasive Essay

What are some issues or problems that truly matter to you? A good way to get people to agree with your opinion is to put it in writing and back it up with solid evidence. To get started, study the **Writer's Road Map.**

WRITER'S ROAD MAP

Persuasive Essay

WRITING PROMPT 1

Writing for the Real World What makes you angry or concerned? Choose an issue that you feel strongly about. Write a persuasive essay in which you explain the issue and attempt to persuade your readers to agree with your point of view.

Issues to Explore

- searches of backpacks at school
- a ban on skateboards in certain areas
- restrictions on television viewing at home

WRITING PROMPT 2

Writing from Literature Sometimes you read something that makes you think about an issue in a new way. Using a selection in this unit as a springboard, write a persuasive essay about an issue that interests you.

Issues and Selections to Explore

- violence in video games ("The Violent Side of Video Games")
- humane treatment of animals ("Should Wild Animals Be Kept as Pets?")
- whether television commercials should be more closely regulated ("Persuasive Techniques in Commercials")

WRITING TOOLS
For prewriting, revision, and editing tools, visit the **Writing Center** at **ClassZone.com.**

KEY TRAITS

1. IDEAS

- Presents an opinion on a clearly identified issue in a **thesis statement**
- Uses **convincing details** to support the position
- Answers **opposing arguments**

2. ORGANIZATION

- **Introduces** the issue in a memorable way
- Uses **transitions** to show how ideas are related
- **Concludes** by summarizing the position and issuing a call to action or call to agreement

3. VOICE

- Reflects the **writer's strong belief** in his or her opinion

4. WORD CHOICE

- Uses **persuasive language** effectively

5. SENTENCE FLUENCY

- Varies the **lengths of sentences** to keep the reader interested

6. CONVENTIONS

- Uses **correct grammar, spelling, and punctuation**

Part 1: Analyze a Student Model

Jamie Barrett
East Salem Junior High School

Keep Your Dog on a Leash

Have you ever had that dream about a big animal chasing you, and you're so happy when you wake up and realize it didn't happen? Well, last month, I would have been happy to wake up and know I was dreaming, but I wasn't. While I was walking in the park, a dog that was
5　running free attacked me. I got away in time and wasn't hurt, but some people may not be so lucky. That experience really scared me, and now I strongly believe that a dog should not be allowed in a public place unless it is on a leash.

Dogs that are allowed to run free can be dangerous to people, to
10　other dogs, and even to themselves. If the owner doesn't control it, a dog could chase any person going by. Even if the dog doesn't bite or scratch, it could cause the person to fall and get hurt. The dog could also attack another dog and bite it or get bitten. Finally, it could run out into the street and get hit by a car or even cause a traffic accident. Having dogs
15　on leashes could prevent all this from happening.

This is a simple solution, but some people still believe that dogs should be allowed to run free. They say that tying something around a dog's neck and keeping it under control is cruel. It can make the dog try to run away or fight. If owners trained their dogs to walk quietly
20　and not run after anything, leashes wouldn't be necessary, they believe. To these people, the problem is the dog owners, not the dogs.

My response to that argument is that not all dog owners are good trainers, and not all dogs can be trained. Also, even trained dogs are not perfect all the time. All it takes is a dog breaking away from its owner
25　one time to cause a serious injury. It's much better to use a leash and be safe than to be sorry after the dog bites someone.

KEY TRAITS IN ACTION

Introduces the topic powerfully by referring to a dream that many people have had.

Clear **thesis statement** gives the writer's opinion.

Uses **convincing details** to explain why dogs should be kept on leashes.

The **transition** *but* introduces an opinion that doesn't agree with the writer's.

Answers **opposing arguments** in a way that shows the **writer's strong belief** in leash laws.

Nineteen states and many cities already have leash laws. Some of these laws don't allow unleashed dogs anywhere. Others apply only to certain areas, such as city parks, or to certain kinds of dogs. Making
30 laws is only the beginning, though. Somebody has to enforce them. Many leash laws say that dog owners who don't obey them will be fined or even put in jail. Unfortunately, people don't usually report unleashed dogs until someone is hurt.

Here's what you can do. First, find out about your community's
35 laws. If leash laws exist where you are, help enforce them by reporting unleashed dogs to the local animal control office. If no law exists, work to get one passed. That way, being chased by unleashed dogs may one day be only a bad dream.

Different **sentence lengths** keep the essay from becoming choppy or boring.

Concludes with a call to action using **persuasive language,** including the active verbs *enforce* and *work*.

Creates a feeling of completion by reminding readers of the introduction.

2

Part 2: Apply the Writing Process

PREWRITING

| What Should I Do? | What Does It Look Like? |

1. Analyze the prompt.
Choose one of the prompts on page 918 and read it at least twice. <u>Underline</u> the type of writing you will be doing. (Circle) other important information, such as your purpose and audience. Make notes about any thoughts that come to mind.

▶ **WRITING PROMPT** What makes you angry or concerned? Choose (an issue that you feel strongly about.) Write a <u>persuasive essay</u> in which you (explain the issue) and attempt to (persuade your readers) to agree with your point of view.

> *My readers will be my teacher and classmates. I should think of topics that would interest them and that are important to me.*

2. Brainstorm issues that you care about.
Make a chart or a list of worthwhile issues. Include questions or comments about each issue. If you chose Prompt 2, you should also include the names of selections from this unit. Put a ⬚box⬚ around the topic that you want to write about.

> **TIP** Be sure to choose an issue that has two sides. You can't be persuasive if everyone already agrees with you.

▶

Issue	Comments
too many chores at home	interesting to teacher and classmates?
leash laws for dogs	really important and interesting
violence	not a good topic because nobody favors violence— also too broad for a short essay

3. Draft your thesis.
Write a sentence explaining the main point you want to make in your essay. It doesn't need to be perfect—you can rework it as you continue writing.

▶ **Working thesis statement**
Dogs should always be on a leash when they are out in public.

4. Gather support.
Having a strong opinion on an issue isn't enough. What facts, statistics, expert opinions, or reasons explain your viewpoint on this issue?

▶ **Dangers of unleashed dogs**
- *to people: bites, scratches, falls*
- *to other dogs: fights*
- *to themselves: fights, getting hit by a car*

What Should I Do?	What Does It Look Like?

1. Organize your ideas.
Here are two ways to present your ideas:

Pattern 1: Explain all the reasons to support your point of view. Then explain all the reasons to oppose your point of view. This is the pattern the writer of the model used.

Pattern 2: Discuss both sides of each point or reason as you present it.

PATTERN 1

Reasons for leashes
- *protect people*
- *protect dogs*

Reasons against leashes
- *owners should train their dogs*
- *make dogs want to fight or run*

PATTERN 2

Protect people
- *for: prevent attacks*
- *against: owners should train their dogs*

Protect dogs
- *for: prevent fights*
- *against: make dogs want to fight or run*

2. Choose persuasive words.
State your opinions confidently. Use words that appeal to your audience's emotions. The writer of the student model used *attacked, enforce, serious, safe,* and many others. Also, include a few **imperative sentences**—ones that tell your audience what to do.

See page 886: The Power of Persuasion

While I was walking in the park, a dog that was running free attacked me.

Find out about your community's laws. If leash laws exist where you are, help enforce them by reporting unleashed dogs to the local animal control office.

3. Include details to support your ideas.
Give facts, statistics, or the opinions of experts to back up your statements. Be sure to explain how each detail supports your opinion.

Dogs that are allowed to run free can be dangerous. —Key idea

If the owner doesn't control it, a dog could chase any person going by. —Support

4. Explain why you disagree with each opposing argument.
Clearly show readers why they should agree with you and not with someone on the other side of the issue.

Opposing argument: Leash laws aren't necessary if owners train their dogs properly.

Not all dog owners are good trainers, and not all dogs can be trained.

REVISING AND EDITING

| *What Should I Do?* | *What Does It Look Like?* |

1. Correct overgeneralizations.
- Look for **overgeneralizations**—statements that are too broad. They often include words like *everybody, everywhere, always, none, nobody,* or *never.*
- Delete overgeneralizations or revise them to include words like *many, some,* and *often.*

See page 924: Mistakes in Logic

▶ ~~Dogs are always dangerous.~~
Even trained dogs are not perfect all the time.

~~There are leash laws everywhere.~~
Nineteen states and many cities already have leash laws.

2. Fully explain your supporting details.
- Have a peer reader (circle) the details you used to support each reason.
- If there aren't many circles, or if the circled information doesn't make sense, add details or explain your ideas more clearly.

See page 924: Ask a Peer Reader

▶ Some people still believe that dogs should be allowed to run free. (They say that tying something around a dog's neck and keeping it under control is cruel.) It can make the dog try to run away or fight. If owners trained their dogs to walk quietly and not run after anything, leashes wouldn't be necessary, they believe. To these people, the problem is the dog owners, not the dogs.

3. Replace vague language.
- Underline vague words, such as *kind of, really, something, things, stuff, nice,* and *bad.*
- Replace these words with terms that give readers precise, persuasive information.

▶ Even if the dog doesn't bite or scratch, it could ~~do something really bad to the person.~~ cause the person to fall and get hurt.

4. Finish strongly and clearly.
- Does your conclusion summarize your opinion? Does it tell readers what to do?
- If not, add a summary and a call to action. (If you prefer, you can add a call to agreement. That's when you tell your reader what to think instead of what to do.)

▶ ~~In conclusion, that's why leash laws are important.~~
Here's what you can do. First, find out about your community's laws. If leash laws exist where you are, help enforce them by reporting unleashed dogs to the local animal control office. If no law exists, work to get one passed. That way, being chased by unleashed dogs may one day be only a bad dream.

Preparing to Publish

Persuasive Essay

Apply the Rubric

A strong persuasive essay . . .

- ☑ begins with an attention-getting introduction
- ☑ gives the writer's opinion in a thesis statement
- ☑ supports the opinion with convincing details
- ☑ states and answers opposing arguments
- ☑ expresses the writer's strong beliefs
- ☑ uses precise, persuasive language
- ☑ shows how ideas are related by using appropriate transitions
- ☑ varies sentence lengths
- ☑ concludes with a summary and either a call to action or a call to agreement

Ask a Peer Reader

- Why is this issue so important to me?
- Did I present supporting evidence clearly? If not, where could I make improvements?
- How can I strengthen my conclusion?

Mistakes in Logic

- **Circular reasoning**—supporting a statement by just repeating it in different words ("Dogs should be on leashes because controlling pets is important.")
- **False cause**—thinking that one event causes another just because it happens first ("I fed my dog a different brand of dog food and he started to behave better.")
- **Either/or fallacy**—a statement that suggests there are only two choices available in a situation ("Either leash laws are passed everywhere, or dogs will attack children.")

Check Your Grammar

Make sure pronouns agree with their antecedents. They must agree both in person (first, second, or third) and in number (singular or plural).

> I strongly believe that a dog shouldn't be allowed in a public place unless ~~they are~~ *it is* on a leash.

See page R52: Agreement with Antecedent

Writing Online

PUBLISHING OPTIONS
For publishing options, visit the **Writing Center** at ClassZone.com.

ASSESSMENT PREPARATION
For writing and grammar assessment practice, go to the **Assessment Center** at ClassZone.com.

Delivering a Persuasive Speech

Make your written words even more persuasive by presenting your essay as a speech.

Planning the Speech

1. **Use your essay to create a script.** Underline or highlight the sentences you want to include. You may want to make your sentences shorter and your language less formal.

2. **Decide how you want to begin.** You can use the introduction from your essay or think of another way to capture listeners' attention. The writer of the student model began her speech with a brief video clip of a barking, growling dog.

3. **Create a visual aid.** Write the points you want to make on a poster, transparencies for an overhead projector, or a flip chart. If you prefer, you can create a power presentation instead. That's a series of slides that you create on a computer and project on a screen. Whatever

type of visual you decide to use, be sure to include details to support each point. Make the text large enough to be read at the back of the room.

4. **Choose words that are strong and specific.** Make sure it's clear what your opinion is, how you want your listeners to feel, and what you want them to do.

Delivering the Speech

1. **Follow the guidelines for delivering a speech.** Read the guidelines on pages R76–R78 of the **Speaking and Listening Handbook.** Practice alone or in front of your parents or friends before giving your speech.

2. **Refer to your visuals.** Place your visuals so that all audience members can see them. You might want to point to the specific information you are discussing as you speak.

Reading Comprehension

DIRECTIONS *Read these selections and answer the questions that follow.*

Fighting Is Never a Good Solution

Sylvia Cassedy

A fight broke out on the playground yesterday because of a torn jacket. Some members of Miss Goldstein's class took José's goose-down jacket without his permission and used it for second base. When Dolores scored a double, the jacket tore and most of its feathers spilled out.

At first there was just a lot of arguing. Pretty soon, though, kids started hitting and punching one another. By the time the fight was over, two kids were injured, David with a bent finger and Alison with a bloody nose. Agnes had to be sent home because she has asthma and is allergic to feathers.

10   When a fight breaks out, nobody gains. José still has no jacket, Dolores's double was never counted, a lot of kids who used to be friends are now enemies, and the whole class has been punished by having to give up a week of recess.

We think that the damage of a fight like this is greater than a torn coat or a week spent indoors. Lots of times countries go to war with each other because their leaders don't know how to settle arguments peacefully. Ten years from now the people in this class will be grown up. If they don't learn now how to settle disagreements without hitting each other over the head, what will they be like when they are old enough to use guns and
20 drop bombs?

Where Do You Stand?

from **The Kids' Guide to Working Out Conflicts**

Naomi Drew

You may have heard teachers or other kids talk about *conflict resolution.* This is another term for solving or resolving conflicts. When it comes to conflict resolution, where do you stand right now? What are you doing to be a conflict solver? Take this quick self-test to find out. Respond yes or no to each statement:

When I have a conflict . . .
✓ I try to calm down before I react.
✓ I do my best to avoid physical fighting.
✓ I believe I have more to gain by working things out.
10 ✓ I listen to what the other person has to say.
✓ I try to see how I'm responsible instead of just blaming the other person.
✓ I look for ways to solve the problem rather than win the argument.
✓ I'm willing to compromise.
✓ I avoid using put-downs.
✓ I speak my truth, but I do it respectfully.
✓ I try to put myself in the other person's place instead of only focusing on my own stuff.

How many times did you answer yes?
• **Five or more?** If so, you're already a conflict solver a good part of the
20 time. Keep at it! Also know that you'll become an even better conflict solver by working to turn your "no" answers into "yeses."
• **Fewer than five?** You're not there yet . . . but you can get there. Choose one new idea to try and do it until it starts to come more easily. Then choose another. Also continue doing whatever you said yes to.
• **If you answered yes to the third statement,** you've already made an important start. Being willing to work out conflicts is the first big step on the road to becoming a conflict solver.

Comprehension

DIRECTIONS *Answer these questions about "Fighting Is Never a Good Solution."*

1. Which statement from the article identifies the author's claim?

   A "Fighting Is Never a Good Solution" (the title)

   B "When Dolores scored a double, the jacket tore and most of its feathers spilled out." (lines 3–4)

   C "At first there was just a lot of arguing." (line 5)

   D "Ten years from now the people in this class will be grown up." (lines 16–17)

2. The support the author gives in lines 5–9 can best be described as

   A an emotional description

   B a factual description

   C an irrelevant list

   D a few overgeneralizations

3. The statement in line 10 that "When a fight breaks out, nobody gains" is

   A the author's position in the argument

   B an example of irrelevant support

   C a reason that supports the claim

   D a counterargument

4. Which phrase is an overgeneralization that could weaken the author's argument?

   A "most of its feathers" (line 4)

   B "At first" (line 5)

   C "We think" (line 14)

   D "Lots of times" (line 15)

5. Which statement is a strongly worded opinion that supports the claim?

   A "A fight broke out on the playground yesterday because of a torn jacket."

   B "At first there was just a lot of arguing."

   C "Agnes had to be sent home because she has asthma and is allergic to feathers."

   D "We think that the damage of a fight like this is greater than a torn coat or a week spent indoors."

6. By writing in lines 12–13 that "the whole class has been punished by having to give up a week of recess," the author appeals to the reader's sense of

   A kindness   C fairness

   B worry   D curiosity

7. The persuasive technique used in lines 17–20 can best be characterized as

   A an appeal to expert authorities

   B an emotional appeal to fear

   C words with positive connotations

   D an irrelevant example

8. Which statement best summarizes the argument in this article?

   A Adults' arguments end up in physical fights more often than children's do.

   B After José's jacket was used for second base, a fight broke out on the playground.

   C Physical fighting can make an argument even worse.

   D It isn't worthwhile to fight because you might get punished.

DIRECTIONS *Answer these questions about "Where Do You Stand?"*

9. The title "Where Do You Stand?" serves to

   A reveal information about the topic

   B introduce the topic in a challenging way

   C summarize the main idea of the article

   D argue a point with reasons and evidence

10. The subheading in line 6, "When I have a conflict . . . ," introduces a

   A caption for a photograph

   B checklist of items

   C sidebar of statements

   D summary of the article

11. Which text feature helps you find your score?

   A captions   C drawings

   B bullets   D checklists

12. Which statement best summarizes the article?

   A To find out if you are good at resolving conflicts, have your teacher give you a test.

   B Good conflict solvers need to tell the truth about an argument.

   C You can work on your behavior to become a better conflict solver.

   D Students who answered "yes" fewer than five times on the self-test can memorize the list of suggestions in the article.

DIRECTIONS *Answer this question about both selections.*

13. Which statement supports the main idea of both selections?

   A It is better to hide my angry feelings when there is a conflict.

   B My feelings about a conflict are more important than anyone else's feelings.

   C How I act when I am angry can make a situation better or worse.

   D It is easy to get into a fight, but I can run away if it gets bad.

Written Response

SHORT RESPONSE *Write two or three sentences to answer this question.*

14. Identify one persuasive technique used in "Fighting Is Never a Good Solution." Give line references to support your answer.

EXTENDED RESPONSE *Write a short paragraph to answer this question.*

15. Reread the checklist in the self-test from "Where Do You Stand?" Summarize the advice on how to be a good conflict solver.

GO ON

Vocabulary

DIRECTIONS *Use context clues to answer the following questions about words in "Fighting Is Never a Good Solution."*

1. Which nearby word gives the best clue to the meaning of *double* as it is used in line 4?

   A scored   **C** tore

   B jacket   **D** spilled

2. What is the meaning of the word *injured* as it is used in line 7?

   A upset   **C** harmed

   B unhappy   **D** defeated

3. The word *allergic* in line 8 means having

   A an illness with flu-like symptoms that is passed from person to person through the air

   B a condition in which a rash or sickness appears after one comes into contact with something that doesn't affect most people

   C a strong dislike of anything that is annoying or unpleasant to taste

   D an interest in the makeup of a naturally occurring material or substance

4. What is the meaning of the word *damage* as it is used in line 14?

   A something that helps

   B possible cause

   C money paid

   D bad result

DIRECTIONS *Use the prefixes and suffixes in the chart to help you answer the following questions about words in both selections.*

Prefix	Meaning
com-	together or with
dis-	not; absence of
in-	into; within
re-	again; in return

Suffix	Meaning
-ment	the act or result of
-ion	the act or condition of
-ful	full of
-ible	capable of; tending to

5. Which word means "the result of not having the same opinion"?

   A recess   **C** instead

   B statement   **D** disagreement

6. Which word means "to settle differences together by having each side give up something"?

   A argument   **C** permission

   B compromise **D** already

7. Which word means "to do or say something in return"?

   A react   **C** responsible

   B resolution **D** respectfully

Writing & Grammar

DIRECTIONS *Use your knowledge of the rules of punctuation and capitalization to answer the following questions.*

1. Choose the correct way to punctuate and capitalize the following short story title:

> trapped in a comic book

    A "Trapped In A Comic Book "
    B *Trapped in A Comic Book*
    C "Trapped in a Comic Book"
    D *Trapped in a comic Book*

2. Choose the correct way to punctuate and capitalize the following book title:

> where the sidewalk ends

    A *Where The Sidewalk Ends*
    B "Where the sidewalk Ends"
    C "Where The Sidewalk ends"
    D *Where the Sidewalk Ends*

3. Choose the correct way to punctuate and capitalize the following poem title.

> hector the collector

    A "Hector the collector"
    B *Hector the Collector*
    C *Hector The Collector*
    D "Hector the Collector"

4. Choose the correct way to punctuate and capitalize the following magazine article title.

> ways we can protect the environment

    A *Ways we can protect the Environment*
    B "Ways We Can Protect the Environment"
    C *Ways We Can Protect The Environment*
    D "Ways we can protect the environment"

5. Choose the correct way to punctuate and capitalize the following book title.

> the tomb robbers

    A "The tomb robbers"
    B *The tomb Robbers*
    C *The Tomb Robbers*
    D "the Tomb Robbers"

6. Choose the correct way to punctuate and capitalize the following short story title.

> girl at the window

    A *Girl At the Window*
    B "Girl at the Window"
    C *Girl at the Window*
    D "Girl At The Window"

7. Choose the correct way to punctuate and capitalize the following magazine article title.

> meltdown in the alps

    A *Meltdown In The Alps*
    B "Meltdown In the Alps"
    C *Meltdown in the Alps*
    D "Meltdown in the Alps"

Ideas for Independent Reading

Which questions from Unit 8 made an impression on you?
Continue exploring with these books.

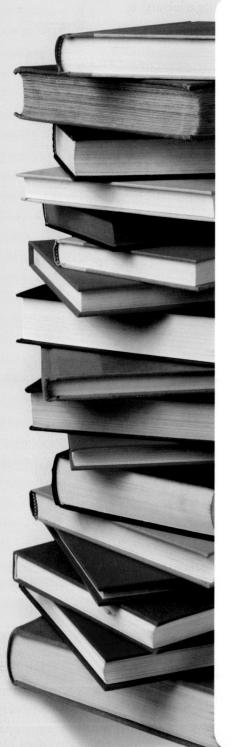

How smart are animals?

The Chimpanzees I Love
by Jane Goodall

Goodall has studied one community of chimpanzees in Tanzania for over 40 years. She has seen them use sticks as tools and watched as they pass on skills like hunting and child-rearing from one generation to the next.

Exploding Ants: Amazing Facts About How Animals Adapt
by Joanne Settel, PhD.

Why does a cuckoo chick push the other babies out of the nest? If an owl doesn't chew, how does it eat? Animals find all kinds of ways to survive in various circumstances.

Wild Horses I Have Known
by Hope Ryden

All horses were wild before people caught and tamed them. About 400 years ago, some horses in the United States got loose and have been roaming free ever since. How have they survived?

How can we uncover the past?

Buttons, Bones, and the Organ-Grinder's Monkey: Tales of Historical Archaeology
by Meg Greene

Some people search for clues about the past in books. Others look in old trash pits or ancient cellars to find evidence of how people really lived.

Curse of the Pharaohs
by Zahi Hawass

The mummy's curse warns that anyone who disturbs the pharaohs' tombs will be haunted by their spirits. Egyptian archeologist Zahi Hawass says he doesn't believe that, but strange things have happened to him on the job.

Secrets from the Rocks
by Albert Marrin

Roy Chapman Andrews led the first archaeological expedition into Mongolia in 1922. His team found dinosaur eggs and evidence of the first mammal, along with a large deposit of other fossils.

What's the full news story?

Phineas Gage
by John Fleischman

In 1848, an iron rod shot straight through Phineas Gage's brain. He survived, but his family said he wasn't the same man afterward. Doctors studied Phineas to find out more about how the human brain works.

Remember: The Journey to School Integration
by Toni Morrison

Imagine having to walk through an angry mob just to go to school. This is what life was like for thousands of children when the Supreme Court ended segregation in 1954.

Where the Action Was
by Penny Colman

During World War II, women weren't allowed near combat. However, 127 brave female journalists managed to get around the rules and report on some of the most important events during the war.

The Power of Research

RESEARCH WORKSHOPS

- Research Strategies
- Writing Research Reports

What is RESEARCH?

Research is using sources to find answers. You do research in your everyday life. For example, if you want to know what the weather will be like tomorrow, you can turn on the television or go online. In this unit, you will learn to find and use sources of information to answer more complex and challenging questions.

ACTIVITY Work with a partner to list some questions that you often answer by doing research, either at home or at school. Explain where you get the answers.

What I Research	Where I Find Answers

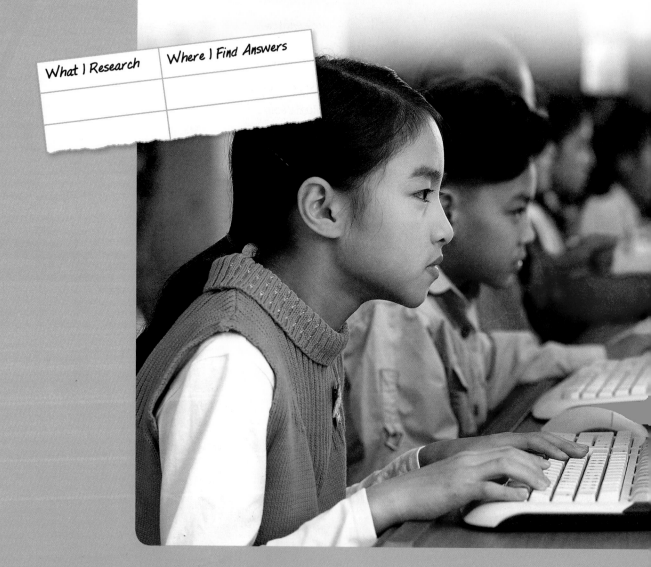

Preview Unit Goals

DEVELOPING RESEARCH SKILLS	• Plan research • Develop research questions • Use library and media center resources • Evaluate information and sources, including nonfiction books, periodicals, and Web sites • Collect your own data
WRITING	• Write a research report • Narrow your research topic • Locate and evaluate sources • Take notes • Make source cards • Summarize and paraphrase • Quote directly and avoid plagiarism • Document sources • Prepare a Works Cited list • Format your paper
SPEAKING, LISTENING, AND VIEWING	• Create a multimedia report
ACADEMIC VOCABULARY	• research topic • plagiarism • research report • documentation • resources • Works Cited • sources • multimedia report • source cards

How do I answer my QUESTIONS?

KEY IDEA Questions don't always have easy answers. Sometimes you will **research** a topic and find that you have even more questions about it than when you started. This unit explains where to look for answers and how to tell which sources are reliable.

QUICKWRITE You might do research for a school assignment or just to satisfy your own curiosity. In this unit, you will follow a student who is curious about coyotes because her uncle keeps seeing them in his suburban backyard. She also saw a news program about coyotes in urban and suburban areas. If you were this student, what questions would you ask? Create a cluster diagram like this one but with your own questions about coyotes.

Beginning the Research Process

Good planning makes research easier and faster. Take a few minutes to think about what you want to accomplish before you dive in.

DECIDE ON A GOAL

What do you want to find out? Begin by writing down some goals—general and specific ones. Here's how one student listed her goals.

> **General goal:** I want to learn more about coyotes.
>
> **Questions:**
>
> - **Why do coyotes interest me?** It seems weird that they would live near people.
> - **What do I want to learn about them?** I wonder if lots of them live in cities and suburbs.
>
> **Specific goal:** I want to learn more about how many coyotes live in cities and suburbs, and I want to know why they live there.

FIND SOME GENERAL INFORMATION

Now that you have a specific goal in mind, it's time to start your search. Try some or all of these ideas.

- **Talk with people.** Find someone who knows about your topic. Ask the person what interests him or her about it.
- **Try the Internet.** Type the name of your topic into a search engine. Visit one or two Web sites to get an overview.
- **Go to the library.** Read an encyclopedia article or a magazine article on your topic, or skim a nonfiction book on the subject.
- **Talk to a librarian.** Get more suggestions for books, magazines, or online sources. Use these sources to list even more ideas.

NARROW YOUR TOPIC

Smaller, more specific topics are easier to research than big ones. This chart shows how one student narrowed her topic as she learned more about it.

Specific Topic	More Specific	Even More Specific
coyotes that live in cities or suburbs	why coyotes have moved to my suburb	why coyotes have moved to my suburb and what people are doing about it

RESEARCH TOOLS
For research tools and strategies, visit the **Research Center** at **ClassZone.com.**

CREATE RESEARCH QUESTIONS

The next step is to guide your research by writing some research questions. Here are some questions on the topic of coyotes in the suburbs. Notice that most can't be answered with just a yes or a no.

> • Where do coyotes normally live? What is their habitat?
>
> • What do coyotes eat? What is their prey?
>
> • Are more coyotes living in cities or suburbs now? Are they dangerous to people or pets?

After you write your research questions, highlight important words or phrases in them. You will type these **keywords** into library catalogs, databases, and search engines.

PREPARE TO TAKE NOTES

If you stay organized as you research, you will be able to get more done in less time. Taking notes is a great way to stay organized. If you are doing research as part of a class assignment, using note cards can be helpful. You will learn more about note cards on page 961.

For other types of research, consider using different note-taking tools, such as lists or charts. Ask yourself what kinds of information you are looking for and which format would be best for that information. The student who was interested in coyotes made a chart to keep track of her sources.

Source of Information on Coyotes	Notes About Source
my uncle	He has seen coyotes in his backyard twice this spring.
newspaper article	Last week's <u>Montgomery Reporter</u> had an article about coyote sightings.
radio news story	This morning my mom heard a news reporter talking about coyotes, deer, and other wild animals in the suburbs.
the Web	I tried a search engine and got millions of results. There's lots of information about coyotes, but how can I find exactly what I need?

Many researchers begin their searches online. The next pages will show you how to use the Internet effectively.

Using the Internet

The World Wide Web is part of the **Internet,** a huge system of linked computers. The Web includes hundreds of millions of Web sites and billions of Web pages.

EXPLORE THE WEB

Begin by clicking on your search engine or browser. **Search engines** are Web sites that organize information based on keywords, titles, and other content. You can choose from many search engines. Because search engines select and organize information differently, no two will give you exactly the same results.

USE KEYWORDS AND ADVANCED SEARCHES

Type some of your keywords into a search engine. The best results turn up when you combine specific keywords.

Different search engines allow you to modify your search in different ways. Click on your search engine's "Advanced Search" or "Search Tips" link to find out more. Here are some examples of search modifiers:

- Try putting a phrase in quotation marks. A search for *"coyote habitat"* finds only pages that mention both terms, in that order, right next to each other.

- Some search engines allow you to use the terms AND, NOT, and OR. For example, a search for *coyote AND suburbs* results in a list of Web pages that contain both terms, but not necessarily right next to each other.

- Other search engines let you put a plus sign next to words or phrases that you want included and a minus sign next to words and phrases that you don't want included. If a search for *coyote* results in many Web pages about a movie with that word in the title, you may want to modify your search to *+coyote -movie*.

Notice how the more specific terms below bring more specific results.

YOU TYPE IN...	YOU GET...	THIS IS...
coyote	17,600,000 results	much too broad, so you add another keyword
+coyote +habitat	451,000 results	still too broad, so you try again
"coyotes in the suburbs"	294 results	best, because the results are specific to the topic

ACADEMIC VOCABULARY FOR THE INTERNET

You will use these terms when discussing online research:

- keyword
- Web site
- Web page
- search engine
- Web address
- home page
- hyperlink
- icon

TIP The research questions that you wrote will help you think of keywords.

EXAMINE SEARCH ENGINE RESULTS

One search can bring up many pages of results. Follow these guidelines for examining the first page of results:

1. Don't just click on the first result. It may not be the most useful one for you.

2. Read the description for each result, including the Web address. Many Web addresses include the abbreviations *.com* or *.net.* Sites with these addresses are usually created by individuals or by companies that are trying to sell products. Sites created by the government or by nonprofit organizations generally have *.gov* or *.org* in their addresses.

3. If a description matches your goal or keywords, click on it. If not, go to the next result or to the next page of results. You can also think of ways to improve your search terms and try again.

4. Don't print a Web page until you have skimmed the text and looked at the images. Printing dozens of Web sites may make you feel that you have done lots of research. However, if the sites you print are off-topic or repeat the same information many times over, all you are doing is wasting paper.

TIP Because most *.gov* and *.org* sites are the work of large groups and are frequently reviewed, they are often more reliable than other sites. Be aware, however, that organizations like political parties also have *.org* addresses.

TRY IT OUT! *Choose Search Engine Results*

These are the first results that showed up in an online search.

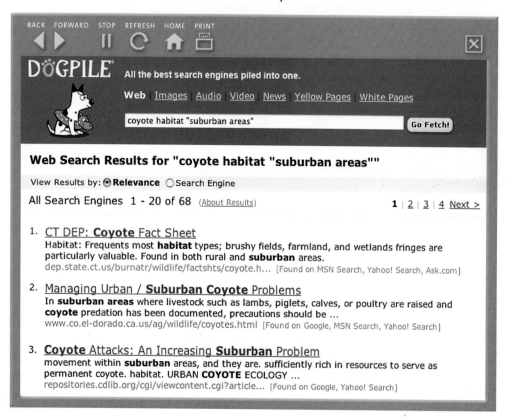

Close Read

1. Which terms did the searcher use? How do you know?

2. Is this search too broad, too narrow, or just right? Give reasons for your answer.

3. Which of these results would you click on first? Why?

NAVIGATE A WEB SITE

To get the most from your search results, you need to know the features that Web pages have.

- **Home page**—A **home page** is the main page or organizing page of a Web site. It welcomes you to the site, gives general information, and helps you get where you want to go.

- **Menus and Hyperlinks**—**Menus** show the main categories of information on the site. Click on a menu item to find out more about that category. Sometimes menu items are **hyperlinks,** which are underlined words, terms, or Web addresses. Click on hyperlinks (sometimes just called links) to get to information on another page or on a different site.

- **Icons**—Click on **icons,** which are small pictures or symbols, to find information.

- **Sponsor and Credits**—A **sponsor** is a company, organization, or individual that pays for and owns the site. **Credits** tell where the information on a Web site came from. Sometimes credits tell who wrote and designed the site. They might also tell when the site was last updated.

TRY IT OUT! *Examine a Web Site*

Is this a useful Web site for someone who wants to learn about coyotes?

Close Read

1. Where are the icons on this page?

2. Which icon would you click to find out where in the world coyotes live?

3. Who created this site, and when was it last updated? Why is that information important?

A Home page   **B** Menus   **C** Icons   **D** Sponsor and Credits

These terms will come
in handy as you use the
library or media center:

- fiction
- nonfiction
- reference work
- library catalog
- primary source
- secondary source
- table of contents
- bibliography
- glossary
- index

Using the Library or Media Center

The Internet can be an excellent source of information. However, don't forget about the resources available at your local public library or at your school's media center. Most libraries have different sections for adults, young adults, and children. Some libraries also have special sections, such as areas devoted to business or to family history. Computer terminals throughout the library can help you find information within the library, use online sources such as databases and electronic bulletin boards, send e-mails, and write reports.

LIBRARY AND MEDIA CENTER RESOURCES

BOOKS

Fiction—Novels and short stories are fiction. Works of fiction come from writers' imaginations, but they may be based on real people, places, and events.

Nonfiction—Biographies, diaries, newspaper and magazine articles, cookbooks, speeches, history books, science books, procedural manuals, and how-to books are nonfiction. They tell about real people, places, events, and ideas.

REFERENCE

Reference desk—You can ask for help with your research here.

Reference works—This section of the library contains encyclopedias, dictionaries, atlases, almanacs, collections of biographical articles, and other works that you can use only in the library.

NEWSPAPERS AND PERIODICALS

Newspapers and magazines—Your library or media center has current issues and may also have older copies in print or on microfilm.

AUDIO AND VIDEO RESOURCES

DVDs—Documentaries or instructional films may provide helpful information.

Audio—You may find music, books, plays, poems, or speeches recorded on CDs.

E-RESOURCES

Electronic collections—Ask a librarian about databases, CD-ROMs, e-books, e-audiobooks, podcasts, and MP3s.

USE THE LIBRARY CATALOG

The **library catalog** lists the library's or library network's holdings. The reference librarian can also show you the best and fastest ways to search it.

You can search a library catalog in a variety of ways.

- **Author**—Usually, you type the author's last name first, like this: *Soto, Gary*. If you don't get results, try the first name first: *Gary Soto*. Make sure you spell both names correctly.

- **Title**—You may be able to do a successful title search even if you don't know the full title of the book or other resource you are searching for. Try typing in a partial title and see what the results are.

- **Keyword (sometimes called Subject)**—As you learned on page 939, you should try to make your keywords very specific. You may need to try a variety of words to find the information you need. For example, if the keywords *coyote habitat* bring you few useful results, try *coyote migration* or *coyote control*. Keep trying until you find the right results.

TRY IT OUT! *Search a Library Catalog*

To get to the catalog page below, a student searched for the keywords *coyote control*.

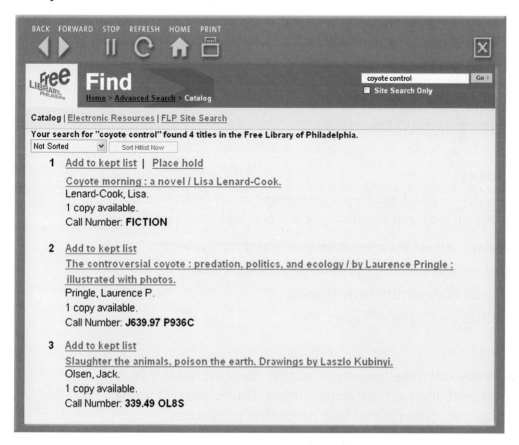

Close Read

1. Is the first choice listed a useful one for someone who wants to learn about coyotes in the suburbs? Explain.

2. Which of the three books shown here would be most useful to someone looking for information on coyote habitats? Why?

3. How could the user find out more about each of these books?

Selecting Sources

The millions of choices on the Internet and at the library can be confusing. Learning more about the different types of nonfiction resources can help.

PRIMARY AND SECONDARY SOURCES

Every nonfiction work is either a primary source or a secondary source.

PRIMARY SOURCES	SECONDARY SOURCES
WHAT THEY ARE	**WHAT THEY ARE**
firsthand accounts created by people who took part in or witnessed events	**records of events created by people who were not directly involved in or present at the events**
Examples: letters, e-mails, diaries, journals, speeches, autobiographies, advertisements, interviews, first-person newspaper and magazine articles, public documents such as birth certificates	*Examples:* textbooks, reference works, biographies, third-person newspaper and magazine articles, documentaries
▼	▼
WHEN TO USE THEM	**WHEN TO USE THEM**
• to learn about witnesses' and participants' thoughts, feelings, and reactions • to gather important and interesting details of a time period *Remember, however, that primary sources often give just one person's limited view.*	• for an overview of a topic based on many sources • to gain a broad understanding of a topic over time *Remember, however, that any source can contain errors or be one-sided.*

REFERENCE WORKS

To get an overview of your topic, try using electronic or print reference works. Depending on your topic, you might consult one or more of these works:

- **Encyclopedias,** such as the *Oxford American Children's Encyclopedia*
- **Dictionaries,** such as the *American Heritage Student Dictionary*
- **Almanacs,** such as the *TIME for Kids Almanac*
- **Atlases,** such as the *Kingfisher Student Atlas*

DATABASES

Databases are electronic collections of information. Some databases, such as the Internet Movie Database, focus on one subject. Others, such as InfoTrac Junior (see page 946), gather articles from hundreds of publications.

Your school or local library offers many databases for free. Use them when you have narrowed your topic considerably and are looking for very specific information. Ask your librarian for help.

NONFICTION BOOKS

Nonfiction books are good sources of in-depth information. Here's how to decide whether a specific book matches your research goal.

1. Read the **title** and **subtitle** to get a general idea of what the book is about. If there are entire books on your exact topic, you may have selected a topic that is too broad. If so, go back to page 937 and narrow your topic.

2. Turn to the **copyright page.** Look for the copyright date. Focus on the latest date shown, and decide if the book is up to date.

3. Look at the **table of contents.** Part and chapter headings will give you an overview of what the book covers. This page will also tell you whether the book has other useful features. For example, it may have a **bibliography** (a list of sources used), a list of **further reading,** or a **glossary** (a list of specialized terms and their definitions).

4. Check the **index** for specific topics or terms that interest you. Make sure the book has many pages on your topic rather than just a mention.

TIP Is the book that you are looking at older than you are? If so, you may want to choose a different book—unless you are researching a historical topic and want to find out what people thought of it many years ago.

TRY IT OUT! *Examine the Parts of a Book*

Which parts of a book are shown here?

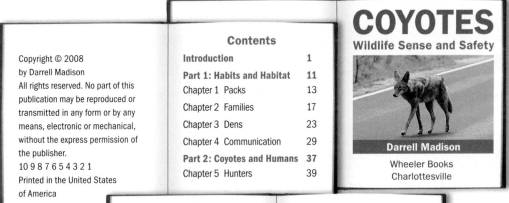

Copyright © 2008
by Darrell Madison
All rights reserved. No part of this publication may be reproduced or transmitted in any form or by any means, electronic or mechanical, without the express permission of the publisher.
10 9 8 7 6 5 4 3 2 1
Printed in the United States of America

Contents

Introduction	1
Part 1: Habits and Habitat	**11**
Chapter 1 Packs	13
Chapter 2 Families	17
Chapter 3 Dens	23
Chapter 4 Communication	29
Part 2: Coyotes and Humans	**37**
Chapter 5 Hunters	39

COYOTES
Wildlife Sense and Safety

Darrell Madison

Wheeler Books
Charlottesville

Recommended Reading

Baumgartner, Will. *Wildlife in the Suburbs and City.* Denver: High Sierra Books, 2008.

Gadski, Mary Ellen. *Coyotes, Controversy, and Control.* New York: Solstice Environmental Books, 2007.

Reid, Catherine. *Coyote: Seeking the Hunter in Our Midst.* Boston: Houghton Mifflin, 2004.

Index

A
adaptations, 37–38, 53, 83
alpha pair, 13–15, 18
animal control programs, 110

B
barking, 30–31
bobcats, 101
bounties, 156

C
cattle, 102
communication, 29–36
courtship, 18
coyote hunters, 39

D
dens, 23–28
dogs and coyotes, comparing, 41

Close Read

1. What is the subtitle of this book? What does it tell you about the book?

2. Does this book include information about dens? How about animal control programs? How do you know?

3. Is this book up to date? How do you know?

NEWSPAPERS AND PERIODICALS

Newspapers are publications that contain news and advertising. They are published daily, weekly, or very frequently. **Periodicals** are publications that are issued on a regular basis of more than one day apart. They contain news, advice, fiction, or a combination of these. Magazines are the most common type of periodical.

Recent newspaper and periodical articles can provide current information on your topic. Many articles present information briefly in a way that is easy to understand.

- **Examples of Newspapers**—*Washington Post, Los Angeles Times, Indianapolis Star, Baltimore Sun, Dallas Morning News, Arizona Republic*
- **Examples of Magazines**—*Sports Illustrated, U.S. News & World Report, Teen Ink, Next Step, HowStuffWorks Express*

You can search for magazine and newspaper articles on your topic by using a database such as InfoTrac. The page below comes from a periodical database called InfoTrac Junior. It is for students in grades 5 through 12.

TRY IT OUT! *Finding a Newspaper or Magazine Article*

A search for *coyote population* brought up these results. Clicking on the underlined title of the article or the underlined words *Check Out* brings up the text of the article.

Close Read

1. What keywords were used in this search?

2. What three search options does this database provide? (Hint: Look at the menu on the left.)

3. If you were hunting for information on coyotes in people's backyards, which two entries would probably be most helpful? Why?

4. Which entry is not related to the topic of coyotes in the suburbs? How do you know?

Evaluating Sources

Some sources are more trustworthy than others, so you should evaluate every source you find. **Evaluating** a source means asking and answering questions about its reliability.

The questions below apply to all sources. On pages 948–950, you will find questions to ask about specific types of sources.

WHAT TO ASK	WHY IT MATTERS
What is the date of the information?	Up-to-date information is especially important when you are researching subjects related to medicine, technology, science, and sports. Even when you are researching something that happened long ago, up-to-date sources often contain the latest findings and insights.
Who is the author?	Not every author is an expert. Look for information on the author's other publications. What kind of education, job, or experience does he or she have that relates to the topic? Has the author won any awards?
Who is the publisher?	Some publishers are more careful and accurate than others. For example, popular magazines and newspapers with fads and gossip in their headlines can be unreliable. Ask a librarian for help finding reputable sources.
What is the purpose of the information?	Some publications and Web sites may be trying to sell you a product. Others may want you to donate money or support a political idea. Some may present an issue that has two sides as if there were only one side. Look for information about the author and the publisher. Does the author's purpose affect the reliability of the information?
Is this information useful to me?	Check the table of contents or menus and links for your keywords or other words and phrases that relate to your research goals. Also, be sure the source is written at a level that's not too high or too low for you.

EVALUATE WEB SITES

Most books have an author, one or more editors, a publisher, and reviewers. In contrast, a Web site may be the work of just one individual. The information on a site may not have been checked or verified by anyone else.

When you visit a Web site, ask yourself these questions:

- **Who created the site?** Look for details about the author, information about a sponsoring organization, and a "last updated" reference.

- **Why was the site created?** Do the creators want to inform you about something? Do they want to entertain you? Are they trying to persuade you to support or oppose an issue? Maybe they want to sell you a product or service. Some sites are created for more than one purpose.

- **Do you notice problems with the site?** Do some hyperlinks lead nowhere? If you find mistakes in facts, grammar, or spelling, the site may have been put together quickly and sloppily.

- **Could you find more accurate or more useful information somewhere else?** Use a variety of sources, such as encyclopedias, almanacs, magazines, newspapers, interviews with experts, and documentaries.

TRY IT OUT! *Examine a Personal Web Site*

What do you think is useful here? What errors or problems do you see?

BACK FORWARD STOP REFRESH HOME PRINT

www.coyoteworld.net

Coyote World

You're guide to the amazing world of the coyote!

INSTANT WINNER click now!

Cool Coyote Sites

Cool Coyote Facts

Attacks	Pups	Dens
Dens	Habits	Map
Homes	Tracks	Wolfs
Coydogs	Diet	Dog family

Back to Anna Marie's home page
©2000 by A.M. Behrens

Close Read

1. Who created this site? When was it created?

2. What is the purpose of this site?

3. Name three problems with this site.

EVALUATE NONFICTION BOOKS

Books often provide even more information than Web sites do. To evaluate a nonfiction book, ask these questions:

- **Is this book up to date?** You learned on page 945 why the copyright page is important. Check the copyright page and the book jacket for dates and for words such as "all new" or "revised and updated." A book that has been through many updates and printings is more likely to be reliable.

- **Is the book carefully researched?** The book jacket may quote reviewers and state their qualifications. Look inside the book for **footnotes** and **end notes** that tell you where the author got information. Check the back of the book to see if there is an **appendix** with extra material, such as maps, charts, and tables.

- **What does the book say about the author?** Look for an author biography on the book jacket, at the beginning of the book, or at the end of the book. Read the biography for information about the author's education, profession, and other publications. Also, look for a **preface** near the front. This short introductory essay may provide clues to the author's background and a statement of his or her purpose.

TRY IT OUT! **Examine a Nonfiction Book**

Use what you have learned about nonfiction books and about the parts of a book (page 945) to decide whether this book is a good source for someone who is researching coyote habitats.

*Revised for 2008!
3rd Edition*

About the Author
Guinevere O'Brien is one of the country's leading authorities on coyote habitats. In this book, she explores the facts and fictions surrounding the most common large predator in North America. Dr. O'Brien is also the author of *The Coyote and the Wolf*. She has taught at several universities and is currently an associate professor of ecology.

Close Read
1. What is this book about?
2. Is the author qualified to write about this topic? Why or why not?
3. How up to date is this information? How do you know?
4. What other parts of this book should someone evaluate to be sure it is right for his or her research goal? (Hint: See page 945.)

EVALUATE NEWSPAPERS AND PERIODICALS

Your library may offer some newspapers and periodicals in hard copy (in other words, printed on paper) and many others online or on microfilm. Ask these questions when evaluating an article:

- **Is this magazine or newspaper well-known and respected?** Most large-circulation newspapers and magazines are reliable. Avoid newspapers and magazines that focus on fads, space aliens, and celebrity gossip.

- **When was it published?** Usually, up-to-date sources are best. There are exceptions, however. For example, if you are researching the civil rights era, a newspaper article from 1961 could be an excellent source.

- **Who is the author?** Sometimes, magazines and newspapers provide information about the writer's qualifications and his or her other publications. Staff writers and contributing editors tend to be reliable.

- **Can the facts be verified?** Does the author say where his or her facts came from? You should be able to verify every fact in at least one other source.

TRY IT OUT! *Examine a Newspaper Article*

Ask questions about the periodical, the author, the facts, and other content to evaluate this article.

from the **Montgomery Reporter**

Local Coyotes Are Getting Bold

BY MARTIN HERZOG, STAFF WRITER

Don't leave your food, your trash, or your house pets outside. That's the advice of Sharon DiSanti, Loomis County's animal control officer. The reason is coyotes.

"People think of coyotes as wild animals, but they're in the suburbs, and they're getting bolder," DiSanti explains.

In recent years, coyotes in Loomis County have become more bold, and, probably, more numerous. Once it was unusual to see coyotes anywhere except in rural or forested areas. Now coyotes are showing up in backyards and even in urban areas around the country.

SAFETY TIPS

1. Do not leave pet food outside.
2. Cover and secure all trash and compost.
3. Bring in cats and other pets.
4. Never try to become friendly with a wild animal.

Coyotes once lived only in regions west of the Mississippi. In fact, coyotes were never spotted in this part of the country until the early 1950s. At that time sightings were extremely rare, and the coyote's range was thought to be

See COYOTE, page B3

Close Read

1. How well is this article related to the research topic "coyotes in the suburbs"?

2. Would you call the information in this article reliable? Why or why not?

3. The reporter's e-mail address appeared at the end of this article when it was printed. Why would having that e-mail address be useful to a researcher?

Gathering Your Own Facts

The library and the Internet are both rich sources of information, but you can collect data in other places as well. For instance, you can visit museums and historical societies. You can conduct interviews. You can even do field research.

INTERVIEWS

Interviews can be excellent ways to gather information. To learn whether coyotes live in your area, you might interview a neighbor who works for the local parks department or a relative who works for your community's animal control office. You can interview someone in person, by telephone, by e-mail, or by letter. The most important part of an interview is preparing for it. See page R81–R82 to learn more about preparing for and conducting an interview.

FIELD RESEARCH AND OBSERVATION

When you observe with a research goal in mind, you are doing **field research.** A wildlife specialist might collect data about when and where coyotes were sighted over a particular time period. If you are studying coyotes, you might go to a zoo and make observations. You might take notes about what coyotes look like and how they move or sound. Also, you might make observations about a coyote's size and features by looking at a stuffed coyote in a natural history museum or a science museum.

Another way to gather your own facts about coyotes is by visiting the office of an animal control officer or a wildlife management office. Your notes might look like this.

> *Notes on Visit to Loomis County Wildlife Office, 5/1/2008*
>
> - *Tracking charts show 44 coyote sightings in 2007, 32 so far in 2008.*
> - *State map shows movement from rural areas to the suburbs and the city between 1998 and 2008.*
> - *So far in 2008, department has received 11 calls from residents:*
>
>   *3 unconfirmed sightings*
>   *4 confirmed sightings of coyotes in yards or near trash bins*
>   *2 pet attacks (1 fatal)*
>   *1 livestock attack (1 fatal)*
>   *1 human interaction (no harm done)*

Research Tips and Strategies

Start Searching

Learn about your options for finding information on the Web. Here are just a few.

Search Engines

Use more than one search engine. Here are a few to try:

- Ask for Kids (www.askforkids.com)
- Google (www.google.com)
- Yahoo! (www.yahoo.com)
- All the Web (alltheweb.com)

Metasearch Tools

A metasearch tool searches many search engines at a time and combines the results.

- Dogpile (dogpile.com)
- Metacrawler (metacrawler.com)

Directories

Directories put Internet resources into categories. You can try these directories:

- KidsClick! (www.kidsclick.org)
- Yahooligans! (yahooligans.yahoo.com)

Virtual Libraries

Virtual libraries contain information in encyclopedias, directories, and indexes.

- Internet Public Library Kidspace (www.ipl.org/div/kidspace/)
- KidsWeb (www.npac.syr.edu/textbook/kidsweb/)

Other Web Resources

- Smithsonian for Kids (www.smithsonianeducation.org/students/)
- Databases: ProQuest K–12, InfoTrac Junior Edition

Checklist for Evaluating a Source

- ☑ Is the information clearly related to your topic?
- ☑ Is the author an expert on the topic?
- ☑ Is the information up to date?
- ☑ Is the information trustworthy? Think about whether the source is regularly reviewed and updated. Also, consider whether a reliable institution, such as a U.S. government agency, created it.
- ☑ Can you verify the facts in at least one other source?
- ☑ Is the writing at your level? Avoid books for very young children as well as works designed for college students and scholars.

Understanding Web Addresses

A Web address contains clues to the site's author and purpose.

WEB ABBREVIATIONS AND MEANINGS

.COM	commercial—businesses, products, and many personal Web sites
.EDU	education—schools and universities, including teachers' and students' personal sites
.GOV	U.S. government—U.S. government sites, such as whitehouse.gov, cia.gov, and www.census.gov
.MIL	military—U.S. armed forces and related sites
.NET	network—product information and sales
.ORG	organizations—sites of charities, libraries, and other nonprofit groups; also political parties

Navigating the Library or Media Center

Fiction is usually easy to find in a library or media center. It is alphabetized according to the author's last name.

Nonfiction is different. It is organized by category or topic. Most media centers and public libraries use the Dewey decimal system. Most university and research libraries use the Library of Congress system.

DEWEY DECIMAL SYSTEM

000–099	General works
100–199	Philosophy and psychology
200–299	Religion
300–399	Social sciences
400–499	Language
500–599	Natural sciences and mathematics
600–699	Technology (applied sciences)
700–799	Art and recreation
800–899	Literature and rhetoric
900–999	Geography and history

LIBRARY OF CONGRESS SYSTEM

A	General works	**M**	Music
B	Philosophy, psychology, religion	**N**	Fine arts
C–D	History	**P**	Language and literature
E–F	American history	**Q**	Science
G	Geography, anthropology, recreation	**R**	Medicine
H	Social sciences	**S**	Agriculture
J	Political science	**T**	Technology
K	Law	**U**	Military science
L	Education	**V**	Naval science
		Z	Bibliography and library science

Writing Workshop

Research Report

Now it's time to combine the research process with the writing process. Follow the **Writer's Road Map** to find out how to write an informative, memorable report.

WRITER'S ROAD MAP

Research Report

WRITING PROMPT 1

Writing for the Real World Write a research report that investigates a topic that you have always wanted to know more about. Your report should include information from at least three sources.

Topics to Consider

- How and why does an earthquake happen?
- What is life on a space station like?
- How did the game of basketball get started?
- Were there ever any female pirates?

WRITING PROMPT 2

Writing from Literature Did a work of fiction or nonfiction that you read this year make you think of a topic that you would like to explore? Write a research report that explores the topic in detail. Your report should include data from at least three sources as well as your own ideas.

Topics to Consider

- a natural disaster ("The Dog of Pompeii")
- sharks or another type of sea creature ("Ghost of the Lagoon")
- the life of an explorer ("Matthew Henson at the Top of the World")

 RESEARCH TOOLS
For research help and citation guidelines, go to the **Research Center** at **ClassZone.com.**

KEY TRAITS

1. IDEAS

- Presents a **thesis statement** that clearly identifies the main idea of the report
- Supports the thesis with **evidence,** such as examples, facts, statistics, and expert opinions
- Combines information from **multiple sources**
- Provides informative **quotations** and **paraphrases**
- Includes the **writer's own ideas**

2. ORGANIZATION

- Follows a clear **organizational pattern**
- Uses **transitions** to connect ideas
- Includes a strong **introduction** and a satisfying **conclusion**

3. VOICE

- Maintains a serious, formal **tone**

4. WORD CHOICE

- Uses **precise words** to explain ideas

5. SENTENCE FLUENCY

- Varies the **lengths of sentences**

6. CONVENTIONS

- Uses **correct grammar, spelling, and punctuation**
- Credits sources
- Uses **correct formats and style**

Part 1: Analyze a Student Model

Melissa Hensley
Mrs. Weiss
English 6
14 April 2008

Cats in Ancient Egypt

Cats didn't always brush up against people's legs and purr. A long
time ago, cats were fierce, wild animals. Over time, they got closer to
people and became pets. Eventually, some people even worshiped cats.
Cats became truly powerful in ancient Egypt when they went from
5 being wild animals to useful animals to sacred animals.

Before about 4000 B.C. in Egypt, cats were wild. They were also
bigger than the pet cats we know today (Bisno). When Egyptians began
to farm, they had to store their grain, but mice and rats got into the
grain and ate it. Cats attacked the mice and rats (Bisno; Fogle 20).
10 People realized that cats could help keep grain safe. For that reason, cats
became valuable to people.

Big, wild cats also killed poisonous snakes (Fogle 21). People must
have noticed this and then figured out that it would be good to keep
cats around their homes. People began to feed the cats to make sure
15 that they stayed around. At some point, they probably began to pet and
enjoy them, too. Bisno says that the cats "found a good source of food
living around people's homes" and that cats and people started to have a
friendly relationship. By 2000 B.C., many cats were pets instead of wild
animals (Bisno).

KEY TRAITS IN ACTION

Uses **correct formats and style,** including the header information and page numbering that this teacher requires.

Has a clear, fact-filled **introduction.** The **thesis statement** is highlighted.

Includes **paraphrases** and a **quotation** from sources. The **writer's own idea** is highlighted.

Cats and people interacted for a few thousand years before people
started thinking of cats as sacred. That happened beginning about
1000 B.C. (Bisno). At that time, ancient Egyptians began to believe
that cats were the special favorites of a goddess named Bastet. In fact,
in some works of art, Bastet has a female body and the head of a cat
("Egypt"). According to Trumble, the cat became Bastet's "sacred
animal" (11). As a result, people started to worship cats ("Egypt").

Art from ancient Egypt shows the importance of the cat. In statues
and paintings, some cats wear earrings and other jewelry ("Egypt").
They look taken care of instead of wild. Their fur looks brushed, and
they look well fed (Fogle 26).

People had great respect for cats. Trumble explains that visitors to
holy places brought cat statues to offer to the goddess Bastet (13). Some
cats were made into mummies. This probably means that Egyptians
thought cats would have an afterlife just as people would ("Egypt").

Cats aren't sacred in Egypt anymore. That's because different
groups of people conquered Egypt. They brought new religions that
didn't include animals. For example, when the Romans conquered
Egypt, they brought Christianity. Later, the Arabs brought Islam
(Trumble 39–40, 48). Beliefs changed, and over time, cats were just cats
once again. This timeline shows the changes between 4000 B.C. and
A.D. 1000. The dates are estimates.

Sources: "Egypt"; Trumble 39–40; Bisno.

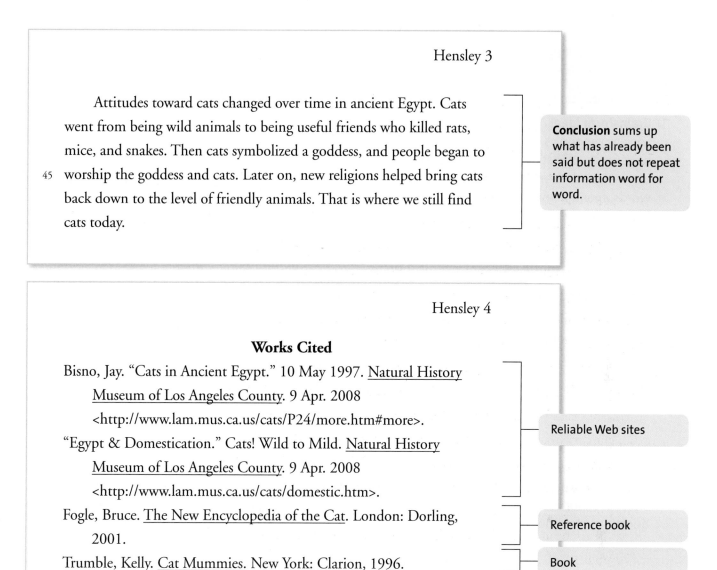

Hensley 3

Attitudes toward cats changed over time in ancient Egypt. Cats went from being wild animals to being useful friends who killed rats, mice, and snakes. Then cats symbolized a goddess, and people began to
45 worship the goddess and cats. Later on, new religions helped bring cats back down to the level of friendly animals. That is where we still find cats today.

> **Conclusion** sums up what has already been said but does not repeat information word for word.

Hensley 4

Works Cited

Bisno, Jay. "Cats in Ancient Egypt." 10 May 1997. <u>Natural History Museum of Los Angeles County</u>. 9 Apr. 2008 <http://www.lam.mus.ca.us/cats/P24/more.htm#more>.

"Egypt & Domestication." Cats! Wild to Mild. <u>Natural History Museum of Los Angeles County</u>. 9 Apr. 2008 <http://www.lam.mus.ca.us/cats/domestic.htm>.

Fogle, Bruce. <u>The New Encyclopedia of the Cat</u>. London: Dorling, 2001.

Trumble, Kelly. <u>Cat Mummies</u>. New York: Clarion, 1996.

> Reliable Web sites

> Reference book

> Book

Part 2: Apply the Writing Process

PREWRITING

What Should I Do?	What Does It Look Like?

1. Brainstorm ideas.
Look at the topics on page 954 or at a topic or general subject area that your teacher has assigned. Start freewriting—in other words, spend a few minutes listing whatever ideas come into your head. When you are finished, (circle) an idea that you would like to research.

▶ *I think I want to write about pets. Jamal has an iguana. That's a strange pet because it doesn't seem to care about him. I like cats. I wonder how cats and people first got to be friends. (How did wild cats become pets?) Angie's cat Tigerwoman is still pretty wild! My cat Minky is much sweeter.*

2. Ask research questions.
Focus on the idea you circled. Ask some specific questions about it. These questions will help you focus on what you really want to know.

See page 938: Create Research Questions

▶ *My Research Questions*
- *Were cats always tame?*
- *What made people start liking cats?*

3. Read and learn.
Learn about your topic by reading an encyclopedia article or by exploring Web sites. Look for answers to your research questions. Jot down notes.

▶ *My Answers and Other Notes*
- *Cats helped people by catching mice—people liked cats for doing that!*
- *Some ancient Egyptians worshiped cats and made mummies out of them.*
- *There's lots of information about cats in ancient Egypt. Maybe that's what I should write about.*

4. Narrow your topic.
Your report needs to fit into a few pages. If there is a whole book on your topic, then your topic is too broad. Try to find just one small angle of your topic to explore.

▶ *Narrowing My Topic*

Cats (way too broad)

↓

Cat mummies (narrower, but there's a whole book about it)

↓

How people saw cats in ancient Egypt (narrow topic)

RESEARCHING

What Should I Do?	What Does It Look Like?

1. Locate sources.

After you have narrowed your topic, you can begin the research process. Find sources by typing **keywords** (specific words and phrases that are important to your topic) into an Internet search engine or a library catalog. See pages 939–943 to learn how to search on the Internet or in a library.

Keep track of what you have found by creating a chart like this one.

TIP If you are having trouble finding information, ask a librarian for help. He or she can suggest the best sources for your topic.

Sources	My Comments
Library Encyclopedias	
"Cats," <u>World Book Encyclopedia</u>	not much about cats in Egypt
<u>New Encyclopedia of the Cat</u> (Ref 636.8 F656)	several interesting pages about cats in Egypt
Library Books	
<u>Cat Mummies</u> by Kelly Trumble (J932 T77lc)	lots on mummies and the cat goddess
<u>The Ancient Egyptians</u> by Elton LeChavre (932 LEC)	three chapters on Egyptian religion
Web Sites	
"Cool Cats of Egypt"	no information about the author, and the links don't work
"Cats in Ancient Egypt" (bookmarked on Kelly's computer)	lots of good facts, exactly on my topic, and the site was created by a museum

2. Evaluate your sources.

For each source you find, ask yourself: Should I use this source?

Do not use a source if

- it is too high-level or low-level for you

- it might not be accurate (For example, Web sites without an author, sponsor, or working links may not have been checked or updated by anyone.)

See pages 947–950: Evaluating Sources

Sources I Won't Use

1. "Cats," <u>World Book Encyclopedia</u> (not enough information on my topic)

2. <u>The Ancient Egyptians</u> (too hard to understand)

3. "Cool Cats of Egypt" (information may not be correct)

What Should I Do?	What Does It Look Like?

3. Make source cards.
Write the information below on each card. Then number each card in the top right corner.

Online encyclopedia
- author (if given) and title of the article
- date the information was published (if given)
- publisher's name
- date you accessed the article
- the complete Web address, also called a URL

Print or CD-ROM encyclopedia
- author (if given) and title of the article
- name and year of encyclopedia
- if a CD-ROM, the term "CD-ROM," plus the publisher and the place of publication

Web site
- author (if given) and title of page or article
- Web site date (if given)
- name of the organization that sponsored or created the site (if given)
- date you accessed the article
- the complete Web address
- if the site comes from a print publication, list the publisher, place of publication, and year of publication

Book
- author or editor
- title
- publisher, place of publication, and year of publication
- library call number

Online encyclopedia

> ①
>
> "Cat, domestic." *Encyclopaedia Britannica.* 2006. Encyclopaedia Britannica Online. 6 Apr. 2008 <http://searchebcom/eb/article-9106124>.

Print encyclopedia

> ②
>
> "Cats." *The World Book Encyclopedia.* 2006 ed.

Web site

> ③
>
> Bisno, Jay. "Cats in Ancient Egypt." 10 May 1997. *Natural History Museum of Los Angeles County.* 9 Apr. 2008 <http://www.lammuscaus/cats/P24/more.htm#more>

Book

> ④
>
> Trumble, Kelly. *Cat Mummies.* New York: Clarion, 1996.
> j932 T77lc

RESEARCHING

What Should I Do?	What Does It Look Like?

4. Make note cards.

Note cards help you keep track of the information you are learning from your sources. Each note card should contain:

- the source number (This is the same number you wrote on your source card.)
- a specific heading
- the fact, opinion, or quotation that you want to include in your report
- the page number, if there is one

▶

Wild cats long ago	③

Wild cats were bigger than cats are now (no page number).

How wild cats helped people	⑤

They killed mice and rats (20).

They also killed poisonous snakes (21).

5. Take careful, honest notes.

Use these three ways to record information from a source.

- To **quote** the source, copy the important phrase, sentence, or paragraph word for word. Put quotation marks before and after what you have copied.
- To **paraphrase** the source, write what the source says, but express it in your own words. A paraphrase states an idea in about the same number of words as the original source does.
- To **summarize** the source, use your own words to record only the key ideas. A summary states an idea in fewer words than the original source.

TIP Most of your notes should be paraphrases and summaries. Use quotations only for information that you cannot state as clearly or precisely as the source does.

▶

Original source

Artisans made thousands of small bronze sculptures of cats. They sold them to people who worshiped Bastet. These worshipers offered the bronze cats at temples and shrines and hoped for an answer to their prayers.

Trumble, Kelly, *Cat Mummies*

Paraphrase

Cat statues in ancient Egypt	

Artists created cat statues out of bronze. Followers of Bastet bought the statues and took them to holy places. They offered them to the goddess so that she would help them with what they asked for (13).

Summary

Cat statues in ancient Egypt	

Visitors to holy places brought cat statues to offer to the goddess Bastet (13).

What Should I Do?	What Does It Look Like?

6. Do not plagiarize.

If you use someone else's words or ideas and don't tell where you got them, you are plagiarizing. Plagiarism is dishonest and can cause you to fail the assignment.

How can you give credit to the sources you use?

- **As you take notes, summarize and paraphrase as much as possible.** This takes longer than copying does, but it helps you think through and understand what you are reading.

- **Don't overuse one source.** Be sure to get your information from at least three sources. Doing this will help you learn about different ideas and develop your own opinions.

- **Every time you copy something exactly, put quotation marks around it.** Even if you paraphrase most of a sentence but just copy a few key words, put quotation marks around any words you took directly from the source.

- **When you write your draft, put your sources away.** Use only your note cards.

Original source

Cats . . . found a good source of food living around people's homes and farms as well as affection from their human friends.

Bisno, Jay, "Cats in Ancient Egypt"

Plagiarized

Cats found food by living near people's homes, and they also got affection from their human friends.

Correctly documented

Cats "found a good source of food living around people's homes," and cats and people started to have a friendly relationship (Bisno).

Original source

Depictions of cats often show them with jewelry such as earrings and necklaces, so it is likely that Egyptians adorned their pets.

"Egypt & Domestication," Cats! Wild to Mild

Plagiarized

Pictures of cats often show them with jewelry like earrings and necklaces, so Egyptians probably put jewelry on their pets.

Properly credited

In statues and paintings, some cats wear earrings and other jewelry ("Egypt").

RESEARCHING

What Should I Do?	**What Does It Look Like?**

7. Write a thesis statement.

A thesis statement is the main idea that your report is about. Everything in your report should help explain and prove your thesis statement.

Be sure that your thesis statement names your writing topic and says something about it.

TIP Don't worry if your thesis isn't perfect now. You can revise it after you draft.

▶

My topic:

Cats in Ancient Egypt

↓

What I will say about the topic:

What people thought of cats changed.

↓

My working thesis statement:

In ancient Egypt, people's ideas about cats changed over time.

8. Make an organizational plan.

Use your note cards to make a writing plan.

- Group all your note cards that have the same or similar headings.

- Look at your groups and decide on an order that fits your thesis. For example, if your thesis is about how people's ideas about cats changed over time, a logical order is the earliest ideas to the latest ones.

- Use your groups of cards to write an outline of your report.

TIP You can create a graphic organizer instead of a formal outline. Try a flow chart or a sequence chain.

▶

Cats in Ancient Egypt

I. Changes in how people viewed cats

   A. Once were wild animals

   B. Became pets

   C. In Egypt, became sacred animals

II. Wild cats

   A. Bigger than pet cats we know today

   B. Killed mice, rats, and snakes

   C. Became important to ancient Egyptians

III. Sacred cats

   A. Bastet, the cat goddess

   B. Earrings and other jewelry for cats

   C. Cat statues as presents for Bastet

   D. Cat mummies

IV. Cats no longer sacred

   A. Different rulers in Egypt

   B. Different beliefs

What Should I Do?	What Does It Look Like?

1. Start writing your first draft.
Use your outline or graphic organizer plus your note cards to tell your reader what you learned.

▶

Outline

II. Wild cats
   A. Bigger than pet cats we know today
   B. Killed mice, rats, and snakes
   C. Became important to ancient Egyptians

First draft

In the year 4000 B.C., cats were wild. Mice and rats started eating the grain that Egyptian farmers stored. Cats killed the mice and rats, so people liked that. The cats killed poisonous snakes, too. People fed the cats to make sure that they stayed around.

2. Weave your sources into your sentences.
Here are some ways to tell your reader where you got your information.
   • "According to Bisno, . . ."
   • "Trumble explains . . ."
   • "In *The Encyclopedia of Cats,* Fogle writes . . ."

▶

According to Trumble,

The cat became Bastet's "sacred animal." (11).
~~This information comes from Kelly Trumble and is on page 11 of her book.~~

3. Consider creating a graphic.
You can sum up or show information by creating a graphic and blending it into your report. For instance, you might include a labeled diagram, a cause-effect chart, a graph, or a timeline. Be sure to include a source line that tells where you found the facts in your graphic.

▶

Dates for timeline:

4000 B.C.—Wild cats catch mice.

2000 B.C.—Cats become pets.

1000 B.C.—Cat goddess

400 B.C.—Cat worship at its peak

A.D. 200—New religions come to Egypt.

A.D. 1000—Cats no longer sacred

Sources: "Egypt"; Trumble 39–40; Bisno.

DRAFTING

What Should I Do?	What Does It Look Like?

4. Credit your sources.
If you got an idea or a fact from someone else, you need to tell your reader that. Show the source of each idea in parentheses at the end of the sentence. This is called **parenthetical documentation** and usually includes the author's last name and a page number, like this: (Fogle 21). Here are some exceptions to this rule:

- **Author already mentioned in the sentence**—use only the page number: (21)
- **Web site with no page numbers**—use only the author's name: (Bisno)
- **Source with no author and no page numbers**—use a short form of the title: ("Egypt")
- **More than one source supporting an idea**—separate the information for each source with a semicolon: (Fogle 20; Trumble 11)

> They look taken care of instead of wild. Their fur looks brushed, and they look well fed (Fogle 26).
>
> — Author and page number

> Trumble explains that visitors to holy places brought cat statues to honor the goddess Bastet (13).
>
> — Author is mentioned in sentence

> When Egyptians began to farm, they had to store their grain, but mice and rats got into the grain and ate it. Cats attacked the mice and rats (Bisno; Fogle 20).
>
> — Information from two sources

5. Make a Works Cited list.
Put your source cards in alphabetical order by the author's last name. If a source does not include the name of its author, alphabetize that source by title instead. Use the examples here for common types of sources. See page 968 of this book or the *MLA Handbook for Writers of Research Papers* for other kinds of entries.

Works Cited

Bisno, Jay. "Cats in Ancient Egypt." 10 May 1997. <u>Natural History Museum of Los Angeles County</u>. 9 Apr. 2008 <http://www.lammus.ca.us/cats/P24/more.htm#more>.

"Egypt & Domestication." Cats! Wild to Mild. <u>Natural History Museum of Los Angeles County</u>. 9 Apr. 2008 <http://www.lammus.ca.us/cats/domestic.htm>.

Fogle, Bruce. <u>The New Encyclopedia of the Cat</u>. London: Dorling, 2001.

Trumble, Kelly. <u>Cat Mummies</u>. New York: Clarion, 1996.

What Should I Do?	What Does It Look Like?

1. Make your introduction an attention-getter.
- Highlight the first two sentences of your introduction. Do they make you want to keep reading?
- Think about starting with an intriguing description, a short and vivid quotation, or a thought-provoking question.

▶ Cats didn't always brush up against people's legs and purr. A long time ago, cats were fierce, wild animals. ~~My report is about cats. The dictionary says that a cat is "a small mammal domesticated for many centuries."~~ Some people even worshiped cats. Cats had real power in ancient Egypt because they went from being wild animals to useful animals to sacred animals.

2. Be sure that you are giving your reader enough information.
- Ask a peer reader to (circle) sentences or paragraphs that don't have enough support.
- Add explanations, details, facts, or examples as needed. Credit your sources.

See page 968: Ask a Peer Reader

▶ Cats aren't sacred in Egypt anymore. That's because different groups of people conquered Egypt. (They brought new religions that didn't include animals.) Beliefs changed, and over time, cats were just cats once again.

For example, when the Romans conquered Egypt, they brought Christianity. Later, the Arabs brought Islam (Trumble 38–40, 48).

3. Add original comments and ideas.
- Does your report contain your own thinking, or have you just put together information and ideas from other people?
- Look for places where you can comment on one or more ideas from your sources.

▶ Big, wild cats also killed poisonous snakes (Fogle 21). People must have noticed this and then figured out that it would be good to keep cats around their homes.

4. Take out unnecessary details.
- Reread your report. Look for information that is off-topic or unrelated to your thesis.
- Revise or delete these passages so that your report is clear and focused.

▶ Some cats were made into mummies. ~~The Egyptians made baboons, crocodiles, and other animals into mummies, too.~~ This probably means that Egyptians thought ~~animals~~ would have an afterlife just as people would (19–20). cats

REVISING AND EDITING

What Should I Do?	What Does It Look Like?

5. Add transitions where they are needed.
- Check your report to see if one idea flows smoothly into the next.
- If necessary, add transitions to connect paragraphs and to show how one sentence leads to the next.

> ▶ *Then*
> Cats went from being wild animals to being useful friends who killed rats, mice, and snakes. ^Cats symbolized a goddess, and people worshiped the goddess and cats.^New religions helped bring cats back down to the level of friendly animals.
> *Later on,*

6. Focus on sentence length.
- If you have many short, choppy sentences, try combining two or more red.
- If you have many long sentences, try varying the rhythm by including a few short sentences.

> ▶ **Combining sentences**
>
> *before*
> Cats and people interacted for a few thousand years. ^Then people started thinking of cats as sacred. That happened beginning about 1000 B.C. (Bisno).

> **Shortening sentences**
>
> People realized that cats could keep grain safe₍.₎ ~~and~~ for that reason, cats became valuable to people.

7. Improve your conclusion.
- Don't repeat word for word what you have already said. Instead, summarize your key ideas using fresh, new words.
- Consider adding a final interesting idea. The writer of the student model added a sentence that brings the topic up to the present day.

> ▶ Attitudes toward cats changed over time in ancient Egypt. Cats went from being wild animals to being useful friends who killed rats, mice, and snakes. Then cats symbolized a goddess, and people worshiped the goddess and cats. Later on, new religions helped bring cats back down to the level of friendly animals. *That is where we still find cats today.*

Apply the Rubric

A strong research report . . .

☑ has an attention-getting or thought-provoking introduction

☑ presents a clear thesis statement

☑ uses evidence to support the thesis

☑ summarizes, paraphrases, and quotes multiple sources

☑ includes the writer's own comments and ideas

☑ follows a clear pattern of organization

☑ uses precise words and varied sentence lengths

☑ maintains a formal tone

☑ has a fresh, effective conclusion

Ask a Peer Reader

• Is my thesis clear? If not, how can I improve it?

• Should I add more support? If so, where?

• Where have I left out credit for my sources, or where have I made mistakes in giving credit?

• What did you learn from my report?

Citing Sources

If you need to cite one of the types of sources below, follow these examples.

CD-ROM encyclopedia
"Cats." Britannica Student Encyclopedia. 2004 ed. CD-ROM. Chicago: Encyclopaedia Britannica, 2004.

Newspaper or magazine article
Sorenson, Tanya. "On the Trail of Cats in Ancient Egypt." Detroit Free Press 15 June 2008: B6+.

Interview you conducted with an expert
LaGuerre, Nicole. Personal interview. 31 Mar. 2008.

Book with editor
DiFazio, Martin, ed. The Cat Through History. New York: Wonders, 2008.

Film or documentary
Mummies Made in Egypt. Dir. Larry Lancit. DVD. GPN, 2004.

For more examples plus help with margins, tabs, and spacing, see the *MLA Handbook for Writers of Research Papers.*

Writing Online

PUBLISHING OPTIONS
For publishing options, visit the **Writing Center** at ClassZone.com.

ASSESSMENT PREPARATION
For writing and grammar assessment practice, go to the **Assessment Center** at ClassZone.com.

Cats

Creating a Multimedia Report

Congratulations—you are an expert on your research subject! Share what you have learned by producing a multimedia report.

Planning the Presentation

1. **Reread your report, thinking about sights and sounds.** Circle parts of your report that you could express with pictures, photographs, drawings, music, or sound effects. Make notes about what images and sounds you would like to include.

2. **Outline your presentation.** List the ideas that lend themselves to sights and sounds. Make an outline that puts those ideas in a logical order.

3. **Storyboard the show.** Map out everything your audience will see and hear by making a storyboard.

(Sound: fierce sound of wildcat)
Narrator: Cats attacked the mice and rats.

(Sound: a cat meowing)
Narrator: People realized that cats could keep grain safe.

Producing the Presentation

1. **Gather your images and sounds.** If you drew your own pictures, scan them into a computer. Also record or download your music and sound effects.

2. **Put it all together.** Use an editing software program to assemble your presentation. Make a title screen that includes your name. You should also make a final screen that credits the sources of your ideas, images, and sounds.

Student Resource Bank

Short stories, poems, magazine articles, newspapers, and Web pages are all different types of texts that require some different strategies to be understood. For example, you might plot the events of a short story on a diagram, whereas you may use text features to spot main ideas in a magazine article. You should also identify patterns of organization in the text. Using these strategies will help you read different kinds of texts with ease.

1 Reading Literary Texts

Literary texts include short stories, novels, poems, and dramas. Literary texts can also be biographies, autobiographies, and essays. To appreciate and analyze literary texts, you will need to understand the characteristics of each type of text.

1.1 READING A SHORT STORY
Strategies for Reading

- Read the **title.** As you read the story, you may notice that the title has a special meaning.

- Keep track of **events** as they happen. Plot the events on a diagram like this one.

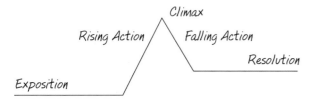

- From the details the writer provides, **visualize** the characters. **Predict** what they might do next.

- Look for specific adjectives that help you visualize the **setting**—the time and place in which events occur.

1.2 READING A POEM
Strategies for Reading

- Notice the **form** of the poem, or the number of lines and their arrangement on the page.

- Read the poem aloud a few times. Listen for **rhyme** and **rhythm.**

- **Visualize** the images and comparisons.

- **Connect** with the poem by asking yourself what message the poet is trying to send.

- Create a word web or another **graphic organizer** to record your reactions and questions.

1.3 READING A PLAY
Strategies for Reading

- Read the stage directions to help you **visualize** the setting and characters.

- **Question** what the title means and why the playwright chose it.

- Identify the main conflict (struggle or problem) in the play. To **clarify** the conflict, make a chart that shows what the conflict is and how it is resolved.

- **Analyze** the characters. What do they want? How do they change during the play? You may want to make a chart that lists each character's name, appearance, and traits.

1.4 READING LITERARY NONFICTION
Strategies for Reading

- If you are reading a biography or an autobiography, a family tree or word web can help you keep track of the people mentioned.

- When reading an essay, **evaluate** the writer's ideas. Is there a clear main idea? Does the writer use appropriate details to support the main idea?

❷ Reading Informational Texts: Text Features

An **informational text** is writing that provides factual information. Informational materials—such as chapters in textbooks and articles in magazines, encyclopedias, and newspapers—usually contain elements that help the reader recognize their purpose, pattern of organization, and key ideas. These elements are known as **text features.**

2.1 UNDERSTANDING TEXT FEATURES

Text features are design elements of a text that indicate its pattern of organization or otherwise make its key ideas and information understandable. Text features include titles, headings, subheadings, boldface type, bulleted and numbered lists, and graphic aids, such as charts, graphs, illustrations, and photographs. Notice how the text features help you find key information on the textbook page shown.

Ⓐ The **title** or **main heading** identifies the topic.

Ⓑ A **subheading** indicates the start of a new topic or section and identifies that section's focus.

Ⓒ **Questions** may be used to focus your understanding of the text.

Ⓓ A **bulleted list** shows items of equal importance.

Ⓔ **Graphic aids,** such as illustrations, photographs, charts, diagrams, maps, and timelines, often make ideas in the text clearer.

Ⓕ A **caption,** or the text that accompanies a graphic aid, gives information about the graphic aid that isn't necessarily obvious from the image itself.

PRACTICE AND APPLY

1. What is the second subheading following the title?

2. What is a dynasty?

3. Which text feature tells you about the structures shown in the photograph?

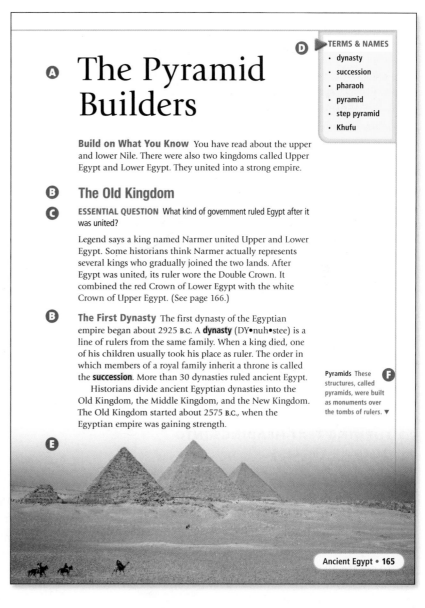

Ⓓ ▶TERMS & NAMES
- dynasty
- succession
- pharaoh
- pyramid
- step pyramid
- Khufu

Ⓐ The Pyramid Builders

Build on What You Know You have read about the upper and lower Nile. There were also two kingdoms called Upper Egypt and Lower Egypt. They united into a strong empire.

Ⓑ The Old Kingdom

Ⓒ ESSENTIAL QUESTION What kind of government ruled Egypt after it was united?

Legend says a king named Narmer united Upper and Lower Egypt. Some historians think Narmer actually represents several kings who gradually joined the two lands. After Egypt was united, its ruler wore the Double Crown. It combined the red Crown of Lower Egypt with the white Crown of Upper Egypt. (See page 166.)

Ⓑ The First Dynasty The first dynasty of the Egyptian empire began about 2925 B.C. A **dynasty** (DY•nuh•stee) is a line of rulers from the same family. When a king died, one of his children usually took his place as ruler. The order in which members of a royal family inherit a throne is called the **succession.** More than 30 dynasties ruled ancient Egypt.

Historians divide ancient Egyptian dynasties into the Old Kingdom, the Middle Kingdom, and the New Kingdom. The Old Kingdom started about 2575 B.C., when the Egyptian empire was gaining strength.

Pyramids These structures, called pyramids, were built as monuments over the tombs of rulers. ▼ **Ⓕ**

Ⓔ

Ancient Egypt • **165**

2.2 USING TEXT FEATURES

You can use text features to locate information, to help you understand it, and to take notes. Just use the following strategies when you encounter informational text.

Strategies for Reading

- **Preview** the text by looking at the title, headings, and subheadings to get an idea of the main concepts and the way the text is organized.

- Before you begin reading the text more thoroughly, **skim** it—read it quickly—to get an overview.

- Read any **questions** that appear at the end of a lesson or chapter. Doing this will help you set a purpose for your reading.

- Turn subheadings into questions. Then use the text below the subheadings to answer the questions. Your answers will be a **summary** of the text.

- **Take notes** by turning headings and subheadings into main ideas. You might use a chart like the following.

The Pyramid Builders		Main heading
The Old Kingdom	Notes: 1. Upper and Lower Egypt united by Narmer 2. Ruler wore double crown 3. Egypt ruled by dynasties	Subheading

- To locate particular facts or details, **scan** the text. In other words, look for key words and phrases as you move slowly down the page.

2.3 TURNING TEXT HEADINGS INTO OUTLINE ENTRIES

After you have read a selection at least once, you can use text features to take notes in outline form. The following outline shows how one student used text headings from the textbook sample on page R3. Study the outline and use the strategies that follow to create an outline based on text features.

Strategies for Using Text Headings

- Preview the headings and subheadings in the text to get an idea of what different kinds there are and what their positions might be in an outline.

- Be consistent. Note that subheadings that are the same size and color should be used consistently in Roman-numeral or capital-letter entries in the outline. If you decide that a chapter heading should appear with a Roman numeral, then that's the level at which all other chapter headings should appear.

- Write the main headings and subheadings that you will use as your Roman-numeral and capital-letter entries first. As you read, fill in numbered details from the text under the headings and subheadings in your outline.

PRACTICE AND APPLY

Reread "The Violent Side of Video Games," pages 895–896. Use text features in the selection to take notes in outline form.

Preview the headings and subheadings in the text to get an idea of the different kinds. Decide which main headings, titles, and subheadings you will use to create your Roman-numeral and capital-letter entries. Then fill in the details.

2.4 GRAPHIC AIDS

Information is communicated not only with words but also with graphic aids, such as graphs, diagrams, charts, maps, and timelines. **Graphic aids** are visual representations of verbal statements that make complex information easier to understand. For that reason, they are often used to organize, simplify, and summarize information for easy reference.

Graphs

Graphs are used to illustrate statistical information. A **graph** is a drawing that shows the relative values of numerical quantities. Different kinds of graphs are used to show different numerical relationships.

Strategies for Reading

Ⓐ Read the title.

Ⓑ Find out what is being represented or measured.

Ⓒ In a circle graph, compare the sizes of the parts.

Ⓓ In a line graph, study the slant of the line. The steeper the line, the faster the rate of change.

Ⓔ In a bar graph, compare the lengths of the bars.

A **circle graph,** or **pie graph,** shows the relationships of parts to a whole. The entire circle equals 100 percent. The parts of the circle represent percentages of the whole.

MODEL: CIRCLE GRAPH

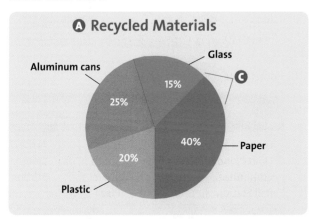

Line graphs show changes in numerical quantities over time and can be used to present trends such as global temperature change. A line graph is made on a grid. On the following line graph, the vertical axis indicates average global temperature, and the horizontal axis shows the number of years ago. The line connecting the data points shows a trend or pattern.

MODEL: LINE GRAPH

Source: *Ice Ages: Solving the Mystery*

In a **bar graph,** vertical or horizontal bars are used to show or compare categories of information, such as the sizes of different empires. The lengths of the bars indicate quantities—in this case, size.

MODEL: BAR GRAPH

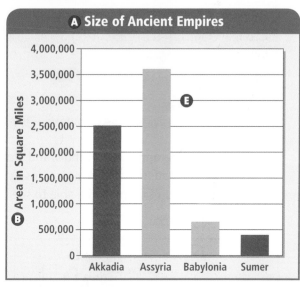

Source: *Institute for Research on World Systems*

WATCH OUT! Evaluate information presented in graphs carefully. The way you interpret the information depends on the graph form. For example, circle graphs show major differences well but tend to reduce the importance of smaller differences.

Diagrams

A **diagram** is a drawing that shows how something works or how its parts relate to one another.

Strategies for Reading

Ⓐ Read the title.

Ⓑ Read each label and look at the part it identifies.

Ⓒ Follow any arrows or numbers that show the order of steps or direction of movement.

A **picture diagram** is a picture or drawing of the subject being discussed.

MODEL: PICTURE DIAGRAM

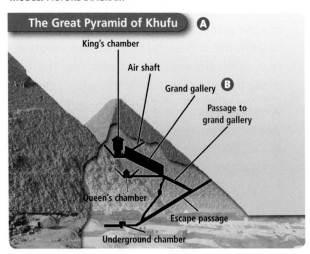

The Great Pyramid of Khufu Ⓐ

King's chamber

Air shaft

Grand gallery Ⓑ

Passage to grand gallery

Queen's chamber

Escape passage

Underground chamber

In a **schematic diagram,** lines, symbols, and words are used to help readers visualize processes or objects they wouldn't normally be able to see.

MODEL: SCHEMATIC DIAGRAM

Coil rotates and lifts water Ⓒ

Water Ⓑ

▲ Archimedes' Water-Lifting Device Ⓐ

Charts and Tables

A **chart** presents information, shows a process, or makes comparisons, usually in rows or columns.

A **table** is a specific type of chart that presents a collection of facts in rows and columns and shows how the facts relate to one another.

Strategies for Reading

Ⓐ Read the title to learn what information the chart or table covers.

Ⓑ Study column headings and row labels to determine the categories of information presented.

Ⓒ Look down columns and across rows to find specific information.

MODEL: CHART

Greek and Roman Gods Ⓐ		
Description	Greek Ⓑ	Roman
Supreme god	Zeus	Jupiter Ⓒ
Supreme goddess	Hera (wife of Zeus)	Juno (wife of Jupiter)
God of the sea	Poseidon	Neptune
God of music and poetry	Apollo	Apollo

MODEL: TABLE

Route 238 Ⓐ	Quincy Center Station—Holbrook/Randolph Commuter Rail Station via Crawford Square		
Leave Ⓑ Holb./Rand. Commuter Rail Station	Leave Crawford Square	Leave South Shore Plaza	Arrive Quincy Station
6:25 A	6:29 A	6:42 A	7:08 A
6:50	6:54	7:07	7:35 Ⓒ
7:20	7:25	7:38	8:06
7:50	7:55	8:08	8:36
8:25	8:30	8:43	9:11
8:55	9:00	9:13	9:41
9:25	9:30	9:46	10:14

Maps

A **map** visually represents a geographic region, such as a state or country. It provides information about areas through lines, colors, shapes, and symbols. There are different kinds of maps.

- **Political maps** show political features, such as national borders.
- **Physical maps** show the landforms in an area.
- **Road or travel maps** show roads and highways.
- **Thematic maps** show information on a specific topic, such as climate, weather, or natural resources.

Strategies for Reading

Ⓐ Read the title to find out what kind of map it is.

Ⓑ Read the labels to get an overall sense of what the map shows.

Ⓒ Look at the **key** or **legend** to find out what the symbols and colors on the map stand for.

MODEL: PHYSICAL MAP

MODEL: THEMATIC MAP

Timelines

A timeline shows events in the order in which they occurred. Events are listed along a horizontal or vertical line and are usually labeled with the year in which they happened.

November 1860—Abraham Lincoln is elected president of the United States.	December 1860—South Carolina secedes from the Union; other states follow.
1860 A.D.	**1861 A.D.**
February 1861— Southern states form the Confederacy.	April 1861—Confederate soldiers attack Fort Sumter.

PRACTICE AND APPLY

Use the graphic aids shown on pages R5–R7 to answer the following questions:

1. According to the circle graph, is more glass or plastic recycled?

2. For how many years did the average global temperature decrease?

3. According to the bar graph, what was the approximate area of Babylonia?

4. How many chambers did the Great Pyramid of Khufu contain?

5. What did the coil in Archimedes' water-lifting device do?

6. Use the chart to find the name of the Roman god of the sea.

7. According to the train schedule, if you took the 7:25 A.M. train from Crawford Square, when would you arrive at Quincy Station?

8. What Australian desert is partially below sea level?

9. According to the thematic map of Australia, what part of the country has the highest risk of desertification?

10. Use information in the timeline to make a prediction about what might happen in May 1861.

❸ Reading Informational Texts: Patterns of Organization

Reading any type of writing is easier once you recognize how it is organized. Writers usually arrange ideas and information in ways that best show how they are related. There are several common patterns of organization:

- main idea and supporting details
- chronological order
- cause-effect organization
- compare-and-contrast organization
- problem-solution order

Writers try to present their arguments in ways that will help readers follow their reasoning. For more about common ways of organizing and presenting arguments, see *Analyzing Logic and Reasoning,* page R22.

3.1 MAIN IDEA AND SUPPORTING DETAILS

Main idea and supporting details is a basic pattern of organization in which a central idea about a topic is supported by details. The **main idea** is the most important idea about a topic that a particular text or paragraph conveys. **Supporting details** are words, phrases, or sentences that tell more about the main idea. The main idea may be directly stated at the beginning and then followed by supporting details, or it may merely be implied by the supporting details. It may also be stated after it has been implied by supporting details.

Strategies for Reading

- To find a stated main idea in a paragraph, identify the paragraph's topic. The topic is what the paragraph is about and can usually be summed up in one or two words. The word, or synonyms of it, will usually appear throughout the paragraph. Headings and subheadings are also clues to the topics of paragraphs.
- Ask: What is the topic sentence? The topic sentence states the most important idea, message, or information the paragraph conveys about this topic. It is often the first sentence in a paragraph; however, it may appear at the end.
- To find an implied main idea, ask yourself: Whom or what did I just read about? What do the details suggest about the topic?
- Formulate a sentence stating this idea and add it to the paragraph. Does your sentence express the main idea?

Notice how the main idea is expressed in each of the following models.

MODEL: MAIN IDEA AS THE FIRST SENTENCE

Technology consists of all the ways in which people apply knowledge, tools, and inventions to meet their needs. Technology dates back to early humans. At least 2 million years ago, people made stone tools for cutting. Around 1,500 B.C., early humans also made carrying bags, stone hand axes, awls (tools for piercing holes in leather or wood), and drills.

> **Main idea**
>
> **Supporting details**

MODEL: MAIN IDEA AS THE LAST SENTENCE

In time, humans developed more complex tools, such as hunting bows made of wood. They learned to make flint spearheads and metal tools. Early humans used tools to hunt and butcher animals and to construct simple forms of shelter. Technology—these new tools—gave humans more control over their environment and set the stage for a more settled way of life.

> **Supporting details**
>
> **Main idea**

MODEL: IMPLIED MAIN IDEA

Prehistoric art exists in Africa, Asia, Europe, Australia, and the Americas. Cave paintings thousands of years old show lively images of bulls, stallions, and bison. Prehistoric jewelry and figurines also have been found. Early humans may have worn these items. Other items may have had religious meaning.

> **Implied main idea:** Early humans created art and art objects for many purposes.

Read each paragraph, and then do the following:

1. Identify the main idea in the paragraph, using one of the strategies discussed on the previous page.

2. Identify whether the main idea is stated or implied in the paragraph.

> Late on the night of April 18, 1775, Boston patriot Joseph Warren learned of a British military operation planned for the next day. To warn John Hancock and Samuel Adams, who were across the Charles River in Lexington, Warren dispatched two riders, Paul Revere and William Dawes. . . . Revere's ride has been celebrated in poems and textbooks, but Dawes' role was at least as important.
> —PBS Online, "The Other Riders"

> I passed out of the house. Day was trying to dawn through the smoke-pall. A sickly light was creeping over the face of things. Once only the sun broke through the smoke-pall, blood-red, and showing a quarter its usual size. The smoke-pall itself, viewed from beneath, was a rose color that pulsed and fluttered with lavender shades. Then it turned to mauve and yellow and dun. There was no sun. And so dawned the second day on stricken San Francisco.
> —Jack London, "The Story of an Eyewitness"

3.2 CHRONOLOGICAL ORDER

Chronological order is the arrangement of events in the order in which they happen. This type of organization is used in short stories and novels, historical writing, biographies, and autobiographies. To show the order of events, writers use order words, such as *before, after, next,* and *later,* and time words and phrases that identify specific times of day, days of the week, and dates, such as *the next morning, Friday,* and *on June 6, 2006.*

Strategies for Reading

- Look in the text for headings and subheadings that may indicate a chronological pattern of organization, such as *Early Life* or *The Later Years.*

- Look for words and phrases that identify times, such as *in a year, three weeks later, in 79 A.D.,* and *the next day.*

- Look for words that signal order, such as *first, afterward, then, during,* and *finally,* to see how events or steps are related.

- Note that a paragraph or passage in which ideas and information are arranged chronologically will have several words or phrases that indicate time order, not just one.

- Ask yourself: Are the events in the paragraph or passage presented in time order?

Notice the words and phrases that signal time in the first two paragraphs of the following model.

> The great Chinese teacher Confucius was born in 551 B.C. His father died when he was 3 years old. Although Confucius came from a very poor family, he studied hard and became well-educated.
>
> By the time he was 15, in 536 B.C., Confucius' heart was set on learning. In his 30s, Confucius started his teaching career. He later became one of the most important teachers in history. One of his teachings was that people should treat each other the way they would like to be treated. His teachings still seem wise after 2,500 years.
>
> When Confucius died in 479 B.C., he had many followers. About 100 years later, one of his followers, Mencius, began spreading Confucius' ideas. Mencius extended these ideas and added some of his own. He taught that people are basically good and that everyone has equal value. For that reason, he believed that rulers are no

Events

Time phrase

better than their subjects. A good king, he said, must treat his people well.

After Mencius died in 289 B.C., Hsun-tzu carried on Confucius' teachings. Hsun-tzu lived from about 300 to 230 B.C. He did not agree with Mencius that people were basically good. Instead, he taught that human nature was evil. He did believe that education and strong laws and governments could help people become good. Some people say that Hsun-tzu's teachings about strong government later helped the dictator Shih Huang Ti to conquer China and set up the Ch'in Dynasty in 221 B.C.

Order word

PRACTICE AND APPLY

Reread the preceding model and then do the following:

1. List at least four words or phrases in the last three paragraphs that indicate time or order.

2. List all the events in Confucius' life that are mentioned in the model.

3. Create a timeline, beginning with Confucius' birth and ending in 479 B.C., that shows all the events you listed for question 2.

3.3 CAUSE-EFFECT ORGANIZATION

Cause-effect organization is a pattern of organization that shows the relationships between events, ideas, and trends. Cause-effect relationships may be directly stated or merely implied by the order in which the information is presented. Writers often use the cause-effect pattern in historical and scientific writing. Cause-effect relationships may have several forms.

One cause with one effect

One cause with multiple effects

Multiple causes with a single effect

A chain of causes and effects

Strategies for Reading

- Look for headings and subheadings that indicate a cause-effect pattern of organization, such as "Effects of Food Allergies."

- To find the effect or effects, read to answer the question "What happened?"

- To find the cause or causes, read to answer the question "Why did it happen?"

- Look for words and phrases that help you identify specific relationships between events, such as *because, since, had the effect of, led to, as a result, resulted in, for that reason, due to, therefore, if . . . then,* and *consequently.*

- Look closely at each cause-effect relationship. Do not assume that because one event happened before another, the first event caused the second event.

- Use graphic organizers like the diagrams shown to record cause-effect relationships as you read.

Notice the words that signal causes and effects in the following model.

MODEL

Watch Out for Mosquitoes

If you spend any time outdoors in the summer, at some point you will probably find yourself covered with mosquito bites. Mosquitoes can transmit serious diseases such as yellow fever, encephalitis, and malaria. Usually, though, mosquito bites just cause people to develop raised, red bumps that itch.

> Cause
>
> Effect
>
> Cause
>
> Signal word
>
> Effect

This is what happens. Female mosquitoes need blood to nourish their eggs. Consequently, they zero in on living things whose blood they can suck. Once they find a likely victim, the attack begins.

This attack is not really a bite, since a mosquito isn't able to open her jaws. Instead, she punctures the victim's skin with sharp stylets inside her mouth. The mosquito's saliva then flows into these puncture wounds. Because the saliva keeps the victim's blood from clotting, the mosquito can drink her fill.

Meanwhile, the mosquito's saliva causes the person to have an allergic reaction. As a result, the person develops the itchy swelling we call a mosquito bite. Ironically, if the mosquito finishes eating before the victim slaps her or brushes her off, there will be less saliva left in the skin. Therefore, the redness and itching will not be so severe.

PRACTICE AND APPLY

1. Make a graphic organizer like the sample illustrated on page R10 to show the chain of causes and effects described in the text.

2. List three words or phrases that the writer uses to signal cause-effect relationships in the last two paragraphs.

3.4 COMPARE-AND-CONTRAST ORGANIZATION

Compare-and-contrast organization is a pattern of organization that provides a way to look at similarities and differences in two or more subjects. A writer may use this pattern of organization to compare the important points or characteristics of two or more subjects. These points or characteristics are called **points of comparison.** The compare-and-contrast pattern of organization may be developed in either of two ways:

Point-by-point organization—The writer discusses one point of comparison for both subjects, then goes on to the next point.

Subject-by-subject organization—The writer covers all points of comparison for one subject and then all points of comparison for the next subject.

Strategies for Reading

- Look in the text for headings, subheadings, and sentences that may suggest a compare-and-contrast pattern of organization, such as "Plants Share Many Characteristics," to help you identify where similarities and differences are addressed.

- To find similarities, look for words and phrases such as *like, similarly, both, all, every, also,* and *in the same way.*

- To find differences, look for words and phrases such as *unlike, but, on the other hand, more, less, in contrast,* and *however.*

- Use a graphic organizer, such as a Venn diagram or a compare-and-contrast chart, to record points of comparison and similarities and differences.

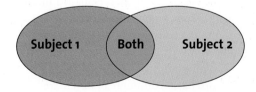

	Subject 1	Subject 2
Point 1		
Point 2		
Point 3		

Read the following models. As you read, use the signal words and phrases to identify the similarities and differences between the subjects and how the details are organized in each text.

MODEL 1

Pass the Bread, Please

There are as many varieties of bread as there are countries. Two kinds that you can enjoy today—from Paris, France, to Paris, Texas, and from Cairo, Illinois, to Cairo, Egypt—are the baguette and the bagel.

Both baguettes and bagels are made from the same basic ingredients, which may include flour, water, yeast, butter, eggs, and salt. Different methods are used to prepare them, however. In each case, bakers first mix the dough, knead it, and leave it to rise. Unlike baguettes, though, bagels are boiled in water before they are baked. This process makes them heavy and chewy and gives them a very light crust. Baguettes, on the other hand, are soft in the center and have a crisp, crunchy crust.

Another difference between the two types of bread is their shape. The word *baguette* means "wand" or "stick" in French. That describes what the bread looks like, too. Baguettes are thin and usually about two feet long. In some places, you can find shorter and fatter versions as well.

The bagel, in contrast, is shaped like a ring. Some legends say that it was originally created to honor a Polish king. It was made to look like a stirrup as a symbol of his victories in battle on horseback. Although all bagels are round, their size can vary greatly. You can choose from minibagels that are only a couple of inches in diameter to larger bagels six inches or more across.

Comparison word

Subjects

Contrast word

Standard baguettes and bagels are both made from white flour. Nowadays, you can choose from a whole universe of variations, however. Baguettes come in sourdough, rye, or whole-wheat varieties.

Bagels come in all those varieties, too. In addition, though, they are available in flavors ranging from apple and blueberry to spinach and tomato. Inside, you might find raisins, nuts, or even chocolate chips. And they might be topped with poppy seeds, sunflower seeds, or sesame seeds.

So the next time you get a craving for crispy, light bread, try a baguette. But for chewy bread with tasty flavors and fillings, choose a bagel.

MODEL 2

What Kind of Person Are You?

There are definitely two types of people in the world—cat people and dog people. About the only thing they share is the fact that they like pets. Aside from that, they are as different as the pets they favor. Comparing these pets might help you figure out what kind of person you are.

Cat people tend to be very independent. They don't like to be controlled or to control anything else. So they don't want an animal that needs a lot of attention. Cats are their perfect pets since they almost take care of themselves.

You can leave cats alone for days at a time. Just set out bowls of food and water, and they will eat and drink only what they want.

Cats also groom themselves without your help. They can be quite affectionate, but only on their own terms. A cat will snuggle with you— when and if it feels like it.

Subjects

Comparison word

Contrast word

Dog people, on the other hand, enjoy feeling needed and don't mind having a pet that is more dependent on them. And dogs definitely are dependent.

Contrast words and phrases

Unlike cats, dogs need a lot of attention daily. They can't be left alone for more than several hours because they have to be fed and walked regularly. You can't just leave food out for them, because they'll eat it all at once. Dogs also generally need a lot of interaction with people. Many of them seem to think their only purpose in life is to please their owners.

As different as cats and dogs are, the good news is that there are plenty of each to go around. So what kind of person are you?

PRACTICE AND APPLY

Refer to the preceding models to answer the following questions:

1. Which model is organized by subject? Which model is organized by points of comparison?

2. Identify two words or phrases in each model that signal a compare-and-contrast pattern of organization.

3. List two points that the writer of each model compares and contrasts.

4. For one of the two models, use a Venn diagram or a compare-and-contrast chart to identify two or more points of comparison and the similarities and differences shown.

3.5 PROBLEM-SOLUTION ORDER

Problem-solution order is a pattern of organization in which a problem is stated and analyzed and then one or more solutions are proposed and examined. This pattern of organization is often used in persuasive writing, such as editorials or proposals.

Strategies for Reading

• Look for an explanation of the problem in the first or second paragraph.

• Look for words, such as *problem* and *reason*, that may signal an explanation of the problem.

• To find the solution, ask: What suggestion does the writer offer to solve the problem?

• Look for words, such as *propose, conclude,* and *answer*, that may signal a solution.

MODEL

It happened again last night. Two cars collided at the corner of West Avenue and Beach Street. This is the sixth accident that has taken place at that intersection in the past year. Luckily, no one has been seriously injured or killed so far. But we need to do something before it's too late. How many crashes do there have to be before we make the streets safer for everyone?

This intersection is so dangerous because West Avenue bends around just before it crosses Beach Street. This means that drivers or cyclists aren't able to see traffic approaching on West Avenue until they're entering the intersection. They have to just take their chances and hope they make it to the other side. Too many times, they don't.

One action that would help solve this problem would be to put a stoplight at the intersection. This would allow drivers and cyclists to move safely through the intersection in both directions. It would also slow traffic down and force people to pay more attention to their driving. Although it would cost the community some money to put in the stoplight, think how much it would save in car repairs, personal injuries, and possibly even lives.

Here's what you can do to help solve this problem. First, talk to your friends and neighbors about it. Then, go to the village hall and sign the petition!

PRACTICE AND APPLY

Reread the model and then answer the following questions:

1. According to the model, what is the cause of the problem?

2. What solution does the writer offer? What words are a clue?

4 Reading Informational Texts: Forms

Magazines, newspapers, Web pages, and consumer, public, and workplace documents are all examples of informational materials. To understand and analyze informational texts, pay attention to text features and patterns of organization.

4.1 READING A NEWSPAPER ARTICLE

Because people often skim newspapers, newspaper publishers use devices to attract attention to articles.

Strategies for Reading

A Consider whether **graphic aids** or quotations are attracting your attention. **Pull quotes**—engaging quotations pulled from the body of the text and reprinted in larger type—are often used to get readers interested in an article.

B Once you decide that you're interested in the article, read the **title** and other **headings** to find out more about its topic and organization.

C Notice whether the article has a **byline,** a line naming the author.

D A **caption,** or text accompanying a graphic aid, may provide information or examples that add to the meaning of the article and are not obvious from the graphic aid.

PRACTICE AND APPLY

1. Who wrote this article?
2. What does the pull quote tell you?
3. How does the photograph relate to the article?

MODEL: NEWSPAPER ARTICLE

Metro · Region

B Peers Talk It Out

SPECIAL REPORT

C by Janis Leibs Dworkis

Does a 10-year-old really know enough to help other students solve their problems? Can he understand more than one side of an issue? Can she be fair and impartial if she knows the students involved?

About 10 percent of the 85,000 schools in the United States offer some form of peer mediation. The Dallas Independent School District offers peer

A "If they had been sent to an adult, . . . they would probably just have been told not to do a fight."

mediation in about half of its almost 200 schools. And almost every school district in the Dallas–Fort Worth area offers a similar program in at least some of its schools.

The peer mediation concept is simple: two or more students who have a disagreement talk over their problem in front of one or two of their peers, with no adults present. The peer mediators, who remain neutral, help the students come to a mutually agreeable solution. . . .

At the Nathaniel Hawthorne Elementary School, sixth graders Earnestine Glosson (front left) and Rocio De Leon (front right) mediate a misunderstanding between fourth graders Laura Rios and Quaniqua Davis (back, left and right). **D**

Sixth-grader Rocio De Leon is serving her third year as a student mediator at Hawthorne. She says, . . . "If they had been sent to an adult, instead of coming to mediation, they would probably just have been told not to do a fight. But the adult wouldn't really understand them. It's a lot easier for a child to understand because you're talking to a person who is actually your age and having some of the same problems as you are."

Those who work with peer mediation hope that, in the long run, these problem-solving skills will lessen the occurrence of fighting—not only at school, but elsewhere, too.

4.2 READING A TEXTBOOK

Each textbook that you use has its own system of organization based on the content in the book. Often an introductory unit will explain the book's organization and special features. If your textbook has such a unit, read it first.

Strategies for Reading

Ⓐ Before you begin reading a lesson or chapter, read any **questions** that appear at the beginning or end of it. Then use the questions to set your purpose for reading.

Ⓑ Read slowly and carefully to better understand and remember the ideas presented in the text. When you come to an unfamiliar word, first try to figure out its meaning from **context clues.** If necessary, find the meaning of the word in a **glossary** in the textbook, or in a dictionary. Avoid interrupting your reading by constantly looking up words in a dictionary.

*For more information on context clues and glossaries, see the **Vocabulary and Spelling Handbook,** pages R68 and R72.*

Ⓒ Use the book's special features, such as sidebars, to increase your understanding of the text. A **sidebar** is a short presentation of additional information. It is usually set off in a box on the page.

Ⓓ Take notes as you read. Use text features such as **subheadings** and boldfaced terms to help you organize your notes. Record your notes in graphic organizers, such as cause-effect charts, to help you clarify relationships among ideas.

MODEL: TEXTBOOK PAGE

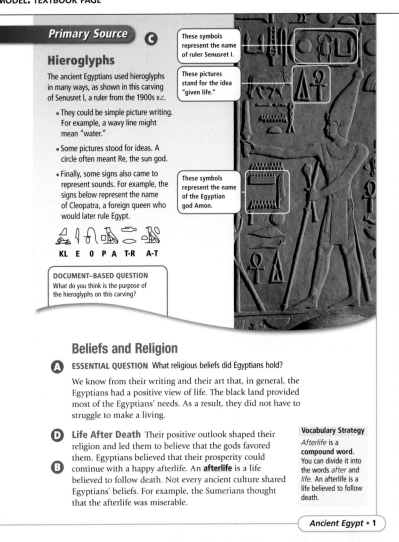

Primary Source **Ⓒ**

Hieroglyphs

The ancient Egyptians used hieroglyphs in many ways, as shown in this carving of Senusret I, a ruler from the 1900s B.C.

- They could be simple picture writing. For example, a wavy line might mean "water."
- Some pictures stood for ideas. A circle often meant Re, the sun god.
- Finally, some signs also came to represent sounds. For example, the signs below represent the name of Cleopatra, a foreign queen who would later rule Egypt.

KL E O P A T-R A-T

These symbols represent the name of ruler Senusret I.

These pictures stand for the idea "given life."

These symbols represent the name of the Egyptian god Amon.

DOCUMENT–BASED QUESTION
What do you think is the purpose of the hieroglyphs on this carving?

Beliefs and Religion

Ⓐ **ESSENTIAL QUESTION** What religious beliefs did Egyptians hold?

We know from their writing and their art that, in general, the Egyptians had a positive view of life. The black land provided most of the Egyptians' needs. As a result, they did not have to struggle to make a living.

Ⓓ **Life After Death** Their positive outlook shaped their religion and led them to believe that the gods favored them. Egyptians believed that their prosperity could **Ⓑ** continue with a happy afterlife. An **afterlife** is a life believed to follow death. Not every ancient culture shared Egyptians' beliefs. For example, the Sumerians thought that the afterlife was miserable.

Vocabulary Strategy
Afterlife is a **compound word.** You can divide it into the words *after* and *life.* An afterlife is a life believed to follow death.

Ancient Egypt • 1

PRACTICE AND APPLY

Reread the textbook page and answer the following questions:

1. Does the sidebar on hieroglyphs give more details about the other text on this page, or does it add new information?

2. Where do you find the definition and additional information for the word *afterlife?*

3. What is the answer to the Essential Question?

4.3 READING A CONSUMER DOCUMENT

Consumer documents are printed materials that accompany products and services. They usually provide information about the use, care, operation, or assembly of the products they accompany. Some common consumer documents are contracts, warranties, manuals, instructions, and schedules.

Strategies for Reading

A Read the **heading** to see what information the document covers. Read the **subheadings** to learn what process each section of the instructions explains.

B Read the directions all the way through at least once. Look carefully for sections that require information such as a signature or a date.

C Look for **numbers** or **letters** that indicate the order in which the steps should be followed. You can also look for signal words such as *first* and *finally*.

D Words that appear in **boldface** or in all **capital letters** often indicate areas that require your attention.

E Look for **verbs that describe actions** you should take, such as *show*, *complete*, and *sign*.

F Pay attention to **notes** that give extra information.

PRACTICE AND APPLY

Reread the library card application and the instructions for applying. Use these documents to answer the questions.

1. How might you apply for a library card if you do not have a driver's license?

2. Who is responsible for borrowed materials if the library card owner is under the age of 14?

MODEL: INSTRUCTIONS

Milton Valley Public Library **A**

Applying for a Library Card A

Residents of Milton Valley can apply for a library card at either the Central or South Milton branch. To apply:

1. Present two forms of identification. Acceptable forms of identification are:
   C Student ID
   Valid Driver's License
   State ID Card
   Passport

2. If you do not have a driver's license or State ID, you must show proof of residency. This can be any one of the following:
   Driver's Learning Permit
   Bank Statement
   Utility or Credit Card Bill
   Lease or Housing Contract

3. Complete a registration form by providing the following information: name, address, telephone number, previous address (if you have lived at your current residence for less than three years), and signature.

4. If you are under the age of 14, you will need to have your parent or guardian sign **E** the application.

5. Finally, submit your application and wait to have a picture taken for your library card. Cards will be ready for pickup in half an hour.

MODEL: APPLICATION

Milton Valley Public Library Card Application

PLEASE PRINT. USE BLACK OR BLUE INK. **D**

NAME: _____

ADDRESS: _____ CITY: _____

STATE:_____ ZIP CODE/POSTAL CODE: _____

PREVIOUS ADDRESS: _____

HOME PHONE: (____)_____ MOBILE PHONE: (____)_____

DATE OF BIRTH (dd/mm/yyyy): _____

I agree to be responsible for any materials borrowed from Milton Valley Public Library in my name.

SIGNATURE:_____ DATE: ____ **B**

For cardholders under the age of 14: You must have permission of a parent or guardian along with a signature. Parents: Your signature indicates that you are responsible for any materials borrowed under your child's name. **F**

PARENT SIGNATURE: _____ DATE: _____

PLEASE PRINT NAME: _____ **B**

Office Use Only

Card No. _____ Date Issued _____ Expires _____

4.4 READING A PUBLIC DOCUMENT

Public documents are documents that are written for the public to provide information that is of public interest or concern. These documents are often free. They can be federal, state, or local government documents. They can be speeches or historical documents. They may even be laws, posted warnings, signs, or rules and regulations.

Strategies for Reading

Ⓐ The **title** tells you about the message of the document.

Ⓑ The **rows** and **columns** of the chart help you find the specific information you need.

- **Column 1:** Your age, situation, and special needs
- **Column 2:** When you should get your flu shot

Ⓒ The **contact information** at the bottom of the page tells you what number to call or Web site to consult if you have questions or need more information.

MODEL: PUBLIC NOTICE

Ⓐ When should YOU get your flu shot?

	Ⓑ OCT	NOV	DEC or later
People at high risk of severe illness ▪ **65 years old or older**—Even if you're in great health! ▪ **Children 6-23 months old**—Children younger than 2 years old have one of the highest rates of hospitalizations from influenza ▪ **Adults and children with a chronic health condition**—Such as heart disease, diabetes, kidney disease, asthma, cancer, and HIV/AIDS ▪ **More than 3 months pregnant during flu season**—Typically November through March	Best Time		Not too late!
People who can give the flu to those at high risk ▪ **Household contact or care-giver of someone at high risk** ▪ **Health care workers** ▪ **Household contact or care-giver of a child under 2 years old**—Infants younger than 6 months old can't get a flu shot, but they can get the flu	Best Time		Not too late!
Your child's very first flu shot ▪ **Children 6 months – 8 years old** getting the very first flu shot need a booster shot one month after the first dose of vaccine	Best Time		Not too late!
Healthy people 50-64 years old		Best Time	Not too late!
Anyone who wants to prevent the flu		Best Time	Not too late!

A flu shot is your best protection against the flu.

Ⓒ For more information: Ask your health care provider or call the CDC Immunization Hot Line.
English: 1-800-232-2522   Español: 1-800-232-0233   www.cdc.gov/nip/flu

CDC
Immunization
SAFER·HEALTHIER·PEOPLE™

Fight the Flu

PRACTICE AND APPLY

Refer to the public notice to answer the following questions:

1. Who can't get a flu shot?

2. When is the best time for healthy people 50 to 64 years old to get their flu shots?

3. What phone number should you call to get information in Spanish?

4.5 READING A WORKPLACE DOCUMENT

Workplace documents are materials that are produced or used within a workplace, for business purposes. Some documents, such as minutes of a meeting or a sales report, may be generated by a business to monitor itself. Others may explain company policies or make requests. Workplace documents include memos, e-mails, business letters, job applications, and résumés.

Strategies for Reading

A Read the header to learn basic information about the e-mail.

    To: This line shows the e-mail address of the recipient.

    Subject: This line tells the reader what the e-mail is about.

B Read the document carefully, as it may contain details that should not be overlooked.

C Look for features, such as **bullet points,** that ask you to take action or find specific information. Take notes to help you remember what actions are required.

D Pay attention to the **signature line.** The signature line will often tell you how to contact the sender if you have any questions.

MODEL: BUSINESS E-MAIL

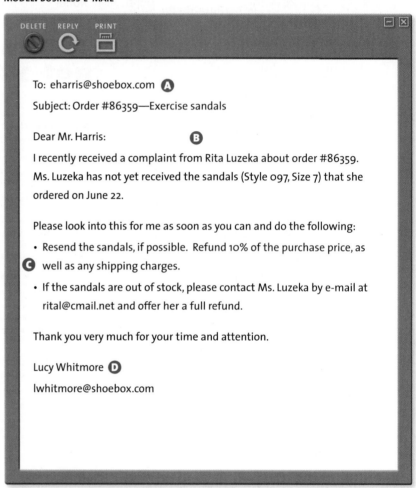

DELETE   REPLY   PRINT

To: eharris@shoebox.com **A**

Subject: Order #86359—Exercise sandals

Dear Mr. Harris: **B**

I recently received a complaint from Rita Luzeka about order #86359. Ms. Luzeka has not yet received the sandals (Style 097, Size 7) that she ordered on June 22.

Please look into this for me as soon as you can and do the following:

- Resend the sandals, if possible. Refund 10% of the purchase price, as well as any shipping charges. **C**
- If the sandals are out of stock, please contact Ms. Luzeka by e-mail at rital@cmail.net and offer her a full refund.

Thank you very much for your time and attention.

Lucy Whitmore **D**

lwhitmore@shoebox.com

PRACTICE AND APPLY

Read the business e-mail and answer the following questions:

1. What is this e-mail about?

2. Who sent the e-mail, and who received it?

3. When did the customer order her shoes?

4. What should Mr. Harris do if the sandals are out of stock?

5. How can Mr. Harris contact Ms. Luzeka?

4.6 READING ELECTRONIC TEXT

Electronic text is any text that is in a form that a computer can store and display on a screen. Electronic text can be part of Web pages, CD-ROMs, search engines, and documents that you create with your computer software. Like books, Web pages often provide aids for finding information. However, each Web page is designed differently, and information is not in the same location on each page. It is important to know the functions of different parts of a Web page so that you can easily find the information you want.

Strategies for Reading

Ⓐ First look at the **title** of a page to determine what topics it covers. The title is different from the **Web address,** or URL, which usually begins with *http://.*

Ⓑ Look for a **menu bar** along the top, bottom, or side of a Web page. Clicking on an item in a menu bar will take you to another part of the Web site.

Ⓒ Notice any **hyperlinks** to related pages. Hyperlinks are often underlined or highlighted in a contrasting color. You can click on a hyperlink to get to another page—one that may or may not have been created by the same person or organization.

Ⓓ For information that you want to keep for future reference, save documents on your computer or print them. For online sources, you can pull down the **Favorites** or **Bookmarks** menu and bookmark pages so that you can easily return to them or print the information you need. Printing the pages will allow you to highlight key ideas on a hard copy.

MODEL: WEB PAGE

PRACTICE AND APPLY

1. What is the Web address, or URL, of this Web page?

2. Which menu items would you click on to help plan your family's visit to Yosemite?

3. How could you use this Web site to find information about another national park?

5 Reading Persuasive Texts

5.1 ANALYZING AN ARGUMENT

An **argument** expresses a position on an issue or problem and supports it with reasons and evidence. Being able to analyze and evaluate arguments will help you distinguish between claims you should accept and those you should not. A sound argument should appeal strictly to reason. However, arguments are often used in texts that also contain other types of persuasive devices. An argument includes the following elements:

- A **claim** is the writer's position on an issue or problem.

- **Support** is any material that serves to prove a claim. In an argument, support usually consists of reasons and evidence.

- **Reasons** are declarations made to justify an action, decision, or belief—for example, "My reason for bringing my umbrella is that the weather forecast predicted rain."

- **Evidence** can be the specific references, quotations, facts, examples, and opinions that support a claim. Evidence may also consist of statistics, reports of personal experience, or the views of experts.

- A **counterargument** is an argument made to oppose another argument. A good argument anticipates the opposition's objections and provides counterarguments to disprove or answer them.

Claim	We have too much homework.
Reason	There's no time for other activities.
Evidence	I had to drop out of the Eagle Scouts.
Counterargument	Students need to do homework to practice and learn their subjects, but too much overwhelms us and makes learning harder.

Read the following editorial and use a chart like the one shown to identify the claim, reasons, evidence, and counterargument.

Our School Needs to Get in the Swim
by Maria Lopez

This school needs a swimming pool. Swimming is an important life skill and one of the best forms of exercise there is. It is one of the few activities that won't harm the body and can actually improve circulation, breathing, and mobility. I believe it is the responsibility of the school to provide this essential part of students' lifelong education.

The school's mission is to educate the whole person—mind and body—and to prepare students to be productive citizens. In addition to our academic subjects, we are taught how to eat right and budget our money. But we don't learn the water safety skills that could someday save our lives.

The community and school board obviously don't feel the same way about this issue as I do, however. They repeatedly have refused to fund the building of a pool. In the opinion of one board member, "Students can take swimming lessons at the local health club." Other school officials think that the school has more important needs—repairing the sagging gym floor and installing new lockers, for example.

In my opinion, these reasons are not valid. First, most students cannot afford swimming lessons at the health club. Even those who have the money don't have the time. They're busy with homework and other activities during the school year and have to work or go to summer school during vacation.

I agree that the gym floor should be replaced and wouldn't mind having a new locker. But I believe that the educational needs of the students should come first. Even if knowing how to swim never saves your life, it can improve its quality. Isn't that what an education is all about?

5.2 RECOGNIZING PERSUASIVE TECHNIQUES

Persuasive texts typically rely on more than just the **logical appeal** of an argument to be convincing. They also rely on ethical and emotional appeals and other **persuasive techniques**—devices that can convince you to adopt a position or take an action.

Ethical appeals establish a writer's credibility and trustworthiness with an audience. When a writer links a claim to a widely accepted value, the writer not only gains moral support for that claim but also establishes him- or herself as a reputable, moral person readers can and should trust. For example, with the following appeal the writer reminds readers of a value they should accept and aligns himself or herself with the reader: "Most of us think it's important to be informed about current events, but we don't spend much time reading newspapers."

The chart shown here explains several other methods by which a writer may attempt to persuade you to adopt his or her position. If you learn to recognize these techniques, you are less likely to be influenced by them.

Persuasive Technique	Example
Appeals by Association	
Bandwagon appeal Suggests that a person should believe or do something because "everyone else" does	Don't be the last person in town to be connected to Neighbor Net.
Testimonial Relies on endorsements from well-known people or satisfied customers	Start your day with the vitamins recommended by four out of five doctors—Superstrength Vigorvites.
Snob appeal Taps into people's desire to be special or part of an elite group	You deserve to eat like a king. Join the distinguished diners at Marco's Palace.
Appeal to loyalty Relies on people's affiliation with a particular group	Show your support for the community by marching in our local Memorial Day parade!
Emotional Appeals	
Appeals to pity, fear, or vanity Use strong feelings, rather than facts, to persuade	If you don't see a dentist regularly, your teeth will rot.
Word Choice	
Glittering generality A generalization that includes a word or phrase with positive connotations, to promote a product, a person, or an idea	Serve your family George's farm-fresh eggs, because fresh is always better.

Identify the persuasive techniques used in this model.

Learn While You Sleep

Join the increasing number of with-it people who are making every hour of their day—and night—count. No matter whether they're awake or asleep, they keep going, growing, and improving themselves every minute. Impossible? Not according to college basketball superstar Jordan Navarro, whose grade-point average went from a 2.5 to a 4.0 after just one month on the program. "As amazing as it sounds, my free-throw average shot up, too," he said. Stop wasting time and start becoming the smart and effective person you always dreamed of being. Just call 555-ZZ-LEARN and sign up right now.

5.3 ANALYZING LOGIC AND REASONING

While persuasive techniques may sway you to side with a writer, they should not be enough to convince you that an argument is sound. To determine the soundness of an argument, you really need to examine the argument's claim and support and the logic or reasoning that links them. To do this, it is helpful to identify the writer's mode of reasoning.

The Inductive Mode of Reasoning

When a writer moves from specific evidence to a general principle or generalization, that writer is using **inductive reasoning.** Here is an example of inductive reasoning.

SPECIFIC FACTS

Fact 1 Allison's eyes swell and she has trouble breathing when she's around cats.

Fact 2 Roses make her sister Lucy sneeze.

Fact 3 Max gets an allergic reaction from eating peanuts.

GENERALIZATION

People can be allergic to animals, plants, and foods.

Strategies for Determining the Soundness of Inductive Arguments

Ask yourself the following questions to evaluate an inductive argument:

- **Is the evidence valid and sufficient support for the conclusion?** Inaccurate facts lead to inaccurate conclusions.

- **Does the conclusion follow logically from the evidence?** From the facts listed above, the conclusion that *all* animals, plants, and foods cause allergic reactions would be too broad.

- **Is the evidence drawn from a large enough sample?** These three facts are enough to support the generalization. However, if you wanted to support a conclusion that most people are allergic to something, you would need a larger sample.

The Deductive Mode of Reasoning

When a writer arrives at a conclusion by applying a general principle to a specific situation, the writer is using **deductive reasoning.** Here's an example.

Spiders have eight legs, a body, and a head.	General principle or premise

This bug has a body and a head, but only six legs.	Specific situation

This bug is not a spider. It must be something else.	Specific conclusion

Strategies for Determining the Soundness of Deductive Arguments

Ask yourself the following questions to evaluate a deductive argument:

- **Is the general principle actually stated, or is it implied?** Note that writers often use deductive reasoning in arguments without stating the general principle. They just assume that readers will recognize and agree with the principle. So you may want to identify the general principle for yourself.

- **Is the general principle sound?** Don't just assume the general principle is sound. Ask yourself whether it is really true.

- **Is the conclusion valid?** To be valid, a conclusion in a deductive argument must follow logically from the general principle and the specific situation.

The following chart shows two conclusions drawn from the same general principle.

The whole basketball team went to the school picnic.	
Accurate Deduction	**Inaccurate Deduction**
Carl is on the team; therefore, Carl went to the picnic.	Nabu went to the school picnic; therefore, Nabu is on the basketball team.

People other than those on the basketball team might have gone to the school picnic.

PRACTICE AND APPLY

Identify the mode of reasoning used in the following paragraph.

> I was doing my homework in my room last night when the light went out. Going out into the hall, I saw that the lights were still on in the kitchen and in my parents' room. That told me the problem was just in my room. The lamp was still plugged in, so I tried putting in a new light bulb. Luckily, that worked.

Identifying Faulty Reasoning

Sometimes an argument at first appears to make sense but isn't valid because it is based on an unsupported inference. An **unsupported inference** is a statement that is not backed up by facts. An argument may also not be valid if it is based on a fallacy. A **fallacy** is an error in logic. Learn to recognize these common fallacies.

TYPE OF FALLACY	DEFINITION	EXAMPLE
Circular reasoning	Supporting a statement by simply repeating it in different words	I forgot my lunch because **I didn't remember to bring it.**
Either/or fallacy	A statement that suggests that there are only two choices available in a situation that really offers more than two options	**Either** you get an A in English this year **or** you'll get an F.
Oversimplification	An explanation of a complex situation or problem as if it were much simpler than it is	**Just be a good listener** and you'll have lots of friends.
Overgeneralization	A generalization that is too broad. You can often recognize overgeneralizations by the use of words such as *all, everyone, every time, anything, no one,* and *none.*	I **always** say the wrong thing.
Hasty generalization	A conclusion drawn from too little evidence or from evidence that is biased	**We all must have done badly on the test,** because Ms. Chen looked angry at the beginning of class today.
Stereotyping	A dangerous type of overgeneralization. Stereotypes are broad statements about people on the basis of their gender, ethnicity, race, or political, social, professional, or religious group.	**Boys** are better at sports than **girls** are.
Attacking the person or name-calling	An attempt to discredit an idea by attacking the person or group associated with it	Only **immature** people like animated movies.
Evading the issue	Responding to an objection with arguments and evidence that do not address its central point	I didn't tell you I broke the statue, **but you said you never liked it anyway.**
False cause	The mistake of assuming that because one event occurred after another event in time, the first event caused the second one	Ellie studied really hard for the test, **so the teacher cancelled it.**

evading the issue. The speaker points a finger at his opponent's voting record without addressing his own.

EXAMPLE: *My opponent is lying when he says I don't care about the people. He says he represents the people's needs, but his voting record shows that he really only cares about rich businessmen.* (The speaker does not include the fact that he voted the same way as his opponent on 80 percent of the issues.)

For more information on logical fallacies, see **Identifying Faulty Reasoning,** *page R24.*

Strategies for Evaluating Evidence

It is important to have a set of standards by which you can evaluate persuasive texts. Use the questions below to help you critically assess facts and opinions that are presented as evidence.

- **Are the facts presented verifiable?** Facts can be proven by eyewitness accounts, authoritative sources such as encyclopedias and almanacs, experts, or research.

- **Are the opinions presented well informed?** Any opinions offered should be supported by facts, be based on research or eyewitness accounts, or be the opinions of experts on the topic.

- **Is the evidence thorough?** Thorough evidence leaves no reasonable questions unanswered. If a choice is offered, background for making the choice should be provided. If taking a side is called for, all sides of the issue should be presented.

- **Is the evidence balanced?** Be alert to evidence that is weighted unfairly or contains loaded language—two signs of bias.

- **Is the evidence authoritative?** The people, groups, or organizations that provided the evidence should have credentials that support their authority.

- **Is it important that the evidence be current?** Where timeliness is crucial, as in the areas of medicine and technology, the evidence should reflect the latest developments in the areas.

PRACTICE AND APPLY

Look for examples of logical fallacies in the following argument. Identify each one and explain why you identified it as such.

> My parents can't understand me because they just don't get it. Adults are like robots and just keep doing things the way they were taught. For example, all my friends are allowed to stay up as late as they want on weekends, but I have to be in bed by 9:00. Why? Because that's how my parents were raised. I've tried to explain to them that if I can't stay up later, I'll lose all my friends. They just say I'll understand when I'm a parent. Well, I guess I'll never understand, because I'll never have kids.

5.4 EVALUATING PERSUASIVE TEXTS

Learning how to evaluate persuasive texts and identify bias will help you become more selective when doing research and also help you improve your own reasoning and arguing skills. **Bias** is an inclination for or against a particular opinion or viewpoint. A writer may reveal a strongly positive or negative opinion on an issue by presenting only one way of looking at it or by heavily weighting the evidence on one side of the argument. The presence of the following is often a sign that a writer is biased:

Loaded language consists of words with strongly positive or negative connotations that are intended to influence a reader's attitude.

EXAMPLE: *This movie insults my intelligence. It was so ridiculous that I walked out before it was done.* (*Insults* and *ridiculous* have very negative connotations.)

Propaganda is any form of communication that is so distorted that it conveys false or misleading information. Some politicians create and distribute propaganda. Many logical fallacies, such as name-calling, the either/or fallacy, and false causes, are often used in propaganda. The following example includes name-calling and

Read the argument below. Identify the facts, opinions, and elements of bias.

Lewis Middle School doesn't care about students' needs. I know the school board voted to remove our lockers so we can't hide dangerous items there. We don't deserve this lack of respect and suspicion, though. The lockers gave us a place to store our books, jackets, lunches, and other gear when we weren't using them. It's not fair to make us haul our stuff around all day. After all, my textbooks alone weigh over 70 pounds—as much as I do. Would you board members want to carry me around on your back all day?

Strategies for Determining a Strong Argument

Make sure that all or most of the following statements are true:

- The argument presents a claim or thesis.

- The claim is connected to its support by a general principle that most readers would readily agree with. Valid general principle: *People are responsible for treating others with kindness.* Invalid general principle: *People are responsible for making other people happy.*

- The reasons make sense.

- The reasons are presented in a logical and effective order.

- The claim and all reasons are adequately supported by sound evidence.

- The evidence is adequate, accurate, and appropriate.

- The logic is sound. There are no instances of faulty reasoning.

- The argument offers counterarguments to address possible reader concerns and counterclaims.

Use the preceding criteria to evaluate the strength of the following proposal.

MODEL

Summary of Proposal

I propose that the town put trash containers at bus stops, train stations, playgrounds, parks, beaches, and all other public areas.

Need

The community is littered with paper, food and drink containers, and other garbage. This situation doesn't make us feel good about ourselves or where we live.

Proposed Solution

Making trash containers available in places where people gather will help create a cleaner environment and restore our pride in our community.

Everybody would be willing to throw their bottles, cans, newspapers, gum wrappers, bags, and other garbage in a container if there was one available. Most people aren't willing to carry their trash with them until they find a proper place to throw it, however. Many citizens are such slobs that they won't even walk across the street to throw something away rather than just dropping it on the ground.

I know that installing these trash containers will cost money. Workers also will have to be paid to empty them regularly. Another objection might be that kids sometimes overturn trash containers or enjoy rolling them around.

These objections are ridiculous, though. None of us really believe that having a clean, pleasant community wouldn't be worth the few dollars this would cost. And a simple— and cheap—way to prevent kids from playing with the containers would be to chain them to a pole or fence.

Either the town council votes to approve this proposal and put it into effect right away, or they should be voted out of office.

6 Adjusting Reading Rate to Purpose

You may need to change the way you read certain texts in order to understand them. To adjust the way you read, you first need to be aware of what you want to get out of what you are reading. Then you can adjust the speed at which you read in response to your purpose and the difficulty of the material.

Determine Your Purpose for Reading

You read different types of materials for different purposes. You may read a novel for enjoyment. You may read a textbook unit to learn a new concept or to master the content for a test. When you read for enjoyment, you naturally read at a pace that is comfortable for you. When you read for information, you need to read material more slowly and thoroughly. When you are being tested on material, you may think you have to read fast, especially if the test is being timed. However, you can actually increase your understanding of the material if you slow down.

Determine Your Reading Rate

The rate at which you read most comfortably is called your **independent reading level.** It is the rate at which you read materials that you enjoy. To learn to adjust your reading rate to read materials for other purposes, you need to be aware of your independent reading level. You can figure out your reading level by following these steps:

1. Select a passage from a book or story you enjoy.
2. Have a friend or classmate time you as you begin reading the passage silently.
3. Read at the rate that is most comfortable for you.
4. Stop when your friend or classmate tells you one minute has passed.
5. Determine the number of words you read in that minute and write down the number.
6. Repeat the process at least two more times, using different passages.
7. Add the numbers and divide the sum by the number of times your friend timed you.

Reading Techniques for Informational Material

You can use the following techniques to adapt your reading for informational texts, to prepare for tests, and to better understand what you read:

- **Skimming** is reading quickly to get the general idea of a text. To skim, read the title, headings, graphic aids, highlighted words, and first sentence of each paragraph. Also, read any introduction, conclusion, or summary. Skimming can be especially useful when taking a test. Before reading a passage, you can skim questions that follow it in order to find out what is expected and better focus on the important ideas in the text.

  When researching a topic, skimming can help you decide whether a source has information that is related to your topic.

- **Scanning** is reading quickly to find a specific piece of information, such as a fact or a definition. When you scan, your eyes sweep across a page, looking for key words that may lead you to the information you want. Use scanning to review for tests and to find answers to questions.

- **Changing pace** is increasing or decreasing the rate at which you read parts of a particular text. When you come across explanations of familiar concepts, you might be able to speed up without misunderstanding them. When you encounter unfamiliar concepts or material presented in a new way, however, you may need to slow down to understand the information.

WATCH OUT! Reading too slowly can affect your ability to understand what you read. Make sure you aren't just reading one word at a time. Practice reading phrases.

PRACTICE AND APPLY

Find an article in a magazine or textbook. Skim the article. Then answer the following questions:

1. What did you notice about the organization of the article from skimming it?
2. What is the main idea of the article?

Writing is a process that can help you explore your thoughts, experiment with ideas, and make connections. Through writing, you can examine and record your thoughts, feelings, and ideas for yourself alone, or you can communicate them to an audience.

WRITING TOOLS
Go to the **Writing Center** at **ClassZone.com** for interactive models, publishing ideas, and other support.

1 The Writing Process

The writing process consists of the following stages: prewriting, drafting, revising and editing, proofreading, and publishing. These are not stages that you must complete in a set order. Rather, you may return to an earlier stage at any time to improve your writing.

1.1 PREWRITING

In the prewriting stage, you explore what you want to write about, what your purpose for writing is, whom you are writing for, and what form you will use to express your ideas. Ask yourself the following questions to get started.

Topic	• Is my topic assigned, or can I choose it? • What would I be interested in writing about?
Purpose	• Am I writing to entertain, to inform, to persuade, to argue, to request, or for some combination of these purposes? • What effect do I want to have on my readers?
Audience	• Who is the audience? • What might the audience members already know about my topic? • What about the topic might interest them?
Format	• Which format will work best? Personal letter? Letter to the editor? Essay? Poem? Speech? Short story? Article? Report? Research paper? Review?

Find Ideas for Writing

• Browse through magazines, newspapers, and Web sites.

• Start a file or notebook of articles you want to save for future reference.

• With a group, brainstorm a list of ideas.

• Write down further ideas as they come to you.

• Interview someone who is an expert on a particular topic.

• Use graphic organizers to explore other ideas that relate to a general topic.

Organize Ideas

Once you've chosen a topic, you will need to compile and organize your ideas. If you are writing a description, you may need to gather sensory details. For an essay or a research paper, you may need to record information from different sources. To record notes from sources you read or view, use any or all of these methods:

• **Summarize**—Briefly retell the main ideas of a piece of writing in your own words.

• **Paraphrase**—Restate all of the information in your own words.

• **Quote**—Record the author's exact words.

Depending on what form your writing takes, you may also need to arrange your ideas in a certain pattern.

*For more information, see the **Writing Handbook**, pages R34–R41.*

1.2 DRAFTING

In the drafting stage, you put your ideas on paper and allow them to develop and change as you write. Don't worry about correct grammar and spelling at this stage. There are two ways that you can draft.

Discovery drafting is a good approach when you are not quite sure what you think about your subject. You just start writing and let your feelings and ideas lead you in developing the topic.

Planned drafting may work better if you know that your ideas have to be arranged in a certain way, as in a research paper. Try making a writing plan or an informal outline before you begin drafting.

1.3 REVISING AND EDITING

The revising and editing stage allows you to polish your draft and make changes to its content, organization, and style. Use the questions that follow to spot problems and determine what changes would improve your work:

- Does my writing have a **main idea** or central focus? Is my thesis clear?
- Have I used **precise** nouns, verbs, and modifiers?
- Have I included enough **details** and **evidence?** Where can I add details, statistics, or examples?
- Do all ideas and details support my main idea?
- Is my writing clear and **coherent?** Do sentences connect to one another smoothly and logically?
- Have I used a consistent **point of view?**
- Do I need to add **transitional words, phrases,** or **sentences** to explain relationships among ideas?
- Have I used a variety of **sentence types?** Are my sentences well constructed? Would combining sentences improve the rhythm of my writing?
- Does my **tone** fit my audience and purpose?

1.4 PROOFREADING

When you are satisfied with your revision, proofread your paper for mistakes in grammar, usage, and mechanics. Dictionaries, handbooks, and other resources will help you correct errors. You may want to do this several times, looking for a different type of mistake each time. Ask:

- Have I made any errors in **subject-verb agreement** and **pronoun-antecedent agreement?**
- Have I checked for errors in **confusing word pairs,** such as *it's/its, than/then,* and *too/to?*
- Have I corrected any **run-on sentences** and **sentence fragments?**
- Have I followed rules for **correct capitalization** and used **punctuation marks** correctly?
- Have I checked the **spellings** of unfamiliar words in the dictionary?
- Have I checked for errors in **possessive form** or in the **comparative** and **superlative forms** of adverbs and adjectives?

TIP If possible, don't begin proofreading right after you've finished writing. Put your work away for at least a few hours. When you return to it, you will find it easier to identify and correct mistakes.

*For more information, see the **Grammar Handbook** and the **Vocabulary and Spelling Handbook**, pages R46–R75.*

Use the proofreading symbols in the chart to mark changes on your draft.

Proofreading Symbols	
⋀ Add letters or words.	/ Make a capital letter lowercase.
⊙ Add a period.	⌗ Begin a new paragraph.
☰ Capitalize a letter.	⌒ Delete letters or words.
⌒ Close up space.	∿ Switch the positions of letters or words.
⋀ Add a comma.	

1.5 PUBLISHING AND REFLECTING

Always consider sharing your finished writing with a wider audience. Another good way to finish a project is to reflect on your writing.

Publishing Ideas

- Post your writing on a Weblog.
- Create a multimedia presentation and share it with classmates.
- Publish your writing in a school newspaper, local newspaper, or literary magazine.
- Present your work orally in a report, speech, reading, or dramatic performance.

Reflecting on Your Writing

Think about your writing process and whether you would like to add what you have written to your writing portfolio. Ask yourself:

- What did I learn about myself and my subject during this writing project?
- What was the biggest problem I faced during the writing process? How did I solve the problem?
- Which parts of the writing process did I most and least enjoy?
- What did I learn about my own process that I can use the next time I write?

1.6 PEER RESPONSE

Peer response consists of the suggestions and comments you make about the writing of your peers and also the comments and suggestions they make about your writing. You can ask a peer reader for help at any time in the writing process.

Using Peer Response as a Writer

- Tell readers where you are in the writing process and whether you would prefer feedback about your ideas or about your writing.

- Ask questions that will help you get specific information about your writing. Open-ended questions, which require more than yes-or-no answers, are more likely to give you information that will help you revise.

- Give your readers plenty of time to respond thoughtfully to your writing.

- Encourage your readers to be honest.

Being a Peer Reader

- Respect the writer's feelings.

- Offer positive reactions first.

- Make sure you understand what kind of feedback the writer is looking for and respond accordingly.

For more information on the writing process, see the **Introductory Unit,** *pages 1–19.*

2 Building Blocks of Good Writing

Whatever your purpose is for writing, you need to capture your reader's interest and organize your thoughts clearly.

2.1 INTRODUCTIONS

An introduction should capture your reader's attention. It may also contain the thesis statement or introduce a main idea.

Kinds of Introductions

There are many different ways to write an introduction. The one you choose depends on who the audience is and on your purpose for writing.

Make a Surprising Statement Beginning with a startling statement or an interesting fact can stir your reader's curiosity about a subject, as in the following model.

> **MODEL**
>
> A male Kodiak bear may weigh 1,500 pounds, measure 10 feet long, and run up to 30 miles an hour. Protected within Alaska's Kodiak National Wildlife Refuge, nearly 3,000 of these bears share 100-mile-long Kodiak Island, where they feast on fish, berries, and whale and seal carcasses.

Provide a Description A vivid description sets a mood and brings a scene to life for your reader.

Here, details about running on a track set the mood for a narrative about a race.

> **MODEL**
>
> In the pale morning light, the shadowy track was still. Rounding the curve, the athlete locked her eyes on the single floodlight at the far end of the track, her every muscle straining toward it.

Ask a Question Beginning with a question can make your reader want to read on to find out the answer. The following introduction asks a question about the importance of a particular person.

> **MODEL**
>
> Why does Danielle Del Ferraro hold a special place in the history of the Soap Box Derby? Since the derby began in 1934, she has been the only participant ever to win twice.

Relate an Anecdote Beginning with an anecdote, or brief story, can hook your reader and help you make a point in a dramatic way. The following anecdote introduces a firsthand account of a memorable event.

> **MODEL**
>
> Dressed in my best clothes, I rushed outside, late for my sister's wedding. I waited impatiently for the light to change at the corner. Then, from out of nowhere came an out-of-control in-line skater. The result was a head-on collision.

Address the Reader Speaking directly to your reader establishes a friendly, informal tone and involves the reader in your topic.

> **MODEL**
>
> Find out how you can get in shape and have fun at the same time. Come to a free demonstration of Fit for Life on Friday night at 7:00 P.M.

Begin with a Thesis Statement A thesis statement expressing a main idea may be woven into both the beginning and the end of a piece of nonfiction writing.

> **MODEL**
>
> Although the names of the Greek and Roman gods were different, the things the gods did were very similar.

TIP To write the best introduction for your paper, you may want to try more than one of the methods and then decide which is the most effective for your purpose and audience.

2.2 PARAGRAPHS

A paragraph is made up of sentences that work together to develop an idea or accomplish a purpose. Whether or not it contains a topic sentence stating the main idea, a good paragraph must have unity and coherence.

Unity

A paragraph has unity when all the sentences support and develop one stated or implied idea. Use the following technique to create unity in your paragraphs:

Write a Topic Sentence A topic sentence states the main idea of the paragraph; all other sentences in the paragraph provide supporting details. A topic sentence is often the first sentence in a paragraph, as shown in the model that follows.

However, it may also appear later in a paragraph or at the end, to summarize or reinforce the main idea.

> **MODEL**
>
> The most important rule for a beginning photographer is this: check before you click. Is the film loaded? Is your subject well lighted or will you need a flash? Have you framed your picture carefully? Are you holding the camera still? Checking the basics will go a long way toward making your snapshots memorable.

TIP Paying attention to topic sentences when you read literature can help you craft your own topic sentences. Notice the use of strong topic sentences in "Matthew Henson at the Top of the World" on page 768. For example, the fourth paragraph on page 770 begins, "Although Matthew Henson's early life seems harsh, in many ways he was very lucky." The rest of the paragraph then explains some of the advantages Henson had while he was growing up.

Coherence

A paragraph is coherent when all its sentences are related to one another and each flows logically to the next. Use the following techniques to make your paragraphs more coherent:

- Present your ideas in the most logical order.
- Use pronouns, synonyms, and repeated words to connect ideas.
- Use transitional words to show relationships among ideas.

In the model shown here, the writer used several techniques to create a coherent paragraph.

> **MODEL**
>
> Most scientists believe that all of Earth's land once formed one supercontinent. Over 200 million years ago, this supercontinent began to break into two large masses of land. Since that time, the plates on which continents rest have continued to move.

2.3 TRANSITIONS

Transitions are words and phrases that show connections between details. Clear transitions help show how your ideas relate to one another.

Kinds of Transitions

The types of transitions you choose depend on the ideas you want to convey.

Time or Sequence Some transitions help to clarify the sequence of events over time. When you are telling a story or describing a process, you can connect ideas with such transitional words as *first, second, always, then, next, later, soon, before, finally, after, earlier, afterward,* and *tomorrow.*

> **MODEL**
>
> During the Revolutionary War, many of the colonists who remained loyal to the British monarchy lost their houses and land by force. After the war, between 80,000 and 100,000 of these Loyalists went to England or emigrated elsewhere.

Spatial Order Transitional words and phrases such as *in front, behind, next to, along, nearest, lowest, above, below, underneath, on the left,* and *in the middle* can help your reader visualize a scene.

> **MODEL**
>
> As I waited, I stared at the bleachers across the rink. My family was lined up in the front row. Behind this group and to the right were friends from school, and next to my friends were three of my teachers.

Degree of Importance Transitional words such as *mainly, strongest, weakest, first, second, most important, least important, worst,* and *best* may be used to rank ideas or to show degrees of importance.

> **MODEL**
>
> Why do I read mysteries? Mainly I read them because I enjoy suspense. Second, I like meeting characters who are different from anybody I know in real life. Least important, but still a reason, is that I enjoy reading about interesting places.

Compare and Contrast Words and phrases such as *similarly, likewise, also, like, as, neither . . . nor,* and *either . . . or* show similarity between details. *However, by contrast, yet, but, unlike, instead, whereas,* and *while* show difference. Note the use of transitions showing contrast in the model.

> **MODEL**
>
> Matthew Henson was not recognized as the co-discoverer of the North Pole until 1944, although he and Robert Peary had reached it together on April 9, 1909. By contrast, the achievement of Roald Amundsen's team, which made it to the South Pole in December 1911, was recognized almost immediately.

TIP Both *but* and *however* can be used to join two independent clauses. When *but* is used as a coordinating conjunction, it is preceded by a comma. When *however* is used as a conjunctive adverb, it is preceded by a semicolon and followed by a comma.

> **EXAMPLE**
>
> A greenbottle fly is small, but its eyes contain many lenses.
>
> You can try to quietly sneak up on a fly with a swatter; however, the fly, with its compound eyes, will still be able to see the motion of the swatter.

Cause-Effect When you are writing about a cause-effect relationship, use transitional words and phrases such as *since, because, thus, therefore, so, due to, for this reason,* and *as a result* to help explain that relationship and make your writing coherent.

> **MODEL**
>
> Because a tree fell across the electric wires Monday night, we lost our electricity for four hours.

2.4 CONCLUSIONS

A conclusion should leave readers with a strong final impression.

Kinds of Conclusions

Good conclusions sum up ideas in a variety of ways. Here are some techniques you might try:

Restate Your Thesis A good way to conclude an essay is by restating your thesis, or main idea, in different words. The following conclusion restates the thesis introduced on page R31.

> **MODEL**
>
> It may surprise you to hear that two very different cultures might have very similar gods, but this comparison of Zeus and Jupiter shows how similar the Greek and Roman gods could be.

Ask a Question Try asking a question that sums up what you have said and gives your reader something new to think about. This question concludes a piece of persuasive writing and suggests a course of action.

> **MODEL**
>
> More and more people are biking to school and work and are riding for exercise. Doesn't it make sense to create safe bike lanes throughout our city?

Make a Recommendation When you are persuading your audience to take a position on an issue, you can conclude by recommending a specific course of action.

> **MODEL**
>
> You can make your research easier by taking advantage of the Internet. Develop a list of key words that will help you narrow your search.

Offer an Opinion Leave your reader with something to think about by offering your personal opinion on the topic. The following model offers an opinion about draining wetlands.

> **MODEL**
>
> Even though the developers draining the wetlands hope to bring in new business, the health of the environment is more important than any economic gains.

End with the Last Event If you're telling a story, you may end with the last thing that happens. Here, the ending includes an embarrassing moment for the narrator.

> **MODEL**
>
> When I pulled myself out of the pool, he growled, "You just set a new record for the 22-meter free. Too bad it was the wrong event." Suddenly, I realized I had swum four extra laps! It was one victory I never celebrated.

2.5 ELABORATION

Elaboration is the process of developing an idea by providing specific supporting details that are relevant and appropriate to the purpose and form of your writing.

Facts and Statistics A fact is a statement that can be verified, and a statistic is a fact expressed as a number. Make sure the facts and statistics you supply are from reliable, up-to-date sources.

> **MODEL**
>
> Women have aided U.S. military efforts for more than a century. Today, more than 200,000 women are on active military duty.

Sensory Details Details that show how something looks, sounds, tastes, smells, or feels can make readers feel they are actually experiencing what you are describing. Which senses does the writer appeal to in the following model?

> **MODEL**
>
> Anna Hawk got off her bike and sat beside the muddy road. The rain on her poncho made the only sound, and nothing on the prairie moved. Anna took a sip of warm, sweet cocoa from her thermos bottle.

Incidents From our earliest years, we are interested in hearing "stories." One way to illustrate a point powerfully is to relate an incident or tell a story, as shown in the example.

> **MODEL**
>
> Some of our most valuable sources of historical knowledge come from tragic events. The eruption of the volcano Vesuvius in A.D. 79 was a nightmare for the people of Pompeii. About 2,000 inhabitants may have died, and their homes were buried under tons of volcanic ash.

Examples An example can help make an abstract idea concrete or can serve to clarify a complex point for your reader.

> **MODEL**
>
> Realistic fiction is imaginative writing set in the real, modern world. For example, the short story "Tuesday of the Other June" is set in a realistic city, and its characters deal with ordinary human problems.

Quotations Choose quotations that clearly support your points, and be sure that you copy each quotation word for word. Always remember to credit the source.

> **MODEL**
>
> In Avi's short story "Scout's Honor," one of the characters tries to come up with an excuse for not crossing a scary-looking bridge. "I'm not so sure we should go," he says. "Maybe it doesn't have another side."

3 Descriptive Writing

Descriptive writing allows you to paint word pictures about anything, from events of global importance to the most personal feelings. It is an essential part of almost every piece of writing.

> **RUBRIC: Standards for Writing**
>
> **Successful descriptive writing should**
>
> - have a clear focus and sense of purpose
> - use sensory details and precise words to create a vivid image, establish a mood, or express emotion
> - present details in a logical order

*For more information, see **Writing Workshop: Describing a Person**, page 288.*

3.1 KEY TECHNIQUES

Consider Your Goals What do you want to accomplish with your description? Do you want to show why something is important to you? Do you want to make a person or scene more memorable? Do you want to explain an event?

Identify Your Audience Who will read your description? How familiar are they with your subject? What background information will they need? Which details will they find most interesting?

Think Figuratively What figures of speech might help make your description vivid and interesting? What similes, metaphors, or analogies come to mind? What imaginative comparisons can you make? What living thing does an inanimate object remind you of?

Gather Sensory Details Which sights, smells, tastes, sounds, and textures make your subject come alive? Which details stick in your mind when you observe or recall your subject? Which senses does it most strongly affect?

You might want to use a chart like the one shown here to collect sensory details about your subject.

Sights	Sounds	Textures	Smells	Tastes

Organize Your Details Details that are presented in a logical order help the reader form a mental picture of the subject. Descriptive details may be organized in spatial order, by order of impression, in order of importance, or in chronological order.

3.2 OPTIONS FOR ORGANIZATION

Option 1: Spatial Order Spatial order describes a space or scene and all of the objects or people in that space. Either of the following options will help readers "see" the place you are describing.

*For more information, see **Transitions**, page R32.*

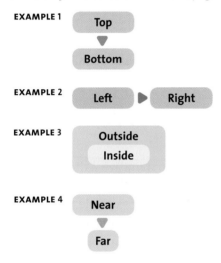

MODEL

Arthur and Chantal came to the bicycle race to cheer on their friends. As the first group of cyclists approached the finish line, Arthur and Chantal cheered wildly when they saw that their friend Lindsey was leading the pack. Another friend, Charles, was just behind her. Far off in the distance, they could just make out their friend Georgia's red bike.

Option 2: Order of Impression Order of impression is the order in which you notice details.

MODEL

Mike descended the stairs slowly, so we saw his shoes first—polished to a gleaming black so that they looked almost like patent leather. Then, the satin stripe on each trouser leg told us he was dressed for a formal event. Finally, we saw the white bow tie, just below the grin.

TIP Use transitions that help readers understand the order of the impressions you are describing. Some useful transitions are *after, next, during, first, before, finally,* and *then.*

*For more information, see **Transitions**, page R32.*

Option 3: Order of Importance You can use the order of importance as the organizing structure for a description.

MODEL

Most impressionist paintings were created outdoors. The paintings feature bright colors and loose brushwork. The painters used these techniques to portray the effects of sunlight on objects. The goal of the impressionists was to capture their immediate "impression" of a brief moment in time.

Option 4: Chronological Order You can use chronological order as the organizing structure for a description. See section 4.2 on page R36 for an example of how this is done.

❹ Narrative Writing

Narrative writing tells a story. If you write a story from your imagination, it is a fictional narrative. A true story about actual events is a nonfictional narrative. Narrative writing can be found in short stories, novels, news articles, personal narratives, and biographies.

RUBRIC: Standards for Writing

A successful narrative should

- hook the reader's attention with a strong introduction
- include descriptive details and dialogue to develop the characters, setting, and plot
- have a clear beginning, middle, and end
- have a logical organization, with clues and transitions that help the reader understand the order of events
- use a consistent tone and point of view
- use language that is appropriate to the audience
- demonstrate the significance of events or ideas

*For more information, see **Writing Workshop: Short Story**, page 158, and **Writing Workshop: Personal Narrative**, page 824.*

4.1 KEY TECHNIQUES

Identify the Main Events What are the most important events in your narrative? Is each event needed to tell the story? Consider organizing events in a way that builds suspense and keeps readers guessing about what will happen next.

Describe the Setting When do the events occur? Where do they take place? How can you use setting to create mood and to set the stage for the characters and their actions?

Depict Characters Vividly What do your characters look like? What do they think and say? How do they act? What details can show what they are like?

TIP One method of developing characters is to include dialogue. When writing dialogue, choose words that express the characters' personalities. Dialogue should show how characters feel about one another and about events in the narrative.

4.2 OPTIONS FOR ORGANIZATION

Option 1: Chronological Order One way to organize a piece of narrative writing is to arrange the events in chronological order, as shown.

EXAMPLE

Aunt Jessica gives Danielle her first horse to train.

He's a horse Danielle doesn't like. He's stubborn, and when Danielle tries to train him, nothing happens.

Danielle sees the horse running in the field. He looks proud and independent.

Aunt Jessica asks Danielle if she would like a different horse to train. Danielle says she wants to keep the horse she has. Aunt Jessica smiles warmly at her.

> **Introduction**
> *Characters and setting*
> ▼
> **Event 1**
> ▼
> **Event 2**
> ▼
> **End**
> *Perhaps showing the significance of the events*

Option 2: Flashback In narrative writing, you may want to include events that happened before the beginning of the story. For example, you can hook your reader's interest by opening a story with an exciting event. After your introduction, you can use a flashback to show how past events led up to the present situation or to provide background about a character or an event. Use clue words such as *last summer, as a young girl, the previous school year,* and *his earliest memories* to let your reader know that you are interrupting the main action to describe earlier events.

Notice how the flashback interrupts the action in the model.

MODEL

As he helped his sister prepare the turkey, his mind drifted back to the years when they had spent the holidays in the country with their grandparents. The farmhouse kitchen had always been so warm and welcoming, filled with good smells.

Option 3: Focus on Conflict When a fictional narrative focuses on a central conflict, the story's plot may be organized as in the following example.

EXAMPLE

Danielle lives on the Kansas prairie near her Aunt Jessica. Danielle excels at everything she does and is a little spoiled. She looks up to her aunt, who is quiet and thoughtful.

When Danielle asks for a horse to train, Jessica deliberately gives her a horse that will be hard to train.

- Danielle and Aunt Jessica have always been very close.
- Danielle is hurt that her aunt has given her a horse she dislikes.
- Danielle wants to train the horse quickly so that she can ride him in a competition.

By dealing with the challenge of training a difficult horse, Danielle becomes more mature. She and her aunt are brought closer together.

> **Describe main characters and setting**
>
> **Present conflict**
>
> **Relate events that create conflict and cause characters to change**
> ▼
> **Present resolution or outcome of conflict**

⑤ Expository Writing

Expository writing informs and explains. You can use it to explain how to cook spaghetti or to compare two pieces of literature. There are many types of expository writing. Think about your topic and select the type that presents the information most clearly.

5.1 COMPARISON AND CONTRAST

Compare-and-contrast writing examines the similarities and differences between two or more subjects. You might, for example, compare and contrast two short stories, the main characters in a novel, or two movies.

RUBRIC: Standards for Writing

Successful compare-and-contrast writing should

- hook the reader's attention with a strong introduction
- clearly identify the subjects that are being compared
- include specific, relevant details
- follow a clear plan of organization
- use language and details appropriate to the audience
- use transitional words and phrases to clarify similarities and differences

For more information, see **Writing Workshop: Comparison-Contrast Essay,** *page 526.*

Options for Organization

Compare-and-contrast writing can be organized in different ways. The examples that follow demonstrate point-by-point organization and subject-by-subject organization.

Option 1: Point-by-Point Organization

EXAMPLE

I. Similarities in Appearance   **Point 1**

   Subject A. Domestic honeybees are about five-eighths of an inch long.

   Subject B. Africanized bees, contrary to rumor, are about the same size as domestic bees.

II. Differences in Temperament   **Point 2**

   Subject A. Domestic honeybees are bred to be gentle.

   Subject B. The Africanized bee is a "wild" bee that is quick-tempered around animals and people.

Option 2: Subject-by-Subject Organization

EXAMPLE

I. Domestic Honeybees   **Subject A**

  Point 1. Domestic honey-bees are about five-eighths of an inch long.

  Point 2. Domestic honeybees are bred to be gentle.

II. Africanized Bees   **Subject B**

  Point 1. Africanized bees are about five-eighths of an inch long.

  Point 2. The Africanized bee is a "wild" bee that is quick-tempered around animals and people.

5.2 CAUSE AND EFFECT

Cause-effect writing explains why something happened, why certain conditions exist, or what resulted from an action or a condition. You might use cause-effect writing to explain a character's actions, the progress of a disease, or the outcome of a war.

RUBRIC: Standards for Writing

Successful cause-effect writing should

- hook the reader's attention with a strong introduction
- clearly state the cause-and-effect relationship
- show clear connections between causes and effects
- present causes and effects in a logical order and use transitions effectively
- use facts, examples, and other details to illustrate each cause and effect
- use language and details appropriate to the audience

Options for Organization

Your organization will depend on your topic and your purpose for writing.

Option 1: Effect-to-Cause Organization If you want to explain the causes of an event, such as the threat of Africanized bees to commercial beekeeping, you might first state the effect and then examine its causes.

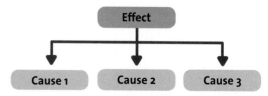

Option 2: Cause-to-Effect Organization If your focus is on explaining the effects of an event, such as the appearance of Africanized bees in the United States, you might first state the cause and then explain the effects.

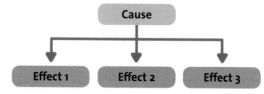

Option 3: Cause-Effect Chain Organization Sometimes you'll want to describe a chain of cause-and-effect relationships to explore a topic such as the myths about the Africanized honeybee.

TIP Don't assume that a cause-effect relationship exists just because one event follows another. Look for evidence that the later event could not have happened if the first event had not caused it.

5.3 PROBLEM-SOLUTION

Problem-solution writing clearly states a problem, analyzes the problem, and proposes a solution to the problem. It can be used to identify and solve a conflict between characters, investigate global warming, or explain why a soccer team keeps losing games.

RUBRIC: Standards for Writing

Successful problem-solution writing should

- hook the reader's attention with a strong introduction
- identify the problem and help the reader understand the issues involved
- analyze the causes and effects of the problem
- include quotations, facts, and statistics
- explore possible solutions to the problem and recommend the best one(s)
- use language, details, and a tone appropriate to the audience

*For more information, see **Writing Workshop: Problem-Solution Essay,** page 742.*

Options for Organization

How you organize a problem-solution piece will depend on your goal, your intended audience, and the specific problem you have chosen to address. The following organizational methods are effective for different kinds of problem-solution writing.

Option 1: Simple Problem-Solution

Option 2: Deciding Between Solutions

5.4 ANALYSIS

In writing an analysis, you explain how something works, how it is defined, or what its parts are.

RUBRIC: Standards for Writing

A successful analysis should

- hook the reader's attention with a strong introduction
- clearly define the subject and its parts
- follow a specific organization to provide a logical flow of information
- show connections among facts and ideas through transitional words and phrases
- use language and details appropriate for the audience

Options for Organization

Different types of analysis will require diffferent methods of organization. Be sure that you organize details in an order that makes sense for the kind of analysis you are writing. Use one of the following options:

Option 1: Process Analysis What are the important steps or stages of a process? A process analysis is usually organized chronologically, with steps or stages in the order in which they occur. You might use a process analysis to explain how to program a cell phone or prepare for a test, or to explain the different stages of development in an insect's life.

MODEL

Keep your house safe from dangerous bees.

Some types of bees, like the Africanized honeybee, can be a threat to your safety.

Step 1: Fill in common nesting sites, such as holes in trees and walls.

Step 2: Look for active hives around your home and contact a beekeeper to remove them.

Step 3: Watch for new hives in the spring and fall, when bees form new colonies.

> Introduce process.

> Give background.

> Explain steps.

Option 2: Definition Analysis What are the most important characteristics of a subject? Use a definition analysis to explain a quality (such as beauty), the characteristics of a limerick, or the characteristics of insects. You can organize the details of a definition analysis in order of importance or impression.

MODEL

What is an Africanized honeybee?

An Africanized honeybee is a cross between a domestic honeybee and an aggressive African bee.

Feature 1: The aggressiveness of the African bee ancestors comes out in the hybrid bees.

Feature 2: The Africanized bee is not comfortable around animals or humans.

Feature 3: An individual who threatens the bees may receive hundreds of stings, and even die.

> Introduce term and definition.

> Explain features.

Option 3: Parts Analysis What are the parts, groups, or types that make up your subject? The following parts analysis explains the significance of the beekeeping industry.

MODEL

The beekeeping industry is a complex and productive industry.

Part 1: The primary product is honey. The United States produces 250 million pounds of honey per year.

Part 2: Other products are beeswax and royal jelly.

Part 3: Honeybees pollinate more than 90 different types of crops, affecting every third bite of food that people eat.

> Introduce subject.

> Explain parts.

6 Persuasive Writing

Persuasive writing allows you to use the power of language to inform and influence others. It includes speeches, persuasive essays, newspaper editorials, advertisements, and critical reviews.

> **RUBRIC: Standards for Writing**
>
> **Successful persuasive writing should**
>
> - hook the reader's attention with a strong introduction
> - state the issue and the writer's position
> - give opinions and support them with facts or reasons
> - have a reasonable and respectful tone
> - answer opposing views
> - use sound logic and effective language
> - conclude by summing up reasons or calling for action

For more information, see **Writing Workshop: Persuasive Essay,** *page 918.*

6.1 KEY TECHNIQUES

Clarify Your Position What do you believe about the issue? How can you express your opinion most clearly?

Know Your Audience Who will read your writing? What do they already know and believe about the issue? What objections to your position might they have? What additional information might they need to understand your argument? What tone and approach would be most effective?

Support Your Opinion Why do you feel the way you do about the issue? What facts, statistics, examples, quotations, anecdotes, or expert opinions support your view? What reasons will convince your readers? What evidence can answer their objections?

Ways to Support Your Argument	
Statistics	facts that are stated in numbers
Examples	specific instances that explain points
Observations	events or situations you yourself have seen
Anecdotes	brief stories that illustrate points
Quotations	direct statements from authorities

*For more information, see **Identifying Faulty Reasoning,** page R24.*

Begin and End with a Bang How can you hook your readers and make a lasting impression? What memorable quotation, anecdote, or statistic will catch their attention at the beginning or stick in their minds at the end? What strong summary or call to action can you use as a conclusion?

MODEL

Beginning

Whether you are a bicyclist, a driver, or even a pedestrian, chances are you've been put in a dangerous situation because bikes must use the same lanes as cars.

End

Please help improve safety for everyone in our community by supporting the creation of bike lanes on all major streets.

6.2 OPTIONS FOR ORGANIZATION

In a two-sided persuasive essay, you want to show the weaknesses of other opinions as you explain the strengths of your own.

Option 1: Reasons for Your Opinion

Introduction states issue and your position on it.
▼
Reason 1 with evidence and support
▼
Reason 2 with evidence and support
▼
Reason 3 with evidence and support
▼
Objections to whole argument
▼
Response to objections
▼
Conclusion restates your position and suggests a course of action.

Option 2: Point-by-Point Basis

Introduction states issue and your position on it.
▼
Reason 1 with evidence and support
▼
Objections and responses for reason 1
▼
Reason 2 with evidence and support
▼
Objections and responses for reason 2
▼
Reason 3 with evidence and support
▼
Objections and responses for reason 3
▼
Conclusion restates your position and suggests a course of action.

7 Workplace and Technical Writing

Business writing is writing done in a workplace to support the work of a company or business. You may need to do business writing to request information or complain about a product or service. Several types of formats, such as memos, letters, e-mails, and applications, have been developed to make communication easier.

> **RUBRIC: Standards for Writing**
> **Successful business writing should**
> - be courteous
> - use language that is appropriate for its audience
> - state the purpose clearly in the opening sentences or paragraph
> - have a formal tone and not contain slang, contractions, or sentence fragments
> - use precise words
> - present only essential information
> - present details in a logical order
> - conclude with a summary of important points

7.1 KEY TECHNIQUES OF WORKPLACE WRITING

Think About Your Purpose Why are you writing? Do you want to order or complain about a product?

Identify Your Audience Who will read your writing? What background information will they need? What tone or language is appropriate?

Use a Pattern of Organization That Is Appropriate to the Content If you have to compare and contrast two products in a letter, you can use the same compare-and-contrast organization that you would use in an essay.

Support Your Points What specific details might clarify your ideas? What reasons do you have for your statements?

Finish Strongly How can you best sum up your statements? What is your main point? What action do you want the recipients to take?

Revise and Proofread Your Writing Just as you are graded on the quality of an essay you write for a class, you will be judged on the quality of your writing in the workplace.

7.2 MATCH THE FORMAT TO THE OCCASION

Memos, e-mail messages, and letters have similar purposes but are used in different situations. The chart shows how each format can be used.

Format	Occasion
Memo	Use to send correspondence **inside** the workplace only.
E-mail message	Use to send correspondence **inside or outside** the company.
Letter	Use to send correspondence **outside** the company.

TIP Memos are often sent as e-mail messages in the workplace. Remember that both require formal language and standard spelling, capitalization, and punctuation.

Technical writing is used for detailed instructions or descriptions of items and processes. It is important to a variety of fields, such as science, government, and industry. At work, at school, or in everyday life, you may have to use technical writing to leave instructions for another person.

> **RUBRIC: Standards for Writing**
> **Instructions should**
> - present only essential information
> - present steps in a logical order
> - include sentences that are short and simple
> - include definitions of unfamiliar terms if necessary
> - use transitions and/or numbered steps
> - use verbs that describe actions
> - use the present tense

7.3 KEY TECHNIQUES OF TECHNICAL WRITING

Think About Your Organization As you write, make sure you are presenting your information in a sensible order. For example, your instructions would probably list any necessary tools and materials early on. Then you would present the steps in the order in which they should be followed.

Keep Your Audience in Mind Explain what readers who are unfamiliar with the activity or process will need to know. Sometimes making a comparison to something the reader is familiar with can help. Graphics, such as pictures and maps, can also help make instructions easier to understand.

Use Transitions as Needed Transitions such as *first, next, after,* and *last* and numbered steps can make the order of steps clear and guide your reader from one step to the next.

Review Your Ending You can simply end with the last step, or you can end by describing the result or outcome of following the directions.

Evaluate Your Instructions Have a friend follow your instructions to make sure they are clear.

7.4 FORMATS

Business letters usually have a formal tone and a specific format as shown below. The key to writing a business letter is to get to the point as quickly as possible and to present your information clearly.

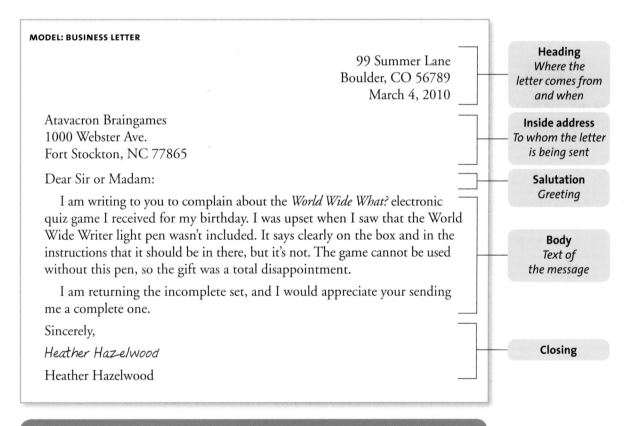

MODEL: BUSINESS LETTER

99 Summer Lane
Boulder, CO 56789
March 4, 2010

Heading
Where the letter comes from and when

Atavacron Braingames
1000 Webster Ave.
Fort Stockton, NC 77865

Inside address
To whom the letter is being sent

Dear Sir or Madam:

Salutation
Greeting

I am writing to you to complain about the *World Wide What?* electronic quiz game I received for my birthday. I was upset when I saw that the World Wide Writer light pen wasn't included. It says clearly on the box and in the instructions that it should be in there, but it's not. The game cannot be used without this pen, so the gift was a total disappointment.

I am returning the incomplete set, and I would appreciate your sending me a complete one.

Body
Text of the message

Sincerely,

Heather Hazelwood

Heather Hazelwood

Closing

PRACTICE AND APPLY

1. Draft a response to the letter. Then revise your letter as necessary according to the rubric at the beginning of page R42. Make sure you have included the necessary information and have written in an appropriate tone.

2. Proofread your letter for grammatical errors and spelling mistakes. Follow the format of the model and use appropriate spacing between each part.

Memos and e-mail messages are often used in workplaces as a way of sending information in a direct and concise manner. They can be used to announce or summarize meetings and to request actions or specific information.

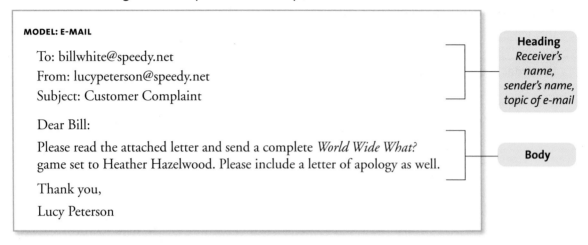

MODEL: E-MAIL

To: billwhite@speedy.net
From: lucypeterson@speedy.net
Subject: Customer Complaint

Dear Bill:

Please read the attached letter and send a complete *World Wide What?* game set to Heather Hazelwood. Please include a letter of apology as well.

Thank you,

Lucy Peterson

Heading
Receiver's name, sender's name, topic of e-mail

Body

TIP Don't forget to write the topic of your e-mail in the subject line. This will help the receiver determine the importance of your message.

PRACTICE AND APPLY

Write an e-mail in response to the e-mail shown here. Tell the receiver what actions you have taken. Follow the format of the model.

When filling out an application, be sure to skim the form before writing anything. Watch for any sections that you are not required to fill in or questions that you do not need to answer. Pay special attention to places that require a signature.

Millwood Public Library Card Application

Please print clearly.

(for office use only) **CARD NO.** _____

NAME _____
 Last   First   Middle

LOCAL ADDRESS _____

CITY _____ **STATE** _____ **ZIP CODE** _____

HOME PHONE ( ) _____ **WORK PHONE** ( ) _____

SEX _____ _____ **BIRTH DATE** _____/_____/_____
 Male   Female   Month Day Year

I agree to be responsible for all materials borrowed from the Millwood Public Library in my name.

SIGNATURE _____ **DATE** _____

---

for office use only

STAFF INITIALS_____ **REGISTRATION CLASS** _____

MI   CH   NS   OTHER   FEE STAFF   ISU   KE   NL   TE

Instructions present information in such a way that the reader can use them to complete a task, such as assembling an item or performing an experiment. Instructions should provide all essential information in the proper order. They should not contain any extra or unnecessary information.

MODEL: INSTRUCTIONS

What are some signs of chemical change?

MATERIALS

- graduated cylinder
- water
- 2 clear plastic cups
- 2 eyedroppers
- iodine solution
- cornstarch
- spoon
- vitamin C tablet

TIME

15 minutes

PROCEDURE

1. Measure 80 mL of water and pour it into one of the cups.
2. Add 3 full droppers of iodine solution. Record your observations.
3. Add 1 spoonful of cornstarch to the iodine solution and stir. Record your observations.
4. Measure 50 mL of water and pour it into the second cup.
5. Using a clean eyedropper, add 4 full droppers of the iodine/cornstarch solution to the second cup.
6. Drop a vitamin C tablet into the second cup and stir the liquid with a clean spoon until the tablet is dissolved. Record your observations.

PRACTICE AND APPLY

Think about something you might want someone else to do because you won't be at home, such as do laundry or prepare dinner. Follow the rubric at the end of page R42 to write instructions. Be sure to include the following:

- an opening statement that describes what needs to be done
- a list of tools and materials needed to perform the task
- the steps needed to perform the task
- transition words and/or numbered steps if the order is important
- any special notes or warnings about a tool or step in the process

Writing that has a lot of mistakes can confuse or even annoy a reader. Punctuation errors in a letter might lead to a miscommunication or delay a reply. A sentence fragment might lower your grade on an essay. Paying attention to grammar, punctuation, and capitalization rules can make your writing clearer and easier to read.

Quick Reference: Parts of Speech

PART OF SPEECH	FUNCTION	EXAMPLES
Noun	names a person, a place, a thing, an idea, a quality, or an action	
Common	serves as a general name, or a name common to an entire group	subway, fog, puzzle, tollbooth
Proper	names a specific, one-of-a-kind person, place, or thing	Mrs. Price, Pompeii, China, Meg
Singular	refers to a single person, place, thing, or idea	onion, waterfall, lamb, sofa
Plural	refers to more than one person, place, thing, or idea	dreams, commercials, men, tortillas
Concrete	names something that can be perceived by the senses	jacket, teacher, caterpillar, aroma
Abstract	names something that cannot be perceived by the senses	friendship, opportunities, fear, stubbornness
Compound	expresses a single idea through a combination of two or more words	jump rope, paycheck, Chinese-American, pine needles
Collective	refers to a group of people or things	colony, family, clan, flock
Possessive	shows who or what owns something	Mama's, Tito's, children's, waitresses'
Pronoun	takes the place of a noun or another pronoun	
Personal	refers to the person making a statement, the person(s) being addressed, or the person(s) or thing(s) the statement is about	I, me, my, mine, we, us, our, ours, you, your, yours, she, he, it, her, him, hers, his, its, they, them, their, theirs
Reflexive	follows a verb or preposition and refers to a preceding noun or pronoun	myself, yourself, herself, himself, itself, ourselves, yourselves, themselves
Intensive	emphasizes a noun or another pronoun	(same as reflexives)
Demonstrative	points to one or more specific persons or things	this, that, these, those
Interrogative	signals a question	who, whom, whose, which, what
Indefinite	refers to one or more persons or things not specifically mentioned	both, all, most, many, anyone, everybody, several, none, some
Relative	introduces an adjective clause by relating it to a word in the clause	who, whom, whose, which, that

PART OF SPEECH	FUNCTION	EXAMPLES
Verb	expresses an action, a condition, or a state of being	
Action	tells what the subject does or did, physically or mentally	run, reaches, listened, consider, decides, dreamed
Linking	connects the subject to something that identifies or describes it	am, is, are, was, were, sound, taste, appear, feel, become, remain, seem
Auxiliary	precedes the main verb in a verb phrase	be, have, do, can, could, will, would, may, might
Transitive	directs the action toward someone or something; always has an object	The storm **sank** the ship.
Intransitive	does not direct the action toward someone or something; does not have an object	The ship **sank**.
Adjective	modifies a noun or pronoun	**strong** women, **two** epics, **enough** time
Adverb	modifies a verb, an adjective, or another adverb	walked **out, really** funny, **far** away
Preposition	relates one word to another word	at, by, for, from, in, of, on, to, with
Conjunction	joins words or word groups	
Coordinating	joins words or word groups used the same way	and, but, or, for, so, yet, nor
Correlative	used as a pair to join words or word groups used the same way	both . . . and, either . . . or, neither . . . nor
Subordinating	introduces a clause that cannot stand by itself as a complete sentence	although, after, as, before, because, when, if, unless
Interjection	expresses emotion	wow, ouch, hurrah

Quick Reference: The Sentence and Its Parts

The diagrams that follow will give you a brief review of the essentials of a sentence and some of its parts.

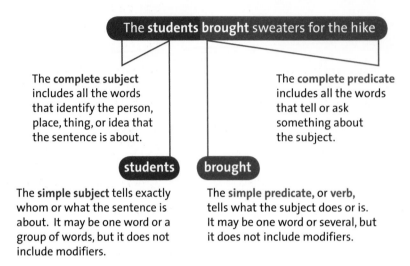

The **students brought** sweaters for the hike

The **complete subject** includes all the words that identify the person, place, thing, or idea that the sentence is about.

The **complete predicate** includes all the words that tell or ask something about the subject.

students

The **simple subject** tells exactly whom or what the sentence is about. It may be one word or a group of words, but it does not include modifiers.

brought

The **simple predicate**, or **verb**, tells what the subject does or is. It may be one word or several, but it does not include modifiers.

Every word in a sentence is part of a complete subject or a complete predicate.

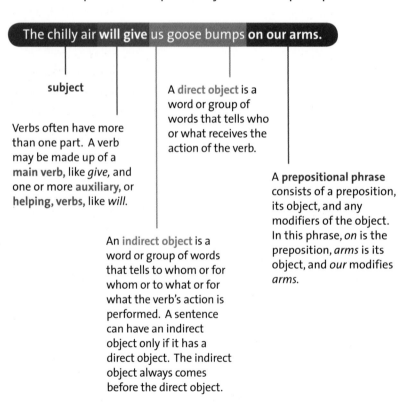

The chilly air **will give** us goose bumps **on our arms.**

subject

Verbs often have more than one part. A verb may be made up of a **main verb**, like *give*, and one or more **auxiliary**, or **helping**, **verbs**, like *will*.

A **direct object** is a word or group of words that tells who or what receives the action of the verb.

A **prepositional phrase** consists of a preposition, its object, and any modifiers of the object. In this phrase, *on* is the preposition, *arms* is its object, and *our* modifies *arms*.

An **indirect object** is a word or group of words that tells to whom or for whom or to what or for what the verb's action is performed. A sentence can have an indirect object only if it has a direct object. The indirect object always comes before the direct object.

Quick Reference: Punctuation

MARK	FUNCTION	EXAMPLES
End Marks period, question mark, exclamation point	ends a sentence	We can start now. When would you like to leave? What a fantastic hit!
period	follows an initial or abbreviation **Exception:** postal abbreviations of states	Mrs. Dorothy Parker, McDougal Littell Inc., C. P. Cavafy, P.M., A.D., lb., oz., Blvd., Dr. NE (Nebraska), NV (Nevada)

period	follows a number or letter in an outline or a list	I. Volcanoes
		  A. Central-vent
		    1. Shield

Comma	separates parts of a compound sentence	I had never disliked poetry, but now I really love it.
	separates items in a series	She is brave, loyal, and kind.
	separates adjectives of equal rank that modify the same noun	The slow, easy route is best.
	sets off a term of address	Maria, how can I help you? You must do something, soldier.
	sets off a parenthetical expression	Hard workers, as you know, don't quit. I'm not a quitter, believe me.
	sets off an introductory word, phrase, or dependent clause	Yes, I forgot my key. At the beginning of the day, I feel fresh. While she was out, I was here. Having finished my chores, I went out.
	sets off a nonessential phrase or clause	Ed Pawn, the captain of the chess team, won. Ed Pawn, who is the captain, won. The two leading runners, sprinting toward the finish line, finished in a tie.
	sets off parts of dates and addresses	Mail it by May 14, 2010, to the Hauptman Company, 321 Market Street, Memphis, Tennessee.
	follows the salutation and closing of a letter	Dear Jim, Sincerely yours,
	separates words to avoid confusion	By noon, time had run out. What the minister does, does matter. While cooking, Jim burned his hand.
Semicolon	separates items in a series that contain commas	We spent the first week of summer vacation in Chicago, Illinois; the second week in St. Louis, Missouri; and the third week in Albany, New York.
	separates parts of a compound sentence that are not joined by a coordinating conjunction	The last shall be first; the first shall be last. I read the Bible; however, I have not memorized it.
	separates parts of a compound sentence when the parts contain commas	After I ran out of money, I called my parents; but only my sister was home, unfortunately.

MARK	FUNCTION	EXAMPLES
Colon	introduces a list	Those we wrote were the following: Dana, John, and Will.
	introduces a long quotation	Abraham Lincoln wrote: "Four score and seven years ago, our fathers brought forth on this continent a new nation...."
	follows the salutation of a business letter	To Whom It May Concern: Dear Leonard Atole:
	separates certain numbers	1:28 P.M., Genesis 2:5
Dash	indicates an abrupt break in thought	I was thinking of my mother—who is arriving tomorrow—just as you walked in.
Parentheses	enclose less important material	It was so unlike him (John is always on time) that I began to worry. The last World Series game (did you see it?) was fun.
Hyphen	joins parts of a compound adjective before a noun	That's a not-so-happy face.
	joins parts of a compound with *all-, ex-, self-,* or *-elect*	The ex-firefighter helped rescue him. Our president-elect is self-conscious.
	joins parts of a compound number (to ninety-nine)	My bicycle wheel has twenty-six spokes.
	joins parts of a fraction	My cup is one-third full.
	joins a prefix to a word beginning with a capital letter	Were your grandparents born post-World War II? The mid-April snowstorm surprised everyone.
	indicates that a word is divided at the end of a line	How could you have any reasonable expectations of getting a new computer?
Apostrophe	used with *s* to form the possessive of a noun or an indefinite pronoun	my friend's book, my friends' books, anyone's guess, somebody else's problem
	replaces one or more omitted letters in a contraction or numbers in a date	don't (omitted *o*), he'd (omitted *woul*), the class of '99 (omitted *19*)
	used with *s* to form the plural of a letter	I had two A's on my report card.
Quotation Marks	set off a speaker's exact words	Sara said, "I'm finally ready." "I'm ready," Sara said, "finally." Did Sara say, "I'm ready"? Sara said, "I'm ready!"
	set off the title of a story, an article, a short poem, an essay, a song, or a chapter	I like Bradbury's "All Summer in a Day" and Collins's "On Turning Ten." I learned to play Paul Simon's song "I Am a Rock."
Ellipses	replace material omitted from a quotation	"Early one morning, Mrs. Bunnin wobbled into the classroom lugging a large cardboard box. ... Robert was at his desk scribbling a ballpoint tattoo ... on the tops of his knuckles."
Italics	indicate the title of a book, a play, a magazine, a long poem, an opera, a film, or a TV series, or the name of a ship	*In Search of Pompeii, The Phantom Tollbooth, Time,* the *Iliad, The Marriage of Figaro, Lemony Snicket's A Series of Unfortunate Events, American Idol, Titanic*

Quick Reference: Capitalization

CATEGORY	EXAMPLES
People and Titles	
Names and initials of people	Maya Angelou, E. E. Cummings
Titles used before a name	Mrs. Price, Scoutmaster Brenkman
Deities and members of religious groups	Jesus, Allah, Buddha, Zeus, Baptists, Roman Catholics
Names of ethnic and national groups	Hispanics, Jews, African Americans
Geographical Names	
Cities, states, countries, continents	Philadelphia, Kansas, Japan, Europe
Regions, bodies of water, mountains	the South, Lake Baikal, Mount Everest
Geographic features, parks	Great Basin, Yellowstone National Park
Streets and roads, planets	318 East Sutton Drive, Charles Court, Jupiter, Mars
Organizations, Events, Etc.	
Companies, organizations, teams	Ford Motor Company, Boy Scouts of America, St. Louis Cardinals
Buildings, bridges, monuments	Empire State Building, Eads Bridge, Washington Monument
Documents, awards	Declaration of Independence, Stanley Cup
Special named events	Mardi Gras, World Series
Government bodies, historical periods and events	U.S. Senate, House of Representatives, Middle Ages, Vietnam War
Days and months, holidays	Thursday, March, Thanksgiving, Labor Day
Specific cars, boats, trains, planes	Porsche, *Carpathia, Southwest Chief,* Concorde
Proper Adjectives	
Adjectives formed from proper nouns	French cooking, Spanish omelet, Edwardian age, Western movie
First Words and the Pronoun *I*	
First word in a sentence or quotation	This is it. He said, "Let's go."
First word of sentence in parentheses that is not within another sentence	The spelling rules are covered in another section. (Consult that section for more information.)
First words in the salutation and closing of a letter	Dear Madam, Very truly yours,
First word in each line of most poetry Personal pronoun *I*	Then am I A happy fly If I live Or if I die.
First word, last word, and all important words in a title	"Alone in the Nets," *Under the Royal Palms*

1 Nouns

A **noun** is a word used to name a person, a place, a thing, an idea, a quality, or an action. Nouns can be classified in several ways.

*For more information on different types of nouns, see **Quick Reference: Parts of Speech**, page R46.*

1.1 COMMON NOUNS

Common nouns are general names, common to entire groups.

1.2 PROPER NOUNS

Proper nouns name specific, one-of-a-kind people, places, and things.

Common	Proper
volcano, student, country, president	Mount Vesuvius, June, China, President Cleveland

*For more information, see **Quick Reference: Capitalization**, page R51.*

1.3 SINGULAR AND PLURAL NOUNS

A noun may take a singular or a plural form, depending on whether it names a single person, place, thing, or idea or more than one. Make sure you use appropriate spellings when forming plurals.

Singular	Plural
walrus, bully, lagoon, goose	walruses, bullies, lagoons, geese

*For more information, see **Forming Plural Nouns**, page R73.*

1.4 POSSESSIVE NOUNS

A **possessive noun** shows who or what owns something.

*For more information, see **Forming Possessives**, page R74.*

2 Pronouns

A **pronoun** is a word that is used in place of a noun or another pronoun. The word or word group to which the pronoun refers is called its **antecedent.**

2.1 PERSONAL PRONOUNS

Personal pronouns change their form to express person, number, gender, and case. The forms of these pronouns are shown in the following chart.

	Nominative	Objective	Possessive
Singular			
First person	I	me	my, mine
Second person	you	you	your, yours
Third person	she, he, it	her, him, it	her, hers, his, its
Plural			
First person	we	us	our, ours
Second person	you	you	your, yours
Third person	they	them	their, theirs

2.2 AGREEMENT WITH ANTECEDENT

Pronouns should agree with their antecedents in number, gender, and person.

If an antecedent is singular, use a singular pronoun.
> **EXAMPLE:** *That **poem** was fun to read. **It** rhymed.*

If an antecedent is plural, use a plural pronoun.
> **EXAMPLES:** ***Poets** choose **their** words carefully.*
> *I like **poems,** but Mischa doesn't care for **them.***

The gender of a pronoun must be the same as the gender of its antecedent.
> **EXAMPLE:** ***Eve Merriam's** creativity makes **her** poems easy to remember.*

The person of the pronoun must be the same as the person of its antecedent. As the chart in Section 2.1 shows, a pronoun can be in first-person, second-person, or third-person form.
> **EXAMPLE:** ***We** each have **our** favorite poets.*

Rewrite each sentence so that the underlined pronoun agrees with its antecedent.

1. The speaker in Maya Angelou's poem "Life Doesn't Frighten Me" talks about <u>their</u> fears.

2. When I read this poem, <u>we</u> felt braver already.

3. Scary things lose <u>its</u> power.

4. Even frogs and snakes don't seem as bad as <u>you</u> usually do.

5. I want to know how to be unafraid in <u>her</u> life.

2.3 PRONOUN FORMS

Personal pronouns change form to show how they function in sentences. The three forms are the subject form, the object form, and the possessive form. For examples of these pronouns, see the chart in Section 2.1.

A **subject pronoun** is used as a subject in a sentence.

EXAMPLE: *"All Summer in a Day" was written by Ray Bradbury. He chose Venus as the setting.*

Also use the subject form when the pronoun follows a linking verb.

EXAMPLE: *The girl in the closet was she.*

An **object pronoun** is used as a direct object, an indirect object, or the object of a preposition.

SUBJECT   OBJECT
They locked her in it.
OBJECT OF PREPOSITION

A **possessive pronoun** shows ownership. The pronouns *mine, yours, hers, his, its, ours,* and *theirs* can be used in place of nouns.

EXAMPLE: *The poem about the sun was hers.*

The pronouns *my, your, her, his, its, our,* and *their* are used before nouns.

EXAMPLE: *The other children got their revenge on Margot.*

WATCH OUT! Many spelling errors can be avoided if you watch out for *its* and *their.* Don't confuse the possessive pronoun *its* with the contraction *it's,* meaning "it is" or "it has." The homonyms *they're* (a contraction of *they are*) and *there* ("in that place") are often mistakenly used for *their.*

TIP To decide which pronoun to use in a comparison, such as "He tells better tales than (I *or* me)," fill in the missing word(s): *He tells better tales than I tell.*

GRAMMAR PRACTICE

Write the correct pronoun form to complete each sentence.

1. The children saw the sun in (their, they) dreams.

2. Margot really remembered that yellow flower and (its, her) warmth.

3. Margot was different, and the others feared (she, her).

4. The children thought, "(We, Us) will punish you."

5. The sun came out, but Margot didn't see (them, it).

2.4 REFLEXIVE AND INTENSIVE PRONOUNS

These pronouns are formed by adding *-self* or *-selves* to certain personal pronouns. Their forms are the same, and they differ only in how they are used.

A **reflexive pronoun** follows a verb or preposition and reflects back on an earlier noun or pronoun.

EXAMPLES: *He likes himself too much.*
She is now herself again.

Intensive pronouns intensify or emphasize the nouns or pronouns to which they refer.

EXAMPLES: *They themselves will educate their children.*
You yourself did it.

WATCH OUT! Avoid using *hisself* or *theirselves.* Standard English does not include these forms.

NONSTANDARD: *The children congratulated theirselves.*

STANDARD: *The children congratulated themselves.*

2.5 DEMONSTRATIVE PRONOUNS

Demonstrative pronouns point out things and persons near and far.

	Singular	Plural
Near	this	these
Far	that	those

2.6 INDEFINITE PRONOUNS

Indefinite pronouns do not refer to specific persons or things and usually have no antecedents. The chart shows some commonly used indefinite pronouns.

Singular	Plural	Singular or Plural	
another	both	all	none
anybody	few	any	some
no one	many	more	most
neither			

TIP Indefinite pronouns that end in *one, body,* or *thing* are always singular.

> INCORRECT: *Did everybody play their part well?*

If the indefinite pronoun might refer to either a male or a female, *his or her* may be used to refer to it, or the sentence may be rewritten.

> CORRECT: *Did everybody play his or her part well?*
> *Did all the students play their parts well?*

2.7 INTERROGATIVE PRONOUNS

An **interrogative pronoun** tells a reader or listener that a question is coming. The interrogative pronouns are *who, whom, whose, which,* and *what.*

> EXAMPLES: *Who is going to rehearse with you?*
> *From whom did you receive the script?*

TIP *Who* is used as a subject; *whom,* as an object. To find out which pronoun you need to use in a question, change the question to a statement.

> QUESTION: *(Who/Whom) did you meet there?*
> STATEMENT: *You met (?) there.*

Since the verb has a subject (*you*), the needed word must be the object form, *whom.*

> EXAMPLE: *Whom did you meet there?*

WATCH OUT! A special problem arises when you use an interrupter, such as *do you think,* within a question.

> EXAMPLE: *(Who/Whom) do you think will win?*

If you eliminate the interrupter, it is clear that the word you need is *who.*

2.8 RELATIVE PRONOUNS

Relative pronouns relate, or connect, adjective clauses to the words they modify in sentences. The noun or pronoun that a relative clause modifies is the antecedent of the relative pronoun. Here are the relative pronouns and their uses.

	Subject	Object	Possessive
Person	who	whom	whose
Thing	which	which	whose
Thing/Person	that	that	whose

Often, short sentences with related ideas can be combined by using a relative pronoun to create a more effective sentence.

> SHORT SENTENCE: *Lewis Carroll wrote "The Walrus and the Carpenter."*
> RELATED SENTENCE: *"The Walrus and the Carpenter" is a poem in his book* Through the Looking Glass.
> COMBINED SENTENCE: *Lewis Carroll wrote "The Walrus and the Carpenter," which is a poem in his book* Through the Looking Glass.

GRAMMAR PRACTICE

Write the correct form of each incorrect pronoun.

1. Whom eats the Oysters in Lewis Carroll's poem?
2. The Carpenter doesn't feel sympathy for who?
3. Everybody enjoys their walk.
4. Few of the Oysters believe what is happening to it.
5. The Walrus cries but eats the biggest Oysters hisself.

2.9 PRONOUN REFERENCE PROBLEMS

You should always be able to identify the word a pronoun refers to. Avoid problems by rewriting sentences.

An **indefinite reference** occurs when the pronoun *it, you,* or *they* does not clearly refer to a specific antecedent.

> UNCLEAR: *They told me how the story ended, and it was annoying.*

> CLEAR: *They told me how the story ended, and I was annoyed.*

A **general reference** occurs when the pronoun *it, this, that, which,* or *such* is used to refer to a general idea rather than a specific antecedent.

> UNCLEAR: *I'd rather not know what happens. That keeps me interested.*

> CLEAR: *I'd rather not know what happens. Not knowing keeps me interested.*

Ambiguous means "having more than one possible meaning." An **ambiguous reference** occurs when a pronoun could refer to two or more antecedents.

> UNCLEAR: *Jan told Danielle that she would read her story aloud.*

> CLEAR: *Jan told Danielle that she would read Danielle's story aloud.*

GRAMMAR PRACTICE

Rewrite the following sentences to correct indefinite, ambiguous, and general pronoun references.

1. In the story "Ghost of the Lagoon," it said even talking about Tupa could bring bad luck.
2. The shark came close to Afa. That made Mako throw the spear.
3. Mako told Afa that he would rescue him.
4. After Mako killed Tupa, they cheered.

---

❸ Verbs

A **verb** is a word that expresses an action, a condition, or a state of being.

*For more information, see **Quick Reference: Parts of Speech**, page R47.*

3.1 ACTION VERBS

Action verbs express mental or physical activity.

> EXAMPLE: *Lucy ran several miles every day.*

3.2 LINKING VERBS

Linking verbs join subjects with words or phrases that rename or describe them.

> EXAMPLE: *After a few months, her shoes were worn out.*

3.3 PRINCIPAL PARTS

Action and linking verbs typically have four principal parts, which are used to form verb tenses. The principal parts are the **present,** the **present participle,** the **past,** and the **past participle.**

Action verbs and some linking verbs also fall into two categories: regular and irregular. A **regular verb** is a verb that forms its past and past participle by adding *-ed* or *-d* to the present form.

Present	Present Participle	Past	Past Participle
jump	(is) jumping	jumped	(has) jumped
solve	(is) solving	solved	(has) solved
grab	(is) grabbing	grabbed	(has) grabbed
carry	(is) carrying	carried	(has) carried

An **irregular verb** is a verb that forms its past and past participle in some other way than by adding *-ed* or *-d* to the present form.

Present	Present Participle	Past	Past Participle
begin	(is) beginning	began	(has) begun
break	(is) breaking	broke	(has) broken
go	(is) going	went	(has) gone

3.4 VERB TENSE

The **tense** of a verb indicates the time of the action or the state of being. An action or state of being can occur in the present, the past, or the future. There are six tenses, each expressing a different range of time.

The **present tense** expresses an action or state that is happening at the present time, occurs regularly, or is constant or generally true. Use the present part.

> NOW: *This apple is rotten.*
> REGULAR: *I eat an apple every day.*
> GENERAL: *Apples are round.*

The **past tense** expresses an action that began and ended in the past. Use the past part.

> EXAMPLE: *They settled the argument.*

The **future tense** expresses an action or state that will occur. Use *shall* or *will* with the present part.

> EXAMPLE: *You will understand someday.*

The **present perfect tense** expresses an action or state that (1) was completed at an indefinite time in the past or (2) began in the past and continues into the present. Use *have* or *has* with the past participle.

> EXAMPLE: *These buildings have existed for centuries.*

The **past perfect tense** expresses an action in the past that came before another action in the past. Use *had* with the past participle.

> EXAMPLE: *I had told you, but you forgot.*

The **future perfect tense** expresses an action in the future that will be completed before another action in the future. Use *shall have* or *will have* with the past participle.

> EXAMPLE: *She will have found the note by the time I get home.*

TIP A past-tense form of an irregular verb is not used with an auxiliary, or helping, verb, but a past-participle main irregular verb is always used with an auxiliary verb.

> INCORRECT: *He has did that too many times.* (*Did* is the past-tense form of an irregular verb and shouldn't be used with *has*.)
> INCORRECT: *He done that too many times.* (*Done* is the past participle of an irregular verb and shouldn't be used without an auxiliary verb.)
> CORRECT: *He has done that too many times.*

3.5 PROGRESSIVE FORMS

The progressive forms of the six tenses show ongoing actions. Use forms of *be* with the present participles of verbs.

> PRESENT PROGRESSIVE: *Angelo is taking the test.*
> PAST PROGRESSIVE: *Angelo was taking the test.*
> FUTURE PROGRESSIVE: *Angelo will be taking the test.*
> PRESENT PERFECT PROGRESSIVE: *Angelo has been taking the test.*
> PAST PERFECT PROGRESSIVE: *Angelo had been taking the test.*
> FUTURE PERFECT PROGRESSIVE: *Angelo will have been taking the test.*

WATCH OUT! Do not shift from tense to tense needlessly. Watch out for these special cases.

- In most compound sentences and in sentences with compound predicates, keep the tenses the same.

> INCORRECT: *She smiled and shake his hand.*
> CORRECT: *She smiled and shook his hand.*

- If one past action happens before another, do shift tenses.

> INCORRECT: *He remembered what he studied.*
> CORRECT: *He remembered what he had studied.*

Rewrite each sentence, using a form of the verb in parentheses. Identify each form that you use.

1. Helen Keller (become) blind and deaf before she (be) two.

2. A wonderful teacher (change) her life.

3. Anne Sullivan (be) almost blind before she (have) an operation.

4. Even now, Keller (be) an inspiration to everyone with a disability.

5. People (remember) both Helen and her teacher for years to come.

Rewrite each sentence to correct an error in tense.

1. Helen Keller writes a book about her life.

2. She described how she learns to understand language.

3. She felt like she knew it once and forgotten it.

4. Anne Sullivan was a determined teacher and does not give up.

5. Helen had began a life of learning.

3.6 ACTIVE AND PASSIVE VOICE

The voice of a verb tells whether its subject performs or receives the action expressed by the verb. When the subject performs the action, the verb is in the **active voice.** When the subject is the receiver of the action, the verb is in the **passive voice.**

Compare these two sentences:

ACTIVE: *May Swenson wrote "Analysis of Baseball."*

PASSIVE: *"Analysis of Baseball" was written by May Swenson.*

To form the passive voice, use a form of *be* with the past participle of the verb.

WATCH OUT! Use the passive voice sparingly. It can make writing awkward and less direct.

AWKWARD: *"Analysis of Baseball" is a poem that was written by May Swenson.*

BETTER: *May Swenson wrote the poem "Analysis of Baseball."*

There are occasions when you will choose to use the passive voice because

• you want to emphasize the receiver: *The king was shot.*

• the doer is unknown: *My books were stolen.*

• the doer is unimportant: *French is spoken here.*

4 Modifiers

Modifiers are words or groups of words that change or limit the meanings of other words. Adjectives and adverbs are common modifiers.

4.1 ADJECTIVES

Adjectives modify nouns and pronouns by telling which one, what kind, how many, or how much.

WHICH ONE: *this, that, these, those*
EXAMPLE: *This poem moves along quickly.*

WHAT KIND: *square, dirty, fast, regular*
EXAMPLE: *Fast runners make baseball exciting.*

HOW MANY: *some, few, both, thousands*
EXAMPLE: *Thousands of fans cheer in the stands.*

HOW MUCH: *more, less, enough, as much*
EXAMPLE: *I had more fun watching the game than I expected.*

4.2 PREDICATE ADJECTIVES

Most adjectives come before the nouns they modify, as in the examples above. A **predicate adjective,** however, follows a linking verb and describes the subject.

EXAMPLE: *Baseball players are strong.*

Be especially careful to use adjectives (not adverbs) after such linking verbs as *look, feel, grow, taste,* and *smell.*

EXAMPLE: *Exercising feels good.*

4.3 ADVERBS

Adverbs modify verbs, adjectives, and other adverbs by telling where, when, how, or to what extent.

WHERE: *The children played outside.*

WHEN: *The author spoke yesterday.*

HOW: *We walked slowly behind the leader.*

TO WHAT EXTENT: *He worked very hard.*

Adverbs may occur in many places in sentences, both before and after the words they modify.

EXAMPLES: *Suddenly the wind shifted.*

The wind suddenly shifted.

The wind shifted suddenly.

4.4 ADJECTIVE OR ADVERB?

Many adverbs are formed by adding *-ly* to adjectives.

EXAMPLES: *sweet, sweetly; gentle, gently*

However, *-ly* added to a noun will usually yield an adjective.

EXAMPLES: *friend, friendly; woman, womanly*

4.5 COMPARISON OF MODIFIERS

Modifiers can be used to compare two or more things. The form of a modifier shows the degree of comparison. Both adjectives and adverbs have **comparative** and **superlative** forms.

The **comparative form** is used to compare two things, groups, or actions.

EXAMPLES: *Today's weather is hotter than yesterday's.*

The boy got tired more quickly than his sister did.

The **superlative form** is used to compare more than two things, groups, or actions.

EXAMPLES: *This has been the hottest month ever recorded.*

Older people were most affected by the heat.

4.6 REGULAR COMPARISONS

Most one-syllable and some two-syllable adjectives and adverbs have comparatives and superlatives formed by adding *-er* and *-est*. All three-syllable and most two-syllable modifiers have comparatives and superlatives formed with *more* or *most.*

Modifier	Comparative	Superlative
messy	messier	messiest
quick	quicker	quickest
wild	wilder	wildest
tired	more tired	most tired
often	more often	most often

WATCH OUT! Note that spelling changes must sometimes be made to form the comparatives and superlatives of modifiers.

EXAMPLES: *friendly, friendlier* (Change *y* to *i* and add the ending.)

sad, sadder (Double the final consonant and add the ending.)

4.7 IRREGULAR COMPARISONS

Some commonly used modifiers have irregular comparative and superlative forms. They are listed in the following chart. You may wish to memorize them.

Modifier	Comparative	Superlative
good	better	best
bad	worse	worst
far	farther *or* further	farthest *or* furthest
little	less *or* lesser	least
many	more	most
well	better	best
much	more	most

4.8 PROBLEMS WITH MODIFIERS

Study the tips that follow to avoid common mistakes:

Farther* and *Further Use *farther* for distances; use *further* for everything else.

Double Comparisons Make a comparison by using *-er/-est* or by using *more/most.* Using *-er* with *more* or using *-est* with *most* is incorrect.

INCORRECT: *I like her more better than she likes me.*

CORRECT: *I like her better than she likes me.*

Illogical Comparisons An illogical or confusing comparison results when two unrelated things are compared or when something is compared with itself. The word *other* or the word *else* should be used when comparing an individual member to the rest of a group.

ILLOGICAL: *I like "Fog" more than any poem.* (implies that "Fog" isn't a poem)

LOGICAL: *I like "Fog" more than any other poem.* (identifies that "Fog" is a poem)

Bad vs. Badly *Bad,* always an adjective, is used before a noun or after a linking verb. *Badly,* always an adverb, never modifies a noun. Be sure to use the right form after a linking verb.

INCORRECT: *I felt badly that I missed the game.*

CORRECT: *I felt bad that I missed the game.*

Good vs. Well *Good* is always an adjective. It is used before a noun or after a linking verb. *Well* is often an adverb meaning "expertly" or "properly." *Well* can also be used as an adjective after a linking verb when it means "in good health."

INCORRECT: *I wrote my essay good.*

CORRECT: *I wrote my essay well.*

CORRECT: *I didn't feel well when I wrote it, though.*

Double Negatives If you add a negative word to a sentence that is already negative, the result will be an error known as a double negative. When using *not* or *-n't* with a verb, use *any-* words, such as *anybody* or *anything,* rather than *no-* words, such as *nobody* or *nothing,* later in the sentence.

INCORRECT: *The teacher didn't like nobody's paper.*

CORRECT: *The teacher didn't like anybody's paper.*

Using *hardly, barely,* or *scarcely* after a negative word is also incorrect.

INCORRECT: *My friends couldn't hardly catch up.*

CORRECT: *My friends could hardly catch up.*

Misplaced Modifiers Sometimes a modifier is placed so far away from the word it modifies that the intended meaning of the sentence is unclear.

Prepositional phrases and participial phrases are often misplaced. Place modifiers as close as possible to the words they modify.

MISPLACED: *We found the child in the park who was missing.*

CLEARER: *We found the child who was missing in the park.* (The child was missing, not the park.)

Dangling Modifiers Sometimes a modifier doesn't appear to modify any word in a sentence. Most dangling modifiers are participial phrases or infinitive phrases.

DANGLING: *Looking out the window, his brother was seen driving by.*

CLEARER: *Looking out the window, Josh saw his brother driving by.*

GRAMMAR PRACTICE

Choose the correct word or words from each pair in parentheses.

1. According to Gary Paulsen, bears were a (bad, badly) problem in the woods.

2. The (worse, worst) time of year was spring.

3. The bears didn't have (any, no) interest in the yard animals.

4. They stalked the dogs really (good, well), though.

5. Scarface was (more, most) daring than any other bear in the forest.

GRAMMAR PRACTICE

Rewrite each sentence that contains a misplaced or dangling modifier. Write "correct" if the sentence is written correctly.

1. Coyotes know how to survive in the wild.

2. Hunting their prey, we have seen them in the forest.

3. Looking out the window, a coyote was seen in the yard.

4. My brother and I found books about coyotes at the library.

5. We learned that wolves are their natural enemies reading about them.

5 The Sentence and Its Parts

A **sentence** is a group of words used to express a complete thought. A complete sentence has a subject and a predicate.

For more information, see **Quick Reference: The Sentence and Its Parts,** *page R48.*

5.1 KINDS OF SENTENCES

There are four basic types of sentences.

Type	Definition	Example
Declarative	states a fact, a wish, an intent, or a feeling	Avi remembers being young.
Interrogative	asks a question	Have you read "Scout's Honor"?
Imperative	gives a command or direction	Find a copy.
Exclamatory	expresses strong feeling or excitement	It's really funny!

5.2 COMPOUND SUBJECTS AND PREDICATES

A compound subject consists of two or more subjects that share the same verb. They are typically joined by the coordinating conjunction *and* or *or.*

> EXAMPLE: *A short story or novel will keep you interested.*

A compound predicate consists of two or more predicates that share the same subject. They too are usually joined by a coordinating conjunction: *and, but,* or *or.*

> EXAMPLE: *The class finished all the poetry but did not read the short stories.*

5.3 COMPLEMENTS

A **complement** is a word or group of words that completes the meaning of a sentence. Some sentences contain only a subject and a verb. Most sentences, however, require additional words placed after the verb to complete the meaning of the sentence. There are three kinds of complements: direct objects, indirect objects, and subject complements.

Direct objects are words or word groups that receive the action of action verbs. A direct object answers the question *what* or *whom.*

> EXAMPLES: *Daria caught the ball.* (Caught what?)
> *She tagged the runner.* (Tagged whom?)

Indirect objects tell to whom or what or for whom or what the actions of verbs are performed. Indirect objects come before direct objects. In the examples that follow, the indirect objects are highlighted.

> EXAMPLES: *The audience gave us a standing ovation.* (Gave to whom?)
> *We offered the newspaper an interview.* (Offered to what?)

Subject complements come after linking verbs and identify or describe the subjects. A subject complement that names or identifies a subject is called a **predicate nominative.** Predicate nominatives include **predicate nouns** and **predicate pronouns.**

> EXAMPLES: *The students were happy campers.*
> *The best actor in the play is he.*

A subject complement that describes a subject is called a **predicate adjective.**

> EXAMPLE: *The coach seemed thrilled.*

6 Phrases

A **phrase** is a group of related words that does not contain a subject and a predicate but functions in a sentence as a single part of speech.

6.1 PREPOSITIONAL PHRASES

A **prepositional phrase** is a phrase that consists of a preposition, its object, and any modifiers of the object. Prepositional phrases that modify nouns or pronouns are called **adjective phrases.** Prepositional phrases that modify verbs, adjectives, or adverbs are **adverb phrases.**

> ADJECTIVE PHRASE: *The central character of the story is a villain.*

> ADVERB PHRASE: *He reveals his nature in the first scene.*

6.2 APPOSITIVES AND APPOSITIVE PHRASES

An **appositive** is a noun or pronoun that identifies or renames another noun or pronoun. An **appositive phrase** includes an appositive and modifiers of it. An appositive usually follows the noun or pronoun it identifies.

An appositive can be either **essential** or **nonessential**. An **essential appositive** provides information that is needed to identify what is referred to by the preceding noun or pronoun.

> EXAMPLE: *Aesop's story is about the characters Ant and Grasshopper.*

A **nonessential appositive** adds extra information about a noun or pronoun whose meaning is already clear. Nonessential appositives and appositive phrases are set off with commas.

> EXAMPLE: *The story, a fable, has an important message.*

7 Verbals and Verbal Phrases

A **verbal** is a verb form that is used as a noun, an adjective, or an adverb. A **verbal phrase** consists of a verbal along with its modifiers and complements. There are three kinds of verbals: infinitives, participles, and gerunds.

7.1 INFINITIVES AND INFINITIVE PHRASES

An **infinitive** is a verb form that usually begins with *to* and functions as a noun, an adjective, or an adverb. An **infinitive phrase** consists of an infinitive plus its modifiers and complements.

> NOUN: *To be happy is not easy.* (subject)
> *I want to have fun.* (direct object)
> *My hope is to enjoy every day.* (predicate nominative)
> ADJECTIVE: *That's a goal to be proud of.* (adjective modifying *goal*)
> ADVERB: *I'll work to achieve it.* (adverb modifying *work*)

Because *to*, the sign of the infinitive, precedes infinitives, it is usually easy to recognize them. However, sometimes *to* may be omitted.

> EXAMPLE: *No one can help me [to] achieve my goal.*

7.2 PARTICIPLES AND PARTICIPIAL PHRASES

A **participle** is a verb form that functions as an adjective. Like adjectives, participles modify nouns and pronouns. Most participles are present-participle forms, ending in *-ing*, or past-participle forms ending in *-ed* or *-en*. In the examples below, the participles are highlighted.

> MODIFYING A NOUN: *The waxed floor was sticky.*
> MODIFYING A PRONOUN: *Sighing, she mopped up the mess.*

Participial phrases are participles with all their modifiers and complements.

> MODIFYING A NOUN: *The girls working on the project are very energetic.*
> MODIFYING A PRONOUN: *Having finished his work, he took a nap.*

7.3 DANGLING AND MISPLACED PARTICIPLES

A participle or participial phrase should be placed as close as possible to the word that it modifies. Otherwise the meaning of the sentence may not be clear.

> MISPLACED: *The boys were looking for squirrels searching the trees.*
> CLEARER: *The boys searching the trees were looking for squirrels.*

A participle or participial phrase that does not clearly modify anything in a sentence is called a **dangling participle.** A dangling participle causes confusion because it appears to modify a word that it cannot sensibly modify. Correct a dangling participle by providing a word for the participle to modify.

> DANGLING: *Waiting for the show to start, the phone rang.* (The phone wasn't waiting.)
> CLEARER: *Waiting for the show to start, I heard the phone ring.*

7.4 GERUNDS AND GERUND PHRASES

A **gerund** is a verb form ending in *-ing* that functions as a noun. Gerunds may perform any function nouns perform.

> SUBJECT: *Cooking is a good way to relax.*
> DIRECT OBJECT: *I enjoy cooking.*

INDIRECT OBJECT: *They should give* cooking *a chance.*

SUBJECT COMPLEMENT: *My favorite pastime is* cooking.

OBJECT OF PREPOSITION: *A love of* cooking *runs in the family.*

Gerund phrases are gerunds with all their modifiers and complements.

SUBJECT: Depending on luck *never got me far.*

OBJECT OF PREPOSITION: *I will finish before* leaving the office.

APPOSITIVE: *Her hobby,* training horses, *finally led to a career.*

GRAMMAR PRACTICE

Rewrite each sentence, adding the type of phrase shown in parentheses.

1. "The Jacket" is by Gary Soto. (appositive phrase)

2. He needed a new jacket. (infinitive phrase)

3. He didn't like it and was embarrassed. (prepositional phrase)

4. It brought him bad luck. (gerund phrase)

5. The ugly jacket was like a brother. (participial phrase)

8 Clauses

A **clause** is a group of words that contains a subject and a predicate. There are two kinds of clauses: independent clauses and subordinate clauses.

8.1 INDEPENDENT AND SUBORDINATE CLAUSES

An **independent clause** can stand alone as a sentence, as the word *independent* suggests.

INDEPENDENT CLAUSE: *I read "Night Journey."*

A sentence may contain more than one independent clause.

EXAMPLE: *I read it once, and I liked it.*

In the preceding example, the coordinating conjunction *and* joins two independent clauses.

For more information, see **Coordinating Conjunctions,** *page R47.*

A **subordinate (dependent) clause** cannot stand alone as a sentence. It is subordinate to, or dependent on, an independent clause.

EXAMPLE: After I finished it, *I read it again.*

The highlighted clause cannot stand by itself.

8.2 ADJECTIVE CLAUSES

An **adjective clause** is a subordinate clause used as an adjective. It usually follows the noun or pronoun it modifies.

EXAMPLE: *The journey* that Roethke describes *is a train trip.*

EXAMPLE: *The speaker,* who is in a train berth, *watches the scenery.*

Adjective clauses are typically introduced by the relative pronouns *who, whom, whose, which,* and *that.*

For more information, see **Relative Pronouns,** *page R54.*

An adjective clause can be either essential or nonessential. An **essential adjective clause** provides information that is necessary to identify the preceding noun or pronoun.

EXAMPLE: *He sees the mist* that hides the mountains.

A **nonessential adjective clause** adds additional information about a noun or pronoun whose meaning is already clear. Nonessential clauses are set off with commas.

EXAMPLE: *The rain,* which moved in from the east, *kept him awake all night.*

8.3 ADVERB CLAUSES

An **adverb clause** is a subordinate clause that is used to modify a verb, an adjective, or an adverb. It is introduced by a subordinating conjunction.

For examples of subordinating conjunctions, see **Quick Reference: Parts of Speech,** *page R47.*

Adverb clauses typically occur at the beginning or end of sentences.

MODIFYING A VERB: *When your present arrives, I'll bring it to you.*

MODIFYING AN ADVERB: *Wait here where I can find you.*

MODIFYING AN ADJECTIVE: *I hope you are happy when you see it.*

TIP An adverb clause should be followed by a comma when it comes before an independent clause. When an adverb clause comes after an independent clause, a comma may not be needed.

8.4 NOUN CLAUSES

A **noun clause** is a subordinate clause that is used as a noun. A noun clause may be used as a subject, a direct object, an indirect object, a predicate nominative, or the object of a preposition. Noun clauses are introduced either by pronouns, such as *that, what, who, whoever, which,* and *whose,* or by subordinating conjunctions, such as *how, when, where, why,* and *whether.*

For more subordinating conjunctions, see **Quick Reference: Parts of Speech,** *pages R46 and R47.*

TIP Because the same words may introduce adjective and noun clauses, you need to consider how a clause functions within its sentence. To determine if a clause is a noun clause, try substituting *something* or *someone* for the clause. If you can do it, it is probably a noun clause.

EXAMPLES: *I don't remember whose CD this is.* ("I don't remember *something.*" The clause is a noun clause, direct object of the verb *remember.*)

Will you take it to whoever lost it? ("Will you take it to *someone*?" The clause is a noun clause, object of the preposition *to.*)

GRAMMAR PRACTICE

Add descriptive details to each sentence by writing the type of clause indicated in parentheses.

1. We look forward to summer vacation. (adverb clause)

2. Interesting adventures keep us busy. (adjective clause)

3. People think we're wasting time. (adjective clause)

4. We don't mind. (noun clause)

5. We're having fun. (noun clause)

---

9 The Structure of Sentences

When classified by their structure, there are four kinds of sentences: simple, compound, complex, and compound-complex.

9.1 SIMPLE SENTENCES

A **simple sentence** is a sentence that has one independent clause and no subordinate clauses.

EXAMPLES: *Seth drove to the station.*

Chloe looked for the train.

A simple sentence may contain a compound subject or a compound verb.

EXAMPLES: *Seth and Chloe drove to the train station. (compound subject)*

They waved and shouted as the train pulled in. (compound verb)

9.2 COMPOUND SENTENCES

A **compound sentence** consists of two or more independent clauses. The clauses in compound sentences are joined with commas and coordinating conjunctions (*and, but, or, nor, yet, for, so*) or with semicolons. Like simple sentences, compound sentences do not contain any subordinate clauses.

EXAMPLES: *We all get older, but not everyone gets wiser.*

Some young people don't want to grow up; others grow up too quickly.

WATCH OUT! Do not confuse compound sentences with simple sentences that have compound parts.

EXAMPLE: *Change can be scary and often challenging.*

(Here *and* joins parts of a compound predicate, not a compound sentence.)

9.3 COMPLEX SENTENCES

A **complex sentence** consists of one independent clause and one or more subordinate clauses.

EXAMPLES: *I often wonder what I'll be like in ten years.*

When I think about the future, I see a canvas that has nothing on it.

9.4 COMPOUND-COMPLEX SENTENCES

A **compound-complex sentence** contains two or more independent clauses and one or more subordinate clauses. Compound-complex sentences are, simply, both compound and complex. If you start with a compound sentence, all you need to do to form a compound-complex sentence is add a subordinate clause.

COMPOUND: *All the students knew the answer, yet they were too shy to volunteer.*

COMPOUND-COMPLEX: *All the students knew the answer that their teacher expected, yet they were too shy to volunteer.*

9.5 PARALLEL STRUCTURE

When you write sentences, make sure that coordinate parts are equivalent, or **parallel,** in structure.

NOT PARALLEL: *He forgot his lunch and to bring his homework.* (*Lunch* is a noun; *to bring his homework* is an infinitive phrase.)

PARALLEL: *He forgot his lunch and his homework.* (*Lunch* and *homework* are both nouns.)

NOT PARALLEL: *Writing, to play the piano, and sleep were her favorite pastimes.*
(*Writing* is a gerund, *to play the piano* is an infinitive phrase, and *sleep* is a noun.)

PARALLEL: *Writing, playing the piano, and sleeping were her favorite pastimes.*
(*Writing, playing* and *sleeping* are all gerunds.)

🔟 Writing Complete Sentences

Remember, a sentence is a group of words that expresses a complete thought. In writing that you wish to share with a reader, try to avoid both sentence fragments and run-on sentences.

10.1 CORRECTING FRAGMENTS

A **sentence fragment** is a group of words that is only part of a sentence. It does not express a complete thought and may be confusing to a reader or listener. A sentence fragment may be lacking a subject, a predicate, or both.

FRAGMENT: *Didn't care about sports.* (no subject)

CORRECTED: *The lawyer didn't care about sports.*

FRAGMENT: *Her middle-school son.* (no predicate)

CORRECTED: *Her middle-school son played on the soccer team.*

FRAGMENT: *Before every game.* (neither subject nor predicate)

CORRECTED: *Before every game, he tried to teach his mom the rules.*

In your writing, fragments may be a result of haste or incorrect punctuation. Sometimes fixing a fragment will be a matter of attaching it to a preceding or following sentence.

FRAGMENT: *She made an effort. But just couldn't make sense of the game.*

CORRECTED: *She made an effort but just couldn't make sense of the game.*

10.2 CORRECTING RUN-ON SENTENCES

A **run-on sentence** is made up of two or more sentences written as though they were one. Some run-ons have no punctuation within them. Others may have only commas where conjunctions or stronger punctuation marks are necessary.

Use your judgment in correcting run-on sentences, as you have choices. You can change a run-on to two sentences if the thoughts are not closely connected. If the thoughts are closely related, you can keep the run-on as one sentence by adding a semicolon or a conjunction.

RUN-ON: *Most parents watched the game his mother read a book instead.*

MAKE TWO SENTENCES: *Most parents watched the game. His mother read a book instead.*

RUN-ON: *Most parents watched the game they played sports themselves.*

USE A SEMICOLON: *Most parents watched the game; they played sports themselves.*

ADD A CONJUNCTION: *Most parents watched the game since they played sports themselves.*

WATCH OUT! When you form compound sentences, make sure you use appropriate punctuation: a comma before a coordinating conjunction, a semicolon when there is no coordinating conjunction. A very common mistake is to use a comma without a conjunction or instead of a semicolon. This error is called a **comma splice.**

INCORRECT: *He finished the job, he left the village.*

CORRECT: *He finished the job, and he left the village.*

11 Subject-Verb Agreement

The subject and verb in a clause must agree in number. Agreement means that if the subject is singular, the verb is also singular, and if the subject is plural, the verb is also plural.

11.1 BASIC AGREEMENT

Fortunately, agreement between subjects and verbs in English is simple. Most verbs show the difference between singular and plural only in the third person of the present tense. In the present tense, the third-person singular form ends in *-s.*

Present-Tense Verb Forms	
Singular	**Plural**
I sleep	we sleep
you sleep	you sleep
she, he, it sleeps	they sleep

11.2 AGREEMENT WITH *BE*

The verb *be* presents special problems in agreement, because this verb does not follow the usual verb patterns.

Forms of *Be*			
Present Tense		**Past Tense**	
Singular	**Plural**	**Singular**	**Plural**
I am	we are	I was	we were
you are	you are	you were	you were
she, he, it is	they are	she, he, it was	they were

11.3 WORDS BETWEEN SUBJECT AND VERB

A verb agrees only with its subject. When words come between a subject and a verb, ignore them when considering proper agreement. Identify the subject and make sure the verb agrees with it.

EXAMPLES: *The poem I read describes a moose. The moose in the poem searches for a place where he belongs.*

11.4 AGREEMENT WITH COMPOUND SUBJECTS

Use plural verbs with most compound subjects joined by the word *and.*

EXAMPLE: *My father and his friends play chess every day.*

To confirm that you need a plural verb, you could substitute the plural pronoun *they* for *my father and his friends.*

If a compound subject is thought of as a unit, use a singular verb. Test this by substituting the singular pronoun *it.*

EXAMPLE: *A bagel and cream cheese [it] is my usual breakfast.*

Use a singular verb with a compound subject that is preceded by *each, every,* or *many a.*

> EXAMPLE: *Each novel and short story seems grounded in personal experience.*

When the parts of a compound subject are joined by *or, nor,* or the correlative conjunctions *either . . . or* or *neither . . . nor,* make the verb agree with the noun or pronoun nearest the verb.

> EXAMPLES: *Cookies or ice cream is my favorite dessert.*
>
> *Either Cheryl or her parents are being invited.*
>
> *Neither ice storms nor snow is predicted today.*

11.5 PERSONAL PRONOUNS AS SUBJECTS

When using a personal pronoun as a subject, make sure to match it with the correct form of the verb *be.* (See the chart in Section 11.2.) Note especially that the pronoun *you* takes the forms *are* and *were,* regardless of whether it is singular or plural.

WATCH OUT! *You is* and *you was* are nonstandard forms and should be avoided in writing and speaking. *We was* and *they was* are also forms to be avoided.

> INCORRECT: *You was a good student.*
>
> CORRECT: *You were a good student.*
>
> INCORRECT: *They was starting a new school.*
>
> CORRECT: *They were starting a new school.*

11.6 INDEFINITE PRONOUNS AS SUBJECTS

Some indefinite pronouns are always singular; some are always plural.

Singular Indefinite Pronouns			
another	either	neither	one
anybody	everybody	nobody	somebody
anyone	everyone	no one	someone
anything	everything	nothing	something
each	much		

> EXAMPLES: *Each of the writers was given an award.*
>
> *Somebody in the room upstairs is sleeping.*

Plural Indefinite Pronouns			
both	few	many	several

> EXAMPLES: *Many of the books in our library are not in circulation.*
>
> *Few have been returned recently.*

Still other indefinite pronouns may be either singular or plural.

Singular or Plural Indefinite Pronouns		
all	more	none
any	most	some

The number of the indefinite pronoun *any* or *none* often depends on the intended meaning.

> EXAMPLES: *Any of these stories has an important message.* (any one story)
>
> *Any of these stories have important messages.* (all of the many stories)

The indefinite pronouns *all, some, more, most,* and *none* are singular when they refer to quantities or parts of things. They are plural when they refer to numbers of individual things. Context will usually give a clue.

> EXAMPLES: *All of the flour is gone.* (referring to a quantity)
>
> *All of the flowers are gone.* (referring to individual items)

11.7 INVERTED SENTENCES

A sentence in which the subject follows the verb is called an **inverted sentence.** A subject can follow a verb or part of a verb phrase in a question; a sentence beginning with *here* or *there;* or a sentence in which an adjective, an adverb, or a phrase is placed first.

> EXAMPLES: *Here comes the scariest part.*
>
> *There goes the hero with a flashlight.*
>
> *Then, into the room rushes a big black cat!*

TIP To check subject-verb agreement in some inverted sentences, place the subject before the verb. For example, change *There are many people* to *Many people are there.*

11.8 SENTENCES WITH PREDICATE NOMINATIVES

In a sentence containing a predicate noun (nominative), the verb should agree with the subject, not the predicate noun.

> **EXAMPLES:** *Ogden Nash's limericks are a source of laughter.* (*Limericks* is the subject—not *source*—and it takes the plural verb *are.*)
>
> *One source of laughter is Ogden Nash's limericks.* (The subject is *source*—not *limericks*—and it takes the singular verb *is.*)

11.9 *DON'T* AND *DOESN'T* AS AUXILIARY VERBS

The auxiliary verb *doesn't* is used with singular subjects and with the personal pronouns *she, he,* and *it.* The auxiliary verb *don't* is used with plural subjects and with the personal pronouns *I, we, you,* and *they.*

> **SINGULAR:** *The humor doesn't escape us.*
>
> *Doesn't the limerick about Dougal MacDougal make you laugh?*
>
> **PLURAL:** *We don't usually forget such funny images.*
>
> *Don't people like to recite limericks?*

11.10 COLLECTIVE NOUNS AS SUBJECTS

Collective nouns are singular nouns that name groups of persons or things. *Team,* for example, is a collective name of a group of individuals. A collective noun takes a singular verb when the group acts as a single unit. It takes a plural verb when the members of the group act separately.

> **EXAMPLES:** *The class creates a bulletin board of limericks.* (The class as a whole creates the board.)
>
> *The faculty enjoy teaching poetry.* (The individual members enjoy teaching poetry.)

11.11 RELATIVE PRONOUNS AS SUBJECTS

When the relative pronoun *who, which,* or *that* is used as a subject in an adjective clause, the verb in the clause must agree in number with the antecedent of the pronoun.

> **SINGULAR:** *The **myth** from ancient Greece that interests me most is "Apollo's Tree."*

The antecedent of the relative pronoun *that* is the singular *myth;* therefore, *that* is singular and must take the singular verb *interests.*

> **PLURAL:** *Rafe Martin and Judith Ortiz Cofer are **writers** who tell folk tales.*

The antecedent of the relative pronoun *who* is the plural subject *writers.* Therefore *who* is plural, and it takes the plural verb *tell.*

GRAMMAR PRACTICE

Locate the subject of each verb in parentheses in the sentences below. Then choose the correct verb form.

1. Jim Haskins's "Matthew Henson at the Top of the World" (describes, describe) Henson's adventures in the Arctic.

2. The stories of the sea (is, are) inspiring to the young boy.

3. Nobody else (has, have) such courage and adventurousness.

4. Many of his experiences (brings, bring) danger and hardship, though.

5. The fishing boat's captain and crew (acts, act) cruel to Henson.

6. There (is, are) visions of hope when the explorer Robert Peary offers him a job.

7. With Peary, Henson (makes, make) five expeditions to the Arctic.

8. Henson's talents, such as his hunting ability, (endears, endear) him to the Eskimos.

9. None of his other achievements (equals, equal) his reaching the North Pole with Peary.

10. (Doesn't, Don't) the government feel ashamed for not recognizing Henson's contribution for so many years?

The key to becoming an independent reader is to develop a tool kit of vocabulary strategies. By learning and practicing the strategies, you'll know what to do when you encounter unfamiliar words while reading. You'll also know how to refine the words you use for different situations—personal, school, and work.

Being a good speller is important when communicating your ideas in writing. Learning basic spelling rules and checking your spelling in a dictionary will help you spell words that you may not use frequently.

> **VOCABULARY PRACTICE**
> For more practice, go to the **Vocabulary Center** at ClassZone.com.

1 Using Context Clues

The context of a word is made up of the punctuation marks, words, sentences, and paragraphs that surround the word. A word's context can give you important clues about its meaning.

1.1 GENERAL CONTEXT

Sometimes you need to determine the meaning of an unfamiliar word by reading all the information in a passage.

> *Kevin set out the broom, a dustpan, and three trash bags before beginning the* monumental *task of cleaning his room.*

You can figure out from the context that *monumental* means "huge."

1.2 SPECIFIC CONTEXT CLUES

Sometimes writers help you understand the meanings of words by providing specific clues such as those shown in the chart. When reading content area materials, use word, sentence, and paragraph clues to help you figure out meanings.

1.3 IDIOMS, SLANG, AND FIGURATIVE LANGUAGE

Use context clues to figure out the meanings of idioms, slang, and figurative language.

An **idiom** is an expression whose overall meaning differs from the meaning of the individual words.

> *The mosquitos* drove us crazy *on our hike.* (Drove us crazy *means "irritated.")*

Slang is informal language that features made-up words and ordinary words that are used to mean something different from their meanings in formal English.

> *That's a really* cool *backpack you're wearing.* (Cool *means "excellent.")*

Figurative language is language that communicates meaning beyond the literal meaning of the words.

> *Like a plunging horse, my car kicked up dirt, moved ahead quickly, and made a loud noise when I hit the gas.* (Kicked up dirt, moved ahead, *and* made a loud noise *describe a plunging horse.)*

Specific Context Clues		
Type of Clue	**Key Words/ Phrases**	**Example**
Definition or restatement of the meaning of the word	or, which is, that is, in other words, also known as, also called	In 1909, a French inventor flew a *monoplane*, or a **single-winged plane.**
Example following an unfamiliar word	such as, like, as if, for example, especially, including	The stunt pilot performed *acrobatics*, such as **dives and wing-walking.**
Comparison with a more familiar word or concept	as, like, also, similar to, in the same way, likewise	The doctor prescribed a *bland* diet, similar to the **rice and potatoes** he was already eating.
Contrast with a familiar word or experience	unlike, but, however, although, on the other hand, on the contrary	The moon will *diminish* at the end of the month; however it **will grow** during the first part of the month.
Cause-and-effect relationship in which one term is familiar	because, since, when, consequently, as a result, therefore	Because their general was *valiant*, the rest of the soldiers **showed courage** in battle.

For more information, see **Vocabulary Strategy: Context Clues**, pages 252 and 907, **Vocabulary Strategy: Idioms**, page 778, **Vocabulary Strategy: Slang**, page 363, and **Vocabulary Strategy: Figurative Language**, pages 98 and 220.

2 Analyzing Word Structure

Many words can be broken into smaller parts. These word parts include base words, roots, prefixes, and suffixes.

2.1 BASE WORDS

A **base word** is a word part that by itself is also a word. Other words or word parts can be added to base words to form new words.

For more information, see **Vocabulary Strategy: Recognizing Base Words**, page 740.

2.2 ROOTS

A **root** is a word part that contains the core meaning of the word. Many English words contain roots that come from older languages such as Greek and Latin. Knowing the meanings of a word's root can help you determine the word's meaning.

Root	Meaning	Example
auto (Greek)	self, same	**auto**mobile
hydr (Greek)	water	**hydr**ant
cent (Latin)	hundred	**cent**ury
circ (Latin)	ring	**circ**le
port (Latin)	carry	**port**able

For more information, see **Vocabulary Strategy: Word Roots**, pages 120, 264, 326, 476, 601.

2.3 PREFIXES

A **prefix** is a word part attached to the beginning of a word. Most prefixes come from Greek, Latin, or Old English.

Prefix	Meaning	Example
dis-	not	**dis**honest
pre-	before	**pre**face
un-	the opposite of, not	**un**happy
re-	carry, back	**re**pay

For more information, see **Vocabulary Strategy: Prefixes**, page 120.

2.4 SUFFIXES

A **suffix** is a word part that appears at the end of a root or base word to form a new word. Some suffixes do not change word meaning. These suffixes are
- added to nouns to change the number of persons or objects
- added to verbs to change the tense
- added to modifiers to change the degree of comparison

Suffix	Meaning	Example
-s, -es	to change the number of a noun	lock + s = locks
-d, -ed, -ing	to change verb tense	stew + ed = stewed
-er, -est	to indicate comparison in modifiers	mild + er = milder soft + est = softest

Other suffixes can be added to the root or base to change the word's meaning. These suffixes can also determine a word's part of speech.

Suffix	Meaning	Example
-ion	process of	transporta**tion**
-able	capable of	read**able**
-ness	quality of, condition	sad**ness**

For more information, see **Vocabulary Strategy: Suffixes**, page 60, and **Vocabulary Strategy: Noun-Forming Suffixes**, page 346.

3 Understanding Word Origins

Strategies for Understanding Unfamiliar Words

- Look for any prefixes or suffixes. Remove them so that you can concentrate on the base word or the root.
- See if you recognize any elements—prefix, suffix, root, or base—of the word. You may be able to guess its meaning by analyzing one or two elements.

- Think about the way the word is used in the sentence. Use the context and the word parts to make a logical guess about the word's meaning.
- Look in a dictionary to see whether you are correct.

3.1 ETYMOLOGIES

Etymologies show the origin and historical development of a word. When you study a word's history and origin, you can find out when, where, and how the word came to be.

> **em•per•or** (ĕm′pər-ər) *n.* **1.** The male ruler of an empire. **2a.** The emperor butterfly. **b.** The emperor moth. [Middle English *emperour,* from Old French *empereor,* from Latin *imperātor,* from *imperāre,* to command *: in-,* in; see EN–[1] + *parāre,* to prepare.]

3.2 WORD FAMILIES

Words that have the same root make up a word family and have related meanings. The following chart shows a common Greek and a common Latin root. Notice how the meanings of the example words are related to the meanings of their roots.

Latin Root	*man:* "hand"
English	**manual** by hand
	manage handle
	manuscript document written by hand

Greek Root	*phon:* "sound"
English	**telephone** an instrument that transmits sound
	phonograph machine that reproduces sound
	phonetic representing sounds of speech

3.3 FOREIGN WORDS IN ENGLISH

The English language includes words from other languages, such as French, Dutch, Spanish, Italian, and Chinese. Many words have stayed the way they were in their original language.

French	Dutch	Spanish	Italian
ballet	boss	canyon	diva
vague	caboose	rodeo	cupola
mirage	dock	bronco	spaghetti

PRACTICE AND APPLY

Look up the origin and meaning of each word listed in the preceding chart. Then use each word in a sentence.

4 Synonyms and Antonyms

4.1 SYNONYMS

A **synonym** is a word with a meaning similar to that of another word. You can find synonyms in a thesaurus or a dictionary. In a dictionary, synonyms are often given as part of the definition of a word. The following word pairs are synonyms:

satisfy/please   occasionally/sometimes

rob/steal   schedule/agenda

*For more information, see **Vocabulary Strategy: Synonyms,** pages 72 and 898.*

4.2 ANTONYMS

An **antonym** is a word with a meaning opposite that of another word. The following word pairs are antonyms:

accurate/incorrect   similar/different

fresh/stale   unusual/ordinary

5 Denotation and Connotation

5.1 DENOTATION

A word's dictionary meaning is called its **denotation.** For example, the denotation of the word *thin* is "having little flesh; spare; lean."

5.2 CONNOTATION

The images or feelings you connect to a word add a finer shade of meaning, called **connotation.** The connation of a word goes beyond its basic dictionary definition. Writers use connotations of words to communicate positive or negative feelings.

Positive	Negative
slender	scrawny
thrifty	cheap
young	immature

Make sure you understand the denotation and connotation of a word when you read it or use it in your writing.

*For more information, see **Vocabulary Strategy: Denotations and Connotations,** pages 40, 707, 913.*

6 Analogies

An **analogy** is a comparison between two things that are similar in some way but are otherwise not alike. Analogies are sometimes used in writing when unfamiliar subjects or ideas are explained in terms of familiar ones. Analogies often appear on tests as well. In an analogy problem, the analogy is expressed using two groups of words. The relationship between the first pair of words is the same as the relationship between the second pair of words. Some analogy problems are expressed like this:

love : hate :: war: _____
a. soldier   **b.** peace   **c.** battle   **d.** argument

Follow these steps to determine the correct answer:

- Read the problem as "*Love* is to *hate* as **war** is to...."

- Ask yourself how the words *love* and *hate* are related. (*Love* and *hate* are antonyms.)

- Ask yourself which answer choice is an antonym of *war*. (*Peace* is an antonym of *war*, therefore *peace* is the best answer.)

*For more information, see **Vocabulary Strategy: Analogies,** page 794.*

7 Homonyms, Homographs, and Homophones

7.1 HOMONYMS

Homonyms are words that have the same spelling and sound but have different meanings.

The snake shed its skin in the shed behind the house.

Shed can mean "to lose by natural process," but an identically spelled word means "a small structure."

Sometimes only one of the meanings of a homonym may be familiar to you. Use context clues to help you figure out the meaning of an unfamiliar word.

*For more information, see **Vocabulary Strategy: Homonyms,** page 686.*

7.2 HOMOGRAPHS

Homographs are words that are spelled the same but have different meanings and origins. Some are also pronounced differently, as in these examples:

Please close the door. (clōz)
That was a close call. (clōs)

If you see a word used in a way that is unfamiliar to you, check a dictionary to see if it is a homograph.

7.3 HOMOPHONES

Homophones are words that sound alike but have different meanings and spellings. The following homophones are frequently misused:

it's/its	they're/their/there
to/too/two	stationary/stationery

Many misused homophones are pronouns and contractions. Whenever you are unsure whether to write *your* or *you're* and *who's* or *whose*, ask yourself if you mean *you are* and *who is/has*. If you do, write the contraction. For other homophones, such as *fair* and *fare*, use the meaning of the word to help you decide which one to use.

8 Words with Multiple Meanings

Over time, some words have acquired additional meanings that are based on the original meaning.

I had to be replaced in the cast of the play because of the cast on my arm.

These two uses of *cast* have different meanings, but both of them have the same origin. You will find all the meanings of *cast* listed in one entry in the dictionary. Context can also help you figure out the meaning of the word.

*For more information, see **Vocabulary Strategy: Multiple-Meaning Words,** page 376.*

9 Specialized Vocabulary

Specialized vocabulary is a group of terms suited to a particular field of study or work. For example, science, mathematics, and history all have their own technical or specialized vocabularies. To figure out specialized terms, you can use context clues and reference sources, such as dictionaries on specific subjects, atlases, or manuals.

*For more information, see **Vocabulary Strategy: Specialized Vocabulary,** page 565.*

10 Using Reference Sources

10.1 DICTIONARIES

A **general dictionary** will tell you not only a word's definitions but also its pronunciation, parts of speech, history, and origin.

tan·gi·ble (tăn′jə-bəl) *adj.* **1a.** Discernible by the touch; palpable. **b.** Possible to touch. **c.** Possible to be treated as fact; real or concrete. **2.** Possible to understand or realize. **3.** *Law* That can be valued monetarily [Late Latin *tangibilis,* from Latin *tangere,* to touch.]

1 Entry word
2 Pronunciation
3 Part of speech
4 Definitions
5 Etymology

A **specialized dictionary** focuses on terms related to a particular field of study or work. Use a dictionary to check the spelling of any word you are unsure of in your reading.

*For more information, see **Vocabulary Strategy: Dictionary Usage Labels,** page 487.*

10.2 THESAURI

A **thesaurus** (plural, *thesauri*) is a dictionary of synonyms. A thesaurus can be especially helpful when you find yourself using the same modifiers over and over again.

10.3 SYNONYM FINDERS

A **synonym finder** is often included in word-processing software. It enables you to highlight a word and be shown a display of its synonyms.

10.4 GLOSSARIES

A **glossary** is a list of specialized terms and their definitions. It is often found in the back of a book and sometimes includes pronunciations. Many textbooks contain glossaries. In fact, this textbook has three glossaries: the **Glossary of Literary Terms,** the **Glossary of Reading & Informational Terms,** and the **Glossary of Vocabulary in English & Spanish.** Use these glossaries to help you understand how terms are used in this textbook.

*For more information, see **Vocabulary Strategy: Use Reference Aids,** page 668.*

11 Spelling Rules

11.1 WORDS ENDING IN A SILENT *E*

Before adding a suffix beginning with a vowel or *y* to a word ending in a silent *e,* drop the *e* (with some exceptions).

> amaze + -ing = amazing
> love + -able = lovable
> create + -ed = created
> nerve + -ous = nervous

Exceptions: *change + -able = changeable; courage + -ous = courageous*

When adding a suffix beginning with a consonant to a word ending in a silent *e,* keep the *e* (with some exceptions).

> late + -ly = lately
> spite + -ful = spiteful
> noise + -less = noiseless
> state + -ment = statement

Exceptions: *truly, argument, ninth, wholly, awful,* and others

When a suffix beginning with *a* or *o* is added to a word with a final silent *e,* the final *e* is usually retained if it is preceded by a soft *c* or a soft *g.*

> bridge + -able = bridgeable
> peace + -able = peaceable
> outrage + -ous = outrageous
> advantage + -ous = advantageous

When a suffix beginning with a vowel is added to words ending in *ee* or *oe,* the final, silent *e* is retained.

> agree + -ing = agreeing   free + -ing = freeing
> hoe + -ing = hoeing   see + -ing = seeing

11.2 WORDS ENDING IN Y

Before adding most suffixes to a word that ends in *y* preceded by a consonant, change the *y* to *i.*

> easy + -est = easiest
> crazy + -est = craziest
> silly + -ness = silliness
> marry + -age = marriage

Exceptions: *dryness, shyness,* and *slyness*

However, when you add *-ing,* the *y* does not change.

> empty + -ed = emptied   but
> empty + -ing = emptying

When adding a suffix to a word that ends in *y* preceded by a vowel, the *y* usually does not change.

> play + -er = player
> employ + -ed = employed
> coy + -ness = coyness
> pay + -able = payable

11.3 WORDS ENDING IN A CONSONANT

In one-syllable words that end in one consonant preceded by one short vowel, double the final consonant before adding a suffix beginning with a vowel, such as *-ed* or *-ing.* These are sometimes called 1+1+1 words.

> dip + -ed = dipped   set + -ing = setting
> slim + -est = slimmest   fit + -er = fitter

The rule does not apply to words of one syllable that end in a consonant preceded by two vowels.

> feel + -ing = feeling   peel + -ed = peeled
> reap + -ed = reaped   loot + -ed = looted

In words of more than one syllable, double the final consonant when (1) the word ends with one consonant preceded by one vowel and (2) when the word is accented on the last syllable.

> be•gin´   per•mit´   re•fer´

In the following examples, note that in the new words formed with suffixes, the accent remains on the same syllable:

> be•gin´ + -ing = be•gin´ning = beginning
> per•mit´ + -ed = per•mit´ted = permitted

Exceptions: In some words with more than one syllable, though the accent remains on the same syllable when a suffix is added, the final consonant is nevertheless not doubled, as in the following examples:

> tra´vel + er = tra´vel•er = traveler
> mar´ket + er = mar´ket•er = marketer

In the following examples, the accent does not remain on the same syllable; thus, the final consonant is not doubled:

> re•fer´ + -ence = ref´er•ence = reference
> con•fer´ + -ence = con´fer•ence = conference

11.4 PREFIXES AND SUFFIXES

When adding a prefix to a word, do not change the spelling of the base word. When a prefix creates a double letter, keep both letters.

> dis- + approve = disapprove
> re- + build = rebuild
> ir- + regular = irregular
> mis- + spell = misspell
> anti- + trust = antitrust
> il- + logical = illogical

When adding *-ly* to a word ending in *l,* keep both *l*'s. When adding *-ness* to a word ending in *n,* keep both *n*'s.

> careful + -ly = carefully
> sudden + -ness = suddenness
> final + -ly = finally
> thin + -ness = thinness

11.5 FORMING PLURAL NOUNS

To form the plural of most nouns, just add *-s.*

> prizes   dreams   circles   stations

For most singular nouns ending in *o,* add *-s.*

> solos   halos   studios   photos   pianos

For a few nouns ending in *o*, add *-es*.

heroes   tomatoes   potatoes   echoes

When a singular noun ends in *s, sh, ch, x,* or *z*, add *-es*.

waitresses   brushes   ditches
axes   buzzes

When a singular noun ends in *y* with a consonant before it, change the *y* to *i* and add *-es*.

army—armies   candy—candies
baby—babies   diary—diaries
ferry—ferries   conspiracy—conspiracies

When a vowel (*a, e, i, o, u*) comes before the *y*, just add *-s*.

boy—boys   way—ways
array—arrays   alloy—alloys
weekday—weekdays   jockey—jockeys

For most nouns ending in *f* or *fe*, change the *f* to *v* and add *-es* or *-s*.

life—lives   loaf—loaves
calf—calves   knife—knives
thief—thieves   shelf—shelves

For some nouns ending in *f*, add *-s* to make the plural.

roofs   chiefs   reefs   beliefs

Some nouns have the same form for both singular and plural.

deer   sheep   moose   salmon   trout

For some nouns, the plural is formed in a special way.

man—men   goose—geese
ox—oxen   woman—women
mouse—mice   child—children

For a compound noun written as one word, form the plural by changing the last word in the compound to its plural form.

stepchild—stepchildren   firefly—fireflies

If a compound noun is written as a hyphenated word or as two separate words, change the most important word to the plural form.

brother-in-law—brothers-in-law
life jacket—life jackets

11.6 FORMING POSSESSIVES

If a noun is singular, add *'s*.

mother—my mother's car   Ross—Ross's desk

Exception: An apostrophe alone is used to indicate the possessive case with the names Jesus and Moses and with certain names in classical mythology (such as Zeus). These possessive forms can thus be pronounced easily.

If a noun is plural and ends with *s*, just add an apostrophe.

parents—my parents' car
the Santinis—the Santinis' house

If a noun is plural but does not end in *s*, add *'s*.

people—the people's choice
women—the women's coats

11.7 SPECIAL SPELLING PROBLEMS

Only one English word ends in *-sede: supersede*. Three words end in *-ceed: exceed, proceed,* and *succeed*. All other verbs ending in the sound "seed" are spelled with *-cede*.

concede   precede   recede   secede

In words with **ie** or **ei**, when the sound is long *e* (as in *she*), the word is spelled *ie* except after *c* (with some exceptions).

i before *e*	thief	relieve	field
	piece	grieve	pier
except after *c*	conceit	perceive	ceiling
	receive	receipt	
Exceptions:	either	neither	weird
	leisure	seize	

⓬ Commonly Confused Words

WORDS	DEFINITIONS	EXAMPLES
accept/except	The verb *accept* means "to receive" or "to believe." *Except* is usually a preposition meaning "excluding."	Did the teacher **accept** your report? Everyone smiled for the photographer **except** Jody.
advice/advise	*Advise* is a verb. *Advice* is a noun naming that which an *adviser* gives.	I **advise** you to take that job. Whom should I ask for **advice?**
affect/effect	As a verb, *affect* means "to influence." *Effect* as a verb means "to cause." If you want a noun, you will almost always want *effect.*	How deeply did the news **affect** him? The students tried to **effect** a change in school policy. What **effect** did the acidic soil produce in the plants?
all ready/already	*All ready* is an adjective meaning "fully ready." *Already* is an adverb meaning "before" or "by this time."	He was **all ready** to go at noon. I have **already** seen that movie.
desert/dessert	*Desert* (děz´ərt) means "a dry, sandy, barren region." *Desert* (dĭ-zûrt´) means "to abandon." *Dessert* (dĭ-zûrt´) is a sweet, such as cake.	The Sahara, in North Africa, is the world's largest **desert.** The night guard did not **desert** his post. Alison's favorite **dessert** is chocolate cake.
among/between	*Between* is used when you are speaking of only two things. *Among* is used for three or more.	**Between** ice cream and sherbet, I prefer the latter. Gary Soto is **among** my favorite authors.
bring/take	*Bring* is used to denote motion toward a speaker or place. *Take* is used to denote motion away from such a person or place.	**Bring** the books over here, and I will **take** them to the library.
fewer/less	*Fewer* refers to the number of separate, countable units. *Less* refers to bulk quantity.	We have **less** literature and **fewer** selections in this year's curriculum.
leave/let	*Leave* means "to allow something to remain behind." *Let* means "to permit."	The librarian will **leave** some books on display but will not **let** us borrow any.
lie/lay	To *lie* is "to rest or recline." It does not take an object. *Lay* always takes an object.	Rover loves to **lie** in the sun. We always **lay** some bones next to him.
loose/lose	*Loose* (lōōs) means "free, not restrained." *Lose* (lōōz) means "to misplace" or "to fail to find."	Who turned the horses **loose?** I hope we won't **lose** any of them.
passed/past	*Passed* is the past tense of *pass* and means "went by." *Past* is an adjective that means "of a former time." *Past* is also a noun that means "time gone by."	We **passed** through the Florida Keys during our vacation. My **past** experiences have taught me to set my alarm. Ebenezer Scrooge is a character who relives his **past.**
than/then	Use *than* in making comparisons. Use *then* on all other occasions.	Ramon is stronger **than** Mark. Cut the grass and **then** trim the hedges.
two/too/to	*Two* is the number. *Too* is an adverb meaning "also" or "very." Use *to* before a verb or as a preposition.	Meg had **to** go **to** town, **too.** We had **too** much reading **to** do. **Two** chapters is **too** many.
their/there/they're	*Their* means "belonging to them." *There* means "in that place." *They're* is the contraction for "they are."	**There** is a movie playing at 9 P.M. **They're** going to see it with me. Sakara and Jessica drove away in **their** car after the movie.

*For more information, see **Vocabulary Strategy: Easily Confused Words,** page 189.*

Good speakers and listeners do more than just talk and hear. They use specific techniques to present their ideas effectively, and they are attentive and critical listeners. Effective oral communication occurs when the audience understands a message the way the speaker intends it.

1 Speech

In school, in business, and in community life, speaking directly to a live audience is an effective way to present information.

1.1 AUDIENCE, PURPOSE, AND OCCASION

When preparing and presenting a speech, think about your purpose in speaking as well as your audience's knowledge of and interest in your subject. Understanding your audience can help you choose a focus, a method of organization, and a point of view for your speech that will best express your message.

- **Know Your Audience** What kind of group are you presenting to? Fellow classmates? A group of teachers? What are their interests and backgrounds? Understanding their different points of view can help you organize the information so that they understand and are interested in it.

- **Understand Your Purpose for Speaking** Are you trying to persuade the audience to do something? Perhaps you simply want to entertain them by sharing a story or an experience. Your purpose for speaking should affect your tone. Decide whether a serious or a humorous tone is more appropriate for your purpose.

- **Know the Occasion** Are you speaking at a special event? Is it formal? Will others be giving speeches besides you? Knowing what the occasion is will help you choose the proper language and the right length for your speech.

1.2 WRITING YOUR SPEECH

Once you understand your purpose and audience, use the following guidelines to help you write your speech:

- **Create a Unified Speech** Do this first by organizing your speech into paragraphs, each of which develops a single main idea. Make sure that all the sentences in a paragraph support the main idea of the paragraph. Then make sure all the paragraphs support the main idea of the whole speech.

- **Clarify Your Ideas** Make sure that you show clear relationships between ideas. Transition words can help listeners follow your ideas.

*For more information on transitions, see the **Writing Handbook,** page R32.*

- **Use Appropriate Language** The subject of your speech—and the way you choose to present it—should be appropriate for your audience, your purpose, and the occasion. For example, if you are telling a funny story to your classmates, you might use informal language, such as slang. However, if you are giving a speech at a school assembly, you will want to use formal, standard American English. In an informative presentation, be sure to explain any terms that might be unfamiliar to the audience.

- **Provide Evidence** Include relevant facts, statistics, and incidents; quote experts to support your ideas and opinions. Elaborate— provide specific details, perhaps with visual or media displays—to clarify what you are saying.

- **Arrange Details and Evidence Effectively** In a good presentation, your main thesis statement should be supported by clearly stated evidence. The evidence can be presented as details, reasons, descriptions, or examples. Use the following chart to help you arrange your ideas.

Introduction	• Focus on one strong example or statistic. • Make sure your evidence is intense or even surprising, so that it grabs the audience's attention.
Main Body	• Try to provide at least one piece of evidence for every new idea you introduce. • Define unfamiliar terms clearly. • When possible, include well-labeled diagrams or illustrations.
Conclusion	• Leave your audience with one strong piece of evidence or a powerful detail.

- **Use Figurative Language** Help your audience follow the main ideas of your speech by using similes, metaphors, analogies, and sensory images to draw attention to important points.

- **Use Precise Language** Use precise language to express your ideas and give your sentences variety. Words that suggest strong emotions will capture the audience's attention. Asking questions will help you connect your experience or information with that of your audience.

- **Start Strong, Finish Strong** As you begin your speech, consider using a "hook"—an interesting question or statement that captures your audience's attention. At the end of the speech, restate your main ideas simply and clearly. Perhaps conclude with a powerful example or anecdote to reinforce your message.

- **Revise Your Speech** After you write your speech, revise, edit, and proofread it as you would a written report. Use a variety of sentence structures to achieve a natural rhythm. Check for correct subject-verb agreement and consistent verb tense. Correct run-on sentences and sentence fragments. Use parallel structure to emphasize ideas. Make sure you use complete sentences and correct punctuation and capitalization, even if no one else will see it. Your written speech should be clear and error free. If you notice an error in your notes during the speech, you may not remember what you actually wanted to say.

1.3 DELIVERING YOUR SPEECH

Confidence is the key to a successful presentation. Use these techniques to help you prepare and present your speech:

Prepare

- **Review Your Information** Reread your notes and review any background research. This will help you feel more confident during your speech.

- **Organize Your Notes** Some people prefer to write down only key points. Others prefer an entire script. Write each main point, or each paragraph, of your speech on a separate numbered index card. Be sure to include your most important evidence and examples.

- **Plan Your Visual Aids** If you are planning to use visual aids, such as slides, posters, charts, graphs, video clips, overhead transparencies, or media displays, now is the time to design them and decide how to work them into your speech.

Practice

- **Rehearse** Rehearse your speech several times, possibly in front of a practice audience. Maintain good posture by standing with your shoulders back and your head up. If you are using visual aids, arrange them in the order in which you will need them. Adapt your rate of speaking, pitch, and tone of voice to your audience and setting. Glance at your notes to refresh your memory, but avoid reading them word for word. Your style of performance should express the purpose of your speech. Use the following chart to help you.

Purpose	Pace	Pitch	Tone
to persuade	fast but clear	same throughout	urgent
to inform	using plenty of pauses	same throughout	authoritative
to entertain	usually building to a "punch"	varied to create characters or drama	funny or dramatic

- **Use Audience Feedback** If you had a practice audience, ask them specific questions about your delivery: Did I use enough eye contact? Was my voice at the right volume? Did I stand straight, or did I slouch? Use the audience's comments to evaluate the effectiveness of your delivery and to set goals for future rehearsals.

- **Evaluate Your Performance** When you have finished each rehearsal, evaluate your performance. Did you pause to let an important point sink in and use gestures for emphasis? Make a list of the aspects of your presentation that you wish to improve.

Present

- **Begin Your Speech** Try to look relaxed and smile.

- **Make Eye Contact** Try to make eye contact with as many audience members as possible. This will establish personal contact and help you determine if the audience understands your speech.

- **Remember to Pause** A slight pause after important points will provide emphasis and give your audience time to think about and connect with what you're saying.

- **Speak Clearly** Speak loudly enough to be heard clearly, but not so loud that your voice is overwhelming. Use a conversational tone.

- **Maintain Good Posture** Stand up straight and avoid nervous movements that may distract the audience's attention from what you are saying.

- **Use Expressive Body Language** Use facial expressions to show your feelings toward your topic. Lean forward when you make an important point; move your hands and arms for emphasis. Use body language to show your own style and reflect your personality.

- **Watch the Audience for Responses** If they start fidgeting or yawning, speak a little louder or get to your conclusion a little sooner. Use what you learn to evaluate the effectiveness of your speech and to decide what areas need improvement.

Respond to Questions

Depending on the content of your speech, your audience may have questions. Follow these steps to make sure that you answer questions in an appropriate manner:

- Think about what your audience may ask, and prepare answers before your speech.

- Tell your audience at the beginning of your speech that you will take questions at the end. This helps avoid audience interruptions that may make your speech hard to follow.

- Call on audience members in the order in which they raise their hands.

- Repeat each question before you answer it to ensure that everyone has heard it. This step also gives you time to prepare your answer.

2 Different Types of Oral Presentations

2.1 INFORMATIVE SPEECH

When you deliver an informative speech, you give the audience new information, provide a better understanding of information, or enable the audience to use the information in a new way. An informative speech is presented in an objective way.

Use the following questions to evaluate the presentation of a peer or a public figure, or your own presentation.

Evaluate an Informative Speech

- Did the speaker explain the purpose of the presentation?
- Did the speaker take the audience's previous knowledge into consideration?
- Did the speaker emphasize important points to help the audience follow the main ideas?
- Did the speaker cite a variety of sources for the information?
- Did the speaker communicate the information in a balanced, unbiased way?
- Did the speaker explain all unfamiliar terms?
- Did the speaker use visual aids effectively?

2.2 PERSUASIVE SPEECH

When you deliver a persuasive speech, you offer a thesis or clear statement on a subject, you provide relevant evidence to support your position, and you attempt to convince the audience to accept your point of view.

*For more information, see **Speaking and Listening: Delivering a Persuasive Speech,** page 925.*

Use the following guidelines to evaluate a persuasive presentation.

Evaluate a Persuasive Speech

- Did the speaker present a clear thesis or argument?
- Did the speaker anticipate and address audience concerns, biases, and counterarguments?
- Did the speaker use sound logic and reasoning in developing the argument?
- Did the speaker support the argument with convincing evidence, examples, facts, expert opinions, and quotations?
- Did the speaker hold the audience's interest with an effective voice and with effective facial expressions and gestures?
- Is your reaction to the speech similar to other audience members'?

2.3 PROBLEM-SOLUTION PRESENTATION

When delivering a presentation on problems and solutions, you need to be organized, logical, and persuasive.

- **Identify the Problem** Define the problem for your audience. Provide background information: How long has this problem existed? What are its causes?

- **Make Connections** Think about how similar or related problems have been solved. How might this information help solve the current problem?

- **Propose Solutions** Offer at least two or three possible solutions. Back them up with persuasive evidence and logical analysis of how they would work.

- **Encourage Discussion** Ask your audience if they have any questions or alternative suggestions. Have them discuss and evaluate what you said.

Use the following guidelines to evaluate a problem-solution presentation.

Evaluate a Problem-Solution Speech

- Did the speaker provide a clear introduction to the problem?
- Did the speaker give enough background information?
- Did the speaker explore other similar or related problems?
- Did the speaker offer several reasonable, well-supported solutions?
- Did the speaker invite the audience to respond, participate, and discuss ideas?

PRACTICE AND APPLY

Listen as a classmate gives a presentation on a problem and its possible solutions. Use the preceding guidelines to evaluate it.

2.4 DESCRIPTIVE SPEECH

Most presentations will involve some description. In a descriptive speech, you describe a subject that you are personally involved with. Use the following questions to evaluate a speaker or your own presentation.

Evaluate a Descriptive Speech

- Did the speaker clearly express his or her point of view about the subject being described?
- Did the speaker use sensory details, figurative language, and factual details?
- Did the speaker use tone and pitch to emphasize important details?
- Did the speaker use facial expressions to emphasize his or her feelings toward the subject?

2.5 NARRATIVE SPEECH

A narrative speech tells a story or presents a subject using a story-type format. A good narrative keeps an audience informed and entertained. It also delivers a message in a creative way.

*For more information, see **Speaking and Listening: Telling a Story,** page 165.*

Use the following guidelines to evaluate a speaker or your own presentation.

Evaluate a Narrative Speech

- Does the plot flow well?
- Did the speaker choose a setting, context, and point of view that make sense and contribute to a believable narrative?
- Were the characters—and their points of view—memorable and realistic?
- Did the speaker use words that express the appropriate mood and tone?
- Did the speaker use sensory details to help the audience experience the sights, sounds, and smells of a scene and the actions, gestures, and thoughts of the characters?
- Did the speaker use narrative devices, such as dialogue, tension, and suspense, to keep the audience interested?

2.6 ORAL INTERPRETATION

When you read a poem, play, or story aloud, your voice can bring the literature to life. In a dramatic reading, several speakers participate in the reading of a play or other work.

Oral Reading

An oral reading can be a monologue, during which you assume the voice of a character, the narrator, or the speaker in a poem. Or it may be a dialogue, during which you take the roles of two or more characters.

Use these techniques when giving an oral reading:

- **Speak Clearly** As you speak, pronounce your words carefully and clearly.
- **Control Your Volume** Make sure that you are loud enough to be heard, but do not shout.
- **Pace Yourself** Read at a moderate rate, but vary your pace if it seems appropriate to the emotions of the character or to the action.
- **Vary Your Voice** Use a different voice for each character. Stress important words and phrases.

*For more information, see **Speaking and Listening: Oral Interpretation of a Poem**, page 629.*

Use the following questions to evaluate an artistic performance by a peer, a media presentation, or your own performance.

Evaluate an Oral Interpretation

- Did the speaker speak clearly?
- Did the speaker maintain eye contact with the audience?
- Was the speaker's voice the right volume?
- Did the speaker vary the rate of speech appropriately to express emotion, mood, and action?
- Did the speaker use different voices for the different characters in the piece?
- Did the speaker stress important words or phrases?
- Did the speaker use voice, tone, and gestures to enhance meaning?
- How did the audience react to the performance?

PRACTICE AND APPLY

Listen to an oral reading by a classmate or view a dramatic performance in a theater or on television. Use the preceding guidelines to evaluate it.

2.7 ORAL RESPONSE TO LITERATURE

An oral response to literature is your own personal interpretation of a piece written by someone else. It is a way to show an audience what a piece means to you.

- **Choose Carefully** In choosing a piece, think about the assignment, your interests, and the audience.
- **Exhibit Understanding** Develop an interpretation that shows careful reading, understanding, and insight. Direct the audience's attention to specific words, sentences, or phrases that are rich with meaning. Discuss the writer's techniques in developing plot, characterization, setting, or theme and how they contribute to your interpretation.
- **Organize Clearly** Organize your presentation around several clear ideas or images. What elements of the literature are most important? How do they relate to the piece as a whole and help provide meaning? Support your interpretation with examples from the selection.

Use the following questions to evaluate a speaker or your own presentation.

Evaluate an Oral Response to Literature

- Did the speaker choose an interesting piece that he or she enjoys and understands?
- Did the speaker engage in in-depth analysis and demonstrate his or her understanding of the piece?
- Did the speaker analyze the effects of any figurative language used in the piece?
- Did the speaker direct the audience to specific parts of the piece that support the interpretation?
- Did the speaker present ideas in a clear, well-organized manner?

2.8 ORAL SUMMARY

An oral summary includes the main ideas of a book or article. It also includes the most important details or evidence.

Use the following questions to evaluate a speaker or your own presentation.

Evaluate an Oral Summary

- Did the speaker introduce the subject clearly?
- Did the speaker present the main ideas early in the presentation?
- Did the speaker discuss the supporting details?
- Did the speaker show the audience that he or she really understood the piece?

3 Other Types of Communication

3.1 CONVERSATION

Conversations are informal, but they are an important form of communicating. When two or more people exchange messages, it is important for each person to contribute and actively listen.

3.2 GROUP DISCUSSION

Successful groups assign a role to each member. These roles distribute responsibility among the members and help keep discussions focused.

Role	Responsibilities
Chairperson	• Introduces topic • Explains goal or purpose • Participates in discussion and keeps it on track • Helps resolve conflicts • Helps group reach goal
Recorder	• Takes notes on discussion • Reports on suggestions and decisions • Organizes and writes up notes • Participates in discussion
Participants	• Contribute relevant facts or ideas to discussion • Respond constructively to one another's ideas • Reach agreement or vote on final decision

Guidelines for Discussion

- Be informed about the topic.
- Participate in the discussion; ask questions, and respond appropriately to questions.
- Don't talk while someone else is talking.
- Support statements and opinions with facts and examples.
- Listen attentively; be courteous and respectful of others' viewpoints.
- Work toward the goal; avoid getting sidetracked by unrelated topics.

For more information, see Speaking and Listening: Holding a Discussion, page 405.

3.3 INTERVIEW

An **interview** is a formal type of conversation with a definite purpose and goal. Use the following guidelines to conduct a successful interview:

Prepare for the Interview

- Carefully select the person you want to interview. Identify who has the kind of knowledge and experience you are looking for.
- Set a time, a date, and a place. Ask permission to tape-record the interview.

- Learn all you can about the person you will interview and the subjects you will discuss.

- Prepare a list of questions. Create questions that encourage detailed responses instead of yes-or-no answers. Arrange your questions in order from most important to least important.

Conduct the Interview

- Ask your questions clearly and listen to the responses carefully. Give the person whom you are interviewing plenty of time to answer.

- Be flexible; follow up on interesting responses.

- Avoid arguments; be tactful and polite.

- Even if you tape the interview, take notes on important points.

- Thank the person for the interview, and ask if you can call with any follow-up questions.

Follow Up on the Interview

- Summarize your notes or make a written transcript of the tape recording as soon as possible.

- If any points are unclear or if information is missing, call and ask more questions.

- Select quotations to support your ideas.

- If possible, have the person you interviewed review your work to make sure you haven't misrepresented what he or she said.

- Send a thank-you note to the person in appreciation of his or her time and effort.

For more information, see **Speaking and Listening: Conducting an Interview,** *page 295.*

Evaluate an Interview

You can determine how effective your interview was by asking yourself these questions:

- Was the person being interviewed focused on the subject throughout the interview?
- Were your most important questions answered?
- Did you get the information you were looking for?

4 Active Listening

Active listening means receiving, interpreting, evaluating, and responding to a message. Whether you are listening to a class discussion or a formal speech, use the following strategies to get as much as you can from the message.

Listening with a Purpose		
Situation	**Reason for Listening**	**How to Listen**
Your grandfather tells a story about his childhood.	For enjoyment	Maintain eye contact; react to the story.
You are watching a demonstration on television.	To follow step-by-step instructions	Listen for words such as *first, second, next,* and *finally;* take notes that you can refer to later.

Before Listening

- Learn what the topic is beforehand. You may need to read background information about the topic or learn new terms in order to understand the speaker's message.

- Think about what you know or want to know about the topic.

- Have a pen and paper to take notes.

- Establish a purpose for listening.

While Listening

- Focus your attention on the speaker. Make eye contact, and use facial expressions and body language to demonstrate your interest in the topic. Try to ignore noises and other distractions.

- Listen for the speaker's purpose (usually stated at the beginning), which alerts you to main ideas. Note any ideas that are repeated for emphasis.

- To help you understand the speaker's message, listen for words or phrases that signal important points, such as *to begin with, in addition, most important, finally,* and *in conclusion.*

- Listen for explanations of unfamiliar terms. Use these terms to help you understand the speaker's message.

- Take notes on the most important points. You may want to organize your notes using an outline or list.
- Note comparisons and contrasts, causes and effects, or problems and solutions.
- Note how the speaker uses word choice, voice pitch, posture, and gestures to convey meaning.

After Listening

- Review your notes right away to make sure you understand what was said.
- Ask questions to clarify anything that was unclear or confusing.
- Summarize and paraphrase the main points.
- Ask other listeners if they had the same understanding of the message that you did.

4.1 CRITICAL LISTENING

Critical listening involves analyzing a speaker's message in order to judge whether the message is accurate and reliable. Use the following strategies as you listen to public speakers:

- **Determine the Speaker's Purpose** Think about the background, viewpoint, and possible motives of the speaker. Separate facts from opinions. Listen carefully to details and evidence that a speaker uses to support the message.

- **Listen for the Main Idea** Figure out the speaker's main message before allowing yourself to be distracted by seemingly convincing details.

- **Recognize the Use of Persuasive Techniques** Pay attention to a speaker's choice of words. Speakers may present information in a particular way to persuade you to accept an idea. Persuasive devices such as glittering generalities, either/or reasoning, and bandwagon or snob appeal may represent faulty reasoning and provide misleading information.

  For more information, see Recognizing Persuasive Techniques, page R21.

- **Recognize Rhetorical Devices** Rhetorical devices can be a clue to the speaker's purpose. For example, a speaker may draw attention to important ideas with **repetition** of words

and phrases or by changing the **cadence,** or rhythm and timing, of the speech. **Rhetorical questions,** or questions with assumed answers, involve the audience in the topic. A speaker may also make **allusions,** or indirect references, to something the audience will recognize. **Onomatopoeia,** a sound device in which words sound like the thing or action they represent, can help express ideas more creatively.

- **Observe Verbal and Nonverbal Messages** Note the speaker's movements, gestures, and posture. Compare your impressions of the speaker's appearance with his or her tone of voice to see if both support the message.

- **Give Appropriate Feedback** An effective speaker looks for verbal and nonverbal cues from his or her listeners to see how the message is being received. For example, if you agree with the speaker's message, you might nod your head.

4.2 VERBAL FEEDBACK

You may be asked to give a speaker feedback on a presentation's delivery and content.

Evaluate Delivery

- Did the speaker speak clearly and distinctly?
- Did the speaker pronounce words correctly?
- Did the speaker vary his or her rate of speaking?
- Did the speaker's voice sound natural and not strained?
- Was the speaker's voice loud enough?

Evaluate Content

Here's how to give constructive suggestions:

Be Specific Don't make statements like "Your examples need work." Offer concrete advice, such as "Consider dropping one of the last two examples, since they are very similar."

Discuss Only the Most Important Points Some points to focus on are:

- Is the topic appropriate for the audience?
- Are the supporting details and evidence well organized?
- Is the conclusion strong enough?

Give Balanced Feedback Tell the speaker what worked, as well as what didn't.

Movies, television, radio, newspapers, the Internet—media are all around us. You see hundreds of media images and messages every day. How can you be a smart media consumer? A person who is media literate *is familiar with the different types of media, their purposes, and how they are created. If you are media literate, you are able to analyze and evaluate media messages and the effects they have on you and your world. This section introduces the tools you will need to study media messages.*

MEDIA TOOLS
For more information, visit the **Media Center** at **ClassZone.com.**

1 Five Core Concepts in Media Literacy

from The Center for Media Literacy

The five core concepts of media literacy provide you with the basic ideas you can consider when examining media messages.

All media messages are "constructed." All media messages are made by someone. In fact, they are carefully thought out and researched and have attitudes and values built into them. Much of the information that you use to make sense of the world comes from the media. Therefore, it is important to know how a medium is put together so you can better understand the message it conveys.

Media messages are constructed using a creative language with its own rules. Each means of communication—whether it is film, television, newspapers, magazines, radio, or the Internet—has its own language and design. Therefore, the message must use the language and design of the medium that delivers the message. Thus, the medium actually shapes the message. For example, a horror film may use music to heighten suspense, or a newspaper may use a big headline to signal the importance of a story. Understanding the language of each medium can increase your enjoyment of it as well as help you recognize any subtle attempt to persuade you.

Different people experience the same media messages differently. Personal factors such as age, education, and experience will affect the way a person responds to a media message. How many times has your interpretation of a film or book differed from that of a friend? Everyone interprets media messages differently.

Media have embedded values and points of view. Media messages carry underlying values, which are purposely built into them by the creators of the message. For example, a commercial's main purpose may be to persuade you to buy something, but the commercial may also aim to convince you that the product is important to a particular way of life. Understanding not only the main message but also any other points of view will help you decide whether to accept or reject the message.

Most media messages are constructed to gain profit and/or power. The creators of media messages often provide a commodity, such as information or entertainment, in order to make money. The bigger the audience, the more the media outlet can charge for advertising. Consequently, media outlets want to build large audiences in order to bring in more revenue from advertising. For example, a television network will create programming to appeal to the largest audience possible, in the hope that the viewer ratings will attract more advertising dollars.

2 Media Basics

2.1 MESSAGE

When a film or TV show is created, it becomes a media product. Each media product is created to send a **message,** or an expression of a belief or opinion, that serves a specific purpose. In order to understand the message, you will need to deconstruct it.

Deconstruction of a media presentation is the process of analyzing it. To analyze a media presentation you will need to ask why and how it was created, who created it, and whom it is trying to influence.

2.2 AUDIENCE

A **target audience** is the specific group of people at whom a product or presentation is aimed. The members of a target audience usually have certain characteristics in common, such as age, gender, ethnic background, values, or lifestyle. For example, a target audience may be kids ages 8 to 12 who like chewing gum.

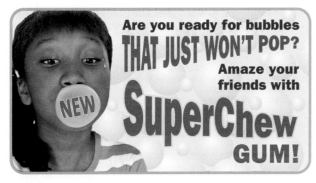

Demographics are the characteristics of a population, including age, gender, profession, income, education, ethnicity, and geographical location. Media decision makers use demographics to shape their product's content to suit the needs and tastes of a target audience.

2.3 PURPOSE

The **purpose,** or intent, of a media presentation is the reason it was made. All media products—from news programs to video games—are created for a specific purpose. Identifying why a media product was invented is the first step in understanding how it can influence you. The following chart shows purposes of different media products.

Purposes of Media Products	
Purpose	**Example**
To Inform	news reports and articles, public service announcements, some Web sites
To Persuade	advertisements, editorials, reviews, political cartoons
To Entertain	most TV shows, films, recorded music, video games, talk shows

Most media products have more than one purpose. For example, a documentary's main purpose is to inform people about a subject, but it also tries to entertain its audience. If you aren't aware of all of a media product's different purposes, you may become influenced without knowing it. This chart shows some examples of media products that have multiple purposes.

Multiple Purposes in Media		
Media Product	**Main Purpose**	**Other Purposes**
News Broadcast	to inform	to persuade you that an issue or idea is important
Advertisement	to persuade	to entertain you; to inform you about a product
Sports Coverage	to entertain	to inform you about sports or athletes

2.4 TYPES AND GENRES OF MEDIA

The term *media* refers to television, newspapers, magazines, radio, movies, and the Internet. Each is a **medium,** or means for carrying information, entertainment, and advertisements to a large audience.

Each type of media has different characteristics, strengths, and weaknesses. The following chart shows how several types of media deliver their messages.

Type of Media	Characteristics
Newspaper Article	• Provides detailed information and dramatic photographs • Uses **headlines** and **subheads** to give main ideas • Can't be updated until next edition or next day
Television News Report	• Uses an **announcer,** or "anchor," to guide viewers through the news report • Uses **video footage** to bring news to life or clarify what happened • Uses **graphics** to give information at a glance • Can be updated quickly
Documentary	• Tells about historic people and places, major events, and important social, political, or environmental issues • Uses **footage,** or shots of photographs, interviews, news reports, and film clips, to help viewers understand the subject • Features **interviews** of experts or people directly involved with the subject • Uses a **voice-over narrator,** the voice of an unseen speaker, who tells viewers why the subject is important and how the information about the subject is organized
Web Site	• Gives in-depth information on specialized subjects • Uses **text, still images,** and **video** • Allows users to select the information they want to receive by clicking on links • Allows users to see when the site was last updated • Can be updated quickly

2.5 PRODUCERS AND CREATORS

People who control the media are known as **gatekeepers.** Gatekeepers decide what information to share with the public and the ways it will be presented. The following diagram gives some examples.

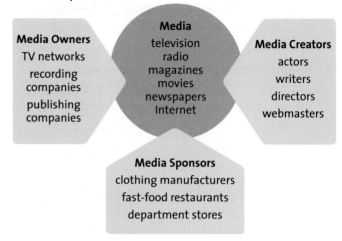

Media sponsors are companies that pay for their products to be advertised. It's important to be aware of sponsors and other gatekeepers, because they control much of what you see and hear. For example, if a fast-food chain sponsors a television show, you probably won't see characters on that show eating food from a competing restaurant.

2.6 INFLUENCE OF MEDIA

Everywhere you go, you're bombarded by media—advertisements, newspapers, magazines, radio, and television. Different kinds of media are all competing for your attention, telling you, "Buy this product. Listen to this music. Read this story. Look at this image. Think about this opinion." The creators of these media products are selling messages. But they may also be sending subtle messages about values that they want you to believe in.

For example, an ad for sneakers is meant to sell you shoes, but if you examine the ad more closely, you will see that it uses a set of values, such as athletic skill, to make the shoes more appealing. The ad suggests that if you buy the shoes, your athletic skills will improve. It also sends the message that athletic skill is a good thing to have. TV shows, movies, and news programs also convey values and beliefs.

Media can also shape your opinions about the world. For example, news about crime shapes our understanding of how much and what type of crime is common in the world around us. TV news items, magazine interviews, and commercials may shape what we think of a political candidate, a celebrity, an ethnic group, a country, or a region. As a result, our knowledge of a person or a place could be completely based on the information we receive from the media.

3 Film and TV

Films and television programs come in a variety of types. Films include comedies, dramas, documentaries, and animated features. Televison programs include dramas, sitcoms, talk shows, reality shows, and newscasts. Producers of films and producers of television programs rely on many of the same elements to make the action and settings seem real and also to affect the emotions of their audience members. Among these elements are scripts, visual and sound elements, special effects, and editing.

3.1 SCRIPT AND WRITTEN ELEMENTS

The writer and editor develop a story for television or film using a script and a storyboard. A **script** is the text, or words, of a film or television show. A **storyboard** is used to plan the shooting of a movie or TV show. A storyboard is made up of drawings and brief descriptions of what is happening in each shot of a scene. This helps a director visualize how a finished scene might look before the scene is filmed. Following are two scenes from a storyboard that a student created.

Long shot of the approaching train. The music is fast and exciting.

The train rumbles by loudly. Medium shot of Klaus and Violet.

For more information, see **Media Study: Produce Your Own Media,** *page 109.*

3.2 VISUAL ELEMENTS

Visual elements in film and television include camera shots and angles. A **camera shot** is a single, continuous view taken by a camera. A **camera angle** is the angle at which the camera is positioned during the recording of a shot or image. Each is carefully planned to create a certain effect. This chart shows what different shots are used for.

Camera Shot/Angle	Effect
Establishing shot introduces viewers to the location of a scene, usually by presenting a wide view of an area	establishes the setting of a film or television show
Close-up shot shows a close view of a person or object	helps to create emotion and make viewers feel as if they know the character
Medium shot shows a view wider than a close-up but narrower than an establishing or long shot	shows part of an object, or a character from the knees or waist up
Long shot gives a wide view of a scene, showing the full figure(s) of a person or group and the surroundings	allows the viewer to see the "big picture" and shows the relationship between characters and the environment
Reaction shot shows in some way what a character sees	allows the viewer to see how the character feels in order to create empathy in the viewer
Low-angle shot looks up at an object or person	makes a character, object, or scene appear more important or threatening
High-angle shot looks down on an object or person	makes a character, object, or scene seem weak or unimportant
Point-of-view (POV) shot shows a part of the story through a character's eyes	helps viewers identify with that character

3.3 SOUND ELEMENTS

Sound elements in film and television include music, voice-over, and sound effects.

Music may be used to create an atmosphere and mood in a scene. Music can have a powerful effect on the way viewers feel about a story. For example, fast-paced music can help give an action scene a mood of excitement and danger.

Voice-over is the voice of the unseen commentator or narrator of a film, TV program, or commercial.

Sound effects are the sounds added to films, TV programs, and commercials during the editing process. Sound effects, such as laugh tracks or the sounds of punches in a fight scene, can create humor, emphasize a point, or contribute to the mood.

3.4 SPECIAL EFFECTS

Special effects include computer-generated animation, altered video images, and fast- or slow-motion sequences in films, TV programs, and commercials.

Animation on film involves the frame-by-frame photography of a series of drawings or objects. When these frames are projected—at a rate of 24 per second—the illusion of movement is achieved.

A **split screen** is a special-effects shot in which two or more separate images are shown in the same frame. One example is when two people, actually a distance apart, are shown talking to each other.

3.5 EDITING

Editing is the process of selecting and arranging shots in a sequence. Moviemakers put shots together in ways that help you follow the action of a story. The editor decides which scenes or shots to use, as well as the length of each shot, the number of shots, and their sequence.

Cut is the transition from one shot to another. To create excitement, editors often use quick cuts, which are a series of short shots strung together.

Dissolve is a device in which one scene fades into another.

Fade-in is a device in which a white or black shot fades in to reveal the beginning of a new scene.

Fade-out is a device in which a shot fades to darkness to end a scene.

Jump cut is an abrupt and jarring change from one shot to another. A jump cut shows a break in time.

Pace is the length of time each shot stays on the screen and the rhythm that is created by the transitions between shots. Short, quick cuts create a fast pace in a story. Long cuts slow down a story.

4 News

The **news** is information on events, people, and places in your community, the region, the nation, and the world. It can be found in local newspapers, newscasts, online wire services, magazines, and documentaries. It would be impossible to publish all the news that happens in one day in any one source, though, so journalists have to make decisions about which stories will appear in each day's newspapers and on newscasts. Several factors help determine which events are "news."

4.1 CHOOSING THE NEWS

Newsworthiness is the importance of an event or action that makes it worthy of media reporting. Journalists and their editors often use the following guidelines in determining which stories are newsworthy:

Timeliness is the quality of being very current. Timely events usually take priority over previously reported events. For example, information about an election will be timely on the day the voting occurs. Election results may appear on the front page of a newspaper once the votes are counted.

Widespread impact is a characteristic of an event that could affect a number of people. The more widespread the impact of an event, the more likely it is to be newsworthy.

Proximity measures the nearness of an event to a particular city, region, or country. People tend to be more interested in stories that take place close to where they live and thus may affect them directly.

Human interest is a quality of stories that cause readers or listeners to feel emotions such as happiness, anger, or sadness. People are interested in reading or hearing stories about other people.

Uniqueness is the condition of being the only one of a kind. Unique or uncommon events or circumstances are likely to be interesting to an audience.

Compelling video and **photographs** grab people's attention and stay in their minds.

4.2 REPORTING THE NEWS

When developing a news story, a journalist must decide how to construct the story—what information to include, and how to organize it. The following elements are commonly used in news stories:

5 *W*'s and *H* are the six questions reporters answer when writing news stories—*who, what, when, where, why,* and *how*. It is a journalist's job to answer these questions in any type of news report. These questions also provide a structure for writing and editing a story.

Inverted pyramid is a way of organizing information in the order of importance. In an inverted-pyramid organization, the most important information (the answers to the 5 *W*'s and *H*) appears at the top of the pyramid. The less important details appear at the bottom. Not all stories are reported using the inverted-pyramid form. However, this form helps a reader to get the most important information without having to read the entire story. Following is an example of inverted-pyramid organization.

This week, local officials passed a law making it illegal to ride a bicycle without a helmet.

The mayor hopes this law will reduce bicycle-related injuries.

Several other cities are planning to pass similar laws this summer.

Angle or slant is the point of view from which a story is written. Even an objective report must have an angle.

Consider these two headlines that describe the same tornado.

City Sends Tornado Warning Too Late

Tornado Strikes Downtown Area

PHOENIX March 17 — After

The headline on the right focuses on a fact. The headline on the left focuses on an opinion and has a negative slant.

Standards for News Reporting

The ideal of journalism is to present news in a way that is objective, accurate, and thorough. The best news stories contain the following elements:

- **Objectivity**—The story takes a balanced point of view on the issues. It is not biased, nor does it reflect a specific attitude or opinion.
- **Accuracy**—The story presents factual information that can be verified.
- **Thoroughness**—The story presents all sides of an issue. It includes background information, telling *who, what, when, where, why,* and *how*.

Balanced Versus Biased Reporting

Objectivity in news reporting can be measured by how balanced or biased the story is.

Balanced reporting presents all sides of an issue equally and fairly.

A balanced news story

- represents people and subjects in a neutral light
- treats all sides of an issue equally
- does not include inappropriate questions, such as "Will you seek counseling to help you recover from this terrible tragedy?"

- does not show stereotypes or prejudice toward people of a particular race, gender, age, religion, or other group
- does not leave out important background information that is needed to establish a context or perspective

Biased reporting is reporting in which one side is favored over another or in which the subject is unfairly represented. Biased reporting may show an overly negative view of a subject, or it may encourage racial, gender, or other stereotypes and prejudices. Sometimes biased reporting is apparent in the journalist's choice of sources.

Sources are the people interviewed for the news report, and also any written materials the journalist used for background information. From each source, the journalist gets a different point of view. To decide whether news reporting is balanced or biased, you will need to pay attention to the sources. Consider a magazine article about the safety of a new kind of car. If the journalist only interviews a spokesperson for the car company, then the article may be biased. If, on the other hand, the journalist also includes information from a neutral person, such as an engineer who studies automobile safety, the article might be more balanced. The following chart shows which sources are reliable.

Sources for News Stories	
Reliable Sources	**Weak Sources**
• experts in a field or subject area • people directly affected by the reported event (eyewitnesses) • published reports that are specifically mentioned or shown	• unnamed or anonymous sources • people who are not involved in the reported event (for example, people who heard about a story from a friend) • research, data, or reports that are not specifically named or are referred to only in vague terms (for example, "Research shows that …")

5 Advertising

Advertising is a sponsor's paid use of various media to promote products, services, or ideas. Some common forms of advertising are shown in the chart.

Type of Ad	Description
Billboard	a large outdoor advertising sign
Print Ad	an ad that appears in magazines and newspapers; typically uses eye-catching graphics and persuasive copy
Flyer	a print ad that is circulated by hand or mail
Infomercial	an extended ad on TV that includes detailed product information, demonstrations, and testimonials
Public Service Announcement	a message aired on radio or TV to promote ideas that are considered to be in the public interest
Political Ad	a message broadcast on radio or TV to promote political candidates
Trailer	a short film promoting an upcoming movie, TV show, or video game

Marketing is the process of transferring products and services from producer to consumer. It involves determining the packaging and pricing of a product, how it will be promoted and advertised, and where it will be sold. One way companies market their products is by becoming media sponsors.

Sponsors pay for their products to be advertised. These companies hire advertising agencies to create and produce specific campaigns for their products. They then buy television or radio airtime or magazine, newspaper, or billboard space to feature ads where the target audience is sure to see them. Because selling time and space to advertisers produces much of the income the media need to function, the media need advertisers just as much as advertisers need the media.

Product placement is the intentional and identifiable featuring of brand-name products in movies, television shows, video games, and other media. The intention is to have viewers feel positive about a product because they see a favorite character using it. Another purpose may be to promote product recognition.

5.1 PERSUASIVE TECHNIQUES

Persuasive techniques are the methods used to convince an audience to buy a product or adopt an idea. Advertisers use a combination of visuals, sound, special effects, and words to persuade their target audience. Recognizing the following techniques can help you evaluate persuasive media messages and identify misleading information:

Emotional appeals use strong feelings, such as fear and pity, rather than facts to persuade consumers. An example is "Our shelter has dozens of lonely puppies looking for homes. Won't you give one of them a chance?"

Bandwagon appeals use the argument that a person should believe or do something because "everyone else" does. These appeals take advantage of people's desire to be socially accepted by other people. An example of a bandwagon appeal is "Don't be left out! See why everyone's buying the new album by Gopher Broke."

Slogans are memorable phrases used in advertising campaigns. Slogans substitute catchy phrases for facts.

Logical appeals rely on logic and facts, appealing to a consumer's reason and his or her respect for authority. Two examples of logical appeals are expert opinions and product comparison.

Celebrity ads use one of the following two categories of spokesperson:

- **Celebrity authorities** are experts in a particular field. Advertisers hope that audiences will transfer the respect or admiration they have for the person to the product. For example, suppose a famous Hollywood hairstylist endorses, or recommends, a brand of shampoo. The shampoo manufacturer wants you to think that the product is good enough for even the best professionals.

- **Celebrity spokespeople** are famous people who endorse a product. Advertisers hope that audiences will associate the product with the celebrity.

Product comparison is comparing between a product and its competition. Often mentioned by name, the competing product is portrayed as inferior. The intended effect is for people to question the quality of the competing product and to believe the featured product is better.

6 Elements of Design

The design of a media product is just as important as the words are in conveying the message. Like words, visual elements are used to persuade, inform, and entertain.

Graphics and images, such as charts, diagrams, maps, timelines, photographs, illustrations, and symbols, present information that can be quickly and easily understood. The following basic elements are used to give meaning to visuals:

Color can be used to highlight important elements such as headlines and subheads. It can also create mood, because many colors have strong emotional or psychological impacts on the reader or viewer. For example, warm colors are often associated with happiness and comfort. Cool colors are often associated with feelings of peace and contentment or sometimes with sadness.

Lines—strokes or marks—can be thick or thin, long or short, and smooth or jagged. They can focus attention and create a feeling of depth. They can frame an object. They can also direct a viewer's eye or create a sense of motion.

Texture is the apparent surface quality of an object. For example, an object's texture can be rough, wet, or shiny. Texture can be used to create contrast. It can also be used to make an object look "real." For example, a pattern on wrapping paper can create a feeling of depth even though the texture is only visual and cannot be felt.

Shape is the external outline of an object. Shapes can be used to symbolize living things or geometric objects. They can emphasize visual elements and add interest. Shapes can also symbolize ideas.

Notice how this movie poster uses design elements.

Lines The reader's eyes are led downward from the main image by the lamppost, to the smaller images around the edges of the poster.

Color Deep blues and bright golds suggest a dramatic story and hint at a conflict.

Shape The large image of the lion catches the reader's attention. The images surrounding the lion draw the eye to the film's title.

7 Evaluating Media Messages

By looking closely at media products, you can see how their messages influence your opinions and your buying habits. Here are six questions to ask about any media message:

Who made—and who sponsored—this message, and for what purpose? The source of the message is a clue to its purpose. If the source of the message is a private company, that company may be trying to sell you a product. If the source is a government agency, that agency may be trying to promote a program or particular point of view. To discover the purpose, think about why its creator paid for and produced the message.

Who is the target audience and how is the message specifically tailored to it? Think about the age group, ethnic group, gender, and/or profession the message is targeting. Decide how it relates to you.

What are the different techniques used to inform, persuade, entertain, and attract attention? Analyze the elements, such as humor, music, special effects, and graphics, that have been used to create the message. Think about how visual and sound effects, such as symbols, color, photographs, words, and music, support the purpose behind the message.

What messages are communicated (and/or implied) about certain people, places, events, behaviors, lifestyles, and so forth? The media try to influence who we are, what we believe in, how we view things, and what values we hold. Look or listen closely to determine whether certain types of behavior are being shown and if judgments or values are communicated through those behaviors. What are the biases in the message?

How current, accurate, and believable is the information in this message? Think about the reputation of the source. Note the broadcast or publication date of the message and whether the message might change quickly. If a report or account is not supported by facts, authoritative sources, or eyewitness accounts, you should question the message.

What is left out of this message that might be important to know? Think about what the message is asking you to believe. Also think about what questions come to mind as you watch, read, or listen to the message.

Strategies and Practice for State and Standardized Tests

The test questions in this section are modeled after many different kinds of tests that you may have to take while you are a student. The tips and strategies presented here will help you prepare for answering multiple-choice, short-response, and extended-response questions in critical reading and writing. This section also includes guidelines for writing an essay, as well as a sample essay. Read the tips in the margin, and then apply them to the practice questions. You can also apply the tips to the Assessment Practice *tests in this book.*

❶ General Test-Taking Strategies

Getting Ready

- Arrive on time and be prepared. Be sure to bring either sharpened pencils with erasers or pens—whichever you are told to bring.

- If you have any questions, ask them before the test begins. Make sure you understand how to mark the answers, how much time you will have to take the test, and other test rules.

- Read the test directions carefully. Look at the passages and the types of questions to get an idea of what is expected.

Reading the Test

- Focus on one question at a time rather than thinking about the whole test.

- Look for main ideas as you read passages. They are often stated at the beginning or the end of a paragraph. Sometimes the main idea is implied, or suggested, rather than stated.

- Refer back to the passage as needed. For example, if a question asks about an author's attitude, you might have to reread a passage for clues.

Marking Your Answers

- If you are not sure of your answer, make a logical guess. You can often arrive at the correct answer by reasoning and rejecting wrong answers.

- As you fill in answers on your answer sheet, make sure you match each test item to its numbered space on the answer sheet.

- Don't look for patterns in the positions of correct choices.

- Only change an answer if you are sure your original choice is incorrect. If you do change an answer, erase your original choice neatly and thoroughly.

- Check your answers and reread your essay.

❷ Critical Reading

In middle school, you will read many different types of writing, both fiction and nonfiction. You will read novels, persuasive essays, poems, historical documents, and scientific or technical information. Tests will measure your ability to read and analyze these kinds of writing.

Directions: Read the passage and then answer the questions that follow.

PASSAGE

Did you ever see an Egyptian mummy in a museum? Or statues dug from ancient cities? If so, you already have been introduced to archaeology. ❷

Archaeology is a science. It is the study of very old objects such as buildings, bones, and tools.

The scientists who find and study old objects are called archaeologists. They look for objects that are many hundreds or thousands of years old. They study old objects to learn how people lived in ancient times.

Up until the 1700s, people had little interest in studying things from the past. When they found ancient objects (called artifacts), they kept the ones
10 made of gold. Less valuable ones were often thrown away!

In 1748 a farmer digging in a field in Italy struck an underground wall. A digging crew then unearthed an ancient city. It was Pompeii, which had been destroyed by a volcano nearly 1,700 years earlier. The excavation (digging) at Pompeii was one of the first done in an organized way. But ❸ archaeologists of the 1700s still mainly sought treasure. They tossed aside many other artifacts in search of it.

Sir Flinders Petrie (1853–1942) was one of the first archaeologists to study everything he found. Petrie worked in Egypt during the late 1800s. When Petrie dug, he searched the earth "inch by inch," as he described it.
20 Petrie found pottery, tools, and other items used by Egyptians in their daily life. Because he worked so carefully, Petrie is called the "Father of Modern Archaeology."

Today's archaeologists use the "inch by inch" method. They keep detailed records of everything they find. They know that the smallest artifact can help us understand how ancient people lived.

The world is a big place. How do archaeologists know where to look for ancient relics? They don't just guess. Like detectives, they search for clues.

Old books often provide good clues. The Bible, the works of Homer, and other old manuscripts describe ancient towns. Some of those towns are ❹
30 still there—buried under layers of dirt. Archaeologists study the books to determine where the ancient sites may be located.

People often tell stories about past events. For example, people may tell of a sunken ship. Archaeologists listen to such stories for clues about the ship's location.

Tips: Reading Text

❶ Before you begin reading a passage, quickly skim over the questions that follow it to get an idea of the number and kinds of questions you will be answering.

❷ Look for key ideas as you read. The way in which the science of archaeology changed over time is a key idea in this passage. It is expressed in the opening lines.

❸ Watch for specialized or technical vocabulary words. This passage introduces *excavation* and *artifacts,* two terms used in archaeology.

❹ Pay attention to comparisons. In this passage, the author compares archaeologists to detectives because both follow clues to find what they are looking for.

Archaeologists often use photographs taken from airplanes. They show things that can't be seen from the ground. An aerial photo may show a piece of land to be more fertile than nearby land. This may be because ancient people worked the soil there. Cameras are also used to spot undersea wrecks.

40   Archaeologists have many other tools to help them decide where to work. These include magnets, metal detectors, soil studies, and electrical tests of the ground.

—from *Archaeology*
by Dennis B. Fradin

Directions: Answer these questions about the passage from *Archaeology.*

1. What is the author's purpose in this passage? ❷

    A to describe how ancient people lived

    B to encourage readers to become archaeologists

    C to explain the science and practice of archaeology

    D to compare ancient and modern cities

2. From the details in lines 11–16, you can infer that archaeology in the 1700s was

    A popular among Italian farmers

    B concerned mainly with finding treasure

    C a good way to become rich and famous

    D a dangerous new branch of science

3. As explained in lines 28–31, archaeologists often use old books to

    A distinguish fact from science

    B find ancient sites to excavate ❹

    C learn how much artifacts are worth

    D prove how archaeology has changed

4. Archaeologists use the "inch by inch" method of excavation to

    A search a site very carefully

    B calculate how deep to dig

    C measure artifacts that are found

    D sharpen their tiny digging tools

Tips: Multiple Choice

A multiple-choice question consists of a stem and a set of answer choices. The stem is in the form of a question or an incomplete sentence. One of the choices correctly answers the question or completes the sentence. Many tests offer four answer choices, but no matter how many choices are given, you can use the same strategies to guide you to the best answer.

❶ Read the stem carefully and try to answer the question before you look at the choices.

❷ Pay attention to key words in the stem. They may direct you to the correct answer. Note that question 1 is looking for the *author's purpose,* or the author's reason for writing the passage.

❸ Read all the answer choices before you decide which one is correct. For example, in question 2, you might be tempted to stop at choice A, because the passage mentions a farmer in Italy, but that is not the correct answer.

❹ Look for clues in the passage. Question 3 asks about the role of old books in archaeology. The passage says that archaeologists study old books "to determine where the ancient sites may be located." It says nothing about using books to establish historical facts, monetary values, or archaeological practices.

Answers: 1. C, **2.** B, **3.** B, **4.** A

3 Vocabulary

Most standardized tests include questions about the meanings of words. Some questions might be about words in a passage you just read, while others might be about words in a sentence or paragraph, followed by the answer choices.

1. Which word from the passage on pages R94–R95 has a negative connotation? ❶
   A   objects (line 3)
   B   artifacts (line 9)
   C   underground (line 11)
   D   tossed (line 15)

2. Which word from the passage comes from the Latin words that mean "written by hand"?
   A   artifacts (line 9)
   B   organized (line 14)
   C   records (line 24)
   D   manuscripts (line 29) ❷

3. Which line from the passage contains a simile? ❸
   A   The scientists who find and study old objects are called archaeologists. (line 5)
   B   Because he worked so carefully, Petrie is called the "Father of Modern Archaeology." (lines 21–22)
   C   Like detectives, they search for clues. (line 27)
   D   People often tell stories about past events. (line 32)

4. Read this dictionary entry for the word *spot*. Which definition best matches the meaning of the word *spot* as it is used in line 38 of the passage?

   DEFINITION

   spot *noun.* **1.** A dirty area. **2.** A small place. **3.** A location.
   verb. **1.** To stain. **2.** To locate. **3.** To schedule at a particular time.

   A   *noun* meaning 1
   B   *noun* meaning 2
   C   *verb* meaning 1
   D   *verb* meaning 2 ❹

Tips: Word Meaning

❶ Connotation is the suggestion or feeling a word or phrase carries beyond its literal meaning. *Objects* is a neutral word, while *artifacts* is more positive, suggesting something valuable. The word *tossed*, which is part of the phrase "tossed aside," has a negative connotation.

❷ If you don't know the exact meaning of a word, look for clues in nearby sentences. For the word *manuscripts* in line 29, read the sentence it appears in and the one before it. The information about books is a clue that manuscripts are written records.

❸ A simile is a figure of speech. The words *like* and *as* are clues that a comparison is a simile.

❹ Eliminate any answers that are not the same part of speech as the word as it is used in the passage. *Spot* is used as a verb in the passsage, so you can rule out answer choices A and B.

Answers: 1. D, **2.** D, **3.** C, **4.** D

4 Writing and Grammar

You will be asked to write essays and even research papers in middle school. When it comes to writing, good ideas aren't enough. You need to know how to express them. That requires knowledge of English grammar, sentence structure, and usage. To measure this knowledge, many standardized tests ask you to identify errors or to improve sentences and paragraphs.

Directions: Read this passage and then answer the questions.

PASSAGE

(1) Their is nothing better than a morning bike ride. (2) You should leave just as the sun rises. (3) It will be quiet with very little traffic. (4) The silence will allow you to enjoy the early morning sounds of nature. (5) When was the last time you heard the wind whispering through the trees? (6) The birds will be just waking up and trying out its songs soon. (7) Rising off the grass, you'll also see the mist. (8) As you pedal along, you'll feel free and happy.

1. What change, if any, should be made to sentence 1?
   A   Change *Their* to *There*
   B   Change *than* to *then*
   C   Change *better* to *more better*
   D   Make no change

2. The correct conjunction to join sentences 2 and 3 is
   A   but
   B   unless
   C   because
   D   nor

3. What change, if any, should be made to sentence 6?
   A   Change *trying* to *tried*
   B   Change *waking* to *has woken*
   C   Change *its* to *their*
   D   Make no change

4. What is the best way to rewrite sentence 7?
   A   You'll also, rising off the grass, see the mist.
   B   Rising off the grass, the mist you'll also see.
   C   Also rising off the grass, you'll see the mist.
   D   You'll also see the mist rising off the grass.

Tips: Grammar

❶ Read the entire passage to grasp its overall meaning. Pay particular attention to any underlined parts.

❷ Some items will test your knowledge of commonly confused words. In test item 1, choice A is a possible revision.

❸ In test items 1 and 3, choice D says, "Make no change." Choose this answer only if the sentence is correct as it is originally written.

❹ If you are asked to combine sentences, think about how the ideas relate to each other. When you understand the connection between the thoughts, you will know how to join them. The word *but* (choice A) can be used to show how two different ideas are related, but it is not the right word to express the cause-and-effect relationship between sentences 2 and 3.

❺ Some items will test your knowledge of language conventions. Make sure that pronouns agree with antecedents and that verbs agree with subjects.

❻ Before choosing a revision, read through all of the choices to decide which one is best. Your answer should produce a sentence that is grammatically correct.

Answers: 1. A, **2.** C, **3.** C, **4.** D

5 Responding to Writing Prompts

Not all tests are multiple choice. Sometimes you have to develop your ideas into a paragraph or a short essay. You might be asked to interpret, summarize, or react to a reading selection.

> **Directions:** Reread the passage from *Archaeology* on pages R94–R95 and follow the directions for the short and extended responses.

SHORT RESPONSE

Write a well-organized paragraph comparing and contrasting archaeology before the 1700s with archaeology today. Base your response on the information given in the passage.

SAMPLE SHORT RESPONSE

Today, archaeology is practiced very differently than it was in the 1700s. In the 1700s, people usually did not search carefully for old objects or try to learn about ancient people. They were mainly interested in finding treasure and threw away anything that wasn't gold. Today, in contrast, archaeologists use the slow, careful "inch by inch" method developed by Sir Flinders Petrie. Modern archaeologists must pay close attention to everything they find, because anything can be a clue about ancient people and their lives.

❶ ❷

EXTENDED RESPONSE

What sources and tools do archaeologists use to help them make new discoveries? Express your ideas in two or three paragraphs.

SAMPLE EXTENDED RESPONSE

One of the most important tools archaeologists need is curiosity about the way people lived long ago. In addition to this, they rely upon both high-tech and low-tech resources to help them in their search.

❸

Old written records, such as the Bible or the works of Homer, can give clues about the locations of ancient cities or objects. Local legends and stories can also be a source of information and ideas for the scientists.

❹ Modern archaeologists also use technology in their work. Photographs taken underwater and from airplanes show features that can't be seen from the ground. Magnets and metal detectors can locate hidden metal objects. Electrical tests on the ground also can show the scientists where to begin digging for relics.

Tips: Responding to Writing Prompts

❶ Short-response prompts are often fact based rather than interpretive. Get right to the point in your answer, and stick to the facts.

❷ Make sure that you write about the assigned topic. Support your answer with details from the passage, such as a quotation, a paraphrase, or an example.

❸ Express your ideas clearly so that the reader will understand your viewpoint. You may also want to include any inferences you have made from your reading.

❹ When you are writing an extended response, build your paragraphs around clear topic sentences that will pull your ideas together.

❺ Proofread your response for errors in capitalization, punctuation, spelling, or grammar.

⑥ Writing an Essay

Many tests will ask you to read a prompt and write an essay in response to it. You might be asked to write a narrative, persuasive, or expository essay. You might be asked to write a story, summarize an article, or respond to a piece of writing. It is important to read the prompt carefully and look for direction words that tell you what to write about. Because you will have a limited amount of time, this essay will represent a first draft. Even so, it should be complete. Essays are scored according to the following guidelines:

- **Focus** Establish a point of view in the opening paragraph. Stay with that focus throughout the essay.
- **Organization** Connect ideas and present information logically.
- **Support for ideas** Use details and examples to develop an argument or line of thinking.
- **Style/word choice** Use words accurately and vary sentences.
- **Grammar** Use standard English and proofread for errors.

WRITING PROMPT

Many stories, books, and movies make predictions about the future, describing a world with a changed environment or new technology. What do you think the world will be like when you are grown up? Describe your predictions in an essay of four or five paragraphs.

SAMPLE DESCRIPTIVE ESSAY

Today, I turned 60 years old. So many things have changed since I was in middle school! At the same time, some things haven't changed that much.

I stop in the doorway of my apartment and look at my street. It's a busy street in a big city, humming with activity. Dozens of glittering glass buildings tower over the mechanical sidewalks as they carry people along. My building is the tallest, at just over 400 stories. I live on the 385th floor. When I was a kid, just 50 stories seemed dizzying! **②**

① Down the street is a garage where the city stores cars. Nobody has their own car anymore; they ride on the high-speed train or borrow a car from the city for a day. The garage looks like an enormous greenhouse—that's because **③** of the thousands of solar panels that cover its curved rooftop. The panels are used to charge the cars' batteries. All of our cars run on solar power, so they create much less pollution.

① At the end of my street is the river. Unfortunately, no one can swim in it. The water is sour smelling and greenish brown, and it foams at the edges. **②** This pollution has gotten much worse over the last 50 years, although we are working hard to fix it.

All in all, though the world now still has some of the old problems I remember from my childhood, in many ways it has become a cleaner, safer place. **④**

Tips: Writing an Essay

Before you begin writing, take a minute or two to gather your thoughts. You don't need to prepare a complete outline, but write the main points you want to make. In the futuristic essay here, pollution and transportation are key issues.

❶ When writing a descriptive essay, be sure to present your details in a logical order. In this essay, the information is arranged in spatial order, which describes all the details of a space or scene.

❷ Sensory details make your subject come to life, no matter what the topic is. Use them in the body of your essay to create memorable images and experiences for your reader.

❸ Figures of speech, such as similes, metaphors, and analogies, will help clarify your meaning to readers and strengthen your descriptions. In this essay, the author uses a simile to describe a futuristic building.

❹ Make sure your essay has a conclusion, even if it's just a single sentence. A conclusion pulls your ideas together and lets the reader know you have finished.

❺ Allow time to reread what you have written. If you have to make a correction, do so neatly and legibly.

Glossary of Literary Terms

Act An act is a major division within a play, similar to a chapter in a book. Each act may be further divided into smaller sections, called scenes.

Adventure Story An adventure story is a literary work in which action is the main element. An **adventure novel** usually focuses on a main character who is on a mission and faces many challenges and choices.

Alliteration Alliteration is the repetition of consonant sounds at the beginning of words. Note the repetition of the *w* sound in this line.

> To the gull's <u>w</u>ay and the <u>w</u>hale's <u>w</u>ay where the <u>w</u>ind's like a <u>w</u>hetted knife;
>
> —John Masefield, "Sea-Fever"

See pages 546, 581.

Allusion An allusion is a reference to a famous person, place, event, or work of literature. In the personal essay "Role-Playing and Discovery," Jerry Pinkney makes an allusion to such men as movie cowboy Roy Rogers and pioneer Daniel Boone.

Analogy An analogy is a comparison between two things that are alike in some way. Often, writers use analogies to explain unfamiliar subjects or ideas in terms of familiar ones.
See also **Metaphor; Simile.**

Anecdote An anecdote is a short account of an event that is usually intended to entertain or make a point. In the short story "The All-American Slurp" by Lensey Namioka, the story's narrator uses a humorous anecdote about her family loudly slurping soup in a restaurant to show one of the many cultural differences her Chinese family faced after their immigration to the United States.
See page 803.

Antagonist The antagonist is a force working against the protagonist, or main character, in a story, play, or novel. The antagonist is usually another character but can be a force of nature, society itself, or an internal force within the main character. In Fan Kissen's dramatization of the Greek legend "Damon and Pythias," the king is the antagonist.
See also **Protagonist.**

Assonance Assonance is the repetition of vowel sounds within nonrhyming words. An example of assonance is the repetition of the $\overline{oo}$ sound in the following lines.

> I'm Nobody! Wh<u>o</u> are y<u>ou</u>?
> Are y<u>ou</u>—Nobody—T<u>oo</u>?
> —Emily Dickinson, "I'm Nobody! Who are You?"

Audience The audience of a piece of writing is the group of readers that the writer is addressing. A writer considers his or her audience when deciding on a subject, a purpose, a tone, and a style in which to write.

Author's Perspective An author's perspective is the combination of ideas, values, feelings, and beliefs that influences the way the writer looks at a topic. **Tone,** or attitude, often reveals an author's perspective. Helen Keller wrote "The Story of My Life" from the perspective of an adult looking back at an important moment that changed the course of her life.
See page 267.
See also **Author's Purpose; Tone.**

Author's Purpose A writer usually writes for one or more of these purposes: to express thoughts or feelings, to inform or explain, to persuade, or to entertain. For example, in "SuperCroc," author Peter Winkler's purpose was to inform readers about an important archaeological discovery.
See also **Author's Perspective.**

Autobiography An autobiography is a writer's account of his or her own life. In almost every case, it is told from the first-person point of view. An autobiography focuses on the most important events and people in the writer's life over a period of time. Helen Keller's "The Story of My Life" is an autobiography.
See pages 760, 762, 787.
See also **Memoir.**

Ballad A ballad is a type of narrative poem that tells a story and was originally meant to be sung or recited. Because it tells a story, a ballad has a setting, a plot, and characters. **Folk ballads** were composed orally and handed down by word of mouth from generation to generation.

Biography A biography is the true account of a person's life, written by another person. As such, biographies are usually told from a third-person point of view. The writer of a biography—a **biographer**—usually researches his or her subject in order to present accurate information. The best biographers strive for honesty and balance in their accounts of their subjects' lives. Jim Haskins's "Matthew Henson at the Top of the World" is an example of a biography.

Cast of Characters In the script of a play, a cast of characters is a list of all the characters in the play, usually in order of appearance. It may include a brief description of each character.

Character Characters are the people, animals, or imaginary creatures who take part in the action of a work of literature. Like real people, characters display certain qualities, or **character traits,** that develop and change over time, and they usually have **motivations,** or reasons, for their behaviors.

> **Main character:** Main characters are the most important characters in literary works. Generally, the plot of a short story focuses on one main character, but a novel may have several main characters.
> **Minor characters:** The less important characters in a literary work are known as minor characters. The story is not centered on them, but they help carry out the action of the story and help the reader learn more about the main character.
> **Dynamic character:** A dynamic character is one who undergoes important changes as a plot unfolds. The changes occur because of the character's actions and experiences in the story. The changes are usually internal and may be good or bad. Main characters are usually, though not always, dynamic.
> **Static character:** A static character is one who remains the same throughout a story. The character may experience events and interact with other characters, but he or she is not changed because of them.

See pages 24, 176, 229, 255, 349.
See also **Characterization; Character Traits.**

Character Development Characters that change during a story are said to undergo character development. Any character can change, but main characters usually develop the most. For example, in "President Cleveland, Where Are You?" Jerry changes from acting selfishly to acting on behalf of others.

See also **Character: Dynamic Character.**

Characterization The way a writer creates and develops characters is known as characterization. There are four basic methods of characterization:

- The writer may make direct comments about a character through the voice of the narrator.
- The writer may describe the character's physical appearance.
- The writer may present the character's own thoughts, speech, and actions.
- The writer may present the thoughts, speech, and actions of other characters.

See pages 178, 205, 817.
See also **Character; Character Traits.**

Character Traits Character traits are the qualities shown by a character. Traits may be physical (tall) or expressions of personality (confidence). Writers reveal the traits of their characters through methods of characterization. Sometimes writers directly state a character's traits, but more often readers need to infer traits from a character's words, actions, thoughts, appearance, and relationships. Examples of words that describe traits include *brave, considerate,* and *rude.*

Climax The climax stage is the point of greatest interest in a story or play. The climax usually occurs toward the end of a story, after the reader has understood the **conflict** and become emotionally involved with the characters. At the climax, the conflict is resolved and the outcome of the plot usually becomes clear.

See pages 26, 31.
See also **Plot.**

Comedy A comedy is a dramatic work that is light and often humorous in tone, usually ending happily with a peaceful resolution of the main conflict.

Conflict A conflict is a struggle between opposing forces. Almost every story has a main conflict—a conflict that is the story's focus. An **external conflict** involves a character who struggles against a force outside him- or herself, such as nature, a physical obstacle, or another character. An **internal conflict** is one that occurs within a character.
Examples: In Armstrong Sperry's "The Ghost of the Lagoon," young Mako becomes involved in a conflict with a shark. In Sandra Cisneros's "Eleven," it is Rachel's birthday, and she is torn between the idea of growing older and yet still feeling like a little girl.

See pages 24, 31, 43, 107, 143, 337.
See also **Plot.**

Connotation A word's connotations are the ideas and feelings associated with the word, as opposed to its dictionary definition. For example, the word *bread*, in addition to its basic meaning ("a baked food made from flour and other ingredients"), has connotations of life and general nourishment.

See also **Denotation.**

Couplet A couplet is a rhymed pair of lines. A couplet may be written in any rhythmic pattern.

> Before the coming of the night
> The moon shows papery white;
> —Christina Rossetti, "Is the Moon Tired?"

See also **Rhyme; Stanza.**

Critical Essay *See* **Essay.**

Cultural Values Cultural values are the behaviors that a society expects from its people.

Denotation A word's denotation is its dictionary definition. *See also* **Connotation.**

Description Description is writing that helps a reader to picture events, objects, and characters. To create descriptions, writers often use **imagery**—words and phrases that appeal to the reader's senses.

Dialect A dialect is a form of a language that is spoken in a particular place or by a particular group of people. Dialects may feature unique pronunciations, vocabulary, and grammar. For example, the narrator in Walter Dean Myers's short story "Jeremiah's Song" uses dialect that reflects the community in which he lives. This dialect includes informal grammar.

> When he said that, Deacon Turner's wife started crying and goin' on and I give her a hard look, but she just went on.
> —Walter Dean Myers, "Jeremiah's Song"

Dialogue Dialogue is written conversation between two or more characters. Writers use dialogue to bring characters to life and to give readers insights into the characters' qualities, traits, and reactions to other characters. In fiction, dialogue is usually set off with quotation marks. In drama, stories are told primarily through dialogue.

Diary A diary is a daily record of a writer's thoughts, experiences, and feelings. As such, it is a type of autobiographical writing. A *journal* is another term for a diary.

Drama A drama, or play, is a form of literature meant to be performed by actors in front of an audience. In a drama, the characters' dialogue and actions tell the story. The written form of a drama is called a script. A script usually includes dialogue, a cast of characters, and stage directions that give instructions about performing the drama. The person who writes the drama is known as the playwright or dramatist.

Epic Poem An epic poem is a long narrative poem about the adventures of a hero whose actions reflect the ideals and values of a nation or a group of people.

Essay An essay is a short work of nonfiction that deals with a single subject. There are many types of essays. An **expository essay** presents or explains information and ideas. A **persuasive essay** attempts to convince the reader to adopt a certain viewpoint. A **critical essay** evaluates a situation or a work of art. A **personal essay** usually reflects the writer's experiences, feelings, and personality. "The First Skateboard in the History of the World" by Betsy Byars is an example of a personal essay.

See page 259.

Exaggeration An extreme overstatement of an idea is called an exaggeration. It is often used for purposes of emphasis or humor. In "Uncle Septimus's Beard," author Herbert Shippey exaggerates the length and uses of Septimus's beard in order to create a humorous, larger-than-life description of Septimus.

Exposition Exposition is the first stage of a typical story plot. The exposition provides important background information and introduces the setting and the important characters. The conflict the characters face may also be introduced in the exposition, or it may be introduced later, in the rising action.

See pages 26, 31.
See also **Plot.**

Expository Essay *See* **Essay.**

External Conflict *See* **Conflict.**

Fable A fable is a brief tale told to illustrate a moral or teach a lesson. Often the moral of a fable appears in a distinct and memorable statement near the tale's beginning or end. "Ant and Grasshopper" by Aesop is an example of a fable.

See also **Moral.**

Falling Action The falling action is the stage of the plot in which the story begins to draw to a close. The falling action comes after the **climax** and before the **resolution.** Events in the falling action show the results of the important decision or action that happened at the climax. Tension eases as the falling action begins; however, the final outcome of the story is not yet fully worked out at this stage.

See pages 26, 31.

See also **Climax; Plot.**

Fantasy Fantasy is a type of fiction that is highly imaginative and portrays events, settings, or characters that are unrealistic. The setting might be a nonexistent world, the plot might involve magic or the supernatural, and the characters might have superhuman powers.

Fiction Fiction is prose writing that tells an imaginary story. The writer of a short story or novel might invent all the events and characters or might base parts of the story on real people and events. The basic elements of fiction are plot, character, setting, and theme. Different types of fiction include realistic fiction, historical fiction, science fiction, and fantasy.

See also **Novel; Novella; Short Story.**

Figurative Language In figurative language, words are used in an imaginative way to express ideas that are not literally true. "Megan has a bee in her bonnet" is an example of figurative language. The sentence does not mean that Megan is wearing a bonnet, nor that there is an actual bee in it. Instead, it means that Megan is angry or upset about something. Figurative language is used for comparison, emphasis, and emotional effect.

See pages 548, 595.

See also **Metaphor; Onomatopoeia; Personification; Simile.**

First-Person Point of View *See* **Point of View.**

Flashback In a literary work, a flashback is an interruption of the action to present events that took place at an earlier time. A flashback provides information that can help a reader better understand a character's current situation.

Example: In "Aaron's Gift," Myron Levoy uses a flashback to explain some of the experiences and behavior of Aaron's grandmother. It also helps readers understand the significance of Aaron's use of the word *Cossacks* to fight off his attackers.

Folklore The traditions, customs, and stories that are passed down within a culture are known as its folklore. Folklore includes various types of literature, such as legends, folk tales, myths, trickster tales, and fables.

See also **Fable; Folk Tale; Myth.**

Folk Tale A folk tale is a story that has been passed down from generation to generation by word of mouth. Folk tales may be set in the distant past and involve supernatural events. The characters in them may be animals, people, or superhuman beings. "The Crane Maiden" by Rafe Martin is an example of a folk tale.

Foreshadowing Foreshadowing occurs when a writer provides hints that suggest future events in a story. Foreshadowing creates suspense and makes readers eager to find out what will happen. For example, in Joan Aiken's short story "Lob's Girl," references to the steep hill near the Pengellys' house hint that it will play a part in the story's plot.

Form The structure or organization of a written work is often called its form. The form of a poem includes the arrangement of its words and lines on the page.

Free Verse Poetry without regular patterns of rhyme and rhythm is called free verse. Some poets use free verse to capture the sounds and rhythms of ordinary speech. The poem "On Turning Ten" by Billy Collins is written in free verse.

> This is the beginning of sadness, I say to myself,
> as I walk through the universe in my sneakers.
> It is time to say good-bye to my imaginary friends,
> time to turn the first big number.
> —Billy Collins, "On Turning Ten"

See page 603.

See also **Rhyme, Rhythm.**

Genre The term *genre* refers to a category in which a work of literature is classified. The major genres in literature are fiction, nonfiction, poetry, and drama.

Haiku Haiku is a form of Japanese poetry in which 17 syllables are arranged in three lines of 5, 7, and 5 syllables. The rules of haiku are strict. In addition to following the syllabic count, the poet must create a clear picture that will evoke a strong emotional response in the reader. Nature is a particularly important source of inspiration for Japanese haiku poets, and details from nature are often the subjects of their poems.

> Winter solitude—
> in a world of one color
> the sound of the wind.
> —Bashō

Hero A hero is a main character or protagonist in a story. In older literary works, heroes tend to be better than ordinary humans. They are typically courageous, strong, honorable, and intelligent. They are protectors of society who hold back the forces of evil and fight to make the world a better place. In modern literature, a hero may simply be the most important character in a story. Such a hero is often an ordinary person with ordinary problems.

Historical Fiction A short story or a novel can be called historical fiction when it is set in the past and includes real places and real events of historical importance. The short story "The Dog of Pompeii" by Louis Untermeyer is an example of historical fiction.

See pages 100, 313.

Humor Humor is a quality that provokes laughter or amusement. Writers create humor through exaggeration, amusing descriptions, irony, and witty and insightful dialogue. In the short story "The All-American Slurp," author Lensey Namioka uses humor to tell the story of a Chinese immigrant family learning to adjust to American culture.

See pages 423, 439, 462, 503, 699.

Idiom An idiom is an expression that has a meaning different from the meaning of its individual words. For example, "to let the cat out of the bag" is an idiom meaning "to reveal a secret or surprise."

Imagery Imagery consists of words and phrases that appeal to a reader's five senses. Writers use sensory details to help the reader imagine how things look, feel, smell, sound, and taste.

> The winter
> still stings
> clean and cold and white
> as it did last year.
>   —Charlotte Zolotow, "Change"

See pages 418, 495, 567, 817.

Internal Conflict *See* **Conflict.**

Interview An interview is a conversation conducted by a writer or reporter, in which facts or statements are elicited from another person, recorded, and then broadcast or published. This book includes an interview with Ji-li Jiang.

See page 276.

Irony Irony is a contrast between what is expected and what actually exists or happens. Exaggeration and sarcasm are techniques writers use to express irony.

Journal *See* **Diary.**

Legend A legend is a story handed down from the past about a specific person, usually someone of heroic accomplishments. Legends usually have some basis in historical fact. "The Chenoo" by Joseph and James Bruchac is a Native-American legend.

Limerick A limerick is a short, humorous poem made up of five lines. It usually has the rhyme scheme *aabba*, created by two rhyming couplets followed by a fifth line that rhymes with the first couplet. A limerick typically has a sing-song rhythm.

> There was an Old Man with a beard,   *a*
> Who said, "It is just as I feared!"—   *a*
> Two Owls and a Hen,   *b*
> Four Larks and a Wren,   *b*
> Have all built their nests in my beard!"   *a*
>   —Edward Lear

Literary Nonfiction *See* **Narrative Nonfiction.**

Lyric Poetry Lyric poetry is poetry that presents the personal thoughts and feelings of a single speaker. Most poems, other than narrative poems, are lyric poems. Lyric poetry can be in a variety of forms and cover many subjects, from love and death to everyday experiences. Lilian Moore's "Message from a Caterpillar" is an example of a lyric poem.

Main Character *See* **Character.**

Memoir A memoir is a form of autobiographical writing in which a writer shares his or her personal experiences and observations of important events or people. Often informal in tone, memoirs usually give readers information about the impact of historical events on people's lives. "The Red Guards" by Ji-li Jiang is a memoir.

See pages 123, 479, 796.

See also **Autobiography.**

Metaphor A metaphor is a comparison of two things that are basically unlike but have some qualities in common. Unlike a simile, a metaphor does not contain the word *like* or *as.* In "Mooses" by Ted Hughes, a moose's body is compared to a house frame, his ears to palms reaching out, and his front legs to a lectern.

See pages 548, 595.

See also **Figurative Language; Simile.**

Meter In poetry, meter is the regular pattern of stressed (ˊ) and unstressed (ˇ) syllables. Although poems have rhythm, not all poems have regular meter. Each unit of meter is known as a **foot** and is made up of one stressed syllable and one or two unstressed syllables. Notice the meter marked in the following line.

> Ĭ mús̀t go̊ dŏwn tŏ thĕ séas ăgáin, tŏ thĕ lónĕly̆ séa ănd thĕ sk̊y,
>
> —John Masefield, "Sea-Fever"

See also **Rhythm.**

Minor Character *See* **Character.**

Mood Mood is the feeling or atmosphere that a writer creates for the reader. Descriptive words, imagery, and figurative language all influence the mood of a work. In "The Morning Walk," Mary Oliver creates a mood of thankfulness and contentment.

See pages 416, 495.

Moral A moral is a lesson that a story teaches. A moral is often stated at the end of a fable. For example, the moral of the fable "Ant and Grasshopper" is "In good times prepare for when the bad times come."

See also **Fable.**

Motivation Motivation is the reason why a character acts, feels, or thinks in a certain way. A character may have more than one motivation for his or her actions. Understanding these motivations helps readers get to know the character.

Myth A myth is a traditional story that attempts to answer basic questions about human nature, origins of the world, mysteries of nature, and social customs. For example, "The Story of Ceres and Proserpina" is a classical myth that explains the reason for the change of seasons.

Narrative Writing that tells a story is called a narrative. The events in a narrative may be real or imagined. Autobiographies and biographies are narratives that deal with real people or events. Fictional narratives include short stories, fables, myths, and novels. A narrative may also be in the form of a poem.

Narrative Nonfiction Narrative nonfiction is writing that reads much like fiction, except that the characters, setting, and plot are real rather than imaginary. Narrative nonfiction includes autobiographies, biographies, and memoirs. "The First Emperor" by Daniel Cohen is an example of narrative nonfiction.

Narrative Poetry Poetry that tells a story is called narrative poetry. Like fiction, a narrative poem contains characters, a setting, and a plot. It might also contain such elements of poetry as rhyme, rhythm, imagery, and figurative language. Lewis Carroll's "The Walrus and the Carpenter" is a narrative poem.

Narrator The narrator is the voice that tells a story. Sometimes the narrator is a character in the story. At other times, the narrator is an outside voice created by the writer. The narrator is not the same as the writer.

See also **Point of View.**

Nonfiction Nonfiction is writing that tells about real people, places, and events. Unlike fiction, nonfiction is mainly written to convey factual information. Nonfiction includes a wide range of writing—newspaper articles, letters, essays, biographies, movie reviews, speeches, true-life adventure stories, advertising, and more.

Novel A novel is a long work of fiction. Like a short story, a novel is the product of a writer's imagination. Because a novel is considerably longer than a short story, a novelist can develop the characters and story line more thoroughly.

See also **Fiction.**

Novella A novella is a work of fiction that is longer than a short story but shorter than a novel. Due to its shorter length, a novella generally includes fewer characters and a less complex plot than a novel.

See also **Fiction; Novel; Short Story.**

Ode An ode is a type of lyric poem that deals with serious themes, such as justice, truth, or beauty.

Onomatopoeia Onomatopoeia is the use of words whose sounds echo their meanings, such as *buzz*, *whisper*, *gargle*, and *murmur*. In "The All-American Slurp," onomatopoeia is used to indicate the sound made as the Lin family pulls the strings out of celery stalks.

> I pulled the strings out of my stalk. *Z-z-zip, z-z-zip.*
>
> —Lensey Namioka, "The All-American Slurp"

Oral Literature Oral literature, or the oral tradition, consists of stories that have been passed down by word of mouth from generation to generation. Oral literature includes folk tales, legends, and myths. In more recent times, some examples of oral literature have been written down or recorded so that the stories can be preserved.

Parody A parody is a humorous imitation of another writer's work. Parodies can take the form of fiction, drama, or poetry. Jon Scieszka's "The True Story of the Three Little Pigs" is an example of a parody.

Personal Essay *See* **Essay.**

Personification The giving of human qualities to an animal, object, or idea is known as personification. In "Ant and Grasshopper," for example, the insects are personified. They have conversations with each other as if they were human.

> "Why haven't you saved anything up?" asked Ant. "*I* worked hard all through the summer, storing food for the winter. Very glad I am too, for as you say, it's bitterly cold."
> "I wasn't idle last summer, either," said Grasshopper.
>
> —Aesop, "Ant and Grasshopper"

See pages 548, 595.
See also **Figurative Language.**

Persuasive Essay *See* **Essay.**

Play *See* **Drama.**

Playwright *See* **Drama.**

Plot The series of events in a story is called the plot. The plot usually centers on a **conflict,** or struggle, faced by the main character. The action that the characters take to solve the problem builds toward a **climax** in the story. At this point, or shortly afterward, the problem is solved and the story ends. Most story plots have five stages: exposition, rising action, climax, falling action, and resolution.
See pages 26, 31, 143.
See also **Climax; Exposition; Falling Action; Rising Action.**

Poetry Poetry is a type of literature in which words are carefully chosen and arranged to create certain effects.

Poets use a variety of sound devices, imagery, and figurative language to express emotions and ideas.
See also **Alliteration; Assonance; Ballad; Free Verse; Imagery; Meter; Narrative Poetry; Rhyme; Rhythm; Stanza.**

Point of View Point of view refers to how a writer chooses to narrate a story. When a story is told from the **first-person** point of view, the narrator is a character in the story and uses first-person pronouns, such as *I, me,* and *we.* In a story told from the **third-person** point of view, the narrator is not a character. A writer's choice of narrator affects the information readers receive.
See pages 176, 183, 191.
See also **Narrator.**

Prop The word *prop,* originally an abbreviation of the word *property,* refers to any physical object that is used in a drama. In the play based on Norton Juster's *The Phantom Tollbooth,* the props include a clock and a toy car.

Prose The word *prose* refers to all forms of writing that are not in verse form. The term may be used to describe very different forms of writing—short stories as well as essays, for example.

Protagonist A protagonist is the main character in a story, play, or novel. The protagonist is involved in the main conflict of the story. Usually, the protagonist undergoes changes as the plot runs its course. In "The Good Deed" by Marion Dane Bauer, Heather is the protagonist.

Pun A pun is a play on words based on similar senses of two or more words, or on various meanings of the same word. A pun is usually made for humorous effect.
Example: The fisherman was fired for playing hooky.

Radio Play A radio play is a drama that is written specifically to be broadcast over the radio. Because the audience is not meant to see a radio play, sound effects are often used to help listeners imagine the setting and the action. The stage directions in the play's script indicate the sound effects. Fan Kissen's drama *Damon and Pythias* was originally written as a radio play.

Realistic Fiction Realistic fiction is fiction that is set in the real, modern world. The characters behave like real people and use human abilities to cope with modern life's problems and conflicts. "Tuesday of the Other June" by Norma Fox Mazer is an example of realistic fiction.

Recurring Theme *See* **Theme.**

Refrain   A refrain is one or more lines repeated in each stanza of a poem.

See also **Stanza.**

Repetition   Repetition is a technique in which a sound, word, phrase, or line is repeated for emphasis or unity. Repetition often helps to reinforce meaning and create an appealing rhythm. Note how the use of repetition in the following lines emphasizes the rhythm of windshield wipers.

> fog smog   fog smog
> tissue paper   tissue paper
> clear the blear   clear the smear
> —Eve Merriam, "Windshield Wiper"

See pages 546, 567, 581.

See also **Alliteration; Sound Devices.**

Resolution   *See* **Falling Action.**

Rhyme   Rhyme is the repetition of sounds at the end of words. Words rhyme when their accented vowels and the letters that follow have identical sounds. *Pig* and *dig* rhyme, as do *reaching* and *teaching.* The most common type of rhyme in poetry is called **end rhyme,** in which rhyming words come at the ends of lines. Rhyme that occurs within a line of poetry is called **internal rhyme.** The following lines are examples of end rhyme.

> Shadows on the wall
> Noises down the hall
> Life doesn't frighten me at all
> —Maya Angelou, "Life Doesn't Frighten Me"

See pages 546, 559.

Rhyme Scheme   A rhyme scheme is a pattern of end rhymes in a poem. A rhyme scheme is noted by assigning a letter of the alphabet, beginning with *a,* to each line. Lines that rhyme are given the same letter.

> Is the moon tired? she looks so pale   *a*
> Within her misty veil: *a*
> She scales the sky from east to west,   *b*
> And takes no rest.   *b*
> —Christina Rossetti, "Is the Moon Tired?"

See pages 559.

Rhythm   Rhythm is a pattern of stressed and unstressed syllables in a line of poetry. Poets use rhythm to bring out the musical quality of language, to emphasize ideas, and to create moods. Devices such as alliteration, rhyme, and assonance often contribute to creating rhythm.

See pages 546, 559.

See also **Meter.**

Rising Action   The rising action is the stage of the plot that develops the **conflict,** or struggle. During this stage, events occur that make the conflict more complicated. The events in the rising action build toward a **climax,** or turning point.

See pages 26, 31.

See also **Plot.**

Scene   In drama, the action is often divided into acts and scenes. Each scene presents an episode of the play's plot and typically occurs at a single place and time. The play based on Mark Twain's *The Prince and the Pauper* has eight scenes.

See also **Act.**

Scenery   Scenery is a painted backdrop or other structures used to create the setting for a play.

Science Fiction   Science fiction is fiction in which a writer explores unexpected possibilities of the past or the future, combining scientific information with his or her creative imagination. Most science fiction writers create believable worlds, although some create fantasy worlds that have familiar elements. Ray Bradbury, the author of "All Summer in a Day," is a famous writer of science fiction.

See also **Fantasy.**

Script   The text of a play, film, or broadcast is called a script.

Sensory Details   Sensory details are words and phrases that appeal to the reader's senses of sight, hearing, touch, smell, and taste. Note the sensory details in the following line. These details appeal to the sense of touch.

> But they were running and turning their faces up
> to the sky and feeling the sun on their cheeks like
> a warm iron; they were taking off their jackets and
> letting the sun burn their arms.
> —Ray Bradbury, "All Summer in a Day"

See also **Imagery.**

Setting The setting of a story, poem, or play is the time and place of the action. Sometimes the setting is clear and well-defined. At other times, it is left to the reader's imagination. Elements of setting include geographic location, historical period (past, present, or future), season, time of day, and culture.

See pages 24, 63, 107, 111.

Short Story A short story is a work of fiction that centers on a single idea and can be read in one sitting. Generally, a short story has one main conflict that involves the characters and keeps the story moving.

See also **Fiction.**

Simile A simile is a figure of speech that makes a comparison between two unlike things using the word *like* or *as*.

> To find out, we studied the system map, which looked like a noodle factory hit by a bomb.
> —Avi, "Scout's Honor"

See pages 548, 595.
See also **Figurative Language; Metaphor.**

Sound Devices Sound devices are ways of using words for the sound qualities they create. Sound devices can help convey meaning and mood in a writer's work. Some common sound devices include **alliteration, assonance, meter, onomatopoeia, repetition, rhyme,** and **rhythm.**

See pages 546, 581.
See also **Alliteration; Assonance; Meter; Onomatopoeia; Repetition; Rhyme; Rhythm.**

Speaker In poetry the speaker is the voice that "talks" to the reader, similar to the narrator in fiction. The speaker is not necessarily the poet. For example, in Sandra Cisneros's "Good Hotdogs," the experiences described may or may not have happened to the poet.

See pages 281, 385, 544.

Speech A speech is a talk or public address. The purpose of a speech may be to entertain, to explain, to persuade, to inspire, or any combination of these purposes. Mawi Asgedom's speech "No Thought of Reward" was written to persuade people to give of themselves without expecting anything in return.

See page 909.

Stage Directions In the script of a play, the instructions to the actors, director, and stage crew are called the stage directions. Stage directions might suggest scenery, lighting, sound effects, and ways for actors to move and speak. Stage directions often appear in parentheses and in italic type.

> *(Suddenly he notices the package. He drags himself over to it, and disinterestedly reads the label.)*
> —Susan Nanus, *The Phantom Tollbooth*

See pages 143, 503.

Stanza A stanza is a group of two or more lines that form a unit in a poem. Each stanza may have the same number of lines, or the number of lines may vary.

See also **Couplet; Form; Poetry.**

Stereotype In literature, characters who are defined by a single trait are known as stereotypes. Such characters do not usually demonstrate the complexities of real people. Familiar stereotypes in popular literature include the absent-minded professor and the busybody.

Structure The structure of a work of literature is the way in which it is put together. In poetry, structure involves the arrangement of words and lines to produce a desired effect. One structural unit in poetry is the stanza. In prose, structure involves the arrangement of such elements as sentences, paragraphs, and events. **Sentence structure** refers to the length and types of sentences used in a work.

Style A style is a manner of writing. It involves how something is said rather than what is said. For example, "The First Skateboard in the History of the World" by Betsy Byars is written in a style that uses a humorous tone and realistic dialogue.

Subject The subject of a literary work is its focus or topic. In an autobiography, for example, the subject is the life of the person telling the story. Subject differs from **theme** in that theme is a deeper meaning, whereas the subject is the main situation or set of facts described by the text.

Surprise Ending A surprise ending is an unexpected plot twist at the end of a story. The surprise may be a sudden turn in the action or a piece of information that gives a different perspective to the entire story.

Suspense Suspense is a feeling of growing tension and excitement felt by a reader. Suspense makes a reader curious about the outcome of a story or an event within a story. A writer creates suspense by raising questions in the reader's mind. The use of **foreshadowing** is one way that writers create suspense.

See pages 26, 83.

See also **Foreshadowing.**

Symbol A symbol is a person, a place, an object, or an activity that stands for something beyond itself. For example, a flag is a colored piece of cloth that stands for a country. A white dove is a bird that represents peace.

Example: In "The Red Guards" by Ji-li Jiang, the photo album represents the Jiang family's history. To the Red Guards, it represents the past and "old ways," which are forbidden.

See page 267.

Tall Tale A tall tale is a humorously exaggerated story about impossible events, often involving the supernatural abilities of the main character. Stories about folk heroes such as Pecos Bill and Paul Bunyan are typical tall tales.

Teleplay A teleplay is a play written for television. In a teleplay, scenes can change quickly and dramatically. The camera can focus the viewer's attention on specific actions. The camera directions in teleplays are much like the stage directions in stage plays.

Theme A theme is a message about life or human nature that the writer shares with the reader. In many cases, readers must infer what the writer's message is. One way of figuring out a theme is to apply the lessons learned by the main characters to people in real life. For example, a theme of "Nadia the Willful" by Sue Alexander is that people we love live on in our memories even after they are gone.

Recurring themes are themes found in a variety of works. For example, authors from different backgrounds might express similar themes having to do with the importance of family values. **Universal themes** are themes that are found throughout the literature of all time periods. For example, Cinderella stories contain a universal theme relating to goodness being rewarded.

See pages 306, 308, 313, 337, 349, 385, 391, 723.

See also **Moral.**

Third-Person Point of View *See* **Point of View.**

Title The title of a piece of writing is the name that is attached to it. A title often refers to an important aspect of the work. For example, "President Cleveland, Where Are You?" refers to the remaining trading card that the boys in the story are trying to find.

Tone The tone of a literary work expresses the writer's attitude toward his or her subject. Words such as *angry, sad,* and *humorous* can be used to describe different tones. For example, the tone of Betsy Byars's memoir "The First Skateboard in the History of the World" is humorous.

See pages 416, 423, 469, 609.

See also **Author's Perspective.**

Tragedy A tragedy is a dramatic work that presents the downfall of a character or characters. The events in a tragic plot are set in motion by a decision that is often an error in judgment on the part of the hero. Events are linked in a cause-and-effect relationship and lead to a disastrous conclusion, usually death.

Traits *See* **Character.**

Turning Point *See* **Climax.**

Universal Theme *See* **Theme.**

Voice The term *voice* refers to a writer's unique use of language that allows a reader to "hear" a human personality in the writer's work. Elements of style that contribute to a writer's voice can reveal much about the author's personality, beliefs, and attitudes.

Word Choice The success of any writing depends on the writer's choice of words. Words not only communicate ideas but also help describe events, characters, settings, and so on. Word choice can make a writer's work sound formal or informal, serious or humorous. A writer must choose words carefully depending on the goal of the piece of writing. For example, a writer working on a science article would probably use technical, formal words; a writer trying to establish the setting in a short story would probably use more descriptive words. Word choice is sometimes referred to as diction.

See also **Style.**

Glossary of Reading and Informational Terms

Almanac *See* **Reference Works.**

Analogy An analogy is a comparison between two things that are alike in some way. Often, writers use analogies in nonfiction to explain an unfamiliar subject or idea by showing how it is like a familiar one.

Appeal to Authority An appeal to authority is an attempt to persuade an audience by making reference to people who are experts on a subject.

Argument An argument is speaking or writing that expresses a position on a problem and supports it with reasons and evidence. An argument often takes into account other points of view, anticipating and answering objections that opponents might raise.
See also **Claim; Counterargument; Evidence.**

Assumption An assumption is an opinion or belief that is taken for granted. It can be about a specific situation, a person, or the world in general. Assumptions are often unstated.

Author's Message An author's message is the main idea or theme of a particular work.
See also **Main Idea; Theme,** *Glossary of Literary Terms, page R109.*

Author's Perspective *See Glossary of Literary Terms, page R100.*

Author's Position An author's position is his or her opinion on an issue or topic.
See also **Claim.**

Author's Purpose *See Glossary of Literary Terms, page R100.*

Autobiography *See Glossary of Literary Terms, page R100.*

Bias In a piece of writing, the author's bias is the side of an issue that he or she favors. Words with extremely positive or negative connotations are often a signal of an author's bias.

Bibliography A bibliography is a list of related books and other materials used to write a text. Bibliographies can be good sources for further study on a subject.
See also **Works Consulted.**

Biography *See Glossary of Literary Terms, page R100.*

Business Correspondence Business correspondence is written business communications such as business letters, e-mails, and memos. In general, business correspondence is brief, to the point, clear, courteous, and professional.

Cause and Effect Two events are related by cause and effect when one event brings about, or causes, the other. The event that happens first is the **cause;** the one that follows is the **effect.** Cause and effect is also a way of organizing an entire piece of writing. It helps writers show the relationships between events or ideas.
See also **False Cause,** *Reading Handbook, page R24.*

Chronological Order Chronological order is the arrangement of events by their order of occurrence. This type of organization is used in fictional narratives and in historical writing, biography, and autobiography.

Claim In an argument, a claim is the writer's position on an issue or problem. Although an argument focuses on supporting one claim, a writer may make more than one claim in a text.

Clarify Clarifying is a reading strategy that helps readers understand or make clear what they are reading. Readers usually clarify by rereading, reading aloud, or discussing.

Classification Classification is a pattern of organization in which objects, ideas, and/or information are presented in groups, or classes, based on common characteristics.

Cliché A cliché is an overused expression. "Better late than never" and "hard as nails" are common examples. Good writers generally avoid clichés unless they are using them in dialogue to indicate something about a character's personality.

Compare and Contrast To compare and contrast is to identify the similarities and differences of two or more subjects. Compare and contrast is also a pattern of organizing an entire piece of writing.

Conclusion A conclusion is a statement of belief based on evidence, experience, and reasoning. A valid conclusion is one that logically follows from the facts or statements upon which it is based.

Connect Connecting is a reader's process of relating the content of a text to his or her own knowledge and experience.

Consumer Documents Consumer documents are printed materials that accompany products and services. They usually provide information about the use, care, operation, or assembly of the product or service they accompany. Some common consumer documents are applications, contracts, warranties, manuals, instructions, labels, brochures, and schedules.

Context Clues When you encounter an unfamiliar word, you can often use context clues to understand it. Context clues are the words or phrases surrounding the word that provide hints about the word's meaning.

Counterargument A counterargument is an argument made to oppose another argument. A good argument anticipates opposing viewpoints and provides counterarguments to disprove them.

Credibility Credibility is the believability or trustworthiness of a source and the information it provides.

Critical Review A critical review is an evaluation or critique by a reviewer, or critic. Types of reviews include film reviews, book reviews, music reviews, and art show reviews.

Database A database is a collection of information that can be quickly and easily accessed and searched and from which information can be easily retrieved. It is frequently presented in an electronic format.

Debate A debate is an organized exchange of opinions on an issue. In school settings, debate is usually a formal contest in which two opposing teams defend and attack a proposition.
See also **Argument.**

Deductive Reasoning Deductive reasoning is a way of thinking that begins with a generalization, presents a specific situation, and then moves forward with facts and evidence toward a logical conclusion. The following passage has a deductive argument embedded in it: "All students in the math class must take the quiz on Friday. Since Lana is in the class, she had better show up." This deductive argument can be broken down as follows: generalization—All students in the math class must take the quiz on Friday; specific situation—Lana is a student in the math class; conclusion— Therefore, Lana must take the math quiz.
See also **Analyzing Logic and Reasoning,** *Reading Handbook, page R22.*

Diary *See Glossary of Literary Terms, page R102.*

Dictionary *See* **Reference Works.**

Draw Conclusions To draw a conclusion is to make a judgment or arrive at a belief based on evidence, experience, and reasoning.

Editorial An editorial is an opinion piece that usually appears on the editorial page of a newspaper or as part of a news broadcast. The editorial section of the newspaper presents opinions rather than objective news reports.
See also **Op/Ed Piece.**

Either/Or Fallacy An either/or fallacy is a statement that suggests that there are only two choices available in a situation when in fact there are more than two.
See also **Identifying Faulty Reasoning,** *Reading Handbook, page R24.*

Emotional Appeal An emotional appeal is a message that creates strong feelings in order to make a point. An appeal to fear is a message that taps into people's fear of losing their safety or security. An appeal to pity is a message that taps into people's sympathy and compassion for others to build support for an idea, a cause, or a proposed action. An appeal to vanity is a message that attempts to persuade by tapping into people's desire to feel good about themselves.
See also **Recognizing Persuasive Techniques,** *Reading Handbook, page R21.*

Encyclopedia *See* **Reference Works.**

Essay *See Glossary of Literary Terms, page R102.*

Ethical Appeal In an ethical appeal, a writer links a claim to a widely accepted value in order to gain moral support for the claim. The appeal also creates an image of the writer as a trustworthy, moral person.
See also **Recognizing Persuasive Techniques,** *Reading Handbook, page R21.*

Evaluate To evaluate is to examine something carefully and to judge its value or worth. Evaluating is an important skill. A reader can evaluate the actions of a particular character, for example. A reader can also form opinions about the value of an entire work.

Evidence Evidence is a specific piece of information that supports a claim. Evidence can take the form of a fact, a quotation, an example, a statistic, or a personal experience, among other things.

Expository Essay *See* **Essay,** *Glossary of Literary Terms, page R102.*

Fact Versus Opinion A **fact** is a statement that can be proved, or verified. An opinion, on the other hand, is a statement that cannot be proved because it expresses a person's beliefs, feelings, or thoughts.
See also **Generalization; Inference.**

Fallacy A fallacy is an error of reasoning. Typically, a fallacy is based on an incorrect inference or a misuse of evidence.
See also **Either/Or Fallacy; Logical Appeal; Overgeneralization.**
See also **Identifying Faulty Reasoning,** *Reading Handbook, page R24.*

Faulty Reasoning *See* **Fallacy.**

Feature Article A feature article is an article in a newspaper or magazine about a topic of human interest or lifestyles.

Generalization A generalization is a broad statement about a class or category of people, ideas, or things based on a study of, or a belief about, only some of its members.
See also **Overgeneralization; Stereotyping.**

Government Publications Government publications are documents produced by government organizations. Pamphlets, brochures, and reports are just some of the many forms these publications take. Government publications can be good resources for a wide variety of topics.

Graphic Aid A graphic aid is a visual tool that is printed, handwritten, or drawn. Charts, diagrams, graphs, photographs, and maps are examples of graphic aids.
See also **Graphic Aids,** *Reading Handbook, page R4.*

Graphic Organizer A graphic organizer is a "word picture"—a visual illustration of a verbal statement—that helps a reader understand a text. Charts, tables, webs, and diagrams can all be graphic organizers. Graphic organizers and graphic aids can look the same. However, graphic organizers and graphic aids do differ in how they are used. Graphic aids help deliver important information to students using a text. Graphic organizers are actually created by students themselves. They help students understand the text or organize information.

Historical Document Historical documents are writings that have played a significant role in human events. The Declaration of Independence, for example, is a historical document.

How-To Book A how-to book explains how to do something—usually an activity, a sport, or a household project.

Implied Main Idea *See* **Main Idea.**

Index The index of a book is an alphabetized list of important topics covered in the book and the page numbers on which they can be found. An index can be used to quickly find specific information about a topic.

Inductive Reasoning Inductive reasoning is the process of logical reasoning that starts with observations, examples, and facts and moves on to a general conclusion or principle.
See also **Analyzing Logic and Reasoning,** *Reading Handbook, page R22.*

Inference An inference is a logical guess that is made based on facts and one's own knowledge and experience.

Informational Text Informational text is writing that provides factual information. It often explains an idea or teaches a process. Examples include news reports, a science textbook, software instructions, and lab reports.

Internet The Internet is a global, interconnected system of computer networks that allows for communication through e-mail, listservs, and the World Wide Web. The Internet connects computers and computer users throughout the world.

Journal A journal is a periodical publication issued by a legal, medical, or other professional organization. The term may also be used to refer to a diary or daily record.

Loaded Language Loaded language consists of words with strongly positive or negative connotations, intended to influence a reader's or listener's attitude.

Logical Appeal A logical appeal is a way of writing or speaking that relies on logic and facts. It appeals to people's reasoning or intellect rather than to their values or emotions. Flawed logical appeals—that is, errors in reasoning—are called logical fallacies.
See also **Fallacy.**

Logical Argument A logical argument is an argument in which the logical relationship between the support and claim is sound.

Main Idea The main idea is the central or most important idea about a topic that a writer or speaker conveys. It can be the central idea of an entire work or of just a paragraph. Often, the main idea of a paragraph is expressed in a topic sentence. However, a main idea may just be implied, or suggested, by details. A main idea is typically supported by details.

Make Inferences *See* **Inference.**

Monitor Monitoring is the strategy of checking your comprehension as you read and modifying the strategies you are using to suit your needs. Monitoring often includes the following strategies: questioning, clarifying, visualizing, predicting, connecting, and rereading.

Narrative Nonfiction *See Glossary of Literary Terms, page R105.*

News Article A news article is writing that reports on a recent event. In newspapers, news articles are usually brief and to the point, presenting the most important facts first, followed by more detailed information.

Nonfiction *See Glossary of Literary Terms, page R105.*

Op/Ed Piece An op/ed piece is an opinion piece that typically appears opposite ("op") the editorial page of a newspaper. Unlike editorials, op/ed pieces are written and submitted by readers.

Organization *See* **Pattern of Organization.**

Overgeneralization An overgeneralization is a generalization that is too broad. You can often recognize overgeneralizations by the appearance of words and phrases such as *all, everyone, every time, any, anything, no one,* or *none.* An example is "None of the city's workers really cares about keeping the environment clean." In all probability, there are many exceptions. The writer can't possibly know the feelings of every city worker.
See also **Identifying Faulty Reasoning,** *Reading Handbook, page R24.*

Overview An overview is a short summary of a story, a speech, or an essay.

Paraphrase Paraphrasing is the restating of information in one's own words.
See also **Summarize.**

Pattern of Organization The term *pattern of organization* refers to the way ideas and information are arranged and organized. Patterns of organization include cause and effect, chronological, compare and contrast, classification, and problem-solution, among others.
See also **Cause and Effect; Chronological Order; Classification; Compare and Contrast; Problem-Solution Order; Sequential Order.**
See also **Reading Informational Texts: Patterns of Organization,** *Reading Handbook, page R8.*

Periodical A periodical is a magazine or other publication that is issued on a regular basis.

Personal Essay *See* **Essay,** *Glossary of Literary Terms, page R102.*

Persuasion Persuasion is the art of swaying others' feelings, beliefs, or actions. Persuasion normally appeals to both the mind and the emotions of readers.
See also **Appeal to Authority; Emotional Appeal; Ethical Appeal; Loaded Language; Logical Appeal.**
See also **Recognizing Persuasive Techniques,** *Reading Handbook, page R21.*

Predict Predicting is a reading strategy that involves using text clues to make a reasonable guess about what will happen next in a story.

Primary Source *See* **Sources.**

Prior Knowledge Prior knowledge is the knowledge a reader already possesses about a topic. This information might come from personal experiences, expert accounts, books, films, or other sources.

Problem-Solution Order Problem-solution order is a pattern of organization in which a problem is stated and analyzed and then one or more solutions are proposed and examined.

Propaganda Propaganda is any form of communication that is so distorted that it conveys false or misleading information to advance a specific belief or cause.

Public Document Public documents are documents that were written for the public to provide information that is of public interest or concern. They include government documents, speeches, signs, and rules and regulations.
See also **Government Publications.**

Reference Work Reference works are sources that contain facts and background information on a wide range of subjects. Most reference works are good sources of reliable information because they have been reviewed by experts. The following are some common reference works: encyclopedias, dictionaries, thesauri, almanacs, atlases, and directories.

Review *See* **Critical Review.**

Rhetorical Question Rhetorical questions are those that have such obvious answers that they do not require a reply. Writers often use them to suggest that their claim is so obvious that everyone should agree with it.

Scanning Scanning is the process used to search through a text for a particular fact or piece of information. When you scan, you sweep your eyes across a page, looking for key words that may lead you to the information you want.

Scope Scope refers to a work's focus. For example, an article about Austin, Texas, that focuses on the city's history, economy, and residents has a broad scope. An article that focuses only on the restaurants in Austin has a narrower scope.

Secondary Source *See* **Source.**

Sequential Order Sequential order is a pattern of organization that shows the order of steps or stages in a process.

Setting a Purpose The process of establishing specific reasons for reading a text is called setting a purpose. Readers can look at a text's title, headings, and illustrations to guess what it might be about. They can then use these guesses to figure out what they want to learn from reading the text.

Sidebar A sidebar is additional information set in a box alongside or within a news or feature article. Popular magazines often make use of sidebars.

Signal Words In a text, signal words are words and phrases that help show how events or ideas are related. Some common examples of signal words are *and, but, however, nevertheless, therefore,* and *in addition.*

Source A source is anything that supplies information. **Primary sources** are materials created by people who witnessed or took part in the event they supply information about. Letters, diaries, autobiographies, and eyewitness accounts are primary sources. **Secondary sources** are those made by people who were not directly involved in the event or even present when it occurred. Encyclopedias, textbooks, biographies, and most news articles are examples of secondary sources.

Speech *See Glossary of Literary Terms, page R108.*

Stereotyping Stereotyping is a dangerous type of overgeneralization. It can lead to unfair judgments of people based on their ethnic background, beliefs, practices, or physical appearance.

Summarize To summarize is to briefly retell the main ideas of a piece of writing in one's own words. *See also* **Paraphrase.**

Support Support is any information that helps to prove a claim.

Supporting Detail *See* **Main Idea.**

Synthesize To synthesize information means to take individual pieces of information and combine them in order to gain a better understanding of a subject.

Text Feature Text features are elements of a text, such as boldface type, headings, and subheadings, that help organize and call attention to important information. Italic type, bulleted or numbered lists, sidebars, and graphic aids such as charts, tables, timelines, illustrations, and photographs are also considered text features. *See also* **Understanding Text Features,** *Reading Handbook, page R3.*

Thesaurus *See* **Reference Works.**

Thesis Statement A thesis statement is the main proposition that a writer attempts to support in a piece of writing.

Topic Sentence The topic sentence of a paragraph states the paragraph's main idea. All other sentences in the paragraph provide supporting details.

Treatment The way a topic is handled in a work is referred to as its treatment. Treatment includes the form the writing takes as well as the writer's purpose and tone.

Visualize Visualizing is the process of forming a mental picture based on written or spoken information.

Web Site A Web site is a collection of "pages" on the World Wide Web that is usually devoted to one specific subject. Pages are linked together and accessed by clicking hyperlinks or menus, which send the user from page to page within a Web site. Web sites are created by companies, organizations, educational institutions, branches of the government, the military, and individuals.

Workplace Document Workplace documents are materials that are produced or used within a work setting, usually to aid in the functioning of the workplace. They include job applications, office memos, training manuals, job descriptions, and sales reports.

Works Cited The term *works cited* refers to a list of all the works a writer has referred to in his or her text. This list often includes not only books and articles but also Internet sources.

Works Consulted The term *works consulted* refers to a list of all the works a writer consulted in order to create his or her text. It is not limited just to those works cited in the text. *See also* **Bibliography.**

Glossary of Vocabulary in English & Spanish

acclaim (ə-klām′) *n.* enthusiastic praise
aclamación *s.* elogio entusiasta

accusation (ăk′yōō-zā′shən) *n.* the act of charging someone with wrongdoing
acusación *s.* acción de imputar un delito o maldad

acrid (ăk′rĭd) *adj.* harsh and sharp in taste or odor
acre *adj.* de sabor u olor áspero y picante

administer (ăd-mĭn′ĭ-stər) *v.* to give or apply
administrar *v.* dar o aplicar

affliction (ə-flĭk′shən) *n.* a cause of pain, suffering, or worry
aflicción *s.* causa de dolor, sufrimiento o preocupación

aggressively (ə-grĕs′ĭv-lē) *adv.* in a manner showing readiness to attack
agresivamente *adv.* de modo dispuesto a atacar

agility (ə-jĭl′ĭ-tē) *n.* quickness or ease of movement
agilidad *s.* rapidez o facilidad de movimiento

agitated (ăj′ĭ-tāt′əd) *adj.* disturbed; upset **agitate** *v.*
inquieto *adj.* perturbado; alterado **inquietar** *v.*

agonize (ăg′ə-nīz′) *v.* to suffer extreme physical or mental pain
padecer *v.* sufrir dolor físico o mental extremo

alley (ăl′ē) *n.* a narrow street behind or between buildings
callejón *s.* calle angosta entre edificios o casas

allot (ə-lŏt′) *v.* to parcel out; distribute
repartir *v.* asignar; distribuir

ancestor (ăn′sĕs′tər) *n.* a person from whom another person or group is descended
antepasado *s.* persona de la que descendemos

apparatus (ăp′ə-răt′əs) *n.* a device or set of equipment used for a specific purpose
aparato *s.* instrumento o conjunto de instrumentos usados con un fin específico

appreciate (ə-prē′shē-āt′) *v.* to admire or value
apreciar *v.* admirar o valorar

archaeological (är′kē-ə-lŏj′ĭ-kəl) *adj.* relating to the study of past human life and culture
arqueológico *adj.* relacionado con el estudio de la vida y la cultura humana en el pasado

ardent (är′dnt) *adj.* having strong enthusiasm or devotion
ardiente *adj.* que tiene mucho entusiasmo o devoción

assassinate (ə-săs′ə-nāt′) *v.* to murder by surprise attack for political reasons
asesinar *v.* matar por razones políticas en un ataque sorpresa

assert (ə-sûrt′) *v.* to put into words with force or confidence; maintain
afirmar *v.* expresar en palabras con fuerza o confianza; sostener

assume (ə-sōōm′) *v.* to take on
asumir *v.* adoptar

atone (ə-tōn′) *v.* to seek pardon; to make up for
expiar *v.* pedir perdón; reparar una culpa

banish (băn′ĭsh) *v.* to send away; to exile
desterrar *v.* expulsar; exilar

banquet (băng′kwĭt) *n.* a dinner honoring a particular guest or occasion
banquete *s.* cena en honor de un invitado o de una ocasión

barbarian (bär-bâr′ē-ən) *n.* a person considered by those of another group to have a primitive culture
bárbaro *s.* persona de cultura primitiva desde el punto de vista de otro grupo

barren (băr′ən) *adj.* unable to produce or without vegetation
estéril *adj.* yermo o árido

blunder (blŭn′dər) *v.* to move clumsily
andar a ciegas *v.* andar a tropezones

brawny (brô′nē) *adj.* strong and muscular
musculoso *adj.* fuerte y muscular

cackle (kăk′əl) *v.* to make a sound of shrill laughter or chatter
chillar *v.* emitir un sonido agudo de risa o parloteo

captivate (kăp′tə-vāt′) *v.* to attract and hold interest
cautivar *v.* atraer y conservar interés

captivity (kăp-tĭv′ĭ-tē) *n.* the condition of being confined or not free
cautiverio *s.* encarcelamiento o privación de la libertad

certify (sûr′tə-fī′) *v.* to confirm as true or genuine
certificar *v.* confirmar la autenticidad

chariot (chăr′ē-ət) *n.* two-wheeled vehicle used in ancient times
　carroza *s.* carro antiguo de dos ruedas

clan (klăn) *n.* a family group; a group united by common interests or qualities
　clan *s.* grupo familiar; grupo unido por intereses o cualidades comunes

clarity (klăr′ĭ-tē) *n.* the quality of being clear
　claridad *s.* calidad de claro

clearing (klîr′ĭng) *n.* an open area of land, as in the middle of a forest
　claro *s.* terreno despejado, por ejemplo en medio de un bosque

coherent (kō-hîr′ənt) *adj.* clear; logical
　coherente *adj.* claro; lógico

collapse (kə-lăps′) *v.* to fall down
　derrumbarse *v.* caerse

commence (kə-mĕns′) *v.* to begin
　comenzar *v.* empezar

complexity (kəm-plĕk′sĭ-tē) *n.* the quality of being complicated
　complejidad *s.* calidad de complicado

complicate (kŏm′plĭ-kāt′) *v.* to make difficult or complex
　complicar *v.* hacer difícil o complejo

condition (kən-dĭsh′ən) *n.* a disease or state of health
　afección *s.* enfermedad

confiscate (kŏn′fĭ-skāt′) *v.* to take and keep something that belongs to someone else
　confiscar *v.* quitarle a una persona sus bienes

congeal (kən-jēl′) *v.* to make into a solid mass
　cuajar *v.* volverse sólido

consciousness (kŏn′shəs-nĭs) *n.* awareness of one's own thoughts
　conciencia *s.* reconocimiento de los pensamientos propios

console (kən-sōl′) *v.* to ease someone's sorrow; to comfort
　consolar *v.* aliviar la pena; confortar

consumption (kən-sŭmp′shən) *n.* the act of taking in, eating, or drinking **consume** *v.*
　consumo *s.* acción de comer o beber **consumir** *v.*

contempt (kən-tĕmpt′) *n.* the feeling produced by something disgraceful or worthless; scorn
　desprecio *s.* sentimiento que produce algo vergonzoso o sin valor; desdén

contribute (kən-trĭb′yōōt) *v.* to offer a gift or a service
　contribuir *v.* ofrecer un regalo o servicio

cope (kōp) *v.* to struggle to overcome difficulties
　sobrellevar *v.* esforzarse por superar dificultades

corrupt (kə-rŭpt′) *v.* to cause something to change from good to bad
　corromper *v.* hacer que algo se dañe

crag (krăg) *n.* a steep, rugged formation of rock
　risco *s.* peñasco escarpado

daze (dāz) *n.* a condition in which one cannot think clearly
　aturdimiento *s.* ofuscación que no permite pensar con claridad

dazzling (dăz′lĭng) *adj.* beautiful; amazing **dazzle** *v.*
　deslumbrante *adj.* hermoso; llamativo **deslumbrar** *v.*

decisively (dĭ-sī′sĭv′lē) *adv.* in a clear, definite way
　terminantemente *adv.* de modo claro y definitivo

dedicate (dĕd′ĭ-kāt′) *v.* to set apart for a particular use
　dedicar *v.* destinar a cierto uso

dedication (dĕd′ĭ-kā′shən) *n.* commitment or devotion
　dedicación *s.* compromiso o devoción

dejectedly (dĭ-jĕk′tĭd-lē) *adv.* unhappily; in a disheartened way
　abatidamente *adv.* afligidamente

desperately (dĕs′pər-ĭt-lē) *adv.* urgently
　desesperadamente *adv.* urgentemente

destination (dĕs′tə-nā′shən) *n.* the place to which a person is going
　destino *s.* lugar a donde va una persona

devise (dĭ-vīz′) *v.* to plan or design
　ingeniar *v.* planear o idear

devoted (dĭ-vō′tĭd) *adj.* very loyal; faithful **devote** *v.*
　devoto *adj.* muy leal; fiel **dedicarse** *v.*

diagnosis (dī′əg-nō′sĭs) *n.* the identification of a disease through examination of a patient
　diagnóstico *s.* identificación de una enfermedad por medio de un examen

discard (dǐ-skärd′) *v.* to throw away
  descartar *v.* tirar

disintegrate (dǐs-ǐn′tǐ-grāt′) *v.* to break down into smaller parts
  desintegrar *v.* romper en partes pequeñas

dislodge (dǐs-lǒj′) *v.* to move from a settled position
  desastascar *v.* mover de una posición fija

distorted (dǐ-stôrt′əd) *adj.* twisted out of shape; misshapened
  distorsionado *adj.* torcido; deformado

divulge (dǐ-vǔlj′) *v.* to reveal, especially something private or secret
  divulgar *v.* revelar, especialmente algo privado o secreto

domesticate (də-mĕs′tǐ-kāt′) *v.* to tame a wild species of animal over generations
  domesticar *v.* amansar una especie a lo largo de generaciones

dreary (drîr′ē) *adj.* dismal, bleak, or boring
  deprimente *adj.* triste, pesado o aburrido

eject (ǐ-jĕkt′) *v.* to throw out from inside
  expulsar *v.* arrojar hacia fuera

eldest (ĕl′dǐst) *adj.* oldest
  mayor *adj.* más viejo

embrace (əm-brās′) *v.* to hold close
  abrazar *v.* rodear con los brazos

emerald (ĕm′ər-əld) *adj.* of a rich green color
  esmeralda *adj.* de color verde profundo

emerge (ǐ-mûrj′) *v.* to come into view
  emerger *v.* salir a la vista

engage (ĕn-gāj′) *v.* to involve; participate
  meterse *v.* participar

enhance (ĕn-hăns′) *v.* to increase in value or quality
  realzar *v.* aumentar el valor o la calidad

erupt (ǐ-rǔpt′) *v.* to release one's anger or enthusiasm in a sudden, noisy way
  estallar *v.* expresar furia o entusiasmo de modo repentino y explosivo

etiquette (ĕt′ǐ-kĕt′) *n.* the practice of social manners
  etiqueta *s.* práctica de buenos modales

excavation (ĕk′skə-vā′shən) *n.* the act or process of exposing by digging away a covering
  excavación *s.* acción o proceso de destapar lo que está cubierto de tierra

except (ǐk-sĕpt′) *prep.* but; however
  excepto *prep.* pero; sin embargo

expedition (ĕk′spǐ-dǐsh′ən) *n.* a journey taken by a group with a definite goal
  expedición *s.* viaje en que se embarca un grupo con una meta definida

expert (ĕk′spûrt′) *n.* one who is skilled in or knowledgeable about a particular thing
  experto *s.* persona que domina un campo de conocimiento

exquisite (ĕk′skwǐ-zǐt) *adj.* of extraordinary beauty or charm
  exquisito *adj.* de extraordinaria belleza o encanto

extinct (ǐk-stǐngkt′) *adj.* no longer existing
  extinto *adj.* que ya no existe

feasibility (fē′zə-bǐl-ə-tē′) *n.* the possibility of something being accomplished
  viabilidad *s.* posibilidad de realizarse

ferocious (fə-rō′shəs) *adj.* savage; fierce
  feroz *adj.* salvaje; fiero

fertile (fûr′tl) *adj.* able to produce farm crops or other vegetation
  fértil *adj.* bueno para cultivar

fossil (fŏs′əl) *n.* the remains of a living thing, preserved in soil or rock
  fósil *s.* restos de un organismo preservados en el suelo o en la roca

frenzied (frĕn′zēd) *adj.* wildly excited; frantic
  frenético *adj.* sumamente agitado

frugal (froo′gəl) *adj.* avoiding waste; thrifty
  frugal *adj.* moderado; económico

gait (gāt) *n.* manner of walking or moving on foot
  paso *s.* modo de andar

generic (jə-nĕr′ǐk) *adj.* having no particularly distinctive or noteworthy quality
  genérico *adj.* que no tiene características distintivas o destacadas

glistening (glĭs′ən-ĭng) *adj.* sparkling
　　reluciente *adj.* brillante

graciousness (grā′shəs-nəs) *n.* the condition of being pleasant, courteous, and generous
　　gentileza *s.* simpatía, cortesía y generosidad

harsh (härsh) *adj.* rough; cruel
　　duro *adj.* severo; cruel

hibernation (hī′bər-nā′shən) *n.* the state of being inactive through the winter
　　hibernación *s.* estado de inactividad durante el invierno

hospitality (hŏs′pĭ-tăl′ĭ-tē) *n.* the friendly, generous treatment of guests
　　hospitalidad *s.* tratamiento amistoso y generoso de huéspedes

immense (ĭ-mĕns′) *adj.* extremely big; huge
　　inmenso *adj.* sumamente grande; enorme

immensely (ĭ-mĕns′lē) *adv.* extremely; very
　　inmensamente *adv.* sumamente; muy

immigrant (ĭm′ĭ-grənt) *n.* a person who leaves one country to live in another
　　inmigrante *s.* persona que llega a vivir a otro país

immortality (ĭm′ôr-tăl′ĭ-tē) *n.* endless life
　　inmortalidad *s.* vida eterna

impaired (ĭm-pârd′) *adj.* being in a less than perfect condition
　　deteriorado *adj.* que no está en perfectas condiciones

imposing (ĭm-pō′zĭng) *adj.* impressive; grand
　　imponente *adj.* impresionante; grandioso

impostor (ĭm-pŏs′tər) *n.* a person who uses a false name or identity
　　impostor *s.* persona que usa un nombre o una identidad falsos

impressionable (ĭm-prĕsh′ə-nə-bəl) *adj.* easily influenced
　　impresionable *adj.* fácil de influenciar

incident (ĭn′sĭ-dənt) *n.* a single event or occurrence
　　incidente *s.* suceso u ocurrencia

incredibly (ĭn-krĕd′ə-blē) *adv.* unbelievably
　　increíblemente *adv.* de modo imposible de creer

incredulous (ĭn-krĕj′ə-ləs) *adj.* unbelieving
　　incrédulo *adj.* que no cree

indignantly (ĭn-dĭg′nənt-lē) *adv.* angrily; in annoyance
　　con indignación *adv.* con furia

indistinct (ĭn′dĭ-stĭngkt′) *adj.* not clearly recognizable or understandable
　　indistinto *adj.* que no se distingue o diferencia

inefficient (ĭn′ĭ-fĭsh′ənt) *adj.* not able to produce without wasting time or energy
　　ineficaz *adj.* que desperdicia tiempo o energía

inevitable (ĭn-ĕv′ĭ-tə-bəl) *adj.* impossible to avoid or prevent
　　inevitable *adj.* que no se puede evitar o prevenir

inspect (ĭn-spĕkt′) *v.* to examine carefully
　　inspeccionar *v.* examinar con cuidado

inspiration (ĭn′spə-rā′shən) *n.* something that motivates or influences
　　inspiración *s.* algo que motiva o influencia

instinctive (ĭn-stĭngk′tĭv) *adj.* of or about the natural behaviors of a type of animal
　　instintivo *adj.* relativo a la conducta natural de un animal

intensity (ĭn-tĕn′sĭ-tē) *n.* extreme amount of energy or feeling
　　intensidad *s.* cantidad extrema de energía o sentimiento

intolerable (ĭn-tŏl′ər-ə-bəl) *adj.* unbearable; too much to be endured
　　intolerable *adj.* inaguantable; insoportable

invisible (ĭn-vĭz′ə-bəl) *adj.* not able to be seen
　　invisible *adj.* que no se ve

khaki (kăk′ē) *n.* cloth made of light yellowish brown cotton or wool
　　caqui *s.* tela de algodón o de lana de color pardo amarillento

lagoon (lə-gōōn′) *n.* a shallow body of water separated from a larger body of water by sandbars or other barriers
　　laguna *s.* masa de agua separada de una masa mayor por bancos de arena u otras barreras

lavishly (lăv′ĭsh-lē) *adv.* in a rich or plentiful way; abundantly
　　profusamente *adv.* derrochadoramente; abundantemente

lean (lēn) *adj.* having little to spare; thin
  flaco *adj.* delgado; escaso

lectern (lĕk'tərn) *n.* a stand that holds books, a computer, or papers for someone giving a speech or lecture
  atril *s.* soporte para sostener libros, una computadora o papeles al dar un discurso o conferencia

leisurely (lē'zhər-lē) *adj.* done slowly; unhurried
  despacio *adj.* pausadamente; sin prisa

leniency (lē'nē-ən-sē) *n.* tolerance; gentleness
  lenidad *s.* indulgencia; suavidad

manifestation (măn'ə-fĕ-stā'shən) *n.* evidence that something is present
  manifestación *s.* expresión pública

massacre (măs'ə-kər) *n.* the act of killing a number of helpless humans or animals
  masacre *s.* matanza de personas o animales indefensos

melancholy (mĕl'ən-kŏl'ē) *adj.* sad; gloomy
  melancólico *adj.* triste; abatido

mimic (mĭm'ĭk) *n.* one who imitates the speech and gestures of others
  imitador *s.* persona que imita las palabras y los gestos de otros

mortified (môr'tə-fīd') *adj.* ashamed, humiliated **mortify** *v.*
  avergonzado *adj.* apenado, humillado **avergonzar** *v.*

mournful (môrn'fəl) *adj.* feeling or expressing sorrow or grief
  afligido *adj.* triste, dolorido

narrative (năr'ə-tĭv) *n.* a story
  narrativa *s.* relato

nocturnal (nŏk-tûr'nəl) *adj.* active at night
  nocturno *adj.* activo de noche

novelty (nŏv'əl-tē) *n.* something new and unusual
  novedad *s.* algo nuevo y poco común

obscure (ŏb-skyŏŏr') *adj.* far from cities or other areas of human population
  alejado *adj.* lejos de ciudades u otros centros de población

obsess (əb-sĕs') *v.* to occupy the mind of
  obsesionar *v.* ocupar la mente

obstacle (ŏb'stə-kəl) *n.* something that stands in the way or prevents progress
  obstáculo *s.* algo que presenta un inconveniente o dificultad

obstinacy (ŏb'stə-nə-sē) *n.* the act of being stubborn or disobedient
  obstinación *s.* terquedad; persistencia

ominous (ŏm'ə-nəs) *adj.* threatening; frightening
  ominoso *adj.* amenazante; siniestro

pauper (pô'pər) *n.* someone who is extremely poor
  indigente *s.* persona muy pobre

perception (pər-sĕp'shən) *n.* an impression or feeling
  percepción *s.* impresión o sentimiento

persuade (pər-swād') *v.* to win someone over; convince
  persuadir *v.* convencer

pert (pûrt) *adj.* offensively bold; saucy
  descarado *adj.* insolente; fresco

petrify (pĕt'rə-fī') *v.* to paralyze with astonishment or fear
  petrificar *v.* paralizar de sorpresa o miedo

ponder (pŏn'dər) *v.* to think seriously about; reflect on
  ponderar *v.* examinar; reflexionar

precise (prĭ-sīs') *adj.* exact or correct
  preciso *adj.* exacto o correcto

predator (prĕd'ə-tər) *n.* an animal that feeds on other animals
  depredador *s.* animal que se alimenta de otros animales

preservation (prĕz'ər-vā'shən) *n.* the state of being mostly unchanged or kept from harm
  preservación *s.* protección contra algún daño

prestige (prĕ-stēzh') *n.* recognition; fame
  prestigio *s.* reconocimiento; fama

proceed (prō-sēd') *v.* to go forward or onward; continue
  proceder *v.* avanzar; continuar

proclaim (prō-klām') *v.* to announce publicly; declare
  proclamar *v.* anunciar públicamente; declarar

profile (prō'fīl') *n.* a side view of an object, especially of the human head
  perfil *s.* vista lateral de un objeto, especialmente de una cabeza humana

profound (prə-found′) *adj.* very deep or great
  profundo *adj.* intenso, fuerte o muy grande

prop (prŏp) *n.* an object an actor uses in a play
  utilería *s.* accesorio que usa un actor en una obra

propeller (prə-pĕl′ər) *n.* a spinning blade used to move a boat or airplane forward **propel** *v.*
  hélice *s.* palas rotativas que impulsa un bote o avión propulsar *v.*

protest (prə-tĕst′) *v.* to argue about or object to something
  protestar *v.* expresar disconformidad o queja

pursuit (pər-sōōt′) *n.* the act of following or chasing
  persecución *s.* acción de seguir o perseguir

raggedy (răg′ĭ-dē) *adj.* tattered or worn out
  rasgado *adj.* andrajoso o gastado

recollection (rĕk′ə-lĕk′shən) *n.* something remembered
  recuerdo *s.* memoria

reconstruction (rē′kən-strŭk′shən) *n.* the act of building or assembling again
  reconstrucción *s.* acción de volver a armar o construir

reef (rēf) *n.* a ridge of rocks, sand, or coral that rises to the surface of a body of water
  arrecife *s.* saliente de rocas, arena o coral que se ve en la superficie del agua

relentless (rĭ-lĕnt′lĭs) *adj.* refusing to stop or give up
  implacable *adj.* que no para ni cede

reluctant (rĭ-lŭk′tənt) *adj.* unwilling
  reacio *adj.* mal dispuesto

repentance (rĭ-pĕn′təns) *n.* sorrow or regret
  arrepentimiento *s.* pena o remordimiento

repose (rĭ-pōz′) *n.* freedom from work or worry; rest
  reposo *s.* descanso y tranquilidad

resilient (rĭ-zĭl′yənt) *adj.* flexible and springy
  elástico *adj.* flexible y adaptable

resounding (rĭ-zound′ĭng) *adj.* unmistakable; loud
  resonante *adj.* inconfundible; fuerte

resourcefulness (rĭ-sôrs′fəl-nĕs) *n.* the ability to act effectively, even in difficult situations
  ingenio *s.* capacidad de responder debidamente, inclusive en situaciones difíciles

restless (rĕst′lĭs) *adj.* unable to sleep or rest
  inquieto *adj.* que no puede dormir ni descansar

retort (rĭ-tôrt′) *v.* to reply, especially in a quick or unkind way
  replicar *v.* contestar, especialmente a una ofensa

retrieve (rĭ-trēv′) *v.* to get back again
  recuperar *v.* recobrar

revolting (rĭ-vōl′tĭng) *adj.* causing disgust **revolt** *v.*
  repugnante *adj.* nauseabundo repugnar *v.*

rigid (rĭj′ĭd) *adj.* stiff; not moving
  rígido *adj.* tieso; que no se mueve

sacred (sā′krĭd) *adj.* worthy of great respect; holy
  sagrado *adj.* que merece gran respeto; santo

sane (sān) *adj.* mentally healthy; reasonable
  cuerdo *adj.* sensato; razonable

savor (sā′vər) *v.* to take great pleasure in
  deleitarse *v.* gozar; apreciar

scavenge (skăv′ənj) *v.* to search for discarded scraps
  hurgar *v.* escarbar la basura

sensation (sĕn-sā′shən) *n.* a feeling
  sensación *s.* sentimiento

setback (sĕt′băk′) *n.* an unexpected stop in progress; a change from better to worse
  revés *s.* contratiempo o fracaso; desmejora

shrivel (shrĭ′vəl) *v.* to shrink or wrinkle
  secarse *v.* arrugarse o marchitarse

shrouded (shroud′əd) *adj.* concealed or hidden
  velado *adj.* envuelto u oculto

sibling (sĭb′lĭng) *n.* brother or sister
  hermano/a *s.* hijo o hija de los mismos padres

simulate (sĭm′yə-lāt′) *v.* to imitate
  simular *v.* imitar

simultaneously (sī′məl-tā′nē-əs-lē) *adv.* at the same time
  simultáneamente *adv.* al mismo tiempo

sinewy (sĭn′yōō-ē) *adj.* lean
  fibroso *adj.* flaco

skirmish (skûr′mĭsh) *n.* a minor battle or conflict
  reyerta *s.* batalla o conflicto menor

slacken (slăk′ən) *v.* to slow down or lessen
   aflojar *v.* disminuir o relajar

smirk (smûrk) *v.* to smile in an insulting way
   regodearse *v.* sonreír con suficiencia

snare (snâr) *n.* a trap for catching small animals and birds
   lazo *s.* trampa para animales pequeños y aves

species (spē′shēz) *n.* a variety or type of something
   especie *s.* variedad o tipo

stalemate (stāl′māt′) *n.* a situation in which no one playing a game is able to win
   punto muerto *s.* situación en que ninguno de los jugadores puede ganar

stealthily (stĕl′thə-lē) *adv.* secretly; sneakily
   clandestinamente *adv.* secretamente; furtivamente

stroke (strōk) *n.* a sudden, severe attack; a sudden loss of blood flow to the brain, often leading to physical or mental damage
   apoplejía *s.* derrame cerebral que suele causar daño físico o mental

successor (sək-sĕs′ər) *n.* a person who follows another, taking on his or her rights or duties
   sucesor *s.* persona que sucede a otra en el desempeño de un cargo

succumb (sə-kŭm′) *v.* to give in; die
   sucumbir *v.* ceder; morir

surmise (sər-mīz′) *v.* to make a guess
   suponer *v.* hacer una conjetura

surpass (sər-păs′) *v.* to become greater than; to go beyond
   sobrepasar *v.* superar; aventajar

tangible (tăn′jə-bəl) *adj.* possible to touch; real
   tangible *adj.* que se puede tocar; real

taunt (ônt) *v.* to mock or insult
   ridiculizar *v.* mofar o insultar

tense (ĕns) *adj.* nervous; feeling strain
   tenso *adj.* nervioso; tirante

torment (tôr′mĕnt′) *v.* to cause severe distress to the body or mind
   atormentar *v.* causar profundo dolor físico o mental

trite (trīt) *adj.* boring because overused; not fresh or original
   gastado *adj.* trillado y trivial

truce (trōōs) *n.* an agreement to end an argument or fight
   tregua *s.* acuerdo que termina una discusión o una pelea

tumultuously (tōō-mŭl′chōō-əs′lē) *adv.* in a wild or disorderly way
   tumultuosamente *adv.* de modo desordenado y ruidoso

tyrant (tī′rənt) *n.* a ruler who governs in a cruel manner
   tirano *s.* gobernante que abusa del poder

uncomprehending (ŭn′kŏm-prĭ-hĕn′dĭng) *adj.* not understanding
   atónito *adj.* que no entiende

unsuitable (ŭn-sōō′tə-bəl) *adj.* not appropriate or fitting
   impropio *adj.* inservible o inadecuado

vagrant (vā′grənt) *adj.* wandering from place to place; unrestrained
   vagabundo *adj.* que va de un lugar a otro

variation (vâr′ē-ā′shən) *n.* a slightly different form of something
   variación *s.* forma ligeramente distinta

vicious (vĭsh′əs) *adj.* severe or fierce
   feroz *adj.* malo; salvaje

vulnerable (vŭl′nər-ə-bəl) *adj.* open to attack or damage
   vulnerable *adj.* fácil de atacar o dañar

zealous (zĕl′əs) *adj.* eager and enthusiastic
   fervoroso *adj.* entusiasta

Pronunciation Key

Symbol	Examples		Symbol	Examples		Symbol	Examples
ă	at, gas		m	man, seem		v	van, save
ā	ape, day		n	night, mitten		w	web, twice
ä	father, barn		ng	sing, hanger		y	yard, lawyer
âr	fair, dare		ŏ	odd, not		z	zoo, reason
b	bell, table		ō	open, road, grow		zh	treasure, garage
ch	chin, lunch		ô	awful, bought, horse		ə	awake, even, pencil, pilot, focus
d	dig, bored		oi	coin, boy		ər	perform, letter
ĕ	egg, ten		ŏŏ	look, full			
ē	evil, see, meal		ōō	root, glue, through			
f	fall, laugh, phrase		ou	out, cow			
g	gold, big		p	pig, cap			
h	hit, inhale		r	rose, star			
hw	white, everywhere		s	sit, face			
ĭ	inch, fit		sh	she, mash			
ī	idle, my, tried		t	tap, hopped			
îr	dear, here		th	thing, with			
j	jar, gem, badge		*th*	then, other			
k	keep, cat, luck		ŭ	up, nut			
l	load, rattle		ûr	fur, earn, bird, worm			

Sounds in Foreign Words

Symbol	Examples
KH	*German* ich, auch; *Scottish* loch
N	*French* entre, bon, fin
œ	*French* feu, cœur; *German* schön
ü	*French* utile, rue; *German* grün

Stress Marks

ʹ This mark indicates that the preceding syllable receives the primary stress. For example, in the word *language*, the first syllable is stressed: lăngʹgwĭj.

ˌ This mark is used only in words in which more than one syllable is stressed. It indicates that the preceding syllable is stressed, but somewhat more weakly than the syllable receiving the primary stress. In the word *literature*, for example, the first syllable receives the primary stress, and the last syllable receives a weaker stress: lĭtʹər-ə-chŏŏrˌ.

Adapted from *The American Heritage Dictionary of the English Language,* fourth edition. Copyright © 2000 by Houghton Mifflin Company. Used with the permission of Houghton Mifflin Company.

Index of Skills

symbols, 267–277, 475, 600, 685, R109

theme, 309–311, 313–325, 337–345, 349–362, 406, 564, 685, 731, R109

themes, recurring, 391–397, R109

themes, universal, 723–731, 739, R109

tone, 416–417, 423–434, 469–475, 609–620, R109

topic, 313–325

word choice, 418, 449, 575–579, 586, 620, R109

Literary nonfiction, 8, 75, 76, 80, 110 122, 133, 223, 258, 265, 266, 276, 329, 334, 365, 437, 468, 478, 489, 557, 589, 671, 687, 766, 781, 786, 792, 796, 832, 845, 846, 856, 864, 872, 888, 892, 895, 900, 908, 926, 927, R14, R15, R16, R17, R18, R110, R112, R113. *See also* Narrative nonfiction.

Literary techniques. *See* Literary elements and devices.

Literary works
  comparing, 59, 119, 219

Loaded language, 886, 901, R25, R112

Logic. *See* Arguments; Fallacies; Reasoning.

Logical appeals, R91, R112

Logical fallacy. *See* Fallacies.

Lyric poetry, 574, 558, 570, 594, 597, 608, 614, 816, 821, R104

M

Magazine articles, 76, 265, 557, 822, 845, 846, 872, R14
  strategies for reading, 75

Magazines, 942, 946, 949. *See also* References.

Main characters, 24, 219, 229–241, 251, R101

Main ideas, 803–809, 832, R112. *See also* Patterns of organization.
  identifying, 670–675, 844, 857–861
  and supporting details, 670–675, 832, 844, 857–861, R29, R35

Making inferences. *See* Inferences, making.

Maps, 687, R7

Media, 4, R84–R92. *See also* Advertising; Films; Media elements and techniques; Media genres and types; Media messages; Viewing skills and strategies.
  accuracy of, R89
  audience of, R85
  background, 106, 254, 522
  core concepts in media literacy, R84
  demographics, 914, R85
  gatekeepers in, R86
  influence of, R86

newsworthiness, R88

persuasion in, 887, 914–917, R90, R92

producers and creators of, R84, R86, R92

purpose of, R85

reporting, R89–R90

sponsors of, R90

strategies for reading, 10

target audience, 914–915, R85

Media center, 942–943

Media elements and techniques. *See also* Camera shots in film and video; Editing, of film and video; Visual design, elements of.
  animation, R88
  camera movement, 255
  camera shot/angle, 107, 255, R87
  characterization, 254–256
  costumes, 255
  design, R91–R92
  dialogue, 107
  editing, R88
  emotional appeal, 901, R91, R111
  footage, 813
  graphics, R91
  illustrations, 80, 523, 525
  interviews, 813
  music, 969, R88
  pace, R88
  script, 83, R871
  setting and conflict, 107
  sound, 107, 969, R87–R88
  special effects, R88
  storyboards, 109, 831, 917, 969, R87
  voice-over narration, 813, R88

Media genres and types, R85–R91
  advertising, 10, 914–917, R90–R91
  documentaries, 813, R87–R88
  films, 10, 106–109, 812–815, R87–R88
  magazines, 942, 946, R112–R114
  news media, 10, 880–883, R88–R90
  photographs, 969
  television, 10, 880–883, 914–917, R84, R85, R86, R87–R88, R90
  Web sites, 941, R86

Media literacy, 107, 255, 523, 813, 881, R84–R92

Media messages, R84–R92
  deconstructing, R85
  purpose of, R85
  viewing strategies for, 813, R92

Media presentations and products. *See also* Multimedia presentations.
  casting for, 255
  creating a character gallery for, 257
  designing, 109, 257, 815, 525, 883
  illustration, 525

newscast, 883

photo documentary, 815

print ad, R90

producing, 109

sound effects, 107, 969, R88

storyboard, 109, 831, 917, R87

video presentation, 831

Memoirs, 110, 122, 266, 468, 478, 781, 796, 832, R104. *See also* Autobiography.
  analyzing, 486, 796–801

Menus, Web site, 941, R19, R114

Message. *See* Author's message.

Metaphor, 548, 579, 595–600, 630, R104–R105

Metasearch engines, 952

Meter, 546–547, R105. *See also* Rhythm.
  foot, R105

Microfilm, 942, 950

Minor characters, 24, 188, 241, R101

MLA citation guidelines, 968

Modes of reasoning. *See* Reasoning.

Modifiers, R47, R48, R57–R59. *See also* Adjectives; Adverbs; Commonly confused words.
  clauses, R62
  comparative and superlative forms of, 279, 296, R58
  dangling, R59
  essential adjective clauses, R62
  irregular comparison of, R58
  misplaced, 899, R59, R61
  nonessential adjective clauses, R62
  phrases, 899, R60
  placement of, R59, R60
  problems with, R58–R59
  regular comparison of, R58

Monitoring, 12, 31–39, 287, 449–459, 603–607, 787–793, R112

Monologue, writing, 721

Mood, 416–417, 459, 495–500, 534, R105

Motivation, of characters, 241, 251, R105

Movies. *See* Films.

Multimedia presentations, 969, R29. *See also* Media presentations and products; Oral presentations.
  planning, 533, 969
  power presentation, 533
  producing, 533, 969

Multiple-choice questions, R95

Multiple-meaning words, 376, 406, R71

Multiple-step instructions. *See* Instructions.

Myths, 644, 646, 656, 662, 750, 751, R105. *See also* Oral tradition.
  analysis of, 647–653, 750
  cultural values in, 642, 657–667, 750

progressive forms of, R56–R57

in reading consumer documents, R16

regular, R55–R56

singular, R65–R67

transitive, R47

vivid, R108

voice of, R57

Verb tense, 296, R56–R57

future, 221, R56

future perfect, R56

past, 164, 221, 296, R56

past perfect, R56

present, 221, 296, R56

present perfect, R56

progressive forms, R56

shifting, R56–R57

Verb voice, R57

Verifying information, R24, R33

Video. *See* Media genres and types;
Technology.

Video presentations, 831

Viewing skills and strategies

analyzing techniques, 107, 255, 523, 813,
881, R92

compare and contrast audience, R85

considering purpose, R92

core concepts in media literacy, R84

deconstructing media, R85

message analysis, 10, R84

Viewpoint. *See* Author's perspective; Bias.

Virtual libraries, 952

Visual aids. *See also* Graphic aids.

in oral presentations, R77, R78

in persuasive speech, 925

Visual design, elements of, 523, R91–R92.
See also Media elements and
techniques.

color, 523, R91–R92

lines, 523, R91–R92

shape, 523, R92

texture, 523, R91

Visualizing, 12, 135–141, 205–219, 296,
385–389, 503–521, 575–579,
699–706, R2, R112, R114

Visuals, analysis of, 32, 37, 44, 48, 54, 64,
84, 86, 91, 95, 112, 114, 124, 128,
136, 184, 192, 195, 199, 206, 209,
214, 230, 237, 242, 263, 268, 272,
275, 314, 316, 321, 322, 338, 342,
350, 353, 358, 368, 371, 372, 424,
427, 431, 440, 446, 450, 454, 457,
470, 473, 480, 496, 568, 570, 648,
651, 658, 661, 662, 666, 678, 681,
684, 700, 710, 713, 716, 724, 728,
730, 732, 735, 737

Vocabulary. *See also* Vocabulary skills and
strategies.

assessment practice, 170, 300, 410, 538,
634, 754, 836, 930, R96

building, 15

in context, 40, 43, 60, 63, 72, 83, 98,
111, 120, 123, 132, 143, 183, 189,
191, 202, 205, 220, 229, 252, 264,
267, 278, 313, 326, 337, 346, 349,
363, 367, 376, 423, 435, 439, 449,
460, 474, 476, 479, 487, 503, 559,
565, 595, 601, 647, 654, 657, 668,
677, 686, 689, 707, 709, 720, 723,
740, 767, 778, 787, 794, 810, 847,
854, 857, 865, 878, 891, 898, 901,
907, 909, 913

in writing, 40, 60, 72, 98, 120, 132,
189, 202, 220, 252, 264, 278, 326,
346, 363, 376, 435, 460, 476, 487,
565, 601, 654, 668, 686, 707, 720,
740, 778, 794, 810, 854, 878, 898.
907, 913

Vocabulary skills and strategies

analogies as context clues, 794

antonyms, R70

base words, 740, R69

commonly confused words, R75

compound words, 460

connotation, 40, 707, 750, 913, R70,
R102

context clues, 252, 296, 654, 720, 907,
R68

denotation, 40, 707, 750, R70, R102

dictionary usage labels, 487

easily confused words, 189, 296

figurative language in context, 220, R68

foreign words in English, 810, 832, R70

glossaries, 945, R15, R72

homographs, R71

homonyms, 686, R71

homophones, R71

idioms, 778, R68, R104

Latin roots, 120, 264, 326, 476, 601,
630, R69

literal and figurative, 98

multiple-meaning words, 376, 406, R71

prefixes, 230, 278, R69

reference aids, 668

root words, R69

similes as context clues, 435

slang, 363, R68

specialized vocabulary, 565, 630, R72,
R94

suffixes, 60, 346, 406, R69

synonym finder, 668, R72

synonyms, 72, 166, 668, 898, R70

thesaurus, 72, 668, R72

word families, R70

word origins, 132, 854, R69

word parts. *See* Word parts.

word roots. *See* Word roots.

words connected with water, 202

Voice (of verbs)

active, R57

passive, R57

Volume. *See* Speaking strategies.

W

Web address (URL), 940, 952, R19

Webs (graphics), 82, 182, 384, 478, 564,
574, 600, 602, 688, 766, 823

Web sites, 941, 960, R19, R86, R114.
See also Internet; References.

credits, 941

evaluating, 948

home page, 941

hyperlinks, 941

icons, 941

menus, 941

reading, R19

sponsors, 941

Word choice, 418, 449, 534, R109

persuasive techniques and, R21, R83

in poetry, 575–579, 586, 620

in writing, 158, 288, 954, R29

Word derivations. *See* Word families;
Word parts; Word roots.

Word origins, 132, 832, 854, R69–R70.
See also Word roots.

Word parts, R69

base words, 60, 120, 278, 346, 740, 878,
R69, R73

prefixes, 120, 278, 740, 832, 878, 926,
R69–R70, R73

roots, 120, 264, 326, 476, 601, 630,
R69–R70

suffixes, 60, 166, 346, 406, 740, 878,
R69–R70, R72–R73

Word roots, R69–R70

Greek, R70

Latin, 120, 264, 326, 476, 601, 630, R70

Word structure. *See* Word parts.

Workplace and technical writing, R42–R45,
R114. *See also* Business writing.

audience for, R43

business letter, 779, 863, R43, R110

e-mail, R44

formats for, R43–R45

instructions, 493, R44

key techniques, R42, R43

INDEX OF TITLES & AUTHORS

Page numbers that appear in italics refer to biographical information.

ACKNOWLEDGMENTS

UNIT 1

Viking Penguin: Excerpt from *Trouble River* by Betsy Byars. Copyright © 1969 by Betsy Byars. Used by permission of Viking Penguin, a division of Penguin Young Readers Group, a member of Penguin Group (USA) Inc., 345 Hudson Street, New York, NY 10014. All rights reserved.

HarperCollins: Excerpt from "Zlateh the Goat" from *Zlateh the Goat and Other Stories* by Isaac Bashevis Singer. Copyright © 1966 by Isaac Bashevis Singer, copyright renewed 1994 by Alma Singer. Reprinted by permission of HarperCollins Publishers.

Bancroft Library: Excerpt from "The Bracelet" by Yoshiko Uchida from *The Scribner Anthology for Young People*, edited by Anne Diven. Copyright © 1976 by Charles Scribner's Sons. Reprinted courtesy of the Bancroft Library, the University of California, Berkeley.

Brandt & Hochman Literary Agents, Inc.: Excerpt from "You're Not a Winner Unless Your Picture's in the Paper" by Avi from *The Color of Absence: 12 Short Stories About Loss and Hope*, Atheneum Books. Copyright © 2001 by Avi. Reprinted by permission of Brandt and Hochman Literary Agents, Inc. Any copying or distribution of this text is expressly forbidden.

Simon & Schuster: "Boar Out There" by Cynthia Rylant from *Every Living Thing*. Copyright © 1985 by Cynthia Rylant. Reprinted with the permission of Atheneum Books for Young Readers, an imprint of Simon & Schuster Children's Publishing Division.

Random House, Inc.: "The School Play" by Gary Soto from *Funny You Should Ask,* edited by David Gale. Copyright © 1992 by Gary Soto. Used by permission of Dell Publishing, a division of Random House, Inc.

Marion Dane Bauer: "The Good Deed" by Marion Dane Bauer from *Shelf Life: Stories by the Book* edited by Gary Paulsen. Copyright © 2003 by Marion Dane Bauer. Reprinted by permission of the author.

Henry Holt and Company, LLC: "The Pasture" from *The Poetry of Robert Frost* by Robert Frost, edited by Edward Connery Lathem. Copyright © 1939, 1967, 1969 by Henry Holt and Company. Reprinted by permission of Henry Holt and Company, LLC.

Don Congdon Associates: "All Summer in a Day" by Ray Bradbury, published in *Magazine of Fantasy and Science Fiction,* March 1954. Copyright © 1954, renewed 1982 by Ray Bradbury. Reprinted by permission of Don Congdon Associates, Inc.

Carus Publishing Company: "Weather That's Out of this World!" adapted from "Getting Caught Up in Earth's Atmosphere" by Alan Dyer from *Odyssey*, April 1993. Copyright © 1993 by Cobblestone Publishing, 30 Grove Street, Suite C, Peterborough, NH 03458. Used by permission of Carus Publishing Company.

NASA: "What Is an Orbital Space Colony?" by Al Globus. Copyright © NASA. Reprinted by courtesy of NASA.

Brandt & Hochman Literary Agents, Inc.: "Lob's Girl" from *A Whisper in the Night: Tales of Terror and Suspense* by Joan Aiken. Copyright © 1984 by Joan Aiken Enterprises, Ltd., published by Delacorte Press. Used by permission of Brandt & Hochman Literary Agents, Inc.

Random House Children's Books: Excerpt from *Bud, Not Buddy* by Christopher Paul Curtis. Copyright © 1999 by Christopher Paul Curtis. Used by permission of Random House Children's Books, a division of Random House, Inc.

Simon & Schuster: Excerpt from *Woodsong* by Gary Paulsen. Copyright © 1990 by Gary Paulsen. Reprinted with the permission of Simon & Schuster Books for Young Readers, an imprint of Simon & Schuster Children's Publishing Division.

NI Syndication: "A Life in the Day of Gary Paulsen" by Caroline Scott from the *Sunday Times,* November 15, 1998. Copyright © 1998 NI Syndication. Reprinted by permission of NI Syndication Ltd.

HarperCollins: "The Horse Snake" from *The Land I Lost* by Huynh Quang Nhuong. Copyright © 1982 by Huynh Quang Nhuong. Reprinted by permission of HarperCollins Publishers.

PLAYS/Sterling Partners Inc.: "The Prince and the Pauper" by Mark Twain, adapted by Joellen Bland, from *Stage Plays from the Classics* and *PLAYS, The Drama Magazine for Young People.* Copyright © 1987, reprinted 1994 and 2005 and © 2000. Reprinted with the permission of the publisher PLAYS/Sterling Partners, Inc., P.O. Box 60016, Newton, MA 02460.

Scholastic: "Fish Story" by Mary Lou Brooks from *Scholastic Action*, May 6, 1983. Copyright © 1983 by Scholastic Inc. Reprinted by permission.

UNIT 2

HarperCollins: Excerpt from *Walk Two Moons* by Sharon Creech, Copyright © 1994 by Sharon Creech. Reprinted by permission of HarperCollins Publishers.

Harcourt, Inc.: Excerpt from "How Becky Garza Learned to Golf" from *Help Wanted* by Gary Soto. Copyright © 2005 by Gary Soto. Reprinted by permission of Harcourt, Inc. This material may not be reproduced in any form or by any means without the prior written permission of the publisher.

Ralph M. Vicinanza, Ltd.: Excerpt from "The Fable of the Three Princes" from *Magic: The Final Fantasy Collection* by Isaac Asimov. Copyright © 1996 by Nightfall, Inc./The Estate of Isaac Asimov. Reprinted with the permission of Ralph M. Vicinanza, Ltd.

Scholastic Inc.: Excerpt from "Ta-Na-E-Ka" by Mary Whitebird, published in *Scholastic Voice,* December 13, 1973. Copyright © 1973 by Scholastic Inc. Reprinted by permission.

Philomel Books: Excerpt from *Cousins* by Virginia Hamilton. Copyright © 1990 by Virginia Hamilton. Used by permission of Philomel Books, a division of Penguin Young Readers Group, a member of Penguin Group (USA) Inc., 345 Hudson Street, New York, NY 10014. All rights reserved.

Curtis Brown, Ltd.: Excerpt from "The King's Dragon" from *Spaceships & Spells* by Jane Yolen, published by Harper & Row. Copyright © 1987 by Jane Yolen. Reprinted by permission of Curtis Brown, Ltd.

Houghton Mifflin: Excerpt from *Anastasia Krupnik* by Lois Lowry. Copyright © 1979 by Lois Lowry. Reprinted by permission of Houghton Mifflin Company. All rights reserved.

Susan Bergholz Literary Services: "Eleven" from *Woman Hollering Creek* by Sandra Cisneros. Copyright © 1991 by Sandra Cisneros. Published by Vintage Books, a division of Random House, Inc., and originally in hardcover by Random House, Inc. Reprinted by permission of Susan Bergholz Literary Services, New York. All rights reserved.

Barry N. Malzberg: "Ghost of the Lagoon" by Armstrong Sperry from *Children's Stories to Read or Tell*. Copyright © 1961 by Armstrong Sperry. Copyright © 1961 by the Estate of Armstrong Sperry. Reprinted by permission of Barry N. Malzberg.

Elaine Markson Agency: "Tuesday of the Other June" by Norma Fox Mazer from *Short Takes,* selected by Elizabeth Segel. Copyright © 1986 by Norma Fox Mazer. Reprinted by permission of the Elaine Markson Agency. All rights reserved.

W. W. Norton & Company: "Primer" from *Mother Love* by Rita Dove. Copyright © 1995 by Rita Dove. Used by permission of the author and W. W. Norton & Company, Inc.

Scholastic Inc.: Adapted from "The Problem with Bullies" by Sean Price, from *Junior Scholastic*, February 9, 2004. Copyright © 2004 by Scholastic Inc. Used by permission.

Random House, Inc.: "President Cleveland, Where Are You?" from *Eight Plus One* by Robert Cormier. Copyright © 1965 by Robert Cormier. Used by permission of Random House Children's Books, a division of Random House, Inc.

HarperCollins Publishers: "Aaron's Gift" from *The Witch of Fourth Street and Other Stories* by Myron Levoy. Copyright © 1972 by Myron Levoy. Used by permission of HarperCollins Publishers.

Sheldon Fogelman Agency, Inc.: "Role-Playing and Discovery" by Jerry Pinkney, published as part of the anthology *Guys Write for Guys Read* by Viking Books for Young Readers. Copyright © 2005 by Jerry Pinkney. All rights reserved. Used by permission of Sheldon Fogelman Agency, Inc.

Carus Publishing Company: Excerpt from "Invisible Hero" by Bill Gwaltney, adapted from *Footsteps* March/April 1999 Issue: Black Cowboys. Copyright © 2005 by Carus Publishing. Published by Cobblestone Publishing, 30 Grove Street, suite C, Peterborough, NH 03458. Used by permission of the publisher.

HarperCollins Publishers: Excerpt from *Red Scarf Girl: A Memoir of the Cultural Revolution* by Ji-li Jiang. Copyright © 1997 by Ji-li Jiang. Foreward copyright © 1997 by HarperCollins Publishers. Reprinted by permission of HarperCollins Publishers.

Excerpt from "An Interview with Ji-li Jiang" by Ji-li Jiang. Copyright © 2002 by HarperCollins Publishers. Reprinted by permission of HarperCollins Publishers. All rights reserved.

Random House, Inc.: "Life Doesn't Frighten Me" from *And Still I Rise* by Maya Angelou. Copyright © 1978 by Maya Angelou. Used by permission of Random House, Inc.

University of Pittsburgh Press: "On Turning Ten" from *The Art of Drowning* by Billy Collins. Copyright © 1995 by Billy Collins. Reprinted by permission of the University of Pittsburgh Press.

Curtis Brown, Ltd.: Excerpt from "Phoenix Farm" by Jane Yolen first appeared in *Bruce Coville's Book of Magic,* published by Scholastic, now appears in *Twelve Impossible Things Before Breakfast* by Jane Yolen, published by Harcourt Brace. Copyright © 1996 by Jane Yolen. Reprinted by permission of Curtis Brown, Ltd.

HarperCollins Publishers: Excerpt from *Ruby Holler* by Sharon Creech. Copyright © 2002 by Sharon Creech. Used by permission of HarperCollins Publishers.

UNIT 3

RP/Courage Books: "The Dog and His Reflection" by Aesop from *The Classic Treasury of Aesop's Fables*, illustrated by Don Daily. Copyright © 1999 by Running Press. Reprinted by permission of RP/Courage Books, a member of Perseus Books L.L.C.

Marian Reiner: "The Stray Cat" from *Catch a Little Rhyme* by Eve Merriam. Copyright © 1966 by Eve Merriam, renewed 1994. Used by permission of Marian Reiner.

Bancroft Library: Excerpt from "Gombei and the Wild Ducks" from *The Sea of Gold and Other Tales from Japan* adapted by Yoshiko Uchida. Copyright © 1965 by Yoshiko Uchida. Used by courtesy of the Bancroft Library, the University of California, Berkeley.

Professional Publishing Services Company: Excerpt from *The Donkey of God* by Louis Untermeyer. Copyright © 1932 by Harcourt, Brace and Company, Inc. Reprinted by arrangement with the Estate of Louis Untermeyer, Norma Anchin Untermeyer c/o Professional Publishing Services. The reprint is granted with the expressed permission by Laurence S. Untermeyer.

Hachette Children's Books: Excerpt from *In Search of Pompeii* by Giovanni Caselli, Copyright © 1999 by Giovanni Caselli. Reprinted by permission of Hachette Children's Books.

USA Today: Excerpt from "Italians trying to prevent a modern Pompeii" by Ellen Hale from USA Today.com, October 20, 2003. Copyright © 2003 by USA Today. Reprinted with permission.

Curtis Brown, Ltd.: *Nadia the Willful* by Sue Alexander, first published by Alfred A. Knopf. Copyright © 1983 by Sue Alexander. Reprinted by permission of Curtis Brown, Ltd.

Brandt & Hochman Literary Agents, Inc.: "Scout's Honor" from *When I Was Your Age: Original Stories About Growing Up* by Avi. Copyright © 1996 by Avi. Reprinted by permission of Brandt & Hochman Literary Agents, Inc.

Boy Scouts of America: "Wilderness Survival Merit Badge Requirements" by the Boy Scouts of America. Copyright © 1979 the Boy Scouts of America. Reprinted by courtesy of the Boy Scouts of America.

Laura Cecil Literary Agency: "Ant and Grasshopper" by Aesop, retold by James Reeves from *Fables from Aesop*. Copyright © 1961 by James Reeves. Reprinted by permission of the James Reeves Estate.

Doubleday: "The Richer, the Poorer," from *The Richer, the Poorer: Stories, Sketches, and Reminiscences* by Dorothy West. Copyright © 1995 by Dorothy West. Used by permission of Doubleday, a division of Random House, Inc.

Scholastic Inc.: Excerpt from *Esperanza Rising* by Pam Muñoz Ryan. Copyright © 2000 by Pam Muñoz Ryan, published by Scholastic Inc. Reprinted by permission.

Random House, Inc.: "Dreams" and "Words Like Freedom" from *The Collected Poems of Langston Hughes* by Langston Hughes. Copyright © 1994 by the Estate of Langston Hughes. Used by permission of Alfred A. Knopf, a division of Random House, Inc.

Arte Publico Press: "Same Song" from *Borders* by Pat Mora. Copyright ©1986 by Pat Mora. Reprinted by permission of Arte Publico Press—University of Houston.

Harcourt, Inc.: "Without Commercials" from *Horses Make a Landscape Look More Beautiful: Poems by Alice Walker.* Copyright © 1984 by Alice Walker. Reprinted by permission of Harcourt, Inc. This material may not be reproduced in any form or by any means without the prior written permission of the publisher.

UNIT 4

Farrar, Straus and Giroux, LLC: Excerpt from "The Black Thing" from *A Wrinkle in Time* by Madeleine L'Engle. Copyright © 1962, renewed 1990 by Madeleine L'Engle Franklin. Reprinted by permission of Farrar, Straus and Giroux, LLC.

Random House, Inc.: Excerpt from "Caesar the Giant" from *My Life in Dog Years* by Gary Paulsen. Copyright © 1998 by Gary Paulsen. Used by permission of Bantam Doubleday Dell Books for Young Readers, a division of Random House, Inc.

Simon & Schuster: Excerpt from *From the Mixed-up Files of Mrs. Basil E. Frankweiler* by E. L. Konigsburg. Copyright © 1967 by E. L. Konigsburg. Reprinted with the permission of Antheneum Books for Young readers, an imprint of Simon & Schuster Children's Publishing.

HarperCollins Publishers: Excerpt from *Julie of the Wolves* by Jean Craighead George. Copyright © 1972 by Jean Craighead George. Used by permission of HarperCollins Publishers.

Excerpt from *Dragonwings* by Laurence Yep. Copyright 1975 by Laurence Yep. Used by permission of HarperCollins Publishers.

HarperCollins Publishers: Excerpt from *Dragonwings* by Laurence Yep. Copyright © 1975 by Laurence Yep. Used by permission of HarperCollins Publishers.

Random House, Inc.: Excerpt from *Knots in My Yo-Yo String* by Jerry Spinelli. Copyright © 1998 by Jerry Spinelli. Used by permission of Alfred A. Knopf, a division of Random House, Inc.

Ashley Grayson Literary Agency: Excerpt from "Duffy's Jacket" by Bruce Coville from *Oddly Enough: Stories by Bruce Coville.* Copyright © 1989 by Bruce Coville, originally published in *Things That Go Bump in the Night* (HarperCollins). Reprinted by permission of Ashley Grayson Literary Agency.

Farrar, Straus and Giroux, LLC: Excerpt from *Tuck Everlasting* by Natalie Babbitt. Copyright © 1975, renewed 2003 by Natalie Babbitt. Reprinted by permission of Farrar, Straus and Giroux, LLC.

Jewel Parker Rhodes: Excerpt from "Block Party" by Jewel Parker Rhodes. Copyright © 1993 by Jewel Parker Rhodes. Reprinted by permission of the author.

Ruth Cohen, Inc.: "All-American Slurp" by Lensey Namioka from *Visions: Nineteen Short Stories for Outstanding Writers,* edited by Donald R. Gallo. Copyright © 1987 by Lensey Namioka. Reprinted by permission of Lensey Namioka. All rights reserved.

Project Harmony: Excerpt from "American Lifestyles & Habits" by Project Harmony. Copyright © by Project Harmony. Reprinted by permission of Project Harmony (www.projectharmony.org).

Viking Penguin: *The True Story of the Three Little Pigs* by Jon Scieska, illustrated by Lane Smith. Text Copyright © 1989 by Jon Scieska, illustrations Copyright © 1989 by Lane Smith. Used by permission of Viking Penguin, a Division of Penguin Young Readers Group, a Member of Penguin Group (USA) Inc., 345 Hudson Street, New York, NY 10014. All rights reserved.

Dell Publishing: "Jeremiah's Song" by Walter Dean Myers from *Visions: Nineteen Short Stories for Outstanding Writers,* edited by Donald R. Gallo. Copyright © 1987 by Donald R. Gallo. Used by permission of Dell Publishing, a division of Random House, Inc.

Ray Lincoln Literary Agency: Excerpt from *Maniac Magee* by Jerry Spinelli. Copyright © 1990 by Jerry Spinelli. Reprinted by permission of the Ray Lincoln Literary Agency.

Da Capo Press: "The Jacket" by Gary Soto from *The Effects of Knut Hamsun on a Fresno Boy: Recollections and Short Essays.* Copyright © 1983, 2001 by Gary Soto. Reprinted by permission of Da Capo Press, a member of Persea Books, Inc. (New York).

Betsy Byars: "The First Skateboard in the History of the World" from *The Moon and I* by Betsy Byars. Copyright © 1991 by Betsy Byars. Reprinted by permission of the author.

Exploratorium: Excerpt from "Skateboard Science" by Pearl Tesler and Paul Doherty. Copyright © Exploartorium. Reprinted by permission of Exploratorium (www.exploratorium.edu).

Perseus Book Group: "The Morning Walk" from *Long Life: Essays and Other Writings* by Mary Oliver. Copyright © 2004 by Mary Oliver. Reprinted courtesy of Da Capo Press, a division of the Perseus Books Group.

Tall Mountain Estate: "There Is No Word for Goodbye" from *There Is No Word for Goodbye* by Mary Tall Mountain. Copyright © 1994 by Tall Mountain Estate. Reprinted by permission of the Tall Mountain Estate. All rights reserved.

Samuel French, Inc.: *The Phantom Tollbooth* by Susan Nanus and Norton Juster. Copyright © 1977 by Susan Nanus and Norton Juster. Reprinted by permission of Samuel French, Inc. **Caution:** Professionals and amateurs are hereby warned that *The Phantom Tollbooth,* being fully protected under the copyright laws of the United States of America, the British Commonwealth countries, including Canada, and the other countries of the Copyright Union, is subject to a royalty. All rights, including professional, amateur, motion picture, recitation, public reading, radio, television, and cable broadcasting, and the rights of translation into foreign languages, are strictly reserved. Any inquiry regarding the availability of performance rights, or the purchase of individual copies of the authorized acting edition, must be directed to Samuel French, Inc., 45 West 25th Street, New York, NY 10010, with other locations in Hollywood and Toronto, Canada.

Farrar, Straus and Giroux, LLC: Excerpt from "Alan Mendelsohn, the Boy from Mars" from *Five Novels* by Daniel Pinkwater. Copyright © 1997 by Daniel Pinkwater. Reprinted by permission of Farrar, Straus and Giroux, LLC.

Diana Nightingale: "Sparky" from *Earl Nightingale's Greatest Discovery* by Earl Nightingale. Copyright © 1987 by Earl Nightingale. Reprinted by courtesy of Diana Nightingale, widow of Earl Nightingale.

UNIT 5

HarperCollins: "A Fine Head of Lettuce" from *A Pizza the Size of the Sun* by Jack Prelutsky. Copyright © 1996 by Jack Prelutsky. Reprinted by permission of HarperCollins Publishers.

Simon & Schuster: "Losing Face" from *Good Luck Gold and Other Poems* by Janet S. Wong. Copyright © 1994 by Janet S. Wong. Reprinted with the permission of Margaret K. McElderry Books, an imprint of Simon & Schuster Children's Publishing Division.

Scott Treimel NY: "People" from *All That Sunlight* by Charlotte Zolotow. Copyright © 1967 by Charlotte Zolotow, copyright renewed 1995. Used by permission of Scott Treimel NY.

Random House, Inc.: Excerpt from "April Rain Song" from *The Collected Poems of Langston Hughes* by Langston Hughes. Copyright © 1994 by the Estate of Langston Hughes. Used by permission of Alfred A. Knopf, a division of Random House, Inc.

Brooks Permissions: "Pete at the Zoo" from *The Bean Eaters* by Gwendolyn Brooks. Copyright © 1950, 1959, 1960 by Gwendolyn Brooks. Reprinted by consent of Brooks Permissions.

Farrar, Straus and Giroux, LLC: "fireworks," from *more small poems* by Valerie Worth. Copyright © 1976 by Valerie Worth. Reprinted by permission of Farrar, Straus and Giroux, LLC.

W. W. Norton & Company: "Poem" from *The Really Short Poems of A. R. Ammons* by A. R. Ammons. Copyright © 1990 by A. R. Ammons. Used by permission of the author and W. W. Norton & Company, Inc.

Marian Reiner: Excerpt from "December Leave" from *Don't Ever Cross a Crocodile and Other Poems* by Kaye Starbird. Copyright © 1963, 1991 by Kaye Starbird. All rights reserved. Used by permission of Marian Reiner.

"New Sounds" from *Something new begins* by Lilian Moore. Copyright © 1967, 1969, 1972, 1975, 1980, 1982 by Lilian Moore. This poem originally appeared in *Little Raccoon and Poems from the Woods* by Lilian Moore. Used by permission of Marian Reiner.

"Like Bookends" from *If Only I Could Tell You* by Eve Merriam. Copyright © 1983 by Eve Merriam. Used by permission of Marian Reiner.

Rozanne Knudson: "Analysis of Baseball" from *More Poems to Solve* by May Swenson. Copyright © 1954 by May Swenson. Copyright renewed 1963, 1967, 1970, 1971 by May Swenson. Used with permission of the Literary Estate of May Swenson.

Arnold Adoff: "Alone in the Nets" by Arnold Adoff from *Sports Pages*. Copyright 1986 by Arnold Adoff. Reprinted by permission of the author.

Scholastic Inc.: Adaption of "Teen Athletes: Many Kids Dream of Playing in the Big Leagues. But at What Cost?" by Victor Landauro. Published in *Junior Scholastic*, October 18, 2004. Copyright © 2004 by Scholastic Inc. All rights reserved. Used by permission.

Simon & Schuster: "Something Told the Wild Geese" from *Branches Green* by Rachel Field. Copyright © 1934 by Macmillan Publishing Company; copyright renewed 1962 by Arthur S. Pederson. Reprinted with the permission of Simon & Schuster Books for Young Readers, an imprint of Simon & Schuster Children's Publishing Division.

Scott Treimel NY: "Change" from *River Winding* by Charlotte Zolotow. Copyright © 1970 by Charlotte Zolotow. Used by permission of Scott Treimel NY.

Marian Reiner: "Message from a Caterpillar" from *Little Raccoon and Poems from the Woods* by Lilian Moore. Copyright © 1975 by Lilian Moore. All rights renewed and reserved. Used by permission of Marian Reiner.

Harcourt, Inc.: "Fog" from *Chicago Poems* by Carl Sandburg. Copyright © 1916 by Holt, Rinehart and Winston and renewed 1944 by Carl Sandburg. Reprinted by permission of Harcourt, Inc. This material may not be reproduced in any form or by any means without the prior written permission of the publisher.

HarperCollins: "Winter solitude" and "A field of cotton" by Bashō from *The Essential Haiku: Versions of Basho, Buson & Issa*, edited and with an introduction by Robert Haas. Copyright © 1994 by Robert Haas. Reprinted by permission of HarperCollins Publishers.

Marian Reiner: "Windshield Wiper" from *Chortles: New and Selected Wordplay Poems* by Eve Merriam. Copyright © 1962, 1964, 1973, 1976, 1989 by Eve Merriam. Used by permission of Marian Reiner.

Doubleday: "Night Journey" from *The Collected Poems of Theodore Roethke* by Theodore Roethke. Copyright © 1940 by Theodore Roethke. Used by permission of Doubleday, a division of Random House, Inc.

Walker & Co.: Excerpt from *A Long Hard Journey: The Story of the Pullman Porter* by Patricia and Frederick McKissack. Copyright © 1989 by Patricia and Frederick McKissack. Published by agreement with Walker & Co.

Harvard University Press: "I'm Nobody! Who are you?" from *The Poems of Emily Dickinson*, Thomas H. Johnson, editor, Cambridge, Mass. Copyright © 1951, 1955, 1979, 1983 by the President and Fellows of Harvard College. Reprinted with the permission of Harvard University Press and the Trustees of Amherst College.

Viking Penguin: "Mooses" from *Under the North Star* by Ted Hughes. Copyright © 1981 by Ted Hughes. Used by permission of Viking Penguin, a division of Penguin Group (USA) Inc.

Liveright Publishing Corporation: "who knows if the moon's" from *Complete Poems: 1904–1962* by E. E. Cummings, edited by George J. Firmage. Copyright © 1923, 1925, 1951, 1953, 1991 by the Trustees for the E. E. Cummings Trust. Copyright © 1976 by George James Firmage. Used by permission of Liveright Publishing Corporation.

Curtis Brown, Ltd.: "A bugler named Dougal MacDougal" from *Lots of Limericks* by Ogden Nash. Copyright 1934 by Ogden Nash. Reprinted by permission of Curtis Brown, Ltd.

Susan Bergholz Literary Services: "Good Hot Dogs" and "Ricos Hot Dogs" from *My Wicked Wicked Ways* by Sandra Cisneros, published by Third Woman Press and in hardcover by Alfred A. Knopf. Copyright © 1987 by Sandra Cisneros. Reprinted by permission of Third Woman Press and Susan Bergholz Literary Services, New York. All rights reserved.

Simon & Schuster: "Ode to an Artichoke" by Pablo Neruda from *The Yellow Canary Whose Eye Is So Black,* by Pablo Neruda, translated by Cheli Durán. Copyright © 1977 by Cheil Durán Ryan. Reprinted with the permission of Simon & Schuster Books for Young Readers, an imprint of Simon & Schuster Children's Publishing Division.

Agencia Literaria: "Oda a la Alcachofa," from *Pablo Nerudo Poesía I* by Pablo Neruda. Copyright © 1954 by Pablo Neruda. Reprinted by permission of Agencia Literaria Carmen Balcells.

Little, Brown and Company: "Rain in Ohio" from *American Primitive* by Mary Oliver. Copyright © 1978, 1979, 1980, 1981, 1982, 1983 by Mary Oliver. By permission of Little, Brown and Co., Inc.

UNIT 6

Virginia Pounds Brown: "How Day and Night Came" from *Southern Indian Myths and Legends,* edited by Virginia Pounds Brown and Laurella Owens. Copyright © 1985 by Virginia Pounds Brown and Laurella Owens. Reprinted by permission of Virginia Pounds Brown and Laurella Owens. All rights reserved.

Penguin Group (USA) Inc.: Excerpt from "Sal Fink" from *Cut from the Same Cloth* by Robert D. San Souci. Copyright © 1993 by Robert D. San Souci, text. Used by permission of Philomel Books, a Division of Penguin Young Readers Group, a Member of Penguin Group (USA) Inc., 345 Hudson Street, New York, NY 10014. All rights reserved.

Gail B. Graham: Excerpt from *The Beggar In the Blanket & Other Vietnamese Tales* by Gail B. Graham. Copyright © 1970 by Gail B. Graham. Reprinted by permission of Gail B. Graham.

Houghton Mifflin: Excerpt from "Baucis and Philemon" by Olivia Coolidge from *Greek Myths.* Copyright © 1949 by Olivia E. Coolidge. Adapted by permission of Houghton Mifflin Company. All rights reserved.

HarperCollins: Excerpt from *Robin Hood Of Sherwood Forest* told by Ann McGovern. Copyright

Simon & Schuster: "Orion" from *The Macmillan Book of Greek Gods and Heroes* by Alice Low. Copyright © 1985 by Macmillan Publishing Company. Reprinted with the permission of Simon & Schuster Books for Young Readers, an imprint of Simon & Schuster Children's Publishing Division.

Scholastic Inc.: "The Story of Ceres and Proserpina" and "Apollo's Tree: The Story of Daphne and Apollo" retold by Mary Pope Osborne from *Favorite Greek Myths.* Copyright © 1989 by Mary Pope Osborne. Reprinted by permission of Scholastic Inc.

Houghton Mifflin: "Arachne" by Olivia Coolidge from *Greek Myths.* Copyright © 1949 by Olivia E. Coolidge, copyright renewed 1977 by Olivia E. Coolidge. Adapted by permission of Houghton Mifflin Company. All rights reserved.

BioKids Project: Excerpt from "Spider Webs" by BioKids Project (http://www.biokids.umich.edu) of the Animal Diversity Web (http://animaldiversity.org). Reprinted by permission of the BioKids Project.

Walker & Co.: "The Chenoo," by Joseph and James Bruchac from *When the Chenoo Howls: Native American Tales of Terror.* Copyright © 1998 by Jospeh and James Bruchac. Reprinted by permission of Walker & Co.

Houghton Mifflin: "The Legend of Damon and Pythias" by Fan Kissen from *The Bag of Fire and Other Plays.* Copyright © 1964 by Houghton Mifflin Company, renewed 1993 by John Kissen Heaslip. Reprinted by permission of Houghton Mifflin Company. All rights reserved.

Cricket Magazine: "Uncle Septimus's Beard" by Herbert Shippey from *Cricket,* August 2002, Vol. 29 No. 12. Copyright © 2002 by Herbert P. Shippey. Reprinted by permission of *Cricket* magazine.

Penguin Group (USA) Inc.: "The Crane Maiden" from *Mysterious Tales of Japan* by Rafe Martin, text. Copyright © 1996 by Rafe Martin. Used by permission of G. P. Putnam's Sons, a Division of Penguin Young Readers Group, a Member of Penguin Group (USA) Inc., 345 Hudson Street, New York, NY 10014. All rights reserved.

Judith Ortiz Cofer: "Aunty Misery" retold by Judith Ortiz Cofer from *Third World: Pig Iron No. 15.* Copyright © Judith Ortiz Cofer. Reprinted by permission of Judith Ortiz Cofer (www.english.uga.edu/~jcofer).

Penguin Group (USA) Inc.: *Yeh-Shen: A Cinderella Story from China* by Ai-Ling Louie, text. Copyright © 1982 by Ai-Ling Louie. Used by permission of Philomel Books, a Division of Penguin Young Readers Group, a Member of Penguin Group (USA) Inc., 345 Hudson Street, New York, NY 10014. All rights reserved.

Random House Children's Books: from *Sootface* by Robert D. San Souci. Copyright © 1994 by Robert D. San Souci. Used by permission of Random House Children's Books, a division of Random House, Inc.

Simon & Schuster: "Cassiopeia" and "Castor and Pollux" from *The Macmillan Book of Greek Gods and Heroes* retold by Alice Low. Copyright © 1995 by Macmillan Publishing Company. Reprinted with the permission of Simon & Schuster Books for Young Readers, an imprint of Simon & Schuster Children's Publishing Division.

UNIT 7

The Gale Group: Excerpt from *J.K. Rowling* by Bradley Steffens. Copyright © 2002 by Lucent Books. Reprinted by permission of The Gale Group.

HarperCollins: Excerpt from *No Pretty Pictures: A Child of War* by Anita Lobel. Copyright © 1998 by Anita Lobel. Reprinted by permission of HarperCollins Publishers.

Sports Illustrated: Excerpt from "Chairman of the Board" by Armen Keteyian, *Sports Illustrated,* November 24, 1986. Copyright © 1986 by Time Inc. Reprinted by permission of *Sports Illustrated.* All rights reserved.

Houghton Mifflin Company: Excerpt from *The Voice That Challenged a Nation: Marian Anderson and the Struggle for Equal Rights* by Russell Freedman. Copyright © 2004 by Russell Freedman. Reprinted by permission of Clarion Books, an imprint of Houghton Mifflin Company. All rights reserved.

Penguin Group (USA) Inc.: Excerpt from "Easter Sunday" from *My Lord, What a Morning* by Marian Anderson. Copyright © 1956 by Marian Anderson. Copyright renewed 1984. Used by permission of Viking Penguin, a division of Penguin Group (USA) Inc.

The Estate of James Haskins: Excerpt from "Matthew Henson at the Top of the World" from *Against All Opposition: Black Explorers in America* by James Haskins. Copyright © 1992 by James Haskins. Reprinted by permission of the Estate of James Haskins.

Scholastic Inc.: Excerpt from *Over the Top of the World: Explorer Will Steger's Trek Across the Arctic* by Will Steger and Jon Bowermaster, published by Scholastic Press/Scholastic Inc. Copyright © 1997 by Expeditions Unlimited Inc. Used by permission.

Simon & Schuster: Excerpt from *Under the Royal Palms* by Alma Flor Ada. Copyright © 1998 by Alma Flor Ada. Reprinted with the permission of Atheneum Books for Young Readers, an imprint of Simon & Schuster Children's Publishing Division.

Tom Lalicki: Excerpt from *Spellbinder: The Life of Harry Houdini* by Tom Lalicki. Copyright © 2000 by Tom Lalicki. Reprinted by permission of the author.

Chronicle Books: "In a Neighborhood in Los Angeles" from *Body in Flames/Cuerpo en Llamas* by Francisco X. Alarcón. Copyright © 1990 by Francisco X. Alarcón. Used with permission of Chronicle Books LLC, San Francisco. Visit ChronicleBooks.com.

University of Georgia Press: "For Gwen, 1969" from *This Is My Century: New and Collected Poems* by Margaret Walker. Copyright © 1989 by Margaret Walker Alexander. Reprinted by permission of the University of Georgia Press, Athens, Georgia, 30602. All rights reserved.

Carus Publishing Company: Excerpt from "A Way with Words" by James C. Hall, adapted from *Footsteps* March/April 2005 Issue: Women Writers. Copyright © 2005 by Carus Publishing. Published by Cobblestone Publishing, 30 Grove Street, Suite C, Peterborough, NH 03458. Used by permission of the publisher.

UNIT 8

National Geographic Society: Excerpt from "Super Croc" by Peter Winkler from *National Geographic for Kids,* March 2002. Copyright © 2002 by National Geographic. Reprinted by permission of National Geographic Society.

Gareth Huw Davies: Excerpt from "Bird Brains" by Gareth Huw Davies from www.pbs.org. Copyright © Gareth Huw Davies. Reprinted by permission of the author.

Henry Morrison, Inc.: Excerpt from *The Tomb Robbers* by Daniel Cohen. Copyright © 1980 by Daniel Cohen. Reprinted by permission of the author and his agents, Henry Morrison, Inc.

Carus Publishing Company: Excerpt from "Digging Up the Past: Discovery and Excavation of Shi-Huangdi's Tomb" by Helen Wieman Bledsoe adapted from *Calliope,* October 1997 issue: China's First Emperor: Shi-Huangdi. Copyright © 1997 by Cobblestone Publishing, 30 Grove Street, Suite C, Peterborough, NH 03458. All rights reserved. Used by permission of Carus Publishing Company.

Science News: Excerpts from "The Violent Side of Video Games" and "What Video Games Can Teach Us" by Emily Sohn from *Science News for Kids* (www.sciencenewsforkids.org). Copyright © 2004 by *Science News for Kids.* Reprinted by permission of *Science News for Kids.*

The Humane Society of the United States: "Should Wild Animals Be Kept as Pets?" from www.hsus.org. Copyright © 2005 the Humane Society of the United States. Reprinted by permission of the Humane Society of the United States (www.hsus.org).

Little, Brown and Company: "No Thought of Reward" from *The Code: The 5 Secrets of Teen Success* by Mawi Asgedom. Copyright © 2003 by Mawi Asgedom. By permission of Little, Brown and Co., Inc.

www.zillions.org: "Food Ad Tricks" from www.ConsumerReports.org., Copyright © 2000 by Consumers Union of U.S. Inc., Yonkers, NY 10703–1057, a nonprofit organization. Reprinted with permission from www.zillions.org for educational purposes only. No commercial use or reproduction permitted (www.ConsumerReports.org).

National Geographic Society: "Swimmers Beware: Jellyfish Are Everywhere" by Susan Jaques from *National Geographic Kids* magazine, August 1996. Copyright © August 1996 by *National Geographic World* magazine. Reprinted by permission of National Geographic Society.

"Flying into the Eye of a Hurricane" by Susan Jaques from *National Geographic Kids* magazine, September 2002. Copyright © 2002 by *National Geographic World* magazine. Reprinted by permission of National Geographic Society.

National Association for Humane and Environmental Education: "Power in Numbers" by the National Association for Humane and Environmental Education (NAHEE) from www.humaneteen.org. Copyright © 2006 by NAHEE. Reprinted by permission of NAHEE.

The editors have made every effort to trace the ownership of all copyrighted material found in this book and to make full acknowledgment for its use. Omissions brought to our attention will be corrected in a subsequent edition.

ART CREDITS

CONSULTANTS

Title page © Getty Images; Photo © Duane McCubrey; Photo © Mark Schmidt; Photo © Bruce Forrester; Photo © McDougal Littell; Photo © Howard Gollub; Photo © Tamra Stallings; Photo © Mark Schmidt; Photo © Robert J. Marzano; Photo © McDougal Littell; Photo © Dawson & Associates Photography; Photo © Gitchell's Studio; Photo © Michael Romeo; Photo © Monica Ani; Photo © William McBride; Photo © Bill Caldwell; Photo © Gabriel Pauluzzi; Photo © Steven Scheffler.

TABLE OF CONTENTS

Contents in Brief verso *top* © Chris North/Travel-Ink; *bottom, La Bendicion en el Dia de la Boda* 1993), Carmen Lomas Garza. Alkyds on canvas, 24″ × 32″. © 1993 Carmen Lomas Garza. Collection of Smith College Museum, Northampton, Massachusetts. Photo by M. Lee Fatherree; **recto** *top* © Stuart Westmorland/Corbis; *bottom* © LWA-JDC/Corbis; **Unit 1 verso** *top left* NASA; *top right background* © John and Lisa Merrill/Corbis; *top right* © Mark Kostich Photography; *bottom* Courtesy American Library Association **recto** © PunchStock; **Unit 2 verso** *left* © David Alan Harvey/Magnum Photos; *right* © James Yang; **recto** © PunchStock; **Unit 3 verso** *left, La Grande Famille* (1947), René Magritte. Oil on canvas, 100 cm × 81 cm. Private collection. © Photothèque R. Magritte-ADAGP/Art Resource, New York. © 2008 C. Herscovici, Brussels/Artists Rights Society (ARS), New York; *right* Detail of *Bessie's Blues: The American Collection #5* (1997), Faith Ringgold. Acrylic on canvas, painted, tie-dyed, and pieced fabric, 76⅞″ × 79¼″. Robert Allerton Endowment, 2002.381, The Art Institute of Chicago. © Faith Ringgold; **recto** *top* Courtesy American Library Association; *bottom* © PunchStock; **Unit 4 verso** *top left* © Veer; *inset left* © Hans Neleman/Getty Images; *top right, La Llorona* (1989), Carmen Lomas Garza. Gouache, 18″ × 26″. © 1989 Carmen Lomas Garza. Collection of Sonia Saldivar-Hull and Felix Hull, Austin, Texas. Photo by Wolfgang Dietze; *bottom* Courtesy American Library Association; **recto** © PunchStock; **Unit 5 verso** *left* © Grant V. Faint/Getty Images; *right, The Masterpiece on the Mysteries* (1955), René Magritte. Oil on canvas. © 2008 C. Herscovici, Brussels/Artists Rights Society (ARS), New York. © Christies's Images/SuperStock; **recto** © PunchStock; **Unit 6 verso** *left* Illustration by Daniel San Souci, © 1994 by Daniel San Souci, from *Sootface* by Robert D. San Souci. Used by permission of Random House Children's Books, a division of Random House, Inc.; *right* © Kate Thompson/Getty Images; **recto** © PunchStock; **Unit 7 verso** *top left, Handcuff King Poster*, 1906.The Granger Collection, New York; *top right* © willsteger.com; *bottom* Courtesy American Library Association; **recto** © PunchStock; **Unit 8 verso** *left* © Mike Hettwer/Project Exploration; *right* © ImagineChina; **recto** © PunchStock; **Unit 9 verso** *left* © Stock4B/Getty Images; *right foreground* © Tobin Rogers/Alamy Images; *right background* © Harrison Smith/Alamy Images.

INTRODUCTORY UNIT

1 *left, The Son of Man* (1964), René Magritte. © 2008 C. Herscovici, Brussels/Artists Rights Society (ARS), New York. © Christie's Images/Corbis; *top right* © Time Life Pictures/Getty Images; *bottom right* Detail of *Room 13, Los Estudiantes* (2004), José Ramirez. Mixed media on canvas, 47″ × 19″; **2** *left* Illustration by Keiler Sensenbrenner; *right* Illustration by Juliette Borda; **3** *left* © Kathy Collins/Getty Images; *left inset* © Staffan

Andersson/Age Fotostock America, Inc.; *right* © Bart Bemus/Getty Images; **8** *top left* © Bettmann/Corbis; *center left* © SuperStock/Age Fotostock America, Inc.; *bottom left* Harvard News Office; *top right* AP/WideWorld Photos; *center right* © Jim Gensheimer/Getty Images; *bottom right* © Thomas Northcut/Getty Images; **9** *top* NASA; *center* © Chad Baker/Getty Images; *bottom* © The Macovich Collection/epa/Corbis; **10** © Warner Bros./Courtesy Everett Collection; *upper center* © Bill Stormont/Corbis; *lower center* © Apple Computer, Inc. Used with permission. All rights reserved. Apple® and the Apple logo are registered trademarks of Apple Computer, Inc. *bottom image* © Michael S. Quinton/National Geographic Image Collection; *bottom website* © National Geographic. com Kids. Reprinted by permission of National Geographic; **11** © Ali Jarekji/Reuters/Corbis; **12** © Al Francekevich/Corbis; **13** © Stockbyte; **15** © PhotoDisc; **16** *left* © Jose Luis Pelaez, Inc./Getty Images; *center* © Dirk Anshultz/Getty Images; *right top* © PhotoDisc; *right center* Courtesy National Geographic Kids magazine; *right center left* © Erik Dreyer/Getty Images; **17** *left* © Google; *right* © Image Source/Getty Images; **18** © Jason Ernst/Age Fotostock America, Inc.; **19** *left* © Siede Preis/Getty Images; *center* © Corbis; *right* © Wizdata, Inc./Alamy Images.

UNIT 1

21 *left* Illustration by Sir John Tenniel from *Through the Looking-Glass* by Lewis Carroll. Reprinted by permission of St. Martin's Press, New York; *right, Lemony Snicket's A Series of Unfortunate Events* Courtesy of Paramount Pictures; **22–23** © Michael S. Yamashita/Corbis; **22** *left* Public Domain; *right, Alice at the Mad Hatter's Tea Party*. Illustration by John Tenniel. From *The Nursery Alice* by Lewis Carroll. 1890 edition. Photo© Mary Evans Picture Library; **26** © Getty Images; **30** © Robert Llewellyn/Corbis; **31** © Photo courtesy of Gary Soto; **33** *left* © Randy Faris/Corbis; *right* © Rubberball; *background* © William Whitehurst/Corbis; **37** *left* © Rubberball; *right* © Getty Images; **42** *left* © Sean Murphy/Getty Images; *right* © Gary Rhijnsburger/Masterfile; *background* © Lisa M. Robinson/Getty Images; **43** Courtesy of the author; **45** *Alex Reading* (2000), Erik Slutsky. Oil on canvas. © Eric Stutsky/SuperStock; **51** *Dream Hydrangea II* (1995), John Bunker. Water color on paper. Private collection. © John Bunker/ SuperStock; **54** *Muchacha en la Ventana* (2000), Graciela Genoves. Oil on canvas. Zurbanan Galeria, Buenos Aires, Argentina. Photo © Zubaran Galleria/SuperStock **62** © Universal/The Kobal Collection; **63** © Bassouls Sophie/Corbis Sygma; **65** © Josh Westrich/zefa/Corbis; **66** © NASA/Roger Ressmeyer/Corbis; **69** © Jon Arnold/Getty Images; **71** *left* © NASA/Corbis; *right* © NASA/Roger Ressmeyer/Corbis; **74** © Josh Westrich/zefa/Corbis; **75** NASA; **76** Digital image © 1996 Corbis; Original image courtesy of NASA/Corbis; **77–79** *background* © Phil Banko/Getty Images; **78** *left top to bottom* NASA; **79** *top* © Roger Ressmeyer/Corbis; *center* NASA; *bottom* © Phil Banko/Getty Images; **80** NASA; **82** © Age Fotostock America, Inc.; **83** © Beth Gwinn; **86** © GeoNova LLC; **100** *top* © Les Cunliffe/Age Fotostock America, Inc.; *bottom* © Time Life Pictures/Getty Images; **100–101** AP/Wide World Photos; **101** *top right* Courtesy American Library Association; *lower right* Cover of *Bud, Not Buddy* by Christopher Paul Curtis. © 1999 by Christopher Paul Curtis. Cover art by Ernie Norcia. Reprinted by permission of Random House Children's Books, a division of Random House, Inc.; **102–103** The Granger Collection, New York; **104–105** © David Harriman/Getty Images; **106, 107** *Lemony*

Snicket's A Series of Unfortunate Events Courtesy of Paramount Pictures; **108** *background* © Sadik Demiroz/Getty Images; *left, Lemony Snicket's A Series of Unfortunate Events* Courtesy of Paramount Pictures; **110** © Mark Laricchia/Corbis; **111** © C. E. Mitchell/stockphoto.com; **116** © Corbis; **118** © NI Syndication. Reprinted by permission of NI Syndication; **122** © Paul King/Getty Images; **123** Huynh Quang Nhuong, Papers, 1956-2000, Western Historical Manuscript Collection, Columbia, Missouri; **125** *foreground* © Mark Kostich Photography; *mid ground* © John and Lisa Merrill/Corbis; *background* © Alison Wright/Corbis; **127** © GeoNova LLC; **128** *foreground* © Martyn Chillmaid/Oxford Scientific Films Ltd.; *background* © Oxford Scientific Films Ltd.; *bottom* © Robert Francis/Getty Images; **129** © Michael Pole/Corbis; **130** *foreground* © Chris Rainier/Corbis; *mid ground* © Joson/zefa/Corbis; *background* © Frans Lanting/Corbis; **133** *left* Courtesy The Voice of Vietnam; *right* © Jerry Redfern/www.onasia.com; **134** © Julian Beever; **135** © Bettmann/Corbis; **142** *left* © Randy Faris/Corbis; *right* © Rubberball/Superstock; **143** Library of Congress; **145, 147, 148, 150, 155** Crown Media Distribution, LLC. Sparrowhawk Distribution Limited; **157** The Granger Collection, New York; **158, 164** © Craig Aurness/Corbis; **165** © Bob Daemmrich/PhotoEdit; **172** © Siede Preis/Photodisc/Getty Images.

UNIT 2

173 *left* Detail of *Fire and Ice* (2004), Brian Calvin. Courtesy of Anton Kern Gallery. New York © Brian Calvin; *right* © Veer; **174** *The Complete Classic Alex Toth Zorro*, Number 1, May1999. Published by Image Comics, Inc. Berkeley, California. www.imagecomics.com. ZORRO (TM). © 2006 Zorro Productions, Inc. All rights reserved; **174–175** © Corbis Sygma; **182** © Age Fotostock/SuperStock; **183** © Gene Blevins/Corbis; **190** © Getty Images; **191** Courtesy of Barry Malzberg, for the estate of Armstrong Sperry; **194** © GeoNova LLC; **196** © Andrew J. Martinez/Photo Researchers, Inc.; **197** © Galen Rowell/Corbis; **199** © Images.com/Corbis; **205** © 2005 Judith S. Buck; **209** Left panel of *Le Plongeur (Paper Pool 18)* (1978), David Hockney. Coloured and pressed paper pulp. 72″ x 171″. © David Hockney/Bradford Art Galleries and Museums, West Yorkshire, United Kingdom /Bridgeman Art Library; **213** Courtesy of Beth Reitmeyer; **218** © Robert Daly/Getty Images; **222** Detail of *Fire and Ice* (2004), Brian Calvin. Acrylic on canvas, 48″ x 60″. Courtesy of Anton Kern Gallery, New York. © Brian Calvin; **223, 225, 226** © James Yang; **228** Courtesy of Beth Reitmeyer; **229** *top* © Richard Howard Photography; *bottom* Courtesy of the author; **231** Library of Congress, Prints and Photographs Division; **232** Courtesy Smoky Mountain Knife Works; **234** *top, Whelan's Drug Store, 44th Street and Eighth Avenue, Manhattan* (February 7, 1936), Berenice Abbott. Gelatin silver print, 8″ x 10″. Photography collection, Miriam and Ira D. Wallach Division of Art, Prints and Photographs. The New York Public Library. © Berenice Abbott/Commerce Graphics Ltd., New York. © The New York Public Library/Art Resource, New York; *bottom* © Comstock Images/Age Fotostock America; **237** *left* Library of Congress, Prints and Photographs Division; *right* © Corbis; **238** Public Domain; **244** © Talent Factory/Age Fotostock America; **245** © GeoNova LLC; **246** *La Colombe*, Pablo Picasso. Embossed, cut out and painted copper, pencil strokes, 15 3/4″ x 10 3/4″. © 2008 Estate of Pablo Picasso/Artists Rights Society (ARS), New York; **248** *Head with a Bird II* (1971), Pablo Picasso. Oil on canvas, 55 cm x 46 cm. Private collection. © Bridgeman Art Library © 2008 Estate of Pablo Picasso/Artists Rights Society (ARS), New York; **254** © Matthias Clamer/Getty Images; **255** *top* © Warner Bros./Courtesy Everett Collection; bottom © The WB/Warner Bros./Photofest; **256** *background* © David Madison/Getty Images; *top left* © Warner Bros./Courtesy Everett Collection; **257** © Rubberball Productions/Getty

Images; **258** © Kobi Israel/Alamy Images; **259** © Myles Pinkey; **262** *left* © Bettmann/Corbis; *center, right* The Granger Collection, New York; **263** © Bettmann/Corbis; **265** *top left* © Bill Manns/The Art Archive; *top center* © Historical Museum of Souther Florida/Bridgeman Art Library; *top right* © Bill Manns/The Art Archive; *center left* Photo of Bill Pickett. Private collection. © Bridgeman Art Library; *right side #1* © MPI/Getty Images; *right side #2* © Bill Manns/The Art Archive; *right side #3* © Bettmann/Corbis; *bottom left* © Bettman/Corbis; *bottom center* © UTSA's Institute of Texan Cultures, No. 088-0076, Courtesy of the John Wildenthal Family; *bottom right* © Bill Manns/The Art Archive; *inset in middle* © Elizabeth Simpson/Getty Images; **266** © Gary Moon/Age Fotostock America, Inc.; **267** © Ronald J. Saunders; **277** © Liu Liqun/Corbis; **280** © Photodisc Photography/Veer; **281** *top* © Getty Images; *bottom* © Christopher Felver/Corbis; **283** © David Alan Harvey/Magnum Photos; **285** © Comstock Images; **288, 294** © Joseph Sohm; ChromoSohm Inc./Corbis; **295** © Michael Newman/PhotoEdit; **302** © Siede Preis/Photodisc/Getty Images.

UNIT 3

303 *left* © Images.com/Corbis; *right* © Chris North/Travel-Ink; **304** © DAJ/Getty Images; **306** © Louis Psihoyos/Corbis; **312** © Phillippe Eranian/Corbis; **313** © Getty Images; **315, 316** Illustration © 1997 by Greg Ruhl. From *The Buried City of Pompeii* by Shelley Tanaka. A Hyperion/Madison Press Book. Published by permission of Madison Press Books, Toronto; **317** © GeoNova LLC; **321, 322** Illustration © 1997 by Greg Ruhl. From *The Buried City of Pompeii* by Shelley Tanaka. A Hyperion/Madison Press Book. Published by permission of Madison Press Books, Toronto; **323** AP/Wide World Photos; **328** Illustration © 1997 by Greg Ruhl. From *The Buried City of Pompeii* by Shelley Tanaka. A Hyperion/Madison Press Book. Published by permission of Madison Press Books, Toronto; **329** © O. Louis Mazzatenta/National Geographic Image Collection; **330** *top* © Werner Forman/Art Resource, New York; *bottom left* © Scala/Art Resource, New York; *bottom right* © Erich Lessing/Art Resource, New York; **330–331** Illustration by Albert Lorenz; **331** © Scala/Art Resource, New York; **332–333** Illustration by Garry Hincks; **333** *Pliny the Younger*, Annunzio da Lurago. Facade sculpture. South Abbondio, Como, Italy. © Alinari/Art Resource, New York; **336** © Corbis; **337** © 2003 Nancy Yamin; **338** © Gary Godby/ShutterStock; **339** © Christine Osborne Pictures; **340** © Jean-Luc Manaud/Rapho/ImageState; **341** © Keren Su/Corbis; **342** © Chris North/Travel-Ink; **343** Scimitar (1616). Turkish. Victoria and Albert Museum, London. © Victoria and Albert Museum, London/Art Resource, New York; **348** © David Pu'u/Corbis; **349** Photo by Russ Wright/Courtesy of the author; **351** *11th Floor Water Towers Looking East* (2005), Sonya Sklaroff. Oil on panel, 48″ x 48″. © Sonya Sklaroff 2005/www.goartline.com; **352** © GeoNova LLC; **354** © Tom Schierlitz/Getty Images; **365** *Boy Scout Handbook, Tenth Edition* © 1990. Boy Scouts of America, Irving, Texas; **366** © Robert Rathe/Getty Images; **367** *top, Aesop.* Ancient marble bust. Museo di Villa Albani, Rome. Photo © Alinari/Art Resource, New York; *bottom* © Photo by Alison Shaw; **369** From *Aesop's Fables.* © 2000 by Jerry Pinkney. Used with permission of Chronicle Books LLC. San Francisco. From Aesop's Fables. Illustration © 2000 by Jerry Pinkney. Published by Chronicle book LLC. All rights reserved. Used with permission; **371** *left, Woman in Calico* (1944), William H. Johnson. Oil on paperboard, 26½″ x 20 ½″. Gift of the Harmon Foundation. 1967.59.10144. © Smithsonian American Art Museum, Washington, D.C./Art Resource, New York; *right, Mom and Dad* (1944), William H. Johnson. Oil on paperboard, 31″ x 25⅜″. Gift of the Harmon Foundation. Smithsonian American Art Museum,

Washington, D.C. © Smithsonian American Art Museum, Washington, D.C./Art Resource, New York; **372** *Street Life, Harlem* (1940), William H. Johnson. Smithsonian American Art Museum, Washington, D.C. © Smithsonian American Art Museum, Washington, D.C./Art Resource, New York; **378** *top* © Les Cunliffe/Age Fotostock America, Inc.; *bottom* © Steve Thanos Photography; **378–379** © Garry Black/Masterfile; **379** *top* Courtesy American Library Association; *bottom* From *Esperanza Rising* by Pam Muñoz Ryan. Cover art by Joe Cepeda. Reprinted by permission of Scholastic Inc.; **380–381** © Robert Stahl/Getty Images; **382–383** © Creatas/Superstock; **384** © Veer; **385** © Corbis; **387** © Images.com/Corbis; **388** *La Grande Famille* (1947), René Magritte. Oil on canvas, 100 cm x 81 cm. Private collection. Photo © Photothèque R. Magritte-ADAGP/Art Resource, New York © 2008 C. Herscovici, Brussels/ Artists Rights Society (ARS), New York; **390** *foreground* © Warner Brothers/The Kobal Collection; *background* © WizData, Inc./Alamy Images; **391** *top* Courtesy Pat Mora/Photo by Cheron Bayna; *bottom* © Getty Images; **398, 404** © Daryl Benson/Masterfile; **405** © David Young-Wolff/PhotoEdit; **412** © Siede Preis/Photodisc/Getty Images.

UNIT 4

413 *left* From *The True Story of the 3 Little Pigs* by John Scieszka, illustrated by Lane Smith. Text © 1989 by John Scieszka. Illustrations © 1989 by Lane Smith. Used by permission of Viking Penguin, a division of Penguin Young Readers Group, a member of Penguin Group (USA) Inc., 345 Hudson Street, New York, NY 10014. All rights reserved; *right* © Christoph Wilhelm/Getty Images; **414–415** © Photodisc; **416** *left* © Wilfried Krecichwost/Getty Images; *right* © Stockbyte/Getty Images; **418** *left* Cover of *From the Mixed-up Files of Mrs. Basil E. Frankweiler* by E. L. Konigsburg. © 1967, 1995 & 2002 by E. L . Konigsburg. Cover photo © 2002 by Barry David Marcus. Cover designed by Russell Gordon. Reprinted by permission of Simon Pulse, an imprint of Simon & Schuster Children's Publishing Division, New York; *right* Cover from *Julie of the Wolves* by Jean Craighead George. © 1972 by Jean Craighead George. Cover art © 1995 by Wendell Minor. Cover © 1995 by Harper Collins Publishers. Newberry Medal reproduced with permission of the American Library Association. Used by permission of HarperCollins Publishers; **423** © Richard McNamee; **425** © Christoph Wilhelm/Getty Images; **427** © Romilly Lockyer/Getty Images; **428** © Beaconstox/Alamy Images; **431** © Owen Franken/Corbis; **432** © Food Collection/Age Fotostock America, Inc.; **438** © Ron Chapple/Alamy Images; **439** © Getty Images; **441, 442, 444, 445, 446** From *The True Story of the 3 Little Pigs* by John Scieszka, illustrated by Lane Smith. Text © 1989 by John Scieszka. Illustrations © 1989 by Lane Smith. Used by permission of Viking Penguin, a division of Penguin Young Readers Group, a member of Penguin Group (USA) Inc., 345 Hudson Street, New York, NY 10014. All rights reserved; **447** Photograph by Sharon Hoogstraten; Public Domain; **448** © Corbis; **449** © Jerry Bauer; **453** © GeoNova LLC; **459** © Getty Images; **462** *top* © Cully Craft Photography; **462–463** © Andrew Gunners/Getty Images; **463** *top* Courtesy American Library Association; *bottom* © McDougal Littell; **464–465** © André Jenny/Alamy Images; **466** © age fotostock/SuperStock; **466–467** © Jack Hollingsworth/Getty Images; **467** © Comstock/Superstock; **468** © Alistair Berg/Getty Images; **469** © Gary Soto; **471** *background* © Veer; *foreground* © Hans Neleman/Getty Images; **473** © Thomas Barwick/Getty Images; **474** Photograph by Sharon Hoogstraten; **479** © Ed Byars/Betsy Byars; **488** Illustration by Juliette Borda; **489** © Al Fuchs/NewSport/Corbis; **492** © Terry Husebye/Getty Images; **494** AP/Wide World Photos; **495** *top* © Barbara Savage Cheresh/Molly Malone Cook Literary Agency;

bottom © Lance Woodruff; **502** © Eureka/Alamy Images; **503** © Paul Franz; **522** © Dan Lim/Masterfile; **524** *left, Father and Son* (2003), Benny Andrews. From *Pictures for Miss Josie* by Sandra Belton. © 2004 by Sandra Belton. Reprinted by permission of Greenwillow Books, an imprint of HarperCollins Publishers, New York *bottom* © Masterfile; **525** © David Young-Wolff/PhotoEdit; **526, 532** © Richard Sisk/Jupiter Images; **533** *left* © David Young-Wolff/PhotoEdit; *right* © Illustration Works; **540** © Siede Preis/Photodisc/Getty Images.

UNIT 5

541 *left, Splash,* Nancy Glazier. Oil, 26″ × 34″; *right, Spoonbridge and Cherry* (1988), Claes Oldenburg and Coosje van Bruggen. Stainless steel and aluminum painted with polyurethane enamel, 29′6″ × 51′6″ × 13′6″. Minneapolis Sculpture Garden, Walker Art Center, Minneapolis. © Claes Oldenburg and Coosje van Bruggen. Photo by Attlio Maranzano; **542–543** © Age-Fotostock/SuperStock; **544** © Turbo/zefa/Corbis; **548** © Mark Wiens/Masterfile; **550** © Getty Images; **551** *top* © The Literary Estate of Mary Swenson; *bottom* © 2006 by Arnold Adoff, used by permission of Arnold Adoff; **553** © Corbis; **554** © Lisa Pines/Getty Images; **558** © Corbis; **559** *top* The Granger Collection, New York; *bottom* © Stock Montage; **566** © Canopy Productions/Veer; **567** *top* AP/Wide World Photos; *bottom* © Andrew Kilgore; **569** © Bart Bemus/Getty Images; **574** © Michael Keller/Corbis; **575** *top* Photo © Joan Glazer, 1985; *center* © Bettmann/Corbis; *bottom, Portrait of Basho,* Kameda Bosai. Hanging scroll in ink and color on paper. Gift of an anonymous donor. © New Orleans Museum of Art (80.181); **576** © Scott Tysick/Masterfile; **576–577** © Grant V. Faint/Getty Images; **578** © Ray Juno/Corbis; **580** © Tim McGuire/Corbis; **581** *top* © The Schlesinger Library, Radcliffe Institute, Harvard University; *bottom* © Bettmann/Corbis; **583** © Grant Faint/Getty Images; **585, 588** © Sylvia de Swaan/Jupiter Images; **589** © Getty Images; **591** Courtesy Archives of the Historic Pullman Foundation, Inc.; **592** Library of Congress, Prints and Photographs Division; **595** *top* The Granger Collection, New York; *center* © Bettmann/Corbis; *bottom* © UPPA/Topham/The Image Works, Inc.; **596** *The Son of Man* (1964), René Magritte. © 2008 C. Herscovici, Brussels © Artists Rights Society (ARS), New York © Christie's Images /Corbis; **597** *The Masterpiece on the Mysteries* (1955), René Magritte. Oil on canvas. © 2008 C. Herscivici, Brussels/ Artists Rights Society (ARS), New York © Christies's Images /SuperStock; **602** © Ron Chapple/Getty Images; **603** *top* © Bettmann/Corbis; *center* © National Portrait Gallery, London; *bottom* © Time Life Pictures/Getty Images; **605, 606** Illustration by Kurt Devlaeminck; **608** © Jupiterimages Corporation; **609** *top* © Gene Blevins/Corbis; *bottom* © Getty Images; **610–611** © Jim Ballard/Getty Images; **612–613** © Ingram Publishing/Age Fotostock America, Inc.; **614, 615** © Noel/FoodPix/Jupiter Images; **616, 617** © photocuisine/Corbis; **622, 628** © Daryl Benson/Masterfile; **629** © Corbis; **636** © Siede Preis/Photodisc/Getty Images.

UNIT 6

637 *left* Illustration by Joel Priddy; *right* © Jean-Yves Bruel/Masterfile; **638–639** © Catherine Karnow/Corbis; **640** *left* (Detail of) *Prometheus Carrying Fire,* Jan Cossiers. Museo del Prado, Madrid, Spain/Art Resource, New York; *center* Illustration by Walter Crane in *King Arthur's Knights* by Henry Gilbert, 1911 © Edwin Wallace/Mary Evans Picture Library; *right* Illustration by Joel Priddy; **642** Photograph by Sharon Hoogstraten; **644** © Phil Banko/Getty Images; **646** © Joy Tessman/Getty Images; **647** © Paul Coughlin; **649** *Proserpina and Pluto in Chariot,* Leonid Gore. From

The Pomegranate Seeds retold by Laura Geringer. Illustrations © 1995 by Leonid Gore. Used by permission of Houghton Mifflin Company, Boston; **651** *Ceres and Proserpina Reunited*, Leonid Gore. From *The Pomegranate Seeds* retold by Laura Geringer. Illustrations © 1995 by Leonid Gore. Used by permission of Houghton Mifflin Company, Boston; **652** *Ceres*, Leonid Gore. From *The Pomegranate Seeds* retold by Laura Geringer. Illustrations © 1995 by Leonid Gore. Used by permission of Houghton Mifflin Company, Boston; **656** Courtesy of Photofest; **657** *top* © Paul Coughlin; *bottom* Courtesy of Julian Coolidge; **663** From *Arachne Speaks* by Kate Hovey, illustrated by Blair Drawson. Illustration © 2000 Blair Drawson. Reprinted with the permission of Margaret K. McElderry Books, an imprint of Simon & Schuster Children's Publishing Division, New York; **664** © Alistair Dove/Alamy Images; **666, 670** From *Arachne Speaks* by Kate Hovey, illustrated by Blair Drawson. Illustration © 2000 Blair Drawson. Reprinted with the permission of Margaret K. McElderry Books, an imprint of Simon & Schuster Children's Publishing Division, New York; **671** *top* © Anselm Spring/Getty Images; *bottom* © José Fuste Raga/Corbis; **672** *top* © Jerry Young/Dorling Kindersley; *bottom* © Adam Jones/Photo Researchers, Inc.; **673** *top* © Theo Allofs/Getty Images; *bottom* © Nancy Rotenberg/Animals Animals; **674** *top* © Hans Pfletschinger/Peter Arnold, Inc.; *bottom* © Kim Taylor/naturepl.com; **676** © Zia Soleil/Getty Images; **677** Photo by Carol Bruchac © Joseph Bruchac; **679** © Kate Thompson/Getty Images; **680** © Bettmann/Corbis; **681** © Per Eriksson/Getty Images; **682** © Chase Jarvis/Getty Images; **684** *collaged on top* © Staffan Andersson/Age Fotostock America, Inc.; *collaged on bottom* © Kathy Collins/Getty Images; **687** *background* © GeoNova LLC; *top* Photograph by Sharon Hoogstraten; *right* Canoe model (1905), Tomah Joseph. Passamaquoddy. Peter Dana Point, Maine. L. 50½" × 10½". Eugene and Clair Thaw Collection, Fenimore Art Museum, Cooperstown, New York. © John Bigelow Taylor/Art Resource, New York; **689** Courtesy of John Heaslip; **698** © John Lund/Getty Images; **699** © Daniel Shippey; **705** © Adrian Davies/naturepl.com; **708** © Natalie Fobes/Getty Images; **709** *top* Courtesy of the author © Moira Speer; *bottom* Photo of Judith Ortiz Cofer is reprinted with permission from the publisher Arte Publico Press. © 2005, University of Houston, Houston, Texas; **711** *Crane* (about 1800), Kano Yosen'in Korenobu. Hanging scroll, inkand color on silk, 129 cm × 53 cm. Japanese, Edo Period. William Sturgis Bigelow Collection. © Museum of Fine Arts, Boston. Photo © 2007 Museum of Fine Arts, Boston; **722** *The Wizard of Oz*, 1939. Everett Collection; **723** *top* © Nat Solomon; *bottom* Courtesy of the author; **733** Illustration by Daniel San Souci, © 1994 by Daniel San Souci, from *Sootface* by Robert D. San Souci., © 1994 by Robert D. San Souci. Used by permission of Random House Children's Books, a division of Random House, Inc.; **734** © Corbis; **735, 737** Illustration by Daniel San Souci, © 1994 by Daniel San Souci, from *Sootface* by Robert D. San Souci, © 1994 by Robert D. San Souci. Used by permission of Random House Children's Books, a division of Random House, Inc.; **738** © Fred Espenak/Photo Researchers, Inc.; **742, 748** © J. David Andrews/Masterfile; **749** *left* © Ed Kashi/Corbis; *right* © Nancy R. Cohen/Getty Images; **756** © Siede Preis/Photodisc/Getty Images.

UNIT 7

757 *left* © Chris Noble/Getty Images; *right* © Bettmann/Corbis; *collage* © Kevin Jones/Getty Images; © Peter Turnley/Corbis; © Stockbyte/Getty Images; **758–759** *collage background* © Digital Vision Photography/Veer; © Peter Turnley/Corbis; *foreground* © Stockbyte/Getty Images; **763** © 2006 Matt Stroshane/Getty Images; **765** © Time Life Pictures/Getty Images; **766** NASA; **767** Jane Dominguez, UF CLAS News & Publications; **769** © Bettmann/Corbis; **771** Library of Congress; **773**

© GeoNova LLC; **774** *left* National Archives; *right* © Stockdisc/Getty Images; **780** © Bettmann/Corbis; **781–782** © willsteger.com; **786** AP/Wide World Photos; **787** © Bettmann/Corbis; **789** © Courtesy of Perkins School for the Blind; © 1995 Photo by Larry Gillentine; **792** *top, bottom* The Granger Collection, New York; **796** *top* © Les Cunliffe/Age Fotostock America, Inc.; *bottom* © F. Isabel Campoy; **796–797** © Bob Krist/Corbis; **797** *top right* Courtesy American Library Association; *bottom right* Cover photograph by Alma Flor Ada. © 1998 by Alma Flor Ada. Photograph used by permission of the author and BookStop Literary Agency. All rights reserved; **798–799** Photo © J. Richard Abbott; **800–801** © Ian Pert/Travel-Ink; **802** © Robert Daly/Getty Images; **803** © Photo by Barbara Lalicki; **807** The Granger Collection, New York; **809** Library of Congress; **812** © Deborah Davis/Getty Images; **813** *left* Courtesy of A & E Television Networks; *right* © Library of Congress, Prints and Photographs Division; **814** *top* The Granger Collection, New York; *bottom* © Bettmann/Corbis; **815** *top left* © Steve Dunwell/Getty Images; *top center, top right, bottom left* © Hans Neleman/Getty Images; *bottom center* © Teubner/Getty Images; *bottom right* © Brooklyn Productions/Corbis; **816** © Garry Black/Masterfile; **817** *top* Photo by Neil Michel/Axiom; *bottom* © Tom Roster; **819, 820** *Provence Kitchen*, Josephine Trotter. © Josephine Trotter/SuperStock; **822** National Archives; **824, 830** © Jason Ernst/Age Fotostock America, Inc.; **831** © Michael Newman/PhotoEdit; **838** © Siede Preis/Photodisc/Getty Images.

UNIT 8

839 *left* © Raul Martin/Project Exploration; *right* © Mike Hettwer, courtesy Project Exploration; **840–841** © Matthias Kulka/Corbis; **842** *top* © G. Biss/Masterfile; *center, bottom* © Getty Images; **843** © Lee Foster/Getty Images; **845** © J. Silver/SuperStock; **846** © Vo Trung Dung/Corbis Sygma; **847** © National Geographic Image Collection; **848** *top* © National Geographic Image Collection; *bottom* © GeoNova LLC; **849** © Mike Hettwer/Project Exploration; **850** *top* © Raul Martin/Project Exploration; *bottom* © Mike Hettwer/Project Exploration; **851** *inset, Illustration by Precision Graphics*; © Mike Hettwer, courtesy Project Exploration; **852** © Reuters/Corbis; **856** © John Lund/Getty Images; **857** Courtesy of the author; **858** © Miles Barton/naturepl.com; **859** © Rick Friedman/Corbis; **861** © James R. Page/Valan Photos; **864** © Michael Melford/Getty Images; **865** *top* Courtesy of Daniel Cohen; *bottom* © www.legendportraits.com; **866** © PhotoDisc/PunchStock; **867** © GeoNova LLC; **870** © O. Louis Mazzatenta/National Geographic Image Collection; **872** © ImagineChina; **874** *left* © akg-images; *right* Illustration by Precision Graphics; **875, 876** © O. Louis Mazzatenta/National Geographic Image Collection; **880, 881** *right* AP/Wide World Photos; **882** *background* © Stuart Westmorland/Corbis; *top left, bottom left* Courtesy of ABC News; **883** © Hiroshi Yoshii/Getty Images; **885** © Michael Doolittle/The Image Works, Inc.; **887** © Ole Graf/zefa/Corbis; **888** © Julia Fishkin/Getty Images; **889** © Karl Weatherly/Getty Images; **890** AP/Wide World Photos; **891** © David McLain/Aurora Photos; **892** © SuperStock/Age Fotostock America, Inc.; **900** © Corbis; **901** © Mike Buckley/Fremont Tribune/AP/Wide World Photos; **902** © Scott C. Schulman/Getty Images; **904** © JoSon/Getty Images; **905** © Gloria H. Chomica/Masterfile; **906** AP/Wide World Photos; **908** Photograph by Sharon Hoogstraten; **909** © Mawi, Inc. 2005; **910** © Brand X Pictures/PunchStock; **914** © GDT/Getty Images; **915** *left* © Apple Computer, Inc. Used with permission. All rights reserved. Apple © and the Apple logo are registered trademarks of Apple Computer, Inc. *right* Microsoft Stephanie commercial. Courtesy of McCann Worldgroup/Microsoft; **916** *top left* © Apple Computer, Inc. Used with permission. All rights reserved. Apple

© and the Apple logo are registered trademarks of Apple Computer, Inc.; *bottom left* Microsoft Start Something Ad Campaign. Courtesy of McCann Worldgroup/Microsoft; *background* © Alan Towse; Ecoscene/Corbis; **918, 924** © Alain Choisnet/Getty Images; **925** *left* © SW Productions/ Getty Images; *right* © Martin Rugner/Age Fotostock; **932** © Siede Preis/ Photodisc/Getty Images.

UNIT 9 RESEARCH UNIT

933 *left* © LWA-JDC/Corbis; *right* Photograph by Sharon Hogstraten; **934–935** © Wizdata, Inc./Alamy Images; **936** *foreground* © Tobin Rogers/Alamy Images; *background* © Harrison Smith/Alamy Images; **940** © 2007 Infospace, Inc. All rights reserved. Reprinted with permission of Infospace, Inc.; **941** © Michael S. Quinton/National Geographic Image Collection; **943** Image from www.library.phila.gov, The Free Library of Philadelphia; **945** © Jim Gensheimer/Getty Images; **946** From *InfoTrac* (Website & CD-ROM usage) by Gale Group. Reprinted by permission of the Gale Group; **948** © Malcolm Schuyl/Alamy Images; **949** *left* © Larry Michael/naturepl.com; *right* © WireImageStock/Masterfile; **953** © Stock4B/Getty Images; **954, 968** © Sam Barricklow/Workbookstock. com; **969** © Michael J. Doolittle/The Image Works, Inc.; © Jean Fujita/ McDougal Littell.

STUDENT RESOURCE BANK

R03 © Jon Arnold/Alamy Images; **R06** *top* © David Sutherland/Getty Images; *bottom* The Granger Collection, New York; **R07** © GeoNova LLC; **R14** *left* © The Dallas Morning News. Reprinted with the permission of The Dallas Morning News; *right* Beatriz Terrazas/The Dallas Morning News; **R15** © Roger Wood/Corbis; **R17, R19** Public Domain; **R85** © Digital Vision Ltd./Superstock; **R92** © Walt Disney Pictures/Walden Media/The Kobal Collection.

BACK COVER

© Getty Images.